THE A & P

EVERYDAY COOK

AND

RECIPE BOOK.

Containing more than Two Thousand Practical Recipes for Cooking every kind of Meat, Fish, Poultry, Game, Soups, Broths, Vegetables and Salads. Also for making all kinds of Plain and Fancy Breads, Pastries, Puddings, Cakes, Creams, Ices, Jellies, Preserves, Marmalades, etc., together with Various Miscellaneous Recipes for Preparation of Food and Attention to Invalids, all carefully prepared and practically tested.

By MISS E. NEIL.

THE GREAT ATLANTIC AND PACIFIC TEA CO.,
PUBLISHERS:
35 & 37 VESEY STREET,
NEW YORK.
200 Stores in the United States.

THE EVERYDAY COOK-BOOK.

Of all the arts upon which the physical well-being of man, in his social state, is dependent, none has been more neglected than that of cookery, though none is more important, for it supplies the very fountain of life. The preparation of human food, so as to make it at once wholesome, nutritive, and agreeable to the palate, has hitherto been beset by imaginary difficulties and strong prejudices.

Many persons associate the idea of wealth with culinary perfection; others consider unwholesome, as well as expensive, everything that goes beyond the categories of boiling, roasting, and the gridiron. All are aware that wholesome and luxurious cookery is by no means incompatible with limited pecuniary means; whilst in roasted, boiled, and broiled meats which constitute what is termed true American fare, much that is nutritive and agreeable is often lost for want of skill in preparing them. Food of every description is wholesome and digestible in proportion as it approaches nearer to the state of complete digestion, or, in other words, to that state termed *chyme*, whence the chyle or milky juice that afterwards forms blood is absorbed, and conveyed to the heart. Now nothing is further from this state than raw meat and raw vegetables. Fire is therefore necessary to soften them, and thereby begin that elaboration which is consummated in the stomach. The preparatory process, which forms the cook's art, is more or les perfect in proportion as the aliment is softened, withou losing any of its juices or flavor—for flavor is not only a agreeable but a necessary accompaniment to wholesome foo Hence it follows, that meat very much underdone, whethe roasted or boiled, is not so wholesome as meat well don but retaining all its juices. And here comes the necessit for the cook's skill, which is so often at fault even in thes simple modes of preparing human nourishment.

Pork, veal, lamb, and all young meats, when not tho oughly cooked, are absolute poison to the stomach; and half-raw beef or mutton are often eaten with impunity, must not be inferred that they are unwholesome in their sem crude state, but only less wholesome than the young meat

Vegetables, also, half done, which is the state in whic they are often sent to the table, are productive of gre gastric derangement, often of a predisposition to cholera.

A great variety of relishing, nutritive, and even elega dishes, may be prepared from the most homely material which may not only be rendered more nourishing, but b made to go much farther in a large family than they usual do. The great secret of all cookery, except in roasting an broiling, is a judicious use of butter, flour, and herbs, an the application of a very slow fire—for good cooking re quires only gentle simmering, but no boiling up, which onl renders the meat hard. Good roasting can only be acquire by practice, and the perfection lies in cooking the who joint thoroughly without drying up the juice of any pa of it. This is also the case with broiling; while a joint un der process of broiling, as we have said, should be allowe to simmer gently.

With regard to *made dishes*, as the horrible imitatio of French cookery prevalent in America are termed, w must admit that they are very unwholesome. All th juices are boiled out of the meat which is swimming in heterogeneous compound, disgusting to the sight, and seasoned so strongly with spice and Cayenne pepper enough to inflame the stomach of an ostrich.

French cookery is generally mild in seasoning, and free from grease; it is formed upon the above-stated principle of reducing the aliment as near to the state of chyme as possible, without injury to its nutritive qualities, rendering it at once easy of digestion and pleasant to the taste.

HINTS ON MARKETING.

In the first place, the housewife ought, where it is possible, to do her marketing herself, *and pay ready money for everything she purchases.* This is the only way in which she can be sure of getting the best goods at the lowest price. We repeat that this is the only way compatible with economy; because, if a servant be entrusted with the buying, she will, if she is not a good judge of the quality of articles, bring home those she can get for the least money (and these are seldom the cheapest); and even if she is a good judge, it is ten to one against her taking the trouble to make a careful selection.

When the ready-money system is found inconvenient, and an account is run with a dealer, the mistress of the house ought to have a pass-book in which she should write down all the orders herself, leaving the dealer to fill in only the prices. Where this is not done, and the mistress neglects to compare the pass-book with the goods ordered every time they are brought in, it sometimes happens, either by mistake, or the dishonesty of the dealer, or the servant, that goods are entered which were never ordered, perhaps never had, and that those which were ordered are overcharged; and if these errors are not detected at the time, they are sure to be difficult of adjustment afterwards. For these and other economic reasons, the housewife should **avoid running accounts, and pay ready money.**

RULES FOR EATING.

Dr. Hall, on this important subject, gives the following advice:

1. Never sit down to table with an anxious or disturbed mind; better a hundred times intermit that meal, for there will then be that much more food in the world for hungrier stomachs than yours; and besides, eating under such circumstances can only, and will always, prolong and aggravate the condition of things.

2. Never sit down to a meal after any intense mental effort, for physical and mental injury are inevitable, and no one has a right to deliberately injure body, mind, or estate.

3. Never go to a full table during bodily exhaustion—designated by some as being worn out, tired to death, used up, over done, and the like. The wisest thing to be done under such circumstances is to take a cracker and a cup of warm tea, either black or green, and no more. In ten minutes you will feel a degree of refreshment and liveliness which will be pleasantly surprising to you; not of the transient kind which a glass of liquor affords, but permanent; but the tea gives present stimulus and a little strength, and before it subsides, nutriment begins to draw from the sugar, and cream, and bread, thus allowing the body gradually, and by safe degrees, to regain its usual vigor. Then, in a couple of hours, a full meal may be taken, provided that it does not bring it later than two hours before sundown; if later, then take nothing for that day in addition to the cracker and tea, and the next day you will feel a freshness and vigor not recently known.

No lady will require to be advised a second time, who will conform to the above rules; while it is a fact of no unusual observation among intelligent physicians, that eating heartily and under bodily exhaustion, is not unfrequently the cause of alarming and painful illness, and sometimes sudden death. These things being so, let every family make it a point to assemble around the table with kindly feelings—with a cheerful humor, and a courteous spirit; and let that member of it be sent from it in disgrace who presumes to mar the reunion by sullen silence, or impatient look, or angry tone, or complaining tongue. Eat ever in thankful gladness, or away with you to the kitchen, you "ill-tempered thing, that you are." There was good philosophy in the old-time custom of having a buffoon or music at the dinner-table.

HOW TO CHOOSE MEAT.

Ox-beef, when it is young, will have a fine open grain, and a good red color; the fat should be white, for when it is of a deep yellow color, the meat is seldom very good. The grain of cow-beef is closer, the fat whiter, and the lean scarcely so red as that of ox-beef. When you see beef, of which the fat is hard and skinny, and the lean of a deep red, you may be sure that it is of an inferior kind; and when the meat is old, you may know it by a line of horny texture running through the meat of the ribs.

Mutton must be chosen by the firmness and fineness of the grain, its good color, and firm white fat. It is not considered prime until the sheep is about five years old.

Lamb will not keep long after it is killed. It can be discovered by the neck end in the fore-quarter if it has been killed too long, the veins in the neck being bluish when the meat is fresh, but green when it is stale. In the hind quarter, the same discovery may be made by examining the kidney and the knuckle, for the former has a slight smell, and the knuckle is not firm when the meat has been killed too long.

Pork should have a thin rind; and when it is fresh, the

meat is smooth and cool; but, when it looks flabby, and is clammy to the touch, it is not good; and pork, above all meat, is disagreeable when it is stale. If you perceive many enlarged glands, or, as they are usually termed, kernels, in the fat of the pork, you may conclude that the pork cannot be wholesome.

Veal is generally preferred of a delicate whiteness, but it is more juicy and well-flavored when of a deeper color. Butchers bleed calves profusely in order to produce this white meat; but this practice must certainly deprive the meat of some of its nourishment and flavor. When you choose veal, endeavor to look at the loin, which affords the best means of judging of the veal generally, for if the kidney, which may be found on the under side of one end of the loin, be deeply enveloped in white and firm-looking fat, the meat will certainly be good; and the same appearance will enable you to judge if it has been recently killed. The kidney is the part which changes the first; and then the suet around it becomes soft, and the meat flabby and spotted.

Bacon, like pork, should have a thin rind; the fat should be firm, and inclined to a reddish color; and the lean should firmly adhere to the bone, and have no yellow streak in it. When you are purchasing a ham, have a knife stuck into it to the bone, which, if the ham be well cured, may be drawn out again without having any of the meat adhering to it, and without your perceiving any disagreeable smell. A short ham is reckoned the best.

HOW TO CHOOSE FISH.

TURBOT, which is in season the greater part of the year should have the underside of a yellowish white, for when it is very transparent, blue, or thin, it is not good; the whole fish should be thick and firm.

SALMON should have a fine red flesh and gills; the scales should be bright, and the whole fish firm. Many persons think that salmon is improved by keeping a day or two.

COD should be judged by the redness of the gills, the whiteness, stiffness, and firmness of the flesh, and the clear freshness of the eyes; these are the infallible proofs of its being good. The whole fish should be thick and firm.

WHITE-FISH may be had good almost throughout the year; but the time in which they are in their prime is early in the year. The white-fish is light and delicate, and in choosing it you must examine whether the fins and flesh be firm.

FRESH-WATER FISH may be chosen by similar observations respecting the firmness of the flesh, and the clear appearance of the eyes, as salt-water fish.

In a LOBSTER lately caught, you may put the claws in motion by pressing the eyes; but when it has been long caught, the muscular action is not excited. The freshness of boiled lobsters may be determined by the elasticity of the tail, which is flaccid when they have lost any of their wholesomeness. Their goodness, independent of freshness, is determined by their weight.

CRABS, too, must be judged of by their weight, for when they prove light, the flesh is generally found to be wasted and watery. If in perfection, the joints of the legs will be stiff, and the body will have an agreeable smell. The eyes, by a dull appearance, betray that the crab has been long caught.

HOW TO CHOOSE POULTRY.

In the choice of poultry the age of the bird is the chief point to which you should attend.

A young Turkey has a smooth black leg; in an old one the legs are rough and reddish. If the bird be fresh killed the eyes will be full and fresh, and the feet moist.

Fowls, when they are young, the combs and the legs will be smooth, and rough when they are old.

In Geese, when they are young, the bills and the feet are yellow and have a few hairs upon them, but they are red if the bird be old. The feet of a goose are pliable when the bird is fresh killed, and dry and stiff when it has been killed some time. Geese are called green till they are two or three months old.

Ducks should be chosen by their feet, which should be supple; and they should also have a plump and hard breast. The feet of a tame duck are yellowish, those of a wild one, reddish.

Pigeons should always be eaten while they are fresh; when they look flabby and discolored about the under part, they have been kept too long. The feet, like those of poultry, show the age of the bird; when they are supple, it is young; when stiff, it is old. Tame pigeons are larger than wild ones.

HOW TO CHOOSE GAME.

Venison, when young, will have the fat clear and bright, and this ought also to be of a considerable thickness. When you do not wish to have it in a very high state, a knife plunged into either haunch or the shoulder, and drawn out, will by the smell enable you to judge if the venison is sufficiently fresh.

With regard to venison, which, as it is not an every-day

article of diet, it may be convenient to keep for some time after it has begun to get high or tainted, it is useful to know that the animal putrefaction is checked by fresh burnt charcoal; by means of which, therefore, the venison may be prevented from getting worse, although it cannot be restored to its original freshness. The meat should be placed in a hollow dish, and the charcoal powder strewed over it until it covers the joint to the thickness of half an inch.

HARES and RABBITS, when the ears are dry and tough, the haunch thick, and the claws blunt and rugged, they are old. Smooth and sharp claws, ears that readily tear, and a narrow cleft in the lip, are the marks of a young hare. Hares may be kept for some time after they have been killed; indeed, many people think they are not fit for the table until the inside begins to turn a little. Care, however, should be taken to prevent the inside from becoming musty, which would spoil the flavor of the stuffing.

PARTRIDGES have yellow legs and a dark-colored bill when young. They are not in season till after the first of September.

HOW TO CHOOSE EGGS.

In putting the hand round the egg, and presenting to the light, the end which is not covered, it should be transparent. If you can detect some tiny spots, it is not newly laid, but may be very good for all ordinary purposes except boiling soft. If you see a large spot near the shell, it is bad, and should not be used on any account. The white of a newly-laid egg boiled soft is like milk; that of an egg a day old, is like rice boiled in milk; and that of an old egg, compact, tough, and difficult to digest. A cook ought not to give eggs two or three days old to people who really care for fresh eggs, under the delusion that they will not find any difference; for an amateur will find it out in a moment, not only by the appearance, but also by the taste.

CARVING.

The seat for the carver should be somewhat elevated above the other chairs; it is extremely ungraceful to carve standing, and it is rarely done by any person accustomed to the business. Carving depends more on skill than on strength. We have seen very small women carve admirably sitting down; and very tall men who knew not how to cut a piece of beefsteak without rising on their feet to do it.

The carving-knife should be very sharp, and not heavy; and it should be held firmly in the hand; also the dish should not be too far from the carver. It is customary to help the fish with a fish-trowel, and not with a knife. The middle part of a fish is generally considered the best. In helping it, avoid breaking the flakes, as that will give it a mangled appearance.

In carving ribs or sirloin of beef begin by cutting thin slices off the side next to you. Afterwards you may cut from the tenderloin, or cross-part near the lower end. Do not send anyone the outside piece, unless you know they particularly wish it.

In helping beefsteak put none of the bone on the plate. In cutting a round of corned beef begin at the top; but lay aside the first cut or outside piece, and send it to no one, as it is always dry and hard. In a round of *beef a-la mode* the outside is frequently preferred.

A leg of mutton begin across the middle, cutting the slices quite down to the bone. The same with a leg of pork or a ham. The latter should be cut in very thin slices, as its flavor is spoiled when cut thick.

To taste well, tongue should be cut crossways in round slices. Cutting it lengthwise (though the practice at many tables) injures the flavor. The middle part of the tongue is the best. Do not help anyone to a piece of the root; that, being by no means a favored part, is generally left in the dish.

In carving a fore-quarter of lamb first separate the shoulder part from the breast and ribs by passing the knife under, and then divide the ribs. If the lamb is large, have another dish brought to put the shoulder in.

For a loin of veal begin near the smallest end, and separate the ribs; helping a part of the kidney (as far as it will go) with each piece. Carve a loin of pork or mutton in the same manner.

In carving a fillet of veal begin at the top. Many persons prefer the first cut or outside piece. Help a portion of the stuffing with each slice.

In a breast of veal there are two parts very different in quality, the ribs and the brisket. You will easily perceive the division; enter your knife at it and cut through, which will separate the two parts. Ask the person you are going to help whether they prefer a rib or a piece of the brisket.

For a haunch of vension first make a deep incision by passing your knife all along the side, cutting quite down to the bone. This is to let out the gravy. Then turn the broad end of the haunch toward you, and cut it as deep as you can in thin slices, allowing some of the fat to each person.

For a saddle of venison, or of mutton, cut from the tail to the other end on each side of the backbone, making very thin slices, and sending some fat with each. Venison and roast mutton chill very soon. Currant jelley is an indispensable appendage to venison, and to roast mutton, and to ducks.

A young pig is most generally divided before it comes to table, in which case it is not customary to send in the head, as to many persons it is a revolting spectacle after it is cut off. When served up whole, first separate the head from the shoulders, then cut off the limbs, and then divide the ribs. Help some of the stuffing with each piece.

To carve a fowl, begin by sticking your fork in the pinion, and draw it towards the leg; and then passing your knife underneath take off the wing at the joint. Next, slip your knife between the leg and the body, to cut through the joint; and with the fork turn the leg back, and the joint will give way. Then take off the other wing and leg. If the fowl has been trussed (as it ought to be) with the liver and gizzard, help the liver with one wing, and the gizzard with the other. The liver-wing is considered the best. After the limbs are taken off enter your knife into the top of the breast, and cut under the merry-thought, so as to loosen it, lifting it with your fork. Afterwards cut slices from both sides of the breast. Next take off the collar-bones, which lie on each side of the merry-thought, and then separate the side-bones from the back. The breast and wings are considered the most delicate part of the fowl; the back, as the least desirable, is generally left in the dish. Some persons, in carving a fowl, find it more convenient to take it on a plate, and as they separate it return each part to the dish, but this is not the usual way.

A turkey is carved in the same manner as a fowl; except that the legs and wings, being larger, are separated at the lower joint. The lower part of the leg (or drum-stick, as it is called), being hard, tough, and stringy, is never helped to any one, but allowed to remain in the dish. First cut off the wing, leg, and breast from one side; then turn the turkey over, and cut them off from the other.

To carve a goose, separate the leg from the body, by putting the fork into the small end of the limb; pressing it close to the body, and then passing the knife under, and turning the leg back, as you cut through the joint. To take off the wing, put your fork into the small end of the pinion, and press it closely to the body; then slip the knife under, and separate the joint. Next cut under the merry-thought, and take it off; and then cut slices from the breast. Then turn the goose, and dismember the other side. Take off the two upper side-bones that are next to the wings, and then the two lower side-bones. The breast and legs of a goose afford the finest pieces. If a goose is old there is no fowl so tough; and, if difficult to carve, it will be still more difficult to eat.

Partridges, pheasants, grouse, etc., are carved in the same manner as fowls. Quails, woodcocks, and snipes are merely split down the back; so also are pigeons, giving a half to each person.

In helping any one to gravy, or to melted butter, do not pour it *over* their meat, fowl, or fish, but put it to one side on a vacant part of the plate, that they may use just as much of it as they like. In filling a plate never heap one thing on another.

In helping vegetables, do not plunge the spoon down to the bottom of the dish, in case they should not have been perfectly well drained, and the water should have settled there.

By observing carefully how it is done you may acquire a knowledge of the joints, and of the process of carving, which a little daily practice will soon convert into dexterity. If a young lady is ignorant of this useful art, it will be well for her to take lessons of her father, or her brother, and a married lady can easily learn from her husband. Domestics who wait at table may soon, from looking on daily, become so expert that, when necessary, they can take a dish to the side-table and carve it perfectly well.

At a dinner-party, if the hostess is quite young, she is frequently glad to be relieved of the trouble of carving by the gentleman who sits nearest to her; but if she is familiar with the business she usually prefers doing it herself.

SOUPS.

GENERAL REMARKS.

Be careful to proportion the quantity of water to that of the meat. Somewhat less than a quart of water to a pound of meat is a good rule for common soups. Rich soups, intended for company, may have a still smaller allowance of water.

Soup should always be made entirely of fresh meat that has not been previously cooked. An exception to this rule may sometimes be made in favor of the remains of a piece of roast beef that has been *very much* under-done in roasting. This may be *added* to a good piece of raw meat. Cold ham, also, may be occasionally put into white soups.

Soup, however, that has been originally made of raw meat entirely is frequently better the second day than the first, provided it is reboiled only for a very short time, and that no additional water is added to it.

Unless it has been allowed to boil too hard, so as to exhaust the water, the soup-pot will not require replenishing. When it is found absolutely necessary to do so, the additional water must be boiling-hot when poured in; if lukewarm or cold, it will entirely spoil the soup.

Every particle of fat should be carefully skimmed from the surface. Greasy soup is disgusting and unwholesome. The lean of meat is much better for soup than the fat.

Long and slow boiling is necessary to extract the strength from the meat. If boiled fast over a large fire, the meat becomes hard and tough, and will not give out its juices.

Potatoes, if boiled in the soup, are thought by some to render it unwholesome, from the opinion that the water in which potatoes have been cooked is almost a poison. As potatoes are a part of every dinner, it is very easy to take a few out

Green Peas
Artichokes
Tomatoes
Potatoes
Spanish Onions
Salad
Vegetable Marrow
Lima Beans
Cauliflowers
Asparagus
Sea Kale
Carrots
Brussels Sprouts
French Beans

of the pot in which they have been boiled by themselves. and to cut them up and add them to the soup just before it goes to table. Remove all shreds of meat and bone.

The cook should season the soup but very slightly with salt and pepper. If she puts in too much it may spoil it for the taste of most of those who are to eat it; but if too little it is easy to add more to your own plate.

SOUPS.

STOCK.

Four pounds of shin of beef, or four pounds of knuckle of veal, or two pounds of each; any bones, trimmings of poultry, or fresh meat, quarter pound of lean bacon or ham, two ounces of butter, two large onions, each stuck with cloves; one turnip, three carrots, one head of celery, three lumps of sugar, two ounces of salt, half a teaspoonful of whole pepper, one large blade of mace, one bunch of savory herbs, four quarts and half pint of cold water.

Cut up the meat and bacon, or ham, into pieces of about three inches square; rub the butter on the bottom of the stewpan; put in half a pint of water, the meat, and all the other ingredients. Cover the stewpan, and place it on a sharp fire, occasionally stirring its contents. When the bottom of the pan becomes covered with a pale, jelly-like substance, add the four quarts of cold water, and simmer very gently for five hours. As we have said before, do not let it boil quickly. Remove every particle of scum while it is doing, and strain it through a fine hair sieve.

This stock is the basis of many of the soups afterwards mentioned, and will be found quite strong enough for ordinary purposes.

Time: five and one-half hours. Average cost, twenty-five cents per quart.

WHITE STOCK SOUP.

Six pounds knuckle of veal, half pound lean bacon, two tablespoonfuls of butter rubbed in one of flour, two onions, two carrots, two turnips, three cloves stuck in an onion, one blade of mace, bunch of herbs, six quarts of water, pepper and salt, one cup of boiling milk.

Cut up the meat and crack the bones. Slice carrots, turnips, and one onion, leaving that with the cloves whole. Put on with mace, and all the herbs except the parsley, in two quarts of cold water. Bring to a slow boil; take off the scum, as it rises, and at the end of an hour's stewing, add the rest of the cold water—one gallon. Cover and cook steadily, always gently, four hours. Strain off the liquor, of which there should be about five quarts; rub the vegetables through the colander, and pick out bones and meat. Season these highly and put, as is your Saturday custom, into a wide-mouth jar, or a large bowl. Add to them three quarts of stock, well salted, and, when cold, keep on ice. Cool to-day's stock; remove the fat, season, put in chopped parsley, and put over the fire. Heat in a saucepan a cup of milk, stir in the floured butter; cook three minutes. When the soup has simmered ten minutes after the last boil, and been carefully skimmed, pour into the tureen, and stir in the hot, thickened milk.

SHIN OF BEEF SOUP.

Get a shin-bone of beef weighing four or five pounds; let the butcher saw it in pieces about two inches long, that the marrow may become the better incorporated with the soup, and so give it greater richness.

Wash the meat in cold water; mix together of salt and pepper each a tablespoonful, rub this well into the meat, then put into a soup-pot; put to it as many quarts of water as there are pounds of meat, and set it over a moderate fire, until it comes to a boil, then take off whatever scum may have risen, after which cover it close, and set it where it will boil very gently for two hours longer, then skim it again, and add to it the proper vegetables, which are these—

one large carrot grated, one large turnip cut in slices (the yellow or ruta baga is best),one leek cut in slices, one bunch of parsley cut small, six small potatoes peeled and cut in half, and a teacupful of pearl barley well washed, then cover it and let it boil gently for one hour, at which time add another tablesponful of salt and a thickening made of a tablespoonful of wheat flour and a gill of water, stir it in by the spoonful; cover it for fifteen minutes and it is done.

Three hours and a half is required to make this soup; it is the best for cold weather. Should any remain over the first day, it may be heated with the addition of a little boiling water, and served again.

Take the meat from the soup, and if to be served with it, take out the bones, and lay it closely and neatly on a dish, and garnish with sprigs of parsley; serve made mustard and catsup with it. It is very nice pressed and eaten with mustard and vinegar or catsup.

MUTTON SOUP WITH TAPIOCA.

Three pounds perfectly lean mutton. The scrag makes good soup and costs little. Two or three pounds of bones, well pounded, one onion, two turnips, two carrots, two stalks of celery, a few sprigs of parsley; if you have any tomatoes left from yesterday, add them, four tablespoonfuls of pearl or granulated tapioca (not heaping spoonfuls),four quarts of water.

Put on the meat, cut in small pieces, with the bones,in two quarts of cold water. Heat very slowly, and when it boils, pour in two quarts of hot water from the kettle. Chop the vegetables, cover with cold water. So soon as they begin to simmer, throw off the first water, replenishing with hot, and stew until they are boiled to pieces. The meat should cook steadily, never fast, five hours, keeping the pot-lid on. Strain into a great bowl; let it cool to throw the fat to the surface; skim and return to the fire. Season with pepper and salt, boil up, take off the scum; add the vegetables with their liquor. Heat together ten minutes, strain again, and bring to a slow boil before the tapioca goes in. This should have been soaked for one hour in cold water, then cooked in the same within another vessel of boiling water until each grain is clear. It is necessary to stir up often from the bottom while cooking. Stir gradually into the soup until the tapioca is dissolved.

Send around grated cheese with this soup.

VEAL SOUP.

To about three pounds of a joint of veal, which must be well broken up, put four quarts of water and set it over to boil. Prepare one-fourth pound of macaroni by boiling it by itself, with sufficient water to cover it; add a little butter to the macaroni when it is tender, strain the soup and season to taste with salt and pepper, then add the macaroni in the water in which it is boiled. The addition of a pint of rich milk or cream and celery flavor is relished by many.

OX-TAIL SOUP.

Take two ox tails and two whole onions, two carrots, a small turnip, two tablespoonfuls of flour, and a little white pepper, add a gallon of water, let all boil for two hours; then take out the tails and cut the meat into small pieces, return the bones to the pot, for a short time, boil for another hour, then strain the soup, and rinse two spoonfuls of arrowroot to add to it with the meat cut from the bones, and let all boil for a quarter of an hour.

VEGETABLE SOUP.

Two pounds of coarse, lean beef, cut into strips, two pounds of knuckle of veal chopped to pieces, two pounds of mutton bones, and the bones left from your cold veal cracked to splinters, pound of lean ham, four large carrots, two turnips, two onions, bunch of herbs, three tablespoonfuls of butter, and two of flour, one tablespoonful of sugar, salt and pepper, seven quarts of water.

Put on meat, bones, herbs and water, and cook slowly five hours. Strain the soup, of which there should be five quarts. Season meat and bones, and put into the stock-pot with three quarts of liquor. Save this for days to come. While the soup for to-day is cooling that you may take off the fat, put the butter into a frying pan with sliced carrots, turnips and onions, and fry to a light brown. Now, add a pint of the skimmed stock, and stew the vegetables tender, stir in the flour wet with water, and put all, with your cooled stock, over the fire in the soup-kettle. Season with sugar, Cayenne and salt, boil five minutes, rub through a colander, then a soup-sieve, heat almost to boiling, and serve.

MACARONI SOUP.

To a rich beef or other soup, in which there is no seasoning other than pepper or salt, take half a pound of small pipe macaroni, boil it in clear water until it is tender, then drain it and cut it in pieces of an inch in length, boil it for fifteen minutes in the soup and serve.

VERMICELLI SOUP.

Swell quarter of a pound of vermicelli in a quart of warm water, then add it to a good beef, veal, lamb or chicken soup or broth with quarter of a pound of sweet butter; let the soup boil for fifteen minutes after it is added.

CHICKEN CREAM SOUP.

Boil an old fowl, with an onion, in four quarts of cold water, until there remain but two quarts. Take it out and let it get cold. Cut off the whole of the breast, and chop very fine. Mix with the pounded yolks of two hard-boiled eggs, and rub through a colander. Cool, skim, and strain the soup into a soup-pot. Season, add the chicken-and-egg mixture, simmer ten minutes, and pour into the tureen. Then add a small cup of boiling milk.

MOCK-TURTLE SOUP.

Clean and wash a calf's head, split it in two, save the brains, boil the head until tender in plenty of water; put a slice of fat ham, a bunch of parsley cut small, a sprig of thyme, two leeks cut small, six cloves, a teaspoonful of pepper, and three ounces of butter, into a stew-pan, and fry them a nice brown; then add the water in which the head was boiled, cut the meat from the head in neat square pieces, and put them to the soup; add a pint of Madeira and one lemon sliced thin, and Cayenne pepper and salt to taste; let it simmer gently for two hours, then skim it clear and serve.

Make a forcemeat of the brains as follows: put them in a stew-pan, pour hot water over, and set it over the fire for a few minutes, then take them up, chop them small, with a sprig of parsley, a saltspoonful of salt and pepper each, a tablespoonful of wheat flour, the same of butter, and one well-beaten egg; make it in small balls, and drop them in the soup fifteen minutes before it is taken from the fire; in making the balls, a little more flour may be necessary. Egg-balls may also be added.

HARD PEA SOUP.

Many persons keep the bones of their roast in order to convert them into stock for pea soup, which is, to my taste, one of the most relishable of all soups, and a famous dish for cold weather, with this advantage in its favor, that it may be made from almost anything. Capital stock for pea soup can be made from a kuckle of ham or from a piece of pickled-pork. Supposing that some such stock is at hand to the extent of about two quarts, procure, say, two pounds of split peas, wash them well, and then soak them for a night in water to which a very little piece of soda has been added (the floating peas should be all thrown away), strain out the peas and place them in the stock, adding a head of celery, a cut-down carrot and a large onion or two, and season with a pinch of curry powder, or half an eggspoonful of Cayenne pepper. Boil with a lid on the pot till all is soft, skimming off the scum occasionally, and then carefully strain into a well-warmed tureen, beating the pulp through the strainer with a spoon. Serve as hot as possible, placing a breakfastcupful of crumbled toast (bread) into the tureen before the soup is dished. Much of the success in preparing this soup lies in the "straining," which ought to be carefully attended to. A wire sieve is best; but an active housewife must never stick. If she has not a sieve made for the purpose, she can fold a piece of net two or three times, and use that. When a knuckle of ham has been used to make the stock it should form a part of the dinner, with potatoes, or it may be used as a breakfast or supper relish.

GREEN PEA SOUP.

Wash a small quarter of lamb in cold water, and put it into a soup-pot with six quarts of cold water; add to it two tablespoonfuls of salt, and set it over a moderate fire—let it boil gently for two hours, then skim it clear, add a quart of shelled peas, and a teaspoonful of pepper; cover it, and let it boil for half an hour, then having scraped the skins from a quart of small young potatoes, add them to the soup; cover the pot, and let it boil for half an hour longer; work quarter of a pound of butter, and a dessert spoonful of flour together, and add them to the soup ten or twelve minutes before taking it off the fire.

Serve the meat on a dish with parsley sauce over, and the soup in a tureen.

POTATO SOUP.

Potato soup is suitable for a cold day. Make it in the following manner: Get as many beef or ham bones as you can, and smash them into fragments. Add a little bit of lean ham to give flavor. Boil the bone and ham for two hours and a half at least. The bone of a roast beef is excellent. Strain off the liquor carefully, empty the bones and *debris* of the ham, restore the liquor to the pot; and place again on the fire. Having selected, washed, and pared some nice potatoes, cut them into small pieces, and boil them in the stock till they melt away. An onion or two may also be boiled among the bones to help the flavor. I do not like thick potato soup, and I usually strain it through a hair sieve, after doing so placing it again on the fire, seasoning it with pepper and salt to taste. A stick of celery boiled with the bones is an improvement. Make only the quantity required for the day, as potato soup is best when it is newly made.

TOMATO SOUP.

Tomato soup is a much relished American dish, and is prepared as follows: Steam, or rather stew slowly, a mess of turnips, carrots, and onions, also a stalk of celery, with half a pound of lean ham and a *little bit* of fresh butter over a slow fire for an hour or so. Then add two quarts of diluted stock or of other liquor in which meat has been boiled, as also eight or ten ripe tomatoes. Stew the whole for an hour and a half, then pass through the sieve into the pan again; add a little pepper and salt, boil for ten minutes and serve hot.

GAME SOUP.

Two grouse or partridges, or if you have neither, use a pair of rabits; half a pound of lean ham; two medium-sized onions; one pound of lean beef; fried bread; butter for frying; pepper, salt, and two stalks of white celery cut into inch lengths; three quarts of water.

Joint your game neatly; cut the ham and onions into small pieces, and fry all in butter to a light brown. Put into a soup-pot with the beef, cut into strips, and a little pepper. Pour on the water; heat slowly, and stew gently two hours. Take out the pieces of bird, and cover in a bowl; cook the soup an hour longer; strain; cool; drop in the celery, and simmer ten minutes. Pour upon fried bread in the tureen.

CELERY SOUP.

Celery soup may be made with *white stock*. Cut down the white of half a dozen heads of celery into little pieces and boil it in four pints of white stock, with a quarer of a pound of lean ham and two ounces of butter. Simmer gently for a full hour, then drain through a sieve, return the liquor to pan and stir in a few spoonfuls of cream with great care. Serve with toasted bread, and, if liked, thicken with a little flour. Season to taste.

OYSTER SOUP.

Two quarts of oysters, one quart of milk, two tablespoonfuls of butter, one teacupful hot water; pepper, salt.

Strain all the liquor from the oysters; add the water and heat. When near the boil, add the seasoning, then the oysters. Cook about five minutes from the time they begin to simmer, until they "ruffle." Stir in the butter, cook one minute and pour into the tureen. Stir in the boiling milk, and send to table.

LOBSTER SOUP.

Procure a large hen fish, boiled, and with all its coral, if possible. Cut away from it all the meat in neat little pieces; beat up the fins and minor claws in a mortar, then stew the results in a stew-pan, slowly, along with a little white stock; season this with a bunch of sweet herbs; a small onion, a little bit of celery, and a carrot may be placed in the stock as also the toasted crust of a French roll. Season to taste with salt and a little Cayenne. Simmer the whole for about an hour; then strain and return the liquor to the saucepan; place in it the pieces of lobster, and having beat up the coral in a little flour and gravy, stir it in. Let the soup remain on the fire for a few minutes without boiling and serve hot. A small strip of the rind of a lemon may be boiled in the stock, and a little nutmeg may be added to the seasoning. This is a troublesome soup to prepare, but there are many who like it when it is well made.

EGG BALLS FOR SOUP.

Boil four eggs; put into cold water; mash yolks with yolk of one raw egg, and one teaspoonful of flour, pepper, salt and parsley; make into balls and boil two minutes.

NOODLES FOR SOUP.

Rub into two eggs as much sifted flour as they will absorb; then roll out until thin as a wafer; dust over a little flour, and then roll over and over into a roll, cut off thin slices from the edge of the roll, and shake out into long strips; put them into the soup lightly and boil for ten minutes; salt should be added while mixing with the flour—about a saltspoonful.

IRISH STEW.—STOVED POTATOES.

These form excellent and nutritious dishes. The former dish can be made from a portion of the back ribs or neck of mutton, the fleshy part of which must be cut into cutlets. Flatten these pieces of meat with a roller, and dip them in a composition of pepper, salt and flour. Peel potatoes and slice them to the extent of two pounds of potatoes for every pound of meat. An onion or two sliced into small bits will be required. Before building the materials into a goblet, melt a little suet or dripping in it, then commence by laying in the pot a layer of potatoes, which dust well with pepper and salt, then a layer of meat sprinkled with the chopped onions, and so on till the goblet is pretty full. Fill in about a breakfast-cupful of gravy, if there be any in the house; if not, water will do. Finish off with a treble row of potatoes on the top. Let the mess stew slowly for about three hours, taking great care to keep the lid so tight that none of the virtue can escape—letting away the steam is just letting away the flavor. Shake the pot occasionally with some force, to prevent burning. Some cooks in preparing this dish, boil the potatoes for some time, and then pour and dry them well; others add a portion of kidney to the stew; while extravagent people throw in a few oysters, a slice or two of lean ham, or a ham shank. Irish stew should be served as hot as possible. It is a savory and inexpensive dish for cold weather.—*Stoved potatoes* are prepared much in the same way. Cut down what of the Sunday's roast is left, and proceed with it just as you would with the neck of mutton. Some cooks would stew the bones of the roast, in order to make a gravy in which to stove the meat and potatoes, but the bones will make excellent potato soup. Irish stew is an excellent dish for skaters and curlers. It is sometimes known as "hot pot."

TO GET UP A SOUP IN HASTE.

Chop some cold cooked meat fine, and put a pint into a stew-pan with some gravy, season with pepper and salt and a little butter if the gravy is not rich, add a little flour moistened with cold water, and three pints boiling water, boil moderately half an hour. Strain over some rice or nicely toasted bread, and serve. Uncooked meat may be used by using one quart of cold water to a pound of chopped meat, and letting it stand half before boiling. Celery root may be grated in as seasoning, or a bunch of parsley thrown in.

TO COLOR SOUPS.

A fine amber color is obtained by adding finely-grated carrot to the clear stock when it is quite free from scum.

Red is obtained by using red skinned tomatoes from which the skin and seeds have been strained out.

Only white vegetables should be used in white soups, as chicken.

Spinach leaves, pounded in a mortar, and the juice expressed, and added to the soups, will give a green color.

Black beans make an excellent brown soup. The same color can be gotten by adding burnt sugar or browned flour to clear stock.

FISH.

Fish are good, when the gills are red, eyes are full, and the body of the fish is firm and stiff. After washing them well, they should be allowed to remain for a short time in salt water sufficient to cover them; before cooking wipe them dry, dredge lightly with flour, and season with salt and pepper. Salmon trout and other small fish are usually fried or broiled; all large fish should be put in a cloth, tied closely with twine, and placed in cold water, when they may be put over the fire to boil. When fish are baked, prepare the fish the same as for boiling, and put in the oven on a wire gridiron, over a dripping pan.

BOILED SALMON.

The middle slice of salmon is the best. Sew up neatly in a mosquito-net bag, and boil a quarter of an hour to the pound in hot, salted water. When done, unwrap with care, and lay upon a hot dish, taking care not to break it. Have ready a large cupful of drawn butter, very rich, in which has been stirred a tablespoonful of minced parsley and the juice of a lemon. Pour half upon the salmon, and serve the rest in a boat. Garnish with parsley and sliced eggs.

Here is a recipe for a nice *pickle for cold salmon* made out of the liquor in which the fish has been boiled, of which take as much as you wish, say three breakfast-cupfuls, to which add vinegar to taste (perhaps a teacupful will be enough), a good pinch of pepper, a dessert-spoonful of salt. Boil for a few minutes with a sprig or two of parsley and a little thyme. After it has become quite cold, pour it over the fish.

BROILED SALMON.

Cut some slices about an inch thick, and broil them over a gentle bright fire of coals, for ten or twelve minutes. When both sides are done, take them on to a hot dish; butter each slice well with sweet butter; strew over each a very little salt and pepper to taste, and serve.

BAKED SALMON.

Clean the fish, rinse it, and wipe it dry; rub it well outside and in, with a mixture of pepper and salt, and fill it with a stuffing made with slices of bread, buttered freely and moistened with hot milk or water (add sage or thyme to the seasoning if liked); tie a thread around the fish so as to keep the stuffing in (take off the thread before serving); lay muffin-rings, or a trivet in a dripping-pan, lay bits of butter over the fish, dredge flour over, and put it on the rings; put a pint of hot water in the pan, to baste with; bake one hour if a large fish, in a quick oven; baste frequently. When the fish is taken up, having cut a lemon in very thin slices, put them in the pan, and let them fry a little; then dredge in a teaspoonful of wheat flour; add a small bit of butter; stir it about, and let it brown without burning for a little while then add half a teacupful or more of boiling water stir it smooth, take the slices of lemon into the gravy boat, and strain the gravy over. Serve with boiled potatoes. The lemon may be omitted if preferred, although generally it will be liked.

SALMON-TROUT.

Dressed the same as salmon.

SPICED SALMON (PICKLED).

Boil a salmon, and after wiping it dry, set it to cool; take of the water in which it was boiled, and good vinegar each equal parts, enough to cover it; add to it one dozen cloves, as many small blades of mace, or sliced nutmeg, one teaspoonful of whole pepper, and the same of alspice; make it boiling hot, skim it clear, add a small bit of butter (the size of a small egg), and pour it over the fish; set it in a cool place. When cold, it is fit for use, and will keep for a long time, covered close, in a cool place. Serve instead of pickled oysters for supper.

A fresh cod is very nice, done in the same manner, as is also a striped sea bass.

SALMON AND CAPER SAUCE.

Two slices of salmon, one quarter pound butter, one half teaspoonful of chopped parsley, one shalot; salt, pepper and grated nutmeg to taste.

Mode: Lay the salmon in a baking-dish, place pieces of butter over it, and add the other ingredients, rubbing a little of the seasoning into the fish; baste it frequently; when done, take it out and drain for a minute or two; lay it in a dish; pour caper sauce over it, and serve; salmon dressed in this way, with tomato sauce, is very delicious.

SALMON CUTLETS.

Cut the slices one inch thick, and season them with pepper and salt; butter a sheet of white paper, lay each slice on a separate piece, with their ends twisted; boil gently over a clear fire, and serve with anchovy or caper sauce. When higher seasoning is required, add a few chopped herbs and a little spice.

DRIED OR SMOKED SALMON.

Cut the fish down the back, take out the entrails, and roe, scale it, and rub the outside and in with common salt, and hang it to drain for twenty-four hours.

Pound three ounces of saltpetre, two ounces of coarse salt and two of coarse brown sugar; mix these well together, and rub the salmon over every part with it; then lay it on a large dish for two days; then rub it over with common salt, and in twenty-four hours it will be fit to dry. Wipe it well, stretch it open with two sticks, and hang it in a chimney, with a smothered wood fire, or in a smoke house, or in a dry, cool place.

Shad done in this manner are very fine.

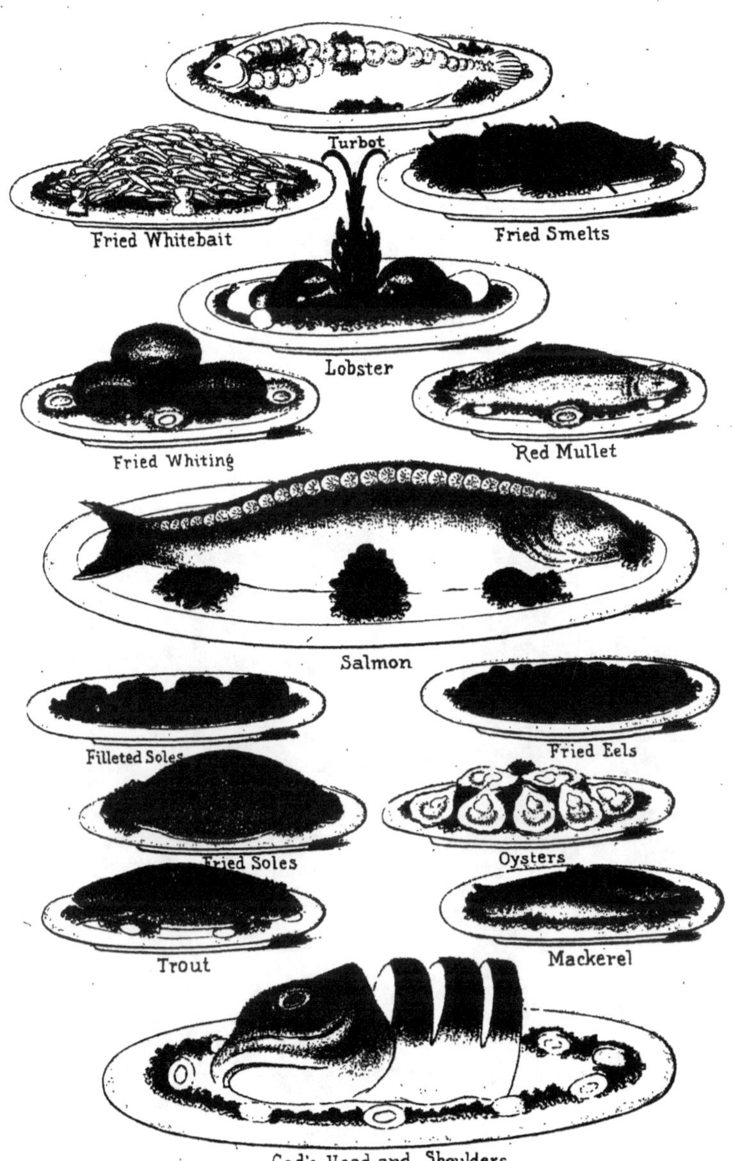
Turbot
Fried Whitebait
Fried Smelts
Lobster
Fried Whiting
Red Mullet
Salmon
Filleted Soles
Fried Eels
Fried Soles
Oysters
Trout
Mackerel
Cod's Head and Shoulders

BOILED COD.

Lay the fish in cold water, a little salt, for half an hour. Wipe dry, and sew up in a linen cloth, coarse and clean fitted to the shape of the piece of cod. Have but one fold over each part. Lay in the fish-kettle, cover with boiling water, salted at discretion. Allow nearly an hour for a piece weighing four pounds.

COD PIE.

Any remains of cold cod, twelve oysters, sufficint melted butter to moisten it; mashed potatoes enough to fill up the dish.

Mode: Flake the fish from the bone, and carefully take away all the skin. Lay it in a pie-dish, pour over the melted butter and oysters (or oyster sauce, if there is any left), and cover with mashed potatoes. Bake for half an hour, and send to table of a nice brown color.

DRIED CODFISH.

This should always be laid in soak at least one night before it is wanted; then take off the skin and put it in plenty of cold water; boil it gently (skimming it meanwhile) for one hour, or tie it in a cloth and boil it.

Serve with egg sauce; garnish with hard-boiled eggs cut in slices, and sprigs of parsley. Serve plain boiled or mashed potatoes with it.

STEWED SALT COD.

Scald some soaked cod by putting it over the fire in boiling water for ten minutes; then scrape it white, pick it in flakes, and put it in a stew-pan, with a tablespoonful of butter worked into the same of flour, and as much milk as will moisten it; let it stew gently for ten minutes; add pepper to taste, and serve hot; put it in a deep dish, slice hard-boiled eggs over, and sprigs of parsley around the edge.

This is a nice relish for breakfast, with coffe and tea, and rolls or toast.

CODFISH CAKES.

First boil soaked cod, then chop it fine, put to it an equal quantity of potatoes boiled and mashed; moisten it with beaten eggs or milk, and a bit of butter and a little pepper; form it in small, round cakes, rather more than a half inch thick; flour the outside, and fry in hot lard or beef drippings until they are a delicate brown; like fish, these must be fried gently, the lard being boiling hot when they are put in; when one side is done turn the other. Serve for breakfast.

BOILED BASS.

Put enough water in the pot for the fish to swim in, easily, Add half a cup of vinegar, a teaspoonful of salt, an onion, a dozen black peppers, and a blade of mace. Sew up the fish in a piece of clean net, fitted to its shape. Heat slowly for the first half hour, then boil eight minutes, at least, to the pound, quite fast. Unwrap, and pour over it a cup of drawn butter, based upon the liquor in which the fish was boiled, with the juice of half a lemon stirred into it. Garnish with sliced lemon.

FRIED BASS.

Clean, wipe dry, inside and out, dredge with flour, and season with salt. Fry in hot butter, beef-dripping, or sweet lard. Half-butter, half-lard is a good mixture for frying fish. The moment the fish are done to a good brown, take them from the fat and drain in a hot colander. Garnish with parsley.

TO FRY OR BROIL FISH PROPERLY.

After the fish is well cleansed, lay it on a folded towel and dry out all the water. When well wiped and dry, roll it in wheat flour, rolled crackers, grated stale bread, or Indian meal, whichever may be preferred; wheat flour will generally be liked.

Have a thick-bottomed frying-pan or spider, with plenty of sweet lard salted (a tablespoonful of salt to each pound of lard), for fresh fish which have not been previously salted; let it become boiling not, then lay the fish in and let it fry gently, until one side is a fine delicate brown, then turn the other; when both are done, take it up carefully and serve quickly, or keep it covered with a tin cover, and set the dish where it will keep hot.

BAKED BLACK BASS.

Eight good-sized onions chopped fine; half that quantity of bread-crumbs; butter size of hen's egg; plenty of pepper and salt, mix thoroughly with anchovy sauce until quite red. Stuff your fish with this compound and pour the rest over it, previously sprinkling it with a little red pepper. Shad, pickerel, and trout are good the same way. Tomatoes can be used instead of anchovies, and are more economical. If using them take pork in place of butter and chop fine.

BROILED MACKEREL.

Pepper and salt to taste, a small quantity of oil. Mackerel should never be washed when intended to be broiled, but merely wiped very clean and dry after taking out the gills and inside. Open the back, and put in a little pepper, salt, and oil; broil it over a clear fire, turn it over on both sides, and also on the back. When sufficiently cooked, the flesh can be detached from the bone, which will be in about ten minutes for a small mackerel. Chop a little parsley, work it up in the butter, with pepper and salt to taste, and a squeeze of lemon-juice, and put it in the back. Serve before the butter is quite melted.

Mode: Scale and clean the pike, and fasten the tail in its mouth by means of a skewer. Lay it in cold water, and when it boils, throw in the salt and vinegar. The time for boiling depends, of course, on the size of the fish; but a middling-sized pike will take about half an hour. Serve with Dutch or anchovy sauce, and plain melted butter.

Mackerel baked will be found palatable. Clean and trim the fish nicely, say four large ones, or half a dozen small ones, bone them and lay neatly in a baking dish, or a bed of potato chips well dusted with a mixture of pepper and salt; on the potatoes place a few pieces of butter. Dust the fish separately with pepper and salt, and sprinkle slightly with a diluted mixture of anchovy sauce and catsup. Bake three quarters of an hour.

SALT MACKEREL WITH CREAM SAUCE.

Soak over night in lukewarm water, changing this in the morning for ice-cold. Rub all the salt off, and wipe dry. Grease your gridiron with butter, and rub the fish on both sides with the same, melted. Then broil quickly over a clear fire, turning with a cake-turner so as not to break it. Lay upon a hot water dish, and cover until the sauce is ready.

Heat a small cup of milk to scalding. Stir into it a teaspoonful of corn-starch wet up with a little water. When this thickens, add two tablespoonfuls of butter, pepper, salt, and chopped parsley. Beat an egg light, pour the sauce gradually over it, put the mixture again over the fire, and stir one minute, not more. Pour upon the fish, and let all stand, covered, over the hot water in the chafing dish.

Put fresh boiling water under the dish before sending to table.

BOILED EELS.

Four small eels, sufficient water to cover them; a large bunch of parsley.

Choose small eels for boiling, put them on a stewpan with the parsley, and just sufficient water to cover them; simmer till tender. Take them out, pour a little parsley and butter over them, and serve some in a tureen.

FRICASSEED EELS.

After skinning, clearing, and cutting five or six eels in pieces of two inches in length, boil them in water nearly to cover them, until tender; then add a good-sized bit of butter, with a teaspoonful of wheat flour or rolled cracker, worked into it, and a little scalded and chopped parsley; add salt and pepper to taste, and a wine-glass of vinegar if liked; let them simmer for ten minutes and serve hot.

FRIED EELS.

After cleaning the eels well, cut them in pieces two inches long; wash them and wipe them dry; roll them in wheat flour or rolled cracker, and fry as directed for other fish, in hot lard or beef dripping, salted. They should be browned all over and thoroughly done,

Eels may be prepared in the same manner and broiled.

COLLARED EELS.

One large eel, pepper and salt to taste; two blades of mace, two cloves, a little allspice very finely pounded, six leaves of sage, and a small bunch of herbs minced very small.

Mode: Bone the eel and skin it; split it, and sprinkle it over with the ingredients, taking care that the spices are very finely pounded, and the herbs chopped very small. Roll it up and bind with a broad piece of tape, and boil it in water, mixed with a little salt and vinegar, till tender. It may either be served whole or cut in slices; and when cold, the eel should be kept in the liquor it was boiled in but with a little more vingar put to it.

FRIED TROUT.

They must, of course, be nicely cleaned and trimmed all round, but do not cut off their heads. Dredge them well with flour, and fry in a pan of boiling hot fat or oil. Turn them from side to side till they are nicely browned, and quite ready. Drain off all the fat before sending the fish to table; garnish them with a few sprigs of parsley, and provide plain melted butter. If preferred, the trout can be larded with beaten egg, and be then dipped in bread crumb. The frying will occupy from five to eight minutes, acccording to size. Very large trout can be cut in pieces.

TROUT IN JELLY (or other Fish).

This is a beautiful supper dish, and may be arranged as follows: Turn the fish into rings, with tail in mouth, prepare a seasoned water in which to boil the trout; the water should have a little vinegar and salt in it, and may be flavored with a shallot or clove or garlic. When the water is cold, place the trout in it, and boil them very gently, so as not to hash or break them. When done, lift out and drain. Baste with fish jelly, for which a recipe is given elsewhere, coat ofter coat, as each coat hardens. Arrange neatly, and serve.

BOILED TROUT.

Let the water be thoroughly a-boil before you put in the fish. See that it is salt, and that a dash of vinegar has been put in it. Remove all scum as it rises, and boil the fish till their eyes protrude. Lift them without breaking, drain off the liquor, and serve on a napkin if you like. To be eaten with a sauce according to taste, that is, if it can be made of either anchovies or shrimps.

BROILED TROUT.

Clean and split them open, season with a little salt and Cayenne; dip in whipped egg, dredge with flour and brander over a clear fire. Serve with sauce.

BAKED HADDOCK.

Choose a nice fish of about six pounds, which trim and scrape nicely, gutting it carefully, fill the vacuum with a stuffing of veal, chopped ham, and bread-crumbs, sew up with strong thread, and shape the fish round, putting its tail into its mouth, or, if two are required, lay them along the dish reversed—that is, tail to head; rub over with plenty of butter, or a batter of eggs and flour, and then sprinkle with bread-crumbs. Let the oven be pretty hot when put in. In about on hour the fish will be ready. Serve on the tin or aisset in which they have been baked, placing them on a larger dish for that purpose. Mussel sauce is a good accompaniment.

CURRIED HADDOCK.

Curried haddock is excellent. Fillet the fish and curry it in a pint of beef stock slightly diluted with water, and thickened with a tablespoonful of curry powder. Some cooks chop up an onion to place in the stew. It will take an hour to ready this fish. If preferred, fry the fish for a few minutes in clean lard oil before stewing it in the curry.

RIZZARED HADDOCK.

First, of course, procure your fish, clean them thoroughly, rub them well with salt, and let them lie for one night, after which hang them in the open air, to dry, in a shady place. In two days they will be ready for the gridiron. Before cooking them take out the backbone and skin them, if desired (I never do *skin* them), broil till ready, eat with a little fresh butter.

Haddocks can be boiled with advantage: all that is necessary is plenty of salt in the water, and not to serve them till they are well done. As a general rule, it may be ascertained when fish is sufficiently cooked by the readiness with which the flesh lifts from the bone. Stick a fork into the shoulder of a cod or haddock and try it. If living sufficiently near the sea, procure sea water in which to boil your haddocks.

BROILED WHITE-FISH—FRESH.

Wash and drain the fish; sprinkle with pepper and lay with the inside down upon the gridiron, and broil over fresh bright coals. When a nice brown, turn for a moment on the other side, then take up and spread with butter. This is a very nice way of broiling all kinds of fish, fresh or salted. A little smoke under the fish adds to its flavor. This may be made by putting two or three cobs under the gridiron.

BAKED WHITE-FISH.

Fill the fish with a stuffing of fine bread-crumbs and a little butter; sew up the fish; sprinkle with butter, pepper and salt. Dredge with flour and bake one hour, basting often. and serving with parsley sauce or egg sauce.

TO CHOOSE LOBSTERS.

These are chosen more by weight than size, the heaviest are best; a good, small-sized one will not unfrequently be found to weigh as heavily as one much larger. If fresh, a lobster will be lively and the claws have a strong motion when the eyes are pressed with the finger.

The male is best for boiling; the flesh is firmer, and the shell a brighter red; it may be readily distinguished from the female; the tail is narrower, and the two uppermost fins within the tail are stiff and hard. Those of the hen lobster are not so, and the tail is broader.

Hen lobsters are preferred for sauce or salad, on account of their coral. The head and small claws are never used.

BOILED LOBSTER.

These crustaceans are usually sold ready-boiled. When served, crack the claws and cut open the body, lay neatly on a napkin-covered dish, and garnish with a few sprigs of parsley. Lobster so served is usually eaten cold.

CURRIED LOBSTER.

Pick out the meat of two *red* lobsters from the shells into a shallow sauce-pan, in the bottom of which has been placed a thin slice of tasty ham, with a little Cayenne pepper and a teaspoonful of salt. Mix up half a cupful of white soup and half a cupful of cream and pour over the meat. Put it on the fire and let it simmer for about an hour, when you will add a dessert-spoonful of curry, and another of flour rubbed smooth in a little of the liquor taken out of the pot; in three minutes the curry will be ready to dish. Some add a dash of lemon to this curry (I don't), and the cream can be dispensed with if necessary. Put a rim of well-boiled rice round the dish if you like, or serve the rice separately.

LOBSTER CHOWDER.

Four or five pounds of lobster, chopped fine; take the green part and add to it four pounded crackers; stir this into one quart of boiling milk; then add the lobster, a piece of butter one-half the size of an egg, a little pepper and salt, and bring it to a boil.

CHOWDER.

Cut some slices of pork very thin, and fry them out dry in the dinner-pot; then put in a layer of fish cut in slices on the pork, then a layer of onions, and then potatoes, all cut in exceedingly thin slices; then fish, onions, potatoes again, till your materials are all in, putting some salt and pepper on each layer of onions; split some hard biscuits, dip them in water, and put them round the sides and over the top; put in water enough to come up in sight; stew for over half an hour, till the potatoes are done; add half a pint of milk, or a teacup of sweet cream, five minutes before you take it up.

TO FRY SMELTS.

Egg and bread-crumbs, a little flour, boiling lard. Smelts should be very fresh, and not washed more than is necessary to clean them. Dry them in a cloth, lightly flour, dip them in egg, and sprinkle over with very fine bread-crumbs, and put them into boiling lard. Fry of a nice pale brown, and be careful not to take off the light roughness of the crumbs, or their beauty will be spoiled. Dry them before the fire on a drainer, and serve with plain melted butter.

TO BAKE SMELTS.

Smelts, bread-crumbs, one-quarter pound of fresh butter, two blades of pounded mace; salt and Cayenne to taste.

Wash, and dry the fish thoroughly in a cloth, and arrange them nicely in a flat baking-dish. Cover them with fine bread-crumbs, and place little pieces of butter all over them. Season and bake for fifteen minutes. But before serving, add a squeeze of lemon-juice, and garnish with fried parsley and cut lemon.

RED HERRINGS or YARMOUTH BLOATERS.

The best way to cook these is to make incisions in the skin across the fish, because they do not then require to be so long on the fire, and will be far better than when cut open. The hard roe makes a nice relish by pounding it in a mortar, with a little anchovy, and spreading it on toast.

If very dry, soak in warm water, one hour before dressing.

POTTED FISH.

Take out the backbone of the fish; for one weighing two pounds take a tablespoonful of allspice and cloves mixed; these spices should be put into little bags of not too thick muslin; put sufficient salt directly upon each fish; then roll in a cloth, over which sprinkle a little Cayenne pepper; put alternate layers of fish, spice and sago in an earthen jar; cover with the best cider-vinegar; cover the jar closely with a plate and over this put a covering of dough, rolled out to twice the thickness of pie crust. Make the edges of paste, to adhere closely to the sides of the jar, so as to make it air-tight. Put the jar into a pot of cold water and let it boil from three to five hours, according to quantity. Ready when cold.

OYSTERS ON THE SHELL.

Wash the shells and put them on hot coals or upon the top of a hot stove, or bake them in a hot oven; open the shells with an oyster-knife, taking care to lose none of the liquor, and serve quickly on hot plates, with toast. Oysters may be steamed in the shells, and are excellent eaten in the same manner.

OYSTERS STEWED WITH MILK.

Take a pint of fine oysters, put them with their own liquor, and a gill of milk into a stew pan, and if liked, a blade of mace, set it over the fire, take off any scum which may rise; when they are plump and white turn them into a deep plate; add a bit of butter, and pepper to taste. Serve crackers and dressed celery with them. Oysters may be stewed in their own liquor without milk.

OYSTERS FRIED IN BATTER.

Half pint of oysters, two eggs, half pint of milk, sufficient flour to make the batter; pepper and salt to taste; when liked, a little nutmeg; hot lard. Scald the oysters in their own liquor, beard them, and lay them on a cloth, to drain thoroughly. Break the eggs into a basin, mix the flour with them, add the milk gradually, with nutmeg and seasoning, and put the oysters in a batter. Make some lard hot in a deep frying-pan, put in the oysters, one at a time; when done, take them up with a sharp-pointed skewer, and dish them on a napkin. Fried oysters are frequently used for garnishing boiled fish, and then a few bread-crumbs should be added to the flour.

SCALLOPED OYSTERS.

Two tablespoonfuls of white stock, two tablesponfuls of cream; pepper and salt to taste; bread-crumbs, oiled butter. Scald the oysters in their own liquor, take them out, beard them, and strain the liquor free from grit. Put one ounce of butter into a stewpan; when melted, dredge in sufficient flour to dry it up; add the stock, cream and strained liquor, and give one boil. Put in the oysters and seasoning; let them gradually heat through, but not boil. Have ready the scallop-shells buttered; lay in the oysters, and as much of the liquid as they will hold; cover them over with bread-crumbs, over which drop a little oiled butter. Brown them in the oven, or before the fire, and serve quickly, and very hot.

FRIED OYSTERS.

Take large oysters from their own liquor on to a thickly folded napkin to dry them off; then make a tablespoonful of lard or beef fat hot, in a thick bottomed frying-pan, add to it half a saltspoonful of salt; dip each oyster in wheat flour, or cracker rolled fine, until it will take up no more, then lay them in the pan, hold it over a gentle fire until one side is a delicate brown; turn the other by sliding a fork under it; five minutes will fry them after they are in the pan. Oysters may be fried in butter but it is not so good, lard and butter half and half is very nice for frying. Some persons like a very little of the oyster liquid poured in the pan after the oysters are done; let it boil up, then put it in the dish with the oysters; when wanted for breakfast, this should be done.

Oysters to be fried, after drying as directed, may be dipped into beaten egg first, then into rolled cracker.

OYSTER PATTIES.

Make some rich puff paste and bake it in very small tin patty pans; when cool, turn them out upon a large dish; stew some large fresh oysters with a few cloves, a little mace and nutmeg; then add the yolk of one egg, boiled hard and grated; add a little butter, and as much of the oyster liquid as will cover them. When they have stewed a little while, take them out of the pan and set them to cool.

When quite cold, lay two or three oysters in each shell of puff paste.

BROILED OYSTERS.

Drain the oysters well and dry them with a napkin. Have ready a griddle hot and well buttered; season the oysters; lay them to griddle and brown them on both sides. Serve them on a hot plate with plenty of butter.

CLAM FRITTERS.

Take fifty small or twenty-five large sand clams from their shells; if large, cut each in two, lay them on a thickly folded napkin; put a pint bowl of wheat flour into a basin, add to it two well-beaten eggs, half a pint of sweet milk, and nearly as much of their own liquor; beat the batter until it is smooth and perfectly free from lumps; then stir in the clams. Put plenty of lard or beef fat into a thick-bottomed frying pan, let it become boiling hot; put in the batter by the spoonful; let them fry gently; when one side is a delicate brown, turn the other.

SOFT-SHELLED CLAMS.

These are very fine if properly prepared. They are good only during cold weather and must be perfectly fresh.

Soft-shelled clams may be boiled from the shells, and served with butter, pepper and salt over.

TO BOIL SOFT-SHELL CLAMS.

Wash the shells clean, and put the clams, the edges downwards, in a kettle; then pour about a quart of boiling water over them; cover the pot and set it over a brisk fire for three quarters of an hour; pouring boiling water on them causes the shells to open quickly and let out out the sand which may be in them.

Take them up when done, take off the black skin which covers the hard part, trim them clean, and put them into a stew-pan; put to them some of the liquor in which they were boiled; put to it a good bit of butter and pepper and salt to taste; make them hot; serve with cold butter and rolls.

CLAM CHOWDER.

Butter a deep tin basin, strew it thickly with grated bread-crumbs, or soaked cracker; sprinkle some pepper over and bits of butter the size of a hickory nut, and, if liked, some finely chopped parsley; then put a double layer of clams, season with pepper, put bits of butter over, then another layer of soaked cracker; after that clams and bits of butter; sprinkle pepper over; add a cup of milk or water, and lastly a layer of soaked crackers. Turn a plate over the basin, and bake in a hot oven for three-quarters of an hour; use half a pound of soda biscuit, and quarter of a pound of butter with fifty clams.

MEATS.

ROAST BEEF.

Prepare for the oven by dredging lightly with flour, and seasoning with salt and pepper; place in the oven, and baste frequently while roasting. Allow a quarter of an hour for a pound of meat, if you like it rare; longer if you like it well done. Serve with a sauce made from the drippings in the pan, to which has been added a tablespoon of Harvey or Worcestershire sauce, and a tablespoon of tomato catsup.

ROUND OF BEEF BOILED.

See that it is not too large, and that it is tightly bound all round. About twelve pounds or fourteen pounds form a convenient size, and a joint of that weight will require from three hours to three hours and a quarter to boil. Put on with cold water—as the liquor is valuable for making pea-soup—and let it come slowly to the boil. Boil carefully but not rapidly, and skim frequently; as a rule, keep the lid of the pot well fixed. The meat may be all the better if taken out once or twice in the process of cooking. Carrots and turnips may be boiled to serve with the round; they will, of course, cook in about a third of the time necessary to boil the beef.

BEEF SALTED, OR CORNED, RED,

To Keep for Years.

Cut up a quarter of beef. For each hundredweight take half a peck of coarse salt, quarter of a pound of saltpetre,

Veal Cutlets
Leg of Pork
Leg of Lamb
Roast Pig
Fillet of Veal
Boiled Beef
Sirloin of Beef
Cutlets & Peas
Calf's Head
Calf's Heart
Sausages
Kidneys
Haunch of Mutton
Fore Quarter of Lamb
Saddle of Mutton

the same weight of saleratus, and a quart of molasses, or two pounds of coarse brown sugar. Mace, cloves and allspice may be added for spiced beef.

Strew some of the salt in the bottom of a pickle-tub or barrel; then put in a layer of meat, strew this with salt, then add another layer of meat, and salt and meat alternately, until all is used. Let it remain one night. Dissolve the saleratus and saltpetre in a little warm water, and put it to the molasses or sugar; then put it over the meat, add water enough to cover the meat, lay a board on it to keep it under the brine. The meat is fit for use after ten days. This receipt is for winter beef. Rather more salt may be used in warm weather.

Towards spring take the brine from the meat, make it boiling hot, skim it clear, and when it is cooled, return it to the meat.

Beef tongues and smoking pieces are fine pickled in this brine. Beef liver put in this brine for ten days and then wiped dry and smoked, is very fine. Cut it in slices, and fry or broil it. The brisket of beef, after being corned, may be smoked, and is very fine for boiling.

Lean pieces of beef, cut properly from the hind quarter, are the proper pieces for being smoked. There may be some fine pieces cut from the fore-quarter.

After the beef has been in brine ten days or more wipe it dry, and hang it in a chimney where wood is burnt, or make a smothered fire of sawdust or chips, and keep it smoking for ten days; then rub fine black pepper over every part, to keep the flies from it, and hang it in a dry, dark, cool place. After a week it is fit for use. A strong, coarse brown paper, folded around beef, and fastened with paste, keeps it nicely.

Tongues are smoked in the same manner. Hang them by a string put through the root end. Spiced brine for smoked beef or tongues will be generally liked.

For convenience make a pickle as mentioned for beef, keep it in the cellar, ready for pickling beef at any time. Beef may remain in three or four or more days.

TO BOIL CORNED BEEF.

Put the beef in water enough to cover it, and let it heat slowly, and boil slowly, and be careful to take off the grease. Many think it much improved by boiling potatoes, turnips, and cabbages with it. In this case the vegetables must be peeled and *all* the grease carefully skimmed as fast as it rises. Allow about twenty minutes of boiling for each pound of meat.

A NICE WAY TO SERVE COLD BEEF.

Cut cold roast beef in slices, put gravy enough to cover them, and a wineglass of catsup or wine, or a lemon sliced thin; if you have not gravy, put hot water and a good bit of butter, with a teaspoonful or more of browned flour; put it in a closely covered stew-pan, and let it simmer gently for half an hour. If you choose, when the meat is down, cut a leek in thin slices, and chop a bunch of parsley small, and add it; serve boiled or mashed potatoes with it. This is equal to beef-a-la-mode.

Or, cold beef may be served cut in neat slices, garnished with sprigs of parsley, and made mustard, and tomato catsup in the castor; serve mashed, if not new potatoes, with it, and ripe fruit, or pie, or both, for dessert, for a small family dinner.

SPICED BEEF.

Four pounds of round of beef chopped fine; take from it all fat; add to it three dozen small crackers rolled fine, four eggs, one cup of milk, one tablespoon ground mace, two tablespoons of black pepper, one tablespoon melted butter; mix well and put in any tin pan that it will just fill, packing it well; baste with butter and water, and bake two hours in a slow oven.

BROILED BEEFSTEAK.

Lay a thick tender steak upon a gridiron over hot coals, having greased the bars with butter before the steak has been put upon it (a steel gridiron with slender bars is to be preferred, the broad flat iron bars of gridirons commonly used fry and scorch the meat, imparting a disagreeable flavor). When done on one side, have ready your platter warmed, with a little butter on it; lay the steak upon the platter with the cooked side down, that the juices which have gathered may run on the platter, but do not press the meat; then lay your beefsteak again upon the gridiron quickly and cook the other side. When done to your liking, put again on the platter, spread lightly with butter, place where it will keep warm for a few moments, but not to let the butter become oily (over boiling steam is best); and then serve on hot plates. Beefsteak should never be seasoned with salt and pepper while cooking. If your meat is tough, pound *well* with a steak mallet on both sides.

FRIED BEEFSTEAKS.

Cut some of the fat from the steak, and put it in a frying pan and set it over the fire; if the steaks are not very tender, beat them with a rolling pin, and when the fat is boiling hot, put the steak evenly in, cover the pan and let it fry briskly until one side is done, sprinkle a little pepper and salt over, and turn the other; let it be rare or well done as may be liked; take the steak on a hot dish, add a wineglass or less of boiling water or catsup to the gravy; let it boil up once, and pour it in the dish with the steak.

BEEFSTEAK PIE.

Take some fine tender steaks, beat them a little, season with a saltspoonful of pepper and a teaspoonful of salt to a two-pound steak; put bits of butter, the size of a hickory nut, over the whole surface, dredge a teaspoonful of flour over, then roll it up and cut it in pieces two inches long; put a rich pie paste around the sides and bottom of a tin basin; put in the pieces of steak, nearly fill the basin with water, add a piece of butter the size of a large egg, cut small, dredge in a teaspoonful of flour, add a little pepper and salt, lay skewers across the basin, roll a top crust to half an inch thickness, cut a slit in the center; dip your fingers in flour and neatly pinch the top and side crust together all around the edge. Bake one hour in a quick oven.

BOILED LEG OF MUTTON.

Mutton, water, salt. A leg of mutton for boiling should not hang too long, as it will not look a good color when dressed. Cut off the shank-bone, trim the knuckle and wash and wipe it very clean; plunge it into sufficient boiling water to cover it; let it boil up, then draw the saucepan to the side of the fire, where it should remain till the finger can be borne in the water. Then place it sufficiently near the fire, that the water may gently simmer, and be very careful that it does not boil fast, or the meat will be hard. Skim well, add a little salt, and in about two and one quarter hours after the water begins to simmer, a moderate-sized leg of mutton will be done. Serve with carrots and mashed turnips, which may be boiled with the meat, and send caper sauce to table with it in a tureen.

ROAST LOIN OF MUTTON.

Loin of mutton, a little salt. Cut and trim off the superfluous fat, and see that the butcher joints the meat properly, as thereby much annoyance is saved to the carver, when it comes to table. Have ready a nice clear fire (it need not be a very wide, large one), put down the meat, dredge with flour, and baste well until it is done.

BROILED MUTTON CHOPS.

Loin of mutton, pepper and salt, a small piece of butter. Cut the chops from a well-hung, tender loin of mutton, remove a portion of the fat, and trim them into a nice shape; slightly beat and level them; place the gridiron over a bright, clear fire, rub the bars with a little fat, and lay on the chops. While broiling, frequently turn them, and in about eight minutes they will be done. Season with pepper and salt, dish them on a very hot dish, rub a small piece of butter on each chop, and serve very hot and expeditiously.

MUTTON CHOP FRIED.

Cut some fine mutton chops without much fat, rub over both sides with a mixture of salt and pepper, dip them in wheat flour or rolled crackers, and fry in hot lard or beef drippings; when both sides are a fine brown, take them on a hot dish, put a wineglass of hot water in the pan, let it become hot, stir in a teaspoonful of browned flour, let it boil up at once, and serve in the pan with the meat.

ROAST FORE-QUARTER OF LAMB.

Lamb, a little salt. To obtain the flavor of lamb in perfection it should not be long kept; time to cool is all that is required; and though the meat may be somewhat thready, the juices and flavor will be infinitely superior to that of lamb that has been killed two or three days. Make up the fire in good time, that it may be clear and brisk when the joint is put down. Place it at sufficient distance to prevent the fat from burning, and baste it constantly till the moment of serving. Lamb should be very thoroughly done without being dried up, and not the slightest appearance of red gravy should be visible, as in roast mutton; this rule is applicable to all young white meats. Serve with a little gravy made in the dripping-pan, the same as for other roasts, and send to table with a tureen of mint sauce.

LAMBS' SWEETBREADS.

Two or three sweetbreads, one-half pint of veal stock, white pepper and salt to taste, a small bunch of green onions, one blade of pounded mace, thickening of butter and flour, two eggs, nearly one-half pint of cream, one teaspoonful of minced parsley, a very little grated nutmeg.

Mode: Soak the sweetbreads in lukewarm water, and put them into a saucepan with sufficient boiling water to cover them, and let them simmer for ten minutes; then take them out and put them into cold water. Now lard them, lay them in a stewpan, add the stock, seasoning, onions, mace, and a thickening of butter and flour, and stew gently for one-quarter of an hour or twenty minutes. Beat up the egg with the cream, to which add the minced parsley and very little grated nutmeg. Put this to the other ingredients; stir it well till quite hot, but do not let it boil after the cream is added, or it will curdle. Have ready some asparagus-tops, boiled; add these to the sweetbreads, and serve.

Lamb-Steak dipped in egg, and then in biscuit or bread-crumbs, and fried until it is brown, helps to make variety for the breakfast table. With baked sweet potatoes, good coffee, and buttered toast or corn muffins, one may begin the day with courage.

TO ROAST VEAL.

Rinse the meat in cold water; if any part is bloody, wash it off; make a mixture of pepper and salt, allowing a large teaspoonful of salt and a saltspoonful of pepper for each pound of meat; wipe the meat dry; then rub the seasoning into every part, shape it neatly, and fasten it with skewers, and put it on a spit, or set it on a trivet or muffin rings, in a pan; stick bits of butter over the whole upper surface; dredge a little flour over, put a pint of water in the pan to baste with, and roast it before the fire in a Dutch oven or reflector, or put it into a hot oven; baste it occasionally, turn it if necessary that every part may be done; if the water wastes add more, that the gravy may not burn; allow fifteen minutes for each pound of meat; a piece weighing four or five pounds will then require one hour, or an hour and a quarter.

VEAL CHOPS.

Cut veal chops about an inch thick; beat them flat with a rolling-pin, put them in a pan, pour boiling water over them, and set them over the fire for five minutes; then take them up and wipe them dry; mix a tablespoonful of salt and a teaspoonful of pepper for each pound of meat; rub each chop over with this, then dip them, first into beaten egg, then into rolled crackers as much as they will take up; then finish by frying in hot lard or beef drippings; or broil them. For the broil have some sweet butter on a steak dish; broil the chops until well done, over a bright clear fire of coals; (let them do gently that they may be well done,) then take them on to the butter, turn them carefully once or twice in it, and serve. Or dip the chops into a batter, made of one egg beaten with half a teacup of milk and as much wheat flour as may be necessary. Or simply dip the chops without parboiling into wheat flour; make some lard or beef fat hot in a frying-pan; lay the chops in, and when one side is a fine delicate brown, turn the other. When all are done, take them up, put a very little hot water into the pan, then put it in the dish with the chops.

Or make a flour gravy thus: After frying them as last directed, add a tablespoonful more of fat to that in the pan, let it become boiling hot; make a thin batter, of a small tablespoonful of wheat flour and cold water; add a little more salt and pepper to the gravy, then gradually stir in the batter; stir it until it is cooked and a nice brown; then put it over the meat, or in the dish with it; if it is thicker than is liked, add a little boiling water.

VEAL CUTLETS.

Two or three pounds of veal cutlets, egg and bread-crumbs, two tablespoonfuls of minced savory herbs, salt and pepper to taste, a little grated nutmeg.

Cut the cutlets about three-quarters of an inch in thickness, flatten them, and brush them over with the yolk of an egg; dip them into bread-crumbs and minced herbs, season with pepper and salt and grated nutmeg, and fold each cutlet in a piece of buttered paper. Broil them, and send them to table with melted butter or a good gravy.

STUFFED FILLET OF VEAL WITH BACON.

Take out the bone from the meat, and pin into a round with skewers. Bind securely with soft tapes. Fill the cavity left by the bone with a force-meat of crumbs, chopped pork, thyme, and parsley, seasoned with pepper, salt, nutmeg and a pinch of lemon-peel. Cover the top of the fillet with thin slices of cold *cooked*, fat bacon or salt pork, tying them in place with twines crossing the meat in all directions. Put into a pot with two cups of boiling water, and cook slowly and steadily two hours. Then take from the pot and put into a dripping-pan. Undo the strings and tapes. Brush the meat all over with raw egg, sift rolled cracker thickly over it, and set in the oven for half an hour, basting often with gravy from the pot. When it is well browned, lay upon a hot dish with the pork about it. Strain and thicken the gravy, and serve in a boat.

If your fillet be large, cook twice as long in the pot. The time given above is for one weighing five pounds.

VEAL CAKE (a Convenient Dish for a Picnic).

A few slices of cold roast veal, a few slices of cold ham, two hard boiled eggs, two tablespoonfuls of minced parsley, a little pepper, good gravy, or stock No. 109.

Cut off all the brown outside from the veal, and cut the eggs into slices. Procure a pretty mold; lay veal, ham, eggs, and parsley in layers, with a little pepper between each, and when the mold is full, get some *strong* stock, and fill up the shape. Bake for one half-hour, and when cold, turn it out.

VEAL PIE.

Cut a breast of veal small, and put it in a stewpan, with hot water to cover it; add to it a tablespoonful of salt, and set it over the fire; take off the scum as it rises; when the meat is tender, turn it into a dish to cool; take out all the small bones, butter a tin or earthen basin or pudding-pan, line it with a pie paste, lay some of the parboiled meat in to half fill it; put bits of butter the size of a hickory nut all over the meat; shake pepper over, dredge wheat flour over until it looks white; then fill it nearly to the top with some of the water in which the meat was boiled; roll a cover for the top of the crust, puff paste it, giving it two or three turns, and roll it to nearly half an inch thickness; cut a slit in the center, and make several small incisions on either side of it; lay some skewers across the pie, put the crust on, trim the edges neatly with a knife; bake one hour in a quick oven. A breast of veal will make two two-quart basin pies; half a pound of nice corned pork, cut in thin slices and parboiled with the meat, will make it very nice, and very little, if any butter, will be required for the pie; when pork is used, no other salt will be necessary.

BOILED CALF HEAD (without the skin).

Calf's head, water, a little salt, four tablespoonfuls of melted butter, one tablespoonful of minced parsley, pepper and salt to taste, one tablespoonful of lemon-juice.

After the head has been thoroughly cleaned, and the brains removed, soak it in warm water to blanch it. Lay the brains also into warm water to soak, and let them remain for about an hour. Put the head into a stewpan, with sufficient cold water to cover it, and when it boils, add a little salt; take off every particle of scum as it rises, and boil the head until perfectly tender. Boil the brains, chop them, and mix with them melted butter, minced parsley, pepper, salt, and lemon-juice in the above proportion. Take up the head, skin the tongue, and put it on a small dish with the brains round it. Have ready some parsley and butter, smother the head with it, and the remainder send to table in a tureen. Bacon, ham, pickled pork, or a pig's cheek are indispensable with calf's head. The brains are sometimes chopped with hard-boiled eggs.

CALF'S HEAD CHEESE.

Boil a calf's head in water enough to cover it, until the meat leaves the bones, then take it with a skimmer into a wooden bowl or tray; take from it every particle of bone; chop it small; season with pepper and salt; a heaping tablespoonful of salt, and a teaspoonful of pepper will be sufficient; if liked, add a tablespoonful of finely chopped sweet herbs; lay a cloth in a colander, put the minced meat into it, then fold the cloth closely over it, lay a plate over, and on it a gentle weight. When cold it may be sliced thin for supper or sandwiches. Spread each slice with made mustard.

BOILED CALF'S FEET AND PARSLEY BUTTER.

Two calf's feet, two slices of bacon, two ounces of butter, two tablespoonfuls of lemon-juice, salt and whole pepper to taste, one onion, a bunch of savory herbs, four cloves, one blade of mace, water, parsley and butter.

Procure two white calf's feet; bone them as far as the first joint, and put them into warm water to soak for two hours. Then put the bacon, butter, lemon-juice, onion, herbs, spices, and seasoning into a stewpan; lay in the feet, and pour in just sufficient water to cover the whole. Stew gently for about three hours; take out the feet, dish them, and cover with parsley and butter.

The liquor they were boiled in should be strained and put by in a clean basin for use; it will be found very good as an addition to gravies, etc., etc.

CALF'S LIVER AND BACON.

Two or three pounds of liver, bacon, pepper and salt to taste, a small piece of butter, flour, two tablespoonfuls of lemon-juice, one-quarter pint of water.

Cut the liver in thin slices, and cut as many slices of bacon as there are of liver; fry the bacon first, then put that on a hot dish before the fire. Fry the liver in the fat which comes from the bacon, after seasoning it with pepper and salt, and dredging over it a very little flour. Turn the liver occasionally to prevent its burning, and when done, lay it round the dish with a piece of bacon between each. Pour away the bacon fat, put in a small piece of butter, dredge in a little flour, add the lemon-juice and water, give one boil, and pour it in the *middle* of the dish.

SWEETBREAD.

Three sweetbreads, egg, and bread-crumbs, oiled butter, three slices of toast, brown gravy.

Choose large white sweetbreads; put them into warm water to draw out the blood, and to improve the color; let them remain for rather more than one hour; then put them into boiling water, and allow them to simmer for about ten minutes, which renders them firm. Take them up, drain them, brush over the egg, sprinkle with bread-crumbs; dip them in egg again, and then into more bread-crumbs. Drop on them a little oiled butter, and put the sweetbreads into a moderately heated oven, and let them bake for nearly three-quarters of an hour. Make three pieces of toast; place the sweetbreads on the toast, and pour round, but not over them, a good brown gravy.

EGGED VEAL HASH.

Chop fine remnants of coal roast veal. Moisten with the gravy or water. When hot, break into it three or four eggs, according to the quantity of veal. When the eggs are cooked, stir into it a spoonful of butter, and serve quickly. If to your taste, shake in a little parsley. Should you lack quantity, half a cup of fine stale bread-crumbs are no disadvantage.

ROAST BEEF, WITH YORKSHIRE PUDDING.

Have your meat ready for roasting on Saturday, always. Roast upon a grating of several clean sticks (not pine) laid over the dripping-pan. Dash a cup of boiling water over the beef when it goes into the oven; baste often, and see that the fat does not scorch. About three-quarters of an hour before it is done, mix the pudding.

YORKSHIRE PUDDING.

One pint of milk, four eggs, whites and yolks beaten separately; two cups of flour—prepared flour is best; one teaspoonful of salt.

Use less flour if the batter grows too stiff. Mix quickly; pour off the fat from the top of the gravy in the dripping pan, leaving just enough to prevent the pudding from sticking to the bottom. Pour in the batter and continue to roast the beef, letting the dripping fall upon the pudding below. The oven should be brisk by this time. Baste the meat with the gravy you have taken out to make room for the batter. In serving, cut the pudding into squares and lay about the meat in the dish. It is very delicious.

BEEF HEART BAKED OR ROASTED.

Cut a beef heart in two, take out the strings from the inside; wash it with warm water, rub the inside with pepper and salt, and fill it with a stuffing made of bread and butter moistened with water, and seasoned with pepper and salt, and, if liked, a sprig of thyme made fine; put it together and tie a string around it, rub the outside with pepper and salt; stick bits of butter on, then dredge flour over and set it on a trivet, or muffin rings, in a dripping-pan; put a pint of water in to baste with, then roast it before a hot fire, or in a hot oven; turn it around and baste frequently. One hour will roast or bake it; when done, take it up, cut a lemon in thick slices, and put it in the pan with a bit of butter, dredged in a teaspoonful of flour; let it brown; add a small teacup of boiling water, stir it smooth, and serve in a gravy tureen.

BEEF KIDNEY.

Cut the kidney into thin slices, flour them, and fry of a nice brown. When done, make a gravy in the pan by pouring away the fat, putting in a small piece of butter, one-quarter pint of boiling water, pepper and salt, and a tablespoonful of mushroom catsup. Let the gravy just boil up, pour over the kidney, and serve.

POTTED BEEF.

Two pounds of lean beef, one tablespoonful of water, one-quarter pound of butter, a seasoning to taste of salt, Cayenne, pounded mace, and black pepper. Procure a nice piece of lean beef, as free as possible from gristle, skin, etc., and put it into a jar (if at hand, one with a lid) with one teaspoonful of water. Cover it *closely*, and put the jar into a saucepan of boiling water, letting the water come within two inches of the top of the jar. Boil gently for three and a half hours, then take the beef, chop it very small with a chopping-knife, and pound it thoroughly in a mortar. Mix with it by degrees, all, or a portion of the gravy that will have run from it, and a little clarified butter: add the seasoning, put it in small pots for use, and cover with a little butter just warmed and poured over. If much gravy is added to it, it will keep but a short time; on the contrary, if a large proportion of butter is used, it may be preserved for some time.

BOILED TONGUE.

One tongue, a bunch of savory herbs, water. In choosing a tongue, ascertain how long it has been dried or pickled, and select one with a smooth skin, which denotes its being young and tender. If a dried one, and rather hard, soak it at least for twelve hours previous to cooking it; if, however, it is fresh from the pickle, two or three hours will be sufficient for it to remain in soak. Put the tongue into a stewpan with plenty of cold water and a bunch of savory herbs; let it gradually come to a boil, skim well, and simmer very gently until tender. Peel off the skin, garnish with tufts of cauliflowers or Brussels sprouts, and serve. Boiled tongue is frequently sent to table with boiled poultry, instead of ham, and is, by many persons, preferred. If to serve cold, peel it, fasten it down to a piece of board by sticking a fork through the root, and another through the top, to straighten it. When cold, glaze it, and put a paper ruche round the root, and garnish with tufts of parsley.

FRICASSEED TRIPE.

Cut a pound of tripe in narrow strips, put a small cup of water or milk to it, add a bit of butter the size of an egg, dredge in a large teaspoonful of flour, or work it with the butter; season with pepper and salt, let it simmer gently for half an hour, serve hot. A bunch of parsley cut small and put with it is an improvement.

BROILED TRIPE.

Prepare tripe as for frying; lay it on a gridiron over a clear fire of coals, let it broil gently; when one side is a fine brown, turn the other side (it must be nearly done through before turning); take it up on a hot dish, butter it, and if liked, add a little catsup or vinegar to the gravy.

ROAST RABBIT.

Empty, skin, and thoroughly wash the rabbit; wipe it dry, line the inside with sausage-meat and force-meat (the latter of bread-crumbs, well-seasoned, and worked up). Sew the stuffing inside, skewer back the head between the shoulders, cut off the fore joints of the shoulders and legs, bring them close to the body, and secure them by means of a skewer. Wrap the rabbit in buttered paper, keep it well basted, and a few minutes before it is done remove the paper, flour and froth it, and let it acquire a nice brown color. It should be done in three-quarters of an hour. Take out the skewers, and serve with brown gravy and red-currant jelly. To bake the rabbit, proceed in the same manner as above; in a good oven it will take about the same time as roasting. Most cooks garnish the rabbit with slices of lemon and serve up with currant jelly. Sometimes the head is cut off before sending to the table; but this is a matter of individual taste.

STEWED RABBIT, Larded.

One rabbit, a few strips of bacon, rather more than one pint of good broth or stock, a bunch of savory herbs, salt and pepper to taste, thickening of butter and flour, one glass of sherry. Well wash the rabbit, cut it into quarters, lard them with slips of bacon, and fry them; then put them into a stewpan with the broth, herbs, and a seasoning of pepper and salt; simmer gently until the rabbit is tender, then strain the gravy, thicken it with butter and flour, add the sherry, give one boil, pour it over the rabbit, and serve. Garnish with slices of cut lemon.

FRICASSEED RABBITS.

The best way of cooking rabbits is to fricassee them. Cut them up, or disjoint them. Put them into a stewpan; season them with Cayenne pepper, salt and some chopped parsley. Pour in a pint of warm water (or of veal broth, if you have it) and stew it over a slow fire till the rabbits are quite tender; adding (when they are about half done) some bits of butter rolled in flour. Just before you take it from the fire, enrich the gravy with a gill or more of thick cream with some nutmeg grated into it. Stir the gravy well, but take care not to let it boil after the cream is in, lest it curdle. Put the pieces of rabbit on a hot dish, and pour the gravy over them.

A PRETTY DISH OF VENISON.

Cut a breast of venison in steaks, make quarter of a pound of butter hot, in a pan, rub the steaks over with a mixture of a little salt and pepper, dip them in wheat flour, or rolled crackers, and fry a rich brown; when both sides are done, take them up on a dish, and put a tin cover over; dredge a heaping teaspoonful of flour into the butter in the pan, stir it with a spoon until it is brown, without burning, put to it a small teacup of boiling water, with a tablespoonful of currant jelly dissolved into it, stir it for a few minutes, then strain it over the meat and serve. A glass of wine, with a tablespoonful of white sugar dissolved in it, may be used for the gravy, instead of the jelly and water. Venison may be boiled, and served with boiled vegetables, pickled beets, etc., and sauce.

TO BOIL VENISON STEAKS.

Let the gridiron become hot, rub the bars with a bit of suet, then lay on the steaks, having dipped them in rolled crackers or wheat flour, and set it over a bright, clear, but not fierce fire of coals; when one side is done, take the steak carefully over the steak dish, and hold it so that the blood may fall into the dish, then turn them on the gridiron, let it broil nicely; set a steak dish where it will become hot, put on a bit of butter the size of an egg for each pound of venison, put to it a saltspoon of salt, and the same of black pepper, put to it a tablespoonful of currant jelly, made liquid with a tablespoonful of hot water or wine, lay the steaks on, turn them once or twice in the gravy, and serve hot. Or they may be simply broiled, and served with butter, pepper, and salt; or having broiled one side, and turned the steaks, lay thin slices of lemon over, and serve in the dish with the steaks.

BEEFSTEAK AND KIDNEY PUDDING.

Two pounds of rump-steak, two kidneys, seasoning to taste of salt and black pepper, suet crust made with milk (*see* PASTRY), in the proportion of six ounces of suet to each one pound of flour.

Mode: Procure some tender rump-steak (that which has been hung a little time), and divide it into pieces about an inch square, and cut each kidney into eight pieces. Line the dish (of which we have given an engraving) with crust made with suet and flour in the above proportion, leaving a small piece of crust to overlap the edge. Then cover the bottom with a portion of the steak and a few pieces of kidney; season with salt and pepper (some add a little flour to thicken the gravy, but it is not necessary), and then add another layer of steak kidney, and seasoning. Proceed in this manner till the dish is full, when pour in sufficient water to come within two inches of the top of the basin. Moisten the edges of the crust, cover the pudding over, press the two crusts together, that the gravy may not escape, and turn up the overhanging paste. Wring out a cloth in hot water, flour it, and tie up the pudding; put it into boiling water, and let it boil for at least four hours. If the water diminishes, always replenish with some, hot in a jug, as the pudding should be kept covered all the time, and not allowed to stop boiling. When the cloth is removed, cut a round piece in the top of the crust, to prevent the pudding bursting, and send it to table in the basin, either in an ornamental dish, or with a napkin pinned round it. Serve quickly.

BREAKFAST DISHES.

HASHED COLD MEAT.

Take your bones, and stew them in a little water with an onion, some salt and pepper, and, if you like, a little savory herbs; when the goodness is all out of the bones, and it tastes nice, thicken the gravy with a teaspoonful of corn starch, and if it is not very strong put in a bit of butter, then place your stewpan on the hot hearth, and put in your slices of meat. Warm but not boil. Serve with toasted bread.

POTATO AND BEEF HASH.

Mince some cold beef, a little fat with the lean, put to it as much cold boiled potatoes chopped as you like, (the quantity as of meat or twice as much), season with pepper and salt; add as much gravy or hot water as will make it moist, then put in a stewpan over a gentle fire; dredge in a small quantity of wheat flour; stir it about with a spoon, cover the stewpan, and let it simmer for half an hour—take care that it does not burn. Dish it with or without a slice of toast under it, for breakfast. This hash may be made without potatoes, if water is used instead of gravy, a bit of butter may be added, more or less, according to the proportion of fat with the lean meat.

DRIED BEEF.

The most common way of serving dried or smoked beef is to shave it into thin slices or chips, raw; but a more savory relish may be made of it with little trouble. Put the slices of uncooked beef into a frying pan with just enough boiling water to cover them; set them over the fire for ten minutes, drain off all the water, and with a knife and fork cut the meat into small bits. Return to the pan, which should be hot, with a tablespoonful of butter and a little pepper. Have ready some well-beaten eggs, allowing four to a half pound of beef; stir them into the pan with the minced meat and toss and stir the mixture for about two minutes. Send to table in a covered dish.

CHICKEN CUTLETS.

Season pieces of cold chicken or turkey with salt and pepper. Dip in melted butter; let this cool on the meat, and dip in beaten egg and in fine bread-crumbs. Fry in butter till a delicate brown. Serve on slices of hot toast, with either a white or curry sauce poured around. Pieces of cold veal make a nice dish, if prepared in this manner.

BEEF PATTIES.

Chop fine some cold beef; beat two eggs and mix with the meat and add a little milk, melted butter, and salt and pepper. Make into rolls and fry.

JELLIED VEAL.

Boil the veal tender, pick it up fine, put in a mold, add the water it was boiled in, and set it in a cold place; season with salt and pepper to taste; a layer of hard-boiled eggs improves it.

RICE AND MEAT CROQUETTES.

One cupful of boiled rice, one cupful of finely-chopped cooked meat—any kind; one teaspoonful of salt, a little pepper, two tablespoonfuls of butter, half a cupful of milk, one egg. Put the milk on to boil, and add the meat, rice and seasoning. When this boils, add the egg, well beaten; stir one minute. After cooling, shape, dip in egg and crumbs, and fry as before directed.

AMERICAN TOAST.

To one egg thoroughly beaten, put one cup of sweet milk and a little salt. Slice light bread and dip into the mixture, allowing each slice to absorb some of the milk; then brown on a hot buttered griddle; spread with butter, and serve hot.

MEAT AND POTATOES.

Mince beef or mutton, small, with onions, pepper and salt; add a little gravy, put into scalloped shells or small cups, making them three parts full, and fill them up with potatoes mashed with a little cream, put a bit of butter on the top and brown them in an oven.

BREADED SAUSAGES.

Wipe the sausages dry. Dip them in beaten egg and bread-crumbs. Put them in the frying-basket and plunge into boiling fat. Cook ten minutes. Serve with a garnish of toasted bread and parsley.

HAM CROQUETTES.

One cupful of finely-chopped cooked ham, one of bread-crumbs, two of hot mashed potatoes, one large tablespoonful of butter, three eggs, a speck of Cayenne. Beat the ham, Cayenne, butter, and two of the eggs into the potato. Let the mixture cool slightly, and shape it like croquettes. Roll in the bread-crumbs, dip in beaten egg and again in crumbs, put in the frying-basket and plunge into boiling fat. Cook two minutes. Drain, and serve.

A NICE BREAKFAST DISH.

Chopped cold meat well seasoned; wet with gravy, if convenient, put it on a platter; then take cold rice made moist with milk and one egg, seasoned with pepper and salt; if not sufficient rice, add powdered bread-crumbs; place this around the platter quite thick; set in oven to heat and brown.

CHICKEN IN JELLY.

A little cold chicken (about one pint), one cupful of water or stock, one-fifth of a box of gelatine, half a teaspoonful of curry powder, salt, pepper. Cut the meat from the bones of a chicken left from dinner. Put the bones on with water to cover, and boil down to one cupful. Put the gelatine to soak in one-fourth of a cupful of cold water. When the stock is reduced as much as is necessary, strain and season. Add the curry and chicken. Season and simmer ten minutes; then add the gelatine, and stir on the table until it is dissolved. Turn all into a mold, and set away to harden. This makes a nice relish for tea or lunch. If you have mushrooms, omit the curry, and cut four of them into dice. Stir into the mixture while cooking. This dish can be varied by using the whites of hard-boiled eggs, or bits of boiled ham. To serve: Dip the mold in warm water, and turn out on the dish. Garnish with parsley.

A GOOD DISH.

Minced cold beef or lamb; if beef put in a pinch of pulverized cloves; if lamb, a pinch of summer savory to season it, very little pepper and some salt, and put it in a baking-dish; mash potatoes and mix them with cream and butter and a little salt, and spread them over the meat; beat up an egg with cream or milk, a very little, spread it over the potatoes, and bake it a short time, sufficient to warm it through and brown the potatoes.

POULTRY, GAME, ETC.

In choosing poultry, the best way to determine whether it is young, is to try the skin under the leg or wing; if it is easily broken, it is young; or, turn the wing backwards; if the joint yields readily, it is tender; a fat fowl is best for any purpose.

After a chicken or fowl is killed, plunge it into a pot of scalding hot water; then pluck off the feathers, taking care not to tear the skin; when it is picked clean, roll up a sheet of white wrapping paper, set fire to it, singe off all the hairs. Poultry should be carefully picked, and nicely singed.

If a fowl is fresh killed, the vent will be close, and the flesh have a pleasant smell.

ROAST TURKEY.

Carefully pluck the bird, singe it with white paper, and wipe it thoroughly with a cloth; draw it, preserve the liver and gizzard, and be particular not to break the gall-bag, as no washing will remove the bitter taste it imparts where it once touches. Wash it *inside* well, and wipe it thoroughly with a dry cloth; the *outside* merely requires wiping nicely. Cut off the neck close to the back, but leave enough of the crop-skin to turn over; break the leg-bones close below the knee; draw out the strings from the thighs, and flatten the breast-bone to make it look plump. Have ready your dressing of bread-crumbs, mixed with butter, pepper, salt, thyme or sweet marjoram; fill the breast with this, and sew the neck over to the back. Be particular that the turkey is firmly trussed. Dredge it lightly with flour, and put a piece of butter into the basting-ladle; as the butter melts, baste the bird with it. When of a nice brown and well-frothed, serve with a tureen of good brown gravy and one of bread-sauce. The liver should be put under one pinion, and the gizzard under the other. Fried sausages are a favorite addition to roast turkey; they make a pretty garnish, besides adding much to the flavor. When these are not at hand, a few force-meat balls should be placed round the dish as a garnish. Turkey may also be stuffed with sausage-meat, and a chestnut force-meat with the same sauce is, by many persons, much esteemed as an accompaniment to this favorite dish.

Second Recipe.—After drawing and cleansing the turkey, prepare a dressing of chopped sausage and bread-crumbs, mixing in butter, pepper, salt and thyme to flavor. Fill the craw and the body of the turkey with this, and sew up carefully. Dredge with flour and put in the oven to roast, basting freely first with butter and water, then with the gravy from the pan. The time it takes to roast will depend both on the age and the weight of the turkey. If you have a good fire, you will be safe to allow ten minutes or so to the pound. Roast to a fine brown, and serve with the chopped giblets, which should be well stewed; add cranberry sauce.

BOILED TURKEY.

Hen turkeys are the best for boiling. They are the whitest, and if nicely kept, tenderest. Of course the sinews must be drawn, and they ought to be trussed with the legs out, so as to be easily carved. Take care to clean the animal well after it has been singed. Place the fowl in a sufficiently large pot with clean water sufficient to cover it, and little more; let the fire be a clear one, but not too fierce, as the slower the turkey boils the plumper it will be. Skim carefully and constantly, and simmer for two hours and a half in the case of a large fowl, and two hours for a smaller beast, and from an hour and ten to forty minutes for still smaller turkeys. Some people boil their turkeys in a floured cloth. I don't; the whiteness being mostly in the animal itself. My stuffing for a boiled turkey is thought good. I prepare it of crumbs of stale bread, with a little marrow or butter, some finely-shred parsley, and two dozen of small oysters, minus their beards, of course, and neatly trimmed. Stuff with this and a little chopped ham in addition, if desired.

TO ROAST A FOWL OR CHICKEN.

Have a bright, clear, and steady fire for roasting poultry; prepare it as directed; spit it, put a pint of hot water in the dripping-pan, add to it a small tablespoonful of salt, and a small teaspoonful of pepper, baste frequently, and let it roast quickly, without scorching; when nearly done, put a piece of butter the size of a large egg to the water in the pan; when it melts, baste with it, dredge a little flour over, baste again, and let it finish; half an hour will roast a full grown chicken, if the fire is right. When done take it up, let the giblets (heart, liver, and gizzard) boil tender, and chop them very fine, and put them in the gravy; add a tablespoonful of browned flour and a bit of butter, stir it over the fire for a few minutes, then serve in a gravy tureen. Or put the giblets in the pan and let them roast.

BOILED CHICKENS.

Clean, wash, and stuff as for roasting. Baste a floured cloth around each, and put into a pot with enough boiling water to cover them well. The hot water cooks the skin at once, and prevents the escape of the juices. The broth will not be so rich as if the fowls are put on in cold water, but this is proof that the meat will be more nutritious and better flavored. Stew very slowly, for the first half hour especially. Boil an hour or more, guiding yourself by size and toughness. Serve with egg or bread sauce.

BROILED CHICKEN.

Prepare in the same way as for boiling, cut them in two through the back, and flatten them; place on a cold grid-iron over a nice red fire. After a little time, when they have become thoroughly hot, set them on a plate or other dish, and lard them well with a piece of butter; pepper and salt them to taste, chiefly on the inside, then place them on the brander and continue turning till done—they will take fully twenty minutes. Serve hot, with a little dab of butter and plenty of stewed mushrooms—a delightful dish.

FRIED CHICKEN.

Cut the chicken in pieces, lay it in salt and water, which change several times; roll each piece in flour; fry in very hot lard or butter; season with salt and pepper; fry pars-ley with them also. Make a gravy of cream seasoned with salt, pepper, and a little mace, thickened with a little flour in the pan in which the chickens were fried, pouring off the lard.

FRICASSEE OF CHICKEN.

Cut into joints, scald and skin, place in a stewpan, with two raw onions cut into eight parts, a little chopped parsley, salt and pepper, and the least squeeze of lemon-juice. Add a bit of butter as large as an egg, and fill in a pint of water. Stew for an hour under a very close lid, then lift and strain off the gravy, into which beat gradually a teacupful of cream and the yolks of two eggs; heat up the gravy, taking care that it does not boil, and pour it over the fricassee.

TO CURRY CHICKEN.

Slice an onion and brown in a little butter; add a spoonful of curry powder; allow it to remain covered for a few minutes to cook; add a little more butter and put in chicken, veal, etc., etc.; cut up small, thicken with a little flour. This is excellent.

PRESSED CHICKEN.

Cut up the fowls and place in a kettle with a tight cover, so as to retain the steam; put about two teacups of water and plenty of salt and pepper over the chicken, then let it cook until the meat cleaves easily from the bones; cut or chop all the meat (freed from skin, bone and gristle) about as for chicken salad; season well, put into a dish and pour the remnant of the juice in which it was cooked over it. This will jelly when cold, and can then be sliced or set on the table in shape. Nice for tea or lunch. The knack of making this simple dish is not having too much water; it will not jelly if too weak, or if the water is allowed to boil away entirely while cooking.

CHICKEN POT-PIE.

Skin and cut up the fowls into joints, and put the neck, legs and back bones in a stew pan, with a little water, an onion, a bunch of savory herbs, and a blade of mace; let these stew for an hour, and, when done, strain off the liquor; this is for gravy. Put a layer of fowl at the bottom of a pie-dish, then a layer of ham, then one of force-meat and hard-boiled eggs, cut in rings; between the layers put a seasoning of pounded mace, nutmeg, pepper and salt. Pour in about half a pint of water, border the edge of dish with puff-crust, put on the cover, ornament the top and glaze it by brushing over it the yolk of an egg. Bake for about an hour and a half, and, when done, pour in at the top the gravy made from the bones.

A CHICKEN SALAD.

Take a fine white bunch of celery (four or five heads), scrape and wash it white; reserve the delicate green leaves; shred the white part like straws, lay this in a glass, or white china dish, in the form of a nest. Mince all the white meat of a boiled, or white stewed fowl, without the skin, and put it in the nest.

Make a salad dressing thus: Rub the yolks of two hard-boiled eggs to a smooth paste, with a dessertspoonful of salad oil, or melted butter; add to it two teaspoonfuls of made mustard, and a small teaspoonful of fine white sugar, and put to it gradually (stirring it in) a large cup of strong vinegar.

Make a wreath of the most delicate leaves of the celery, around the edge of the nest, between it and the chicken; pour the dressing over the chicken, when ready to serve; if the dressing is poured over too soon it will discolor the celery.

White heart lettuce may be used for the nest instead of celery.

JELLIED CHICKEN.

Boil a fowl until it will slip easily from the bones; let the water be reduced to about one pint in boiling; pick the meat from the bones in good sized pieces, taking out all gristle, fat, and bones; place in a wet mold; skim the fat from the liquor; a little butter; pepper and salt to the taste, and one-half ounce of gelatine. When this dissolves, pour it hot over the chicken. The liquor must be seasoned pretty high, for the chicken absorbes.

CHICKEN PATES.

Mince chicken that has been previously roasted or boiled, and season well; stir into this a sauce made of half a pint of milk, into which while boiling a teaspoonful of corn starch has been added to thicken, season with butter, about a teaspoonful, and salt and pepper to taste. Have ready small pate pans lined with a good puff paste. Bake the crust in a brisk oven; then fill the pans and set in the oven a few minutes to brown very slightly.

SAGE-AND-ONION STUFFING, FOR GEESE, DUCKS AND PORK.

Four large onions, ten sage-leaves, one-quarter pound of bread-crumbs, one and one-half ounce of butter, salt and pepper to taste, one egg. Peel the onions, put them into boiling water, let them simmer for five minutes or rather longer, and, just before they are taken out, put in the sage-leaves for a minute or two to take off their rawness. Chop both these very fine, add the bread, seasoning, and butter, and work the whole together with the yolk of an egg, when the stuffing will be ready for use. It should be rather highly seasoned, and the sage-leaves should be very finely chopped. Many cooks do not parboil the onions in the manner just stated, but merely use them raw. The stuffing then, however, is not nearly so mild, and, to many tastes, its strong flavor would be very objectionable. When made for goose, a portion of the liver of the bird, simmered for a few minutes and very finely minced, is frequently added to this stuffing; and where economy is studied, the egg may be dispensed with.

TO ROAST A GOOSE.

Having drawn and singed the goose, wipe out the inside with a cloth, and sprinkle in some pepper and salt. Make a stuffing of four good-sized onions, minced fine, and half their quantity of green sage-leaves, minced also, a large teacupful of grated bread-crumbs, a piece of butter the size of a walnut, and the beaten yolks of two eggs, with a little pepper and salt. Mix the whole together, and incorporate them well. Put the stuffing into the goose, and press it in hard; but do not entirely fill up the cavity, as the mixture will swell in cooking. Tie the goose securely round with a greased or wetted string; and paper the breast to prevent it from scorching. The fire must be brisk and well kept up. It will require from two hours to two and a half to roast. Baste it at first with a little salt and water, and then with its own gravy. Take off the paper when the goose is about half done, and dredge it with a little flour towards the last. Having parboiled the liver and heart, chop them and put them into the gravy, which must be skimmed well and thickened with a little brown flour.

Send apple sauce to table with the goose; also mashed potatoes.

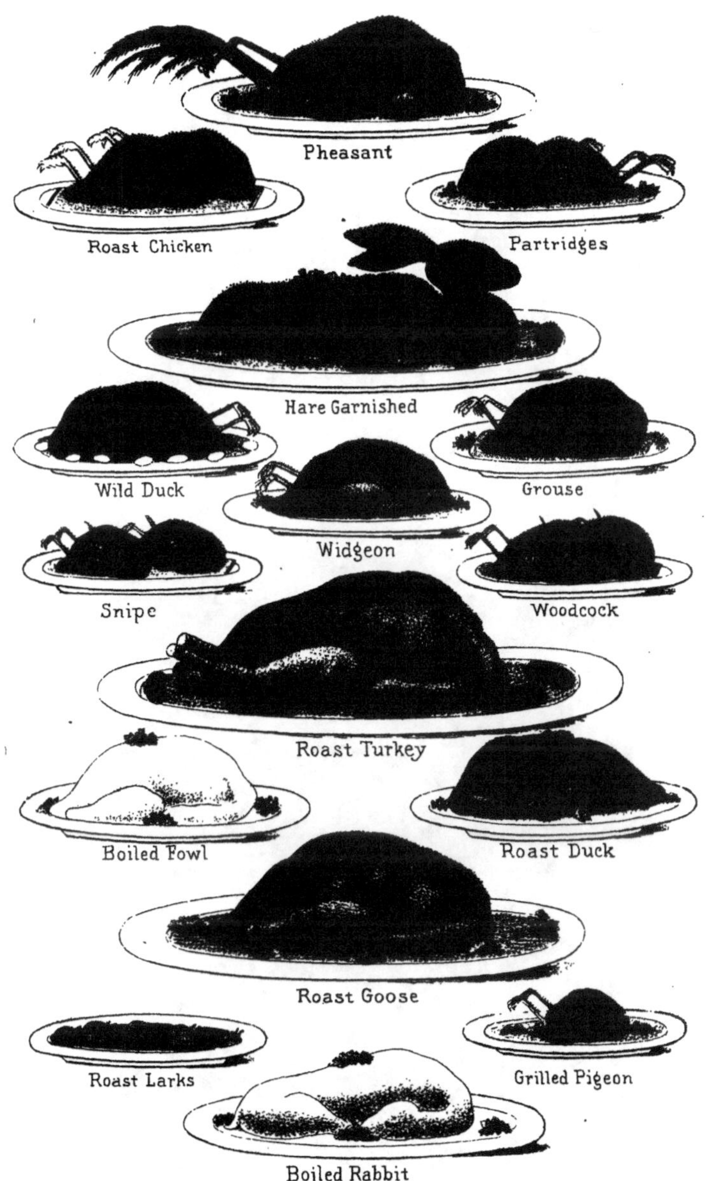
Pheasant
Roast Chicken
Partridges
Hare Garnished
Wild Duck
Grouse
Widgeon
Snipe
Woodcock
Roast Turkey
Boiled Fowl
Roast Duck
Roast Goose
Roast Larks
Grilled Pigeon
Boiled Rabbit

A goose may be stuffed entirely with potatoes, boiled and mashed with milk, butter, pepper and salt.

You may make a gravy of the giblets, that is the neck, pinions, liver, heart and gizzard, stewed in a little water, thickened with butter, rolled in flour, and seasoned with pepper and salt. Before you send it to table, take out all but the liver and heart; mince them and leave them in the gravy. This gravy is by many preferred to that which comes from the goose in roasting. It is well to have both.

If a goose is old it is useless to cook it, as when hard and tough it cannot be eaten.

ROAST DUCKS.

Wash and dry the ducks carefully. Make a stuffing of sage and onion; insert, and sew up completely that the seasoning may not escape. If tender, ducks do not require more than an hour to roast. Keep them well basted, and a few minutes before serving, dredge lightly with flour, to make them froth and look plump. Send to table hot, with a good brown gravy poured not *round* but *over* them. Accompany with currant jelly, and, if in season, green peas.

ROAST PIGEONS.

Clean the pigeons, and stuff them the same as chickens; leave the feet on, dip them into scalding water, strip off the skin, cross them, and tie them together below the breastbone; or cut them off; the head may remain on; if so, dip it in scalding water, and pick it clean; twist the wings back, put the liver between the right wing and the body, and turn the head under the other; rub the outside of each bird with a mixture of pepper and salt; spit them, and put some water in the dripping-pan; for each bird put a bit of butter the size of a small egg, put them before a hot fire, and let them roast quickly; baste frequently; half an hour will do them; when nearly done, dredge them with wheat flour and baste with the butter in the pan; turn them, that they may be nicely and easily browned; when done, take them up, set the pan over the fire, make a thin batter of a teaspoonful of wheat flour, and cold water; when the gravy is boiling hot, stir it in; continue to stir it for a few minutes, until it is brown, then pour it through a gravy sieve into a tureen, and serve with the pigeons.

TO MAKE A BIRD'S NEST.

Boil some yellow macaroni gently, until it is quite swelled out and tender, then cut it in pieces, the length of a finger, and lay them on a dish like a straw nest.

Truss pigeons with the heads on, (having scalded and picked them clean), turned under the left wing, leave the feet on, and having stewed them, arrange them as in a nest; pour the gravy over and serve.

The nest may be made of boiled rice, or bread cut in pieces, the length and thickness of a finger, and fried a nice brown in hot lard, seasoned with pepper and salt. Or, make it of bread, toasted a yellow brown. Any small birds may be stewed or roasted, and served in this way.

PIGEONS IN JELLY.

Wash and truss one dozen pigeons. Put them in a kettle with four pounds of the shank of veal, six cloves, twenty-five pepper-corns, an onion that has been fried in one spoonful of butter, one stalk of celery, a bouquet of sweet herbs and four and a half quarts of water. Have the veal shank broken in small pieces. As soon as the contents of the kettle come to a boil, skim carefully, and set for three hours where they will just simmer. After they have been cooking one hour, add two tablespoonfuls of salt. When the pigeons are done, take them up, being careful not to break them, and remove the strings. Draw the kettle forward, where it will boil rapidly, and keep there for forty minutes; then strain the liquor through a napkin, and taste to see if seasoned enough. The water should have boiled down to two and a half quarts. Have two molds that will each hold six pigeons. Put a thin layer of the jelly in these, and set on ice to harden. When hard, arrange the pigeons in them, and cover with the jelly, which must be cold, but liquid. Place in the ice-chest for six, or, better still, twelve hours. There should be only one layer of the pigeons in the mold.

To serve: Dip the mold in a basin of warm water for one minute, and turn on a cold dish. Garnish with pickled beets and parsley. A Tartare sauce can be served with this dish.

If squabs are used, two hours will cook them. All small birds, as well as partridge, grouse, etc., can be prepared in the same manner. Remember that the birds must be cooked tender, and that the liquor must be so reduced that it will become jellied.

PIGEON PIE.

Clean and truss three or four pigeons, rub the outside and in with a mixture of pepper and salt; rub the inside with a bit of butter, and fill it with a bread-and-butter stuffing, or mashed potatoes; sew up the slit, butter the sides of a tin basin or pudding-dish, and line (the sides only) with pie paste, rolled to quarter of an inch thickness; lay the birds in; for three large tame pigeons, cut quarter of a pound of sweet butter and put it over them, strew over a large teaspoonful of salt, and a small teaspoonful of pepper, with a bunch of finely-cut parsley, if liked; dredge a large tablespoonful of wheat flour over; put in water to nearly fill the pie; lay skewers across the top, cover with a puff paste crust; cut a slit in the middle, ornament the edge with leaves, braids, or shells of paste, and put it in a moderately hot or quick oven, for one hour; when nearly done, brush the top over with the yolk of an egg beaten with a little milk, and finish. The pigeons for this pie may be cut in two or more pieces, if preferred.

Any small birds may be done in this manner.

WILD DUCKS.

Nearly all wild ducks are liable to have a fishy flavor, and when handled by inexperienced cooks, are sometimes uneatable from this cause. Before roasting them guard against this by parboiling them with a small carrot, peeled, put within each. This will absorb the unpleasant taste. An onion will have the same effect; but unless you mean to use onion in the stuffing, the carrot is preferable. In my own kitchen, I usually put in the onion, considering a suspicion of garlic a desideratum in roast duck, whether wild or tame.

ROAST WILD DUCK.

Parboil as above directed; throw away the carrot or onion, lay in fresh water half an hour; stuff with bread-crumbs seasoned with pepper, salt, sage, and onion, and roast until brown and tender, basting for half the time with butter and water, then with the drippings. Add to the gravy, when you have taken up the ducks, a teaspoonful of currant jelly, and a pinch of Cayenne. Thicken with browned flour and serve in a tureen.

WILD TURKEY.

Draw and wash the inside very carefully, as with all game. Domestic fowls are, or should be, kept up without eating for at least twelve hours before they are killed; but we must shoot wild when we can get the chance, and of course it often happens that their crops are distended by a recent hearty meal of rank or green food. Wipe the cavity with a dry, soft cloth before you stuff. Have a rich force-meat, bread-crumbs, some bits of fat pork, chopped fine, pepper and salt. Moisten with milk, and beat in an egg and a couple of tablespoonfuls of melted butter. Baste with butter and water for the first hour, then three or four times with gravy; lastly, five or six times with melted butter. A generous and able housekeeper told me once that she always allowed a pound of butter for basting a large wild turkey. This was an extravagant quantity, but the meat is drier than that of the domestic fowl, and not nearly so fat. Dredge with flour at the last, froth with butter, and when he is of a tempting brown, serve. Skim the gravy, add a little hot water, pepper, thicken with the giblets chopped fine and browned flour, boil up, and pour into a tureen. At the South the giblets are not put in the gravy, but laid whole, one under each wing, when the turkey is dished. Garnish with small fried sausages, not larger than a dollar, crisped parsley between them. Send around currant jelly and cranberry sauce with it.

TO ROAST SNIPES, WOODCOCKS, OR PLOVERS.

Pick them immediately; wipe them, and season them slightly with pepper and salt. Cut as many slices of bread as you have birds. Toast them brown, butter them, and lay them in the pan. Dredge the birds with flour, and put them in the oven with a brisk fire. Baste them with lard or fresh butter. They will be done in twenty or thirty minutes. Serve them up laid on the toast, and garnish with sliced orange, or with orange jelly.

ROAST PARTRIDGE.

Choose young birds, with dark-colored bills and yellowish legs, and let them hang a few days, or there will be no flavor to the flesh, nor will it be tender. The time they should be kept entirely depends on the taste of those for whom they are intended, as what some persons would consider delicious, would be to others disgusting and offensive. They may be trussed with or without the head, the latter mode is now considered the most fashionable. Pluck, draw, and wipe the partridge carefully inside and out; cut off the head, leaving sufficient skin on the neck to skewer back; bring the legs close to the breast, between it and the side-bones, and pass a skewer through the pinions and thick part of the thighs. When the head is left on, it should be brought round and fixed on to the point of the skewer. When the bird is firmly and plumply trussed, roast it before a nice bright fire; keep it well basted, and a few minutes before serving, flour and froth it well. Dish it, and serve with gravy and bread-sauce, and send to table hot and quickly. A little of the gravy should be poured over the bird.

ROAST QUAIL.

Pluck and draw the birds, rub a little butter over them, tie a strip of bacon over the breasts, and set them in the oven for twenty or twenty-five minutes.

ROAST PRAIRIE CHICKEN.

The bird being a little strong, and its flesh when cooked a little dry, it should be either larded or wide strips of bacon or pork placed over its breast. A mild seasoned stuffing will improve the flavor of old birds. Dust a little flour over them, baste occasionally, and serve. Pheasants may be managed in the same manner.

LARDED GROUSE.

Clean and wash the grouse. Lard the breast and legs. Put a small skewer into the legs and through the tail. Tie firmly with twine. Dredge with salt, and rub the breast with soft butter; then dredge thickly with flour. Put into a quick oven. If to be very rare, cook twenty minutes; if wished better done, thirty minutes. The former time, as a general thing, suits gentlemen better, but thirty minutes is preferred by ladies. If the birds are cooked in a tin-kitchen, it should be for thirty or thirty-five minutes. When done, place on a hot dish, on which has been spread bread-sauce. Sprinkle fried crumbs over both grouse and sauce. Garnish with parsley. The grouse may, instead, be served on a hot dish, with the parsley garnish, and the sauce and crumbs served in separate dishes. The first method is the better, however, as you get in the sauce all the gravy that comes from the birds.

PORK, HAMS, ETC.

To Choose Pork.—If the rind of pork is tough and thick, and cannot easily be impressed with the finger, it is old.

If fresh, the flesh will look cool and smooth; when moist or clammy it is stale. The knuckle is the first to become tainted.

Pork is often what is called measly, and is then almost poisonous; measly pork may easily be detected, the fat being full of small kernels. Swill or still-fed pork is not fit for curing; either dairy or corn-fed is good.

Fresh pork is in season from October to April.

In cutting up a large hog, it is first cut in two down the back and belly. The chine or back-bone should be cut out from each side the whole length, and is either boiled or roasted. The chine is considered the prime part. The sides of the hog are made into bacon, and the inside or ribs is cut with very little meat; this is the spare-rib.

CURING HAMS.

Hang up the hams a week or ten days, the longer the tenderer and better, if kept perfectly sweet; mix for each good-sized ham, one teacup of salt, one tablespoon of molasses, one ounce of saltpetre; lay the hams in a clean dry tub; heat the mixture and rub well into the hams, especially around the bones and recesses; repeat the process once or twice, or until all the mixture is used; then let the hams lie two or three days, when they must be put for three weeks in brine strong enough to bear an egg; then soak eight hours in cold water; hang up to dry in the kitchen or other more convenient place for a week or more; smoke from three to five days, being careful not to heat the hams. Corn-cobs and apple-tree wood are good for smoking. The juices are better retained if smoked with the hock down. Tie up carefully in bags for the summer.

TO ROAST A LEG OF PORK.

Take a sharp knife and score the skin across in narrow strips (you may cross it again so as to form diamonds) and rub in some powdered sage. Raise the skin at the knuckle and put in a stuffing of minced onion and sage, bread-crumbs, pepper, salt, and beaten yolk of egg. Fasten it down with a buttered string, or with skewers. You may make deep incisions in the meat of the large end of the leg, and stuff them also, pressing in the filling very hard. Rub a little sweet oil all over the skin with a brush or a goose feather, to make it crisp and of a handsome brown. A leg of pork will require from three to four hours to roast.

Moisten it all the time by brushing it with sweet oil, or with fresh butter tied in a rag. To baste it with its own drippings will make the skin tough and hard. Skim the fat carefully from the gravy, which should be thickened with a little flour.

A roast leg of pork should always be accompanied by apple sauce, and by mashed potatoes and mashed turnips.

PORK AND BEANS.

Pick over carefully a quart of beans and let them soak over night; in the morning wash and drain in another water, put on to boil in cold water with half a teaspoon of soda; boil about thirty minutes (when done, the skin of a bean will crack if taken out and blown upon), drain, and put in an earthen pot first a slice of pork and then the beans, with two or three tablespoons of molasses. When the beans are in the pot, put in the centre half or three-fourths of a pound of well-washed salt pork with the rind scored in slices or squares, and uppermost; season with pepper and salt if needed; cover all over with hot water, and bake six hours or longer in a moderate oven, adding hot water as needed; they cannot be baked too long. Keep covered so that they will not burn on the top, but remove cover an hour or two before serving, to brown the top and crisp the pork.

PORK SAUSAGES.

Take such a proportion of fat and lean pork as you like; chop it quite fine, and for every ten pounds of meat take four ounces of fine salt, and one of fine pepper; dried sage, or lemon thyme, finely powdered, may be added if liked; a teaspoonful of sage, and the same of ground allspice and cloves, to each ten pounds of meat. Mix the seasoning through the meat; pack it down in stone pots or put in muslin bags. Or fill the hog's or ox's guts, having first made them perfectly clean, thus: empty them, cut them in lengths, and lay them three or four days in salt and water, or weak lime water; turn them inside out once or twice, scrape them; then rinse them, and fill with the meat.

If you do not use the skins or guts, make the sausage meat up to the size and shape of sausages, dip them in beaten egg, and then into wheat flour, or rolled crackers, or simply into wheat flour, and fry in hot lard. Turn them, that every side may be a fine color. Serve hot, with boiled potatoes or hominy; either taken from the gravy, or after they are fried, pour a little boiling water into the gravy in the pan, and pour it over them; or first dredge in a teaspoonful of wheat flour, stir it until it is smooth and brown; then add a little boiling water, let it boil up once, then put it in the dish with the sausages.

Chopped onion and green parsley may be added to the sausage meat, when making ready to fry.

Or sausage meat may be tied in a muslin bag, and boiled, and served with vegetables; or let it become cold, and cut in slices.

PORK CHOPS, STEAKS AND CUTLETS.

Fry or stew pork chops, after taking off the rind or skin, the same as for veal.

Cutlets and steaks are also fried, broiled, or stewed, the same as veal.

ROAST PIG.

Thoroughly clean the pig, then rinse it in cold water, wipe it dry; then rub the inside with a mixture of salt and pepper, and if liked, a little pounded and sifted sage; make a stuffing thus: cut some wheat bread in slices half an inch thick, spread butter on to half its thickness, sprinkled with pepper and salt, and if liked, a little pounded sage and minced onion; pour enough hot water over the bread to make it moist or soft, then fill the body with it and sew it together, or tie a cord around it to keep the dressing in, then spit it; put a pint of water in the dripping-pan, put into it a tablespoonful of salt, and a teaspoonful of pepper, let the fire be hotter at each end than in the middle, put the pig down at a little distance from the fire, baste it as it begins to roast, and gradually draw it nearer; continue to baste occasionally; turn it that it may be evenly cooked; when the eyes drop out it is done; or a better rule is to judge by the weight, fifteen minutes for each pound of meat, if the fire is right.

Have a bright clear fire, with a bed of coals at the bottom; first put the roast at a little distance, and gradually draw it nearer; when the pig is done stir up the fire, take a coarse cloth with a good bit of butter in it, and wet the pig all over with it, and when the crackling is crisp take it up; dredge a little flour into the gravy, let it boil up once, and having boiled the heart, liver, etc., tender, and chopped it fine, add it to the gravy, give it one boil, then serve.

PIG'S CHEEK,

Is smoked and boiled like ham with vegetables; boiled cabbage or fried parsnips may be served with it.

ROAST SPARE-RIB.

Trim off the rough ends neatly, crack the ribs across the middle, rub with salt and sprinkle with pepper, fold over, stuff with turkey-dressing, sew up tightly, place in dripping-pan with pint of water, baste frequently, turning over once so as to bake both sides equally until a rich brown.

PORK FRITTERS.

Have at hand a thick batter of Indian meal and flour; cut a few slices of pork and fry them in the frying-pan until the fat is fried out; cut a few more slices of the pork, dip them in the batter, and drop them in the bubbling fat, seasoning with salt and pepper; cook until light brown, and eat while hot.

BAKED HAM.

Cover your ham with cold water, and simmer gently just long enough to loosen the skin, so that it can be pulled off. This will probably be from two to three hours, according to the size of your ham. When skinned, put in a dripping-pan in the oven, pour over it a teacup of vinegar and one of hot water, in which dissolve a teaspoonful of English mustard, bake slowly, basting with the liquid, for two hours. Then cover the ham all over to the depth of one inch with coarse brown sugar, press it down firmly, and do not baste again until the sugar has formed a thick crust, which it will soon do in a very slow oven. Let it remain a full hour in, after covering with the sugar, until it becomes a rich golden brown. When done, drain from the liquor in the pan and put on a dish to cool. When it is cool, but not cold, press by turning another flat dish on top, with a weight over it. You will never want to eat ham cooked in any other way when you have tasted this, and the pressing makes it cut firmly for sandwiches or slicing.

TO BOIL A HAM.

Wash thoroughly with a cloth. Select a small size to boil, put it in a large quantity of cold water, and boil twenty minutes for each pound, allowing it to boil slowly;

take off the rind while hot and put in the oven to brown half an hour; remove and trim.

TO BROIL HAM.

Cut some slices of ham, quarter of an inch thick, lay them in hot water for half an hour, or give them a scalding in a pan over the fire; then take them up, and lay them on a gridiron, over bright coals; when the outside is browned, turn the other; then take the slices on a hot dish, butter them freely, sprinkle pepper over and serve. Or, after scalding them, wipe them dry, dip each slice in beaten egg, and then into rolled crackers, and fry or broil.

FRIED HAM AND EGGS (a Breakfast Dish).

Cut the ham into slices, and take care that they are of the same thickness in every part. Cut off the rind, and if the ham should be particularly hard and salt, it will be found an improvement to soak it for about ten minutes in hot water, and then dry it in a cloth. Put it into a cold frying-pan, set it over the fire, and turn the slices three or four times whilst they are cooking. When done, place them on a dish, which should be kept hot in front of the fire during the time the eggs are being poached. Poach the eggs; slip them on to the slices of ham, and serve quickly.

HAM TOAST.

Mince finely a quarter of a pound of cooked ham with an anchovy boned and washed; add a little Cayenne and pounded mace; beat up two eggs; mix with the mince, and add just sufficient milk to keep it moist; make it quite hot, and serve on small rounds of toast or fried bread.

HEAD CHEESE.

Having thoroughly cleaned a hog's head or pig's head, split it in two with a sharp knife, take out the eyes, take out the brains, cut off the ears, and pour scalding water over them and the head, and scrape them clean. Cut off any part of the nose which may be discolored so as not to be scraped clean; then rinse all in cold water, and put it into a large kettle with hot (not boiling) water to cover it, and set the kettle (having covered it) over the fire; let it boil gently, taking off the scum as it rises; when boiled so that the bones leave the meat readily, take it from the water with a skimmer into a large wooden bowl or tray; take from it every particle of bone; chop the meat small and season to taste with salt and pepper, and if liked, a little chopped sage or thyme; spread a cloth in a colander or sieve; set it in a deep dish, and put the meat in, then fold the cloth closely over it, lay a weight on which may press equally the whole surface (a sufficiently large plate will serve). Let the weight be more or less heavy, according as you may wish the cheese to be fat or lean; a heavy weight by pressing out the fat will of course leave the cheese lean. When cold, take the weight off; take it from the colander or sieve, scrape off whatever fat may be found on the outside of the cloth, and keep the cheese in the cloth in a cool place, to be eaten sliced thin, with or without mustard, and vinegar or catsup. After the water is cold in which the head was boiled, take off the fat from it, and whatever may have drained from the sieve, or colander, and cloth; put it together in some clean water, give it one boil; then strain it through a cloth, and set it to become cold; then take off the cake of fat. It is fit for any use.

PIGS' FEET SOUSED.

Scald and scrape clean the feet; if the covering of the toes will not come off without, singe them in hot embers, until they are loose, then take them off. Many persons lay them in weak lime water to whiten them. Having scraped them clean and white, wash them and put them in a pot of hot (not boiling) water, with a little salt, and let them boil gently, until by turning a fork in the flesh it will easily break and the bones are loosened. Take off the scum as it rises. When done, take them from the hot water into cold vinegar, enough to cover them, add to it one-third as much of the water in which they were boiled; add whole pepper and allspice, with cloves and mace if liked, put a cloth and a tight-fitting cover over the pot or jar. Soused feet may be eaten cold from the vinegar, split in two from top to toe, or having split them, dip them in wheat flour and fry in hot lard; or broil and butter them. In either case, let them be nicely browned.

TO MAKE LARD.

Take the leaf fat from the inside of a bacon hog, cut it small, and put it in an iron kettle, which must be perfectly free from any musty taste; set it over a steady, moderate fire, until nothing but scraps remain of the meat; the heat must be kept up, but gentle, that it may not burn the lard; spread a coarse cloth in a wire sieve, and strain the liquid into tin basins which will hold two or three quarts; squeeze out all the fat from the scraps. When the lard in the pans is cold, press a piece of new muslin close upon it, trim it off at the edge of the pan, and keep it in a cold place. Or it may be kept in wooden kegs with close covers. Lard made with one-third as much beef suet as fat is supposed by many persons to keep better.

TO TELL GOOD EGGS.

Put them in water—if the large end turns up, they are not fresh. This is an infallible rule to distinguish a good egg from a bad one.

KEEPING EGGS FRESH.

"All it is necessary to do to keep eggs through summer is to procure small, clean wooden or tin vessels, holding from ten to twenty gallons, and a barrel, more or less, of common, fine-ground land plaster. Begin by putting on the bottom of the vessel two or three inches of plaster, and then, having fresh eggs, with the yolks unbroken, set them up, small end down, close to each other, but not crowding, and make the first layer. Then add more plaster and enough so the eggs will stand upright, and set up the second layer; then another deposit of plaster, followed by a layer of eggs, till the vessel is full, and finish by covering the top layer with plaster. Eggs so packed and subjected to a temperature of at least 85 degrees, if not 90 degrees, during August and September, came out fresh, and if one could be certain of not having a temperature of more than 75 degrees to contend with, I am confident eggs could be kept by these means all the year round. Observe that the eggs must be fresh laid, the yolks unbroken, the packing done in small vessels, and with clean, fine-ground land plaster, and care must be taken that no egg so presses on another as to break the shell."

Eggs may be kept good for a year in the following manner:

To a pail of water, put of unslacked lime and coarse salt each a pint; keep it in a cellar, or cool place, and put the eggs in, as fresh laid as possible.

It is well to keep a stone pot of this lime water ready to

receive the eggs as soon as laid; make a fresh supply every few months. This lime water is of exactly the proper strength; strong lime water will cook the eggs. Very strong lime water will eat the shell.

POACHED EGGS.

Two eggs, two tablespoonfuls of milk, half a teaspoonful of salt, half a teaspoonful of butter. Beat the eggs, and add the salt and milk. Put the butter in a small saucepan, and when it melts, add the eggs. Stir over the fire until the mixture thickens, being careful not to let it cook hard. About two minntes will cook it. The eggs, when done, should be soft and creamy. Serve immediately.

DROPPED EGGS.

Have one quart of boiling water and one tablespoonful of salt in a frying-pan. Break the eggs, one by one, to a saucer, and slide carefully into the salted water. Cook until the white is firm, and lift out with a griddle-cake turner and place on toasted bread. Serve immediately.

STUFFED EGGS.

Six hard-boiled eggs cut in two, take out the yolks and mash fine; then add two teaspoonfuls of butter, one of cream, two or three drops of onion-juice, salt and pepper to taste. Mix all thoroughly and fill the eggs with this mixture; put them together. Then there will be a little of the filling left, to which add one well-beaten egg. Cover the eggs with this mixture, and then roll in cracker-crumbs. Fry a light brown in boiling fat. Plain baked eggs make a quite pretty breakfast dish. Take a round white-ware dish thick enough to stand the heat of the oven, put into it sufficient fresh butter, and break as many eggs in it as are desirable, putting a few bits of butter on the top, and set in a rather slow oven until they are cooked. Have a dish of nicely made buttered toast arranged symmetrically on a plate, and garnish it and the dish of eggs with small pieces of curled parsley.

EGGS A LA SUISSE.

Spread the bottom of a dish with two ounces of fresh butter; cover this with grated cheese; break eight whole eggs upon the cheese without breaking the yolks. Season with red pepper and salt if necessary; pour a little cream on the surface, strew about two ounces of grated cheese on the top, and set the eggs in a moderate oven for about a quarter of an hour. Pass a hot salamander over the top to brown it.

EGGS BROUILLÉ.

Six eggs, half a cupful of milk, or, better still, of cream; two mushrooms, one teaspoonful of salt, a little pepper, three tablespoonfuls of butter, a slight grating of nutmeg. Cut the mushrooms into dice, and fry them for one minute in one tablespoonful of the butter. Beat the eggs, salt, pepper, and cream together, and put them in a saucepan. Add the butter and mushrooms to these ingredients. Stir over a moderate heat until the mixture begins to thicken. Take from the fire and beat rapidly until the eggs become quite thick and creamy. Have slices of toast on a hot dish. Heap the mixture on these, and garnish with points of toast. Serve immediately.

CURRIED EGGS.

Slice two onions aud fry in butter, add a tablespoon curry-powder and one pint good broth or stock, stew till onions are quite tender, add a cup of cream thickened with arrowroot or rice flour, simmer a few moments, then add eight or ten hard-boiled eggs, cut in slices, and beat them well, but do not boil.

CREAMED EGGS.

Boil six eggs twenty minutes. Make one pint of cream sauce. Have six slices of toast on a hot dish. Put a layer of sauce on each one, and then part of the whites of the eggs, cut in thin strips; and rub part of the yolks through a sieve on to the toast. Repeat this, and finish with a third layer of sauce. Place in the oven for about three minutes. Garnish with parsley, and serve.

SOFT-BOILED EGGS.

Place the eggs in a warm saucepan, and cover with *boiling* water. Let them stand where they will keep hot, but *not* boil, for ten minutes. This method will cook both whites and yolks.

EGGS UPON TOAST.

Put a good lump of butter into a frying-pan. When it is hot, stir in four or five well-beaten eggs, with pepper, salt, and a little parsley. Stir and toss for three minutes. Have ready to your hand some slices of buttered toast (cut round with a tin cake cutter before they are toasted); spread thickly with ground or minced tongue, chicken, or ham. Heap the stirred egg upon these in mounds, and set in a hot dish garnished with parsley and pickled beets.

DUTCH OMELET.

Break eight eggs into a basin, season with pepper and salt, add two ounces of butter cut small, beat these well together, make an ounce of butter hot in a frying-pan, put the eggs in, continue to stir it, drawing it away from the sides, that it may be evenly done, shake it now and then to free it from the pan; when the under side is a little browned, turn the omelet into a dish, and serve; this must be done over a moderate fire.

EGGS POACHED IN BALLS.

Put three pints of boiling water into a stewpan; set it on a hot stove or coals; stir the water with a stick until it runs rapidly around, then having broken an egg into a cup, taking care not to break the yolk, drop it into the whirling water; continue to stir it until the egg is cooked; then take it into a dish with a skimmer and set it over a pot of boiling water; boil one at a time, until you have enough. These will remain soft for a long time.

OMELET AU NATURAL.

Break eight or ten eggs into a basin; add a small teaspoonful of salt and a little pepper, with a tablespoonful of cold water; beat the whole well with a spoon or whisk. In the meantime put some fresh sweet butter into an omelet pan, and when it is nearly hot, put in an omelet; while it is frying, with a skimmer spoon raise the edges from the pan that it may be properly done. When the eggs are set and one side is a fine brown, double it half over and serve hot. These omelets should be put quite thin in the pan; the butter required for each will be about the size of a small egg.

OMELET IN BATTER.

Fry an omelet; when done, cut it in squares or diamonds; dip each piece in batter made of two eggs and a pint of milk, with enough wheat flour, and fry them in nice salted lard to a delicate brown. Serve hot.

SCRAMBLED EGGS.

Four eggs, one tablespoonful of butter, half a teaspoonful of salt. Beat the eggs and add the salt to them. Melt the butter in a saucepan. Turn in the beaten eggs, stir quickly over a hot fire for one minute, and serve.

OMELET (SPLENDID).

Six eggs, whites and yolks beaten separately; half pint milk, six teaspoons corn starch, one teaspoon baking powder, and a little salt; add the whites, beaten to stiff froth, last; cook in a little butter.

VEGETABLES.

BOILED POTATOES.

Old potatoes are better for being peeled and put in cold water an hour before being put over to boil. They should then be put into fresh cold water, when set over the fire. New potatoes should always be put in a boiling water, and it is best to prepare them just in time for cooking. Are better steamed than boiled.

MASHED POTATOES.

Potatoes are not good for mashing until they are full grown; peel them, and lay them in water for an hour or more before boiling, for mashing.

Old potatoes, when unfit for plain boiling, may be served mashed; cut out all imperfections, take off all the skin, and lay them in cold water for one hour or more; then put them into a dinner-pot or stewpan, with a teaspoonful of salt; cover the stewpan, and let them boil for half an hour, unless they are large, when three-quarters of an hour will be required; when they are done, take them up with a skimmer into a wooden bowl or tray, and mash them fine with a potato beetle; melt a piece of butter, the size of a large egg, into half a pint of hot milk; mix it with the mashed potatoes until it is thoroughly incorporated, and a smooth mass; then put it in a deep dish, smooth the top over, and mark it neatly with a knife; put pepper over and serve. The quantity of milk used must be in proportion to the quantity of potatoes.

Mashed potatoes may be heaped on a flat dish; make it in a crown or pineapple; stick a sprig of green celery or parsley in the top; or first brown it before the fire or in an oven.

Mashed potatoes may be made a highly ornamental dish; after shaping it, as taste may direct, trim the edge of the plate with a wreath of celery leaves or green parsley; or first brown the outside in an oven or before the fire.

FRIED POTATOES.

Peel and cut the potatoes into thin slices, as nearly the same size as possible; make some butter or dripping quite hot in a frying-pan; put in the potatoes, and fry them on both sides to a nice brown. When they are crisp and done, take them up, place them on a cloth before the fire to drain the grease from them, and serve very hot, after sprinkling them with salt. These are delicious with rump-steak, and in France are frequently served thus as a breakfast dish. The remains of cold potatoes may also be sliced and fried by the above recipe, but the slices must be cut a little thicker.

BROILED POTATOES.

Cut cold boiled potatoes in slices lengthwise, quarter of an inch thick; dip each slice in wheat flour, and lay them on a gridiron over a bright fire of coals; when both sides are browned nicely, take them on a hot dish, put a bit of butter, pepper and salt to taste over, and serve hot.

POTATOES AND CREAM.

Mince cold boiled potatoes fine; put them into a spider with melted butter in it; let them fry a little in the butter, well covered; then put in a fresh piece of butter, seasoned with salt and pepper, and pour over cream or rich milk; let it boil up once and serve.

POTATO PUFFS.

Prepare the potatoes as directed for mashed potato. While *hot*, shape in balls about the size of an egg. Have a tin sheet well buttered, and place the balls on it. As soon as all are done, brush over with beaten egg. Brown in the oven. When done, slip a knife under them and slide them upon a hot platter. Garnish with parsley, and serve immediately.

POTATO SNOW.

Choose large white potatoes, as free from spots as possible; boil them in their skin in salt and water until perfectly tender, drain and *dry them thoroughly* by the side of the fire, and peel them. Put a hot dish before the fire, rub the potatoes through a coarse sieve on to this dish; do not touch them afterwards, or the flakes will fall, and serve as hot as possible.

POTATO BORDER.

Six potatoes, three eggs, one tablespoonful of butter, one of salt, half a cupful of boiling milk. Pare, boil and mash the potatoes. When fine and light, add the butter, salt and pepper and two well-beaten eggs. Butter the border mold and pack the potato in it. Let this stand on the kitchen table ten minutes; then turn out on a dish and brush over with one well-beaten egg. Brown in the oven.

WHIPPED POTATOES.

Instead of mashing in the ordinary way whip with a fork until light and dry; then whip in a little melted butter, some milk, and salt to taste, whipping rapidly until creamy. Pile as lightly and irregularly as you can in a hot dish.

SCALLOPED POTATOES.

Prepare in this proportion: Two cups of mashed potatoes, two tablespoonfuls of cream or milk, and one of melted butter; salt and pepper to taste. Stir the potatoes, butter, and cream together, adding one raw egg. If the potatoes seem too moist, beat in a few fine bread-crumbs. Bake in a hot oven for ten minutes, taking care to have the top a rich brown.

POTATO CROQUETTES.

Pare, boil, and mash six good-sized potatoes. Add one tablespoonful of butter, two-thirds of a cupful of hot cream or milk, the whites of two eggs well beaten, salt and pepper to taste. When cool enough to handle, work into shape, roll in eggs and bread-crumbs, and fry in hot lard.

POTATOES A LA CREME.

Heat a cupful of milk; stir in a heaping tablespoonful of butter cut up in as much flour. Stir until smooth and thick; pepper and salt, and add two cupfuls of cold boiled potatoes, sliced, and a little very finely-chopped parsley. Shake over the fire until the potatoes are hot all through, and pour into a deep dish.

TO BOIL SWEET POTATOES.

Wash them perfectly clean, put them into a pot or stew-pan, and pour boiling water over to cover them; cover the pot close, and boil fast for half an hour, or more if the potatoes are large; try them with a fork; when done, drain off the water, take off the skins, and serve.

Cold sweet potatoes may be cut in slices across or lengthwise, and fried or broiled as common potatoes; or they may be cut in half and served cold.

ROASTED SWEET POTATOES.

Having washed them clean, and wiped them dry, roast them on a hot hearth as directed for common potatoes; or put them in a Dutch oven or tin reflector. Roasted or baked potatoes should not be cut, but broken open and eaten from the skin, as from a shell.

TO BAKE SWEET POTATOES.

Wash them perfectly clean, wipe them dry, and bake in a quick oven, according to their size—half an hour for quite small size, three-quarters for larger, and a full hour for the largest. Let the oven have a good heat, and do not open it, unless it is necessary to turn them, until they are done.

FRENCH FRIED SWEET POTATOES.

Prepare and fry the same as the white potatoes. Or they can first be boiled half an hour, and then pared, cut and fried as directed. The latter is the better way, as they are liable to be a little hard if fried when raw.

TURNIPS.

Boil until tender; mash and season with butter, pepper, salt, and a little rich milk or cream.

SPINACH.

An excellent way to serve spinach is to first look it over carefully; wash it in two or three waters. If the stalks are not perfectly tender, cut the leaves from the stalk. Boil for twenty minutes in water with enough salt dissolved in it to salt the spinach sufficiently. When done let it drain, then chop it fine, put it on the stove in a saucepan, with a lump of butter, salt, and pepper, and enough milk to moisten it. When the butter is melted and spinach steaming, take from the fire and put it in the dish in which it is going to the table. Garnish with hard-boiled eggs cut in slices or in rings—that is, with the yolk removed and rings of the white only left.

BEETS.

Clean these nicely, but do not pare them, leaving on a short piece of the stalk. Then put over to boil in hot water. Young beets will cook tender in an hour; old beets require several hours' boiling. When done, skin quickly while hot, slice thin into your vegetable dish, put on salt, pepper, and a little butter, put over a little vinegar, and serve hot or cold.

TO PRESERVE VEGETABLES FOR WINTER USE.

Green string beans must be picked when young; put a layer three inches deep in a small wooden keg or half barrel; sprinkle in salt an inch deep, then put another layer of beans, then salt, and beans and salt in alternate layers, until you have enough; let the last be salt; cover them with a piece of board which will fit the inside of the barrel or keg, and place a heavy weight upon it; they will make a brine.

When wanted for use, soak them one night or more in plenty of water, changing it once or twice, until the salt is out of them, then cut them, and boil the same as when fresh.

Carrots, beans, beet-roots, parsnips, and potatoes

keep best in dry sand or earth in a cellar; turnips keep best on a cellar bottom, or they may be kept the same as carrots, etc. Whatever earth remains about them when taken from the ground, should not be taken off.

When sprouts come on potatoes or other stored vegetables, they should be carefully cut off. The young sprouts from turnips are sometimes served as a salad, or boiled tender in salt and water, and served with butter and pepper over.

Celery may be kept all winter by setting it in boxes filled with earth; keep it in the cellar; it will grow and whiten in the dark; leeks may also be kept in this way.

Cabbage set out in earth, in a good cellar, will keep good and fresh all winter. Small close heads of cabbage may be kept many weeks by taking them before the frost comes, and laying them on a stone floor; this will whiten them, and make them tender.

Store onions are to be strung, and hung in a dry, cold place.

DELICATE CABBAGE.

Remove all defective leaves, quarter and cut as for coarse slaw, cover well with cold water, and let remain several hours before cooking, then drain and put into pot with enough boiling water to cover; boil until thoroughly cooked (which will generally require about forty-five minutes), add salt ten or fifteen minutes before removing from fire, and when done, take up into a colander, press out the water well, and season with butter and pepper. This is a good dish to serve with corned meats, but should not be cooked with them; if preferred, however, it may be seasoned by adding some of the liquor and fat from the boiling meat to the cabbage while cooking. Drain, remove, and serve in a dish with drawn butter or a cream dressing poured over it.

RED CABBAGE.

Select two small, solid heads of hard red cabbage; divide them in halves from crown to stem; lay the split side down, and cut downwards in thin slices. The cabbage will then be in narrow strips or shreds. Put into a saucepan a tablespoonful of clean drippings, butter, or any nice fat; when fat is hot, put in cabbage, a teaspoonful of salt, three tablespoonfuls vinegar (if the latter is very strong, use but two), and one onion, in which three or four cloves have been stuck, buried in the middle; boil two hours and a half; if it becomes too dry and is in danger of scorching, add a very *little* water. This is very nice.

CAULIFLOWER.

Boil a fine cauliflower, tied up snugly in coarse tarlatan, in hot water, a little salt. Drain and lay in a deep dish, flower uppermost. Heat a cup of milk; thicken with two tablespoonfuls of butter, cut into bits, and rolled in flour. Add pepper, salt, the beaten white of an egg, and boil up one minute, stirring well. Take from the fire, squeeze the juice of a lemon through a hair sieve into the sauce, and pour half into a boat, the rest over the cauliflower.

MASHED CARROTS.

Scrape, wash, lay in cold water half an hour; then cook tender in boiling water. Drain well, mash with a wooden spoon, or beetle, work in a good piece of butter, and season with pepper and salt. Heap up in a vegetable dish, and serve very hot.

BOILED GREEN CORN.

Choose young sugar-corn, full grown, but not hard; test with the nail. When the grain is pierced, the milk should escape in a jet, and not be thick. Clean by stripping off the outer leaves, turn back the innermost covering carefully, pick off every thread of silk, and re-cover the ear with the thin husk that grew nearest it. Tie at the top with a bit of thread, put boiling water salted, and cook fast from twenty minutes to half an hour, in proportion to size and age. Cut off the stalks close to the cob, and send whole to table wrapped in a napkin.

Or you can cut from the cob while hot and season with butter, pepper, and salt. Send to table in a vegetable dish.

GREEN PEAS.

Shell and lay in cold water fifteen minutes. Cook from twenty to twenty-five minutes in boiling salted water. Drain, put into a deep dish with a good lump of butter; pepper and salt to taste.

TO BOIL ONIONS.

Take off the tops and tails, and the thin outer skin; but no more, lest the onions should go to pieces. Lay them on the bottom of a pan which is broad enough to contain them without piling one on another; just cover them with water, and let them simmer slowly till they are tender all through, but not till they break.

Serve them up with melted butter.

FRIED ONIONS.

Cut them in thin slices and season them; have a piece of fat bacon frying to get the juice, take it out, and put the onions in and stir until a pretty brown.

BOILED PARSNIPS.

Wash the parsnips, scrape them thoroughly, and with the point of a knife, remove any black spots about them, and should they be very large, cut the thick part into quarters. Put them into a saucepan of boiling water, salted in the above proportion, boil them rapidly until tender, which may be ascertained by thrusting a fork into them; take them up, drain them, and serve in a vegetable dish. This vegetable is usually served with salt fish, boiled pork, or boiled beef; when sent to table with the latter, a few should be placed alternately with carrots round the dish as a garnish.

PARSNIPS FRIED IN BUTTER.

Scrape the parsnips and boil gently forty-five minutes. When cold, cut in long slices about one-third of an inch thick. Season with salt and pepper. Dip in melted butter and in flour. Have two tablespoonfuls of butter in the frying-pan, and as soon as hot, put in enough parsnips to cover the bottom. Fry brown on both sides and serve on a hot dish.

CREAMED PARSNIPS.

Boil tender, scrape, and slice lengthwise. Put over the fire with two tablespoonfuls of butter, pepper, and salt, and a little minced parsley. Shake until the mixture boils. Dish the parsnips, add to the sauce three tablespoonfuls of cream in which has been stirred a quarter spoonful of flour. Boil once, and pour over the parsnips.

PARSNIP FRITTERS.

Boil four or five parsnips; when tender, take off the skin and mash them fine, add to them a teaspoonful of wheat flour and a beaten egg; put a tablespoonful of lard or beef dripping in a frying-pan over the fire, add to it a saltspoonful of salt; when boiling hot, put in the parsnips, make it in small cakes with a spoon; when one side is a delicate brown, turn the other; when both are done, take them on a dish, put a very little of the fat in which they were fried over, and serve hot. These resemble very nearly the taste of the salsify or oyster plant, and will generally be preferred.

SALSIFY, OR VEGETABLE OYSTER.

Boil and serve as directed for parsnips, either plain boiled, or fried, or made fritters.

BOILED VEGETABLE MARROW.

Have ready a saucepan of boiling water, properly salted; put in the marrows after peeling them, and boil them until quite tender. Take them up with a slice; halve, and, should they be very large, quarter them. Dish them on toast, and send to table with them a tureen of melted butter, or, in lieu of this, a small pat of salt butter. Large vegetable marrows may be preserved throughout the winter by storing them in a dry place; when wanted for use, a few slices should be cut and boiled in the same manner as above; but, when once begun, the marrow must be eaten quickly, as it keeps but a short time after it is cut. Vegetable marrows are also very delicious mashed; they should be boiled, then drained, and mashed smoothly with a wooden spoon. Heat them in a saucepan, add a seasoning of salt and pepper, and a small piece of butter, and dish with a few snippets of toasted bread placed round as a garnish.

Vegetable marrows are delightful when sliced and fried for ten minutes in butter. Before being fried they may be dipped in a batter of flour and water, seasoned with a little salt. Vegetable marrows may also be dressed as follows: Boil one, and when it is about ready, cut it in pieces, which place in a fresh saucepan, covered with soup stock, either white or brown; add a little salt in stewing. Serve in a deep dish when thoroughly tender. Vegetable marrows are very nice plain boiled, and served upon buttered toast. Peel them and cut them so as to be able to remove the seeds. Marrows will take from twenty minutes to an hour to boil, according to size and age. After being parboiled, they may be sliced down, dipped in egg, and then rubbed among bread-crumbs, and fried; serve them as hot as possible.

Tomatoes may be sliced thin, and served with salt, pepper, and vinegar over, for breakfast; or sliced, and strewn with sugar and grated nutmeg, for tea; for dinner they may be stewed or broiled, or baked.

Tomatoes may be preserved in sugar, or as catsup, when out of season. Such as like them, declare them to be equally excellent in each and every form or dressing.

STEWED TOMATOES.

Pour boiling water over six or eight large tomatoes, or a greater number of smaller ones; let them remain for a few minutes, then peel off the skins, squeeze out the seeds, and some of the juice, by pressing them gently in the hand; put them in a well-tinned stewpan, with a teaspoonful of salt, a saltspoonful of pepper, a bit of butter, half as large as an egg, and a tablespoonful of grated bread or rolled crackers; cover the stewpan close, and set it over the fire for nearly an hour; shake the stewpan occasionally, that they may not burn; serve hot.

This is decidedly the best manner of stewing tomatoes; they may be done without the bread-crumbs, and with less stewing if preferred.

BAKED TOMATOES.

Wash five or six smooth tomatoes; cut a piece from the stem end, the size of a twenty-five cent piece; put a saltspoonful of salt, half as much pepper, and a bit of butter the size of a nutmeg, in each; set them in a dish or pan, and bake in a moderate oven for nearly one hour.

STUFFED TOMATOES.

Twelve large, smooth tomatoes, one teaspoonful of salt, a little pepper, one tablespoonful of butter, one of sugar, one cupful of bread-crumbs, one teaspoonful of onion-juice. Arrange the tomatoes in a baking-pan. Cut a thin slice from the smooth end of each. With a small spoon, scoop out as much of the pulp and juice as possible without injuring the shape. When all have been treated in this way, mix the pulp and juice with the other ingredients, and fill the tomatoes with this mixture. Put on the tops, and bake slowly three-quarters of an hour. Slide the cake turner under the tomatoes and lift gently on to a flat dish. Garnish with parsley, and serve.

SCALLOPED TOMATOES.

Turn nearly all the juice off from a can of tomatoes. Salt and pepper this, by the way, and put aside in a cool place for some other day's soup. Put a layer of bread-crumbs in the bottom of a buttered pie-dish; on them one of tomatoes; sprinkle with salt, pepper, and some bits of butter, also a little sugar. Another layer of crumbs, another of tomatoes —seasoned—then a top layer of very fine, dry crumbs. Bake covered until bubbling hot, and brown quickly.

TO PEEL TOMATOES.

Put the tomatoes in a frying basket and plunge them into boiling water for about three minutes. Drain and peel.

BAKED BEANS.

Pick one quart of beans free from stones and dirt. Wash and soak in cold water over night. In the morning pour off the water. Cover with hot water, put two pounds of corned beef with them, and boil until they begin to split open (the time depends upon the age of the beans, but it will be from thirty to sixty minutes). Turn them into the colander, and pour over them two or three quarts of cold water. Put about half of the beans in a deep earthen pot, then put in the beef, and finally the remainder of the beans. Mix one teaspoonful of mustard and one tablespoonful of molasses with a little water. Pour this over the beans, and then add boiling water to just cover. Bake *slowly* ten hours. Add a little water occasionally.

STRING BEANS.

String, snap and wash two quarts beans, boil in plenty of water about fifteen minutes, drain off and put on again in about two quarts boiling water; boil an hour and a half, and add salt and pepper just before taking up, stirring in one and a half tablespoons butter, rubbed into two tablespoons flour and half pint sweet cream. Or boil a piece of salted pork one hour, then add beans and boil an hour and a half. For shelled beans boil half an hour in water enough to cover, and dress as above.

BUTTER BEANS.

With a knife cut off the ends of pods and strings from both sides, being very careful to remove every shred; cut every bean lengthwise, in two or three strips, and leave them for half an hour in cold water. Much more than cover them with boiling water; boil till perfectly tender.

It is well to allow three hours for boiling. Grain well, return to kettle, and add a dressing of half a gill of cream, one and a half ounces butter, one even teaspoon salt, and half a teaspoon pepper. This is sufficient for a quart of cooked beans.

ASPARAGUS WITH EGGS.

Boil a bunch of asparagus twenty minutes; cut off the tender tops and lay in a deep pie-plate, buttering, salting, and peppering well. Beat four eggs just enough to break up the yolks, add a tablespoonful of melted butter, with pepper and salt, and pour upon the asparagus. Bake eight minutes in a quick oven, and serve immediately.

ASPARAGUS UPON TOAST.

Tie the bunch of asparagus up with soft string, when you have cut away the wood, and cook about twenty-five minutes in salted boiling water. Have ready some slices of crustless toast; dip each in the asparagus liquor; butter well while hot and lay upon a heated dish. Drain the asparagus, and arrange upon the toast. Pepper, salt, and butter generously.

MUSHROOMS, STEWED.

If fresh, let them lie in salt and water about an hour, then put them in the stewpan, cover with water and let them cook two hours gently. Dress them with cream, butter and flour as oysters, and season to taste.

MUSHROOMS, FRIED.

When peeled put them into hot butter and let them heat thoroughly through—too much cooking toughens them. Season well with butter, pepper and salt. Serve on buttered toast; a teaspoon of wine or vinegar on each mushroom is a choice method.

BAKED MUSHROOMS.

Place some large flat ones nicely cleaned and trimmed on thin slices of well-buttered toast, putting a little nudgel of butter in each, as also a snuff of pepper and salt; lay them on a baking-tray, and cover them carefully; heap the hot ashes upon them, and let them bake on the hearth for fifteen or twenty minutes.

BROILED MUSHROOMS.

Choose the largest sort, lay them on a small gridiron over bright coals; the stalk upwards. Broil quickly, and serve, with butter, pepper, and salt over.

MASHED SQUASH.

Peel, seed and slice fresh summer squashes. Lay in cold water ten minutes; put into boiling water, a little salt, and cook tender. Twenty minutes will suffice if the squash be young. Mash in a colander, pressing out all the water; heap in a deep dish, seasoning with pepper, salt and butter. Serve hot.

BAKED SQUASH.

Cut in pieces, scrape well, bake from one to one and a half hours, according to the thickness of the squash; to be eaten with salt and butter as sweet potatoes.

FRIED SQUASHES.

Cut the squash into thin slices, and sprinkle it with salt; let it stand a few moments; then beat two eggs, and dip the squash into the egg; then fry it brown in butter.

STEWED CELERY

Is an excellent winter dish, and is very easily cooked. Wash the stalks thoroughly, and boil in well-salted water till tender, which will be in about twenty minutes. After it is made ready as above, drain it thoroughly, place it on toasted bread, and pour over it a quantity of sauce. A sauce of cream, seasoned with a little mace, may be served over the celery. It may also be served with melted butter.

STUFFED EGG-PLANT.

Cut the egg-plant in two; scrape out all the inside and put it in a saucepan with a little minced ham; cover with water and boil with salt; drain off the water; add two tablespoonfuls grated crumbs, tablespoonful butter, half a minced onion, salt and pepper; stuff each half of the hull with the mixture; add a small lump of butter to each, and bake fifteen minutes.

SAUCES FOR MEATS, FISH, POULTRY OR VEGETABLES.

TO MAKE DRAWN BUTTER.

Put half a pint of milk in a perfectly clean stewpan, and set it over a moderate fire; put into a pint bowl a heaping tablespoonful of wheat flour, quarter of a pound of sweet butter, and a saltspoonful of salt; work these well together with the back of a spoon, then pour into it, stirring it all the time, half a pint of boiling water; when it is smooth, stir it into the boiling milk, let it simmer for five minutes or more, and it is done.

Drawn butter made after this receipt will be found to be most excellent; it may be made less rich by using less butter.

PARSLEY SAUCE.

Make a drawn butter as directed, dip a bunch of parsley into boiling water, then cut it fine, and stir into the drawn butter a few minutes before taking it up.

EGG SAUCE.

Make a drawn butter; chop two hard-boiled eggs quite fine, the white and yolk separately, and stir it into the sauce before serving. This is used for boiled fish or vegetables.

ONION SAUCE.

Peel some nice white onions, and boil them tender; press the water from them; chop them fine, and put them to a half pint of hot milk; add a bit of butter, and a teaspoonful of salt, and pepper to taste. Serve with boiled veal, or poultry, or mutton.

ANCHOVY SAUCE.

Make the butter sauce, and stir into it four tablespoonfuls of essence of anchovy and one of lemon-juice.

BREAD SAUCE.

One pint milk, one cup bread-crumbs (very fine), one onion, sliced, a pinch of mace, pepper and salt to taste, three tablespoonfuls butter. Simmer the sliced onion in the milk until tender; strain the milk and pour over the bread-crumbs, which should be put into a saucepan. Cover and soak half an hour; beat smooth with an egg-whip, add the seasoning and butter; stir in well, boil up once, and serve in a tureen. If it is too thick, add boiling water and more butter.

This sauce is for roast poultry. Some people add some of the gravy from the dripping-pan, first straining it and beating it well in with the sauce.

TOMATO SAUCE

Can be cheaply made either from the fresh fruit or from the canned tomatoes, which are on sale in every grocer's shop. Squeeze as much as you require through a sieve, and then simmer slowly for a little time in a few tablespoonfuls of beef gravy, season with pepper and salt. Excellent for chops and cutlets, or for roasted beef.

TOMATO MUSTARD.

One peck of ripe tomatoes; boiled with two onions, six red peppers, four cloves of garlic, for one hour; then add a half pint or half pound salt, three tablespoons black pepper, half ounce ginger, half ounce allspice, half ounce mace, half ounce cloves; then boil again for one hour longer, and when cold add one pint of vinegar and a quarter pound of mustard; and if you like it very hot, a tablespoonful of Cayenne.

MINT SAUCE.

Mix one tablespoon of white sugar to half a teacup of good vinegar; add the mint and let it infuse for half an hour in a cool place before sending to the table. Serve with roast lamb or mutton.

CELERY SAUCE.

Mix two tablespoons of flour with half a teacup of butter; have ready a pint of boiling milk; stir the flour and butter into the milk; take three heads of celery, cut into small bits, and boil for a few minutes in water, which strain off; put the celery into the melted butter, and keep stirred over the fire for five or ten minutes. This is very nice with boiled fowl or turkey.

GOVERNOR'S SAUCE.

One peck green tomatoes, four large onions, six red peppers, one teacup grated horseradish, one teaspoon Cayenne and one of black pepper, one teaspoon mustard, half cup sugar; slice the tomatoes and sprinkle one teacup salt on, and lay all night; drain well in the morning, then simmer all together till cooked through

CREAM SAUCE.

One cupful of milk; a teaspoonful of flour and a tablespoonful of butter, salt and pepper. Put the butter in a small frying-pan, and when hot, but not brown, add the flour. Stir until smooth; then gradually add the milk. Let it boil up once. Season to taste with salt and pepper, and serve. This is nice to cut cold potatoes into and let them just heat through. They are then creamed potatoes. It also answers as a sauce for other vegetables, omelets, fish and sweetbreads, or, indeed, for anything that requires a white sauce. If you have plenty of cream, use it, and omit the butter.

RUSSIAN SAUCE.

(Piquant) may be thus made: Grated horseradish, four tablespoonfuls, weak mustard, one spoonful, sugar, half a spoonful, a little salt, two or three grains of Cayenne, and a spoonful or two of vinegar. Mix thoroughly, and serve to cold meat. When wanted for fish, let it be added to melted butter—two parts butter to one of sauce.

MAYONNAISE SAUCE.

Mix in a two-quart bowl one even teaspoon ground mustard, one of salt, and one and a half of vinegar; beat in the yolk of a raw egg, then add very gradually half a pint pure olive oil (or melted butter), beating briskly all the time. The mixture will become a very thick batter. Flavor with vinegar or fresh lemon-juice. Closely covered, it will keep for weeks in a cold place, and is delicious.

OYSTER SAUCE.

Take a pint of oysters, and save out a little of their liquor. Put them with their remaining liquor, and some mace and nutmeg, into a covered saucepan, and simmer them on hot coals about ten minutes. Then drain them. Oysters for sauce should be large. Having prepared in a saucepan some drawn or melted butter (mixed with oyster liquid instead of water), pour it into a sauceboat, add the oysters to it, and serve it up with boiled poultry, or with boiled fresh fish. Celery, first boiled and then chopped, is an improvement to oyster sauce.

LOBSTER SAUCE.

Put the coral and spawn of a boiled lobster into a mortar, with a tablespoonful of butter, pound it to a smooth mass, then rub it through a sieve; melt nearly a quarter of a pound of sweet butter, with a wineglass of water, or vinegar; add a teaspoonful of made mustard, stir in the coral and spawn, and a little salt and pepper; stir it until it is smooth, and serve. Some of the meat of the lobster may be chopped fine, and stirred into it.

CAPER SAUCE.

Make a butter sauce, and stir into it one tablespoonful of lemon-juice, two of capers, and one of essence of anchovy.

MUSTARD SAUCE.

Stir three tablespoonfuls of mixed mustard and a speck of Cayenne into a butter sauce. This is nice for devilled turkey and broiled smoked herrings.

CURRY SAUCE.

One tablespoonful of butter, one of flour, one teaspoonful of curry powder, one large slice of onion, one large cupful of stock, salt and pepper to taste. Cut the onion fine, and fry brown in the butter. Add the flour and curry powder. Stir for one minute, add the stock, and season with salt and pepper. Simmer five minutes; then strain, and serve. This sauce can be served with a broil or *saute* of meat or fish.

CRANBERRY SAUCE.

After removing all soft berries, wash thoroughly, place for about two minutes in scalding water, remove, and to every pound of fruit add three-quarters of a pound of granulated sugar and a half pint water; stew together over a moderate but steady fire. Be careful to *cover* and *not to stir* the fruit, but occasionally shake the vessel, or apply a gentler heat if in danger of sticking or burning. If attention to these particulars be given, the berries will retain their shape to a considerable extent, which adds greatly to their appearance on the table. Boil from five to seven minutes, remove from fire, turn into a deep dish, and set aside to cool. If to be kept, they can be put up at once in air-tight jars. Or, for strained sauce, one and a half pounds of fruit should be stewed in one pint of water for ten or twelve minutes, or until quite soft, then strained through a colander or fine wire sieve, and three-quarters of a pound of sugar thoroughly stirred into the pulp thus obtained; after cooling it is ready for use. Serve with roast turkey or game. When to be kept for a long time without sealing, more sugar may be added, but its too free use impairs the peculiar cranberry flavor. For dinner sauce half a pound is more economical, and really preferable to three-quarters, as given above. It is better, though not necessary, to use a porcelain kettle.

Some prefer not to add the sugar till the fruit is almost done, thinking this plan makes it more tender, and preserves the color better.

PORT WINE SAUCE FOR GAME.

Half a tumbler of currant jelly, half a tumbler of port wine, half a tumbler of stock, half a teaspoonful of salt, two tablespoonfuls of lemon-juice, four cloves, a speck of Cayenne. Simmer the cloves and stock together for half an hour. Strain on the other ingredients, and let all melt together. Part of the gravy from the game may be added to it.

CURRANT JELLY SAUCE.

Three tablespoonfuls of butter, one onion, one bay leaf, one sprig of celery, two tablespoonfuls of vinegar, half a cupful of currant jelly, one tablespoonful of flour, one pint of stock, salt, pepper. Cook the butter and onion until the latter begins to color. Add the flour, and herbs. Stir until brown; add the stock, and simmer twenty minutes. Strain, and skim off all the fat. Add the jelly, and stir over the fire until it is melted. Serve with game.

APPLE SAUCE.

Peel, quarter, and core, rich tart apples; put to them a very little water, cover them, and set them over the fire; when tender, mash them smooth, and serve with roasted pork, goose, or any other gross meat.

BREAD AND BREAKFAST CAKES.

YEAST.

Put two quarts of water and two tablespoonfuls of hops on to boil. Pare and grate six large potatoes. When the hops and water *boil* strain the water on the grated potatoes, and stir well. Place on the stove and boil up once. Add half a cupful of sugar and one-fourth of a cupful of salt. Let the mixture get blood-warm; then add one cupful of yeast, or one cake of compressed yeast, and let it rise in a warm place five or six hours. When well-risen turn into a stone jug. Cork this tightly, and set in a cool place.

PLAIN WHITE FAMILY BREAD.

Take one pint of flour and half a pint of good hop yeast and stir it together about five o'clock in the afternoon; at nine put one-half gallon of flour in a tray, put the sponge in the middle of the flour with a piece of lard as large as a walnut. Knead it all up with tepid water made salt with two teaspoonfuls or more to taste; work it well, and put it in a jar to rise. Next morning knead it over with a little flour; make it in two loaves; and set it in a warm place or oven until ready; then put it to bake, and when done, wrap it in a nice coarse towel. If you have no sugar in the yeast you use, stir a large teaspoonful in it before putting it in the flour.

GRAHAM BREAD.

Take a little over a quart of warm water, one-half cup brown sugar or molasses, one-fourth cup hop yeast, and one and one-half teaspoons salt; thicken the water with unbolted flour to a thin batter; add sugar, salt and yeast, and stir in more flour until quite stiff. In the morning add a small teaspoon soda, and flour enough to made the batter stiff as can be stirred with a spoon, put it into pans and let rise again; then bake in even oven, not too hot at first; *keep warm while rising;* smooth over the loaves with a spoon or knife dipped in water.

BOSTON BROWN BREAD.

One heaping coffee-cup each of corn, rye and Graham meal. The rye meal should be as fine as the Graham, or rye flour may be used. Sift the three kinds together as closely as possible, and beat together thoroughly with two cups New Orleans or Porto Rico molasses, two cups sweet milk, one cup sour milk, one dessertspoon soda, one teaspoon salt; pour into a tin form, place in a kettle of *cold* water, put on and boil four hours. Put on to cook as soon as mixed. It may appear to be too thin, but it is not, as this receipt has never been known to fail. Serve warm, with baked beans or Thanksgiving turkey. The bread should not quite fill the form (or a tin pail with a cover will answer), as it must have room to swell. See that the water does not boil up to the top of the form; also take care it does not boil entirely away or stop boiling. To serve it, remove the lid and set it a few moments into the open oven to dry the top, and it will then turn out in perfect shape. This bread can be used as a pudding, and served with a sauce made of thick *sour* cream, well sweetened and seasoned with nutmeg, or it is good toasted the next day.

CORN BREAD.

Sift three quarts of corn meal, add a tablespoonful of salt, one teaspoonful baking powder, and mix sufficient water with it to make a thin batter. Cover it with a bread-cloth and set it to rise. When ready to bake stir it well, pour it into a baking-pan, and bake slowly. Use cold water in summer and hot water in winter.

STEAMED BROWN BREAD.

One quart each of milk and Indian meal, one pint rye meal, one cup of molasses, two tablespoonfuls of soda. Add a little salt and steam four hours.

PARKER HOUSE ROLLS.

One teacup home-made yeast, a little salt, one tablespoon sugar, a piece of lard size of an egg, one pint milk, flour sufficient to mix. Put the milk on the stove to scald, with the lard in it. Prepare the flour with salt, sugar and yeast. Then add the milk, not too hot. Knead thoroughly when mixed at night; in the morning but very slight kneading is necessary. Then roll out and cut with large biscuit cutter. Spread a little butter on each roll and lap together. Let them rise very light, then bake in a quick oven.

FRENCH ROLLS.

One pint of milk, scalded; put into it while hot half a cup of sugar and one tablespoon of butter. When the milk is cool, add a little salt and half a cup of yeast, or one compressed yeast cake; stir in flour to make a stiff sponge, and when light, mix as for bread. Let it rise until light, punch it down with the hand, and let it rise again—repeat two or three times, then turn the dough on to the molding-board and pound with the rolling-pin until thin enough to cut. Cut out with a tumbler, brush the surface of each one with melted butter, and fold over. Let the rolls rise on the tins; bake, and while warm brush over the surface with melted butter to make the crust tender.

BUNS.

Break one egg into a cup and fill with sweet milk; mix with it half cup yeast, half cup butter, one cup sugar, enough flour to make a soft dough; flavor with nutmeg. Let it rise till very light, then mold into biscuits with a few currants. Let rise a second time in pan; bake, and when nearly done, glaze with a little molasses and milk. Use the same cup, no matter about the size, for each measure.

BISCUIT.

Dissolve one rounded tablespoon of butter in a pint of hot milk; when lukewarm stir in one quart of flour, and one beaten egg, a little salt, and a teacup of yeast; work into dough until smooth. If winter, set in a warm place; if summer, a cool one to rise. In the morning work softly and roll out one-half inch and cut into biscuit and set to rise for thirty minutes, when they will be ready to bake. These are delicious.

TO MAKE RUSKS.

To every pound of flour add two ounces of butter, one-quarter pint of milk, two ounces of loaf sugar, three eggs, one tablespoonful of yeast. Put the milk and butter into a saucepan, and keep shaking it round until the latter is melted. Put the flour into a basin with the sugar, mix these well together, and beat the eggs. Stir them with the yeast to the milk and butter, and with this liquid work the flour into a smooth dough. Cover a cloth over the basin, and leave the dough to rise by the side of the fire; then knead it, and divide it into twelve pieces; place them in a brisk oven, and bake for about twenty minutes. Take the rusks out, break them in half, and then set them in the oven to get crisp on the other side. When cold, they should be put into tin canisters to keep them dry; and, if intended for the cheese course, the sifted sugar should be omitted.

SWEET MILK GEMS.

Beat an egg well, add a pint new milk, a little salt, and Graham flour until it will drop off the spoon nicely; heat and butter the gem-pans before dropping in the dough; bake in a hot oven twenty minutes.

BREAKFAST GEMS.

One cup sweet milk, one and a half cups flour, one egg, one teaspoon salt, one teaspoon baking powder, beaten together five minutes; bake in hot gem-pans in a hot oven about fifteen minutes.

GRAHAM BREAKFAST CAKES.

Two cups of Graham flour, one cup of wheat flour, two eggs well beaten; mix with sweet milk, to make a very thin batter; bake in gem-irons; have the irons hot, then set them on the upper grate in the oven; will bake in fifteen minutes.

BUCKWHEAT CAKES.

One quart buckwheat flour; four tablespoonfuls yeast; one teaspoonful salt; one handful Indian meal; two tablespoonfuls molasses—*not* syrup. Warm water enough to make a thin batter. Beat very well and set to rise in a warm place. If the batter is in the least sour in the morning, stir in a very little soda dissolved in hot water. Mix in an earthen crock, and leave some in the bottom each morning—a cupful or so—to serve as sponge for the next night, instead of getting fresh yeast. In cold weather this plan can be successfully pursued for a week or ten days without setting a new supply. Of course you add the usual quantity of flour, etc., every night, and beat up well. Do not make your cakes too small. Buckwheats should be of generous size. Some put two-thirds buckwheat, one-third oat-meal, omitting the Indian.

FLANNEL CAKES.

Beat six eggs very light, stir in them two pounds of flour, one gill of yeast, small spoonful of salt, and sufficient milk to make a thick batter. Make them at night for breakfast, and at ten in the morning for tea. Have your griddle hot, grease it well, and bake as buckwheat. Butter and send them hot to the table, commencing after the family are seated.

RICE GRIDDLE-CAKES.

Boil half a cup rice; when cold, mix one quart sweet milk, the yolks of four eggs, and flour sufficient to make a stiff batter; beat the whites to a froth, stir in one teaspoon soda, and two of cream tartar; add a little salt, and lastly, the whites of eggs; bake on a griddle. A nice way to serve is to spread them while hot with butter, and almost any kind of preserves or jelly; roll them up neatly, cut off the ends, sprinkle them with sugar, and serve immediately.

FRENCH PANCAKES.

Two eggs, two ounces of butter, two ounces of sifted sugar, two ounces of flour, half pint of new milk. Beat the eggs thoroughly, and put them into a basin with the butter, which should be beaten to a cream; stir in the sugar and flour, and when these ingredients are well mixed, add the milk; keep stirring and beating the mixture for a few minutes; put it on buttered plates, and bake in a quick oven for twenty minutes. Serve with a cut lemon and sifted sugar, or pile the pancakes high on a dish, with a layer of preserve or marmalade between each.

PANCAKES.

Two cups of prepared flour; six eggs; one saltspoonful of salt; milk to make a *thin* batter. Beat the eggs light; add salt, two cups of milk, then the whites and flour alternately with milk, until the batter is of the right consistency. Run a teaspoonful of lard over the bottom of a hot frying-pan, pour in a large ladleful of batter and fry quickly. Roll the pancake up like a sheet of paper; lay upon a hot dish; put in more lard, and fry another pancake. Keep hot over boiling water, sending half a dozen to the table at a time.

BREAD FRITTERS.

One quart milk—boiling hot; two cups fine bread-crumbs; three eggs; one teaspoonful nutmeg; one tablespoonful butter—melted; one saltspoonful salt, and the same of soda, dissolved in hot water. Soak the bread in the boiling milk ten minutes, in a covered bowl. Beat to a smooth paste; add the whipped yolks, the butter, salt, soda, and finally the whites, whipped stiff.

QUICK SALLY LUNN.

One cup of sugar, half cup of butter; stir well together, and then add one or two eggs; put in one good pint of sweet milk, and with sufficient flour to make a batter about as stiff as cake; put in three teaspoons of baking powder; bake and eat hot with butter, for tea or breakfast.

BREAKFAST CAKE.

One pint of flour, three tablespoons of butter, three tablespoons of sugar, one egg, one cup sweet milk, one teaspoon cream tartar, half teaspoon soda; to be eaten with butter.

QUICK WAFFLES.

Two pints sweet milk, one cup butter (melted), sifted flour to make a soft batter; add the well-beaten yolks of six eggs, then the beaten whites, and lastly (just before baking), four teaspoons baking powder, beating very hard and fast for a few minutes. These are very good with four or five eggs, but much better with more.

JOHNNY CAKE.

Two-thirds teaspoon soda, three tablespoons sugar, one teaspoon cream tartar, one egg, one cup sweet milk, six tablespoons Indian meal, three tablespoonfuls flour, and a little salt. This makes a thin batter.

MUSH.

Indian or oatmeal mush is best made in the following manner: Put fresh water in a kettle over the fire to boil, and put in some salt; when the water boils, stir in handful by handful corn or oatmeal until thick enough for use. In order to have excellent mush, the meal should be allowed to cook well and long as possible while thin, and before the final handful is added. When desired to be fried for breakfast, turn into an earthen dish and set away to cool. Then cut in slices when you wish to fry; dip each piece in beaten eggs and fry on a hot griddle.

CORN MUSH.

Put four quarts fresh water in a kettle to boil, salt to suit the taste; when it begins to boil stir in one and a half quarts meal, letting it sift through the fingers slowly to prevent lumps, adding it a little faster at the last, until as thick as can be conveniently stirred with one hand; set in the oven in the kettle, (or take out into a pan), bake an hour, and it will be thoroughly cooked. It takes corn meal so long to cook thoroughly that it is very difficult to boil it until done without burning. Excellent for frying when cold. Use a hard wood paddle, two feet long, with a blade two inches wide and seven inches long, to stir with. The thorough cooking and baking in oven afterwards takes away all the raw taste that mush is apt to have, and adds much to its sweetness and delicious flavor.

GRAHAM MUSH.

Sift meal slowly into boiling salted water, stirring briskly until it is as thick as can be stirred with one hand; serve with milk, or cream and sugar, or butter and syrup. It is much improved by removing from the kettle to a pan as soon as thoroughly mixed, and steaming for three or four hours. It may also be eaten cold, or sliced and fried like corn mush.

SALADS, PICKLES AND CATSUP.

LETTUCE.

The early lettuce, and first fine salad, are five or six leaves in a cluster; their early appearance is their greatest recommendation; cabbage or white-heart lettuce is later and much more delicate; break the leaves apart one by one from the stalk and throw them into a pan of cold water; rinse them well, lay them into a salad bowl or a deep dish, lay the largest leaves first, put the next size upon them, then lay on the finest white leaves; cut hard-boiled eggs in slices or quarters and lay them at equal distances around the edge and over the salad; serve with vinegar, oil, and made mustard in the castor. Or, having picked and washed the lettuce, cut the leaves small; put the cut salad in a glass dish or bowl, pour a salad dressing over and serve; or, garnish with small red radishes, cut in halves or slices, and hard-boiled eggs cut in quarters or slices; pour a salad dressing over when ready to serve. Serve with boiled lobster, boiled fowls, or roasted lamb or veal.

LETTUCE SALAD.

Take the yolks of three hard-boiled eggs, add salt and mustard to taste; mash it fine; make a paste by adding a dessertspoon of olive oil or melted butter (use butter always when it is difficult to get *fresh* oil); mix thoroughly, and then dilute by adding *gradually* a teacup of vinegar, and pour over the lettuce. Garnish by *slicing* another egg and laying over the lettuce. This is sufficient for a moderate-sized dish of lettuce.

SALMON SALAD.

One quart of cooked salmon, two heads of lettuce, two tablespoonfuls of lemon-juice, one of vinegar, two of capers, one teaspoonful of salt, one-third of a teaspoonful of pepper, one cupful of mayonnaise dressing, or the French dressing. Break up the salmon with two silver forks. Add to it the salt, pepper, vinegar and lemon-juice. Put in the ice-chest or some other cold place, for two or three hours. Prepare the lettuce as directed for lobster salad. At serving time, pick out leaves enough to border the dish. Cut or tear the remainder in pieces, and arrange these in the centre of a flat dish. On them heap the salmon lightly, and cover with the dressing. Now sprinkle on the capers. Arrange the whole leaves at the base; and, if you choose, lay one-fourth of a thin slice of lemon on each leaf.

LOBSTER SALAD.

Put a large lobster over the fire in boiling water slightly salted; boil rapidly for about twenty minutes; when done it will be of a bright red color, and should be removed, as if boiled too long it will be tough; when cold, crack the claws, after first disjointing, twist off the head (which is used in garnishing), split the body in two lengthwise, pick out the meat in bits not too fine, saving the coral separate; cut up a large head of lettuce slightly, and place on a dish over which lay the lobster, putting the coral around the outside. For dressing, take the yolks of three eggs, beat well, add four tablespoons salad oil, dropping it in very slowly, beating all the time; then add a little salt, Cayenne pepper, half teaspoon mixed mustard, and two tablespoons vinegar. Pour this over the lobster, just before sending to table.

TOMATO SALAD.

Take the skin, juice and seeds from nice, fresh tomatoes, chop what remains with celery, and add a good salad-dressing.

SALAD DRESSING.

Yolks of two hard-boiled eggs rubbed very fine and smooth, one teaspoon English mustard, one of salt, the yolks of two raw eggs beaten into the other, dessertspoon of fine sugar. Add very fresh sweet oil poured in by very small quantities, and beaten as long as the mixture continues to thicken, then add vinegar till as thin as desired. If not hot enough with mustard, add a little Cayenne pepper.

SARDINE SALAD.

Arrange one quart of any kind of cooked fish on a bed of crisp lettuce. Split six sardines, and if there are any bones, remove them. Cover the fish with the sardine dressing. Over this put the sardines, having the ends meet in the center of the dish. At the base of the dish make a wreath of thin slices of lemon. Garnish with parsley or lettuce, and serve immediately.

FRENCH SALAD DRESSING.

Three tablespoonfuls of oil, one of vinegar, one saltspoonful of salt, one-half a saltspoonful of pepper. Put the salt and pepper in a cup, and add one tablespoonful of the oil. When thoroughly mixed, add the remainder of the oil and the vinegar. This is dressing enough for a salad for six persons. If you like the flavor of onion, grate a little juice into the dressing. The juice is obtained by first peeling the onion, and then grating with a coarse grater, using a good deal of pressure. Two strokes will give about two drops of juice.

CREAM DRESSING FOR COLD SLAW.

Two tablespoons whipped sweet cream, two of sugar, and four of vinegar; beat well and pour over cabbage, previously cut very fine and seasoned with salt.

CHICKEN SALAD.

Boil one chicken tender; chop moderately fine the whites of twelve hard-boiled eggs and the chicken; add equal quantities of chopped celery and cabbage; mash the yolks fine, add two tablespoons butter, two of sugar, one teaspoon mustard; pepper and salt to taste; and lastly, one-half cup good cider vinegar; pour over the salad, and mix thoroughly. If no celery is at hand, use chopped pickled cucumbers or lettuce and celery seed. This may be mixed two or three days before using.

RED VEGETABLE SALAD.

One pint of cold boiled potatoes, one pint of cold boiled beets, one pint of uncooked red cabbage, six tablespoonfuls of oil, eight of red vinegar (that in which beets have been pickled), two teaspoonfuls of salt (unless the vegetables have been cooked in salted water), half a teaspoonful of pepper. Cut the potatoes in *thin* slices and the beets fine, and slice the cabbage as thin as possible. Mix all the ingredients. Let stand in a cold place one hour; then serve. Red cabbage and celery may be used together.

CELERY SALAD.

One boiled egg, one raw egg, one tablespoonful salad oil, one teaspoonful white sugar, one saltspoonful of salt, one saltspoon of pepper, four tablespoonfuls of vinegar, one teaspoonful made mustard. Prepare the dressing as for tomato salad; cut the celery into bits half an inch long, and season. Eat at once, before the vinegar injures the crispness of the vegetable.

COLD SLAW.

Chop or shred a small white cabbage. Prepare a dressing in the proportion of one tablespoonful of oil to four of vinegar, a teaspoonful of made mustard, the same quantity of salt and sugar, and half as much pepper. Pour over the salad, adding, if you choose, three tablespoonfuls of minced celery; toss up well and put into a glass bowl.

SALAD DRESSING (Excellent).

Four eggs, one teaspoonful of mixed mustard, one-quarter teaspoonful of white pepper, half that quantity of Cayenne, salt to taste, four tablespoonfuls of cream, vinegar.

Boil the eggs until hard, which will be in about one-quarter hour or twenty minutes; put them into cold water, take off the shells, and pound the yolks in a mortar to a smooth paste. Then add all the other ingredients, except the vinegar, and stir them well until the whole are thoroughly incorporated one with the other. Pour in sufficient vinegar to make it of the consistency of cream, taking care to add but little at a time. The mixture will then be ready for use.

PICKLED CUCUMBERS.

Wash and wipe six hundred small cucumbers and two quarts of peppers. Put them in a tub with one and a half cupfuls of salt and a piece of alum as large as an egg. Heat to the boiling point three gallons of cider vinegar and three pints of water. Add a quarter of a pound each of whole cloves, whole allspice and stick cinnamon, and two ounces of white mustard seed, and pour over the pickles.

TO PICKLE ONIONS.

Peel the onions until they are white, scald them in strong salt and water, then take them up with a skimmer; make vinegar enough to cover them, boiling hot; strew over the onions whole pepper and white mustard seed, pour the vinegar over to cover them; when cold, put them in wide-mouthed bottles, and cork them close. A tablespoonful of sweet oil may be put in the bottles before the cork. The best sort of onions for pickling are the small white buttons.

PICKLED CAULIFLOWERS.

Two cauliflowers, cut up; one pint of small onions, three medium-sized red peppers. Dissolve half a pint of salt in water enough to cover the vegetables, and let these stand over night. In the morning drain them. Heat two quarts of vinegar with four tablespoonfuls of mustard, until it boils. Add the vegetables, and boil for about fifteen minutes, or until a fork can be thrust through the cauliflower.

RED CABBAGE.

Procure a firm good-sized cabbage, and after taking off any straggling or soiled leaves, cut it in very narrow slices, which, after you sprinkle them well with salt, lay aside for forty-eight hours. Next drain off the salt liquor which has formed, and pour over the cabbage a well-seasoned pickle of boiling hot vinegar; black pepper and ginger are best for seasoning. Cover the pickle jars till the cabbage is cold, and then cork.

TO PICKLE TOMATOES.

Take the round, smooth green tomatoes, put them in salt and water, cover the vessel and put them over the fire to scald; that is, to let the water become boiling hot; then set the kettle off; take them from the pot into a basin of cold water; to enough cold vinegar to cover them, put whole pepper and mustard seed; when the tomatoes are cold take them from the water, cut each in two across, shake out the seeds and wipe the inside dry with a cloth, then put them into glass jars, and cover with the vinegar; cork them close or with a close-fitting tin cover.

RIPE TOMATO PICKLES.

To seven pounds of ripe tomatoes add three pounds sugar, one quart vinegar; boil them together fifteen minutes, skim out the tomatoes and boil the syrup a few minutes longer. Spice to suit the taste with cloves and cinnamon.

CHOPPED PICKLE.

One peck of green tomatoes, two quarts of onions and two of peppers. Chop all fine, separately, and mix, adding three cupfuls of salt. Let them stand over night, and in the morning drain well. Add half a pound of mustard seed, two tablespoonfuls of ground allspice, two of ground cloves and one cupful of grated horseradish. Pour over it three quarts of boiling vinegar.

CHOW CHOW.

One peck of green tomatoes, half peck string beans, quarter peck small white onions, quarter pint green and red peppers mixed, two large heads cabbage, four tablespoons white mustard seed, two of white or black cloves, two of celery seed, two of allspice, one small box yellow mustard, pound brown sugar, one ounce of turmeric; slice the tomatoes and let stand over night in brine that will bear an egg; then squeeze out brine, chop cabbage, onions and beans; chop tomatoes separately, mix with the spices, put all in porcelain kettle, cover with vinegar and boil three hours.

PICCALILLI.

One peck of green tomatoes; (if the flavor of onions is desired, take eight, but it is very nice without any); four green peppers; slice all, and put in layers, sprinkle on one cup of salt, and let them remain over night; in the morning press dry through a sieve, put it in a porcelain kettle and cover with vinegar; add one cup of sugar, a tablespoon of each kind of spice; put into a muslin bag; stew slowly about an hour, or until the tomatoes are as soft as you desire.

PICKLED WALNUTS (Very Good).

One hundred walnuts, salt and water. To each quart of vinegar allow two ounces of whole black pepper, one ounce of allspice, one ounce of bruised ginger. Procure the walnuts while young; be careful they are not woody, and prick them well with a fork; prepare a strong brine of salt and water (four pounds of salt to each gallon of water), into which put the walnuts, letting them remain nine days, and changing the brine every third day; drain them off, put them on a dish, place it in the sun until they become perfectly black, which will be in two or three days; have ready dry jars, into which place the walnuts, and do not quite fill the jars. Boil sufficient vinegar to cover them, for ten minutes, with spices in the above proportion, and pour it hot over the walnuts, which must be quite covered with the pickle; tie down with bladder, and keep in dry place. They will be fit for use in a month, and will keep good two or three years.

GREEN TOMATO PICKLE.

One peck green tomatoes sliced, six large onions sliced, one teacup of salt over both; mix thoroughly and let it remain over night; pour off liquor in the morning and throw it away; mix two quarts of water and one of vinegar, and boil twenty minutes; drain and throw liquor away; take three quarts of vinegar, two pounds of sugar, two tablespoons each of allspice, cloves, cinnamon, ginger, and mustard, and twelve green peppers chopped fine; boil from one to two hours. Put away in a stone crock.

CHILI SAUCE.

Eight quarts tomatoes, three cups of peppers, two cups of onions, three cups of sugar, one cup of salt, one and a half quarts of vinegar, three teaspoonfuls of cloves; same quantity of cinnamon, two teaspoonfuls each of ginger and nutmeg; boil three hours; chop tomatoes, peppers, and onions very fine; bottle up and seal.

MIXED PICKLES.

Three hundred small cucumbers, four green peppers sliced fine, two large or three small heads cauliflower, three heads white cabbage shaved fine, nine large onions sliced, one large root horseradish, one quart green beans cut one inch long, one quart green tomatoes sliced; put this mixture in a pretty strong brine twenty-four hours; drain three hours, then sprinkle in a quarter pound black and a quarter pound white mustard seed; also one tablespoon black ground pepper; let it come to a good boil in just vinegar enough to cover it, adding a little alum. Drain again, and when cold, mix in a half pint ground mustard; cover the whole with good cider vinegar; add turmeric enough to color, if you like.

PICKLED MUSHROOMS.

Sufficient vinegar to cover the mushrooms, to each quart of mushrooms, two blades pounded mace, one ounce ground pepper; salt to taste. Choose some nice young button-mushrooms for pickling, and rub off the skin with a piece of flannel and salt, and cut off the stalks; if very large, take out the red inside, and reject the black ones, as they are too old. Put them in a stewpan, sprinkle salt over them, with pounded mace and pepper in the above proportion; shake them well over a clear fire until the liquor flows, and keep them there until it is all dried up again; then add as much vinegar as will cover them; just let it simmer for one minute, and store it away in stone jars for use. When cold, tie down with bladder, and keep in a dry place; they will remain good for a length of time, and are generally considered delicious.

FAVORITE PICKLES.

One quart raw cabbage chopped fine; one quart boiled beets chopped fine; two cups sugar, tablespoon salt, one teaspoon black pepper, a quarter teaspoon red pepper, one teacup grated horseradish; cover with cold vinegar and keep from the air.

TOMATO MUSTARD.

Slice and boil for an hour, with six small red peppers, half bushel of ripe tomatoes; strain through a colander and boil for an hour with two tablespoonfuls of black pepper, two ounces of ginger, one ounce allspice, half ounce cloves, one-eighth ounce mace, quarter pound salt. When cold add two ounces mustard, two ounces curry powder, and one pint of vinegar.

INDIAN CHETNEY.

Eight ounces of sharp, sour apples, pared and cored, eight ounces of tomatoes, eight ounces of salt, eight ounces of brown sugar, eight ounces of stoned raisins, four ounces of Cayenne, four ounces of powdered ginger, two ounces of garlic, two ounces of shalots, three quarts of vinegar, one quart of lemon-juice. Chop the apples in small square pieces, and add to them the other ingredients. Mix the whole well together, and put in a well-covered jar. Keep this in a warm place, and stir every day for a month, taking care to put on the lid after this operation; strain, but do not squeeze it dry; store it away in clean jars or bottles for use, and the liquor will serve as an excellent sauce for meat or fish.

PICKLED CHERRIES.

Five pounds of cherries, stoned or not; one quart of vinegar, two pounds of sugar, one-half ounce of cinnamon, one-half ounce of cloves, one-half ounce of mace, boil the sugar and vinegar and spices together (grind the spices and tie them in a muslin bag), and pour hot over the cherries.

PICKLED PLUMS.

To seven pounds plums, four pounds sugar, two ounces stick cinnamon, two ounces cloves, one quart vinegar, add a little mace; put in the jar first a layer of plums, then a layer of spices alternately; scald the vinegar and sugar together, pour it over the plums; repeat three times for plums (only once for cut apples and pears), the fourth time scald all together, put them into glass jars and they are ready for use.

SPICED PLUMS.

Make a syrup, allowing one pound of sugar to one of plums, and to every three pounds of sugar a scant pint of vinegar. Allow one ounce each of ground cinnamon, cloves, mace, and allspice to a peck of plums. Prick the plums. Add the spices to the syrup, and pour, boiling, over the plums. Let these stand three days; then skim them out, and boil down the syrup until it is quite thick, and pour hot over the plums in the jar in which they are to be kept. Cover closely.

PEACHES, PEARS, AND SWEET APPLES.

For six pounds of fruit use three of sugar, about five dozen cloves, and a pint of vinegar. Into each apple, pear, or peach, stick two cloves. Have the syrup hot, and cook until tender.

TOMATO CATSUP.

Take one gallon of skinned tomatoes, four tablespoonfuls of salt, four ditto of whole black pepper, half a spoonful of allspice, eight pods of red pepper, and three spoonfuls of mustard, boil them together for one hour, then strain it through a sieve or coarse cloth, and when cold, bottle for use; have the best velvet corks.

WALNUT CATSUP.

Bruise to a mass one hundred and twenty green walnuts, gathered when a pin could pierce one; put to it three-quarters of a pound of salt and a quart of good vinegar; stir them every day for a fortnight, then strain and squeeze the liquor from them through a cloth, and set it aside, put to the husks half a pint of vinegar, and let it stand all night, then strain and squeeze them as before; put the liquor from them to that which was put aside, add to it one ounce and a quarter of whole pepper, forty cloves, half an ounce of nutmeg sliced, and half an ounce of ginger, and boil it for half an hour closely covered, then strain it; when cold, bottle it for use. Secure the bottles with new corks, and dip them in melted rosin.

MUSHROOM CATSUP.

To each peck of mushrooms one-half pound of salt; to each quart of mushroom liquor one-quarter ounce of Cayenne, one-half ounce of allspice, one-half ounce of ginger, two blades of pounded mace. Choose full-grown mushroom-flaps, and take care they are perfectly *fresh-gathered* when the weather is tolerably dry; for, if they are picked during very heavy rain the catsup from which they are made is liable to get musty, and will not keep long. Put a layer of them in a deep pan, sprinkle salt over them, and then another layer of mushrooms, and so on alternately. Let them remain for a few hours, then break them up with the hand; put them in a nice cool place for three days, occasionally stirring and mashing them well to extract from them as much juice as possible. Now measure the quantity of liquor without straining, and to each quart allow the above proportion of spices, etc. Put all into a stone jar, cover it up very closely, put it in a saucepan of boiling water, set it over the fire, and let it boil for three hours.

Have ready a nice clean stewpan; turn into it the contents of the jar, and let the whole simmer very gently for half an hour; pour into a jug, where it should stand in a cool place till next day; then pour it off into another jug, and strain it into very dry, clean bottles, and do not squeeze the mushrooms. To each pint of catsup add a few drops of brandy. Be careful not to shake the contents, but leave all the sediment behind in the jug; cork well, and either seal or rosin the cork, so as perfectly to exclude the air. When a very clear, bright catsup is wanted, the liquor must be strained through a very fine hair-sieve, or flannel bag, *after* it has been very gently poured off; if the operation is not successful, it must be repeated until you have quite a clear liquor. It should be examined occasionally, and if it is spoiling should be reboiled with a few peppercorns.

BRINE THAT PRESERVES BUTTER A YEAR

To three gallons of brine strong enough to bear an egg, add one-quarter pound good loaf sugar, and one tablespoonful of saltpetre; boil the brine, and when it is cold strain carefully. Pack butter closely in small jars, and allow the brine to cover the butter to the depth of at least four inches. This completely excludes the air. If practicable make your butter into small rolls, wrap each carefully in a clean muslin cloth, tying up with a string; place a weight over the butter to keep it all submerged in the brine. This mode is most recommended by those who have tried both.

BUTTER IN HASTE,

FROM WINTER CREAM, OR FROM THE MILK OF ONE COW.

Take milk fresh from the cow, strain it into clean pans, set it over a gentle fire until it is scalding hot; do not let it boil; then set it aside; when it is cold skim off the cream; the milk will still be fit for any ordinary use; when you have enough cream, put it into a clean earthen basin; beat it with a wooden spoon until the butter is made, which will not be long; then take it from the milk and work with a little cold water, until it is free from milk, then drain off the water, put a small tablespoonful of fine salt to each pound of butter, and work it in. A small teaspoonful of fine white sugar, worked in with the salt, will be found an improvement—sugar is a great preservative. Make the butter in a roll; cover with a bit of muslin, and keep it in a cool place.

This receipt was obtained from one who practiced it for several winters.

PUDDINGS.

GENERAL REMARKS.

All boiled pudding should be put on in *boiling water*, which must not be allowed to stop simmering, and the pudding must always be covered with the water; if requisite the saucepan should be kept filled up. To prevent a pudding boiled in a cloth from sticking to the bottom of the saucepan, place a small plate or saucer underneath it, if a mold is used, this precaution is not necessary; but care must be taken to keep the pudding well covered with water. For dishing a boiled pudding as soon as it comes out of the pot, dip it into a basin of cold water, and the cloth will then not adhere to it. Great expedition is necessary in sending puddings to table, as, by standing, they quickly become heavy, batter puddings particularly. For baked or boiled puddings, the molds, cups, or basins should be always buttered before the mixture is put into them, and they should be put into the saucepan directly they are filled.

CHRISTMAS PLUM PUDDING.

One pound butter, one pound suet, freed from strings and chopped fine, one pound sugar, two and a half pounds flour, two pounds raisins, seeded, chopped and dredged with flour, two pounds currants, picked over carefully after they are washed, one-quarter pound citron, shred fine, twelve eggs, whites and yolks beaten separately, one pint milk, one cup brandy, one-half ounce cloves, one-half ounce mace, two grated nutmegs. Cream the butter and sugar, beat in the yolks when you have whipped them smooth and light; next put in the milk, then the flour, alternately with the beaten whites, then the brandy and spice, lastly the fruit, well dredged with flour. Mix all thoroughly wring out your pudding-cloth in hot water, flour well inside, pour in the mixture and boil five hours.

BOILED BATTER PUDDING.

Three eggs, one ounce butter, one pint milk, three tablespoonfuls flour, a little salt. Put the flour into a basin, and add sufficient milk to moisten it; carefully rub down all the lumps with a spoon, then pour in the remainder of the milk, and stir in the butter, which should be previously melted; keep beating the mixture, add the eggs and a pinch of salt, and when the batter is quite smooth, put it into a well-buttered basin, tie it down very tightly, and put it into boiling water; move the basin about for a few minutes after it is put into the water, to prevent the flour settling in any part, and boil for one and one-quarter hours. This pudding may also be boiled in a floured cloth that has been wetted in hot water; it will then take a few minutes less than when boiled in a basin. Send these puddings very quickly to table, and serve with sweet sauce, wine sauce, stewed fruit, or jam of any kind; when the latter is used, a little of it may be placed round the dish in small quantities, as a garnish.

BATTER PUDDING.

One quart milk, four eggs, six ounces flour, a little soda and salt. Mix the flour very carefully with a little milk so it will not be lumpy. Bake twenty minutes. Serve immediately.

MADEIRA PUDDING.

One-half pound cheap suet, three-quarters of a pound bread-crumbs, six ounces moist sugar, one-quarter pound flour, two eggs, two wineglasses sherry; mix the suet, bread-crumbs, sugar and flour well together. When these ingredients are well-mixed, add the eggs and two glasses of sherry, to make a thick batter; boil three hours and a half. Serve with wine sauce.

APPLE SAGO PUDDING.

One cup sago in a quart of tepid water, with a pinch of salt, soaked for one hour; six or eight apples, pared and cored, or quartered, and steamed tender, and put in the pudding dish; boil and stir the sago until clear, adding water to make it thin, and pour it over the apples; this is good hot with butter and sugar, or cold with cream and sugar.

QUEEN OF PUDDINGS.

One large cup of fine bread-crumbs soaked in milk, three-quarters cup sugar, one lemon, juice and grated rind, six eggs, one-half pound stale sponge cake, one-half pound macaroons—almond, one-half cup jelly or jam, and one small tumbler sherry wine, one-half cup milk poured upon the bread-crumbs, one tablespoonful melted butter. Rub the butter and sugar together; put the beaten yolks in next, then the soaked bread-crumbs, the lemon, juice and rind, and beat to a smooth, light paste before adding the whites. Butter your mold *very* well, and put in the bottom a light layer of dry bread-crumbs, upon this one of macaroons, laid evenly and closely together. Wet this with wine, and cover with a layer of the mixture, then with slices of sponge cake, spread thickly with jelly or jam; next macaroons, wet with wine, more custard, sponge-cake and jàm, and so on until the mold is full, putting a layer of the mixture at the top. Cover closely, and steam in the oven three-quarters of an hour; then remove the cover to brown the top. Turn out carefully into a dish, and pour over it a sauce made of currant jelly warmed, and beaten up with two tablespoonfuls melted butter and a glass of pale sherry.

ORANGE PUDDING.

Peel and cut five sweet oranges into thin slices, taking out the seeds, pour over them a coffee-cup of white sugar; let a pint of milk get boiling hot, by setting it in a pot of boiling water; add the yolks of three eggs well beaten, one tablespoonful of corn starch, made smooth with a little cold milk: stir all the time; as soon as thickened pour over the fruit. Beat the whites to a stiff froth, adding a tablespoonful of sugar, and spread over the top for frosting; set it in the oven for a few minutes to harden; eat cold or hot (better cold), for dinner and supper. Berries or peaches can be substituted for oranges.

CORN STARCH PUDDING.

One pint sweet milk, whites of three eggs, two tablespoons corn starch, three of sugar, a little salt. Put the milk in a pan or small bucket, set in a kettle of hot water on the stove, and when it reaches the boiling point add the sugar, then the starch dissolved in a little cold milk, and lastly the whites of eggs whipped to a stiff froth; beat it, and let cook for a few minutes, then pour into teacups, filling about half full, and set in cool place. For sauce, make a boiled custard as follows: Bring to boiling point one pint of milk, add three tablespoons sugar, then the beaten yolks thinned by adding one tablespoon milk, stirring all the time till it thickens; flavor with two teaspoons lemon or two of vanilla, and set to cool. In serving, put one of the molds in a saucedish for each person, and pour over it some of the boiled custard. Or the pudding may be made in one large mold.

To make a chocolate pudding, flavor the above pudding with vanilla, remove two-thirds of it, and add half a cake of chocolate softened, mashed, and dissolved in a little milk. Put a layer of half the white pudding into the mold, then the chocolate, then the rest of the white; or two layers of chocolate may be used with a white between; or the centre may be cocoa (made by adding half a cocoanut grated fine), and the outside chocolate; or pineapple chopped fine (if first cooked in a little water, the latter makes a nice dressing), or strawberries may be used.

FRENCH PUDDING.

One quart of milk, three tablespoons of corn starch, yolks of four eggs, half cup sugar and a little salt; put part of the milk, salt and sugar on the stove and let it boil; dissolve the corn starch in the rest of the milk; stir into the milk, and while boiling add the yolks. Flavor with vanilla.

FROSTING.—Whites of four eggs beaten to a stiff froth, half a cup of sugar; flavor with lemon; spread it on the pudding, and put it into the oven to brown, saving a little of the frosting to moisten the top; then put on grated cocoanut to give it the appearance of snow-flake.

BELLE'S PUDDING.

Soak for an hour in a pint of cold water one box of Cox's sparkling gelatine, and add one pint of boiling water, one pint of wine, the juice of four lemons, and three large cupfuls of sugar. Beat the whites of four eggs to a stiff froth, and stir into the jelly when it begins to thicken. Pour into a large mold, and set in ice-water in a cool place. When ready to serve, turn out as you would jelly, only have the pudding in a deep dish. Pour one quart of soft custard around it, and serve.

CREAM TAPIOCA PUDDING.

Soak three tablespoons of tapioca in water over night; put the tapioca into a quart of boiling milk, and boil half an hour; beat the yolks of four eggs with a cup of sugar; add three tablespoons of prepared cocoanut; stir in and boil ten minutes longer; pour into a pudding-dish; beat the whites of four eggs to a stiff froth, stir in three tablespoons of sugar; put this over the top and sprinkle cocoanut over the top and brown for five minutes.

A BACHELOR'S PUDDING.

Four ounces of grated bread, four ounces of currants, four ounces of apples, two ounces of sugar, three eggs, a few drops of essence of lemon, a little grated nutmeg. Pare, core, and mince the apples very finely, sufficient, when minced, to make four ounces; add to these the currants, which should be well washed, the grated bread, and sugar; whisk the eggs, beat these up with the remaining ingredients, and, when all is thoroughly mixed, put the pudding into a buttered basin, tie it down with a cloth, and boil for three hours.

MACARONI PUDDING.

One-half pound macaroni broken into inch lengths, two cups boiling water, one teaspoonful butter, one large cup milk, two tablespoonfuls sugar, grated peel of half a lemon, a little cinnamon and salt. Boil the macaroni in the water until it is tender, and has soaked up the liquid. It must be cooked in a farina-kettle. Add the butter and salt. Cover for five minutes without cooking. Put in the rest of the ingredients. Simmer, after the boil begins, ten minutes longer, before serving in a deep dish. Be careful, in stirring, not to break the macaroni. Eat with butter and powdered sugar, or cream and sugar.

BAKED INDIAN PUDDING.

Two quarts scalded milk with salt, one and one-half cups Indian meal (yellow); one tablespoon ginger, letting this stand twenty minutes; one cup molasses, two eggs (saleratus if no eggs), a piece of butter the size of a common walnut. Bake two hours. Splendid.

BOILED INDIAN PUDDING.

Warm a pint of molasses and pint of milk, stir well together, beat four eggs, and stir gradually into molasses and milk; add a pound beef suet chopped fine, and Indian meal sufficient to make a thick batter; add a teaspoon pulverized cinnamon, nutmeg and a little grated lemon-peel, and stir all together thoroughly; dip cloth into boiling water, shake, flour a little, turn in the mixture, tie up, leaving room for the pudding to swell, and boil three hours; serve hot with sauce made of drawn butter, wine and nutmeg.

MARMALADE PUDDINGS.

Half pound suet, half pound grated bread-crumbs, half pound sugar, three ounces orange marmalade; mix these ingredients together with four eggs; boil four hours. Lay a few raisins open in the bottom of the mold. Sauce: Two ounces butter, and two ounces white sugar; beat to a cream and flavor with brandy or lemon.

BOILED APPLE DUMPLINGS.

Add to two cups sour milk one teaspoon soda, and one salt, half cup butter, lard, flour enough to make dough a little stiffer than for biscuit; or make a good baking powder crust; peel and core apples, roll out crust, place apples on dough, fill cavity of each with sugar, encase each apple in coating of the crust, press edges tight together, (it is nice to tie a cloth around each one), put into kettle of boiling water slighted salted, boil half an hour, taking care that the water covers the dumplings. They are also very nice steamed. To bake, make in same way, using a soft dough, place in a shallow pan, bake in a hot oven, and serve with cream and sugar, or place in a pan which is four or five inches deep (do not have the dumplings touch each other); then pour in hot water, just leaving top of dumplings uncovered. To a pan of four or five dumplings, add one teacup sugar and half a teacup butter; bake from half to three-quarters of an hour. If water cooks away too much, add more. Serve dumplings on platter and the liquid in sauce-boat for dressing. Fresh or canned peaches may be made in the same way.

NELLY'S PUDDING.

Half pound flour, half pound treacle, half pound suet, the rind and juice of one lemon, a few strips of candied lemon-peel; three tablespoonfuls cream, two eggs. Chop the suet finely; mix with it the flour, treacle, lemon-peel minced, and candied lemon-peel; add the cream, lemon-juice, and two well-beaten eggs; beat the pudding well, put it into a buttered basin, tie it down with a cloth, and boil from three and a half to four hours.

RICH BAKED APPLE PUDDING.

Half pound the pulp of apples, half pound loaf sugar, six ounces butter, the rind one lemon, six eggs, puff paste. Peel, core and cut the apples, as for sauce; put them into a stewpan, with only just sufficient water to prevent them from burning, and let them stew until reduced to a pulp. Weigh the pulp, and to every half pound add sifted sugar, grated lemon-rind, and six well-beaten eggs. Beat these ingredients well together; then melt the butter, stir it to the other things, put a border of puff paste round the dish, and bake for rather more than half an hour. The butter should not be added until the pudding is ready for the oven.

SNOW BALLS.

Pick all imperfections from a half pint of rice, put it in water, and rub it between the hands; then pour that water off, put more on, stir it about in it, let the rice settle, then drain the water off; put the rice in a two-quart stewpan, with a teaspoonful of salt, and a quart of water; cover the stewpan, and set it where it will boil gently for one hour, or until the water is all absorbed; dip some teacups into cold water, fill them with the boiled rice, press it to their shape; then turn them out on a dish, and serve with butter and sugar, or wine sauce.

RICE PUDDING.

One teacup rice, one teacup sugar, one teacup raisins, small piece butter, a little salt, two quarts milk. Bake from an hour and a half to two hours. Serve with sauce.

APPLE CHARLOTTE.

Cut slices of wheat bread or rolls, and having rubbed the bottom and sides of a basin with a bit of butter, line it with the sliced bread or rolls; peel tart apples, cut them small, and nearly fill the pan, strewing bits of butter and sugar between the apples; grate a small nutmeg over; soak as many slices of bread or rolls as will cover it; over which put a plate, and a weight, to keep the bread close upon the apples; bake two hours in a quick oven, then turn it out. Quarter of a pound of butter, and half a pound of sugar, to half a peck of tart apples.

GROUND RICE PUDDING.

This is an economical pudding, made with two pints of sweet milk, a teacupful of ground rice, two tablespoonfuls of sugar, three eggs, and a little ground nutmeg. Bring half the quantity of milk to the boiling point, with the nutmeg or any other flavoring matter, and sugar. In the other half of the milk beat up the rice flour into a thin batter, adding to it through a strainer the hot seasoned milk, stirring all the time. The eggs well-whisked should next be added. A sprinkling of salt is an improvement. Bake this mixture in a moderate oven for a little over an hour, say seventy minutes, or boil in a buttered basin or shape. Serve with apricot preserve, or marmalade, or indeed any kind of jam.

FIG PUDDING.

One-half pound figs, one-quarter pound grated bread, two and a half ounces powdered sugar, three ounces butter, two eggs, one teacup of milk. Chop the figs small and mix first with the butter, then all the other ingredients by degrees; butter a mold, sprinkle with bread-crumbs, cover it tight and boil for three hours.

BREAD AND BUTTER PUDDING.

Place as many slices of thin cut bread and butter as you like in a pie-dish, say ten or twelve slices, sprinkle a few well-washed currants between the layers, beat up half a dozen of eggs in two pints of new milk, adding sugar to taste and a little flavoring, such as nutmeg or cinnamon, and pour over the bread and butter. Bake for an hour and ten minutes, and send it to table in the dish it has been baked in.

CABINET PUDDING.

One quart of milk, four eggs, four tablespoonfuls of sugar, half a teaspoonful of salt, one tablespoonful of butter, three pints of stale sponge cake, one cupful of raisins, chopped citron and currants. Have a little more of the currants than of the two other fruits. Beat the eggs, sugar, and salt together, and add the milk. Butter a three-pint pudding mold (the melon shape is nice), sprinkle the sides and bottom with the fruit, and put in a layer of cake. Again sprinkle in fruit, and put in more cake. Continue this until all the materials are used. Gradually pour on the custard. Let the pudding stand two hours, and steam an hour and a quarter. Serve with wine or creamy sauce.

SNOW PUDDING.

One half package Cox's gelatine; pour over it a cup of cold water and add one and one-half cups of sugar; when soft, add one cup boiling water, juice of one lemon and the whites of four well-beaten eggs; beat all together until very light; put in a glass dish and pour over it custard made as

PUDDINGS & PASTRY

follows: One pint milk, yolks of four eggs, and grated rind of one lemon; boil. Splendid.

CARROT PUDDING.

One pound grated carrots, three-fourths pound chopped suet, half pound each raisins and currants, four tablespoons sugar, eight tablespoons flour, and spices to suit the taste. Boil four hours, place in the oven for twenty minutes, and serve with wine sauce.

LEMON PUDDING.

Half pound of sugar, half pound of butter, five eggs, half gill brandy, rind and juice of one large lemon; beat well the butter and sugar, whisk the eggs, add them to the lemon, grate the peel, line a dish with puff-paste, and bake in a moderate oven.

ROLY-POLY.

Take one quart of flour; make good biscuit crust; roll out one-half inch thick and spread with any kind of fruit, fresh or preserved; fold so that the fruit will not run out; dip cloth into boiling water, and flour it and lay around the pudding closely, leaving room to swell; steam one and one-half hours; serve with boiled sauce; or lay in steamer without a cloth, and steam for one hour.

COTTAGE PUDDING.

One-half cup of sugar, one cup of milk, one pint of flour, three tablespoonfuls of melted butter, one teaspoonful soda, two of cream of tartar, two eggs, a little salt; bake one-quarter of an hour in small pans.

COCOANUT PUDDING.

Beat two eggs with one cupful of new milk; add one-quarter of a pound of grated cocoanut; mix with it three tablespoonfuls each of grated bread and powdered sugar, two ounces of melted butter, five ounces of raisins, and one teaspoonful of grated lemon-peel; beat the whole well together; pour the mixture into a buttered dish, and bake in a slow oven; then turn it out, dust sugar over it, and serve. This pudding may be either boiled or baked.

CREAM PUDDING.

Stir together one pint cream, three ounces sugar, the yolks of three eggs, and a little grated nutmeg; add the well-beaten whites, stirring lightly, and pour into a buttered pie-plate on which has been sprinkled the crumbs of stale bread to about the thickness of an ordinary crust; sprinkle over the top a layer of bread-crumbs, and bake.

TAPIOCA PUDDING.

Cover three tablespoons tapioca with water; stand over night; add one quart milk, a small piece of butter, a little salt, and boil; beat the yolks of three eggs with a cup of sugar, and boil the whole to a very thick custard, flavor with vanilla; when cold cover with whites of eggs beaten.

COMMON CUSTARD.

Beat either four or five fresh eggs light; then stir them into a quart of milk; sweeten to taste; flavor with a teaspoonful of peach-water, or extract of lemon, or vanilla, and half a teaspoonful of salt; rub butter over the bottom and sides of a baking-dish or tin basin; pour in the custard, grate a little nutmeg over, and bake in a quick oven. Three-quarters of an hour is generally enough. Try whetber it is done by putting a teaspoon handle into the middle of it; if it comes out clean, it is enough.

Or butter small cups; set them into a shallow pan of hot water, reaching nearly to the top of the cups; nearly fill them with the custard mixture; keep the water boiling until they are done. The pan may be set in an oven, or hot shovel.

PUDDING SAUCES.

RICH WINE SAUCE.

One cupful of butter, two of powdered sugar, half a cupful of wine. Beat the butter to a cream. Add the sugar gradually, and when very light add the wine, which has been made hot, a little at a time. Place the bowl in a basin of hot water and stir for two minutes. The sauce should be smooth and foamy.

WHIPPED CREAM SAUCE.

Whip a pint of thick sweet cream, add the beaten whites of two eggs, sweeten to taste; place pudding in centre of dish, and surround with the sauce; or pile up in centre and surround with molded blanc-mange, or fruit puddings.

LEMON SAUCE.

One cup of sugar, half a cup of butter, one egg, one lemon, juice and grated rind, three tablespoonfuls of boiling water; put in a tin pail and thicken over steam.

JELLY SAUCE.

Melt one ounce of sugar and two tablespoons grape jelly over the fire in a half pint of boiling water, and stir into it half a teaspoon corn starch dissolved in a half cup cold water; let it come to a boil, and it will be ready for use. Any other fruit jelly may be used instead of grape.

CABINET PUDDING SAUCE.

Take the yolks of five eggs and whip them lightly; express the juice of a lemon and grate down a little of the peel. The other ingredients are a tablespoon of butter, a cup of sugar, a glass of good wine, and a little spice. Mix the sugar and butter, adding the yolks, spice, and lemon-juice. Beat fifteen minutes, then add the wine, and stir hard. Immerse in a saucepan of boiling water, beating while it heats.

FOAMING SAUCE

Beat whites of three eggs to a stiff froth; melt teacup of sugar in a little water, let it boil, stir in one glass of wine, and then the whites of the three eggs; serve at once.

SPANISH SAUCE.

One half cup of boiling water, one tablespoon corn starch, two tablespoonfuls vinegar, one tablespoonful of butter, one cup sugar, one-half nutmeg.

HARD SAUCE.

Beat to a cream a quarter of a pound of butter, add gradually a quarter of a pound of sugar; heat it until very white; add a little lemon-juice, or grate nutmeg on top.

PUDDING SAUCE

One cup of sugar, one-half cup of butter, yolks of three eggs; one teaspoon of corn starch or arrow-root; stir the whole until very light; add sufficient boiling water to make the consistency of thick cream; wine or brandy to suit the taste.

SAUCE FOR PLUM PUDDING.

The yolks of three eggs, one tablespoonful of powdered sugar, one gill of milk, a very little grated lemon-rind, two small wineglassfuls of brandy. Separate the yolks from the whites of three eggs, and put the former into a stew-pan; add the sugar, milk, and grated lemon-rind, and stir over the fire until the mixture thickens; but do *not* allow it to *boil*. Put in the brandy; let the sauce stand by the side of the fire, to get quite hot; keep stirring it, and serve in a boat or tureen separately, or pour it over the pudding.

VANILLA SAUCE.

The whites of two eggs and the yolk of one, half a cupful of powdered sugar, one teaspoonful of vanilla, three table-spoonfuls of milk. Beat the whites of the eggs to a stiff froth, next beat in the sugar, and then the yolk of the egg and the seasoning. Serve immediately. This sauce is for light puddings.

PASTRY.

VERY GOOD PUFF-PASTE.

To every pound of flour allow one pound of butter, and not quite one-half pint of water. Carefully weigh the flour and butter, and have the exact proportion; squeeze the butter well, to extract the water from it, and afterwards wring it in a clean cloth, that no moisture may remain. Sift the flour; see that it is perfectly dry, and proceed in the following manner to make the paste, using a very *clean* paste-board and rolling-pin. Supposing the quantity to be one pound of flour, work the whole into a smooth paste, with not quite one-half pint of water, using a knife to mix it with; the proportion of this latter ingredient must be regulated by the discretion of the cook; if too much be added, the paste, when baked, will be tough. Roll it out until it is of an equal thickness of about an inch; break four ounces of the butter into small pieces; place these on the paste, sift over it a little flour, fold it over, roll out again, and put another four ounces of butter. Repeat the rolling and buttering until the paste has been rolled out four times, or equal quantities of flour and butter have been used. Do not omit, every time the paste is rolled out, to dredge a little flour over that and the rolling-pin, to prevent both from sticking. Handle the paste as lightly as possible, and do not press heavily upon it with the rolling-pin. The next thing to be considered is the oven, as the baking of pastry requires particular attention. Do not put it into the oven until it is sufficiently hot to raise the paste; for the best-prepared paste, if not properly baked, will be good for nothing. Brushing the paste as often as rolled out, and the pieces of butter placed thereon, with the white of an egg, assists it to rise in *leaves* or *flakes*. As this is the great beauty of puff-paste, it is as well to try this method.

PLAINER PASTE.

One pound of flour, a little more for rolling-pin and board, and half a pound of butter and half a pound of lard. Cut the butter and lard through the flour (which should be sifted), and mix with sufficient ice-water to roll easily. Avoid kneading it, and use the hands as little as possible in mixing.

SUET CRUST, FOR PIES OR PUDDINGS.

To every pound of flour allow five or six ounces of beef suet, one-half pint of water. Free the suet from skin and shreds; chop it extremely fine, and rub it well into the flour; work the whole to a smooth paste with the above proportion of water; roll it out, and it is ready for use. This crust is quite rich enough for ordinary purposes; but when a better one is desired, use from one-half to three-quarters pound of suet to every pound of flour. Some cooks, for rich crusts, pound the suet in a mortar, with a small quantity of butter. It should then be laid on the paste in small pieces, the same as for puff-crust, and will be found exceedingly nice for hot tarts. Five ounces of suet to every pound of flour will make a very good crust; and even one-quarter pound will answer very well for children, or where the crust is wanted very plain.

TO ICE PASTRY.

To ice pastry, which is the usual method adopted for fruit tarts and sweet dishes of pastry, put the white of an egg on a plate, and with the blade of a knife beat it to a stiff froth. When the pastry is nearly baked, brush it over with this, and sift over some pounded sugar; put it back into the oven to set a glaze, and in a few minutes it will be done. Great care should be taken that the paste does not catch or burn in the oven, which it is very liable to do after the icing is laid on.

TO GLAZE PASTRY.

To glaze pastry, which is the usual method adopted for meat or raised pies, break an egg, separate the yolk from the white, and beat the former for a short time. Then, when the pastry is nearly baked, take it out of the oven, brush it over with this beaten yolk of egg, and put it back in the oven to set the glaze.

MINCE-MEAT.

Take five or six pounds scraggy beef—a neck piece will do—and put to boil in water enough to cover it; take off the scum that rises when it reaches the boiling point, add hot water from time to time until it is tender, then remove the lid from the pot, salt, let boil till almost dry, turning the meat over occasionally in the liquor, take from the fire, and let stand over night to get thoroughly cold; pick bones, gristle, or stringy bits from the meat, chop very fine, mincing at the same time three pounds of nice beef suet; seed and cut four pounds raisins, wash and dry four pounds currants, slice thin a pound of citron, chop fine four quarts good cooking tart apples; put into a large pan together, add two ounces cinnamon, one of cloves, one of ginger, four nutmegs, the juice and grated rind of two lemons, one tablespoon salt, one teaspoon pepper, and two pounds sugar. Put in a porcelain kettle one quart boiled cider, or, better still, one quart currant or grape-juice (canned when grapes are turning from green to purple), one quart nice molasses or syrup, also a good lump of butter; let it come to boiling point, and pour over the ingredients in the pan after having first mixed them well, then mix again thoroughly. Pack in jars and put in a cool place, and, when cold, pour molasses over the top an eighth of an inch in thickness, and cover tightly. This will keep two months. For baking, take some out of the jar; if not moist enough add a little hot water, and strew a few whole raisins over each pie. Instead of boiled beef, a beef's heart or roast meat may be used; and a good proportion for a few pies is one-third chopped meat and two-thirds apples, with a little suet, raisins, spices, butter, and salt.

MOCK MINCE PIE.

One egg, three or four large crackers, or six or eight small ones, one-half cup of molasses, one-half cup sugar, one-half cup vinegar, one-half cup strong tea, one cup chopped raisins, a small piece butter, spice and salt.

APPLE CUSTARD PIE.

Peel sour apples and stew until soft and not much water is left in them, and rub through a colander. Beat three eggs for each pie. Put in proportion of one cup butter and one of sugar for three pies. Season with nutmeg.

APPLE MERINGUE PIE.

Pare, slice, stew and sweeten ripe, tart and juicy apples, mash and season with nutmeg (or stew lemon-peel with them for flavor), fill crust and bake till done; spread over the apple a thick meringue made by whipping to froth whites of three eggs for each pie, sweetening with three tablespoons powdered sugar; flavor with vanilla, beat until it will stand alone, and cover pie three-quarters of an inch thick. Set back in a quick oven till well "set," and eat cold. In their season substitute peaches for apples.

APPLE PIE.

Stew green or ripe apples, when you have pared and cored them. Mash to a smooth compote, sweeten to taste, and, while hot, stir in a teaspoon butter for each pie. Season with nutmeg. When cool, fill your crust, and either cross-bar the top with strips of paste, or bake without cover. Eat cold, with powdered sugar strewed over it.

LEMON PIE.

The juice and rind of one lemon, two eggs, eight heaping tablespoonfuls of sugar, one small teacupful of milk, one teaspocnful of corn starch. Mix the corn starch with a little of the milk. Put the remainder on the fire, and when boiling, stir in the corn starch. Boil one minute. Let this cool, and add the yolks of the eggs, four heaping tablespoonfuls of the sugar, and the grated rind and juice of the lemon, all well beaten together. Have a deep pie-plate lined with paste, and fill with this mixture. Bake slowly half an hour. Beat the whites of the eggs to a stiff froth, and gradually beat into them the remainder of the sugar. Cover the pie with this, and brown slowly.

CUSTARD PIE.

Make a custard of the yolks of three eggs with milk, season to the taste; bake it in ordinary crust; put it in a quick oven, that the crust may not be heavy, and as soon as that is heated remove it to a place in the oven of a more moderate heat, that the custard may bake slowly and not curdle; when done, beat the whites to a froth; add sugar and spread over the top, and return to the oven to brown slightly; small pinch of salt added to a custard heightens the flavor; a little soda in the crust prevents it from being heavy. Very nice.

COCOANUT PIE.

One-half pound grated cocoanut, three-quarters pound of white sugar (powdered), six ounces of butter, five eggs, the whites only, one glass of white wine, two tablespoonfuls rose-water, one tablespoonful of nutmeg. Cream the butter and sugar, and when well-mixed, beat very light, with the wine and rose-water. Add the cocoanut with as little and as light beating as possible; finally, whip in the stiffened whites of the eggs with a few skillful strokes, and bake at once in open shells. Eat cold, with powdered sugar sifted over them.

LEMON TARTS.

Mix well together the juice and grated rind of two lemons, two cups of sugar, two eggs, and the crumbs of sponge cake; beat it all together until smooth; put into twelve patty-pans lined with puff-paste, and bake until the crust is done.

PASTRY SANDWICHES.

Puff-paste, jam of any kind, the white of an egg, sifted sugar.

Roll the paste out thin; put half of it on a baking-sheet or tin, and spread equally over it apricot, greengage, or any preserve that may be preferred. Lay over this preserve another thin paste, press the edges together all round, and mark the paste in lines with a knife on the surface, to show where to cut it when baked. Bake from twenty minutes to half an hour; and, a short time before being done, take the pastry out of the oven, brush it over with the white of an egg, sift over pounded sugar, and put it back in the oven to color. When cold, cut it into strips; pile these on a dish pyramidically, and serve. These strips, cut about two inches long, piled in circular rows, and a plateful of flavored whipped cream poured in the middle, make a very pretty dish.

CHERRY PIE.

Line the dish with a good crust, and fill with ripe cherries, regulating the quantity of sugar you scatter over them by their sweetness. Cover and bake.

Eat cold, with white sugar sifted over the top.

SQUASH PIE.

Two teacups of boiled squash, three-fourths teacup of brown sugar, three eggs, two tablespoons of molasses, one tablespoon of melted butter, one tablespoon of ginger, one teaspoon of cinnamon, two teacups of milk, a little salt. Make two plate pies.

CREAM PIE.

Pour a pint of cream upon a cup and a half powdered sugar; let stand until the whites of three eggs have been beaten to a stiff froth; add this to the cream, and beat up thoroughly; grate a little nutmeg over the mixture and bake in two pies without upper crusts.

TARTLETS.

Puff-paste, the white of an egg, pounded sugar.

Mode: Roll some good puff-paste out thin, and cut it into two and a half inch squares; brush each square over with the white of an egg, then fold down the corners, so that they all meet in the middle of each piece of paste;

slightly press the two pieces together, brush them over with the egg, sift over sugar, and bake in a nice quick oven for about a quarter of an hour. When they are done, make a little hole in the middle of the paste, and fill it up with apricot jam, marmalade, or red-currant jelly. Pile them high in the centre of a dish, on a napkin, and garnish with the same preserve the tartlets are filled with.

PEACH PIE.

Line a pie-tin with puff-paste, fill with pared peaches in halves or quarters, well covered with sugar; put on upper crust and bake; or make as above without upper crust, bake until done, remove from the oven, and cover with a meringue made of the whites of two eggs, beaten to a stiff froth with two tablespoons powdered sugar; return to oven and brown slightly. Canned peaches may be used instead of fresh, in the same way.

TART SHELLS.

Roll out thin a nice puff-paste, cut out with a glass or biscuit cutter, with a wine-glass or smaller cup cut out the centre of two out of three of these, lay the rings thus made on the third, and bake immediately; or shells may be made by lining patty-pans with paste. If the paste is light, the shell will be fine, and may be used for tarts or oyster patties. Filled with jelly and covered with meringue (tablespoon sugar to white of one egg) and browned in oven, they are very nice to serve for tea.

PUMPKIN PIE.

One quart of stewed pumpkin, pressed through a sieve; nine eggs, whites and yolks beaten separately; two scant quarts of milk, one teaspoonful of mace, one teaspoonful of cinnamon, and the same of nutmeg; one and a half cups of white sugar, or very light brown. Beat all well together, and bake in crust without cover.

MINCE PIES.

Three pounds of raisins, stone and chop them a little; three pounds of currants, three pounds of sugar, three pounds of suet chopped very fine, two ounces candied lemon-peel, two ounces of candied orange-peel, six large apples grated, one ounce of cinnamon, two nutmegs, the juice of three lemons and the rinds grated, and half a pint of brandy. Excellent.

CAKES.

WHITE LADY-CAKE.

Beat the whites of eight eggs to a high froth, add gradually a pound of white sugar finely ground, beat quarter of a pound of butter to a cream, add a teacup of sweet milk with a small teaspoonful of powdered volatile salts or saleratus dissolved in it; put the eggs to butter and milk, add as much sifted wheat flour as will make it as thick as pound cake mixture, and a teaspoon of orange-flower water or lemon extract, then add a quarter of a pound of shelled almonds, blanched and beaten to a paste with a little white of egg; beat the whole together until light and white; line a square tin pan with buttered paper, put in the mixture an inch deep, and bake half an hour in a quick oven. When done take it from the pan; when cold take the paper off, turn it upside down on the bottom of the pan and ice the side which was down; when the icing is nearly hard mark it in slices the width of a finger, and two inches and a half long.

MACAROONS.

One-half pound of sweet almonds, one-half pound of sifted loaf sugar, the whites of three eggs, wafer-paper. Blanch, skin, and dry the almonds, and pound them well with a little orange-flower water or plain water; then add to them the sifted sugar and the whites of the eggs, which should be beaten to a stiff froth, and mix all the ingredients well together. When the paste looks soft, drop it at equal distances from a biscuit-syringe on to sheets of wafer-paper; put a strip of almond on the top of each; strew some sugar over, and bake the macaroons in rather a slow oven, of a light brown color. When hard and set, they are done, and must not be allowed to get very brown, as that would spoil their appearance. If the cakes, when baked, appear heavy, add a little more white of egg, but let this always be well-whisked before it is added to the other ingredients. We have given a recipe for making these cakes, but we think it almost or quite as economical to purchase such articles as these at a good confectioner's.

ALMOND ICING.

Whites of four eggs; one pound sweet almonds; one pound powdered sugar; a little rose-water. Blanch the almonds by pouring boiling water over them and stripping off the skins. When dry, pound them to a paste, a few at a time, in a Wedgewood mortar, moistening it with rose-water as you go on. When beaten fine and smooth, beat gradually into icing. Put on very thick, and, when nearly dry, cover with plain icing.

TO MAKE ICING FOR CAKES.

Beat the whites of two small eggs to a high froth; then add to them quarter of a pound of white sugar, ground fine, like flour; flavor with lemon extract, or vanilla; beat it until it is light and very white, but not quite so stiff as kiss mixture; the longer it is beaten the more firm it will become. No more sugar must be added to make it so. Beat the frosting until it may be spread smoothly on the cake. This quantity will ice quite a large cake over the top and sides.

LOAF CAKE.

One pound of butter beaten to a cream, two pounds of sugar rolled fine, three pounds of sifted flour, six well-beaten eggs, three teaspoonfuls of powdered saleratus, dissolved in a little hot water, one tablespoonful of ground cinnamon, and half a nutmeg grated; add one pound of currants, well washed and dried, one pound of raisins stoned and cut in two; work the whole well together, divide it in three loaves, put them in buttered basins, and bake one hour in a moderate oven.

RICH BRIDE-CAKE.

Take four pounds of sifted flour, four pounds of sweet, fresh butter, beaten to a cream, and two pounds of white powdered sugar; take six eggs for each pound of flour, an ounce of ground mace or nutmegs, and a tablespoonful of lemon extract or orange-flower water.

LADY FINGERS.

Take eight eggs; whip the whites to a firm snow. In the meantime, have the yolks beaten up with six ounces of powdered sugar. Each of these operations should be performed at least one hour. Then mix all together with six ounces of sifted flour; and when well incorporated, stir in half a pint of rose or orange-flower water; stir them together for some time.

Have ready some tin plates, rubbed with white wax; take a funnel with three or four tubes; fill it with the paste, and press out the cakes upon the plates, to the size and length of a finger; grate white sugar over each; let them lay until the sugar melts, and they shine; then put them in a moderate oven, until they have a fine color; when cool, take them from the tins, and lay them together in couples, by the backs. These cakes may be formed with a spoon, on sheets of writing paper. Half this quantity will be trouble enough at one time.

QUEEN CAKE.

Beat one pound of butter to a cream, with a tablespoonful of rose-water; then add one pound of fine white sugar, ten eggs, beaten very light, and a pound and a quarter of sifted flour; beat the cake well together; then add half a pound of shelled almonds, blanched, and beaten to a paste; butter tin round basins, line them with white paper; put in the mixture an inch and a half deep; bake one hour in a quick oven.

CHOCOLATE MACAROONS.

Put three ounces of plain chocolate in a pan and melt on a slow fire; then work it to a thick paste with one pound of powdered sugar and the whites of three eggs; roll the mixture down to the thickness of about one-quarter of an inch; cut it in small, round pieces with a paste-cutter, either plain or scalloped; butter a pan slightly, and dust it with flour and sugar in equal quantities; place in it the pieces of paste or mixture, and bake in a hot but not quick oven.

CARAMEL CAKE.

One cup of butter, two of sugar, a scant cup milk, one and a half cups flour, cup corn starch, whites of seven eggs, three teaspoons baking powder in the flour; bake in a long pan. Take half pound brown sugar, scant quarter pound chocolate, half cup milk, butter size of an egg, two teaspoons vanilla; mix thoroughly and cook as syrup until stiff enough to spread; spread on cake and set in the oven to dry.

POUND CAKE.

One pound of butter, one and one-quarter pounds of flour, one pound of pounded loaf sugar, one pound of currants, nine eggs, two ounces of candied peel, one-half ounce of citron, one-half ounce of sweet almonds; when liked, a little pounded mace. Work the butter to a cream; dredge in the flour; add the sugar, currants, candied peel, which should be cut into neat slices, and the almonds, which should be blanched and chopped, and mix all these well together; whisk the eggs, and let them be thoroughly blended with the dry ingredients. Beat the cake well for twenty minutes, and put it into a round tin, lined at the bottom and sides with a strip of white buttered paper. Bake it from one and one-half to two hours, and let the oven be well heated when the cake is first put in, as, if this is not the case, the currants will all sink to the bottom of it. To make this preparation light, the yolks and whites of the eggs should be beaten separately and added separately to the other ingredients. A glass of wine is added to the mixture; but this is scarcely necessary, as the cake will be found quite rich enough without it.

COCOANUT SPONGE CAKE.

Beat the yolks of six eggs with half a pound of sugar and a quarter of a pound of flour, add a teaspoonful of salt, a teaspoonful of lemon essence, and half a nutmeg, grated; beat the whites of the eggs to a froth, and stir them to the yolks, etc., and the white meat of a cocoanut, grated; line square tin pans with buttered paper, and having stirred the ingredients well together, put the mixture in an inch deep in the pans; bake in a quick oven half an hour; cut it in squares, to serve with or without icing.

COCOANUT POUND CAKE.

Beat half a pound of butter to a cream; add gradually a pound of sifted flour, one pound of powdered sugar, two teaspoonfuls baking powder, a pinch of salt, a teaspoonful of grated lemon-peel, quarter of a pound of prepared cocoanut, four well-beaten eggs, and a cupful of milk; mix thoroughly; butter the tins, and line them with buttered paper; pour the mixture in to the depth of an inch and a half, and bake in a good oven. When baked take out, spread icing over them, and return the cake to the oven a moment to dry the icing.

COCOANUT CUP CAKE.

Two cups of sugar, two cups of butter, one cup of milk, one teaspoonful of essence of lemon, half a nutmeg grated, four well-beaten eggs and the white meat of a cocoanut grated; use as much sifted wheat flour as will make a rather stiff batter; beat it well, butter square tin pans, line them with white paper, and put in the mixture an inch deep; bake in a moderate oven half an hour, or it may require ten minutes longer. When cold, cut in small squares or diamonds; this is a rich cake and is much improved by a thin icing. This cake should be made with fine white sugar.

COCOANUT DROPS.

Break a cocoanut in pieces, and lay it in cold water, then cut off the dark rind, and grate the white meat on a coarse grater; put the whites of four eggs with half a pound of powdered white sugar; beat it until it is light and white, then add to it a teaspoonful of lemon extract, and gradually as much grated cocoanut as will make it as thick as can be stirred easily with a spoon; lay it in heaps the size of a large nutmeg on sheets of white paper, place them the distance of half an inch apart; when the paper is full, lay it on a baking-tin, set them in a quick oven; when they begin to look yellowish, they are done; let them remain on the paper until nearly cold, then take them off with a thin-bladed knife.

CITRON HEART CAKES.

Beat half a pound of butter to a cream, take six eggs, beat the whites to a froth, and the yolks with half a pound of sugar, and rather more than half a pound of sifted flour, beat these well together, add a wineglass of brandy, and quarter of a pound of citron cut in thin slips, bake it in small heart-shaped tins, or a square tin pan, rubbed over with a bit of sponge dipped in melted butter; put the mixture in half an inch deep, bake fifteen or twenty minutes in a quick oven. These are very fine cakes. Shred almonds may be used instead of citron.

IMPERIAL CAKE.

One pound of flour, half a pound of butter, three-quarters of a pound of sugar, four eggs, half a pound of currants, well-washed and dredged, half a teaspoonful of soda dissolved in hot water, half a lemon, grated rind and juice, one teaspoonful of cinnamon. Drop from a spoon upon well-buttered paper, lining a baking-pan. Bake quickly

PLUM CAKE.

Make a cake of two cups of butter, two cups of molasses, one cup of sweet milk, two eggs, well-beaten, one teaspoonful of powdered saleratus, dissolved with a little hot water, one teaspoonful of ground mace or nutmeg, one teaspoonful of ground allspice, a tablespoonful of cinnamon, and a gill of brandy; stir in flour to make a batter as stiff as may be stirred easily with a spoon; beat it well until it is light, then add two pounds of raisins, stoned, and cut in two, two pounds of currants, picked, washed, and dried, and half a pound of citron, cut in slips. Bake in a quick oven. This is a fine, rich cake, easily made, and not expensive.

GOLD AND SILVER CAKE.

Gold Part.—Yolks of eight eggs, scant cup butter, two of sugar, four of flour, one of sour milk, teaspoon soda, tablespoon corn starch; flavor with lemon and vanilla.

Silver Part.—Two cups sugar, one of butter, four (scant) of flour, one of sour milk, teaspoon soda, tablespoon corn starch, whites of eight eggs; flavor with almond or peach. Put in pan, alternately, one spoonful of gold and one of silver.

TO MAKE SMALL SPONGE CAKES.

The weight of five eggs in flour, the weight of eight in pounded loaf sugar; flavor to taste. Let the flour be perfectly dry, and the sugar well pounded and sifted. Separate the whites from the yolks of the eggs, and beat the latter up with the sugar; then whisk the whites until they become rather stiff, and mix them with the yolks, but do not stir them more than is just necessary to mingle the ingredients well together. Dredge in the flour by degrees, add the flavoring; butter the tins well, pour in the batter, sift a little sugar over the cakes, and bake them in rather a quick oven, but do not allow them to take too much color, as they should be rather pale. Remove them from the tins before they get cold, and turn them on their faces, where let them remain until quite cold, when store them away in a closed tin canister or wide-mouthed glass bottle.

LEMON CHEESE CAKE.

Two cups sugar, half cup butter, three-quarters cup sweet milk, whites of six eggs, three cups flour, three teaspoons baking powder.

Sauce for Lemon Cheese Cake.—Grated rind and juice of two lemons, yolks of three eggs, half cup butter, one cup sugar; mix all together, and set on stove, and cook till thick as sponge, stirring all the time; then use like jelly between the cakes.

SNOW CAKE.

One pound of arrowroot, half pound pounded white sugar, half pound butter, the whites of six eggs; flavoring to taste, of essence of almonds, or vanilla, or lemon.

Mode: Beat the butter to a cream; stir in the sugar and arrowroot gradually. at the same time beating the mixture. Whisk the whites of the eggs to a stiff froth, add them to the other ingredients, and beat well for twenty minutes. Put in whichever of the above flavoring may be preferred; pour the cake into a buttered mold or tin and bake it in a moderate oven from one to one and a half hours.

TILDEN CAKE.

One cup butter, two of pulverized sugar, one of sweet milk, three of flour, half cup corn starch, four eggs, two teaspoons baking powder, two of lemon extract. This is excellent.

CORN STARCH CAKE.

Whites of six eggs, one cup of butter, two cups of flour, one cup of corn starch, two cups of sugar, one cup of sweet milk, one-half teaspoonful of soda, one of cream of tartar.

BIRTHDAY CAKE.

One pound and a half of fine sugar, one pound and a half of butter, three pounds and a half of currants, two pounds of flour, one-half pound candied peel, one-half pound almonds, two ounces spices, the grated rind of three lemons, eighteen eggs, one gill of brandy. Paper the hoops, and bake three hours. Ice when cold.

NAPLES BISCUIT.

Beat eight eggs light; add to them one pound of fine white sugar, and one pound of sifted wheat flour; flavor with a teaspoonful of salt, and essence of lemon or orange-flower water; beat it until it rises in bubbles; bake in a quick oven.

CAKE TRIFLE.

Bake a Naples biscuit; cut out the inside about one inch from the edge and bottom, leaving the shell. In place of the inside, put a custard made of the yolks of four eggs, beaten with a pint of boiling milk, sweetened, and flavored with half a teaspoonful of peach-water; lay on it some jelly, or jam; beat the whites of two eggs, with white ground sugar, until it will stand in a heap; put it on the jelly, and serve.

SAVOY CAKE.

The weight of four eggs in pounded loaf-sugar, the weight of seven in flour, a little grated lemon-rind, or essence of almonds, or orange-flower water. Break the seven eggs, putting the yolks into one basin and the whites into another. Whisk the former, and mix with them the sugar, the grated lemon-rind, or any other flavoring to taste; beat them well together, and add the whites of the eggs, whisked to a froth. Put in the flour by degrees, continuing to beat the mixture for one-quarter of an hour, butter a mold, pour in the cake, and bake it from one and a quarter to one and a half hours. This is a very nice cake for dessert, and may be iced for a supper table, or cut into slices and spread with jam, which converts it into sandwiches.

COMPOSITION CAKE.

Five cups of flour, two cups of butter, three of sugar, one of milk, five eggs, one teaspoon of soda; two of cream of tartar, fruit as you please, cinnamon, nutmeg and clove to taste.

ALMOND CREAM CAKE.

On beaten whites of ten eggs sift one and a half goblets pulverized sugar, and a goblet of flour, through which has been stirred a heaping teaspoon cream tartar; stir very gently and do not heat it; bake in jelly-pans. For cream, take a half pint of sweet cream, yolks of three eggs, tablespoon pulverized sugar, teaspoon corn starch; dissolve starch smoothly with a little milk, beat yolks and sugar together with this, boil the cream, and stir these ingredients in as for any cream cake filling, only make a little thicker; blanch and chop fine a half pound almonds and stir into the cream. Put together like jelly cake while icing is soft, and stick in a half pound of almonds, split in two.

ICE-CREAM CAKE.

Make good sponge cake, bake half an inch thick in jelly-pans, and let them get perfectly cold; take a pint thickest sweet cream, beat until it looks like ice-cream, make very sweet, and flavor with vanilla; blanch and chop a pound almonds, stir into cream, and put very thick between each layer. This is the queen of all cakes.

ECONOMICAL CAKE.

One pound of flour, one-quarter pound of sugar, one-quarter pound of butter or lard, one-half pound of currants, one teaspoonful of carbonate of soda, the whites of four eggs, one-half pint of milk. In making many sweet dishes, the whites of eggs are not required, and if well beaten and added to the above ingredients, make an excellent cake, with or without currants. Beat the butter to a cream, well whisk the whites of the eggs, and stir all the ingredients together but the soda, which must not be added until all is well mixed, and the cake is ready to be put into the oven. When the mixture has been well beaten, stir in the soda, put the cake into a buttered mold, and bake it in a moderate oven for one and a half hours.

DELICATE CAKE.

Three cups of flour, two of sugar, three-fourths cup of sweet milk, whites of six eggs, half cup butter, teaspoon cream tartar, half teaspoon of soda. Flavor with lemon.

ORANGE CAKE.

One cup of sugar, half a cup of butter, half a cup of sweet milk, two cups of flour, three eggs, one and a half teaspoonfuls of baking powder; bake in jelly-tins.

Orange Frosting for Same.—One orange, grate off the outside, and mix with juice, and add sugar until quite stiff, and make like jelly cake; make four layers of the cake.

FRIED CAKES.

One cup of sugar, two eggs, half a cup of shortening, one teaspoon of soda, one cup of sour milk, cut in rings; have your lard very hot, in which place a peeled potato to keep lard from burning, and drop in your cakes; they will come to the top of lard when light; fry a dark brown; when taken out sprinkle sugar over them.

JELLY KISSES.

Kisses to be served for dessert at a large dinner, with other suitable confectionery, may be varied in this way: Having made the kisses, put them in a moderate oven, until the outside is a little hardened; then take one off carefully, as before directed; take out the soft inside with the handle of a spoon, and put it back with the mixture, to make more; then lay the shell down. Take another, and prepare it likewise; fill the shells with currant jelly, or jam; join two together, cementing them with some of the mixture; so continue until you have enough. Make kisses, cocoanut drops, and such like, the day before they are wanted.

COCOANUT KISSES.

Make a kiss mixture; add to it half of a cocoanut, grated (the white meat only); finish as directed for kisses.

FIG CAKE.

Silver Part.—Two cups sugar, two-thirds cup butter, not quite two-thirds cup sweet milk, whites of eight eggs, three heaping teaspoons baking powder, thoroughly sifted, with three cups flour; stir sugar and butter to a cream, add milk and flour, and last whites of eggs.

Gold Part.—One cup sugar, three-fourths cup butter, half

cup sweet milk, one and a half teaspoons baking powder sifted in a little more than one and a half cups flour, yolks of seven eggs thoroughly beaten, and one whole egg, one teaspoon allspice, and cinnamon until you can taste it; bake the white in two long pie-tins. Put half the gold in a pie-tin, and lay on one pound halved figs (previously sifted over with flour), so that they will just touch each other; put on the rest of the gold, and bake. Put the cakes together with frosting while warm, the gold between the white ones, and cover with frosting.

CALIFORNIA CAKE.

Two cups of sugar, one cup butter, one cup milk, two eggs, three teaspoons baking powder, put in three cups sifted flour, flavor and add fruit. This recipe makes two cakes.

WHITE MOUNTAIN CAKE.

One cup sugar, one-half cup of butter, one-half cup sweet milk, one-half cup corn starch, one cup flour, whites of six eggs, a little vanilla, two teaspoonfuls baking powder. Bake in layers.

Frosting for Above.—Whites of five eggs, twenty tablespoonfuls sifted sugar, beaten very light; a little vanilla. Spread between layers and outside of cake.

LEMON CAKE.

One-half cup of sugar, one teaspoon butter, one tablespoonful of milk, three eggs, one cup flour, one teaspoon baking powder; bake in jelly-tins, put between two apple and one lemon, grated together with a little sugar.

STRAWBERRY SHORTCAKE.

Make good biscuit crust; bake in two tins of same shape and size; mix berries with plenty of sugar; open the shortcake, butter well and place berries in layers, alternated with the crust; have the top layer of berries and over all put charlotte russe or whipped cream.

MARBLE CAKE.

White Part.—Whites of seven eggs, three cups white sugar, one of butter, one of sour milk, four of flour, sifted and heaping, one teaspoon soda; flavor to taste.

Dark Part.—Yolks of seven eggs, three cups brown sugar, one of butter, one of sour milk, four of flour, sifted and heaping, one tablespoon each of cinnamon, allspice and cloves, one teaspoon soda; put in pans a spoonful of white part and then a spoonful of dark, and so on. Bake an hour and a quarter. Use coffee cups to measure. This will make one large and one medium cake. The white and dark parts are alternated, either putting in a spoonful of white, then of dark, or a layer of white and then of dark part, being careful that the cake may be nicely "marbleized."

WHITE POUND CAKE.

One pound sugar, one of flour, half pound butter, whites of sixteen eggs, teaspoon baking powder sifted thoroughly with the flour; put in cool oven with gradual increase of heat. For boiled icing for the cake, take three cups sugar boiled in one of water until clear; beat whites of three eggs to very stiff froth, and pour over them the boiling liquid, beating all the time for ten minutes; froth while both cake and icing are warm.

NELLY'S CHOCOLATE CAKE.

One cup of butter, two of sugar, five eggs, leaving out two of the whites, one scant cup of milk, two full teaspoons of baking powder; mix well in three cups flour; bake in two long shallow tins. Dressing: Beat the whites of two eggs to a stiff froth, add a scant cup and a half of sugar; flavor with vanilla, add six tablespoons of grated chocolate; add the dressing when the cake is cold, and cut in diamond slices.

RICE CAKE.

One cupful of butter, two of sugar, two and one-fourth of rice flour, six eggs, the juice and rind of a lemon. Beat the butter to a cream; then gradually beat in the sugar, and add the lemon. Beat the yolks and whites separately, and add them to the beaten sugar and butter. Add also the rice flour. Pour into a shallow pan, to the depth of about two inches. Bake from thirty-five to forty-five minutes in a moderate oven.

CREAM CAKE.

Two eggs, one cup of sugar, one cup of cream, two cups of flour, one teaspoonful of cream of tartar, and one teaspoonful of soda.

DOUGHNUTS.

One cup of sugar, two eggs, two tablespoons of melted butter, two-thirds cup of milk, two even teaspoons of cream tartar, one even teaspoon of soda, flour enough to roll, salt and nutmeg.

SPONGE CAKE.

One pound sugar, one of flour, ten eggs. Stir yolks of eggs and sugar till perfectly light; beat whites of eggs and add them with the flour after beating together lightly; flavor with lemon. Three teaspoons baking powder in the flour will add to its lightness, but it never fails without. Bake in a moderate oven.

COFFEE CAKE.

Two cups brown sugar, one of butter, one of molasses, one of strong coffee as prepared for the table, four eggs, one teaspoon saleratus, two of cinnamon, two of cloves, one of grated nutmeg, pound raisins, one of currants, four cups flour.

SOFT GINGERBREAD.

Six cupfuls of flour, three of molasses, one of cream, one of lard or butter, two eggs, one teaspoonful of saleratus, and two of ginger. This is excellent.

SPICE CAKE.

One and one-half cups of sugar, half cup butter, half of sour milk, two cups of raisins chopped, three eggs, half a nutmeg, one teaspoon cinnamon, one of cloves, one saleratus; mix rather stiff; bake in loaf tins in moderate oven.

SWEET STRAWBERRY SHORTCAKE.

Three eggs, one cupful sugar, two of flour, one tablespoonful of butter, a teaspoonful, heaped, of baking powder. Beat the butter and sugar together, and add the eggs well-beaten. Stir in the flour and baking powder well sifted together. Bake in deep tin plates. This quantity will fill four plates. With three pints of strawberries mix a cupful of sugar. Spread the fruit between the layers of cake. The top layer of strawberries may be covered with a meringue made with the white of an egg and a tablespoonful of powdered sugar.

GINGER NUTS.

One and three-quarter pounds of syrup, one pound of moist sugar, one pound of butter, two and three-quarter pounds of flour, one and a half ounces of ground ginger, one and a half ounces of allspice, one and a half ounces of coriander seed, sal volatile size of a bean, a little Cayenne, flour enough to roll out, but not thin, cut with a wineglass or roll between your hands into small balls, and pinch.

RIBBON CAKE.

Two cupfuls of sugar, one of butter, one of milk, four of flour (rather scant), four eggs, half a teaspoonful of soda, one of cream of tartar. Beat the butter to a cream. Add the sugar gradually, beating all the while; then the flavoring (lemon or nutmeg). Beat the eggs very light. Add them and the milk. Measure the flour after it has been sifted. Return it to the sieve, and mix the soda and cream of tartar with it. Sift this into the bowl of beaten ingredients. Beat quickly and vigorously, to thoroughly mix, and then stop. Take three sheet pans of the same size, and in each of two put one-third of the mixture, and bake. To the other third add four teaspoonfuls of cinnamon, a cupful of currants and about an eighth of a pound of citron, cut fine. Bake this in the remaining pan. When done, take out of the pans. Spread the light cake with a thin layer of jelly, while warm. Place on this the dark cake, and spread with jelly. Place the other sheet of light cake on this. Lay a paper over all, and then a thin sheet, on which put two irons. The cake will press in about two hours.

JELLY ROLL.

Make the sponge cake mixture as for lady-fingers, and bake in one shallow pan twenty minutes. While it is yet warm cut off the edges, and spread the cake with any kind of jelly. Roll up, and pin a towel around it. Put in a cool place until serving time. Cut in slices with a sharp knife.

DELICATE CRULLERS.

Take four eggs, four tablespoonfuls of lard, four tablespoonfuls of sugar, a teaspoonful of salt, and half a nutmeg grated, a teaspoonful of lemon extract may be added; work into these as much sifted flour as will make a nice dough, roll it to about an eighth of an inch thickness, and fry as directed for doughnuts and crullers.

To make little baskets, cut the paste in strips an inch and a half wide, and three inches long, and with a giggling iron cut slices across it from one side to the other, within a quarter of an inch of either edge, and quarter of an inch apart; then join the two ends together in a circle, forming the basket; press it down slightly, that the strips may bulge, and so form the basket, like those made for fly-traps of paper; so soon as they are taken from the fat (five minutes will do them), grate white sugar over.

DESSERT AND TEA DISHES.

BOILED CUSTARD.

One quart milk, eight eggs, one-half pound of sugar; beat to a good froth the eggs and sugar. Put the milk in a tin pail and set it in boiling water; pour in the eggs and sugar and stir it until it thickens.

LEMON CUSTARD.

Beat the yolks of eight eggs till they are white, add pint boiling water, the rinds of two lemons grated, and the juice sweetened to taste; stir this on the fire till it thickens, then add a large glass of rich wine, and one-half glass brandy; give the whole a good boil, and put in glasses. To be eaten cold. Or, put the thin yellow rind of two lemons, with the juice of three, and sugar to taste, into one pint of warm water. As lemons vary in size and juiciness, the exact quantity of sugar cannot be given. Ordinary lemons require three gills. It will be safe to begin with that quantity, more may be added if required. Beat the whites to a stiff froth, then the yolks; then beat both together, pour in gradually while beating the other ingredients; put all in a pail, set in a pot of boiling water, and stir until thick as boiled custard; strain it in a deep dish; when cool place on ice. Serve in glasses.

SNOW CUSTARD.

Half a package of Cox's gelatine, three eggs, two cups of sugar, juice of one lemon; soak the gelatine one hour in a teacup of cold water, add one pint boiling water, stir until thoroughly dissolved, add two-thirds of the sugar and the lemon-juice; beat the whites of the eggs to a stiff froth, and when the gelatine is quite cold whip it into the whites, a spoonful at a time from half an hour to an hour. Whip steadily and evenly, and when all is stiff pour in a mold, or in a dozen egg-glasses previously wet with cold water, and set in a cold place. In four or five hours turn into a glass dish. Make a custard of one and a half pints milk, yolks of eggs, and remainder of the sugar, flavor with vanilla, and when the meringue or snowballs are turned out of the mold, pour this around the base.

TAPIOCA PUDDING.

Three ounces of tapioca, one quart of milk, two ounces of butter, quarter of a pound of sugar, four eggs, flavoring of vanilla or bitter almonds. Wash the tapioca, and let it stew gently in the milk by the side of the stove for quarter of an hour, occasionally stirring it; then let it cool; mix with it the butter, sugar, and eggs, which should be well beaten, and flavor with either of the above ingredients. Butter a pie-dish, and line the edges with puff-paste; put in the pudding, and bake in a moderate oven for an hour. If the pudding is boiled, add a little more tapioca, and boil it in a buttered basin one and a half hours.

BLANC-MANGE.

One quarter pound of sugar, one quart of milk, one and a half ounces of isinglass, the rind of half a lemon, four laurel leaves. Put all the ingredients into a lined saucepan, and boil gently until the isinglass is dissolved; taste it occasionally to ascertain when it is sufficiently flavored with the laurel leaves; then take them out, and keep stirring the mixture over the fire for about ten minutes. Strain it through a fine sieve into a jug, and, when nearly cold, pour it into a well-oiled mold, omitting the sediment at the bottom. Turn it out carefully on a dish, and garnish with preserves, bright jelly, or a compote of fruit.

IVORY BLANC-MANGE.

Soak one ounce of gelatine for ten minutes in a little cold milk and pour over the gelatine, and stir it constantly until it is all dissolved; it may be placed in the dish and set on top of a boiling teakettle for a few minutes; remove it and add a small cupful of sugar and two tablespoonfuls of sherry wine. Strain into molds.

RICE BLANC-MANGE.

One-quarter pound of ground rice, three ounces of loaf sugar, one ounce of fresh butter, one quart of milk, flavoring of lemon-peel, essence of almonds or vanilla, or laurel leaves. Mix the rice to a smooth batter with about one-half pint of milk, and the remainder put into a saucepan, with the sugar, butter, and whichever of the above flavorings may be preferred; bring the milk to the boiling point, quickly stir in the rice, and let it boil for about ten minutes, or until it comes easily away from the saucepan, keeping it well stirred the whole time. Grease a mold with pure salad oil; pour in the rice, and let it get perfectly set, when it should turn out quite easily; garnish it with jam, or pour round a compote of any kind of fruit, just before it is sent to table. This blanc-mange is better for being made the day before it is wanted, as it then has time to become firm. If laurel leaves are used for flavoring, steep three of them in the milk, and take them out before the rice is added;

about eight drops of essence of almonds, or from twelve to sixteen drops of essence of vanilla, would be required to flavor the above proportion of milk.

APPLE TRIFLE.

Ten good-sized apples, the rind of one-half lemon, six ounces of pounded sugar, one-half pint of milk, one-half pint of cream, two eggs, whipped cream. Peel, core, and cut the apples into thin slices; and put them into a saucepan, with two tablespoonfuls of water, the sugar, and minced lemon-rind. Boil all together until quite tender, and pulp the apples through a sieve; if they should not be quite sweet enough, add a little more sugar, and put them at the bottom of the dish to form a thick layer. Stir together the milk, cream and eggs, with a little sugar, over the fire; and let the mixture thicken, but do not allow it to reach the boiling point. When thick, take it off the fire; let it cool a little, then pour it over the apples. Whip some cream with sugar, lemon-peel, etc., the same as for other trifles; heap it high over the custard, and the dish is ready for table. It may be garnished, as fancy dictates, with strips of bright apple jelly, slices of citron, etc.

LEMON TRIFLE.

Juice of two lemons and grated peel of one, one pint cream, well sweetened and whipped stiff, one cup of sherry, a little nutmeg. Let sugar, lemon-juice and peel lie together two hours before you add wine and nutmeg. Strain through double tarlatan, and whip gradually into the frothed cream. Serve very soon, heaped in small glasses. Pass cake with this, as well as with the tea.

FLOATING ISLAND.

Take a quart of rich cream, and divide it in half. Sweeten one pint of it with loaf sugar, and stir it into sufficient currant jelly, to color it of a fine pink. Put it into a glass bowl, and place in the centre a pile of sliced almond sponge cake, or lady cake; every slice spread thickly with raspberry jam or marmalade, and laid evenly one on another. Have ready the other pint of cream, flavored with the juice of two lemons, and beaten to a stiff froth. Heap it all over the pile of cake so as entirely to cover it. Both creams must be made very sweet.

APPLE SNOW

Forms a showy, sweet dish, and may be made as follows: Ten or a dozen apples prepared as before, flavoring with a little lemon-juice; when reduced to a pulp let them stand to cool for a little time, meanwhile beat up the whites of ten or a dozen eggs to a froth, and stir into the apples, as also some sifted sugar, say a teacupful; stir till the mixture begins to stiffen, and then heap it up in a glass dish or serve in custard cups, ornamented with spots of red currant jelly. Thick cream should at table be ladled out to the snow.

TROPICAL SNOW.

Ten sweet oranges, one cocoanut, pared and grated, two glasses sherry, one cup powdered sugar, six bananas. Peel and cut the oranges small, taking out the seeds. Put a layer in a glass bowl and wet with wine, then strew with sugar. Next, put a layer of grated cocoanut, slice the bananas thin, and cover the cocoanut with them. When the dish has been filled in this order, heap with cocoanut. Eat soon or the oranges will toughen.

SWISS CREAM.

One-quarter pound of macaroons or six small sponge-cakes, one pint of cream, five ounces of lump sugar, two tablespoonfuls of arrowroot, the rind of one lemon, the juice of half lemon, three tablespoonfuls of milk. Lay the macaroons or sponge-cakes in a glass dish, and pour over them as much sherry as will cover them, or sufficient to cover them well. Put the cream into a lined saucepan, with the sugar and lemon-rind, and let it remain by the side of the fire until the cream is well-flavored, when take out the lemon-rind. Mix the arrowroot smoothly with the cold milk; add this to the cream, and let it boil gently for about three minutes, keeping it well stirred. Take it off the fire, stir till nearly cold, when add the lemon-juice, and pour the whole over the cakes. Garnish the cream with strips of angelica, or candied citron cut thin, or bright-colored jelly or preserve. This cream is exceedingly delicious, flavored with vanilla instead of lemon; when this flavoring is used, the sherry may be omitted, and the mixture poured over the *dry* cakes.

ITALIAN CREAM.

Take one quart of cream, one pint of milk sweetened very sweet, and highly seasoned with sherry wine and vanilla; beat it with a whip dasher, and remove the froth as it rises, until it is all converted into froth. Have ready one box of Cox's sparkling gelatine dissolved in a little warm water; set the frothed cream into a tub of ice; pour the gelatine into it, and stir constantly until it thickens, then pour into molds, and set in a cool place.

WHIPPED CREAM.

Mix one pint of cream with nine tablespoons of fine sugar and one gill of wine in a large bowl; whip these with the cream dasher, and as the froth rises, skim into the dish in which it is to be served. Fill the dish full to the top, and ornament with kisses or macaroons.

TIPSY CAKE.

One molded sponge or Savoy cake, sufficient sweet wine or sherry to soak it, six tablespoonfuls of brandy, two ounces of sweet almonds, one pint of rich custard. Procure a cake that is three or four days old—either sponge, Savoy, or rice answering for the purpose of a tipsy cake. Cut the bottom of the cake level, to make it stand firm in the dish; make a small hole in the centre, and pour in and over the cake sufficient sweet wine or sherry, mixed with the above proportion of brandy, to soak it nicely. When the cake is well soaked, blanch and cut the almonds into strips, stick them all over the cake, and pour round it a good custard, allowing eight eggs instead of five to the pint of milk. The cakes are sometimes crumbled and soaked, and a whipped cream heaped over them, the same as for trifles.

SNOW PYRAMIDS.

Beat to a stiff foam the whites of half a dozen eggs, add a small teacupful of currant jelly, and whip all together again. Fill as many saucers as you have guests half full of cream, dropping in the centre of each saucer a tablespoonful of the beaten eggs and jelly in the shape of a pyramid.

AN EXCELLENT DESSERT.

One can or twelve large peaches, two coffeecups of sugar, one pint of water, and the whites of three eggs; break the peaches with and stir all the ingredients together; freeze the whole into form; beat the eggs to a froth.

APPLE FRITTERS.

One teacup of sweet milk, one tablespoon sweet light dough dissolved in milk, three eggs beaten separately, one teaspoon of salt, one and a half teacups of flour, one tablespoon of sugar, and the grated peel of a lemon, peeled apples sliced without the core; drop into hot lard with a piece of apple in each one; sprinkle with powdered or spiced sugar. Let them stand after making and they will be lighter. Good.

JELLY CAKE FRITTERS.

Some stale sponge, or *plain* cup cake, cut into rounds with a cake cutter. Hot lard, strawberry or other jam, or jelly, a little boiling milk. Cut the cake carefully and fry a nice brown. Dip each slice for a second in a bowl of boiling milk, draining this off on the side of the vessel; lay on a hot dish and spread thickly with strawberry jam, peach jelly, or other delicate conserve. Pile them neatly and send around hot, with cream to pour over them. This is a nice way of using up stale cake, and if rightly prepared, the dessert is almost equal to Neapolitan pudding.

PEACH MERINGUE.

Pare and quarter (removing stones) a quart of sound, ripe peaches, place them all in a dish that it will not injure to set in the oven and yet suitable to place on the table. Sprinkle the peaches with sugar, and cover them well with the beaten whites of three eggs. Stand the dish in the oven until the eggs have become a delicate brown, then remove and, when cool enough, set on a dish of ice, in a very cool place. Take the yolks of the eggs, add to them a pint of milk, sweeten and flavor and boil same in a custard kettle, being careful to keep the eggs from curdling. When cool, pour into a glass pitcher and serve with the meringue when ready to use.

CHARLOTTE RUSSE.

Whip one quart rich cream to a stiff froth, and drain well on a nice sieve. To one scant pint of milk add six eggs beaten very light; make very sweet; flavor high with vanilla. Cook over hot water till it is a thick custard. Soak one full ounce Cox's gelatine in a very little water, and warm over hot water. When the custard is very cold, beat in lightly the gelatine and the whipped cream. Line the bottom of your mold with buttered paper, the sides with sponge cake or lady-fingers fastened together with the white of an egg. Fill with the cream, put in a cold place or in summer on ice. To turn out, dip the mold for a moment in hot water. In draining the whipped cream, all that drips through can be rewhipped.

JELLIED GRAPES.

A very delicate dish is made of one-third of a cup of rice, two cups of grapes, half a cup of water, and two spoons of sugar. Sprinkle the rice and sugar among the grapes, while placing them in a deep dish; pour on the water, cover close and simmer two hours slowly in the oven. Serve warm as sauce, or cold as pudding. If served warm as pudding, increase slightly the proportion of rice and sugar.

JELLY AND CUSTARD.

One-half package of gelatine, soaked in water enough to cover it; when soaked pour one pint of boiling water over it, then add one cup of white sugar and squeeze the juice of one large lemon into it and a little essence of lemon and set aside to stiffen.

Make a custard with a pint and a half of milk, the yolks

of three eggs, one tablespoonful of corn starch; sugar and flavoring. When the jelly is set, and just before using, cut the jelly into squares, laying them in layers at intervals in the bottom of the dish, then pour in some of the cold custard, another layer of jelly, and so on until the custard is all used. Beat the whites of the eggs to a stiff froth, adding two or three teaspoonfuls of confectioner's sugar and lay on in pieces with jelly between. All these recipes are better when prepared in a tin set inside of another in which there is a little water to prevent danger of burning.

LEMON TOAST.

Take the yolks of six eggs, beat them well and add three cups of sweet milk; take baker's bread not too stale and cut into slices; dip them into the milk and eggs, and lay the slices into a spider, with sufficient melted butter, hot, to fry a nice delicate brown; take the whites of six eggs, and beat them to a froth, adding a large cup of white sugar; add the juice of two lemons, heating well, and adding two cups boiling water. Serve over the toast as a sauce, and you will find it a very delicious dish.

DISH OF SNOWWHIPPED CREAM.

To the whites of three eggs beaten to a froth, add a pint of cream and four tablespoonfuls of sweet wine, with three of fine white sugar and a teaspoonful of extract of lemon or vanilla; whip it to a froth and serve in a glass dish; serve jelly or jam with it. Or lay lady-fingers or sliced sponge cake in a glass dish, put spoonfuls of jelly or jam over, and heap the snow upon it.

OMELET FOR DESSERT.

Beat six eggs light, add a teaspoonful of salt, and four or five macaroons pounded fine, beat them well together; fry as usual; strew plentifully with sugar, and serve.

JELLY FRITTERS.

Make a batter of two eggs, a pint of milk, and a pint bowl of wheat flour or more, beat it light; put a tablespoonful lard or beef fat in a frying or omelet-pan, add a saltspoonful of salt, make it boiling hot, put in the batter by the large spoonful, not too close; when one side is a delicate brown, turn the other; when done, take them on to a dish with a doily over it, put a dessertspoonful of firm jelly on each, and serve.

PRESERVES, CANNED FRUITS, JELLY.

TO PRESERVE PLUMS WITHOUT THE SKINS.

Pour boiling water over large egg or magnum bonum plums, cover them until it is cold, then pull off the skins. Make a syrup of a pound of sugar and a teacup of water for each pound of fruit, make it boiling hot, and pour it over; let them remain for a day or two, then drain it off and boil again; skim it clear and pour it hot over plums; let them remain until the next day, then put them over the fire in the syrup, boil them very gently until clear; take them from the syrup with a skimmer into the pots or jars; boil the syrup until rich and thick, take off any scum which may rise, then let it cool and settle, and pour it over the plums. If brown sugar is used, which is quite as good, except for greengages, clarify it as directed.

TO PRESERVE PURPLE PLUMS.

Make a syrup of clean brown sugar, clarify it as directed in these recipes; when perfectly clear and boiling hot, pour it over the plums, having picked out all unsound ones, and stems; let them remain in the syrup two days, then drain it off; make it boiling hot, skim it and pour it over again; let them remain another day or two, then put them in a preserving-kettle over the fire and simmer gently until the syrup is reduced and thick or rich. One pound of sugar for each pound of plums. Small damsons are very fine, preserved as cherries or any other ripe fruit; clarify the syrup and when boiling hot put in the plums, let them boil very gently until they are cooked and the syrup rich. Put them in pots or jars; the next day secure as directed.

PRESERVED GREENGAGES IN SYRUP.

To every pound of fruit allow one pound of loaf-sugar, one-quarter pint of water. Boil the sugar and water together for about ten minutes; divide the greengages, take out the stones, put the fruit into the syrup, and let it simmer gently until nearly tender. Take it off the fire, put it into a large pan, and, the next day, boil it up again for about ten minutes with the kernels from the stones, which should be blanched. Put the fruit carefully into jars, pour it over the syrup, and, when cold, cover down, so that the air is quite excluded. Let the syrup be well skimmed both the first and second day of boiling, otherwise it will not be clear.

TO PRESERVE CHERRIES IN SYRUP.

Four pounds of cherries, three pounds of sugar, one pint of white-currant juice. Let the cherries be as clear and as transparent as possible, and perfectly ripe; pick off the stalks, and remove the stones, damaging the fruit as little as you can. Make a syrup with the above proportion of sugar, mix the cherries with it, and boil them for about fifteen minutes, carefully skimming them; turn them gently into a pan, and let them remain till the next day; then drain the cherries on a sieve, and put the syrup and white-currant juice into the preserving-pan again. Boil these together until the syrup is somewhat reduced and rather thick; then put in the cherries, and let them boil for about five minutes;

take them off the fire, skim the syrup, put the cherries into small pots or wide-mouthed bottles; pour the syrup over, and when quite cold, tie them down carefully, so that the air is quite excluded.

PRESERVED PEARS.

To six pounds of pears, four pounds of sugar, two coffee-cups of water, the juice of two lemons, and the rind of one, a handful of whole ginger; boil all together for twenty minutes, then put in your pears and boil till soft, say about a quarter of an hour; take them out and boil your syrup a little longer; then put back your fruit and give it a boil; bottle while hot; add a little cochineal to give them a nice color.

TO PRESERVE PEACHES.

Peaches for preserving may be ripe but not soft; cut them in halves, take out the stones, and pare them neatly; take as many pounds of white sugar as of fruit, put to each pound of sugar a teacup of water; stir it until it is dissolved, set it over a moderate fire, when it is boiling hot, put in the peaches, let them boil gently until a pure, clear, uniform color; turn those at the bottom to the top carefully with a skimmer several times; do not hurry them; when they are clear, take each half up with a spoon, and spread the halves on flat dishes to become cold; when all are done, let the syrup boil until it is quite thick, pour it into a large pitcher, and let it set to cool and settle. When the peaches are cold, put them carefully into jars, and pour the syrup over them, leaving any sediment which has settled at the bottom, or strain the syrup. Some of the kernels from the peach stones may be put in with the peaches while boiling. Let them remain open one night, then cover.

TO PRESERVE CITRON.

Pare the citrons and cut them into slices about an inch and a half thick, then into strips the same thickness, leaving them the full length of the fruit; take out all the seeds with a small knife, then weigh, and to each pound of citron put a pound of white sugar, make a syrup; to ten pounds put a pint of water, and simmer gently for twenty minutes; then put in the citron and boil for one hour, or until tender; before taking off the fire put in two lemons, sliced thin, seeds taken out, and two ounces of root ginger; do not let them boil long after the lemon and ginger are put in; do not stir them while boiling. The above is very fine if carefully attended to.

CRAB-APPLES.

To each pound of fruit allow half a pound of sugar, and a pint of water to three pounds of sugar. When the syrup is boiling hot, drop in the apples. They will cook very quickly. When done, fill a jar with the fruit, and fill it up with syrup.

PINEAPPLE.

Pare the fruit, and be sure you take out all the eyes and discolored parts. Cut in slices, and cut the slices in small bits, taking out the core. Weigh the fruit, and put in a pan with half as many pounds of sugar as of fruit. Let it stand over night. In the morning put it over the fire and let it boil rapidly for a minute only, as cooking long discolors it. Put it in the jars as directed.

GOOSEBERRY JAM.

To every eight pounds of red, rough, ripe gooseberries, allow one quart of red-currant juice, five pounds of loaf-sugar. Have the fruit gathered in dry weather, and cut off the tops and tails. Prepare one quart of red-currant juice, the same as for red-currant jelly; put it into a preserving-pan with the sugar, and keep stirring until the latter is dissolved. Keep it boiling for about five minutes; skim well; then put in the gooseberries, and let them boil from one-half to three-quarters of an hour; then turn the whole into an earthen pan, and let it remain for two days. Boil the jam up again until it looks clear; put it into pots, and when cold cover with oiled paper, and over the jars put tissue paper, brushed over on both sides with the white of an egg, and store away in a dry place. Care must be taken in making this to keep the jam well stirred and well skimmed, to prevent it burning at the bottom of the pan, and to have it very clear.

BLACK-CURRANT JAM.

Pick the currants carefully, and take equal quantities of fruit and sugar. Pounded loaf-sugar is best. Dissolve it over or mix it with the currants. Put in a very little water or red-currant juice, boil and skim for twenty-five minutes.

RASPBERRY JAM.

To five or six pounds of fine red raspberries (not too ripe) add an equal quantity of the finest quality of white sugar. Mash the whole well in a preserving-kettle; add about one quart of currant juice (a little less will do), and boil gently until it jellies upon a cold plate; then put into small jars; cover with brandied paper, and tie a thick white paper over them. Keep in a dark, dry, and cool place.

QUINCE PRESERVE.

Pare, core, and quarter your fruit, then weigh it and allow an equal quantity of white sugar. Take the parings and cores and put in a preserving-kettle; cover them with water and boil for half an hour; then strain through a hair sieve and put the juice back into the kettle and boil the quinces in it a little at a time until they are tender; lift out as they are done with a drainer and lay on a dish; if the liquid seems scarce add more water. When all are done throw in the sugar and allow it to boil ten minutes before putting in the quinces; let them boil until they change color, say one hour and a quarter, on a slow fire; while they are boiling occasionally slip a silver spoon under them to see that they do not burn, but on no account stir them. Have two fresh lemons cut in thin slices, and when the fruit is being put in jars lay a slice or two in each.

RED-CURRANT JELLY.

Red-currants; to every pint of juice allow three-quarter pounds of loaf-sugar. Have the fruit gathered in fine weather; pick it from the stalks, put it into a jar, and place this jar in a saucepan of boiling water over the fire, and let it simmer gently until the juice is well drawn from the currants; then strain them through a jelly-bag of fine cloth, and, if the jelly is washed very clear, do not squeeze them *too much*, as the skin and pulp from the fruit will be pressed through with the juice, and so make the jelly muddy. Measure the juice, and to each pint allow three-quarter pounds of loaf-sugar; put these into a preserving-pan, set it over the fire, and keep stirring the jelly until it is done, carefully removing every particle of scum as it rises, using a wooden or silver spoon for the purpose, as metal or iron ones would spoil the color of the jelly. When it has boiled from twenty minutes to a half hour, put a little of the jelly on a plate, and if firm, when cool, it is done. Take it off the fire, pour it into small gallipots, cover each of the pots with an oiled paper, and then with a piece of tissue paper brushed over on both sides with the white of an egg. Label the pots, adding the year when the jelly was made, and store it away in a dry place. A jam may be made with the currants, if they are not squeezed too dry, by adding a few fresh raspberries, and boiling all together with sufficient sugar to sweeten it nicely. As this preserve is not worth storing away, but is only for immediate eating, a smaller proportion of sugar than usual will be found enough; it answers very well for children's puddings, or for a nursery preserve.

APPLE JELLY.

Apples, water; to every pint of syrup allow three-quarters of a pound of loaf-sugar. Pare and cut the apples into pieces, remove the cores, and put them in a preserving-pan with sufficient cold water to cover them. Let them boil for an hour; then drain the syrup from them through a hair sieve or jelly-bag, and measure the juice; to every pint allow three-quarters of a pound of loaf-sugar, and boil these together for three-quarters of an hour, removing every particle of scum as it rises, and keeping the jelly well stirred, that it may not burn, A little lemon-rind may be boiled with the apples, and a small quantity of strained lemon-juice may be put in the jelly, just before it is done, when the flavor is liked. This jelly may be ornamented with preserved greengages, or any other preserved fruit, and will turn out very prettily for dessert. It should be stored away in small pots.

BLACK-CURRANT JELLY.

Pick each currant individually, and heat the lot in a jar set in boiling water, squeeze as before, and allow a pint of juice to a pound of sugar, a little water may be added if thought proper, or a little red-currant juice. Boil for half an hour, carefully removing the skimmings. Another way: Clarify the sugar, and add the fruit to it whole, boil for twenty minutes, and strain, then boil a few minutes additional. Pot it and paper it when cool. The refuse berries may be kept as black-currant jam, for tarts, dumplings, etc.

CRAB-APPLE JELLY.

Wash the fruit clean, put in a kettle, cover with water, and boil until thoroughly cooked. Then pour it into a sieve, and let it drain. Do not press it through. For each pint of this liquor allow one pound of sugar. Boil from twenty minutes to half an hour.

OTHER JELLIES.

Jellies can be made from quinces, peaches and apples by following the directions for crab-apple jelly.

WINE JELLY.

One box of Cox's gelatine, dissolved in one pint of cold water, one pint of wine, one quart of boiling water, one quart of granulated sugar, and three lemons.

CALVES' FEET JELLY

Should be made at any rate the day before it is required. It is a simple affair to prepare it. Procure a couple of feet and put them on the fire in three quarts of water; let them boil for five hours, during which keep skimming. Pass the liquor through a hair sieve into a basin, and let it firm, after which remove all the oil and fat. Next take a teacupful of water, two wineglassfuls of sherry, the juice of half a dozen lemons and the rind of one, the whites and shells of five eggs, half a pound of fine white sugar, and whisk the whole till the sugar be melted, then add the jelly, place the whole on the fire in an enameled stewpan, and keep actively stirring till the composition comes to the boil; pass it twice through a jelly-bag, and then place in the molds.

ORANGE MARMALADE.

Allow pound for pound. Pare half the oranges and cut the rind into shreds. Boil in three waters until tender, and set aside. Grate the rind of the remaining oranges; take off and throw away every bit of the thick white inner skin; quarter all the oranges and take out the seeds. Chop, or cut them into small pieces; drain all the juice that will come away, without pressing them, over the sugar; heat this, stirring until the sugar is dissolved, adding a *very* little water, unless the oranges are very juicy. Boil and skim five or six minutes; put in the boiled shreds, and cook ten minutes; then the chopped fruit and grated peel, and boil twenty minutes longer. When cold, put into small jars, tied up with bladder or with paper next the fruit, cloths dipped in wax over all. A nicer way still is to put away in tumblers with self-adjusting metal tops. Press brandied tissue paper down closely to the fruit.

LEMON MARMALADE

Is made as you would prepare orange—allowing a pound and a quarter of sugar to a pound of the fruit, and using but half the grated peel.

QUINCE MARMALADE.

Gather the fruit when fully ripe; pare, quarter and core it; boil the skins with as many teacupfuls of water as you have pounds of quinces; when they are soft, mash them, and strain the water from them, and put it to the quinces; boil them until they are soft enough to mash them fine; rub them through a sieve; put to the pulp as many pounds of sugar; stir them together, and set them over a gentle fire, until it will fall from a spoon, like jelly; or try some in a saucer. If it jellies when cold, it is enough.

Put it in pots or tumblers, and when cold, secure as directed for jelly.

PEACH MARMALADE.

Peel ripe peaches, stone them, and cut them small; weigh three-quarters of a pound of sugar for each pound of cut fruit, and a teacup of water for each pound of sugar; set it over the fire; when it boils, skim it clear, then put in the peaches, let them boil quite fast; mash them fine, and let them boil until the whole is a jellied mass, and thick, then put it in small jars or tumblers; when cold, secure it as directed for jellies. Half a pound of sugar for a pound of fruit will make nice marmalade.

APPLE BUTTER.

Boil one barrel of new cider down half, peel and core three bushels of good cooking apples; when the cider has boiled to half the quantity, add the apples, and when soft, stir constantly for from eight to ten hours. If done it will adhere to an inverted plate. Put away in stone jars (not earthen ware), covering first with writing-paper cut to fit the jar, and press down closely upon the apple butter; cover the whole with thick brown paper snugly tied down.

LEMON BUTTER.

Beat six eggs, one-fourth pound butter, one pound sugar, the rind and juice of three lemons; mix together and set in a pan of hot water to cook. Very nice for tarts, or to eat with bread.

PEACH BUTTER.

Take pound for pound of peaches and sugar; cook peaches alone until they become soft, then put in one-half the sugar, and stir for one-half hour; then the remainder of the sugar, and stir an hour and a half. Season with cloves and cinnamon.

APPLE GINGER.

(A DESSERT DISH).

Two pounds of any kind of hard apples, two pounds of loaf-sugar, one and one-half pints of water, one ounce of tincture of ginger. Boil the sugar and water until they form a rich syrup, adding the ginger when it boils up. Pare, core, and cut the apples into pieces; dip them in cold water to preserve the color, and boil them in the syrup until transparent; but be careful not to let them break. Put the pieces of apple into jars, pour over the syrup, and carefully exclude the air, by well covering them. It will remain good for some time, if kept in a dry place.

ICED CURRANTS.

One-quarter pint of water, the whites of two eggs, currants, pounded sugar. Select very fine bunches of red or white currants, and well beat the whites of the eggs. Mix these with water; then take the currants, a bunch at a time, and dip them in; let them drain for a minute or two, and roll them in very finely-pounded sugar. Lay them to dry on paper, when the sugar will crystallize round each currant, and have a very pretty effect. All fresh fruit may be prepared in the same manner; and a mixture of various fruits iced in this manner, and arranged on one dish, looks very well for a summer dessert.

TO BOTTLE FRESH FRUIT.

(VERY USEFUL IN WINTER).

Fresh fruit, such as currants, raspberries, cherries, gooseberries, plums of all kinds, damsons, etc.; wide-mouthed glass bottles, new corks to fit them tightly. Let the fruit be full grown, but not too ripe, and gathered in dry weather. Pick it off the stalks without bruising or breaking the skin, and reject any that is at all blemished; if gathered in the damp, or if the skins are cut at all, the fruit will mold. Have ready some *perfectly dry* glass bottles, and some nice *new* soft corks or bungs; burn a match in each bottle, to exhaust the air, and quickly place the fruit in to be preserved; gently cork the bottles, and put them into a very *cool* oven, where let them remain until the fruit has shrunk away a fourth part. Then take the bottles out, *do not open them*, but immediately beat the corks in tight, cut off the tops, and cover them with melted rosin. If kept in a dry place, the fruit will remain good for months; and on this principally depends the success of the preparation, for if stored away in a place that is the least damp, the fruit will soon spoil.

TO GREEN FRUIT FOR PRESERVING IN SUGAR OR VINEGAR.

Apples, pears, limes, plums, apricots, etc., for preserving or pickling, may be greened thus: Put vine-leaves under, between, and over the fruit in a preserving-kettle; put small bits of alum, the size of a pea, say a dozen bits to a kettleful; put enough water to cover the fruit, cover the kettle close to exclude all outer air, set it over a gentle fire, let them simmer; when they are tender drain off the water; if they are not a fine green let them become cold, then put vine-leaves and a bit of saleratus or soda with them, and set them over a slow fire until they begin to simmer; a bit of soda or saleratus the size of a small nutmeg will have the desired effect; then spread them out to cool, after which finish as severally directed.

TO COLOR PRESERVES PINK.

By putting in with it a little cochineal powdered fine, then finish in the syrup.

TO COLOR FRUIT YELLOW.

Boil the fruit with fresh skin lemons in water to cover them, until it is tender; then take it up, spread it on dishes to cool, and finish as may be directed.

CANNED STRAWBERRIES.

After the berries are pulled, let as many as can be put carefully in the preserve kettle at once be placed on a platter. To each pound of fruit add three-fourths of a pound of sugar; let them stand two or three hours, till the juice is drawn from them; pour it in the kettle and let it come to a boil, and remove the scum which rises; then put in the berries very carefully. As soon as they come thoroughly to a boil put them in warm jars, and seal while boiling hot. Be sure the cans are air-tight.

CANNED PEACHES.

Select some fine, free-stone peaches; pare, cut in two and stone them. Immerse in cold water, taking care not to break the fruit. See that the peaches are not over ripe. Place in the kettle, scattering sugar between the layers—the sugar should be in the proportion of a full tablespoonful to a quart of fruit. To prevent burning put a little water in the kettle. Heat slowly to a boil, then boil for three or four minutes. Can and seal the fruit.

CANNED PEARS.

Prepare and can precisely like peaches in preceding recipe, except that they require longer cooking. When done they are easily pierced with a silver fork.

CANNED PLUMS.

To every pound of fruit allow three-quarters of a pound of sugar; for the thin syrup, a quarter of a pound of sugar to each pint of water. Select fine fruit, and prick with a needle to prevent bursting. Simmer gently in a syrup made with the above proportion of sugar and water. Let them boil not longer than five minutes. Put the plums in a jar, pour in the hot syrup, and seal. Greengages are also delicious done in this manner.

CANNED CURRANTS.

Look them over carefully, stem and weigh them, allowing a pound of sugar to every one of fruit; put them in a kettle, cover, and leave them to heat slowly and stew gently for twenty or thirty minutes; then add the sugar, and skake the kettle occasionally to make it mix with the fruit; do not allow it to boil, but keep as hot as possible until the sugar is dissolved, then pour it in cans and secure the covers at once. White currants are beautiful preserved in this way.

CANNED PINEAPPLE.

For six pounds of fruit when cut and ready to can make syrup with two and a half pounds of sugar and nearly three pints of water; boil syrup five minutes and skim or strain if necessary; then add the fruit, and let it boil up; have cans hot, fill and shut up as soon as possible. Use the best white sugar. As the cans cool, keep tightening them up.

TO CAN QUINCES.

Cut the quinces into thin slices like apples for pies. To one quart jarful of quince take a coffee-saucer and a half of sugar and a coffeecup of water; put the sugar and water on the fire, and when boiling put in the quinces; have ready the jars with their fastenings, stand the jars in a pan of boiling water on the stove, and when the quince is clear and tender put rapidly into the jars, fruit and syrup together. The jars must be filled so that the syrup overflows, and fastened up tight as quickly as possible.

CANNING TOMATOES.

Scald your tomatoes, remove the skins, cut in small pieces, put in a porcelain kettle, salt to taste, and boil fifteen minutes; have tin cans filled with hot water; pour the water out and fill with tomatoes; solder tops on immediately with shellac and rosin melted together.

CANNED CORN.

Dissolve an ounce of tartaric acid in half teacup water,

and take one tablespoon to two quarts of sweet corn; cook, and while boiling hot, fill the cans, which should be tin. When used turn into a colander, rinse with cold water, add a little soda and sugar while cooking, and season with butter, pepper and salt.

ICES, ICE-CREAM, CANDY.

CURRANT ICE.

One pint of currant-juice, one pound of sugar, and pint of water; put in freezer, and when partly frozen add the whites of three eggs well beaten.

STRAWBERRY OR RASPBERRY ICE.

One quart of berries. Extract the juice and strain; one pint of sugar, dissolved in the juice; one lemon, juice only; half pint water.

ORANGE AND LEMON ICES.

The rind of three oranges grated and steeped a few moments in a little more than a pint of water; strain one pint of this on a pound of sugar and then add one pint of orange or lemon-juice; pour in a freezer, and when half frozen add the whites of four eggs beaten to a stiff froth.

ICE-CREAM.

One quart of new milk, two eggs, two tablespoons of corn starch; heat the milk in a dish set in hot water, then stir in the corn starch mixed smooth in a little of the milk; let it boil for one or two minutes, then remove from stove and cool, and stir in the egg and half a pound of sugar. If to be extra nice, add a pint of rich cream, and one-fourth pound of sugar, strain the mixture, and when cool add the flavoring, and freeze as follows: Prepare freezer in the usual manner, turn the crank one hundred times, then pour upon the ice and salt a quart of boiling water from the tea-kettle. Fill up again with ice and salt, turn the crank fifty times one way and twenty-five the other (which serves to scrape the cream from sides of freezer); by this time it will turn very hard, indicating that the cream is frozen sufficiently.

VANILLA OR LEMON ICE-CREA

Take two drachms of vanilla or lemon-peel, o milk, half a pound of sugar, one pint of crear yolks of three eggs; beat the yolks well, and stir t the milk, then add the other ingredients; set . moderate fire, and stir it constantly with a silver until it is boiling hot, then take out the lemon-peel or nilla, and, when cold, freeze it.

STRAWBERRY ICE-CREAM.

Sprinkle strawberries with sugar, wash well and rub through a sieve; to a pint of the juice add half a pint of good cream; make it very sweet; freeze, and when beginning to set, stir lightly one pint of cream whipped, and lastly a handful of whole strawberries, sweetened. It may then be put in a mold and imbedded in ice, or kept in the freezer; or mash with a potato pounder in an earthen bowl one quart of strawberries with one pound of sugar, rub it through a colander, add one quart of sweet cream and freeze. Or, if not in the strawberry season, use the French bottled strawberries (or any canned ones), mix juice with half a pint of cream, sweeten and freeze; when partially set add whipped cream and strawberries.

CHOCOLATE ICE-CREAM.

Take six ounces of chocolate, a pint of cream, half a pint of new milk, and half a pint of sugar. Rub the chocolate down into the milk and mix thoroughly, adding the cream and sugar. The milk should be heated almost to boiling. Heat until it thickens, stirring constantly. Strain and set aside to cool, afterwards freeze. This makes perhaps the ɑst favorite of ice-creams.

CREAM CANDIES.

nd one-half pounds of sugar to one and one-half water; dissolve in the water before putting with one-quarter of an ounce of fine white gum-arabic, n added to the sugar put in one teaspoon of cream ar. The candy should not be boiled quite to the le stage. The proper degree can be ascertained if, en a small skimmer is put in and taken out, when blowing through the holes of the skimmer, the melted sugar is forced through in feather filaments; remove from the fire at this point and rub the syrup against the sides of the dish with an iron spoon. If it is to be a chocolate candy, add two ounces of chocolate finely sifted and such flavoring as you may prefer, vanilla, rolls, or orange. If you wish to make cocoanut candy, add this while soft and stir until cold.

PINEAPPLE ICE-CREAM.

Three pints of cream, two large ripe pineapples, two pounds powdered sugar; slice the pineapples thin, scatter the sugar between the slices, cover and let the fruit stand three hours, cut or chop it p in the syrup, and strain through a hair sieve or double bag of coarse lace; beat gradually into the cream, and freeze as rapidly as possible; reserve a few pieces of pineapple unsugared, cut into square bits, and

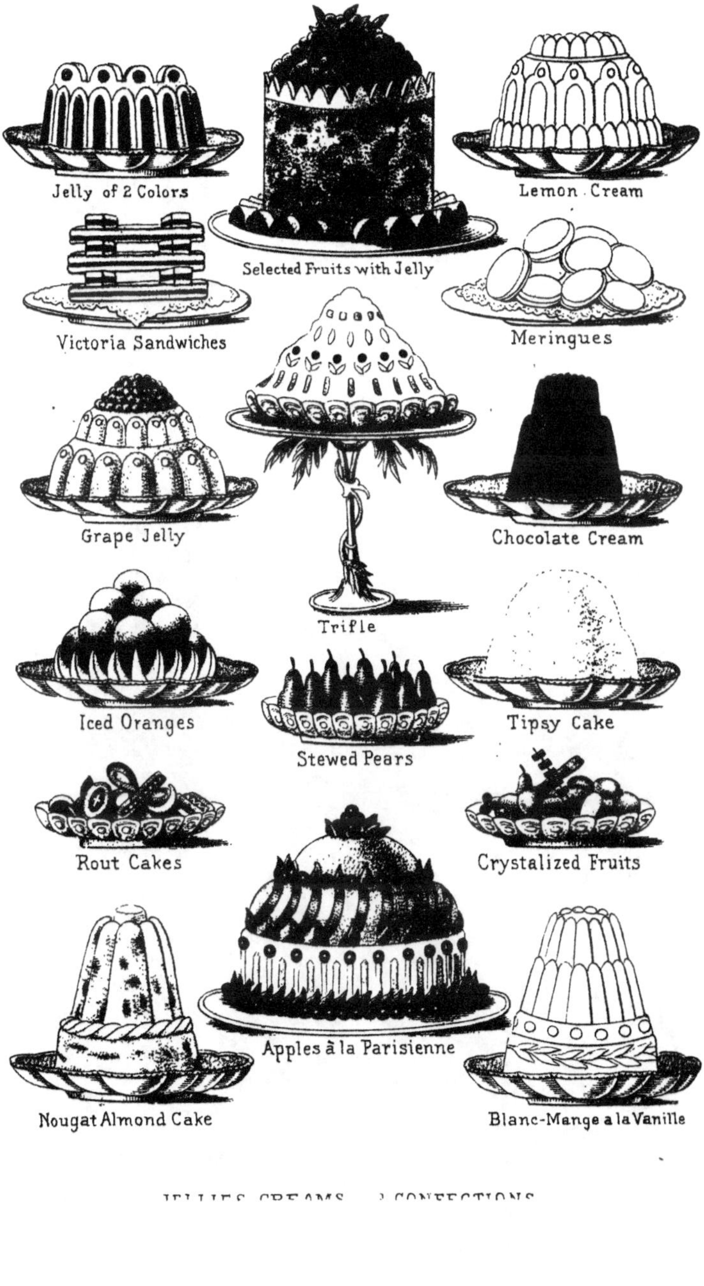

JELLIES, CREAMS, & CONFECTIONS

stir through cream when half frozen, first a pint of well-whipped cream, and then the fruit. Peach ice-cream may be made in the same way.

ITALIAN CREAM.

Put one ounce of soaked isinglass, six ounces of loaf-sugar, half a stick of vanilla, and one pint of milk into a saucepan; boil slowly; and stir all the time until the isinglass is dissolved; strain the mixture, and when a little cool mix with a pint of thick cream. Beat thoroughly until it thickens. Pour into large or individual molds, and put in ice-box until wanted.

TO MAKE BARLEY-SUGAR.

To every pound of sugar allow one-half pint of water, one-half the white of an egg. Put the sugar into a well-tinned saucepan, with the water, and when the former is dissolved, set it over a moderate fire, adding the well-beaten egg before the mixture gets warm, and stir it well together. When it boils, remove the scum as it rises, and keep it boiling until no more appears, and the syrup looks perfectly clear; then strain it through a fine sieve or muslin bag, and put it back into the saucepan. Boil it again like caramel, until it is brittle when a little is dropped into a basin of cold water; it is then sufficiently boiled. Add a little lemon-juice and a few drops of the essence of lemon, and let it stand for a minute or two. Have ready a marble slab or large dish rubbed over with salad oil, pour the sugar on it, and cut it into strips with a pair of scissors; these strips should then be twisted, and the barley-sugar stored away in a very dry place. It may be formed into lozenges or drops, by dropping the sugar in a very small quantity at a time on to the oiled slab or dish.

TO MAKE EVERTON TOFFEE.

One pound of powdered loaf-sugar, one teacupful of water, one-quarter pound of butter, six drops of essence of lemon. Put the water and sugar into a brass pan, and beat the butter to a cream. When the sugar is dissolved, add the butter, and keep stirring the mixture over the fire until it sets when a little is poured on to a buttered dish; and just before the toffee is done add the essence of lemon. Butter a dish or tin, pour on it the mixture, and when cool it will easily separate from the dish. Butter-Scotch, an excellent thing for coughs, is made with brown, instead of white sugar, omitting the water, and flavored with one-half ounce of ginger. It is made in the same manner as toffee.

COCOANUT DROPS.

To one grated cocoanut add half its weight of sugar and the white of one egg, cut to a stiff froth; mix thoroughly and drop on buttered white paper or tin sheets. Bake fifteen minutes.

MOLASSES CANDY.

One cup of molasses, two cups of sugar, one tablespoon vinegar, a little butter and vanilla, boil ten minutes, then cool it enough to pull.

CHOCOLATE CARAMELS.

Two cups of brown sugar, one cup molasses, one cup chocolate grated fine, one cup of boiled milk, one tablespoon of flour; butter the size of a large English walnut; let it boil slowly and pour on flat tins to cool; mark off while warm.

LEMON CANDY.

Put into a kettle three and one-half pounds of sugar, one and one-half pints of water, and one teaspoon of cream of tartar. Let it boil until it becomes brittle when dropped in cold water; when sufficiently done take off the fire and pour in a shallow dish which has been greased with a little butter. When this has cooled so that it can be handled, add a teaspoon of tartaric acid and the same quantity of extract of lemon, and work them into the mass. The acid must be fine and free from lumps. Work this in until evenly distributed, and no more, as it will tend to destroy the transparency of the candy. This method may be used for preparing all other candies, as pineapple, etc., using different flavors.

DRINKS.

TO MAKE GREEN TEA.

Have ready a kettle of water boiling fast, pour some into the teapot, let it remain for a few minutes, then throw it out; measure a teaspoonful of tea for each two persons, put it in the pot, pour on it about a gill of boiling water, cover it close for five minutes, then fill it up; have a covered pitcher of boiling water with it; when two cups are poured from it, fill it up; you will thus keep the strength good and equal. If the company is large, it is best to have some of the tea drawn in the covered pitcher, and replenish the teapot or urn when it is exhausted.

TO MAKE BLACK TEA.

Make as directed for green tea.

ICED TEA.

Prepare tea in the morning, making it stronger and sweeter than usual; strain and pour into a clean stone jug or glass bottle, and set aside in the ice-chest until ready to use. Drink from goblets without cream. Serve ice broken in small pieces on a platter nicely garnished with well-washed grape-leaves. Iced tea may be prepared from either green or black alone, but it is considered an improvement to mix the two. Tea made like that for iced tea (or that left in the teapot after a meal), with sugar to taste, a slice or two of lemon, a little of the juice, and some pieces of cracked ice, makes a delightful drink. Serve in glasses.

TO MAKE COFFEE.

Take a good-sized cupful of ground coffee, and pour into a quart of boiling water, with the white of an egg and the crushed shell. Stir well together, adding a half-cupful of cold water to clear. Put into the coffee-boiler and boil for about a quarter of an hour; after standing for a little while to settle, pour into your coffeepot, which should be well scalded, and send to the table. The coffee should be stirred as it boils. To make *coffee au lait,* take a pint each of hot *made* coffee and boiling milk; strain through thin muslin into coffeepot, to get rid of the grounds, and serve hot.

CHOCOLATE.

Take six tablespoons scraped chocolate, or three of chocolate and three of cocoa, dissolve in a quart of boiling water, boil hard fifteen minutes, add one quart of rich milk, let scald and serve hot; this is enough for six persons. Cocoa can also be made after this receipt. Some boil either cocoa or chocolate only one minute and then serve, while others make it the day before using, boiling it for one hour, and when cool skimming off the oil, and when wanted for use, heat it to the boiling point and add the milk. In this way it is equally good and much more wholesome. Cocoa is from the seed of the fruit of a small tropical tree. There are several forms in which it is sold, the most nutritious and convenient being chocolate, the next cocoa, then cocoa nibs, and last cocoa shells. The ground bean is simply cocoa; ground fine and mixed with sugar it is chocolate; the beans broken into bits are "nibs." The shells are the shells of the bean, usually removed before grinding. The beans are roasted like coffee, and ground between hot rollers.

LEMON SYRUP.

Take the juice of twelve lemons, grate the rind of six in it, let it stand over night, then take six pounds of white sugar, and make a thick syrup. When it is quite cool, strain the juice into it, and squeeze as much oil from the grated rind as will suit the taste. A tablespoonful in a goblet of water will make a delicious drink on a hot day, far superior to that prepared from the stuff commonly sold as lemon syrup.

STRAWBERRY SYRUP.

Take fine ripe strawberries, crush them in a cloth, and press the juice from them; to each pint of it put a pint of simple syrup, boil gently for one hour, then let it become cold, and bottle it; cork and seal it. When served reduce it to taste with water, set it on ice, and serve in small tumblers half filled.

RASPBERRY SYRUP.

Make as directed for strawberry.

STRAWBERRY SHERBET.

Take fourteen ounces of picked strawberries, crush them in a mortar, then add to them a quart of water; pour this into a basin, with a lemon sliced, and a teaspoonful of orange-flower water; let it remain for two or three hours. Put eighteen ounces of sugar into another basin, cover it with a cloth, through which pour the strawberry-juice; after as much has run through as will, gather up the cloth, and squeeze out as much juice as possible from it; when the sugar is all dissolved, strain it again; set the vessel containing it on ice, until ready to serve.

RASPBERRY VINEGAR.

To four quarts red raspberries, put enough vinegar to cover, and let them stand twenty-four hours; scald and strain it; add a pound of sugar to one pint of juice; boil it twenty minutes, and bottle; it is then ready for use and will keep years. To one glass of water add a great spoonful. It is much relished by the sick. Very nice.

LEMONADE.

Take half a pound of loaf-sugar and reduce it to a syrup with one pint of water; add the rind of five lemons and let stand an hour; remove the rinds and add the strained juice of the lemons; add one bottle of "Apollinaris" water, and a block of ice in centre of bowl. Peel one lemon and cut it up into thin slices, divide each slice in two, and put in lemonade. Claret or fine cordials may be added if desired. Serve with a piece of lemon in each glass.

EGG-NOG.

Whip the whites and yolks of six eggs into a stiff cream, adding a half cupful of sugar. Pour into a quart of rich milk, adding a half pint of good brandy, and a little flavoring of nutmeg. Stir up and thoroughly mix the ingredients, and add the whites of three additional eggs well whipped.

RAISIN WINE.

Take two pounds of raisins, seed and chop them, a lemon, a pound of white sugar, and about two gallons of boiling water. Pour into a stone jar, and stir daily for six or eight days. Strain, bottle, and put in a cool place for ten days or so, when the wine will be ready for use.

CURRANT WINE.

The currants should be quite ripe. Stem, mash, and strain them, adding a half pint of water, and less than a pound of sugar, to a quart of the mashed fruit. Stir well up together and pour into a clean cask, leaving the bung-hole open, or covered with a piece of lace. It should stand for a month to ferment, when it will be ready for bottling.

GINGER WINE.

One-half pound of cinnamon bark, four ounces of pimento, two ounces of mace, three-quarters of an ounce of capsicum, three-quarters of a pound of ginger root, five gallons of alcohol; macerate and strain or filter, after standing fifteen days. Now make syrup, thirty pounds of white sugar, half pound of tartaric acid, one and a half pounds of cream tartar, dissolved with warm water, clarify with whites of two eggs, and add soft water to make forty gallons. Color with cochineal and let it stand six months before use.

FINE MILK PUNCH.

Pare off the yellow rind of four large lemons, and steep it for twenty-four hours in a quart of brandy or rum. Then mix with it the juice of the lemons, a pound and a half of loaf-sugar; two grated nutmegs, and a quart of water. Add a quart of rich unskimmed milk, made boiling hot, and strain the whole through a jelly-bag. You may either use it as soon as it is cold, or make a larger quantity (in the above proportion), and bottle it. It will keep several months.

CLARET CUP.

One quart bottle of claret, one bottle of soda water, one lemon cut very thin, four tablespoons of powdered sugar, quarter of a teaspoon of grated nutmeg, one liquor glass of brandy, one wineglass of sherry wine. Half an hour before it is to be used, put in a large piece of ice, so that it may get perfectly cold.

ROMAN PUNCH.

Grate the yellow rinds of four lemons and two oranges upon two pounds of loaf-sugar. Squeeze on the juice of the lemons and oranges; cover it, and let it stand till next day. Then strain it through a sieve, add a bottle of champagne, and the whites of eight eggs beaten to a froth. You may freeze it or not.

CREAM NECTAR.

Dissolve two pounds of crushed sugar in three quarts of water; boil down to two quarts; drop in the white of an egg while boiling; then strain, and put in the tartaric acid; when cold drop in the lemon to your taste; then bottle and cork. Shake two or three times a day.

RED-CURRANT CORDIAL.

To two quarts of red-currants put one quart of whiskey; let it stand twenty-four hours, then bruise and strain through a flannel bag. To every two quarts of this liquor, add one pound of loaf-sugar, add quarter of a pound of ginger well bruised and boiled; let the whole stand to settle, then strain or filter; bottle and cork, seal the corks tightly. It is an improvement to have half red-raspberry juice if the flavor is liked. The above is fit for use in a month.

ELDERBERRY SYRUP.

Take elderberries perfectly ripe, wash and strain them, put a pint of molasses to a pint of the juice, boil it twenty minutes, stirring constantly, when cold add to each quart a pint of French brandy; bottle and cork it tight. It is an excellent remedy for a cough.

INVALID COOKERY.

PORT WINE JELLY.

Melt in a little warm water an ounce of isinglass; stir it into a pint of port wine, adding two ounces of sugar candy, an ounce of gum-arabic, and half a nutmeg, grated. Mix all well and boil it ten minutes; or till everything is thoroughly dissolved. Then strain it through muslin and set it away to get cold.

TAPIOCA JELLY.

Wash the tapioca carefully in two or three waters, then soak it for five or six hours, simmer it then in a stewpan until it becomes quite clear, add a little of the juice of a lemon, wine if desired.

ARROWROOT WINE JELLY.

One cup boiling water, two heaping teaspoons arrowroot, two heaping teaspoons white sugar, one tablespoonful brandy *or* three tablespoonfuls of wine. An excellent corrective to weak bowels.

JELLIED CHICKEN.

Cook six chickens in a small quantity of water, until the meat will part from the bone easily; season to taste with salt and pepper; just as soon as cold enough to handle, remove bones and skin; place meat in a deep pan or mold, just as it comes from the bone, using gizzard, liver and heart, until the mold is nearly full. To the water left in the kettle, add three-fourths of a box of Cox's gelatine (some add juice of lemon), dissolved in a little warm water, and boil until it is reduced to a little less than a quart, pour over the chicken in the mold, leave to cool, cut with a very sharp knife and serve. The slices will not easily break up if directions are followed.

CHICKEN BROTH.

Half fowl, or the inferior joints of a whole one, one quart of water, one blade of mace, half onion, a small bunch of sweet herbs, salt to taste, ten peppercorns. If a young one be used for this broth, the inferior joints may be put in the broth, and the best pieces reserved for dressing in some other manner. Put the fowl into a saucepan, with all the ingredients, and simmer gently for one and a half hours, carefully skimming the broth well. When done, strain, and put by in a cool place until wanted; then take all the fat off the top, warm up as much as may be required, and serve. This broth is, of course, only for those invalids whose stomachs are strong enough to digest it, with a flavoring of herbs, etc. It may be made in the same manner as beef-tea, with water and salt only; but the preparation will be but tasteless and insipid. When the invalid cannot digest this chicken broth with the flavoring, we would recommend plain beef tea in preference to plain chicken tea, which it would be without the addition of herbs, onions, etc.

TO MAKE GRUEL.

One tablespoonful of Robinson's patent groats, two tablespoonfuls of cold water, one pint of boiling water. Mix the prepared groats smoothly with the cold water in a basin; pour over them the boiling water, stirring it all the time. Put it into a very clean saucepan; boil the gruel for ten minutes, keeping it well stirred; sweeten to taste, and serve. It may be flavored with a small piece of lemon-peel, by boiling it in the gruel, or a little grated nutmeg may be put in; but in these matters the taste of the patient should be consulted. Pour the gruel in a tumbler and serve. When wine is allowed to the invalid, two tablespoonfuls of sherry or port make this preparation very nice. In cases of colds, the same quantity of spirits is sometimes added instead of wine.

BARLEY WATER.

Put a large tablespoonful of well-washed pearl barley into a pitcher; pour over it boiling water; cover it, and let it remain till cold; then drain off the water; sweeten to taste, and, if liked, add the juice of a lemon, and grated nutmeg.

ARROWROOT BLANC-MANGE.

Put a quart of milk to boil, take an ounce of Bermnda arrowroot ground fine, make it a smooth batter with cold milk, add a teaspoonful of salt; when the milk is boiling hot, stir the batter into it, continue to stir it over a gentle fire (that it may not be scorched) for three or four minutes, sweeten to taste with double refined sugar, and flavor with lemon extract or orange-flower water, or boil a stick of cinnamon or vanilla bean in the milk before putting in the arrowroot; dip a mold into cold water, strain the blancmange through a muslin into the mold, when perfectly cold turn it out; serve currant jelly or jam with it.

LEMONADE FOR INVALIDS.

One-half a lemon, lump sugar to taste, one pint of boiling water. Pare off the rind of the lemon thinly; cut the lemon into two or three thick slices, and remove as much as possible of the white outside pith, and all the pips. Put the slices of lemon, the peel, and lump sugar into a jug; pour over the boiling water; cover it closely, and in two hours it will be fit to drink. It should either be strained or poured off from the sediment.

MUTTON BROTH

Is frequently ordered as a preparation for invalids. For the sick-room such broth must be made as plainly as possible, and so as to secure the juice of the meat. Boil slowly a couple of pounds of lean mutton for two hours, skim it very carefully as it simmers, and do not put in very much salt. If the doctor permits, some vegetable as seasoning may be added, and for some broths a little fine barley or rice is added.

FLAX SEED LEMONADE.

Four tablespoons flax seed (whole), one quart boiling water poured on the flax seed, juice of two lemons, leaving out the peel. Sweeten to taste; stew three hours in a covered pitcher. If too thick, put in cold water with the lemon-juice and sugar. Ice for drinking. It is splendid for colds.

ARROWROOT.

This is very nourishing and light, either for invalids or infants; make it with milk or water—put a pint of either into a stewpan, make it boiling hot, add a saltspoonful of salt, put a heaped teaspoonful of ground Bermuda arrowroot into a cup, make it smooth with cold milk, stir it into the stewpan, and let it simmer for two or three minutes; then turn it into a bowl, sweeten and grate nutmeg over, if liked; should it be preferred thin, use less arrowroot. This should be made only as much as is wanted at a time, since it will become as thin as water if heated over.

STEWED RABBITS IN MILK.

Two very young rabbits, not nearly half grown; one and one-half pints of milk, one blade of mace, one dessertspoonful of flour, a little salt and Cayenne. Mix the flour very smoothly with four tablespoonfuls of the milk, and when this is well-mixed, add the remainder. Cut up the rabbits into joints, put them into a stewpan with the milk and other ingredients, and simmer them *very gently* until quite tender. Stir the contents from time to time, to keep the milk smooth and prevent it from burning. Half an hour will be sufficient for the cooking of this dish.

SLIPPERY-ELM BARK TEA.

Break the bark into bits, pour boiling water over it, cover and let it infuse until cold. Sweeten, ice, and take for summer disorders, or add lemon-juice and drink for a bad cold.

BEEF TEA.

One pound of *lean* beef, cut into small pieces. Put into a jar without a drop of water; cover tightly, and set in a pot of cold water. Heat gradually to a boil, and continue this steadily for three or four hours, until the meat is like white rags, and the juice all drawn out. Season with salt to taste, and, when cold, skim.

EGG WINE.

One egg, one tablespoonful and one-half glass of cold water, one glass of sherry, sugar and grated nutmeg to taste. Beat the egg, mixing with it a tablespoonful of cold water; make the wine and water hot, but not boiling; pour it on the egg, stirring all the time. Add sufficient lump sugar to sweeten the mixture, and a little grated nutmeg; put all into a very clean saucepan, set it on a gentle fire, and stir the contents one way until they thicken, but *do not allow them to boil.* Serve in a glass with snippets of toasted bread or plain crisp biscuits. When the egg is not warmed, the mixture will be found easier of digestion, but it is not so pleasant a drink.

TOAST WATER.

Slices of toast, nicely browned, without a symptom of burning. Enough boiling water to cover them. Cover closely and let them steep until cold. Strain the water, sweeten to taste, and put a piece of ice in each glassful.

ONION GRUEL

Is excellent for cold. Slice down a few onions and boil them in a pint of new milk, stir in a sprinkle of oatmeal and a very little salt, boil till the onions are quite tender, then sup rapidly and go to bed.

COSMETIQUES.

COMPLEXION WASH.

Put in a vial one drachm of benzoin gum in powder, one drachm nutmeg oil, six drops of orange-blossom tea, or apple-blossoms put in half pint of rain-water and boiled down to one teaspoonful and strained, one pint of sherry wine. Bathe the face morning and night; will remove all flesh worms and freckles, and give a beautiful complexion. Or, put one ounce of powdered gum of benzoin in pint of whiskey; to use, put in water in wash-bowl till it is milky, allowing it to dry without wiping. This is perfectly harmless.

TO CLEAR A TANNED SKIN.

Wash with a solution of carbonate of soda and a little lemon-juice; then with Fuller's earth-water, or the juice of unripe grapes.

OIL TO MAKE THE HAIR CURL.

Olive oil, one pound; oil of organum, one drachm; oil rosemary, one and one-half drachms.

WRINKLES IN THE SKIN.

White wax, one ounce; strained honey, two ounces; juice of lily-bulbs, two ounces. The foregoing melted and stirred together will remove wrinkles.

PEARL WATER FOR THE FACE.

Put half a pound best Windsor soap scraped fine into half a gallon of boiling water; stir it well until it cools, add a pint of spirits of wine and half an ounce of oil of rosemary; stir well. This is a good cosmetique, and will remove freckles.

PEARL DENTIFRICE.

Prepare chalk, one-half pound; powdered myrrh, two ounces; camphor, two drachms; orris-root powdered, two ounces. Moisten the camphor with alcohol and mix all well together.

WASH FOR A BLOTCHED FACE.

Rose water, three ounces; sulphate of zinc, one drachm; mix. Wet the face with it, gently dry it and then touch it over with cold cream, which also gently dry off.

FACE POWDER.

Take of wheat starch, one pound; powdered orris-root, three ounces; oil of lemon, thirty drops; oil of bergamot, oil of cloves, each fifteen drops. Rub thoroughly together.

BANDOLINE.

To one quart of rose-water add an ounce and a half of gum tragacanth; let it stand forty-eight hours, frequently straining it, then strain through a coarse linen cloth; let it stand two days, and again strain; add to it a drachm of oil of roses; used by ladies dressing their hair, to make it lie in any position.

A GOOD WASH FOR THE HAIR.

One pennyworth of borax, half a pint of olive-oil, one pint of boiling water.

Mode: Pour the boiling water over the borax and oil; let it cool; then put the mixture into a bottle. Shake it before using, and apply it with a flannel. Camphor and borax, dissolved in boiling water and left to cool, make a very good wash for the hair; as also does rosemary water mixed with a little borax. After using any of these washes, when the hair becomes thoroughly dry, a little pomatum or oil should be rubbed in, to make it smooth and glossy.

MISCELLANEOUS.

AN EXCELLENT HARD SOAP.

Pour twelve quarts soft boiling water on two and one-half pounds of unslacked lime; dissolve five pounds sal soda in twelve quarts soft hot water; then mix and let them remain from twelve to twenty-four hours. Pour off all the clear fluid, being careful not to allow any of the sediment to run off; boil three and one-half pounds clean grease and three or four ounces of rosin in the above lye till the grease disappears; pour into a box and let it stand a day to stiffen and then cut in bars. It is as well to put the lime in all the water and then add the soda. After pouring off the fluid, add two or three gallons of water and let it stand with the lime and soda dregs a day or two. This makes an excellent washing fluid to boil or soak the clothes in, with one pint in a boiler of water.

TO WASH WOOLEN BLANKETS.

Dissolve soap enough to make a good suds in boiling water, add a tablespoon of aqua ammonia; when scalding hot, turn over your blankets. If convenient, use a pounder, or any way to work thoroughly through the suds without rubbing on a board. Rinse well in hot water. There is usually soap enough from the first suds to make the second soft; if not, add a little soap and ammonia; and after being through the wringer let two persons, standing opposite, pull them into shape; dry in the sun. White flannels may be washed in the same way without shrinking. Calicoes and other colored fabrics can, before washing, be advantageously soaked for a time in a pail of water to which a spoonful of ox gall has been added. It helps to keep the color. A teacup of lye to a pail of water will improve the color of black goods when necessary to wash them, and vinegar in the rinsing water of pink or green will brighten those colors, as will soda for purple and blue.

FOR CLOTHES THAT FADE.

One ounce sugar of lead in a pail of rain water. Soak over night.

LAMP-WICKS.

To insure a good light, wicks must be changed often, as they soon become clogged, and do not permit the free passage of the oil. Soaking wicks in vinegar twenty-four hours before placing in lamp insures a clear flame.

TO MAKE OLD CRAPE LOOK NEARLY EQUAL TO NEW.

Place a little water in a teakettle, and let it boil until there is plenty of steam from the spout; then holding the crape in both hands, pass it to and fro several times through the steam, and it will be clean and nearly equal to new.

A CEMENT FOR STOVES.

If the stove is cracked, a good cement is made for it as follows: Wood ashes and salt in equal proportions, reduced to a paste with cold water, and filled in the cracks when the stove is cool. It will soon harden.

TO CLEAN KID GLOVES.

Rub with very slightly damp bread-crumbs. If not effectual, scrape upon them dry Fuller's earth or French chalk, when on the hands, and rub them quickly together in all directions. Do this several times. Or put gloves of a light color on the hands and wash the hands in a basin of spirits of hartshorn. Some gloves may be washed in a strong lather made of soft soap and warm water or milk; or wash with rice pulp; or sponge them well with turpentine, and hang them in a warm place or where there is a current of air, and all smell of turpentine will be removed.

STAINS AND SPOTS.

Children's clothes, table linens, towels, etc., should be thoroughly examined before wetting, as soap-suds, washing-fluids, etc., will fix almost any stain past removal. Many stains will pass away by being simply washed in pure soft water; or alcohol will remove, before the articles have been in soap-suds, many stains. Ironmold, mildew, or almost any similar spot, can be taken out by dipping in diluted citric acid; then cover with salt, and lay in the bright sun until the stain disappears. If of long standing, it may be necessary to repeat the wetting and the sunlight. Be careful to rinse in several waters as soon as the stain is no longer visible. Ink, fruit, wine, and mildew stains must first be washed in clear, cold water, removing as much of the spots as can be; then mix one teaspoonful of oxalic acid and half a pint of rain water. Dip the stain in this, and wipe off in clear water. Wash at once, if a fabric that will bear washing. A tablespoonful of white-currant juice, if any can be had, is even better than lemon. This preparation may be used on the most delicate articles without injury. Shake it up before using it, and be careful and put out of the reach of meddlers or little folks, as it is poisonous.

TO REMOVE GREASE SPOTS.

An excellent mixture to remove grease spots from boys' and men's clothing particularly, is made of four parts alcohol to one part of ammonia and about half as much ether as ammonia. Apply the liquid to the grease spot, and then rub diligently with a sponge and clear water. The chemistry of the operation seems to be that the alcohol and ether dissolve the grease, and the ammonia forms a soap with it which is washed out with the water. The result is much more satisfactory than when something is used which only seems to spread the spot and make it fainter, but does not actually remove it. If oil is spilt on the carpet, and you immediately scatter corn meal over it, the oil will be absorbed by it. Oil may also be removed from carpets on which you do not dare to put ether and ammonia, by laying thick blotting paper over it and pressing a hot flat-iron on it. Repeat the operation several times, using a clean paper each time.

STAINS ON MARBLE.

Iron-rust stains on marble can usually be removed by rubbing with lemon-juice. Almost all other stains may be taken off by mixing one ounce of finely-powdered chalk, one of pumice stone, and two ounces of common soda. Sift these together through a fine sieve, and mix with water. When thoroughly mixed, rub this mixture over the stains faithfully and the stains will disappear. Wash the marble after this with soap and water, dry and polish with a chamois skin, and the marble will look like new.

A thin coating of three parts lard melted with one part rosin applied to stoves and grates will prevent their rusting in summer.

PAINT OR VARNISH.

Oil of turpentine or benzine will remove spots of paint, varnish, or pitch from white or colored cotton or woolen goods. After using it they should be washed in soap-suds.

TO REMOVE INK FROM CARPETS.

When freshly spilled, ink can be removed from carpets by wetting in milk. Take cotton batting and soak up all of the ink it will receive, being careful not to let it spread. Then take fresh cotton, wet in milk, and sop it up carefully. Repeat this operation, changing cotton and milk each time. After most of the ink has been taken up in this way, with fresh cotton and clean, rub the spot. Continue till all disappears, then wash the spot in clean warm water and a little soap; rinse in clean water, and rub till nearly dry. If the ink is dried in, we know of no way that will not take the color from the carpet as well as the ink, unless the ink is on a white spot. In that case salts of lemon, or soft-soap, starch, and lemon-juice will remove the ink as easily as if on cotton.

TO REMOVE INK FROM PAPER.

Put one pound of cloride of lime to four quarts of water. Shake well together and let it stand twenty-four hours; then strain through a clean cotton cloth. Add one teaspoonful of acetic acid to one ounce of this prepared lime water, and apply to the blot, and the ink will disappear. Absorb the moisture with blotting paper. The remainder may be bottled, closely corked, and set aside for future use.

An occasional feed of hard-boiled eggs made fine and mixed with cracker-crumbs is good for canary birds. Feed a couple of thimblefuls at a time.

INK ON ROSEWOOD OR MAHOGANY.

If ink has been unfortunately spilled on mahogany, rosewood, or black walnut furniture, put half a dozen drops of spirits of nitre into a spoonful of water, and touch the stain with a feather wet in this; as soon as the ink disappears, rub the place immediately with a cloth ready wet in cold water, or the nitre will leave a white spot very difficult to remove, If after washing off the nitre the ink spot still lingers, make the mixture a little stronger and use the second time, and never forget to wash it off at once.

COAL FIRE.

If your coal fire is low, throw on a tablespoon of salt, and it will help it very much.

POLISH FOR BRIGHT STOVES AND STEEL ARTICLES.

One tablespoonful of turpentine; one tablespoonful of sweet oil; emery powder. Mix the turpentine and sweet oil together, stirring in sufficient emery powder to make the mixture of the thickness of cream. Put it on the article with a piece of soft flannel, rub off quickly with another piece, then polish with a little emery powder and clean leather.

TO PREVENT PUMPS FROM FREEZING.

Take out the lower valve in the fall, and drive a tack under it, projecting in such a way that it cannot quite close. The water will then leak back into the well or cistern, while the working qualities of the pump will not be damaged.

To keep starch from sticking to irons rub the irons with a little piece of wax or sperm.

TO KEEP OFF MOSQUITOES.

Rub exposed parts with kerosene. The odor is not noticed after a few minutes, and children especially are much relieved by its use.

TO BRIGHTEN GILT FRAMES.

Take sufficient flour of sulphur to give a golden tinge to about one and one-half pints of water, and in this boil four or five bruised onions or garlic, which will answer the same purpose. Strain off the liquid, and with it, when cold, wash, with a soft brush, any gilding which requires restoring, and when dry it will come out as bright as new work.

TO MAKE HENS LAY IN WINTER.

Keep them warm; keep corn constantly by them, but do not feed it to them. Feed them with meat scraps when lard or tallow has been tried, or fresh meat. Some chop green peppers finely, or mix Cayenne pepper with corn meal to feed them. Let them have a frequent taste of green food, a little gravel and lime, or clam-shells.

TO PRESERVE STEEL PENS.

Steel pens are destroyed by corrosion from acid in the ink. Put in the ink some nails or old steel pens, and the acid will exhaust itself on them, and the pens in use will not corrode.

MICE.

Pumpkin seeds are very attractive to mice, and traps baited with them will soon destroy this little pest.

CAMPHOR

Placed in trunks or drawers will prevent mice from doing them injury.

TO CLEAN COMBS.

If it can be avoided, never wash combs, as the water often makes the teeth split, and the tortoiseshell or horn of which they are made, rough. Small brushes, manufactured purposely for cleaning combs, may be purchased at a trifling cost; with this the comb should be well brushed, and afterwards wiped with a cloth or towel.

FOR CLEANING INK-SPOTS.

Ink-spots on the fingers may be instantly removed by a little ammonia. Rinse the hands after washing in clear water. A little ammonia in a few spoonfuls of alcohol is excellent to sponge silk dresses that have grown "shiny" or rusty, as well as to take out spots. A silk, particularly a black, becomes almost like new when so sponged.

FOR CLEANING JEWELRY.

For cleaning jewelry there is nothing better than ammonia and water. If very dull or dirty, rub a little soap on a soft brush and brush them in this wash, rinse in cold water, dry first in an old handkerchief, and then rub with buck or chamois skin. Their freshness and brilliancy when thus cleaned cannot be surpassed by any compound used by jewelers.

FOR WASHING SILVER AND SILVERWARE

For washing silver, put half a teaspoonful ammonia into the suds; have the water hot; wash quickly, using a small brush, rinse in hot water, and dry with a clean linen towel;

then rub very dry with a chamois skin. Washed in this manner, silver becomes very brilliant, requires no polishing with any of the powders or whiting usually employed, and does not wear out. Silver-plate, jewelry and door-plates can be beautifully cleaned and made to look like new by dropping a soft cloth or chamois skin into a weak preparation of ammonia-water, and rubbing the articles with it. Put half a teaspoonful into clear water to wash tumblers or glass of any kind, rinse and dry well, and they will be beautifully clear.

FOR WASHING GLASS AND GLASSWARE.

For washing windows, looking-glasses, etc., a little ammonia in the water saves much labor, aside from giving a better polish than anything else; and for general house-cleaning it removes dirt, smoke and grease most effectually.

INSECTS AND VERMIN.

Dissolve two pounds of alum in three or four quarts of water. Let it remain over night, till all the alum is dissolved. Then, with a brush, apply, boiling hot, to every joint or crevice in the closet or shelves where Croton bugs, ants, cockroaches, etc., intrude; also to the joints and crevices of bedsteads, as bed bugs dislike it as much as Croton bugs, roaches or ants. Brush all the cracks in the floor and mop-boards. Keep it boiling hot while using.

To keep woolens and furs from moths, two things are to be observed—first, to see that none are in the articles when they are put away, and second, to put them where the parent moth cannot enter. Tin cases, soldered tight, whiskey barrels headed so that not even a liquid can get in or out, have been used to keep out moths. A piece of strong brown paper with not a hole through which even a large pin can enter, is just as good. Put the articles in a close box and cover every joint with paper, or resort to whatever will be a complete covering. A wrapper of common cotton cloth, so put around and secured, is often used. Wherever a knitting needle will pass the parent moth can enter. Carefully exclude the insect and the articles will be safe.

MOTHS IN CARPETS.

Persons troubled with carpet moths may get rid of them by scrubbing the floor with strong hot salt and water before laying the carpet, and sprinkling the carpet with salt once a week before sweeping.

SMOOTH SAD-IRONS.

To have your sad-irons clean and smooth rub them first with a piece of wax tied in a cloth, and afterwards scour them on a paper or thick cloth strewn with coarse salt.

TO SWEETEN MEAT.

A little charcoal thrown into the pot will sweeten meat that is a little old. Not if it is anyway tainted—it is then not fit to eat—but only if kept a little longer than makes it quite fresh.

STOVE POLISH.

Stove lustre, when mixed with turpentine and applied in the usual manner, is blacker, more glossy and more durable than when mixed with any other liquid. The turpentine prevents rust, and when put on an old rusty stove will make it look as well as new.

CLEANING WHITE PAINT.

Spirits of ammonia, used in sufficient quantity to soften the water, and ordinary hard soap, will make the paint look white and clean with half the effort of any other method I ever have tried. Care should be taken not to have too much ammonia, or the paint will be injured.

TO CLEANSE THE INSIDE OF JARS.

This can be done in a few minutes by filling the jars with hot water (it need not be scalding hot), and then stirring in a teaspoonful or more of baking soda. Shake well, then empty the jar at once, and if any of the former odor remains about it, fill again with water and soda; shake well, and rinse out in cold water.

FURNITURE POLISH.

Equal proportions of linseed oil, turpentine, vinegar, and spirits of wine.

Mode: When used, shake the mixture well, and rub on the furniture with a piece of linen rag, and polish with a clean duster. Vinegar and oil, rubbed in with flannel, and the furniture rubbed with a clean duster, produce a very good polish.

Squeaking doors ought to have the hinges oiled by a feather dipped in some linseed oil.

A soft cloth, wetted in alcohol, is excellent to wipe off French plate-glass and mirrors.

A red-hot iron will soften old putty so that it can be easily removed.

TO REMOVE STAINS FROM MATTRESSES.

Make a thick paste by wetting starch with cold water. Spread this on the stain, first putting the mattress in the sun; rub this off after an hour or so, and if the ticking is not clean try the process again.

KALSOMINING.

For plain white use one pound white glue, twenty pounds English whiting; dissolve glue by boiling in about three pints of water; dissolve whiting with hot water; make the consistency of thick batter; then add glue and one cup soft soap. Dissolve a piece of alum the size of a hen's egg, add and mix the whole thoroughly. Let it cool before using. If too thick to spread nicely add more water till it spreads easily. For blue tints add five cents' worth of Prussian blue, and a little Venetian red for lavender. For peach-blow use red in white alone. The above quantity is enough to cover four ceilings, sixteen feet square, with two coats, and will not rub off as the whitewash does made of lime.

PAPERING WHITEWASHED WALLS.

There are many ways, but we mention those that are the most reliable. Take a perfectly clean broom, and wet the walls all over with clean water; then with a small sharp hoe or scraper scrape off all the old whitewash you can. Then cut your paper of the right length, and, when you are all ready to put on the paper, wet the wall with strong vinegar. Another way is to make very thin paste by dissolving one pound of white glue in five quarts of warm water, and wash the walls with it before putting on the paper. A very good way is to apply the paste to both paper and wall. The paste may be made from either wheat or rye flour, but must be put on warm.

HOW TO CLEAN CORSETS.

Take out the steels at front and sides, then scrub thoroughly with tepid or cold lather of white castile soap, using a very small scrubbing brush. Do not lay them in water. When quite clean let cold water run on them freely from the spigot to rinse out the soap thoroughly. Dry without ironing (after pulling lengthwise until they are straight and shapely) in a cool place.

TO CLEAN HAIRBRUSHES.

Do not use soap, but put a tablespoon of hartshorn into the water, having it only tepid, and dip up and down until clean; then dry with the brushes down, and they will be like new ones. If you do not have ammonia, use soda; a teaspoonful dissolved in the water will do very well.

HOW TO WASH FLANNELS.

There are many conflicting theories in regard to the proper way to wash flannels, but I am convinced, from careful observation, that the true way is to wash them in water in which you can comfortably bear your hand. Make suds before putting the flannels in, and do not rub soap on the flannel. I make it a rule to have only one piece of flannel put in the tub at a time. Wash in two suds if much soiled; then rinse thoroughly in clean, weak suds, wring, and hang up; but do not take flannels out of warm water and hang out in a freezing air, as that certainly tends to shrink them. It is better to dry them in the house, unless the sun shines. In washing worsted goods, such as men's pantaloons, pursue the same course, only do not wring them, but hang them up and let them drain; while a little damp bring in and press smoothly with as hot an iron as you can use without scorching the goods. The reason for not wringing them is to prevent wrinkles.

CLEANING LACE.

Cream-colored Spanish lace can be cleaned and made to look like new by rubbing it in dry flour; rub as if you were washing in water. Then take it outdoors and shake all the flour out; if not perfectly clean, repeat the rubbing in a little more clean flour. The flour must be very thoroughly shaken from the lace, or the result will be far from satisfactory. White knitted hoods can be cleaned in this way; babies' socks also, if only slightly soiled.

NEW KETTLES.

The best way to prepare a new iron kettle for use is to fill it with clean potato peelings, boil them for an hour or more, then wash the kettle with hot water; wipe it dry, and rub it with a little lard; repeat the rubbing for half a dozen times after using. In this way you will prevent rust and all the annoyances liable to occur in the use of a new kettle.

TO KEEP FLIES OFF GILT FRAMES.

Boil three or four onions in a pint of water and apply with a soft brush.

TO PREVENT KNIVES FROM RUSTING.

In laying aside knives, or other steel implements, they should be slightly oiled and wrapped in tissue paper to prevent their rusting. A salty atmosphere will in a short time quite ruin all steel articles, unless some such precaution is taken.

CEMENT FOR GLASSWARE.

For mending valuable glass objects, which would be disfigured by common cement, chrome cement may be used. This is a mixture of five parts of gelatine to one of a solution of acid chromate of lime. The broken edges are covered with this, pressed together and exposed to sunlight, the effect of the latter being to render the compound insoluble even in boiling water.

WATERPROOF PAPER.

Excellent paper for packing may be made of old newspapers; the tougher the paper of course the better. A mixture is made of copal varnish, boiled linseed oil and turpentine, in equal parts. It is painted on the paper with a flat varnish brush an inch and a half wide, and the sheets are laid out to dry for a few minutes. This paper has been very successfully used for packing plants for sending long distances, and is probably equal to the paper commonly used by nurserymen.

RECIPE FOR VIOLET INK.

To make one gallon, take one ounce of violet analine; dissolve it in one gill of hot alcohol. Stir it a few moments. When thoroughly dissolved add one gallon of boiling water, and the ink is made. As the analine colors vary a great deal in quality, the amount of dilution must vary with the sample used and the shade determined by trial.

PERSPIRATION.

The unpleasant odor produced by perspiration is frequently the source of vexation to persons who are subject to it. Nothing is simpler than to remove this odor much more effectually than by the application of such costly unguents and perfumes as are in use. It is only necessary to procure some of the compound spirits of ammonia, and place about two tablespoonfuls in a basin of water. Washing the face, hands, and arms with this leaves the skin as clean, sweet and fresh as one could wish. The wash is perfectly harmless and very cheap. It is recommended on the authority of an experienced physician.

RENEWING OLD KID GLOVES.

Make a thick mucilage by boiling a handful of flax-seed; add a little dissolved toilet soap; then, when the mixture cools, put the glove on the hands and rub them with a piece of white flannel wet with the mixture. Do not wet the gloves through.

COLOGNE WATER.

Take a pint of alcohol and put in thirty drops of oil of lemon, thirty of bergamot, and half a gill of water. If musk or lavender is desired, add the same quantity of each. The oils should be put in the alcohol and shaken well before the water is added. Bottle it for use.

TO CLEANSE A SPONGE.

By rubbing a fresh lemon thoroughly into a soured sponge and rinsing it several times in lukewarm water, it will become as sweet as when new.

ICY WINDOWS.

Windows may be kept free from ice and polished by rubbing the glass with a sponge dipped in alcohol.

To remove blood stains from cloth, saturate with kerosene, and after standing a little, wash in warm water.

CAMPHOR ICE.

One ounce of lard, one ounce of spermaceti, one ounce of camphor, one ounce of almond oil, one-half cake of white wax; melt and turn into molds.

STARCH POLISH.

Take one ounce of spermaceti and one ounce of white wax, melt and run it into a thin cake on a plate. A piece the size of a quarter dollar added to a quart of prepared starch gives a beautiful lustre to the clothes and prevents the iron from sticking.

TO CLEAN FEATHERS.

Cover the feathers with a paste made of pipe-clay and water, rubbing them one way only. When quite dry, shake off all the powder and curl with a knife. Grebe feathers may be washed with white soap in soft water.

TO TEST NUTMEGS.

To test nutmegs prick them with a pin, and if they are good the oil will instantly spread around the puncture.

TO CLEAN MICA.

Mica in stoves, when smoked, is readily cleaned by taking it out and thoroughly washing with vinegar a little diluted. If the black does not come off at once, let it soak a little.

TO SOFTEN HARD WATER.

Add half a pound of the best quick lime, dissolved in water to every hundred gallons. Smaller proportions may be more conveniently managed, and if allowed to stand a short time the lime will have united with the carbonate of lime and been deposited at the bottom of the receptacle. Another way is to put gallon of lye into a barrelful of water.

TO DESTROY VERMIN IN THE HAIR.

Powdered cevadilla one ounce, powdered staves-acre one ounce, powdered panby seed one ounce, powdered tobacco one ounce. Mix well and rub among the roots of the hair thoroughly.

TO REMOVE BRUISES FROM FURNITURE.

Wet the bruised spot with warm water. Soak a piece of brown paper of several thicknesses in warm water, and lay over the place. Then apply a warm flat-iron until the moisture is gone. Repeat the process if needful, and the bruise will disappear.

PEARL SMELLING SALTS.

Powdered carbonate of ammonia, one ounce; strong solution of ammonia, half a fluid ounce; oil of rosemary, ten drops; oil of bergamot, ten drops. Mix, and while moist put in a wide-mouthed bottle which is to be well closed.

POUNDED GLASS.

Pounded glass, mixed with dry corn-meal, and placed within the reach of rats, it is said, will banish them from the premises; or sprinkle Cayenne pepper in their holes.

POLISH FOR BOOTS.

Take of ivory-black and treacle each four ounces; sulphuric acid, one ounce; best olive oil, two spoonfuls, best white-wine vinegar, three half pints; mix the ivory-black and treacle well in an earthen jar; then add the sulphuric acid, continuing to stir the mixture; next pour in the oil, and, lastly, add the vinegar, stirring it in by degrees until thoroughly incorporated.

TO CLEAN PLATE.

Wash the plate well to remove all grease, in a strong lather of common yellow soap and boiling water, and wipe it quite dry; then mix as much hartshorn powder as will be required, into a thick paste, with cold water or spirits of wine; smear this lightly over the plate with a piece of soft rag, and leave it for some little time to dry. When perfectly dry, brush it off quite clean with a soft plate-brush, and polish the plate with a dry leather. If the plate be very dirty, or much tarnished, spirits of wine will be found to answer better than water for mixing the paste.

TO CLEAN DECANTERS.

Roll up in small pieces some soft brown or blotting paper; wet them, and soap them well. Put them into the decanters about one-quarter full of warm water; shake them well for a few moments, then rinse with clear cold water; wipe the outsides with a nice dry cloth, put the decanters to drain, and when dry they will be almost as bright as new ones.

SPOTS ON TOWELS AND HOSIERY.

Spots on towels and hosiery will disappear with little trouble if a little ammonia is put into enough water to soak the articles, and they are left in it an hour or two before washing; and if a cupful is put into the water in which white clothes are soaked the night before washing, the ease with which the articles can be washed, and their great whiteness and clearness when dried will be very gratifying. Remembering the small sum paid for three quarts of ammonia of common strength, one can easily see that no bleaching preparation can be more cheaply obtained.

No articles in kitchen use are so likely to be neglected and abused as the dish-cloths and dish-towels; and in washing these, ammonia, if properly used, is a greater comfort than anywhere else. Put a teaspoonful into the water in which these cloths are, or should be washed every day; rub soap on the towels. Put them in the water; let them stand a half hour or so, then rub them out thoroughly, rinse faithfully, and dry out-doors in clear air and sun, and dish-cloths and towels need never look gray and dingy—a perpetual discomfort to all housekeepers.

CROUP.

Croup, it is said, can be cured in one minute, and the remedy is simply alum and sugar. The way to accomplish the deed is to take a knife or grater, and shave off in small particles about a teaspoonful of alum; then mix it with twice its amount of sugar, to make it palatable, and administer it as quickly as possible. Almost instantaneous relief will follow.

In the summer season it is not an uncommon thing for persons going into the woods to be poisoned by contact with dogwood, ivy, or the poisoned oak. The severe itching and smarting which is thus produced may be relieved by first washing the parts with a solution of saleratus, two teaspoonfuls to the pint of water, and then applying cloths wet with extract of hamammellis. Take a dose of Epsom salts internally or a double Rochelle powder.

CONVULSION FITS.

Convulsion fits sometimes follow [the feverish restlessness produced by these causes; in which case a hot bath should be administered without delay, and the lower parts of the body rubbed, the bath being as hot as it can be without scalding the tender skin.

BURNS AND SCALDS.

A burn or scald is always painful; but the pain can be instantly relieved by the use of bi-carbonate of soda, or common baking soda (saleratus). Put two tablespoonfuls of soda in a half cup of water. Wet a piece of linen cloth in the solution and lay it on the burn. The pain will disappear as if by magic. If the burn is so deep that the skin has peeled off, dredge the dry soda directly on the part affected.

CUTS.

For a slight cut there is nothing better to control the hemorrhage than common unglazed brown wrapping paper, such as is used by marketmen and grocers; a piece to be bound over the wound.

COLD ON THE CHEST.

A flannel dipped in boiling water, and sprinkled with turpentine, laid on the chest as quickly as possible, will relieve the most severe cold or hoarseness.

BLEEDING FROM THE NOSE.

Many children, especially those of a sanguineous temperament, are subject to sudden discharges of blood from some part of the body; and as all such fluxes are in general the result of an effort of nature to relieve the system from some overload or pressure, such discharges, unless in excess, and when likely to produce debility, should not be rashly or too abruptly checked. In general, these discharges are confined to the summer or spring months of the year, and follow pains in the head, a sense of drowsiness, languor or oppression, and as such symptoms are relieved by the loss of blood, the hemorrhage should, to a certain extent, be encouraged. When, however, the bleeding is excessive, or returns too frequently, it becomes necessary to apply means to subdue or mitigate the amount. For this purpose the sudden and unexpected application of cold is itself sufficient in most cases to arrest the most active hemorrhage. A wet towel laid suddenly on the back, between the shoulders, and placing the child in a recumbent posture is often sufficient to effect the object; where, however, the effusion resists such simple means, napkins wrung out of cold water must be laid across the forehead and nose, the hands dipped in cold water, and a bottle of hot water applied to the feet. If, in spite of these means, the bleeding continues, a little fine wool or a few folds of lint, tied together by a piece of thread, must be pushed up the nostril from which the blood flows; to act as a plug and pressure on the bleeding vessel. When the discharge has entirely ceased, the plug is to be pulled out by means of the thread. To prevent a repetition of the hemorrhage, the body should be sponged every morning with cold water, and the child put under a course of steel wine, have open-air exercise, and, if possible, salt water bathing. For children, a key suddenly dropped down the back between the skin and clothes, will often immediately arrest a copious bleeding.

CHILBLAINS.

Chilblains are most irritating to children. The following is an infallible cure for unbroken chilblains: Hydrochloric acid, diluted, one-quarter ounce; hydrocyanic acid, diluted, 30 drops; camphor-water, six ounces. This chilblain lotion cures mild cases by one application. It is a deadly poison, and should be kept under lock and key. A responsible person should apply it to the feet of children. This must not be applied to broken chilblains.

TO CURE A STING OF BEE OR WASP.

Mix common earth with water to about the consistency of mud. Apply at once.

FOR TOOTHACHE.

Alum reduced to an impalpable powder, two drachms; nitrous spirit of ether, seven drachms; mix and apply to the tooth.

CHOKING.

A piece of food lodged in the throat may sometimes be pushed down with the finger, or removed with a hairpin quickly straightened and hooked at the end, or by two or three vigorous blows on the back between the shoulders.

A very excellent carminative powder for flatulant infants may be kept in the house, and employed with advantage, whenever the child is in pain or griped, by dropping five grains of oil of aniseed and two of peppermint on half an ounce of lump sugar, and rubbing it in a mortar, with a drachm of magnesia, into a fine powder. A small quantity of this may be given in a little water at any time, and always with benefit.

CUBEB BERRIES FOR CATARRH.

A new remedy for catarrh is crushed cubeb berries smoked in a pipe, emitting the smoke through the nose; after a few trials this will be easy to do. If the nose is stopped up so that it is almost impossible to breath, one pipeful will make the head as clear as a bell. For sore throat, asthma, and bronchitis, swallowing the smoke effects immediate relief. It is the best remedy in the world for offensive breath, and will make the most foul breath pure and sweet. Sufferers from that horrid disease, ulcerated catarrh, will find this remedy unequaled, and a month's use will cure the most obstinate case. A single trial will convince anyone. Eating the uncrushed berries is also good for sore throat and all bronchial complaints. After smoking, do not expose yourself to cold air for at least fifteen minutes.

DIARRHŒA.

For any form of diarrhœa that, by excessive action, demands a speedy correction, the most efficacious remedy that can be employed in all ages and conditions of childhood is the tincture of kino, of which from ten to thirty drops, mixed with a little sugar and water in a spoon, are to be given every two or three hours till the undue action has been checked. Often the change of diet to rice, milk, eggs, or the substitution of animal for vegetable food *vice versa,* will correct an unpleasant and almost chronic state of diarrhœa.

If it is not convenient to fill flannel bags for the sick room with sand, bran will answer the purpose very well, and will retain the heat a long time.

BITES OF DOGS.

The only safe remedy in case of a bite from a dog suspected of madness, is to burn out the wound thoroughly with red-hot iron, or with lunar caustic, for fully eight seconds, so as to destroy the entire surface of the wound. Do this as soon as possible, for no time is to be lost. Of course it will be expected that the parts touched with the caustic will turn black.

MEASLES AND SCARLATINA.

Measles and scarlatina much resemble each other in their early stages; headache, restlessness, and fretfulness are the symptoms of both. Shivering fits, succeeded by a hot skin; pains in the back and limbs, accompanied by sickness, and, in severe cases, sore throat; pain about the jaws, difficulty in swallowing, running at the eyes, which become red and inflamed, while the face is hot and flushed, often distinguish scarlatina from scarlet fever, of which it is only a mild form. While the case is doubtful, a dessertspoonful of spirit of nitre diluted in water, given at bedtime, will throw the child into a gentle perspiration, and will bring out the rash in either case. In measles, this appears first on the face; in scarlatina, on the chest; and in both cases, a doctor should be called in. In scarlatina, tartar-emetic powder or ipecacuhana may be administered in the meantime.

STYE IN THE EYE.

Styes are little abscesses which form between the roots of the eyelashes, and are rarely larger than a small pea. The best way to manage them is to bathe them frequently with warm water; or in warm poppy-water, if very painful. When they have burst, use an ointment composed of one part of citron ointment and four of spermaceti, well rubbed together, and smear along the edge of the eyelid. Give a grain or two of calomel with five or eight grains of rhubarb, according to the age of the child, twice a week. The old-fashioned and apparently absurd practice of rubbing the stye with a ring, is as good and speedy a cure as that by any process of medicinal application; though the number of times it is rubbed, or the quality of the ring and direction of the strokes, has nothing to do with its success. That pressure and the friction excite the vessels of the part, and cause an absorption of the effused matter under the eyelash. The edge of the nail will answer as well as a ring.

FOR CONSTIPATION.

One or two figs eaten fastly is sufficient for some, and they are especially good in the case of children, as there is no trouble in getting them to take them. A spoon of wheaten bran in a glass of water is a simple remedy and quite effective.

LEANNESS

Is caused generally by lack of power in the digestive organs to digest and assimilate the fat-producing elements of food. First restore digestion, take plenty of sleep, drink all the water the stomach will bear in the morning on rising, take moderate exercise in the open air, eat oatmeal, cracked wheat, Graham mush, baked sweet apples, roasted and broiled beef, cultivate jolly people, and bathe daily.

SUPERFLUOUS HAIRS

Are best left alone. Shaving only increases the strength of the hair, and all depilatories are dangerous and sometimes disfigure the face. The only sure plan is to spread on a piece of leather equal parts of garbanum and pitch plaster, lay it on the hair as smoothly as possible, let it remain three or four minutes, then remove it with the hairs, root and branch. This is severe, but effective. Kerosene will also remove them. If sore after using, rub on sweet oil.

THE BREATH.

Nothing makes one so disagreeable to others as a bad breath. It is caused by bad teeth, diseased stomach, or disease of the nostrils. Neatness and care of the health will prevent and cure it.

THE QUININE CURE FOR DRUNKENNESS.

Pulverize one pound of fresh quill-red Peruvian bark, and soak it in one pint of diluted alcohol. Strain and evaporate down to one-half pint. For the first and second days give a teaspoonful every three hours. If too much is taken, headache will result, and in that case the doses should be diminished. On the third day give one-half a teaspoonful; on the fourth reduce the dose to fifteen drops, then to ten, and then to five. Seven days, it is said, will cure average cases, though some require a whole month.

FOR SORE THROAT.

Cut slices of salt pork or fat bacon; simmer a few moments in hot vinegar, and apply to throat as hot as possible. When this is taken off, as the throat is relieved, put around a bandage of soft flannel. A gargle of equal parts of borax and alum, dissolved in water, is also excellent. To be used frequently.

A GOOD CURE FOR COLDS.

Boil two ounces of flaxseed in one quart of water; strain and add two ounces of rock candy, one-half pint of honey, juice of three lemons; mix, and let all boil well; let cool, and bottle. *Dose:* One cupful on going to bed, one-half cupful before meals. The hotter you drink it the better.

TO STOP BLEEDING.

A handful of flour bound on the cut.

A HEALTHFUL APPETIZER.

How often we hear women who do their own cooking say that by the time they have prepared a meal, and it is ready for the table, they are too tired to eat. One way to mitigate this is to take, about half an hour before dinner, a raw egg, beat it until light, put in a little sugar and milk, flavor it, and "drink it down;" it will remove the faint, tired-out feeling, and will not spoil your appetite for dinner.

TO REMOVE DISCOLORATION FROM BRUISES.

Apply a cloth wrung out in very hot water, and renew frequently until the pain ceases. Or apply raw beefsteak.

EARACHE.

There is scarcely any ache to which children are subject so hard to bear and difficult to cure as the earache; but there is a remedy never known to fail. Take a bit of cotton batting, put upon it a pinch of black pepper, gather it up and tie it, dip in sweet oil and insert into the ear; put a flannel bandage over the head to keep it warm. It will give immediate relief. As soon as any soreness is felt in the ear, let three or four drops of the tincture of arnica be poured in and the orifice be filled with a little cotton wool to exclude the air. If the arnica be not resorted to until there is actual pain, then the cure may not be as speedy, but it is just as certain, although it may be necessary to repeat the operation. It is a sure preventive against gathering in the ear, which is the usual cause of earache.

TO CURE TOOTHACHE.

The worst toothache, or neuralgia coming from the teeth, may be speedily and delightfully ended by the application of a bit of clean cotton, saturated in a solution of ammonia, to the defective tooth. Sometimes the late sufferer is prompted to momentary laughter by the application, but the pain will disappear.

FOR FELON.

Take common rock salt, as used for salting down pork or beef, dry in an oven, and pound it fine and mix with spirits of turpentine in equal parts; put it in a rag and wrap it around the parts affected; as it gets dry put on more, and in twenty-four hours you are cured. The felon will be dead.

Coffee pounded in a mortar and roasted on an iron plate; sugar burned on hot coals, and vinegar boiled with myrrh and sprinkled on the floor and furniture of a sick room, are excellent deodorizers.

The skin of a boiled egg is the most efficacious remedy that can be applied to a boil. Peel it carefully, wet and apply to the part affected. It will draw off the matter, and relieve the soreness in a few hours.

TO CURE A WHITLOW.

As soon as the whitlow has risen distinctly, a pretty large piece should be snipped out, so that the watery matter may readily escape, and continue to flow out as fast as produced. A bread and water poultice should be put on for a few days, when the wound should be bound up lightly with some mild ointment, when a cure will be speedily completed. Constant poulticing both before and after the opening of the whitlow is the only practice needed; but as the matter lies deep, when it is necessary to open the abscess, the incision must be made *deep* to reach the suppuration.

TAPE-WORMS.

Tape-worms are said to be removed by refraining from supper and breakfast, and at eight o'clock taking one-third part of two hundred minced pumpkin seeds, the shells of which have been removed by hot water; at nine take another third, at ten the remainder, and follow it at eleven with strong dose of castor oil.

FOR A CAKED BREAST.

Bake large potatoes, put two or more in a woolen stocking; crush them soft and apply to the breast as hot as can be borne; repeat constantly till relieved.

A good remedy for blistered feet from long walking is to rub the feet at going to bed with spirits mixed with tallow dropped from a lighted candle into the palm of the hand.

A lady writes that sufferers from asthma should get a muskrat skin and wear it over their lungs, with the fur side next to the body. It will bring certain relief.

CHAPPED HANDS.

Powdered starch is an excellent preventive of chapping of the hands, when it is rubbed over them after washing and drying them thoroughly. It will also prevent the needle in sewing from sticking and becoming rusty. It is therefore advisable to have a small box of it in the work-box or basket, and near your wash-basin.

LUNAR CAUSTIC.

Lunar caustic, carefully applied so as not to touch the skin, will destroy warts.

CURE FOR RHEUMATISM AND BILIOUS HEADACHE.

Finest Turkey rhubarb, half an ounce; carbonate magnesia, one ounce; mix intimately; keep well corked in glass bottle. *Dose:* One teaspoonful, in milk and sugar, the first thing in the morning; repeat till cured. Tried with success.

FEVER AND AGUE.

Four ounces galangal-root in a quart of gin, steeped in a warm place; take often.

For a simple fainting fit a horizontal position and fresh air will usually suffice. If a person receive a severe shock caused by a fall or blow, handle carefully without jarring. A horizontal position is best. Loosen all tight clothing from the throat, chest, and waist. If the patient can swallow, give half teaspoonful aromatic spirits of ammonia in a little water. If that cannot be procured, give whiskey or brandy and water. Apply warmth to the feet and bowels.

TO RESTORE FROM STROKE OF LIGHTNING.

Shower with cold water for two hours; if the patient does not show signs of life, put salt in the water, and continue to shower an hour longer.

RELIEF FOR INFLAMED FEET.

The first thing to be done is to take off and throw away tight-fitting boots, which hurt the tender feet as much as if they were put into a press. Then take one pint of wheat bran and one ounce of saleratus, and put it into a foot-bath, and add one gallon of hot water. When it has become cool enough put in the feet, soak them for fifteen minutes, and the relief will be almost immediate. Repeat this every night for a week, and the cure will be complete. The burning, prickly sensation is caused by the pores of the skin being closed up so tightly by the pressure of the boots that they cannot perspire freely.

WARM WATER.

Warm water is preferable to cold water as a drink to persons who are subject to dyspeptic and bilious complaints, and it may be taken more freely than cold water, and consequently answers better as a diluent for carrying off bile, and removing obstructions in the urinary secretion, in cases of stone and gravel. When water of a temperature equal to that of the human body is used for drink, it proves considerably stimulant, and is particularly suited to dyspetic, bilious, gouty, and chlorotic subjects.

CLEANING HOUSE.

SITTING AND DINING-ROOMS.

By the time the upper part of the house is well cleaned and in good order, if it has been taken one room at a time, and leisurely, probably, the dining-room can be torn up on a warm and pleasant day, and, unless the alterations are to be extensive, scoured and gotten to rights again before nightfall. And the sitting-room on another day. House-cleaning, unless conducted on some plan which occasions little if any disturbance in the general domestic arrangement, is a nuisance, particularly to the males of the household. Nothing can be (next to a miserable dinner) more exasperating to a tired man, than to come home and find the house topsy-turvy. And it certainly raises his opinion of his wife's executive ability to find everything freshened and brightened, and that without his having been annoyed by the odor of the soapsuds, or yet having been obliged to betake himself to the kitchen for his meals.

But if the order of work is well laid out the night beforehand, the breakfast as leisurely eaten as usual, and the family dispersed in their various ways before commencing operations, then by working with a will wonders can be accomplished in a very short time. It is not worth while to undertake a thorough cleaning of all extra china, silver and glassware, which may be stored in the china closet in addittition to the room itself. They can readily wait over until another morning, as can the examination of table-linen. In cleaning any room after the furniture and carpets have been taken out and the dust swept out with a damp broom, the proper order is to begin with the ceiling, then take the walls and windows, and lastly the floor. Kalsomining or whitewash dries most quickly when exposed to free draughts of air, the windows being thrown wide open for the purpose; this process can also be aided by lighting a fire in the room, either in the stove left for the purpose, or in the grate. These means are equally good for drying a freshly-scoured floor.

In lieu of regular carpet wadding, layers of newspapers are very good padding under a carpet, or better yet, sheets of thick brown paper will answer very well. Matting and green linen shades are delightfully cool in either sitting or dining-room for summer use, or all through the hottest weather if the dining-room can be left with a bare floor, and lightly washed off with cold water before breakfast each day it will add greatly to the coolness of the room. A fireplace can be arranged with a screen before it, or it can be left open, the fixtures taken away, and a large stone or pottery jar filled with fresh flowers daily set into it. Very showy flowers can in this way be made effective in decorating a room. Jars covered with pictures of delcalcomania are tawdry-looking. Better far to paint them a dull black or bottle-green; or a brick-red, with a plain band or geometric design traced in some contrasting color.

In dining-room furniture oak wood with green trimmings and light paint are good contrasting colors, while black walnut or mahogany, with red carpet and shades of red predominating about the room, look well with dark paint.

In arranging a sitting-room large spaces left empty look more comfortable and are more convenient in every way than a room huddled too full of furniture. A home is not a furniture wareroom nor a fancy bazaar, but a place for people to live in, and to grow in, and to move about in.

House-cleaning time presents an opportunity for disposing of many ostensibly ornamental articles which only serve to fill up place, without being either beautiful or well-made of their kind.

An empty wall looks better than one hung with daubs. Good engravings and plain cheap frames are now obtained at such a trifling cost that almost every one can afford one or two excellent ones in their sitting-room. People living at a distance can easily send to some large city for an engraving or two, or, if they prefer colored pictures, to some well-known establishment for two or three good chromos

I have seen some of the best newspaper engravings pinned upon the sitting-room wall, framed in pressed ferns, with very good effect indeed. Once a very simple bracket held a glass bumper of unique pattern, from which was trailed cypress vines, and mingled with them, a bunch of scarlet lychnis. Against the white wall of the room they looked brilliant, and the effect was really beautiful.

When the sitting-room is torn up frequently an array of newspapers, missing books, etc., are found huddled together in some corner. In settling the room these should find their proper places, and it would be a good thing to keep them there ever after, for, no matter how thorough the cleaning process, untidiness and litter will soon make any room appear nearly as badly as before it was scoured.

HOW TO DUST A ROOM.

Soft cloths make the best of dusters. In dusting any piece of furniture begin at the top and dust down, wiping carefully with the cloth, which can be frequently shaken. A good many people seem to have no idea what dusting is intended to accomplish, and instead of wiping off and removing the dust it is simply flirted off into the air and soon settles down upon the articles dusted again. If carefully taken up by the cloth it can be shaken off out of the window into the open air. If the furniture will permit the use of a damp cloth, that will more easily take up the dust, and it can be washed out in a pail of soapsuds. It is far easier to save work by covering up nice furniture while sweeping, than to clean the dust out, besides leaving the furniture looking far better in the long run. The blessing of plainness in decoration is appreciated by the thorough housekeeper who does her own work while dusting.

GIRLS, LEARN TO COOK.

Yes, yes, learn how to cook, girls; and learn how to cook well. What right has a girl to marry and go into a house of her own unless she knows how to superintend every branch of housekeeping, and she cannot properly superintend unless she has some practical knowledge herself. It is sometimes asked, sneeringly, "What kind of a man is he who would marry a cook?" The fact is, that men do not think enough of this; indeed, most men marry without thinking whether the woman of his choice is capable of cooking him a meal, and it is a pity he is so shortsighted, as his health, his cheerfulness, and, indeed, his success in life, depend in a very great degree on the kind of food he eats; in fact, the whole household is influenced by the diet. Feed them on fried cakes, fried meats, hot bread and other indigestible viands, day after day, and they will need medicine to make them well.

Let all girls have a share in housekeeping at home before they marry; let each superintend some department by turns. It need not occupy half the time to see that the house has been properly swept, dusted, and put in order, to prepare puddings and make dishes, that many young ladies spend in reading novels which enervate both mind and body and unfit them for every-day life. Women do not, as a general rule, get pale faces doing housework. Their sedentary habits, in overheated rooms, combined with ill-chosen food, are to blame for bad health. Our mothers used to pride themselves on their housekeeping and fine needlework. Let the present generation add to its list of real accomplishments the art of properly preparing food for the human body.

TEACH THE LITTLE ONES.

There is scarcely a busy home mother in the land who

has not at some time or other felt how much easier it would be to do all the work herself than to attempt to teach a child to assist her, whether it be in household matters or in sewing. Now, we would speak particularly of the latter. But it seems almost the right of every little girl to be taught to sew neatly, even if it does cost the mother some self-sacrifice. Very few grown women are wholly exempt from ever using a needle. On the contrary, almost every woman must take more or less care of her own wardrobe, even if she has no responsibility for that of any one's around her. Machines cannot sew up rips in gloves, replace missing buttons, or make or mend without any needlework by hand. Some stitches must be taken, and how to sew neatly is an accomplishment quite as necessary, if not more so, to the happiness of a majority of women than any other. If a little girl be early taught how to use her needle, it very soon becomes a sort of second nature to her, and very little ones can learn to thread the needle and take simple stitches. Only the mother must be patient and painstaking with them, not letting poor work receive praise or permitting the child to slight what she undertakes. The stint can be a very short one with very little children. It is usually best so, but frequent lessons should be given.

CHILDREN LOVE GAMES.

Take advantage of this to give them physical training. Furnish them the aparatus for games which requires a good deal of muscular exercise. Those curious little affairs which require them to sit on the floor or gather about the table and remain in a cramped position, are not advisable.

It is particularly desirable that the games should call them into the open air and sunshine. In this way children lay in a stock of health and strength. Remember that, particularly in our early years, this is infinitely more important than all adornments of the person or study of books.

Let it not be forgotten that symmetrical development of the body is of the utmost importance. A child, for example, is *weak* and *round-shouldered.* It is important that he should be made strong. It is not less important that he should be made straight. Every conceivable exercise may tend to increase the strength, but only special exercises tend to draw the shoulders back, and thus secure the rectitude which is the basis of spinal and visceral tone. It is not difficult to give children such games and sports as will have this special tendency.

TEACH YOUR OWN CHILDREN.

Some parents allow their children to acquire the very rude and unmannerly habit of breaking in upon their conversation and those of older persons with questions and remarks of their own. It is very uncivil to allow them to do so. So, even among their own brothers and sisters and schoolmates, of their own age, let them speak without interrupting. If one begins to tell a story or bit of news, teach them to let him finish it; and if he makes mistakes that ought to be corrected, do it afterwards. Don't allow them to acquire the habit of being interrupters. Most of those who allow their own children to form this disagreeable habit will be exceedingly annoyed at the same conduct in other folks' children. The fault is that of the parents in not teaching their children. If they interrupt at home, tell them to wait till they can converse without annoying, and see that they do it.

CULTIVATING SELFISHNESS IN CHILDREN.

The mother who in the fullness of generous love runs hither and thither continually to do for the various members of the family those things which they should do themselves, comes to be regarded as a useful piece of machinery, suited to minister to their wants, but she is not regarded with one whit more of love or reverence, rather the reverse. By and by, when the mother is worn out in body and spirit, when the child, grown older, feels no need of her as its slave, it finds other more attractive playmates and companions.

The mother has necessarily far more labor, care, and anxiety than any other member of the household. She is continually occupied, and her work seems to have no end. Neither husband nor children will love her the more for sacrificing herself wholly to them, as many a sad, weary mother has learned to her cost. Let her be just to herself. Not that she should make slaves of the children any more than they should make a slave of her. But children like to be useful, like to feel that they are a real help to older persons, and if a little praise and perhaps, too, a little money is given them, they will learn to enjoy the pleasure of helping mother and of earning something for themselves, and early taught the dignity of labor as well as save their mother a little time to keep herself in advance of them in study and thought, in general information, and in spiritual growth, so as to be always reverenced as their intellectual and spiritual guide and friend and counsellor.

It has been truly said by Miss Sewell, author of an excellent work on education, that "Unselfish mothers make selfish children." This may seem startling, but the truth is, that the mother who is continually giving up her own time, money, strength, and pleasure for the gratification of her children teaches them to expect it always. They learn to be importunate in their demands, and to expect more and more. If the mother wears an old dress that her daughter may have a new one, if she work that her daughter may play, she is helping to make her vain, selfish, and ignorant, and very likely she will be ungrateful and disrespectful, and this is equally true of the husband, and other members of the family. Unselfish wives make selfish husbands.

PACKING AWAY FURS.

All furs should be well switched and beaten lightly, free from dust and loose hairs, well wrapped in newspaper, with bits of camphor laid about them and in them, and put away in a cool dark place. If a cedar closet or chest is to be had, laid into that. In lieu of that new cedar chips may be scattered about. It is never well to delay packing furs away until quite late in the season, for the moth will early commence depredations. In packing them they should not be rolled so tightly as to be crushed and damaged.

COURAGE.

One may possess physical courage, so that in times of danger, a railroad accident, a steamboat collision or a runaway horse, the heart will not be daunted or the cheek paled, while on the other hand, one may be morally brave, not afraid to speak a word for the right in season, though unwelcome, to perform a disagreeable duty unflinchingly or to refuse to do a wrong act, and yet be a physical coward, trembling and terrified in a thunder-storm, timid in the dark, and even scream at the sight of a mouse. Courage, both moral and physical, is one of the finest attributes of character, and both can be cultivated and gained if desired and sought after. Some girls think it interesting and attractive to be terrified at insects, and will shriek with fright if they happen to be chased a few rods by a flock of geese, but they only excite laughter and do not gain the admiration which a brave girl who tries to help herself would deserve.

THE ART OF BEAUTY IN DRESS.

It is far easier to find fault with existing customs than to devise and put in practice other and better ones.

Ladies do not like to appear singular, and make themselves conspicuous by wearing such articles of dress as are laughed at, possibly, certainly not worn by any other persons in the city or county in which she may belong. And so the matter goes on. Manufacturers, dry goods dealers, and milliners, and dressmakers, carry the day with a high hand. Yet there is always some choice, and as, thanks to our civilized habits, a full-length mirror is obtainable by most ladies, given the resolution to make the most and best of themselves, the greater number of women can so study the art of dressing well as to produce some excellent results.

It will hardly do to copy the old masters of painting in the arrangement of drapery, at least anyways closely, for no matter how well the voluminous folds may look painted, they certainly would be very much in the way in real life, and impede any free action of the muscles somewhat, while the length of sweeping gowns certainly looks more in place on painted canvas than it can do on an ordinary walking dress. Ladies have realized this fact, however, and the short walking-skirt, at once pretty and convenient, has been the result.

In some places the common sense shoe can be found, and this permits the muscles of the foot, if not the freest, yet fair play. One great mistake in the dressing of the feet is in getting the covering too short. It will throw back the toe joints, and a bunion is only too frequently the result. If the soles of the shoes are too thin, the feet become chilled, and disease ensues. Yet in repeated instances they have been known to draw the feet and made them exceedingly tender and sore. A light cork sole sewed to a knitted worsted slipper will give a foot covering, equally light and far less injurious in its results.

There are ladies who wholly ignore woolen hosiery, preferring lisle thread, cotton or silk. Yet in winter time, particularly for children, woolen stockings are almost a necessity, particularly if woolen is worn over the rest of the body. There are some people who can not abide the feeling of woolen garments next the skin, and they are obliged to get their warmth of clothing in other than their undergarments. Heavy outside garments are not quite so graceful as those of softer and lighter material. But if they must be worn they will bear a plainer cut than such clothes as are naturally clinging, and adapt themselves to the figure.

Solid and plain colors have a greater richness than mixed shades. If combined tints are used, they should only be such as harmonize well, and in the full-length figure give a good personal effect. Probably more ladies err in getting good general effects than in any other one particular. They have various garments, pretty enough, possibly, in themselves, yet which do not harmonize well together, either in material, color or cut, or possibly with their particular style of figure and shade of hair and complexion. For example, the skirt will have one style of trimming, the waist another, the bonnet may look exceedingly well with one suit, and be quite out of keeping with another. A short dumpy person will wear flounces, a tall slim one stripes, while some red-haired woman will fancy an exquisite shade of pink, while green or blue would have been much more becoming.

Black generally makes people look smaller, and white larger. A very pale person can bear a certain amount of bright red. Any delicate complexion looks well with soft ruchings or laces at neck and wrist. Lace is so expensive that it cannot be so generally worn as it might be, with excellent effect. Probably no prettier head covering has ever been designed than the veils worn by the Spanish women. Certainly they are infinitely more graceful than a modern poke bonnet.

Dress goods cut up into little bits and sewed together into fantastical shapes called trimmings, are apt if too freely used to give an air of fussiness to the dress, and be withal a source of endless annoyance in catching dust and dirt. The former ideas of a border or hem to finish has become the greater part of the garment.

Nothing is gained in grace by making any outside garment skin-tight, while much is lost in comfort by so doing. A sleeve, for instance, to be serviceable and look well, should be loose and adapt itself somewhat to the curve of the arm. Likewise a dress waist looks far better a little loose, as well as being more healthful and wearing better.

Large, stout persons can add to their appearance much by wearing all outside skirts buttoned on to fitted under-garments below the hips several inches, for gathers about the waist only add to their stoutness of look, and are uncomfortable to carry about. A yoked petticoat answers the purpose very well in lieu of the buttoned skirts.

A wrapper for a tall slim person can have a Spanish flounce, while a slashed skirt with kilt inserts is more becoming to a short figure. Large folds are always more graceful than small pleats and puckers. One very great fault of our dressmaking lies in not allowing the goods to fall in large and natural folds, but in bunching and pleating it in folding, and pressing the goods down into fantastic and inartistic shapes. Added to this, paniers, and padding, bustles, and hoops, until an ordinary woman is forced to appear like a stuffed figure instead of a living human being.

Every woman can modify, and arrange, and simplify, and that without becoming either ultra or conspicuous. It will take time. That cannot be helped, yet possibly the saving in comfort and expense may fully compensate for the few hours spent in studying her own dress with the mirror before her and with the determination to make the very best and most of herself.

HOME DRESSMAKING.

The art of dressmaking in America has been of late years so simplified that almost anyone with a reasonable degree of executive ability can manufacture a fashionable costume by using an approved pattern and following the directions printed upon it, selecting a new pattern for each distinct style; while in Europe many ladies adhere to the old plan of cutting one model and using it for everything, trusting to personal skill or luck to gain the desired formation. However, some useful hints are given which are well worth offering after the paper pattern has been chosen.

The best dressmakers here and abroad use silk for lining, but nothing is so durable or preserves the material as well as a firm slate twill. This is sold double width and should be laid out thus folded: place the pattern upon it with the upper part towards the cut end, the selvedge for the fronts. The side pieces for the back will most probably be got out of the width, while the top of the back will fit in the intersect of the front. A yard of good stuff may be often saved by laying the pattern out and well considering how one part cuts into another. Prick the outline on to the lining; these marks serve as a guide for the tacking.

In forming the front side plaits be careful and do not allow a fold or crease to be apparent on the bodice beyond where the stitching commences. To avoid this, before beginning stick a pin through what is to be the top of the plait. The head will be on the right side, and holding the point, one can begin pinning the seam without touching the upper part of the bodice. To ascertain the size of the buttonholes put a piece of card beneath the button to be used and cut it an eighth of an inch on either side beyond. Having turned down the piece in front on the buttonhole side run a thread a sixteenth of an inch from the extreme edge, and again another the width of the card. Begin to cut the first buttonhole at the bottom of the bodice, and continue at equal distances. The other side of the bodice is left wide enough to come well under the buttonholes. The buttonholes must be laid upon it and a pin put through the centre of each to mark where the button is to be placed. In sewing on the buttons put the stitches in horizontally; if perpendicularly they are likely to pucker that side of the bodice so much that it will be quite drawn up, and the buttons will not match the buttonholes.

A WOMAN'S SKIRTS.

Observe the extra fatigue which is insured to every woman in merely carrying a tray upstairs, from the skirts of the dress. Ask any young women who are studying to pass examinations whether they do not find loose clothes a *sine qua non* while poring over their books, and then realize the harm we are doing ourselves and the race by habitually lowering our powers of life and energy in such a manner. As a matter of fact it is doubtful whether any persons have ever been found who would say that their stays were at all tight; and, indeed, by a muscular contraction they can apparently prove that they are not so by moving them about on themselves, and thus probably believe what they say. That they are in error all the same they can easily assure themselves by first measuring round the waist outside the stays; then take them off, let them measure while they take a deep breath, with the tape merely laid on the body as if measuring for the quantity of braid to go round a dress, and mark the result. The injury done by stays is so entirely internal that it is not strange that the maladies caused by wearing them should be attributed to every reason under the sun except the true one, which is, briefly, that all the internal organs, being by them displaced, are doing their work imperfectly and under the least advantageous conditions; and are, therefore, exactly in the state most favorable to the development of disease, whether hereditary or otherwise.—*Maxmillan's Magazine.*

TO MAKE THE SLEEVES.

As to sleeves. Measure from the shoulder to the elbow and again from elbow to the wrist. Lay these measurements on any sleeve patterns you may have, and lengthen or shorten accordingly. The sleeve is cut in two pieces, the top of the arm and the under part, which is about an inch narrower than the outside. In joining the two together, if the sleeve is at all tight, the upper part is slightly fulled to the lower at the elbow. The sleeve is sown to the armhole with no cordings now, and the front seam should be about two inches in front of the bodice.

Bodices are now worn very tight-fitting, and the French stretch the material well on the cross before beginning to cut out, and in cutting allow the lining to be slightly pulled, so that when on, the outside stretches to it and insures a better fit. An experienced eye can tell a French-cut bodice at once, the front side pieces being always on the cross. In dress cutting and fitting, as in everything else, there are failures and discouragements, but practice overrules these little matters, and "trying again" brings a sure reward in success.

A sensible suggestion is made in regard to the finish in necks of dresses for morning wear. Plain colors have rather a stiff appearance, tulle or crepe lisse frilling are expensive and frail, so it is a good idea to purchase a few yards of really good washing lace, about an inch and a half in depth; quill or plait and cut into suitable lengths to tack around the necks of dresses. This can be easily removed and cleaned when soiled. A piece of soft black Spanish lace, folded loosely around the throat close to the frillings, but below it, looks very pretty; or you may get three yards of scarf lace, trim the ends with frillings, place it around the neck, leaving nearly all the length in the right hand, the end lying upon the left shoulder being about half a yard long. Wind the larger piece twice around the throat, in loose, soft folds, and festoon the other yard and a half, and fasten with brooch or flower at the side.—*Philadelphia Times.*

ALL ABOUT KITCHEN WORK.

A lady who for a time was compelled to do all of her own kitchen work says: "If every iron, pot, pan, kettle or any utensil used in the cooking of food, be washed as soon as emptied, and while still hot, half the labor will be saved." It is a simple habit to acquire, and the washing of pots and kettles by this means loses some of its distasteful aspects. No lady seriously objects to washing and wiping the crystal and silver, but to tackle the black, greasy, and formidable-looking ironware of the kitchen take a good deal of sturdy brawn and muscle as well as common-sense.

If the range be wiped carefully with brown paper, after cooking greasy food, it can be kept bright with little difficulty.

Stoves and ranges should be kept free from soot in all compartments. A clogged hot-air passage will prevent any oven from baking well.

When the draught is imperfect the defect frequently

arises from the chimney being too low. To remedy the evil the chimney should be built up, or a chimney-pot added.

It is an excellent plan for the mistress to acquaint herself with the practical workings of her range, unless her servants are exceptionally good, for many hindrances to well-cooked food arises from some misunderstanding of, or imperfection in, this article.

A clean, tidy kitchen can only be secured by having a place for everything and everything in its place, and by frequent scourings of the room and utensils.

A hand-towel and basin are needed in every kitchen for the use of the cook or house-worker.

Unless dish-towels are washed, scalded and thoroughly dried daily, they become musty and unfit for use, as also the dish-cloth.

Cinders make a very hot fire—one particularly good for ironing days.

Milk keeps from souring longer in a shallow pan than in a milk pitcher. Deep pans make an equal amount of cream.

Hash smoothly plastered down will sour more readily than if left in broken masses in the chopping bowl, each mass being well exposed to the air.

Sauce, plain, and for immediate use, should not be put into a jar and covered when warm, else it will change and ferment very quickly. It will keep some days with care in the putting up. Let it stand until perfectly cold, then put into a stone jar.

To scatter the Philadelphia brick over the scouring board on to the floor, to leave the soap in the bottom of the scrubbing pail, the sapolio in the basin of water, and to spatter the black lead or stove polish on the floor are wasteful, slatternly habits.

A clock in the kitchen is both useful and necessary.

A NICE CLOTHES FRAME.

Our kitchen is very small; too small, in fact, to be very comfortable in, and, moreover, has to serve the double purpose of kitchen and laundry. There was no room to spare for the large clothes-horse we had been accustomed to use, nor even for a smaller clothes-screen we thought of purchasing. In this emergency we happened upon a nice frame, which consists of bars of wood secured at one end in an iron clamp, which screws on the side of a window frame. These bars move freely around, and quite a respectable sized ironing can be aired upon them. We found they were invented and made by a dealer in the country who had no patent upon them, and so, of course, his sales must be limited, yet they are very convenient. The clothes are hung quite out of the way, and yet can be well aired.

KEEP THE CELLAR CLEAN.

A great deal of the sickness families suffer could be easily traced to the cellar. The cellar not unusually opens into the kitchen, the kitchen is heated, and the cellar is not. Following natural laws, the colder air of the cellar will rush to take the place of the warmer, and, therefore, lighter air of the kitchen. This would be well enough if the cellar air was pure, but often it is not; partly decayed vegetables may be there, or rotten wood, etc. A day should be taken to throw out and carry away all dirt, rotten woods, decaying vegetables, and other accumulations which have gathered there. Brush down the cobwebs, and with a bucket of lime give the walls and ceiling a good coat of whitewash. If a whitewash brush is not at hand take an old broom that the good wife has worn out, and spread the whitewash on thick and strong. It will sweeten up the air in the cellar, the parlor, and the bedrooms, and it may save the family from the afflictions of fevers, diphtheria and doctors.

SUNLIT ROOMS.

No article of furniture should be put in a room that will not stand sunlight, for every room in a dwelling should have the windows so arranged that some time during the day a flood of sunlight will force itself into the apartments. The importance of admitting the light of the sun freely to all parts of our dwellings cannot be too highly estimated. Indeed, perfect health is nearly as much dependent on pure sunlight as it is on pure air. Sunlight should never be excluded except when so bright as to be uncomfortable to the eyes. And walks should be in bright sunlight, so that the eyes are protected by veil or parasol when inconveniently intense. A sun-bath is of more importance in preserving a healthful condition of the body than is generally understood.

A sun-bath costs nothing, and that is a misfortune, for people are deluded with the idea that those things only can be good or useful which cost money. But remember that pure water, fresh air and sunlit homes kept free from dampness, will secure you from many heavy bills of the doctors and give you health and vigor, which no money can procure. It is a well established fact that people who live much in the sun are usually stronger and more healthy than those whose occupations deprive them of sunlight. And certainly there is nothing strange in the result, since the same law applies with nearly equal force to every animate thing in nature. It is quite easy to arrange an isolated dwelling so that every room may be flooded with sunlight some time in the day, and it is possible many town houses could be so built as to admit more light than they now receive.

PLEASANT HOMES.

Handsome furniture will not, unaided, make rooms cheerful. The charm of a cosy home rests principally with its mistress. If she is fortunate enough to have sunny rooms, her task is half done. In apartments into which the sun never shines recourse must be had to various devices to make up, so far as may be, for this grave lack. A sunless room should have bright and joyous color in its furnishings. The walls should be warmly tinted, the curtains give a roseate glow to the light that passes through them. An open fire may diffuse the sunshine but lately imprisoned in oak or hickory, or ages ago locked up in anthracite. Ferneries and shade-loving plants may contribute their gentle cheer to the room and suggest quiet forest nooks. An attractive room need not be too orderly. A book left lying on the table, a bit of needle-work on the window-sill, an open piano, may indicate the tastes and occupations of the inmates, without suggesting that there is not a place for everything in that room. There is such a thing as being too neat and nice to take comfort in everyday life, and this is anything but cheerful. And then there is such a thing as being so disorderly and negligent that comfort and cheer are impossible. If the house-mother cannot rest while there is a finger-mark on the paint or a spot on the window-panes, she may make a neat room, but her splint will keep it from ever being cheerful. If she has no care for the "looks of things" her failure will be equally sure. A bird singing in the window, an aquarium on the table in some corner, plants growing and blooming, domestic pets moving about as if at home, these give life and brightness to an apartment, and afford constant opportunities for the pleasantest occupation and companionship. Books people a room, and pictures on the walls, if selected with taste, are ever fresh sources of enjoyment. You may gauge the refinement and cultivation of a family by these infallible tests, unless they have been selected by some outsider. Bits of embroidery, of scroll-work, and a thousand tasteful devices may contribute to the charm of a room and make it irresistibly attractive.

HOW TO BE HANDSOME.

Where is the woman who would not be beautiful? If such there be—but no, she does not exist. From that memorable day when the Queen of Sheba made a formal call on the late lamented King Solomon until the recent advent of the Jersey Lily, the power of beauty has controlled the fate of dynasties and the lives of men. 'How to be beautiful, and consequently powerful, is a question of far greater inportance to the feminine mind than predestination or any other abstract subject. If women are to govern, control, manage, influence, and retain the adoration of husbands, fathers, brothers, lovers, or even cousins, they must look their prettiest at all times.

All women cannot have good features, but they can look well, and it is possible to a great extent to correct deformity and develop much of the figure. The first step to good looks is good health, and the first element of health is cleanliness. Keep clean—wash freely, bathe regularly. All the skin wants is leave to act, and it takes care of itself. In the matter of baths we do not strongly advocate a plunge in ice-cold water; it takes a woman with some of the clear grit that Robert Collyer loves to dilate on and a strong constitution to endure it. If a hot bath be used, let it come before retiring, as there is less danger of taking cold afterwards; and, besides, the body is weakened by the ablution and needs immediate rest. It is well to use a flesh-brush, and afterwards rinse off the soap-suds by briskly rubbing the body with a pair of coarse toilet gloves. The most important part of a bath is the drying. Every part of the body should be rubbed to a glowing redness, using a coarse crash towel at the finish. If sufficient friction cannot be given, a small amount of bay rum applied with the palm of the hand will be found efficacious. Ladies who have ample leisure and who lead methodical lives take a plunge or sponge bath three times a week, and a vapor or sun bath every day. To facilitate this very beneficial practice a south or east apartment is desirable. The lady denudes herself, takes a seat near the window, and takes in the warm rays of the sun. The effect is both beneficial and delightful. If, however, she be of a restless disposition, she may dance, instead of basking, in the sunlight. Or, if she be not fond of dancing, she may improve the shining hours by taking down her hair and brushing it, using sulphur water, pulverized borax dissolved in alcohol, or some similar dressing. It would be surprising to many ladies to see her carefully wiping the separate locks on a clean, white towel until the dust of the previous day is entirely removed. With such care it is not necessary to wash the head, and the hair under this treatment is invariably good.

One of the most useful articles of the toilet is a bottle of ammonia, and any lady who has once learned its value will never be without it. A few drops in the water takes the place of the usual amount of soap, and cleans out the pores of the skin as well as a bleach will do. Wash the face with a flesh-brush, and rub the lips well to tone their color. It is well to bathe the eyes before putting in the spirits, and if it is desirable to increase their brightness, this may be done by dashing soapsuds into them. Always rub the eyes, in washing, toward the nose. If the eyebrows are inclined to spread irregularly, pinch the hairs together where thickest. If they show a tendency to meet, this contact may be avoided by pulling out the hairs every morning before the toilet.

The dash of Orientalism in costume and lace now turns a lady's attention to her eyelashes, which are worthless if not long and drooping. Indeed, so prevalent is the desire for this beautiful feature that hair-dressers and ladies' artists have scores of customers under treatment for invigorating their stunted eyelashes and eyebrows. To obtain these fringed curtains, anoint the roots with a balsam made of two drachms of nitric oxide of mercury mixed with one of leaf lard. After an application wash the roots with a camel's hair brush dipped in warm milk. Tiny scissors are used, with which the lashes are carefully but slightly trimmed every other day. When obtained, refrain from rubbing or even touching the lids with the finger-nails. There is more beauty in a pair of well-kept eyebrows and full, sweeping eyelashes than people are aware of, and a very inattractive and lustreless eye assumes new beauty when it looks out from beneath elongated fringes. Many ladies have a habit of rubbing the corners of their eyes to remove the dust that will frequently accumulate there. Unless this operation is done with little friction it will be found that the growth of hair is very spare, and in that case it will become necessary to pencil the barren corners. Instead of putting cologne water on the handkerchief, which has come to be considered a vulgarism among ladies of correct tastes, the perfume is spent on the eyebrows and lobes of the ears.

If commenced in youth, thick lips may be reduced by compression, and thin linear ones are easily modified by suction. This draws the blood to the surfaces, and produces at first a temporary and, later, a permanent inflation. It is a mistaken belief that biting the lips reddens them. The skin of the lips is very thin, rendering them extremely susceptible to organic derangement, and if the atmosphere does not cause chaps or parchment, the result of such harsh treatment will develop into swelling or the formation of scars. Above all things, keep a sweet breath.

Everybody cannot have beautiful hands, but there is no plausible reason for their being ill-kept. Red hands may be overcome by soaking the feet in hot water as often as possible. If the skin is hard and dry, use tar or oat-meal soap, saturate them with glycerine, and wear gloves in bed. Never bathe them in hot water, and wash no oftener than is necessary. There are dozens of women with soft, white hands who do not put them in water once a month. Rubber gloves are worn in making the toilet, and they are cared for by an ointment of glycerine and rubbed dry with chamois-skin or cotton flannel. The same treatment is not unfrequently applied to the face with the most successful results. If such methods are used, it would be just as well to keep the knowledge of it from the gentlemen. We know of one beautiful lady who has not washed her face for three years, yet it is always clean, rosy, sweet, and kissable. With some of her other secrets she gave it to her lover for safe keeping. Unfortunately, it proved to be her last gift to that gentleman, who declared in a subsequent note that "I cannot reconcile my heart and my manhood to a woman who can get along without washing her face."

SOME OF THE SECRETS OF BEAUTY.

There is as much a "fashion" in complexion as there is in bonnets or boots. Sometime nature is the mode, sometimes art. Just now the latter is in the ascendant, though, as a rule, only in that inferior phase which has not reached the "concealment of art"—the point where extremes meet and the perfection of artifice presents all the appearance of artlessness. No one of an observant turn of mind, who is accustomed to the sight of English maids and matrons, can deny that making-up, as at present practiced, partakes of the amateurish element. Impossible reds and whites grow still more impossibly red and white from week to week under the unskilled hands of the wearer of "false colors," who does not like to ask for advice on so delicate a subject, for, even were she willing to confess to the practice, the imputation of experience conveyed in the asking for counsel might be badly received, and would scarcely be in good taste.

The prevalent and increasing short-sightedness of our times is, perhaps, partly the cause of the excessive use of rouge and powder. The wielder of the powder puff sees herself afar off, as it were. She knows that she cannot judge of the effect of her complexion with her face almost touching its reflection in the glass, and, standing about a yard off, she naturally accentuates her roses and lilies in a way that looks very pleasing to her, but is rather startling to any one with longer sight. Nor can she tone down her rouge with the powdered hair that softened the artificial coloring of her grandmother when she had her day. Powder is only occasionally worn with evening dress, and it is by daylight that those dreadful bluish reds and whites look their worst.

On the other hand, there are some women so clever at making up their faces that one almost feels inclined to condone the practice in admiration of the result. These are the small minority, and are likely to remain so, for their secret is of a kind unlikely to be shared. The closest inspection of these cleverly managed complexions reveals no trace of art.

Notwithstanding the reticence of these skilled artists, an occasional burst of confidence has revealed a few of their means of accomplishing the great end of looking pretty. "Do you often do that?" said one of those clever ones, a matron of 37, who looked like a girl of 19, to a friend who was vigorously rubbing her cheeks with a coarse towel after a plentiful application of cold water.

"Yes, every time I come in from a walk, ride, or drive. Why?"

"Well, no wonder you look older than you are. You are simply wearing your face out!"

"But I must wash?"

"Certainly, but not like that. Take a leaf out of my book; never wash your face just before going out into the fresh air, or just after coming in. Nothing is more injurious to the skin. Come to the glass. Do you notice a drawn look about your eyes and a general streakiness in the cheeks? That is the result of your violent assault upon your complexion just now. You look at this moment ten years older than you did twenty minutes ago in the park."

"Well, I really do. I look old enough to be your mother; but then, you are wonderful. You always look so young and fresh!"

"Because I never treat my poor face so badly as you do yours. I use rain-water, and if I cannot get that, I have the water filtered. When I dress for dinner I always wash my face with milk, adding just enough hot water to make it pleasant to use. A very soft sponge and very fine towel take the place of your terrible huckaback arrangement."

Two or three years ago a lady of Oriental parentage on her father's side spent a season in London society. Her complexion was brown, relieved by yellow, her features large and irregular, but redeemed by a pair of lovely and expressive eyes. So perfect was her taste in dress that she always attracted admiration wherever she went. Dressed in rich dark brown or dullest crimsons or russets, so that no one ever noticed much what she wore, she so managed that suggestions and hints—no more—of brilliant amber or pomegranate scarlet should appear just where they imparted brilliancy to her deep coloring, and abstract the yellow from her skin. A knot of old gold satin under the rim of her bonnet, another at her throat, and others in among the lace at her wrists, brightened up the otherwise subdued tinting of her costume, so that it always looked as though it had been designed expressly for her by some great colorist. Here rouge was unnecessary. The surroundings were arranged to suit the complexion, instead of the complexion to suit the surroundings. There can be no doubt as to which is the method which best becomes the gentlewoman.

In addition to the disagreeable sensation of making-up, it must be remembered that the use of some of the white powders eventually destroys the texture of the skin, rendering it rough and coarse. Rimmel, the celebrated perfumer, in his "Book of Perfumes," says that rouge, being composed of cochineal and saffron, is harmless, but that white cosmetics consist occasionally of deleterious substances which may injure the health. He advises actors and actresses to choose cosmetics, especially the white, with the greatest care, and women of the world, who wish to preserve the freshness of their complexion, to observe the following recipe: Open air, rest, exercise, and cold water. In another part of this pleasant book the author says that *schonada*, a cosmetic used among the Arabs, is quite innocuous and at the same time effectual. "This cream, which consists of sublimated benzoin, acts upon the skin as a slight stimulant, and imparts perfectly natural colors during some hours without occasioning the inconveniences with which European cosmetics may justly be reproached." It is a well-known fact that bismuth, a white powder containing sugar of lead, injures the nerve-centres when constantly employed, and occasionally causes paralysis itself.

In getting up the eyes, nothing is injurious that is not dropped into them. The use of *kohl* or *kohol* is quite harmless, and, it must be confessed, very effective when applied —as the famous recipe for salad dressing enjoins with regard to the vinegar—by the hand of a miser. Modern Egyptian ladies make their *kohol* of the smoke produced by burning almonds. A small bag holding the bottle of *kohol*, and a pin, with a rounded point with which to apply it, form part of the toilet paraphernalia of all the beauties of Cairo, who make the immense mistake of getting up their eyes in an exactly similar manner, thus trying to reduce the endless variety of nature to one common pattern, a mistake that may be accounted for by the fact that the Arabs believe *kohol* to be a sovereign specific against ophthalmia. Their English sisters often make the same mistake without the same excuse. A hairpin steeped in lampblack is the usual method of darkening the eyes in England, retribution following sooner or later in the shape of a total loss of the eyelashes. Eau de Cologne is occasionally dropped into the eyes, with the effect of making them brighter. The operation is painful, and it is said that half a dozen drops of whiskey and the same quantity of Eau de Cologne, eaten on a lump of sugar, is quite as effective.

HEADACHE.

One of our English contemporaries has wisely been devoting some thought and space to the common and distressing fact that a great many English women suffer from headache. The same trouble prevails in America, and men, no matter how selfish they may be, are deeply concerned about it, for a wife with a headache cannot be companionable; the best of sweethearts with a headache is sure to be unreasonable, while a lady who has neither husband or other special cavalier to engross her attention can ruin the peace of mind of every one she meets while she has a headache of perceptible size. No amount of masculine grumbling is likely to change all this, but women themselves might change it if they would comprehend the causes of the malady, and then apply their nimble wits to the work of prevention or cure.

The trouble is that all American women who have headaches live indoors, where the best air is never good and the worst is poison, and they have none of the exercises which saves man from the popular feminine malady. Were a strong man to eat breakfast at any ordinary American table and then sit down at a work-table or even move about briskly from one room to another, he would have a splitting headache before noon, and the chatter of his innocent children would seem to be the jargon of fiends. The midday meal would increase his wretchedness, and by dusk he would be stretched in misery upon his bed, with one hand moping his forehead with ice-water, while the other would threaten with a club or pistol any one who dared to enter the room or make a noise outside. There is no reason why women should not suffer just as severely for similar transgressions of physical law. True, indoor life is compulsory for a large portion every day, but special physical exercise in a well-aired room is within the reach of almost every woman, and so is a brisk walk in garments not so tight as to prevent free respiration. There is very little complaint at summer resorts, where windows are always open and games and excursions continually tempt women who do not value complexion more than health. Girls who ride, row, sail, and shoot, seldom have headaches; neither do those unfortunate enough to be compelled to hoe potatoes or play Maud Muller in hay-fields. Let women of all social grades remember that the human machine must have reasonable treatment, and be kept at work or play, to keep it from rusting, then headaches will be rare enough to be interesting.

HIGH-HEELED BOOTS MUST GO.

A lady looks infinitely taller and slimmer in a long dress than she does in a short costume, and there is always a way of showing the feet, if desired, by making the front quite short, which gives, indeed, a more youthful appearance to a train dress. The greatest attention must, of course, be paid to the feet with these short dresses, and I may here at once state that high heels are absolutely forbidden by fashion. Doctors, are you content? Only on cheap shoes and boots are they now made, and are only worn by common people. A good bootmaker will not make high heels now, even if paid double price to do so. Ladies—that is, real ladies—now wear flat-soled shoes and boots, *a la* Cinderella. For morning walking, boots or high Moliere shoes are worn.

If you wear boots you may wear any stockings you like, for no one sees them. But if you wear shoes you must adapt your stockings to your dress. Floss silk, Scotch thread, and even cotton stockings are worn for walking, silk stockings have returned into exclusively evening wear. Day stockings should be of the same color as the dress, but they may be shaded, or stripped, or dotted, just as you please. White stockings are absolutely forbidden for day wear—no one wears them—no one dares wear them under fashion's interdiction.

DON'T STOOP.

Grandmother has noticed that some of her boys lately have acquired a very bad habit. They go about with their backs bent, as if they were fifty years old, and were bearing the responsibilities of age on their shoulders. This is all wrong. Stand up straight, boys; don't go around with a "stoop in your back," as if you had a curvature of the pine. If you *do*, depend upon it, you will have it sure enough long before you get to be old. Always stand erect, and when you walk, throw back your shoulders, and take that kink out of your backbone. This is easier said than done, isn't it? Grandmother will tell you just how you can do it, and remember every word she says, for she has been through it all herself, and has straightened up many a grandchild in more respects than one. Here is her rule:

"THROW UP YOUR CHIN!"

The whole secret of standing and walking erect consists in keeping the chin well away from the breast. This throws the head upward and backward, and the shoulders will naturally settle backward and in their true position. Those who stoop in walking generally look downward. The proper way is to look straight ahead, upon the same level with your eyes, or if you are inclined to stoop, until that tendency is overcome, look rather above than below the level. Mountaineers are said to be as "straight as an arrow," and the reason is because they are obliged to look upward so much. It is simply impossible to stoop in walking if you will heed and practice this rule. You will notice that all round-shouldered persons carry the chin near the breast and pointed downward. Take warning in time, and heed grandmother's advice, for a bad habit is more easily prevented than cured. The habit of stooping when one walks or stands is a bad habit and especially hard to cure.

MAKE HOME PLEASANT.

A cheerful, happy home is the greatest safeguard against temptations for the young. Parents should spare no pains to make home a cheerful spot. There should be pictures to adorn the walls, flowers to cultivate the finer sensibilities, dominoes, checkers, and other games, entertaining books and instructive newspapers and periodicals. These things, no doubt, cost money, but not a tithe the amount that one of the lesser vices will cost—vices which are sure to be acquired away from home, but seldom there. Then there should be social pleasure—a gathering of young and old around the hearthstone, a warm welcome to the neighbor who drops in to pass a pleasant hour. There should be music and amusements and reading. The tastes of all should be consulted, until each member of the family looks forward to the hour of reunion around the hearth as the brightest one in the twenty-four. Wherever there is found a pleasant, cheerful, neat, attractive, inexpensive home there you may be sure to find the abode of the domestic virtues; there will be no dissipated husbands, no discontented or discouraged wives, no "fast" sons or frivolous daughters.

DINNER-TABLE FANCIES.

To be thoroughly good form at dinner is the very inflorescence of civilized life. Like many other regulations of social life, dinner-table etiquette is arbitrary, but not to know certain things is to argue yourself unknown so far as society life goes. To take soup pushing the spoon from rather than toward yourself; to touch the napkin as little as possible; to accept or decline what is offered instantly and quietly; these and other trifles characterize the well-bred diner-out. The attempts to introduce too much color in dinner-table decorations are rather declining. The finest white damask still holds the preference, and the centre-piece of plush or velvet underlace is little used now. Fewer flowers, too, are seen, and those in very low forms. The dessert plates come in deep tones in Dresden china, and the doyley on which the finger-bowl rests should be immediately removed with the bowl, on reaching the guest. The latest fashion in ice-cream plates is the Bohemian glass in oval form with small handles. Menu cards, hand-painted, hold the preference, but many are seen on tinted cardboard with engraved vignette in one corner and the date in another.

THE USE OF AMMONIA IN BAKING POWDERS.

The recent discoveries in science and chemistry are fast revolutionizing our daily domestic economies. Old methods are giving way to the light of modern investigation, and the habits and methods of our fathers and mothers are stepping down and out, to be succeeded by the new ideas, with marvelous rapidity. In no department of science, however, have more rapid strides been made than its relations to the preparation and preservation of human food. Scientists, having discovered how to traverse space, furnish heat, and beat time itself, by the application of natural forces, and to do a hundred other things promotive of the comfort and happiness of the human kind, are naturally turning their attention to the development of other agencies and powers that shall add to the years during which man may enjoy the blessings set before him.

Among the recent discoveries in this direction, none is more important than the uses to which common ammonia can be properly put as a leavening agent, and which indicate that this familiar salt is hereafter to perform an active part in the preparation of our daily food.

The carbonate of ammonia is an exceedingly volatile substance. Place a small portion of it upon a knife and hold over a flame, and it will almost immediately be entirely developed into gas and pass off into the air. The gas thus formed is a simple composition of nitrogen and hydrogen. No residue is left from the ammonia. This gives it its superiority as a leavening power over soda and cream tartar when used alone, and has induced its use as a supplement to these articles. A small quantity of ammonia in the dough is effective in producing bread that will be lighter, sweeter, and more wholesome than that risen by any other leavening agent. When it is acted upon by the heat of baking, the leavening gas that raises the dough is liberated. In this act it uses itself up, as it were; the ammonia is entirely diffused, leaving no trace of residuum whatever. The light, fluffy, flaky appearance, so desirable in biscuits, etc., and so sought after by professional cooks, is said to be imparted to them only by the use of this agent.

The bakers and baking powder manufacturers producing the finest goods have been quick to avail themselves of this useful discovery, and the handsomest and best bread and cake are now largely risen by the aid of ammonia, combined, of course, with other leavening material.

Ammonia is one of the best known products of the laboratory. If, as seems to be justly claimed for it, the application of its properties to the purposes of cooking results in giving us lighter and more wholesome bread, biscuit, and cake, it will prove a boon to dyspeptic humanity, and will speedily force itself into general use in the new field to which science has assigned it.

LAUGHTER.

"The laughter of girls is, and ever was, among the most delightful sounds of earth." Truly there is nothing sweeter or pleasanter to the ear than the merry laugh of a happy, joyous girl, and nothing dissipates gloom and sadness quicker, and drives dull care away like a good, hearty laugh. We do not laugh enough; nature should teach us this lesson, it is true; the earth needs the showers, but if it did not catch and hold the sunshine, too, where would be the brightness and beauty it lavishes upon us? Laugh heartily, laugh often, girls; not boisterously, but let the gladness of your hearts bubble up once in a while, and overflow in a glad, mirthful laugh.

ITEMS WORTH REMEMBERING.

A sun-bath is of more worth than much warming by the fire.

Books exposed to the atmosphere keep in better condition than if confined in a book-case.

Pictures are both for use and ornament. They serve to recall pleasant memories and scenes; they harmonize with the furnishing of the rooms. If they serve neither of these purposes they are worse than useless; they only help fill space which would look better empty, or gather dust and make work to keep them clean.

A room filled with quantities of trifling ornaments has the look of a bazar and displays neither good taste nor good sense. Artistic excellence aims to have all the furnishings of a high order of workmanship combined with simplicity, while good sense understands the folly of dusting a lot of rubbish.

A poor book had best be burned to give place to a better, or even to an empty shelf, for the fire destroys its poison, and puts it out of the way of doing harm.

Better economize in the purchasing of furniture or carpets than scrimp in buying good books or papers.

Our sitting-rooms need never be empty of guests or our libraries of society if the company of good books is admitted to them.

THOSE UNGRACEFUL HABITS.

A public conveyance brings one awkwardly near the faces of strangers. Perhaps from sheer inanity one is apt to take undue notice of his fellow-passengers. When glances meet, the gaze is lowered to the flounces of the lady seated near, or to the trim, polished boot of a gent at the far end of the car. There are nice people everywhere, and if one is artistic in taste, there will ever be a looking for beauty of face or form, in dress, or carriage, or manner, or speech; but "why is the fresh girl face so often marred by the ugly habit of cribbing?" "A beautiful woman," whispered a friend, and the eye was attracted toward a grand looking lady with wide, white forehead, from which the brown glossy hair was smoothed away without the ghost of a crimp; there were pretty arching brows, shading lashes, shapely nose, but, alas! for the ruby lips bitten and moistened so often as to prevent the possibility of catching the outline—the profile so needful to the sketcher of beauty. A poet has somewhere said that "affectation begins with the mouth," but "who would charge the gentle sex with vanity!"

What! To redden by biting, or brighten by wetting; that folly could not be. Let us rather suppose the fair one had by some mishap forgotten to lunch, and all this is due to the gnawings of hunger. While thus seeking to palliate the fair cribber, a young man becomes noticeable by persistently pulling at the ends of his moustache, chewing them in a hungry way, now changing the exercise by twisting them to needle-like points which he seemed to be coaxing upward.

"From whence has come *this* ugly habit?" one is fain to ask. Certainly not from pride. A fine flowing beard and full moustache ought not to be a cause of folly to the owner. The hairs of the face, given to protect the throat and lungs, never to be shorn in the cold seasons, can it be that there is nutriment in them? While thus questioning, the writer's two hands were suddenly jerked from his side pockets, where they had been comfortably resting. The wife's gentle remonstrance had been brought to mind by the entrance of an awkward fellow, with hands deeply thrust in the pockets of his torn pants. A caricature of one's self is often a tacit reproof. That very morning the dear wife had said: "Those torn side-pockets are the most difficult of tears to mend." And the inward monitor asked: "From whence has come this indolent habit? From love of ease or want of mittens, which? Perhaps indifference of the patient mender's." And again the monitor asked:

"What of that habit not comparable to weeds for growth?"

"What mean you?" was meekly asked.

"That of looking well to one's own faults, that lesson the hardest and the latest learned: to know thyself." Then the writer realized that he, too, was not quite perfect.

INDEX.

BREAD AND BREAKFAST DISHES.

PAGE.

Yeast........ 130
Plain White Family Bread........ 130
Graham Bread........ 131
Boston Brown Bread........ 131
Corn Bread........ 132
Steamed Brown Bread........ 132
Parker House Rolls........ 132
French Rolls........ 132
Buns........ 133
Biscuits........ 133
To Make Rusks........ 133
Sweet Milk Gems........ 134
Breakfast Gems........ 134
Graham Breakfast Cakes........ 134
Buckwheat Cakes........ 134
Flannel Cakes........ 135
Rice Griddle Cakes........ 136
French Pancakes........ 136
Pancakes........ 136
Bread Fritters........ 136
Quick Sally Lunn........ 137
Breakfast Cake........ 137
Quick Waffles........ 137
Johnny Cake........ 137
Mush........ 137
Corn Mush........ 138
Graham Mush........ 138

CAKES.

White Lady Cake........ 180
Macaroons........ 180
Almond Icing........ 181
To Make Icing for Cakes........ 181
Loaf Cake........ 182
Rich Bride Cake........ 182
Lady-Fingers........ 182
Queen Cake........ 183
Chocolate Macaroons........ 183
Caramel Cake........ 183
Pound Cake........ 184
Cocoanut Sponge Cake........ 184
Cocoanut Pound Cake........ 185

PAGE.

Cocoanut Cup Cake........ 185
Cocoanut Drops........ 185
Citron Heart Cakes........ 186
Imperial Cakes........ 186
Plum Cakes........ 186
Gold and Silver Cakes........ 187
To Make Small Sponge Cakes........ 187
Lemon Cheese Cakes........ 188
Snow Cakes........ 188
Tilden Cakes........ 188
Corn Starch Cakes........ 188
Birthday Cakes........ 189
Naples Biscuit........ 189
Cake Trifles........ 189
Savoy Cake........ 189
Composition Cake........ 190
Almond Cream Cake........ 190
Ice-Cream Cake........ 190
Economical Cake........ 191
Delicate Cake........ 191
Orange Cake........ 191
Jelly Kisses........ 192
Fig Cake........ 192
Fried Cake........ 192
Cocoanut Kisses........ 192
California Cake........ 193
White Mountain Cake........ 193
Lemon Cake........ 193
Strawberry Short Cake........ 193
Marble Cake........ 194
White Pound Cake........ 194
Nelly's Chocolate Cake........ 194
Rice Cake........ 195
Cream Cake........ 195
Sponge Cake........ 195
Doughnuts........ 195
Coffee Cake........ 196
Spice Cake........ 196
Soft Ginger Bread........ 196
Sweet Strawberry Short Cake........ 196
Ginger Nuts........ 196
Ribbon Cake........ 197
Jelly Roll........ 197
Delicate Crullers........ 198

MISCELLANEOUS.

PAGE.
An Excellent Hard Soap........ 248
To Wash Woolen Blankets........ 248
For Clothes that Fade........ 249
Lamp Wicks........ 249
To Make Old Crape Look Nearly Equal to New........ 249
A Cement for Stoves........ 249
To Clean Kid Gloves........ 250
Stains and Spots........ 250
To Remove Grease Spots........ 251
Stains on Marble........ 251
Paint or Varnish........ 252
To Remove Ink from Carpets........ 252
To Remove Ink from Paper........ 252
Feed for Canary Birds........ 252
Ink on Rosewood or Mahogany........ 253
Coal Fire........ 253
Polish for Bright Stoves and Steel Articles........ 253
To Prevent Pumps from Freezing........ 253
To Keep Starch from Sticking........ 253
To Keep off Mosquitoes........ 254
To Brighten Gilt Frames........ 254
To Make Hens Lay in Winter........ 254
To Preserve Steel Pens........ 254
Mice........ 254
Camphor........ 255
To Clean Combs........ 255
For Cleaning Jewelry........ 255
For Washing Silver and Silverware 255
For Washing Glass and Glassware.. 256
Insects and Vermin........ 256
Moths in Carpets........ 257
Smooth Sad Irons........ 257
To Sweeten Meat........ 257
Stove Polish........ 257
Cleaning White Paint........ 258
To Cleanse the Inside of Jars........ 258
Furniture Polish........ 258
Squeaking Doors........ 258
For Cleaning Mirrors........ 258
To Soften Putty........ 258
To Remove Stains from Mattresses. 259
Kalsomining........ 259
Papering Whitewashed Walls........ 259
How to Clean Corsets........ 260
To Clean Hairbrushes........ 260
How to Wash Flannels........ 260
Cleaning Lace........ 261
New Kettles........ 261
To Keep Flies off Gilt Frames........ 261
To Prevent Knives from Rusting... 261

PAGE
Cement for Glassware........ 262
Waterproof Paper........ 262
Recipe for Violet Ink........ 262
Perspiration........ 262
Renewing Old Kid Gloves........ 263
Cologne Water........ 263
To Cleanse a Sponge........ 263
Icy Windows........ 263
To Remove Blood from Cloth........ 263
Camphor Ice........ 264
Starch Polish........ 264
To Clean Feathers........ 264
To Test Nutmegs........ 264
To Clean Mica........ 264
To Soften Hard Water........ 264
To Destroy Vermin in the Hair........ 265
To Remove Bruises from Furniture 265
Pearl Smelling Salts........ 265
Pounded Glass........ 265
Polish for Boots........ 265
To Clean Plate........ 266
To Clean Decanters........ 266
Spots on Towels and Hosiery........ 266
Croup........ 267
Poison Ivy or Oak........ 267
Convulsion Fits........ 268
Burns and Scalds........ 268
Cuts........ 268
Cold on the Chest........ 268
Bleeding from the Nose........ 268
Chilblains........ 269
To Cure a Sting of Bee or Wasp........ 270
For Toothache........ 2
Choking........
Excellent Carminative Powder f
Flatulent Infants........
Cubeb Berries for Catarrh........
Diarrhœa........
For Sick Room........
Bites of Dogs........
Measles and Scarlatina........
Stye in the Eye........
For Constipation........
Leanness........ 2.
Superfluous Hairs........ 27
The Breath........ 274
The Quinine Cure for Drunkenness 274
For Sore Throat........ 274
A Good Cure for Colds........ 274
To Stop Bleeding........ 275
A Health Appetizer........ 275
To Remove Discoloration from Bruises........ 275

PAGE.
Earache ... 275
To Cure Toothache ... 276
For Felon ... 276
Excellent Deodorizers ... 276
To Cure a Boil ... 276
To Cure a Whitlow ... 277
Tape Worms ... 277
For a Caked Breast ... 277
Remedy for Blistered Feet ... 277
Relief for Asthma ... 277
Chapped Hands ... 278
Lunar Caustic ... 278
Rheumatism and Headache ... 278
Fever and Ague ... 278
For a Fainting Fit ... 278
To Restore from Stroke of Lightning ... 279
Relief for Inflamed Feet ... 279
Warm Water ... 279
Cleaning House, Sitting and Dining Room ... 279
How to Dust a Room ... 282
Girls Learn to Cook ... 283
Teach the Little Ones ... 283
Children Love Games ... 284
Teach Your Own Children ... 285
Cultivating Selfishness in Children 285
Packing Away Furs ... 287
Courage ... 287
The Art of Beauty in Dress ... 288
Home Dressmaking ... 290
Woman's Skirts ... 292
Make Sleeves ... 293
bout Kitchen Work ... 294
Clothes Frame ... 296
ooms ... 297
Homes ... 298
e Handsome ... 299
he ... 306
Heeled Boots ... 308
Home Pleasant ... 309
er Table Fancies ... 310
Use of Ammonia ... 311
ughter ... 312
ems Worth Remembering ... 313
hose Ungraceful Habits ... 313

PUDDINGS.

Remarks ... 154
Christmas Plum Pudding ... 154
Boiled Batter Pudding ... 155
Batter Pudding ... 155
Madeira Pudding ... 156
Apple Sauce Pudding ... 156
Queen of Puddings ... 156
Orange Pudding ... 157
Corn Starch Pudding ... 157
French Pudding ... 158
Belle's Pudding ... 158
Cream Tapioca Pudding ... 159
A Bachelor's Pudding ... 159
Macaroni Pudding ... 159
Baked Indian Pudding ... 160
Boiled Indian Pudding ... 160
Marmalade Pudding ... 160
Boiled Apple Pudding ... 161
Nelly's Pudding ... 161
Rich Baked Apple Pudding ... 162
Snow Balls ... 162
Rice Pudding ... 162
Apple Charlotte ... 163
Ground Rice Pudding ... 163
Fig Pudding ... 163
Bread and Butter Pudding ... 164
Cabinet Pudding ... 164
Snow Pudding ... 164
Carrot Pudding ... 165
Lemon Pudding ... 165
Roly-Poly Pudding ... 165
Cottage Pudding ... 165
Cocoanut Pudding ... 166
Cream Pudding ... 166
Tapioca Pudding ... 166
Common Custard ... 166

PUDDING SAUCES.

Rich Wine Sauce ... 168
Whipped Cream Sauce ... 168
Lemon Sauce ... 168
Jelly Sauce ... 168
Cabinet Pudding Sauce ... 169
Foaming Sauce ... 169
Spanish Sauce ... 169
Hard Sauce ... 169
Pudding Sauce ... 169
Sauce for Plum Pudding ... 170
Vanilla Sauce ... 170

PASTRY.

Very Good Puff Paste ... 171
Plainer Paste ... 172
Suet Crusts for Pies or Puddings ... 172
To Ice Pastry ... 172
To Graze Pastry ... 173
Mince Meat ... 173
Mock Mince Pie ... 174

PAGE.
Apple Custard Pie........ 174
Apple Meringue Pie........ 174
Apple Pie........ 175
Lemon Pie........ 175
Custard Pie........ 175
Cocoanut Pie........ 176
Lemon Tarts........ 176
Pastry Sandwiches........ 176
Cherry Pie........ 177
Squash Pie........ 177
Cream Pie........ 177
Tartlets........ 177
Peach Pie........ 178
Pumpkin Pie........ 178
Tart Shells........ 178
Mince Pies........ 179

PRESERVES, CANNED FRUITS, JELLY.

To Preserve Plums Without the Skins........ 210
To Preserve Purple Plums........ 210
Preserved Greengages in Syrup........ 211
Preserved Cherries in Syrup........ 211
Preserved Pears........ 212
Preserved Peaches........ 212
Preserved Citron........ 213
Crab Apples Preserved........ 213
Pineapples Preserved........ 213
Gooseberry Jam........ 213
Black Currant Jam........ 214
Raspberry Jam........ 214
Quince Preserve........ 214
Red Currant Jelly........ 215
Apple Jelly........ 216
Black Currant Jelly........ 216
Crab Apple Jelly........ 217
Other Jellies........ 217
Wine Jelly........ 217
Calves' Feet Jelly........ 217
Orange Marmalade........ 218
Lemon Marmalade........ 218
Quince Marmalade........ 218
Peach Marmalade........ 219
Apple Butter........ 219
Lemon Butter........ 219
Peach Butter........ 220

PRESERVED AND CANNED FRUITS.

Apple Ginger (A Dessert Dish)........ 220
Iced Currants........ 220
To Bottle Fresh Fruit........ 221

PAGE.
To Green Fruit for Preserving in Sugar or Vinegar........ 221
To Color Preserves Pink........ 222
To Color Fruit Yellow........ 222
Canned Peaches........ 222
Canned Strawberries........ 222
Canned Pears........ 223
Canned Plums........ 223
Cannd Currants........ 223
Canned Pineapple........ 224
Canned Quinces........ 224
Canned Tomatoes........ 224
Canned Corn........ 224

POULTRY, GAME, ETC.

Roast Turkey........ 77
Boiled Turkey........ 78
To Roast a Fowl or Chicken........ 79
Boiled Chicken........ 80
Broiled Chicken........ 80
Fried Chicken........ 80
Fricassee of Chicken........ 81
To Curry Chicken........ 81
Pressed Chicken........ 81
Chicken Pot-Pie........ 82
Chicken Salad........ 82
Chicken, Jellied........ 83
Chicken Pates........ 83
Sage and Onion Stuffing for Geese, Ducks and Pork........ 83
To Roast a Goose........ 84
Roast Ducks........ 85
Roast Pigeons........ 85
To Make a Bird's Nest........ 86
Pigeons in Jelly........ 86
Pigeon Pie........ 87
Wild Ducks........
Roast Wild Duck........
Wild Turkey........
To Roast Snipe, Woodcock, an Plover........
Roast Partridge........
Roast Quail........
Roast Prairie Chicken........ 9
Larded Grouse........ 9

PORK, HAM AND EGGS.

To Choose Pork........ 91
Curing Hams........ 92
To Roast a Leg of Pork........ 92
Pork and Beans........ 93
Pork Sausages........ 93
Pork Chops, Steaks and Cutlets........ 94

PAGE.
Roast Pig.................................... 94
Pigs' Cheek.................................... 95
Roast Spare Rib.................................... 95
Pork Fritters.................................... 96
Baked Ham.................................... 96
To Boil a Ham.................................... 96
To Broil a Ham.................................... 97
Fried Ham and Eggs.................................... 97
Ham Toast.................................... 97
Head Cheese.................................... 98
Pigs' Feet Soused.................................... 99
To Make Lard.................................... 99
To Tell Good Eggs.................................... 100
Keeping Eggs Fresh.................................... 100
Poached Eggs.................................... 101
Dropped Eggs.................................... 101
Stuffed Eggs.................................... 101
Eggs a la Suisse.................................... 102
Eggs Brouille.................................... 102
Eggs Curried.................................... 102
Eggs Creamed.................................... 103
Soft Boiled Eggs.................................... 103
Eggs Upon Toast.................................... 103
Dutch Omelet.................................... 103
Eggs Poached in Balls.................................... 104
Omelet au Natural.................................... 104
Omelet in Batter.................................... 104
Scrambled Eggs.................................... 105
Omelet (Splendid).................................... 105

SOUPS.

Remarks on Soups.................................... 20
Stock Soups.................................... 22
White Stock.................................... 22
Shin of Beef.................................... 23
Mutton with Tapioca.................................... 24
.... 25
ail.................................... 25
table.................................... 25
aroni.................................... 26
rmiceili.................................... 26
hicken Cream.................................... 26
lock Turtle.................................... 27
Hard Pea.................................... 27
Green Pea.................................... 28
Potato.................................... 29
Tomato.................................... 29
Game.................................... 30
Celery.................................... 30
Oyster.................................... 30
Lobster.................................... 31
Egg Balls for Soup.................................... 31
Noodles.................................... 31

PAGE.
Irish Stew.................................... 32
To get up Soup in Haste.................................... 33
To Color Soups.................................... 33

SAUCES FOR MEATS, ETC.

To Make Drawn Butter.................................... 123
Parsley Sauce.................................... 123
Egg Sauce.................................... 123
Onion Sauce.................................... 124
Anchovy Sauce.................................... 124
Bread Sauce.................................... 124
Tomato Sauce.................................... 124
Tomato Mustard.................................... 125
Mint Sauce.................................... 125
Celery Sauce.................................... 125
Governor's Sauce.................................... 125
Cream Sauce.................................... 126
Russian Sauce.................................... 126
Mayonnaise Sauce.................................... 126
Oyster Sauce.................................... 127
Lobster Sauce.................................... 127
Caper Sauce.................................... 127
Mustard Sauce.................................... 127
Curry Sauce.................................... 128
Cranberry Sauce.................................... 128
Port Wine Sauce for Game.................................... 129
Currant Jelly Sauce.................................... 129
Apple Sauce.................................... 129

SALADS, PICKLES AND CATSUP.

Lettuce.................................... 139
Lettuce Salad.................................... 139
Salmon Salad.................................... 140
Lobster Salad.................................... 140
Tomato Salad.................................... 141
Sardine Salad.................................... 141
Salad Dressing.................................... 141
French Salad Dressing.................................... 141
Cream Dressing for Cold Slaw.................................... 142
Chicken Salad.................................... 142
Red Vegetable Salad.................................... 142
Celery Salad.................................... 143
Cold Slaw.................................... 143
Salad Dressing (Excellent).................................... 143
Pickled Cucumbers.................................... 144
To Pickle Onions.................................... 144
Pickled Cauliflowers.................................... 144
Red Cabbage.................................... 144
To Pickle Tomatoes.................................... 145
Ripe Tomato Pickles.................................... 145
Chopped Pickle.................................... 145

	PAGE.
Chow-Chow	146
Piccalilli	146
Pickled Walnuts (very good)	146
Green Tomato Pickle	147
Chili Sauce	147
Mixed Pickles	147
Pickled Mushrooms	148
Favorite Pickles	148
Tomato Mustard	149
Indian Chetney	149
Pickled Cherries	149
Pickled Plums	150
Spiced Plums	150
Peaches, Pears and Sweet Apples	150
Tomato Catsup	150
Walnut Catsup	151
Mushroom Catsup	151
Brine that Preserves Butter a Year.	152
Butter in Haste	152

VEGETABLES.

Boiled Potatoes	106
Mashed Potatoes	106
Fried Potatoes	107
Broiled Potatoes	107
Potatoes and Cream	107
Potato Puffs	108
Potato Snow	108
Potato Border	108
Potatoes, Whipped	108
Potatoes, Scalloped	109
Potato Croquettes	109
Potatoes a la Cream	109
To Boil Sweet Potatoes	109
Roasted Sweet Potatoes	110
Baked Sweet Potatoes	110
French Fried	110

	PAGE.
Turnips	110
Spinach	110
Beets	111
To Preserve Vegetables for Winter.	111
Delicate Cabbage	112
Red Cabbage	113
Cauliflowers	113
Mashed Carrots	113
Boiled Green Corn	113
Green Peas	114
To Boil Onions	114
Fried Onions	114
Boiled Parsnips	114
Parsnips Fried in Butter	115
Parsnips Creamed	115
Parsnip Fritters	115
Salsify, or Vegetable Oyster	116
Broiled Vegetable Marrow	116
Stewed Tomatoes	117
Baked Tomatoes	117
Stuffed Tomatoes	118
Scalloped Tomatoes	118
To Peal Tomatoes	118
Baked Beans	119
String Beans	119
Butter Beans	119
Asparagus with Eggs	120
Asparagus upon Toast	120
Mushrooms, Stewed	120
Mushrooms, Fried	120
Mushrooms, Baked	121
Mushrooms, Broiled	121
Mashed Squash	121
Baked Squash	121
Fried Squash	121
Stewed Celery	122
Stuffed Egg Plant	122

www.ingramcontent.com/pod-product-compliance
Lightning Source LLC
LaVergne TN
LVHW020616110826
845149LV00002B/488

* 9 7 8 1 4 1 8 1 8 7 9 6 5 *

ŒUVRES

DE

CHARLES HERMITE.

43600 PARIS. — IMPRIMERIE GAUTHIER-VILLARS,
Quai des Grands-Augustins, 55.

Cliché Pirou Héliog. L. Schutzenberger

ŒUVRES

DE

CHARLES HERMITE

PUBLIÉES

SOUS LES AUSPICES DE L'ACADÉMIE DES SCIENCES

Par **ÉMILE PICARD**,

MEMBRE DE L'INSTITUT.

TOME III.

PARIS,

GAUTHIER-VILLARS, IMPRIMEUR-LIBRAIRE

DU BUREAU DES LONGITUDES, DE L'ÉCOLE POLYTECHNIQUE,

Quai des Grands-Augustins, 55.

1912

AVERTISSEMENT.

La publication des Œuvres d'Hermite se poursuit dans les mêmes conditions, grâce au zèle dévoué de M. Henry Bourget qui me continue son précieux concours, et aux soins de M. Gauthier-Villars.

Les Mémoires ici reproduits vont de 1872 à 1880. Ce Volume commence toutefois par un travail inédit *Sur l'extension du théorème de Sturm à un système d'équations simultanées*, datant de la jeunesse d'Hermite, retrouvé récemment dans les papiers de Liouville. On lira aussi dans ce Tome divers Chapitres empruntés au *Cours d'Analyse de l'École Polytechnique*, une Note publiée dans l'*Algèbre supérieure* de Serret sur les équations résolubles par radicaux, et enfin une Leçon sur *l'équation de Lamé*, faite à l'École Polytechnique pendant l'hiver de 1872-1873, qui, à notre connaissance, contient les premières recherches d'Hermite sur une question qu'il devait approfondir quelques années plus tard. Le portrait placé au commencement du Volume représente Hermite vers l'âge de soixante-cinq ans.

Dans le Tome IV et dernier, nous publierons la fin de l'œuvre mathématique d'Hermite, ainsi que divers articles et discours.

ÉMILE PICARD.

ŒUVRES

DE

CHARLES HERMITE.

TOME III.

SUR

L'EXTENSION DU THÉORÈME DE M. STURM

A UN SYSTÈME D'ÉQUATIONS SIMULTANÉES (¹).

Mémoire inédit.

J'ai présumé longtemps que la question traitée dans ce Mémoire dépendait de l'extension des principes du calcul des résidus aux fonctions de plusieurs variables. On sait, en effet, que Cauchy a tiré de ce calcul son beau théorème sur la détermination du nombre des racines imaginaires d'une équation à une inconnue qui sont renfermées dans un contour donné. En réfléchissant sur les méthodes de l'illustre géomètre, il me semblait que des théorèmes analogues pour des équations simultanées devraient résulter de l'état des

(¹) Nous publions ici un Mémoire présenté à l'Académie par Hermite, le 12 juillet 1852, et retrouvé dans les papiers de Liouville par sa fille Mme de Blignières, qui a bien voulu nous le donner pour cette édition. Ce Mémoire avait été renvoyé à une Commission composée de Cauchy, Liouville et Sturm. Aucun Rapport n'a été fait; une Note a seulement été publiée dans les *Comptes rendus* et elle se trouve reproduite dans le Tome I de ces *Œuvres* (p. 281). E. P.

diverses valeurs que peut prendre une même intégrale double, lorsqu'en conservant les limites on substitue des fonctions imaginaires quelconques aux variables réelles de l'intégration. C'est ainsi qu'en désignant par $F(z, z')$, $\Phi(z, z')$ les premiers membres de deux équations simultanées, j'ai été conduit à la recherche des valeurs multiples de l'intégrale $\displaystyle\int\int \frac{\frac{dF}{dz}\frac{d\Phi}{dz'} - \frac{d\Phi}{dz}\frac{dF}{dz'}}{F\Phi}\, dz\, dz'$, qui me semblait devoir jouer un rôle analogue à celui de l'intégrale simple $\int \frac{F'_z}{F}\, dz$ dans la théorie des équations à une inconnue. Un grand nombre d'autres questions que je ne puis indiquer ici et qui se rapportent aux fonctions périodiques de plusieurs variables, m'amenaient encore à cette même recherche, et je ne puis douter qu'elles n'ouvrent un jour à l'analyse le plus vaste champ de découvertes. Mais, arrêté à plusieurs reprises par des difficultés qui me semblent bien au-dessus de mes forces, je ne sais s'il me sera jamais donné d'y faire quelque progrès. Aussi est-ce à d'autres principes que se rattachent les considérations développées dans ce Mémoire. Je dois indiquer d'abord les belles expressions découvertes par M. Sylvester pour les fonctions auxiliaires qui figurent dans le théorème de M. Sturm, et celles que M. Cayley en a déduites, comme m'ayant ouvert une voie nouvelle. Ce sont, en effet, des formules analogues à celles de ces deux savants géomètres qui seront posées *a priori* pour des équations simultanées, et dont on conclut avec facilité des propriétés toutes semblables à celles des fonctions de M. Sturm.

I. Nous considérerons en premier lieu une équation à une inconnue $F(x) = 0$, et nous désignerons ses racines par $x_1, x_2, \ldots, x_m$. Soit encore S_i la somme symétrique des puissances semblables $x_1^i + x_2^i + \ldots + x_m^i$; avec les quantités $S_1, S_2, \ldots, S_{2m-1}$ et une indéterminée λ, composons le système linéaire :

$$(1)\quad \left\{\begin{array}{lllll} S_1-\lambda, & S_2, & S_3, & \ldots, & S_m, \\ S_2, & S_3-\lambda, & S_4, & \ldots, & S_{m+1}, \\ S_3, & S_4, & S_5-\lambda, & \ldots, & S_{m+2}, \\ \ldots, & \ldots, & \ldots\ldots, & \ldots, & \ldots\ldots, \\ S_m, & S_{m+1}, & S_{m+2}, & \ldots, & S_{2m-1}-\lambda. \end{array}\right.$$

Le déterminant de ce système sera un polynome entier en λ du degré m, que nous représenterons ainsi :

$$\Lambda = \Lambda_0 + \lambda \Lambda_1 + \lambda^2 \Lambda_2 + \ldots + (-1)^m \lambda^m.$$

Comme le système (1) est symétrique, l'équation $\Lambda = 0$ aura toujours ses racines réelles ; cette propriété importante, démontrée pour la première fois par M. Cauchy dans ses recherches sur les inégalités séculaires du mouvement elliptique des planètes, sera fondamentale dans ce Mémoire. Mais voici d'abord la forme nouvelle sous laquelle nous présentons le théorème de M. Sturm.

Soit $\Lambda(\xi)$ ce que devient le polynome Λ, lorsqu'on considère l'équation $F(x+\xi) = 0$, au lieu de la proposée, et ν_ξ le nombre de ses variations pour une valeur donnée de la quantité ξ ; le nombre des racines réelles de l'équation $F(x) = 0$, qui sont comprises entre deux limites quelconques ξ_0 et ξ_1, sera représenté en supposant $\xi_1 > \xi_0$ par la différence $\nu_{\xi_0} - \nu_{\xi_1}$.

Les coefficients des diverses puissances de λ, dans le polynome $\Lambda(\xi)$, sont ainsi des fonctions entières de ξ, qui forment un système non identique, mais analogue à celui des fonctions auxiliaires de M. Sturm et qui conduisent absolument au même résultat.

Considérons en second lieu deux équations à deux inconnues

$$F(x, y) = 0, \qquad \Phi(x, y) = 0,$$

que nous supposerons d'abord générales et du degré m chacune ; soient

$$\begin{array}{llll} x = x_1, & x = x_2, & \ldots, & x = x_{m^2}, \\ y = y_1, & y = y_2, & \ldots, & y = y_{m^2}, \end{array}$$

leurs diverses solutions simultanées, et $S_{i,j}$ la somme symétrique $x_1^i y_1^j + x_2^i y_2^j + \ldots + x_{m^2}^i y_{m^2}^j$; nous représenterons pour abréger par (ω) le système linéaire

$$\begin{array}{llll l} S_{1\omega}, & S_{2\omega}, & S_{3\omega}, & \ldots, & S_{m\omega}, \\ S_{2\omega}, & S_{3\omega}, & S_{4\omega}, & \ldots, & S_{m+1\omega}, \\ S_{3\omega}, & S_{4\omega}, & S_{5\omega}, & \ldots, & S_{m+2\omega}, \\ \ldots, & \ldots, & \ldots, & \ldots, & \ldots\ldots, \\ S_{m\omega}, & S_{m+1\omega}, & S_{m+2\omega}, & \ldots, & S_{2m-1\omega}. \end{array}$$

En attribuant à l'indice ω les valeurs $1, 2, \ldots, m$, on aura un système que nous réunirons de la manière suivante :

$$\begin{array}{lllll}
(1), & (2), & (3), & \ldots, & (m),\\
(2), & (3), & (4), & \ldots, & (m+1),\\
(3), & (4), & (5), & \ldots, & (m+2),\\
\ldots, & \ldots, & \ldots, & \ldots, & \ldots\ldots,\\
(m), & (m+1), & (m+2), & \ldots, & (2m-1),
\end{array}$$

ce qui donne un système à m^2 colonnes dont la loi est facile à saisir. Cela posé, retranchons des termes en diagonale une même quantité λ, et formons le déterminant; nous obtiendrons un polynome en λ du degré m^2 que nous représenterons ainsi :

$$\Lambda = \Lambda_0 + \lambda\Lambda_1 + \lambda^2\Lambda_2 + \ldots + (-1)^{m^2}\lambda^{m^2},$$

et qui nous conduira à étendre le théorème de M. Sturm à deux équations simultanées.

Considérons pour cela les deux inconnues x et y, comme l'abscisse et l'ordonnée d'un point rapporté à deux axes rectangulaires, de sorte qu'à chaque solution des équations proposées, telle que

$$x = x_i,$$
$$y = y_i,$$

corresponde un point déterminé. L'objet de notre proposition est de déterminer le nombre de ces points qui sont renfermés dans l'intérieur d'un rectangle donné. A cet effet, soit $\Lambda(\xi, \eta)$ ce que devient Λ lorsqu'on considère les équations

$$F(x+\xi, y+\eta) = 0, \qquad \Phi(x+\xi, y+\eta) = 0,$$

au lieu des proposées, et $v_{\xi,\eta}$ le nombre de ses variations pour des valeurs données de ξ et η.

Le nombre des solutions renfermées dans l'intérieur du rectangle ayant pour coordonnées de ses sommets

$$\begin{array}{llll}
x = \xi_0, & x = \xi_0, & x = \xi_1, & x = \xi_1,\\
y = \eta_0, & y = \eta_1, & y = \eta_0, & y = \eta_1,
\end{array}$$

sera donnée par l'expression

$$\frac{v_{\xi_1,\eta_1} + v_{\xi_0,\eta_0} - v_{\xi_0,\eta_1} - v_{\xi_1,\eta_0}}{2}.$$

II. La démonstration des théorèmes que nous venons d'énoncer repose, dans le cas des équations à une inconnue comme dans le cas des équations simultanées, sur l'expression en fonction des racines des deux premiers termes Λ_0 et Λ_1 des fonctions Λ. Voici d'abord cette recherche pour les équations à une inconnue, en suivant la méthode propre au second cas et dont on verra ainsi le principe avec plus de facilité.

La quantité Λ_0 est évidemment la valeur du polynome Λ pour $\lambda = 0$; c'est donc le déterminant du système

$$\begin{array}{lllll} S_1, & S_2, & S_3, & \ldots, & S_m, \\ S_2, & S_3, & S_4, & \ldots, & S_{m+1}, \\ S_3, & S_4, & S_5, & \ldots, & S_{m+2}, \\ \ldots, & \ldots, & \ldots, & \ldots, & \ldots\ldots, \\ S_m, & S_{m+1}, & S_{m+2}, & \ldots, & S_{2m-1}. \end{array}$$

Quant à Λ_1, il suffit d'un peu d'attention pour reconnaître que c'est la somme prise en signe contraire de tous les déterminants à $m-1$ colonnes que fournit le système précédent, lorsqu'on fait abstraction d'une colonne horizontale de rang quelconque telle que $S_i, S_{i+1}, \ldots, S_{i+m-2}$, et de la colonne verticale composée des mêmes termes. D'après cela, si l'on considère le système des équations linéaires

$$(1)\quad \left\{ \begin{array}{l} S_1 z_1 + S_2 z_2 + S_3 z_3 + \ldots + S_m z_m = Z_1, \\ S_2 z_1 + S_3 z_2 + S_4 z_3 + \ldots + S_{m+1} z_m = Z_2, \\ S_3 z_1 + S_4 z_2 + S_5 z_3 + \ldots + S_{m+2} z_m = Z_3, \\ \ldots\ldots\ldots\ldots\ldots\ldots\ldots\ldots, \\ S_m z_1 + S_{m+1} z_2 + S_{m+2} z_3 + \ldots + S_{2m-1} z_m = Z_m, \end{array} \right.$$

et qu'on le résolve par rapport aux quantités z, de manière à obtenir

$$\begin{array}{l} z_1 = A_1^1 Z_1 + A_2^1 Z_2 + A_3^1 Z_3 + \ldots + A_m^1 Z_m, \\ z_2 = A_1^2 Z_1 + A_2^2 Z_2 + A_3^2 Z_3 + \ldots + A_m^2 Z_m, \\ z_3 = A_1^3 Z_1 + A_2^3 Z_2 + A_3^3 Z_3 + \ldots + A_m^3 Z_m, \\ \ldots\ldots\ldots\ldots\ldots\ldots\ldots\ldots, \\ z_m = A_1^m Z_1 + A_2^m Z_2 + A_3^m Z_3 + \ldots + A_m^m Z_m. \end{array}$$

Λ_0 sera le dénominateur commun des quantités A, et $\frac{\Lambda_1}{\Lambda_0}$ sera la valeur changée de signe de la somme des termes en diagonale $A_1^1 + A_2^2 + A_3^3 + \ldots + A_m^m$.

Cela posé, nous observerons qu'en introduisant m inconnues auxiliaires $\zeta_1, \zeta_2, \ldots, \zeta_m$, on peut remplacer le système des équations (1) par les deux suivants :

$$(2)\quad \left\{\begin{array}{l} \zeta_1 + \zeta_2 + \zeta_3 + \ldots + \zeta_m = Z_1, \\ x_1\zeta_1 + x_2\zeta_2 + x_3\zeta_3 + \ldots + x_m\zeta_m = Z_2, \\ x_1^2\zeta_1 + x_2^2\zeta_2 + x_3^2\zeta_3 + \ldots + x_m^2\zeta_m = Z_3, \\ \ldots\ldots\ldots\ldots\ldots\ldots\ldots\ldots\ldots\ldots, \\ x_1^{m-1}\zeta_1 + x_2^{m-1}\zeta_2 + x_3^{m-1}\zeta_3 + \ldots + x_m^{m-1}\zeta_m = Z_m, \end{array}\right.$$

et

$$(3)\quad \left\{\begin{array}{l} \zeta_1 = x_1 z_1 + x_1^2 z_2 + x_1^3 z_3 + \ldots + x_1^m z_m, \\ \zeta_2 = x_2 z_1 + x_2^2 z_2 + x_2^3 z_3 + \ldots + x_2^m z_m, \\ \zeta_3 = x_3 z_1 + x_3^2 z_2 + x_3^3 z_3 + \ldots + x_3^m z_m, \\ \ldots\ldots\ldots\ldots\ldots\ldots\ldots\ldots\ldots\ldots, \\ \zeta_m = x_m z_1 + x_m^2 z_2 + x_m^3 z_3 + \ldots + x_m^m z_m, \end{array}\right.$$

comme on le voit immédiatement par la substitution des valeurs des quantités ζ. De là résulte d'abord, par l'une des propositions élémentaires de la théorie des déterminants, que Λ_0 sera le produit des déterminants relatifs aux équations (2) et (3); or il est visible que le second n'est autre que le premier multiplié par le produit $x_1 x_2 x_3 \ldots x_m$; ainsi, nous avons cette égalité :

$$\Lambda_0 = \begin{vmatrix} S_1 & S_2 & S_3 & \ldots & S_m \\ S_2 & S_3 & S_4 & \ldots & S_{m+1} \\ S_3 & S_4 & S_5 & \ldots & S_{m+2} \\ \ldots & \ldots & \ldots & \ldots & \ldots \\ S_m & S_{m+1} & S_{m+2} & \ldots & S_{2m-1} \end{vmatrix}$$

$$= x_1 x_2 x_3 \ldots x_m \begin{vmatrix} 1 & 1 & 1 & \ldots & 1 \\ x_1 & x_2 & x_3 & \ldots & x_m \\ x_1^2 & x_2^2 & x_3^2 & \ldots & x_m^2 \\ \ldots & \ldots & \ldots & \ldots & \ldots \\ x_1^{m-1} & x_2^{m-1} & x_3^{m-1} & \ldots & x_m^{m-1} \end{vmatrix}^2 .$$

Si nous n'avions en vue que les équations à une inconnue, nous pourrions nous arrêter ici, car on sait que le carré du déterminant par lequel se trouve exprimé Λ_0, est le produit des différences des racines x, prises deux à deux, de toutes les manières possibles, mais cette donnée nous manquera dans la question analogue relative aux équations simultanées; aussi nous allons, dès à présent, recourir à la méthode suivante. Introduisant un nouveau système de quantités auxiliaires $\eta_0, \eta_1, \eta_2, \ldots, \eta_{m-1}$, nous poserons

$$(4)\quad \left\{\begin{aligned}
\zeta_1 &= \frac{\eta_0 + x_1\eta_1 + x_1^2\eta_2 + \ldots + x_1^{m-1}\eta_{m-1}}{F'(x_1)},\\
\zeta_2 &= \frac{\eta_0 + x_2\eta_1 + x_2^2\eta_2 + \ldots + x_2^{m-1}\eta_{m-1}}{F'(x_2)},\\
\zeta_3 &= \frac{\eta_0 + x_3\eta_1 + x_3^2\eta_2 + \ldots + x_3^{m-1}\eta_{m-1}}{F'(x_3)},\\
&\ldots\ldots\ldots\ldots\ldots\ldots,\\
\zeta_m &= \frac{\eta_0 + x_m\eta_1 + x_m^2\eta_2 + \ldots + x_m^{m-1}\eta_{m-1}}{F'(x_m)},
\end{aligned}\right.$$

$F'(x)$ désignant la dérivée du premier membre de l'équation proposée $F(x) = 0$; maintenant, si l'on substitue les nouvelles inconnues η aux quantités ζ dans les équations (2), il viendra

$$(5)\quad \left\{\begin{aligned}
&\eta_0\sum\frac{1}{F'} + \eta_1\sum\frac{x}{F'} + \eta_2\sum\frac{x^2}{F'} + \ldots + \eta_{m-1}\sum\frac{x^{m-1}}{F'} = Z_1,\\
&\eta_0\sum\frac{x}{F'} + \eta_1\sum\frac{x^2}{F'} + \eta_2\sum\frac{x^3}{F'} + \ldots + \eta_{m-1}\sum\frac{x^{m}}{F'} = Z_2,\\
&\eta_0\sum\frac{x^2}{F'} + \eta_1\sum\frac{x^3}{F'} + \eta_2\sum\frac{x^4}{F'} + \ldots + \eta_{m-1}\sum\frac{x^{m+1}}{F'} = Z_3,\\
&\ldots\ldots\ldots\ldots\ldots\ldots\ldots\ldots\ldots,\\
&\eta_0\sum\frac{x^{m-1}}{F'} + \eta_1\sum\frac{x^m}{F'} + \eta_2\sum\frac{x^{m+1}}{F'} + \ldots + \eta_{m-1}\sum\frac{x^{2m-2}}{F'} = Z_m,
\end{aligned}\right.$$

en représentant, pour abréger, la somme

$$\frac{x_1^\mu}{F'(x_1)} + \frac{x_2^\mu}{F'(x_2)} + \frac{x_3^\mu}{F'(x_3)} + \ldots + \frac{x_m^\mu}{F'(x_m)}$$

par

$$\sum\frac{x^\mu}{F'}.$$

Mais on sait que cette somme est nulle pour toutes les valeurs de μ moindres que $m-1$, et qu'elle est l'unité pour $\mu = m-1$ si le coefficient de x^m dans $F(x)$ est lui-même égal à 1. Pour les valeurs supérieures de μ, elle représentera une fonction rationnelle et entière des coefficients du polynome $F(x)$, de sorte qu'en faisant

$$\sum\frac{x^{m-1+i}}{F'} = \sigma_i,$$

les équations (5) prendront la forme

$$(6)\quad \begin{cases} \eta_{m-1} = Z_1, \\ \eta_{m-2} + \sigma_1 \eta_{m-1} = Z_2, \\ \eta_{m-3} + \sigma_1 \eta_{m-2} + \sigma_2 \eta_{m-1} = Z_3, \\ \dots\dots\dots\dots, \\ \eta_0 + \sigma_1 \eta_1 + \sigma_2 \eta_2 + \dots + \sigma_{m-2} \eta_{m-2} + \sigma_{m-1} \eta_{m-1} = Z_m, \end{cases}$$

et ne contiendront plus les racines $x_1, x_2, \dots, x_m$. Mais, comme on le voit, le déterminant relatif à un pareil système est simplement $(-1)^{\frac{m(m+1)}{2}}$; il est d'ailleurs égal au produit des déterminants relatifs aux systèmes (2) et (4); le système (4) lui-même donne pour déterminant celui du système (2), divisé par le produit $F'(x_1) F'(x_2) F'(x_3) \dots F'(x_m)$; on en conclut l'expression suivante que nous voulions obtenir, savoir

$$\Lambda_0 = (-1)^{\frac{m(m+1)}{2}} x_1 x_2 \dots x_m F'(x_1) F'(x_2) \dots F'(x_m).$$

III. L'introduction des inconnues η n'avait pas seulement pour objet de nous conduire à la valeur de Λ_0; elle nous servira aussi à la résolution des équations (1) et, par suite, à la détermination des quantités A et à celle de $\frac{\Lambda_1}{\Lambda_0}$. J'observerai d'abord que les équations (3) peuvent être mises absolument sous la même forme que les équations (6). Multiplions-les respectivement par les quantités $\frac{1}{x_1 F'(x_1)}, \frac{1}{x_2 F'(x_2)}, \dots, \frac{1}{x_m F'(x_m)}$, en les ajoutant et se servant, pour abréger, du signe $\sum$, comme plus haut; il viendra d'abord

$$z_m = \frac{\zeta_1}{x_1 F'_{x_1}} + \frac{\zeta_2}{x_2 F'_{x_2}} + \dots + \frac{\zeta_m}{x_m F'_{x_m}} = \sum \frac{\zeta}{x F'(x)},$$

et si l'on continue de même en prenant pour multiplicateurs les quantités $\frac{x^\mu}{F'_x}$, on arriva au système suivant :

$$(7)\quad \begin{cases} z_m = \sum \frac{\zeta}{x F'_x}, \\ z_{m-1} + \sigma_1 z_m = \sum \frac{x\zeta}{x F'_x}, \\ z_{m-2} + \sigma_1 z_{m-1} + \sigma_2 z_m = \sum \frac{x^2 \zeta}{x F'_x}, \\ \dots\dots\dots\dots, \\ z_1 + \sigma_1 z_2 + \sigma_2 z_3 + \dots + \sigma_{m-2} z_{m-1} + \sigma_{m-1} z_m = \sum \frac{x^{m-1} \zeta}{x F'_x}. \end{cases}$$

Cela posé, il est facile de voir que la résolution des équations (6) donne des résultats de cette forme, savoir :

$$\begin{aligned}
\eta_0 &= Z_m + \omega_1 Z_{m-1} + \omega_2 Z_{m-2} + \ldots + \ldots\ldots\ldots + \omega_{m-2} Z_2 + \omega_{m-1} Z_1,\\
\eta_1 &= Z_{m-1} + \omega_1 Z_{m-2} + \omega_2 Z_{m-3} + \ldots + \ldots\ldots\ldots + \omega_{m-2} Z_1,\\
\eta_2 &= Z_{m-2} + \omega_1 Z_{m-3} + \omega_2 Z_{m-4} + \ldots + \omega_{m-3} Z_1,\\
&\ldots\ldots\ldots\ldots\ldots\ldots\ldots\ldots\ldots\ldots,\\
\eta_{m-2} &= Z_2 + \omega_1 Z_1,\\
\eta_{m-1} &= Z_1.
\end{aligned}$$

Les quantités ω étant des fonctions rationnelles et entières des quantités σ, et, par suite, des coefficients de l'équation $F(x) = 0$. Si donc on fait

$$\begin{aligned}
\Omega_1(x) &= x^{m-1} + \omega_1 x^{m-2} + \omega_2 x^{m-3} + \ldots + \omega_{m-2} x + \omega_{m-1},\\
\Omega_2(x) &= x^{m-2} + \omega_1 x^{m-3} + \omega_2 x^{m-4} + \ldots + \omega_{m-2},\\
&\ldots\ldots\ldots\ldots\ldots\ldots\ldots\ldots\ldots\ldots,\\
\Omega_{m-1}(x) &= x^2 + \omega_1 x + \omega_2,\\
\Omega_m(x) &= x + \omega_1,
\end{aligned}$$

on trouvera, par la substitution des quantités η dans les équations (4), les valeurs suivantes :

$$\begin{aligned}
\zeta_1 &= \frac{\Omega_1(x_1)Z_1 + \Omega_2(x_1)Z_2 + \ldots + \Omega_{m-1}(x_1)Z_{m-1} + Z_m}{F'(x_1)},\\
\zeta_2 &= \frac{\Omega_1(x_2)Z_1 + \Omega_2(x_2)Z_2 + \ldots + \Omega_{m-1}(x_2)Z_{m-1} + Z_m}{F'(x_2)},\\
&\ldots\ldots\ldots\ldots\ldots\ldots\ldots\ldots\ldots\ldots,\\
\zeta_m &= \frac{\Omega_1(x_m)Z_1 + \Omega_2(x_m)Z_2 + \ldots + \Omega_{m-1}(x_m)Z_{m-1} + Z_m}{F'(x_m)}.
\end{aligned}$$

Maintenant la résolution des équations (7) par rapport aux inconnues z s'effectuera comme celle des équations (6), et donnera les valeurs

$$\begin{aligned}
z_1 &= \sum \frac{\Omega_1(x)\zeta}{x F'_x} = \frac{\Omega_1(x_1)\zeta_1}{x_1 F'(x_1)} + \frac{\Omega_1(x_2)\zeta_2}{x_2 F'(x_2)} + \ldots + \frac{\Omega_1(x_m)\zeta_m}{x_m F'(x_m)},\\
z_2 &= \sum \frac{\Omega_2(x)\zeta}{x F'_x} = \frac{\Omega_2(x_1)\zeta_1}{x_1 F'(x_1)} + \frac{\Omega_2(x_2)\zeta_2}{x_2 F'(x_2)} + \ldots + \frac{\Omega_2(x_m)\zeta_m}{x_m F'(x_m)},\\
&\ldots\ldots\ldots\ldots\ldots\ldots\ldots\ldots\ldots\ldots,\\
z_{m-1} &= \sum \frac{\Omega_{m-1}(x)\zeta}{x F'_x} = \frac{\Omega_{m-1}(x_1)\zeta_1}{x_1 F'(x_1)} + \frac{\Omega_{m-1}(x_2)\zeta_2}{x_2 F'(x_2)} + \ldots + \frac{\Omega_{m-1}(x_m)\zeta_m}{x_m F'(x_m)},\\
z_m &= \sum \frac{\zeta}{x F'_x} = \frac{\zeta_1}{x_1 F'(x_1)} + \frac{\zeta_2}{x_2 F'(x_2)} + \ldots + \frac{\zeta_m}{x_m F'(x_m)},
\end{aligned}$$

enfin, si l'on substitue les valeurs des inconnues ζ précédemment trouvées, il viendra, en employant toujours le signe $\sum$ pour indiquer une somme relative aux racines $x_1, x_2, \ldots, x_m$,

$$z_1 = \sum \frac{\Omega_1(x)[\Omega_1(x)Z_1 + \Omega_2(x)Z_2 + \ldots + \Omega_{m-1}(x)Z_{m-1} + Z_m]}{x\,F'^2(x)},$$

$$z_2 = \sum \frac{\Omega_2(x)[\Omega_1(x)Z_1 + \Omega_2(x)Z_2 + \ldots + \Omega_{m-1}(x)Z_{m-1} + Z_m]}{x\,F'^2(x)},$$

. . . . ,

$$z_{m-1} = \sum \frac{\Omega_{m-1}(x)[\Omega_1(x)Z_1 + \Omega_2(x)Z_2 + \ldots + \Omega_{m-1}(x)Z_{m-1} + Z_m]}{x\,F'^2(x)},$$

$$z_m = \sum \frac{\Omega_1(x)Z_1 + \Omega_2(x)Z_2 + \ldots + \Omega_{m-1}(x)Z_{m-1} + Z_m}{x\,F'^2(x)}.$$

Ce sont là les formules auxquelles nous voulions arriver pour la résolution des équations (1) du paragraphe précédent; on aurait pu les obtenir par une méthode plus directe et plus rapide, mais qu'il n'eût pas été possible d'appliquer aux équations analogues composées avec les solutions simultanées d'un système de deux équations à deux inconnues que nous rencontrerons plus tard; elles donnent, comme on voit, sous une forme élégante, les quantités désignées précédemment par A_k^i, savoir :

$$A_k^i = \sum \frac{\Omega_i(x)\,\Omega_k(x)}{x\,F'^2(x)}$$

et l'on en tire, pour la valeur de $\frac{\Lambda_1}{\Lambda_0}$, cette expression dont le numérateur est une somme de carrés

$$\frac{\Lambda_1}{\Lambda_0} = -(A_1^1 + A_2^2 + \ldots + A_m^m) = -\sum \frac{\Omega_1^2(x) + \Omega_2^2(x) + \ldots + \Omega_{m-1}^2(x) + 1}{x\,F'^2(x)}.$$

IV. Nous avons désigné par $\Lambda(\xi)$ au commencement, ce que devenait le polynome Λ, lorsqu'on considère au lieu de l'équation $F(x) = 0$, la suivante $F(x+\xi) = 0$, et nous avons posé

$$\Lambda(\xi) = \Lambda_0(\xi) + \lambda\,\Lambda_1(\xi) + \ldots + (-1)^m \lambda^m;$$

or, il est facile de passer des valeurs précédemment trouvées de Λ_0 et $\frac{\Lambda_1}{\Lambda_0}$, à celles de $\Lambda_0(\xi)$ et $\frac{\Lambda_1(\xi)}{\Lambda_0(\xi)}$. Et d'abord, comme on le voit de suite, les valeurs de la dérivée $F'(x+\xi)$, lorsqu'on mettra pour x

les racines de l'équation transformée $F(x+\xi)=0$, ne différeront point des quantités $F'(x_1)$, $F'(x_2)$, etc., de sorte qu'on aura

$$\Lambda_0(\xi)=(-1)^{\frac{m(m+1)}{2}}(x_1-\xi)(x_2-\xi)\ldots(x_m-\xi)\times F'(x_1)F'(x_2)\ldots F'(x_m).$$

Quant aux polynomes $\Omega_1(x)$, $\Omega_2(x)$, ..., ils deviendront des fonctions rationnelles et entières de ξ; ainsi en posant

$$\Omega_1^2(x)+\Omega_2^2(x)+\ldots+\Omega_{m-1}^2(x)+1=\mathfrak{F}(\xi, x),$$

la fonction $\mathfrak{F}$ correspondant à une racine x réelle ne pourra jamais ni s'évanouir ni changer de signe pour aucune valeur de ξ. Ces préliminaires posés, nous allons démontrer que les coefficients des diverses puissances de λ dans le polynome $\Lambda(\xi)$ possèdent les mêmes propriétés que les fonctions qui figurent dans le théorème de M. Sturm. En premier lieu, l'équation $\Lambda(\xi)=0$, ayant toujours toutes ses racines réelles, il suit d'une conséquence de la règle des signes de Descartes, que les coefficients de deux puissances consécutives de λ ne pourront jamais être supposés nuls en même temps, et que si un coefficient s'évanouit, ceux de la puissance précédente et suivante de λ seront de signes contraires. Si donc on fait croître ξ d'une manière continue de ξ_0 à ξ_1, des changements dans le nombre des variations de $\Lambda(\xi)$ ne pourront survenir qu'autant que ce sera le dernier terme qui viendra à s'annuler. Mais, d'après l'expression obtenue pour ce dernier terme, les valeurs de ξ qui peuvent l'annuler sont uniquement les racines de l'équation proposée. Cela étant, considérons le rapport $\frac{\Lambda_1(\xi)}{\Lambda_0(\xi)}$ dont nous avons obtenu l'expression, savoir :

$$\frac{\Lambda_1(\xi)}{\Lambda_0(\xi)}=-\sum\frac{\mathfrak{F}(\xi, x)}{(x-\xi)F'^2(x)}=\sum\frac{\mathfrak{F}(\xi, x)}{(\xi-x)F'^2(x)}.$$

Pour une valeur de ξ voisine d'une racine quelconque x, le signe de ce rapport dépendra du seul terme $\frac{\mathfrak{F}(\xi, x)}{(\xi-x)F'^2(x)}$; donc, d'après ce que nous avons remarqué sur le numérateur, il sera négatif pour une valeur de ξ un peu inférieure à x, et positif pour une valeur un peu supérieure. Nous voyons donc que la quantité ξ croissant d'une manière continue de ξ_0 à ξ_1, le polynome $\Lambda(\xi)$ perd autant de variations qu'il y a de racines réelles de l'équation $F(x)=0$, comprises entre ces limites; le nombre de ces racines est donc bien $v_{\xi_0} - v_{\xi_1}$, comme nous l'avons annoncé.

V. Dans la démonstration du théorème analogue au précédent pour deux équations, nous supposons ces équations les plus générales de leur degré, pour n'avoir pas lieu de discuter les cas particuliers qui pourraient s'offrir et où nos formules seraient en défaut. Ces cas particuliers se trouveront d'ailleurs complètement évités dans une autre forme sous laquelle nous présenterons plus tard notre théorème, et qui, moins symétrique à la vérité, se prête plus facilement aux applications numériques. Nous avons pensé utile de présenter d'abord pour deux équations du second degré les calculs des quantités Λ_0 et Λ_1 ; on peut, en effet, écrire alors en entier les formules qui, en général, sont représentées d'une manière abrégée, et l'on en saisira très facilement le sens.

Nous avons employé, en commençant, le symbole (ω) pour représenter le système

$$\begin{matrix} S_{1\omega}, & S_{2\omega}, & S_{3\omega}, & \ldots, & S_{m\omega}, \\ S_{2\omega}, & S_{3\omega}, & S_{4\omega}, & \ldots, & S_{m+1\,\omega}, \\ S_{3\omega}, & S_{4\omega}, & S_{5\omega}, & \ldots, & S_{m+2\,\omega}, \\ \ldots, & \ldots, & \ldots, & \ldots, & \ldots\ldots, \\ S_{m\omega}, & S_{m+1\,\omega}, & S_{m+2\,\omega}, & \ldots, & S_{2m-1\,\omega}. \end{matrix}$$

Si l'on suppose $m = 2$, ce système se réduira à

$$\begin{matrix} S_{1\omega}, & S_{2\omega}, \\ S_{2\omega}, & S_{3\omega}, \end{matrix}$$

de sorte que la fonction Λ sera le déterminant suivant à quatre colonnes, savoir :

$$\Lambda = \begin{vmatrix} S_{11} - \lambda & S_{21} & S_{12} & S_{22} \\ S_{21} & S_{31} - \lambda & S_{22} & S_{32} \\ S_{12} & S_{22} & S_{13} - \lambda & S_{23} \\ S_{22} & S_{32} & S_{23} & S_{33} - \lambda \end{vmatrix}.$$

Cela posé, formons le système des équations linéaires :

$$(8) \qquad \left\{ \begin{aligned} S_{11} z_1 + S_{21} z_2 + S_{12} z_3 + S_{22} z_4 &= Z_1, \\ S_{21} z_1 + S_{31} z_2 + S_{22} z_3 + S_{32} z_4 &= Z_2, \\ S_{12} z_1 + S_{22} z_2 + S_{13} z_3 + S_{23} z_4 &= Z_3, \\ S_{22} z_1 + S_{32} z_2 + S_{23} z_3 + S_{33} z_4 &= Z_4. \end{aligned} \right.$$

Le dénominateur commun des valeurs des inconnues z sera Λ_0, et si ces valeurs sont représentées par les formules

$$\begin{aligned} z_1 &= A_1^1 Z_1 + A_2^1 Z_2 + A_3^1 Z_3 + A_4^1 Z_4,\\ z_2 &= A_1^2 Z_1 + A_2^2 Z_2 + A_3^2 Z_3 + A_4^2 Z_4,\\ z_3 &= A_1^3 Z_1 + A_2^3 Z_2 + A_3^3 Z_3 + A_4^3 Z_4,\\ z_4 &= A_1^4 Z_1 + A_2^4 Z_2 + A_3^4 Z_3 + A_4^4 Z_4, \end{aligned}$$

on aurait, comme précédemment,

$$\frac{\Lambda_1}{\Lambda_0} = -(A_1^1 + A_2^2 + A_3^3 + A_4^4).$$

Or, en introduisant quatre inconnues auxiliaires $\zeta_1, \zeta_2, \zeta_3, \zeta_4$, nous pourrons remplacer les équations (8) par les suivantes :

$$(9)\quad \left\{\begin{aligned} \zeta_1 + \quad \zeta_2 + \quad \zeta_3 + \quad \zeta_4 &= Z_1,\\ x_1\zeta_1 + x_2\zeta_2 + x_3\zeta_3 + x_4\zeta_4 &= Z_2,\\ y_1\zeta_1 + y_2\zeta_2 + y_3\zeta_3 + y_4\zeta_4 &= Z_3,\\ x_1y_1\zeta_1 + x_2y_2\zeta_2 + x_3y_3\zeta_3 + x_4y_4\zeta_4 &= Z_4, \end{aligned}\right.$$

et

$$(10)\quad \left\{\begin{aligned} \zeta_1 &= x_1y_1(z_1 + x_1z_2 + y_1z_3 + x_1y_1z_4),\\ \zeta_2 &= x_2y_2(z_1 + x_2z_2 + y_2z_3 + x_2y_2z_4),\\ \zeta_3 &= x_3y_3(z_1 + x_3z_2 + y_3z_3 + x_3y_3z_4),\\ \zeta_4 &= x_4y_4(z_1 + x_4z_2 + y_4z_3 + x_4y_4z_4), \end{aligned}\right.$$

Donc Λ_0, qui est le déterminant relatif aux équations (8) aura pour valeur le produit des déterminants propres aux deux systèmes (9) et (10), ce qui donnera très facilement l'égalité suivante

$$\Lambda_0 = \begin{vmatrix} S_{11} & S_{21} & S_{12} & S_{22}\\ S_{21} & S_{31} & S_{22} & S_{32}\\ S_{12} & S_{22} & S_{13} & S_{23}\\ S_{22} & S_{32} & S_{23} & S_{33} \end{vmatrix}$$

$$= x_1x_2x_3x_4y_1y_2y_3y_4 \begin{vmatrix} 1 & 1 & 1 & 1\\ x_1 & x_2 & x_3 & x_4\\ y_1 & y_2 & y_3 & y_4\\ x_1y_1 & x_2y_2 & x_3y_3 & x_4y_4 \end{vmatrix}^2.$$

Cela posé, représentons par $\Delta(x,y)$ la déterminante fonctionnelle relative aux premiers membres de nos deux équations du second degré, $F(x,y) = 0$, $\Phi(x,y) = 0$, c'est-à-dire l'expression

$\frac{\partial F}{\partial y}\frac{\partial \Phi}{\partial x} - \frac{\partial F}{\partial x}\frac{\partial \Phi}{\partial y}$, et introduisons les nouvelles quantités auxiliaires $\eta_1, \eta_2, \eta_3, \eta_4$ par ces formules :

$$(11)\quad \begin{cases} \zeta_1 = \dfrac{\eta_1 + x_1\eta_2 + y_1\eta_3 + x_1 y_1 \eta_4}{\Delta(x_1, y_1)}, \\ \zeta_2 = \dfrac{\eta_1 + x_2\eta_2 + y_2\eta_3 + x_2 y_2 \eta_4}{\Delta(x_2, y_2)}, \\ \zeta_3 = \dfrac{\eta_1 + x_3\eta_2 + y_3\eta_3 + x_3 y_3 \eta_4}{\Delta(x_3, y_3)}, \\ \zeta_4 = \dfrac{\eta_1 + x_4\eta_2 + y_4\eta_3 + x_4 y_4 \eta_4}{\Delta(x_4, y_4)}. \end{cases}$$

On trouvera, par la substitution dans les équations (9), qu'elles se transforment ainsi :

$$\begin{aligned} \eta_1\sum\frac{1}{\Delta} + \eta_2\sum\frac{x}{\Delta} + \eta_3\sum\frac{y}{\Delta} + \eta_4\sum\frac{xy}{\Delta} &= Z_1, \\ \eta_1\sum\frac{x}{\Delta} + \eta_2\sum\frac{x^2}{\Delta} + \eta_3\sum\frac{xy}{\Delta} + \eta_4\sum\frac{x^2y}{\Delta} &= Z_2, \\ \eta_1\sum\frac{y}{\Delta} + \eta_2\sum\frac{xy}{\Delta} + \eta_3\sum\frac{y^2}{\Delta} + \eta_4\sum\frac{xy^2}{\Delta} &= Z_3, \\ \eta_1\sum\frac{xy}{\Delta} + \eta_2\sum\frac{x^2y}{\Delta} + \eta_3\sum\frac{xy^2}{\Delta} + \eta_4\sum\frac{x^2y^2}{\Delta} &= Z_4. \end{aligned}$$

en représentant pour abréger, par exemple, la somme symétrique $\frac{1}{\Delta(x_1, y_1)} + \frac{1}{\Delta(x_2, y_2)} + \ldots$, par $\sum\frac{1}{\Delta}$. Mais, d'après un théorème de M. Jacobi, les sommes $\sum\frac{1}{\Delta}$, $\sum\frac{x}{\Delta}$ et $\sum\frac{y}{\Delta}$ s'évanouissent ; ainsi nos équations en η deviennent plus simplement

$$(12)\quad \begin{cases} \eta_4\sum\dfrac{xy}{\Delta} = Z_1, \\ \eta_2\sum\dfrac{x^2}{\Delta} + \eta_3\sum\dfrac{xy}{\Delta} + \eta_4\sum\dfrac{x^2y}{\Delta} = Z_2, \\ \eta_2\sum\dfrac{xy}{\Delta} + \eta_3\sum\dfrac{y^2}{\Delta} + \eta_4\sum\dfrac{xy^2}{\Delta} = Z_3, \\ \eta_1\sum\dfrac{xy}{\Delta} + \eta_2\sum\dfrac{x^2y}{\Delta} + \eta_3\sum\dfrac{xy^2}{\Delta} + \eta_4\sum\dfrac{x^2y^2}{\Delta} = Z_4. \end{cases}$$

Dans ce système, le déterminant n'est plus l'unité comme nous l'avons trouvé plus haut pour des équations analogues ; on obtient aisément pour sa valeur

$$\left(\sum \frac{xy}{\Delta}\right)^2 \left[\left(\sum \frac{xy}{\Delta}\right)^2 - \sum \frac{x^2}{\Delta} \sum \frac{y^2}{\Delta}\right],$$

dont voici l'expression en fonction des coefficients des équations proposées. A cet effet, soit

$$\begin{aligned} F(x, y) &= a x^2 + 2 b xy + c y^2 + \ldots, \\ \Phi(x, y) &= \alpha x^2 + 2 \beta xy + \gamma y^2 + \ldots, \end{aligned}$$

les termes non écrits étant d'un degré inférieur; posons, pour abréger,

$$\begin{aligned} A &= \beta c - b\gamma, \\ B &= \alpha c - a\gamma, \\ C &= \alpha b - a\beta, \\ B^2 - 4AC &= \mathfrak{D} \quad (^1). \end{aligned}$$

On trouvera par un calcul facile

$$\sum \frac{x^2}{\Delta} = -\frac{2A}{\mathfrak{D}}, \qquad \sum \frac{xy}{\Delta} = \frac{B}{\mathfrak{D}}, \qquad \sum \frac{y^2}{\Delta} = -\frac{2C}{\mathfrak{D}};$$

donc

$$\left(\sum \frac{xy}{\Delta}\right)^2 \left[\left(\sum \frac{xy}{\Delta}\right)^2 - \sum \frac{x^2}{\Delta} \sum \frac{y^2}{\Delta}\right] = \frac{B^2}{\mathfrak{D}^3}.$$

Le cas d'exception à nos formules se présenterait lorsque B ou $\mathfrak{D}$ s'évanouissent, mais, en général, ils seront différents de zéro; alors la quantité précédente représentant le produit des déterminants relatifs aux systèmes (9) et (11), on arrivera à cette égalité

$$\begin{vmatrix} 1 & 1 & 1 & 1 \\ x_1 & x_2 & x_3 & x_4 \\ y_1 & y_2 & y_3 & y_4 \\ x_1 y_1 & x_2 y_2 & x_3 y_3 & x_4 y_4 \end{vmatrix}^2 = \frac{B^2}{\mathfrak{D}^3} \Delta(x_1, y_1) \Delta(x_2, y_2) \Delta(x_3, y_3) \Delta(x_4, y_4),$$

d'où l'on conclut la valeur de Λ_0, sous la forme suivante :

$$\Lambda_0 = x_1 x_2 x_3 x_4 y_1 y_2 y_3 y_4 \frac{B^2}{\mathfrak{D}^3} \Delta(x_1, y_1) \Delta(x_2, y_2) \Delta(x_3, y_3) \Delta(x_4, y_4).$$

---

(1) Cette quantité $\mathfrak{D}$ est le coefficient de la puissance la plus élevée dans l'équation finale en x ou en y quand on a fait disparaître les dénominateurs.

On retrouve bien ici la propriété connue de la fonction Δ de s'évanouir pour deux solutions égales, car si l'on suppose, par exemple, $x_1 = x_2$ et $y_1 = y_2$, deux colonnes du déterminant deviennent identiques et il s'annule.

VI. Résolvons, par rapport aux inconnues η, les équations (12), leurs valeurs auront la forme suivante :

$$\begin{aligned}
\eta_1 &= \alpha Z_1 + \beta Z_2 + \gamma Z_3 + \delta Z_4,\\
\eta_2 &= \alpha' Z_1 + \beta' Z_2 + \gamma' Z_3,\\
\eta_3 &= \alpha'' Z_1 + \beta'' Z_2 + \gamma'' Z_3,\\
\eta_4 &= \alpha''' Z_1,
\end{aligned}$$

et l'on pourrait même démontrer qu'on a ces relations

$$\beta = \alpha', \qquad \gamma = \alpha'', \qquad \delta = \alpha''', \qquad \gamma' = \beta'';$$

mais, pour abréger, nous éviterons de les employer en modifiant légèrement la marche suivie précédemment dans le calcul analogue pour les équations à une inconnue. Posons d'abord

$$\begin{aligned}
\Omega_1(x, y) &= \alpha + \alpha' x + \alpha'' y + \alpha''' xy,\\
\Omega_2(x, y) &= \beta + \beta' x + \beta'' y,\\
\Omega_3(x, y) &= \gamma + \gamma' x + \gamma'' y,
\end{aligned}$$

on trouvera, par la substitution des quantités η dans les équations (11),

$$(14)\quad \left\{\begin{aligned}
\zeta_1 &= \frac{\Omega_1(x_1, y_1)Z_1 + \Omega_2(x_1, y_1)Z_2 + \Omega_3(x_1, y_1)Z_3 + \delta Z_4}{\Delta(x_1, y_1)},\\
\zeta_2 &= \frac{\Omega_1(x_2, y_2)Z_1 + \Omega_2(x_2, y_2)Z_2 + \Omega_3(x_2, y_2)Z_3 + \delta Z_4}{\Delta(x_2, y_2)},\\
\zeta_3 &= \frac{\Omega_1(x_3, y_3)Z_1 + \Omega_2(x_3, y_3)Z_2 + \Omega_3(x_3, y_3)Z_3 + \delta Z_4}{\Delta(x_3, y_3)},\\
\zeta_4 &= \frac{\Omega_1(x_4, y_4)Z_1 + \Omega_2(x_4, y_4)Z_2 + \Omega_3(x_4, y_4)Z_3 + \delta Z_4}{\Delta(x_4, y_4)}.
\end{aligned}\right.$$

Or, en multipliant les équations (9) respectivement par z_1, z_2, z_3, z_4, et les ajoutant, il viendra en ayant égard aux équations (10),

$$\frac{1}{x_1 y_1}\zeta_1^2 + \frac{1}{x_2 y_2}\zeta_2^2 + \frac{1}{x_3 y_3}\zeta_3^2 + \frac{1}{x_4 y_4}\zeta_4^2 = z_1 Z_1 + z_2 Z_2 + z_3 Z_3 + z_4 Z_4.$$

Qu'on substitue maintenant dans le second membre à z_1, z_2, ..., leurs valeurs en fonction linéaire de $Z_1, Z_2, \ldots$; valeurs que nous avons plus haut représentées ainsi :

$$\begin{aligned} z_1 &= A_1^1 Z_1 + A_2^1 Z_2 + A_3^1 Z_3 + A_4^1 Z_4, \\ z_2 &= A_1^2 Z_1 + A_2^2 Z_2 + A_3^2 Z_3 + A_4^2 Z_4, \\ z_3 &= A_1^3 Z_1 + A_2^3 Z_2 + A_3^3 Z_3 + A_4^3 Z_4, \\ z_4 &= A_1^4 Z_1 + A_2^4 Z_2 + A_3^4 Z_3 + A_4^4 Z_4. \end{aligned}$$

La relation obtenue existera identiquement quelles que soient les quantités $Z_1, Z_2, \ldots$, et, si l'on compare en particulier les coefficients des carrés dans les deux membres, on trouvera de suite la formule à laquelle nous voulions arriver, savoir :

$$A_1^1 + A_2^2 + A_3^3 + A_4^4 = \sum \frac{\Omega_1^2(x, y) + \Omega_2^2(x, y) + \Omega_3^2(x, y) + \delta^2}{xy\,\Delta^2(x, y)} = -\frac{\Lambda_1}{\Lambda_0},$$

le signe $\sum$ se rapportant aux divers couples de solutions $x_1, y_1, x_2, y_2, \ldots$.

VII. Arrêtons-nous un instant, avant d'aller plus loin, sur une conséquence remarquable des calculs précédents. Rapprochant des équations (9) les équations (14) qui en donnent la résolution, nous voyons que les premières sont satisfaites en annulant ζ_2, ζ_3, ζ_4 et faisant

$$\zeta_1 = Z_1, \qquad x_1\zeta_1 = Z_2, \qquad y_1\zeta_1 = Z_3, \qquad x_1y_1\zeta_1 = Z_4;$$

donc, dans ces hypothèses, il en sera de même des secondes. Or, il suit de là qu'en posant

$$\Omega(x, y) = \Omega_1(x, y) + x_1\,\Omega_2(x, y) + y_1\,\Omega_3(x, y) + \delta x_1 y_1,$$

on aura à la fois

$$\Omega(x_2, y_2) = 0, \qquad \Omega(x_3, y_3) = 0, \qquad \Omega(x_4, y_4) = 0$$

et

$$\Omega(x_1, y_1) = \Delta(x_1, y_1).$$

On voit donc que l'équation $\Omega(x, y) = 0$ admet toutes les solutions des équations $F(x, y) = 0$, $\Phi(x, y) = 0$, sauf une seule. Les coefficients de cette équation dépendent d'ailleurs rationnellement de ceux des équations proposées et de la solution écartée

x_1, y_1; ainsi le polynome $\Omega(x, y)$ peut être regardé comme analogue au quotient de la division du premier membre d'une équation à une seule inconnue par l'inconnue diminuée d'une racine. La relation

$$\Omega(x_1, y_1) = \Delta(x_1, y_1)$$

confirme encore cette analogie, la déterminante fonctionnelle jouant dans cette circonstance comme dans tant d'autres le rôle d'une dérivée. Enfin, nous remarquerons qu'en joignant à l'équation $\Omega(x, y) = 0$ une combinaison linéaire des proposées où le carré de l'une des inconnues ait été éliminé, le système ainsi obtenu conduira à une équation finale en x ou en y, du troisième degré seulement; c'est ce qu'on vérifiera très facilement par l'application de la règle de M. Minding, ou même directement par l'élimination.

VIII. Nous allons maintenant revenir au cas de deux équations $F(x, y) = 0$, $\Phi(x, y) = 0$ du degré m, pour présenter de la manière la plus générale des calculs entièrement semblables aux précédents, et qu'il sera bien facile de saisir. Désignant par les mêmes lettres affectées d'indices simples ou doubles, les quantités analogues, nous considérons en premier lieu entre deux groupes de quantités, ζ et Z, un système de m^2 équations linéaires, déduites de la suivante :

$$(9') \qquad \sum_{1}^{m^2}{}_{\omega} x_\omega^p y_\omega^q \zeta_\omega = Z_{p,q},$$

en attribuant successivement aux exposants p et q toutes les valeurs $0, 1, 2, \ldots, m-1$. Ces équations seront, comme on voit, les analogues des équations (9); nous établirons aussi un second système de m^2 équations entre les mêmes quantités ζ et un nouveau groupe d'inconnues z, qu'on déduira de la suivante :

$$(10') \qquad \zeta_\omega = x_\omega y_\omega \sum_{1}^{m-1}{}_{i,j} x_\omega^i y_\omega^j z_{i,j},$$

en attribuant à l'indice ω les valeurs $1, 2, \ldots, m^2$, et ces équations correspondront aux équations (10). Cela posé, l'élimination des quantités ζ donnera m^2 équations entre les inconnues z et Z dont voici le type :

$$\sum_1^{m^2}{}_\omega x_\omega^p y_\omega^q x_\omega y_\omega \sum_0^{m-1}{}_{i,j} x_\omega^i y_\omega^j z_{i,j} = \mathrm{Z}_{p,q},$$

ou bien encore

$$\sum_1^{m^2}{}_\omega \sum_0^{m-1}{}_{i,j} x_\omega^{p+1+i} y_\omega^{q+1+j} z_{i,j} = \mathrm{Z}_{p,q},$$

et, en intervertissant l'ordre des deux sommations,

$$\sum_0^{m-1}{}_{i,j} z_{i,j} \sum_1^{m^2}{}_\omega x_\omega^{p+1+i} y_\omega^{q+1+j} = \mathrm{Z}_{p,q}.$$

Mais nous avons déjà introduit la notation $\mathrm{S}_{a,b}$ pour désigner la somme symétrique $\sum x^a y^b$, de sorte que nous écrirons plus simplement

$$(8') \qquad \sum_0^{m-1}{}_{i,j} z_{i,j} \mathrm{S}_{p+1+i,\, q+1+j} = \mathrm{Z}_{p,q}.$$

Nous fixerons l'ordre dans lequel toutes les équations du système se déduiront de celle-là en attribuant d'abord à q la valeur zéro, et à p la série des valeurs $0, 1, 2, \ldots, m-1$, puis à q la valeur 1, et à p la même série que précédemment, et ainsi de suite. Cela étant, la fonction Λ se déduira du déterminant relatif au système ainsi formé après que des termes en diagonale on aura retranché une même quantité λ, de sorte que Λ sera un polynome entier du degré m^2 :

$$\Lambda = \Lambda_0 + \lambda \Lambda_1 + \lambda^2 \Lambda^2 + \ldots + (-1)^{m^2} \lambda^{m^2},$$

et ce qu'il nous faut calculer présentement ce sont les deux premiers coefficients Λ_0 et Λ_1, ou plutôt le rapport $\frac{\Lambda_1}{\Lambda_0}$.

Et d'abord Λ_0 sera le produit des déterminants des systèmes (9′) et (10′), et en désignant par $\mathfrak{D}$ le premier on trouvera de suite l'équation

$$\Lambda_0 = x_1 y_1 x_2 y_2 \ldots x_{m^2} y_{m^2} \mathfrak{D}^2.$$

Le déterminant $\mathfrak{D}$ appartiendrait également au système déduit de l'équation suivante :

$$\zeta_\omega = \sum_{i,j}^{m-1}{}_{0} x_\omega^i y_\omega^j z_{i,j},$$

puisqu'il ne diffère du système (9') que par l'échange des colonnes horizontales et verticales, mais nous verrons ainsi plus facilement une propriété essentielle de ce déterminant, celle de ne pas changer de valeur lorsqu'on met respectivement $x_\omega - \xi$ et $y_\omega - \eta$ à la place de x_ω et y_ω, c'est-à-dire lorsqu'on considère, au lieu des équations

$$F(x, y) = 0, \qquad \Phi(x, y) = 0,$$

les suivantes :

$$F(x + \xi, y + \eta) = 0, \qquad \Phi(x + \xi, y + \eta) = 0.$$

Qu'on fasse en effet pour un instant

$$\Pi(x, y) = \sum_{i,j}^{m-1}{}_{0} x^i y^j z_{i,j},$$

le changement en question reviendra à mettre à la place de $z_{i,j}$ une fonction linéaire des quantités z, donnée par le coefficient de $x^i y^j$ dans le développement de l'expression

$$\Pi(-\xi + x, -\eta + y)$$

suivant les puissances de x et y, de sorte que si l'on fait

$$\Pi(-\xi + x, -\eta + y) = \sum_{i,j}^{m-1}{}_{0} x^i y^j z'_{i,j},$$

ce sera précisément la quantité $z'_{i,j}$ qu'il faudra substituer à $z_{i,j}$. Mais si l'on met dans l'équation précédente $x + \xi$ et $y + \eta$ à la place de x et y, le premier membre redevenant $\Pi(x, y)$, on voit que les quantités z s'exprimeront inversement par les quantités z', sans introduire aucun dénominateur; donc le déterminant relatif à la substitution des z' aux z ne peut être que l'unité.

Cette remarque nous permet immédiatement de passer de l'équation

$$\Lambda_0 = x_1 y_1 x_2 y_2 \ldots x_{m^2} y_{m^2} \mathfrak{D}^2$$

à la suivante :

$$\Lambda_1(\xi, \eta) = (x_1 - \xi)(y_1 - \eta)(x_2 - \xi)(y_2 - \eta)\ldots(x_{m^2} - \xi)(y_{m^2} - \eta)\mathcal{D}^2$$

sur laquelle nous nous fonderons plus tard.

La détermination du rapport $\frac{\Lambda_1}{\Lambda_0}$ dépend, comme nous l'avons vu, de la résolution des équations (8′) par rapport aux inconnues z, de sorte que si l'on représente les valeurs de ces quantités par la formule générale

$$z_{i,j} = \sum_{p,q}^{m-1} {}_0\, \mathrm{A}_{p,q}^{i,j} \mathrm{Z}_{p,q},$$

on aura

$$\frac{\Lambda_1}{\Lambda_0} = -\sum_{0\;p,q}^{m-1} \mathrm{A}_{p,q}^{p,q}.$$

Pour effectuer sous la forme convenable la résolution des équations (8′), introduisons les quantités η en posant

$$\zeta_\omega = \sum \frac{\sum_{0\;i,j}^{m-1} x_\omega^i y_\omega^j \eta_{i,j}}{\Delta(x_\omega, y_\omega)};$$

il viendra, par la substitution dans les équations (9′),

$$\sum_{0\;i,j}^{m-1} \eta_{i,j} \sum_{1\;\omega}^{m^2} \frac{x_\omega^{p+i} y_\omega^{q+j}}{\Delta(x_\omega, y_\omega)} = \mathrm{Z}_{p,q}, \tag{12′}$$

et dans ce nouveau système on devra, d'après le théorème déjà cité de M. Jacobi, annuler toutes les sommes

$$\sum_{1\;\omega}^{m^2} \frac{x_\omega^{p+i} y_\omega^{q+j}}{\Delta(x_\omega, y_\omega)},$$

dans lesquelles on aura

$$p + q + i + j = \text{ou} < 2m - 3.$$

Ainsi, en particulier dans la première équation où l'on doit supposer

$$p = q = 0,$$

toutes les inconnues disparaîtront, sauf la dernière $z_{m-1,m-1}$ multipliée par la somme non évanouissante en général, $\sum_{1}^{m^2}\omega \frac{x_\omega^{m-1} y_\omega^{m-1}}{\Delta(x_\omega, y_\omega)}$. Mais ce qu'il importe surtout de remarquer, c'est que les coefficients qui ne disparaissent pas sont des fonctions rationnelles des coefficients des équations proposées, fonctions que M. Jacobi a appris à calculer dans son admirable Mémoire intitulé *Theoremata nova algebraica circa systema duarum æquationum inter duas variabiles propositarum* (¹). Quant au déterminant de ce système il est le produit des déterminants relatifs aux systèmes (9′) et (11′); si donc on le désigne par δ, on arrivera à la relation

$$\mathfrak{D}^2 = \delta\,\Delta(x_1, y_1)\,\Delta(x_2, y_2)\ldots\Delta(x_{m^2}, y_{m^2}),$$

équation remarquable et analogue à celle que nous avons précédemment trouvée pour les équations à une inconnue. Nous ne pouvons nous occuper ici d'une détermination plus complète de δ dont nous avons fait le calcul ci-dessus dans le cas de $m = 2$; nous observerons seulement qu'en passant des équations proposées à leurs transformées en $x - \xi$, $y - \eta$, δ ne change pas. Cette propriété vient déjà d'être établie pour le déterminant $\mathfrak{D}$, et il est très facile de voir qu'elle a lieu également pour toutes les quantités $\Delta(x_\omega, y_\omega)$, en se rapportant à l'expression de $\Delta(x, y)$ où ne figurent que les dérivées partielles des fonctions $F(x, y)$, $\Phi(x, y)$. Cela posé, résolvons, par rapport aux inconnues η, les équations (12′) et soit

$$\eta_{i,j} = \frac{\sum_{0}^{m-1}{}_{p,q}\, \omega_{p,q}^{i,j} Z_{p,q}}{\delta},$$

les quantités ω étant des fonctions entières des coefficients des équations proposées. Si nous posons

$$\Omega_{p,q}(x, y) = \sum_{0}^{m-1}{}_{i,j}\, x^i y^j \omega_{p,q}^{i,j},$$

(¹) Jacobi, *Gesammelte Werke*, t. III, p. 285-294.

on trouvera, par la substitution dans les équations (11'),

$$\zeta_\omega = \sum_{0}^{m-1}{}_{p,q} \frac{\Omega_{p,q}(x_\omega, y_\omega) Z_{p,q}}{\delta\, \Delta(x_\omega, y_\omega)}.$$

Or, des équations (9') et (10') nous tirons la relation

$$\sum_{1}^{m^2}{}_\omega \frac{1}{x_\omega y_\omega} \zeta_\omega^2 = \sum_{0}^{m-1}{}_{i,j} z_{i,j} Z_{i,j},$$

qui existera identiquement par rapport aux quantités Z, lesquelles entrent seules dans le premier membre. Quant au second membre, si l'on y remplace $z_{i,j}$ par la formule posée plus haut, savoir

$$z_{i,j} = \sum_{0}^{m-1}{}_{p,q} A_{p,q}^{i,j} Z_{p,q},$$

il ne dépendra plus de même que des quantités Z, et, en égalant les carrés de $Z_{p,q}$ dans les deux membres, on trouvera

$$A_{p,q}^{p,q} = \sum_{1}^{m^2}{}_\omega \frac{\Omega_{p,q}^2(x_\omega, y_\omega)}{x_\omega y_\omega \delta^2 \Delta^2(x_\omega, y_\omega)},$$

d'où l'on conclut enfin

$$\frac{\Lambda_1}{\Lambda_0} = -\sum_{0}^{m-1}{}_{p,q} A_{p,q}^{p,q} = -\sum_{1}^{m^2}{}_\omega \frac{\sum_{0}^{m-1}{}_{p,q} \Omega_{p,q}^2(x_\omega, y_\omega)}{x_\omega y_\omega \delta^2 \Delta^2(x_\omega, y_\omega)}.$$

IX. De l'analyse précédente résulte un théorème analogue à celui que nous avons donné précédemment pour deux équations du second degré, et qui consiste en ce que le polynome

$$\Omega(x, y) = \sum_{0}^{m-1}{}_{p,q} \Omega_{p,q}(x, y) x_1^p y_1^q$$

vérifie l'équation

$$\Omega(x_1, y_1) = \delta\, \Delta(x_1, y_1),$$

et s'annule quand on y remplace x et y par toutes les solutions simultanées différentes de la solution

$$x = x_1, \qquad y = y_1.$$

Comme cela est très facile à vérifier, nous ne nous y arrêterons pas, et nous arrivons de suite à la démonstration de notre théorème. Précédemment nous avons obtenu l'équation

$$\Lambda_0(\xi, \eta) = (x_1 - \xi)(y_1 - \eta)(x_2 - \xi)(y_2 - \eta)\ldots(x_{m^2} - \xi)(y_{m^2} - \eta)\mathfrak{D}^2,$$

et de la valeur trouvée pour $\frac{\Lambda_1}{\Lambda_0}$ résulte aussi

$$\frac{\Lambda_1(\xi, \eta)}{\Lambda_0(\xi, \eta)} = -\sum_1^{m^2}{}_{\omega} \frac{\mathfrak{F}(x_\omega, y_\omega, \xi, \eta)}{(x_\omega - \xi)(y_\omega - \eta)\,\delta^2\Delta^2(x_\omega, y_\omega)},$$

le numérateur $\mathfrak{F}(x_\omega, y_\omega, \xi, \eta)$ désignant ce que devient l'expression $\sum \Omega_{p,q}^2(x_\omega, y_\omega)$ lorsqu'on substitue aux équations proposées leurs transformées en $x + \xi$ et $y + \eta$. Or, il est évident que la fonction $\mathfrak{F}$ correspondante à deux solutions simultanées réelles ne changera jamais de signe pour aucune valeur des quantités ξ et η. Ces préliminaires posés, nous allons, en premier lieu, rechercher comment se modifie le nombre des variations du polynome

$$\Lambda(\xi, \eta) = \Lambda_0(\xi, \eta) + \lambda\Lambda_1(\xi, \eta) + \ldots + (-1)^{m^2}\lambda^{m^2}$$

lorsqu'on y fait croître η d'une manière continue de η_0 à η_1, la quantité ξ restant constante et égale à une valeur déterminée ξ_0. Et, d'abord, les coefficients de deux puissances consécutives de λ ne pourront jamais s'évanouir en même temps, et si un coefficient s'annule, le précédent et le suivant seront de signes contraires. C'est, comme nous l'avons déjà dit, une conséquence du théorème de Descartes et de ce que l'équation $\Lambda(\xi, \eta) = 0$ a toujours toutes ses racines réelles.

Ainsi des changements dans le nombre des variations ne pourront survenir qu'autant que ce sera le dernier terme qui viendra à s'annuler. Mais, d'après l'expression de ce dernier terme, les valeurs de η qui peuvent l'annuler sont uniquement les racines y du système des équations proposées, qui sont comprises entre les limites η_0 et η_1.

Cela étant, considérons le rapport

$$\frac{\Lambda_1(\xi, \eta)}{\Lambda_0(\xi, \eta)} = -\sum \frac{\mathfrak{F}(x_\omega, y_\omega, \xi, \eta)}{(x_\omega - \xi)(y_\omega - \eta)\delta^2 \Delta^2(x_\omega, y_\omega)}$$
$$= \sum \frac{\mathfrak{F}(x_\omega, y_\omega, \xi, \eta)}{(x_\omega - \xi)(\eta - y_\omega)\delta^2 \Delta^2(x_\omega, y_\omega)}$$

pour une valeur de η voisine d'une racine y_ω; son signe dépendra du seul terme $\frac{\mathfrak{F}(x_\omega, y_\omega, \xi, \eta)}{(x_\omega - \xi)(\eta - y_\omega)\delta^2 \Delta^2(x_\omega, y_\omega)}$, ou, d'après ce que nous avons établi relativement au numérateur, du seul facteur $\frac{1}{(x_\omega - \xi)(\eta - y_\omega)}$. Or, deux cas sont à distinguer; en premier lieu, si $x_\omega - \xi_0$ est positif, ce rapport sera négatif pour une valeur de η un peu inférieure à y_ω, et positif pour une valeur un peu supérieure; donc alors une variation se change en permanence dans le polynome $\Lambda(\xi, \eta)$, lorsque η atteint et dépasse la racine y_ω. Mais si nous supposons en second lieu $x_\omega - \xi_0$ négatif, c'est évidemment le contraire qui arrive : c'est une variation qui s'introduit dans $\Lambda(\xi, \eta)$ lorsque η franchit la valeur y_ω. Il est facile de conclure de là la signification de la différence $v_{\xi_0, \eta_0} - v_{\xi_0, \eta_1}$, c'est-à-dire des séries du nombre des variations du polynome $\Lambda(\xi_0, \eta_0)$, sur le nombre des variations de $\Lambda(\xi_0, \eta_1)$. Considérons x_ω comme l'abscisse et y_ω comme l'ordonnée d'un point rapporté à deux axes rectangulaires dans un certain plan, de sorte qu'à chaque solution du système de nos équations corresponde un point déterminé. Cela étant, si nous menons deux parallèles à l'axe des abscisses par les points dont les coordonnées seraient

$$x = \xi_0, \qquad x = \xi_0,$$
$$y = \eta_0, \qquad y = \eta_1,$$

les points auxquels correspondent des solutions et qui seront compris dans l'intérieur des deux parallèles se partageront en deux groupes ξ_0, selon que leurs abscisses seront plus grandes ou plus petites que ξ_0. On voit que ceux du premier groupe seront à droite de l'ordonnée verticale menée par le point (ξ_0, η_0), et les autres à gauche. Donc, lorsque la quantité η varie d'une manière continue de η_0 à η_1, le polynome $\Lambda(\xi, \eta)$ perd autant de variations qu'il existe de points dans le premier groupe, et en gagne autant qu'il en existe dans le second. Soient donc respectivement $\mathfrak{N}$ et $\mathfrak{N}'$ le nombre de ces points, on aura la relation

$$v_{\xi_0,\eta_0} - v_{\xi_0,\eta_1} = \mathfrak{N} - \mathfrak{N}',$$

Cela posé, si la quantité ξ_0 devient ξ_1, $\mathfrak{N}$ s'accroîtra du nombre des points renfermés dans l'intérieur du rectangle, ayant pour coordonnées de ses sommets

$$\begin{array}{llll} x = \xi_0, & x = \xi_0, & x = \xi_1, & x = \xi_1, \\ y = \eta_0, & y = \eta_1, & y = \eta_0, & y = \eta_1, \end{array}$$

et $\mathfrak{N}'$ sera diminué du même nombre. En le désignant par n, nous aurons donc

$$v_{\xi_1,\eta_0} - v_{\xi_1,\eta_1} = (\mathfrak{N} + n) - (\mathfrak{N}' - n) = \mathfrak{N} - \mathfrak{N}' + 2n.$$

Or, cette relation jointe à la précédente conduit immédiatement à notre théorème qui consiste dans l'équation

$$\frac{v_{\xi_0,\eta_0} + v_{\xi_1,\eta_1} - v_{\xi_0,\eta_1} - v_{\xi_1,\eta_0}}{2} = n.$$

X. On a pu remarquer dans les calculs précédents que les deux inconnues x et y étaient traitées de la même manière; c'est cette symétrie qui nous a engagés à nous occuper ainsi avec détail de deux équations générales du degré m. Mais on va voir que les mêmes principes conduisent à une analyse plus simple lorsqu'on considère deux équations de la forme

$$\begin{aligned} F(x) &= 0, \\ \Phi(x) &= y, \end{aligned}$$

$F(x)$ étant un polynome entier et $\Phi(x)$ une fonction rationnelle quelconque de x. On obtient d'ailleurs des formules d'une application numérique très facile, et qui n'offrent aucune exception. Nous admettrons seulement qu'on ait enlevé, dans le polynome $F(x)$, les facteurs qui lui seraient communs avec le dénominateur de $\Phi(x)$, de sorte que toutes les racines y soient des quantités finies. Cela étant, nommons $x_1, x_2, \ldots, x_m$ les racines de l'équation $F(x) = 0$; $y_1, y_2, \ldots, y_m$, les valeurs correspondantes de y, et T la somme symétrique $y_1 x_1^i + y_2 x_2^i + \ldots + y_m x_m^i$; notre fonction $\Lambda(\xi, \eta)$, sera ce que devient le déterminant

$$\Lambda = \begin{vmatrix} T_1 - \lambda & T_2 & T_3 & \dots & T_m \\ T_2 & T_3 - \lambda & T_4 & \dots & T_{m+1} \\ T_3 & T_4 & T_5 - \lambda & \dots & T_{m+2} \\ \dots & \dots & \dots & \dots & \dots \\ T_m & T_{m+1} & T_{m+2} & \dots & T_{2m-1} - \lambda \end{vmatrix}$$

lorsqu'on substitue $x + \xi$ et $y + \eta$, à la place de x et y, dans les équations proposées, et le nombre des solutions simultanées comprises dans l'intérieur d'un rectangle sera encore donné par la même formule que ci-dessus :

$$\frac{\nu_{\xi_1, \eta_1} + \nu_{\xi_0, \eta_0} - \nu_{\xi_1, \eta_0} - \nu_{\xi_0, \eta_1}}{2}.$$

XI. La démonstration repose toujours sur le calcul du terme indépendant et du coefficient de la première puissance de λ dans la fonction Λ; nous le présenterons de la manière suivante.

Formons en premier lieu, entre les quantités ζ et Z, les m équations :

$$(2')\quad \left\{ \begin{aligned} \zeta_1 + \zeta_2 + \dots + \zeta_m &= Z_1, \\ x_1 \zeta_1 + x_2 \zeta_2 + \dots + x_m \zeta_m &= Z_2, \\ x_1^2 \zeta_1 + x_2^2 \zeta_2 + \dots + x_m^2 \zeta_m &= Z_3, \\ \dots\dots\dots\dots\dots\dots&\dots, \\ x_1^{m-1} \zeta_1 + x_2^{m-1} \zeta_2 + \dots + x_m^{m-1} \zeta_m &= Z_m, \end{aligned} \right.$$

semblables aux équations (2) du paragraphe II, puis, entre les quantités ζ et Z, les suivantes analogues aux équations (3), savoir :

$$(3')\quad \left\{ \begin{aligned} \zeta_1 &= y_1 (x_1 z_1 + x_1^2 z_2 + \dots + x_1^m z_m), \\ \zeta_2 &= y_2 (x_2 z_1 + x_2^2 z_2 + \dots + x_2^m z_m), \\ \zeta_3 &= y_3 (x_3 z_1 + x_3^2 z_2 + \dots + x_3^m z_m), \\ \dots&\dots\dots\dots\dots\dots\dots, \\ \zeta_m &= y_m (x_m z_1 + x_m^2 z_2 + \dots + x_m^m z_m); \end{aligned} \right.$$

on trouvera d'abord, par l'élimination des quantités ζ, les relations

$$(1')\quad \left\{ \begin{aligned} S_1 z_1 + S_2 z_2 + \dots + S_m z_m &= Z_1, \\ S_2 z_1 + S_3 z_2 + \dots + S_{m+1} z_m &= Z_2, \\ S_2 z_1 + S_4 z_2 + \dots + S_{m+2} z_m &= Z_3, \\ \dots\dots\dots\dots\dots\dots&\dots, \\ S_m z_1 + S_{m+1} z_2 + \dots + S_{2m-1} z_m &= Z_m, \end{aligned} \right.$$

la quantité S_i désignant la somme $y_1 x_1^i + y_2 x_2^i + \ldots + y_m x_m^i$.

Donc le déterminant de ce dernier système, c'est-à-dire précisément Λ_0, sera le produit des déterminants relatifs aux équations (2′) et (1′), ce qui donnera la relation

$$\Lambda_0 = \begin{vmatrix} S_1 & S_2 & \ldots & S_m \\ S_2 & S_3 & \ldots & S_{m+1} \\ S_3 & S_4 & \ldots & S_{m+2} \\ \ldots & \ldots & \ldots & \ldots \\ S_m & S_{m+1} & \ldots & S_{2m-1} \end{vmatrix}$$

$$= x_1 y_1 x_2 y_2 \ldots x_m y_m \begin{vmatrix} 1 & 1 & \ldots & 1 \\ x_1 & x_2 & \ldots & x_m \\ x_1^2 & x_2^2 & \ldots & x_m^2 \\ \ldots & \ldots & \ldots & \ldots \\ x_1^{m-1} & x_2^{m-1} & \ldots & x_m^{m-1} \end{vmatrix}^2,$$

ou, évidemment,

$$\Lambda_0 = x_1 y_1 x_2 y_2 \ldots x_m y_m \, F'(x_1) \, F'(x_2) \ldots F'(x_m).$$

Donc, désignant par $\Lambda(\xi, \eta)$ ce que devient la fonction Λ, par rapport aux équations en $x + \xi$ et $y + \eta$, et faisant comme ci-dessus

$$\Lambda(\xi, \eta) = \Lambda_0(\xi, \eta) + \lambda \, \Lambda_1(\xi, \eta) + \ldots + (-1)^m \lambda^m,$$

on aura

$$\Lambda_0(\xi, \eta) = (x_1 - \xi)(y_1 - \eta)(x_2 - \xi)(y_2 - \eta) \ldots$$
$$\times (x_m - \xi)(y_m - \eta) \, F'(x_1) \, F'(x_2) \ldots F'(x_m).$$

Le calcul du rapport $\frac{\Lambda_1}{\Lambda_0}$ dépend, comme nous l'avons déjà vu, de la résolution des équations (1′); soit donc

$$\begin{aligned} z_1 &= A_1^1 Z_1 + A_2^1 Z_2 + \ldots + A_m^1 Z_m, \\ z_2 &= A_1^2 Z_1 + A_2^2 Z_2 + \ldots + A_m^2 Z_m, \\ z_3 &= A_1^3 Z_1 + A_2^3 Z_2 + \ldots + A_m^3 Z_m, \\ &\ldots\ldots\ldots\ldots\ldots\ldots, \\ z_m &= A_1^m Z_1 + A_2^m Z_2 + \ldots + A_m^m Z_m, \end{aligned}$$

on aura

$$\frac{\Lambda_1}{\Lambda_0} = -(A_1^1 + A_2^2 + \ldots + A_m^m).$$

Maintenant, pour effectuer cette résolution, nous introduirons un système de quantités auxiliaires η par les formules

$$(4') \quad \left\{ \begin{aligned} \zeta_1 &= \frac{\eta_0 + x_1\eta_1 + x_1^2\eta_2 + \ldots + x_1^{m-1}\eta_{m-1}}{F'(x_1)}, \\ \zeta_2 &= \frac{\eta_0 + x_2\eta_1 + x_2^2\eta_2 + \ldots + x_2^{m-1}\eta_{m-1}}{F'(x_2)}, \\ &\ldots\ldots\ldots\ldots\ldots\ldots\ldots\ldots\ldots, \\ \zeta_m &= \frac{\eta_0 + x_m\eta_1 + x_m^2\eta_2 + \ldots + x_m^{m-1}\eta_{m-1}}{F'(x_m)}. \end{aligned} \right.$$

En substituant dans les équations (2'), il viendra

$$\begin{aligned} &\eta_0 \sum \frac{1}{F'} + \eta_1 \sum \frac{x}{F'} + \ldots + \eta_{m-1} \sum \frac{x^{m-1}}{F'} = Z_1, \\ &\eta_0 \sum \frac{x}{F'} + \eta_1 \sum \frac{x^2}{F'} + \ldots + \eta_{m-1} \sum \frac{x^m}{F'} = Z_2, \\ &\eta_0 \sum \frac{x^2}{F'} + \eta_1 \sum \frac{x^3}{F'} + \ldots + \eta_{m-1} \sum \frac{x^{m+1}}{F'} = Z_3, \\ &\ldots\ldots\ldots\ldots\ldots\ldots\ldots\ldots\ldots\ldots, \\ &\eta_0 \sum \frac{x^{m-1}}{F'} + \eta_1 \sum \frac{x^m}{F'} + \ldots + \eta_{m-1} \sum \frac{x^{2m-2}}{F'} = Z_m. \end{aligned}$$

Or ces équations se résolvent immédiatement comme on va le voir. Soit, en effet,

$$F(x) = x^m + a_1 x^{m-1} + a_2 x^{m-2} + \ldots + a_{m-1} x + a_m.$$

On vérifiera sans peine les valeurs suivantes que nous avons omis de donner explicitement dans le paragraphe III, savoir :

$$\begin{aligned} \eta_0 &= Z_m + a_1 Z_{m-1} + a_2 Z_{m-2} + \ldots + a_{m-2} Z_2 + a_{m-1} Z_1, \\ \eta_1 &= Z_{m-1} + a_1 Z_{m-2} + a_2 Z_{m-3} + \ldots + a_{m-2} Z_1, \\ &\ldots\ldots\ldots\ldots\ldots\ldots\ldots\ldots\ldots\ldots, \\ \eta_{m-2} &= Z_2 + a_1 Z_1, \\ \eta_{m-1} &= Z_1. \end{aligned}$$

Que l'on pose donc

$$\begin{aligned} \Omega_1(x) &= x^{m-1} + a_1 x^{m-2} + a_2 x^{m-3} + \ldots + a_{m-2} x + a_{m-1}, \\ \Omega_2(x) &= x^{m-2} + a_1 x^{m-3} + a_2 x^{m-4} + \ldots + a_{m-2}, \\ &\ldots\ldots\ldots\ldots\ldots\ldots\ldots\ldots\ldots\ldots, \\ \Omega_{m-2}(x) &= x^2 + a_1 x + a_2, \\ \Omega_{m-1}(x) &= x + a_1, \end{aligned}$$

on trouvera, par la substitution des quantités η dans les équations (4′), les valeurs

$$\zeta_1 = \frac{\Omega_1(x_1)Z_1 + \Omega_2(x_1)Z_2 + \ldots + \Omega_{m-1}(x_1)Z_{m-1} + Z_m}{F'(x_1)},$$
$$\zeta_2 = \frac{\Omega_1(x_2)Z_1 + \Omega_2(x_2)Z_2 + \ldots + \Omega_{m-1}(x_2)Z_{m-1} + Z_m}{F'(x_2)},$$
$$\ldots\ldots\ldots\ldots\ldots\ldots\ldots\ldots\ldots\ldots,$$
$$\zeta_m = \frac{\Omega_1(x_m)Z_1 + \Omega_2(x_m)Z_2 + \ldots + \Omega_{m-1}(x_m)Z_{m-1} + Z_m}{F'(x_m)}.$$

Cela posé, les relations (2′) et (3′) donnent la suivante :

$$\frac{1}{x_1 y_1}\zeta_1^2 + \frac{1}{x_2 y_2}\zeta_2^2 + \ldots + \frac{1}{x_m y_m}\zeta_m^2 = z_1 Z_1 + z_2 Z_2 + \ldots + z_m Z_m,$$

et si l'on met dans le second membre, à la place des quantités z, leurs valeurs en fonction linéaire des quantités Z, on trouvera, en comparant les carrés de Z_1, Z_2, ..., les expressions auxquelles nous voulions parvenir, savoir

$$A_i^i = \frac{\Omega_i^2(x_1)}{x_1 y_1 F'^2(x_1)} + \frac{\Omega_i^2(x_2)}{x_2 y_2 F'^2(x_2)} + \ldots + \frac{\Omega_i^2(x_m)}{x_m y_m F'^2(x_m)};$$

elles donnent immédiatement

$$\frac{A_1}{A_0} = -(A_1^1 + A_2^2 + \ldots + A_m^m) = -\sum \frac{\Omega_1^2(x) + \Omega_2^2(x) + \ldots + \Omega_{m-1}^2(x) + 1}{xy\, F'^2(x)},$$

le signe $\sum$ se rapportant aux diverses solutions simultanées. On en conclut qu'en passant des équations proposées à leurs transformées en $x+\xi$ et $y+\eta$, il viendra

$$\frac{A_1(\xi, \eta)}{A_0(\xi, \eta)} = -\sum \frac{\mathfrak{F}(x, \xi)}{(x-\xi)(y-\eta)\, F'^2(x)},$$

expression dans laquelle le numérateur désigné par $\mathfrak{F}(x, \xi)$ ne pourra jamais ni s'évanouir ni changer de signe quel que soit ξ, lorsque la racine x sera réelle, puisqu'elle représente une somme de carrés. Nous pouvons donc appliquer exactement la démonstration employée précédemment pour la détermination du nombre des solutions simultanées qui sont comprises dans l'intérieur d'un rectangle ayant ses côtés parallèles aux axes coordonnés. Seulement on voit de suite la possibilité d'obtenir par le calcul des quantités S_1, S_2, ..., les divers coefficients de la fonction $\Lambda(\xi, \eta)$, qui jouent dans cette question le rôle de fonctions auxiliaires du théorème de M. Sturm. D'ailleurs aucun cas d'exception ne peut ici se présenter à moins que l'équation $F(x) = 0$ n'ait des racines égales. Mais, même alors, nous pouvons conserver la fonction $\Lambda(\xi, \eta)$, dont le premier terme $\Lambda_0(\xi, \eta)$ disparaît, car les deux suivants Λ_1 et Λ_2, s'il existe par exemple deux racines égales, se trouvent prendre la même forme analytique et jouer le même rôle que les deux premiers. Nous développerons ce qui se rapporte à ce sujet dans un autre Mémoire.

XII. Il suffira d'un peu d'attention pour reconnaître qu'on peut étendre à un nombre quelconque d'équations simultanées les principes appliqués précédemment à deux équations à deux inconnues. Nons en donnerons un exemple en considérant le système suivant :

$$
\begin{aligned}
F(x) &= 0,\\
\Phi(x) &= y,\\
\Psi(x) &= z,
\end{aligned}
$$

où nous supposerons que les fonctions Φ et Ψ sont rationnelles et ne deviennent infinies pour aucune valeur satisfaisant à la première équation $F(x) = 0$. Soient toujours $x_1, x_2, \ldots, x_m$ les racines de cette équation, $y_1, z_1, y_2, z_2, \ldots, y_m, z_m$ les déterminations correspondantes des inconnues y et z, et U_i la somme symétrique

$$y_1 z_1 x_1^i + y_2 z_2 x_2^i + \ldots + y_m z_m x_m^i,$$

nous considérerons encore le déterminant

$$\Lambda = \begin{vmatrix} U_1 - \lambda & U_2 & U_3 & \ldots & U_m \\ U_2 & U_3 - \lambda & U_4 & \ldots & U_{m+1} \\ U_3 & U_4 & U_5 - \lambda & \ldots & U_{m+2} \\ \ldots & \ldots & \ldots & \ldots & \ldots \\ U_m & U_{m+1} & U_{m+2} & \ldots & U_{2m-1} - \lambda \end{vmatrix},$$

de même forme analytique que les précédents. Cela posé, si l'on substitue $x + \xi$, $y + \eta$, $z + \zeta$ aux inconnues proposées, il deviendra fonction de ξ, η, ζ, et nous le représenterons par

$$\Lambda(\xi, \eta, \zeta) = \Lambda_0(\xi, \eta, \zeta) + \lambda \Lambda_1(\xi, \eta, \zeta) + \ldots + (-1)^m \lambda^m.$$

Or, on trouvera les expressions suivantes, savoir :

$$\Lambda_0(\zeta, \eta, \zeta) = (x_1 - \xi)(y_1 - \eta)(z_1 - \zeta)(x_2 - \xi)(y_2 - \eta)(z_2 - \zeta)\ldots \times F'(x_1) F'(x_2)\ldots F'(x_m),$$

$$\frac{\Lambda_1(\xi, \eta, \zeta)}{\Lambda_0(\xi, \eta, \zeta)} = -\sum \frac{\mathcal{F}(x, \xi)}{(x-\xi)(y-\eta)(z-\zeta)F'^2(x)},$$

le signe $\sum$ s'étendant aux diverses solutions et le numérateur $\mathcal{F}(x, \xi_0)$ étant la fonction déjà considérée dans les cas des équations à une seule et à deux inconnues. Cela posé, soit, pour un système donné de valeurs de ξ, η, ζ, $v(\xi, \eta, \zeta)$ le nombre des variations du polynome $\Lambda(\xi, \eta, \zeta)$, nous allons en premier lieu donner la signification de la différence $v(\xi, \eta, \zeta_0) - v(\xi, \eta, \zeta_1)$ où nous supposons $\zeta_1 > \zeta_0$. Considérons en effet x, y, z comme les coordonnées rectangulaires d'un point situé dans l'espace, de sorte qu'à chaque solution des trois équations proposées corresponde un point déterminé.

Les deux plans $z = \zeta_0$ et $z = \zeta_1$ comprendront dans leur intervalle un certain nombre des points figurant ainsi des solutions; nous les partagerons en quatre groupes de la manière suivante. Menant dans le plan des xy des parallèles aux axes des x et des y par le point dont les coordonnées sont $x = \xi$, $y = \eta$, on voit que ces droites détermineront quatre régions, que nous désignerons par A, B, C, D, et les points dont nous formerons un même groupe seront ceux qui le projettent dans une même région, ou, si l'on veut, dans l'intérieur d'un même angle. Soient A et C d'une part, B et D de l'autre, les angles opposés par le sommet; dans les deux premiers, les expressions $(x-\xi)(y-\eta)$ seront de même signe et, pour fixer les idées, seront positives; tandis qu'elles seront négatives dans B et D. D'après cela, on voit de suite qu'en nommant respectivement a, b, c, d, les nombres de points qui appartiennent aux régions A, B, C, D, la différence

$$v(\xi, \eta, \zeta_0) - v(\xi, \eta, \zeta_1)$$

aura pour valeur

$$a + c - b - d.$$

Considérons en second lieu deux valeurs de η, η_0 et η_1, en laissant constante la quantité ξ. Les deux droites $y = \eta_0$, $y = \eta_1$

comprendront dans leur intervalle un certain nombre des projections des points racines; nous les séparerons encore en deux groupes, suivant qu'elles se trouveront à droite ou à gauche de la parallèle à l'axe des y, $x=\xi$, et nous désignerons par $\mathfrak{N}$ le nombre des projections contenues dans le premier groupe et par $\mathfrak{N}'$ le nombre des projections contenues dans le second.

Cela posé, il est clair qu'en passant de η_0 à η_1, a et d deviendront respectivement $a+\mathfrak{N}'$ et $d-\mathfrak{N}'$; b et c en même temps se changeront en $b+\mathfrak{N}$ et $c-\mathfrak{N}$. Nous aurons donc, d'une part,

$$v(\xi, \eta_0, \zeta_0) - v(\xi, \eta_0, \zeta_1) = a + c - b - d,$$

et de l'autre

$$v(\xi, \eta_1, \zeta_0) - v(\xi, \eta_1, \zeta_1) = a + c - b - d + 2(\mathfrak{N}' - \mathfrak{N}),$$

et, par suite,

$$v(\xi, \eta_0, \zeta_0) + v(\xi, \eta_1, \zeta_1) - v(\xi, \eta_0, \zeta_1) - v(\xi, \eta_1, \zeta_0) = 2(\mathfrak{N} - \mathfrak{N}').$$

Il ne nous reste plus maintenant qu'à faire varier la quantité ξ; or, en passant de ξ_0 à ξ_1, $\mathfrak{N}'$ s'augmentera du nombre des projections renfermées dans le rectangle ayant pour sommets

$$\begin{matrix} x=\xi_0, & x=\xi_0, & x=\xi_1, & x=\xi_1, \\ y=\eta_0, & y=\eta_1, & y=\eta_0, & y=\eta_1, \end{matrix}$$

et $\mathfrak{N}$ diminuera du même nombre. Désignons par n ce nombre, il représentera évidemment combien se trouvent de points figurant des couples de solution dans l'intérieur du parallélépipède ayant pour projection verticale le rectangle dont nous venons de parler et terminé par les plans $z=\zeta_0$, $z=\zeta_1$. Or, nous avons à la fois les relations

$$v(\xi_0, \eta_0, \zeta_0) + v(\xi_0, \eta_1, \zeta_1) - v(\xi_0, \eta_0, \zeta_1) - v(\xi_0, \eta_1, \zeta_0) = 2(\mathfrak{N} - \mathfrak{N}'),$$
$$v(\xi_1, \eta_0, \zeta_0) + v(\xi_1, \eta_1, \zeta_1) - v(\xi_1, \eta_0, \zeta_1) - v(\xi_1, \eta_1, \zeta_0) = 2(\mathfrak{N} - \mathfrak{N}') - 4n.$$

d'où l'on conclut

$$n = \frac{\left[\begin{matrix} v(\xi_0, \eta_0, \zeta_0) + v(\xi_0, \eta_1, \zeta_1) + v(\xi_1, \eta_0, \zeta_1) + v(\xi_1, \eta_1, \zeta_0) \\ - v(\xi_0, \eta_0, \zeta_1) - v(\xi_0, \eta_1, \zeta_0) - v(\xi_1, \eta_0, \zeta_0) - v(\xi_1, \eta_1, \zeta_1) \end{matrix}\right]}{4}.$$

On aura un énoncé plus simple si l'on convient de désigner par

(M) le nombre des variations du polynome $\Lambda(\xi, \eta, \zeta)$, M étant le point de l'espace dont les coordonnées rectangulaires sont ξ, η, ζ. Nommant alors $pqrs$ la base inférieure et $p'q'r's'$ la base supérieure du parallélépipède, de sorte que les points p et p', q et q', ..., appartiennent respectivement aux mêmes ordonnées verticales et que les droites pq, ps soient parallèles aux parties positives des x et des y, on aura la valeur suivante :

$$n = \frac{1}{4}\{[(p)-(p')]-[(q)-(q')]+[(r)-(r')]-[(s)-(s')]\}.$$

INTÉGRATION

DES

FONCTIONS RATIONNELLES (1).

Nouvelles Annales de Mathématiques, 2e série, t. XI, 1872, p. 145-148.
Annales de l'École Normale supérieure, 1re série, t. I, 1872, p. 215-218.
Cours d'Analyse de l'École Polytechnique, 1873, p. 268 et suiv.

Soient $F(x)$ et $F_1(x)$ deux polynomes entiers; en posant, pour mettre en évidence l'ordre de multiplicité des divers facteurs,

$$F(x) = (x-a)^{\alpha+1}(x-b)^{\beta+1}\ldots(x-l)^{\lambda+1},$$

en admettant pour simplifier que le degré du numérateur soit moindre que le degré de $F(x)$, la décompositon en fractions simples donne la formule générale

$$\begin{aligned}\frac{F_1(x)}{F(x)} = {} & \frac{A}{x-a} + \frac{A_1}{(x-a)^2} + \ldots + \frac{A_\alpha}{(x-a)^{\alpha+1}} \\ & + \frac{B}{x-b} + \frac{B_1}{(x-b)^2} + \ldots + \frac{B_\beta}{(x-b)^{\beta+1}} \\ & \ldots\ldots\ldots\ldots\ldots\ldots\ldots\ldots \\ & + \frac{L}{x-l} + \frac{L_1}{(x-l)^2} + \ldots + \frac{L_\lambda}{(x-l)^{\lambda+1}},\end{aligned}$$

(1) Nous publions ici un extrait du *Cours d'Analyse de l'École Polytechnique* Paris, Gauthiers-Villars, 1873) relatif à l'intégration des fonctions rationnelles; antérieurement, la question avait été traitée d'une manière plus sommaire par Hermite dans deux Notes des *Nouvelles Annales* et des *Annales de l'École Normale* que nous ne reproduisons pas. E. P.

ou, pour abréger l'écriture [1],

$$\frac{F_1(x)}{F(x)} = \sum \frac{A}{x-a} + \sum \frac{A_1}{(x-a)^2} + \ldots + \sum \frac{A_n}{(x-a)^{n+1}}.$$

On en déduit immédiatement cette expression de l'intégrale de toute fonction rationnelle

$$\int \frac{F_1(x)}{F(x)}\,dx = \sum A \log(x-a) - \sum \frac{A_1}{x-a} - \ldots - \frac{1}{n} \sum \frac{A_n}{(x-a)^n},$$

où l'on voit figurer une partie transcendante et une partie algébrique qui donnent lieu aux remarques suivantes.

I. Nous observerons d'abord qu'en supposant réels les polynomes $F(x)$ et $F_1(x)$, les racines du dénominateur peuvent être imaginaires, de sorte qu'il est nécessaire de mettre le résultat obtenu sous une forme explicitement réelle. Or, on sait que les racines imaginaires seront conjuguées deux à deux; de plus, qu'elles seront de même ordre de multiplicité, et qu'en les désignant par a et b les numérateurs des fractions simples correspondantes

$$\frac{A_i}{(x-a)^{i+1}}, \quad \frac{B_i}{(x-b)^{i+1}}$$

seront respectivement exprimés de la même manière en fonction rationnelle de a et b. Ce seront donc aussi des quantités imaginaires conjuguées, et les termes qui en résultent dans la partie algébrique de l'intégrale, à savoir

$$-\frac{1}{i}\frac{A_i}{(x-a)^i}, \quad -\frac{1}{i}\frac{B_i}{(x-b)^i},$$

donnent, par les réductions ordinaires, une somme réelle. Mais, dans la partie transcendante, il sera nécessaire, pour effectuer cette réduction, d'employer l'expression des logarithmes des quantités imaginaires

$$\log(x-\alpha-\beta\sqrt{-1}) = \frac{1}{2}\log[(x-\alpha)^2+\beta^2] + \sqrt{-1}\,\text{arc tang}\,\frac{x-\alpha}{\beta};$$

---

[1] On supposera que n soit le plus grand des nombres α, β, ..., λ, et qu'on attribue des valeurs nulles à ceux des numérateurs A_n, B_n, ..., L_n dont les indices surpasseraient respectivement α, β, ..., λ.

et, en faisant

$$a = \alpha + \beta\sqrt{-1}, \qquad A = P + Q\sqrt{-1},$$
$$b = \alpha - \beta\sqrt{-1}, \qquad B = P - Q\sqrt{-1},$$

on trouvera facilement

$$\begin{aligned} &A \log(x - a) + B \log(x - b) \\ &\quad = P \log[(x - \alpha)^2 + \beta^2] - 2Q \operatorname{arc\,tang} \frac{x - \alpha}{\beta}. \end{aligned}$$

Ce résultat peut également s'obtenir par l'intégration directe de la somme des fractions imaginaires conjuguées

$$\frac{P + Q\sqrt{-1}}{x - \alpha - \beta\sqrt{-1}} + \frac{P - Q\sqrt{-1}}{x - \alpha + \beta\sqrt{-1}} = \frac{2P(x - \alpha) - 2Q\beta}{(x - \alpha)^2 + \beta^2}.$$

Écrivant, en effet,

$$\int \frac{2P(x - \alpha) - 2Q\beta}{(x - \alpha)^2 + \beta^2}\, dx = P \int \frac{2(x - \alpha)\, dx}{(x - \alpha)^2 + \beta^2} - 2Q \int \frac{\beta\, dx}{(x - \alpha)^2 + \beta^2},$$

on a d'abord

$$\int \frac{2(x - \alpha)\, dx}{(x - \alpha)^2 + \beta^2} = \int \frac{d[(x - \alpha)^2 + \beta^2]}{(x - \alpha)^2 + \beta^2} = \log[(x - \alpha)^2 + \beta^2];$$

faisant ensuite $x - \alpha = \beta z$, il viendra

$$\int \frac{\beta\, dx}{(x - \alpha)^2 + \beta^2} = \int \frac{dz}{z^2 + 1} = \operatorname{arc\,tang} z,$$

et, par suite,

$$\int \frac{\beta\, dx}{(x - \alpha)^2 + \beta^2} = \operatorname{arc\,tang} \frac{x - \alpha}{\beta},$$

de sorte que nous aurons, comme précédemment,

$$\int \frac{2P(x - \alpha) - 2Q\beta}{(x - \alpha)^2 + \beta^2}\, dx = P \log[(x - \alpha)^2 + \beta^2] - 2Q \operatorname{arc\,tang} \frac{x - \alpha}{\beta}.$$

II. La formule

$$\int \frac{F_1(x)}{F(x)}\, dx = \sum A \log(x - a) - \sum \frac{A_1}{x - a} - \ldots - \frac{1}{n} \sum \frac{A_n}{(x - a)^n}$$

montre que le second membre sera simplement algébrique, lorsque les constantes A, B, ..., L seront toutes nulles. Ces conditions, qui sont suffisantes, sont évidemment nécessaires; car, si l'on égale pour un instant à une fraction rationnelle la quantité

$$\sum A \log(x-a) = \int \sum \frac{A}{x-a}\,dx,$$

et qu'on prenne la dérivée de cette fonction rationnelle après l'avoir décomposée en fractions simples, on fera ainsi disparaître toutes les fractions partielles dont les dénominateurs sont du premier degré. On ne pourra donc reproduire l'expression $\sum \frac{A}{x-a}$, la décomposition en fractions simples n'étant possible que d'une seule manière.

Remarquons aussi que la partie algébrique de l'intégrale est de la forme $\frac{\mathfrak{F}(x)}{(x-a)^\alpha (x-b)^\beta \ldots (x-l)^\lambda}$, $\mathfrak{F}(x)$ étant un polynome entier qu'on peut facilement obtenir, comme on va le voir, à l'aide des développements en série suivant les puissances décroissantes de la variable, de l'intégrale et de la partie transcendante. On forme le premier en supposant qu'on ait, par la division algébrique,

$$\frac{F_1(x)}{F(x)} = \frac{\omega}{x} + \frac{\omega_1}{x^2} + \frac{\omega_2}{x^3} + \ldots;$$

de là, nous tirons, en effet, en intégrant les deux membres,

$$\int \frac{F_1(x)}{F(x)}\,dx = \omega \log x - \frac{\omega_1}{x} - \frac{\omega_2}{2x^2} - \ldots.$$

Quant au second, il suffit d'employer la série élémentaire

$$\frac{1}{x-a} = \frac{1}{x} + \frac{a}{x^2} + \frac{a^2}{x^3} + \ldots,$$

pour en conclure

$$\sum \frac{A}{x-a} = \frac{\Sigma A}{x} + \frac{\Sigma A a}{x^2} + \frac{\Sigma A a^2}{x^3} + \ldots,$$

puis, en intégrant,

$$\Sigma A \log(x-a) = \Sigma A \log x - \frac{\Sigma A a}{x} - \frac{\Sigma A a^2}{2x^2} - \ldots$$

Nous obtenons ainsi la relation

$$\frac{\mathfrak{F}(x)}{(x-a)^\alpha(x-b)^\beta\ldots(x-l)^\lambda}$$
$$=(\Sigma\mathrm{A}-\omega)\log x+\frac{\omega_1-\Sigma\mathrm{A}a}{x}+\frac{\omega_2-\Sigma\mathrm{A}a^2}{2x^2}+\ldots,$$

où le terme logarithmique, dans le second membre, doit nécessairement disparaître, un tel terme ne pouvant provenir du développement d'une fonction rationnelle suivant les puissances descendantes de la variable. Nous avons donc la condition

$$\Sigma\mathrm{A}=\omega,$$

dont il est souvent fait usage, surtout dans le cas où le degré de $\mathrm{F}_1(x)$ étant inférieur de deux unités à celui de $\mathrm{F}(x)$, on a $\omega=0$ (¹).

Soit maintenant, pour abréger,

$$\frac{\omega_n-\Sigma\mathrm{A}a^n}{n}=\pi_n,$$

le polynome $\mathfrak{F}(x)$, que nous nous proposons de déterminer, sera donné par cette expression

$$\mathfrak{F}(x)=(x-a)^\alpha(x-b)^\beta\ldots(x-l)^\lambda\left(\frac{\pi_1}{x}+\frac{\pi_2}{x^2}+\frac{\pi_3}{x^3}+\ldots\right),$$

où il est nécessaire que les termes en nombre infini contenant x en dénominateur se détruisent, de sorte qu'il suffira d'en extraire la partie entière. Soit, à cet effet,

$$(x-a)^\alpha(x-b)^\beta\ldots(x-l)^\lambda=x^m+p_1x^{m-1}+p_2x^{m-2}+\ldots+p_m;$$

on trouve sur-le-champ

$$\mathfrak{F}(x)=\pi_2(x^{m-1}+p_1x^{m-2}+\ldots+p_{m-1})$$
$$+\pi_2(x^{m-2}+p_1x^{m-3}+\ldots+p_{m-2})+\ldots+\pi_{m-1}(x+p_1)+\pi_m,$$

et nous voyons qu'on pourra s'arrêter dans les développements de

(¹) Les quantités A, B, ..., L étant les résidus de la fonction $\frac{\mathrm{F}_1(x)}{\mathrm{F}(x)}$ correspondant aux diverses racines du dénominateur, la somme $\Sigma\mathrm{A}$ a reçu de Cauchy la dénomination de *résidu intégral* de cette fonction.

l'intégrale et de la partie transcendante aux termes en $\frac{1}{x^m}\cdot$ Mais nous allons reprendre, par une méthode plus approfondie, cette recherche importante de la partie algébrique de l'intégrale

$$\int \frac{F_1(x)}{F(x)}\,dx.$$

Nous nous proposons, en effet, de la déterminer de manière à obtenir la somme effectuée des fractions simples données par la formule générale, de sorte que la connaissance des racines de l'équation $F(x) = 0$ ne sera plus nécessaire que pour former la partie transcendante $\sum A \log(x-a)$.

III. Dans ce but, on commencera par mettre le dénominateur au moyen de la théorie des racines égales, sous la forme

$$F(x) = N^{n+1} P^{p+1} Q^{q+1} \ldots S^{s+1},$$

N, P, Q, ..., S étant des polynomes tels que l'équation

$$NPQ\ldots S = 0$$

n'ait que des racines simples. Nous remplaçons ensuite la décomposition en fractions simples par celle-ci :

$$\frac{F_1(x)}{F(x)} = \frac{\mathfrak{N}}{N^{n+1}} + \frac{\mathfrak{P}}{P^{p+1}} + \frac{\mathfrak{Q}}{Q^{q+1}} + \ldots + \frac{\mathfrak{S}}{S^{s+1}},$$

où $\mathfrak{N}$, $\mathfrak{P}$, $\mathfrak{Q}$, ..., $\mathfrak{S}$ sont des fonctions entières qu'on obtient par la méthode suivante.

Je me fonderai sur le procédé algébrique que je vais rappeler, et par lequel, étant donnés deux polynomes premiers entre eux U et V, on peut en déterminer deux autres A et B, tels qu'on ait

$$AV + BU = 1,$$

et, par conséquent,

$$\frac{A}{U} + \frac{B}{V} = \frac{1}{UV}.$$

Effectuons sur U et V la recherche du plus grand commun diviseur de manière à obtenir ces relations, où Q, Q_1, Q_2, ... sont les quotients, et R, R_1, R_2, ... les restes successifs, savoir

$$\begin{aligned} U &= VQ + R, \\ V &= RQ_1 + R_1, \\ R &= R_1 Q_2 + R_2. \\ &\ldots\ldots\ldots \end{aligned}$$

Les valeurs qu'on en tire, savoir

$$\begin{aligned} R &= U - VQ, \\ R_1 &= V(1 + QQ_1) - UQ_1, \\ &\ldots\ldots\ldots, \end{aligned}$$

montrent qu'un reste de rang quelconque s'exprime an moyen des polynomes U et V par une combinaison de la forme

$$AV + BU,$$

où A et B sont des fonctions entières. Or, le dernier de ces restes est, dans l'hypothèse admise, une simple constante, ce qui démontre et donne le moyen de former la relation annoncée.

Cela posé, soit

$$U = N^{n+1}, \qquad V = P^{p+1} Q^{q+1} \ldots S^{s+1};$$

nous pouvons écrire

$$\frac{1}{UV} = \frac{1}{F(x)} = \frac{A}{N^{n+1}} + \frac{B}{P^{p+1} Q^{q+1} \ldots S^{s+1}},$$

puis, en multipliant par $F_1(x)$, et faisant $\mathfrak{N} = AF_1(x)$,

$$\frac{F_1(x)}{F(x)} = \frac{\mathfrak{N}}{N^{n+1}} + \frac{BF_1(x)}{P^{p+1} Q^{q+1} \ldots S^{s+1}}.$$

Maintenant il est clair qu'en opérant sur la fraction

$$\frac{BF_1(x)}{P^{p+1} Q^{q+1} \ldots S^{s+1}},$$

comme sur la proposée, on la décomposera pareillement en un terme $\frac{\mathfrak{P}}{P^{p+1}}$ et une nouvelle fraction dont le dénominateur ne renfermera que les facteurs de $F(x)$ autres que N^{n+1} et P^{p+1}. Continuant donc les mêmes opérations jusqu'à l'épuisement complet de ces facteurs, on réalisera ainsi la décomposition que nous voulions obtenir de $\frac{F_1(x)}{F(x)}$ sous la forme

$$\frac{F_1(x)}{F(x)} = \frac{\mathfrak{N}}{N^{n+1}} + \frac{\mathfrak{P}}{P^{p+1}} + \ldots + \frac{\mathfrak{S}}{S^{s+1}}.$$

On en tire

$$\int \frac{F_1(x)}{F(x)} dx = \int \frac{\mathfrak{N}}{N^{n+1}} dx + \int \frac{\mathfrak{P}}{P^{p+1}} dx + \ldots + \int \frac{\mathfrak{S}}{S^{s+1}} dx,$$

les intégrations portant, comme on voit, sur des expressions toutes semblables, qu'on traite de la manière suivante.

IV. J'observe que N, n'ayant pas de facteurs multiples, est premier avec la dérivée N'; de sorte qu'on pourra déterminer deux polynomes A et B remplissant la condition

$$BN - N'A = 1.$$

Cela étant, nous formerons deux séries de fonctions entières

$$\begin{array}{llll} V_0, & V_1, & \ldots, & V_{n-1}, \\ \mathfrak{N}_1, & \mathfrak{N}_2, & \ldots, & \mathfrak{N}_n, \end{array}$$

par ces relations, où $K, K_1, \ldots, K_{n-1}$ sont des polynomes entièrement arbitraires, savoir

$$\begin{aligned} nV_0 &= A\mathfrak{N} - NK, \\ (n-1)V_1 &= A\mathfrak{N}_1 - NK_1, \\ (n-2)V_2 &= A\mathfrak{N}_2 - NK_2, \\ &\ldots\ldots\ldots\ldots\ldots\ldots, \\ V_{n-1} &= A\mathfrak{N}_{n-1} - NK_{n-1}, \end{aligned}$$

puis, en second lieu,

$$\begin{aligned} \mathfrak{N}_1 &= B\mathfrak{N} - N'K - V'_0, \\ \mathfrak{N}_2 &= B\mathfrak{N}_1 - N'K_1 - V'_1, \\ &\ldots\ldots\ldots\ldots\ldots\ldots, \\ \mathfrak{N}_n &= B\mathfrak{N}_{n-1} - N'K_{n-1} - V'_{n-1}. \end{aligned}$$

Je vais maintenant prouver qu'en faisant

$$U = \mathfrak{N}_n,$$
$$V = V_0 + NV_1 + N^2V_2 + \ldots + N^{n-1}V_{n-1},$$

on a identiquement

$$\frac{\mathfrak{N}}{N^{n+1}} = \frac{U}{N} + \frac{d}{dx}\left(\frac{V}{N^n}\right),$$

d'où

$$\int \frac{\mathfrak{N}}{N^{n+1}}\,dx = \int \frac{U}{N}\,dx + \frac{V}{N^n},$$

de sorte que $\frac{V}{N^n}$ est la partie algébrique de l'intégrale, et $\int \frac{U}{N}\,dx$ la partie transcendante.

Éliminons, à cet effet, A et B entre les trois égalités

$$(n-i)V_i = A\,\mathfrak{N}_i - NK_i,$$
$$\mathfrak{N}_{i+1} = B\,\mathfrak{N}_i - N'K_i - V'_i,$$
$$1 = BN - N'A,$$

ce qui donne

$$N\,\mathfrak{N}_{i+1} = \mathfrak{N}_i + (n-i)N'V_i - NV_i.$$

Nous mettrons cette relation sous la forme suivante :

$$\frac{\mathfrak{N}_i}{N^{n-i+1}} - \frac{\mathfrak{N}_{i+1}}{N^{n-i}} = \frac{d}{dx}\left(\frac{V_i}{N^{n+i}}\right),$$

et, supposant ensuite $i = 0, 1, 2, \ldots, n-1$, nous en conclurons, en ajoutant membre à membre,

$$\frac{\mathfrak{N}}{N^{n+1}} - \frac{\mathfrak{N}_n}{N} = \frac{d}{dx}\left(\frac{V_0}{N^n} + \frac{V_1}{N^{n-1}} + \ldots + \frac{V_{n-1}}{N}\right),$$

ce qui fait bien voir qu'on satisfait à la condition proposée

$$\frac{\mathfrak{N}}{N^{n+1}} = \frac{U}{N} + \frac{d}{dx}\left(\frac{V}{N^n}\right).$$

par les expressions

$$U = \mathfrak{N}_n,$$
$$V = V_0 + NV_1 + N^2V_2 + \ldots + N^{n-1}V_{n-1},$$

comme il s'agissait de le démontrer.

J'ai dit que les polynomes $K, K_1, \ldots, K_{n-1}$ étaient arbitraires; on pourra donc en disposer de manière que les degrés de $V_0, V_1, \ldots, V_{n-1}$ soient moindres que le degré de N; on pourra aussi les supposer tous nuls, ce qui donne, par exemple,

$$n V_0 = \mathfrak{M} A,$$
$$n(n-1) V_1 = \mathfrak{M} A(nB - A') - \mathfrak{M}' A^2,$$
$$\cdots\cdots\cdots\cdots$$

Ces deux suppositions se concilient dans le cas de l'intégrale

$$\int \frac{dx}{(x^2-1)^{n+1}},$$

que je choisis comme application de la méthode. Nous aurons alors

$$N = x^2 - 1, \qquad N' = 2x,$$
$$A = -\frac{x}{2}, \qquad B = -1,$$

puis successivement

$$n V_0 = -\frac{x}{2},$$
$$(n-1) V_1 = +\frac{2n-1}{2n}\frac{x}{2},$$
$$(n-2) V_2 = -\frac{(2n-1)(2n-3)}{2n(2n-2)}\frac{x}{2},$$
$$(n-3) V_3 = +\frac{(2n-1)(2n-3)(2n-5)}{2n(2n-2)(2n-4)}\frac{x}{2},$$
$$\cdots\cdots\cdots\cdots,$$

$$\mathfrak{M}_1 = -\frac{2n-1}{2n},$$
$$\mathfrak{M}_2 = +\frac{(2n-1)(2n-3)}{2n(2n-2)},$$
$$\mathfrak{M}_3 = -\frac{(2n-1)(2n-3)(2n-5)}{2n(2n-2)(2n-4)},$$
$$\cdots\cdots\cdots\cdots,$$

d'où ces valeurs, qu'on retrouvera bientôt par une autre voie,

$$U = \mathfrak{M}_n = (-1)^n \frac{(2n-1)(2n-3)\ldots 3.1}{2n(2n-2)\ldots 4.2},$$

$$V = V_0 + NV_1 + N^2 V_2 + \ldots + N^{n-1} V_{n-1}$$
$$= -\frac{x}{2}\left[\frac{1}{n} - \frac{2n-1}{2n}\frac{x^2-1}{n-1} + \frac{(2n-1)(2n-3)}{2n(2n-2)}\frac{(x^2-1)^2}{n-2} - \ldots \right.$$
$$\left. + (-1)^n \frac{(2n-1)(2n-3)\ldots 3}{2n(2n-2)\ldots 4}(x^2-1)^{n-1}\right].$$

De l'intégrale $\int \frac{dx}{(x^2-a^2)^{n+1}}$.

I. Des notions importantes d'Analyse se rattachent à cette expression, qui va nous servir d'exemple pour l'application des méthodes générales d'intégration des fonctions rationnelles. J'observe d'abord qu'on aura pour la partie transcendante et la partie algébrique ces expressions

$$A\log(x-a)+B\log(x+a), \qquad \frac{\mathfrak{F}(x)}{(x^2-a^2)^n},$$

et que, dans la série

$$\frac{\omega}{x}+\frac{\omega_1}{x^2}+\frac{\omega_2}{x^3}+\ldots,$$

les coefficients ω, ω_1, ..., ω_{2n} s'évanouissent. En écrivant, en effet,

$$\frac{1}{(x^2-a^2)^{n+1}}=\frac{1}{x^{2n+2}}\left(1-\frac{a^2}{x^2}\right)^{-(n+1)},$$

la formule du binome donne

$$\frac{1}{(x^2-a^2)^{n+1}}=\frac{1}{x^{2n+2}}+\frac{(n+1)a^2}{x^{2n+4}}+\ldots,$$

d'où

$$\int\frac{dx}{(x^2-a^2)^{n+1}}=-\frac{1}{(2n+1)x^{2n+1}}-\frac{(n+1)a^2}{(2n+3)x^{2n+3}}-\ldots.$$

La première conséquence à tirer de là, c'est qu'ayant

$$A+B=0,$$

la partie transcendante est simplement

$$A\log\frac{x-a}{x+a},$$

et la seconde, c'est que le produit du développement en série de l'intégrale par le facteur $(x^2-a^2)^n$, ne contenant aucune puissance positive de la variable, le polynome $\mathfrak{F}(x)$ se réduit à la partie entière de l'expression $A\log\frac{x-a}{x+a}(x^2-a^2)^n$.

Maintenant A est donné par le coefficient de $\frac{1}{z}$ dans le développement suivant les puissances croissantes de cette quantité, de la fraction $\frac{1}{(x^2-a^2)^{n+1}}$, lorsqu'on y a fait $x = a + z$. Or, ayant

$$\frac{1}{(x^2-a^2)^{n-1}} = \frac{1}{z^{n+1}}(2a+z)^{-n-1},$$

nous sommes amenés à chercher le coefficient de z^n dans le développement de $(2a+z)^{-n-1}$. Partant, à cet effet, de la formule du binome

$$(\alpha+z)^m = \alpha^m + \frac{m}{1}\alpha^{m-1}z + \ldots + \frac{m(m-1)\ldots(m-n+1)}{1.2\ldots n}\alpha^{m-n}z^n + \ldots,$$

il suffira de supposer, dans le terme général,

$$\alpha = 2a, \qquad m = -n-1,$$

pour obtenir la valeur

$$A = \frac{(-1)^n}{(2a)^{2n+1}}\,\frac{(n+1)(n+2)\ldots 2n}{1.2\ldots n},$$

où je remarquerai que le facteur numérique $\frac{(n+1)(n+2)\ldots 2n}{1.2\ldots n}$ est aussi le coefficient du terme moyen dans le développement de la puissance $2n$ du binome. On peut donc lui substituer la quantité $2^{2n}\alpha_n$, en posant

$$\alpha_n = \frac{1.3.5\ldots 2n-1}{2.4.6\ldots 2n},$$

ce qui donnera

$$A = \frac{(-1)^n \alpha_n}{2a^{2n+1}}.$$

Cela posé, il ne nous reste plus qu'à déterminer la partie rationnelle de l'intégrale, en formant le polynome $\mathfrak{F}(x)$ au moyen des termes entiers en x du produit

$$A \log\frac{x+a}{x-a}(x^2-a^2)^n.$$

Mais le calcul et le résultat sont plus simples en employant, à la place de la série

$$\frac{1}{2}\log\left(\frac{x+a}{x-a}\right) = \frac{a}{x} + \frac{1}{3}\frac{a^3}{x^3} + \frac{1}{5}\frac{a^5}{x^5} + \ldots,$$

celle-ci,

$$\frac{1}{2}\log\left(\frac{x+a}{x-a}\right) = x\left[\frac{a}{x^2-a^2} - \frac{2}{3}\frac{a^3}{(x^2-a^2)^2} + \frac{2.4}{3.5}\frac{a^5}{(x^2-a^2)^3} - \frac{2.4.6}{3.5.7}\frac{a^7}{(x^2-a^2)^4} + \ldots\right],$$

qu'on démontre facilement en prenant les dérivées des deux membres, et employant cette identité

$$\frac{d}{da}\left[\frac{a^{2n-1}}{(x^2-a^2)^n}\right] = \frac{(2n-1)a^{2n-2}}{(x^2-a^2)^n} + \frac{2a^{2n}}{(x^2-a^2)^{n+1}}.$$

La partie entière qui résulte de la multiplication par $(x^2-a^2)^n$ se présente, en effet, sous la forme

$$x\left[a(x^2-a^2)^{n-1} - \frac{2}{3}a^3(x^2-a^2)^{n-2} + \frac{2.4}{3.5}a^5(x^2-a^2)^{n-3} - \ldots - (-1)^n\frac{2.4\ldots 2n-2}{3.5\ldots 2n-1}a^{2n-1}\right],$$

et il vient, par suite,

$$\mathfrak{F}(x) = 2Ax\left[(x^2-a^2)^{n-1} - \frac{2}{3}a^2(x^2-a^2)^{n-2} + \frac{2.4}{3.5}a^4(x^2-a^2)^{n-3} - \ldots - (-1)^n\frac{2.4\ldots 2n-2}{3.5\ldots 2n-1}a^{2n-2}\right],$$

ou, en employant le facteur A sous la forme

$$A = \frac{(-1)^n}{2a^{2n+1}}\frac{1.3.5\ldots(2n-1)}{2.4.6\ldots 2n},$$

et renversant l'ordre des termes,

$$\mathfrak{F}(x) = -\frac{x}{2}\left[\frac{1}{na^2} - \frac{2n-1}{2n}\frac{x^2-a^2}{(n-1)a^4} + \frac{(2n-1)(2n-3)}{2n(2n-2)a^6}\frac{(x^2-a^2)^2}{n-2} - \ldots\right];$$

c'est précisément le résultat trouvé précédemment, dans le cas de $a=1$.

II. L'intégrale $\int \frac{dx}{(x^2-a^2)^{n+1}}$ peut encore s'obtenir au moyen d'un changement de variables en posant

$$\frac{x-a}{x+a}=y.$$

Cette substitution donne en effet

$$x=a\frac{1+y}{1-y},\qquad dx=\frac{2a\,dy}{(1-y)^2},$$

d'où, par conséquent,

$$\int\frac{dx}{(x^2-a^2)^{n+1}}=\frac{1}{(2a)^{2n+1}}\int\frac{(y-1)^{2n}\,dy}{y^{n+1}},$$

et l'intégration relative à la nouvelle variable s'effectue aisément comme il suit. Soit en désignant, pour abréger, les coefficients numériques par N_1, N_2, N_3, ...,

$$(y-1)^{2n}=y^{2n}+N_1y^{2n-1}+N_2y^{2n-2}+\ldots+N_1y+1,$$

nous écrirons, en rapprochant les termes équidistants des extrêmes et isolant le terme du milieu y^n,

$$(y-1)^{2n}=(y^{2n}+1)+N_1(y^{2n-1}+y)+N_2(y^{2n-2}+y^2)+\ldots+N_ny^n,$$

de sorte qu'il viendra

$$\frac{(y-1)^{2n}}{y^{n+1}}=\left(y^{n-1}+\frac{1}{y^{n+1}}\right)+N_1\left(y^{n-2}+\frac{1}{y^n}\right)$$
$$+N_2\left(y^{n-3}+\frac{1}{y^{n-1}}\right)+\ldots+\frac{N_n}{y},$$

et, par suite,

$$\int\frac{(y-1)^{2n}\,dy}{y^{n+1}}=\frac{1}{n}\left(y^n-\frac{1}{y^n}\right)+\frac{N_1}{n-1}\left(y^{n-1}-\frac{1}{y^{n-1}}\right)$$
$$+\frac{N_2}{n-2}\left(y^{n-2}-\frac{1}{y^{n-2}}\right)+\ldots+N_n\log y.$$

Cette formule doit coïncider, en y remplaçant y par $\frac{x-a}{x+a}$, avec celle que donne la première méthode, et, en effet, la partie logarithmique est la même, car le coefficient moyen N_n de la puissance $(y-1)^{2n}$ a précisément pour valeur

$$(-1)^n\frac{(n+1)(n+2)\ldots2n}{1.2\ldots n}.$$

Quant à l'égalité des parties rationnelles, elle conduit, en posant

$$x = a\sqrt{-1}\cot\frac{1}{2}\varphi,$$

d'où

$$y = \cos\varphi + \sqrt{-1}\sin\varphi,$$

à l'identité suivante :

$$\begin{aligned}\frac{\sin n\varphi}{n} &+ N_1\frac{\sin(n-1)\varphi}{n-1} + N_2\frac{\sin(n-2)\varphi}{n-2} + \ldots \\ &= (-1)^{n-1}\frac{(n+1)(n+2)\ldots 2n}{1.2\ldots n}\cot\frac{1}{2}\varphi \\ &\times\left(\sin^2\frac{1}{2}\varphi + \frac{2}{3}\sin^4\frac{1}{2}\varphi + \frac{2.4}{3.5}\sin^6\frac{1}{2}\varphi + \ldots\right. \\ &\left.+\frac{2.4\ldots(2n-2)}{3.5\ldots(2n-1)}\sin^{2n}\frac{1}{2}\varphi\right);\end{aligned}$$

mais, sans m'y arrêter, voici un troisième procédé entièrement différent des précédents, et qui servira de transition pour arriver aux méthodes propres essentiellement à l'intégration des fonctions algébriques.

Soit $u = (x^2 - a^2)^m$, l'exposant m étant quelconque, on aura, en différentiant deux fois de suite,

$$\frac{1}{2m}\frac{du}{dx} = x(x^2 - a^2)^{m-1},$$

$$\frac{1}{2m}\frac{d^2u}{dx^2} = (x^2 - a^2)^{m-1} + (2m-2)x^2(x^2-a^2)^{m-2}.$$

Or, on peut écrire

$$\begin{aligned}\frac{1}{2m}\frac{d^2u}{dx^2} &= (x^2-a^2)^{m-1} + (2m-2)(x^2-a^2+a^2)(x^2-a^2)^{m-2} \\ &= (2m-1)(x^2-a^2)^{m-1} + a^2(2m-2)(x^2-a^2)^{m-2}.\end{aligned}$$

de sorte qu'il vient, en multipliant les deux membres par dx et intégrant,

$$\begin{aligned}\frac{1}{2m}\frac{du}{dx} &= x(x^2-a^2)^{m-1} \\ &= (2m-1)\int(x^2-a^2)^{m-1}\,dx + a^2(2m-2)\int(x^2-a)^{m-2}\,dx.\end{aligned}$$

Faisons maintenant

$$m = 1 - n,$$

et l'on obtiendra

$$\frac{x}{(x^2-a^2)^n} = -(2n-1)\int \frac{dx}{(x^2-a^2)^n} - 2na^2 \int \frac{dx}{(x^2-a^2)^{n+1}},$$

ou bien

$$2na^2 \int \frac{dx}{(x^2-a^2)^{n+1}} = -(2n-1)\int \frac{dx}{(x^2-a^2)^n} - \frac{x}{(x^2-a^2)^n},$$

et, par conséquent, pour $n = 1, 2, 3, \ldots$,

$$2a^2 \int \frac{x}{(x^2-a^2)^2} = -\int \frac{dx}{x^2-a^2} - \frac{x}{x^2-a^2},$$

$$4a^2 \int \frac{dx}{(x^2-a^2)^3} = -3\int \frac{dx}{(x^2-a^2)^2} - \frac{x}{(x^2-a^2)^2},$$

$$6a^2 \int \frac{dx}{(x^2-a^2)^4} = -5\int \frac{dx}{(x^2-a^2)^3} - \frac{x}{(x^2-a^2)^3},$$

....

Ces relations successives conduisent évidemment à exprimer l'intégrale relative à un exposant quelconque $\int \frac{dx}{(x^2-a^2)^{n+1}}$, au moyen de celle-ci $\int \frac{dx}{x^2-a^2}$, et d'une fonction rationnelle de x; un calcul facile donne en effet pour résultat

$$a^{2n} \int \frac{dx}{(x^2-a^2)^{n+1}} = (-1)^n \frac{1.3.5\ldots(2n-1)}{2.4.6\ldots 2n}\left[\int \frac{dx}{x^2-a^2} + f_n(x)\right],$$

en posant

$$f_n(x) = x\left[\frac{1}{x^2-a^2} - \frac{2}{3}\frac{a^2}{(x^2-a^2)^2} + \frac{2.4}{3.5}\frac{a^4}{(x^2-a^2)^3} - \ldots \right.$$
$$\left. - (-1)^n \frac{2.4\ldots(2n-2)}{3.5\ldots(2n-1)}\frac{a^{2n-2}}{(x^2-a^2)^n}\right].$$

Et, si l'on veut le démontrer, on observera qu'en changeant n en $n-1$, il vient

$$a^{2n-2} \int \frac{dx}{(x^2-a^2)^n} = (-1)^{n-1} \frac{1.3\ldots(2n-3)}{2.4\ldots(2n-2)}\left[\int \frac{dx}{x^2-a^2} + f_{n-1}(x)\right],$$

de sorte qu'en substituant dans la relation générale

$$2na^2 \int \frac{dx}{(x^2-a^2)^{n+1}} = -(2n-1)\int \frac{dx}{(x^2-a^2)^n} - \frac{x}{(x^2-a^2)^n},$$

nous obtenons la condition

$$f_n(x) = f_{n-1}(x) - (-1)^n \frac{2.4\ldots(2n-2)}{3.5\ldots(2n-1)} \frac{a^{2n-2}x}{(x^2-a^2)^n},$$

qui est satisfaite d'elle-même. La fonction $f_n(x)$ donne ainsi, pour la partie rationnelle de l'intégrale proposée, l'intégrale

$$\frac{(-1)^n}{a^{2n}} \frac{1.3.5\ldots(2n-1)}{2.4.6\ldots2n} \frac{x}{(x^2-a^2)^n}$$
$$\times \left[(x^2-a^2)^{n-1} - \frac{2}{3}a^2(x^2-a^2)^{n-2} + \frac{2.4}{3.5}a^4(x^2-a^2)^{n-3} - \ldots\right],$$

qui, d'après l'expression du coefficient A, coïncide bien avec celle qui a été obtenue précédemment sous la forme $\dfrac{\mathfrak{F}(x)}{(x^2-a^2)^n}$, et quant à la partie transcendante, l'identité

$$\frac{2a}{x^2-a^2} = \frac{1}{x-a} - \frac{1}{x+a}$$

donne sur-le-champ

$$\int \frac{dx}{x^2-a^2} = \frac{1}{2a} \log \frac{x-a}{x+a}.$$

III. La détermination du polynome $\mathfrak{F}(x)$, dans l'équation

$$\int \frac{dx}{(x^2-a^2)^{n+1}} = \text{A} \log \frac{x-a}{x+a} + \frac{\mathfrak{F}(x)}{(x^2-a^2)^n},$$

a été obtenue par cette remarque très simple qu'en l'écrivant ainsi

$$\mathfrak{F}(x) = \text{A}(x^2-a^2)^n \log \frac{x+a}{x-a} + (x^2-a^2)^n \int \frac{dx}{(x^2-a^2)^{n+1}},$$

le développement suivant les puissances descendantes de la variable de l'expression $(x^2-a^2)^n \int \frac{dx}{(x^2-a^2)^{n+1}}$ est de la forme $\frac{\alpha}{x} + \frac{\beta}{x^2} + \ldots$, sans contenir aucune partie entière en x. Or, il résulte encore de cette remarque une conséquence importante que voici. Faisons, pour plus de simplicité, $a = 1$, et prenons les dérivées d'ordre n des deux membres dans la relation

$$\mathfrak{F}(x) = \text{A}(x^2-1)^n \log \frac{x+1}{x-1} + \frac{\alpha}{x} + \frac{\beta}{x^2} + \ldots.$$

A l'égard du produit $(x^2 - 1)^n \log \frac{x+1}{x-1}$, il faudra, en posant

$$U = (x^2 - 1)^n, \qquad V = \log \frac{x+1}{x-1},$$

appliquer la formule

$$\frac{d^n UV}{dx^n} = \frac{d^n U}{dx^n} V + \frac{n}{1} \frac{d^{n-1} U}{dx^{n-1}} \frac{dV}{dx} + \frac{n(n-1)}{1.2} \frac{d^{n-2} U}{dx^{n-2}} \frac{d^2 V}{dx^2} + \ldots,$$

dont le premier terme $\frac{d^n (x^2 - 1)^n}{dx^n} \log \frac{x+1}{x-1}$ sera seul à dépendre du logarithme, les autres étant tous rationnels et même entiers. On a effectivement

$$\begin{aligned} \frac{d^a \log \frac{x+1}{x-1}}{dx^a} &= \frac{d^a}{dx^a} [\log(x+1) - \log(x-1)] \\ &= (-1)^{a-1} 1.2 \ldots (a-1) \left[\frac{1}{(x+1)^a} - \frac{1}{(x-1)^a} \right], \end{aligned}$$

et comme $\frac{d^{n-a} (x^2 - 1)^n}{dx^{n-a}}$ contient en facteur $(x^2 - 1)^a$, le produit est entier en x. Réunissant ces termes au polynome $\frac{d^n \mathfrak{F}(x)}{dx^n}$, en les faisant passer dans le premier membre, que je désignerai alors par $F_n(x)$, nous parviendrons à cette relation.

$$\begin{aligned} F_n(x) = {} & A \frac{d^n (x^2 - 1)^n}{dx^n} \log \frac{x+1}{x-1} \\ & + (-1)^n 1.2 \ldots n \left[\frac{\alpha}{x^{n+1}} - \frac{(n+1)\beta}{x^{n+2}} + \ldots \right], \end{aligned}$$

à laquelle je m'arrêterai un moment. Elle montre qu'en multipliant par le polynome du $n^{\text{ième}}$ degré $\frac{d^n (x^2 - 1)^n}{dx^n}$ la série infinie

$$\log \frac{x+1}{x-1} = 2 \left(\frac{1}{x} + \frac{1}{3x^3} + \frac{1}{5x^5} + \ldots \right),$$

le produit manque des puissances $\frac{1}{x}, \frac{1}{x^2}, \frac{1}{x^3}, \ldots, \frac{1}{x^n}$, et il en résulte qu'en divisant $F_n(x)$ par $\frac{d^n (x^2 - 1)^n}{dx^n}$, le quotient, ordonné par rapport aux puissances décroissantes de la variable, coïncide avec cette série, aux termes près de l'ordre $\frac{1}{x^{2n+1}}$. Cet exemple de l'approximation d'une transcendante par une fonction rationnelle, qui est intéressant en lui-même, recevra plus tard une application importante. Il met en évidence une propriété entièrement caractéristique des expressions $\frac{d^n(x^2-1)^n}{dx^n}$ auxquelles on donne le nom de *polynomes de Legendre*, et qu'on désigne par X_n en posant

$$X_n = \frac{1}{2.4.6\ldots 2n}\frac{d^n(x^2-1)^n}{dx^n}.$$

Ces fonctions, introduites en Analyse par l'illustre géomètre à l'occasion de ses recherches sur l'attraction des sphéroïdes et la figure des planètes, sont d'une grande importance, et donnent lieu à plusieurs théorèmes remarquables, dont l'un nous servira de nouvelle application du procédé de l'intégration par parties, fondé sur la formule

$$\int U\frac{d^{n+1}V}{dx^{n+1}}\,dx = \Theta - (-1)^n\int V\frac{d^{n+1}U}{dx^{n+1}}\,dx$$

où

$$\Theta = U\frac{d^nV}{dx^n} - \frac{dU}{dx}\frac{d^{n-1}V}{dx^{n-1}} + \frac{d^2U}{dx^2}\frac{d^{n-2}V}{dx^{n-2}} + \ldots.$$

Soit, en effet, $V = (x^2-1)^{n+1}$, en supposant que U soit un polynome arbitraire de degré n, l'intégrale du second membre disparaîtra, et nous obtiendrons d'abord

$$\int U\frac{d^{n+1}(x^2-1)^{n+1}}{dx^{n+1}}\,dx = \Theta.$$

J'observe ensuite que, les dérivées successives de $(x^2-1)^{n+1}$ jusqu'à celle d'ordre n, contenant en facteur x^2-1, Θ s'évanouit pour $x=1$ et $x=-1$, et il en résulte que l'intégrale définie

$$\int_{-1}^{+1} U\frac{d^{n+1}(x^2-1)^{n+1}}{dx^{n+1}}\,dx,$$

différence des valeurs de Θ pour $x=1$ et $x=-1$, est nulle.

Le théorème exprimé par l'équation

$$\int_{-1}^{+1} UX_{n+1}\,dx = 0$$

appartient exclusivement aux polynomes de Legendre; car, en

désignant un moment par $F(x)$ une autre fonction entière de degré $n+1$, telle que l'on ait aussi

$$\int_{-1}^{+1} UF(x)\,dx = 0,$$

on en conclurait, quelle que soit la constante k,

$$\int_{-1}^{+1} UF(x)\,dx - k\int_{-1}^{+1} UX_{n+1}\,dx = 0,$$

ou bien

$$\int_{-1}^{+1} U[F(x) - kX_{n+1}]\,dx = 0.$$

Or, en prenant k, de manière que $F(x) - kX_{n+1}$ s'abaisse au $n^{\text{ième}}$ degré, en posant alors

$$U = F(x) - kX_{n+1},$$

nous trouvons la condition suivante :

$$\int_{-1}^{+1} U^2\,dx = 0.$$

Elle exige évidemment que U s'évanouisse identiquement; car autrement, l'intégrale ne serait jamais nulle, tous les éléments étant positifs, et il en résulte

$$F(x) = kX_{n+1}.$$

INTÉGRATION

DES

FONCTIONS TRANSCENDANTES.

Sur l'intégrale des fonctions circulaires (*Proceedings of the London mathematical Society*, t. IV, 1872, pp. 164-175).
Cours d'Analyse de l'École Polytechnique, 1873, pp. 320-351.

En désignant par $f(x)$ une fonction rationnelle de la variable, et par $f(\sin x, \cos x)$ une fonction rationnelle de $\sin x$ et $\cos x$, les seules expressions, dans le champ infini des quantités transcendantes, dont nous puissions aborder l'intégration sont celles-ci :

$$f(\sin x, \cos x), \quad e^{\omega x} f(x), \quad e^{\omega x} f(\sin x, \cos x),$$

et nous n'aurons point, pour parvenir à notre but, à exposer des principes nouveaux, ni des méthodes propres qui en soient la conséquence. On va retrouver, en effet, d'une part la décomposition en fractions simples, et de l'autre le procédé pour obtenir, lorsqu'elle est possible sous forme algébrique, l'intégrale d'une fonction dépendant de la racine carrée d'un polynome. Il ne sera pas toutefois sans profit d'employer ainsi, dans des conditions différentes, les méthodes qui nous sont déjà familières ; elles recevront de ces applications un nouveau jour qui en fera mieux saisir la portée et le caractère. On verra surtout comment cette recherche des procédés d'intégration conduit naturellement à approfondir, au point de vue de l'Analyse générale, la nature des expressions $(f \sin x, \cos x)$, qui sont le type des fonctions périodiques, en préparant ainsi ce que nous aurons à dire, dans la seconde partie du Cours, des fonctions à double période.

De l'intégrale $\int f(\sin x, \cos x)\, dx$.

1. Nous partirons de la transformation en une fonction rationnelle de la quantité transcendante $f(\sin x, \cos x)$, qu'on obtient en posant

$$e^{x\sqrt{-1}} = z.$$

De là résulte, en effet,

$$\sin x = \frac{z^2 - 1}{2z\sqrt{-1}}, \qquad \cos x = \frac{z^2 + 1}{2z},$$

de sorte qu'on peut faire

$$f(\sin x, \cos x) = \frac{F_1(z)}{F(z)};$$

$F(z)$ et $F_1(z)$ désignent des polynomes entiers en z. Cela posé, je vais montrer que de la décomposition en fractions simples de la fraction rationnelle $\frac{F_1(z)}{F(z)}$ résulte une décomposition en éléments simples, de la fonction transcendante qui en donnera semblablement et d'une manière immédiate l'intégration. Considérant, dans ce but, la quantité $\frac{1}{(z-a)^n}$, qui est le type des fractions simples, je pose

$$a = e^{\alpha\sqrt{-1}},$$

ce qui sera toujours possible en exceptant le cas de $a = 0$, et je remarque qu'on aura

$$\frac{1}{z-a} = \frac{1}{e^{x\sqrt{-1}} - e^{\alpha\sqrt{-1}}} = \frac{e^{-\alpha\sqrt{-1}}}{2}\left(-1 - i\cot\frac{x-\alpha}{2}\right);$$

c'est une conséquence, en effet, de la relation

$$\cot\frac{x}{2} = \sqrt{-1}\,\frac{e^{x\sqrt{-1}} + 1}{e^{x\sqrt{-1}} - 1},$$

mise sous la forme

$$\frac{1}{e^{x\sqrt{-1}} - 1} = \frac{1}{2}\left(- \quad - i\cot\frac{x}{2}\right),$$

quand on y change x en $x-\alpha$. De là résulte une première transformation du groupe des fractions partielles

$$\frac{A}{z-a}+\frac{A}{(z-a)^2}+\ldots+\frac{A_n}{(z-a)^{n+1}}$$

en un polynome entier et du degré $n+1$ en $\cot\frac{x-\alpha}{2}$; mais nous pouvons faire

$$\cot^2 x = -1-\frac{d\cot x}{dx},$$

$$\cot^3 x = -\cot x+\frac{1}{2}\frac{d^2\cot x}{dx^2},$$

$$\ldots\ldots\ldots\ldots\ldots\ldots\ldots\ldots,$$

et la relation identique

$$\cot^{k+1}x = -\cot^{k-1}x-\frac{1}{k}\frac{d\cot^k x}{dx}$$

montre que, de proche en proche, on exprimera linéairement $\cot^n x$ au moyen des dérivées successives de $\cot x$ jusqu'à celle d'ordre $n-1$. Nous parvenons donc à ce nouveau résultat, savoir

$$\frac{A}{z-a}+\frac{A_1}{(z-a)^2}+\ldots+\frac{A_n}{(z-a)^{n+1}}$$
$$= C+\mathcal{A}\cot\frac{1}{2}(x-\alpha)+\mathcal{A}_1\frac{d\cot\frac{1}{2}(x-\alpha)}{dx}+\ldots+\mathcal{A}_n\frac{d^n\cot\frac{1}{2}(x-\alpha)}{dx^n},$$

les constantes $C, \mathcal{A}, \mathcal{A}_1, \ldots, \mathcal{A}_n$ dépendant linéairement des divers numérateurs $A, A_1, \ldots, A_n$. Ce point établi, je mettrai en évidence, si elles existent, les racines nulles du polynome $F(z)$ en faisant

$$F(z) = z^{m+1}(z-a)^{n+1}(z-b)^{p+1}\ldots(z-l)^{s+1},$$

et je modifierai la formule générale de décomposition en fractions simples en réunissant à la partie entière du quotient $\frac{F_1(z)}{F(z)}$ les fractions partielles en $\frac{1}{z}, \frac{1}{z^2}, \ldots, \frac{1}{z^{m-1}}$, de manière à avoir

$$\begin{aligned}\frac{F_1(z)}{F(z)} = \mathfrak{F}(z)&+\frac{A}{z-a}+\frac{A_1}{(z-a)^2}+\ldots+\frac{A_n}{(z-a)^{n+1}}\\ &+\frac{B}{z-b}+\frac{B_1}{(z-b)^2}+\ldots+\frac{B_p}{(z-b)^{p+1}}\\ &\ldots\ldots\ldots\ldots\ldots\ldots\ldots\ldots\\ &+\frac{L}{z-l}+\frac{L_1}{(z-l)^2}+\ldots+\frac{L_s}{(z-l)^{s+1}},\end{aligned}$$

où $\mathfrak{F}(z)$ sera, par conséquent, de la forme $\sum a_k z^k$ avec des puissances entières, mais positives ou négatives, de z. Maintenant nous conclurons de cette formule élémentaire, en revenant à la valeur $z = e^{x\sqrt{-1}}$, l'expression suivante de la fonction $f(\sin x, \cos x)$. La quantité $\mathfrak{F}(x)$, devenant d'abord

$$a_k e^{kx\sqrt{-1}} = \Sigma a_k(\cos kx + \sqrt{-1}\sin kx),$$

nous donne une première partie, que je désignerai par $\Pi(x)$, et qui en sera considérée comme la partie entière. Les fractions partielles donnent ensuite une seconde partie $\Phi(x)$, qui, en posant

$$a = e^{\alpha\sqrt{-1}}, \qquad b = e^{\beta\sqrt{-1}}, \qquad \ldots, \qquad l = e^{\lambda\sqrt{-1}},$$

aura la forme suivante :

$$\begin{aligned}\Phi(x) = \text{const.} &+ \mathcal{A}\cot\tfrac{1}{2}(x-\alpha) + \mathcal{A}_1\frac{d\cot\frac{1}{2}(x-\alpha)}{dx} + \ldots + \mathcal{A}_n\frac{d^n\cot\frac{1}{2}(x-\alpha)}{dx^n}\\ &+ \mathcal{B}\cot\tfrac{1}{2}(x-\beta) + \mathcal{B}_1\frac{d\cot\frac{1}{2}(x-\beta)}{dx} + \ldots + \mathcal{B}_p\frac{d^p\cot\frac{1}{2}(x-\beta)}{dx^p}\\ &\ldots\ldots\ldots\ldots\ldots\ldots\ldots\ldots\ldots\ldots\ldots\ldots\\ &+ \mathcal{L}\cot\tfrac{1}{2}(x-\lambda) + \mathcal{L}_1\frac{d\cot\frac{1}{2}(x-\lambda)}{dx} + \ldots + \mathcal{L}_s\frac{d^s\cot\frac{1}{2}(x-\lambda)}{dx^s}.\end{aligned}$$

La détermination des coefficients $\mathcal{A}$, $\mathcal{B}$, ..., $\mathcal{L}$, $\mathcal{A}_1$, $\mathcal{B}_1$, ... rendra plus complète encore l'analogie de la formule que nous venons d'obtenir

$$f(\sin x, \cos x) = \Pi(x) + \Phi(x),$$

avec celle de la décomposition des fractions rationnelles en fractions simples.

II. Je ferai, dans ce but, en ayant en vue le groupe des coefficients $\mathcal{A}$, $\mathcal{A}_1$, ..., $\mathcal{A}_n$, $x = \alpha + h$, et je développerai les deux membres suivant les puissances croissantes de h. Or, les séries provenant ainsi de la partie entière et de $\cot\frac{1}{2}(x-\beta)$, ..., $\cot\frac{1}{2}(x-\lambda)$ ne contiendront que des puissances entières et positives de h, tandis que la quantité $\cot\frac{1}{2}(x-\alpha)$ et ses dérivées donneront un nombre fini et limité de puissances négatives. Nous avons, en effet,

$$\cot\frac{x-\alpha}{2}=\cot\frac{h}{2}=\frac{2}{h}-\frac{h}{6}-\frac{h^3}{360}-\ldots,$$

et, comme la dérivée de h prise par rapport à x est l'unité, on déduira successivement de cette relation

$$\frac{d\cot\frac{1}{2}(x-\alpha)}{dx}=-\frac{2}{h^2}-\frac{1}{6}-\frac{h^2}{120}-\ldots,$$

$$\frac{d^2\cot\frac{1}{2}(x-\alpha)}{dx^2}=+\frac{4}{h^3}-\frac{h}{60}-\ldots;$$

et, en général, si l'on n'écrit point les puissances positives de h,

$$\frac{d^n\cot\frac{1}{2}(x-\alpha)}{dx^n}=(-1)^n 1.2\ldots n\frac{2}{h^{n+1}}.$$

Le développement du second membre $\Pi(x)+\Phi(x)$ se composant ainsi des termes

$$2\left[\frac{\mathcal{A}}{h}-\frac{\mathcal{A}_1}{h^2}+\frac{1.2\mathcal{A}_2}{h^3}-\ldots+(-1)^n\frac{1.2\ldots n\mathcal{A}_n}{h^{n+1}}\right]$$

et d'une série infinie de puissances positives de h, nous obtiendrons les coefficients $\mathcal{A}$, $\mathcal{A}_1$, ..., $\mathcal{A}_n$, en formant la partie du développement du premier membre $f(\sin x,\cos x)$ qui est composée des seules puissances négatives de h. Supposons à cet effet

$$f[\sin(\alpha+h),\cos(\alpha+h)]=\frac{A}{h}-\frac{A_1}{h^2}+\frac{1.2A_2}{h^3}-\ldots+(-1)^n\frac{1.2\ldots nA_n}{h^{n+1}},$$

on aura immédiatement

$$\mathcal{A}=\frac{1}{2}A,\qquad \mathcal{A}_1=\frac{1}{2}A_1,\qquad \ldots,\qquad \mathcal{A}_n=\frac{1}{2}A_n,$$

et j'ajoute que, si l'on multiplie membre à membre l'égalité précédente avec celle-ci, que donne le théorème de Taylor,

$$\cot\frac{1}{2}(x-\alpha-h)$$
$$=\cot\frac{1}{2}(x-\alpha)-\frac{h}{1}\frac{d\cot\frac{1}{2}(x-\alpha)}{dx}+\frac{h^2}{1.2}\frac{d^2\cot\frac{1}{2}(x-\alpha)}{dx^2}-\ldots$$
$$+(-1)^n\frac{h^n}{1.2\ldots n}\frac{d^n\cot\frac{1}{2}(x-\alpha)}{dx^n}+\ldots,$$

on trouve pour le coefficient divisé par deux, du terme en $\frac{1}{h}$, précisément

$$\mathcal{A}\cot\frac{1}{2}(x-\alpha)+\mathcal{A}_1\frac{d\cot\frac{1}{2}(x-\alpha)}{dx}+\ldots+\mathcal{A}_n\frac{d^n\cot\frac{1}{2}(x-\alpha)}{dx^n}.$$

Le groupe total des *éléments simples*, se rapportant à la quantité $x=\alpha$ qui rend infinie la fonction proposée, est ainsi le demi-résidu correspondant à $h=0$, de l'expression

$$f[\sin(\alpha+h),\ \cos(\alpha+h)]\cot\frac{x-\alpha-h}{2};$$

résultat analogue, comme on voit, à un théorème de Lagrange.

III. Après avoir jusqu'ici suivi pas à pas la théorie de la décomposition des fractions rationnelles en fractions simples, nous allons introduire une considération nouvelle qui a son origine dans la propriété caractéristique de la transcendante $f(\sin x, \cos x)$ d'être périodique. Je remarque que, d'après la relation

$$\cot\frac{x}{2}=\cot x+\operatorname{coséc} x,$$

la fonction $\Phi(x)$ s'exprime en termes de deux formes, à savoir

$$\frac{d^n\cot(x-\alpha)}{dx^n}\quad\text{et}\quad\frac{d^n\operatorname{coséc}(x-\alpha)}{dx^n},$$

les premiers ayant pour période π et les autres se reproduisant en signe contraire lorsqu'on change x en $x+\pi$. Or, à l'égard de

$$\Pi(x)=\Sigma a_k(\cos kx+\sqrt{-1}\sin kx),$$

si l'on fait

$$\theta(x) = \Sigma a_{2k}(\cos 2kx + \sqrt{-1}\sin 2kx)$$

et

$$\eta(x) = \Sigma a_{2k+1}\left[\cos(2k+1)x + \sqrt{-1}\sin(2k+1)x\right],$$

en réunissant d'une part les termes contenant les multiples pairs, et de l'autre les multiples impairs de la variable, on aura de même

$$\theta(x+\pi) = \theta(x), \qquad \eta(x+\pi) = -\eta(x).$$

De là résulte la décomposition de la fonction proposée en deux parties $\Theta(x)$, $\mathrm{H}(x)$, de sorte qu'on aura

$$f(\sin x, \cos x) = \Theta(x) + \mathrm{H}(x),$$

avec les conditions

$$\Theta(x+\pi) = \Theta(x), \qquad \mathrm{H}(x+\pi) = -\mathrm{H}(x),$$

les expressions des nouvelles fonctions introduites étant

$$\begin{aligned}\Theta(x) = \theta(x) &+ \mathcal{A}\cot(x-\alpha) + \mathcal{A}_1\frac{d\cot(x-\alpha)}{dx} + \ldots + \mathcal{A}_n\frac{d^n\cot(x-\alpha)}{dx^n}\\ &+ \mathcal{B}\cot(x-\beta) + \mathcal{B}_1\frac{d\cot(x-\beta)}{dx} + \ldots + \mathcal{B}_p\frac{d^p\cot(x-\beta)}{dx^p}\\ &\ldots\ldots\ldots\ldots\ldots\ldots\ldots\ldots\ldots\ldots\ldots\ldots\\ &+ \mathcal{L}\cot(x-\lambda) + \mathcal{L}_1\frac{d\cot(x-\lambda)}{dx} + \ldots + \mathcal{L}_s\frac{d^s\cot(x-\lambda)}{dx^s}\end{aligned}$$

et

$$\begin{aligned}\mathrm{H}(x) = \eta(x) &+ \mathcal{A}\,\mathrm{coséc}(x-\alpha) + \mathcal{A}_1\frac{d\,\mathrm{coséc}(x-\alpha)}{dx} + \ldots + \mathcal{A}_n\frac{d^n\,\mathrm{coséc}(x-\alpha)}{dx^n}\\ &+ \mathcal{B}\,\mathrm{coséc}(x-\beta) + \mathcal{B}_1\frac{d\,\mathrm{coséc}(x-\beta)}{dx} + \ldots + \mathcal{B}_p\frac{d^p\,\mathrm{coséc}(x-\beta)}{dx^p}\\ &\ldots\ldots\ldots\ldots\ldots\ldots\ldots\ldots\ldots\ldots\ldots\ldots\\ &+ \mathcal{L}\,\mathrm{coséc}(x-\lambda) + \mathcal{L}_1\frac{d\,\mathrm{coséc}(x-\lambda)}{dx} + \ldots + \mathcal{L}_s\frac{d^s\,\mathrm{coséc}(x-\lambda)}{dx^s}.\end{aligned}$$

Nous voyons donc apparaître deux éléments simples distincts, $\cot x$ et $\mathrm{coséc}\,x$ ou $\frac{1}{\sin x}$, appartenant en propre aux fonctions dont la périodicité est celle de $\Theta(x)$ ou $\mathrm{H}(x)$, au lieu de $\cot\frac{x}{2}$ qui, dans le cas général, a le rôle de la quantité $\frac{1}{x}$ à l'égard des fonctions rationnelles. C'est par les applications qu'on reconnaîtra surtout l'utilité de ces distinctions et, pour commencer par un cas facile, j'envisagerai d'abord la fonction $\frac{1}{\cos\alpha - \cos x}$.

J'observe en premier lieu qu'en introduisant la variable $z = e^{x\sqrt{-1}}$, il vient

$$\frac{1}{\cos\alpha - \cos x} = \frac{2z}{2z\cos\alpha - 1 - z^2}.$$

Or, les racines du dénominateur sont évidemment les quantités $e^{\alpha\sqrt{-1}}$, $e^{-\alpha\sqrt{-1}}$, le numérateur est seulement du premier degré ; ainsi la partie entière $\Pi(z)$ n'existe point, et nous aurons

$$\frac{1}{\cos\alpha - \cos x} = \mathrm{C} + \mathcal{A}\cot\frac{x-\alpha}{2} + \mathcal{B}\cot\frac{x+\alpha}{2}.$$

Calculant maintenant les résidus pour $x = \alpha$ et $x = -\alpha$, j'obtiens les quantités

$$\frac{1}{\sin\alpha}, \qquad -\frac{1}{\sin\alpha},$$

et, par suite, en divisant par 2 les valeurs

$$\mathcal{A} = \frac{1}{2\sin\alpha}, \qquad \mathcal{B} = -\frac{1}{2\sin\alpha},$$

de sorte qu'il vient

$$\frac{1}{\cos\alpha - \cos x} = \mathrm{C} + \frac{1}{2\sin\alpha}\left(\cot\frac{x-\alpha}{2} - \cot\frac{x+\alpha}{2}\right).$$

On trouve d'ailleurs sans peine que $\mathrm{C} = 0$; mais voici, pour des cas moins faciles, une détermination directe et immédiate de cette constante. Supposons, en général,

$$f(\sin x, \cos x) = \frac{\mathrm{F}_1(z)}{\mathrm{F}(z)};$$

$\mathrm{F}(z)$ ne contenant point le facteur z et étant de degré au moins égal à celui de $\mathrm{F}_1(z)$, la partie désignée par $\Phi(x)$ existera seule dans l'expression de la fonction, qui sera ainsi

$$\begin{aligned} f(\sin x, \cos x) = C &+ \mathcal{A} \cot \frac{1}{2}(x-\alpha) + \mathcal{A}_1 \frac{d \cot \frac{1}{2}(x-\alpha)}{dx} + \ldots \\ &+ \mathcal{B} \cot \frac{1}{2}(x-\beta) + \mathcal{B}_1 \frac{d \cot \frac{1}{2}(x-\beta)}{dx} + \ldots \\ &\ldots\ldots\ldots\ldots\ldots\ldots\ldots\ldots\ldots\ldots \\ &+ \mathcal{L} \cot \frac{1}{2}(x-\lambda) + \mathcal{L}_1 \frac{d \cot \frac{1}{2}(x-\lambda)}{dx} + \ldots . \end{aligned}$$

Or, je dis qu'en appelant G et H les valeurs de $\frac{F_1(z)}{F(z)}$ pour z nul et infini, on aura

$$C = \frac{1}{2}(G + H).$$

En effet, la relation

$$\cot \frac{x-\alpha}{2} = \sqrt{-1}\, \frac{e^{(x-\alpha)\sqrt{-1}} + 1}{e^{(x-\alpha)\sqrt{-1}} - 1} = \sqrt{-1}\, \frac{z e^{-\alpha\sqrt{-1}} + 1}{z e^{-\alpha\sqrt{-1}} - 1}$$

fait voir qu'en supposant z nul et infini toutes les quantités $\cot \frac{x-\alpha}{2}$ se réduisent à $-\sqrt{-1}$ et $+\sqrt{-1}$; elle montre aussi que leurs dérivées des divers ordres s'évanouissent; nous avons donc

$$\begin{aligned} G &= C - (\mathcal{A} + \mathcal{B} + \ldots + \mathcal{L})\sqrt{-1}, \\ H &= C + (\mathcal{A} + \mathcal{B} + \ldots + \mathcal{L})\sqrt{-1}, \end{aligned}$$

et, par conséquent,

$$\mathcal{A} + \mathcal{B} + \ldots + \mathcal{L} = -\frac{G - H}{2}\sqrt{-1}, \qquad C = \frac{G + H}{2}.$$

Dans l'exemple considéré tout à l'heure, on trouve sur-le-champ $G = 0$, $H = 0$, de sorte que C est nul comme nous l'avons dit.

Soit, en second lieu, l'expression

$$\frac{\sin mx}{\sin nx} = z^{n-m} \frac{z^{2m} - 1}{z^{2n} - 1},$$

les nombres m et n étant entiers. Si l'on suppose $m > n$, on voit qu'il existera une partie entière $\mathrm{H}(x)$, dont voici le calcul. Partant de cette identité

$$z^{n-m}\frac{z^{2m}-1}{z^{2n}-1} = z^{m-n}+z^{n-m}+z^{m-3n}+z^{3n-m}+\ldots$$
$$+z^{m-(2k-1)n}+z^{(2k-1)n-m}+\frac{z^{(2k+1)n-m}-z^{m-(2k-1)n}}{z^{2n}-1},$$

je prends pour k l'entier immédiatement supérieur à $\frac{m-n}{2n}$, de sorte qu'on ait

$$k=\frac{m-n}{2n}+\varepsilon,$$

ε étant positif et moindre que l'unité. Il en résulte que

$$(2k+1)n-m=2\varepsilon n \qquad \text{et} \qquad m-(2k-1)n=2(1-\varepsilon)n;$$

ainsi, dans la fraction du second membre, le numérateur est de degré inférieur au dénominateur. L'identité employée se vérifie d'ailleurs sur-le-champ, car, en remplaçant z par l'exponentielle $e^{x\sqrt{-1}}$, elle se transforme dans l'équation bien connue

$$\frac{\sin mx}{\sin nx}=2\cos(m-n)x+2\cos(m-3n)x+\ldots$$
$$+2\cos[m-(2k-1)n]x-\frac{\sin(2kn-m)x}{\sin nx}.$$

Nous obtenons ainsi

$$\mathrm{H}(x)=2\cos(m-n)x+2\cos(m-3n)x+\ldots+2\cos[m-(2k-1)n]x$$

et

$$\Phi(x)=-\frac{\sin(2kn-m)x}{\sin nx},$$

ou simplement

$$\Phi(x)=-\frac{\sin mx}{\sin nx},$$

en supposant maintenant m inférieur à n, en valeur absolue.

Cela établi, les racines de l'équation $z^{2n}-1=0$ sont données par la formule $z=e^{\frac{k\pi}{n}\sqrt{-1}}$, k prenant les valeurs $0, 1, 2, \ldots, 2n-1$, et si l'on fait $\alpha=\frac{k\pi}{n}$, le résidu de la fonction $\frac{\sin mx}{\sin nx}$ correspondant à $x=\alpha$ sera $\frac{\sin m\alpha}{\sin n\alpha}=\frac{(-1)^k\sin m\alpha}{n}$; et nous obtenons, par conséquent,

$$\frac{\sin mx}{\sin nx} = \frac{1}{2n}\sum(-1)^k \sin m\alpha \cot\frac{1}{2}(x-\alpha).$$

Mais ayant

$$\Phi(x+\pi) = (-1)^{m+n}\Phi(x),$$

la fonction appartiendra à l'espèce $\Theta(x)$ ou $\mathrm{H}(x)$, suivant que $m+n$ sera pair ou impair, de sorte qu'il vient, pour le premier cas,

$$\frac{\sin nx}{\sin mx} = \frac{1}{2n}\sum(-1)^k \sin m\alpha \cot(x-\alpha),$$

et pour le second,

$$\frac{\sin mx}{\sin nx} = \frac{1}{2n}\sum\frac{(-1)^k \sin m\alpha}{\sin(x-\alpha)}.$$

Or, dans les deux cas, les termes des sommes qui correspondent aux valeurs k et $k+n$ sont égaux; on peut donc, en doublant, se borner à prendre $k=1, 2, \ldots, n-1$, le résidu relatif à $k=0$ étant nul.

Soit encore l'expression

$$\cot(x-\alpha)\cot(x-\beta)\ldots\cot(x-\lambda);$$

en désignant par n le nombre des quantités $\alpha, \beta, \ldots, \varkappa, \lambda$ et faisant $a=e^{\alpha\sqrt{-1}}$, $b=e^{\beta\sqrt{-1}}$, ..., $l=e^{\lambda\sqrt{-1}}$, on aura, pour transformée en z,

$$(\sqrt{-1})^n\frac{(z^2+a^2)(z^2+b^2)\ldots(z^2+l^2)}{(z^2-a^2)(z^2-b^2)\ldots(z^2-l^2)}.$$

On voit que le numérateur et le dénominateur sont de même degré; ainsi il n'existe pas de partie entière et nous avons seulement à calculer $\Phi(x)$. Or, les $2n$ racines du dénominateur sont, d'une part, $e^{\alpha\sqrt{-1}}$, $e^{\beta\sqrt{-1}}$, ..., $e^{\lambda\sqrt{-1}}$, et, en outre, ces mêmes quantités changées de signe, c'est-à-dire $e^{(\alpha+\pi)\sqrt{-1}}$, $e^{(\beta+\pi)\sqrt{-1}}$, $e^{(\lambda+\pi)\sqrt{-1}}$; d'ailleurs, ayant $\Phi(x+\pi)=\Phi(x)$, la fonction proposée appartient au type $\Theta(x)$ et ses éléments simples, où figurent les arguments α et $\alpha+\pi$, β et $\beta+\pi$, ..., se réduiront à ceux-ci :

$$\cot(x-\alpha),\quad \cot(x-\beta),\quad \ldots,\quad \cot(x-\lambda).$$

Nous aurons, en conséquence,

$$\Phi(x) = C + \mathcal{A} \cot(x-\alpha) + \mathcal{B} \cot(x-\beta) + \ldots + \mathcal{L} \cot(x-\lambda),$$

$\mathcal{A}, \mathcal{B}, \ldots, \mathcal{L}$ étant les résidus de $\Phi(x)$ pour $x=\alpha$, $x=\beta$, ..., $x=\lambda$, c'est-à-dire

$$\begin{aligned}
\mathcal{A} &= \cot(\alpha-\beta)\cot(\alpha-\gamma)\ldots\cot(\alpha-\lambda),\\
\mathcal{B} &= \cot(\beta-\alpha)\cot(\beta-\gamma)\ldots\cot(\beta-\lambda),\\
&\ldots\ldots\ldots\ldots\ldots\ldots\ldots\ldots,\\
\mathcal{L} &= \cot(\lambda-\alpha)\cot(\lambda-\beta)\ldots\cot(\lambda-\varkappa).
\end{aligned}$$

Enfin la constante C s'obtient par l'équation établie page 63, $C = \frac{1}{2}(G+H)$, au moyen des valeurs

$$G = (-\sqrt{-1})^n, \qquad H = (\sqrt{-1})^n,$$

que prend la transformée en z, pour z nul et infini, ce qui donne simplement $C = \cos\frac{n\pi}{2}$.

On traitera de la même manière l'expression plus générale

$$\frac{F(\sin x, \cos x)}{\sin(x-\alpha)\sin(x-\beta)\ldots\sin(x-\lambda)},$$

où le numérateur est un polynome entier en $\sin x$ et $\cos x$, et, si nous supposons qu'il soit homogène et de degré $n-1$, on sera amené à la relation suivante :

$$\begin{aligned}
&\frac{F(\sin x, \cos x)}{\sin(x-\alpha)\sin(x-\beta)\ldots\sin(x-\lambda)}\\
&\quad= \frac{F(\sin\alpha, \cos\alpha)}{\sin(\alpha-\beta)\sin(\alpha-\gamma)\ldots\sin(\alpha-\lambda)}\,\frac{1}{\sin(x-\alpha)}\\
&\quad+ \frac{F(\sin\beta, \cos\beta)}{\sin(\beta-\alpha)\sin(\beta-\gamma)\ldots\sin(\beta-\lambda)}\,\frac{1}{\sin(x-\beta)}\\
&\quad\ldots\ldots\ldots\ldots\ldots\ldots\ldots\ldots\\
&\quad+ \frac{F(\sin\lambda, \cos\lambda)}{\sin(\lambda-\alpha)\sin(\lambda-\beta)\ldots\sin(\lambda-\varkappa)}\,\frac{1}{\sin(x-\lambda)}.
\end{aligned}$$

Nous en déduirons, en chassant le dénominateur,

$$\begin{aligned}
F(\sin x, \cos x) = {}& \frac{\sin(x-\beta)\sin(x-\gamma)\ldots\sin(x-\lambda)}{\sin(\alpha-\beta)\sin(\alpha-\gamma)\ldots\sin(\alpha-\lambda)} F(\sin\alpha, \cos\alpha)\\
&+ \frac{\sin(x-\alpha)\sin(x-\gamma)\ldots\sin(x-\lambda)}{\sin(\beta-\alpha)\sin(\beta-\gamma)\ldots\sin(\beta-\lambda)} F(\sin\beta, \cos\beta)\\
&\ldots\ldots\ldots\ldots\ldots\ldots\ldots\ldots\\
&+ \frac{\sin(x-\alpha)\sin(x-\beta)\ldots\sin(x-\varkappa)}{\sin(\lambda-\alpha)\sin(\lambda-\beta)\ldots\sin(\lambda-\varkappa)} F(\sin\lambda, \cos\lambda),
\end{aligned}$$

résultat qui se rapporte à la théorie de l'interpolation comme donnant l'expression de la fonction $F(\sin x, \cos x)$, où entrent n coefficients arbitraires, au moyen de n valeurs qu'elle prend pour $x = \alpha, x = \beta, \ldots, x = \lambda$.

V. C'est pour obtenir l'intégrale de la fonction transcendante $f(\sin x, \cos x)$ qu'a été établie la formule de décomposition en éléments simples, dont je ne multiplierai pas davantage les applications; sous ce point de vue, voici maintenant les conséquences à tirer de la formule générale

$$f(\sin x, \cos x) = \Pi(x) + \Phi(x).$$

En premier lieu, et à l'égard de

$$\mathrm{H}(x) = \Sigma a_k(\cos kx + \sqrt{-1}\sin kx),$$

nous observons qu'on a

$$\frac{d\sin kx}{dx} = k\cos kx, \qquad \frac{d\cos kx}{dx} = -k\sin kx,$$

d'où, par conséquent,

$$\int \cos kx\, dx = \frac{\sin kx}{k}, \qquad \int \sin kx\, dx = -\frac{\cos kx}{k}.$$

Ainsi l'intégration reproduit une expression de même forme que la fonction proposée, sauf un terme proportionnel à la variable provenant de la partie constante qu'elle peut contenir.

Soit, par exemple, $\Pi(x) = \cos^n x$; l'égalité $2\cos x = \frac{z^2+1}{z}$ donnera, en l'élevant à la puissance n, et rapprochant les termes équidistants des extrêmes,

$$2^n \cos^n x = z^n + \frac{1}{z^n} + \frac{n}{1}\left(z^{n-2} + \frac{1}{z^{n-2}}\right) + \frac{n(n-1)}{1.2}\left(z^{n-4} + \frac{1}{z^{n-4}}\right) + \ldots$$

Distinguons maintenant les deux cas de n pair et impair; nous aurons, dans le premier, avec le terme constant,

$$2^{n-1}\cos^n x = \cos nx + \frac{n}{1}\cos(n-2)x + \frac{n(n-1)}{1.2}\cos(n-4)x + \ldots$$
$$+ \frac{1}{2}\,\frac{n(n-1)\ldots\left(\frac{n}{2}+1\right)}{1.2\ldots\frac{n}{2}},$$

et, par conséquent,

$$2^{n-1}\int \cos^n x\,dx = \frac{\sin nx}{n} + \frac{n}{1}\,\frac{\sin(n-2)x}{n-2} + \frac{n(n-1)}{1.2}\,\frac{\sin(n-4)x}{n-4} + \dots$$

$$+ \frac{1}{2}\,\frac{n(n-1)\dots\left(\frac{n}{2}+1\right)}{1.2\dots\frac{n}{2}}\,x;$$

dans le second, il viendra

$$2^{n-1}\cos^n x = \cos nx + \frac{n}{1}\cos(n-2)x + \frac{n(n-1)}{1.2}\cos(n-4)x + \dots$$

$$+ \frac{n(n-1)\dots\left(\frac{n+1}{2}+1\right)}{1.2\dots\frac{n-1}{2}}\cos x,$$

d'où cette formule où la variable ne sort plus du signe sinus

$$2^{n-1}\int \cos^n x\,dx = \frac{\sin nx}{n} + \frac{n}{1}\,\frac{\sin(n-2)x}{n-2} + \dots$$

$$+ \frac{n(n-1)\dots\left(\frac{n+1}{2}+1\right)}{1.2\dots\frac{n-1}{2}}\sin x.$$

On traitera de même l'expression plus générale

$$\sin^a x \cos^b x = \left(\frac{z^2-1}{2z\sqrt{-1}}\right)^a \left(\frac{z^2+1}{2z}\right)^b;$$

mais l'intégrale $\int \sin^a \cos^b x\,dx$ s'obtient encore par un autre procédé fondé sur l'identité suivante :

$$\begin{aligned}\frac{d\sin^{a-1}x\cos^{b+1}x}{dx} &= (a-1)\sin^{a-2}x\cos^{b+2}x - (b+1)\sin^a x\cos^b x\\ &= (a-1)\sin^{a-2}x\cos^b x(1-\sin^2 x) - (b+1)\sin^a x\cos^b x\\ &= (a-1)\sin^{a-2}x\cos^b x - (a+b)\sin^a x\cos^b x.\end{aligned}$$

Nous tirons en effet

$$(a+b)\int \sin^a x\cos^b x\,dx = (a-1)\int \sin^{a-2}x\cos^b x\,dx - \sin^{a-1}x\cos^{b+1}x,$$

ce qui permettra de ramener, de proche en proche, la quantité

$$\int \sin^a x \cos^b x \, dx$$

à celle-ci

$$\int \sin^{a-2n} \cos^b x \, dx,$$

où n est un entier quelconque. Si l'on suppose a impair, le calcul est terminé, car, en faisant $a = 2n + 1$, on obtient immédiatement

$$\int \sin x \cos^b x \, dx = -\frac{\cos^{b+1} x}{b+1}.$$

Dans le cas de a pair, nous prendrons $2n = a$, et l'on opérera ensuite sur l'intégrale $\int \cos^b x \, dx$, au moyen de la relation

$$b \int \cos^b x \, dx = (b-1) \int \cos^{b-2} x \, dx + \sin x \cos^{b-1} x,$$

qui ramène, soit à $\int \cos x \, dx = \sin x$, soit à $\int dx = x$.

En considérant en second lieu l'expression $\int \Phi(x) \, dx$, j'écrirai pour abréger, comme à propos des fonctions rationnelles, p. 36,

$$\Phi(x) = C + \sum \mathcal{A} \cot \frac{1}{2}(x - \alpha) + \sum \mathcal{A}_1 \frac{d \cot \frac{1}{2}(x-\alpha)}{dx} + \ldots$$
$$+ \sum \mathcal{A}_n \frac{d^n \cot \frac{1}{2}(x-\alpha)}{dx^n};$$

maintenant on voit comment la composition de cette formule conduit immédiatement au résultat. Nous n'avons, en effet, qu'à déterminer la seule intégrale $\int \cot \frac{1}{2}(x-\alpha) \, dx$; or, on a

$$\cot \frac{x-\alpha}{2} = \frac{\cos \frac{1}{2}(x-\alpha)}{\sin \frac{1}{2}(x-\alpha)} = 2 \frac{d \log \sin \frac{1}{2}(x-\alpha)}{dx},$$

et, par conséquent,

$$\int \cot \frac{x-\alpha}{2} \, dx = 2 \log \sin \frac{1}{2}(x-\alpha),$$

de sorte que

$$\int \Phi(x)\,dx = Cx + 2\sum \mathcal{A} \log \sin \frac{1}{2}(x-\alpha) + \sum \mathcal{A}_1 \cot \frac{1}{2}(x-\alpha) + \ldots$$
$$+ \sum \mathcal{A}_n \frac{d^{n-1} \cot \frac{1}{2}(x-\alpha)}{dx^{n-1}}.$$

Les relations

$$\Theta(x) = \sum \mathcal{A} \cot(x-\alpha) + \sum \mathcal{A}_1 \frac{d \cot(x-\alpha)}{dx} + \ldots$$
$$+ \sum \mathcal{A}_n \frac{d^n \cot(x-\alpha)}{dx^n},$$

$$\mathrm{H}(x) = \sum \mathcal{A} \operatorname{cos\acute{e}c}(x-\alpha) + \sum \mathcal{A}_1 \frac{d \operatorname{cos\acute{e}c}(x-\alpha)}{dx} + \ldots$$
$$+ \sum \mathcal{A}_n \frac{d^n \operatorname{cos\acute{e}c}(x-\alpha)}{dx^n}$$

donneront pareillement

$$\int \Theta(x)\,dx = \sum \mathcal{A} \log \sin(x-\alpha) + \sum \mathcal{A}_1 \cot(x-\alpha) + \ldots$$
$$+ \sum \mathcal{A}_n \frac{d^{n-1} \cot(x-\alpha)}{dx^{n-1}},$$

$$\int \mathrm{H}(x)\,dx = \sum \mathcal{A} \log \operatorname{tang} \frac{1}{2}(x-\alpha) + \sum \mathcal{A}_1 \operatorname{cos\acute{e}c}(x-\alpha) + \ldots$$
$$+ \sum \mathcal{A}_n \frac{d^{n-1} \operatorname{cos\acute{e}c}(x-\alpha)}{dx^{n-1}}.$$

En effet, nous avons déjà

$$\int \cot(x-\alpha)\,dx = \log \sin(x-\alpha),$$

et, quant à l'intégrale

$$\int \operatorname{cos\acute{e}c}(x-\alpha)\,dx = \int \frac{dx}{\sin(x-\alpha)},$$

elle s'obtient, soit par l'équation

$$\frac{1}{\sin(x-\alpha)} = \frac{1}{2}\left[\operatorname{tang} \frac{1}{2}(x-\alpha) + \cot \frac{1}{2}(x-\alpha)\right],$$

soit en posant

$$\operatorname{tang} \frac{1}{2}(x-\alpha) = t,$$

car il vient ainsi

$$\frac{1}{\sin(x-\alpha)} = \frac{1+t^2}{2t}, \qquad dx = \frac{2\,dt}{1+t^2},$$

d'où

$$\frac{dx}{\sin(x-\alpha)} = \int \frac{dt}{t} = \log t = \log \operatorname{tang} \frac{1}{2}(x-\alpha).$$

Voici quelques remarques sur ces résultats.

VI. Les expressions qui, en dehors des termes logarithmiques, à savoir

$$\mathcal{A}_1 \cot(x-\alpha) + \mathcal{A}_2 \frac{d\cot(x-\alpha)}{dx} + \ldots + \mathcal{A}_n \frac{d^{n-1}\cot(x-\alpha)}{dx^{n-1}}$$

et

$$\mathcal{A}_1 \operatorname{coséc}(x-\alpha) + \mathcal{A}_2 \frac{d\operatorname{coséc}(x-\alpha)}{dx} + \ldots + \mathcal{A}_n \frac{d^{n-1}\operatorname{coséc}(x-\alpha)}{dx^{n-1}},$$

composent, avec diverses valeurs des constantes $\mathcal{A}$ et α, les intégrales $\int \Theta(x)\,dx$, $\int \mathrm{H}(x)\,dx$, ont respectivement la même périodicité que $\Theta(x)$ et $\mathrm{H}(x)$. La première, comme on l'a vu au paragraphe I, équivaut à un polynome entier du degré n en $\cot(x-\alpha)$, la seconde donne lieu à la transformation suivante. Soit, pour un moment,

$$\operatorname{coséc}(x-\alpha) = u \qquad \text{et} \qquad \cot(x-\alpha) = t;$$

nous remarquerons qu'on peut écrire

$$u = -\sin(x-\alpha)\frac{dt}{dx},$$

de sorte qu'il vient successivement

$$\frac{du}{dx} = -\sin(x-\alpha)\frac{d^2 t}{dx^2} - \cos(x-\alpha)\frac{dt}{dx},$$

$$\frac{d^2 u}{dx^2} = -\sin(x-\alpha)\left(\frac{d^3 t}{dx^3} - \frac{dt}{dx}\right) - 2\cos(x-\alpha)\frac{d^2 t}{dx^2},$$

et, en général,

$$\frac{d^k u}{dx^k} = -\sin(x-\alpha)\left[\frac{d^{k+1} t}{dx^{k+1}} - \frac{k(k-1)}{1.2}\frac{d^{k-1} t}{dx^{k-1}} + \ldots\right]$$
$$- \cos(x-\alpha)\left[\frac{k}{1}\frac{d^k t}{dx^k} - \frac{k(k-1)(k-2)}{1.2.3}\frac{d^{k-2} t}{dx^{k-2}} + \ldots\right].$$

Il en résulte qu'on peut donner à l'expression

$$\mathcal{A}_1 u + \mathcal{A}_2 \frac{du}{dx} + \ldots + \mathcal{A}_n \frac{d^{n-1} u}{dx^{n-1}}$$

d'abord la forme

$$\sin(x-\alpha)\left(G \frac{d^n t}{dx^n} + G_1 \frac{d^{n-1} u}{dx^{n-1}} + \ldots\right)$$
$$+ \cos(x-\alpha)\left(H \frac{d^{n-1} t}{dx^{n-1}} + H_1 \frac{dx^{n-2} t}{dx^{n-2}} + \ldots\right),$$

les coefficients G et H étant constants; ensuite celle-ci

$$\sin(x-\alpha)\,F(t) + \cos(x-\alpha)\,F_1(t),$$

en désignant par $F(t)$ et $F_1(t)$ des polynomes en t des degrés $n+1$ et n; enfin au moyen des valeurs

$$\sin(x-\alpha) = \frac{1}{\sqrt{1+t^2}}, \qquad \cos(x-\alpha) = \frac{t}{\sqrt{1+t^2}},$$

on écrira

$$\mathcal{A}_1 u + \mathcal{A}_2 \frac{du}{dx} + \ldots + \mathcal{A}_n \frac{d^{n-1} u}{dx^{n-1}} = \frac{\mathfrak{F}(t)}{\sqrt{1+t^2}},$$

ce nouveau polynome $\mathfrak{F}(t)$ étant du degré $n+1$. Sous ces formes nouvelles, les quantités qui entrent dans les deux intégrales sont parfois d'une détermination plus facile, et j'en donnerai quelques exemples.

Soit d'abord l'intégrale

$$\int \cot^{n+1} x \, dx,$$

l'exposant n étant entier et positif; d'après la méthode générale, on posera

$$\cot^{n+1} x = C + \mathcal{A}_0 \cot x + \mathcal{A}_1 \frac{d \cot x}{dx} + \ldots + \mathcal{A}_n \frac{d^n \cot x}{dx^n},$$

et les coefficients s'obtiendront, soit au moyen des relations

$$\cot^2 x = -1 - \frac{d \cot x}{dx},$$

$$\cot^3 x = -\cot x + \frac{1}{2} \frac{d^2 \cot x}{dx^2},$$

$$\cot^4 x = 1 + \frac{4}{3} \frac{d \cot x}{dx} - \frac{1}{6} \frac{d^3 \cot x}{dx^3},$$

$$\ldots\ldots\ldots\ldots\ldots\ldots,$$

soit en formant la puissance $n+1$ ainsi que les dérivées de la série

$$\cot x = \frac{1}{x} - \frac{x}{3} - \frac{x^3}{45} - \ldots,$$

et substituant dans l'équation pour identifier.

Or, la variable $\cot x = t$, qui est indiquée par la forme connue d'avance de l'intégrale, en donne facilement la valeur, car ayant

$$\int \cot^{n+1} x\, dx = -\int \frac{t^{n+1}\, dt}{1+t^2},$$

il suffira d'extraire la partie entière de la fraction $\frac{t^{n+1}}{1+t^2}$; si n est impair, on formera ainsi l'égalité

$$\frac{t^{n+1}}{1+t^2} = t^{n-1} - t^{n-3} + t^{n-5} - \ldots + (-1)^{\frac{n-1}{2}} - \frac{(-1)^{\frac{n-1}{2}}}{1+t^2},$$

d'où

$$\int \frac{t^{n+1}\, dt}{1+t^2} = \frac{t^n}{n} - \frac{t^{n-2}}{n-2} + \frac{t^{n-4}}{n-4} - \ldots + (-1)^{\frac{n-1}{2}} t - (-1)^{\frac{n-1}{2}} \operatorname{arc\,tang} t,$$

et, par conséquent,

$$\int \cot^{n+1} x\, dx = -\frac{\cot^n x}{n} + \frac{\cot^{n-2} x}{n-2} - \frac{\cot^{n-4} x}{n-4} - \ldots$$
$$- (-1)^{\frac{n-1}{2}} \cot x - (-1)^{\frac{n-1}{2}} x.$$

Dans le cas de n pair, il viendra semblablement

$$\frac{t^{n+1}}{1+t^2} = t^{n-1} - t^{n-2} + t^{n-5} - \ldots - (-1)^{\frac{n}{2}} t + \frac{(-1)^{\frac{n}{2}} t}{1+t^2};$$

on en conclura alors

$$\int \cot^{n+1} x\, dx = -\frac{\cot^n x}{n} + \frac{\cot^{n-2} x}{n-2} - \frac{\cot^{n-4} x}{n-4} + \ldots$$
$$+ (-1)^{\frac{n}{2}} \frac{\cot^2 x}{2} + (-1)^{\frac{n}{2}} \log \sin x.$$

Rapprochant ces résultats de l'expression donnée par la méthode générale, à savoir :

$$\int \cot^{n+1} x\, dx = Cx + \mathcal{A} \log \sin x + \ldots + \mathcal{A}_1 \cot x + \ldots + \mathcal{A}_n \frac{d^{n-1} \cot x}{dx^{n-1}},$$

nous en tirons cette conséquence qu'on a $\mathcal{A} = (-1)^{\frac{n}{2}}$ ou $\mathcal{A} = 0$, suivant que n est pair ou impair; et je m'y arrêterai un moment pour montrer en peu de mots comment cette seule connaissance du résidu $\mathcal{A}$ relatif à la valeur $x = 0$ de la fonction $\cot^{n+1} x$ suffit pour la détermination complète de la série

$$\cot x = \frac{a}{x} + b + cx + dx^2 + \ldots.$$

Et d'abord, de ce que le terme en $\frac{1}{x}$ manque dans le carré, la quatrième puissance et toutes les puissances paires, on conclut de proche en proche les conditions $b = 0$, $d = 0$, ..., c'est-à-dire que le développement ne contient que des puissances impaires de la variable, et a la forme

$$\cot x = \frac{\alpha}{x} + \beta x + \gamma x^3 + \ldots.$$

De ce que le coefficient du même terme est $+1, -1, +1, \ldots$, dans la première, la troisième, la cinquième puissance, etc., on tire aisément les égalités

$$\alpha = 1, \qquad 3\alpha^2\beta = -1, \qquad 5\alpha^4\gamma + 10\alpha^3\beta^2 = 1, \qquad \ldots,$$

d'où

$$\beta = -\frac{1}{3}, \qquad \gamma = -\frac{1}{45}, \qquad \ldots.$$

Le développement de $\cot x$, auquel nous parvenons ainsi, est d'une grande importance en Analyse; en l'écrivant de cette manière

$$\cot x = \frac{1}{x} - \frac{2^2 B_1 x}{1.2} - \frac{2^4 B_2 x^3}{1.2.3.4} - \frac{2^6 B_3 x^5}{1.2.3.4.5.6} - \ldots,$$

les coefficients

$$B_1 = \frac{1}{6}, \qquad B_2 = \frac{1}{30}, \qquad B_3 = \frac{1}{42}, \qquad \ldots$$

sont appelés les *nombres de Bernoulli* (¹), et l'on a de même

$$\operatorname{tang} x = \frac{2^2(2^2-1)B_1 x}{1.2} + \frac{2^4(2^4-1)B_2 x^3}{1.2.3.4} + \frac{2^6(2^6-1)B_3 x^5}{1.2.3.4.5.6} + \ldots,$$

$$\operatorname{coséc} x = \frac{1}{x} + \frac{(2^2-2)B_1 x}{1.2} + \frac{(2^4-2)B_2 x^3}{1.2.3.4} + \frac{(2^6-2)B_3 x^5}{1.2.3.4.5.6} + \ldots.$$

(¹) BERTRAND, *Traité de calcul différentiel et de calcul intégral*, t. I, p. 347. — SERRET, *Cours de calcul différentiel et intégral*, t. II, p. 217.

Soit encore l'expression $\frac{1}{\sin^{\alpha+1}x\cos^{\beta+1}x}$, qui, en supposant $\alpha+\beta$ un nombre pair, aura, comme la précédente, la périodicité de $\Theta(x)$. Au lieu de déduire l'intégrale

$$\int \frac{dx}{\sin^{\alpha+1}x\cos^{\beta+1}x}$$

de la relation

$$\begin{aligned}\frac{1}{\sin^{\alpha+1}x\cos^{\beta+1}x} = \mathrm{C} + \mathcal{A}\cot x &+ \mathcal{A}_1\frac{d\cot x}{dx} + \ldots + \mathcal{A}_\alpha\frac{d\cot x}{dx}\\ &+ \mathcal{B}\operatorname{tang}x + \mathcal{B}_1\frac{d\operatorname{tang}x}{dx} + \ldots + \mathcal{B}_\beta\frac{d\operatorname{tang}x}{dx},\end{aligned}$$

nous ferons toujours $\cot x = t$, et l'on voit que la transformée

$$\int \frac{(1+t^2)^{\frac{\alpha+\beta}{2}}}{t^{\beta+1}}\,dt$$

s'obtiendra facilement en développant la puissance $(1+t^2)^{\frac{\alpha+\beta}{2}}$, dont l'exposant est entier dans l'hypothèse admise. Si nous faisons en particulier $\beta=-1$, $\alpha=2n+1$, nous trouvons, en désignant par n_1, n_2, ... les coefficients de la puissance n du binome

$$\int\frac{dx}{\sin^{2n+2}x} = -\cot x - \frac{n_1}{3}\cot^3 x - \frac{n_2}{5}\cot^5 x - \ldots - \frac{1}{2n+1}\cot^{2n+1}x,$$

puis, en changeant x en $\frac{\pi}{2}-x$,

$$\int\frac{dx}{\cos^{2n-2}x} = \operatorname{tang}x + \frac{n_1}{3}\operatorname{tang}^3 x + \frac{n_2}{5}\operatorname{tang}^5 x + \ldots + \frac{1}{2n+1}\operatorname{tang}^{2n+1}x.$$

VII. L'intégrale $\int f(\sin x, \cos x)\,dx$ se ramenant par la substitution $\sin x = \mathrm{X}$ à cette forme

$$\int f(\mathrm{X}, \sqrt{1-\mathrm{X}^2})\frac{d\mathrm{X}}{\sqrt{1-\mathrm{X}^2}},$$

qui a été l'objet d'une étude antérieure, nous devrions maintenant comparer les deux procédés d'intégration, et les résultats auxquels ils conduisent. A cet égard, je me bornerai à remarquer qu'en faisant $\sin x = X$ dans la formule générale

$$\int \Phi(x)\,dx = Cx + 2\sum \mathcal{A} \log \sin \frac{1}{2}(x - \alpha)$$

$$+ \sum \mathcal{A}_1 \cot \frac{1}{2}(x - \alpha) + \ldots + \sum \mathcal{A}_n \frac{d^{n-1} \cot \frac{1}{2}(x - \alpha)}{dx^{n-1}},$$

la partie transcendante est donnée par les termes Cx et

$$\int \cot \frac{1}{2}(x - \alpha)\,dx = 2 \log \sin \frac{1}{2}(x - \alpha),$$

dont le dernier prendra la forme suivante. Soient

$$Y = \sqrt{1 - X^2}, \qquad a = \sin\alpha, \qquad b = \cos\alpha,$$

on aura

$$\int \cot \frac{1}{2}(x - \alpha)\,dx = \int \frac{\sin(x - \alpha)}{1 - \cos(x - \alpha)}\,dx = \int \frac{bX - aY}{1 - aX - bY}\frac{dX}{Y},$$

de sorte qu'au lieu de la fonction de troisième espèce amenée par la méthode d'intégration des radicaux carrés, à savoir :

$$\int \frac{b\,dx}{(x - a)y} = \log\left(\frac{1 - ax - by}{x - a}\right),$$

nous sommes conduits à la quantité

$$\int \frac{bx - ay}{1 - ax - by}\frac{dx}{y} = \log(1 - ax - by).$$

Mais j'arrive, sans insister sur ce point (¹), à une dernière considération, à la détermination de l'intégrale définie

$$\int_0^{2\pi} f(\sin x, \cos x)\,dx.$$

(¹) On a, d'une manière plus générale,

$$\int \frac{(cb' - bc')x + (ac' - ca')y + ab' - ba'}{(ax + by + c)(a'x + b'y + c')}\frac{dx}{y} = \log \frac{ax + by + c}{a'x + b'y + c'},$$

et l'on doit remarquer les cas particuliers dans lesquels cette intégrale ne devient indéfinie que pour deux valeurs de la variable. Ils se présentent lorsque les droites $ax + by + c = 0$, $a'x + b'x + c' = 0$ se coupent sur le cercle $x^2 + y^2 = 1$, ou lui sont tangentes.

Reprenant, à cet effet, l'expression

$$f(\sin x, \cos x = \Pi(x) + \Phi(x),$$

j'observe d'abord que la fonction $\Phi(x)$ devra être finie pour toutes les valeurs de la variable comprise de zéro à 2π, c'est-à-dire quel que soit x, puisqu'on a $\Phi(x+2\pi) = \Phi(x)$; ainsi dans les éléments simples $\cot\frac{1}{2}(x-\alpha)$, aucune des constantes α ne sera réelle. Ceci posé, les termes périodiques de l'intégrale indéfinie des fonctions $\Pi(x)$ et $\Phi(x)$, reprenant la même valeur aux limites $x=0$ et $x=2\pi$, ne figureront point dans le résultat, et nous aurons seulement à considérer le terme Cx, ainsi que la partie logarithmique $\sum \mathcal{A} \log\sin\frac{1}{2}(x-\alpha)$. Du premier résulte immédiatement la quantité $C2\pi$; mais les termes transcendants demandent une attention particulière. Comme dans le cas plus simple de l'expression

$$\int_{x_0}^{x_1} \frac{dx}{x-\alpha-\beta\sqrt{-1}},$$

la relation

$$\int \cot\frac{1}{2}(x-\alpha)\,dx = 2\log\sin\frac{x-\alpha}{2}$$

ne détermine pas sur-le-champ, à cause des valeurs multiples des logarithmes, l'intégrale définie prise entre des limites données x_0, x_1, et j'indiquerai d'abord de quelle manière on y parvient avant de supposer $x_0 = 0$ et $x_1 = 2\pi$.

Soient

$$\alpha = a + b\sqrt{-1}, \qquad \sin\frac{1}{2}(x-\alpha) = X + Y\sqrt{-1}.$$

Envisageant X et Y comme les coordonnées OP et MP d'un point M rapporté à deux axes rectangulaires Ox et Oy, je figure la courbe MM′ qui sera le lieu de ces points lorsque la variable x croîtra de x_0 à x_1. De cette manière, le rayon vecteur $OM = R$ et l'angle $MOx = \theta$ seront, à partir du point M, correspondant à $x = x_0$, des fonctions continues entièrement déterminées de la variable x. Remplaçant donc $\cot\frac{1}{2}(x-\alpha)$ par la dérivée logarithmique de

$$\sin\frac{1}{2}(x-\alpha) = X + Y\sqrt{-1} = R(\cos\theta + \sqrt{-1}\sin\theta),$$

il vient

$$\frac{1}{2}\int \cot\frac{1}{2}(x-\alpha)\,dx = \int \frac{dR}{R} + \int d\theta\sqrt{-1},$$

maintenant on a, sans aucune ambiguïté,

$$\int_{x_0}^{x_1} \frac{dR}{R} = \log OM' - \log OM, \qquad \int_{x_0}^{x_1} d\theta = M'Ox - MOx,$$

et l'intégrale proposée se trouve déterminée. Mais arrivons aux limites zéro et 2π; si nous faisons pour un moment

$$A = \cos\frac{b}{2}\sqrt{-1} = \frac{e^b+1}{2e^{\frac{1}{2}b}},$$

$$B = \frac{\sin\frac{b}{2}\sqrt{-1}}{\sqrt{-1}} = \frac{e^b-1}{2e^{\frac{1}{2}b}},$$

nous aurons

$$X = A\sin\frac{1}{2}(x-a), \qquad Y = -B\cos\frac{1}{2}(x-a),$$

d'où

$$\frac{X^2}{A^2} + \frac{Y^2}{B^2} = 1;$$

de sorte que la courbe MM' est une ellipse. Remarquant que A est toujours positif, je distingue deux cas, suivant que B sera positif ou négatif. Dans le premier, je pose

$$\frac{x-a}{2} = \frac{\pi}{2} + \varphi,$$

d'où

$$X = A\cos\varphi, \qquad Y = B\sin\varphi;$$

cela étant, lorsque x croîtra de zéro à 2π, cette ellipse sera décrite dans le sens direct depuis un point M (*fig.* 30) jusqu'au point M' situé sur le prolongement du diamètre OM. En second lieu, lorsque B est négatif, je fais

$$\frac{x-a}{2} = \frac{\pi}{2} - \varphi,$$

ce qui donne

$$X = A\cos\varphi, \qquad Y = -B\sin\varphi;$$

c'est alors du point M au point M' la seconde moitié de la courbe qui sera décrite dans le sens inverse. Cela étant, dans le premier cas, l'angle croît avec x, et nous avons

$$\mathrm{M'O}x = \mathrm{MO}x + \pi;$$

dans le second, au contraire, il décroît, et nous passons de la valeur $\mathrm{MO}x$ à $\mathrm{M'O}x = \mathrm{MO}x - \pi$; les deux rayons vecteurs OM et OM' sont d'ailleurs égaux, ce qui fait disparaître la partie logarithmique; par conséquent, en désignant par (b) une quantité égale à l'unité en valeur absolue et du signe de b, nous aurons

$$\int_0^{2\pi} \cot\frac{1}{2}(x - a - b\sqrt{-1})\,dx = 2(b)\sqrt{-1}.$$

Voici quelques applications de cette formule :

Posons

$$\lambda = \alpha\sqrt{-1}$$

dans la relation

$$\frac{2\sin\lambda}{\cos\lambda - \cos x} = \cot\frac{x-\lambda}{2} - \cot\frac{x+\lambda}{2}$$

établie page 62, et soit $a = e^{\alpha}$; elle prendra cette forme

$$\frac{2(1-a^2)}{1 - 2a\cos x + a^2} = \sqrt{-1}\left(\cot\frac{x - \alpha\sqrt{-1}}{2} - \cot\frac{x + \alpha\sqrt{-1}}{2}\right),$$

et nous en conclurons successivement pour $\alpha < 0$ et $\alpha > 0$, c'est-à-dire en supposant $a < 1$ et $a > 1$,

$$\int_0^{2\pi} \frac{(1-a^2)\,dx}{1 - 2a\cos x + a^2} = 2\pi \quad \text{et} \quad \int_0^{2\pi} \frac{(1-a^2)\,dx}{1 - 2a\cos 2 + a^2} = -2\pi.$$

Le second cas se déduit d'ailleurs immédiatement du premier par le changement de a en $\frac{1}{a}$.

Soit encore l'expression plus générale

$$\frac{\cos mx}{\cos\lambda - \cos x},$$

m étant un nombre entier quelconque; en faisant

$$e^{x\sqrt{-1}} = z,$$

elle devient

$$-\frac{z^{2m}+1}{z^{m-1}(1 - 2z\cos\lambda + z^2)},$$

et contient par conséquent une partie entière qui s'obtient ainsi. Je pars de ces deux identités, faciles à vérifier,

$$\frac{\sin\lambda}{1-2z\cos\lambda+z^2} = \sin\lambda + z\sin 2\lambda + z^2\sin 3\lambda + \ldots$$
$$+ z^{m-2}\sin(m-1)\lambda + z^{m-1}\frac{\sin m\lambda - z\sin(m-1)\lambda}{1-2z\cos\lambda+z^2},$$

$$\frac{\sin\lambda}{1-2z\cos\lambda+z^2} = \frac{\sin\lambda}{z^2} + \frac{\sin 2\lambda}{z^3} + \frac{\sin 3\lambda}{z^4} + \ldots$$
$$+ \frac{\sin m\lambda}{z^{m+1}} + \frac{1}{z^{m+1}}\,\frac{z\sin(m+1)\lambda - \sin m\lambda}{1-2z\cos\lambda+z^2},$$

et je les ajoute membre à membre après avoir divisé la première par z^{m-1}, et multiplié la seconde par z^{m+1}; il vient

$$\frac{(z^{2m}+1)\sin\lambda}{z^{m-1}(1-2z\cos+z^2)} = (z^{m-1}+z^{1-m})\sin\lambda + (z^{m-2}+z^{2-m})\sin 2\lambda + \ldots$$
$$+ (z+z^{-1})\sin(m-1)\lambda + \sin m\lambda$$
$$+ \frac{z[\sin(m+1)\lambda - \sin(m-1)\lambda]}{1-2z\cos\lambda+z^2},$$

et, par conséquent, si l'on remplace z par l'exponentielle $e^{x\sqrt{-1}}$, nous aurons

$$\frac{\cos mx\sin\lambda}{\cos x-\cos\lambda} = \Pi(x) + \frac{\cos m\lambda\sin\lambda}{\cos x-\cos\lambda},$$

en faisant

$$\pi(x) = 2\sin\lambda\cos(m-1)x + 2\sin 2\lambda\cos(m-2)x + \ldots$$
$$+ 2\sin(m-1)\lambda\cos x + \sin m\lambda.$$

Le terme constant de la partie entière est $\sin m\lambda$; on en conclura, en faisant comme plus haut, $\lambda = \alpha\sqrt{-1}$, $e^\alpha = a$, ce qui donne

$$\sin m\lambda = \frac{1-a^{2m}}{2a^m\sqrt{-1}}, \qquad \cos m\lambda = \frac{1+a^{2m}}{2a^m},$$

$$\int_0^{2\pi}\frac{(1-a^2)\cos mx\,dx}{1-2a\cos x+a^2} = 2\pi a^m \qquad \text{pour} \qquad a<1,$$

et

$$\int_0^{2\pi}\frac{(1-a^2)\cos mx\,dx}{1-2a\cos x+a^2} = -\frac{2\pi}{a^m} \qquad \text{pour} \qquad a>1.$$

Je considère en dernier lieu la quantité

$$\frac{\sin^2 x}{(\cos\lambda-\cos x)(\cos\mu-\cos x)};$$

la décomposition en éléments simples conduit d'abord à la relation

$$\frac{\sin^2 x}{(\cos\lambda - \cos x)(\cos\mu - \cos x)} = -1 + \mathcal{A}\left(\cot\frac{x-\lambda}{2} - \cot\frac{x+\lambda}{2}\right)$$
$$+ \mathcal{B}\left(\cot\frac{x-\mu}{2} - \cot\frac{x-\mu}{2}\right),$$

en posant

$$2\mathcal{A} = \frac{\sin\lambda}{\cos\mu - \cos\lambda}, \qquad 2\mathcal{B} = \frac{\sin\mu}{\cos\lambda - \cos\mu}.$$

Faisant encore

$$\lambda = \alpha\sqrt{-1}, \qquad \mu = \beta\sqrt{-1}, \qquad a = e^{\alpha}, \qquad b = e^{\beta},$$

nous trouverons, en nous bornant, pour abréger, au seul cas de $\alpha < 0$, $\beta < 0$,

$$\int_0^{2\pi} \frac{4ab\sin^2 x\,dx}{(1-2a\cos x + a^2)(1-2b\cos x + b^2)}$$
$$= -2\pi - (\mathcal{A} + \mathcal{B})4\pi\sqrt{-1};$$

or, on a facilement

$$\mathcal{A} + \mathcal{B} = \frac{1}{2}\cot\frac{\lambda+\mu}{2} = \frac{1}{2}\sqrt{-1}\,\frac{1+ab}{1-ab},$$

d'où cette formule

$$\int_0^{2\pi} \frac{\sin^2 x\,dx}{(1-2a\cos x + a^2)(1-2b\cos x + b^2)} = \frac{\pi}{1-ab},$$

qui donne un résultat important en développant les deux membres suivant les puissances de a et b. Si nous employons, à cet effet, les relations

$$\frac{\sin x}{1 - 2a\cos x + a^2} = \sum a^m \sin(m+1)x,$$
$$\frac{\sin x}{1 + 2b\cos x + b^2} = \sum b^n \sin(n+1)x,$$

où m et n reçoivent toutes les valeurs entières de zéro à l'infini, on parvient à l'égalité suivante :

$$\sum a^m b^m \int_0^{2\pi} \sin(m+1)x\sin(n+1)x\,dx = \pi(1 + ab + a^2b^2 + \ldots),$$

dont le second membre ne renferme que les puissances du produit ab. Nous avons donc

$$\int_0^{2\pi} \sin mx \sin nx \, dx = 0$$

lorsque m et n sont différents, tandis qu'il vient, si on les suppose égaux,

$$\int_0^{2\pi} \sin^2 mx \, dx = \pi.$$

On trouve d'ailleurs directement ces relations au moyen des identités

$$2 \sin mx \sin nx = \cos(m-n)x - \cos(m+n)x,$$
$$2 \sin^2 mx = 1 - \cos 2mx,$$

qui donnent les intégrales indéfinies

$$\int \sin mx \sin nx \, dx = \frac{\sin(m-n)x}{2(m-n)} - \frac{\sin(m+n)x}{2(m+n)},$$
$$\int \sin^2 mx \, dx = \frac{x}{2} - \frac{\sin 2mx}{4m};$$

et, par suite, comme on voit,

$$\int_0^{2\pi} \sin mx \sin nx \, dx = 0, \qquad \int_0^{2\pi} \sin^2 mx \, dx = \pi.$$

En partant de celles-ci :

$$2 \sin mx \cos nx = \sin(m+n)x + \sin(m-n)x,$$
$$2 \cos mx \cos nx = \cos(m+n)x + \cos(m-n)x,$$

nous aurons semblablement

$$\int_0^{2\pi} \sin mx \cos nx \, dx = 0,$$

même dans le cas de $m = n$, puis

$$\int_0^{2\pi} \cos mx \cos nx \, dx = 0, \qquad \int_0^{2\pi} \cos^2 mx \, dx = \pi.$$

Ces intégrales définies, qu'on obtient si facilement, conduisent, comme nous allons voir, à d'importantes conséquences.

VIII. Les séries qui précèdent suivant les puissances entières et positives d'une ou de plusieurs variables ont pour caractère essentiel d'être continues lorsqu'elles sont convergentes, et c'est en admettant cette condition de continuité qu'elles ont été employées dans les applications géométriques, et en particulier dans les théories du contact et de la courbure des lignes et des surfaces. Mais l'analyse conduit à des séries d'une autre nature, qui, tout en restant convergentes afin d'avoir une limite déterminée, ne sont plus nécessairement continues, et peuvent, lorsque la variable croît par degrés insensibles, représenter diverses successions de valeurs appartenant à des fonctions de formes tout à fait différentes. Un premier exemple en a déjà été donné, et nous avons vu qu'en faisant

$$f(x) = \sin x + \frac{\sin 3x}{3} + \frac{\sin 5x}{5} + \ldots$$

on a

$$f(x) = \frac{\pi}{4},$$

lorsque la variable est comprise entre $2n\pi$ et $(2n+1)\pi$, tandis qu'on obtient

$$f(x) = -\frac{\pi}{4}$$

quand on la suppose comprise entre $(2n-1)\pi$ et $2n\pi$, n étant un nombre entier quelconque. Or, ce résultat se rattache à une formule générale donnant un nouveau mode d'expression des fonctions d'une grande importance en Analyse, et que je vais indiquer succinctement.

Soit $\mathcal{F}(x)$ une fonction donnée entre les limites $x = a$, $x = b$, avec la seule condition d'être toujours finie; la suivante :

$$f(x) = \mathcal{F}\left(a + \frac{b-a}{2\pi}x\right),$$

le sera de même depuis $x = 0$ jusqu'à $x = 2\pi$, et l'on prouve qu'elle peut se représenter de la manière suivante :

$$\begin{aligned} f(x) = A_0 &+ A_1 \cos x + A_2 \cos 2x + \ldots + A_m \cos mx + \ldots \\ &+ B_1 \sin x + B_2 \sin 2x + \ldots + B_m \sin mx + \ldots; \end{aligned}$$

voici maintenant, la possibilité du développement admise ([1]), comment se déterminent les coefficients. Le premier s'obtient en multipliant les deux membres par dx, et intégrant entre les limites zéro et 2π; ayant, en effet,

$$\int_0^{2\pi} \cos mx\, dx = 0, \qquad \int_0^{2\pi} \sin mx\, dx = 0,$$

il vient ainsi

$$2\pi A_0 = \int_0^{2\pi} f(x)\, dx.$$

J'opère ensuite d'une manière analogue en multipliant successivement par les facteurs $\cos mx\, dx$, $\sin mx\, dx$; les relations précédemment établies, à savoir :

$$\int_0^{2\pi} \cos mx \cos nx\, dx = 0, \qquad \int_0^{2\pi} \cos mx \sin nx\, dx = 0$$

montrent que l'intégration entre les limites zéro et 2π éliminera tous les coefficients de la série, sauf A_m et B_m, qui seront respectivement multipliés par les quantités

$$\int_0^{2\pi} \cos^2 mx\, dx = \pi, \qquad \int_0^{2\pi} \sin^2 mx\, dx = \pi,$$

et nous trouverons, par conséquent,

$$\pi A_m = \int_0^{2\pi} f(x) \cos mx\, dx, \qquad \pi B_m = \int_0^{2\pi} f(x) \sin mx\, dx.$$

C'est cette expression de A_m et B_m, au moyen d'intégrales définies, qui donne le moyen de s'affranchir de la condition de continuité que suppose absolument le mode de détermination des coefficients de la série de Maclaurin

$$f(x) = f(x_0) + \frac{x - x_0}{1} f'(x_0) + \frac{(x - x_0)^2}{1.2} f''(x_0) + \ldots,$$

([1]) Je renverrai pour la démonstration rigoureuse au Mémoire célèbre de Dirichlet, sur la convergence des séries trigonométriques qui servent à représenter une fonction arbitraire entre des limites données (*Journal de Crelle*, t. 4, p. 157).

où figurent toutes les dérivées de $f(x)$ pour $x = x_0$. D'après la nature même de l'opération d'intégration, rien n'empêche, en effet, d'admettre qu'entre les limites zéro et 2π, et dans un nombre quelconque d'intervalles de zéro à x_1, x_1 à x_2, ..., x_{n-1} à 2π, $f(x)$ coïncide successivement avec n fonctions distinctes $f_1(x)$, $f_2(x)$, ..., $f_n(x)$, les expressions des coefficients devenant alors

$$2\pi A_0 = \int_0^{x_1} f_1(x)\,dx + \int_{x_1}^{x_2} f_2(x)\,dx + \ldots + \int_{x_{n-1}}^{2\pi} f_n(x)\,dx,$$

$$\pi A_m = \int_0^{x_1} f_1(x)\cos mx\,dx + \int_{x_1}^{x_2} f_2(x)\cos mx\,dx + \ldots + \int_{x_{n-1}}^{2\pi} f_n(x)\cos mx\,dx,$$

$$\pi B_m = \int_0^{x_1} f_1(x)\sin mx\,dx + \int_{x_1}^{x_2} f_2(x)\sin mx\,dx + \ldots + \int_{x_{n-1}}^{2\pi} f_n(x)\sin mx\,dx.$$

Une circonstance qu'il importe aussi de ne pas omettre, c'est qu'à la limite de séparation de deux intervalles, pour $x = x_1$, par exemple, la série ne présente point l'ambiguïté de la fonction et a pour valeur $\frac{1}{2}[f_1(x_1) + f_2(x_1)]$; mais je me bornerai à énoncer ces résultats et à en faire l'application au cas d'une fonction $f(x)$ successivement égale à $+\frac{\pi}{4}$ entre $x = 0$, $x = \pi$, et à $-\frac{\pi}{4}$ entre $x = \pi$, $x = 2\pi$. On trouve alors immédiatement $A_0 = 0$; observant ensuite qu'on a

$$\int_0^{\pi} \cos mx\,dx = 0, \qquad \int_{\pi}^{2\pi} \cos mx\,dx = 0,$$

nous en concluons semblablement $A_m = 0$; enfin les expressions

$$\int_0^{\pi} \sin mx\,dx = \frac{1 - \cos m\pi}{m}, \qquad \int_{\pi}^{2\pi} \sin mx\,dx = \frac{\cos m\pi - 1}{m}$$

donnent

$$\pi B_m = 2\,\frac{1 - \cos m\pi}{m},$$

et l'on retrouve bien la série

$$f(x) = \sin x + \frac{\sin 3x}{3} + \frac{\sin 5x}{5} + \ldots,$$

comme nous l'avions obtenue par une autre voie.

De l'intégrale $\int e^{\omega x} f(x)\,dx$.

I. Je me fonderai sur cette remarque que l'expression

$$e^{\omega x}\left(\mathrm{A}\,u + \mathrm{A}_1\frac{du}{dx} + \mathrm{A}_2\frac{d^2u}{dx^2} + \ldots + \mathrm{A}_n\frac{d^nu}{dx^n}\right),$$

où u est une fonction quelconque de x, prend, si l'on pose

$$e^{\omega x}u = v,$$

la forme suivante :

$$\mathcal{A}\,v + \mathcal{A}_1\frac{dv}{dx} + \mathcal{A}_2\frac{d^2v}{dx^2} + \ldots + \mathcal{A}_n\frac{d^nv}{dx^n}.$$

En effet, nous avons successivement $u = e^{-\omega x}v$,

$$\frac{du}{dx} = e^{-\omega x}\left(-\omega v + \frac{dv}{dx}\right), \quad \frac{d^2u}{dx^2} = e^{-\omega x}\left(\omega^2 v - 2\omega\frac{dv}{dx} + \frac{d^2v}{dx^2}\right), \quad \ldots,$$

et la substitution conduit au résultat annoncé, les quantités $\mathcal{A}$, $\mathcal{A}_1$, ... ayant ces valeurs

$$\begin{aligned}
\mathcal{A} &= \mathrm{A} - \mathrm{A}_1\omega + \mathrm{A}_2\omega^2 - \mathrm{A}_3\omega^3 + \ldots,\\
\mathcal{A}_1 &= \mathrm{A}_1 - 2\mathrm{A}_2\omega + 3\mathrm{A}_3\omega^2 - \ldots = -\frac{d\mathcal{A}}{d\omega},\\
\mathcal{A}_2 &= \mathrm{A}_2 - 3\mathrm{A}_3\omega + \ldots = \frac{1}{2}\frac{d^2\mathcal{A}}{d\omega^2},\\
&\ldots\ldots\ldots\ldots\ldots\ldots\ldots,
\end{aligned}$$

qu'on obtient directement comme il suit. La fonction u étant quelconque, faisons en particulier $u = e^{hx}$, on en conclura $v = e^{(\omega+h)x}$, et la relation

$$\begin{aligned}
&e^{\omega x}\left(\mathrm{A}\,u + \mathrm{A}_1\frac{du}{dx} + \mathrm{A}_2\frac{d^2u}{dx^2} + \ldots + \mathrm{A}_n\frac{d^nv}{dx^n}\right)\\
&= \mathcal{A}\,v + \mathcal{A}_1\frac{dv}{dx} + \mathcal{A}_2\frac{d^2v}{dx^2} + \ldots + \mathcal{A}_n\frac{d^nv}{dx^n}
\end{aligned}$$

donne ainsi, après avoir supprimé dans les deux membres le facteur exponentiel,

$$\begin{aligned} &A + A_1 h + A_2 h^2 + \ldots + A_n h^n \\ &= \mathcal{A} + \mathcal{A}_1(\omega + h) + \mathcal{A}_2(\omega + h)^2 + \ldots + \mathcal{A}_n(\omega + h)^n. \end{aligned}$$

Changeons maintenant h en $h - \omega$; nous en concluons

$$\begin{aligned} &A + A_1(-\omega + h) + A_2(-\omega + h)^2 + \ldots + A_n(-\omega + h)^n \\ &= \mathcal{A} + \mathcal{A}_1 h + \mathcal{A}_2 h^2 + \ldots + \mathcal{A}_n h^n, \end{aligned}$$

et l'on voit que le développement du premier membre suivant les puissances de h donne bien pour les coefficients $\mathcal{A}$, $\mathcal{A}_1$, ... les valeurs précédemment obtenues.

Cela posé, nous tirerons de la décomposition en fractions simples de la fraction rationnelle $f(x)$ la transformation suivante de l'expression $e^{\omega x} f(x)$. Soit, à cet effet, en désignant la partie entière par $F(x)$,

$$f(x) = F(x) + \sum \frac{A}{x - a} + \sum \frac{A_1}{(x - a)^2} + \ldots + \sum \frac{A_n}{(x - a)^{n+1}},$$

ou plutôt, après avoir modifié convenablement les constantes A_1, A_2, ..., A_n,

$$\begin{aligned} f(x) = F(x) &+ \sum A(x - a)^{-1} \\ &+ \sum A_1 \frac{d(x - a)^{-1}}{dx} + \ldots + \sum A_n \frac{d^n(x - a)^{-1}}{dx^n}; \end{aligned}$$

je ferai, d'après la remarque précédente,

$$\begin{aligned} &e^{\omega x}\left[A(x - a)^{-1} + A_1 \frac{d(x - a)^{-1}}{dx} + \ldots + A_n \frac{d^n(x - a)^{-1}}{dx^n}\right] \\ &= \mathcal{A}[e^{\omega x}(x - a)^{-1}] + \mathcal{A}_1 \frac{d}{dx}[e^{\omega x}(x - a)^{-1}] + \ldots \\ &\qquad + \mathcal{A}_n \frac{d^n}{dx^n}[e^{\omega x}(x - a)^{-1}]. \end{aligned}$$

Or, en ajoutant membre à membre les relations de même nature qui correspondent aux divers groupes de fractions simples, on trouvera cette expression

$$\begin{aligned} e^{\omega x} f(x) = e^{\omega x} \mathrm{F}(x) + \sum \mathcal{A} [e^{\omega x}(x-a)^{-1}] \\ + \sum \mathcal{A}_1 \frac{d}{dx} [e^{\omega x}(x-a)^{-1}] + \ldots \\ + \sum \mathcal{A}_n \frac{d^n}{dx^n} [e^{\omega x}(x-a)^{-1}], \end{aligned}$$

où les quantités $\frac{e^{\omega x}}{x-a}$ se montrent comme ayant, à l'égard de la fonction transcendante $e^{\omega x} f(x)$, le même rôle d'éléments simples que les fractions $\frac{1}{x-a}$ par rapport à la fonction rationnelle $f(x)$. Il en résulte que l'intégrale $\int e^{\omega x} f(x)\, dx$ se trouve exprimée d'une part au moyen de celle-ci $\int e^{\omega x} \mathrm{F}(x)\, dx$, précédemment obtenue sous cette forme :

$$\int e^{\omega x} \mathrm{F}(x)\, dx = e^{\omega x} \left[\frac{\mathrm{F}(x)}{\omega} - \frac{\mathrm{F}'(x)}{\omega^2} + \frac{\mathrm{F}''(x)}{\omega^3} - \ldots \right];$$

en second lieu, par les expressions également explicites

$$\sum \mathcal{A}_1 [e^{\omega x}(x-a)^{-1}], \qquad \sum \mathcal{A}_2 \frac{d}{dx} [e^{\omega x}(x-a)^{-1}], \qquad \ldots,$$

et, enfin, par la quantité

$$\sum \mathcal{A} \int e^{\omega x}(x-a)^{-1}\, dx,$$

où figure au fond, comme nous allons voir, une seule et unique transcendante.

Soit, à cet effet, pour un instant,

$$\varphi(z) = \int \frac{e^z\, dz}{z};$$

en faisant

$$z = \omega(x-a),$$

on aura

$$\varphi[\omega(x-a)] = \int \frac{e^{\omega(x-a)}\, dx}{x-a},$$

d'où

$$\int \frac{e^{\omega x}\, dx}{x-a} = e^{\omega a} \varphi[\omega(x-a)],$$

et, par conséquent,

$$\sum \mathcal{A} \int \frac{e^{\omega x}\,dx}{x-a} = \sum \mathcal{A} e^{\omega a} \varphi[\omega(x-a)].$$

La transcendante $\int \frac{e^z\,dz}{z}$, si l'on fait $e^z = x$, prend la forme $\int \frac{dx}{\log x}$ et reçoit la dénomination de *logarithme intégral*. On a démontré l'impossibilité de la représenter par des combinaisons en nombre fini de fonctions algébriques, logarithmiques et exponentielles, d'où résulte qu'on doit l'envisager comme un élément analytique *sui generis*, dont la notion première s'est offerte, ainsi que celle des transcendantes elliptiques et abéliennes, par la voie du Calcul intégral. Elle a été l'objet de nombreux travaux, mais nous nous bornerons à mentionner à son égard une propriété singulière qui en montrera le rôle dans l'Arithmétique supérieure. Elle consiste en ce que l'intégrale définie $\int_a^b \frac{dx}{\log x}$ donne approximativement la valeur N du nombre des nombres premiers compris entre a et b, l'approximation étant d'autant plus grande que b est plus grand par rapport à a, et étant ainsi caractérisée que la limite du rapport de l'intégrale au nombre N est l'unité pour b infini.

II. Il existe une infinité de cas dans lesquels l'intégrale

$$\int e^{\omega x} f(x)\,dx$$

s'obtient sous forme finie explicite; il suffit pour cela que les diverses constantes $\mathcal{A}$ s'évanouissent. J'ajoute que ces conditions sont nécessaires si l'on veut que $\int e^{\omega x} f(x)\,dx$ s'exprime au moyen d'une fonction rationnelle multipliée par $e^{\omega x}$. Il est aisé, en effet, de reconnaître l'impossibilité d'une relation de la forme suivante :

$$\sum \mathcal{A} \int \frac{e^{\omega x}\,dx}{x-a} = e^{\omega x} \mathfrak{F}(x),$$

$\mathfrak{F}(x)$ étant en général une fonction algébrique, car en faisant $x = a + h$, et développant suivant les puissances croissantes de h, le premier membre contiendra la quantité $\mathcal{A} e^{\omega a} \log h$, et aucun terme logarithmique ne pourra, dans l'hypothèse admise, provenir du second membre. On voit par là toute l'importance des constantes $\mathcal{A}$; aussi nous allons en donner une détermination nouvelle, en déduisant à la fois et directement de la formule

$$e^{\omega x} f(x) = e^{\omega x} \mathrm{F}(x) + \sum \mathcal{A}[e^{\omega x}(x-a)^{-1}] + \sum \mathcal{A}_1 \frac{d}{dx}[e^{\omega x}(x-a)^{-1}] + \ldots$$

le groupe de coefficients $\mathcal{A}, \mathcal{A}_1, \ldots, \mathcal{A}_n$.

Soit à cet effet $x = a + h$; développons, comme tout à l'heure, suivant les puissances négatives; posons

$$e^{\omega h} f(a+h) = \mathrm{A} h^{-1} + \mathrm{A}_1 \frac{dh^{-1}}{dh} + \mathrm{A}_2 \frac{dh^{-2}}{dh^2} + \ldots,$$

d'où, par conséquent,

$$e^{\omega(a+h)} f(a+h) = e^{\omega a}\left(\mathrm{A} h^{-1} + \mathrm{A}_1 \frac{dh^{-1}}{dh} + \mathrm{A}_2 \frac{dh^{-2}}{dh^2} + \ldots\right).$$

Or, dans le second membre, les termes en $\frac{1}{h}, \frac{1}{h^2}, \cdots$ ne peuvent provenir que de la quantité $e^{\omega x}(x-a)^{-1}$ et de ses dérivées, qui donnent, en effet, en négligeant les puissances positives,

$$\begin{aligned} e^{\omega x}(x-a)^{-1} &= e^{\omega a} h^{-1} + \ldots, \\ \frac{d}{dx}[e^{\omega x}(x-a)^{-1}] &= e^{\omega a} \frac{dh^{-1}}{dh} + \ldots, \\ \frac{d^2}{dx^2}[e^{\omega x}(x-a)^{-1}] &= e^{\omega a} \frac{d^2 h^{-1}}{dh^2} + \ldots, \\ &\ldots\ldots\ldots\ldots\ldots\ldots, \end{aligned}$$

attendu que la dérivée de h par rapport à x est l'unité. L'expression suivante

$$e^{\omega a}\left(\mathcal{A} h^{-1} + \mathcal{A}_1 \frac{dh^{-1}}{dh} + \mathcal{A}_2 \frac{d^2 h^{-1}}{dh^2} + \ldots\right)$$

représente, par conséquent, la portion du développement du second membre qui renferme les puissances négatives de h, et l'on voit qu'on a

$$\mathcal{A} = \mathrm{A}, \qquad \mathcal{A}_1 = \mathrm{A}_1, \qquad \mathcal{A}_2 = \mathrm{A}_2, \qquad \ldots.$$

Soit, par exemple,

$$f(x) = \left(1 - \frac{1}{ax}\right)\left(1 - \frac{1}{bx}\right),$$

et prenons

$$\omega = a + b;$$

on multipliera le développement de l'exponentielle

$$e^{(a+b)h} = 1 + (a+b)h + (a+b)^2\frac{h^2}{2} + \ldots$$

par la quantité

$$f(h) = \frac{1}{abh^2} - \frac{a+b}{abh} + 1,$$

ce qui donne

$$e^{(a+b)h} f(h) = \frac{1}{abh^2} - \frac{a^2+b^2}{2ab} + \ldots.$$

Or, le terme en $\frac{1}{h}$ manquant, nous sommes assurés que l'intégrale est possible sous forme finie explicite; on a, en effet,

$$\int e^{(a+b)x}\left(1 - \frac{1}{ax}\right)\left(1 - \frac{1}{bx}\right)dx = e^{(a+b)x}\left(\frac{1}{a+b} - \frac{1}{abx}\right),$$

et l'on trouvera semblablement

$$\begin{aligned}
&\int e^{(a+b)x}\left(1 - \frac{3}{ax} + \frac{3}{a^2x^2}\right)\left(1 - \frac{3}{bx} + \frac{3}{b^2x^2}\right)dx \\
&= \frac{e^{(a+b)x}}{a+b} + \frac{3(a^2+b^2)}{2a^2b^2}\,\frac{e^{(a+b)x}}{x} - \frac{3}{2a^2b^2}\,\frac{d^2}{dx^2}\left(\frac{e^{(a+b)x}}{x}\right) \\
&= e^{(a+b)x}\left[\frac{1}{a+b} - \frac{3}{abx} + \frac{3(a+b)}{a^2b^2x^2} - \frac{3}{a^2b^2x^3}\right].
\end{aligned}$$

III. J'ajouterai succinctement, en vue des intégrales

$$\int \cos\omega x\, f(x)\,dx, \qquad \int \sin\omega x\, f(x)\,dx;$$

les conséquences auxquelles conduit la relation générale

$$e^{\omega x} f(x) = e^{\omega x}\,\mathrm{F}(x) + \sum \mathcal{A}[e^{\omega x}(x-a)^{-1}] + \ldots,$$

lorsqu'on y change ω en $\omega\sqrt{-1}$. En supposant pour plus de simplicité que dorénavant ω soit réel, ainsi que $f(x)$ et les quantités a, je remplacerai les coefficients $\mathcal{A}$, $\mathcal{A}_1$, ... par $\mathcal{A}+\mathcal{A}'\sqrt{-1}$, $\mathcal{A}_1+\mathcal{A}'_1\sqrt{-1}$, ... Cette équation donne alors les deux suivantes :

$$\begin{aligned}
&\cos\omega x\, f(x)\\
&\quad=\cos\omega x\,\mathrm{F}(x)+\sum\mathcal{A}[\cos\omega x(x-a)^{-1}]-\sum\mathcal{A}'[\sin\omega x(x-a)^{-1}]\\
&\qquad+\sum\mathcal{A}_1\frac{d}{dx}[\cos\omega x(x-a)^{-1}]-\sum\mathcal{A}'_1\frac{d}{dx}[\sin\omega x(x-a)^{-1}]\\
&\qquad\ldots\ldots\ldots\ldots\ldots\ldots\ldots\ldots,
\end{aligned}$$

$$\begin{aligned}
&\sin\omega x\, f(x)\\
&\quad=\sin\omega x\,\mathrm{F}(x)+\sum\mathcal{A}[\sin\omega x(x-a)^{-1}]+\sum\mathcal{A}'[\cos\omega x(x-a)^{-1}]\\
&\qquad+\sum\mathcal{A}_1\frac{d}{dx}[\sin\omega x(x-a)^{-1}]+\sum\mathcal{A}'_1\frac{d}{dx}[\cos\omega x(x-a)^{-1}]\\
&\qquad\ldots\ldots\ldots\ldots\ldots\ldots\ldots\ldots
\end{aligned}$$

On voit donc que les intégrales

$$\int\cos\omega x\, f(x)\,dx,\qquad \int\sin\omega x\, f(x)\,dx$$

s'expriment en général par les transcendantes

$$\int\frac{\cos\omega x\,dx}{x-a},\quad \int\frac{\sin\omega x\,dx}{x-a},$$

qui elles-mêmes se réduisent à celles-ci :

$$\int\frac{\cos z\,dz}{z},\quad \int\frac{\sin z\,dz}{z}.$$

Nous voyons aussi qu'on obtiendra à la fois pour l'une et pour l'autre, des valeurs sous forme finie explicite, lorsque les divers coefficients $\mathcal{A}$ et $\mathcal{A}'$ s'évanouiront. Or, $\mathcal{A}+\mathcal{A}'\sqrt{-1}$ étant le coefficient de $\frac{1}{h}$ dans le développement de

$$e^{\omega h\sqrt{-1}}f(a+h)=(\cos\omega h+\sqrt{-1}\sin\omega h)\,f(a+h),$$

il en résulte qu'en supposant réelles, comme nous l'avons admis, les quantités ω et a, ainsi que la fonction $f(x)$, $\mathcal{A}$ et $\mathcal{A}'$ seront aussi, à l'égard des fonctions

$$\cos\omega h\, f(a+h),\qquad \sin\omega h\, f(a+h),$$

les coefficients des termes en $\frac{1}{h}$.

Soit, comme application, l'intégrale

$$\int\left(\cos ax - \frac{\sin ax}{ax}\right)\left(\cos bx - \frac{\sin bx}{bx}\right)dx;$$

j'écrirai d'abord

$$\begin{aligned} &2\left(\cos ax - \frac{\sin ax}{ax}\right)\left(\cos bx - \frac{\sin bx}{bx}\right) \\ &= \cos(a+b)x\left(1 - \frac{1}{abx^2}\right) - \sin(a+b)x\,\frac{a+b}{abx} \\ &\quad + \cos(a-b)x\left(1 + \frac{1}{abx^2}\right) + \sin(a-b)x\,\frac{a-b}{abx}, \end{aligned}$$

et nous serons conduits à une combinaison linéaire des quatre quantités

$$\int\frac{\cos(a+b)x\,dx}{x^2}, \quad \int\frac{\sin(a+b)x\,dx}{x},$$
$$\int\frac{\cos(a-b)x\,dx}{x^2}, \quad \int\frac{\sin(a-b)x\,dx}{x},$$

dont aucune ne peut s'obtenir, l'expression proposée s'exprimant néanmoins sous forme finie explicite. Supposons, en effet, dans les formules précédentes,

$$f(x) = \frac{1}{x^2}, \qquad \omega = a+b;$$

on aura

$$\frac{\cos(a+b)x}{x^2} = -(a+b)\frac{\sin(a+b)x}{x} - \frac{d}{dx}\left[\frac{\cos(a+b)x}{x}\right],$$

puis, en changeant b en $-b$,

$$\frac{\cos(a-b)x}{x^2} = -(a-b)\frac{\sin(a-b)x}{x} - \frac{d}{dx}\left[\frac{\cos(a-b)x}{x}\right].$$

Il en résulte, en intégrant,

$$\int\left[\frac{\cos(a+b)x}{x^2} + (a+b)\frac{\sin(a+b)x}{x}\right]dx = -\frac{\cos(a+b)x}{x},$$
$$\int\left[\frac{\cos(a-b)x}{x^2} + (a-b)\frac{\sin(a-b)x}{x}\right]dx = -\frac{\cos(a-b)x}{x},$$

et, par conséquent, ce résultat

$$2\int\left(\cos ax - \frac{\sin ax}{ax}\right)\left(\cos bx - \frac{\sin bx}{bx}\right)dx$$
$$= -\frac{\sin(a+b)x}{a+b} + \frac{\cos(a+b)x}{abx}$$
$$-\frac{\sin(a-b)x}{a-b} - \frac{\cos(a-b)x}{abx}.$$

C'est le cas le plus simple d'une proposition générale concernant les réduites successives

$$\frac{x}{1},\quad \frac{3x}{3-x^2},\quad \frac{15x-x^3}{15-6x^2},\quad \ldots$$

de la fraction continue de Lambert

$$\operatorname{tang} x = \cfrac{x}{1 - \cfrac{x^2}{3 - \cfrac{x^2}{5 - \ldots}}}$$

Soit, en général, $\frac{P}{Q}$ la $n^{\text{ième}}$ réduite, P et Q étant des polynomes entiers en x, et posons

$$\varphi(x) = \frac{P\cos x - Q\sin x}{x^n};$$

l'intégrale $\int\varphi(ax)\,\varphi(bx)\,dx$ pourra toujours être obtenue sous forme finie explicite. La fonction $\varphi(x)$ donne aussi ce résultat

$$\int\frac{dx}{\varphi^2(x)} = \frac{P\sin x + Q\cos x}{P\cos x + Q\sin x};$$

c'est, sous une forme très simple, la valeur d'une intégrale que nous n'avons point de méthode pour aborder, car elle n'appartient à aucune des catégories considérées jusqu'ici; on verra comment on y parvient facilement, dans le seconde partie du Cours.

Je remarquerai enfin que, en désignant par $F(\sin x, \cos x)$ un polynome entier en $\sin x$ et $\cos x$, l'intégrale

$$\int F(\sin x, \cos x)\,f(x)\,dx$$

rentre dans celles que nous venons de traiter, ce polynome pouvant être transformé en une fonction linéaire des sinus et cosinus des multiples de la variable. La quantité $\int \frac{\sin^n x}{x^m} dx$, par exemple, étant d'abord, abstraction faite d'un facteur constant, mise sous la forme

$$\int \sin^n x \frac{d^m (x^{-1})}{dx^m} dx,$$

sera immédiatement ramenée, au moyen de l'intégration par parties, à celle-ci :

$$\int \frac{d^m \sin^n x}{dx^m} \frac{dx}{x}.$$

Or, $\frac{d^m \sin^n x}{dx^m}$ est une somme de cosinus ou une somme de sinus de multiples de x, suivant que $m+n$ est pair ou impair ; dans le premier cas, l'intégrale se réduit donc à $\int \frac{\cos z\, dz}{z}$, et dans le second à $\int \frac{\sin z}{z} dz$.

De l'intégrale $\int e^{\omega x} f(\sin x, \cos x)\, dx$.

I. La propriété caractéristique de la transcendante

$$e^{\omega x} f(\sin x, \cos x),$$

où $f(\sin x, \cos x)$ désigne une fonction rationnelle de $\sin x$ et $\cos x$, consiste en ce qu'elle se reproduit multipliée par un facteur constant $e^{2\omega\pi}$, lorsqu'on y change x en $x + 2\pi$. Elle se rapproche ainsi des fonctions périodiques, et le procédé d'intégration résultera encore d'une décomposition en éléments simples, qu'on obtient comme il suit. Je pars, à cet effet, de la relation générale établie page 58, à savoir

$$f(\sin x, \cos x) = \Pi(x) + \Phi(x);$$

elle nous donne dans la fonction proposée une première partie $e^{\omega x}\Pi(x)$, qui en sera semblablement regardée comme la partie entière et dont l'intégration est immédiate. En effet, $\Pi(x)$ étant composée linéairement des quantités $\cos kx$, $\sin kx$, il suffit d'employer les formules

$$\int e^{\omega x}\cos kx\,dx = \frac{e^{\omega x}(\omega\cos kx + k\sin kx)}{\omega^2+k^2},$$

$$\int e^{\omega x}\sin kx\,dx = \frac{e^{\omega x}(\omega\sin kx - k\cos kx)}{\omega^2+k^2}.$$

Maintenant nous parviendrons aux éléments simples, propres à la nouvelle transcendante, en appliquant la relation de la page 86 à la seconde partie $e^{\omega x}\Phi(x)$, c'est-à-dire aux quantités suivantes :

$$e^{\omega x}\left[\mathcal{A}\cot\frac{1}{2}(x-\alpha)+\mathcal{A}_1\frac{d\cot\frac{1}{2}(x-\alpha)}{dx}+\ldots+\mathcal{A}_n\frac{d^n\cot\frac{1}{2}(x-\alpha)}{dx^n}\right],$$

qui, en conséquence, prendront cette nouvelle forme

$$\mathfrak{A}e^{\omega x}\cot\frac{1}{2}(x-\alpha)+\mathfrak{A}_1\frac{d}{dx}\left[e^{\omega x}\cot\frac{1}{2}(x-\alpha)\right]+\ldots$$
$$+\mathfrak{A}_n\frac{d^n}{dx^n}\left[e^{\omega x}\cot\frac{1}{2}(x-\alpha)\right].$$

Or, en faisant la somme d'expressions semblables, pour les différents systèmes de valeurs constantes $\mathfrak{A}$ et $\mathfrak{B}$, nous trouverons pour formule de décomposition

$$\begin{aligned}
&e^{\omega x}f(\sin x,\cos x)\\
&= e^{\omega x}(x)+\mathfrak{A}\left[e^{\omega x}\cot\frac{1}{2}(x-\alpha)\right]+\mathfrak{A}_1\frac{d}{dx}\left[e^{\omega x}\cot\frac{1}{2}(x-\alpha)\right]+\ldots\\
&\qquad+\mathfrak{B}\left[e^{\omega x}\cot\frac{1}{2}(x-\beta)\right]+\mathfrak{B}_1\frac{d}{dx}\left[e^{\omega x}\cot\frac{1}{2}(x-\beta)\right]+\ldots\\
&\qquad\ldots\ldots\ldots\ldots\ldots\ldots\ldots\ldots\ldots\ldots\ldots\ldots\\
&\qquad+\mathfrak{L}\left[e^{\omega x}\cot\frac{1}{2}(x-\lambda)\right]+\mathfrak{L}_1\frac{d}{dx}\left[e^{\omega x}\cot\frac{1}{2}(x-\lambda)\right]+\ldots.
\end{aligned}$$

C'est, à l'égard de notre fonction, l'équivalent de la décomposition en fractions simples des fractions rationnelles; les quantités qui jouent le rôle d'éléments simples étant

$$e^{\omega x}\cot\frac{1}{2}(x-\alpha),\quad e^{\omega x}\cot\frac{1}{2}(x-\beta),\quad\ldots,\quad e^{\omega x}\cot\frac{1}{2}(x-\lambda),$$

il en résulte qu'en faisant pour un instant

$$\varphi(x)=\int e^{\omega x}\cot\frac{1}{2}x\,dx,$$

l'intégrale

$$\int e^{\omega x} f(\sin x, \cos x)\, dx$$

sera exprimée, d'une part, par la somme

$$\mathfrak{A} e^{\omega\alpha} \varphi(x-\alpha) + \mathfrak{B} e^{\omega\beta} \varphi(x-\beta) + \ldots + \mathfrak{L} e^{\omega\lambda} \varphi(x-\lambda),$$

et de l'autre, au moyen des fonctions explicites de la variable. Les conditions $\mathfrak{A} = 0$, $\mathfrak{B} = 0$, $\ldots$, $\mathfrak{L} = 0$ sont donc suffisantes pour que la partie non explicite disparaisse, et la valeur même de l'intégrale sera connue au moyen des divers coefficients $\mathfrak{A}_1$, $\mathfrak{A}_2$, $\ldots$, $\mathfrak{B}_1$, $\mathfrak{B}_2$, ... Il importe donc d'en avoir une détermination directe, et on l'obtient comme il suit.

II. En ayant, en vue, pour fixer les idées, le groupe des quantités $\mathfrak{A}$, $\mathfrak{A}_1$, $\ldots$, $\mathfrak{A}_n$, nous ferons $x = \alpha + h$ dans la fonction proposée, et développant suivant les puissances ascendantes de h, nous représenterons les termes affectés des puissances négatives de cette quantité sous cette forme

$$\begin{aligned} & e^{\omega(\alpha+h)} f[\sin(\alpha+h), \cos(\alpha+h)] \\ & = e^{\omega\alpha}\left(\mathrm{A} h^{-1} + \mathrm{A}_1 \frac{dh^{-1}}{dh} + \ldots + \mathrm{A}_n \frac{d^n h^{-1}}{dh^n}\right) + \ldots. \end{aligned}$$

Or, la relation

$$\begin{aligned} & e^{\omega x} f(\sin x, \cos x) \\ & = e^{\omega x}\Pi(x) + \mathfrak{A}\left[e^{\omega x}\cot\frac{1}{2}(x-\alpha)\right] + \mathfrak{A}_1 \frac{d}{dx}\left[e^{\omega x}\cot\frac{1}{2}(x-\alpha)\right] + \ldots \\ & \quad + \mathfrak{B}\left[e^{\omega x}\cot\frac{1}{2}(x-\beta)\right] + \mathfrak{B}_1 \frac{d}{dx}\left[e^{\omega x}\cot\frac{1}{2}(x-\beta)\right] + \ldots \\ & \ldots\ldots\ldots\ldots\ldots\ldots\ldots\ldots\ldots\ldots\ldots\ldots \end{aligned}$$

montre que, pour $x = \alpha + h$, la partie suivante du second membre, savoir

$$\mathfrak{A}\left[e^{\omega x}\cot\frac{1}{2}(x-\alpha)\right] + \mathfrak{A}_1 \frac{d}{dx}\left[e^{\omega x}\cot\frac{1}{2}(x-\alpha)\right] + \ldots$$

sera seule à donner des puissances négatives de h. Maintenant on trouve

$$e^{\omega x}\cot\frac{1}{2}(x-\alpha) = e^{\omega\alpha}\left(\frac{2}{h} + 2\omega - \frac{h}{6} + \ldots\right),$$

puis, abstraction faite des puissances positives,

$$\frac{d^n}{dx^n}\left[e^{\omega x}\cot\frac{1}{2}(x-\alpha)\right] = 2e^{\omega\alpha}\frac{d^n h^{-1}}{dh^n},$$

la dérivée de h par rapport à x étant l'unité; nous en conclurons que l'expression

$$2e^{\omega\alpha}\left(\mathfrak{A}h^{-1} + \mathfrak{A}_1\frac{dh^{-1}}{dh} + \ldots + \mathfrak{A}_n\frac{d^n h^{-1}}{dh^n}\right)$$

représente dans le développement du second membre tous les termes contenant des puissances négatives de h, de sorte que l'on aura

$$\mathfrak{A} = \frac{1}{2}A, \qquad \mathfrak{A}_1 = \frac{1}{2}A_1, \qquad \ldots, \qquad \mathfrak{A}_n = \frac{1}{2}A_n.$$

Pour faire une application de ce résultat, nous considérerons la fonction

$$e^{(a+b)x}\left(a - \frac{1}{2}\cot\frac{x}{2}\right)\left(b - \frac{1}{2}\cot\frac{x}{2}\right),$$

qui devient infinie pour la seule valeur $x = 0$, de sorte qu'il suffira de la développer suivant les puissances ascendantes de la variable. Or, on a

$$e^{ax}\left(a - \frac{1}{2}\cot\frac{x}{2}\right) = \left(1 + ax + \frac{a^2x^2}{2} + \ldots\right)\left(-\frac{1}{x} + a + \frac{x}{12} + \ldots\right)$$
$$= -\frac{1}{x} + \frac{1+6a^2}{12}x + \ldots,$$

et pareillement

$$e^{bx}\left(b - \frac{1}{2}\cot\frac{x}{2}\right) = -\frac{1}{x} + \frac{1+6b^2}{12}x + \ldots;$$

d'où, en multipliant membre à membre,

$$e^{(a+b)x}\left(a - \frac{1}{2}\cot\frac{x}{2}\right)\left(b - \frac{1}{2}\cot\frac{x}{2}\right) = \frac{1}{x^2} + \ldots.$$

Le terme en $\frac{1}{x}$ manque, ainsi $A = 0$; mettant ensuite $\frac{1}{x^2}$ sous la forme $\frac{d(x^{-1})}{dx}$, on en conclut $A_1 = -1$; par conséquent

$$\mathfrak{A} = 0, \qquad \mathfrak{A}_1 = -\frac{1}{2}.$$

Maintenant nous devons calculer la partie entière $\Pi(x)$ de la fonction

$$\left(a - \frac{1}{2}\cot\frac{x}{2}\right)\left(b - \frac{1}{2}\cot\frac{x}{2}\right),$$

qui est simplement une constante. Or on a, d'après la règle établie page 63,

$$G = \left(a + \frac{1}{2}\sqrt{-1}\right)\left(b + \frac{1}{2}\sqrt{-1}\right), \qquad H = \left(a - \frac{1}{2}\sqrt{-1}\right)\left(b - \frac{1}{2}\sqrt{-1}\right),$$

donc

$$\Pi(x) = \frac{G + H}{2} = ab - \frac{1}{4},$$

et nous obtenons, en conséquence, la relation

$$e^{(a+b)x}\left(a - \frac{1}{2}\cot\frac{x}{2}\right)\left(b - \frac{1}{2}\cot\frac{x}{2}\right)$$
$$= e^{(a+b)x}\left(ab - \frac{1}{4}\right) - \frac{1}{2}\frac{d}{dx}\left(e^{(a+b)x}\cot\frac{x}{2}\right),$$

d'où cette expression sous forme finie explicite de l'intégrale du premier membre, savoir

$$\int e^{(a+b)x}\left(a - \frac{1}{2}\cot\frac{x}{2}\right)\left(b - \frac{1}{2}\cot\frac{x}{2}\right)dx = e^{(a+b)x}\left[\frac{4ab - 1}{4(a+b)} - \frac{1}{2}\cot\frac{x}{2}\right].$$

Ce résultat est le cas le plus simple du théorème suivant, auquel nous serons amenés dans la seconde partie du Cours. Soit, en désignant par n un nombre entier quelconque,

$$F(x) = (x-1)^a (x+1)^{-a} \frac{d^n}{dx^n}\left[(x-1)^{n-a}(x+1)^{n+a}\right],$$

il est aisé de voir que $F(x)$ est un polynome entier en x et en a du degré n; cela étant, je représenterai par $\mathcal{F}(x, a)$ ce qu'il devient en y changeant x en $x\sqrt{-1}$ et a en $a\sqrt{-1}$, suppression faite du facteur $(\sqrt{-1})^n$. On aura ainsi pour $n = 1$

$$\mathcal{F}(x) = 2(x - a),$$

pour $n = 2$

$$\mathcal{F}(x) = 4(3x^2 - 3ax + a^2 + 1), \qquad \ldots;$$

or, l'intégrale

$$\int e^{(a+b)x} \mathfrak{F}\left(\cot\frac{x}{2}, 2a\right) \mathfrak{F}\left(\cot\frac{x}{2}, 2b\right) dx,$$

ou encore celle-ci, qui s'y ramène

$$\int e^{(a+b)x} \mathfrak{F}(\cot x, a) \mathfrak{F}(\cot x, b) dx,$$

s'expriment toujours sous forme finie explicite.

De l'intégrale $\int_{-\infty}^{+\infty} f(\sin x, \cos x), f_1(x)\, dx$.

I. Je supposerai que $f(\sin x, \cos x)$ soit une fonction rationnelle de $\sin x$ et $\cos x$, et $f_1(x)$ une fonction rationnelle de x, sans partie entière; faisant ensuite, pour abréger,

$$\varphi(x) = f(\sin x, \cos x) f_1(x),$$

nous éviterons la considération de l'infini *a priori*, comme il s'offre dans l'expression proposée

$$\int_{-\infty}^{+\infty} \varphi(x)\, dx,$$

en la remplaçant par celle-ci

$$\int_{-\varepsilon}^{+\eta} \varphi(x)\, dx,$$

en cherchant sa limite lorsqu'on fait croître indéfiniment ε et η. En adoptant en outre pour ces quantités ces formes particulières

$$\varepsilon = 2m\pi, \qquad \eta = 2(n+1)\pi.$$

où m et n sont des nombres entiers, je me fonderai sur une transformation remarquable et importante qui a été donnée par Legendre dans les *Exercices de Calcul intégral*, et par Poisson dans son *Mémoire sur les intégrales définies* (*Journal de l'École Polytechnique*, XVIIe Cahier, p. 630). Elle consiste à décomposer l'intégrale en une somme d'autres de même forme dont les limites soient des multiples consécutifs de 2π, en écrivant

$$\begin{aligned}\int_{-2m\pi}^{+2(n+1)\pi} \varphi(x)\,dx = & \int_{-2m\pi}^{-2(m-1)\pi} \varphi(x)\,dx \\ & + \int_{-2(m-1)\pi}^{-2(m-2)\pi} \varphi(x)\,dx + \ldots \\ & + \int_{-2\pi}^{0} \varphi(x)\,dx + \int_{0}^{2\pi} \varphi(x)\,dx \\ & + \int_{2\pi}^{4\pi} \varphi(x)\,dx + \ldots + \int_{2n\pi}^{2(n+1)\pi} \varphi(x)\,dx,\end{aligned}$$

ou bien, pour abréger,

$$\int_{-2m\pi}^{+2(n+1)\pi} \varphi(x)\,dx = \sum_{k=-m}^{k=+n} \int_{2k\pi}^{2(k+1)\pi} \varphi(x)\,dx.$$

Cela étant, nous ferons dans le second membre $x = z + 2k\pi$, ce qui donnera

$$\int_{2k\pi}^{2(k+1)\pi} \varphi(x)\,dx = \int_{0}^{2\pi} \varphi(z + 2k\pi)\,dz,$$

et, par conséquent,

$$\int_{-2m\pi}^{+2(n+1)\pi} \varphi(x)\,dx = \sum_{k=-m}^{k=+n} \int_{0}^{2\pi} \varphi(z + 2k\pi)\,dz,$$

ou encore

$$\int_{-2m\pi}^{+2(n+1)\pi} \varphi(x)\,dx = \int_{0}^{2\pi} \Phi(x)\,dx,$$

en posant

$$\Phi(x) = \sum_{k=-m}^{k=+n} \varphi(x + 2k\pi).$$

Nous rencontrons ainsi l'expression analytique d'une fonction périodique qui a été indiquée dans l'Introduction, et sous la condition qu'en faisant croître indéfiniment m et n, la série

$$\begin{aligned}\Phi(x) = \varphi(x) + \varphi(x + 2\pi) + \ldots + \varphi(x + 2n\pi) \\ + \varphi(x - 2\pi) + \ldots + \varphi(x - 2m\pi)\end{aligned}$$

soit convergente, nous aurons

$$\Phi(x+2\pi)=\Phi(x).$$

Or, cette transformation donne la valeur de l'intégrale définie proposée; je dis, en effet, que $\Phi(x)$ s'exprime par une fonction rationnelle de $\sin x$ et $\cos x$, lorsqu'on suppose, comme nous l'avons admis,

$$\varphi(x)=f(\sin x, \cos x)f_1(x).$$

II. Je me servirai pour le faire voir de la formule suivante, qui sera démontrée dans le Cours de seconde année, savoir :

$$\sum_{k=-m}^{k=+n}\frac{1}{x+2k\pi}=\frac{1}{2}\cot\frac{x}{2}+\frac{1}{2\pi}\log\frac{n}{m}+\frac{x+\pi}{4m\pi}+\frac{x-\pi}{4n\pi}+\ldots,$$

où les termes non écrits contiennent en dénominateur le carré et les puissances plus élevées de m et n. Elle fait voir que la série du premier membre appartient à l'espèce des suites semi-convergentes, de sorte qu'elle ne représentera $\frac{1}{2}\cot\frac{x}{2}$ qu'en supposant le rapport $\frac{m}{n}$ égal à l'unité pour m et n infinis. Mais, en général, soit λ la limite de la constante $\frac{1}{2\pi}\log\frac{n}{m}$ lorsqu'on fait croître indéfiniment m et n, ce qui donnera

$$\sum_{k=-m}^{k=+n}\frac{1}{x+2k\pi}=\frac{1}{2}\cot\frac{x}{2}+\lambda;$$

nous remarquerons que cette quantité disparaît dans l'expression des dérivées successives du premier membre, qui sont ainsi des séries absolument convergentes, dont la formule nous donne les valeurs, à savoir :

$$\sum_{k=-m}^{k=+n}\frac{d(x+2k\pi)^{-1}}{dx}=\frac{1}{2}\,\frac{d\cot\frac{x}{2}}{dx},$$

$$\sum_{k=-m}^{k=+n}\frac{d^2(x+2k\pi)^{-1}}{dx^2}=\frac{1}{2}\,\frac{d^2\cot\frac{x}{2}}{dx^2}.$$

Cela étant, il suffit d'observer qu'ayant, par la décomposition en fractions simples,

$$f_1(x) = \sum \frac{A}{x-a} + \sum \frac{A_1}{(x-\alpha)^2} + \ldots + \sum \frac{A_n}{(x-\alpha)^n},$$

ou plutôt

$$f_1(x) = \sum A(x-\alpha)^{-1} + \sum A_1 \frac{d(x-\alpha)^{-1}}{dx} + \ldots + \sum A_n \frac{d^n(x-\alpha)^{-1}}{dx^n},$$

on en conclut sur-le-champ

$$\begin{aligned}\sum_{k=-m}^{k=+n} f_1(x+2k\pi) = \lambda \sum A + \frac{1}{2} \sum A \cot \frac{1}{2}(x-\alpha) \\ + \frac{1}{2} \sum A_1 \frac{d \cot \frac{1}{2}(x-\alpha)}{dx} + \ldots \\ + \frac{1}{2} \sum A_n \frac{d^n \cot \frac{1}{2}(x-\alpha)}{dx^n}.\end{aligned}$$

Nous obtenons ainsi une fonction rationnelle de $\sin x$ et $\cos x$; or, ayant

$$\varphi(x) = f(\sin x, \cos x)\, f_1(x),$$

d'où

$$\Phi(x) = f(\sin x, \cos x) \sum_{k=-m}^{k=+n} f_1(x+2k\pi),$$

on voit que $\Phi(x)$ est aussi une expression de même nature. Ajoutons que, dans l'intégrale $\int_0^{2\pi} \Phi(x)\, dx$, à laquelle se trouve ramenée la proposée, la quantité indéterminée λ a pour coefficient

$$\sum A \int_0^{2\pi} (f \sin x, \cos x)\, dx;$$

elle aura donc une valeur entièrement déterminée sous l'une ou l'autre de ces deux conditions

$$\sum A = 0 \qquad \text{ou} \qquad \int_0^{2\pi} f(\sin x, \cos x)\, dx = 0.$$

Il ne sera pas inutile, avant de faire des applications de ce résultat, de présenter sur l'intégrale indéfinie

$$\int f(\sin x,\ \cos x)\, f_1(x)\, dx$$

quelques remarques qui montreront comment elle diffère de celles que nous avons précédemment considérées.

III. Soit, en partant de la formule de décomposition en éléments simples,

$$f(\sin x,\ \cos x) = \Pi(x) + \Phi(x),$$

nous en conclurons

$$\int f(\sin x,\ \cos x)\, f_1(x)\, dx = \int \Pi(x)\, f_1(x)\, dx + \int \Phi(x)\, f_1(x)\, dx;$$

or, la première partie

$$\int \Pi(x)\, f_1(x)\, dx$$

nous est déjà connue, et il a été établi (p. 92) qu'elle s'exprime au moyen de fonctions explicites et des transcendantes

$$\int \frac{\cos mx\, dx}{x-\alpha},\quad \int \frac{\sin mx\, dx}{x-\alpha},$$

m étant un nombre entier, et les quantités α désignant les racines du dénominateur de $f_1(x)$ égalé à zéro. A l'égard de la seconde intégrale

$$\int \Phi(x)\, f_1(x)\, dx,$$

nous ferons, en admettant pour plus de généralité une partie entière,

$$f_1(x) = \mathrm{F}(x) + \sum \mathrm{A}(x-\alpha)^{-1} + \sum \mathrm{A}_1 \frac{d(x-\alpha)^{-1}}{dx} + \ldots + \sum \mathrm{A}_n \frac{d^n(x-\alpha)^{-1}}{dx^n},$$

et elle se trouvera décomposée en termes de ces deux formes, savoir :

$$\int F(x)\,\Phi(x)\,dx \qquad \text{et} \qquad \int \frac{d^m(x-\alpha)^{-1}}{dx^m}\,\Phi(x)\,dx,$$

Ces deux termes se décomposeront eux-mêmes si l'on emploie la formule

$$\Phi(x) = \sum \mathcal{A} \cot\frac{1}{2}(x-a) + \sum \mathcal{A}_1 \frac{d\cot\frac{1}{2}(x-a)}{dx} + \sum \mathcal{A}_2 \frac{d^2\cot\frac{1}{2}(x-a)}{dx^2} + \ldots,$$

dans les suivants

$$\int F(x)\frac{d^n\cot\frac{1}{2}(x-a)}{dx^n}\,dx, \qquad \int \frac{d^m(x-\alpha)^{-1}}{dx^m}\,\frac{d^n\cot\frac{1}{2}(x-a)}{dx^n}\,dx.$$

On tire enfin de l'intégration par parties, c'est-à-dire de la relation

$$\int U\frac{d^n V}{dx^n}\,dx = \Theta + (-1)^n\int V\frac{d^n U}{dx^n}\,dx$$

une dernière résolution donnant, d'une part, des fonctions explicites de la variable, et de l'autre les intégrales

$$\int \cot\frac{1}{2}(x-a)\frac{d^n F(x)}{dx^n}\,dx, \qquad \int \cot\frac{1}{2}(x-a)\frac{d^{m+n}(x-\alpha)^{-1}}{dx^{m+n}}\,dx.$$

Les éléments simples auxquels nous sommes amenés, si l'on observe que $\frac{d^n F(x)}{dx^n}$ est un polynome entier dont le degré peut être quelconque, sont donc les divers termes de ces deux séries

$$\int \cot\frac{1}{2}(x-a)x\,dx, \quad \int \cot\frac{1}{2}(x-a)x^2\,dx, \quad \int \cot\frac{1}{2}(x-a)x^3\,dx, \quad \ldots,$$

$$\int \frac{\cot\frac{1}{2}(x-a)\,dx}{x-\alpha}, \quad \int \frac{\cot\frac{1}{2}(x-a)\,dx}{(x-\alpha)^2}, \quad \int \frac{\cot\frac{1}{2}(x-a)\,dx}{(x-\alpha)^3}, \quad \ldots,$$

dont les uns rappellent la forme analytique des intégrales elliptiques et abéliennes de première et de seconde espèce, les autres celle des fonctions de troisième espèce. Mais on ne connaît entre eux aucune relation qui permette de les ramener les uns aux autres, et ils constituent sans doute des transcendantes distinctes.

Nous voyons par là combien l'intégrale

$$\int f(\sin x, \cos x) f_1(x)\, dx$$

est d'une nature analytique plus complexe que toutes celles dont nous nous sommes déjà occupés; toutefois, les calculs par lesquels nous la réduisons généralement aux éléments simples définis précédemment en donneront la valeur sous forme finie explicite lorsqu'ils disparaîtront du résultat. On en tire aussi cette conclusion que l'intégrale définie prise entre limites $-\infty$ et $+\infty$ dépend uniquement des quantités

$$\int_{-\infty}^{+\infty} \frac{\cos m x\, dx}{x - \alpha}, \quad \int_{-\infty}^{+\infty} \frac{\sin m x\, dx}{x - \alpha},$$

$$\int_{-\infty}^{+\infty} \cot \frac{1}{2}(x - a) \frac{d^n (x - \alpha)^{-1}}{dx^n}\, dx,$$

en excluant l'intégrale $\int_{-\infty}^{+\infty} \cot \frac{1}{2}(x - \alpha) x^n\, dx$, qui est amenée par la partie entière $F(x)$ de la fonction $f_1(x)$, et dont la valeur serait infinie ou indéterminée. Or on peut leur substituer, comme nous avons vu, celles-ci :

$$\frac{1}{2}\int_0^{2\pi} \cos m x \cot \frac{1}{2}(x - \alpha)\, dx, \qquad \frac{1}{2}\int_0^{2\pi} \sin m x \cot \frac{1}{2}(x - \alpha)\, dx,$$

$$\frac{1}{2}\int_0^{2\pi} \cot \frac{1}{2}(x - a) \frac{d^n \cot \frac{1}{2}(x - \alpha)}{dx^n}\, dx,$$

dont voici la détermination.

IV. Nous considérerons en même temps les deux premières, et j'appliquerai, comme s'il s'agissait d'obtenir les intégrales indéfinies, la méthode générale exigeant qu'on mette sous la forme $\Pi(x) + \Phi(x)$ les fonctions

$$\cos m x \cot \frac{1}{2}(x - a), \quad \sin m x \cot \frac{1}{2}(x - a),$$

afin de donner un dernier exemple de ces transformations. Formant pour cela la combinaison

$$\cos mx \cot\frac{1}{2}(x-a) + \sqrt{-1}\sin mx \cot\frac{1}{2}(x-a),$$

dont la transformée en $z = e^{x\sqrt{-1}}$ sera

$$z^m \frac{z+a_1}{z-a_1}\sqrt{-1},$$

si l'on fait $a_1 = e^{a\sqrt{-1}}$, nous n'aurons qu'à extraire la partie entière de la fraction en écrivant

$$z^m \frac{z+a_1}{z-a_1} = z^m + 2a_1 z^{m-1} + 2a_1^2 z^{m-2} + \ldots + 2a_1^m + \frac{2a_1^{m+1}}{z-a_1}.$$

Qu'on remplace maintenant z et a_1 par leurs valeurs, la quantité $\frac{2a_1^{m+1}}{z-a_1}$ par

$$-a_1^m\left[1 + \sqrt{-1}\cot\frac{1}{2}(x-a)\right],$$

en égalant les parties réelles et les parties imaginaires, il viendra aisément

$$\begin{aligned}\cos mx \cot\frac{1}{2}(x-a) = &+ \sin mx + 2\sin[(m-1)x+a] \\ &+ 2\sin[(m-2)x+2a] + \ldots + 2\sin[x+(m-1)a] \\ &+ \sin ma - \cos ma \cot\frac{1}{2}(x-a),\end{aligned}$$

$$\begin{aligned}\sin mx \cot\frac{1}{2}(x-a) = &- \cos mx - 2\cos[(m-1)x+a] \\ &- 2\cos[(m-2)x+2a] - \ldots - 2\cos[x+(m-1)a] \\ &- \cos ma - \sin ma \cot\frac{1}{2}(x-a).\end{aligned}$$

Nous tirons de ces égalités

$$\int_0^{2\pi} \cos mx \cot\frac{1}{2}(x-a)\,dx = +2\pi\sin ma - \cos ma\int_0^{2\pi}\cot\frac{1}{2}(x-a)\,dx,$$

$$\int_0^{2\pi} \sin mx \cot\frac{1}{2}(x-a)\,dx = -2\pi\cos ma - \sin ma\int_0^{2\pi}\cot\frac{1}{2}(x-a)\,dx.$$

Or on a établi (p. 79) qu'en supposant

$$a = \alpha + \beta\sqrt{-1},$$

l'intégrale

$$\int_0^{2\pi} \cot \frac{1}{2}(x-a)\,dx$$

a pour valeur $+2\pi\sqrt{-1}$ ou $-2\pi\sqrt{-1}$, suivant que β est positif ou négatif; dans le premier cas nous aurons donc

$$\int_0^{2\pi} \cos mx \cot \frac{1}{2}(x-a)\,dx$$
$$= 2\pi(+\sin ma - \sqrt{-1}\cos ma) = -2\pi\sqrt{-1}\,e^{ma\sqrt{-1}},$$
$$\int_0^{2\pi} \sin mx \cot \frac{1}{2}(x-a)\,dx$$
$$= -2\pi(\cos ma + \sqrt{-1}\sin ma) = -2\pi e^{ma\sqrt{-1}},$$

et dans le second

$$\int_0^{2\pi} \cos mx \cot \frac{1}{2}(x-a)\,dx$$
$$= 2\pi(+\sin ma + \sqrt{-1}\cos ma) = +2\pi\sqrt{-1}\,e^{-ma\sqrt{-1}},$$
$$\int_0^{2\pi} \sin mx \cot \frac{1}{2}(x-a)\,dx$$
$$= -2\pi(\cos ma - \sqrt{-1}\sin ma) = -2\pi e^{-ma\sqrt{-1}}.$$

Considérant ensuite l'intégrale

$$\int_0^{2\pi} \cot \frac{1}{2}(x-\alpha) \frac{d^n \cot \frac{1}{2}(x-a)}{dx^n}\,dx,$$

nous partirons, en supposant d'abord $n=0$, de la formule

$$\cot \frac{1}{2}(x-\alpha) \cot \frac{1}{2}(x-a)$$
$$= -1 + \cot \frac{1}{2}(\alpha-a)\left[\cot \frac{1}{2}(x-\alpha) - \cot \frac{1}{2}(x-a)\right];$$

on en tirera, en désignant par (a) et (α) des quantités égales à l'unité en valeur absolue, et du signe des coefficients de $\sqrt{-1}$ dans a et α,

$$\int_0^{2\pi} \cot \frac{1}{2}(x-a) \cot \frac{1}{2}(x-a)\,dx$$
$$= -2\pi + 2\pi \cot \frac{1}{2}(\alpha - a)[(\alpha)-(a)]\sqrt{-1}.$$

Supposant ensuite $n > 0$, la partie entière qui était tout à l'heure une constante n'existe plus, et la décomposition en éléments simples donne l'égalité

$$\cot\frac{1}{2}(x-\alpha)\frac{d^n\cot\frac{1}{2}(x-a)}{dx^n}$$

$$= \mathcal{A}\cot\frac{1}{2}(x-\alpha) + \mathrm{A}\cot\frac{1}{2}(x-a)$$

$$+ \mathrm{A}_1\frac{d\cot\frac{1}{2}(x-a)}{dx} + \ldots + \mathrm{A}_n\frac{d^n\cot\frac{1}{2}(x-a)}{dx^n},$$

d'où

$$\int_0^{2\pi}\cot\frac{1}{2}(x-\alpha)\frac{d^n\cot\frac{1}{2}(x-a)}{dx^n}dx = 2\pi[\mathcal{A}(\alpha) + \mathrm{A}(a)]\sqrt{-1}.$$

Or, la relation générale établie page 63,

$$\mathcal{A} + \mathcal{B} + \ldots + \mathcal{L} = -\frac{\mathrm{G}-\mathrm{H}}{2}\sqrt{-1}.$$

conduit, dans le cas actuel, à la condition $\mathcal{A} + \mathrm{A} = 0$, les quantités G et H étant nulles quand n est égal ou supérieur à l'unité. Ayant donc immédiatement

$$\mathcal{A} = \frac{d^n\cot\frac{1}{2}(\alpha-a)}{d\alpha^n},$$

on en conclut la valeur suivante :

$$\int_0^{2\pi}\cot\frac{1}{2}(x-\alpha)\frac{d^n\cot\frac{1}{2}(x-a)}{dx^n}dx$$

$$= 2\pi\frac{d^n\cot\frac{1}{2}(\alpha-a)}{d\alpha^n}[(\alpha)-(a)]\sqrt{-1}.$$

Mais le cas particulier de $a = \alpha$ fait exception, car alors on doit poser

$$\cot\frac{1}{2}(x-\alpha)\frac{d^n\cot\frac{1}{2}(x-a)}{dx^n}$$

$$= \mathcal{A}\cot\frac{1}{2}(x-\alpha) + \mathcal{A}_1\frac{d\cot\frac{1}{2}(x-\alpha)}{dx} + \ldots + \mathcal{A}_{n+1}\frac{d^{n+1}\cot\frac{1}{2}(x-\alpha)}{dx^{n+1}};$$

or, un calcul très facile donne $\mathcal{A} = 0$, l'intégrale, dans ce cas, est donc toujours nulle, sauf le cas unique de $n = 0$, où la relation

$$\cot^2 \frac{1}{2}(x-\alpha) = -1 - 2\frac{d\cot\frac{1}{2}(x-\alpha)}{dx}$$

conduit à la valeur

$$\int_0^{2\pi} \cot^2 \frac{1}{2}(x-\alpha)\,dx = -2\pi.$$

V. Pour passer des résultats que nous venons d'obtenir aux valeurs des intégrales

$$\int_{-\infty}^{+\infty} \frac{\cos mx\,dx}{x-a}, \quad \int_{-\infty}^{+\infty} \frac{\sin mx\,dx}{x-a},$$

$$\int_{-\infty}^{+\infty} \cot\frac{1}{2}(x-\alpha)\frac{d^n \cot\frac{1}{2}(x-a)}{dx^n}\,dx,$$

il ne nous reste plus qu'à considérer le coefficient de l'indéterminée λ, afin de reconnaître si elles ont, en effet, une valeur entièrement déterminée. Or, à l'égard des deux premières, les facteurs

$$\int_0^{2\pi} \cos mx\,dx, \quad \int_0^{2\pi} \sin mx\,dx$$

étant nuls, ce coefficient s'évanouit, et nous avons par conséquent

$$\int_{-\infty}^{+\infty} \frac{\cos mx\,dx}{x-a} = \frac{1}{2}\int_0^{2\pi} \cos mx \cot\frac{1}{2}(x-a)\,dx = -\pi\sqrt{-1}\,e^{ma\sqrt{-1}},$$

$$\int_{-\infty}^{+\infty} \frac{\sin mx\,dx}{x-a} = \frac{1}{2}\int_0^{2\pi} \sin mx \cot\frac{1}{2}(x-a)\,dx = -\pi e^{ma\sqrt{-1}},$$

ou bien

$$\int_{-\infty}^{+\infty} \frac{\cos mx\,dx}{x-a} = +\sqrt{-1}\,e^{-ma\sqrt{-1}},$$

$$\int_{-\infty}^{+\infty} \frac{\sin mx\,dx}{x-a} = -\pi e^{-ma\sqrt{-1}},$$

suivant que le coefficient de $\sqrt{-1}$ dans a est positif ou négatif.

Relativement à la troisième intégrale, la quantité

$$\int_0^{2\pi} \cot\frac{1}{2}(x-\alpha)\,dx$$

est toujours différente de zéro; mais l'autre facteur, qui est l'unique résidu de $\frac{d^n(x-a)^{-1}}{dx^n}$ est nul pour toute valeur de n, sauf dans le cas de $n=0$; l'intégrale

$$\int_{-\infty}^{+\infty} \frac{\cot\frac{1}{2}(x-\alpha)\,dx}{x-a}$$

est donc seule indéterminée, et l'on a généralement

$$\int_{-\infty}^{+\infty} \cot\frac{1}{2}(x-\alpha)\frac{d^n(x-a)^{-1}}{dx^n}dx = \pi\frac{d^n\cot\frac{1}{2}(\alpha-a)}{d\alpha^n}[(\alpha)-(a)]\sqrt{-1}.$$

Observons enfin que les constantes a et α doivent être imaginaires pour que les quantités

$$\frac{1}{x-a}\cot\frac{1}{2}(x-\alpha)$$

ne deviennent point infinies entre les limites des intégrations. Une exception importante est toutefois à remarquer; elle concerne l'intégrale

$$\int_{-\infty}^{+\infty} \frac{\sin mx}{x}\,dx,$$

la fonction $\frac{\sin mx}{x}$ restant finie pour $x=0$. La valeur qu'on obtient alors, savoir

$$\int_{-\infty}^{+\infty} \frac{\sin mx}{x}\,dx = \pi,$$

offre cette circonstance, qu'il est aisé d'expliquer, d'être indépendante de m. Effectivement, si l'on fait $mx=z$, m disparaît et l'on trouve

$$\int_{-\infty}^{+\infty} \frac{\sin mx}{x}\,dx = \int_{-\infty}^{+\infty} \frac{\sin z}{z}\,dz.$$

La même substitution permet semblablement de ramener les intégrales

$$\int_{-\infty}^{+\infty} \frac{\cos mx\,dx}{x-a}, \quad \int_{-\infty}^{+\infty} \frac{\sin mx\,dx}{x-a},$$

où m est non seulement un nombre entier, mais une quantité réelle quelconque, au seul cas de $m = 1$, car on en déduit

$$\int_{-\infty}^{+\infty} \frac{\cos mx\,dx}{x-a} = \int_{-\infty}^{+\infty} \frac{\cos z\,dz}{z-ma}$$

et

$$\int_{-\infty}^{+\infty} \frac{\sin mx\,dx}{x-a} = \int_{-\infty}^{+\infty} \frac{\sin z\,dz}{z-ma}.$$

Mais, en donnant, comme nous l'avons fait, à la transformée en z les limites $-\infty$ et $+\infty$, nous avons supposé implicitement m positif, et dans l'hypothèse contraire les limites doivent être interverties, de sorte qu'on aura alors

$$\int_{-\infty}^{+\infty} \frac{\sin mx\,dx}{x} = -\int_{-\infty}^{+\infty} \frac{\sin x\,dx}{x} = -\pi.$$

De là ce fait remarquable et important en Analyse, que l'intégrale $\int_{-\infty}^{+\infty} \frac{\sin mx\,dx}{x}$, envisagée comme fonction de m, est constante et égale à $+\pi$ ou à $-\pi$, suivant que la variable est positive ou négative. Mais voici d'autres exemples de fonctions discontinues obtenues sous forme d'intégrales définies. Considérons les expressions

$$\int \frac{\sin ax \sin bx}{x^2}\,dx, \quad \int \frac{\sin ax \sin bx \sin cx}{x^3}\,dx,$$

que je vais d'abord réduire par la méthode générale à des quantités explicites et transcendantes

$$\int \frac{\cos mx\,dx}{x}, \quad \int \frac{\sin mx\,dx}{x},$$

Faisant, à cet effet, pour un instant

$$\mathrm{U} = \sin ax \sin bx, \qquad \mathrm{V} = \sin ax \sin bx \sin cx,$$

j'aurai d'abord

$$\int \frac{\mathrm{U}\,dx}{x^2} = -\int \mathrm{U}\,d(x^{-1}) = -x^{-1} + \int x^{-1}\frac{d\mathrm{U}}{dx}\,dx,$$

$$\int \frac{\mathrm{V}\,dx}{x^3} = \frac{1}{2}\int \mathrm{V}\frac{d^2(x^{-1})}{dx^2}\,dx = \frac{1}{2}\left[\mathrm{V}\frac{d(x^{-1})}{dx} - \frac{d\mathrm{V}}{dx}x^{-1}\right] + \frac{1}{2}\int x^{-1}\frac{d^2\mathrm{V}}{dx^2}\,dx,$$

et les identités

$$2\mathrm{U} = \cos(a-b)x - \cos(a+b)x,$$

$$\begin{aligned}4\mathrm{V} = {} & \sin(a+b-c)x + \sin(b+c-a)x \\ & + \sin(c+a-b)x - \sin(a+b+c)x\end{aligned}$$

donneront immédiatement

$$2\frac{d\mathrm{U}}{dx} = -(a-b)\sin(a-b)x + (a+b)\sin(a+b)x,$$

$$\begin{aligned}4\frac{d^2\mathrm{V}}{dx^2} = {} & -(a+b-c)^2\sin(a+b-c)x - (b+c-a)^2\sin(b+c-a)x \\ & -(c+a-b)^2\sin(c+a-b)x + (a+b+c)^2\sin(a+b+c)x.\end{aligned}$$

Nous tirerons de là, en observant que les quantités en dehors des intégrales s'évanouissent aux limites $x = -\infty$, $x = +\infty$,

$$\begin{aligned}&\int_{-\infty}^{+\infty} \frac{\sin ax \sin bx}{x^2}\,dx \\ &= -\frac{a-b}{2}\int_{-\infty}^{+\infty}\frac{\sin(a-b)x}{x}\,dx + \frac{a+b}{2}\int_{-\infty}^{+\infty}\frac{\sin(a+b)x}{x}\,dx;\end{aligned}$$

or, a et b étant positifs, on en conclura, pour $a - b > 0$,

$$\int_{-\infty}^{+\infty} \frac{\sin ax \sin bx}{x^2}\,dx = -\frac{a-b}{2}\pi + \frac{a+b}{2}\pi = b\pi,$$

et, pour $a - b < 0$,

$$\int_{-\infty}^{+\infty} \frac{\sin ax \sin bx}{x^2}\,dx = \frac{a-b}{2}\pi + \frac{a+b}{2}\pi = a\pi;$$

de sorte que l'intégrale a pour valeur le produit par π du plus petit des nombres a et b.

Maintenant, la relation

$$\begin{aligned}\int_{-\infty}^{+\infty} \frac{\sin ax \sin bx \sin cx}{x^3}\,dx &= -\frac{(a+b-c)^2}{8}\int_{-\infty}^{+\infty}\frac{\sin(a+b-c)x}{x}\,dx \\ &\quad -\frac{(b+c-a)^2}{8}\int_{-\infty}^{+\infty}\frac{\sin(b+c-a)x}{x}\,dx \\ &\quad -\frac{(c+a-b)^2}{8}\int_{-\infty}^{+\infty}\frac{\sin(c+a-b)x}{x}\,dx \\ &\quad +\frac{(a+b+c)^2}{8}\int_{-\infty}^{+\infty}\frac{\sin(a+b+c)x}{x}\,dx\end{aligned}$$

aura semblablement pour conséquence que l'intégrale du premier membre, sous les conditions

$$a+b-c>0, \qquad b+c-a>0, \qquad c+a-b>0,$$

sera la quantité

$$(2ab+2bc+2ca-a^2-b^2-c^2)\frac{\pi}{4};$$

tandis qu'en renversant le premier, le second ou le troisième signe d'inégalité, elle aura pour valeur $ab\pi$, $bc\pi$, ou $ca\pi$. Les hypothèses faites sont d'ailleurs, comme on sait, les seules possibles, en admettant que les constantes a, b, c soient positives.

SUR L'ÉQUATION $x^3 + y^3 = z^3 + u^3$.

Nouvelles Annales de Mathématiques, 2e série, t. XI, 1872, p. 5.

On doit à Euler les formules suivantes, qui vérifient identiquement cette équation :

$$\begin{aligned}
x &= +(f^2 + 3g^2)^2 - (ff' + 3gg' + 3fg' - 3f'g)(f'^2 + 3g'^2),\\
y &= -(f^2 + 3g^2)^2 + (ff' + 3gg' - 3fg' + 3f'g)(f'^2 + 3g'^2),\\
z &= -(f'^2 + 3g'^2)^2 + (ff' + 3gg' - 3fg' + 3f'g)(f^2 + 3g^2),\\
u &= +(f'^2 + 3g'^2)^2 - (ff' + 3gg' + 3fg' - 3f'g)(f^2 + 3g^2),
\end{aligned}$$

et M. Binet, dans une *Note sur une question relative à la théorie des nombres* (*Comptes rendus*, t. XII, p. 248), a observé qu'on pouvait, sans diminuer leur généralité, les réduire aux expressions plus simples :

$$\begin{aligned}
x &= +(a^2 + 3b^2)^2 - a + 3b,\\
y &= -(a^2 + 3b^2)^2 + a + 3b,\\
z &= +(a^2 + 3b^2)(a + 3b) - 1,\\
u &= -(a^2 + 3b^2)(a - 3b) + 1,
\end{aligned}$$

où n'entrent que deux indéterminées a et b. Je me propose de tirer ces résultats comme une conséquence de la propriété générale des surfaces du troisième ordre, consistant en ce que leurs points peuvent se déterminer individuellement. Soit donc $u = 1$; j'observe qu'en désignant par α une racine cubique imaginaire de l'unité, les droites

$$\begin{aligned}
x &= \alpha, & x &= \alpha^2,\\
y &= \alpha^2 z, & y &= \alpha z
\end{aligned}$$

sont entièrement situées sur la surface

$$x^3 + y^3 = z^3 + 1.$$

Cela posé, une autre droite, représentée par les équations

$$x = az + b,$$
$$y = pz + q,$$

rencontrera chacune de ces génératrices, si l'on a les conditions

$$\frac{\alpha - b}{a} = \frac{q}{\alpha^2 - p},$$
$$\frac{\alpha^2 - b}{a} = \frac{q}{\alpha - p};$$

d'où l'on tire

$$p = b, \qquad q = \frac{b^2 + b + 1}{a},$$

et les coordonnées z_1, z_2 des points de rencontre seront respectivement les quantités

$$z_1 = \frac{\alpha - b}{a},$$
$$z_2 = \frac{\alpha^2 - b}{a}.$$

Or l'équation

$$(az + b)^3 + (pz + q)^3 = z^3 + 1$$

devra admettre pour solutions

$$z = z_1, \qquad z = z_2;$$

la troisième racine sera donc une fonction rationnelle des coefficients, qui s'obtient aisément comme il suit.

Développons l'équation en nous bornant aux termes en z^3 et z^2; nous en conclurons, pour la somme des racines, l'expression

$$z + z_1 + z_2 = 3\,\frac{a^2 b + p^3 q}{1 - a^3 - p^3}.$$

Mais on a

$$z_1 + z_2 = \frac{\alpha + \alpha^2 - 2b}{a} = -\,\frac{1 + 2b}{a};$$

donc

$$z = \frac{1 + 2b}{a} + 3\,\frac{a^2 b + p^2 q}{1 - a^3 - p^3}.$$

Il vient ensuite, si l'on remplace p et q par leurs valeurs en a et b,

$$z = \frac{(1 + b + b^2)^2 - a^3(1 - b)}{a(1 - a^3 - b^3)},$$

et de là résultent, pour x et y, les expressions

$$x=\frac{(1+b+b^2)(1+2b)-a^3}{1-a^3-b^3},$$

$$y=\frac{(1+b+b^2)^2-a^3(1+2b)}{a(1-a^3-b^3)}.$$

Elles se simplifient, si l'on écrit, au lieu de a, $\frac{1}{a}$, et au lieu de b, $\frac{b}{a}$, en prenant ces nouvelles formes, savoir :

$$x=\frac{(a^2+ab+b^2)(a+2b)-1}{a^3-b^3-1},$$

$$y=\frac{(a^2+ab+b^2)^2-a-2b}{a^3-b^3-1},$$

$$z=\frac{(a^2+ab+b^2)^2-a+b}{a^3-b^3-1};$$

et, en revenant à l'équation homogène

$$x^3+y^3=z^3+u^3,$$

nous obtenons ainsi pour solution :

$$x=(a^2+ab+b^2)(a+2b)-1,$$
$$y=(a^2+ab+b^2)^2-a-2b,$$
$$z=(a^2+ab+b^2)^2-a+b,$$
$$u=a^3-b^3-1=(a^2+ab+b^2)(a-b)-1.$$

Or il suffit maintenant de changer b en $2b$ et a en $a-b$ pour que ces formules deviennent

$$x=(a^2+3b^2)(a+3b)-1,$$
$$y=(a^2+3b^2)^2-a-3b,$$
$$z=(a^2+3b^2)^2-a+3b,$$
$$u=(a^2+3b^2)(a-3b)-1.$$

Ce sont précisément celles d'Euler, sauf que x, y, z, u sont remplacés par z, $-y$, x, et $-u$.

SUR L'ÉQUATION DE LAMÉ [1].

Extrait des feuilles autographiées du *Cours d'Analyse de l'École Polytechnique,* par M. Hermite, 1re Division, 1872-1873, 32e leçon.

Dans la théorie de la chaleur, Lamé a été conduit à considérer l'équation différentielle suivante :

$$4X\frac{d^2y}{dx^2} + 2X'\frac{dy}{dx} = (ax+b)y,$$

dans laquelle X est un polynome du troisième degré de la forme

$$X = x(1-x)(1-K^2x).$$

Dans le cas où $a = n(n+1)K^2$, n étant un nombre entier, il se trouve qu'on peut satisfaire à l'équation de Lamé en prenant pour y un polynome entier de degré n, pourvu que b ait pour valeur un certain polynome entier également de degré n. Nous ne traiterons pas cette question et nous nous bornerons à supposer $a=n(n+1)K''$, b restant complètement arbitraire.

En appelant u et v deux solutions particulières de l'équation de Lamé, la solution la plus générale de l'équation est

$$y = cu + c'v,$$

c et c' étant deux constantes arbitraires.

Je dis que, si u et v sont convenablement choisies, le produit uv

(1) Nous avons retrouvé dans les feuilles lithographiées destinées aux élèves de l'École Polytechnique, une leçon faite par Hermite pendant l'hiver 1872-1873 sur l'équation de Lamé. Nous reproduisons cette leçon, qui, à notre connaissance, fait connaître les premières recherches de Hermite sur une question qu'il devait approfondir queiques années après. E. P.

est un polynome entier en x. En posant $z = y^2$, ou

$$z = c^2 u^2 + 2cc' uv + c'^2 v^2,$$

je vois qu'il sera démontré que uv est un polynome entier en x, de degré n, si je prouve que z est un polynome entier de degré n, puisque u^2 et v^2 sont des valeurs particulières de z; je pose donc $z = y^2$, et je cherche la transformée en z de l'équation de Lamé, ou, en me plaçant à un point de vue plus général, de l'équation

$$4Ay'' + 2A'y' = By,$$

dans laquelle A et B sont deux polynomes entiers quelconques en x. J'aurai

$$\frac{dz}{dx} = 2yy',$$

$$\frac{d^2 z}{dx^2} = 2(yy'' + y'^2).$$

En multipliant par $2A$,

$$2Az'' = 4Ayy'' + 4Ay'^2 = y(By - 2A'y') + 4Ay'^2,$$

ou

$$2Az'' = Bz - 2A'yy' + 4Ay'^2,$$

et, comme

$$2yy' = z',$$

$$2Az'' + A'z' - Bz = 4Ay'^2.$$

En différentiant de nouveau

$$\begin{aligned}[2Az'' + A'z' - Bz]' &= 8Ay'y'' + 4A'y'^2 \\ &= 2y'(4Ay'' + 2A'y'),\end{aligned}$$

et comme

$$4Ay'' + 2A'y = By,$$

$$[2Az'' + A'z' - Bz]' = 2Byy',$$

$$[2Az'' + A'z' - Bz]' = Bz'.$$

Telle est la transformée en z. Si maintenant je développe le premier membre, il vient

$$2Az''' + 3A'z'' + (A'' - 2B)z' - B'z = 0.$$

Je différentie n fois cette équation, et je pose

$$u = \frac{d^n z}{dx^n}.$$

Il vient, en supposant A du troisième degré et B du premier degré, comme dans l'équation de Lamé,

$$\begin{array}{r|c|l|l}
2\mathrm{A}u''' + 2n\mathrm{A}' & u'' + n(n-1)\mathrm{A}'' & u' + \dfrac{n(n-1)(n-2)}{3}\mathrm{A}''' & u = 0. \\
+ 3n\mathrm{A}' & + 3n\mathrm{A}'' & + \dfrac{3n(n-1)}{2}\mathrm{A}''' & \\
 & + \mathrm{A}'' - 2\mathrm{B} & + n(\mathrm{A}''' - 2\mathrm{B}') & \\
 & & - \ \mathrm{B}' &
\end{array}$$

Considérons le coefficient du terme en u et effectuons les réductions dans ce terme. Il vient

$$n\mathrm{A}'''\left[\frac{(n-1)(n-2)}{3} + \frac{3(n-1)}{2} + 1\right] - (2n+1)\mathrm{B}',$$

$$n\mathrm{A}'''\frac{(n+1)(2n+1)}{6} - (2n+1)\mathrm{B}'.$$

Or, on a

$$\mathrm{A} = x(1-x)(1-\mathrm{K}^2 x),$$

d'où

$$\mathrm{A}''' = \mathrm{K}^2 \times 1.2.3;$$

$$\mathrm{B} = n(n+1)\mathrm{K}^2 x + b,$$

d'où

$$\mathrm{B}' = n(n+1)\mathrm{K}^2.$$

On voit donc que le coefficient de u se réduit à zéro. Par suite, l'équation transformée en u est satisfaite quand on donne à u une valeur constante quelconque. Donc

$$\frac{d^n z}{dx^n} = c.$$

En intégrant n fois, on arrivera pour la valeur de z à un polynome entier de degré n, ce qu'il fallait démontrer. Donc le produit uv de deux solutions particulières convenables de l'équation de Lamé est un polynome entier en x de degré n,

$$uv = \mathrm{F}(x).$$

Nous allons maintenant chercher à déterminer u et v. Considérons le déterminant fonctionnel

$$z = u'v - uv'.$$

D'où

$$z' = u''v - uv'',$$
$$4Az' = v \times 4Au'' - u \times 4Av'',$$
$$4Az' = v(Bu - 2A'u') - u(Bv - 2A'v'),$$

ou

$$4Az' = 2A'(v'u - vu'),$$
$$4Az' = -2A'z,$$
$$2Az' + A'z = 0;$$

A est le polynome figurant dans l'équation de Lamé. Par suite,

$$2Xz' + X'z = 0.$$

Le premier membre est la dérivée de Xz^2; il en résulte que $Xz^2 = \text{const.}$,

$$z = \frac{c}{\sqrt{X}},$$

$$u'v - v'u = \frac{c}{\sqrt{X}}.$$

On a d'ailleurs, puisque $uv = F(x)$,

$$u'v + v'u = F'(x).$$

D'où les deux équations

$$\frac{u'}{u} - \frac{v'}{v} = \frac{c}{F(x)\sqrt{X}},$$
$$\frac{u'}{u} + \frac{v'}{v} = \frac{F'(x)}{F(x)},$$

ou

$$\frac{u'}{u} = \frac{1}{2}\left[\frac{c}{F\sqrt{X}} + \frac{F'}{F}\right],$$
$$\frac{v'}{v} = \frac{1}{2}\left[\frac{-c}{F\sqrt{X}} + \frac{F'}{F}\right].$$

En intégrant

$$\operatorname{Log} u = \operatorname{Log}\sqrt{F} + \frac{1}{2}\int\frac{C\,dx}{F\sqrt{X}},$$
$$\operatorname{Log} v = \operatorname{Log}\sqrt{F} - \frac{1}{2}\int\frac{C\,dx}{F\sqrt{X}},$$

$$u = \sqrt{F(x)}\,e^{\frac{c}{2}\int\frac{dx}{F(x)\sqrt{X}}},$$
$$v = \sqrt{F(x)}\,e^{-\frac{c}{2}\int\frac{dx}{F(x)\sqrt{X}}}.$$

Nous avons donc la solution complète de l'équation de Lamé au moyen des fonctions elliptiques, puisque X est un polynome du troisième degré.

Si l'on pose

$$x = \sin^2 am t,$$

l'équation prend la forme sous laquelle Lamé l'a étudiée.

On aura

$$\frac{dx}{dt} = 2 \sin am t \, \frac{d(\sin am t)}{dt}.$$

Or, en posant

$$u = \sin am t,$$

on a

$$\frac{du}{dt} = \sqrt{(1-u^2)(1-K^2u^2)}.$$

Donc

$$\frac{dx}{dt} = 2u\sqrt{(1-u^2)(1-K^2u^2)} = 2\sqrt{u^2(1-u^2)(1-K^2u^2)} = 2\sqrt{X}.$$

Formons maintenant la transformée en t. On a

$$\frac{dy}{dx} = \frac{dy}{dt}\,\frac{1}{\frac{dx}{dt}} = \frac{dy}{dt}\,\frac{1}{2\sqrt{X}},$$

$$\frac{d^2y}{dx^2} = \frac{d^2y}{dt^2}\,\frac{1}{4X} + \frac{dy}{dt}\,\frac{d\frac{1}{2\sqrt{X}}}{dx}.$$

Or

$$\frac{d\frac{1}{2\sqrt{X}}}{dx} = \frac{-1}{2X}\,\frac{d\sqrt{X}}{dx} = \frac{-1}{2X}\,\frac{X'}{2\sqrt{X}} = \frac{-X'}{4X\sqrt{X}}.$$

D'où

$$\frac{d^2y}{dx^2} = \frac{1}{4X}\,\frac{d^2y}{dt^2} - \frac{X'}{4X\sqrt{X}}\,\frac{dy}{dt}.$$

D'où la transformée

$$4X\left[\frac{1}{4X}\,\frac{d^2y}{dt^2} - \frac{X'}{4X\sqrt{X}}\,\frac{dy}{dt}\right] + 2X'\,\frac{1}{2\sqrt{X}}\,\frac{dy}{dt} = [n(n+1)K^2x + \alpha]y,$$

ou enfin

$$\frac{d^2y}{dt^2} = [n(n+1)K^2 \sin^2 am t + \alpha]y.$$

ON AN APPLICATION

OF THE

THEORY OF UNICURSAL CURVES.

Proceedings of the London mathematical Society, t. IV, p. 343-345.

Extract from a letter to Prof. Cayley (Read May 8th, 1873).

Prof. Cayley communicated to the Society a letter, dated 28th March, 1873, which he had received from M. Hermite. In connexion which some investigations on elliptic functions which Prof. Cayley is engaged with, M. Hermite calls attention to the question of determining all the quantities

$$\operatorname{sinam} \frac{4mK + 4m'iK'}{n}$$

in terms of the $n+1$ roots of the modular equation

$$F(u, v) = 0,$$

without, as said Jacobi, the resolution of any equation. Is it necessary, for this purpose, to make use of the singular equations indicated by Abel between the quantities

$$\operatorname{sinam} \frac{l}{n}(4mK + 4m'iK') \qquad \text{for} \qquad l = 1, 2, \ldots, \overline{n-1}$$

and the nth roots of unity?

And after referring to a remark on the employment of the theory of unicursal curves in his *Cours d'Analyse de l'École Polytechnique*, and noticing that it is not only in the commencement of the Integral Calculus that these find an application, M. Hermite proceeds as follows : I have remarked that they give rise to a method of integration of equations of the form

$$F\left(\frac{du}{dx}, u\right) = 0,$$

treated of by MM. Briot and Bouquet, in the *Journal de l'École Polytechnique.*

Suppose, in fact, that the question is to determine the integral when it is an algebraic function of the independent variable.

The question is easely resolved in all the cases where the number which determines the nature of this function is $= 0$; that is, if it is possible to take rationally

$$u = \varphi(t), \qquad x = \psi(t).$$

In fact, from this hypothesis, it follows that

$$\frac{du}{dx} = \frac{\varphi'(t)}{\psi'(t)},$$

is also rational in t; wherefore it is necessary (although not sufficient) that, assuming

$$\frac{du}{dx} = v,$$

the curve

$$F(v, u) = 0$$

should be unicursal. Deriving then, from this relation the rational expressions

$$v = \Phi(t), \qquad u = \varphi(t),$$

we obtain

$$dx = \frac{du}{v} = \frac{\varphi'(t)}{\Phi(t)}\,dt$$

and thence

$$x = \int \frac{\varphi'(t)}{\Phi(t)}\,dt.$$

But this integral can always be obtained rationally, and, in the case where the logarithms disappear, gives the value of x in the assumed form.

In the case where u is of the form

$$u = \varphi(\operatorname{tang} x),$$

φ being rational; making $\operatorname{tang} x = t$, we obtain

$$\frac{du}{dx} = \varphi'(t)(1+t^2);$$

therefore the equation

$$F(v, u) = 0,$$

must give an unicursal curve; and a solution of this form presents itself when the integral

$$x = \int \frac{\varphi'(t)}{\Phi(t)} dt$$

reduces itself to

$$x = \operatorname{arc} \operatorname{tang} t.$$

Again, lastly, assuming

$$u = \varphi\left(\operatorname{sinam} x, \frac{d \operatorname{sinam} x}{dx}\right)$$

φ denoting a rational function of the sine-amplitude, and its derived function (this being the hypothetis of MM. Briot and Bouquet); it is clear that, writing $\operatorname{sinam} x = t$, the derivative $\frac{du}{dx}$ as well as u must be a rational function of t and of the radical

$$\sqrt{(1-t^2)(1-k^2t^2)}.$$

Consequently, the equation

$$F(v, u) = 0$$

denotes a curve of the species (deficiency) 1.

Thus the example XI of these authors,

$$v^5 + (u^2 - 1)v^4 - a u^2(u^2 - 1)^4 = 0$$

$\left(v \text{ denoting } \frac{du}{dx}\right)$, $\left(\text{where } a = \frac{4^4}{5^5}\right)$ on writing

$$v = (u^2 - 1)t,$$

gives

$$u^2 = \frac{t^5 + t^4}{t^5 + t^4 - a} = \frac{t^5 + t^4}{\left(t + \frac{4}{5}\right)^2 \left(t^3 - \frac{3}{5}t^2 + \frac{8}{5^2}t - \frac{4^2}{5^3}\right)}.$$

If then

$$T = (t+1)\left(t^3 - \frac{3}{5}t^2 + \frac{8}{5^2}t - \frac{4^2}{5^3}\right),$$

we have

$$u = \frac{t^2(t+1)}{t+\frac{4}{5}}\frac{1}{\sqrt{T}}, \qquad \text{then} \qquad v = \frac{4^4}{5^5}\frac{(t+1)t}{\left(t+\frac{4}{5}\right)^2 T},$$

whence

$$dx = \frac{du}{v} = \frac{5}{2}\frac{dt}{\sqrt{T}},$$

whence

$$x = -\frac{5}{2}\int\frac{dt}{\sqrt{T}}.$$

Consequently the question is integrable by elliptic functions The other examples are contained in the type

$$v^3 + 3Pv^2 + 4Q = 0$$

(with the condition $P^3 + Q = R^2$).

P, Q, R being integral functions of u of the degrees 2, 6, 3.

But this equation may be writen

$$(v + 2P)^2(v - P) = -4(P^3 + Q) = -4R^2,$$

and on writing

$$v + 2P = -\frac{2R}{w}$$

becomes simply

$$w^3 - 3Pw - 2R = 0.$$

And this transformed equation being of the degree 3 in w, u, these two quantities, and consequently also v, u, can be expressed as rational functions of t and of an elliptic radical.

The equation $F\left(\frac{d^2u}{dx^2}, u\right)$ gives rise to similar substitutions.

SUR L'IRRATIONALITÉ

DE LA

BASE DES LOGARITHMES HYPERBOLIQUES.

Report of the British Association for Advancement of Science
(43th meeting, p. 22-23, 1873).

On reconnaîtra volontiers que, dans le domaine mathématique, la possession d'une vérité importante ne devient complète et définitive qu'autant qu'on a réussi à l'établir par plus d'une méthode. A cet égard la théorie des fonctions elliptiques offre un exemple célèbre, présent à tous les esprits, mais qui est loin d'être unique dans l'Analyse.

Je citerai encore le théorème de Sturm, resté comme enveloppé d'une sorte de mystère jusqu'à la mémorable découverte de M. Sylvester, qui a ouvert, pour pénétrer au cœur de la question, une voie plus facile et plus féconde que celle du premier inventeur. Telles sont encore, dans l'Arithmétique supérieure, les lois de réciprocité entre deux nombres premiers, auxquelles est attaché le nom à jamais illustre d'Eisenstein. Mais dans cette même science et pour des questions du plus haut intérêt, comme la détermination du nombre des classes de formes quadratiques de même invariant, on a été moins heureux, et jusqu'ici le mérite de la première découverte est resté sans partage à Dirichlet. Enfin, et pour en venir à l'objet de cette Note, je citerai encore dans le champ de l'Arithmétique, la proposition de Lambert sur l'irrationalité du rapport de la circonférence au diamètre, et des puissances de la base des logarithmes hyperboliques. Ayant été récemment conduit à m'occuper de ce dernier nombre, j'ai l'honneur de soumettre à la réunion de l'Association Britannique une démonstration nouvelle du théorème de Lambert, où n'intervient plus le Calcul intégral, et qui, je l'espère, paraîtra entièrement élémentaire. Je pars simplement de la série

$$e^x = 1 + \frac{x}{1} + \frac{x^2}{1.2} + \ldots + \frac{x^n}{1.2\ldots n} + \ldots,$$

et posant pour un instant

$$F(x) = 1 + \frac{x}{1} + \frac{x^2}{1.2} + \ldots + \frac{x^n}{1.2\ldots n},$$

ce qui permet d'écrire

$$\frac{e^x - F(x)}{x^{n+1}} = \frac{1}{1.2\ldots n+1} + \frac{x}{1.2\ldots n+2} + \ldots = \sum \frac{x^k}{1.2\ldots n+k+1},$$

il suffira, comme on va voir, de prendre les dérivées d'ordre n des deux membres de cette relation. Effectivement, on obtient d'abord

$$D_x^n \frac{e^x}{x^{n+1}} = \frac{e^x \Phi(x)}{x^{2n+1}},$$

où $\Phi(x)$ est un polynome à coefficients entiers du degré n, dont il n'est aucunement nécessaire d'avoir l'expression qu'il serait d'ailleurs aisé de former. Nous remarquerons ensuite, à l'égard du terme $\frac{F(x)}{x^{n+1}}$, que la différentiation, effectuée n fois de suite, fait disparaître les dénominateurs des coefficients, de sorte qu'il vient

$$D_x^n \frac{F(x)}{x^{n+1}} = \frac{\Phi_1(x)}{x^{2n+1}},$$

$\Phi_1(x)$ étant un polynome dont tous les coefficients sont des nombres entiers. De la relation proposée, nous tirons donc la suivante :

$$\frac{e^x \Phi(x) - \Phi_1(x)}{x^{2n+1}} = \sum_0^\infty {}_k \frac{(k+1)(k+2)\ldots(k+n)x^k}{1.2\ldots k+2n+1},$$

ou bien sous une autre forme

$$\begin{aligned} e^x \Phi(x) - \Phi_1(x) &= x^{2n+1} \sum \frac{(k+1)(k+2)\ldots(k+n)x^k}{1.2\ldots k+2n+1} \\ &= \frac{x^{2n+1}}{1.2\ldots n} \sum \frac{(k+1)(k+2)\ldots(k+n)x^k}{n+1.n+2\ldots k+2n+1}. \end{aligned}$$

Or je dis qu'en faisant croître n, le second membre qui jamais ne peut s'évanouir deviendra plus petit que toute grandeur donnée. Il en est effectivement ainsi du facteur $\frac{x^{2n+1}}{1.2\ldots n}$, et d'autre part, la série infinie $\sum \frac{(k+1)(k+2)\ldots(k+n)x^k}{n+1.n+2\ldots k+2n+1}$ étant mise sous la forme $\sum \frac{1.2\ldots k+n}{n+1.n+2\ldots k+2n+1}\,\frac{x^k}{1.2\ldots k}$, on reconnaît qu'elle a pour limite supérieure $e^x = \sum \frac{x^k}{1.2\ldots k}$, car le facteur

$$\frac{1.2\ldots k+n}{n+1.n+2\ldots k+2n+1}$$

est inférieur à l'unité.

De là résulte qu'en supposant x un nombre entier, e^x ne peut être une quantité commensurable $\frac{b}{a}$; car on aurait

$$e^x\,\Phi(x) - \Phi_1(x) = \frac{b\,\Phi(x) - a\,\Phi_1(x)}{a},$$

et cette fraction dont le numérateur est essentiellement entier, d'après ce qui a été établi à l'égard des polynomes $\Phi(x)$ et $\Phi_1(x)$, ne peut, sans être nulle, descendre au-dessous de $\frac{1}{a}$.

L'expression découverte par Lambert

$$\frac{e^x - e^{-x}}{e^x + e^{-x}} = \cfrac{x}{1 + \cfrac{x^2}{3 + \ldots}},$$

que j'évite ainsi d'employer, n'en reste pas moins un résultat du plus grand prix et qui ouvre la voie à des recherches curieuses et intéressantes. En supposant par exemple $x = 2$, on peut présumer qu'il restera quelque chose, de la série si simple des fractions intégrantes ayant pour numérateurs le nombre constant 4, dans la fraction continue ordinaire équivalente, dont les numérateurs seraient l'unité.

En effet, il paraît que, de distance en distance, viennent alors s'offrir des quotients incomplets continuellement croissants. C'est du moins ce qu'indique le résultat suivant, dû à M. G. Forestier, ingénieur des Ponts et Chaussées, à Rochefort.

Prenant l'expression que nous avons en vue, à partir du terme où les fractions intégrantes sont inférieures à $\frac{1}{2}$, c'est-à-dire la quantité

$$\cfrac{4}{9+\cfrac{4}{11+\cfrac{4}{13+\dots}}}$$

M. Forestier a trouvé pour la fraction continue ordinaire équivalente

$$\cfrac{1}{q+\cfrac{1}{q'+\cfrac{1}{q''+\dots}}},$$

la série suivante, des quotients incomplets, q, q', q'', ..., à savoir : 2, 2, 1, 20, 1, 10, 19, 1, 2, 11, 7, 1, 3, 1, 5, 1, 1, 1, 20, 3, 1, 3, 67, 2, 2, 3, 1, 5, 1, 3, 3, 147, ...

Or, on y voit figurer les termes 19, 20, 67, 147, qui semblent justifier cette prévision (1).

(1) Les nombres indiqués ne sont pas exacts. M. Bourget, ayant exécuté deux fois les calculs, a trouvé la suite 2, 2, 1, 20, 1, 10, 19, 1, 3, 1, 2, 2, 2, 70, 18, 1, 1, 1, 2, 1, 2, 1, 1, 3, 2, 5, 1, 2, 35, 1, 14, 4, ... E. P.

SUR UNE ÉQUATION TRANSCENDANTE.

Bulletin des Sciences mathématiques et astronomiques, t. IV, 1873, p. 61.

Soit $f(x)$ une fonction rationnelle de la forme suivante :

$$\frac{A}{x-a}+\frac{B}{x-b}+\ldots+\frac{L}{x-l},$$

les quantités $a, b, \ldots, l$ étant toutes réelles, et les coefficients A, B, ..., L réels et positifs ; je dis en premier lieu que l'équation

$$\log\alpha\frac{1+x}{1-x}-f(x)=0,$$

où α est une constante positive, possède $n+1$ racines réelles, n désignant le nombre des quantités $a, b, \ldots, l$, comprises entre -1 et $+1$. Soit, en effet, pour un instant,

$$F(x)=\log\alpha\frac{1+x}{1-x}-f(x),$$

et désignons par g et h deux termes consécutifs de la série

$$a,\quad b,\quad c,\quad \ldots,\quad l,$$

en supposant les termes rangés par ordre croissant de grandeur, de sorte que la fonction rationnelle $f(x)$ soit finie et continue lorsque la variable est comprise entre les limites g et h.

Cela étant, la fonction $\log\alpha\frac{1+x}{1-x}$, et, par suite, $F(x)$ sera elle-même réelle et continue entre ces limites, si on les suppose inférieures en valeur absolue à l'unité; or, ayant pour ε infiniment petit et positif

$$F(g+\varepsilon) = -\frac{G}{\varepsilon}, \qquad F(h-\varepsilon) = +\frac{H}{\varepsilon},$$

c'est-à-dire deux résultats de signes contraires, nous en concluons pour l'équation proposée l'existence d'une racine réelle comprise entre g et h. J'ajoute qu'il n'y en a qu'une; car, en prenant la dérivée de $F(x)$, on obtient cette expression positive pour toutes les valeurs de x entre -1 et $+1$, savoir

$$F'(x) = \frac{2}{1-x^2} + \frac{A}{(x-a)^2} + \frac{B}{(x-b)^2} + \ldots + \frac{L}{(x-l)^2},$$

de sorte que $F(x)$ va continuellement en croissant depuis $-\frac{G}{\varepsilon}$ jusquà $+\frac{H}{\varepsilon}$, et ne s'annule par conséquent qu'une seule fois. En désignant donc par n le nombre des quantités $a, b, \ldots, l$, qui sont comprises entre -1 et $+1$, nous prouvons ainsi que l'équation proposée possède $n-1$ racines réelles; mais ayant

$$F(-1+\varepsilon) = \log\alpha \frac{\varepsilon}{2-\varepsilon},$$

quantité infiniment grande et négative, on voit de plus qu'il existe encore une racine comprise entre -1 et le terme le plus voisin de la suite $a, b, \ldots, l$; enfin une dernière racine se trouve pareillement entre le terme le plus voisin de l'unité et l'unité, attendu que l'expression

$$F(1-\varepsilon) = \log\alpha \frac{2-\varepsilon}{\varepsilon}$$

est infiniment grande et positive.

En second lieu, je dis que l'équation proposée ne peut admettre aucune racine imaginaire dont le module soit inférieur à l'unité. Soit, en effet, $x = \alpha + \beta\sqrt{-1}$ une telle racine; on trouvera d'abord

$$\begin{aligned} f(\alpha+\beta\sqrt{-1}) = {} & \frac{A(\alpha-a)}{(\alpha-a)^2+\beta^2} + \frac{B(\alpha-b)}{(\alpha-b)^2+\beta^2} + \ldots \\ & - \beta\sqrt{-1}\left[\frac{A}{(\alpha-a)^2+\beta^2} + \frac{B}{(\alpha-b)^2+\beta^2} + \ldots\right]. \end{aligned}$$

Pour calculer ensuite la valeur, que l'on sait être unique et entièrement déterminée, de l'expression $\log \frac{1+x}{1-x}$, lorsque, conformément à la supposition faite, le module de $x = \alpha + \beta\sqrt{-1}$ est inférieur à l'unité, j'emploierai la relation, aisée à vérifier,

$$\log \frac{1+x}{1-x} = \int_{-1}^{+1} \frac{dz}{\frac{1}{x} - z}.$$

Or on en déduit, en faisant, pour un moment,

$$\frac{1}{\rho} = \alpha^2 + \beta^2,$$

$$\begin{aligned}\int_{-1}^{+1} \frac{dz}{\frac{1}{x} - z} &= \int_{-1}^{+1} \frac{dz}{\rho(\alpha - \beta\sqrt{-1}) - z} \\ &= \int_{-1}^{+1} \frac{(\rho\alpha - z)\,dz}{(\rho\alpha - z)^2 + \beta^2} + \rho\beta\sqrt{-1}\int_{-1}^{+1} \frac{dz}{(\rho\alpha - z)^2 + \beta^2},\end{aligned}$$

et l'on voit ainsi que le coefficient de $\beta\sqrt{-1}$ est la quantité essentiellement positive

$$\rho\int_{-1}^{+1} \frac{dz}{(\rho\alpha - z)^2 + \beta^2}.$$

Ayant donc, pour ce même coefficient dans l'expression de

$$-f(\alpha + \beta\sqrt{-1}),$$

une quantité qui est également positive, à savoir

$$\frac{A}{(\alpha - a)^2 + \beta^2} + \frac{B}{(\alpha - b)^2 + \beta^2} + \ldots,$$

nous reconnaissons que la partie imaginaire de $F(\alpha + \beta\sqrt{-1})$ ne peut jamais s'évanouir, de sorte que notre équation n'admet, comme nous voulions l'établir, que des racines réelles.

La relation précédemment employée, à savoir

$$\log \frac{1+x}{1-x} = \int_{-1}^{+1} \frac{dz}{\frac{1}{x} - z},$$

donne lieu à cette remarque que, en posant

$$\frac{1+x}{1-x} = a,$$

d'où

$$\log a = \int_{-1}^{+1} \frac{dz}{\dfrac{a+1}{a-1} - z},$$

celle des valeurs en nombre infini du logarithme qui se trouve ainsi représentée par l'intégrale définie est l'intégrale $\int_1^a \frac{dz}{z}$, en supposant que la variable z décrive la ligne droite joignant les deux points qui ont pour affixes 1 et a.

EXTRAIT

D'UNE

LETTRE DE M. CH. HERMITE A M. PAUL GORDAN,

SUR L'EXPRESSION $U \sin x + V \cos x + W$.

Journal de Crelle, t. 76, p. 303-312.

... En attendant, c'est des fractions continues algébriques que je prends la liberté de vous entretenir, ou plutôt d'une extension de cette théorie, ayant cherché le système des polynomes entiers en x, U, V, W, tels que le développement de l'expression à trois termes

$$U \sin x + V \cos x + W$$

commence par la plus haute puissance possible de la variable. Ces polynomes forment une série doublement infinie, ainsi que pouvait le faire présumer l'analogie avec la théorie arithmétique des minima successifs de la quantité

$$x + ay + bz,$$

où a et b sont des constantes numériques, x, y, z des nombres entiers. Ces minima s'obtiennent, en effet, par la réduction continuelle de la forme quadratique ternaire :

$$(x + ay + bz)^2 + \frac{y^2}{\alpha} + \frac{z^2}{\beta},$$

où entrent deux indéterminées α et β auxquelles doivent être attribuées toutes les valeurs de zéro à l'infini. La première série conduira à la fraction continue de Lambert :

$$\operatorname{tang} x = \cfrac{x}{1 - \cfrac{x^2}{3 - \cfrac{x^2}{5 - \dots}}}$$

et s'obtient ainsi.

Soit

$$A = \sin x,$$

puis successivement

$$A_1 = \int_0^x A x\,dx = \sin x - x \cos x,$$

$$A_2 = \int_0^x A_1 x\,dx = (3 - x^2)\sin x - 3x \cos x,$$

$$A_3 = \int_0^x A_2 x\,dx = (15 - 6x^2)\sin x - (15x - x^3)\cos x,$$

$$\dots\dots\dots\dots\dots\dots\dots\dots\dots\dots\dots\dots,$$

et, en général,

$$A_{n+1} = \int_0^x A_n x\,dx.$$

Les formules élémentaires

$$\int \cos x\, F(x)\,dx = \sin x\, \mathfrak{F}(x) + \cos x\, \mathfrak{F}'(x),$$

$$\int \sin x\, F(x)\,dx = \sin x\, \mathfrak{F}'(x) - \cos x\, \mathfrak{F}(x),$$

où l'on suppose $F(x)$ un polynome entier et

$$\mathfrak{F}(x) = F(x) - F''(x) + F^{\text{IV}}(x) - \dots,$$

montrent que A_n est de la forme $U \sin x + V \cos x$, U et V étant des polynomes entiers dont l'un est du degré n et l'autre du degré $n-1$. En second lieu, si l'on part du développement en série :

$$A = \sin x = x - \frac{x^3}{2.3} + \frac{x^5}{2.3.4.5} - \dots,$$

on en conclura aisément

$$A_n = \frac{x^{2n+1}}{1.3.5\dots 2n+1} - \frac{x^{2n+3}}{1.2.3.5\dots 2n+3} + \dots$$

ou encore

$$A_n = x^{2n+1} \sum_{0}^{k} \frac{1}{(2k+1)(2k+3)\ldots(2k+2n+1)} \frac{(-1)^k x^{2k}}{1.2.3\ldots 2k}.$$

Le premier terme de cette série étant en x^{2n+1}, vous voyez que U et V sont bien les polynomes qui résultent de la théorie des fractions continues. Mais on peut y parvenir par une autre voie.

Soit

$$\mathfrak{U} = \frac{\sin x}{x},$$

puis successivement

$$\mathfrak{U}_1 = -\frac{1}{x}\frac{d\mathfrak{U}}{dx} = \frac{\sin x - x\cos x}{x^3},$$

$$\mathfrak{U}_2 = -\frac{1}{x}\frac{d\mathfrak{U}_1}{dx} = \frac{(3-x^2)\sin x - 3x\cos x}{x^5},$$

$$\mathfrak{U}_3 = -\frac{1}{x}\frac{d\mathfrak{U}_2}{dx} = \frac{(15-6x^2)\sin x - (15x - x^3)\cos x}{x^7},$$

et, en général,

$$\mathfrak{U}_{n+1} = -\frac{1}{x}\frac{d\mathfrak{U}_n}{dx}.$$

On reconnaît immédiatement qu'on aura

$$\mathfrak{U}_n = \frac{U\sin x + V\cos x}{x^{2n+1}},$$

U et V étant encore des polynomes dont l'un est de degré n et l'autre de degré $n-1$; on obtient aussi facilement la série

$$\mathfrak{U}_n = \frac{1}{1.3.5\ldots 2n+1} - \frac{x^2}{2.3.5\ldots 2n+3} + \ldots.$$

Il s'ensuit que

$$\mathfrak{U}_n = \frac{A_n}{x^{2n+1}};$$

et, par conséquent,

$$\frac{A_{n+1}}{x^{2n+3}} = -\frac{1}{x}\frac{d}{dx}\left(\frac{A_n}{x^{2n+1}}\right),$$

c'est-à-dire

$$A_{n+1} = (2n+1)A_n - \frac{dA_n}{dx}x;$$

mais

$$\frac{dA_n}{dx} = A_{n-1}x,$$

et nous parvenons entre trois termes consécutifs à la relation

$$A_{n+1} = (2n+1)A_n - A_{n-1}x^2.$$

De là se tire la fraction continue de Lambert, et l'équation différentielle des transcendantes de Bessel. Il suffit, en effet, d'observer que

$$A_{n-1} = \frac{1}{x}\frac{dA_n}{dx}, \qquad A_{n-2} = \frac{1}{x^2}\left(\frac{d^2A_n}{dx^2} - \frac{1}{x}\frac{dA_n}{dx}\right)$$

pour passer de l'égalité

$$A_n = (2n-1)A_{n-1} - A_{n-2}x^2$$

à cette équation si connue

$$\frac{d^2A_n}{dx^2} - \frac{2n}{x}\frac{dA_n}{dx} + A_n = 0,$$

dont une seconde solution est donnée comme il est aisé de le voir par la formule

$$A_n = \mathrm{U}\cos x - \mathrm{V}\sin x.$$

Je vais maintenant sortir du domaine des fractions continues, et définir une seconde série de polynomes U, V, W, en posant

$$B_n = \int_0^x A_n\,dx,$$

puis successivement une troisième, une quatrième, etc., par les relations semblables

$$C_n = \int_0^x B_n\,dx, \qquad D_n = \int_0^x C_n\,dx, \qquad \ldots.$$

Les formules déjà employées

$$\int \cos x\,\mathrm{F}(x)\,dx = \sin x\,\mathfrak{F}(x) + \cos x\,\mathfrak{F}'(x),$$

$$\int \sin x\,\mathrm{F}(x)\,dx = \sin x\,\mathfrak{F}'(x) - \cos x\,\mathfrak{F}(x)$$

donnent la composition de ces quantités, et montrent qu'en désignant par P_n le terme général de la série de rang p, on aura

$$P_n = U\sin x + V\cos x + W,$$

U et V étant des polynomes entiers, l'un du degré n, l'autre du degré $n-1$, et W de degré $p-1$. Or le développement

$$P_n = x^{2n+p}\sum_0^k \frac{(2k+2)(2k+4)\ldots(2k+2n)(-1)^k x^{2k}}{1.2.3\ldots 2k+2n+p},$$

dont le premier terme est de degré $2n+p$, a bien la forme voulue.

Ces mêmes quantités peuvent s'obtenir d'une autre manière comme il suit. Posons, suivant que p est pair ou impair,

$$\mathfrak{P} = \frac{(-1)^{\frac{1}{2}p}}{x^p}\left[\cos x - 1 + \frac{x^2}{1.2} - \frac{x^4}{1.2.3.4} + \ldots + (-1)^{\frac{1}{2}p}\frac{x^{p-2}}{1.2\ldots p-2}\right]$$

ou bien

$$\mathfrak{P} = \frac{(-1)^{\frac{p-1}{2}}}{x^p}\left[\sin x - x + \frac{x^3}{1.2.3} - \ldots + (-1)^{\frac{p-1}{2}}\frac{x^{p-2}}{1.2\ldots p-2}\right]$$

et faisons successivement

$$\mathfrak{P}_1 = -\frac{1}{x}\frac{d\mathfrak{P}}{dx}, \qquad \mathfrak{P}_2 = -\frac{1}{x}\frac{d\mathfrak{P}_1}{dx}, \qquad \ldots, \qquad \mathfrak{P}_{n+1} = -\frac{1}{x}\frac{d\mathfrak{P}_n}{dx}.$$

Cette loi de formation donne très facilement le développement en série de $\mathfrak{P}_n$, en partant du développement de $\mathfrak{P}$, à savoir

$$\mathfrak{P} = \frac{1}{1.2\ldots p} - \frac{x^2}{1.2\ldots p+2} + \frac{x^4}{1.2\ldots p+4}\cdots$$

On retrouve ainsi

$$\mathfrak{P}_n = \sum_0^k \frac{(2k+2)(2k+4)\ldots(2k+2n)(-1)^k x^{2k}}{1.2.3\ldots 2k+2n+p},$$

ce qui conduit à la relation

$$\mathfrak{P}_n = \frac{P_n}{x^{2n+p}},$$

d'où l'on tire, comme pour les quantités A_n, celle-ci :

$$P_{n+1} = (2n+p)P_n - \frac{dP_n}{dx}x.$$

Mais la dérivée $\frac{dP_n}{dx}$ est le $n^{\text{ième}}$ terme de la $(p-1)^{\text{ième}}$ série ; faisant donc

$$p = 2,\ 3,\ 4,\ \ldots,$$

nous aurons successivement

$$\begin{aligned}
B_{n+1} &= (2n+2)\,B_n - A_n x,\\
C_{n+1} &= (2n+3)\,C_n - B_n x,\\
D_{n+1} &= (2n+4)\,D_n - C_n x,\\
&\ldots\ldots\ldots\ldots\ldots\ldots
\end{aligned}$$

J'ai calculé par ces formules et celles qui concernent A_n les valeurs suivantes :

$$\begin{aligned}
A_1 &= \sin x - x\cos x,\\
A_2 &= (3-x^2)\sin x - 3x\cos x,\\
A_3 &= (15-6x^2)\sin x - (15x-x^3)\cos x,\\
A_4 &= (105-45x^2+x^4)\sin x - (105x-10x^3)\cos x,\\
A_5 &= (945-420x^2+15x^4)\sin x - (945x-105x^3+x^5)\cos x,\\
&\ldots\ldots\ldots\ldots\ldots\ldots,
\end{aligned}$$

$$\begin{aligned}
B_0 &= -\cos x + 1,\\
B_1 &= -x\sin x - 2\cos x + 2,\\
B_2 &= -5x\sin x - (8-x^2)\cos x + 8,\\
B_3 &= -(33x-x^3)\sin x - (48-9x^2)\cos x + 48,\\
B_4 &= -(279x-14x^3)\sin x - (384-87x^2+x^4)\cos x + 384,\\
B_5 &= -(2895x-185x^3+x^5)\sin x - (3840-975x^2+20x^4)\cos x + 3840,\\
&\ldots\ldots\ldots\ldots\ldots\ldots,
\end{aligned}$$

$$\begin{aligned}
C_0 &= -\sin x + x,\\
C_1 &= -3\sin x + x\cos x + 2x,\\
C_2 &= -(15-x^2)\sin x + 7x\cos x + 8x,\\
C_3 &= -(105-12x^2)\sin x + (57x-x^3)\cos x + 48x,\\
C_4 &= -(945-141x^2+x^4)\sin x + (561x-18x^3)\cos x + 384x,\\
&\ldots\ldots\ldots\ldots\ldots\ldots,
\end{aligned}$$

$$\begin{aligned}
D_0 &= \cos x - 1 + \frac{x^2}{2},\\
D_1 &= x\sin x + 4\cos x + x^2 - 4,\\
D_2 &= 9x\sin x + (24-x^2)\cos x + 4x^2 - 24,\\
D_3 &= (87x-x^3)\sin x + (192-15x^2)\cos x + 24x^2 - 192,\\
&\ldots\ldots\ldots\ldots\ldots\ldots
\end{aligned}$$

C'est maintenant, Monsieur, que se présente une question arithmétique d'un grand intérêt. Supposons $x = i$, en faisant pour abréger

$$h = \frac{\sin i}{i} = \frac{e - e^{-1}}{2}, \qquad h' = \cos i = \frac{e + e^{-1}}{2};$$

la quantité

$$P_n = U \sin x + V \cos x + W$$

prendra la forme suivante,

$$i^{2n+p}(uh + vh' + w),$$

où u et v sont toujours des nombres entiers, w pouvant être fractionnaire, mais devenant également entier quand n croît au delà d'une certaine limite. On a, en effet,

$$W = -(-1)^{\frac{1}{2}p} \sum \frac{(p-k)(p-k+2)\ldots(p-k+2n-2)(-1)^{\frac{1}{2}k} x^k}{1.2.3\ldots k},$$

en supposant $k = 0, 2, 4, \ldots, p-2$, si p est pair, et

$$W = (-1)^{\frac{p-1}{2}} \sum \frac{(p-k)(p-k+2)\ldots(p-k+2n-2)(-1)^{\frac{k-1}{2}} x^k}{1.2.3\ldots k},$$

en faisant $k = 1, 3, 5, \ldots, p-2$, si p est impair; or, dans les deux cas, il est visible que le coefficient

$$\frac{(p-k)(p-k+2)\ldots(p-k+2n-2)}{1.2.3\ldots k}$$

finit par devenir entier. Cela posé, les divers systèmes des nombres

$$x = u, \qquad y = v, \qquad z = w$$

donneront-ils des minima de la fonction linéaire $xh + yh' + z$?

Vous connaissez la découverte mémorable de Dirichlet sur les minima des fonctions linéaires, à un nombre quelconque d'indéterminées; en arithmétique elle me semble, si je puis dire, aussi importante que la théorie des fonctions elliptiques pour l'Analyse. Mais, tandis que les fractions continues sont d'un emploi usuel, les applications numériques des théorèmes de Dirichlet restent comme impossibles, et à cet égard je reconnais n'avoir encore guère avancé la question, en déduisant ces théorèmes de la considération des formes quadratiques. Me plaçant toutefois en ce moment à mon point de vue, j'envisage les minima de la forme

$$f = (xh + yh' + z)^2 + \frac{x^2}{\alpha} + \frac{y^2}{\beta},$$

où α et β sont positifs et dont l'invariant est $D = \frac{1}{\alpha\beta}$. Ces minima satisfont à la condition $f \leqq \sqrt{2D}$; or le produit $(hx + h'y + z)^2 \frac{x^2}{\alpha} \frac{y^2}{\beta}$ a pour maximum $\left(\frac{f}{3}\right)^3$, d'où cette relation indépendante de α et β, savoir :

$$(hx + h'y + z)xy < \sqrt{\frac{2}{27}}.$$

En appliquant ce critérium aux nombres donnés par les quantités B_n, on reconnaît immédiatement qu'ils ne peuvent convenir; mais dans les séries suivantes je trouve :

$$iC_2 = 16h - 7h' - 8 = \frac{1}{3.5.6.7} + \ldots,$$

$$D_2 = -9h + 25h' - 28 = \frac{1}{3.5.6.7.8} + \ldots,$$

$$D_3 = -88h + 207h' - 216 = -\frac{1}{3.5.7.8.9.10} - \ldots,$$

$$iE_3 = -333h + 124h' - 200 = \frac{1}{3.5.7.8.9.10.11} + \ldots,$$

$$F_3 = 166h - 501h' - 578 = \frac{1}{3.5.7.8.9.10.11.12} + \ldots,$$

$$F_4 = 2327h - 6136h' - 6736 = -\frac{1}{3.5.7.9.10.11.12.13.14} - \ldots,$$

$$\ldots\ldots\ldots\ldots\ldots\ldots\ldots\ldots\ldots\ldots\ldots\ldots,$$

et vous voyez que la condition requise est complètement remplie, le calcul par logarithmes donnant dans le dernier cas

$$\frac{2327.6136}{3.5.7.9.10.11.12.13.14} = 0,06006.$$

Mais je reviens à l'Algèbre, pour considérer les expressions rationnelles approchées de $\sin x$ et $\cos x$ données par deux équations telles que

$$A_n = 0, \qquad B_n = 0$$

ou bien

$$B_n = 0, \qquad C_n = 0; \qquad C_n = 0, \qquad D_n = 0, \qquad \ldots.$$

Dans le premier cas, par exemple, on trouve pour $n = 1, 2, 3$ ces valeurs :

$$\sin x = \frac{2x}{2 + x^2} = \frac{24x}{24 + 4x^2 + x^4} = \frac{720x - 48x^3}{720 + 72x^2 + 6x^4 + x^6},$$

$$\cos x = \frac{2}{2 + x^2} = \frac{24 - 8x^2}{24 + 4x^2 + x^4} = \frac{720 - 288x^2}{720 + 72x^2 + 6x^4 + x^6},$$

et, en général, il est aisé de voir qu'elles seront de la forme

$$\cos x = \frac{S}{R}, \qquad \sin x = \frac{T}{R},$$

R, S et T étant des polynomes entiers dont les premiers renferment seulement des puissances paires et le troisième des puissances impaires de la variable. En déduisant d'abord des relations proposées

$$\cos x + i \sin x = \frac{S + iT}{R},$$

j'observe que, si l'on change x en $-ix$, on se trouve amené à une expression entièrement réelle de l'exponentielle e^x, par une fraction dont le dénominateur ne contient que des puissances paires. Sous ce point de vue plus simple, je remarque qu'en posant

$$\Phi(x) = a_0 + a_1 x^2 + a_2 x^4 + \ldots + a_n x^{2n}$$

on peut, en général, disposer des coefficients $a_0, a_1, \ldots$ de manière que le produit $e^x \Phi(x)$ ordonné suivant les puissances croissantes de x manque des n termes en $x^{n+p+1}, x^{n+p+2}, \ldots, x^{2n+p}$, et soit de la forme

$$e^x \Phi(x) = \Pi(x) + \varepsilon x^{2n+p+1} + \varepsilon' x^{2n+p+2} + \ldots.$$

Il résulte qu'en faisant

$$\Pi_1(x) = \Pi(-x)$$

nous aurons, aux termes près de l'ordre $2n + p + 1$,

$$e^x = \frac{\Pi(x)}{\Phi(x)}, \qquad e^{-x} = \frac{\Pi_1(x)}{\Phi(x)},$$

et il suffira de changer x en ix pour retrouver sous forme réelle les expressions que j'ai eues d'abord en vue

$$\cos x = \frac{S}{R}, \qquad \sin x = \frac{T}{R}.$$

Or, ces polynomes $\Phi(x)$ et $\Pi(x)$, dont la considération me semble indispensable pour approfondir la question arithmétique difficile que j'ai seulement touchée, s'obtiennent comme il suit.

J'applique la formule

$$\int F(t)\,e^{-tx}\,dt = -\,e^{-tx}\,\mathfrak{F}(t),$$

où $F(t)$ est une fonction entière et $\mathfrak{F}$ la quantité

$$\mathfrak{F}(t) = \frac{F(t)}{x} + \frac{F'(t)}{x^2} + \frac{F''(t)}{x^3} + \ldots,$$

à la détermination de l'intégrale définie $\int_0^1 t^n(1-t^2)^p\,e^{-tx}\,dt$. Pour cela je remarque que la relation

$$\int_0^1 F(t)\,e^{-tx}\,dt = \mathfrak{F}(0) - e^{-x}\,\mathfrak{F}(1)$$

met en évidence deux termes, dont le premier se calcule au moyen du développement

$$F(t) = t^n(1-t^2)^p = t^n - \frac{p}{1}\,t^{n+2} + \frac{p(p-1)}{1.2}\,t^{n+4} - \ldots + (-1)^p\,t^{n+2p}$$

qui donne les valeurs des dérivées de $F(t)$ pour $t=0$; on a donc immédiatement

$$\begin{aligned}\mathfrak{F}(0) = {} & \frac{1.2.3\ldots n}{x^{n+1}} - \frac{p}{1}\,\frac{1.2.3\ldots n+2}{x^{n+3}} + \ldots \\ & + (-1)^p\,\frac{1.2.3\ldots n+2p}{x^{n+2p+1}} = \frac{1.2.3\ldots n}{x^{n+2p+1}}\,\Phi(x),\end{aligned}$$

en posant

$$\begin{aligned}\Phi(x) = {} & x^{2p} - \frac{p}{1}(n+1)(n+2)x^{2p-2} \\ & + \frac{p(p-1)}{1.2}(n+1)(n+2)(n+3)(n+4)x^{2p-4} - \ldots.\end{aligned}$$

Soit en second lieu $t = 1 + h$; les dérivées de $F(t)$ pour $t = 1$ s'obtiendront en développant suivant les puissances de h la quantité

$$F(1+h) = (-1)^p h^p (1+h)^n (2+h)^p.$$

Faisons

$$(1+h)^n (2+h)^p = A + Bh + Ch^2 + \ldots + h^{n+p},$$

et l'on en conclura semblablement

$$\mathfrak{f}(1) = \frac{(-1)^p . 1.2.3\ldots p}{x^{n+2p+1}} \Pi(x),$$

en écrivant pour abréger

$$\Pi(x) = A x^{n+p} + p B x^{n+p-1} + p(p+1) C x^{n+p-2} + \ldots.$$

Ceci posé, et, en observant que l'intégrale $\int_0^1 t^n (1-t^2)^p e^{-tx}\, dt$ peut être évidemment développée sous la forme $\varepsilon + \varepsilon_1 x + \varepsilon_2 x^2 + \ldots$, la relation à laquelle nous sommes amenés, à savoir

$$\frac{1.2.3\ldots n}{x^{n+2p+1}} \Phi(x) - e^{-x} \frac{(-1)^p . 1.2.3\ldots p}{x^{n+2p+1}} \Pi(x) = \varepsilon + \varepsilon_1 x + \varepsilon_2 x^2 + \ldots,$$

donne facilement

$$e^x \Phi(x) - (-1)^p \frac{1.2.3\ldots p}{1.2.3\ldots n} \Pi(x) = \varepsilon' x^{n+2p+1} + \varepsilon'' x^{n+2p+2} + \ldots.$$

Les polynomes cherchés sont donc ainsi obtenus d'une manière générale, mais je n'en ai pas jusqu'ici fait l'étude approfondie. J'ai seulement remarqué que l'intégrale définie $\int_0^1 t^n (1-t^2)^p e^{-tx}\, dt$, et ces deux autres

$$\int_0^{-1} t^n (1-t^2)^p e^{-tx}\, dt, \qquad \int_0^{\infty} t^n (1-t^2)^p e^{-tx}\, dt,$$

satisfont à l'équation linéaire du troisième ordre

$$x \frac{d^3 y}{dx^3} + (n + 2p + 3) \frac{d^2 y}{dx^2} - x \frac{dy}{dx} - (n+1) y = 0.$$

EXTRAIT

D'UNE

LETTRE DE M. CH. HERMITE A M. BORCHARDT,

SUR

QUELQUES APPROXIMATIONS ALGÉBRIQUES.

Journal de Crelle, t. 76, p. 342-344, 1873.

... Je ne me hasarderai point à la recherche d'une démonstration de la transcendance du nombre π. Que d'autres tentent l'entreprise, nul ne sera plus heureux que moi de leur succès, mais croyez-m'en, mon cher ami, il ne laissera pas que de leur en coûter quelques efforts. Tout ce que je puis, c'est de refaire ce qu'a déjà fait Lambert, seulement d'une autre manière, au moyen de cette égalité

$$A_n = U \sin x + V \cos x = \frac{x^{2n+1}}{2.4\ldots 2n} \int_0^1 (1 - z^2)^n \cos xz \, dz,$$

où A_n, U et V désignent les mêmes quantités que dans ma lettre à M. Gordan. Vous savez que U est un polynome entier et à coefficients entiers en x^2 du degré $\frac{n}{2}$ ou $\frac{n-1}{2}$ selon que n est pair ou impair; il en résulte dans le premier cas, par exemple, que pour $x = \frac{\pi}{2}$, en supposant que $\frac{\pi^2}{4}$ soit une fraction $\frac{b}{a}$, on aura

$$U = \frac{N}{a^{\frac{1}{2}n}},$$

où N est entier, et la relation proposée donne

$$\frac{N}{a^{\frac{1}{2}n}} = \frac{\left(\frac{b}{a}\right)^{\frac{1}{2}}\left(\frac{b}{a}\right)^{n}}{2.4\ldots 2n} \int_0^1 (1-z^2)^n \cos\frac{\pi z}{2}\, dz$$

ou bien

$$N = \frac{\left(\frac{b}{a}\right)^{\frac{1}{2}}\left(\frac{b}{\sqrt{a}}\right)^{n}}{2.4\ldots 2n} \int_0^1 (1-z^2)^n \cos\frac{\pi z}{2}\, dz.$$

Or, on met immédiatement une impossibilité en évidence, puisque le second membre devient, sans pouvoir jamais s'annuler, plus petit que toute quantité donnée quand n augmente, le premier étant un nombre entier.

Voici une autre conséquence de l'expression de A_n par une intégrale définie; on en tire aisément, sous forme d'intégrales doubles, les quantités

$$B_n = \int_0^x A_n\, dx, \qquad C_n = \int_0^x B_n\, dx, \qquad \ldots,$$

en employant les formules élémentaires

$$\int_0^x dx \int_0^x f(x)\, dx = \int_0^x (x-z) f(z)\, dz = x^2 \int_0^1 (1-\lambda) f(\lambda x)\, d\lambda,$$

$$\begin{aligned}\int_0^x dx \int_0^x dx \int_0^x f(x)\, dx &= \int_0^x \frac{(x-z)^2}{1.2} f(z)\, dz \\ &= \frac{x^3}{1.2} \int_0^1 (1-\lambda)^2 f(\lambda x)\, d\lambda,\end{aligned}$$

....,

et il vient ainsi

$$P_n = \frac{x^{2n+p+1}}{1.2\ldots p - 1.2.4\ldots 2n} \int_0^1 \int_0^1 (1-\lambda^2)^n (1-\lambda_1)^{p-1} \lambda_1^{2n+1} \cos \lambda\lambda_1 x\, d\lambda\, d\lambda_1.$$

Mais, sous un point de vue plus général, supposons les i polynomes : $\Phi_m(x)$, $\Phi_n(x)$, ..., $\Phi_r(x)$ des degrés m, n, ..., r déterminés de manière que le développement suivant les puissances croissantes de la variable de la fonction

$$f(x) = e^{\alpha x}\, \Phi_m(x) + e^{\beta x}\, \Phi_n(x) + \ldots + \Phi_r(x)$$

commence au terme du degré le plus élevé possible en $x^{m+n+\ldots+r+i-1}$. En multipliant par une nouvelle exponentielle, $e^{\omega x}$, et formant la suite des quantités

$$f_1(x) = \int_0^x e^{\omega x} f(x)\,dx, \qquad f_2(x) = \int_0^x f_1(x)\,dx, \qquad \ldots,$$
$$f_{s+1}(x) = \int_0^x f_s(x)\,dx,$$

il est clair que la dernière sera de la forme suivante,

$$f_{s+1}(x) = e^{(\alpha+\omega)x}\,\Psi_m(x) + e^{(\beta+\omega)x}\,\Psi_n(x) + \ldots + e^{\omega x}\,\Psi_r(x) + \Psi_s(x),$$

où $\Psi_m(x)$, $\Psi_n(x)$, ..., $\Psi_s(x)$ seront des polynomes entiers des degrés m, n, ..., s, et que son développement commencera par un terme de degré $m+n+\ldots+s+i$. On en conclut aisément que si l'on pose

$$\Theta(\lambda_1, \lambda_2, \ldots, \lambda_i) = (1-\lambda_1)^n (1-\lambda_2)^p \ldots (1-\lambda_i)^s \lambda_1^m \lambda_2^{m+n+1} \ldots \lambda_i^{m+n+\ldots+r+i-}$$
$$\Lambda = (\alpha-\beta)\lambda_1\lambda_2\ldots\lambda_i + (\beta-\gamma)\lambda_2\lambda_3\ldots\lambda_i + (\gamma-\delta)\lambda_3\lambda_4\ldots\lambda_i + \ldots + \omega\lambda_i$$

on aura la relation

$$\int_0^1\int_0^1\ldots\int_0^1 \Theta(\lambda_1, \lambda_2, \ldots, \lambda_i)e^{\Lambda x}\,d\lambda_1\,d\lambda_2\ldots d\lambda_i$$
$$= \frac{e^{\alpha x}\,\Theta_m(x) + e^{\beta x}\,\Theta_n(x) + \ldots + e^{\omega x}\,\Theta_r(x) + \Theta_s(x)}{x^{m+n+\ldots+s+i}},$$

où $\Theta_m(x)$, $\Theta_n(x)$, ..., $\Theta_s(x)$ sont des polynomes entiers des degrés m, n, ..., s; c'est donc au moyen d'une intégrale multiple la définition du système des polynomes entiers de degrés donnés, qui donnent la plus grande approximation de la fonction linéaire composée avec les exponentielles $e^{\alpha x}$, $e^{\beta x}$, ..., $e^{\omega x}$.

Dans le courant de ces recherches, voici une question arithmétique qui m'a beaucoup préoccupé. En considérant pour une valeur entière de x la fraction continue

$$\frac{e^x-1}{e^x+1} = \cfrac{x}{2+\cfrac{x^2}{6+\ddots}}$$

ne doit-il pas exister quelque caractère spécial, à l'égard de la fraction continue ordinaire équivalente dans laquelle les numérateurs des fractions intégrantes sont l'unité? J'avais présumé qu'au moins de distance en distance, les quotients incomplets iraient en grandissant, et c'est ce qui se trouve jusqu'à un certain point confirmé, par le résultat suivant que je dois à l'obligeance de M. Forestier. Soit $x = 3$, et faisons

$$\frac{e^3-1}{e^3+1} = \cfrac{1}{q + \cfrac{1}{q' + \cfrac{1}{q'' + \ldots}}};$$

la suite des nombres entiers $q, q', q'', \ldots$ est

1, 8, 1, 16, 2, 1, 1, 2, 4, 1, 2, 11, 2, 1, 2, 36, 1, 8, 4, 17, 9, 1, 1, 1, 1, 1, 2, 3, 90, ...

Malheureusement les calculs sont si longs et si pénibles qu'on ne peut espérer trouver quelque loi par la voie de l'induction ([1]).

([1]) Le calcul, après deux vérifications, a donné à M. Bourget la suite différente de celle du texte 1, 9, 1, 1, 5, 2, 1, 8, 1, 1, 12, 2, 1, 7, 1, 3, 8, 4, 6, 1, 1, 6, 1, 1, 1, 1, 1, 2, 1, 2, 1, 1, ... E. P.

SUR

LA FONCTION EXPONENTIELLE.

Comptes rendus de l'Académie des Sciences, t. LXXVII, 1873, p. 18-24, 74-79, 226-233, 285-293.

I. Étant donné un nombre quelconque de quantités numériques $\alpha_1, \alpha_2, \ldots, \alpha_n$, on sait qu'on peut en approcher simultanément par des fractions de même dénominateur, de telle sorte qu'on ait

$$\alpha_1 = \frac{A_1}{A} + \frac{\delta_1}{A\sqrt[n]{A}},$$
$$\alpha_2 = \frac{A_2}{A} + \frac{\delta_2}{A\sqrt[n]{A}},$$
$$\ldots\ldots\ldots\ldots\ldots\ldots,$$
$$\alpha_n = \frac{A_n}{A} + \frac{\delta_n}{A\sqrt[n]{A}},$$

$\delta_1, \delta_2, \ldots, \delta_n$ ne pouvant dépasser une limite qui dépend seulement de n. C'est, comme on voit, une extension du mode d'approximation résultant de la théorie des fractions continues, qui correspondrait au cas le plus simple de $n=1$. Or, on peut se proposer une généralisation semblable de la théorie des fractions continues algébriques, en cherchant les expressions approchées de n fonctions $\varphi_1(x), \varphi_2(x), \ldots, \varphi_n(x)$ par des fractions rationnelles $\frac{\Phi_1(x)}{\Phi(x)}, \frac{\Phi_2(x)}{\Phi(x)}, \ldots, \frac{\Phi_n(x)}{\Phi(x)}$, de manière que les développements en série suivant les puissances croissantes de la variable coïncident jusqu'à une puissance déterminée x^M. Voici d'abord, à cet égard, un premier résultat qui s'offre immédiatement. Supposons que les fonctions $\varphi_1(x)$, $\varphi_2(x)$, ..., $\varphi_n(x)$ soient toutes développables en séries de la forme $\alpha + \beta x + \gamma x^2 + \ldots$ et faisons

$$\Phi(x) = A x^m + B x^{m-1} + \ldots + K x + L.$$

On pourra, en général, disposer des coefficients A, B, ..., L de manière à annuler dans les n produits $\varphi_i(x)\Phi(x)$ les termes en

$$x^M, \quad x^{M-1}, \quad \ldots, \quad x^{M-\mu_i+1},$$

μ_i étant un nombre entier arbitraire. Nous poserons ainsi un nombre d'équations homogènes de premier degré égal précisément à μ_i, et l'on aura

$$\varphi_i(x)\Phi(x) = \Phi_i(x) + \varepsilon_1 x^{M+1} + \varepsilon_2 x^{M+2} + \ldots,$$

ε_1, ε_2, ... étant des constantes, $\Phi_i(x)$ un polynome entier de degré $M - \mu_i$. Or, cette relation donnant

$$\varphi_i(x) = \frac{\Phi_i(x)}{\Phi(x)} + \frac{\varepsilon_1 x^{M+1} + \varepsilon_2 x^{M+2} + \ldots}{\Phi(x)},$$

on voit que les développements en série de la fraction rationnelle et de la fonction seront, en effet, les mêmes jusqu'aux termes en x^M, et, comme le nombre total des équations posées est $\mu_1 + \mu_2 + \ldots + \mu_n$, il suffit d'assujettir à la seule condition

$$\mu_1 + \mu_2 + \ldots + \mu_n = m$$

les entiers μ_i restés jusqu'ici absolument arbitraires. C'est cette considération si simple qui a servi de point de départ à l'étude de la fonction exponentielle que je vais exposer, me proposant d'en faire l'application aux quantités

$$\varphi_1(x) = e^{ax}, \qquad \varphi_2(x) = e^{bx}, \qquad \ldots, \qquad \varphi_n(x) = e^{hx}.$$

II. Soit, pour abréger, $M - m = \mu$; je compose avec les constantes a, b, ..., h le polynome

$$F(z) = z^{\mu}(z-a)^{\mu_1}(z-b)^{\mu_2}\ldots(z-h)^{\mu_n},$$

de degré $\mu + \mu_1 + \ldots + \mu_n = M$, et j'envisage les n intégrales définies

$$\int_0^a e^{-zx} F(z)\,dz, \qquad \int_0^b e^{-zx} F(z)\,dz, \qquad \ldots, \qquad \int_0^h e^{-zx} F(z)\,dz,$$

qu'il est facile d'obtenir sous forme explicite. Faisant, en effet,

$$\mathfrak{F}(z) = \frac{F(z)}{x} + \frac{F'(z)}{x^2} + \ldots + \frac{F^{(M)}(z)}{x^{M+1}},$$

nous aurons

$$\int e^{-zx} F(z)\,dz = -e^{-zx}\mathfrak{F}(z),$$

et, par conséquent,

$$\int_0^a e^{-zx} F(z)\,dz = \mathfrak{F}(0) - e^{-ax}\mathfrak{F}(a),$$

$$\int_0^b e^{-zx} F(z)\,dz = \mathfrak{F}(0) - e^{-bx}\mathfrak{F}(b),$$

$$\ldots\ldots\ldots\ldots\ldots\ldots\ldots\ldots\ldots\ldots$$

Or l'expression de $\mathfrak{F}(z)$ donne immédiatement, sous forme de polynomes ordonnés suivant les puissances croissantes de $\frac{1}{x}$, les diverses quantités $\mathfrak{F}(0)$, $\mathfrak{F}(a)$, $\mathfrak{F}(b)$, ..., et si l'on observe qu'on a

$$F(0) = 0, \qquad F'(0) = 0, \qquad \ldots, \qquad F^{(\mu-1)}(0) = 0,$$

puis successivement,

$$\begin{array}{llll} F(a) = 0, & F'(a) = 0, & \ldots, & F^{(\mu_1-1)}(a) = 0, \\ F(b) = 0, & F'(b) = 0, & \ldots, & F^{(\mu_2-1)}(b) = 0, \\ \ldots\ldots\ldots & \ldots\ldots\ldots & \ldots\ldots & \ldots\ldots\ldots\ldots, \end{array}$$

nous en conclurons les résultats suivants

$$\mathfrak{F}(0) = \frac{\Phi(x)}{x^{M+1}}, \qquad \mathfrak{F}(a) = \frac{\Phi_1(x)}{x^{M+1}}, \qquad \ldots, \qquad \mathfrak{F}(h) = \frac{\Phi_n(x)}{x^{M+1}},$$

où le polynome entier $\Phi(x)$ est du degré $M - \mu = m$, et les autres $\Phi_1(x)$, $\Phi_2(x)$, ..., $\Phi_n(x)$, des degrés $M - \mu_1$, $M - \mu_2$, ..., $M - \mu_n$. Cela posé, nous écrirons

$$e^{ax}\Phi(x) - \Phi_1(x) = x^{M+1}e^{ax}\int_0^a e^{-zx} F(z)\,dz,$$

$$e^{bx}\Phi(x) - \Phi_2(x) = x^{M+1}e^{bx}\int_0^b e^{-zx} F(z)\,dz,$$

$$\ldots\ldots\ldots\ldots\ldots\ldots\ldots\ldots\ldots\ldots,$$

$$e^{hx}\Phi(x) - \Phi_n(x) = x^{M+1}e^{hx}\int_0^h e^{-zx} F(z)\,dz;$$

or, les intégrales définies se développant en séries de la forme $\alpha + \beta x + \gamma x^2 + \ldots$, on voit que les conditions précédemment posées comme définitions du nouveau mode d'approximation des fonctions se trouvent entièrement remplies. Nous avons ainsi obtenu, dans toute sa généralité, le système des fractions rationnelles $\frac{\Phi_1(x)}{\Phi(x)}$, $\frac{\Phi_2(x)}{\Phi(x)}$, $\ldots$, $\frac{\Phi_n(x)}{\Phi(x)}$, de même dénominateur, représentant les fonctions e^{ax}, e^{bx}, $\ldots$, e^{hx}, aux termes près de l'ordre x^{M+1}.

III. Soit, comme application, $n = 1$, et supposons de plus $\mu = \mu_1 = m$, ce qui donnera

$$M = 2m, \qquad F(z) = z^m(z-1)^m;$$

les dérivées de $F(z)$ pour $z = 0$ se tirent sur-le-champ du développement par la formule du binome

$$F(z) = z^{2m} - \frac{m}{1} z^{2m-1} + \frac{m(m-1)}{1.2} z^{2m-2} - \ldots + (-1)^m z^m,$$

et l'on obtient

$$\frac{F^{(2m-k)}(0)}{1.2.3\ldots 2m-k} = \frac{m(m-1)\ldots(m-k+1)}{1.2.3\ldots k}(-1)^k,$$

d'où, par suite,

$$\frac{\Phi(x)}{1.2.3\ldots m} = 2m(2m-1)\ldots(m+1) - (2m-1)(2m-2)\ldots(m+1)\frac{m}{1}x + (2m-2)(2m-3)\ldots(m+1)\frac{m(m-1)}{1.2}x^2 - \ldots + (-1)^m x^m.$$

Pour avoir, en second lieu, les valeurs des dérivées quand on suppose $z = 1$, nous poserons $z = 1 + h$, afin de développer suivant les puissances de h le polynome $F(1+h) = h^m(h+1)^m$. Or les coefficients précédemment obtenus se reproduisant, sauf le signe, on voit qu'on aura

$$\Phi_1(x) = \Phi(-x).$$

Ces résultats conduisent à introduire, au lieu de $\Phi(x)$ et $\Phi_1(x)$, les polynomes

$$\Pi(x) = \frac{\Phi(x)}{1.2.3\ldots m}, \qquad \Pi_1(x) = \frac{\Phi_1(x)}{1.2.3\ldots m},$$

dont les coefficients sont des nombres entiers; on aura ainsi

$$e^x \Pi(x) - \Pi_1(x) = \frac{x^{2m+1}}{1.2.3\ldots m} e^x \int_0^1 e^{-zx} z^m (z-1)^m \, dz$$

$$= (-1)^m \frac{x^{2m+1}}{1.2.3\ldots m} \int_0^1 e^{x(1-z)} z^m (1-z)^m \, dz,$$

et l'on met en évidence que le premier membre peut devenir, pour une valeur suffisamment grande de m, plus petit que toute quantité donnée. Nous savons effectivement que le facteur $\frac{x^{2m+1}}{1.2.3\ldots m}$ a zéro pour limite, et il en est de même de l'intégrale, la quantité $z^m(1-z)^m$ étant toujours inférieure à son maximum $\left(\frac{1}{2}\right)^m$ qui décroît indéfiniment quand m augmente. Il résulte de là qu'en supposant x un nombre entier, l'exponentielle e^x ne peut avoir une valeur commensurable; car si l'on fait $e^x = \frac{b}{a}$, on parvient, après avoir chassé le dénominateur, à l'égalité

$$b\,\Pi(x) - a\,\Pi_1(x) = (-1)^m \frac{a x^{2m+1}}{1.2.3\ldots m} \int^1 e^{x(1-x)} z^m (1-z)^m \, dz,$$

dont le second membre peut devenir moindre que toute grandeur donnée, et sans jamais s'évanouir, tandis que le premier est un nombre entier. Lambert, à qui l'on doit cette proposition, ainsi que la seule démonstration, jusqu'à ce jour obtenue, de l'irrationnalité du rapport de la circonférence au diamètre et de son carré, a tiré ces importants résultats de la fraction continue

$$\frac{e^x - e^{-x}}{e^x + e^{-x}} = \cfrac{x}{1 + \cfrac{x^2}{3 + \cfrac{x^2}{5 + \ldots}}}$$

à laquelle nous parviendrons plus tard. Laissant entièrement de côté le rapport de la circonférence au diamètre, je vais maintenant tenter d'aller plus loin à l'égard du nombre e, en établissant l'impossibilité d'une relation de la forme

$$N + e^a N_1 + e^b N_2 + \ldots + e^h N_n = 0,$$

$a, b, \ldots, h$ étant des nombres entiers, ainsi que les coefficients N, $N_1, \ldots, N_n$.

IV. Je considère, à cet effet, parmi les divers systèmes de fractions rationnelles $\frac{\Phi_1(x)}{\Phi(x)}, \frac{\Phi_2(x)}{\Phi(x)}, \ldots, \frac{\Phi_n(x)}{\Phi(x)}$, celui qu'on obtient lorsqu'on suppose $\mu = \mu_1 = \ldots = \mu_n$, ce qui donne

$$m = n\mu, \qquad M = (n+1)\mu \qquad \text{et} \qquad F(z) = f^{\mu}(z),$$

en faisant

$$f(z) = z(z-a)(z-b)\ldots(z-h).$$

Soit alors, comme tout à l'heure,

$$\Pi(x) = \frac{\Phi(x)}{1.2.3\ldots\mu}, \qquad \Pi_1(x) = \frac{\Phi_1(x)}{1.2.3\ldots\mu}, \qquad \ldots,$$
$$\Pi_n(x) = \frac{\Phi_n(x)}{1.2.3\ldots\mu};$$

ces nouveaux polynomes auront encore, pour leurs coefficients, des nombres entiers, et conduiront aux relations suivantes :

$$(\text{A}) \qquad \begin{cases} e^{ax}\Pi(x) - \Pi_1(x) = \varepsilon_1, \\ e^{bx}\Pi(x) - \Pi_2(x) = \varepsilon_2, \\ \dots\dots\dots\dots\dots\dots, \\ e^{hx}\Pi(x) - \Pi_n(x) = \varepsilon_n, \end{cases}$$

en écrivant, pour abréger,

$$\varepsilon_1 = \frac{x^{M+1}e^{ax}}{1.2.3\ldots\mu}\int_0^a e^{-zx}F(z)\,dz = \int_0^a e^{x(a-z)}\frac{f^{\mu}(z)x^{(n+1)\mu+1}}{1.2.3\ldots\mu}\,dz,$$

$$\varepsilon_2 = \frac{x^{M+1}e^{bx}}{1.2.3\ldots\mu}\int_0^b e^{-zx}F(z)\,dz = \int^b e^{x(b-z)}\frac{f^{\mu}(z)x^{(n+1)\mu+1}}{1.2.3\ldots\mu}\,dz,$$

....

Cela posé, j'observe en premier lieu que $\varepsilon_1, \varepsilon_2, \ldots$ deviennent, pour une valeur suffisamment grande de μ, plus petits que toute quantité donnée; car, le polynome $f(z)$ ne dépassant jamais une certaine limite λ dans l'intervalle parcouru par la variable, le facteur $\frac{f^{\mu}(z)x^{(n+1)\mu+1}}{1.2.3\ldots\mu}$, qui multiplie l'exponentielle sous le signe d'intégration, est constamment inférieur à la quantité $\frac{(\lambda x^{n+1})^{\mu}x}{1.2.3\ldots\mu}$, qui a zéro pour limite.

Je suppose maintenant $x = 1$ dans les équations (A), et, désignant alors par P_i la valeur correspondante de $\Pi_i(x)$ qui sera un nombre entier dans l'hypothèse admise à l'égard de $a, b, \ldots, h$, elles deviendront

$$\begin{aligned} e^a P - P_1 &= \varepsilon_1, \\ e^b P - P_2 &= \varepsilon_2, \\ &\ldots\ldots\ldots\ldots, \\ e^h P - P_n &= \varepsilon_n, \end{aligned}$$

et la relation supposée

$$N + e^a N_1 + e^b N_2 + \ldots + e^h N_n = 0$$

donnera facilement celle-ci,

$$NP + N_1 P_1 + \ldots + N_n P_n = -(N_1 \varepsilon_1 + N_2 \varepsilon_2 + \ldots + N_n \varepsilon_n),$$

dont le premier membre est essentiellement entier, le second, d'après ce qui a été établi relativement à $\varepsilon_1, \varepsilon_2, \ldots$ pouvant, lorsque μ augmente, devenir plus petit que toute grandeur donnée. On aura donc nécessairement, à partir d'une certaine valeur de μ et pour toutes les valeurs plus grandes,

$$NP + N_1 P_1 + \ldots + N_n P_n = 0.$$

Supposons, en conséquence, que, μ devenant successivement $\mu + 1$, $\mu + 2$, $\ldots$, $\mu + n$, P_i se change en $P'_i, P''_i, \ldots, P_i^{(n)}$; on aura de même

$$\begin{aligned} NP' + N_1 P'_n + \ldots + N_n P'_n &= 0, \\ NP'' + N_1 P''_1 + \ldots + N_n P''_n &= 0, \\ &\ldots\ldots\ldots\ldots, \\ NP^{(n)} + N_1 P_1^{(n)} + \ldots + N_n P_n^{(n)} &= 0. \end{aligned}$$

Ces relations entraînent la condition suivante :

$$\begin{vmatrix} P & P_1 & \ldots & P_n \\ P' & P'_1 & \ldots & P'_n \\ P'' & P''_1 & \ldots & P''_n \\ \vdots & \vdots & \vdots & \vdots \\ P^{(n)} & P_1^{(n)} & \ldots & P_n^{(n)} \end{vmatrix} = 0.$$

En prouvant donc que ce déterminant est différent de zéro, on démontrera l'impossibilité de la relation admise

$$N + e^a N_1 + e^b N_2 + \ldots + e^b N_n = 0.$$

J'observerai dans ce but qu'on peut substituer aux termes d'une même ligne horizontale des combinaisons linéaires semblables pour toutes ces lignes, et que j'indiquerai en considérant, par exemple, la première. Elle consiste à remplacer respectivement P, P_1, P_2, ..., P_{n-1}, P_n par $P - e^{-a}P_1$, $e^{-a}P_1 - e^{-b}P_2$, ..., $e^{-g}P_{n-1} - e^{-h}P_n$, $e^{-h}P_n$; il est alors aisé de voir que, si l'on multiplie toutes ces quantités par $1.2.3\ldots\mu$, elles deviennent précisément les intégrales

$$\int_0^a e^{-z} f^\mu(z)\,dz, \quad \int_a^b e^{-z} f^\mu(z)\,dz, \quad \ldots,$$
$$\int_g^h e^{-z} f^\mu(z)\,dz, \quad \int_h^\infty e^{-z} f^\mu(z)\,dz.$$

Maintenant les autres lignes se déduisent de celle-là par le changement de μ en $\mu+1$, $\mu+2$, ..., $\mu+n$, et le déterminant transformé sur lequel nous allons raisonner est le suivant :

$$\Delta = \begin{vmatrix} \int_0^a e^{-z} f^\mu(z)\,dz, & \int_a^b e^{-z} f^\mu(z)\,dz, & \ldots, & \int_h^\infty e^{-z} f^\mu(z)\,dz \\ \int_0^a e^{-z} f^{\mu+1}(z)\,dz, & \int_a^b e^{-z} f^{\mu+1}(z)\,dz, & \ldots, & \int_h^\infty e^{-z} f^{\mu+1}(z)\,dz \\ \ldots\ldots\ldots, & \ldots\ldots\ldots, & \ldots, & \ldots\ldots\ldots \\ \int_0^a e^{-z} f^{\mu+n}(z)\,dz, & \int_a^b e^{-z} f^{\mu+n}(z)\,dz, & \ldots, & \int_h^\infty e^{-z} f^{\mu+n}(z)\,dz \end{vmatrix}.$$

V. Nous devons supposer, comme on l'a vu précédemment, que μ est un grand nombre; c'est ce qui conduit à déterminer, au moyen de la belle méthode donnée par Laplace (*De l'intégration par approximation des différentielles qui renferment des facteurs élevés à de grandes puissances* dans la *Théorie analytique des Probabilités,* p. 88), l'expression asymptotique des intégrales

$$\int_0^a e^{-z} f^\mu(z)\,dz, \quad \int_a^b e^{-z} f^\mu(z)\,dz, \quad \ldots, \quad \int_h^\infty e^{-z} f^\mu(z)\,dz,$$

afin d'en conclure pour Δ une valeur approchée, dont le rapport à la valeur exacte soit l'unité pour μ infini. Admettant, à cet effet, que les nombres entiers $a, b, \ldots, h$ soient tous positifs et rangés par ordre croissant de grandeur, de sorte que, dans chaque intégrale, la fonction $e^{-z} f^{\mu}(z)$, qui s'annule aux limites, ne présente, dans l'intervalle, qu'un seul maximum, je considérerai en premier lieu l'équation

$$\frac{f'(z)}{f(z)} = \frac{1}{\mu},$$

dont dépendent tous ces maxima. Or on sait que ses racines sont réelles et comprises, la première z_1 entre zéro et a, la seconde z_2 entre a et b, et ainsi de suite, la plus grande z_{n+1} étant supérieure à h. Envisagées comme fonctions de μ, il est aisé de voir qu'elles croissent lorsque μ augmente, et qu'en désignant par $p, q, \ldots, s$ les racines de l'équation dérivée $f'(z) = 0$, rangées par ordre croissant de grandeur, on aura, si l'on néglige $\frac{1}{\mu^2}$,

$$z_1 = p + \frac{1}{\mu}\frac{f(p)}{f''(p)}, \qquad z_2 = q + \frac{1}{\mu}\frac{f(q)}{f''(q)}, \qquad \ldots, \qquad z_n = s + \frac{1}{\mu}\frac{f(s)}{f''(s)},$$

et, en dernier lieu,

$$z_{n+1} = (n+1)\mu + \frac{a+b+\ldots+h}{n+1},$$

une approximation plus grande n'étant pas alors nécessaire. Cela posé, si l'on écrit pour un instant

$$\varphi(z) = \frac{f(z)}{\sqrt{f'^2(z) - f(z)f''(z)}},$$

les valeurs cherchées seront

$$\sqrt{\frac{2\pi}{\mu}}\, e^{-z_1} f^{\mu}(z_1)\,\varphi(z_1), \quad \sqrt{\frac{2\pi}{\mu}}\, e^{-z_2} f^{\mu}(z_2)\,\varphi(z_2), \quad \ldots,$$
$$\sqrt{\frac{2\pi}{\mu}}\, e^{-z_{n+1}} f^{\mu}(z_{n+1})\,\varphi(z_{n+1});$$

mais ces quantités se simplifient, comme on va le voir.

Considérant la première pour fixer les idées, j'observe que nous avons

$$z_1 = p + \frac{1}{\mu}\frac{f(p)}{f''(p)},$$

où p satisfait à la condition $f'(p)=0$; on en conclut $f(x_1)=f(p)$, en négligeant seulement $\frac{1}{\mu^2}$. Par conséquent, si l'on pose

$$f(z_1)=f(p)\left(1+\frac{\alpha}{\mu^2}+\frac{\alpha'}{\mu^3}+\ldots\right),$$

puis d'une manière analogue

$$\varphi(z_1)=\varphi(p)\left(1+\frac{\beta}{\mu}+\frac{\beta'}{\mu^2}+\ldots\right),$$

on aura d'abord

$$f^{\mu}(z_1)=f^{\mu}(p)\left(1+\frac{\alpha}{\mu}+\ldots\right),$$

et l'on en tire aisément

$$f^{\mu}(z_1)\varphi(z_1)=f^{\mu}(p)\varphi(p)\left(1+\frac{\gamma}{\mu}+\frac{\gamma'}{\mu^2}+\ldots\right).$$

Ainsi, en négligeant seulement des quantités infiniment petites par rapport au terme conservé, nous pouvons écrire

$$\int_0^a e^{-z}f^{\mu}(z)\,dz=\sqrt{\frac{2\pi}{\mu}}\,e^{-p}f^{\mu}(p)\varphi(p),$$

et l'on aura de même

$$\int_a^b e^{-z}f^{\mu}(z)\,dz=\sqrt{\frac{2\pi}{\mu}}\,e^{-q}f^{\mu}(q)\varphi(q),$$

$$\ldots\ldots\ldots\ldots\ldots\ldots\ldots\ldots\ldots\ldots\ldots\ldots,$$

$$\int_g^h e^{-z}f^{\mu}(z)\,dz=\sqrt{\frac{2\pi}{\mu}}\,e^{-s}f^{\mu}(s)\varphi(s).$$

Mais la dernière intégrale $\int_h^{\infty} e^{-z}f^{\mu}(z)\,dz$ est d'une forme analytique différente, en raison de la valeur $z_{n+1}=(n+1)\mu$ qui devient infinie avec μ. Pour y parvenir, je développerai, suivant les puissances descendantes de la variable, l'expression

$$\log[e^{-z}f^{\mu}(z)\varphi(z)],$$

en négligeant les termes en $\frac{1}{z}$, $\frac{1}{z^2}$, ..., ce qui permet d'écrire

$$\log f(z)=(n+1)\log z,\qquad \log\varphi z=\log\frac{z^{n+1}}{\sqrt{(n+1)z^{2n}+\ldots}}=\log\frac{z}{\sqrt{n+1}},$$

et, par suite,

$$\log[e^{-z}f^{\mu}(z)\,\varphi(z)] = (n\mu+\mu+1)\log z - z - \tfrac{1}{2}\log(n+1).$$

Après avoir substitué la valeur de z_{n+1}, une réduction facile nous donnera, en faisant, pour abréger,

$$\theta(\mu) = (n\mu+\mu+1)\log(n+1)\mu - (n+1)\mu - \tfrac{1}{2}\log(n+1),$$

cette expression semblable à celle des intégrales eulériennes de première espèce

$$\int_h^{\infty} e^{-z}f^{\mu}(z)\,dz = \sqrt{\frac{2\pi}{\mu}}\,e^{\theta(\mu)}.$$

Maintenant on va voir comment les résultats ainsi obtenus conduisent aisément à la valeur du déterminant Δ.

VI. J'effectuerai d'abord une première simplification en supprimant, dans les termes de la ligne horizontale de rang i, le facteur $\sqrt{\dfrac{2\pi}{\mu+i}}$, puis une seconde, en divisant tous les termes d'une même colonne verticale par le premier d'entre eux. Le nouveau déterminant ainsi obtenu, si l'on fait, pour abréger,

$$P=f(p),\qquad Q=f(q),\qquad \ldots,\qquad S=f(s),$$

sera évidemment

$$\begin{vmatrix} 1 & 1 & 1 & 1 \\ P & Q & S & e^{\theta(\mu+1)-\theta(\mu)} \\ P^2 & Q^2 & S^2 & e^{\theta(\mu+2)-\theta(\mu)} \\ \vdots & \vdots & \vdots & \vdots \\ P^n & Q^n & S^n & e^{\theta(\mu+n)-\theta(\mu)} \end{vmatrix}.$$

Or, on voit que μ ne figure plus que dans une colonne, dont les termes croissent d'une telle manière que le dernier $e^{\theta(\mu+n)-\theta(\mu)}$ est infiniment plus grand que tous les autres. Nous avons, en effet,

$$\begin{aligned}\theta(\mu+i) &= \theta(\mu)+i\theta'(\mu)+\frac{i^2}{2}\theta''(\mu)+\ldots\\ &= \theta(\mu)+i\left[\frac{1}{\mu}+(n+1)\log(n+1)\mu\right]\\ &\quad+\frac{i^2}{2}\left(-\frac{1}{\mu^2}+\frac{n+1}{\mu}\right)+\ldots,\end{aligned}$$

et, par conséquent, si l'on néglige $\frac{1}{\mu}$, $\frac{1}{\mu^2}$, ...,

$$\theta(\mu+i)-\theta(\mu)=i(n+1)\log(n+1)\mu,$$

d'où

$$e^{\theta(\mu+i)-\theta(\mu)}=[(n+1)\mu]^{i(n+1)}.$$

En ne conservant donc dans le déterminant que le terme en μ de l'ordre le plus élevé, il se réduit simplement à cette expression

$$[(n+1)\mu]^{n(n+1)}\begin{vmatrix} 1 & 1 & 1 \\ P & Q & S \\ P^2 & Q^2 & S^2 \\ \vdots & \vdots & \vdots \\ P^{n-1} & Q^{n-1} & S^{n-1} \end{vmatrix}.$$

Il en résulte qu'on ne peut, en général, admettre que le déterminant proposé Δ s'annule, car les quantités $P=f(p)$, $Q=f(q)$, ..., fonctions entières semblables des racines p, q, ... de l'équation dérivée $f'(x)=0$, seront, comme ces racines, différentes entre elles. C'est ce qu'il fallait établir pour démontrer l'impossibilité de toute relation de la forme

$$N+e^aN_1+e^bN_2+\ldots+e^hN_n=0,$$

et arriver ainsi à prouver que *le nombre e ne peut être racine d'une équation algébrique de degré quelconque à coefficients entiers*.

Mais une autre voie conduira à une seconde démonstration plus rigoureuse; on peut, en effet, comme on va le voir, étendre aux fractions rationnelles

$$\frac{\Phi_1(x)}{\Phi(x)},\quad \frac{\Phi_2(x)}{\Phi(x)},\quad \ldots,\quad \frac{\Phi_n(x)}{\Phi(x)}$$

le mode de formation des réduites donné par la théorie des fractions continues, et par là mettre plus complètement en évidence le caractère arithmétique d'une irrationnelle non algébrique. Dans cet ordre d'idées, M. Liouville a déjà obtenu un théorème remarquable qui est l'objet de son travail intitulé : *Sur des classes très étendues de quantités dont la valeur n'est ni algébrique, ni même réductible à des irrationnelles algébriques* (¹), et je rappellerai aussi que l'illustre géomètre a démontré le premier la proposition qui est le sujet de ces recherches pour les cas de l'équation du second degré et de l'équation bicarrée [*Note sur l'irrationnalité du nombre e* (*Journal de Mathématiques*, t. V, p. 192)]. Sous le point de vue auquel je me suis placé, voici la première proposition à établir :

VII. *Soient* $F(z)$, $F_1(z)$, ..., $F_{n+1}(z)$ *les polynomes déduits de l'expression*

$$z^{\mu}(z-a)^{\mu_1}(z-b)^{\mu_2}\ldots(z-h)^{\mu_n},$$

lorsqu'on attribue aux exposants $\mu, \mu_1, \ldots, \mu_n$, $n+2$ *systèmes différents de valeurs entières et positives. En représentant, en général, par* $\frac{\Phi_i^k(x)}{\Phi^k(x)}$ *les fractions convergentes vers les exponentielles, qui correspondent à l'un quelconque d'entre eux* $F_k(z)$, *on pourra toujours déterminer les quantités* A, B, C, ..., L *par les équations suivantes :*

$$\begin{aligned}
&A\Phi(x) + B\Phi^1(x) + C\Phi^2(x) + \ldots + L\Phi^{n+1}(x) = 0,\\
&A\Phi_1(x) + B\Phi_1^1(x) + C\Phi_1^2(x) + \ldots + L\Phi_1^{n+1}(x) = 0,\\
&\ldots\ldots\ldots\ldots\ldots\ldots\ldots\ldots\ldots\ldots\ldots\ldots\ldots,\\
&A\Phi_n(x) + B\Phi_n^1(x) + C\Phi_n^2(x) + \ldots + L\Phi_n^{n+1}(x) = 0.
\end{aligned}$$

Mais, au lieu de conclure de telles relations des polynomes $\Phi_i^k(x)$ supposés connus, notre objet est de les obtenir directement et *a priori;* je vais établir pour cela qu'il existe, entre les intégrales indéfinies

$$\int e^{-zx}F(z)\,dz,\quad \int e^{-zx}F_1(z)\,dz,\quad \ldots,\quad \int e^{-zx}F_{n+1}(z)\,dz,$$

une équation de la forme

$$\begin{aligned}
\mathcal{A}\int e^{-zx}F(z)\,dz + \mathcal{B}\int e^{-zx}F_1(z)\,dz + \ldots&\\
+ \mathcal{L}\int e^{-zx}F_{n+1}(z)\,dz &= e^{-zx}\Theta(z),
\end{aligned}$$

(¹) *Comptes rendus*, t. XVIII, p. 883 et 910.

les coefficients $\mathcal{A}$, $\mathcal{B}$, ..., $\mathcal{L}$ étant indépendants de z, et $\Theta(z)$ un polynome entier divisible par $f(z)$. Si l'on fait, en effet,

$$\mathfrak{F}_k(z) = \frac{F_k(z)}{x} + \frac{F'_k(z)}{x^2} + \frac{F''_k(z)}{x^3} + \ldots,$$

on aura

$$\mathcal{A}\int e^{-zx}F(z)\,dz + \mathcal{B}\int e^{-zx}F_1(z)\,dz + \ldots + \mathcal{L}\int e^{-zx}F_{n+1}(z)\,dz$$
$$= -e^{-zx}[\mathcal{A}\mathfrak{F}(z) + \mathcal{B}\mathfrak{F}_1(z) + \ldots + \mathcal{L}\mathfrak{F}_{n+1}(z)],$$

et il est clair que les rapports $\frac{\mathcal{B}}{\mathcal{A}}$, $\frac{\mathcal{C}}{\mathcal{A}}$, ..., $\frac{\mathcal{L}}{\mathcal{A}}$ pourront être déterminés, et d'une seule manière, par la condition supposée que le polynome

$$\Theta(z) = -[\mathcal{A}\mathfrak{F}(z) + \mathcal{B}\mathfrak{F}_1(z) + \ldots + \mathcal{L}\mathfrak{F}_{n+1}(z)]$$

contienne comme facteur

$$f(z) = z(z-a)(z-b)\ldots(z-h).$$

Nous conclurons de là en prenant les intégrales entre les limite $z = 0$ et $z = a$, par exemple,

$$\mathcal{A}\int_0^a e^{-zx}F(z)\,dz + \mathcal{B}\int_0^a e^{-zx}F_1(z)\,dz + \ldots$$
$$+ \mathcal{L}\int_0^a e^{-zx}F_{n+1}(z)\,dz \quad = 0.$$

Maintenant, les relations

$$\int_0^a e^{-zx}F(z)\,dz = \frac{e^{ax}\Phi(x) - \Phi_1(x)}{e^{ax}x^{M+1}},$$

$$\int_0^a e^{-zx}F_1(z)\,dz = \frac{e^{ax}\Phi_1(x) - \Phi'_1(x)}{e^{ax}x^{M_1+1}},$$

....

donneront, en égalant séparément à zéro le terme algébrique et le coefficient de l'exponentielle e^{ax}, si l'on fait, pour abréger,

$$A = \frac{\mathcal{A}}{x^{M+1}}, \qquad B = \frac{\mathcal{B}}{x^{M_1+1}}, \qquad \ldots, \qquad L = \frac{\mathcal{L}}{x^{M_{n+1}+1}},$$

les égalités suivantes :

$$A\,\Phi(x) + B\,\Phi^1(x) + \ldots + L\Phi^{n+1}(x) = 0,$$
$$A\Phi_1(x) + B\Phi_1^1(x) + \ldots + L\Phi_1^{n+1}(x) = 0.$$

Or, on aura de même, en prenant pour limites supérieures des intégrales $z = b, c, \ldots, h$,

$$A\,\Phi_2(x) + B\Phi_2^1(x) + \ldots + L\Phi_2^{n+1}(x) = 0,$$
$$\ldots\ldots\ldots\ldots\ldots\ldots\ldots\ldots\ldots\ldots,$$
$$A\Phi_n(x) + B\,\Phi_n^1(x) + \ldots + L\Phi_n^{n+1}(x) = 0,$$

et il est aisé de voir que les coefficients A, B, ..., L pourront être supposés des polynomes entiers en x. L'intégrale

$$\int_0^1 e^{-zx} z^m (z-1)^m \, dz,$$

qui figure dans la relation précédemment considérée (p. 154),

$$e^x \Pi(x) - \Pi_1(x) = \frac{x^{2m+1} e^x}{1.2.3\ldots m} \int_0^1 e^{-zx} z^m (z-1)^m \, dz,$$

nous servira d'abord d'exemple.

VIII. Dans ce cas facile, où l'on a simplement

$$f(z) = z(z-1),$$

je partirai, en supposant

$$\Theta(z) = x f^{m+1}(z) + (m+1) f^m(z) f'(z),$$

de l'identité suivante :

$$\begin{aligned}\frac{d[e^{-zx}\Theta(z)]}{dz} &= e^{-zx}[\Theta'(z) - x\Theta(z)] \\ &= e^{-zx}[-x^2 f^{m+1}(z) + (m+1) f^m(z) f''(z) \\ &\qquad + m(m+1) f^{m-1} f'^2(z)],\end{aligned}$$

et j'observerai que

$$f'^2(z) = 4z^2 - 4z + 1 = 4f(z) + 1, \qquad f''(z) = 2,$$

ce qui permet de l'écrire ainsi :

$$\begin{aligned}\frac{d[e^{-zx}\Theta(z)]}{dx} &= e^{-zx}[-x^2 f^{m+1}(z) \\ &\quad + (2m+1)(2m+2) f^m(z) + m(m+1) f^{m-1}(z)].\end{aligned}$$

Nous aurons donc, en intégrant,

$$e^{-zx}\Theta(z) = -x^2 \int e^{-zx} f^{m+1}(z)\,dz + (2m+1)(2m+2)\int e^{-zx} f^m(z)\,dz$$
$$+ m(m+1)\int e^{-zx} f^{m-1}(z)\,dz,$$

et ensuite, si nous prenons pour limites $z = 0$ et $z = 1$,

$$x^2 \int_0^1 e^{-zx} f^{m+1}(z)\,dz = (2m+1)(2m+2)\int_0^1 e^{-zx} f^m(z)\,dz$$
$$+ m(m+1)\int_0^1 e^{-zx} f^{m-1}(z)\,dz.$$

Soit maintenant

$$\varepsilon_m = \frac{x^{2m+1} e^x}{1.2\ldots m} \int_0^1 e^{-zx} z^m (z-1)^m\,dz,$$

et cette relation deviendra

$$\varepsilon_{m+1} = (4m+2)\varepsilon_m + x^2 \varepsilon_{m-1}.$$

C'est le résultat auquel nous voulions parvenir; en y supposant successivement $m = 1, 2, 3, \ldots$, les équations qu'on en tire

$$\varepsilon_2 = 6\varepsilon_1 + x^2\varepsilon_0,$$
$$\varepsilon_3 = 10\varepsilon_2 + x^2\varepsilon_1,$$
$$\varepsilon_4 = 14\varepsilon_3 + x^2\varepsilon_2,$$
$$\cdots\cdots\cdots\cdots\cdots$$

donnent aisément la fraction continue

$$\frac{\varepsilon_1}{\varepsilon_0} = -\cfrac{x^2}{6 + \cfrac{x^2}{10 + \cfrac{x^2}{14 + \ldots}}},$$

et il suffit d'employer les valeurs

$$\varepsilon_0 = x e^x \int_0^1 e^{-zx}\,dz = e^x - 1,$$
$$\varepsilon_1 = x^3 e^x \int_0^1 e^{-zx} z(z-1)\,dz = e^x(2-x) - 2 - x,$$

d'où l'on conclut

$$\frac{\varepsilon_1}{\varepsilon_0} = 2 - \frac{e^x + 1}{e^x - 1} x,$$

pour retrouver, sauf le changement de x en $\frac{x}{2}$, le résultat de Lambert ([1])

$$\frac{e^x - 1}{e^x + 1} = \cfrac{x}{2 + \cfrac{x^2}{6 + \cfrac{x^2}{10 + \cfrac{x^2}{14 + \dots}}}}$$

En abordant maintenant le cas général et me proposant d'obtenir, à l'égard des intégrales définies

$$\int_0^a e^{-z} f^m(z)\, dz, \quad \int_0^b e^{-z} f^m(z)\, dz, \quad \dots, \quad \int_0^h e^{-z} f^m(z)\, dz,$$

un algorithme qui permette de les calculer de proche en proche, pour toutes les valeurs du nombre entier m, j'introduirai, afin de rendre les calculs plus symétriques, les modifications suivantes dans les notations précédemment admises. Je ferai

$$f(z) = (z - z_0)(z - z_1)\dots(z - z_n),$$

au lieu de

$$f(z) = z(z - a)(z - b)\dots(z - h),$$

de manière à considérer le polynome le plus général de degré $n+1$; désignant ensuite par Z l'une quelconque des quantités $z_1, z_2, \dots, z_n$, je raisonnerai sur l'intégrale

$$\int_{z_0}^{Z} e^{-z} f^m(z)\, dz,$$

qui donnera évidemment toutes celles que nous avons en vue, en faisant $z_0 = 0$. Cela étant, voici la remarque qui m'a ouvert la voie et conduit à la méthode que je vais exposer.

([1]) Mémoire sur quelques propriétés remarquables des quantités transcendantes circulaires et logarithmiques (*Mémoires de l'Académie des Sciences de Berlin*, année 1761, p. 265). *Voir* aussi la Note IV des *Éléments de Géométrie*, de Legendre, p. 288.

IX. En intégrant les deux membres de la relation identique

$$\frac{d[e^{-z}f^m(z)]}{dz} = e^{-z}[mf^{m-1}(z)f'(z) - f^m(z)],$$

on obtient

$$e^{-z}f^m(z) = m\int e^{-z}f^{m-1}(z)f'(z)\,dz - \int e^{-z}f^m(z)\,dz,$$

et, par conséquent,

$$\int_{z_0}^{Z} e^{-z}f^m(z)\,dz = m\int_{z_0}^{Z} e^{-z}f^{m-1}(z)f'(z)\,dz,$$

ou encore

$$\int_{z_0}^{Z} e^{-z}f^m(z)\,dz = m\int_{z_0}^{Z}\frac{e^{-z}f^m(z)}{z-z_0}\,dz + m\int_{z_0}^{Z}\frac{e^{-z}f^m(z)}{z-z_1}\,dz + \ldots + m\int_{z_0}^{Z}\frac{e^{-z}f^m(z)}{z-z_n}\,dz,$$

d'après la formule

$$\frac{f'(z)}{f(z)} = \frac{1}{z-z_0} + \frac{1}{z-z_1} + \ldots + \frac{1}{z-z_n}.$$

Or ce sont ces nouvelles intégrales

$$\int_{z_0}^{Z}\frac{e^{-z}f^m(z)}{z-z_0}\,dz,\quad \int_{z_0}^{Z}\frac{e^{-z}f^m(z)}{z-z_1}\,dz,\quad \ldots,\quad \int_{z_0}^{Z}\frac{e^{-z}f^m(z)}{z-z_n}\,dz$$

qui donnent lieu à un système de relations récurrentes de la forme

$$\int_{z_0}^{Z}\frac{e^{-z}f^{m+1}(z)}{z-z_0}\,dz = (00)\int_{z_0}^{Z}\frac{e^{-z}f^m(z)}{z-z_0}\,dz + (01)\int_{z_0}^{Z}\frac{e^{-z}f^m(z)}{z-z_1}\,dz + \ldots + (0n)\int_{z_0}^{Z}\frac{e^{-z}f^m(z)}{z-z_n}\,dz,$$

$$\int_{z_0}^{Z}\frac{e^{-z}f^{m+1}(z)}{z-z_1}\,dz = (10)\int_{z_0}^{Z}\frac{e^{-z}f^m(z)}{z-z_0}\,dz + (11)\int_{z_0}^{Z}\frac{e^{-z}f^m(z)}{z-z_1}\,dz + \ldots + (1n)\int_{z_0}^{Z}\frac{e^{-z}f^m(z)}{z-z_n}\,dz,$$

. . . . ,

$$\int_{z_0}^{Z}\frac{e^{-z}f^{m+1}(z)}{z-z_n}\,dz = (n0)\int_{z_0}^{Z}\frac{e^{-z}f^m(z)}{z-z_0}\,dz + (n1)\int_{z_0}^{Z}\frac{e^{-z}f^m(z)}{z-z_1}\,dz + \ldots + (nn)\int_{z_0}^{Z}\frac{e^{-z}f^m(z)}{z-z_n}\,dz,$$

où les coefficients (ik), ainsi que leur déterminant, s'obtiennent d'une manière facile, comme nous verrons.

C'est donc en opérant sur les éléments au nombre de $n+1$, dans lesquels a été décomposée l'intégrale $\int_{z_0}^{Z} e^{-z} f^m(z)\,dz$, que nous parvenons à sa détermination, au lieu de chercher, comme une analogie naturelle aurait paru l'indiquer, une expression linéaire de $\int_{z_0}^{Z} e^{-z} f^{m+n+1}(z)\,dz$, au moyen de

$$\int_{z_0}^{Z} e^{-z} f^m(z)\,dz, \quad \int_{z_0}^{Z} e^{-z} f^{m+1}(z)\,dz, \quad \ldots, \quad \int_{z_0}^{Z} e^{-z} f^{m+n}(z)\,dz.$$

Mais soit, d'une manière plus générale, pour des valeurs entières quelconques des exposants,

$$F(z) = (z-z_0)^{\mu_0}(z-z_1)^{\mu_1}\ldots(z-z_n)^{\mu_n};$$

en intégrant les deux membres de l'identité

$$\frac{d[e^{-z}F(z)]}{dz} = e^{-z}[F'(z) - F(z)],$$

on aura

$$e^{-z}F(z) = \int e^{-z}F'(z)\,dz - \int e^{-z}F(z)\,dz,$$

d'où

$$\int_{z_0}^{Z} e^{-z}F(z)\,dz = \int_{z_0}^{Z} e^{-z}F'(z)\,dz.$$

Maintenant la formule

$$\frac{F'(z)}{F(z)} = \frac{\mu_0}{z-z_0} + \frac{\mu_1}{z-z_1} + \ldots + \frac{\mu_n}{z-z_n}$$

donne la décomposition suivante,

$$\int_{z_0}^{Z} e^{-z}F(z)\,dz = \mu_0 \int_{z_0}^{Z} \frac{e^{-z}F(z)\,dz}{z-z_0}$$
$$+ \mu_1 \int_{z_0}^{Z} \frac{e^{-z}F(z)\,dz}{z-z_1} + \ldots + \mu_n \int_{z_0}^{Z} \frac{e^{-z}F(z)\,dz}{z-z_0},$$

qui conduira pareillement au calcul des divers termes de la suite

$$\int_{z_0}^{Z} e^{-z} F(z)\,dz, \quad \int_{z_0}^{Z} e^{-z} F(z) f(z)\,dz, \quad \ldots, \quad \int_{z_0}^{Z} e^{-z} F(z) f^k(z)\,dz;$$

effectivement, les éléments de décomposition de l'un quelconque d'entre eux s'expriment en fonction linéaire des quantités semblables qui se rapportent au terme précédent, ainsi qu'on va le montrer.

X. J'établirai pour cela qu'on peut toujours déterminer deux polynomes entiers de degré n, $\Theta(z)$ et $\Theta_1(z)$, tels qu'on ait, en désignant par ζ l'une des racines $z_0, z_1, \ldots, z_n$, la relation suivante :

$$\int \frac{e^{-z} F(z) f(z)}{z-\zeta}\,dz = \int \frac{e^{-z} F(z)\Theta_1(z)}{f(z)}\,dz - e^{-z} F(z)\Theta(z).$$

En effet, si, après avoir différentié les deux membres, nous multiplions par le facteur $\frac{f(z)}{F(z)}$, il vient

$$\frac{f(z)}{z-\zeta} f(z) = \Theta_1(z) + \left[1 - \frac{F'(z)}{F(z)}\right] f(z)\Theta(z) - f(z)\Theta'(z).$$

Or, $f(z)$ étant divisible par $z-\zeta$, le premier membre de cette égalité est un polynome entier de degré $2n+1$; le second est du même degré, d'après la supposition admise à l'égard de $\Theta(z)$ et $\Theta_1(z)$, et, puisque chacun de ces polynomes renferme ainsi $n+1$ coefficients indéterminés, on a bien le nombre nécessaire égal à $2n+2$ de constantes arbitraires pour effectuer l'identification. Ce point établi, j'observe qu'en supposant $z = z_i$ la fraction rationnelle $\frac{F'(z) f(z)}{F(z)}$ a pour valeur $\mu_i f'(z_i)$; on a, par conséquent, ces conditions

$$\begin{aligned}
\Theta_1(z_0) &= \mu_0 f'(z_0)\Theta(z_0),\\
\Theta_1(z_1) &= \mu_1 f'(z_1)\Theta(z_1),\\
&\ldots\ldots\ldots\ldots\ldots\ldots,\\
\Theta_1(z_n) &= \mu_n f'(z_n)\Theta(z_n),
\end{aligned}$$

qui permettent, par la formule d'interpolation, de calculer immédiatement $\Theta_1(z)$, lorsque $\Theta(z)$ sera connu. Nous avons de cette manière, en effet, l'expression suivante,

$$\frac{\Theta_1(z)}{f(z)} = \frac{\mu_0\,\Theta(z_0)}{z-z_0} + \frac{\mu_1\,\Theta(z_1)}{z-z_1} + \ldots + \frac{\mu_n\,\Theta(z_n)}{z-z_n},$$

dont nous ferons bientôt usage. Pour obtenir maintenant $\Theta(z)$, je reprends la relation proposée, en divisant les deux membres par $f(z)$, ce qui donne

$$\frac{f(z)}{z-\zeta} = \frac{\Theta_1(z)}{f(z)} + \left[1 - \frac{F'(z)}{F(z)}\right]\Theta(z) - \Theta'(z),$$

et je remarque que, la fraction $\frac{\Theta_1(z)}{f(z)}$ n'ayant pas de partie entière, on est amené à cette conséquence, que le polynome cherché doit être tel que la partie entière de l'expression

$$\left[1 - \frac{F'(z)}{F(z)}\right]\Theta(z) - \Theta'(z)$$

soit égale au quotient $\frac{f(z)}{z-\zeta}$. C'est ce qui conduit aisément à la détermination de $\Theta(z)$. Soit d'abord, à cet effet,

$$f(z) = z^{n+1} + p_1 z^n + p_2 z^{n-1} + \ldots + p_{n+1},$$

ce qui donnera

$$\frac{f(z)}{z-\zeta} = z^n \begin{array}{l} +\,\zeta \\ +\,p_1 \end{array} \left|\; z^{n-1} \begin{array}{l} +\,\zeta^2 \\ +\,p_1\zeta \\ +\,p_2 \end{array} \right|\; z^{n-2} + \ldots + \begin{array}{l} \zeta^n \\ +\,p_1\zeta^{n-1} \\ +\,p_2\zeta^{n-2} \\ \ldots\ldots\ldots \\ +\,p_n, \end{array}$$

ou plutôt

$$\frac{f(z)}{z-\zeta} = z^n + \zeta_1 z^{n-1} + \zeta_2 z^{n-2} + \ldots + \zeta_n,$$

en écrivant, pour abréger,

$$\zeta_i = \zeta^i + p_1\zeta^{i-1} + p_2\zeta^{i-2} + \ldots + p_i.$$

Soit encore

$$\Theta(z) = \alpha_0 z^n + \alpha_1 z^{n-1} + \alpha_2 z^{n-2} + \ldots + \alpha_n,$$

et développons la fonction $\frac{F'(z)}{F(z)}$ suivant les puissances descendantes de la variable, afin d'obtenir la partie entière du produit $\frac{F'(z)}{F(z)}\Theta(z)$. Il viendra ainsi, en posant $s_i = \mu_0 z_0^i + \mu_1 z_1^i + \mu_2 z_2^i + \ldots + \mu_n z_n^i$,

$$\frac{F'(z)}{F(z)} = \frac{s_0}{z} + \frac{s_1}{z^2} + \frac{s_2}{z^3} + \ldots,$$

et, par conséquent,

$$\frac{F'(z)}{F(z)}\Theta(z) = \alpha_0 s_0 z^{n-1} + \left.\begin{matrix}\alpha_1 s_0 \\ +\alpha_0 s_1\end{matrix}\right| z^{n-2} + \left.\begin{matrix}\alpha_2 s_0 \\ +\alpha_1 s_1 \\ +\alpha_0 s_2\end{matrix}\right| z^{n-3} + \ldots.$$

Les équations en $\alpha_0, \alpha_1, \alpha_2, \ldots$, auxquelles nous sommes amené par l'identification, sont donc

$$\begin{aligned}
1 &= \alpha_0, \\
\zeta_1 &= \alpha_1 - \alpha_0(s_0 + n), \\
\zeta_2 &= \alpha_2 - \alpha_1(s_0 + n - 1) - \alpha_0 s_1, \\
\zeta_3 &= \alpha_3 - \alpha_2(s_0 + n - 2) - \alpha_1 s_1 - \alpha_0 s_2, \\
&\ldots\ldots\ldots\ldots\ldots\ldots
\end{aligned}$$

Elles donnent

$$\begin{aligned}
\alpha_0 &= 1, \\
\alpha_1 &= \zeta_1 + s_0 + n, \\
\alpha_2 &= \zeta_2 + (s_0 + n - 1)\zeta_1 + (s_0 + n)(s_0 + n - 1) + s_1, \\
&\ldots\ldots\ldots\ldots\ldots\ldots,
\end{aligned}$$

et montrent que $\alpha_0, \alpha_1, \alpha_2, \ldots$ sont des polynomes en ζ ayant pour coefficients des fonctions entières et à coefficients entiers de $s_0, s_1, s_2, \ldots$ et par suite des racines $z_0, z_1, \ldots, z_n$. On voit de plus que α_i est un polynome de degré i dans lequel le coefficient de ζ^i est égal à l'unité; ainsi, en posant pour plus de clarté

$$\alpha_i = \theta_i(\zeta),$$

et écrivant désormais $\Theta(z, \zeta)$ au lieu de $\Theta(z)$, afin de mettre ζ en évidence, nous aurons

$$\Theta(z, \zeta) = z^n + \theta_1(\zeta) z^{n-2} + \theta_2(\zeta) z^{n-3} + \ldots + \theta_n(\zeta).$$

De là résulte, pour le polynome $\Theta_1(z)$, la formule

$$\frac{\Theta_1(z)}{f(z)} = \frac{\mu_0\,\Theta(z_0, \zeta)}{z - z_0} + \frac{\mu_1\,\Theta(z_1, \zeta)}{z - z_1} + \ldots + \frac{\mu_n\,\Theta(z_n, \zeta)}{z - z_n},$$

et l'on en tire immédiatement le résultat que nous nous sommes proposé d'obtenir. Il suffit, en effet, de prendre les intégrales entre les limites z_0 et Z dans la relation

$$\int \frac{e^{-z}\,\mathrm{F}(z)\,f(z)}{z-\zeta}\,dz = \int \frac{e^{-z}\,\mathrm{F}(z)\,\Theta_1(z)}{f(z)}\,dz - e^{-z}\,\mathrm{F}(z)\,\Theta(z),$$

ce qui donne

$$\begin{aligned}\int_{z_0}^{\mathrm{Z}} \frac{e^{-z}\,\mathrm{F}(z)\,f(z)}{z-\zeta}\,dz &= \int_{z_0}^{\mathrm{Z}} \frac{e^{-z}\,\mathrm{F}(z)\,\Theta_1(z)}{f(z)}\,dz \\ &= \mu_0\,\Theta(z_0,\,\zeta)\int_{z_0}^{\mathrm{Z}} \frac{e^{-z}\,\mathrm{F}(z)}{z-z_0}\,dz, \\ &+ \mu_1\,\Theta(z_1,\,\zeta)\int_{z_0}^{\mathrm{Z}} \frac{e^{-z}\,\mathrm{F}(z)}{z-z_1}\,dz, \\ &\ldots\ldots\ldots\ldots\ldots\ldots\ldots\ldots, \\ &+ \mu_n\,\Theta(z_n,\,\zeta)\int_{z_0}^{\mathrm{Z}} \frac{e^{-z}\,\mathrm{F}(z)}{z-z_n}\,dz.\end{aligned}$$

C'est surtout dans le cas où l'on suppose

$$\mu_0 = \mu_1 = \ldots = \mu_n = m,$$

que nous ferons usage de cette équation ; si l'on fait alors

$$m\,\Theta(z_i,\,z_k) = (ik),$$

et qu'on prenne ζ successivement égal à $z_0, z_1, \ldots, z_n$, on en conclut, comme on voit, les relations précédemment énoncées, qui résultent de celle-ci,

$$\begin{aligned}\int_{z_0}^{\mathrm{Z}} \frac{e^{-z}\,f^{m+1}(z)}{z-z_i}\,dz &= (i0)\int_{z_0}^{\mathrm{Z}} \frac{e^{-z}\,f^{m}(z)}{z-z_0}\,dz \\ &+ (i1)\int_{z_0}^{\mathrm{Z}} \frac{e^{-z}\,f^{m}(z)}{z-z_1}\,dz + \ldots + (in)\int_{z_0}^{\mathrm{Z}} \frac{e^{-z}\,f^{m}(z)}{z-z_n}\,dz,\end{aligned}$$

pour $i = 0, 1, 2, \ldots, n$. Je resterai encore cependant dans le cas général pour établir la proposition suivante :

X. *Soient* Δ *et* δ *les déterminants*

$$\begin{vmatrix} \Theta(z_0,\,z_0) & \Theta(z_1,\,z_0) & \ldots & \Theta(z_n,\,z_0) \\ \Theta(z_0,\,z_1) & \Theta(z_1,\,z_1) & \ldots & \Theta(z_n,\,z_1) \\ \ldots\ldots & \ldots\ldots & \ldots & \ldots\ldots \\ \Theta(z_0,\,z_n) & \Theta(z_1,\,z_n) & \ldots & \Theta(z_n,\,z_n) \end{vmatrix}$$

et

$$\begin{vmatrix} 1 & 1 & \dots & 1 \\ z_0 & z_1 & \dots & z_n \\ z_0^2 & z_1^2 & \dots & z_n^2 \\ \dots & \dots & \dots & \dots \\ z_0^n & z_1^n & \dots & z_n^n \end{vmatrix};$$

je dis qu'on a

$$\Delta = \delta^2.$$

Effectivement, l'expression de $\Theta(z, \zeta)$ sous la forme

$$\Theta(z, \zeta) = z^n + \theta_1(\zeta) z^{n-1} + \theta_2(\zeta) z^{n-2} + \dots + \theta_n(\zeta)$$

montre que Δ est le produit des deux déterminants

$$\begin{vmatrix} 1 & 1 & \dots & 1 \\ z_0 & z_1 & \dots & z_n \\ z_0^2 & z_1^2 & \dots & z_n^2 \\ \dots & \dots & \dots & \dots \\ z_0^n & z_1^n & \dots & z_n^n \end{vmatrix}$$

et

$$\begin{vmatrix} 1 & 1 & \dots & 1 \\ \theta_1(z_0) & \theta_1(z_1) & \dots & \theta_1(z_n) \\ \theta_2(z_0) & \theta_2(z_1) & \dots & \theta_2(z_n) \\ \dots\dots & \dots\dots & \dots & \dots\dots \\ \theta_n(z_0) & \theta_n(z_1) & \dots & \theta_n(z_n) \end{vmatrix}.$$

Mais $\theta_i(\zeta)$ étant un polynome en ζ du degré i seulement, de sorte qu'on peut faire

$$\theta_i(\zeta) = \zeta^i + r\zeta^{i-1} + s\zeta^{i-2} + \dots,$$

cette seconde quantité, d'après les théorèmes connus, se réduit simplement à la première, et l'on a bien, comme nous voulions l'établir,

$$\Delta = \delta^2.$$

Cela posé, soient

$$\varepsilon_m = \frac{1}{1.2\dots m} \int_{z_0}^{Z} e^{-z} f^m(z)\, dz,$$

$$\varepsilon_m^i = \frac{1}{1.2\dots m-1} \int_{z_0}^{Z} \frac{e^{-z} f^m(z)}{z - z_i}\, dz;$$

la relation établie page 167

$$\int_{z_0}^{Z} e^{-z} f^m(z)\,dz = m\int_{z_0}^{Z} \frac{e^{-z} f^m(z)}{z-z_0}\,dz + m\int_{z_0}^{Z} \frac{e^{-z} f^m(z)}{z-z_1}\,dz + \ldots + m\int_{z_0}^{Z} \frac{e^{-z} f^m(z)}{z-z_n}\,dz$$

deviendra plus simplement

$$\varepsilon_m = \varepsilon_m^0 + \varepsilon_m^1 + \ldots + \varepsilon_m^n;$$

et celle-ci,

$$\int_{z_0}^{Z} \frac{e^{-z} f^{m+1}(z)}{z-\zeta}\,dz = m\,\Theta(z_0,\zeta)\int_{z_0}^{Z} \frac{e^{-z} f^m(z)}{z-z_0}\,dz + m\,\Theta(z_1,\zeta)\int_{z_0}^{Z} \frac{e^{-z} f^m(z)}{z-z_1}\,dz + \ldots + m\,\Theta(z_n,\zeta)\int_{z_0}^{Z} \frac{e^{-z} f^m(z)}{z-z_n}\,dz,$$

en supposant successivement $\zeta = z_0, z_1, \ldots, z_n$, nous donnera la substitution suivante, que je désignerai par S_m, à savoir

$$\begin{aligned}
\varepsilon_{m+1}^0 &= \Theta(z_0, z_0)\varepsilon_m^0 + \Theta(z_1, z_0)\varepsilon_m^1 + \ldots + \Theta(z_n, z_0)\varepsilon_m^n,\\
\varepsilon_{m+1}^1 &= \Theta(z_0, z_1)\varepsilon_m^0 + \Theta(z_1, z_1)\varepsilon_m^1 + \ldots + \Theta(z_n, z_1)\varepsilon_m^n,\\
&\ldots\ldots\ldots\ldots\ldots\ldots\ldots\ldots\ldots\ldots,\\
\varepsilon_{m+1}^n &= \Theta(z_0, z_n)\varepsilon_m^0 + \Theta(z_1, z_n)\varepsilon_m^1 + \ldots + \Theta(z_n, z_n)\varepsilon_m^n.
\end{aligned}$$

Si l'on compose maintenant de proche $S_1, S_2, \ldots, S_{m-1}$, on en déduira les expressions de $\varepsilon_m^0, \varepsilon_m^1, \ldots, \varepsilon_m^n$ en $\varepsilon_1^0, \varepsilon_1^1, \ldots, \varepsilon_1^n$, que je représenterai ainsi :

$$\begin{aligned}
\varepsilon_m^0 &= A_0\varepsilon_1^0 + A_1\varepsilon_1^1 + \ldots + A_n\varepsilon_1^n,\\
\varepsilon_m^1 &= B_0\varepsilon_1^0 + B_1\varepsilon_1^1 + \ldots + B_n\varepsilon_1^n,\\
&\ldots\ldots\ldots\ldots\ldots\ldots\ldots,\\
\varepsilon_m^n &= L_0\varepsilon_1^0 + L_1\varepsilon_1^1 + \ldots + L_n\varepsilon_1^n,
\end{aligned}$$

et le déterminant de cette nouvelle substitution, étant égal au produit des déterminants des substitutions composantes, sera $\delta^{2(m-1)}$. Il nous reste encore à remplacer $\varepsilon_1^0, \varepsilon_1^1, \ldots, \varepsilon_1^n$ par leurs valeurs pour avoir les expressions des quantités ε_m^i sous la forme appropriée à notre objet. Ces valeurs s'obtiennent facilement, comme on va voir.

XII. J'applique à cet effet la formule générale

$$\int e^{-z}\,\mathrm{F}(z)\,dz = -\,e^{-z}\,\mathfrak{F}(z),$$

en supposant

$$\mathrm{F}(z) = \frac{f(z)}{z-\zeta},$$

c'est-à-dire

$$\mathrm{F}(z) = z^n + \left.\begin{matrix}\zeta \\ +p_1\end{matrix}\right| z^{n-1} + \left.\begin{matrix}\zeta^2 \\ +p_1\zeta \\ +p_2\end{matrix}\right| z^{n-2} + \ldots.$$

Il est aisé de voir alors que $\mathfrak{F}(z)$ devient une expression entière en z et ζ, entièrement semblable à $\Theta(z, \zeta)$, de sorte que, si on la désigne par $\Phi(z, \zeta)$, on a

$$\Phi(z,\zeta) = z^n + \varphi_1(\zeta)z^{n-1} + \varphi_2(\zeta)z^{n-2} + \ldots + \varphi_n(\zeta),$$

$\varphi_i(\zeta)$ étant un polynome en ζ de degré i, dans lequel le coefficient de ζ^i est l'unité. Ainsi l'on obtient, en particulier,

$$\begin{aligned} \varphi_1(\zeta) &= \zeta + p_1 + n, \\ \varphi_2(\zeta) &= \zeta^2 + (p_1 + n - 1)\zeta + p_2 + (n-1)p_1 + n(n-1), \\ &\ldots\ldots\ldots\ldots\ldots\ldots\ldots\ldots, \end{aligned}$$

et l'analogie de forme avec $\Theta(z, \zeta)$ montre que le déterminant

$$\begin{vmatrix} \Phi(z_0, z_0) & \Phi(z_1, z_0) & \ldots & \Phi(z_n, z_0) \\ \Phi(z_0, z_1) & \Phi(z_1, z_1) & \ldots & \Phi(z_n, z_1) \\ \ldots\ldots & \ldots\ldots & \ldots & \ldots\ldots \\ \Phi(z_0, z_n) & \Phi(z_1, z_n) & \ldots & \Phi(z_n, z_n) \end{vmatrix}$$

est encore égal à δ^2. Cela posé, nous tirons de la relation

$$\int_{z_0}^{Z} \frac{e^{-z} f(z)}{z-\zeta}\,dz = e^{-z_0}\,\Phi(z_0, \zeta) - e^{-Z}\,\Phi(Z, \zeta),$$

en supposant $\zeta = z_i$, la valeur cherchée

$$\varepsilon_1^i = e^{-z_0}\,\Phi(z_0, z_i) - e^{-Z}\,\Phi(Z, z_i).$$

Or, voici les expressions des quantités ε_m^i qui en résultent. Soient

$$\begin{aligned} \mathcal{A} &= \mathrm{A}_0\,\Phi(Z, z_0) + \mathrm{A}_1\,\Phi(Z, z_1) + \ldots + \mathrm{A}_n\,\Phi(Z, z_n), \\ \mathcal{B} &= \mathrm{B}_0\,\Phi(Z, z_0) + \mathrm{B}_1\,\Phi(Z, z_1) + \ldots + \mathrm{B}_n\,\Phi(Z, z_n), \\ &\ldots\ldots\ldots\ldots\ldots\ldots\ldots\ldots, \\ \mathcal{L} &= \mathrm{L}_0\,\Phi(Z, z_0) + \mathrm{L}_1\,\Phi(Z, z_1) + \ldots + \mathrm{L}_n\,\Phi(Z, z_n), \end{aligned}$$

et convenons de représenter par $\mathcal{A}_0$, $\mathcal{B}_0$, ..., $\mathcal{L}_0$ les valeurs obtenues pour $Z = z_0$; on aura

$$\begin{aligned} \varepsilon_m^0 &= e^{-z_0}\mathcal{A}_0 - e^{-Z}\mathcal{A}, \\ \varepsilon_m^1 &= e^{-z_0}\mathcal{B}_0 - e^{-Z}\mathcal{B}, \\ &\dots\dots\dots\dots, \\ \varepsilon_m^n &= e^{-z_0}\mathcal{L}_0 - e^{-Z}\mathcal{L}. \end{aligned}$$

Dans ces formules, Z désigne l'une quelconque des quantités z_1, z_2, ..., z_n; maintenant, si nous voulons mettre en évidence le résultat correspondant à $Z = z_k$, nous conviendrons, en outre, de représenter, d'une part, par $\mathcal{A}_k$, $\mathcal{B}_k$, ..., $\mathcal{L}_k$, et de l'autre par η_k^0, η_k^1, ..., η_k^n les valeurs que prennent, dans ce cas, les coefficients $\mathcal{A}$, $\mathcal{B}$, ..., $\mathcal{L}$ et les quantités ε_m^0, ε_m^1, ..., ε_m^n. On obtient ainsi les équations

$$\begin{aligned} \eta_k^0 &= e^{-z_0}\mathcal{A}_0 - e^{-z_k}\mathcal{A}_k, \\ \eta_k^1 &= e^{-z_0}\mathcal{B}_0 - e^{-z_k}\mathcal{B}_k, \\ &\dots\dots\dots\dots, \\ \eta_k^n &= e^{-z_0}\mathcal{L}_0 - e^{-z_k}\mathcal{L}_k, \end{aligned}$$

qui vont nous conduire à la seconde démonstration que j'ai annoncée de l'impossibilité d'une relation de la forme

$$e^{z_0}N_0 + e^{z_0}N_1 + \dots + e^{z_n}N_n = 0,$$

les exposants z_0, z_1, ..., z_n étant supposés entiers, ainsi que les coefficients N_0, N_1, ..., N_n.

XIII. Je dis en premier lieu que ε_m^i peut devenir plus petit que toute quantité donnée, pour une valeur suffisamment grande de m. Effectivement, l'exponentielle e^{-z} étant toujours positive, on a, comme on sait,

$$\int_{z_0}^{Z} e^{-z}\,F(z)\,dz = F(\xi)\int_{z_0}^{Z} e^{-z}\,dz = F(\xi)(e^{-z_0} - e^{-Z}),$$

$F(z)$ étant une fonction quelconque et ξ une quantité comprise entre les limites z_0 et Z de l'intégrale. Or, en supposant

$$F(z) = \frac{f^m(z)}{z - z_1},$$

on aura cette expression

$$\varepsilon_m^i = \frac{f^{m-1}(\xi)}{1.2\ldots m-1}\,\frac{f(\xi)}{\xi - z_i}(e^{-z_0} - e^{-Z}),$$

qui met en évidence la propriété énoncée. Cela posé, je tire des équations

$$\begin{aligned}\eta_1^0 &= e^{-z_0}\mathcal{A}_0 - e^{-z_1}\mathcal{A}_1,\\ \eta_2^0 &= e^{-z_0}\mathcal{A}_0 - e^{-z_2}\mathcal{A}_2,\\ &\ldots\ldots\ldots\ldots,\\ \eta_n^0 &= e^{-z_0}\mathcal{A}_0 - e^{-z_n}\mathcal{A}_n,\end{aligned}$$

la relation suivante,

$$\begin{aligned}&e^{z_1}\eta_1^0 N_1 + e^{z_2}\eta_2^0 N_2 + \ldots + e^{z_n}\eta_n^0 N_n\\ &\quad = e^{-z_0}(e^{z_1}N_1 + e^{z_2}N_2 + \ldots + e^{z_n}N_n)\mathcal{A}_0\\ &\qquad - (\mathcal{A}_1 N_1 + \mathcal{A}_2 N_2 + \ldots + \mathcal{A}_n N_n).\end{aligned}$$

Si l'on introduit la condition

$$e^{z_0}N_0 + e^{z_1}N_1 + \ldots + e^{z_n}N_n = 0,$$

elle devient

$$\begin{aligned}&e^{z_1}\eta_1^0 N_1 + e^{z_2}\eta_2^0 N_2 + \ldots + e^{z_n}\eta_n^0 N_n\\ &\quad = -(\mathcal{A}_0 N_0 + \mathcal{A}_1 N_1 + \ldots + \mathcal{A}_n N_n).\end{aligned}$$

Or, en supposant que $z_0, z_1, \ldots, z_n$ soient entiers, il en est de même des quantités $\Theta(z_i, z_k)$, $\Phi(z_i, z_k)$, et, par conséquent, de $\mathcal{A}_0, \mathcal{A}_1, \ldots, \mathcal{A}_n$. Nous avons donc un nombre entier

$$\mathcal{A}_0 N_0 + \mathcal{A}_1 N_1 + \ldots + \mathcal{A}_n N_n,$$

qui décroît indéfiniment avec $\eta_1^0, \eta_1^1, \ldots, \eta_1^n$, lorsque m augmente; il en résulte que, à partir d'une certaine valeur de m, et pour toutes les valeurs plus grandes, on aura

$$\mathcal{A}_0 N_0 + \mathcal{A}_1 N_1 + \ldots + \mathcal{A}_n N_n = 0,$$

et, comme on obtient pareillement les conditions

$$\begin{aligned}\mathcal{B}_0 N_0 + \mathcal{B}_1 N_1 + \ldots + \mathcal{B}_n N_n &= 0,\\ \ldots\ldots\ldots\ldots&,\\ \mathcal{L}_0 N_0 + \mathcal{L}_1 N_1 + \ldots + \mathcal{L}_n N_n &= 0,\end{aligned}$$

la relation

$$e^{z_0}N_0 + e^{z_1}N_1 + \ldots + e^{z_n}N_n = 0$$

a pour conséquence que le déterminant

$$\Delta = \begin{vmatrix} \mathcal{A}_0 & \mathcal{A}_1 & \dots & \mathcal{A}_n \\ \mathcal{B}_0 & \mathcal{B}_1 & \dots & \mathcal{B}_n \\ \dots & \dots & \dots & \dots \\ \mathcal{L}_0 & \mathcal{L}_1 & \dots & \mathcal{L}_n \end{vmatrix}$$

doit nécessairement être nul. Mais, d'après les expressions des quantités $\mathcal{A}_k, \mathcal{B}_k, \dots, \mathcal{L}_k$, Δ est le produit de ces deux autres déterminants

$$\begin{vmatrix} A_0 & A_1 & \dots & A_n \\ B_0 & B_1 & \dots & B_n \\ \dots & \dots & \dots & \dots \\ L_0 & L_1 & \dots & L_n \end{vmatrix}$$

et

$$\begin{vmatrix} \Phi(z_0, z_0) & \Phi(z_1, z_0) & \dots & \Phi(z_n, z_0) \\ \Phi(z_0, z_1) & \Phi(z_1, z_1) & \dots & \Phi(z_n, z_1) \\ \dots & \dots & \dots & \dots \\ \Phi(z_0, z_n) & \Phi(z_1, z_n) & \dots & \Phi(z_n, z_n) \end{vmatrix},$$

dont le premier a pour valeur $\delta^{2(m-1)}$, et le second δ^2. On a donc $\Delta = \delta^{2m}$, et il est ainsi démontré, d'une manière entièrement rigoureuse, que la relation supposée est impossible, et que, par suite, le nombre e n'est point compris dans les irrationnelles algébriques.

XIV. Il ne sera pas inutile de donner quelques exemples du mode d'approximation des quantités auquel nous avons été conduits, et je considérerai d'abord le cas le plus simple, où l'on ne considère que la seule exponentielle e^x. En faisant alors $f(z) = z(z-x)$, nous aurons

$$\varepsilon_m = \frac{1}{1.2\dots m}\int_0^x e^{-z} z^m (z-x)^m \, dz$$

et

$$\varepsilon_m^0 = \frac{1}{1.2\dots m-1}\int_0^x e^{-z} z^{m-1} (z-x)^m \, dz,$$

$$\varepsilon_m^1 = \frac{1}{1.2\dots m-1}\int_0^x e^{-z} z^m (z-x)^{m-1} \, dz.$$

Or on obtient immédiatement

$$\Theta(z, \zeta) = z + \zeta + 2m + 1 - x,$$

d'où

$$\Theta(0, 0) = 2m + 1 - x, \qquad \Theta(x, 0) = 2m + 1,$$
$$\Theta(0, x) = 2m + 1, \qquad \Theta(x, x) = 2m + 1 + x,$$

et, par conséquent, ces relations

$$\varepsilon_{m+1}^0 = (2m + 1 - x)\varepsilon_m^0 + (2m + 1)\varepsilon_m^1,$$
$$\varepsilon_{m+1}^1 = (2m + 1)\varepsilon_m^0 + (2m + 1 + x)\varepsilon_m^1.$$

J'observerai maintenant qu'il vient, en retranchant membre à membre,

$$\varepsilon_{m+1}^1 - \varepsilon_{m+1}^0 = x(\varepsilon_m^0 + \varepsilon_m^1),$$

de sorte que, ayant

$$\varepsilon_m = \varepsilon_m^0 + \varepsilon_m^1,$$

on en conclut

$$\varepsilon_{m+1}^1 - \varepsilon_{m+1}^0 = x\varepsilon_m.$$

Joignons à cette équation la suivante :

$$\varepsilon_{m+1}^1 + \varepsilon_{m+1}^0 = \varepsilon_{m+1};$$

nous en déduirons les valeurs

$$\varepsilon_{m+1}^1 = \frac{\varepsilon_{m+1} + x\varepsilon_m}{2}, \qquad \varepsilon_{m+1}^0 = \frac{\varepsilon_{m+1} - x\varepsilon_m}{2},$$

et, si l'on y change m en $m - 1$, une simple substitution, par exemple, dans la relation

$$\varepsilon_{m+1}^0 = (2m + 1 - x)\varepsilon_m^0 + (2m + 1)\varepsilon_m^1,$$

donnera le résultat précédemment obtenu (p. 165),

$$\varepsilon_{m+1} = (4m + 2)\varepsilon_m + x^2\varepsilon_{m-1}.$$

Soient, en second lieu,

$$n = 2, \qquad z_0 = 0, \qquad z_1 = 1, \qquad z_2 = 2,$$

d'où

$$f(z) = z(z - 1)(z - 2) = z^3 - 3z^2 + 2z;$$

on trouvera

$$\Theta(z, \zeta) = z^2 + (\zeta - 1)z + (\zeta - 1)^2 + 3m(z + \zeta + 1) + 9m^2,$$

et, par conséquent,

$$\Theta(0,0)=9m^2+3m+1,\quad \Theta(0,1)=9m^2+6m,\quad \Theta(0,2)=9m^2+9m+1,$$
$$\Theta(1,0)=9m^2+6m+1,\quad \Theta(1,1)=9m^2+9m+1,\quad \Theta(1,2)=9m^2+12m+3,$$
$$\Theta(2,0)=9m^2+9m+3,\quad \Theta(2,1)=9m^2+12m+4,\quad \Theta(2,2)=9m^2+15m+7.$$

En particulier, pour $m=1$, nous aurons

$$\begin{aligned} \varepsilon_2^0 &= 13\varepsilon_1^0+16\varepsilon_1^1+21\varepsilon_1^2,\\ \varepsilon_2^1 &= 15\varepsilon_1^0+19\varepsilon_1^1+25\varepsilon_1^2,\\ \varepsilon_2^2 &= 19\varepsilon_1^0+24\varepsilon_1^1+31\varepsilon_1^2; \end{aligned}$$

d'ailleurs il vient facilement

$$\Phi(z,\zeta)=z^2+(\zeta-1)z+(\zeta-1)^2,$$

ce qui donne

$$\begin{aligned} \varepsilon_1^0 &= 1-e^{-Z}(Z^2-Z+1),\\ \varepsilon_1^1 &= \quad -e^{-Z}Z^2,\\ \varepsilon_1^2 &= 1-e^{-Z}(Z^2+Z+1); \end{aligned}$$

on en conclut

$$\begin{aligned} \varepsilon_2^0 &= 34-e^{-Z}(50Z^2+8Z+34),\\ \varepsilon_2^1 &= 40-e^{-Z}(59Z^2+10Z+40),\\ \varepsilon_2^2 &= 50-e^{-Z}(74Z^2+12Z+50). \end{aligned}$$

De là résulte que

$$\varepsilon_1=\varepsilon_1^0+\varepsilon_1^1+\varepsilon_1^2=2-e^{-Z}(3Z^2+2),$$
$$\varepsilon_2=\varepsilon_2^0+\varepsilon_2^1+\varepsilon_2^2=124-e^{-Z}(183Z^2+30Z+124);$$

et, si l'on fait successivement $Z=1$, $Z=2$, l'expression de ε_1 fournit les valeurs approchées

$$e=\frac{5}{2},\qquad e^2=\frac{14}{2}=7,$$

et l'expression de ε_2 les suivantes :

$$e=\frac{337}{124},\qquad e^2=\frac{916}{124},$$

où l'erreur ne porte que sur les dix-millièmes. En supposant ensuite $m = 2$, ce qui donnera ([1])

$$\varepsilon_3^0 = 43\varepsilon_2^0 + 49\varepsilon_2^1 + 57\varepsilon_2^2,$$
$$\varepsilon_3^1 = 48\varepsilon_2^0 + 55\varepsilon_2^1 + 64\varepsilon_2^2,$$
$$\varepsilon_3^2 = 55\varepsilon_2^0 + 63\varepsilon_2^1 + 73\varepsilon_2^2,$$

nous obtiendrons

$$\varepsilon_3^0 = 6272 - e^{-Z}(\ 9259\,Z^2 + 1518\,Z + 6272),$$
$$\varepsilon_3^1 = 7032 - e^{-Z}(10381\,Z^2 + 1702\,Z + 7032),$$
$$\varepsilon_3^2 = 8040 - e^{-Z}(11869\,Z^2 + 1946\,Z + 8040),$$

d'où

$$\varepsilon_3 = 21344 - e^{-Z}(31509\,Z^2 + 5166\,Z + 21344),$$

et, par suite,

$$e = \frac{58019}{21344}, \qquad e^2 = \frac{157712}{21344},$$

l'erreur portant sur les dix-millionièmes.

([1]) Dans le texte d'Hermite, on trouve au dernier terme du second membre de la troisième ligne le coefficient 75. M. Bourget, en refaisant les calculs, a trouvé le coefficient 73; cette rectification a amené des modifications assez importantes dans les valeurs de e et de e^2, dont l'approximation monte, de ce fait, aux dix-millionièmes. E. P.

EXTRAIT D'UNE LETTRE DE M. CH. HERMITE

SUR L'INTÉGRALE $\int_0^\pi \left(\frac{\sin^2 x}{1-2a\cos x+a^2}\right)^m dx.$

Nouvelle Correspondance mathématique, t. I, 1874, p. 33-35.

Permettez-moi de vous adresser une seconde détermination de l'intégrale de Poisson

$$\int_0^\pi \left(\frac{\sin^2 x}{1-2a\cos x+a^2}\right)^m dx,$$

qui offre l'application la plus importante du théorème de M. Liouville, dont vous avez donné la démonstration.

Soit, pour abréger,

$$f(x) = \frac{\sin^2 x}{1-2a\cos x+a^2}.$$

Je désigne par ε une constante telle que la série

$$\varepsilon f(x) + \varepsilon^2 f^2(x) + \ldots + \varepsilon^m f^m(x) + \ldots$$

soit convergente : elle aura pour somme

$$\frac{\varepsilon f(x)}{1-\varepsilon f(x)};$$

ce qui conduit à chercher la valeur de l'intégrale

$$\int_0^\pi \frac{\varepsilon f(x)\,dx}{1-\varepsilon f(x)},$$

dont il suffira ensuite d'effectuer le développement en série, suivant les puissances croissantes de ε. Or, en faisant pour un moment $\cos x = z$, la décomposition en fractions simples de la fraction rationnelle

$$\frac{\varepsilon f(x)}{1-\varepsilon f(x)} = \frac{\varepsilon(1-z^2)}{1-2az+a^2-\varepsilon(1-z^2)}$$

donne immédiatement le résultat; car, en écrivant

$$\frac{\varepsilon(1-z^2)}{1-2az+a^2-\varepsilon(1-z^2)} = -1+\frac{G}{g-z}+\frac{H}{h-z},$$

vous voyez que nous sommes ramenés à l'intégrale connue

$$\int_0^\pi \frac{dx}{g-\cos x} = \frac{\pi}{\sqrt{g^2-1}}.$$

Cela posé, on obtient, en résolvant l'équation du second degré

$$1-2az+a^2-\varepsilon(1-z^2)=0,$$

$$g = \frac{a+\sqrt{(1-\varepsilon)(a^2-\varepsilon)}}{\varepsilon}, \qquad h = \frac{a-\sqrt{(1-\varepsilon)(a^2-\varepsilon)}}{\varepsilon}.$$

On a ensuite

$$G = \varepsilon\frac{g^2-1}{g-h}, \qquad H = \varepsilon\frac{h^2-1}{h-g},$$

$$\sqrt{g^2-1} = \pm\frac{a\sqrt{1-\varepsilon}-\sqrt{a^2-\varepsilon}}{\varepsilon},$$

$$\sqrt{h^2-1} = \pm\frac{a\sqrt{1-\varepsilon}+\sqrt{a^2-\varepsilon}}{\varepsilon},$$

comme il est facile de le vérifier en élevant les deux membres au carré. Mais il est nécessaire, avant d'employer ces formules, de choisir les signes $\pm$ de manière que les radicaux aient bien les déterminations qui leur conviennent dans les relations

$$\int_0^\pi \frac{dx}{g-\cos x} = \frac{\pi}{\sqrt{g^2-1}}, \qquad \int_0^\pi \frac{dx}{h-\cos x} = \frac{\pi}{\sqrt{h^2-1}}.$$

Revenant, à cet effet, à la condition de convergence de la série $\Sigma\varepsilon^m f^m(x)$, j'observe que le maximum de $f(x)$ est l'unité pour $a<1$, et $\frac{1}{a^2}$ pour $a>1$; on doit donc supposer $\varepsilon<1$ dans le premier cas et $\varepsilon<a^2$ dans le second, de manière à avoir $\varepsilon f(x)<1$, pour toutes les valeurs de la variable. De l'inégalité $1-\varepsilon f(x)>0$, résulte que l'équation

$$1-\varepsilon f(x)=0$$

n'admet aucune racine réelle par rapport à x; cependant on peut toujours supposer g et h réels, en prenant dans les deux cas, ce qui est permis, ε moindre que la plus petite des quantités 1 et a^2. Effectivement le radical $\sqrt{(1-\varepsilon)(a^2-\varepsilon)}$ sera réel, et, si l'on admet que a soit positif ainsi que ε, l'équation

$$1-2az+a^2-\varepsilon(1-z^2)=0$$

fait voir que les racines seront, l'une et l'autre, positives. De là résulte que, dans les relations précédentes,

$$\int_0^\pi \frac{dx}{g-\cos x}=\frac{\pi}{\sqrt{g^2-1}}, \qquad \int_0^\pi \frac{dx}{h-\cos x}=\frac{\pi}{\sqrt{h^2-1}},$$

les radicaux ont le signe $+$; par suite, on doit prendre

$$\sqrt{g^2-1}=\frac{a\sqrt{1-\varepsilon}-\sqrt{a^2-\varepsilon}}{\varepsilon},$$

si l'on suppose $a<1$; et

$$\sqrt{g^2-1}=\frac{\sqrt{a^2-\varepsilon}-a\sqrt{1-\varepsilon}}{\varepsilon},$$

dans le cas de $a>1$. Ayant toujours d'ailleurs

$$\sqrt{h^2-1}=\frac{a\sqrt{1-\varepsilon}+\sqrt{a^2-\varepsilon}}{\varepsilon},$$

on obtient, dans le premier cas,

$$\int_0^\pi \frac{\varepsilon \sin^2 x\, dx}{1-2a\cos x+a^2-\varepsilon\sin^2 x}=\pi\left[-1+(1-\varepsilon)^{-\frac{1}{2}}\right],$$

et, dans le second,

$$\int_0^\pi \frac{\varepsilon \sin^2 x\, dx}{1-2a\cos x+a^2-\varepsilon\sin^2 x}=\pi\left[-1+\left(1-\frac{\varepsilon}{a^2}\right)^{-\frac{1}{2}}\right].$$

Vous voyez que ces formules donnent bien le résultat de Poisson, en faisant usage du développement

$$(1-\varepsilon)^{-\frac{1}{2}}=1+\frac{1}{2}\ +\frac{1.3}{2.4}\varepsilon^2+\ldots+\frac{1.3.5\ldots(2m-1)}{2.4.6\ldots 2m}\varepsilon^m+\ldots.$$

EXTRAIT

D'UNE

LETTRE DE M. Ch. HERMITE A M. BORCHARDT,

SUR LA

TRANSFORMATION DES FORMES QUADRATIQUES
TERNAIRES EN ELLES-MÊMES.

Journal de Crelle, t. 78, 1874, p. 325-328.

Permettez-moi de répondre à une objection très fondée qui a été faite par M. *P. Bachmann,* à mes formules pour la transformation des formes quadratiques ternaires en elles-mêmes, dans son travail intitulé : *Untersuchungen über quadratische Formen,* tome LXXVI de votre journal, page 331. L'analyse indirecte dont j'ai fait usage ne prouve pas en effet qu'elles comprennent, sans aucune exception, toutes les substitutions qui reproduisent une forme donnée; or un point aussi essentiel demande à être complètement éclairci, et c'est ce que je vais essayer de faire. Désignant la forme proposée par $f(x, y, z)$, et posant la condition

$$f(x, y, z) = f(X, Y, Z),$$

je l'écris de la manière suivante :

$$x\frac{df}{dx} + y\frac{df}{dy} + z\frac{df}{dz} = X\frac{df}{dX} + Y\frac{df}{dY} + Z\frac{df}{dZ},$$

ou pour abréger

$$\Sigma x\frac{df}{dx} = \Sigma X\frac{df}{dX}.$$

Cela posé, je joins à cette condition la relation identique

$$\Sigma x \frac{df}{dX} = \Sigma X \frac{df}{dx},$$

et j'ajoute les deux égalités membre à membre, ce qui donnera

$$\Sigma x \left(\frac{df}{dx} + \frac{df}{dX}\right) = \Sigma X \left(\frac{df}{dx} + \frac{df}{dX}\right),$$

ou bien

$$\Sigma (x - X) \left(\frac{df}{dx} + \frac{df}{dX}\right) = 0.$$

Soit maintenant

$$U = x - X, \qquad U' = \frac{df}{dx} + \frac{df}{dX},$$

$$V = y - Y, \qquad V' = \frac{df}{dy} + \frac{df}{dY},$$

$$W = z - Z, \qquad W' = \frac{df}{dz} + \frac{df}{dZ}.$$

Vous voyez que des expressions de x, y, z en X, Y, Z résulteront pour ces diverses quantités des fonctions linéaires de ces trois indéterminées, telles qu'on ait identiquement

$$UU' + VV' + WW' = 0.$$

Cherchons ces fonctions, et pour cela considérons un premier cas dans lequel nous supposerons qu'il soit possible d'obtenir inversement X, Y, Z en U, V, W. Il est clair que U′, V′, W′ seront alors des quantités linéaires en U, V, W, et un calcul facile donne sur-le-champ, pour la solution de l'équation proposée, les formules

$$(1) \qquad \begin{cases} U' = \nu V - \mu W, \\ V' = \lambda W - \nu U, \\ W' = \mu U - \lambda V, \end{cases}$$

où λ, μ, ν sont des constantes. Or on en tire les relations suivantes :

$$(I) \qquad \begin{cases} \mu z - \nu y + \dfrac{df}{dx} = \mu Z - \nu Y - \dfrac{df}{dX}, \\ \nu x - \lambda z + \dfrac{df}{dy} = \nu X - \lambda Z - \dfrac{df}{dY}, \\ \lambda y - \mu x + \dfrac{df}{dz} = \lambda Y - \mu X - \dfrac{df}{dZ}, \end{cases}$$

d'une forme bien différente de celles que j'avais d'abord obtenues, à savoir

$$
\text{(II)} \qquad \left\{
\begin{aligned}
x - \nu\frac{df}{dy} + \mu\frac{df}{dz} &= \mathrm{X} + \nu\frac{df}{d\mathrm{Y}} - \mu\frac{df}{d\mathrm{Z}},\\
y - \lambda\frac{df}{dz} + \nu\frac{df}{dx} &= \mathrm{Y} + \lambda\frac{df}{d\mathrm{Z}} - \nu\frac{df}{d\mathrm{X}},\\
z - \mu\frac{df}{dx} + \lambda\frac{df}{dy} &= \mathrm{Z} + \mu\frac{df}{d\mathrm{X}} - \lambda\frac{df}{d\mathrm{Y}},
\end{aligned}
\right.
$$

et qui résulteraient des équations

$$
\begin{aligned}
\mathrm{U} &= \nu\mathrm{V}' - \mu\mathrm{W}',\\
\mathrm{V} &= \lambda\mathrm{W}' - \nu\mathrm{U}',\\
\mathrm{W} &= \mu\mathrm{U}' - \lambda\mathrm{V}'.
\end{aligned}
$$

Mais un de mes élèves, M. *Tannery*, agrégé de l'Université, a fait la remarque ingénieuse qu'en remplaçant λ, μ, ν par $\frac{1}{\mathrm{D}}\frac{dg}{d\lambda}$, $\frac{1}{\mathrm{D}}\frac{dg}{d\mu}$, $\frac{1}{\mathrm{D}}\frac{dg}{d\nu}$, où $g(\lambda, \mu, \nu)$ désigne la forme adjointe de $f(\lambda, \mu, \nu)$, D son déterminant, et changeant X, Y, Z en $-$X, $-$Y, $-$Z, les équations (I) donnent les relations (II).

Supposons, en second lieu, qu'il ne soit pas possible d'exprimer X, Y, Z en U, V, W; en désignant alors par θ, θ', θ'' trois indéterminées, je proposerai d'une part

$$
\mathrm{U} = \theta, \qquad \mathrm{V} = \theta', \qquad \mathrm{W} = a\theta - b\theta'
$$

et de l'autre

$$
\begin{aligned}
\mathrm{U}' &= \mathrm{A}\theta + \mathrm{A}'\theta' + \mathrm{A}''\theta'',\\
\mathrm{V}' &= \mathrm{B}\theta + \mathrm{B}'\theta' + \mathrm{B}''\theta'',\\
\mathrm{W}' &= \mathrm{C}\theta + \mathrm{C}'\theta' + \mathrm{C}''\theta''.
\end{aligned}
$$

Cela étant, la condition proposée $\mathrm{UU}' + \mathrm{VV}' + \mathrm{WW}' = 0$ donne les relations

$$
\begin{aligned}
\mathrm{A} + a\mathrm{C} &= 0, & \mathrm{B}' - b\mathrm{B}' &= 0,\\
\mathrm{A}'' + a\mathrm{C}'' &= 0, & \mathrm{B}'' - b\mathrm{C}'' &= 0
\end{aligned}
$$

et

$$
\mathrm{A}' + \mathrm{B} + a\mathrm{C}' - b\mathrm{C} = 0.
$$

En remplaçant cette dernière par les deux suivantes, où c est une indéterminée

$$
\mathrm{A}' + a\mathrm{C}' = c, \qquad \mathrm{B} - b\mathrm{C} = -c,
$$

on conclura

$$A = -aC, \qquad B = bC - c,$$
$$A' = -aC' + c, \qquad B' = bC',$$
$$A'' = -aC'', \qquad B'' = bC'',$$

et il en résulte que

$$U' = -a(C\theta + C'\theta' + C''\theta'') + c\theta' = cV - aW',$$
$$V' = \quad b(C\theta + C'\theta' + C''\theta'') - c\theta = bW' - cU.$$

Ayant ailleurs $W = aU - bV$, il est clair que la nouvelle solution obtenue se déduit des équations (1) en permutant W et W′. Or les relations auxquelles elle conduit entre x, y, z et X, Y, Z, à savoir

$$cx + \frac{df}{dy} - b\frac{df}{dz} = cX - \frac{df}{dY} + b\frac{df}{dZ},$$
$$cy - a\frac{df}{dz} - \frac{df}{dx} = cY + a\frac{df}{dZ} + \frac{df}{dX},$$
$$ax - by - z = aX - bY - Z,$$

se ramènent au type (II) si l'on fait

$$a = -\frac{\lambda}{\nu}, \qquad b = \frac{\mu}{\nu}, \qquad c = -\frac{1}{\nu},$$

car l'équation

$$\lambda x + \mu y + \nu z = \lambda X + \mu Y + \nu Z$$

s'en déduit comme conséquence.

Il ne reste plus qu'à examiner un dernier cas dans lequel U, V, W dépendraient d'une seule indéterminée au lieu de deux, de sorte qu'on aurait $U = \alpha W$, $V = \beta W$, et par conséquent $\alpha U' + \beta V' + W' = 0$. Nous aurons alors les relations

$$x - \alpha z = X - \alpha Z,$$
$$y - \beta z = Y - \beta Z,$$
$$\alpha\frac{df}{dx} + \beta\frac{df}{dy} + \frac{df}{dz} = -\alpha\frac{df}{dX} - \beta\frac{df}{dY} - \frac{df}{dZ},$$

qui en remplaçant α et β par $\frac{\alpha}{\gamma}$, $\frac{\beta}{\gamma}$ donnent les formules

$$x = X - \frac{\alpha}{f(\alpha, \beta, \gamma)}\left(\alpha\frac{df}{dX} + \beta\frac{df}{dY} + \gamma\frac{df}{dZ}\right),$$
$$y = Y - \frac{\beta}{f(\alpha, \beta, \gamma)}\left(\alpha\frac{df}{dX} + \beta\frac{df}{dY} + \gamma\frac{df}{dZ}\right)$$
$$z = Z - \frac{\gamma}{f(\alpha, \beta, \gamma)}\left(\alpha\frac{df}{dX} + \beta\frac{df}{dY} + \gamma\frac{df}{dZ}\right)$$

Je m'y arrête un moment pour observer qu'en désignant la substitution ainsi obtenue par S, on aura $S^{-1} = S$, d'où $S^2 = 1$. Cette circonstance m'avait fait penser un instant qu'elles constitueraient une exception au type général, mais j'ai ensuite remarqué que les relations (I) donnant la suivante :

$$\lambda \frac{df}{dx} + \mu \frac{df}{dy} + \nu \frac{df}{dz} = -\lambda \frac{df}{dX} - \mu \frac{df}{dY} - \nu \frac{df}{dZ},$$

il suffisait pour les obtenir de poser $\lambda = \alpha\nu$, $\mu = \beta\nu$, puis de faire ν infini. Je pense, mon cher ami, avoir ainsi rempli la lacune que présentaient mes anciennes recherches.

EXTRAIT

D'UNE

LETTRE DE M. CH. HERMITE A M. BORCHARDT,

SUR LA

RÉDUCTION DES FORMES QUADRATIQUES TERNAIRES.

Journal de Crelle, t. 79, 1874, p. 17-20.

Deux géomètres russes extrêmement distingués, M. *Korkine* et M. *Zolotareff*, ont récemment publié dans les *Annales de Mathématiques*, de M. *Neumann*, des recherches approfondies ayant pour objet, entre autres choses, le théorème de *Seeber*, sur la limitation du produit des coefficients des carrés des variables dans les formes quadratiques ternaires réduites. L'importance du sujet rend peut-être utile de multiplier les points de vue sous lesquels on peut le traiter, et, après la méthode de ces deux auteurs, je proposerai la suivante.

Soit

$$D = aa'a'' + 2bb'b'' - ab^2 - a'b'^2 - a''b''^2;$$

il s'agit d'établir dans deux cas distincts que la condition $aa'a'' < 2D$ est vérifiée, le premier supposant les conditions

$$(\mathrm{I}) \qquad \begin{cases} b > 0, \quad b' > 0, \quad b'' > 0, \\ a < a' < a''; \quad 2b'' < a, \quad 2b' < a, \quad 2b < a', \end{cases}$$

et le second cet autre système

$$(\mathrm{II}) \qquad \begin{cases} b < 0, \quad b' < 0, \quad b'' < 0, \\ a < a' < a'', \quad -2b'' < a, \quad -2b' < a, \quad -2b < a', \\ a + a' + 2(b + b' + b'') > 0. \end{cases}$$

Considérant à cet effet a, a' et a'' comme constants dans l'expression

$$2D - aa'a'' = aa'a'' + 4bb'b'' - 2ab^2 - 2a'b'^2 - 2a''b''^2,$$

j'observe qu'il suffira de prouver qu'elle est positive quand on attribue à b'' par exemple sa plus petite et sa plus grande valeur. Effectivement dans les deux cas que nous avons à traiter, b'' parcourt des valeurs toujours du même signe, positives dans le premier, négatives dans le second, à partir de $b''=0$. Or l'expression est un trinome du second degré en b'' dont le terme du second degré est affecté d'un coefficient négatif, et, si le terme constant qui est donné pour $b''=0$ est positif, ses racines seront réelles et de signes contraires. On voit par là qu'à l'égard d'une série de valeurs du même signe, il suffit bien de vérifier que l'expression est positive aux limites, pour être assuré qu'elle l'est aussi pour les valeurs intermédiaires. Cela posé, faisons en premier lieu $b''=0$ et $b''=\frac{a}{2}$ dans l'expression de $2D-aa'a''$. Je remarque que les quantités auxquelles on sera conduit, et qu'il faut démontrer être positives, seront à l'égard de b' des trinomes du second degré dont le terme du second degré sera encore négatif, et que cette variable sera de même assujettie à parcourir une série de valeurs de même signe, de sorte que le raisonnement précédent leur sera applicable. Sans le répéter davantage, on voit clairement que notre objet est maintenant de donner les limites de ces intervalles que parcourent b, b', b'', sous les conditions (I) et (II), et de calculer les valeurs correspondantes de $2D-aa'a''$. Or elles sont pour le premier cas :

$$b''=0\begin{cases} b'=0 \begin{cases} b=0, & aa'a'', \\ b=\dfrac{a'}{2}, & aa'a''-\dfrac{aa'^2}{2}, \end{cases} \\ b'=\dfrac{a}{2} \begin{cases} b=0, & aa'a''-\dfrac{a^2a'}{2}, \\ b=\dfrac{a'}{2}, & aa'a''-\dfrac{aa'^2}{2}-\dfrac{a^2a'}{2}, \end{cases} \end{cases}$$

$$b''=\frac{a}{2}\begin{cases} b'=0 \begin{cases} b=0, & aa'a''-\dfrac{a^2a''}{2}, \\ b=\dfrac{a'}{2}, & aa'a''-\dfrac{a^2a''}{2}-\dfrac{aa'^2}{2}, \end{cases} \\ b'=\dfrac{a}{2} \begin{cases} b=0, & aa'a''-\dfrac{a^2a'}{2}-\dfrac{a^2a''}{2}, \\ b=\dfrac{a'}{2}, & aa'a''-\dfrac{aa'^2}{2}-\dfrac{a^2a''}{2}. \end{cases} \end{cases}$$

Dans l'autre cas on aura ce second Tableau :

$$
b''=0\begin{cases}
b'=0 & \begin{cases} b=0, & aa'a'', \\ b=-\dfrac{a'}{2}, & aa'a''-\dfrac{aa'^2}{2}, \end{cases} \\
b'=-\dfrac{a}{2} & \begin{cases} b=0, & aa'a''-\dfrac{a^2a'}{2}, \\ b=-\dfrac{a'}{2}, & aa'a''-\dfrac{aa'^2}{2}-\dfrac{a^2a'}{2}, \end{cases}
\end{cases}
$$

$$
b''=-\frac{a}{2}\begin{cases}
b'=0 & \begin{cases} b=0, & aa'a''-\dfrac{a^2a''}{2}, \\ b=-\dfrac{a'}{2}, & aa'a''-\dfrac{a^2a''}{2}-\dfrac{aa'^2}{2}, \end{cases} \\
b'=-\dfrac{a}{2} & \begin{cases} b=0, & aa'a''-\dfrac{a^2a'}{2}-\dfrac{a^2a''}{2}, \\ b=-\dfrac{a'-a}{2}, & aa'a''-\dfrac{aa'^2}{2}-\dfrac{a^2a''}{2}, \end{cases}
\end{cases}
$$

et à première vue on reconnaît que ces quantités sont positives sous les conditions

$$a < a' < a''.$$

Mais cette démonstration toute élémentaire est loin de l'élégance et de la profondeur de celle que *Gauss* tire dans le premier cas, par exemple, de cette identité

$$
\begin{aligned}
2\mathrm{D} = aa'a'' &+ ab(a'-2b)+a'b'(a''-2b')+a''b''(a-2b'') \\
&+ b(a-2b')(a'-2b'')+b'(a'-2b'')(a''-2b) \\
&+ b''(a''-2b)(a-2b')+(a-2b')(a'-2b'')(a''-2b).
\end{aligned}
$$

En réfléchissant à cette étonnante transformation j'ai fait la remarque qu'elle peut être généralisée de cette manière :

$$
\begin{aligned}
2\alpha\alpha'\alpha''\mathrm{D} = (2\alpha\alpha'\alpha''-1)aa'a'' &+ \alpha ab(a'-2\alpha'\alpha''b)+\alpha'a'b'(a''-2\alpha\alpha''b') \\
&+ \alpha''a''b''(a-2\alpha\alpha'b'')+\alpha b(a-2\alpha'b')(a'-2\alpha''b'') \\
&+ \alpha'b'(a'-2\alpha''b'')(a''-2\alpha b)+\alpha''b''(a''-2\alpha b)(a-2\alpha'b') \\
&+ (a-2\alpha'b')(a'-2\alpha''b'')(\alpha''-2\alpha b).
\end{aligned}
$$

On vérifie aisément en effet que le second membre s'évanouit si l'on fait $\alpha=0$; par un changement de lettres on conclut qu'il s'annule aussi pour $\alpha'=0$ et $\alpha''=0$; la formule est donc démontrée en général; puisqu'elle coïncide avec celle de *Gauss*, en supposant $\alpha = 1$, $\alpha' = 1$, $\alpha'' = 1$.

Enfin je remarque qu'en permutant x et y par exemple dans la forme proposée, ce qui revient à échanger a et a' d'une part, b et b' de l'autre, l'invariant conserve la même valeur. Il en résulte que cette seconde relation donnée par *Gauss*

$$\begin{aligned} D = {} & aa'a'' + ab(a'' - 2b) + a'b'(a - 2b') + a''b''(a' - 2b'') \\ & + b(a - 2b'')(a'' - 2b') + b'(a' - 2b)(a - 2b'') \\ & + b''(a'' - 2b')(a' - 2b) + (a - 2b'')(a' - 2b)(a'' - 2b') \end{aligned}$$

est simplement une conséquence de la première et qu'elle se généralise de la même manière.

Saint-Sauveur (Hautes-Pyrénées), 25 juin 1874.

EXTRAIT

D'UNE

LETTRE DE M. CH. HERMITE DE PARIS A M. L. FUCHS DE GÖTTINGUE,

SUR

QUELQUES ÉQUATIONS DIFFÉRENTIELLES LINÉAIRES.

Journal de Crelle, t. 79, 1875, p. 324-338.

... J'ai pris en effet pour point de départ l'intégrale suivante

$$y=\int (z-z_0)^{\mu_0-1}(z-z_1)^{\mu_1-1}\ldots(z-z_n)^{\mu_n-1}(x-z)^{n-p}\,dz,$$

qui comprend les transcendantes hyperelliptiques, et dont je tire facilement une équation linéaire d'ordre $n+1$ analogue à celle qui définit la série de *Gauss*.

Soit en effet

$$f(z)=(z-z_0)(z-z_1)\ldots(z-z_n),$$

puis

$$f_1(z)=\frac{\mu_0 f(z)}{z-z_0}+\frac{\mu_1 f(z)}{z-z_1}+\ldots+\frac{\mu_n f(z)}{z-z_n};$$

on trouve aisément la relation

$$\begin{aligned}f(x)\frac{d^{n+1}y}{dx^{n+1}}&+\frac{p}{1}f'(x)\frac{d^n y}{dx^n}+\frac{p(p-1)}{1.2}f''(x)\frac{d^{n-1}y}{dx^{n-1}}+\ldots\\&-f_1(x)\frac{d^n y}{dx^n}-\frac{(p-1)}{1}f_1'(x)\frac{d^{n-1}y}{dx^{n-1}}-\frac{(p-1)(p-2)}{1.2}f_1''(x)\frac{d^{n-2}y}{dx^{n-2}}-\ldots\\&=\pm(p-1)(p-2)\ldots(p-n)(z-z_0)^{\mu_0}(z-z_1)^{\mu_1}\ldots(z-z_n)^{\mu_n}(x-z)^{-p}.\end{aligned}$$

Or, en supposant les exposants $\mu_0, \mu_1, \ldots, \mu_n$ positifs, le second membre s'évanouit pour $z = z_0, z_1, \ldots, z_n$, et, si l'on convient de désigner par Z l'une quelconque des n quantités $z_1, z_2, \ldots, z_n$, les diverses intégrales

$$\int_0^{Z} \mathfrak{f}(z)(x-z)^{n-p}\,dz,$$

où j'ai écrit pour abréger

$$\mathfrak{f}(z) = (z-z_0)^{\mu_0-1}(z-z_1)^{\mu_1-1}\ldots(z-z_n)^{\mu_n-1},$$

satisfont à l'équation linéaire sans second membre. Mais il est un autre point de vue que celui de l'application de vos théorèmes généraux sous lequel cette équation me paraît encore offrir quelque intérêt. Ces rapports de la théorie des fractions continues avec certaines équations du second ordre que nous ont fait connaître les belles recherches de M. *Heine* et de M. *Christoffel* se trouvent en effet susceptibles d'extension, et vous allez voir comment l'équation linéaire d'ordre $n+1$ se lie aux modes nouveaux d'approximations simultanées de plusieurs fonctions, dont j'ai donné un premier exemple en considérant les quantités e^{ax}, e^{bx}, ... [*Sur la fonction exponentielle* (*Comptes rendus*, 1873)]. Soit d'abord, en effet, en supposant m un nombre entier positif,

$$\mu_0 = \mu_1 = \ldots = \mu_n = m+1$$

et

$$p = m+n+1;$$

on sera conduit à l'équation

$$f(x)\frac{d^{n+1}y}{dx^{n+1}} + nf'(x)\frac{d^n y}{dx^n} - \frac{1}{2}(m+n)(m-n+1)f''(x)\frac{d^{n-1}y}{dx^{n-1}}$$
$$-\frac{1}{2.3}(m+n)(m+n-1)(2m-n+2)f'''(x)\frac{d^{n-2}y}{dx^{n-2}} - \ldots = 0,$$

dont n solutions représentées par les intégrales

$$y = \int_{z_0}^{Z} \frac{f^m(z)}{(x-z)^{m+1}}\,dz$$

s'obtiennent comme il suit sous forme finie explicite. Dans la formule élémentaire

$$\int U \frac{d^m V}{dz^m} dz = \Theta + (-1)^m \int V \frac{d^m U}{dz^m} dz,$$

où

$$\Theta = U \frac{d^{m-1} V}{dz^{m-1}} - \frac{dU}{dz} \frac{d^{m-2} V}{dz^{m-2}} + \ldots + (-1)^{m-1} \frac{d^{m-1} U}{dz^{m-1}} V,$$

je fais

$$U = f^m(z), \qquad V = \frac{1}{x-z},$$

et observant qu'aux limites $z = z_0$, $z = Z$ la quantité Θ s'évanouit, puisque la dérivée d'ordre $m-1$ de $f^m(z)$ contient encore le facteur $f(z)$, j'en tire en négligeant un coefficient numérique

$$y = \int_{z_0}^{Z} \frac{d^m f^m(z)}{dz^m} \frac{dz}{x-z}.$$

Soit pour abréger

$$\Phi(z) = \frac{d^m f^m(z)}{dz^m};$$

on pourra écrire encore

$$y = \int_{z_0}^{Z} \frac{\Phi(z)}{x-z} dz = \Phi(x) \int_{z_0}^{Z} \frac{dz}{x-z} - \int_{z_0}^{Z} \frac{\Phi(x)-\Phi(z)}{x-z} dz,$$

de sorte qu'en désignant par $\Phi_i(x)$ l'intégrale

$$\int_{z_0}^{z_i} \frac{\Phi(x)-\Phi(z)}{x-z} dz,$$

qui est un polynome entier en x d'un degré inférieur d'une unité au degré de $\Phi(x)$, les expressions cherchées sont

$$y_1 = \Phi(x) \int_{z_0}^{z_1} \frac{dz}{x-z} - \Phi_1(x),$$

$$y_2 = \Phi(x) \int_{z_0}^{z_2} \frac{dz}{x-z} - \Phi_2(x),$$

$$\ldots\ldots\ldots\ldots\ldots\ldots,$$

$$y_n = \Phi(x) \int_{z_0}^{z_n} \frac{dz}{x-z} - \Phi_n(x).$$

Cela posé, on voit immédiatement, en revenant à l'intégrale

$$\int_{z_0}^{Z} \frac{f^m(z)}{(x-z)^{m+1}} dz,$$

dont elles ont été déduites, qu'elles donnent des développements suivant les puissances descendantes de la variable commençant par un terme en

$$\frac{1}{x^{m+1}}.$$

Les fractions de même dénominateur

$$\frac{\Phi_1(x)}{\Phi(x)}, \quad \frac{\Phi_2(x)}{\Phi(x)}, \quad \ldots, \quad \frac{\Phi_n(x)}{\Phi(x)}$$

représentent donc les quantités

$$\int_{z_0}^{z_1} \frac{dz}{x-z} = \log\frac{x-z_0}{x-z_1}, \qquad \int_{z_0}^{z_2} \frac{dz}{x-z} = \log\frac{x-z_0}{x-z_2}, \qquad \ldots,$$

$$\int_{z_0}^{z_n} \frac{dz}{x-z} = \log\frac{x-z_0}{x-z_n}$$

aux termes près de l'ordre

$$\frac{1}{x^{mn+m+1}},$$

ou si l'on veut de l'ordre de

$$\frac{1}{\Phi(x)\sqrt[n]{\Phi(x)}},$$

afin de nous rapprocher de l'arithmétique, et elles doivent être regardées comme analogues aux réduites de la théorie des fractions continues. Pour le mieux faire voir, supposons que $\Phi(x)$ représente le polynome le plus général de degré mn; tous les coefficients se trouveront déterminés sauf un facteur constant, en s'imposant pour conditions, que les développements suivant les puissances descendantes de la variable des n fonctions

$$\Phi(x)\int_{z_0}^{z_1} \frac{dz}{x-z}, \quad \Phi(x)\int_{z_0}^{z_2} \frac{dz}{x-z}, \quad \ldots, \quad \Phi(x)\int_{z_0}^{z_n} \frac{dz}{x-z}$$

ne contiennent aucune des puissances

$$\frac{1}{x}, \quad \frac{1}{x^2}, \quad \ldots, \quad \frac{1}{x^m}.$$

Et si l'on désigne les parties entières de ces produits qui sont de degré $mn - 1$, par

$$\Phi_1(x), \quad \Phi_2(x), \quad \ldots, \quad \Phi_n(x),$$

on atteint précisément, mais sans la dépasser, l'approximation que nous avions obtenue pour les quantités

$$\Phi(x)\int_{z_0}^{z_i} \frac{dz}{x-z} - \Phi_i(x),$$

dont les développements commencent par un terme en

$$\frac{1}{x^{m+1}};$$

on voit donc que cette approximation est bien en effet de l'ordre le plus élevé possible, en supposant

$$\Phi(x) = \frac{d^m f^m(x)}{dx^m}.$$

J'achèverai enfin de mettre en évidence le lien de l'équation différentielle avec ce nouveau mode d'approximation des fonctions, en établissant que $\Phi(x)$ en est une solution, et ce sera aussi en un point essentiel compléter son analogie avec le polynome X_n de *Legendre*. Remarquons à cet effet que, rien ne spécifiant, à l'égard de l'intégrale

$$\int_{z_0}^{Z} \frac{f^m(z)\,dz}{(x-z)^{m+1}},$$

le chemin suivi par la variable entre les limites z_0, Z, on est maître d'introduire dans une des solutions, telle que

$$\Phi(x)\int_{z_0}^{z_1} \frac{dz}{x-z} - \Phi_1(x),$$

les déterminations multiples du logarithme. Or on obtient de nouvelles solutions, dont se tire immédiatement, par différence, le polynome $\Phi(x)$.

Des résultats semblables aux précédents s'offrent dans des circonstances un peu moins simples, lorsqu'on fait la supposition suivante :

$$\mu_0 = \mu_1 = \ldots = \mu_n = m + \frac{1}{2}$$

et

$$p = m + n + 1,$$

m étant encore un nombre entier positif. L'équation différentielle est alors

$$f(x)\frac{d^{n+1}y}{dx^{n+1}} + \left(n + \frac{1}{2}\right)f'(x)\frac{d^n y}{dx^n} - \frac{1}{2}(m+n)(m-n)f''(x)\frac{d^{n-1}y}{dx^{n-1}}$$
$$- \frac{1}{2.3}(m+n)(m+n-1)\left(2m - n + \frac{3}{2}\right)f'''(x)\frac{d^{n-2}y}{dx^{n-2}} - \ldots = 0,$$

et elle admet pour solutions les intégrales

$$\int_{z_0}^{Z} \frac{f^{m-\frac{1}{2}}(z)}{(x-z)^{m+1}}\,dz,$$

qui, en opérant comme plus haut, se ramènent à la forme

$$y = \int_{z_0}^{Z} \frac{d^m f^{m-\frac{1}{2}}(z)}{dz^m}\,\frac{dz}{x-z}.$$

Posons

$$\frac{d^m f^{m-\frac{1}{2}}(z)}{dz^m} = \frac{\Phi(z)}{\sqrt{f(z)}},$$

de sorte que $\Phi(z)$ soit un polynome entier de degré mn; la relation suivante

$$y = \int_{z_0}^{Z} \frac{\Phi(z)}{(x-z)\sqrt{f(z)}} = \Phi(x)\int_{z_0}^{Z} \frac{dz}{(x-z)\sqrt{f(z)}} - \int_{z_0}^{Z} \frac{\Phi(x)-\Phi(z)}{x-z}\,\frac{dz}{\sqrt{f(z)}}$$

met en évidence les intégrales hyperelliptiques

$$\int_{z_0}^{Z} \frac{dz}{(x-z)\sqrt{f(z)}} \quad \text{et} \quad \int_{z_0}^{Z} \frac{\Phi(x)-\Phi(z)}{x-z}\,\frac{dz}{\sqrt{f(z)}},$$

que je vais exprimer par leurs éléments simples.

A cet effet et en considérant d'abord la première, soit

$$f(z) = A_0 z^{n+1} + A_1 z^n + \ldots + A_{n+1};$$

posons ensuite pour abréger

$$\lambda_k(z) = (2k+1-n)A_0 z^k + (2k-n)A_1 z^{k-1}$$
$$+ (2k-1-n)A_2 z^{k-2} + \ldots + (k+1-n)A_k$$

et

$$[Z]_i = \frac{1}{2}\int_{z_0}^{Z} \frac{z^i\,dz}{\sqrt{f(z)}};$$

on aura, comme conséquence du théorème sur l'échange de l'argument et du paramètre,

$$\int_{z_0}^{Z} \frac{\sqrt{f(x)}\,dz}{(x-z)\sqrt{f(z)}}$$
$$= [Z]_{n-1}\int_{z_0}^{x} \frac{\lambda_0\,dx}{\sqrt{f(x)}} + [Z]_{n-2}\int_{z_0}^{x} \frac{\lambda_1(x)\,dx}{\sqrt{f(x)}} + \ldots + [Z]_0\int_{z_0}^{x} \frac{\lambda_{n-1}(x)\,dx}{\sqrt{f(x)}}.$$

Quant à la seconde, où figure le polynome entier

$$\frac{\Phi(x)-\Phi(z)}{x-z},$$

elle se ramène au moyen des réductions élémentaires connues à une combinaison linéaire de

$$[Z]_0,\quad [Z]_1,\quad \ldots,\quad [Z]_{n-1},$$

et sera par conséquent de cette forme

$$\int_{z_0}^{Z} \frac{\Phi(x)-\Phi(z)}{x-z}\,\frac{dz}{\sqrt{f(z)}} = [Z]_{n-1}\,\Phi_1(x) + [Z]_{n-2}\,\Phi_2(x) + \ldots + [Z]_0\,\Phi_n(x),$$

$\Phi_1(x)$, $\Phi_2(x)$, ..., $\Phi_n(x)$ étant des polynomes entiers en x de degré $mn - 1$. Ces résultats donnent la transformation cherchée

$$\begin{aligned}\int_{z_0}^{Z} \frac{\Phi(z)\,dz}{(x-z)\sqrt{f(z)}} = {} & [Z]_{n-1}\left[\frac{\Phi(x)}{\sqrt{f(x)}}\int_{z_0}^{x} \frac{\lambda_0\,dx}{\sqrt{f(x)}} - \Phi_1(x)\right] \\ & + [Z]_{n-2}\left[\frac{\Phi(x)}{\sqrt{f(x)}}\int_{z_0}^{x} \frac{\lambda_1(x)\,dx}{\sqrt{f(x)}} - \Phi_2(x)\right] \\ & \ldots\ldots\ldots\ldots\ldots\ldots\ldots\ldots\ldots\ldots \\ & + [Z]_0\left[\frac{\Phi(x)}{\sqrt{f(x)}}\int_{z_0}^{x} \frac{\lambda_{n-1}(x)\,dx}{\sqrt{f(x)}} - \Phi_n(x)\right],\end{aligned}$$

dont voici les conséquences :

Remarquons d'abord que le premier membre conduit, comme on le voit, si l'on revient à l'expression

$$\int_{z_0}^{Z} \frac{f^{m-\frac{1}{2}}(z)\,dz}{(x-z)^{m+1}},$$

à un développement suivant les puissances décroissantes de x, commençant par le terme

$$\frac{1}{x^{m+1}}.$$

Supposons ensuite successivement

$$Z = z_1, \quad Z = z_2, \quad \ldots, \quad Z = z_n,$$

en observant à l'égard des relations ainsi obtenues, que le déterminant

$$\begin{vmatrix} [z_1]_0 & [z_1]_1 & \ldots & [z_1]_{n-1} \\ [z_2]_0 & [z_2]_1 & \ldots & [z_2]_{n-1} \\ \ldots & \ldots & \ldots & \ldots \\ [z_n]_0 & [z_n]_1 & \ldots & [z_n]_{n-1} \end{vmatrix}$$

n'est point nul; on en conclut que le développement des n fonctions

$$y_1 = \frac{\Phi(x)}{\sqrt{f(x)}} \int_{z_0}^{x} \frac{\lambda_0\, dx}{\sqrt{f(x)}} - \Phi_1(x),$$

$$y_2 = \frac{\Phi(x)}{\sqrt{f(x)}} \int_{z_0}^{x} \frac{\lambda_1(x)\, dx}{\sqrt{f(x)}} - \Phi_2(x),$$

$$\ldots\ldots\ldots\ldots\ldots\ldots\ldots\ldots,$$

$$y_n = \frac{\Phi(x)}{\sqrt{f(x)}} \int_{z_0}^{x} \frac{\lambda_{n-1}(x)\, dx}{\sqrt{f(x)}} - \Phi_n(x),$$

commence de même par le terme $\frac{1}{x^{m+1}}$. C'est exactement à l'égard des transcendantes

$$\frac{1}{\sqrt{f(x)}} \int_{z_0}^{x} \frac{\lambda_k(x)}{\sqrt{f(x)}}\, dx$$

le résultat obtenu par la quantité $\log \frac{x - z_0}{x - z_k}$, et il en résulte que les intégrales hyperelliptiques

$$\int_{z_0}^{x} \frac{\lambda_0\, dx}{\sqrt{f(x)}}, \quad \int_{z_0}^{x} \frac{\lambda_1(x)\, dx}{\sqrt{f(x)}}, \quad \ldots, \quad \int_{z_0}^{x} \frac{\lambda_{n-1}(x)\, dx}{\sqrt{f(x)}}$$

sont représentées par les expressions

$$\frac{\Phi_1(x)}{\Phi(x)} \sqrt{f(x)}, \quad \frac{\Phi_2(x)}{\Phi(x)} \sqrt{f(x)}, \quad \ldots, \quad \frac{\Phi_n(x)}{\Phi(x)} \sqrt{f(x)}$$

aux quantités près de l'ordre

$$\frac{1}{x^{\left(m-\frac{1}{2}\right)(n+1)+1}}.$$

Relativement à l'équation différentielle, je remarque enfin que les solutions données en premier lieu par les quantités

$$\int_{z_0}^{Z} \frac{f^{m-\frac{1}{2}}(z)\,dz}{(x-z)^{m+1}}$$

ont été mises ensuite sous la forme

$$y_k = \frac{\Phi(x)}{\sqrt{f(x)}} \int_{z_0}^{x} \frac{\lambda_{k-1}(x)\,dx}{\sqrt{f(x)}} - \Phi_k(x),$$

où il est permis d'introduire les déterminations multiples de l'intégrale

$$\int_{z_0}^{x} \frac{\lambda_{k-1}(x)\,dx}{\sqrt{f(x)}};$$

et cette considération, précédemment employée, conduit à la nouvelle solution purement algébrique

$$\frac{\Phi(x)}{\sqrt{f(x)}}, \qquad \text{ou, si l'on veut,} \qquad \frac{d^m f^{m-\frac{1}{2}}(x)}{dx^m}.$$

En rencontrant ainsi, comme un élément nécessaire de l'intégration de certaines équations linéaires, ces approximations des fonctions par des fractions rationnelles analogues aux réduites de la théorie des fractions continues, j'ai dû songer à chercher à leur égard un algorithme semblable à la loi de formation de ces réduites. Mais avant de m'engager dans cette voie, et pour m'éclairer sur la question, je me suis proposé, dans le cas de ces équations, à savoir

$$(x^2-1)\frac{d^2y}{dx^2} + 2x\frac{dy}{dx} - m(m+1)y = 0,$$

$$(x^2-1)\frac{d^2y}{dx^2} + 3x\frac{dy}{dx} - (m^2-1)y = 0,$$

de tirer directement, des intégrales définies qui y satisfont, les relations propres aux fonctions X_m dans le premier cas, et aux quantités $\frac{\sin m(\arccos x)}{\sqrt{1-x^2}}$ dans le second. Pour plus de généralité, je remplacerai ces équations par les suivantes :

$$f(x)\frac{d^2y}{dx^2}+f'(x)\frac{dy}{dx}-\frac{1}{2}m(m+1)f''(x)y=0,$$

$$f(x)\frac{d^2y}{dx^2}+\frac{3}{2}f'(x)\frac{dy}{dx}-\frac{1}{2}(m^2-1)f''(x)y=0,$$

où je suppose

$$f(x)=(x-a)(x-b),$$

de sorte que les solutions seront

$$y=\int_a^b\frac{f^m(z)}{(x-z)^{m+1}}dz,\qquad y=\int_a^b\frac{f^{m-\frac{1}{2}}(z)}{(x-z)^{m+1}}dz.$$

Cela posé, je pars de ces identités faciles à former :

$$\begin{aligned}\frac{d}{dz}\left[\frac{f(z)}{x-z}\right]^{m+1}&=-2(m+1)\left[\frac{f(z)}{x-z}\right]^m\\&\quad+(m+1)(2x-a-b)\frac{f^m(z)}{(x-z)^{m+1}}+(m+1)\frac{f^{m+1}(z)}{(x-z)^{m+2}},\\\frac{d}{dz}\left[\frac{f^m(z)f'(z)}{(x-z)^m}\right]&=2(m+1)\left[\frac{f(z)}{x-z}\right]^m\\&\quad+m(a-b)^2\frac{f^{m-1}(z)}{(x-z)^m}+m(2x-a-b)\frac{f^m(z)}{(x-z)^{m+1}},\end{aligned}$$

et je les ajoute membre à membre afin d'éliminer le terme $\left(\frac{f(z)}{x-z}\right)^m$. Il vient ainsi

$$\begin{aligned}&\frac{d}{dz}\left[\frac{f(z)+(x-z)f'(z)}{(x-z)^{m+1}}\right]f^m(z)\\&\quad=m(a-b)^2\frac{f^{m-1}(z)}{(x-z)^m}\\&\qquad+(2m+1)(2x-a-b)\frac{f^m(z)}{(x-z)^{m+1}}+(m+1)\frac{f^{m+1}(z)}{(x-z)^{m+2}}.\end{aligned}$$

En intégrant entre les limites $z=a$, $z=b$ et posant

$$\frac{1}{2^m}\int_a^b\frac{f^m(z)}{(x-z)^{m+1}}dz=(-1)^m u_m,$$

on en tire la relation

$$(m+1)u_{m+1} = \left(m+\frac{1}{2}\right)(2x-a-b)u_m - \frac{1}{4}m(a-b)^2 u_{m-1}.$$

C'est bien le résultat connu lorsqu'on suppose

$$f(x) = x^2 - 1,$$

pour le polynome de *Legendre;* mais on voit de plus qu'en faisant

$$u_m = X_m \log\frac{x+1}{x-1} - P_m,$$

elle se partage en deux et que P_m, comme l'a trouvé M. *Christoffel*, satisfait à la même équation.

Je considérerai en second lieu les identités suivantes :

$$\frac{d}{dz}\left[\frac{f^{m+\frac{1}{2}}(z)}{(x-z)^{m+1}}\right] = -(2m+1)\frac{f^{m-\frac{1}{2}}(z)}{(x-z)^m}$$
$$+\left(m+\frac{1}{2}\right)(2x-a-b)\frac{f^{m-\frac{1}{2}}(z)}{(x-z)^{m+1}} + (m+1)\frac{f^{m+\frac{1}{2}}(z)}{(x-z)^{m+2}},$$

$$\frac{d}{dz}\left[\frac{f^{m-\frac{1}{2}}(z)f'(z)}{(x-z)^m}\right] = 2m\frac{f^{m-\frac{1}{2}}(z)}{(x-z)^m}$$
$$+m(2x-a-b)\frac{f^{m-\frac{1}{2}}(z)}{(x-z)^{m+1}} + \left(m-\frac{1}{2}\right)(a-b)^2\frac{f^{m-\frac{3}{2}}(z)}{(x-z)^m}.$$

L'élimination de $\dfrac{f^{m-\frac{1}{2}}(z)}{(x-z)^m}$ donne

$$\frac{d}{dz}\left[\frac{\left(m+\frac{1}{2}\right)f^{m-\frac{1}{2}}(z)f'(z)}{(x-z)^m} + m\frac{f^{m+\frac{1}{2}}(z)}{(x-z)^{m+1}}\right] = \frac{d^2}{dz^2}\left[\frac{f^{m-\frac{1}{2}}(z)}{(x-z)^m}\right]$$
$$= (a-b)^2\left(m^2-\frac{1}{4}\right)\frac{f^{m-\frac{3}{2}}(z)}{(x-z)^m}$$
$$+m(2m+1)(2x-a-b)\frac{f^{m-\frac{1}{2}}(z)}{(x-z)^{m+1}} + m(m+1)\frac{f^{m+\frac{1}{2}}(z)}{(x-z)^{m+2}}.$$

Intégrons de nouveau de $z=a$ à $z=b$; on en déduit, en

posant

$$\frac{1.2\ldots m}{1.3.5\ldots 2m-1}\int_a^b \frac{f^{m-\frac{1}{2}}(z)\,dz}{(x-z)^{m+1}} = (-1)^m v_m,$$

$$v_{m+1} = (2x-a-b)v_m - \frac{1}{4}(a-b)^2 v_{m-1},$$

d'où encore un résultat connu dans le cas de

$$f(z) = z^2 - 1.$$

Je viens maintenant au cas général, en me posant cette question : trouver un algorithme qui permette de calculer de proche en proche les termes de cette série

$$\int_{z_0}^{Z} \frac{\mathfrak{f}(z)\,dz}{(x-z)^{m+1}},\quad \int_{z_0}^{Z} \frac{\mathfrak{f}(z)\,f(z)\,dz}{(x-z)^{m+2}},\quad \ldots,\quad \int_{z_0}^{Z} \frac{\mathfrak{f}(z)\,f^k(z)\,dz}{(x-z)^{m+k+1}},$$

où je suppose

$$\mathfrak{f}(z) = (z-z_0)^{\mu_0-1}(z-z_1)^{\mu_1-1}\ldots(z-z_n)^{\mu_n-1},$$
$$f(z) = (z-z_0)(z-z_1)\ldots(z-z_n).$$

Soit pour abréger

$$F(z) = \mathfrak{f}(z)\,f^k(z) = (z-z_0)^{\nu_0}(z-z_1)^{\nu_1}\ldots(z-z_n)^{\nu_n}$$

et

$$m+k = p,$$

de sorte que le terme général devienne

$$\int_{z_0}^{Z} \frac{F(z)\,dz}{(x-z)^{p+1}};$$

je remarquerai qu'en intégrant entre les limites $z = z_0$ et $z = Z$ les deux membres de cette identité

$$\frac{d}{dz}\left[\frac{F(z)}{(x-z)^p}\right] = \frac{p\,F(z)}{(x-z)^{p+1}} + \frac{F'(z)}{(x-z)^p}$$

on en conclut

$$\int_{z_0}^{Z} \frac{F(z)\,dz}{(x-z)^{p+1}} = -\frac{1}{p}\int_{z_0}^{Z} \frac{F'(z)\,dz}{(x-z)^p},$$

et, par suite, d'après la formule

$$\frac{F'(z)}{F(z)} = \frac{\nu_0}{z - z_0} + \frac{\nu_1}{z - z_1} + \ldots + \frac{\nu_n}{z - z_n},$$

$$\int_{z_0}^{Z} \frac{F(z)\,dz}{(x-z)^{p+1}} = -\frac{\nu_0}{p}\int_{z_0}^{Z} \frac{F(x)}{z - z_0}\,\frac{dz}{(x-z)^p}$$

$$- \frac{\nu_1}{p}\int_{z_0}^{Z} \frac{F(z)}{z - z_1}\,\frac{dz}{(x-z)^p} - \ldots - \frac{\nu_n}{p}\int_{z_0}^{Z} \frac{F(z)}{z - z_n}\,\frac{dz}{(x-z)^p}.$$

De cette manière l'intégrale proposée est décomposée en $n+1$ autres qu'on peut représenter par

$$\int_{z_0}^{Z} \frac{F(z)}{z - \zeta}\,\frac{dz}{(x-z)^p},$$

ζ désignant successivement les racines z_0, z_1, ..., z_n, et il en sera de même de celle-ci

$$\int_{z_0}^{Z} \frac{F(z)\,f(z)\,dz}{(x-z)^{p+1}},$$

qui est le terme suivant dans la série, et qui aura pour éléments les quantités

$$\int_{z_0}^{Z} \frac{F(z)\,f(z)}{z - \zeta}\,\frac{dz}{(x-z)^{p+1}}.$$

Or ce sont les éléments ainsi définis qui donnent lieu à un système de relations récurrentes, faciles à obtenir, comme vous allez voir, en suivant, sans y rien changer en quelque sorte, la méthode que j'ai appliquée aux intégrales

$$\int_{z}^{Z} e^{-z}\,F(z)\,dz.$$

[*Sur la fonction exponentielle* (*Comptes rendus*, 1873).]

Effectivement il suffira de démontrer qu'on peut toujours satisfaire à la relation suivante

$$\int \frac{F(z)\,f(z)}{z - \zeta}\,\frac{dz}{(x-z)^{p+1}} = \int \frac{\Theta_1(z)}{f(z)}\,\frac{F(z)\,dz}{(x-z)^p} - \frac{\Theta(z)\,F(z)}{(x-z)^p},$$

en prenant pour $\Theta(z)$ et $\Theta_1(z)$ deux polynomes entiers du degré n, et c'est ce qu'on reconnaît sur-le-champ; car la différentiation donne, après avoir multiplié par $\frac{f(z)}{F(z)}$,

$$\frac{f^2(z)}{z-\zeta} = (x-z)\Theta_1(z) - p\,\Theta(z)\,f(z)$$
$$-(x-z)\left[\Theta'(z)\,f(z) + \Theta(z)\frac{F'(z)\,f(z)}{F(z)}\right],$$

et l'on a précisément le nombre voulu de $2n+2$ constantes arbitraires, pour identifier les deux membres, qui sont des polynomes entiers de degré $2n+1$. Ce point établi, j'observe qu'en supposant

$$z = z_i$$

on obtient

$$\Theta_1(z_i) = \nu_i\,f(z_i)\,\Theta(z_i),$$

et que par suite $\Theta_1(z)$ se déduira de $\Theta(z)$, qui restera seul à déterminer au moyen de la formule

$$\Theta_1(z) = \nu_0\,\Theta(z_0)\frac{f(z)}{z-z_0} + \nu_1\,\Theta(z_1)\frac{f(z)}{z-z_1} + \ldots + \nu_n\,\Theta(z_n)\frac{f(z)}{z-z_n}.$$

Pour obtenir maintenant $\Theta(z)$, après avoir déduit de la relation ci-dessus proposée la condition

$$\Theta(x) = -\frac{1}{p}\,\frac{f(x)}{x-\zeta},$$

je l'écrirai comme il suit

$$\frac{f(z)}{(z-\zeta)(x-z)} = \frac{\Theta_1(z)}{f(z)} - \Theta(z)\left[\frac{p}{x-z} + \frac{F'(z)}{F(z)}\right] - \Theta'(z),$$

et de cette forme nouvelle, je conclurai en remarquant que la fraction $\frac{\Theta_1(z)}{f(z)}$ n'a pas de partie entière, que le polynome cherché doit être tel que les parties entières de ces deux expressions

$$\Theta(z)\left[\frac{p}{x-z} + \frac{F'(z)}{F(z)}\right] + \Theta'(z)$$

et

$$\frac{f(z)}{(z-\zeta)(z-x)}$$

coïncident. Soit donc pour en faire le calcul

$$\frac{p}{x-z} + \frac{F'(z)}{F(z)} = \frac{s_0}{z} + \frac{s_1}{z^2} + \frac{s_2}{z^3} + \ldots$$

en posant

$$\Theta(z) = \alpha_0 z^n + \alpha_1 z^{n-1} + \ldots + \alpha_n;$$

nous aurons d'abord

$$\Theta(z)\left[\frac{p}{x-z} + \frac{F'(z)}{F(z)}\right] = \alpha_0 s_0 z^{n-1} + \left.\begin{array}{l}\alpha_1 s_0 \\ + \alpha_0 s_1\end{array}\right| z^{n-2} + \left.\begin{array}{l}\alpha_2 s_0 \\ + \alpha_1 s_1 \\ + \alpha_0 s_2\end{array}\right| z^{n-3} + \ldots$$

Soit ensuite

$$\frac{f(z)}{(z-\zeta)(z-x)} = z^{n-1} + p_1 z^{n-2} + p_2 z^{n-3} + \ldots + p_{n-1},$$

et nous obtiendrons les équations suivantes, au nombre de n, à savoir :

$$\begin{aligned}
1 &= \alpha_0(s_0 + n), \\
p_1 &= \alpha_1(s_0 + n - 1) + \alpha_0 s_1, \\
p_2 &= \alpha_2(s_0 + n - 2) + \alpha_1 s_1 + \alpha_0 s_2, \\
&\ldots\ldots\ldots\ldots\ldots\ldots\ldots\ldots\ldots, \\
p_{n-1} &= \alpha_{n-1}(s_0 + 1) + \alpha_{n-2} s_1 + \ldots + \alpha_0 s_{n-2}.
\end{aligned}$$

Elles déterminent de proche les coefficients $\alpha_0, \alpha_1, \alpha_2, \ldots, \alpha_{n-1}$, et quant à α_n, qui seul reste à obtenir, c'est la condition précédemment remarquée

$$\Theta(x) = -\frac{1}{p}\frac{f(x)}{x-\zeta},$$

qui en donne la valeur. Revenant maintenant à la relation

$$\int \frac{F(z) f(z)}{z-\zeta} \frac{dz}{(x-z)^{p+1}} = \int \frac{\Theta_1(z)}{f(z)} \frac{F(z)\,dz}{(x-z)^p} - \frac{\Theta(z) F(z)}{(x-z)^p},$$

nous en déduirons d'abord

$$\int_{z_0}^{Z} \frac{F(z) f(z)}{z-\zeta} \frac{dz}{(x-z)^{p+1}} = \int_{z_0}^{Z} \frac{\Theta_1(z)}{f(z)} \frac{F(z)\,dz}{(x-z)^p},$$

puis, en décomposant $\frac{\Theta_1(z)}{f(z)}$ en fractions simples,

$$\begin{aligned}
\int_{z_0}^{Z} \frac{F(z) f(z)}{z-\zeta} \frac{dz}{(x-z)^{p+1}} = {} & \frac{\Theta_1(z_0)}{f'(z_0)} \int_{z_0}^{Z} \frac{F(z)}{z-z_0} \frac{dz}{(x-z)^p} \\
& + \frac{\Theta_1(z_1)}{f'(z_1)} \int_{z_0}^{Z} \frac{F(z)}{z-z_1} \frac{dz}{(x-z)^p} \\
& + \ldots\ldots\ldots\ldots\ldots\ldots\ldots\ldots \\
& + \frac{\Theta_1(z_n)}{f'(z_n)} \int_{z_0}^{Z} \frac{F(z)}{z-z_n} \frac{dz}{(x-z)^p}.
\end{aligned}$$

Mais on a

$$\vartheta_1(z_i) = \nu_i f'(z_i)\Theta(z_i),$$

et si l'on écrit $\Theta(x, \zeta)$ au lieu de $\Theta(z)$ afin de mettre en évidence ζ, qui entre, comme il est aisé de voir, au premier degré dans α_1, au second dans α_2, et ainsi de suite, nous obtiendrons sous forme entièrement explicite

$$\begin{aligned}\int_{z_0}^{Z} \frac{F(z)f(z)}{z-\zeta}\,\frac{dz}{(x-z)^{p+1}} = \;& \nu_0\,\Theta(z_0, \zeta)\int_{z_0}^{Z} \frac{F(z)}{z-z_0}\,\frac{dz}{(x-z)^p} \\ &+ \nu_1\,\Theta(z_1, \zeta)\int_{z_0}^{Z} \frac{F(z)}{z-z_1}\,\frac{dz}{(x-z)^p} \\ &+ \ldots\ldots\ldots\ldots\ldots\ldots \\ &+ \nu_n\,\Theta(z_n, \zeta)\int_{z_0}^{Z} \frac{F(z)}{z-z_n}\,\frac{dz}{(x-z)^p}.\end{aligned}$$

Je ne ferai point, pour abréger, d'applications de ce résultat; j'observerai seulement qu'en considérant l'intégrale

$$\int_{z_0}^{Z} \frac{f^m(z)}{(x-z)^{m+1}}\,dz,$$

on obtiendra, pour les éléments de décomposition, l'expression suivante :

$$\int_{z_0}^{Z} \frac{f^m(z)}{z-\zeta}\,\frac{dz}{(x-z)^m} = \frac{f(x)}{x-\zeta}\,\Pi(x)\int_{z_0}^{Z} \frac{dz}{x-z} - \Pi_1(x),$$

$\Pi(x)$ et $\Pi_1(x)$ étant des polynomes entiers. On voit ainsi que le développement de l'intégrale suivant les puissances décroissantes de la variable commence par un terme en $\frac{1}{x^m}$, et il est facile de reconnaître que c'est l'ordre le plus élevé qu'on puisse obtenir pour un degré donné de $\Pi(x)$. Quant au facteur

$$\frac{f(x)}{x-\zeta},$$

il se trouve amené par la relation

$$\frac{d^{m-1}}{dx^{m-1}}\left[\frac{f^m(x)}{x-\zeta}\right] = \frac{f(x)}{x-\zeta}\Pi(x),$$

qui définit $\Pi(x)$ à un facteur constant près ([1]).

Les Sables-d'Olonne, 10 octobre 1874.

([1]) La lettre d'Hermite se termine par quelques remarques sur l'intégrale

$$\int_x^\infty \frac{(z-x)^m\,dz}{f^{m+1}(z)}.$$

Nous ne les reproduirons pas, car les résultats ne nous ont pas paru exacts.

E. P.

EXTRAIT

D'UNE

LETTRE DE M. CH. HERMITE A M. BORCHARDT

SUR

LES NOMBRES DE BERNOULLI.

Journal de Crelle, t. 81, 1876, p. 93-95.

... M. Clausen et M. Staudt ont découvert en même temps sur les nombres de Bernoulli une proposition extrêmement remarquable, qui donne pour B_n cette expression

$$(-1)^n B_n = A_n + \frac{1}{2} + \frac{1}{\alpha} + \frac{1}{\beta} + \ldots + \frac{1}{\lambda},$$

dans laquelle, A_n étant entier, les dénominateurs des fractions sont tous des nombres premiers tels que $\frac{\alpha-1}{2}$, $\frac{\beta-1}{2}$, ..., $\frac{\lambda-1}{2}$ soient diviseurs de n. Ce beau théorème dont M. Staudt a donné la démonstration dans le Tome XXI, page 372 de ce journal (*Beweis eines Lehrsatzes, die Bernoullischen Zahlen betreffend*), conduit à rechercher directement les nombres entiers A_n, au moyen des relations qui servent au calcul des nombres de Bernoulli. Employant à cet effet l'équation

$$(2n+1)_2 B_1 - (2n+1)_4 B_2 \\ + (2n+1)_6 B_3 - \ldots + (-1)^{n-1}(2n+1)_{2n} B_n = n - \frac{1}{2},$$

où $(2n+1)_2$, $(2n+1)_4$, ... désignent les coefficients de x^2, x^4, ... dans le développement de la puissance $(1+x)^{2n+1}$, on en tire d'abord, en substituant les expressions de B_1, B_2, B_3, ...,

$$\begin{aligned}&(2n+1)_2\left(A_1+\frac{1}{2}+\frac{1}{3}\right)\\&+(2n+1)_4\left(A_2+\frac{1}{2}+\frac{1}{3}+\frac{1}{5}\right)\\&+(2n+1)_6\left(A_3+\frac{1}{2}+\frac{1}{3}+\frac{1}{7}\right)\\&\ldots\ldots\ldots\ldots\ldots\ldots\ldots\ldots\\&+(2n+1)_{2n}\left(A_n+\frac{1}{2}+\frac{1}{\alpha}+\frac{1}{\beta}+\ldots+\frac{1}{\lambda}\right)\\&+n-\frac{1}{2}=0.\end{aligned}$$

Cela posé, les termes contenant en facteur $\frac{1}{2}$ sont

$$\frac{1}{2}[(2n+1)_2+(2n+1)_4+\ldots+(2n+1)_{2n}-1],$$

et comme on a

$$(2n+1)_2+(2n+1)_4+\ldots+(2n+1)_{2n}=2^{2n}-1,$$

ils se réduisent au nombre entier $2^{2n-1}-1$. Mais considérons, en général, ceux qui sont affectés du facteur $\frac{1}{p}$; ils proviennent des nombres de Bernoulli dont l'indice est un multiple de $\frac{1}{2}(p-1)$, et donnent cette somme

$$S_p=\frac{1}{p}[(2n+1)_{p-1}+(2n+1)_{2p-2}+(2n+1)_{3p-3}+\ldots]$$

que je vais montrer être aussi un nombre entier.

J'observe pour cela que, en désignant par ω les diverses racines de l'équation $x^{p-1}=1$, la somme $\sum(1+\omega)^{2n+1}$ a pour valeur

$$(p-1)[1+(2n+1)_{p-1}+(2n+1)_{2p-2}+(2n+1)_{3p-3}+\ldots].$$

Or, les racines ω, prises suivant le module premier p, sont les nombres entiers

$$1,\quad 2,\quad 3,\quad \ldots,\quad p-1;$$

les quantités $1+\omega$ seront donc

$$2,\quad 3,\quad 4,\quad \ldots,\quad p-1,\quad 0;$$

il en résulte que $\sum(1+\omega)^{2n+1}$ est, en lui ajoutant l'unité, la somme des puissances $2n+1$ des nombres $1, 2, \ldots, p-1$, qui est un multiple de p, attendu que l'exposant $2n+1$ n'est pas divisible par le nombre pair $p-1$. Ayant ainsi

$$\sum(1+\omega)^{2n+1}+1 \equiv 0 \pmod{p},$$

on voit immédiatement que S_p se réduit bien à un nombre entier et nous obtenons pour le calcul direct des nombres A_n la relation suivante :

$$\begin{aligned}(2n+1)_2 A_1 + (2n+1)_4 A_2 + \ldots + (2n+1)_{2n} A_n \\ = 1 - n - 2^{2n-1} - S_3 - S_5 - \ldots - S_p\end{aligned}$$

où les quantités S_3, S_5, ..., S_p se rapportent à tous les nombres premiers jusqu'à $2n+1$.

Soit, par exemple, $n=4$, les nombres premiers jusqu'à 9 étant 3, 5, 7, on aura

$$S_3 = \frac{1}{3}(36+126+84+9) = 85,$$

$$S_5 = \frac{1}{5}(126+9) = 27,$$

$$S_7 = \frac{1}{7}84 = 12,$$

et, par conséquent,

$$36A_1 + 126A_2 + 84A_3 + 9A_4 = -255,$$

ou, en supprimant le facteur 3 commun aux deux membres,

$$12A_1 + 42A_2 + 28A_3 + 3A_4 = -85.$$

Pour $n = 1, 2, 3$, nous trouverions successivement

$$\begin{aligned} A_1 &= -1, \\ 2A_1 + A_2 &= -3, \\ 3A_1 + 5A_2 + A_3 &= -9, \end{aligned}$$

et ces équations donnent facilement les valeurs

$$A_1 = A_2 = A_3 = A_4 = -1;$$

d'où

$$B_1 = 1 - \frac{1}{2} - \frac{1}{3} = \frac{1}{6},$$
$$B_2 = -1 + \frac{1}{2} + \frac{1}{3} + \frac{1}{5} = \frac{1}{30},$$
$$B_3 = 1 - \frac{1}{2} - \frac{1}{3} - \frac{1}{7} = \frac{1}{42},$$
$$B_4 = -1 + \frac{1}{2} + \frac{1}{3} + \frac{1}{5} = \frac{1}{30}.$$

On aura ensuite

$$B_5 = 1 - \frac{1}{2} - \frac{1}{3} - \frac{1}{11} = \frac{5}{66},$$
$$B_6 = -1 + \frac{1}{2} + \frac{1}{3} + \frac{1}{5} + \frac{1}{7} + \frac{1}{13} = \frac{691}{2730},$$
$$B_7 = 2 - \frac{1}{2} - \frac{1}{3} = \frac{7}{6},$$
$$B_8 = 6 + \frac{1}{2} + \frac{1}{3} + \frac{1}{5} + \frac{1}{17} = \frac{3617}{510},$$
$$B_9 = 56 - \frac{1}{2} - \frac{1}{3} - \frac{1}{7} - \frac{1}{19} = \frac{43867}{798},$$
$$\dots\dots\dots\dots\dots\dots\dots\dots\dots\dots\dots\dots$$

Vous remarquerez cette nouvelle fonction numérique attachée au nombre impair $2n+1$

$$S_3 + S_5 + \ldots + S_p,$$

à laquelle conduit le théorème de M. Clausen et de M. Staudt; elle vient se joindre à toutes celles dont la théorie des fonctions elliptiques a donné l'origine et les propriétés et peut être généralisée en substituant à S_p la somme suivante :

$$\mathfrak{S}_p = \frac{x^{2n+1}}{p}\left[\frac{(2n+1)_{p-1}}{x^{p-1}} + \frac{(2n+1)_{2p-2}}{x^{2p-2}} + \frac{(2n+1)_{3p-3}}{x^{3p-3}} + \ldots\right]$$

qui coïncide avec S_p pour $x = 1$. On démontre, en effet, comme plus haut, que $\mathfrak{S}_p$ est un nombre entier pour toute valeur entière de x, p étant un nombre premier quelconque, non supérieur à $2n+1$.

LETTRE DE M. CH. HERMITE A M. BORCHARDT

SUR LA

FONCTION DE JACOB BERNOULLI.

Journal de Crelle, t. 79, 1875, p. 339-344.

Je viens au sujet d'un Mémoire de M. Raabe, sur la fonction de Jacob Bernoulli (t. XLII de ce Journal, p. 348) vous présenter quelques remarques. Soient $B''(x)$ et $B'(x)$ les coefficients de $\frac{\lambda^{2m}}{1.2\ldots 2m}$ et $\frac{\lambda^{2m+1}}{1.2\ldots 2m+1}$ dans le développement suivant les puissances croissantes de λ de la fonction $\frac{e^{\lambda x}-1}{e^{\lambda}-1}$, de sorte que l'on ait

$$B''(x) = \frac{x^{2m+1}}{2m+1} - \frac{1}{2}x^{2m} + \frac{1}{2}(2m)_1 B_1 x^{2m-1} - \frac{1}{4}(2m)_3 B_2 x^{2m-3} + \ldots,$$

$$B'(x) = \frac{x^{2m+2}}{2m+2} - \frac{1}{2}x^{2m+1} + \frac{1}{2}(2m+1)_1 B_1 x^{2m} - \frac{1}{4}(2m+1)_3 B_2 x^{2m-2} + \ldots.$$

L'éminent géomètre donne parmi beaucoup de résultats entièrement nouveaux et d'un grand intérêt, cette expression sous forme d'intégrale définie de $B''(x)$, à savoir

$$(-1)^{m+1}(2\pi)^{2m+1} B''(x) = \sin 2\pi x \int_{-\infty}^{+\infty} \frac{u^{2m}\,du}{e^u + e^{-u} - 2\cos 2\pi x}.$$

Peut-être n'est-il pas inutile de remarquer que la proposition importante démontrée par M. Malmsten (sur la formule

$$hu'_x = \Delta u_x - \frac{1}{2}h\Delta u'_x + \ldots,$$

t. XXXV, p. 55) que ce polynome ne change qu'une fois de signe, entre les limites $x=0$, $x=1$, est immédiatement mise en évidence dans l'expression de M. Raabe. Effectivement, l'intégrale

$$\int_{-x}^{+x} \frac{u^{2m}\,du}{e^u+e^{-u}-2\cos 2\pi x}$$

est une quantité essentiellement positive pour toutes les valeurs de x, de sorte qu'entre les limites considérées, $B''(x)$ aura le signe du facteur $(-1)^{m+1}\sin 2\pi x$, et ne s'annulera que pour $x=\frac{1}{2}$. C'est ce qui m'a engagé à en rechercher une démonstration directe et en même temps à obtenir une expression analogue pour le polynome $B'(x)$, qui mettrait aussi en évidence sa propriété caractéristique, d'être toujours de même signe de $x=0$ à $x=1$.

J'emploierai dans ce but, la forme suivante que prend la fonction $\frac{e^{\lambda x}-1}{e^{\lambda}-1}$, en changeant λ en $2i\lambda$; si l'on pose

$$\varphi(x)=\frac{\sin\lambda+\sin(2x-1)\lambda}{2\sin\lambda},$$

$$\psi(x)=\frac{\cos\lambda-\cos(2x-1)\lambda}{2\sin\lambda},$$

on trouve, en effet,

$$\frac{e^{2i\lambda x}-1}{e^{2i\lambda}-1}=\varphi(x)+i\,\psi(x),$$

et il en résulte que $B''(x)$ et $B'(x)$ peuvent être définis comme les coefficients de $\frac{(-1)^m(2\lambda)^{2m}}{1.2\ldots 2m}$ et de $\frac{(-1)^m(2\lambda)^{2m+1}}{1.2\ldots 2m+1}$ dans les développements de $\varphi(x)$ et $\psi(x)$ suivant les puissances croissantes de λ. La considération de ces fonctions suffit déjà pour démontrer plusieurs des théorèmes de Raabe, au moyen de ces relations entièrement élémentaires, à savoir:

$$\varphi(1-x)=1-\varphi(x), \qquad \psi(1-x)=\psi(x),$$

$$\varphi(x)+\varphi\left(x+\frac{1}{n}\right)+\ldots+\varphi\left(x+\frac{n-1}{n}\right)=\frac{1}{2}n+\frac{\sin(2nx-1)\frac{\lambda}{n}}{2\sin\frac{\lambda}{n}},$$

$$\psi(x)+\psi\left(x+\frac{1}{n}\right)+\ldots+\psi\left(x+\frac{n-1}{n}\right)=\frac{n\cos\lambda}{2\sin\lambda}-\frac{\cos(2nx-1)\frac{\lambda}{n}}{2\sin\frac{\lambda}{n}}.$$

Mais c'est leur expression sous forme d'intégrales définies qu'il importe surtout d'obtenir, et voici comment j'y suis parvenu :

Soit $f(e^x)$ une fonction rationnelle quelconque de e^x, et

$$\Phi(x) = e^{mx} f(e^x).$$

Je ferai usage de la valeur de l'intégrale $\int_{-\infty}^{+\infty} \Phi(x)\,dx$, qui se détermine facilement comme vous allez voir. Ayant posé d'abord

$$\begin{aligned} f(z) = \Pi(z) &+ \frac{A}{z-a} + \frac{A_1}{(z-a)^2} + \ldots + \frac{A_\alpha}{(z-a)^{\alpha+1}} \\ &+ \frac{B}{z-b} + \frac{B_1}{(z-b)^2} + \ldots + \frac{B_\beta}{(z-b)^{\beta+1}} \\ &+ \ldots\ldots\ldots\ldots\ldots\ldots\ldots\ldots \end{aligned}$$

en réunissant dans la quantité $\Pi(z)$, la partie entière ainsi que les fractions en $\frac{1}{z}$, $\frac{1}{z^2}$, ..., s'il en existe, je remarque que l'expression

$$e^{mx}\left[\frac{A}{e^x-a} + \frac{A_1}{(e^x-a)^2} + \ldots + \frac{A_\alpha}{(e^x-a)^{\alpha+1}}\right]$$

peut se mettre sous cette nouvelle forme

$$\mathfrak{A}\left(\frac{e^{mx}}{e^x-a}\right) + \mathfrak{A}_1 D_x\left(\frac{e^{mx}}{e^x-a}\right) + \ldots + \mathfrak{A}_\alpha D_x^\alpha\left(\frac{e^{mx}}{e^x-a}\right).$$

Nous aurons en conséquence

$$\begin{aligned} \Phi(x) = e^{mx}\Pi(x) &+ \mathfrak{A}\left(\frac{e^{mx}}{e^x-a}\right) + \mathfrak{A}_1 D_x\left(\frac{e^{mx}}{e^x-a}\right) + \ldots + \mathfrak{A}_\alpha D_x^\alpha\left(\frac{e^{mx}}{e^x-a}\right) \\ &+ \mathfrak{B}\left(\frac{e^{mx}}{e^x-b}\right) + \mathfrak{B}_1 D_x\left(\frac{e^{mx}}{e^x-b}\right) + \ldots + \mathfrak{B}_\beta D_x^\beta\left(\frac{e^{mx}}{e^x-b}\right) \\ &+ \ldots\ldots\ldots\ldots\ldots\ldots\ldots\ldots, \end{aligned}$$

et cette décomposition entièrement analogue à celle des fractions rationnelles en fractions simples, ramènera l'intégrale $\int \Phi(x)\,dx$ à la transcendante $\int \frac{e^{mx}\,dx}{e^x-a}$, et l'intégrale définie proposée à la quantité $\int_{-\infty}^{+\infty} \frac{e^{mx}\,dx}{e^x-a}$. Avant d'en chercher la valeur, je remarque que la constante a doit être supposée négative quand elle est réelle ; on est amené par là à poser : $a = -e^{g+ih}$, avec la condition que h soit compris entre les limites $-\pi$ et $+\pi$, sans atteindre ces limites. Cela étant, nous aurons

$$\int_{-\infty}^{+\infty} \frac{e^{mx}\,dx}{e^x - a} = e^{-g-ih} \int_{-\infty}^{+\infty} \frac{e^{mx}\,dx}{e^{x-g-ih}+1};$$

puis en remplaçant x par $x+g$

$$\int_{-\infty}^{+\infty} \frac{e^{mx}\,dx}{e^{x-g-ih}+1} = e^{mg} \int_{-\infty}^{+\infty} \frac{e^{mx}\,dx}{e^{x-ih}+1},$$

et cette dernière quantité se détermine comme il suit :

Considérons l'intégrale d'une fonction quelconque effectuée en suivant le contour d'un rectangle ABCD, dont la base est sur l'axe

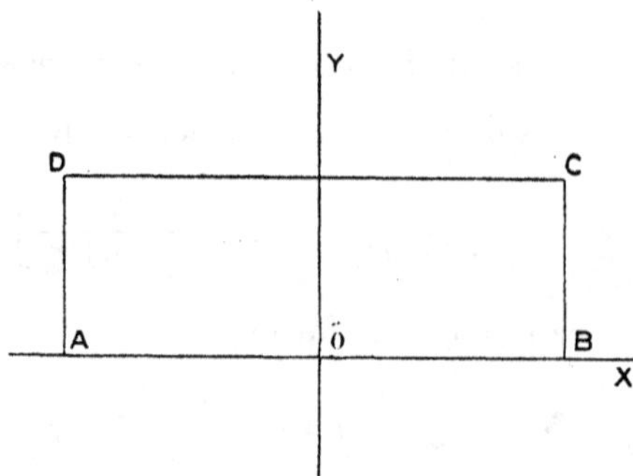

des abscisses, l'origine étant au milieu de cette base, et faisons $OB = a$, $BC = b$. Si l'on désigne par $\Phi(z)$ la fonction et par S la somme de ses résidus qui correspondent aux valeurs de z, comprises à l'intérieur du rectangle, on aura comme on sait

$$\begin{aligned}\int_{-a}^{+a} \Phi(x)\,dx + i\int_0^b \Phi(ix+a)\,dx \\ - \int_{-a}^{+a} \Phi(x+ib)\,dx - i\int_0^b \Phi(ix-a)\,dx = 2i\pi S.\end{aligned}$$

Cela étant, je fais $\Phi(z) = \frac{e^{mz}}{e^z+1}$, et je suppose la hauteur b comprise entre π et 3π, de manière qu'à l'intérieur du rectangle, l'équation $e^z + 1 = 0$ n'ait que la racine $z = i\pi$ et $\Phi(z)$ le seul résidu $-e^{im\pi}$. Faisons maintenant croître indéfiniment la constante a; les deux quantités $\Phi(ix+a)$ et $\Phi(ix-a)$ tendront évidemment vers zéro si m est inférieur en valeur absolue à l'unité, et l'on obtiendra

$$\int_{-\infty}^{+\infty} \Phi(x)\,dx - \int_{-\infty}^{+\infty} \Phi(x+ib)\,dx = -2i\pi e^{im\pi},$$

d'où

$$\int_{-\infty}^{+\infty} \Phi(x+ib)\,dx = \frac{\pi}{\sin m\pi} + 2i\pi e^{im\pi} = \frac{\pi e^{2im\pi}}{\sin m\pi},$$

et par conséquent

$$\int_{-\infty}^{+\infty} \frac{e^{mx}\,dx}{e^{x+ib}+1} = \frac{\pi e^{im(2\pi-b)}}{\sin m\pi}.$$

Mais on peut poser: $b = 2\pi - h$, h étant compris entre $-\pi$ et $+\pi$, et nous trouvons ainsi

$$\int_{-\infty}^{+\infty} \frac{e^{mx}\,dx}{e^{x-ih}+1} = \frac{\pi e^{imh}}{\sin m\pi}.$$

Soit, en second lieu,

$$\Phi(z) = \frac{e^{mz}-e^{nz}}{e^{z}-1},$$

les constantes m et n étant moindres que l'unité, de sorte que $\Phi(ix+a)$ et $\Phi(ix-a)$ soient nulles pour a infini. En supposant $b=\pi$, la fonction proposée restera finie à l'intérieur du rectangle et l'on aura $S = 0$, d'où, par conséquent,

$$\int_{-\infty}^{+\infty} \Phi(x)\,dx = \int_{-\infty}^{+\infty} \Phi(x+i\pi)\,dx.$$

Mais nous avons

$$\Phi(x+i\pi) = -e^{im\pi}\frac{e^{mx}}{e^{x}+1} + e^{in\pi}\frac{e^{nx}}{e^{x}+1},$$

et de cette expression résulte immédiatement la valeur connue

$$\int_{-\infty}^{+\infty} \frac{e^{mx}-e^{nx}}{e^{x}-1}\,dx = \pi\left[\frac{e^{in\pi}}{\sin n\pi} - \frac{e^{im\pi}}{\sin m\pi}\right] = \pi(\cot n\pi - \cot m\pi).$$

J'arrive maintenant à mon objet en appliquant les résultats qui précèdent à la détermination des intégrales,

$$\int_{-\infty}^{+\infty} \frac{e^{mz}\sin h\,dz}{e^{z}+e^{-z}+2\cos h} \quad \text{et} \quad \int_{-\infty}^{+\infty} \frac{(e^{mz}-e^{-mz})(1+\cos h)\,dz}{(e^{z}-1)(e^{z}+e^{-z}+\cos h)}.$$

A l'égard de la première, la relation

$$\frac{\sin h}{e^{z}+e^{-z}+2\cos h}=\frac{1}{2i}\left[\frac{1}{e^{z-ih}+1}-\frac{1}{e^{z+ih}+1}\right]$$

donnera

$$\int_{-\infty}^{+\infty}\frac{e^{mz}\sin h\,dz}{e^{z}+e^{-z}+2\cos h}=\frac{1}{2i}\left[\frac{e^{imh}}{\sin m\pi}-\frac{e^{-imh}}{\sin m\pi}\right]=\frac{\pi\sin mh}{\sin m\pi}.$$

Pour la seconde, j'emploierai la décomposition suivante :

$$\frac{4i\sin h(1+\cos h)}{(e^{z}-1)(e^{z}+e^{-z}+2\cos h)}=\frac{2i\sin h}{e^{z}-1}+\frac{e^{ih}+1}{e^{z+ih}+1}-\frac{e^{-ih}+1}{e^{z-ih}+1},$$

et nous en conclurons au moyen des formules

$$\int_{+\infty}^{+\infty}\frac{e^{mz}-e^{-mz}}{e^{z}-1}\,dz=-2\pi\cot m\pi,\qquad \int_{+\infty}^{+\infty}\frac{e^{mz}-e^{-mz}}{e^{z+ih}+1}\,dz=\frac{2\pi\cos mh}{\sin m\pi},$$

la valeur cherchée

$$\int_{-x}^{+x}\frac{(e^{mz}-e^{-mz})(1+\cos h)}{(e^{z}-1)(e^{z}+e^{-z}+2\cos h)}\,dz=\pi\,\frac{\cos mh-\cos m\pi}{\sin m\pi}.$$

Ramenons encore ces intégrales à avoir pour limites zéro et l'infini, on obtiendra ces formules

$$\frac{\sin mh}{\sin m\pi}=\frac{1}{\pi}\int_{0}^{\infty}\frac{(e^{mz}+e^{-mz})\sin h}{e^{z}+e^{-z}+2\cos h}\,dz,$$

$$\frac{\cos mh-\cos m\pi}{\sin m\pi}=\frac{1}{\pi}\int_{0}^{\infty}\frac{(e^{z}+1)(e^{mz}-e^{-mz})(1+\cos h)}{(e^{z}-1)(e^{z}+e^{-z}+2\cos h)}\,dz,$$

où figurent des fonctions paires de la variable sous les signes d'intégration.

Elles donnent le résultat auquel je voulais arriver en faisant : $m=\frac{\lambda}{\pi}$ et $h=\pi(1-2x)$, de sorte que λ soit compris entre $-\pi$ et $+\pi$ et x entre zéro et l'unité. Il suffit, en effet, de remplacer z par πz, pour avoir

$$\begin{aligned}\varphi(x)&=\frac{\sin\lambda+\sin(2x-1)\lambda}{2\sin\lambda}\\&=\frac{1}{2}+\frac{1}{2}\sin 2\pi x\int_{0}^{\infty}\frac{e^{\lambda z}+e^{-\lambda z}}{e^{\pi z}+e^{-\pi z}-2\cos 2\pi x}\,dz,\end{aligned}$$

et

$$\psi(x) = \frac{\cos\lambda - \cos(2x-1)\lambda}{2\sin\lambda}$$

$$= -\sin^2\pi x \int_0^\infty \frac{(e^{\pi z}+1)(e^{\lambda z}-e^{-\lambda z})}{(e^{\pi z}-1)(e^{\pi z}+e^{-\pi z}-2\cos 2\pi x)}\,dz,$$

et l'on voit immédiatement que le théorème de M. Raabe se tire de de la première égalité en égalant les coefficients de λ^{2m} dans les deux membres. Mais on parvient, en outre, à étendre de la manière suivante, les importantes propositions de M. Malmsten à l'égard des polygones $B''(x)$ et $B(x)$. Remarquant que les dérivées d'un ordre quelconque par rapport à λ, des deux intégrales

$$\int_0^\infty \frac{e^{\lambda z}+e^{-\lambda z}}{e^{\pi z}+e^{-\pi z}-2\cos 2\pi x}\,dz,$$

$$\int_0^\infty \frac{(e^{\pi z}+1)(e^{\lambda z}-e^{-\lambda z})}{(e^{\pi z}-1)(e^{\pi z}+e^{-\pi z}-2\cos 2\pi x)}\,dz,$$

sont essentiellement positives si λ est lui-même positif, nous en concluons, en effet, qu'en supposant λ compris entre zéro et π, si l'on fait croître x de zéro à l'unité, les dérivées de la fonction $\varphi(x)$ par rapport à λ, seront toutes positives de $x=0$ à $x=\frac{1}{2}$ et négatives de $x=\frac{1}{2}$ à $x=1$, tandis que la fonction $\psi(x)$ et ses dérivées par rapport à λ seront toujours négatives de $x=0$ à $x=1$.

Je rattacherai enfin les développements en séries de sinus et de cosinus des arcs multiples de $2\pi x$ que Raabe a donnés pour les fonctions de $B''(x)$ et $B'(x)$, à ces formules connues, et qui subsistent entre les limites $x=0$ et $x=1$:

$$\varphi(x) = \frac{1}{2} + \pi\left[\frac{\sin 2\pi x}{\lambda^2-\pi^2} + \frac{2\sin 4\pi x}{\lambda^2-4\pi^2} + \frac{3\sin 6\pi x}{\lambda^2-9\pi^2} + \ldots\right],$$

$$\psi(x) = \frac{1}{2}\cot\lambda - \frac{1}{2\lambda} - \pi\lambda\left[\frac{\cos 2\pi x}{\lambda^2-\pi^2} + \frac{\cos 4\pi x}{\lambda^2-4\pi^2} + \frac{\cos 6\pi x}{\lambda^2-9\pi^2} + \ldots\right].$$

Il suffit, en effet, pour y arriver, d'égaler les coefficients des mêmes puissances de λ dans les deux membres.

Paris, 1er novembre 1874.

SUR LES

DÉVELOPPEMENTS DE $F(x) = \mathrm{sn}^a x\, \mathrm{cn}^b x\, \mathrm{dn}^c x$

OÙ LES EXPOSANTS SONT ENTIERS.

Académie royale des Sciences de Stockholm, Bihang III, n° 10, 1875, p. 3-10.

Le mode de calcul que je proposerais résulte de la proposition suivante :

Soit $\mathfrak{F}(z)$ une fonction uniforme ayant pour périodes $2K$ et $2iK'$; si l'on considère un rectangle dont les côtés parallèles aux axes Ox et Oy; soient $AB = 2K$, $AD = 2K'$, la somme S des résidus de $\mathfrak{F}(z)$ pour les valeurs de l'argument qui répondent à des points compris dans l'intérieur du rectangle est nulle. C'est ce que donne, en effet, l'intégration de $\mathfrak{F}(z)\,dz$ suivant le contour ABCD, car en appelant p pour un moment l'affixe de A, on obtient ainsi la relation

$$\int_0^{2K} \mathfrak{F}(p+z)\,dz + \int_0^{2iK'} \mathfrak{F}(p+2K+z)\,dz - \int_0^{2iK'} \mathfrak{F}(p+z)\,dz - \int_0^{2K} \mathfrak{F}(p+2iK'+z)\,dz = 2i\pi S$$

ou bien

$$\int_0^{2K} [\mathfrak{F}(p+z) - \mathfrak{F}(p+2iK'+z)]\,dz - \int_0^{2iK'} [\mathfrak{F}(p+z) - \mathfrak{F}(p+2K+z)]\,dz = 2i\pi S,$$

et les conditions

$$\mathfrak{f}(z + 2K) = \mathfrak{f}(z), \qquad \mathfrak{f}(z + 2iK') = \mathfrak{f}(z)$$

donnent sur le champ

$$S = 0.$$

Ce principe posé, je distingue à l'égard de $F(x)$, d'après les relations

$$F(x + 2K) = (-1)^{a+b} F(x), \qquad F(x + 2iK') = (-1)^{b+c} F(x)$$

quatre cas différents, suivant que la périodicité étant celle de $\mathrm{sn}\,x$, $\mathrm{cn}\,x$, $\mathrm{dn}\,x$, $\mathrm{sn}^2 x$, on aura

$$\text{(I)} \quad \begin{cases} F(x + 2K) = -F(x), \\ F(x + 2iK') = +F(x), \end{cases}$$

$$\text{(II)} \quad \begin{cases} F(x + 2K) = -F(x), \\ F(x + 2iK') = -F(x, \end{cases}$$

$$\text{(III)} \quad \begin{cases} F(x + 2K) = +F(x), \\ F(x + 2iK') = -F(x), \end{cases}$$

$$\text{(IV)} \quad \begin{cases} F(x + 2K) = +F(x), \\ F(x + 2iK) = +F(x), \end{cases}$$

et j'en ferai successivement l'application aux fonctions

$$\mathfrak{f}(z) = \frac{F(z)}{\mathrm{sn}(x - z)}, \qquad \frac{F(z)}{\mathrm{cn}(x - z)}, \qquad \frac{F(z)}{\mathrm{dn}(x - z)}, \qquad \frac{F(z)}{\mathrm{sn}^2(x - z)}.$$

Considérant d'abord le premier cas, j'observe que toutes les valeurs de z qui rendent le numérateur infini et le dénominateur nul sont

$$z = iK' + 2mK + 2niK', \qquad z = x + 2mK + 2niK',$$

m et n étant des nombres entiers. On a donc, à l'intérieur du rectangle ABCD, qu'à considérer deux quantités qui peuvent être ramenées à $z = iK'$, $z = x$, pour en déduire les résidus correspondants, c'est-à-dire les coefficients de $\frac{1}{\varepsilon}$ dans les développements suivant les puissances ascendantes de ε, de $F(iK' + \varepsilon)$, $F(x + \varepsilon)$. Soit, à cet effet, en écrivant les seuls termes qui contiennent ε en dénominateur,

$$F(iK'+\varepsilon) = \frac{A}{\varepsilon} + \frac{A_1}{\varepsilon^2} + \ldots + \frac{A_n}{\varepsilon^{n+1}}$$

ou sous une forme préférable

$$F(iK'+\varepsilon) = A\varepsilon^{-1} + A_1 D_\varepsilon \varepsilon^{-1} + \ldots + A_n D_\varepsilon^n \varepsilon^{-1}.$$

En multipliant membre à membre avec l'égalité suivante :

$$\frac{1}{\operatorname{sn}(x - iK' - \varepsilon)} = k\operatorname{sn}(x-\varepsilon) = k\left[\operatorname{sn}x - \frac{\varepsilon}{1} D_x \operatorname{sn}x + \frac{\varepsilon^2}{1.2} D_x^2 \operatorname{sn}x + \ldots \right.$$
$$\left. + (-1)^n \frac{\varepsilon^n}{1.2\ldots n} D_x^n \operatorname{sn}x + \ldots\right],$$

il vient, pour le coefficient de $\frac{1}{\varepsilon}$ dans le produit des seconds membres, l'expression

$$k(A\operatorname{sn}x + A_1 D_x \operatorname{sn}x + \ldots + A_n D_x^n \operatorname{sn}x).$$

L'autre résidu correspondant à $z = x$ étant évidemment $-F(x)$, la relation $S = 0$ donne la formule

$$F(x) = k(A\operatorname{sn}x + A_1 D_x \operatorname{sn}x + \ldots + A_n D_n^n \operatorname{sn}x).$$

Dans le second cas, où $\mathfrak{F}(z) = \frac{F(z)}{\operatorname{cn}(x-z)}$, le développement de $\frac{1}{\operatorname{cn}(x - iK' - \varepsilon)}$ conduit à un calcul tout semblable; mais j'observerai que, ayant

$$\frac{1}{\operatorname{cn}(x - iK')} = -\frac{ik}{k'}\operatorname{cn}(x-K),$$

on peut poser

$$\frac{1}{\operatorname{cn}(x - iK' - \varepsilon)} = -\frac{ik}{k'}\left[\operatorname{cn}(x-K) - \frac{\varepsilon}{1} D_x \operatorname{cn}(x-K) \right.$$
$$\left. + \frac{\varepsilon^2}{1.2} D_x^2 \operatorname{cn}(x-K) - \ldots\right];$$

multipliant membre avec l'égalité précédemment employée

$$F(iK'+\varepsilon) = A\varepsilon^{-1} + A_1 D_\varepsilon \varepsilon^{-1} + A_2 D_\varepsilon^2 \varepsilon^{-1} + \ldots$$

le résidu cherché s'obtient donc sous la forme suivante :

$$-\frac{ik}{k'}[A\operatorname{cn}(x-K)+A_1 D_x \operatorname{cn}(x-K)+\ldots+A_n D_x^n \operatorname{cn}(x-K)].$$

Maintenant, l'équation $\operatorname{cn}(x-z)=0$ donne la solution

$$z = x - K,$$

et le résidu qui lui correspond a pour valeur

$$\frac{F(x-K)}{k'},$$

d'où la relation

$$F(x-K) = ik[A\operatorname{cn}(x-K)+A_1 D_x \operatorname{cn}(x-K)+\ldots],$$

et, en changeant x en $x+K$,

$$F(x) = ik(A\operatorname{cn} x + A_1 D_x \operatorname{cn} x + \ldots + A_n D_x^n \operatorname{cn} x).$$

Le troisième cas, en faisant usage de la relation

$$\frac{1}{\operatorname{dn}(x-iK')} = k' \operatorname{dn}(x-K-iK'),$$

donne de même

$$F(x) = -i(A\operatorname{dn} x + A_1 D_x \operatorname{dn} x + \ldots + A_n D_x^n \operatorname{dn} x);$$

mais la quatrième se présente différemment, le résidu de la fonction $\dfrac{F(z)}{\operatorname{sn}^2(x-z)}$ pour $z=x$ étant $F'(x)$, on obtient, en effet,

$$F'(x) = -k^2(A\operatorname{sn}^2 x + A_1 D_x \operatorname{sn}^2 x + \ldots + A_n D_x^n \operatorname{sn}^2 x).$$

Or, le théorème $S=0$, appliqué à la fonction $F(z)$, remplissant actuellement les conditions

$$F(z+2K) = F(z), \qquad F(z+2iK') = F(z)$$

et qui n'a qu'un seul résidu, fait voir que ce résidu est nul. Ayant ainsi $A=0$, on parvient, en intégrant les deux membres, à la relation cherchée

$$F(z) = \text{const.} - k^2(A_1 \operatorname{sn}^2 x + A_2 D_x \operatorname{sn}^2 x + \ldots + A_n D_x^{n-1} \operatorname{sn}^2 x)$$

qui donnera comme les précédentes, au moyen des coefficients A,

A_1, ..., le développement de $F(x)$ en série de sinus et de cosinus. Ce point établi, je reprends l'égalité

$$F(iK'+\varepsilon) = A\varepsilon^{-1} + A_1 D_\varepsilon \varepsilon^{-1} + \ldots + A_n D_\varepsilon^n \varepsilon^{-1},$$

et, observant que les formules

$$\operatorname{sn}(iK'+x) = \frac{1}{k \operatorname{sn} x},$$

$$\operatorname{cn}(iK'+x) = \frac{\operatorname{dn} x}{ik \operatorname{sn} x} = \frac{k'}{ik \operatorname{sn}\left(k'x, \dfrac{ik'}{k}\right)},$$

$$\operatorname{dn}(iK'+x) = \frac{\operatorname{cn} x}{i \operatorname{sn} x} = \frac{1}{\operatorname{sn}(ix, k')},$$

permettent d'écrire

$$F(iK'+x) = \left(\frac{1}{k}\right)^a \left(\frac{k'}{ik}\right)^b \frac{1}{\operatorname{sn}^a x \operatorname{sn}^b\left(k'x, \dfrac{ik'}{k}\right) \operatorname{sn}^c(ix, k')},$$

je suis amené à m'occuper de développement de $\dfrac{1}{\operatorname{sn} x}$ suivant les puissances ascendantes de la variable. Or, un moyen simple de l'obtenir résulte de la formule suivante :

$$\frac{k+ik'}{\operatorname{sn}\left(\dfrac{k+ik'}{2}x, \dfrac{k-ik'}{k+ik'}\right)} = \frac{1}{\operatorname{sn} x} + \frac{i}{\operatorname{sn}(ix, k')},$$

car, en posant

$$\frac{1}{\operatorname{sn} x} = \frac{1}{x} + \Pi_1(k)x + \Pi_2(k)x^3 + \ldots + \Pi_n(k)x^{2n-1} + \ldots$$

de sorte que

$$\Pi_n(k) = \alpha + \beta k^2 + \gamma k^4 + \ldots + \beta k^{2n-2} + \alpha k^{2n}$$

on en déduira

$$\frac{(k+ik')^{2n}}{2^{2n-1}} \Pi_n\left(\frac{k-ik'}{k+ik'}\right) = \Pi_n(k) + (-1)^n \Pi_n(k'),$$

et cette relation détermine les coefficients β, γ, ... au moyen de α qui est donné d'avance par le développement connu de $\dfrac{1}{\operatorname{sn} x}$.

Soit, par exemple, $n = 4$; en faisant

$$k = \cos\varphi,$$

d'où

$$k' = \sin\varphi, \qquad k + ik' = e^{i\varphi},$$

on aura facilement

$$64[\Pi_4(k) + \Pi_4(k')]$$
$$= 163\alpha + 104\beta + 48\gamma + (28\alpha + 24\beta + 16\gamma)\cos 4\varphi + \alpha\cos 8\varphi,$$

puis

$$(k + ik')^8 \Pi_4\left(\frac{k - ik'}{k + ik'}\right) = 2\alpha\cos 8\varphi + 2\beta\cos 4\varphi + \gamma$$

et, par conséquent, les équations suivantes :

$$\gamma = 2(163\alpha + 104\beta + 48\gamma),$$
$$\beta = 28\alpha + 24\beta + 16\gamma;$$

d'où l'on tire

$$\Pi_4(k) = \frac{127 - 284k^2 + 186k^4 - 284k^6 + 127k^8}{15 \times (2.3.4.5.6.7.8)}.$$

Le développement de $\frac{1}{\operatorname{sn}^2 x}$ me semble aussi mériter une attention particulière, et je remarquerai en premier lieu que, en posant

$$\frac{1}{\operatorname{sn}^2 x} = \frac{1}{x^2} + \Phi_1(k) + \Phi_2(k)x^2 + \ldots + \Phi_n(k)x^{2n-2} + \ldots,$$

le coefficient $\Phi_n(k)$ s'obtient au moyen de $\Pi_n(k)$ comme il suit :

$$(2^{2n-1} - 2)\Phi_n(k) = (2n - 1)\left[2^{2n-1}\Pi_n(k) + (-1)^n(1 + k)^{2n}\Pi_n\left(\frac{1 - k}{1 + k}\right)\right].$$

C'est la conséquence, en effet, de la relation

$$\frac{1}{\operatorname{sn}^2 x} - \frac{1}{\operatorname{sn}^2 \frac{x}{2}} = D_x\left[\frac{1}{\operatorname{sn} x} + \frac{i(1 + k)}{\operatorname{sn}\left(\frac{1 + k}{2} ix, \frac{1 - k}{1 + k}\right)}\right],$$

et inversement en partant de celle-ci

$$2 D_x \frac{1}{\operatorname{sn} x} = \frac{2}{\operatorname{sn}^2 x} - \left[\frac{i(1 + k)}{\operatorname{sn}\left(\frac{1 + k}{2} ix, \frac{1 - k}{1 + k}\right)}\right]^2 - 1 - k^2,$$

on exprimera $\Pi_n(k)$ au moyen de $\Phi_n(k)$.

Voici le système des formules qui conduisent à ces résultats sur $\frac{1}{\operatorname{sn} x}$ et $\frac{1}{\operatorname{sn}^2 x}$:

$$\frac{i(1+k)}{\operatorname{sn}\left(\frac{1+k}{2}ix, \frac{1-k}{1+k}\right)} = \frac{\operatorname{cn} x + \operatorname{dn} x}{\operatorname{sn} x},$$

$$\frac{k+ik'}{\operatorname{sn}\left(\frac{k+ik'}{2}x, \frac{k-ik'}{k+ik'}\right)} = \frac{1+\operatorname{cn} x}{\operatorname{sn} x},$$

$$\frac{1+k'}{\operatorname{sn}\left(\frac{1+k'}{2}x, \frac{1-k'}{1+k'}\right)} = \frac{1+\operatorname{dn} x}{\operatorname{sn} x},$$

$$\frac{1}{\operatorname{sn}^2 \frac{x}{2}} = \frac{(1+\operatorname{cn} x)(1+\operatorname{dn} x)}{\operatorname{sn}^2 x};$$

j'en tirerai cette dernière conclusion

$$\left[\frac{i(1+k)}{\operatorname{sn}\left(\frac{1+k}{2}ix, \frac{1-k}{1+k}\right)}\right]^2 + \left[\frac{k+ik'}{\operatorname{sn}\left(\frac{k+ik'}{2}x, \frac{k-ik'}{k+ik'}\right)}\right]^2$$
$$+ \left[\frac{1+k'}{\operatorname{sn}\left(\frac{1+k'}{2}x, \frac{1-k'}{1+k'}\right)}\right]^2 - \frac{2}{\operatorname{sn}^2 \frac{x}{2}} - \frac{4}{\operatorname{sn}^2 x} + 2(1+k^2) = 0,$$

qui donne, pour le calcul direct de $\Phi_n(k)$, la relation

$$(k+ik)^{2n}\Phi_n\left(\frac{k-ik'}{k+ik'}\right) + (1+k')^{2n}\Phi_n\left(\frac{1-k'}{1+k'}\right)$$
$$+ (-1)^n(1+k)^{2n}\Phi_n\left(\frac{1-k}{1+k}\right) = (4^n+2)\,\Phi_n(k).$$

Mais une remarque est d'abord à faire sur la forme algébrique des polynomes $\Phi(k)$. Les égalités

$$\operatorname{sn}\left(kx, \frac{1}{k}\right) = k \operatorname{sn} x, \qquad \frac{1}{\operatorname{sn}^2 x} + \frac{1}{\operatorname{sn}^2(ix, k')} = 1$$

montrent, en effet, que

$$k^{2n}\Phi_n\left(\frac{1}{k}\right) = \Phi_n(k),$$
$$\Phi_n(k') = (-1)^n \Phi_n(k).$$

On est amené à rechercher l'expression la plus générale des polynomes entiers $\varphi(x)$ de degré n satisfaisant aux conditions

$$x^n \varphi\left(\frac{1}{x}\right) = \varphi(x),$$
$$\varphi(1-x) = (-1)^n \varphi(x).$$

Supposons d'abord n impair; en faisant $x = \frac{1}{2}$ dans ces deux égalités et $x = -1$ dans la première seulement, on en conclura

$$\varphi\left(\frac{1}{2}\right) = 0, \qquad \varphi(2) = 0, \qquad \varphi(-1) = 0,$$

par où l'on voit que $\varphi(x)$ contient le facteur

$$(x+1)(2x-1)(x-2).$$

Soit donc, pour un moment,

$$\varphi(x) = (x+1)(2x-1)(x-2)\psi(x);$$

le polynome de degré pair $\psi(x)$ sera réciproque et vérifiera la condition

$$\psi(1-x) = \psi(x),$$

car le produit $(x+1)(2x-1)(x-2)$ change de signe quand on y remplace x par $1-x$. Le cas de n impair est ainsi ramené à celui de n pair que je vais considérer en posant $n = 2m$. J'observe à cet effet que, en posant

$$\varphi_1(x) = \varphi(x) - A(x^2 - x + 1)^m,$$

où A est une constante arbitraire, on aura encore

$$x^{2m} \varphi_1\left(\frac{1}{x}\right) = \varphi_1(x),$$
$$\varphi_1(1-x) = \varphi_1(x).$$

Cela posé, déterminons A de manière que $\varphi_1(x)$ admette la racine $x = 0$; la condition

$$\varphi_1(1-x) = \varphi_1(x)$$

fait voir qu'on introduira en même temps la racine $x = 1$, de sorte qu'on peut faire

$$\varphi_1(x) = x(1-x)\varphi_2(x).$$

Or, on trouve à l'égard du nouveau polynome $\varphi(x)$ les relations

$$\varphi_2(1-x)=\varphi_2(x),$$
$$x^{2m-3}\varphi_2\left(\frac{1}{x}\right)=-\varphi_2(x)$$

qui donnent pour $x=1$

$$\varphi_2(1)=0 \quad \text{et} \quad \varphi_2(0)=0;$$

donc, comme tout à l'heure, $\varphi_2(x)$ admet le facteur $x(1-x)$, par où l'on voit qu'on doit faire

$$\varphi_1(x)=[x(1-x)]^2\,\varphi_3(x),$$

d'où résultera

$$\varphi_3(1-x)=\varphi_3(x),$$
$$x^{2m-6}\varphi_3\left(\frac{1}{x}\right)=\varphi_3(x).$$

Ainsi $\varphi_3(x)$ est un polynome de même nature que $\varphi(x)$, mais du degré $2m-6$, de sorte que, en raisonnant sur le nouveau polynome comme sur le précédent, on arrivera de proche en proche à l'expression cherchée

$$\begin{aligned}\varphi(x)=A(x^2-x+1)^m&+B(x^2-x+1)^{m-3}(x^2-x)^2\\&+C(x^2-x+1)^{m-6}(x^2-x)^4\\&+\ldots\ldots\ldots\ldots\ldots\ldots\\&+L(x^2-x+1)^{m-3p}(x^2-x)^{2p},\end{aligned}$$

p désignant l'entier contenu dans $\frac{m}{3}$, et l'on en conclut, en faisant $x=k^2$,

$$\begin{aligned}\Phi_n(k)&=A(1-k^2k'^2)^m+B(1-k^2k'^2)^{m-3}k^4k'^4\\&+C(1-k^2k'^2)^{m-6}k^8k'^8+\ldots+L(1-k^2k'^2)^{m-3p}k^{4p}k'^{4p}.\end{aligned}$$

Cette forme, canonique si je puis dire, des coefficients du développement de $\frac{1}{\operatorname{sn}^2 x}$ suivant les puissances croissantes de la variable, contiendra au plus, sous forme homogène, deux coefficients inconnus, jusqu'aux limites $n=10$ et $n=13$, suivant que n est pair ou impair. Et si l'on écrit pour abréger

$$\Phi_n(k)=\Sigma H(1-k^2k'^2)^{m-3h}(kk'^4)^{2h},$$

on aura les formules suivantes :

$$(1+k)^{2n}\Phi_n\left(\frac{1-k}{1+k}\right) = \Sigma H(1+14k^2+k^4)^{m-3h}(4kk'^4)^{2h},$$

$$(1+k')^{2n}\Phi_n\left(\frac{1-k'}{1+k'}\right) = \Sigma H(16-16k^2+k^4)^{m-3h}(4k'k^4)^{2h},$$

$$(k+ik')^{2n}\Phi_n\left(\frac{k-ik'}{k+ik'}\right) = \Sigma H(1-16k^2k'^2)^{m-3h}(4ikk')^{2h},$$

qui permettent d'employer la relation

$$(k+ik')^{2n}\Phi_n\left(\frac{k-ik'}{k+ik'}\right) + (1+k')^{2n}\Phi_n\left(\frac{1-k'}{1+k'}\right) + (1+k)^{2n}\Phi\left(\frac{1-k}{1+k}\right) = (4^n+2)\Phi_n(k).$$

Soit, par exemple, $n=6$; on aura

$$\Phi_6(k) = A(1-k^2k'^2)^3 + B(kk')^4,$$

et l'hypothèse particulière

$$k^2k'^2 = 1,$$

d'où l'on tire

$$k^6 = -1,$$

puis

$$1+14k^2+k^4 = 15k^2, \quad 16-16k^2+k^4 = -15k'^2, \quad 1-16k^2+16k^4 = -15,$$

et enfin

$$(4kk'^4)^2 + (4k^4k')^2 + (4ikk')^2 = -48k^4k'^4 = -48,$$

conduira à l'égalité

$$15^3A + 1382B = 0.$$

Soit encore $n=4$; de la valeur $\Phi_4(k) = A(1-k^2k'^2)^2$ qui est immédiatement connue, nous tirerons celle de $\Pi_4(k)$ au moyen de la relation générale

$$2^{2n-1}(2n-1)\Pi_n(k) = 2^{2n-1}\Phi_n(k) - (-1)^n(1+k)^{2n}\Phi_n\left(\frac{1-k}{1+k}\right),$$

et l'expression précédemment calculée se retrouve, en effet, sous la forme suivante :

$$127 - 284k^2 + 186k^4 - 284k^6 + 127k^8 = 2^7(1-k^2+k^4)^2 - (1+14k^2+k^4)^2.$$

SUR UN THÉORÈME D'EISENSTEIN.

Proceedings of the London Mathematical Society, t. VII, p. 173-175.
Read april 13 th, 1876.

M. Heine en donnant la démonstration du théorème célèbre d'Eisenstein, sur les développements en série des racines des équations algébriques, $f(y, x) = 0$, dans le *Journal de Crelle* (t. **48**, p. 267), y a ajouté cette remarque extrêmement importante, qu'on peut ramener les coefficients supposés commensurables d'un tel développement, à être tous entiers, sauf le premier, par le changement de x en kx (¹). C'est une simplification de la méthode employée par l'éminent géomètre, que je me propose d'indiquer en peu de mots. Considérons d'abord l'ensemble des divers développements ordonnés suivant les puissances entières et positives de la variable, qu'on peut tirer de l'équation proposée. J'observerai avec M. Heine, que si deux ou plusieurs d'entre eux, commençant par les mêmes termes, ont la partie commune

$$a + bx + cx^2 + \ldots + kx^p,$$

la transformée

$$F(z, x) = 0,$$

obtenue en posant

$$y = a + bx + cx^2 + \ldots + kx^p + zx^{p+1},$$

(¹) Note added by the permission of M. Hermite. — This remark had already been made by Eisenstein himself: His Words are, *Endlich kann statt x immer ein solches Vielfache von x gesetzt werden, dass alle Coefficienten der Reihe in ganze Zahlen uebergehen* (See Eisenstein's note in the *Monatsberichte* of the Berlin Academy for July, 1852, p. 441; or the extract from it an earlier paper of M. Heine's in *Crelles Journal*, vol. XLV, p. 285). H.-J.-S. Smith.

aura cette propriété que, pour $x=0$, toutes les racines seront nécessairement inégales. Cela étant, et désignant l'une d'elles supposée commensurable par z_0, je raisonnerai sur l'équation

$$F=(z+z_0,x)=0,$$

qui sera par conséquent de la forme suivante :

$$\begin{aligned}
&m_1x+m_2x^2+m_3x^3+\ldots\\
&\quad+z\;(n+n_1x+n_2x^2+\ldots)\\
&\quad+z^2(p+p_1x+p_2x^2+\ldots)\\
&\quad+\ldots\ldots\ldots\ldots\ldots\ldots\ldots\\
&\quad+z^{\mu}(s+s_1x+s_2x^2+\ldots)=0,
\end{aligned}$$

les coefficients étant des nombres entiers et n devant essentiellement être supposé différent de zéro. Soit maintenant $z=nu$ et $x=n^2t$; il viendra, après avoir divisé par n^2,

$$\begin{aligned}
&m_1t+n^2m_2t^2+\ldots\\
&\quad+u(1+nn_1t+n^3n_2t^2+\ldots)\\
&\quad+u^2(p+n^2p_1t+n^4p_2t^2+\ldots)\\
&\quad\ldots\ldots\ldots\ldots\ldots\ldots\ldots\ldots\\
&\quad+u^{\mu}n^{\mu-2}(s+n^2s_1t+n^4s_2t^2+\ldots)=0,
\end{aligned}$$

relation que j'écrirai ainsi

$$\begin{aligned}
u=&-\frac{m_1t+n^2m_2t^2+\ldots}{1+nn_1t+\ldots}\\
&-u^2\frac{p+n^2p_1t+\ldots}{1+nn_1t+\ldots}\\
&\ldots\ldots\ldots\ldots\ldots\\
&-u^{\mu}n^{\mu-2}\frac{s+n^2s_1t+\ldots}{1+nn_1t+\ldots},
\end{aligned}$$

ou encore

$$\begin{aligned}
u=&\,M_1t+M_2t^2+\ldots\\
&+u^2(P+P_1t+P_2t^2+\ldots)\\
&+u^3(Q+Q_1t+Q_2t^2+\ldots)\\
&+\ldots\ldots\ldots\ldots\ldots\ldots\\
&+u^{\mu}(S+S_1t+S_2t^2+\ldots),
\end{aligned}$$

en observant que les séries infinies introduites dans le second membre ont toutes pour coefficients des nombres entiers. Faisant donc

$$u=a_1t+a_2t^2+a_3t^3+\ldots,$$

on obtiendra les relations

$$\begin{aligned} a_1 &= M_1, \\ a_2 &= M_2 + P a_1^2, \\ a_3 &= M_3 + 2 P a_1 a_2 + P_1 a_1^2 + Q a_1^3, \end{aligned}$$

qui de proche en proche donnent les quantités $a_1, a_2, a_3, \ldots$ en fonctions entières et à coefficients entiers de $M_1, M_2, \ldots, P, P_1, P_2, \ldots$. Nous démontrons immédiatement ainsi le résultat découvert par M. Heine, que la série infinie qui satisfait à l'équation algébrique entre t et u a tous ses coefficients entiers. Et si l'on revient aux variables x et z, on aura cette expression

$$z = \frac{a_1}{n} x + \frac{a_2}{n^3} x^2 + \frac{a_3}{n^5} x^3 + \ldots + \frac{a_i}{n^{2i-1}} x^i + \ldots,$$

que je vais considérer à l'égard de la puissance fractionnaire du binome $(1 - x)^{-\frac{m}{n}}$. Nous trouvons alors cette conséquence que

$$\begin{aligned} &\frac{\frac{m}{n}\left(\frac{m}{n}+1\right)\left(\frac{m}{n}+2\right)\ldots\left(\frac{m}{n}+i-1\right)}{1.2.3\ldots i} \\ &\quad = \frac{m(m+n)(m+2n)\ldots[m+(i-1)n]}{1.2.3\ldots i . n^i} = \frac{a_i}{n^{2i-1}}, \end{aligned}$$

c'est-à-dire que l'expression

$$\frac{m(m+n)(m+2n)\ldots[m+(i-1)n]n^{i-1}}{1.2.3\ldots i}$$

est toujours un nombre entier

Le procédé, dont je viens de faire usage, s'applique également aux relations transcendantes. Considérons, par exemple, l'équation de Kepler

$$y = a + x \sin y;$$

on fera $y = a + u$, et on mettra la transformée

$$u = x \sin(a + u),$$

ou plutôt

$$\begin{aligned} u = {} & x \sin a \left(1 - \frac{1}{2} u^2 + \frac{1}{24} u^4 - \ldots\right) \\ & + x \cos a \left(u - \frac{1}{6} u^3 + \frac{1}{120} u^5 - \ldots\right), \end{aligned}$$

sous la forme suivante :

$$u(1 - x\cos a) = x\sin a - u^2\frac{x\sin a}{2} - u^3\frac{x\cos a}{6} - \dots.$$

Nous sommes ainsi amené à introduire, au lieu de x, la quantité $\frac{x\sin a}{1 - x\cos a}$; en la désignant par ζ pour un moment, l'équation devient, en effet,

$$u = \zeta - u^2\frac{\zeta}{2} - u^3\frac{\zeta\cot a}{6}, \quad \dots,$$

et l'on tire très facilement

$$u = \zeta - \frac{1}{2}\zeta^3 - \frac{\cot a}{6}\zeta^4 - \dots,$$

Dans les *Annales de l'Observatoire de Paris*, M. Serret avait déjà fait la remarque, que la valeur très simple $u = \zeta$, c'est-à-dire

$$y = a + \frac{x\sin a}{1 - x\cos a},$$

donnait une solution approchée du problème de Kepler, en négligeant seulement le cube de l'excentricité.

EXTRAIT

D'UNE

LETTRE DE M. CH. HERMITE A M. L. KÖNIGSBERGER.

SUR LE

DÉVELOPPEMENT DES FONCTIONS ELLIPTIQUES

SUIVANT LES PUISSANCES CROISSANTES DE LA VARIABLE.

Journal de Crelle, t. 81, 1876, p. 220-228.

Je me suis occupé de ces polynomes rationnels et entiers par rapport au module, qui se présentent dans les développements des fonctions sin am$x$, cos am$x$ et Δ am$x$ suivant les puissances croissantes de la variable, et dont les premiers seulement ont été calculés. Si l'on pose

$$\begin{aligned}
\sin \operatorname{am} x &= u - \frac{\mathfrak{P}_1 x^3}{1.2.3} + \frac{\mathfrak{P}_2 x^5}{1.2.3.4.5} - \ldots + (-1)^m \frac{\mathfrak{P}_m x^{2m+1}}{1.2\ldots 2m+1} + \ldots,\\
\cos \operatorname{am} x &= 1 - \frac{\mathfrak{Q}_1 x^2}{1.2} + \frac{\mathfrak{Q}_2 x^4}{1.2.3.4} - \ldots + (-1)^m \frac{\mathfrak{Q}_m x^{2m}}{1.2\ldots 2m} + \ldots,\\
\Delta \operatorname{am} x &= 1 - \frac{\mathfrak{R}_1 x^2}{1.2} + \frac{\mathfrak{R}_2 x^4}{1.2.3.4} - \ldots + (-1)^m \frac{\mathfrak{R}_m x^{2m}}{1.2\ldots 2m} + \ldots,
\end{aligned}$$

vous savez qu'on a ces expressions

$$\begin{aligned}
\mathfrak{P}_m &= \quad 1 \quad + P_1 \varkappa^2 + P_2 \varkappa^4 + \ldots + \varkappa^{2m},\\
\mathfrak{Q}_m &= \quad 1 \quad + Q_1 \varkappa^2 + Q_2 \varkappa^4 + \ldots + Q_{m-1} \varkappa^{2m-2},\\
\mathfrak{R}_m &= R_0 \varkappa^2 + R_1 \varkappa^4 + R_2 \varkappa^6 + \ldots + \varkappa^{2m}
\end{aligned}$$

avec les conditions

$$R_0 = Q_{m-1}, \qquad R_1 = Q_{m-2}, \qquad \ldots,$$

qui ramènent $\mathfrak{R}_m$ à $\mathfrak{Q}_m$. Mais ni la formule de Maclaurin ni les relations tirées de la transformation du second ordre, telles que celle-ci

$$(\varkappa + i\varkappa')\cos\operatorname{am}\left[(\varkappa - i\varkappa')x, \frac{\varkappa + i\varkappa'}{\varkappa - i\varkappa'}\right]$$
$$+ (\varkappa - i\varkappa')\cos\operatorname{am}\left[(\varkappa + i\varkappa')x, \frac{\varkappa - i\varkappa'}{\varkappa + i\varkappa'}\right] = 2\varkappa\cos\operatorname{am}(x, \varkappa),$$

que j'ai employée autrefois pour le calcul des quantités $\mathfrak{Q}_m$, ne paraissent pouvoir conduire à l'expression générale en fonction de m, des coefficients des diverses puissances de $\varkappa$. C'est en suivant une autre voie que j'ai obtenu les résultats suivants, qui en montrent la composition arithmétique. Considérant en premier lieu le polynome $\mathfrak{P}_m$, on aura

$$4^2 P_1 = 3^{2m+1} - 8m - 3,$$
$$4^4 P_2 = 5^{2m+1} - (8m - 4)3^{2m+1} + 32m^2 - 32m - 17,$$
$$4^6 P_3 = 7^{2m+1} - (8m - 12)5^{2m+1} + (32m^2 - 88m + 30)3^{2m+1}$$
$$- \frac{1}{3}(256m^3 - 1056m^2 + 752m + 471),$$

. . . .

A l'égard de $\mathfrak{Q}_m$ je trouve semblablement

$$4^2 Q_1 = 3^{2m} - 8m - 1,$$
$$4^4 Q_2 = 5^{2m} - (8m - 8)3^{2m} + 32m^2 - 48m - 9,$$
$$4^6 Q_3 = 7^{2m} - (8m - 16)5^{2m} + (32m^2 - 120m + 82)3^{2m}$$
$$- \frac{1}{3}(256m^3 - 288m^2 + 320m + 297),$$

. . . .

Enfin pour $\mathfrak{R}_m$ on obtient (¹)

$$R_0 = 2^{2m-2},$$
$$R_1 = 2^{2m-6}[2^{2m} - 8m + 4],$$
$$R_2 = 2^{2m-10}[3^{2m} - (8m - 12)2^{2m} + 32m^2 - 88m + 31],$$
$$R_3 = 2^{2m-14}[4^{2m} - (8m - 20)3^{2m} + (32m^2 - 152m + 148)2^{2m}$$
$$- \frac{1}{3}(256m^3 - 1728m^2 + 3080m - 900)],$$

. . . .

(¹) Nous avons lieu de penser, d'après les calculs de M. Bourget, que les formules donnant Q_3 et R_3 ne sont pas exactes; c'est ce que montre la considération des cas particuliers $m = 2, 3$. E. P.

Supposons que m soit un grand nombre; alors nous aurons, lorsque le module est réel et moindre que l'unité, ces valeurs limites, à savoir

$$\frac{\mathfrak{P}_m}{1.2\ldots(2m+1)} = \frac{2}{\varkappa K'^{2m+2}},$$

$$\frac{\mathfrak{Q}_m}{1.2\ldots 2m} = \frac{2}{\varkappa K'^{2m+1}},$$

$$\frac{\mathfrak{R}_m}{1.2\ldots 2m} = \frac{2}{K'^{2m-1}}.$$

Il en résulte que les développements en série, de $\sin \operatorname{am} x$, $\cos \operatorname{am} x$, $\Delta \operatorname{am} x$, tendent de plus en plus à se confondre dans leurs derniers termes, avec ces simples progressions

$$\frac{(-1)^m 2 x^{2m+1}}{\varkappa K'^{2m+2}}\left(1 - \frac{x^2}{K'^2} + \frac{x^4}{K'^4} - \ldots\right),$$

$$\frac{(-1)^m 2 x^{2m}}{\varkappa K'^{2m+1}}\left(1 - \frac{x^2}{K'^2} + \frac{x^4}{K'^4} - \ldots\right),$$

$$\frac{(-1)^m 2 x^{2m}}{K'^{2m+1}}\left(1 - \frac{x^2}{K'^2} + \frac{x^4}{K'^4} - \ldots\right),$$

et par suite seront convergents, lorsque le module de la variable sera moindre que K'.

Voici, après les quantités $\mathfrak{P}_m$, $\mathfrak{Q}_m$, $\mathfrak{R}_m$, deux nouvelles séries de polynomes, $\mathfrak{S}_m$ et $\mathfrak{T}_m$, définies par les relations suivantes :

$$\frac{1}{\sin \operatorname{am} x} = \frac{1}{x} + \mathfrak{S}_1 x + \frac{\mathfrak{S}_2 x^3}{1.2.3} + \ldots + \frac{\mathfrak{S}_m x^{2m-1}}{1.2\ldots(2m-1)} + \ldots,$$

$$\frac{1}{\sin^2 \operatorname{am} x} = \frac{1}{x^2} + \mathfrak{T}_1 + \frac{\mathfrak{T}_2 x^2}{1.2} + \ldots + \frac{\mathfrak{T}_m x^{2m-2}}{1.2\ldots(2m-2)} + \ldots,$$

et qui présentent quelque intérêt, comme j'espère vous le montrer. On a d'abord ces expressions

$$\mathfrak{S}_m = S_0 - S_1 \varkappa^2 + S_2 \varkappa^4 - \ldots + (-1)^m S_m \varkappa^{2m},$$

$$\mathfrak{T}_m = T_0 - T_1 \varkappa^2 + T_2 \varkappa^4 - \ldots + (-1)^m T_m \varkappa^{2m},$$

et les coefficients qui sont toujours commensurables mais non plus entiers comme précédemment, sont donnés par ces formules où B_m

désigne le $m^{\text{ième}}$ nombre de Bernoulli

$$S_0 = \frac{2^{2m-1}-1}{m} B_m,$$

$$4 S_1 = (-1)^m + 2(2^{2m-1}-1) B_m,$$

$$4^3 S_2 = (-1)^m (8m-9) + (8m-14)(2^{2m-1}-1) B_m,$$

$$4^5 S_3 = (-1)^m (32 m^2 - 128 m + 101 + 3^{2m-1}) + \frac{1}{3}(64 m^2 - 336 m + 416)(2^{2m-1}-1) B_m,$$

$$\dots\dots\dots\dots;$$

$$T_0 = \frac{2^{2m-1} B_m}{m},$$

$$T_1 = 2^{2m-2} B_m,$$

$$T_2 = (-1)^m 2^{2m-7} + (4m-7) 2^{2m-6} B_m,$$

$$T_3 = (-1)^m (m-2) 2^{2m-8} + \frac{1}{3}(4m^2 - 21 m + 26) 2^{2m-7} B_m,$$

$$\dots\dots\dots\dots,$$

ces dernières équations relatives à $\mathfrak{T}_m$ devant être appliquées seulement à partir de $m = 2$.

On a, ensuite, en supposant que m soit un grand nombre, les expressions limites

$$\frac{\mathfrak{S}_m}{1.2\ldots(2m-1)} = \frac{2}{(2K)^{2m}} - \frac{(-1)^m}{(2K')^{2m}},$$

$$\frac{\mathfrak{T}_m}{1.2\ldots(2m-2)} = \frac{4m-1}{(2K)^{2m}} + \frac{(-1)^m (4m-1)}{(2K')^{2m}}.$$

Elles montrent que les développements de $\frac{1}{\sin \operatorname{am} x}$, $\frac{1}{\sin^2 \operatorname{am} x}$ sont convergents, tant que le module de la variable est au-dessous de la plus petite des deux quantités $2K$ et $2K'$, ce qui est encore la conclusion, que donne immédiatement le théorème de Cauchy. C'est à l'égard des polynomes $\mathfrak{S}_m$ et $\mathfrak{T}_m$ qu'on tire de la théorie de la transformation de nombreuses propriétés que je vais indiquer succinctement. Les premières et les plus simples résultent des équations

$$\sin \operatorname{am}\left(\varkappa x, \frac{1}{\varkappa}\right) = \varkappa \sin \operatorname{am}(x, \varkappa),$$

$$\frac{1}{\sin^2 \operatorname{am}(ix, \varkappa')} + \frac{1}{\sin^2 \operatorname{am}(x, \varkappa)} = 1,$$

qui donnent, en faisant

$$\mathfrak{S}_m = \Pi(\varkappa), \qquad \mathfrak{T}_m = \Phi(\varkappa),$$

les conditions

$$\varkappa^{2m}\,\Pi\left(\frac{1}{\varkappa}\right) = \Pi(\varkappa),$$

$$\varkappa^{2m}\,\Phi\left(\frac{1}{\varkappa}\right) = \Phi(\varkappa),$$

$$\Phi(\varkappa') = (-1)^m\,\Phi(\varkappa).$$

On en déduit aisément pour $\Phi(\varkappa)$ les conséquences suivantes : supposant en premier lieu que m soit pair et posant $m = 2n$, nous aurons cette expression canonique

$$\begin{aligned}\Phi(\varkappa) = {} & G(1-\varkappa^2+\varkappa^4)^n + G_1(1-\varkappa^2+\varkappa^4)^{n-3}\varkappa^4\varkappa'^4 \\ & + G_2(1-\varkappa^2+\varkappa^4)^{n-6}\varkappa^8\varkappa'^8 + \ldots + G_p(1-\varkappa^2+\varkappa^4)^{n-3p}\varkappa^{4p}\varkappa'^{4p},\end{aligned}$$

où p est l'entier contenu dans $\frac{n}{3}\cdot$ Supposons ensuite $m = 2n+1$; la forme analytique précédente n'est modifiée que par l'introduction du facteur

$$(1+\varkappa^2)(2-\varkappa^2)(1-2\varkappa^2) = \varphi(\varkappa),$$

et l'on obtient

$$\begin{aligned}\Phi(\varkappa) = \varphi(\varkappa)\,[& H(1-\varkappa^2+\varkappa^4)^{n-1} + H_1(1-\varkappa^2+\varkappa^4)^{n-4}\varkappa^4\varkappa'^4 + \ldots \\ & + H_q(1-\varkappa^2+\varkappa^4)^{n-1-3q}\varkappa^{4q}\varkappa'^{4q}],\end{aligned}$$

q étant l'entier contenu dans $\frac{n-1}{3}\cdot$ Si nous continuons de désigner par B_m le $m^{\text{ième}}$ nombre de Bernoulli, les valeurs des premiers coefficients G et H seront

$$G = \frac{2^{4n-2}B_{2n}}{n},$$

$$G_1 = 2^{4n-7} - 15.2^{4n-6}B_{2n},$$

$$G_2 = -2^{8n-16} + (240n - 745)2^{4n-15} - (180n - 9495)^{4n-14}B_{2n},$$

....;

$$H = \frac{2^{4n}B_{2n+1}}{2n+1},$$

$$H_1 = -2^{4n-6} - \frac{(30-93)2^{4n-5}B_{2n-1}}{2n+1},$$

....

Voici maintenant les propriétés algébriques remarquables auxquelles conduit la transformation du second ordre, en partant des relations

$$\frac{1+\varkappa}{\sin\operatorname{am}\left(\frac{1+\varkappa}{2}ix, \frac{1-\varkappa}{1+\varkappa}\right)} = \frac{1}{\sin\operatorname{am}(ix, \varkappa')} + \frac{\varkappa}{\sin\operatorname{am}\left(i\varkappa x, \frac{i\varkappa'}{\varkappa}\right)},$$

$$\frac{1+\varkappa'}{\sin\operatorname{am}\left(\frac{1+\varkappa'}{2}x, \frac{1-\varkappa'}{1+\varkappa'}\right)} = \frac{1}{\sin\operatorname{am}(x, \varkappa)} + \frac{i\varkappa}{\sin\operatorname{am}\left(i\varkappa x, \frac{i\varkappa'}{\varkappa}\right)},$$

$$\frac{\varkappa+i\varkappa'}{\sin\operatorname{am}\left(\frac{\varkappa+i\varkappa'}{2}x, \frac{\varkappa-i\varkappa'}{\varkappa+i\varkappa'}\right)} = \frac{1}{\sin\operatorname{am}(x, \varkappa)} + \frac{i}{\sin\operatorname{am}(ix, \varkappa')}$$

auxquelles je joindrai encore celle-ci

$$\frac{1}{\sin^2\operatorname{am}\frac{x}{2}} = \frac{(1+\cos\operatorname{am}x)(1+\Delta\operatorname{am}x)}{\sin^2\operatorname{am}x};$$

j'en déduis les diverses conséquences suivantes.

Soit d'abord, pour abréger l'écriture,

$$\Pi' = (-1)^m\,\Pi(\varkappa'), \qquad \Pi'' = (-1)^m \varkappa^{2m}\,\Pi\left(\frac{i\varkappa'}{\varkappa}\right),$$

puis

$$\Pi_0 = (-1)^m\,(1+\varkappa)^{2m}\,\Pi\left(\frac{1-\varkappa}{1+\varkappa}\right),$$

$$\Pi_1 = (1+\varkappa')^{2m}\,\Pi\left(\frac{1-\varkappa'}{1+\varkappa'}\right),$$

$$\Pi_2 = (\varkappa+i\varkappa')^{2m}\,\Pi\left(\frac{\varkappa-i\varkappa'}{\varkappa+i\varkappa'}\right);$$

on aura en premier lieu

$$\Pi_0 = 2^{2m-1}(\Pi' + \Pi''),$$

$$\Pi_1 = 2^{2m-1}(\Pi'' + \Pi),$$

$$\Pi_2 = 2^{2m-1}(\Pi + \Pi')$$

et il est aisé de voir que l'une quelconque de ces équations suffit pour déterminer sauf un facteur constant les coefficients du polynome $\Pi(x)$.

Je remarquerai ensuite que $\Phi(x)$ se conclut immédiatement de $\Pi(\varkappa)$; on a, en effet,

$$\Phi(\varkappa) = \frac{(2m-1)2^{2m-2}}{2^{2m-2}-1}(\Pi + \Pi' + \Pi''),$$

et les trois quantités suivantes, à savoir

$$\Phi_0 = (-1)^m (1+\varkappa)^{2m} \Phi\left(\frac{1-\varkappa}{1+\varkappa}\right),$$

$$\Phi_1 = (1+\varkappa')^{2m} \Phi\left(\frac{1-\varkappa'}{1+\varkappa'}\right),$$

$$\Phi_2 = (\varkappa + i\varkappa')^{2m} \Phi\left(\frac{\varkappa - i\varkappa'}{\varkappa + i\varkappa'}\right),$$

s'expriment par ces formules

$$\Phi_0 = \frac{(2m-1)2^{2m-2}}{2^{2m-2}-1} (\Pi_0 + 2\Pi),$$

$$\Phi_1 = \frac{(2m-1)2^{2m-2}}{2^{2m-2}-1} (\Pi_1 + 2\Pi'),$$

$$\Phi_2 = \frac{(2m-1)2^{2m-2}}{2^{2m-2}-1} (\Pi_2 + 2\Pi'').$$

Enfin on peut, d'une manière inverse, déterminer d'abord le polynome $\Phi(\varkappa)$, en employant à cet effet la relation

$$(2^{2m}+2)\Phi(\varkappa) = \Phi_0 + \Phi_1 + \Phi_2,$$

qui est une conséquence des précédentes. On en déduira ensuite

$$\Pi(\varkappa) = \frac{1}{(2m-1)2^{2m-1}} (2^{2m-1}\Phi - \Phi_0),$$

puis

$$\Pi_0 = \frac{1}{2m-1} (\Phi_0 - 2\Phi),$$

$$\Pi_1 = \frac{1}{2m-1} (\Phi_1 - 2\Phi),$$

$$\Pi_2 = \frac{1}{2m-1} (\Phi_2 - 2\Phi).$$

Ces résultats manifestent entre $\Pi(\varkappa)$ et $\Phi(\varkappa)$ une dépendance réciproque, que ne pouvait guère faire prévoir leur origine; ils conduisent aussi à remarquer les deux combinaisons linéaires suivantes :

$$\Theta(\varkappa) = (2^{m-1}+1)\Phi(\varkappa) - (2m-1)2^{m-1}\Pi(\varkappa),$$
$$\Theta_1(\varkappa) = (2^{m-1}-1)\Phi(\varkappa) - (2m-1)2^{m-1}\Pi(\varkappa).$$

Nous aurons, en effet,

$$(1+\varkappa)^{2m}\Theta\left(\frac{1-\varkappa}{1+\varkappa}\right) = (-1)^m 2^m \Theta(\varkappa),$$

$$(1+\varkappa)^{2m}\Theta_1\left(\frac{1-\varkappa}{1+\varkappa}\right) = (-1)^{m+1} 2^m \Theta_1(\varkappa),$$

et de là résulte, comme vous allez voir, une forme canonique pour ces deux nouveaux polynomes.

Je cherche en premier lieu l'expression la plus générale des polynomes entiers $\varphi(x)$, de degré m en x^2, tels qu'on ait

$$(1)\qquad x^{2m}\varphi\left(\frac{1}{x}\right) = \varphi(x),$$

$$(2)\qquad (1+x)^{2m}\varphi\left(\frac{1-x}{1+x}\right) = 2^m\varphi(x),$$

et je ferai d'abord cette remarque que, si $\varphi(x)$ est supposé s'annuler avec la variable, il contient le facteur $x^2(1-x^2)^2$. Soit à cet effet, dans l'équation (2), $x=0$; on en conclut que $\varphi(x)$ s'annule pour $x=1$ et admet par suite le facteur $x^2(1-x^2)$, puisqu'il ne renferme que des puissances paires de la variable. Or, en posant

$$\varphi(x) = x^2(1-x^2)\,\psi(x),$$

l'équation (1) donne

$$x^{2m-6}\psi\left(\frac{1}{x}\right) = -\psi(x),$$

ce qui montre immédiatement que $\psi(x)$ s'évanouit pour $x=\pm 1$. J'ajoute qu'en faisant

$$\psi(x) = (1-x^2)\chi(x)$$

ou bien

$$\varphi(x) = x^2(1-x^2)^2\chi(x),$$

on obtiendra à l'égard de $\chi(x)$

$$x^{2m-8}\chi\left(\frac{1}{x}\right) = \chi(x),$$

$$(1+x)^{2m-8}\chi\left(\frac{1-x}{1+x}\right) = 2^{m-4}\chi(x),$$

c'est-à-dire les équations caractéristiques du polynome proposé $\varphi(x)$, en y changeant m en $m-4$.

Une seconde remarque va maintenant en donner l'expression générale. Soit pour un moment

$$\varphi_1(x) = \varphi(x) - \mathrm{A}(1+x^2)^m,$$

A étant une constante arbitraire; on voit immédiatement qu'on aura

$$x^{2m}\varphi_1\left(\frac{1}{x}\right) = \varphi_1(x),$$

$$(1+x)^{2m}\varphi_1\left(\frac{1-x}{1+x}\right) = 2^m\varphi_1(x).$$

Or, en disposant de A de manière que $\varphi_1(x)$ s'annule avec x, on le ramène, comme nous l'avons vu, au produit d'un polynome de même nature, de degré $2m-8$, multiplié par le facteur $x^2(1-x^2)^2$. Opérant donc sur ce nouveau polynome comme sur le précédent, il est clair qu'on parviendra de proche en proche à l'expression cherchée

$$\begin{aligned}\varphi(x) = {} & \mathrm{A}(1+x^2)^m + \mathrm{A}_1(1+x^2)^{m-4}x^2(1-x^2)^2 \\ & + \mathrm{A}_2(1+x^2)^{m-8}x^4(1-x^2)^4 + \ldots + \mathrm{A}_r(1+x^2)^{m-4r}x^{4r}(1-x^2)^{4r},\end{aligned}$$

r désignant l'entier contenu dans $\frac{m}{4}$. Mais ce résultat ne nous suffit pas et nous avons encore à considérer les polynomes qui satisfont aux conditions,

$$x^{2m}\varphi\left(\frac{1}{x}\right) = \varphi(x),$$

$$(1+x)^{2m}\varphi\left(\frac{1-x}{1+x}\right) = -2^m\varphi(x).$$

Or, en faisant

$$\frac{1-x}{1+x} = x,$$

c'est-à-dire

$$x^2 + 2x - 1 = 0,$$

la seconde équation donne

$$\varphi(x) = 0,$$

de sorte que $\varphi(x)$ est divisible par x^2+2x-1, et, par conséquent, aussi par x^2-2x-1, attendu que $\varphi(-x) = \varphi(x)$. Ayant

$$(x^2+2x-1)(x^2-2x-1) = x^4 - 6x^2 + 1,$$

faisons

$$\varphi(x) = (x^4 - 6x^2 + 1)\psi(x);$$

on trouvera aisément les conditions

$$x^{2m-4}\psi\left(\frac{1}{x}\right) = \psi(x),$$

$$(1+x)^{2m-4}\psi\left(\frac{1-x}{1+x}\right) = 2^{m-2}\psi(x),$$

qui sont celles du premier cas. Nous obtenons ainsi les expressions canoniques des polynomes $\Theta(\varkappa)$, $\Theta_1(\varkappa)$, et, par conséquent, les valeurs de $\Pi(\varkappa)$ et $\Phi(\varkappa)$ sous une forme algébrique semblable. Mais c'est trop m'étendre sur ces polynomes qui m'ont surtout occupé au point de vue de l'usage qu'on peut en faire dans le développement en série des puissances et produits de puissances des fonctions $\sin\operatorname{am}x$, $\cos\operatorname{am}x$, $\Delta\operatorname{am}x$. Cette question déjà traitée par M. C.-O. Meyer (*Entwickelung der elliptischen Functionen*

$$\Delta^{\pm r}\operatorname{am}\frac{2Kx}{\pi}\cos^{\pm s}\operatorname{am}\frac{2Kx}{\pi}\sin^{\pm t}\operatorname{am}\frac{2Kx}{\pi}\int_0^x\Delta^2\operatorname{am}\frac{2Kx}{\pi}\,dx,$$

nach den Sinus und Cosinus der Vielfachen von x, ce journal, t. XXXVII) joue un grand rôle dans la méthode de calcul des perturbations que M. Hugo Gylden a publiée dans les Mémoires de Saint-Pétersbourg (*Studien auf dem Gebiete der Störungstheorie,* 7e série, t. XVI), et où j'ai vu avec le plus vif intérêt les fonctions elliptiques recevoir une application heureuse et habile à la Mécanique céleste....

Lamothe-de-Meursac (Charente-Inférieure), 2 octobre 1875.

EXTRAIT

D'UNE

LETTRE DE M. CH. HERMITE A M. PAUL MANSION.

SUR

UNE FORMULE DE M. DELAUNAY.

Nouvelle Correspondance mathématique, t. II, 1876, p. 54-55.

M. Delaunay, dans sa *Thèse sur la distinction des maxima et minima qui dépendent du calcul des variations* (*Journal de M. Liouville*, t. VI, p. 212) a donné, sans démonstration, la formule suivante :

$$\mathrm{P}\mathrm{D}_x^m \mathrm{Q} = \mathrm{D}_x^m \mathrm{PQ} - m_1 \mathrm{D}_x^{m-1} \mathrm{P}'\mathrm{Q} + m_2 \mathrm{D}_x^{m-2} \mathrm{P}''\mathrm{Q} + \ldots + (-1)^m \mathrm{P}^{(m)}\mathrm{Q},$$

où P et Q sont deux fonctions de x, m_1, m_2, ... étant les coefficients de x, x^2, ... dans la puissance $(1+x)^m$. On peut l'établir facilement, si l'on observe que tous les termes du second membre donnent, en développant les dérivations indiquées, des résultats compris dans cette formule

$$\mathrm{AP}^{(m)}\mathrm{Q} + \mathrm{BP}^{(m-1)}\mathrm{Q}' + \mathrm{CP}^{(m-2)}\mathrm{Q}'' + \ldots + \mathrm{LPQ}^{(m)},$$

les coefficients A, B, C, ..., L dépendant seulement de m. Leur somme peut donc être représentée par l'expression de même nature

$$a\,\mathrm{P}^{(m)}\mathrm{Q} + b\,\mathrm{P}^{(m-1)}\mathrm{Q}' + c\,\mathrm{P}^{(m-2)}\mathrm{Q}'' + \ldots + l\,\mathrm{PQ}^{(m)};$$

et il suffira, pour obtenir les coefficients numériques a, b, ..., l, de faire une hypothèse particulière convenable sur les fonctions P et Q. Soit, à cet effet,

$$P = e^{px}, \qquad Q = e^{qx}.$$

On sera ainsi conduit à l'identité

$$\begin{aligned} &D^m e^{(p+q)x} - m_1 p D^{m-1} e^{(p+q)x} + m_2 p^2 D^{m-2} e^{(p+q)x} - \ldots + (-1)^m p^m e^{(p+q)x} \\ &= e^{(p+q)x}(ap^m + bp^{m-1}q + \ldots + lq^m). \end{aligned}$$

Or, en effectuant les dérivations et supprimant dans les deux membres le facteur exponentiel, elle prend cette forme

$$\begin{aligned} &(p+q)^m - m_1 p(p+q)^{m-1} + m_2 p^2 (p+q)^{m-2} - \ldots + (-1)^m p^m \\ &\quad = ap^m + bp^{m-1} + \ldots + lq^m; \end{aligned}$$

et le premier membre se réduisant à $(p+q-p)^m$, c'est-à-dire simplement à q^m, on voit qu'en effet les coefficients a, b, ... disparaissent, sauf le dernier qui a pour valeur l'unité.

Paris, 25 novembre 1875.

SUR

L'AIRE D'UN SEGMENT DE COURBE CONVEXE.

Nouvelle Correspondance mathématique, t. II, 1876. Question 95.

Théorème. — AMB *étant un arc de courbe plane, convexe, on projette* A *sur la tangente* BA′ *en* B, *et l'on projette* B *sur la tangente* AB′ *en* A. *Cela posé, si l'on néglige les quantités du* cinquième ordre, *le segment* AMB *est équivalent au* $\frac{1}{6}$ *de la somme des triangles rectangles* AA′B, BB′A.

SUR UN EXEMPLE

DE

RÉDUCTION D'INTÉGRALES ABÉLIENNES,

AUX FONCTIONS ELLIPTIQUES.

Annales de la Société scientifique de Bruxelles, 1re année, 1876, p. 1-16.

Dans une Note du Tome 8 du *Journal de Crelle*, p. 416, Jacobi, en généralisant un résultat obtenu par Legendre, a montré que les deux intégrales abéliennes de première espèce $\int \frac{dz}{\sqrt{R(z)}}$ et $\int \frac{z\,dz}{\sqrt{R(z)}}$, où l'on suppose

$$R(z) = z(1-z)(1-abz)(1+az)(1+bz),$$

peuvent être ramenées, aux intégrales elliptiques, par la même substitution

$$\sqrt{z} = \frac{k'+l'}{\sqrt{1-k^2\sin^2\varphi}+\sqrt{1-l^2\sin^2\varphi}},$$

dont on déduit les relations

$$\int_0^z \frac{dz}{\sqrt{R(z)}} = \frac{1}{2}(k'+l')[F(k,\varphi)+F(l,\varphi)],$$

$$\int_0^z \frac{z\,dz}{\sqrt{R(z)}} = \frac{(k'+l')^2}{2(l'-k')}[F(k,\varphi)-F(l,\varphi)].$$

Les valeurs des modules k, l et de leurs compléments k', l' sont données par les formules suivantes, où je pose pour abréger $c = \sqrt{(1+a)(1+b)}$, à savoir :

$$k = \frac{\sqrt{a}+\sqrt{b}}{c}, \qquad l = \frac{\sqrt{a}-\sqrt{b}}{c},$$

$$k' = \frac{1-\sqrt{ab}}{c}, \qquad l' = \frac{1+\sqrt{ab}}{c}.$$

De ce résultat, extrêmement remarquable, ne semble avoir été tiré jusqu'ici d'autre conclusion que celle indiquée par Jacobi lui-même, et qui consiste à obtenir la partie réelle et le coefficient de i, dans l'intégrale $\int_0^\varphi \frac{d\varphi}{\sqrt{1-(e+if)\sin^2\varphi}}$. Si l'on représente cette quantité par $A+iB$, l'illustre géomètre en conclut, en effet, les expressions

$$A = g\int_0^z \frac{dz}{\sqrt{R(z)}}, \qquad B = h\int_0^z \frac{z\,dz}{\sqrt{R(z)}},$$

en prenant pour les paramètres a et b, qui figurent dans $R(z)$, les valeurs

$$a = \frac{\sqrt{(1-e)^2+f^2}+e-1}{\sqrt{e^2+f^2}-e}, \qquad b = \frac{\sqrt{(1-e)^2+f^2}+e-1}{\sqrt{e^2+f^2}+e},$$

et pour les facteurs g et h, celles-ci,

$$g = \left[\sqrt{(1-e)^2+f^2}-e+1\right]^{-\frac{1}{2}}, \qquad h = \frac{\left[\sqrt{(1-e)^2+f^2}+e-1\right]^{\frac{1}{2}}}{\sqrt{(1-e)^2+f^2}+e+1}.$$

Je me propose de faire voir qu'il a une portée beaucoup plus étendue, et qu'il ouvre une voie nouvelle, même après les belles découvertes de Clebsch, dans la recherche difficile des intégrales de différentielles algébriques, qui peuvent se réduire aux fonctions elliptiques. Il offre, en effet, le premier exemple, et le seul connu jusqu'ici, de la réduction d'un type d'intégrales qui contient essentiellement deux fonctions de première espèce, obtenue en introduisant deux intégrales elliptiques de modules différents. J'ai rencontré récemment dans une recherche, où je ne présumais point devoir le trouver, un second exemple qui a appelé mon attention sur les formules de Jacobi, et que je vais indiquer succinctement.

Soit

$$R(z) = (z^2 - a)(8z^3 - 6az - b);$$

on aura en premier lieu

$$\int \frac{dz}{\sqrt{R(z)}} = \frac{1}{3}\int \frac{dx}{\sqrt{(2ax - b)(x^2 - a)}}$$

en prenant

$$x = \frac{4z^3 - 3az}{a},$$

et, si l'on pose ensuite

$$y = \frac{2z^3 - b}{3(z^2 - a)},$$

on obtiendra la relation

$$\int \frac{z\,dz}{\sqrt{R(z)}} = \frac{1}{2\sqrt{3}}\int \frac{dy}{\sqrt{y^3 - 3ay + b}}.$$

On est ainsi, par induction, conduit à croire qu'il existe pour les irrationnelles algébriques, dont le nombre caractéristique, ordinairement désigné par p, est supérieur à l'unité, des cas de réduction de leurs intégrales aux fonctions elliptiques, dans lesquels les p fonctions de première espèce seraient exprimées par autant d'intégrales elliptiques différentes, au moyen de p substitutions. Sans insister sur l'intérêt et la difficulté des recherches qui se présentent afin d'essayer de confirmer cette induction, je me propose, dans cette Note, d'achever, si je puis dire, la réduction aux fonctions elliptiques des intégrales abéliennes considérées par Jacobi, et d'arriver par là à une sorte de jonction entre la théorie des sinus d'amplitude et celles des fonctions de Göpel et de M. Rosenheim, où le rapprochement des formules et des relations qui les concernent pourra donner, ce me semble, des observations utiles.

I.

En posant pour abréger $x = \sin^2\varphi$, je reprends la substitution de Jacobi sous cette autre forme, donnée aussi par le grand géomètre,

$$x = \frac{c^2 z}{(1+az)(1+bz)},$$

et d'où l'on tire facilement

$$1 - x = \frac{(1-z)(1-abz)}{(1+az)(1+bz)},$$

$$1 - k^2 x = \frac{(1-\sqrt{ab}\,z)^2}{(1+az)(1+bz)},$$

et, par suite,

$$(\text{A}) \qquad \Delta(x, k) = \sqrt{\text{R}(z)}\,\frac{c(1-\sqrt{ab}\,z)}{(1+az)^2(1+bz)^2},$$

si l'on écrit pour abréger

$$\Delta(x, k) = \sqrt{x(1-x)(1-k^2 x)}.$$

Cette relation conduit comme conséquence, en y changeant le signe du radical $\sqrt{ab}$, à la suivante :

$$(\text{B}) \qquad \Delta(x, l) = \sqrt{\text{R}(z)}\,\frac{c(1+\sqrt{ab}\,z)}{(1+az)^2(1+bz)^2},$$

où le nouveau module l est déterminé par la condition

$$l = \frac{\sqrt{a}-\sqrt{b}}{c}.$$

Or, ayant

$$\frac{dx}{dz} = \frac{c^2(1-abz^2)}{(1+az)^2(1+bz)^2},$$

on en tire sur-le-champ les deux égalités

$$\frac{dx}{\Delta(x, k)} = \frac{c(1+\sqrt{ab}\,z)\,dz}{\sqrt{\text{R}(z)}},$$

$$\frac{dx}{\Delta(x, l)} = \frac{c(1-\sqrt{ab}\,z)\,dz}{\sqrt{\text{R}(z)}}.$$

Je me propose maintenant d'en poursuivre les conséquences, et, conformément à la nature des intégrales abéliennes de première classe, je chercherai à réduire aux fonctions elliptiques la somme des deux intégrales semblables

$$\int \frac{f(\text{X})\,d\text{X}}{\sqrt{\text{R}(\text{X})}} + \int \frac{f(\text{Y})\,d\text{Y}}{\sqrt{\text{R}(\text{Y})}},$$

en prenant pour X et Y des fonctions algébriques de deux variables indépendantes x et y, et pour $f(X)$ et $f(Y)$ les mêmes fonctions rationnelles de X et Y. On y parvient en considérant l'équation

$$F^2(z) - R(z) = 0,$$

où $F(z)$ est un polynome de troisième degré en z, déterminé de telle manière qu'elle admette comme facteur, d'une part le polynome du second degré

$$\Phi(z) = x(1 + az)(1 + bz) - c^2 z,$$

avec la condition (A),

$$\sqrt{R(z)} = \Delta(x, k)\frac{(1 + az)^2(1 + bz)^2}{c(1 - \sqrt{ab}\,z)};$$

et, en second lieu, le facteur semblable

$$\Phi_1(z) = y(1 + az)(1 + bz) - c^2 z,$$

et avec la condition (B),

$$\sqrt{R(z)} = \Delta(y, l)\frac{(1 + az)^2(1 + bz)^2}{c(1 + \sqrt{ab}\,z)}.$$

Nous allons voir, en effet, que les quantités X et Y seront les racines de l'équation du second degré en z, représentée par le quotient entier

$$\frac{F^2(z) - R(z)}{\Phi(z)\Phi_1(z)} = 0.$$

II.

Je ferai usage, à cet effet, du théorème d'Abel, en supposant la fonction rationnelle $f(x)$ réduite simplement à $\frac{1}{x - g}$, où g est une constante indéterminée, et j'en déduirai la relation suivante. Soient $z = x_0$, $z = x_1$ les racines de l'équation

$$x(1 + az)(1 + bz) - c^2 z = 0;$$

puis $x = y_0$, $z = y_1$ celles de l'équation semblable

$$y(1 + az)(1 + bz) - c^2 z = 0;$$

on aura comme on sait

$$\frac{1}{\sqrt{R(g)}}\log\frac{F(g)+\sqrt{R(g)}}{F(g)-\sqrt{R(g)}}=\int\frac{dx_0}{(x_0-g)\sqrt{R(x_0)}}+\int\frac{dx_1}{(x_1-g)\sqrt{R(x_1)}}$$
$$+\int\frac{dy_0}{(y_0-g)\sqrt{R(y_0)}}+\int\frac{dy_1}{(y_1-g)\sqrt{R(y_1)}}$$
$$+\int\frac{dX}{(X-g)\sqrt{R(X)}}+\int\frac{dY}{(Y-g)\sqrt{R(Y)}}.$$

Maintenant on va voir que les deux sommes d'intégrales

$$\int\frac{dx_0}{(x_0-g)\sqrt{R(x_0)}}+\int\frac{dx_1}{(x_1-g)\sqrt{R(x_1)}}$$

et

$$\int\frac{dy_0}{(y_0-g)\sqrt{R(y_0)}}+\int\frac{dy_1}{(y_1-g)\sqrt{R(y_1)}}$$

se réduisent aux fonctions elliptiques.

Considérons, en effet, la première qui se rapporte aux racines de l'équation

$$\Phi(z)=x(1+az)(1+bz)-c^2z=0$$

et où l'on se rappelle qu'il faut prendre pour chacune de ces racines

$$\sqrt{R(z)}=\Delta(x,k)\frac{(1+az)^2(1+bz)^2}{c(1-\sqrt{ab}\,z)}.$$

Je transformerai d'abord comme il suit cette relation. Après l'avoir mise sous la forme

$$\sqrt{R(z)}\,c(1-\sqrt{ab}\,z)^2=\Delta(x,k)(1+az)^2(1+bz)^2(1-\sqrt{ab}\,z),$$

je multiplie membre à membre avec la suivante :

$$1-k^2x=\frac{(1-\sqrt{ab}\,z)^2}{(1+az)(1+bz)},$$

ce qui donne, en simplifiant,

$$\sqrt{R(z)}\,c(1-k^2x)=\Delta(x,k)(1+az)(1+bz)(1-\sqrt{ab}\,z).$$

On introduit ainsi, dans le second membre, la quantité

$$\frac{d\Phi}{dx}=(1+az)(1+bz),$$

ce qui permet d'écrire

$$\sqrt{R(z)}\,c(1-k^2x)=\Delta(x,k)\left(1-\sqrt{ab}\,z\right)\frac{d\Phi}{dx}.$$

Or, il vient en différentiant l'équation $\Phi(z)=0$:

$$\frac{d\Phi}{dz}dz=-\frac{d\Phi}{dx}dx,$$

et l'on conclut facilement, en divisant membre à membre,

$$\frac{dz}{\sqrt{R(z)}}=\frac{c(1-k^2x)\,dx}{\left(\sqrt{ab}\,z-1\right)\Phi'(z)\,\Delta(x,k)},$$

puis

$$\frac{dz}{(z-g)\sqrt{R(z)}}=\frac{c(1-k^2x)\,dx}{\left(\sqrt{ab}\,z-1\right)(z-g)\,\Phi'(z)\,\Delta(x,k)}.$$

Supposant maintenant $z=x_0$, puis $z=x_1$ et ajoutant membre à membre, on est conduit à calculer la fonction symétrique

$$\frac{1}{\left(\sqrt{ab}\,x_0-1\right)(x_0-g)\,\Phi'(x_0)}+\frac{1}{\left(\sqrt{ab}\,x_1-1\right)(x_1-g)\,\Phi'(x_1)}$$

des racines de l'équation $\Phi(z)=0$, qu'il est aisé d'obtenir. Écrivons, en effet,

$$\frac{1}{\left(\sqrt{ab}\,z-1\right)(z-g)}=\frac{1}{\left(\sqrt{ab}\,g-1\right)}\left(\frac{1}{z-g}-\frac{\sqrt{ab}}{\sqrt{ab}\,z-1}\right),$$

et la valeur cherchée résultera de la formule élémentaire

$$\frac{1}{\Phi(x)}=\frac{1}{(x-x_0)\,\Phi'(x_0)}+\frac{1}{(x-x_1)\,\Phi'(x_1)},$$

en faisant successivement $x=g$ et $x=\frac{1}{\sqrt{ab}}$. Ce calcul, fort simple, conduit à joindre à la constante g une autre h, qui en dépend par la relation

$$h=\frac{c^2g}{(1+ag)(1+bg)},$$

de sorte qu'on a

$$\sqrt{R(g)}=\Delta(h,k)\frac{(1+ag)^2(1+bg)^2}{c\left(1-\sqrt{ab}\,g\right)}.$$

De cette manière on obtient

$$\frac{dx_0}{(x_0-g)\sqrt{R(x_0)}}+\frac{dx_1}{(x_1-g)\sqrt{R(x_1)}}=-\frac{a+b+\sqrt{ab}+abg}{c(1+ag)(1+bg)}\frac{dx}{\Delta(x,k)}$$
$$+\frac{\Delta(h,k)}{\sqrt{R(g)}(x-h)}\frac{dx}{\Delta(x,k)},$$

et, par conséquent,

$$\int\frac{dx_0}{(x_0-g)\sqrt{R(x_0)}}+\int\frac{dx_1}{(x_1-g)\sqrt{R(x_1)}}=-\frac{a+b+\sqrt{ab}+abg}{c(1+ag)(1+bg)}\int\frac{dx}{\Delta(x,k)}$$
$$+\frac{\Delta(h,k)}{\sqrt{R(g)}}\int\frac{dx}{(x-h)\Delta(x,k)}.$$

Enfin, si l'on met la variable y au lieu de x, et qu'on change le signe du radical $\sqrt{ab}$, on aura la réduction aux fonctions elliptiques de la seconde somme d'intégrales, à savoir

$$\int\frac{dy_0}{(y_0-g)\sqrt{R(y_0)}}+\int\frac{dy_1}{(y_1-g)\sqrt{R(y_1)}}=-\frac{a+b-\sqrt{ab}+abg}{c(1+ag)(1+bg)}\int\frac{dy}{\Delta(y,l)}$$
$$+\frac{\Delta(h,l)}{\sqrt{R(g)}}\int\frac{dy}{(y-h)\Delta(y,l)}.$$

Les quantités X et Y, qui ont été obtenues par l'emploi du théorème d'Abel, ont donc le rôle que nous avons annoncé, et le résultat auquel nous venons de parvenir s'accorde bien avec la nature logarithmique des intégrales abéliennes de troisième espèce, car, en multipliant par le facteur $\sqrt{R(g)}$, on obtient cette formule

$$\int\frac{\sqrt{R(g)}\,dX}{(X-g)\sqrt{R(X)}}+\int\frac{\sqrt{R(g)}\,dY}{(Y-g)\sqrt{R(Y)}}$$
$$=\log\frac{F(g)+\sqrt{R(g)}}{F(g)-\sqrt{R(g)}}+A\int\frac{dx}{\Delta(x,k)}+B\int\frac{dy}{\Delta(y,l)}$$
$$-\int\frac{\Delta(h,k)\,dx}{(x-h)\Delta(x,k)}-\int\frac{\Delta(h,l)\,dy}{(y-h)\Delta(y,l)},$$

où les constantes A et B ont pour valeurs

$$A=\frac{a+b+\sqrt{ab}+abg}{c(1+ag)(1+bg)}\sqrt{R(g)},$$
$$B=\frac{a+b-\sqrt{ab}+abg}{c(1+ag)(1+bg)}\sqrt{R(g)}.$$

Je ne chercherai pas ici à la rapprocher des expressions données par M. Weierstrass, et qui sont l'une des plus belles découvertes de l'illustre géomètre; je me bornerai à remarquer qu'il est facile d'en conclure la réduction aux fonctions elliptiques des intégrales plus générales

$$\int \frac{f(X)\,dX}{\sqrt{R(X)}} + \int \frac{f(Y)\,dY}{\sqrt{R(Y)}}.$$

Effectivement, toute fonction rationnelle $f(x)$ s'exprime linéairement, d'une part, au moyen des quantités $\frac{1}{x-g}$, de leurs dérivées par rapport à g et de l'autre par les puissances entières de la variable. Or, on obtiendra ces dernières intégrales qui appartiennent à la catégorie des fonctions de première et de seconde espèce, en égalant dans les deux membres les coefficients de leurs développements suivant les puissances décroissantes de h. C'est le calcul que je vais faire afin de parvenir aux valeurs des fonctions inverses de nos intégrales abéliennes, exprimées par des fonctions algébriques de sinus d'amplitude.

III.

Considérons d'abord le terme

$$\log \frac{F(g)+\sqrt{R(g)}}{F(g)-\sqrt{R(g)}},$$

que j'écrirai ainsi

$$\log\left[1+\frac{\sqrt{R(g)}}{F(g)}\right] - \log\left[1-\frac{\sqrt{R(g)}}{F(g)}\right].$$

Nous avons dit précédemment que $F(g)$ est du troisième degré en g, et, comme $R(g)$ est du cinquième, on voit qu'elle s'évanouit pour g infini. Passons ensuite aux intégrales

$$\int \frac{\Delta(h,k)\,dx}{(x-h)\,\Delta(x,k)}, \quad \int \frac{\Delta(h,l)\,dy}{(y-l)\,\Delta(y,l)};$$

la formule $h = \frac{c^2 g}{(1+ag)(1+bg)}$, donnant $h = \frac{c^2}{ab}$ pour g infini, fait voir que ces quantités sont dans cette supposition l'une et l'autre finies. De la relation proposée, résulte donc, après avoir divisé les deux membres par $\sqrt{R(g)}$, que les termes en $\frac{1}{g}$ et en $\frac{1}{g^2}$ sont les mêmes, dans les développements des quantités

$$\int \frac{dX}{(X-g)\sqrt{R(X)}} + \int \frac{dY}{(Y-g)\sqrt{R(Y)}}$$

et

$$\frac{a+b+\sqrt{ab}}{c(1+ag)(1+bg)}\int \frac{dx}{\Delta(x,k)} + \frac{a+b-\sqrt{ab}}{c(1+ag)(1+bg)}\int \frac{dy}{\Delta(y,l)},$$

suivant les puissances descendantes de g. On obtient ainsi les relations auxquelles nous voulions parvenir, à savoir :

$$\int \frac{dX}{\sqrt{R(X)}} + \int \frac{dY}{\sqrt{R(Y)}} = -\frac{1}{c}\int \frac{dx}{\Delta(x,k)} - \frac{1}{c}\int \frac{dy}{\Delta(y,l)},$$

$$\int \frac{X\,dX}{\sqrt{R(X)}} + \int \frac{Y\,dY}{\sqrt{R(Y)}} = -\frac{1}{c\sqrt{ab}}\int \frac{dx}{\Delta(x,k)} + \frac{1}{c\sqrt{ab}}\int \frac{dy}{\Delta(y,l)}.$$

Qu'on définisse donc les fonctions inverses de nos intégrales abéliennes, en posant les équations

$$\int \frac{c(1+\sqrt{ab}\,X)\,dX}{2\sqrt{R(X)}} + \int \frac{c(1+\sqrt{ab}\,Y)\,dY}{2\sqrt{R(Y)}} = u,$$

$$\int \frac{c(1-\sqrt{ab}\,X)\,dX}{2\sqrt{R(X)}} + \int \frac{c(1-\sqrt{ab}\,Y)\,dY}{2\sqrt{R(Y)}} = v.$$

On voit qu'on aura

$$u = -\int \frac{dx}{\Delta(x,k)}, \qquad v = -\int \frac{dy}{\Delta(y,l)}.$$

Par conséquent, les quantités X et Y, fonctions algébriques de x et y, s'expriment en u et v par des fonctions algébriques de $\sin\operatorname{am}(u,k)$ et de $\sin\operatorname{am}(v,l)$.

Cette conclusion donne beaucoup d'intérêt au calcul des valeurs de X et Y, et je terminerai cette Note en indiquant succinctement la marche que j'ai suivie pour l'effectuer.

Revenons, à cet effet, à l'équation

$$F^2(z) - R(z) = 0,$$

et à la détermination de $F(z)$ par les conditions posées au paragraphe I. Ce polynome étant du troisième degré, je lui donnerai la forme suivante, où P, Q, R, S sont quatre coefficients arbitraires

$$F(z)=\frac{(1+az)(1+bz)}{c}[Pabz+P(a+b)+Q]+c(Rz+S).$$

Cela posé, ces coefficients devront être déterminés de manière à avoir

$$F(z)=\sqrt{R(z)},$$

en prenant pour z, d'abord les racines de l'équation

$$x(1+az)(1+bz)-c^2z=0,$$

avec la condition

$$\sqrt{R(z)}=\Delta(x,k)\frac{(1+az)^2(1+bz)^2}{c(1-\sqrt{ab}z)},$$

qu'on transforme facilement ainsi

$$\sqrt{R(z)}=\Delta(x,k)\frac{cz(1-\sqrt{ab}\,z)}{x(1-k^2x)},$$

puis en second lieu, les racines de l'équation

$$y(1+az)(1+bz)-c^2z=0,$$

avec la condition correspondante

$$\sqrt{R(z)}=\Delta(g,l)\frac{(1+az)^2(1+bz)^2}{c(1+\sqrt{ab}z)},$$

ou plutôt

$$\sqrt{R(z)}=\Delta(y,l)\frac{cz(1+\sqrt{ab}z)}{y(1-l^2y)}.$$

Or, en remplaçant dans le premier membre $\frac{(1+az)(1+bz)}{c}$ par $\frac{cz}{x}$, et z^2 dans le second membre par

$$\frac{1}{ab}\left[-(a+b)z-1+\frac{c^2}{x}\right],$$

on obtient une équation en z du premier degré, qui doit être par conséquent identique, et donne les égalités

$$Sx - P = \frac{\Delta(x, k)}{\sqrt{ab}(1 - k^2 x)},$$

$$Rx + Q + c^2 S = \frac{(a + b + \sqrt{ab})\,\Delta(x, k)}{\sqrt{ab}\,(1 - k^2 x)}.$$

En opérant d'une manière semblable, avec les conditions concernant le second facteur, avec la variable y, on trouve

$$Sy - P = -\frac{\Delta(y, l)}{\sqrt{ab}(1 - l^2 y)},$$

$$Ry + Q + c^2 S = -\frac{(a + b - \sqrt{ab})\,\Delta(y, l)}{\sqrt{ab}\,(1 - l^2 y)}.$$

Ces équations entre les coefficients P, Q, R, S, sont simples et donnent aisément les valeurs suivantes, ou j'écris pour abréger :

$$\Delta(x, k) = \Delta, \qquad \alpha = a + b + \sqrt{ab},$$

$$\Delta(y, l) = \Delta_1, \qquad \beta = a + b - \sqrt{ab},$$

$$P = \frac{y(1 - l^2 y)\Delta + x(1 - k^2 x)\Delta_1}{\sqrt{ab}(1 - k^2 x)(1 - l^2 y)(y - x)},$$

$$Q = \frac{(\alpha y + c^2)(1 - l^2 y)\Delta + (\beta x + c^2)(1 - k^2 x)\Delta_1}{\sqrt{ab}(1 - k^2 x)(1 - l^2 y)(y - x)},$$

$$R = -\frac{\alpha(1 - l^2 y)\Delta + \beta(1 - k^2 x)\Delta_1}{\sqrt{ab}(1 - k^2 x)(1 - l^2 y)(y - x)},$$

$$S = -\frac{(1 - l^2 y)\Delta + (1 - k^2 x)\Delta_1}{\sqrt{ab}(1 - k^2 x)(1 - l^2 y)(y - x)};$$

le polynome $F(z)$ étant connu, j'emploierai l'identité

$$\begin{aligned} F^2(z) - R(z) = {} & C[x(1 + \alpha z)(1 + bz) - c^2 z] \\ & \times [y(1 + az)(1 + bz) - c^2 z] \\ & \times [(z - X)(z - Y)], \end{aligned}$$

où l'on trouve que le facteur constant C a pour valeur

$$C = \frac{1}{xy}\left(\frac{Pab}{c}\right)^2,$$

et je ferai successivement z égal aux diverses racines du polynome R(z), de manière à obtenir les combinaisons des quantités X et Y que M. Weierstrass, en les considérant comme fonctions des variables u et v, représente par $\mathrm{al}(u, v)_\alpha$, avec un indice unique.

Ce calcul m'a donné pour résultat les formules suivantes :

$$\sqrt{ab\mathrm{XY}} = \frac{y(1-l^2y)\Delta - x(1-k^2x)\Delta_1}{y(1-l^2y)\Delta + x(1-k^2x)\Delta_1},$$

$$\begin{aligned}&\sqrt{ab(1-\mathrm{X})(1-\mathrm{Y})}\\ &\quad = \frac{(1-\sqrt{ab})(1-y)(1-l^2y)\Delta - (1+\sqrt{ab})(1-x)(1-k^2x)\Delta_1}{y(1-l^2y)\Delta + x(1-k^2x)\Delta_1}\\ &\quad\quad \times \frac{\sqrt{xy}}{\sqrt{(1-x)(1-y)}},\end{aligned}$$

$$\begin{aligned}&\sqrt{(1-ab\mathrm{X})(1-ab\mathrm{Y})}\\ &\quad = \frac{(1-\sqrt{ab})(1-y)(1-l^2y)\Delta + (1+\sqrt{ab})(1-x)(1-k^2x)\Delta_1}{y(1-l^2y)\Delta + x(1-k^2x)\Delta_1}\\ &\quad\quad \times \frac{\sqrt{xy}}{\sqrt{(1-x)(1-y)}},\end{aligned}$$

$$\begin{aligned}&\sqrt{b(1-a\mathrm{X})(1-a\mathrm{Y})}\\ &\quad = \frac{(\sqrt{a}+\sqrt{b})(1-l^2y)\Delta - (\sqrt{a}-\sqrt{b})(1-k^2x)\Delta_1}{y(1-l^2y)\Delta + x(1-k^2x)\Delta_1}\sqrt{xy},\end{aligned}$$

$$\begin{aligned}&\sqrt{a(1-b\mathrm{X})(1-b\mathrm{Y})}\\ &\quad = \frac{(\sqrt{a}+\sqrt{b})(1-l^2y)\Delta + (\sqrt{a}-\sqrt{b})(1-k^2x)\Delta_1}{y(1-l^2y)\Delta + x(1-k^2x)\Delta_1}\sqrt{xy}.\end{aligned}$$

Elles ouvrent la voie à des recherches sur lesquelles je me propose de revenir dans une autre occasion.

NOTE

SUR UNE FORMULE DE JACOBI.

Mémoires de la Société royale des Sciences de Liége,
2e série, t. VI, 1879, p. 1-7,
et *Mathematische Annalen,* t. X, 1877.

Les belles recherches de M. Tchebichef et de M. Heine sur l'intégrale $\int_0^b \frac{f(z)}{x-z}dz$ ont montré dans les parties élevées de l'Analyse le rôle et l'importance de la théorie élémentaire des fractions continues algébriques. C'est une nouvelle application de cette théorie que j'ai l'honneur de présenter à la Société, et qui aura pour objet la relation importante dont Jacobi a fait la découverte, à savoir

$$\frac{d^n(1-x^2)^{n+\frac{1}{2}}}{dx^n} = C\sin[(n+1)\arccos x],$$

C désignant une constante.

Je rappellerai, d'abord, qu'étant proposée une fonction $f(x)$, développable en série infinie de la forme

$$f(x) = \frac{a}{x} + \frac{a_1}{x^2} + \frac{a_2}{x^3} + \ldots,$$

toute réduite, ou fraction convergente $\frac{F_1(x)}{F(x)}$, dont le dénominateur est un polynome de degré n en x, s'obtient directement comme il suit.

On détermine en premier lieu ce dénominateur par la condition que le produit $f(x)\,F(x)$, étant ordonné suivant les puissances décroissantes de la variable, manque des termes en $\frac{1}{x}, \frac{1}{x^2}, \ldots, \frac{1}{x^n}$; cela fait, le numérateur $F_1(x)$ est donné par la partie entière du même produit, qui est évidemment du degré $n-1$. On voit, en effet, qu'ayant ainsi la relation

$$f(x)\,F(x) = F_1(x) + \frac{\varepsilon_1}{x^{n+1}} + \frac{\varepsilon_2}{x^{n+2}} + \ldots,$$

et, par conséquent,

$$f(x) = \frac{F_1(x)}{F(x)} + \frac{1}{F(x)}\left(\frac{\varepsilon_1}{x^{n+1}} + \frac{\varepsilon_2}{x^{n+2}} + \ldots\right),$$

les développements suivant les puissances décroissantes de la fonction $f(x)$ et de la fraction rationnelle $\frac{F_1(x)}{F(x)}$ coïncideront jusqu'au terme en $\frac{1}{x^{2n+1}}$, le développement de $\frac{1}{F(x)}$ commençant par un terme en $\frac{1}{x^n}$. De plus, les polynomes $F(x)$ et $F_1(x)$, sauf un facteur constant commun, seront déterminés d'une manière unique.

Cela posé, soit, en particulier,

$$f(x) = \frac{1}{\sqrt{x^2-1}} = \frac{1}{x} + \frac{1}{2}\,\frac{1}{x^3} + \frac{1.3}{2.4}\,\frac{1}{x^5} + \ldots;$$

il sera aisé, dans ce cas, de former $F(x)$ et $F_1(x)$ pour toute valeur de n. Soit, pour cela,

$$\left(x + \sqrt{x^2-1}\right)^n = F(x) + \sqrt{x^2-1}\,F_1(x),$$

c'est-à-dire

$$\begin{aligned} F(x) &= \cos n(\operatorname{arc}\cos x), \\ F_1(x) &= \sin n(\operatorname{arc}\cos x); \end{aligned}$$

je dis que ces polynomes entiers de degrés n et $n-1$ donnent précisément les deux termes des réduites. On a, en effet,

$$x - \sqrt{x^2-1} = \frac{1}{x} + \ldots;$$

d'où

$$\left(x - \sqrt{x^2-1}\right)^n = \frac{1}{x^n} + \ldots;$$

l'équation proposée, si l'on y change le signe du radical, donne, par conséquent,

$$\frac{1}{x^n}+\ldots = F(x) - \sqrt{x^2-1}\,F_1(x),$$

et, enfin,

$$\frac{F(x)}{\sqrt{x^2-1}} = F_1(x) + \frac{1}{\sqrt{x^2-1}}\left(\frac{1}{x^n}+\ldots\right) = F_1(x) + \frac{1}{x^{n+1}}+\ldots.$$

La condition posée, comme définition des réduites, se trouve ainsi complètement remplie. Or, on peut encore la réaliser d'une autre manière, comme on va voir. Formons la dérivée d'ordre n de l'expression

$$(x^2-1)^{n-\frac{1}{2}};$$

il est aisé de voir d'abord qu'elle sera de la forme $\frac{P}{\sqrt{x^2-1}}$, P étant un polynome entier en x de degré n. Soit ensuite, en développant suivant les puissances décroissantes de la variable

$$(x^2-1)^{n-\frac{1}{2}} = x^{2n-1} + a x^{2n-3} + \ldots + \lambda x + \frac{\varepsilon}{x} + \frac{\varepsilon_1}{x^3} + \ldots;$$

je remarquerai qu'en prenant la dérivée d'ordre n, la partie entière du second membre conduira à un polynome P_1 de degré $n-1$, tandis que la partie contenant les puissances négatives de la variable donnera une série infinie commençant par un terme en $\frac{1}{x^{n+1}}$.

Nous trouvons donc encore la relation

$$\frac{P}{\sqrt{x^2-1}} = P_1 + \frac{\varepsilon'}{x^{n+1}} + \frac{\varepsilon''}{x^{n+2}} + \ldots$$

qui détermine, sauf un facteur commun constant, comme nous l'avons dit, les polynomes entiers qui y entrent. On en conclut, en désignant par N une constante numérique,

$$P = N\cos n(\operatorname{arc}\cos x),$$

et, par conséquent,

$$\frac{d^n(x^2-1)^{n-\frac{1}{2}}}{dx^n} = \frac{N\cos n(\operatorname{arc}\cos x)}{\sqrt{x^2-1}}.$$

Or le coefficient de x^{n-1} dans le premier membre a pour valeur

$$n(n+1)(n+2)\ldots(2n-1);$$

et comme on a

$$\cos n(\operatorname{arc}\cos x) = 2^{n-1}x^n + \ldots,$$

cette constante se trouve déterminée par la condition

$$n(n+1)(n+2)\ldots(2n-1) = 2^{n-1}\mathrm{N};$$

d'où l'on tire

$$\mathrm{N} = \frac{n(n+1)(n+2)\ldots(2n-1)}{2^{n-1}} = \frac{1.2.3\ldots(2n-1)}{2^{n-1}\,1.2.3\ldots(n-1)},$$

ou encore

$$\mathrm{N} = \frac{1.2.3\ldots(2n-1)}{2.4.6\ldots(2n-2)} = 1.3.5\ldots(2n-1).$$

La formule de Jacobi que nous avions en vue d'établir est une conséquence immédiate de ce résultat; car en mettant la relation obtenue sous la forme suivante :

$$\begin{aligned}\frac{d^n(1-x^2)^{n-\frac{1}{2}}}{dx^n} &= (-1)^n\mathrm{N}\frac{\cos n(\operatorname{arc}\cos x)}{\sqrt{1-x^2}}\\ &= (-1)^{n-1}\mathrm{N}\cos n(\operatorname{arc}\cos x)\frac{d\operatorname{arc}\cos x}{dx},\end{aligned}$$

on en conclut, en intégrant par rapport à x,

$$\frac{d^{n-1}(1-x^2)^{n-\frac{1}{2}}}{dx^{n-1}} = \frac{(-1)^{n-1}\mathrm{N}}{n}\sin n(\operatorname{arc}\cos x).$$

Nous n'ajoutons point de constante, attendu que les deux membres s'évanouissent quand on suppose $x=1$; cela étant, il suffit, comme on voit, de changer n en $n+1$, pour arriver au théorème proposé, la valeur de la constante C étant

$$\mathrm{C} = (-1)^n\frac{1.3.5\ldots(2n+1)}{n+1}.$$

Paris, août 1873.

SUR QUELQUES APPLICATIONS

DES

FONCTIONS ELLIPTIQUES.

Comptes rendus de l'Académie des Sciences, t. LXXXV, 1877, p. 689, 728, 821, 870, 984, 1085, 1185; t. LXXXVI, 1878, p. 271, 422, 622, 777, 850; t. LXXXIX, 1879, p. 1001, 1092; t. XC, 1880, p. 106, 201, 478, 643, 761; t. XCIII, 1881, p. 920, 1098; t. XCIV, 1882, p. 186, 372, 477, 594, 753.

La théorie analytique de la chaleur donne pour l'importante question de l'équilibre des températures d'un corps solide homogène, soumis à des sources calorifiques constantes, une équation aux différences partielles dont l'intégration, dans le cas de l'ellipsoïde, a été l'une des belles découvertes auxquelles est attaché le nom de Lamé. Les résultats obtenus par l'illustre géomètre découlent principalement de l'étude approfondie d'une équation différentielle linéaire du second ordre, que j'écrirai avec les notations de la théorie des fonctions elliptiques, sous la forme suivante :

$$\frac{d^2y}{dx^2} = [n(n+1)k^2 \operatorname{sn}^2 x + h]y,$$

k étant le module, n un nombre entier et h une constante. Lamé a montré que, pour des valeurs convenables de cette constante, on y satisfait par des polynomes entiers en $\operatorname{sn} x$

$$y = \operatorname{sn}^n x + h_1 \operatorname{sn}^{n-2} x + h_2 \operatorname{sn}^{n-4} x + \ldots,$$

dont les termes sont de même parité, puis encore par ces expressions :

$$y = (\operatorname{sn}^{n-1} x + h'_1 \operatorname{sn}^{n-3} x + h'_2 \operatorname{sn}^{n-5} x + \ldots) \operatorname{cn} x,$$
$$y = (\operatorname{sn}^{n-1} x + h''_1 \operatorname{sn}^{n-3} x + h''_2 \operatorname{sn}^{n-5} x + \ldots) \operatorname{dn} x,$$
$$y = (\operatorname{sn}^{n-2} x + h'''_1 \operatorname{sn}^{n-4} x + h'''_2 \operatorname{sn}^{n-6} x + \ldots) \operatorname{cn} x \operatorname{dn} x.$$

M. Liouville a ensuite introduit, dans la question physique, la considération de la seconde solution de l'équation différentielle, d'où il a tiré des théorèmes du plus grand intérêt ([1]). C'est également cette seconde solution, dont la nature et les propriétés ont été approfondies par M. Heine, qui a montré l'analogie de ces deux genres de fonctions de Lamé avec les fonctions sphériques, et leurs rapports avec la théorie des fractions continues algébriques. On doit de plus à l'éminent géomètre une extension de ses profondes recherches à des équations différentielles linéaires du second ordre beaucoup plus générales, qui se rattachent aux intégrales abéliennes, comme celle de Lamé aux fonctions elliptiques ([2]).

Je me suis placé à un autre point de vue en me proposant d'obtenir, quel que soit h, l'intégrale générale de cette équation, et c'est l'objet principal des recherches qu'on va lire. On verra que la solution est toujours, comme dans les cas particuliers considérés par Lamé, une fonction uniforme de la variable, mais qui n'est plus doublement périodique. Elle est, en effet, donnée par la formule

$$y = \mathrm{C\,F}(x) + \mathrm{C'\,F}(-x),$$

où la fonction $\mathrm{F}(x)$, qui satisfait à ces deux conditions

$$\begin{aligned} \mathrm{F}(x+2\mathrm{K}) &= \mu\,\mathrm{F}(x),\\ \mathrm{F}(x+2i\mathrm{K}') &= \mu'\,\mathrm{F}(x), \end{aligned}$$

dans lesquelles les facteurs μ et μ' sont des constantes, s'exprime comme il suit. Soit, pour un moment,

$$\Phi(x) = \frac{\mathrm{H}(x+\omega)}{\Theta(x)}\, e^{\left[\lambda - \frac{\Theta'(\omega)}{\Theta(\omega)}\right]x};$$

nous aurons

$$\mathrm{F}(x) = \mathrm{D}_x^{n-1}\,\Phi(x) - \mathrm{A}_1\,\mathrm{D}_x^{n-3}\,\Phi(x) + \mathrm{A}_2\,\mathrm{D}_x^{n-5}\,\Phi(x) - \ldots;$$

([1]) *Comptes rendus*, 1er sem. 1845, p 1386 et 1609; *Journal de Mathématiques*, t. XI, p. 217 et 261.

([2]) *Journal de Crelle* (*Beitrag zur Theorie des Anziehung und der Warme* t. 29); *Journal de M. Borchardt* (*Ueber die Lameschen Functionen; Einige Eigenschaften der Lameschen Functionen* dans le Tome 56, et *Die Lameschen Functionen verchiedener Ordnungen*, t. 57). Le premier de ces Mémoires, paru en 1845, mais daté du 19 avril 1844, contient une application de la seconde solution de l'équation de Lamé, qui a été par conséquent découverte par M. Heine, indépendamment des travaux de M. Liouville, et à la même époque.

les quantités $\operatorname{sn}^2\omega$ et λ^2 sont des fonctions rationnelles du module et de h, et les coefficients A_1, A_2, ..., des fonctions entières. On a, par exemple,

$$A_1 = \frac{(n-1)(n-2)}{2(2n-1)}\left[h + \frac{n(n+1)(1+k^2)}{3}\right],$$

$$A_2 = \frac{(n-1)(n-2)(n-3)(n-4)}{8(2n-1)(2n-3)}$$
$$\times\left[h^2 + \frac{2n(n+1)(1+k^2)}{3}h + \frac{n^2(n+1)^2}{9}(1+k^2)^2 - \frac{2n(n+1)(2n-1)}{15}(1-k^2+k^4)\right],$$

. . . .

Je m'occuperai, avant de traiter le cas général où le nombre n est quelconque, des cas particuliers de $n=1$ et $n=2$. Le premier s'applique à la rotation d'un corps solide autour d'un point fixe, lorsqu'il n'y a point de forces accélératrices, et nous conduira aux formules données par Jacobi dans son admirable Mémoire sur cette question (*Œuvres complètes*, t. II, p. 139, et *Comptes rendus*, 30 juillet 1849). J'y rattacherai encore la détermination de la figure d'équilibre d'un ressort, qui a été le sujet de travaux de Binet et de Wantzel (*Comptes rendus*, 1er sem. 1844, p. 1115 et 1197). Le second se rapportant au pendule sphérique, j'aurai ainsi réuni quelques-unes des plus importantes applications qui aient été faites jusqu'ici de la théorie des fonctions elliptiques.

I.

La méthode que je vais exposer, pour intégrer l'équation de Lamé, repose principalement sur des expressions, par les quantités $\Theta(x)$, $H(x)$, ..., des fonctions $F(x)$, satisfaisant aux conditions énoncées tout à l'heure

$$F(x+2K) = \mu\, F(x),$$
$$F(x+2iK') = \mu'\, F(x),$$

qui s'obtiennent ainsi :

Soit, en désignant par A un facteur constant,

$$f(x) = A\,\frac{H(x+\omega)\,e^{\lambda x}}{H(x)};$$

les relations fondamentales

$$H(x+2K) = -H(x),$$
$$H(x+2iK') = -H(x)e^{-\frac{i\pi}{K}(x+iK')}$$

donneront celles-ci :

$$f(x+2K) = f(x)e^{2\lambda K},$$
$$f(x+2iK') = f(x)e^{-\frac{i\pi\omega}{K}+2i\lambda K'}.$$

Disposant donc de ω et λ de manière à avoir

$$\mu = e^{2\lambda K},$$
$$\mu' = e^{-\frac{i\pi\omega}{K}+2i\lambda K'},$$

on voit que le quotient $\frac{F(x)}{f(x)}$ est ramené aux fonctions doublement périodiques, d'où cette première forme générale et dont il sera souvent fait usage :

$$F(x) = f(x)\Phi(x),$$

la fonction $\Phi(x)$ n'étant assujettie qu'aux conditions

$$\Phi(x+2K) = \Phi(x), \qquad \Phi(x+2iK') = \Phi(x).$$

En voici une seconde, qui est fondamentale pour notre objet. Je remarque que les relations

$$f(x+2K) = \mu f(x),$$
$$f(x+2iK') = \mu' f(x),$$

ont pour conséquence celles-ci :

$$f(x-2K) = \frac{1}{\mu}f(x),$$
$$f(x-2iK') = \frac{1}{\mu'}f(x),$$

de sorte que le produit

$$\Phi(z) = F(z)f(x-z)$$

sera, quel que soit x, une fonction doublement périodique de z.

Cela étant, nous allons calculer les résidus $\Phi(z)$, pour les diverses valeurs de l'argument qui la rendent infinie, dans l'intérieur du rectangle des périodes ; et, en égalant leur somme à zéro, nous obtiendrons immédiatement l'expression cherchée. Remarquons à cet effet que $f(x)$ ne devient infinie qu'une fois pour $x = 0$, et que, son résidu ayant pour valeur

$$\frac{AH(\omega)}{H'(0)},$$

on peut disposer de A, de manière à le faire égal à l'unité. Posant donc, en adoptant cette détermination,

$$f(x) = \frac{H'(0)\,H(x+\omega)\,e^{\lambda x}}{H(\omega)\,H(x)},$$

on voit que le résidu correspondant à la valeur $z = x$ de $\Phi(z)$ sera $-F(x)$. Ceux qui proviennent des pôles de $F(z)$ s'obtiennent ensuite sous la forme suivante. Soit $z = a$ l'un d'eux, et posons en conséquence, pour ε infiniment petit,

$$\begin{aligned} F(a+\varepsilon) = A\varepsilon^{-1} + A_1 D_\varepsilon \varepsilon^{-1} + A_2 D_\varepsilon^2 \varepsilon^{-1} + \ldots \\ + A_\alpha D_\varepsilon^\alpha \varepsilon^{-1} + a_0 + a_1\varepsilon + a_2\varepsilon^2 + \ldots, \end{aligned}$$

$$\begin{aligned} f(x-a-\varepsilon) = f(x-a) - \frac{\varepsilon}{1} D_x f(x-a) \\ + \frac{\varepsilon^2}{1.2} D_x^2 f(x-a) - \ldots + \frac{(-1)^\alpha \varepsilon^\alpha}{1.2\ldots\alpha} D_x^\alpha f(x-a) + \ldots, \end{aligned}$$

le coefficient du terme en $\frac{1}{\varepsilon}$ dans le produit des seconds membres, qui est la quantité cherchée, se trouve immédiatement, en remarquant que

$$D_\varepsilon^n \varepsilon^{-1} = (-1)^n \frac{1.2\ldots n}{\varepsilon^{n+1}},$$

et a pour expression

$$A f(x-a) + A_1 D_x f(x-a) + A_2 D_x^2 f(x-a) + \ldots + A_\alpha D_x^\alpha f(x-a).$$

La somme des résidus de la fonction $\Phi(z)$, égalée à zéro, nous conduit ainsi à la relation

$$F(x) = \Sigma[A f(x-a) + A_1 D_x f(x-a) + \ldots + A_\alpha D_x^\alpha f(x-a)],$$

où le signe Σ se rapporte, comme il a été dit, à tous les pôles de $F(z)$ qui sont à l'intérieur du rectangle des périodes.

II.

La fonction $F(x)$ comprend les fonctions doublement périodiques; en supposant égaux à l'unité les multiplicateurs μ et μ', je vais immédiatement rechercher ce que l'on tire, dans cette hypothèse, du résultat auquel nous venons de parvenir. Tout d'abord les relations

$$\mu = e^{2\lambda K}, \qquad \mu' = e^{-\frac{i\pi\omega}{K} + 2i\lambda K'}$$

donnant nécessairement $\lambda = 0$ et $\omega = 2mK$, ou, ce qui revient au même, $\omega = 0$, le nombre m étant entier, la quantité

$$f(x) = \frac{H'(0)H(x+\omega)}{H(\omega)H(x)} e^{\lambda x}$$

devient infinie et la formule semble inapplicable. Mais il arrive seulement qu'elle subit un changement de forme analytique, qui s'obtient de la manière la plus facile, comme on va voir. Supposons, en effet, $\lambda = 0$ et ω infiniment petit; on aura, en développant suivant les puissances croissantes de ω,

$$\frac{H'(0)}{H(\omega)} = \frac{1}{\omega} + \left(\frac{1+k^2}{6} - \frac{J}{2K}\right)\omega + \ldots,$$

$$\frac{H(x+\omega)}{H(x)} = 1 + \frac{H'(x)}{H(x)}\omega + \ldots;$$

d'où

$$f(x) = \frac{1}{\omega} + \frac{H'(x)}{H(x)} + \left(\frac{1+k^2}{6} - \frac{J}{2K}\right)\omega + \ldots.$$

D'autre part, observons que les coefficients $A, A_1, \ldots$ doivent être considérés comme dépendants de ω, et qu'on aura en particulier

$$A = \mathrm{a} + \mathrm{a}'\omega + \ldots,$$

$\mathrm{a}, \mathrm{a}', \ldots$ désignant les valeurs de A et de ses dérivées par rapport à ω pour $\omega = 0$. Nous obtenons donc, en n'écrivant point les termes qui contiennent ω en facteur,

$$A f(x-a) = \frac{\mathrm{a}}{\omega} + \mathrm{a}' + \mathrm{a}\frac{H'(x-a)}{H(x-a)} + \ldots$$

et, par conséquent,

$$\Sigma \mathrm{A} f(x-a) = \frac{1}{\omega}\Sigma \mathrm{a} + \Sigma \mathrm{a}' + \Sigma \mathrm{a} \frac{\mathrm{H}'(x-a)}{\mathrm{H}(x-a)} + \ldots.$$

On voit que le coefficient de $\frac{1}{\omega}$ disparaît, les quantités a ayant une somme nulle comme résidus d'une fonction doublement périodique, et la différentiation donnant immédiatement, pour $\omega = 0$,

$$\mathrm{D}_x f(x) = \mathrm{D}_x \frac{\mathrm{H}'(x)}{\mathrm{H}(x)}, \qquad \mathrm{D}_x^2 f(x) = \mathrm{D}_x^2 \frac{\mathrm{H}'(x)}{\mathrm{H}(x)}, \qquad \ldots,$$

nous parvenons à l'expression suivante, où $\mathrm{a}, \mathrm{a}_1, \ldots, \mathrm{a}_\alpha$ sont les valeurs de $\mathrm{A}, \mathrm{A}_1, \ldots, \mathrm{A}_\alpha$ pour $\omega = 0$:

$$\mathrm{F}(x) = \Sigma \mathrm{a}' + \Sigma \left[\mathrm{a} \frac{\mathrm{H}'(x-a)}{\mathrm{H}(x-a)} + \mathrm{a}_1 \mathrm{D}_x \frac{\mathrm{H}'(x-a)}{\mathrm{H}(x-a)} + \ldots + \mathrm{a}_\alpha \mathrm{D}_x^\alpha \frac{\mathrm{H}'(x-a)}{\mathrm{H}(x-a)} \right].$$

C'est la formule que j'ai établie directement, pour les fonctions doublement périodiques, dans une *Note sur la théorie des fonctions elliptiques*, ajoutée à la sixième édition du *Traité de Calcul différentiel et de Calcul intégral* de Lacroix (HERMITE, *Œuvres*, t. II, p. 125).

III.

Revenant au cas général pour donner des exemples de la détermination de la fonction $f(x)$, qui joue le rôle d'élément simple, et du calcul des coefficients $\mathrm{A}, \mathrm{A}_1, \mathrm{A}_2, \ldots$, je considérerai ces deux expressions :

$$\mathrm{F}(x) = \frac{\Theta(x+a)\,\Theta(x+b)\ldots\Theta(x+l)\,e^{\lambda x}}{\Theta^n(x)},$$

$$\mathrm{F}_1(x) = \frac{\mathrm{H}(x+a)\,\mathrm{H}(x+b)\ldots\mathrm{H}(x+l)\,e^{\lambda x}}{\Theta^n(x)},$$

où $a, b, \ldots, l$ sont des constantes au nombre de n. On trouve d'abord aisément leurs multiplicateurs, au moyen des relations

$$\begin{aligned}
\Theta(x+2\mathrm{K}) &= +\Theta(x),\\
\mathrm{H}(x+2\mathrm{K}) &= -\mathrm{H}(x),\\
\Theta(x+2i\mathrm{K}') &= -\Theta(x)\,e^{-\frac{i\pi}{\mathrm{K}}(x+i\mathrm{K}')},\\
\mathrm{H}(x+2i\mathrm{K}') &= -\mathrm{H}(x)\,e^{-\frac{i\pi}{\mathrm{K}}(x+i\mathrm{K}')}.
\end{aligned}$$

Elles montrent qu'en posant

$$\omega = a + b + \ldots + l,$$

puis, comme précédemment,

$$\mu = e^{2\lambda K},$$
$$\mu' = e^{-\frac{i\pi\omega}{K} + 2i\lambda K'},$$

on aura

$$F(x + 2\ K) = \mu\ F(x), \qquad F_1(x + 2K) = (-1)^n \mu\, F_1(x),$$
$$F(x + 2iK') = \mu'\ F(x), \qquad F_1(x + 2iK') = \mu'\ F_1(x).$$

Il en résulte que, quand n est pair, la fonction

$$f(x) = \frac{H'(0)\, H(x + \omega)\, e^{\lambda x}}{H(\omega)\, H(x)},$$

ayant ces quantités μ et μ' pour multiplicateurs, peut servir d'élément simple pour nos deux expressions ; mais il n'en est plus de même relativement à la seconde $F_1(x)$, dans le cas où n est impair : on voit aisément qu'il faut prendre alors pour élément simple la fonction

$$f_1(x) = \frac{H'(0)\, \Theta(x + \omega)\, e^{\lambda x}}{\Theta(\omega)\, H(x)},$$

afin de changer le signe du premier multiplicateur, le résidu correspondant à $x = 0$ étant d'ailleurs égal à l'unité. Cela posé, comme $F(x)$ et $F_1(x)$ ne deviennent infinies que pour $x = iK'$, ce sont les quantités $f(x - iK')$ et $f_1(x - iK')$ qui figureront dans notre formule. Il convient de leur attribuer une désignation particulière, et nous représenterons dorénavant la première par $\varphi(x)$ et la seconde par $\chi(x)$, en observant que les relations

$$\Theta(x + iK') = i\, H(x)\, e^{-\frac{i\pi}{4K}(2x + iK')},$$
$$H(x + iK') = i\, \Theta(x)\, e^{-\frac{i\pi}{4K}(2x + iK')}$$

donnent facilement, après y avoir changé x en $-x$, ces valeurs :

$$\varphi(x) = \frac{H'(0)\, \Theta(x + \omega)\, e^{\lambda x}}{\sqrt{\mu'}\, H(\omega)\, \Theta(x)},$$
$$\chi(x) = \frac{H'(0)\, H(x + \omega)\, e^{\lambda x}}{\sqrt{\mu'}\, \Theta(\omega)\, \Theta(x)}.$$

Nous avons maintenant à calculer dans les développements de $F(iK'+\varepsilon)$ et $F_1(iK'+\varepsilon)$, suivant les puissances croissantes de ε, la partie qui renferme les puissances négatives de cette quantité, et qu'on pourrait, pour abréger, nommer la partie principale. A cet effet, je remarque qu'en faisant, pour un moment,

$$F(x)=\frac{\Pi(x)}{\Theta^n(x)},\qquad F_1(x)=\frac{\Pi_1(x)}{\Theta^n(x)},$$

on aura

$$F(iK'+\varepsilon)=\frac{\sqrt{\mu'}\,\Pi_1(\varepsilon)}{H^n(\varepsilon)},\qquad F_1(iK'+\varepsilon)=\frac{\sqrt{\mu'}\,\Pi(\varepsilon)}{H^n(\varepsilon)}.$$

Nous développerons donc $\Pi(\varepsilon)$ et $\Pi_1(\varepsilon)$, par la formule de Maclaurin, jusqu'aux termes en ε^{n-1}, et nous multiplierons par la partie principale de $\frac{1}{H^n(\varepsilon)}$, qui s'obtient, comme on va voir, au moyen de la fonction de M. Weierstrass :

$$\mathrm{Al}(x)_1=x-\frac{1+k^2}{6}x^3+\frac{1+4k^2+k^4}{120}x^5-\ldots.$$

On a en effet, d'après la définition même de l'illustre analyste,

$$H(x)=H'(0)\,e^{\frac{Jx^2}{2K}}\,\mathrm{Al}(x)_1,$$

et l'on en déduit

$$\begin{aligned}\left[\frac{H'(0)}{H(\varepsilon)}\right]^n &= e^{-\frac{nJ\varepsilon^2}{2K}}\left[\varepsilon-\frac{1+k^2}{6}\varepsilon^3+\frac{1+4k^2+k^4}{120}\varepsilon^5-\ldots\right]^{-n}\\ &= e^{-\frac{nJ\varepsilon^2}{2K}}\left[\frac{1}{\varepsilon^n}+\frac{n(1+k^2)}{6}\,\frac{1}{\varepsilon^{n-2}}+\ldots\right]\\ &= \frac{1}{\varepsilon^n}+n\left(\frac{1+k^2}{6}-\frac{J}{2K}\right)\frac{1}{\varepsilon^{n-2}}+\ldots.\end{aligned}$$

IV.

Je vais appliquer ce qui précède au cas le plus simple, en supposant $n=2$ et $\lambda=0$, ce qui donnera

$$\begin{aligned}F(x)&=\frac{\Theta(x+a)\,\Theta(x+b)}{\Theta^2(x)},\\ F_1(x)&=\frac{H(x+a)\,H(x+b)}{\Theta^2(x)},\end{aligned}$$

et, par conséquent,

$$\mathrm{H}\,(\varepsilon) = \Theta(a)\,\Theta(b) + [\Theta(a)\,\Theta'(b) + \Theta(b)\,\Theta'(a)]\varepsilon + \ldots,$$
$$\mathrm{H}_1(\varepsilon) = \mathrm{H}(a)\,\mathrm{H}(b) + [\mathrm{H}(a)\,\mathrm{H}'(b) + \mathrm{H}(b)\,\mathrm{H}'(a)]\varepsilon + \ldots.$$

Maintenant, la partie principale de $\frac{1}{\mathrm{H}^2(\varepsilon)}$ ne contenant que le seul terme $\frac{1}{\mathrm{H}'^2(0)}\frac{1}{\varepsilon^2}$, on a immédiatement

$$\frac{\mathrm{H}'^2(0)}{\sqrt{\mu'}}\mathrm{F}\,(i\mathrm{K}'+\varepsilon) = \frac{\mathrm{H}(a)\,\mathrm{H}(b)}{\varepsilon^2} + \frac{\mathrm{H}(a)\,\mathrm{H}'(b) + \mathrm{H}(b)\,\mathrm{H}'(a)}{\varepsilon} + \ldots,$$
$$\frac{\mathrm{H}'^2(0)}{\sqrt{\mu'}}\mathrm{F}_1(i\mathrm{K}'+\varepsilon) = \frac{\Theta(a)\,\Theta(b)}{\varepsilon^2} + \frac{\Theta(a)\,\Theta'(b) + \Theta(b)\,\Theta'(a)}{\varepsilon} + \ldots,$$

et, par conséquent, ces deux relations :

$$\frac{\mathrm{H}'^2(0)\,\Theta(x+a)\,\Theta(x+b)}{\sqrt{\mu'}\,\Theta^2(x)} = -\mathrm{H}(a)\,\mathrm{H}(b)\,\varphi'(x) + [\mathrm{H}(a)\,\mathrm{H}'(b) + \mathrm{H}(b)\,\mathrm{H}'(a)]\,\varphi(x),$$
$$\frac{\mathrm{H}'^2(0)\,\mathrm{H}(x+a)\,\mathrm{H}(x+b)}{\sqrt{\mu'}\,\Theta^2(x)} = -\Theta(a)\,\Theta(b)\,\varphi'(x) + [\Theta(a)\,\Theta'(b) + \Theta(b)\,\Theta'(a)]\,\varphi(x).$$

En y remplaçant $\varphi(x)$ par sa valeur $\frac{\mathrm{H}'(0)\,\Theta\,(x+a+b)}{\sqrt{\mu'}\,\mathrm{H}(a+b)\Theta(x)}$, je les écrirai sous la forme suivante, qui est plus simple :

$$\frac{\mathrm{H}'(0)\,\mathrm{H}(a+b)\,\Theta(x+a)\,\Theta(x+b)}{\mathrm{H}(a)\,\mathrm{H}(b)\,\Theta^2(x)}$$
$$= -\mathrm{D}_x\frac{\Theta(x+a+b)}{\Theta(x)} + \left[\frac{\mathrm{H}'(a)}{\mathrm{H}(a)} + \frac{\mathrm{H}'(b)}{\mathrm{H}(b)}\right]\frac{\Theta(x+a+b)}{\Theta(x)},$$
$$\frac{\mathrm{H}'(0)\,\mathrm{H}(a+b)\,\mathrm{H}(x+a)\,\mathrm{H}(x+b)}{\Theta(a)\,\Theta(b)\,\Theta^2(x)}$$
$$= -\mathrm{D}_x\frac{\Theta(x+a+b)}{\Theta(x)} + \left[\frac{\Theta'(a)}{\Theta(a)} + \frac{\Theta'(b)}{\Theta(b)}\right]\frac{\Theta(x+a+b)}{\Theta(x)}.$$

On en tire d'abord, à l'égard des fonctions Θ, cette remarque que, sous la condition

$$a+b+c+d=0,$$

on a l'égalité [1]

$$\begin{aligned}\mathrm{H}'(0)\,\mathrm{H}(a+b)\,\mathrm{H}(a+c)\,\mathrm{H}(b+c) = {} & \Theta'(a)\,\Theta(b)\,\Theta(c)\,\Theta(d)\\ & + \Theta'(b)\,\Theta(c)\,\Theta(d)\,\Theta(a)\\ & + \Theta'(c)\,\Theta(d)\,\Theta(a)\,\Theta(b)\\ & + \Theta'(d)\,\Theta(a)\,\Theta(b)\,\Theta(c).\end{aligned}$$

---

(1) Elle a été donnée par Jacobi, *Journal de Crelle* (*Formulæ novæ in theoria transcendentium ellipticarum fundamentales*, t. 15, p. 199).

Mais c'est une autre conséquence que j'ai en vue, et qu'on obtient en mettant la première, par exemple, sous la forme

$$\Phi(x) = py - y',$$

où $\Phi(x)$ désigne le premier membre, y la fonction $\dfrac{\Theta(x+a+b)}{\Theta(x)}$, et p la constante $\dfrac{H'(a)}{H(a)} + \dfrac{H'(b)}{H(b)}$.

Si nous multiplions par e^{-px}, elle devient, en effet,

$$\Phi(x)\, e^{-px} = -D_x(y\, e^{-px}),$$

d'où

$$\int \Phi(x)\, e^{-px}\, dx = -y\, e^{-px}.$$

Ce résultat appelle l'attention sur un cas particulier des fonctions $\varphi(x)$, où, par suite d'une certaine détermination de λ, elles ne renferment plus qu'un paramètre. On voit qu'en posant

$$\varphi(x, a) = \frac{H'(0)\,\Theta(x+a)}{\sqrt{\mu'}\, H(a)\,\Theta(x)} e^{-\frac{H'(a)}{H(a)}x},$$

ce qui entraîne, pour le multiplicateur μ', la valeur

$$\mu' = e^{-\frac{i\pi a}{K} - 2iK'\frac{H'(a)}{H(a)}},$$

l'intégrale $\int \varphi(x,a)\,\varphi(x,b)\,dx$ s'obtient sous la forme finie explicite. Un calcul facile conduit en effet à la relation

$$\int \varphi(x, a)\,\varphi(x, b)\,dx = -\varphi(x, a+b)\, e^{\left[\frac{H'(a+b)}{H(a+b)} - \frac{H'(a)}{H(a)} - \frac{H'(b)}{H(b)}\right](x - iK')}.$$

Faisons, en second lieu,

$$\chi(x, a) = \frac{H'(0)\, H(x+a)}{\sqrt{\mu'}\,\Theta(a)\,\Theta(x)} e^{-\frac{\Theta'(a)}{\Theta(a)}x},$$

en désignant alors par μ' la quantité

$$\mu' = e^{-\frac{i\pi a}{K} - 2iK'\frac{\Theta'(a)}{\Theta(a)}},$$

et nous aurons semblablement

$$\int \chi(x, a)\,\chi(x, b)\,dx = -\varphi(x, a+b)\, e^{\left[\frac{H'(a+b)}{H(a+b)} - \frac{\Theta'(a)}{\Theta(a)} - \frac{\Theta'(b)}{\Theta(b)}\right](x - iK')}.$$

On en déduit aisément qu'en désignant a et b deux racines, d'abord de l'équation $H'(x)=0$, puis de l'équation $\Theta'(x)=0$, on aura, dans le premier cas,

$$\int_0^{2K} \varphi(x, a)\,\varphi(x, b)\,dx = 0;$$

et dans le second,

$$\int_0^{2K} \chi(x, a)\,\chi(x, b)\,dx = 0,$$

sous la condition que les deux racines ne soient point égales et de signes contraires. Si l'on suppose $b = -a$, nous obtiendrons

$$\int_0^{2K} \varphi(x, a)\,\varphi(x, -a)\,dx = 2\left(J - \frac{K}{\operatorname{sn}^2 a}\right),$$

$$\int_0^{2K} \chi(x, a)\,\chi(x, -a)\,dx = 2\,(J - k^2 K \operatorname{sn}^2 a).$$

On voit les recherches auxquelles ces théorèmes ouvrent la voie et que je me réserve de poursuivre plus tard ; je me borne à les indiquer succinctement, afin de montrer l'importance des fonctions $\varphi(x)$ et $\chi(x)$. Voici maintenant comment on parvient à les définir par des équations différentielles.

V

Nous remarquerons, en premier lieu, que les fonctions $\varphi(x)$ et $\chi(x)$ peuvent être réduites l'une à l'autre; leurs expressions, si l'on y remplace le multiplicateur μ' par sa valeur, étant, en effet,

$$\varphi(x, \omega) = \frac{H'(0)\,\Theta(x+\omega)}{H(\omega)\,\Theta(x)}\,e^{-\frac{H'(\omega)}{H(\omega)}(x - iK') + \frac{i\pi\omega}{2K}},$$

$$\chi(x, \omega) = \frac{H'(0)\,H(x+\omega)}{\Theta(\omega)\,\Theta(x)}\,e^{-\frac{\Theta'(\omega)}{\Theta(\omega)}(x - iK') + \frac{i\pi\omega}{2K}},$$

on en déduit facilement les relations suivantes

$$\varphi(x, \omega + iK') = \chi(x, \omega),$$

$$\chi(x, \omega + iK') = \varphi(x, \omega),$$

dont nous ferons souvent usage. Cette propriété établie, nous rechercherons le développement, suivant les puissances croissantes de ε, de $\chi(iK'+\varepsilon)$, qui jouera plus tard un rôle important, et dont nous allons, comme on va voir, tirer l'équation différentielle que nous avons en vue. Pour le former, je partirai de l'égalité

$$D_x \log\chi(x) = \frac{H'(x+\omega)}{H(x+\omega)} - \frac{\Theta'(x)}{\Theta(x)} - \frac{\Theta'(\omega)}{\Theta(\omega)},$$

d'où l'on déduit

$$D_\varepsilon \log\chi(iK'+\varepsilon) = \frac{\Theta'(\omega+\varepsilon)}{\Theta(\omega+\varepsilon)} - \frac{H'(\varepsilon)}{H(\varepsilon)} - \frac{\Theta'(\omega)}{\Theta(\omega)}.$$

Cela posé, nous aurons d'abord

$$\frac{\Theta'(\omega+\varepsilon)}{\Theta(\omega+\varepsilon)} - \frac{\Theta'(\omega)}{\Theta(\omega)} = \varepsilon D_\omega \frac{\Theta'(\omega)}{\Theta(\omega)} + \frac{\varepsilon^2}{1.2} D_\omega^2 \frac{\Theta'(\omega)}{\Theta(\omega)} + \ldots;$$

mais, l'équation de Jacobi

$$D_x \frac{\Theta'(x)}{\Theta(x)} = \frac{J}{K} - k^2 \operatorname{sn}^2 x$$

donnant en général

$$D_x^{n+1} \frac{\Theta'(x)}{\Theta(x)} = - D_x^n k^2 \operatorname{sn}^2 x,$$

ce développement prend cette nouvelle forme

$$\frac{\Theta'(\omega+\varepsilon)}{\Theta(\omega+\varepsilon)} - \frac{\Theta'(\omega)}{\Theta(\omega)} = \varepsilon\left(\frac{J}{K} - k^2 \operatorname{sn}^2\omega\right)$$
$$- \frac{\varepsilon^2}{1.2} D_\omega k^2 \operatorname{sn}^2\omega - \frac{\varepsilon^3}{1.2.3} D_\omega^2 k^2 \operatorname{sn}^2\omega - \ldots$$

Joignons-y le résultat qu'on tire de l'équation de M. Weierstrass

$$H(\varepsilon) = H'(0)\, e^{\frac{J\varepsilon^2}{2K}} \operatorname{Al}(\varepsilon)_1,$$

en prenant la dérivée logarithmique des deux membres,

$$\frac{H'(\varepsilon)}{H(\varepsilon)} = \varepsilon \frac{J}{K} + \frac{\operatorname{Al}'(\varepsilon)_1}{\operatorname{Al}(\varepsilon)_1},$$

et nous aurons

$$D_\varepsilon \log\chi(iK'+\varepsilon) = -\varepsilon k^2 \operatorname{sn}^2\omega - \frac{\varepsilon^2}{1.2} D_\omega k^2 \operatorname{sn}^2\omega - \ldots - \frac{\operatorname{Al}'(\varepsilon)_1}{\operatorname{Al}(\varepsilon)_1},$$

d'où, par conséquent,

$$(iK'+\varepsilon) = \frac{e^{-\frac{\varepsilon^2}{2}k^2\,\mathrm{sn}^2\omega - \frac{\varepsilon^3}{2.3}D_\omega k^2\,\mathrm{sn}^2\omega - \dots}}{\mathrm{Al}(\varepsilon)_1}$$

$$= e^{-\frac{\varepsilon^2}{2}k^2\,\mathrm{sn}^2\omega - \frac{\varepsilon^3}{2.3}D_\omega k^2\,\mathrm{sn}^2\omega - \dots}\left(\frac{1}{\varepsilon} + \frac{1+k^2}{6}\varepsilon + \frac{7+8k^2+7k^4}{360}\varepsilon^3 + \dots\right),$$

sans qu'il soit besoin d'introduire un facteur constant dans le second membre, puisque le premier terme de son développement est $\frac{1}{\varepsilon}$, comme il le faut d'après la nature de la fonction $\chi(x)$. Cette formule donne le résultat cherché par un calcul facile ; elle montre qu'en posant

$$\chi(iK'+\varepsilon) = \frac{1}{\varepsilon} - \frac{1}{2}\Omega\varepsilon - \frac{1}{3}\Omega_1\varepsilon^2 - \frac{1}{8}\Omega_2\varepsilon^3 - \dots,$$

on aura

$$\Omega = k^2\,\mathrm{sn}^2\omega - \frac{1+k^2}{3},$$

$$\Omega_1 = k^2\,\mathrm{sn}\,\omega\,\mathrm{cn}\,\omega\,\mathrm{dn}\,\omega,$$

$$\Omega_2 = 2k^4\,\mathrm{sn}^4\omega - \frac{2(k^2+k^4)}{3}\,\mathrm{sn}^2\omega - \frac{7-22k^2+7k^4}{45},$$

$$\dots\dots\dots\dots\dots\dots\dots\dots\dots\dots\dots\dots$$

En voici une première application.

VI.

Considérons, pour la décomposer en éléments simples, la fonction $k^2\,\mathrm{sn}^2 x\,\chi(x)$, qui a les multiplicateurs de $\chi(x)$ et ne devient infinie que pour $x = iK'$. On devra, à cet effet, en posant $x = iK'+\varepsilon$, former la partie principale de son développement suivant les puissances croissantes de ε, que nous obtenons immédiatement en multipliant membre à membre les deux égalités

$$\chi(iK'+\varepsilon) = \frac{1}{\varepsilon} - \frac{1}{2}\Omega\varepsilon - \dots,$$

$$\frac{1}{\mathrm{sn}^2\varepsilon} = \frac{1}{\varepsilon^2} + \frac{1}{3}(1+k^2) - \dots.$$

Il vient ainsi

$$k^2 \operatorname{sn}^2(i\mathrm{K}'+\varepsilon)\,\chi(i\mathrm{K}'+\varepsilon) = \frac{1}{\varepsilon^3} + \left[\frac{1}{3}(1+k^2) - \frac{1}{2}\Omega\right]\frac{1}{\varepsilon} + \ldots$$
$$= \frac{1}{2}\mathrm{D}_\varepsilon^2\,\varepsilon^{-1} + \left[\frac{1}{2}(1+k^2) - \frac{1}{2}k^2\operatorname{sn}^2\omega\right]\varepsilon^{-1} + \ldots,$$

et l'on en conclut la formule suivante

$$k^2 \operatorname{sn}^2 x\,\chi(x) = \frac{1}{2}\mathrm{D}_x^2\,\chi(x) + \left[\frac{1}{2}(1+k^2) - \frac{1}{2}k^2\operatorname{sn}^2\omega\right]\chi(x).$$

Elle montre que, en posant $y=\chi(x)$, nous obtenons une solution de l'équation linéaire du second ordre

$$\frac{d^2y}{dx^2} = (2k^2\operatorname{sn}^2 x - 1 - k^2 + k^2\operatorname{sn}^2\omega)y,$$

qui est celle de Lamé dans le cas le plus simple où l'on suppose $n=1$, la constante $h=-1-k^2+k^2\operatorname{sn}^2\omega$ étant quelconque, puisque ω est arbitraire; et, comme cette équation ne change pas lorsqu'on change x en $-x$, la solution obtenue en donne une seconde, $y=\chi(-x)$, d'où, par suite, l'intégrale complète sous la forme

$$y = \mathrm{C}\,\chi(x) + \mathrm{C}'\,\chi(-x).$$

A ce résultat il est nécessaire de joindre ceux qu'on obtient quand on remplace successivement ω par $\omega+i\mathrm{K}'$, $\omega+\mathrm{K}$, $\omega+\mathrm{K}+i\mathrm{K}'$, ce qui conduit aux équations

$$\frac{d^2y}{dx^2} = \left(2k^2\operatorname{sn}^2 x - 1 - k^2 + \frac{1}{\operatorname{sn}^2\omega}\right)y,$$
$$\frac{d^2y}{dx^2} = \left(2k^2\operatorname{sn}^2 x - 1 - k^2 + \frac{k^2\operatorname{cn}^2\omega}{\operatorname{dn}^2\omega}\right)y,$$
$$\frac{d^2y}{dx^2} = \left(2k^2\operatorname{sn}^2 x - 1 - k^2 + \frac{\operatorname{dn}^2\omega}{\operatorname{cn}^2\omega}\right)y,$$

La première, d'après l'égalité $\chi(x,\omega+i\mathrm{K}')=\varphi(x,\omega)$, a pour intégrale

$$y = \mathrm{C}\,\varphi(x) + \mathrm{C}'\,\varphi(-x);$$

et, en introduisant ces nouvelles fonctions, à savoir

$$i\chi_1(x,\omega) = \chi(x,\omega+\mathrm{K}),$$
$$i\varphi_1(x,\omega) = \varphi(x,\omega+\mathrm{K}),$$

nous aurons, sous une forme semblable, pour la seconde et la troisième,

$$y = C\chi_1(x) + C'\chi_1(-x),$$
$$y = C\varphi_1(x) + C'\varphi_1(-x).$$

Les expressions de $\varphi_1(x)$ et $\chi_1(x)$ s'obtiennent aisément à l'aide des fonctions $\Theta_1(x) = \Theta(x+K)$, $H_1(x) = H(x+K)$; on trouve ainsi

$$\varphi_1(x, \omega) = \frac{H'(0)\,\Theta_1(x+\omega)}{H_1(\omega)\,\Theta(x)}\, e^{-\frac{H'_1(\omega)}{H_1(\omega)}(x - iK') + \frac{i\pi\omega}{2K}},$$

$$\chi_1(x, \omega) = \frac{H'(0)\,H_1(x+\omega)}{\Theta_1(\omega)\,\Theta(x)}\, e^{-\frac{\Theta'_1(\omega)}{\Theta_1(\omega)}(x - iK') + \frac{i\pi\omega}{2K}}.$$

Nous allons en voir un premier usage dans la recherche des solutions de l'équation de Lamé par des fonctions doublement périodiques.

VII.

Nous supposons à cet effet $\omega = 0$ dans les équations précédentes, en exceptant toutefois celle où se trouve le terme $\frac{1}{\operatorname{sn}^2\omega}$ qui deviendrait infini. On obtient ainsi, pour la constante h, les déterminations suivantes :

$$h = -1 - k^2, \qquad h = -1, \qquad h = -k^2.$$

Ce sont précisément les quantités qu'on trouve en appliquant la méthode de Lamé ; et en même temps nous tirons des valeurs des fonctions $\chi(x)$, $\chi_1(x)$, $\varphi_1(x)$, pour $\omega = 0$, les solutions auxquelles conduit son analyse

$$y = \sqrt{k}\,\frac{H(x)}{\Theta(x)}, \qquad y = \sqrt{kk'}\,\frac{H_1(x)}{\Theta(x)}, \qquad y = \sqrt{k'}\,\frac{\Theta_1(x)}{\Theta(x)},$$

ou, plus simplement, puisqu'on peut les multiplier par des facteurs constants,

$$y = \operatorname{sn} x, \qquad y = \operatorname{cn} x, \qquad y = \operatorname{dn} x.$$

Mais une circonstance se présente maintenant, qui demande un examen attentif. On ne peut plus, en effet, déduire de ces expressions d'autres qui en soient distinctes par le changement de signe de la variable, et il faut, par suite, employer une nouvelle méthode pour obtenir l'intégrale complète. Représentons, dans ce but, la solution générale de l'une quelconque de nos trois équations, en laissant ω indéterminé, par la formule

$$y = \text{C}\,\text{F}(x, \omega) + \text{C}'\,\text{F}(-x, \omega).$$

Je la mettrai d'abord sous cette forme équivalente

$$y = \text{C}\,\text{F}(x, \omega) + \text{C}'\,\text{F}(x, -\omega);$$

puis, en développant suivant les puissances croissantes de ω, je ferai

$$\text{F}(x, \omega) = \text{F}_0(x) + \omega\,\text{F}_1(x) + \omega^2\,\text{F}_2(x) + \ldots,$$

ce qui permettra d'écrire

$$y = (\text{C} + \text{C}')\,\text{F}_0(x) + \omega(\text{C} - \text{C}')\,\text{F}_1(x) + \omega^2(\text{C} + \text{C}')\,\text{F}_2(x) + \ldots,$$

ou encore

$$y = \text{C}_0\,\text{F}_0(x) + \text{C}_1\,\text{F}_1(x) + \omega\,\text{C}_0\,\text{F}_2(x) + \ldots,$$

en posant, d'après la méthode de d'Alembert,

$$\text{C}_0 = \text{C} + \text{C}', \qquad \text{C}_1 = \omega(\text{C} - \text{C}').$$

Si l'on suppose maintenant $\omega = 0$, on parvient à la formule

$$y = \text{C}_0\,\text{F}_0(x) + \text{C}_1\,\text{F}_1(x),$$

qu'il faudra appliquer en faisant successivement

$$\text{F}(x, \omega) = \chi(x), \qquad \text{F}(x, \omega) = \chi_1(x), \qquad \text{F}(x, \omega) = \varphi_1(x);$$

mais le calcul sera plus simple si l'on prend

$$\text{F}(x, \omega) = \frac{\text{H}(x + \omega)}{\Theta(x)}\,e^{-\frac{\Theta'(\omega)}{\Theta(\omega)}x},$$

$$\text{F}(x, \omega) = \frac{\text{H}_1(x + \omega)}{\Theta(x)}\,e^{-\frac{\Theta'_1(\omega)}{\Theta_1(\omega)}x},$$

$$\text{F}(x, \omega) = \frac{\Theta_1(x + \omega)}{\Theta(x)}\,e^{-\frac{\text{H}'_1(\omega)}{\text{H}_1(\omega)}x},$$

ces quantités ne différant des précédentes que par des facteurs constants. Observant donc que, pour $\omega = 0$, on a

$$D_\omega \frac{\Theta'(\omega)}{\Theta(\omega)} = \frac{J}{K}, \qquad D_\omega \frac{\Theta_1'(\omega)}{\Theta_1(\omega)} = \frac{J}{K} - k^2, \qquad D_\omega \frac{H_1'(\omega)}{H_1(\omega)} = \frac{J}{K} - 1,$$

nous obtenons immédiatement les valeurs que prennent leurs dérivées par rapport à ω, dans cette hypothèse de $\omega = 0$

$$F_1(x) = \frac{H'(x)}{\Theta(x)} - \frac{J\,H(x)}{K\,\Theta(x)}x,$$

$$F_1(x) = \frac{H_1'(x)}{\Theta(x)} - \frac{(J - k^2K)\,H_1(x)}{K\,\Theta(x)}x,$$

$$F_1(x) = \frac{\Theta_1'(x)}{\Theta(x)} - \frac{(J - K)\,\Theta_1(x)}{K\,\Theta(x)}x.$$

La solution générale de l'équation de Lamé, dans les cas particuliers que nous venons de considérer, peut donc se représenter par les formules suivantes :

1° $h = -1 - k^2$, $\quad y = C\,\mathrm{sn}\,x + C'\,\mathrm{sn}\,x\left[\dfrac{H'(x)}{H(x)} - \dfrac{J}{K}x\right]$,

2° $h = -1$, $\quad y = C\,\mathrm{cn}\,x + C'\,\mathrm{cn}\,x\left[\dfrac{H_1'(x)}{H_1(x)} - \dfrac{J - k^2K}{K}x\right]$,

3° $h = -k^2$, $\quad y = C\,\mathrm{dn}\,x + C'\,\mathrm{dn}\,x\left[\dfrac{\Theta_1'(x)}{\Theta_1(x)} - \dfrac{J - K}{K}x\right]$.

VIII.

Un dernier point me reste à traiter avant d'aborder, au moyen des résultats qui viennent d'être obtenus, le problème de la rotation d'un corps autour d'un point fixe, dans le cas où il n'y a point de forces accélératrices. On a vu que les quantités $\varphi(x)$, $\chi(x)$, $\varphi_1(x)$, $\chi_1(x)$ sont les produits d'une exponentielle par les fonctions périodiques

$$\frac{H'(0)\,\Theta(x+\omega)}{H(\omega)\,\Theta(x)}, \quad \frac{H'(0)\,H(x+\omega)}{\Theta(\omega)\,\Theta(x)}, \quad \frac{H'(0)\,\Theta_1(x+\omega)}{H_1(\omega)\,\Theta(x)}, \quad \frac{H'(0)\,H_1(x+\omega)}{\Theta_1(\omega)\,\Theta(x)},$$

développables par conséquent en séries simples de sinus et cosinus de multiples entiers de $\frac{\pi x}{K}$. Ces séries ont été données pour la première fois par Jacobi, à l'occasion même de ses recherches sur la rotation; et, comme l'observe l'illustre auteur, elles sont d'une grande importance dans la théorie des fonctions elliptiques. Je vais montrer comment on peut y parvenir au moyen de l'équation suivante

$$\int_0^{2K} F(x_0+x)\,dx+\int_0^{2iK'} F(x_0+2K+x)\,dx$$
$$-\int_0^{2K} F(x_0+2iK'+x)\,dx-\int_0^{2iK'} F(x_0+x)\,dx=2i\pi S,$$

où, les quatre intégrales étant rectilignes, S représente la somme des résidus de la fonction $F(x)$ qui correspondent aux pôles situés à l'intérieur du rectangle dont les sommets ont pour affixes les quantités $x_0, x_0+2K, x_0+2K+2iK', x_0+2iK'$. Supposons à cet effet qu'on ait

$$F(x+2K)=\mu\,F(x),$$
$$F(x+2iK')=\mu'\,F(x);$$

on obtiendra la relation

$$(1-\mu')\int_0^{2K} F(x_0+x)\,dx-(1-\mu)\int_0^{2iK'} F(x_0+x)\,dx=2i\pi S,$$

et, si l'on admet en outre que le multiplicateur μ soit égal à l'unité, on en conclura le résultat suivant :

$$\int_0^{2K} F(x_0+x)\,dx=\frac{2i\pi S}{1-\mu'}.$$

Cela posé, soit, en désignant par n un nombre entier quelconque,

$$F(x)=\frac{H'(0)\,\Theta(x+\omega)}{H(\omega)\,\Theta(x)}e^{-\frac{i\pi n x}{K}};$$

on aura

$$\mu=1,\qquad \mu'=e^{-\frac{i\pi}{K}(\omega+2niK')},$$

et, en prenant la constante x_0 dans des limites telles que le pôle unique de $F(x)$ qui est à l'intérieur du rectangle soit $x=iK'$, nous obtiendrons pour le résidu correspondant, et par conséquent pour S, la valeur

$$S=e^{-\frac{i\pi}{2K}(\omega+2niK')}.$$

De là résulte, pour l'intégrale définie, l'expression suivante,

$$\int_0^{2K} F(x_0+x)\,dx = \frac{2i\pi\, e^{-\frac{i\pi}{2K}(\omega+2niK')}}{1-e^{-\frac{i\pi}{K}(\omega+2niK')}} = \frac{\pi}{\sin\frac{\pi}{2K}(\omega+2niK')},$$

et l'on voit qu'en posant l'équation

$$\frac{H'(o)\,\Theta(x_0+x+\omega)}{H(\omega)\,\Theta(x_0+x)} = \sum A_n\, e^{\frac{i\pi n(x_0+x)}{K}},$$

on en déduit immédiatement la détermination de A_n. Nous avons, en effet,

$$2K\,A_n = \int_0^{2K} F(x_0+x)\,dx,$$

et, par conséquent,

$$\frac{2K}{\pi} A_n = \frac{1}{\sin\frac{\pi}{2K}(\omega+2niK')}.$$

La constante x_0 que j'ai introduite pour plus de généralité, et aussi pour éviter qu'un pôle de $F(x)$ se trouve sur le contour d'intégration, peut maintenant sans difficulté être supposée nulle. Nous parvenons ainsi à une première formule de développement

$$\frac{2K}{\pi}\,\frac{H'(o)\,\Theta(x+\omega)}{H(\omega)\,\Theta(x)} = \sum \frac{e^{\frac{i\pi n x}{K}}}{\sin\frac{\pi}{2K}(\omega+2niK')},$$

dont les trois autres résultent, comme on va le voir. Qu'on change, en effet, ω en $\omega+iK'$, on en conclura d'abord

$$\frac{2K}{\pi}\,\frac{H'(o)\,H(x+\omega)}{\Theta(\omega)\,\Theta(x)}\,e^{-\frac{i\pi x}{2K}} = \sum \frac{e^{\frac{i\pi n x}{K}}}{\sin\frac{\pi}{2K}[\omega+(2n+1)iK']};$$

puis en multipliant les deux membres par l'exponentielle, et posant $m=2n+1$,

$$\frac{2K}{\pi}\,\frac{H'(o)\,H(x+\omega)}{\Theta(\omega)\,\Theta(x)} = \sum \frac{e^{\frac{i\pi m x}{2K}}}{\sin\frac{\pi}{2K}(\omega+miK')}.$$

Mettons enfin, dans les deux formules que nous venons d'établir, $\omega + K$ à la place de K, et l'on obtiendra les suivantes, qui nous restaient à trouver :

$$\frac{2K}{\pi}\frac{H'(0)\,\Theta_1(x+\omega)}{H_1(\omega)\,\Theta(x)} = \sum \frac{e^{\frac{i\pi n x}{K}}}{\cos\frac{\pi}{2K}(\omega + 2niK')},$$

$$\frac{2K}{\pi}\frac{H'(0)\,H_1(x+\omega)}{\Theta_1(\omega)\,\Theta(x)} = \sum \frac{e^{\frac{i\pi m x}{2K}}}{\cos\frac{\pi}{2K}(\omega + miK')}.$$

Voici à leur sujet quelques remarques.

IX.

Elles sont d'une forme différente de celles de Jacobi et l'on peut s'en servir utilement dans beaucoup de questions que je ne puis aborder en ce moment. Je me contenterai, sans en faire l'étude, d'indiquer succinctement comment on en tire les sommes des séries suivantes

$$\Sigma f(2niK')\,e^{\frac{i\pi n x}{K}}, \qquad \Sigma f(miK')\,e^{\frac{i\pi m x}{2K}},$$

où $f(z)$ est une fonction rationnelle de $\sin\frac{\pi z}{2K}$ et $\cos\frac{\pi z}{2K}$, sans partie entière et assujettie à la condition $f(z+2K) = -f(z)$. Il suffit, en effet, d'employer la décomposition de cette fonction en éléments simples, c'est-à-dire en termes tels que $D_z^{\alpha}\dfrac{1}{\sin\frac{\pi}{2K}(z+\omega)}$, pour obtenir immédiatement la valeur des séries proposées, au moyen de ces deux expressions

$$\Sigma D_\omega^\alpha\left[\frac{1}{\sin\frac{\pi}{2K}(\omega+2niK')}\right]e^{\frac{i\pi n x}{K}} = D_\omega^\alpha\frac{2K}{\pi}\frac{H'(0)\,\Theta(x+\omega)}{H(\omega)\,\Theta(x)},$$

$$\Sigma D_\omega^\alpha\left[\frac{1}{\sin\frac{\pi}{2K}(\omega+miK')}\right]e^{\frac{i\pi m x}{2K}} = D_\omega^\alpha\frac{2K}{\pi}\frac{H'(0)\,H(x+\omega)}{\Theta(\omega)\,\Theta(x)}.$$

J'ajouterai encore qu'on retrouve les résultats de Jacobi, si l'on réunit les termes qui correspondent à des valeurs de l'indice égales et de signes contraires. Il vient ainsi, en effet, en désignant par m un nombre qu'on fera successivement pair et impair,

$$\frac{e^{\frac{i\pi m x}{2K}}}{\sin\frac{\pi}{2K}(\omega+miK')}+\frac{e^{-\frac{i\pi m x}{2K}}}{\sin\frac{\pi}{2K}(\omega-miK')}=\frac{2\cos\frac{m\pi x}{2K}\cos\frac{m\pi iK'}{2K}\sin\frac{\pi\omega}{2K}}{\sin\frac{\pi}{2K}(\omega+miK')\sin\frac{\pi}{2K}(\omega-miK')}$$
$$-i\frac{2\sin\frac{m\pi x}{2K}\sin\frac{m\pi iK'}{2K}\cos\frac{\pi\omega}{2K}}{\sin\frac{\pi}{2K}(\omega+miK')\sin\frac{\pi}{2K}(\omega-miK')};$$

employons ensuite les équations du paragraphe 35 des *Fundamenta*, qui donnent

$$\cos\frac{m\pi iK'}{2K}=\frac{1+q^m}{2\sqrt{q^m}},$$
$$\sin\frac{m\pi iK'}{2K}=i\frac{1-q^m}{2\sqrt{q^m}},$$
$$\sin\frac{\pi}{2K}(\omega+miK')\sin\frac{\pi}{2K}(\omega-miK')=\frac{1-2q^m\cos\frac{\pi\omega}{K}+q^{2m}}{4q^m},$$

et nous parviendrons à cette nouvelle forme

$$\frac{e^{\frac{i\pi m x}{2K}}}{\sin\frac{\pi}{2K}(\omega+miK')}+\frac{e^{-\frac{i\pi m x}{2K}}}{\sin\frac{\pi}{2K}(\omega-miK')}=\frac{4\sqrt{q^m}(1+q^m)\sin\frac{\pi\omega}{2K}}{1-2q^m\cos\frac{\pi\omega}{K}+q^{2m}}\cos\frac{m\pi x}{2K}$$
$$+\frac{4\sqrt{q^m}(1-q^m)\cos\frac{\pi\omega}{2K}}{1-2q^m\cos\frac{\pi\omega}{K}+q^{2m}}\sin\frac{m\pi x}{2K}.$$

C'est celle qu'on voit dans la lettre adressée à l'Académie des Sciences et publiée dans les *Comptes rendus* du 30 juillet 1849; car, en introduisant la constante $b=\frac{i\omega}{K'}$, on peut écrire

$$\sin\frac{\pi\omega}{2K}=\frac{q^{\frac{1}{2}b}-q^{-\frac{1}{2}b}}{2i},$$
$$\cos\frac{\pi\omega}{2K}=\frac{q^{\frac{1}{2}b}+q^{-\frac{1}{2}b}}{2},$$

et

$$1 - 2q^m \cos\frac{\pi\omega}{K} + q^{2m} = (1 - q^{m+b})(1 - q^{m-b}).$$

Mais une faute d'impression, reproduite dans les *Œuvres complètes*, t. II, p. 143, et dans le *Journal de Crelle*, t. XXXIX, p. 297, s'est glissée dans ces formules. Les équations (3), (4), (5), (6) renferment en effet les quantités

$$\sqrt{q(1+q)},\quad \sqrt{q^3(1+q^3)},\quad \ldots \quad \text{et} \quad \sqrt{q(1-q)},\quad \sqrt{q^3(1-q^3)},\quad \ldots,$$

qui doivent être remplacées par

$$\sqrt{q}(1+q),\quad \sqrt{q^3}(1+q^3),\quad \ldots \quad \text{et} \quad \sqrt{q}(1-q),\quad \sqrt{q^3}(1-q^3),\quad \ldots.$$

On peut d'ailleurs parvenir par d'autres méthodes à ces résultats importants. M. Somoff les obtient en décomposant la quantité

$$\frac{(1-qvz)(1-q^3vz)(1-q^5vz)\ldots(1-qv^{-1}z^{-1})(1-q^3v^{-1}z^{-1})(1-q^5v^{-1}z^{-1})\ldots}{(z-1)(1-q^2z)(1-q^4z)\ldots(1-q^2z^{-1})(1-q^4z^{-1})\ldots}$$

en fractions simples

$$\frac{A_0}{z-1} + \sum \frac{A_m}{1-q^{2m}z} + \sum \frac{B_m}{z-q^{2m}}.$$

Le P. Joubert m'a communiqué la remarque qu'on peut, en suivant la même marche, partir de ces expressions finies

$$\frac{z(z-q^{1-b})(z-q^{3-b})\ldots(z-q^{2n-1-b})(1-q^{1+b}z)(1-q^{3+b}z)\ldots(1-q^{2n-1+b}z)}{(z-q)(z-q^3)\ldots(z-q^{2n+1})(1-qz)(1-q^3z)\ldots(1-q^{2n+1}z)},$$

$$\frac{z(z-q^{2-b})(z-q^{4-b})\ldots(z-q^{2n-b})(1-q^{2+b}z)(1-q^{4+b}z)\ldots(1-q^{2n+b}z)}{(z-q)(z-q^3)\ldots(z-q^{2n+1})(1-qz)(1-q^3z)\ldots(1-q^{2n+1}z)},$$

et faire grandir indéfiniment le nombre n.

Enfin, et en dernier lieu, je remarque qu'au moyen de la formule

$$\int_0^{2K} F(x_0+x)\,dx = \frac{2i\pi S}{1-\mu'},$$

qui a été le point de départ de mon procédé, nous pouvons très simplement démontrer les relations établies au paragraphe IV, page 227 :

$$\int_0^{2K} \frac{\Theta(x+a)\,\Theta(x+b)}{\Theta^2(x)}\,dx = 0,$$

$$\int_0^{2K} \frac{H(x+a)H(x+b)}{\Theta^2(x)}\,dx = 0,$$

où a et b désignent, dans la première, deux racines de l'équation $H'(x) = 0$, et dans la seconde, deux racines de l'équation $\Theta'(x) = 0$. Si l'on prend, en effet, successivement

$$F(x) = \frac{\Theta(x+a)\,\Theta(x+b)}{\Theta^2(x)},$$

$$F(x) = \frac{H(x+a)\,H(x+b)}{\Theta^2(x)},$$

on aura $\mu = 1$ et μ' différant de l'unité, sauf la supposition que nous excluons de $b = -a$. On obtient d'ailleurs, dans le premier cas,

$$S = \frac{H(a)\,H'(b) + H(b)\,H'(a)}{H'^2(0)}\sqrt{\mu'},$$

et, dans le second,

$$S = \frac{\Theta(a)\,\Theta'(b) + \Theta(b)\,\Theta'(a)}{H'^2(0)}\sqrt{\mu'},$$

de sorte que, sous les conditions admises, les deux valeurs de S s'évanouissent. Cela étant, nous pouvons, dans la relation ainsi démontrée,

$$\int_0^{2K} F(x_0 + x)\,dx = 0,$$

supposer $x_0 = 0$; car l'intégrale est une fonction continue de x_0, non seulement dans le voisinage de cette valeur particulière, mais dans l'intervalle des deux parallèles à l'axe des abscisses, menées à la même distance K' au-dessus et au-dessous de cet axe.

X.

Dans la théorie de la rotation d'un corps autour d'un point fixe O, le mouvement d'un point quelconque du solide se détermine en rapportant ce point aux axes principaux d'inertie Ox', Oy', Oz', immobiles dans le corps, mais entraînés par lui, et dont on donne la position à un instant quelconque par rapport à des axes fixes Ox, Oy, Oz, le plan des xy étant le plan invariable et l'axe Oz la perpendiculaire de ce plan. Soient donc x, y, z les coordonnées d'un point du corps par rapport aux axes fixes, et ξ, η, ζ les coordonnées par rapport aux axes mobiles ; ces quantités seront liées par les relations

$$x = a\,\xi + b\,\eta + c\,\zeta,$$
$$y = a'\xi + b'\eta + c'\zeta,$$
$$z = a''\xi + b''\eta + c''\zeta,$$

et la question consiste à obtenir en fonction du temps les neuf coefficients a, b, c, ... Jacobi le premier en a donné une solution complète et définitive, qui offre l'une des plus belles applications de calcul à la Mécanique et ouvre en même temps des voies nouvelles dans la théorie des fonctions elliptiques. C'est à l'étude des résultats si importants découverts par l'immortel géomètre que je dois les recherches exposées dans ce travail, et tout d'abord l'intégration de l'équation de Lamé, dans le cas dont je viens de m'occuper, où l'on suppose $n = 1$; on va voir en effet comment la théorie de la rotation, lorsqu'il n'y a point de force accélératrice, se trouve étroitement liée à cette équation.

Pour cela je partirai des relations suivantes, données dans le Tome II du *Traité de Mécanique* de Poisson, page 135 :

$$\frac{da}{dt} = br - cq, \qquad \frac{da'}{dt} = b'r - c'q, \qquad \frac{da''}{dt} = b''r - c''q,$$
$$\frac{db}{dt} = cp - ar, \qquad \frac{db'}{dt} = c'p - a'r, \qquad \frac{db''}{dt} = c''p - a''r,$$
$$\frac{dc}{dt} = aq - bp, \qquad \frac{dc'}{dt} = a'q - b'p, \qquad \frac{dc''}{dt} = a''q - b''p,$$

dans lesquelles p, q, r sont les composantes rectangulaires de la vitesse de rotation, par rapport aux mobiles Ox', Oy', Oz'. Cela étant, des conditions connues

$$p = \alpha a'', \qquad q = \beta b'', \qquad r = \gamma c'',$$

où α, β, γ sont des constantes, on tire immédiatement les équations

$$\frac{da''}{dt} = (\gamma - \beta)b''c'', \qquad \frac{db''}{dt} = (\alpha - \gamma)c''a'', \qquad \frac{dc''}{dt} = (\beta - \alpha)a''b'',$$

dont une première intégrale algébrique est donnée par l'égalité

$$a''^2 + b''^2 + c''^2 = 1,$$

et une seconde intégrale par celle-ci :

$$\alpha a''^2 + \beta b''^2 + \gamma c''^2 = \delta,$$

δ étant une constante arbitraire. Ces quantités α, β, γ, δ sont liées aux constantes A, B, C, h, l du Mémoire de Jacobi par les relations

$$\alpha = \frac{l}{A}, \qquad \beta = \frac{l}{B}, \qquad \gamma = \frac{l}{C}, \qquad \delta = \frac{h}{l};$$

elles sont donc du signe de l qui peut être positif ou négatif, comme représentant le moment d'impulsion dans le plan invariable. Dans ces deux cas, β sera compris entre α et γ, puisqu'on suppose B compris entre A et C ; mais j'admettrai, pour fixer les idées, que l soit positif. On voit de plus que, δ étant une moyenne entre α, β, γ, peut être plus grand ou plus petit que β : la première hypothèse donne $Bh > l^2$, et Jacobi suppose alors $A > B > C$; dans la seconde, on a $Bh < l^2$, avec $A < B < C$; ces conditions prendront, avec nos constantes, la forme suivante :

$$\text{(I)} \qquad \alpha < \beta < \delta < \gamma,$$

$$\text{(II)} \qquad \alpha > \beta > \delta > \gamma,$$

et nous allons immédiatement en faire usage en recherchant les expressions des coefficients a'', b'', c'', par des fonctions elliptiques du temps.

XI.

J'observe, en premier lieu, qu'on obtient, si l'on exprime a'' et c'' au moyen de b'', les valeurs

$$(\gamma - \alpha) a''^2 = \gamma - \delta - (\gamma - \beta) b''^2, \qquad (\gamma - \alpha) c''^2 = \delta - \alpha - (\beta - \alpha) b''^2.$$

Posons maintenant

$$a''^2 = \frac{\gamma - \delta}{\gamma - \alpha} V^2, \qquad b''^2 = \frac{\gamma - \delta}{\gamma - \beta} U^2, \qquad c''^2 = \frac{\delta - \alpha}{\gamma - \alpha} W^2,$$

puis

$$k^2 = \frac{(\beta - \alpha)(\gamma - \delta)}{(\delta - \alpha)(\gamma - \beta)};$$

il viendra plus simplement

$$V^2 = 1 - U^2, \qquad W^2 = 1 - k^2 U^2.$$

Introduisons, en outre, la quantité $n^2 = (\delta - \alpha)(\gamma - \beta)$; l'équation $\frac{db''}{dt} = (\alpha - \gamma) c'' a''$ prend cette forme :

$$\frac{dU}{dt} = n VW,$$

et l'on en conclut, en désignant par t_0 une constante arbitraire,

$$U = \operatorname{sn}[n(t - t_0), k], \qquad V = \operatorname{cn}[n(t - t_0), k], \qquad W = \operatorname{dn}[n(t - t_0), k].$$

J'ajoute que les quantités $\frac{\gamma - \delta}{\gamma - \alpha}, \frac{\gamma - \delta}{\gamma - \beta}, \frac{\delta - \alpha}{\gamma - \alpha}, (\delta - \alpha)(\gamma - \beta)$ sont toutes positives et que k^2 est positif et moindre que l'unité, sous les conditions (I) et (II). A l'égard du module il suffit en effet de remarquer que l'identité

$$(\delta - \alpha)(\gamma - \beta) = (\gamma - \alpha)(\delta - \beta) + (\beta - \alpha)(\gamma - \delta)$$

donne

$$k'^2 = \frac{(\gamma - \alpha)(\delta - \beta)}{(\delta - \alpha)(\gamma - \beta)},$$

de sorte que k^2 et k'^2, étant évidemment positifs, sont par cela même tous deux inférieurs à l'unité. Ce point établi, désignons par $\varepsilon, \varepsilon', \varepsilon''$ des facteurs égaux à ± 1; en convenant de prendre dorénavant les racines carrées avec le signe $+$, nous pourrons écrire

$$a'' = \varepsilon \sqrt{\frac{\gamma - \delta}{\gamma - \alpha}} V, \qquad b'' = \varepsilon' \sqrt{\frac{\gamma - \delta}{\gamma - \beta}} U, \qquad c'' = \varepsilon'' \sqrt{\frac{\delta - \alpha}{\gamma - \alpha}} W,$$

et la substitution dans les équations

$$\frac{da''}{dt} = (\gamma - \beta) b'' c'', \qquad \frac{db''}{dt} = (\alpha - \gamma) c'' a'', \qquad \frac{dc''}{dt} = (\beta - \alpha) a'' b'',$$

donnera les conclusions suivantes. Admettons d'abord les conditions (I) : les trois différences $\beta - \gamma$, $\alpha - \gamma$, $\alpha - \beta$ seront négatives, et l'on trouvera

$$\varepsilon = -\varepsilon' \varepsilon'', \qquad \varepsilon' = -\varepsilon'' \varepsilon, \qquad \varepsilon'' = -\varepsilon \varepsilon';$$

mais sous les conditions (II), ces mêmes quantités étant positives, nous aurons

$$\varepsilon = \varepsilon'\varepsilon'', \qquad \varepsilon' = \varepsilon''\varepsilon, \qquad \varepsilon'' = \varepsilon\varepsilon';$$

ainsi, en faisant, avec Jacobi, $\varepsilon = -1$, $\varepsilon' = +1$, on voit qu'il faudra prendre $\varepsilon'' = +1$ dans le premier cas et la valeur contraire $\varepsilon'' = -1$ dans le second. Cela posé, et en convenant toujours que les racines carrées soient positives, je dis qu'on peut déterminer un argument ω par les deux conditions

$$\operatorname{cn}\omega = \sqrt{\frac{\gamma - \alpha}{\gamma - \delta}}, \qquad \operatorname{dn}\omega = \sqrt{\frac{\gamma - \alpha}{\gamma - \beta}};$$

d'où nous tirons

$$\frac{\operatorname{dn}\omega}{\operatorname{cn}\omega} = \sqrt{\frac{\gamma - \delta}{\gamma - \beta}};$$

ces quantités satisfont en effet à la relation

$$dn^2\omega - k^2 cn^2\omega = k'^2,$$

comme on le vérifie aisément. Je remarque, en outre, que $\operatorname{cn}\omega$ et $\operatorname{dn}\omega$ étant des fonctions paires, on peut encore à volonté disposer du signe de ω. Or, ayant $\frac{\operatorname{sn}^2\omega}{\operatorname{cn}^2\omega} = \frac{\alpha - \delta}{\gamma - \alpha}$, nous fixerons ce signe de manière que, suivant les conditions (I) ou (II), $\frac{\operatorname{sn}\omega}{i\operatorname{cn}\omega}$, qui est une fonction impaire, soit égal à $+\sqrt{\frac{\delta - \alpha}{\gamma - \alpha}}$ ou à $-\sqrt{\frac{\delta - \alpha}{\gamma - \alpha}}$. Nous éviterons, en définissant la constante ω comme on vient de le faire, les doubles signes qui figurent dans les relations de Jacobi ; ainsi, à l'égard de a'', b'', c'', on aura, dans tous les cas, les formules suivantes, où je fais pour abréger $u = n(t - t_0)$:

$$a'' = -\frac{\operatorname{cn} u}{\operatorname{cn}\omega}, \qquad b'' = \frac{\operatorname{dn}\omega \operatorname{sn} u}{\operatorname{cn}\omega}, \qquad c'' = \frac{\operatorname{sn}\omega \operatorname{dn} u}{i\operatorname{cn}\omega}.$$

Enfin il est facile de voir que $\omega = i\upsilon$, υ étant réel ; de la formule $\operatorname{cn}(i\upsilon, k) = \frac{1}{\operatorname{cn}(\upsilon, k')}$, on conclut, en effet, $\operatorname{cn}(\upsilon, k') = \sqrt{\frac{\gamma - \delta}{\gamma - \alpha}}$, valeur qui est dans les deux cas non seulement réelle, mais moindre que l'unité.

XII.

J'aborde maintenant la détermination des six coefficients a, b, c, a', b', c' en introduisant les quantités

$$A = a + ia', \qquad B = b + ib', \qquad C = c + ic',$$

et partant des relations suivantes:

$$\begin{aligned} A a'' + B b'' + C c'' &= 0, \\ i A - B c'' + C b'' &= 0, \end{aligned}$$

qu'il est facile de démontrer. La première est une suite des égalités

$$aa'' + bb'' + cc'' = 0, \qquad a'a'' + b'b'' + c'c'' = 0,$$

et la seconde résulte de celles-ci :

$$a = b'c'' - c'b'', \qquad a' = b''c - c''b, \qquad a'' = bc' - cb', \qquad \ldots.$$

Qu'on prenne, en effet, les valeurs de a et a', on en déduira

$$a + ia' = (b' - ib)c'' - b''(c' - ic),$$

ce qui revient bien à la relation énoncée. Cela posé, je fais usage des équations de Poisson rappelées plus haut, et qui donnent

$$D_t A = B r - C q, \qquad D_t B = C p - A r, \qquad D_t C = A q - B p,$$

puis, en remplaçant p, q, r par $\alpha a''$, $\beta b''$, $\gamma c''$,

$$D_t A = B c'' \gamma - C b'' \beta, \qquad D_t B = C a'' \alpha - A c'' \gamma, \qquad D_t C = A b'' \beta - B a'' \alpha.$$

Mettons maintenant dans la première les expressions de B et C en A, qu'on tire de nos deux relations, à savoir

$$B = \frac{a'' b'' - ic''}{a''^2 - 1} A, \qquad C = \frac{a'' c'' + ib''}{a''^2 - 1} A;$$

on obtiendra aisément

$$\frac{D_t A}{A} = \frac{(\gamma - \beta) a'' b'' c'' - i(\gamma c''^2 + \beta b''^2)}{a''^2 - 1},$$

ou bien encore

$$\frac{D_t A}{A} = \frac{a'' D_t a'' + i(\alpha a''^2 - \delta)}{a''^2 - 1},$$

et, par un simple changement de lettres, on en conclut, sans nouveau calcul,

$$\frac{D_t B}{B} = \frac{b'' D_t b'' + i(\beta b''^2 - \delta)}{b''^2 - 1},$$

$$\frac{D_t C}{C} = \frac{c'' D_t c'' + i(\gamma c''^2 - \delta)}{c''^2 - 1}.$$

Ces formules seront plus simples si l'on fait

$$A = \mathrm{a}\, e^{i\alpha t}, \qquad B = \mathrm{b}\, e^{i\beta t}, \qquad C = \mathrm{c}\, e^{i\gamma t};$$

car il vient ainsi

$$\frac{D_t \mathrm{a}}{\mathrm{a}} = \frac{a'' D_t a'' + i(\alpha - \delta)}{a''^2 - 1},$$

$$\frac{D_t \mathrm{b}}{\mathrm{b}} = \frac{b'' D_t b'' + i(\beta - \delta)}{b''^2 - 1},$$

$$\frac{D_t \mathrm{c}}{\mathrm{c}} = \frac{c'' D_t c'' + i(\gamma - \delta)}{c''^2 - 1}.$$

Cela étant, j'envisage la première, et pour un instant je pose $a''^2 - 1 = \mathfrak{a}^2$, ce qui donnera

$$\frac{D_t \mathrm{a}}{\mathrm{a}} = \frac{\mathfrak{a} D_t \mathfrak{a} + i(\alpha - \delta)}{\mathfrak{a}^2} = \frac{D_t \mathfrak{a}}{\mathfrak{a}} + i\,\frac{\alpha - \delta}{\mathfrak{a}^2}.$$

On en conclut ensuite, en différentiant,

$$\frac{D_t^2 \mathrm{a}}{\mathrm{a}} - \left(\frac{D_t \mathrm{a}}{\mathrm{a}}\right)^2 = \frac{D_t^2 \mathfrak{a}}{\mathfrak{a}} - \left(\frac{D_t \mathfrak{a}}{\mathfrak{a}}\right)^2 - 2i\,\frac{(\alpha - \delta) D_t \mathfrak{a}}{\mathfrak{a}^3};$$

puis encore, par l'élimination de $\dfrac{D_t \mathrm{a}}{\mathrm{a}}$,

$$\frac{D_t^2 \mathrm{a}}{\mathrm{a}} = \frac{D_t^2 \mathfrak{a}}{\mathfrak{a}} - \frac{(\alpha - \delta)^2}{\mathfrak{a}^4};$$

mais, comme conséquence de l'équation différentielle,

$$(D_t a'')^2 = (\gamma - \beta)^2 b''^2 c''^2 = [\delta - \beta - (\alpha - \beta) a''^2][\gamma - \delta - (\gamma - \alpha) a''^2],$$

on a la suivante :

$$\frac{\mathfrak{a}^2}{1 + \mathfrak{a}^2}(D_t \mathfrak{a})^2 = -(\delta - \alpha)^2 - (\delta - \alpha)(\beta + \gamma - 2\alpha)\mathfrak{a}^2 - (\beta - \alpha)(\gamma - \alpha)\mathfrak{a}^4,$$

qui peut s'écrire

$$(D_t\mathfrak{a})^2+\frac{(\delta-\alpha)^2}{\mathfrak{a}^2}$$
$$=-(\delta-\alpha)^2-(\delta-\alpha)(\beta+\gamma-2\alpha)(1+\mathfrak{a}^2)-(\beta-\alpha)(\gamma-\alpha)(\mathfrak{a}^2+\mathfrak{a}^4).$$

Or on en tire, en différentiant et divisant ensuite les deux membres par $2\mathfrak{a}D_t\mathfrak{a}$,

$$\frac{D_t^2\mathfrak{a}}{\mathfrak{a}}-\frac{(\delta-\alpha)^2}{\mathfrak{a}^4}$$
$$=-[(\delta-\alpha)(\beta+\gamma-2\alpha)+(\beta-\alpha)(\gamma-\alpha)]-2(\beta-\alpha)(\gamma-\alpha)\mathfrak{a}^2.$$

Nous avons donc, après avoir remplacé $\mathfrak{a}^2$ par a''^2-1,

$$\frac{D_t^2\mathfrak{a}}{\mathfrak{a}}=(\beta-\alpha)(\gamma-\delta)-(\delta-\alpha)(\gamma-\alpha)-2(\beta-\alpha)(\gamma-\alpha)a''^2;$$

c'est le résultat que j'avais en vue d'obtenir.

XIII.

Deux voies s'ouvrent maintenant pour parvenir aux expressions de A, B, C; voici d'abord la plus élémentaire. Revenant aux formules

$$B=\frac{a''b''-ic''}{a''^2-1}A,\qquad C=\frac{a''c''+ib''}{a''^2-1}A,$$

je remplace a'', b'', c'' par les valeurs obtenues au paragraphe XI, page 293 :

$$a''=-\frac{\operatorname{cn}u}{\operatorname{cn}\omega},\qquad b''=\frac{\operatorname{dn}\omega\operatorname{sn}u}{\operatorname{cn}\omega},\qquad c''=\frac{\operatorname{sn}\omega\operatorname{dn}u}{i\operatorname{cn}\omega},$$

et, au moyen des relations relatives à l'addition des arguments, j'obtiens ces résultats :

$$\frac{a''b''-ic''}{a''^2-1}=\frac{\operatorname{sn}u\operatorname{cn}u\operatorname{dn}\omega+\operatorname{sn}\omega\operatorname{cn}\omega\operatorname{dn}u}{\operatorname{sn}^2u-\operatorname{sn}^2\omega}=\frac{\operatorname{cn}(u-\omega)}{\operatorname{sn}(u-\omega)},$$
$$\frac{a''c''+ib''}{a''^2-1}=\frac{\operatorname{sn}u\operatorname{cn}\omega\operatorname{dn}\omega+\operatorname{sn}\omega\operatorname{cn}u\operatorname{dn}u}{i(\operatorname{sn}^2u-\operatorname{sn}^2\omega)}=\frac{1}{i\operatorname{sn}(u-\omega)},$$

de sorte que nous pouvons écrire

$$B=\frac{\operatorname{cn}(u-\omega)}{\operatorname{sn}(u-\omega)}A,\qquad C=\frac{A}{i\operatorname{sn}(u-\omega)}.$$

Cela posé, j'envisage l'expression

$$\frac{D_t a}{a} = \frac{a'' D_t a'' + i(\alpha - \delta)}{a''^2 - 1} = \frac{(\gamma - \beta) a'' b'' c'' + i(\alpha - \delta)}{a''^2 - 1}$$

et je fais le même calcul, après avoir remplacé $\gamma - \beta$ et $\alpha - \delta$ par les valeurs suivantes :

$$\gamma - \beta = in \frac{\operatorname{cn} \omega}{\operatorname{sn} \omega \operatorname{dn} \omega}, \qquad \alpha - \delta = in \frac{\operatorname{sn} \omega \operatorname{dn} \omega}{\operatorname{cn} \omega},$$

qu'on tire facilement des équations posées page 293 :

$$\operatorname{cn} \omega = \sqrt{\frac{\gamma - \alpha}{\gamma - \delta}}, \qquad \operatorname{dn} \omega = \sqrt{\frac{\gamma - \alpha}{\gamma - \beta}}, \qquad \operatorname{sn} \omega = i \sqrt{\frac{\delta - \alpha}{\gamma - \delta}}$$

et de $n = \sqrt{(\delta - \alpha)(\gamma - \beta)}$. L'expression à laquelle nous parvenons ainsi,

$$\frac{D_t a}{a} = n \frac{\operatorname{sn} u \operatorname{cn} u \operatorname{dn} u + \operatorname{sn} \omega \operatorname{cn} \omega \operatorname{dn} \omega}{\operatorname{sn}^2 u - \operatorname{sn}^2 \omega},$$

nous offre une fonction doublement périodique, dont les périodes sont $2K$, $2iK'$, et qui a deux pôles, $u = \omega$, $u = iK'$. Les résidus correspondant à ces pôles étant $+1$ et -1, la décomposition en éléments simples donne immédiatement

$$\frac{\operatorname{sn} u \operatorname{cn} u \operatorname{dn} u + \operatorname{sn} \omega \operatorname{cn} \omega \operatorname{dn} \omega}{\operatorname{sn}^2 u - \operatorname{sn}^2 \omega} = \frac{H'(u - \omega)}{H(u - \omega)} - \frac{\Theta'(u)}{\Theta(u)} + C,$$

et la constante se détermine en faisant, par exemple, $u = 0$; on obtient de cette manière

$$C = \frac{H'(\omega)}{H(\omega)} - \frac{\operatorname{cn} \omega \operatorname{dn} \omega}{\operatorname{sn} \omega} + \frac{\Theta'(\omega)}{\Theta(\omega)}.$$

Nous pouvons donc écrire, après avoir pris pour variable $u = n(t - t_0)$,

$$\frac{D_u a}{a} = \frac{H'(u - \omega)}{H(u - \omega)} - \frac{\Theta'(u)}{\Theta(u)} + \frac{\Theta'(\omega)}{\Theta(\omega)},$$

et, si l'on désigne par $Ne^{i\nu}$ une nouvelle constante à laquelle nous donnons cette forme, parce qu'elle doit être, en général, supposée imaginaire, on aura

$$a = N e^{i\nu} \frac{H(u - \omega)}{\Theta(u)} e^{\frac{\Theta'(\omega)}{\Theta(\omega)} u}.$$

De cette formule résulte ensuite

$$A = N\, e^{i(\nu+\alpha t_0)} \frac{H(u-\omega)}{\Theta(u)} e^{\left[\frac{i\alpha}{n} + \frac{\Theta'(\omega)}{\Theta(\omega)}\right] u},$$

ou plus simplement, en mettant $\nu - \alpha t_0$ au lieu de ν,

$$A = N\, e^{i\nu} \frac{H(u-\omega)}{\Theta(u)} e^{\left[\frac{i\alpha}{n} + \frac{\Theta'(\omega)}{\Theta(\omega)}\right] u},$$

et l'on en conclut immédiatement

$$B = \frac{\operatorname{cn}(u-\omega)}{\operatorname{sn}(u-\omega)} A = \sqrt{k'}\, N\, e^{i\nu} \frac{H_1(u-\omega)}{\Theta(u)} e^{\left[\frac{i\alpha}{n} + \frac{\Theta'(\omega)}{\Theta(\omega)}\right] u},$$

$$C = \frac{1}{i \operatorname{sn}(u-\omega)} A = \sqrt{k}\, N\, e^{i\nu} \frac{\Theta(u-\omega)}{i\Theta(u)} e^{\left[\frac{i\alpha}{n} + \frac{\Theta'(\omega)}{\Theta(\omega)}\right] u}.$$

Des deux indéterminées N et ν qui figurent dans ces expressions, la dernière seule subsistera comme quantité arbitraire; N, qui est réel et positif, se détermine comme nous allons le montrer.

XIV.

Je fais à cet effet, pour plus de simplicité, dans les expressions précédentes,

$$\frac{i\alpha}{n} + \frac{\Theta'(\omega)}{\Theta(\omega)} = i\lambda,$$

en observant que cette quantité λ est réelle, car on a $\omega = i\upsilon$, ainsi que nous l'avons fait voir (p. 293). Cela étant, nous pouvons écrire

$$A = \sqrt{k}\, N \frac{\Theta(u-\omega)\, e^{i(\lambda u+\nu)}}{\Theta(u)} \operatorname{sn}(u-\omega),$$

$$B = \sqrt{k}\, N \frac{\Theta(u-\omega)\, e^{i(\lambda u+\nu)}}{\Theta(u)} \operatorname{cn}(u-\omega),$$

$$C = \sqrt{k}\, N \frac{\Theta(u-\omega)\, e^{i(\lambda u+\nu)}}{i\Theta(u)},$$

et je remarque tout d'abord que ces formules permettent de vérifier facilement les conditions auxquelles doivent satisfaire les neuf coefficients a, b, c, ... En premier lieu, nous en déduisons

$$A a'' + B b'' + C c'' = \sqrt{k}\, N \frac{\Theta(u-\omega)\, e^{i(\lambda u+\nu)}}{\operatorname{cn}\omega\, \Theta(u)} \times [-\operatorname{cn} u \operatorname{sn}(u-\omega) + \operatorname{dn}\omega \operatorname{sn} u \operatorname{cn}(u-\omega) - \operatorname{sn}\omega \operatorname{dn} u].$$

Or on a

$$\operatorname{cn} u \operatorname{sn}(u-\omega) - \operatorname{dn}\omega \operatorname{sn} u \operatorname{cn}(u-\omega) + \operatorname{sn}\omega \operatorname{dn} u = 0,$$

cette équation étant l'une des relations fondamentales pour l'addition des arguments [Jacobi, *Œuvres complètes*, t. II, p. 325, équation (16)], et nous obtenons ainsi

$$aa'' + bb'' + cc'' = 0, \qquad a'a'' + b'b'' + c'c'' = 0.$$

Je remarque ensuite que la somme des carrés $A^2 + B^2 + C^2$ s'évanouit comme contenant en facteur $\operatorname{sn}^2(u-\omega) + \operatorname{cn}^2(u-\omega) - 1$, et nous en concluons

$$a^2 + b^2 + c^2 = a'^2 + b'^2 + c'^2, \qquad aa' + bb' + cc' = 0.$$

Ayant d'ailleurs

$$a''^2 + b''^2 + c''^2 = \left(\frac{\operatorname{cn} u}{\operatorname{cn}\omega}\right)^2 + \left(\frac{\operatorname{dn}\omega \operatorname{sn} u}{\operatorname{cn}\omega}\right)^2 - \left(\frac{\operatorname{sn}\omega \operatorname{dn} u}{\operatorname{cn}\omega}\right)^2$$
$$= \frac{1-\operatorname{sn}^2 u}{\operatorname{cn}^2\omega} + \frac{(1-k^2\operatorname{sn}^2\omega)\operatorname{sn}^2 u}{\operatorname{cn}^2\omega} - \frac{(1-k^2\operatorname{sn}^2 u)\operatorname{sn}^2\omega}{\operatorname{cn}^2\omega} = 1,$$

les six relations que nous avons en vue seront complètement vérifiées dès que N sera déterminé de manière à obtenir $a^2 + b^2 + c^2 = 1$ (1).

(1) Les équations

$$iA = Bc'' - Cb'', \quad iB = Ca'' - Ac'', \quad iC = Ab'' - Ba'',$$

dont la première a été employée précédemment, page 294, et qui contiennent les suivantes ;

$$a = b'c'' - c'b'', \qquad b = c'a'' - a'c'', \qquad c = a'b'' - b'a'',$$
$$a' = b''c - c''b, \qquad b' = c''a - a''c, \qquad c' = a''b - b''a,$$

se vérifient aussi de la manière la plus facile. Les relations auxquelles elles conduisent, à savoir :

$$\operatorname{cn}\omega = \operatorname{cn} u \operatorname{cn}(u-\omega) + \operatorname{dn}\omega \operatorname{sn} u \operatorname{sn}(u-\omega),$$
$$\operatorname{cn} u = \operatorname{cn}\omega \operatorname{cn}(u-\omega) - \operatorname{dn} u \operatorname{sn} u \operatorname{sn}(u-\omega),$$
$$\operatorname{dn}\omega \operatorname{sn} u = \operatorname{cn}\omega \operatorname{sn}(u-\omega) + \operatorname{sn}\omega \operatorname{dn} u \operatorname{cn}(u-\omega),$$

figurent, en effet, dans le Tableau donné par Jacobi sous les nos 9, 10 et 11.

Formons pour cela les carrés des modules de A, B, C; en remarquant que, par le changement de i en $-i$, ω se change en $-\omega$, on trouve immédiatement

$$a^2+a'^2=k\mathrm{N}^2\frac{\Theta(u+\omega)\Theta(u-\omega)}{\Theta^2(u)}\,\mathrm{sn}(u+\omega)\,\mathrm{sn}(u-\omega),$$

$$b^2+b'^2=k\mathrm{N}^2\frac{\Theta(u+\omega)\Theta(u-\omega)}{\Theta^2(u)}\,\mathrm{cn}(u+\omega)\,\mathrm{cn}(u-\omega),$$

$$c^2+c'^2=k\mathrm{N}^2\frac{\Theta(u+\omega)\Theta(u-\omega)}{\Theta^2(u)};$$

d'où, en ajoutant membre à membre,

$$2=k\mathrm{N}^2\frac{\Theta(u+\omega)\Theta(u-\omega)}{\Theta^2(u)}[\mathrm{sn}(u+\omega)\,\mathrm{sn}(u-\omega)+\mathrm{cn}(u+\omega)\mathrm{cn}(u-\omega)+1].$$

Formons enfin les trois produits

$$(b-ib')(c+ic'),\quad (c-ic')(a+ia'),\quad (a-ia')(b+ib');$$

nous trouverons

$$(b-ib')(c+ic')=-\frac{\Theta(0)\mathrm{H}_1(0)\mathrm{H}_1(u+\omega)\Theta(u-\omega)}{\mathrm{H}_1^2(\omega)\Theta^2(u)}\,i,$$

$$(c-ic')(a+ia')=-\frac{\Theta_1(0)\mathrm{H}_1(0)\Theta(u+\omega)\mathrm{H}(u-\omega)}{i\,\mathrm{H}_1^2(\omega)\Theta^2(u)},$$

$$(a-ia')(b+ib')=\frac{\Theta(0)\Theta_1(0)\mathrm{H}(u+\omega)\mathrm{H}_1(u-\omega)}{\mathrm{H}_1^2(\omega)\Theta^2(u)};$$

or les relations élémentaires

$$\Theta(0)\mathrm{H}_1(0)\mathrm{H}_1(u+\omega)\Theta(u-\omega)=-\mathrm{H}(\omega)\Theta_1(\omega)\mathrm{H}(u)\Theta_1(u)+\mathrm{H}_1(\omega)\Theta(\omega)\Theta(u)\mathrm{H}_1(u),$$
$$\Theta_1(0)\mathrm{H}_1(0)\Theta(u+\omega)\mathrm{H}(u-\omega)=-\mathrm{H}(\omega)\Theta(\omega)\mathrm{H}_1(u)\Theta_1(u)+\mathrm{H}_1(\omega)\Theta_1(\omega)\Theta(u)\mathrm{H}(u),$$
$$\Theta(0)\Theta_1(0)\mathrm{H}(u+\omega)\mathrm{H}_1(u-\omega)=\Theta(\omega)\Theta_1(\omega)\mathrm{H}(u)\mathrm{H}_1(u)+\mathrm{H}(\omega)\mathrm{H}_1(\omega)\Theta(u)\Theta_1(u)$$

conduisent facilement à ces égalités

$$(b-ib')(c+ic')=-b''c''+ia'',$$
$$(c-ic')(a+ia')=-c''a''+ib'',$$
$$(a-ia')(b+ib')=-a''b''+ic'';$$

d'où l'on tire ce nouveau système de conditions :

$$bc+b'c'+b''c''=0,\qquad bc'-cb'=a'',$$
$$ca+c'a'+c''a''=0,\qquad ca'-ac'=b'',$$
$$ab+a'b'+a''b''=0,\qquad ab'-ba'=c''.$$

Or les formules élémentaires

$$\operatorname{sn}(u+\omega)\operatorname{sn}(u-\omega) = \frac{\operatorname{sn}^2 u - \operatorname{sn}^2\omega}{1-k^2\operatorname{sn}^2 u\operatorname{sn}^2\omega},$$

$$\operatorname{cn}(u+\omega)\operatorname{cn}(u-\omega) = -1+\frac{\operatorname{cn}^2 u + \operatorname{cn}^2\omega}{1-k^2\operatorname{sn}^2 u\operatorname{sn}^2\omega},$$

donnent

$$\operatorname{sn}(u+\omega)\operatorname{sn}(u-\omega)+\operatorname{cn}(u+\omega)\operatorname{cn}(u-\omega)+1 = \frac{2\operatorname{cn}^2\omega}{1-k^2\operatorname{sn}^2 u\operatorname{sn}^2\omega};$$

on a d'ailleurs

$$\frac{\Theta^2(0)\,\Theta(u+\omega)\,\Theta(u-\omega)}{\Theta^2(u)\,\Theta^2(\omega)} = 1-k^2\operatorname{sn}^2 u\operatorname{sn}^2\omega;$$

nous obtenons donc

$$1 = kN^2\frac{\Theta^2(\omega)\operatorname{cn}^2\omega}{\Theta^2(0)},$$

et par conséquent, après une réduction facile,

$$N = \frac{\Theta_1(0)}{H_1(\omega)}.$$

On en conclut les résultats de Jacobi, que nous gardons sous la forme suivante :

$$a+ia' = \frac{\Theta_1(0)\,H\,(u-\omega)\,e^{i(\lambda u+\nu)}}{H_1(\omega)\,\Theta(u)},$$

$$b+ib' = \frac{\Theta\,(0)\,H_1(u-\omega)\,e^{i(\lambda u+\nu)}}{H_1(\omega)\,\Theta(u)},$$

$$c+ic' = \frac{H_1(0)\;\Theta(u-\omega)\,e^{i(\lambda u+\nu)}}{iH_1(\omega)\,\Theta(u)},$$

et il ne nous reste plus qu'à y joindre les expressions des vitesses de rotation autour des axes fixes Ox, Oy, Oz.

Ces quantités, que je désignerai par v, v', v'', ont pour valeurs

$$v = a\,p + b\,q + c\,r,$$
$$v' = a'p + b'q + c'r,$$
$$v'' = a''p + b''q + c''r,$$

ou encore, en remplaçant p, q, r, par $\alpha a''$, $\beta b''$, $\gamma c''$,

$$v = \;aa''\alpha + \;bb''\beta + \;cc''\gamma,$$
$$v' = a'a''\alpha + b'b''\beta + c'c''\gamma,$$
$$v'' = \;a''^2\alpha + \;b''^2\beta + \;c''^2\gamma = \delta.$$

Cela posé, soit $v + iv' = \mathrm{V}$; nous pouvons écrire

$$\mathrm{V} = \mathrm{A}a''\alpha + \mathrm{B}b''\beta + \mathrm{C}c''\gamma,$$

et, si nous employons de nouveau les égalités

$$\mathrm{B} = \frac{a''b'' - ic''}{a''^2 - 1}\mathrm{A}, \qquad \mathrm{C} = \frac{a''c'' + ib''}{a''^2 - 1}\mathrm{A},$$

on obtiendra la formule

$$\mathrm{V} = \frac{(\delta - \alpha)a'' + i(\gamma - \beta)b''c''}{a''^2 - 1}\mathrm{A}.$$

Or, au moyen des relations

$$\delta - \alpha = -in\frac{\operatorname{sn}\omega \operatorname{dn}\omega}{\operatorname{cn}\omega}, \qquad \gamma - \beta = in\frac{\operatorname{cn}\omega}{\operatorname{sn}\omega \operatorname{dn}\omega}$$

et des valeurs de a'', b'', c'', il vient

$$\begin{aligned}\frac{(\delta - \alpha)a'' + i(\gamma - \beta)b''c''}{a''^2 - 1} &= -in\frac{\operatorname{sn}\omega \operatorname{cn}u \operatorname{dn}\omega + \operatorname{sn}u \operatorname{cn}\omega \operatorname{dn}u}{\operatorname{sn}^2 u - \operatorname{sn}^2\omega}\\ &= -in\frac{\operatorname{dn}(u-\omega)}{\operatorname{sn}(u-\omega)};\end{aligned}$$

l'expression précédente de A nous donne donc immédiatement

$$\mathrm{V} = -in\frac{\mathrm{H}'(0)\,\Theta_1(u-\omega)\,e^{i(\lambda u + \nu)}}{\mathrm{H}_1(\omega)\,\Theta(u)}.$$

Voici maintenant la seconde méthode que j'ai annoncée pour parvenir à la détermination des quantités A, B, C.

XV.

Je reprends l'équation différentielle du second ordre, obtenue au paragraphe XII, page 296, à savoir :

$$\mathrm{D}_t^2 \mathrm{a} = [(\beta - \alpha)(\gamma - \delta) - (\delta - \alpha)(\gamma - \alpha) - 2(\beta - \alpha)(\gamma - \alpha)a''^2]\mathrm{a},$$

et j'y joins les deux suivantes, qui s'en tirent par un changement de lettres

$$\mathrm{D}_t^2 \mathrm{b} = [(\gamma - \beta)(\alpha - \delta) - (\delta - \beta)(\alpha - \beta) - 2(\gamma - \beta)(\alpha - \beta)b''^2]\mathrm{b},$$
$$\mathrm{D}_t^2 \mathrm{c} = [(\alpha - \gamma)(\beta - \delta) - (\delta - \gamma)(\beta - \gamma) - 2(\alpha - \gamma)(\beta - \gamma)c''^2]\mathrm{c}.$$

Cela posé, au moyen des expressions de a'', b'', c'', en fonction de u, et de ces formules qu'on établit sans peine,

$$\alpha-\beta = in\frac{k^2\,\mathrm{sn}\,\omega\,\mathrm{cn}\,\omega}{\mathrm{dn}\,\omega}, \qquad \beta-\delta = in\frac{k'^2\,\mathrm{sn}\,\omega}{\mathrm{cn}\,\omega\,\mathrm{dn}\,\omega},$$

$$\alpha-\delta = in\frac{\mathrm{sn}\,\omega\,\mathrm{dn}\,\omega}{\mathrm{cn}\,\omega}, \qquad \gamma-\beta = in\frac{\mathrm{cn}\,\omega}{\mathrm{sn}\,\omega\,\mathrm{dn}\,\omega},$$

$$\gamma-\alpha = in\frac{\mathrm{cn}\,\omega\,\mathrm{dn}\,\omega}{\mathrm{sn}\,\omega}, \qquad \gamma-\delta = in\frac{\mathrm{dn}\,\omega}{\mathrm{sn}\,\omega\,\mathrm{cn}\,\omega},$$

nous obtenons, par un calcul facile,

$$\beta-\alpha)(\gamma-\delta)-(\delta-\alpha)(\gamma-\alpha)-2(\beta-\alpha)(\gamma-\alpha)\,a''^2 = n^2[\,2k^2\mathrm{sn}^2u-1-k^2+k^2\,\mathrm{sn}^2\omega\,],$$

$$\gamma-\beta)(\alpha-\delta)-(\delta-\beta)(\alpha-\beta)-2(\gamma-\beta)(\alpha-\beta)\,b''^2 = n^2\left[2k^2\mathrm{sn}^2u-1-k^2+k^2\frac{\mathrm{cn}^2\omega}{\mathrm{dn}^2\omega}\right],$$

$$\alpha-\gamma)(\beta-\delta)-(\delta-\gamma)(\beta-\gamma)-2(\alpha-\gamma)(\beta-\gamma)\,c''^2 = n^2\left[2k^2\mathrm{sn}^2u-1-k^2+\frac{1}{\mathrm{sn}^2\omega}\right].$$

Prenant donc pour variable indépendante u au lieu de t, on aura

$$D_u^2\,\mathrm{a} = [\,2k^2\,\mathrm{sn}^2u-1-k^2+k^2\,\mathrm{sn}^2\omega\,]\,\mathrm{a},$$

$$D_u^2\,\mathrm{b} = \left[2k^2\,\mathrm{sn}^2u-1-k^2+k^2\frac{\mathrm{cn}^2\omega}{\mathrm{dn}^2\omega}\right]\mathrm{b},$$

$$D_u^2\,\mathrm{c} = \left[2k^2\,\mathrm{sn}^2u-1-k^2+\frac{1}{\mathrm{sn}^2\omega}\right]\mathrm{c},$$

et nous nous trouvons, par conséquent, amenés à trois des quatre formes canoniques de l'équation de Lamé, qui ont été considérées au paragraphe VI, page 280. La solution générale de ces équations nous donne donc, en désignant les constantes arbitraires par P, Q, R, P', Q', R',

$$\mathrm{a} = \mathrm{P}\frac{\mathrm{H}(u-\omega)\,e^{\frac{\Theta'(\omega)}{\Theta(\omega)}u}}{\Theta(u)} + \mathrm{P}'\frac{\mathrm{H}(u+\omega)\,e^{-\frac{\Theta'(\omega)}{\Theta(\omega)}u}}{\Theta(u)},$$

$$\mathrm{b} = \mathrm{Q}\frac{\mathrm{H}_1(u-\omega)\,e^{\frac{\Theta'_1(\omega)}{\Theta_1(\omega)}u}}{\Theta(u)} + \mathrm{Q}'\frac{\mathrm{H}_1(u+\omega)\,e^{-\frac{\Theta'_1(\omega)}{\Theta_1(\omega)}u}}{\Theta(u)},$$

$$\mathrm{c} = \mathrm{R}\frac{\Theta(u-\omega)\,e^{\frac{\mathrm{H}'(\omega)}{\mathrm{H}(\omega)}u}}{\Theta(u)} + \mathrm{R}'\frac{\Theta(u+\omega)\,e^{-\frac{\mathrm{H}'(\omega)}{\mathrm{H}(\omega)}u}}{\Theta(u)},$$

et l'on en conclut, si l'on écrit, pour plus de simplicité, P, Q, R,

... au lieu de $\mathrm{P}e^{i\alpha t_0}$, $\mathrm{Q}e^{i\beta t_0}$, $\mathrm{R}e^{it_0}$, ...,

$$\mathrm{A} = \mathrm{P}\frac{\mathrm{H}(u-\omega)}{\Theta(u)}e^{\left[\frac{i\alpha}{n}+\frac{\Theta'(\omega)}{\Theta(\omega)}\right]u} + \mathrm{P}'\frac{\mathrm{H}(u+\omega)}{\Theta(u)}e^{\left[\frac{i\alpha}{n}-\frac{\Theta'(\omega)}{\Theta(\omega)}\right]u},$$

$$\mathrm{B} = \mathrm{Q}\frac{\mathrm{H}_1(u-\omega)}{\Theta(u)}e^{\left[\frac{i\beta}{n}+\frac{\Theta'_1(\omega)}{\Theta_1(\omega)}\right]u} + \mathrm{Q}'\frac{\mathrm{H}_1(u+\omega)}{\Theta(u)}e^{\left[\frac{i\beta}{n}-\frac{\Theta'_1(\omega)}{\Theta_1(\omega)}\right]u},$$

$$\mathrm{C} = \mathrm{R}\frac{\Theta(u-\omega)}{\Theta(u)}e^{\left[\frac{i\gamma}{n}+\frac{\mathrm{H}'(\omega)}{\mathrm{H}(\omega)}\right]u} + \mathrm{R}'\frac{\Theta(u+\omega)}{\Theta(u)}e^{\left[\frac{i\gamma}{n}-\frac{\mathrm{H}'(\omega)}{\mathrm{H}(\omega)}\right]u}.$$

La détermination des six constantes qui entrent dans ces expressions se fait très facilement, comme on va le voir.

Je remarque, en premier lieu, que nous pouvons poser

$$\frac{i\alpha}{n}+\frac{\Theta'(\omega)}{\Theta(\omega)} = \frac{i\beta}{n}+\frac{\Theta'_1(\omega)}{\Theta_1(\omega)} = \frac{i\gamma}{n}+\frac{\mathrm{H}'(\omega)}{\mathrm{H}(\omega)} = i\lambda,$$

λ désignant la quantité déjà considérée au paragraphe XIV, page 298. On a, en effet,

$$\frac{\Theta'_1(\omega)}{\Theta_1(\omega)} - \frac{\Theta'(\omega)}{\Theta(\omega)} = \mathrm{D}_\omega \log \operatorname{dn}\omega = -\frac{k^2 \operatorname{sn}\omega \operatorname{cn}\omega}{\operatorname{dn}\omega},$$

$$\frac{\mathrm{H}'(\omega)}{\mathrm{H}(\omega)} - \frac{\Theta'(\omega)}{\Theta(\omega)} = \mathrm{D}_\omega \log \operatorname{sn}\omega = \frac{\operatorname{cn}\omega \operatorname{dn}\omega}{\operatorname{sn}\omega},$$

et les égalités précédentes sont vérifiées au moyen des relations

$$\alpha - \beta = in\frac{k^2 \operatorname{sn}\omega \operatorname{cn}\omega}{\operatorname{dn}\omega}, \qquad \gamma - \alpha = in\frac{\operatorname{cn}\omega \operatorname{dn}\omega}{\operatorname{sn}\omega},$$

que nous avons données plus haut. Une conséquence importante découle de là : c'est qu'en changeant u en $u + 4\mathrm{K}$, les fonctions $\frac{\mathrm{H}(u-\omega)e^{i\lambda u}}{\Theta(u)}$, $\frac{\mathrm{H}_1(u-\omega)e^{\lambda i u}}{\Theta(u)}$, $\frac{\Theta(u-\omega)e^{i\lambda u}}{\Theta(u)}$ se reproduisent multipliées par le même facteur $e^{4i\lambda\mathrm{K}}$, tandis que les quantités

$$\frac{\mathrm{H}(u+\omega)}{\Theta(u)}e^{\left[\frac{i\alpha}{n}-\frac{\Theta'(\omega)}{\Theta(\omega)}\right]u}, \quad \frac{\mathrm{H}_1(u+\omega)}{\Theta(u)}e^{\left[\frac{i\beta}{n}-\frac{\Theta'_1(\omega)}{\Theta_1(\omega)}\right]u}, \quad \frac{\Theta(u+\omega)}{\Theta(u)}e^{\left[\frac{i\gamma}{n}-\frac{\mathrm{H}'(\omega)}{\mathrm{H}(\omega)}\right]u}$$

sont affectées des facteurs

$$e^{4i\mathrm{K}\left(\frac{2\alpha}{n}-\lambda\right)}, \quad e^{4i\mathrm{K}\left(\frac{2\beta}{n}-\lambda\right)}, \quad e^{4i\mathrm{K}\left(\frac{2\gamma}{n}-\lambda\right)},$$

essentiellement inégaux. Or on a obtenu, pour les quotients $\frac{B}{A}$, $\frac{C}{A}$, des fonctions doublement périodiques, ne changeant point quand on met $u+4K$ au lieu de u; il faut donc que les facteurs qui multiplient A, B, C, lorsqu'on remplace u par $u+4K$, soient les mêmes, ce qui exige qu'on fasse $P'=0$, $Q'=0$, $R'=0$. Ce point établi, j'écris, en modifiant convenablement la forme des constantes P, Q, R,

$$A = P\frac{\Theta(u-\omega)\,e^{i\lambda u}}{\Theta(u)}\,\mathrm{sn}(u-\omega),$$
$$B = Q\frac{\Theta(u-\omega)\,e^{i\lambda u}}{\Theta(u)}\,\mathrm{cn}(u-\omega),$$
$$C = R\frac{\Theta(u-\omega)\,e^{i\lambda u}}{\Theta(u)},$$

et j'emploie la condition $Aa''+Bb''+Cc''=0$, qui conduit à l'égalité

$$-P\,\mathrm{cn}\,u\,\mathrm{sn}(u-\omega)+Q\,\mathrm{dn}\,\omega\,\mathrm{sn}\,u\,\mathrm{cn}(u-\omega)-iR\,\mathrm{sn}\,\omega\,\mathrm{dn}\,u=0.$$

Or, en faisant $u=0$ et $u=\omega$, on en déduit

$$P=Q=iR;$$

de sorte qu'on peut poser

$$P=\sqrt{k}\,N\,e^{i\nu},\qquad Q=\sqrt{k}\,N\,e^{i\nu},\qquad R=\frac{\sqrt{k}\,N\,e^{i\nu}}{i},$$

ce qui nous donne les expressions de A, B, C obtenues au paragraphe XIV, page 298. Le calcul s'achève donc en déterminant, ainsi qu'on l'a fait plus haut, la valeur du facteur N.

XVI.

Les formules que nous venons d'établir ont été le sujet des travaux de plusieurs géomètres; M. Somoff en a donné une démonstration dans un Mémoire du *Journal de Crelle* (¹), peu différente de celle de Jacobi, et qui repose aussi sur l'emploi des trois angles

(¹) *Démonstration des formules de M. Jacobi relatives à la théorie de la rotation d'un corps solide*, t. XLII, p. 95.

d'Euler. M. Brill, dans un excellent travail intitulé : *Sul problema della rotazione dei corpi* (*Annali di Matematica*, série 2e, t. III, p. 33), a employé le premier les équations différentielles de Poisson et les quantités $a + ia'$, $b + ib'$, $c + ic'$ dont j'ai fait usage, mais son analyse est entièrement différente de la mienne. C'est à un autre point de vue que s'est placé M. Chelini ([1]) en déduisant pour la première fois les conséquences analytiques de la belle théorie de Poinsot, que son auteur ni personne n'avait encore données d'une manière aussi approfondie. Je mentionnerai enfin deux récents Mémoires de M. Siacci, professeur à l'Université de Turin, et dont l'auteur a bien voulu, dans la lettre suivante, m'indiquer les points les plus essentiels :

« Turin, 24 décembre 1877.

» Poinsot, à la fin de son *Mémoire sur la rotation des corps*, démontre que la section diamétrale de l'ellipsoïde central, déterminée par le plan parallèle au couple d'impulsion, a son aire constante. Ce théorème a été le point de départ d'un Mémoire ([2]) dont les résultats se rattachent à la théorie des fonctions elliptiques aussi bien qu'à la théorie de la rotation. Je me suis d'abord proposé le problème de déterminer le mouvement des axes de cette section : pour abréger, je l'appellerai *section invariable*, et son plan, *plan invariable*. Une première solution du problème est suggérée par l'homothétie de la section invariable avec l'indicatrice de Dupin, relative à l'extrémité de l'axe instantané (pôle). La rotation d'un système de trois axes rectangulaires, dont les premiers coïncident avec les axes de la section, n'est que la résultante de deux rotations, l'une due au mouvement du pôle sur la poloïde, l'autre due au mouvement de l'ellipsoïde. Soient, sur ces axes, P_1, P_2, P_3 les composantes de la première vitesse angulaire; m_1, m_2, m_3 celles de la seconde. La résultante se composera de $P_1 + m_1$, $P_2 + m_2$, $P_3 + m_3$; et, comme le pôle reste sur un plan, on aura

$$(1) \qquad P_1 + m_1 = 0, \qquad P_2 + m_2 = 0, \qquad P_3 + m_3 = d\psi : dt,$$

([1]) *Determinazione analitica della rotazione dei corpi liberi secundo i concette del signor Poinsot* (*Memorie dell'Accademia delle Scienze dell'Istituto di Bologna*, vol. X).

([2]) *Memorie della Società italiana delle Scienze*, 3e série, t. III.

ψ étant la longitude d'un des axes de la section. Soient $\sqrt{a_1}$, $\sqrt{a_2}$, $\sqrt{a_3}$ les demi-axes de l'ellipsoïde (le troisième est celui qui ne se couche jamais sur le plan invariable); x_1, x_2, x_3 les coordonnées du pôle; λ_1, λ_2, λ_3 ($\lambda_3 = 0$, λ_1, λ_2 sont les demi-axes carrés de la section) les racines de l'équation

$$(\lambda) \equiv \frac{x_1^2}{a_1 - \lambda} + \frac{x_2^2}{a_2 - \lambda} + \frac{x_3^2}{a_3 - \lambda} - 1 = 0.$$

On aura

$$m_r^2 = \frac{(a_1 - \lambda_r)(a_2 - \lambda_r)(a_3 - \lambda_r)}{(\lambda_r - \lambda_s)(\lambda_r - \lambda_{s'})}, \qquad 2P_r\,dt = \frac{m_s m_{s'}}{\lambda_s - \lambda_{s'}}\left(\frac{d\lambda_s}{m_s^2} + \frac{d\lambda_{s'}}{m_{s'}^2}\right)$$

(r, s, s' étant trois nombres de la série 1, 2, 3). Comme $\lambda_1\lambda_2 = \text{const.} = c^2$, on a $m_3 = \text{const.}$ C'est, en effet, la distance du centre O au plan fixe de contact; de même m_1, m_2 sont les distances de O des plans tangents aux surfaces (λ_1) et (λ_2). Au moyen de ces valeurs, les équations (1), qui reviennent en substance aux équations d'Euler, donnent t et ψ en fonction de $x = \lambda_1 + \lambda_2$. En posant $t = nu$ (n expression connue), on obtient

$$(2)\quad \psi = \mp\frac{u}{2}\left(\frac{d\log \operatorname{sn} i\sigma}{d\sigma} + \frac{d\log \operatorname{sn} i\tau}{d\tau}\right) \pm \frac{1}{2i}[\Pi(u, i\sigma) + \Pi(u, i\tau)],$$

$$(3)\quad \psi = \pm\frac{u}{2}\left[\frac{d\log \mathrm{H}(i\sigma)}{d\sigma} + \frac{d\log \mathrm{H}(i\tau)}{d\tau}\right] \pm \frac{1}{4i}\log\frac{\Theta(u - i\sigma)\Theta(u - i\tau)}{\Theta(u + i\sigma)\Theta(u + i\tau)},$$

et l'on prendra le signe supérieur ou inférieur, suivant que $m_3^2 >$ ou $< a_2$.

Le module est

$$k = \sqrt{\frac{a_3(a_2 - a_1)(c^2 - a_1 a_2)}{a_1(a_2 - a_3)(c^2 - a_2 a_3)}},$$

et σ et τ sont ainsi donnés

$$\tau = \int_0^{\mathrm{F}} \frac{d\varphi}{\sqrt{1 - k'^2 \sin^2\varphi}}, \qquad \sigma = \int_0^{\mathrm{G}} \frac{d\varphi}{\sqrt{1 - k'^2 \sin^2\varphi}},$$

$$\cos\left(\frac{\mathrm{F}}{\mathrm{G}}\right) = \frac{c \pm a_3}{a_3 \pm c}\sqrt{\frac{a_3}{a_2}},$$

F étant un angle aigu négatif ou positif, suivant que $m_3^2 \gtrless a_2$ et G un angle positif, qui sera $<$ ou $> \frac{1}{2}\pi$, suivant que la zone entourée par la poloïde comprendra deux ombilics ou aucun : c'est, en effet, ce qui revient aux cas de $G \lesseqgtr \frac{1}{2}\pi$ ou de $\sigma \lesseqgtr K'$. La double expression

$$c\frac{H(i\sigma)\sqrt{\Theta(u+i\tau)\,\Theta(u-i\tau)} \pm H(i\tau)\sqrt{\Theta(u+i\sigma)\,\Theta(u-i\sigma)}}{H(i\sigma)\sqrt{\Theta(u+i\tau)\,\Theta(u-i\tau)} \pm H(i\tau)\sqrt{\Theta(u+i\sigma)\,\Theta(u-i\sigma)}}$$

donne λ_1 et λ_2. L'étude de l'expression (3) démontre que le mouvement moyen des demi-axes de la section est donné par le terme multiplié par u, et l'inégalité par l'autre, lorsque $\sigma < K'$; lorsque $\sigma > K'$, le mouvement moyen et l'inégalité sont donnés par les mêmes termes en y changeant σ en $\sigma - 2K'$; et l'on trouve que, dans le second cas, le mouvement moyen coïncide avec celui des projections des demi-axes $\sqrt{a_1}$ et $\sqrt{a_2}$, et dans le premier avec celui des projections de $\sqrt{a_3}$ et de l'axe instantané.

» On peut tirer ψ de l'expression de la longitude (μ) d'une droite quelconque OR, dont l'extrémité a ξ_1, ξ_2, ξ_3 pour coordonnées. Je trouve ainsi

$$\psi + \operatorname{arc\,tang}\left[\left(\frac{m_2 x_1 \xi_1}{a_1 - \lambda_2} + \frac{m_2 x_2 \xi_2}{a_2 - \lambda_2} + \frac{m_2 x_3 \xi_3}{a_3 - \lambda_2}\right) : \left(\frac{m_1 x_1 \xi_1}{a_1 - \lambda_1} + \frac{m_1 x_2 \xi_2}{a_2 - \lambda_1} + \frac{m_1 x_3 \xi_3}{a_3 - \lambda_1}\right)\right] = (\mu),$$

et je donne aussi l'expression développée de (μ). Comme ξ_1, ξ_2, ξ_3 sont fonctions arbitraires de u, on voit l'infinité de formes qu'on peut donner à l'expression (2) de ψ.

» En faisant coïncider OR avec $\sqrt{a_1}$, $\sqrt{a_2}$, $\sqrt{a_3}$ et avec l'axe instantané, on obtient leurs longitudes μ_1, μ_2, μ_3, μ et l'on a

$$(4) \qquad \psi = \mu_r - \operatorname{arc\,tang}\frac{m_2}{m_1}\frac{a_r - \lambda_1}{a_r - \lambda_2} = \mu - \operatorname{arc\,tang}\frac{m_2}{m_1}.$$

» Ces quatre expressions de ψ contiennent les principaux théorèmes sur la transformation et sur l'addition des paramètres des intégrales elliptiques de troisième espèce, mais sous une forme nouvelle, à cause des termes circulaires.

» Le mouvement des projections des axes du corps et de l'axe instantané a été déterminé par Jacobi : leurs inégalités sont données au moyen d'une constante a, qui se trouve liée avec nos quantités par l'équation $\sigma + \tau = 2a$; mais aux expressions des mouvements moyens concourent les moments d'inertie du corps. Au moyen des quantités σ et τ, elles acquièrent, comme on a vu, une forme plus homogène. Si nous posons $\sigma - \tau = 2b$, les constantes du problème a_1, a_2, a_3, m_3 se transforment en a, b, c, k. Ainsi on a

$$\frac{a_1}{c} = \frac{\operatorname{sn} ia \operatorname{dn} ia \operatorname{cn} ib}{\operatorname{sn} ib \operatorname{dn} ib \operatorname{cn} ia}, \quad \frac{a_2}{c} = \frac{\operatorname{sn} ia \operatorname{cn} ib \operatorname{dn} ib}{\operatorname{sn} ib \operatorname{cn} ia \operatorname{dn} ia}, \quad \frac{a_3}{c} = \frac{\operatorname{sn} ib \operatorname{cn} ib \operatorname{dn} ia}{\operatorname{sn} ia \operatorname{cn} ia \operatorname{dn} ib},$$

$$\frac{x_1^2}{a_1} = \frac{\operatorname{cn}^2 u}{\operatorname{cn}^2 ib}, \quad \frac{x_2^2}{a_2} = \frac{\operatorname{dn}^2 ib}{\operatorname{cn}^2 ib} \operatorname{sn}^2 u, \quad \frac{x_3^2}{a_3} = -\frac{\operatorname{sn}^2 ib}{\operatorname{cn}^2 ib} \operatorname{dn}^2 u;$$

en changeant $x_r^2 : a_r$ en $m_3^2 x_r^2 : a_r^2$, on change b en a.

» J'ajouterai aux résultats de mon Mémoire le cosinus de direction des axes de la section invariable par rapport à l'axe instantané et aux axes du corps; ils sont

$$\frac{m_1}{\sqrt{m_1^2 + m_2^2}} = \mp \frac{\mathrm{Y} \operatorname{dn}(u + ia) - \mathrm{X} \operatorname{dn}(u - ia)}{2i\sqrt{\mathrm{XY}} \operatorname{dn}(u + ia) \operatorname{dn}(u - ia)},$$

$$\frac{m_2}{\sqrt{m_1^2 + m_2^2}} = -\frac{\mathrm{Y} \operatorname{dn}(u + ia) + \mathrm{X} \operatorname{dn}(u - ia)}{2\sqrt{\mathrm{XY}} \operatorname{dn}(u + ia) \operatorname{dn}(u - ia)},$$

$$\frac{m_1 x_1}{a_1 - \lambda_1} = -\frac{\mathrm{Y} \operatorname{sn}(u + ia) + \mathrm{X} \operatorname{sn}(u - ia)}{2 \operatorname{cn} ia \sqrt{\mathrm{XYZ}}}, \quad \frac{m_2 x_1}{a_1 - \lambda_2} = \mp \frac{\mathrm{Y} \operatorname{sn}(u + ia) - \mathrm{X} \operatorname{sn}(u - ia)}{2i \operatorname{cn} ia \sqrt{\mathrm{XYZ}}},$$

$$\frac{m_1 x_2}{a_2 - \lambda_1} = -\frac{\mathrm{Y} \operatorname{cn}(u + ia) + \mathrm{X} \operatorname{cn}(u - ia)}{2 \operatorname{cn} ia \sqrt{\mathrm{XYZ}}}, \quad \frac{m_2 x_2}{a_2 - \lambda_2} = \mp \frac{\mathrm{Y} \operatorname{cn}(u + ia) - \mathrm{X} \operatorname{cn}(u - ia)}{2i \operatorname{cn} ia \sqrt{\mathrm{XYZ}}},$$

$$\frac{m_1 x_3}{a_3 - \lambda_1} = \mp \frac{\mathrm{Y} - \mathrm{X}}{2i \operatorname{cn} ia \sqrt{\mathrm{XYZ}}}, \quad \frac{m_2 x_3}{a_3 - \lambda_2} = -\frac{\mathrm{Y} + \mathrm{X}}{2 \operatorname{cn} ia \sqrt{\mathrm{XYZ}}},$$

où

$$\mathrm{X}^2 = 1 - k^2 \operatorname{sn}^2 ib \operatorname{sn}^2(u + ia), \quad \mathrm{Y}^2 = 1 - k^2 \operatorname{sn}^2 ib \operatorname{sn}^2(u - ia),$$

$$\mathrm{Z}(1 - k^2 \operatorname{sn}^2 ia \operatorname{sn}^2 u) = 1,$$

$$\frac{n}{\sqrt{c}} = \pm \frac{2 \operatorname{sn} i\sigma \operatorname{sn} i\tau}{\sqrt{\operatorname{sn}^2 i\tau - \operatorname{sn}^2 i\sigma}}.$$

Les doubles signes se rapportent aux cas de $m_3^2 \gtrless a_2$, avec la convention que, suivant que $a + b >$ ou $< \mathrm{K}'$, X, Y, ou bien X $\operatorname{sn}(u - ia)$, Y $\operatorname{sn}(u + ia)$ imaginaires conjugués, aient leur partie réelle positive. On tire ces expressions de (4). La substitution directe des valeurs x_1, x_2, x_3; m_1, m_2; λ_1, λ_2, donne des expressions assez simples, mais tout à fait différentes, et leur comparaison donne lieu à des formules remarquables. »

Les résultats dont on vient de voir l'indication succincte sont les premiers qui aient été ajoutés aux travaux de Jacobi dans la théorie de la rotation; mais je dois signaler encore, en raison de l'intérêt que j'y attache, un point non mentionné dans le résumé précédent. Remplaçons, dans le plan invariable, les axes fixes Ox, Oy par deux autres également rectangulaires, mais mobiles, Ox_1, Oy_1, dont le premier soit constamment parallèle à la direction du rayon vecteur de l'erpoloïde; M. Chelini a introduit, en suivant la méthode de Poinsot, les angles des axes d'inertie avec les droites Ox_1, Oy_1, Oz, et donné ce système de formules, où ι désigne le rayon vecteur de l'erpoloïde

$$\cos(x_1 x') = \frac{(\alpha-\delta)a''}{\iota}, \qquad \cos(y_1 x') = \frac{(\gamma-\beta)b''c''}{\iota}, \qquad \cos(z_1 x') = a'',$$

$$\cos(x_1 y') = \frac{(\beta-\delta)b''}{\iota}, \qquad \cos(y_1 y') = \frac{(\alpha-\gamma)c''a''}{\iota}, \qquad \cos(z_1 y') = b'',$$

$$\cos(x_1 z') = \frac{(\gamma-\delta)c''}{\iota}, \qquad \cos(y_1 z') = \frac{(\beta-\alpha)a''b''}{\iota}, \qquad \cos(z_1 z') = c''.$$

C'est le passage des neuf cosinus de M. Chelini à ceux de Jacobi, qu'il était important d'effectuer pour compléter la déduction analytique de la théorie de Poinsot, alors même que, par cette voie, on ne dût peut-être pas y arriver de la manière la plus rapide. Je renverrai, sur ce point essentiel, aux beaux Mémoires de M. Siacci, en me bornant à remarquer les relations suivantes, dans lesquelles $V_1 = v - iv'$,

$$\cos(x_1 x') + i\cos(y_1 x') = \frac{1}{\iota}AV_1,$$

$$\cos(x_1 y') + i\cos(y_1 y') = \frac{1}{\iota}BV_1,$$

$$\cos(x_1 z') + i\cos(y_1 z') = \frac{1}{\iota}CV_1,$$

et j'y ajouterai quelques formules relatives à l'erpoloïde.

XVII.

Si l'on met, au lieu de ξ, η, ζ, dans les équations du paragraphe X, page 290, les quantités suivantes :

$$\xi = p\rho, \qquad \eta = q\rho, \qquad \zeta = r\rho,$$

où p, q, r sont les composantes de la vitesse et ρ une indéterminée, on aura, pour déterminer la position de l'axe instantané de rotation par rapport aux axes fixes, les formules

$$\begin{aligned} x &= (a\,p + b\,q + c\,r)\rho = v\,\rho, \\ y &= (a'p + b'q + c'r)\rho = v'\rho, \\ z &= (a''p + b''q + c''r)\rho = v''\rho, \end{aligned}$$

dont la dernière est simplement $z = \delta\rho$. Or, l'erpoloïde étant la trace de cet axe mobile sur le plan tangent à l'ellipsoïde central, $z = \delta$, on voit qu'il suffit de faire $\rho = 1$ pour obtenir les coordonnées de cette courbe, exprimées en fonction du temps, ou de la variable u. Nous avons ainsi $x = v$, $y = v'$; mais ce sont plutôt les quantités $x + iy$ et $x - iy$ qu'il convient de considérer, et je poserai en conséquence

$$x + iy = -in\frac{\mathrm{H}'(0)\,\Theta_1(u-\omega)\,e^{i(\lambda u+\nu)}}{\mathrm{H}_1(\omega)\,\Theta(u)} = \Phi\,(u),$$

$$x - iy = +in\frac{\mathrm{H}'(0)\,\Theta_1(u+\omega)\,e^{-i(\lambda u+\nu)}}{\mathrm{H}_1(\omega)\,\Theta(u)} = \Phi_1(u),$$

ce qui permettra d'employer les conditions caractéristiques

$$\Phi\,(u+2\mathrm{K}) = \mu\,\Phi\,(u), \qquad \Phi\,(u+2i\mathrm{K}') = -\,\mu'\,\Phi\,(u),$$

$$\Phi_1(u+2\mathrm{K}) = \frac{1}{\mu}\,\Phi_1(u), \qquad \Phi_1(u+2i\mathrm{K}') = -\,\frac{1}{\mu'}\,\Phi_1(u),$$

où j'ai fait

$$\mu = e^{2i\lambda\mathrm{K}}, \qquad \mu' = e^{\frac{i\pi\omega}{\mathrm{K}} - 2\lambda\mathrm{K}'}.$$

Elles montrent, en effet, que les produits $\Phi(u)\Phi_1(u)$, $\mathrm{D}_u\Phi(u)\mathrm{D}_u\Phi_1(u)$, et en général $\mathrm{D}_u^m\Phi(u)\mathrm{D}_u^n\Phi_1(u)$, quels que soient m et n, sont des fonctions doublement périodiques, ayant $2\mathrm{K}$ et $2i\mathrm{K}'$ pour périodes. En particulier, nous envisagerons l'expression

$$\mathrm{D}_u\,\Phi(u)\,\mathrm{D}_u\,\Phi_1(u) = x'^2 + y'^2,$$

puis les coefficients de i dans les suivantes

$$\begin{aligned} \mathrm{D}_u\,\Phi(u) \qquad \Phi_1(u) &= xx' + yy' + i(xy' - yx'), \\ \mathrm{D}_u^2\,\Phi(u)\,\mathrm{D}_u\,\Phi_1(u) &= x'x'' + y'y'' + i(x'y'' - y'x''), \end{aligned}$$

ces fonctions doublement périodiques donnant, par les formules connues, les éléments de l'arc, du secteur et le rayon de courbure. J'emploierai, pour les obtenir, la formule de décomposition en éléments simples, rappelée au commencement de ce travail (§ I, p. 270), et dont l'application sera facile, $\Phi(u)$ et $\Phi_1(u)$ ayant pour pôle unique $u = iK'$. N'ayant ainsi à considérer qu'un seul élément simple, $\frac{\Theta'(u)}{\Theta(u)}$, il suffit d'avoir les développements suivant les puissances croissantes de ε de $\Phi(iK'+\varepsilon)$ et $\Phi_1(iK'+\varepsilon)$; ils s'obtiennent comme on va voir.

Je remarque d'abord que, au moyen de la fonction $\varphi_1(x, \omega)$, définie au paragraphe VI, page 280, on peut écrire

$$\Phi(u) = C\,\varphi_1(u, -\omega)\,e^{\frac{i\delta u}{n}}, \qquad \Phi_1(u) = C_1\,\varphi_1(x, \omega)\,e^{-\frac{i\delta u}{n}},$$

C et C_1, désignant des constantes. C'est ce qu'on voit en joignant aux relations précédemment employées,

$$i\lambda = \frac{i\alpha}{n} + \frac{\Theta'(\omega)}{\Theta(\omega)} = \frac{i\beta}{n} + \frac{\Theta_1'(\omega)}{\Theta_1(\omega)} = \frac{i\gamma}{n} + \frac{H'(\omega)}{H(\omega)},$$

la suivante

$$i\lambda = \frac{i\delta}{n} + \frac{H_1'(\omega)}{H_1(\omega)},$$

qui résulte de la condition $\alpha - \delta = in\frac{\operatorname{sn}\omega\operatorname{dn}\omega}{\operatorname{cn}\omega}$ (§ XV, p. 303), en la mettant sous la forme

$$\frac{i\alpha}{n} - \frac{i\delta}{n} = D_\omega \log \operatorname{cn}\omega = \frac{H_1'(\omega)}{H_1(\omega)} - \frac{\Theta'(\omega)}{\Theta(\omega)}.$$

Cela posé, l'équation $i\varphi_1(u, \omega) = \chi(u, \omega + K + iK')$ montre qu'on a le développement de $\varphi_1(iK'+\varepsilon, \omega)$ en changeant simplement ω en $\omega + K + iK'$ dans la formule de la page 279 :

$$\chi(iK'+\varepsilon, \omega) = \frac{1}{\varepsilon} - \frac{1}{2}\Omega\varepsilon - \frac{1}{3}\Omega_1\varepsilon^2 - \frac{1}{8}\Omega_2\varepsilon^3 + \ldots,$$

et il vient ainsi, en nous bornant aux seuls termes nécessaires,

$$i\varphi_1(iK'+\varepsilon, \omega) = \frac{1}{\varepsilon} - \left(\frac{k'^2}{\operatorname{cn}^2\omega} + \frac{2k^2-1}{3}\right)\frac{\varepsilon}{2} - \frac{k'^2\operatorname{sn}\omega\operatorname{dn}\omega}{\operatorname{cn}^3\omega}\frac{\varepsilon^2}{3} - \ldots.$$

Désignons par S_1, pour abréger, la série du second membre, et par S ce qu'elle devient lorsqu'on change i en $-i$, c'est-à-dire ω en $-\omega$, puisqu'on a $\omega = i\upsilon$; on aura les expressions

$$\Phi(iK'+\varepsilon) = RS\,e^{\frac{i\delta\varepsilon}{n}}, \qquad \Phi_1(iK'+\varepsilon) = R_1 S_1\,e^{-\frac{i\delta\varepsilon}{n}},$$

où R et R_1 sont deux nouvelles constantes, dont la signification se montre d'elle-même. Il est clair, en effet, que ces quantités sont les résidus des fonctions $\Phi(u)$ et $\Phi_1(u)$ pour $u = iK'$, de sorte qu'on trouve immédiatement les valeurs

$$R = -n e^{\frac{i\pi\omega}{2K} - \lambda K' + i\nu}, \qquad R_1 = +n e^{-\frac{i\pi\omega}{2K} + \lambda K' - i\nu},$$

et par suite la relation $RR_1 = -n^2$. Voici maintenant les applications de nos formules.

XVIII.

Je pars des équations suivantes

$$D_\varepsilon \Phi(iK' + \varepsilon) D_\varepsilon \Phi_1(iK' + \varepsilon) = -n^2\left(S' + \frac{i\delta}{n} S\right)\left(S'_1 - \frac{i\delta}{n} S_1\right),$$

$$D_\varepsilon \Phi(iK' + \varepsilon) \quad \Phi_1(iK' + \varepsilon) = -n^2\left(S' + \frac{i\delta}{n} S\right) S_1,$$

$$D_\varepsilon^2 \Phi(iK' + \varepsilon) D_\varepsilon \Phi_1(iK' + \varepsilon) = -n^2\left(S'' + \frac{2i\delta}{n} S' - \frac{\delta^2}{n^2} S\right)\left(S'_1 - \frac{i\delta}{n} S_1\right),$$

et je me borne à la partie principale des développements en faisant, dans les deux dernières, abstraction des termes réels; le calcul donne pour résultats

$$-\frac{P}{\varepsilon^2} - \frac{n^2}{\varepsilon^4}, \quad -\frac{n\delta}{\varepsilon^2}, \quad -\frac{Q}{n\varepsilon^2},$$

si l'on écrit, pour abréger,

$$P = \frac{n^2 k'^2}{\operatorname{cn}^2 \omega} + \frac{n^2(2k^2 - 1)}{3} + \delta^2,$$

$$Q = -\frac{2n^3 k'^2 \operatorname{sn}\omega \operatorname{dn}\omega}{i \operatorname{cn}^3 \omega} + \frac{3\delta n^2 k'^2}{\operatorname{cn}^2 \omega} + \delta n^2(2k^2 - 1) + \delta^3 \text{ (1)}.$$

---

(1) M. Magnus de Sparre a signalé (*C. R.*, t. XCIX, 1889, p. 906) l'oubli du signe — devant le premier terme de la quantité Q. Il en a conclu que l'équation déterminant les points stationnaires pouvait s'écrire

$$\operatorname{sn}^2 u = \beta \frac{\delta - \alpha}{\beta - \alpha} \frac{\beta\gamma + \alpha\beta + \alpha\gamma}{\delta(\beta\gamma + \gamma\alpha + \alpha\beta) - 2\alpha\beta\gamma}$$

et a retrouvé le théorème démontré antérieurement par Hess dans sa thèse (Munich, 1880) que l'erpoloïde n'a pas de points stationnaires réels (Cf. Hess, *Ueber die Herpolodie, Math. Ann.*, t. XXVII, 1886, p. 465). E. P.

Remplaçant donc $\frac{1}{\varepsilon^2}$ et $\frac{1}{\varepsilon^4}$ par $-D_\varepsilon\frac{1}{\varepsilon}$, $-\frac{1}{6}D_\varepsilon^3\frac{1}{\varepsilon}$, on obtiendra, en désignant par C, C′, C″ des constantes,

$$x'^2+y'^2 = C + PD_u\frac{\Theta'(u)}{\Theta(u)}+\frac{1}{6}n^2 D_u^3\frac{\Theta'(u)}{\Theta(u)},$$
$$xy'-yx' = C'+n\delta D_u\frac{\Theta'(u)}{\Theta(u)},$$
$$x'y''-y'x'' = C''+\frac{Q}{n}D_u\frac{\Theta'(u)}{\Theta(u)}.$$

Employons enfin la relation $D_u\frac{\Theta'(u)}{\Theta(u)}=\frac{J}{K}-k^2\operatorname{sn}^2 u$, et nous parviendrons, en modifiant convenablement les constantes, aux expressions suivantes,

$$x'^2+y'^2 = C+\left(n^2-\delta^2-\frac{n^2k'^2}{\operatorname{cn}^2\omega}\right)k^2\operatorname{sn}^2 u-n^2k^4\operatorname{sn}^4 u,$$
$$xy'-yx' = C'-\delta nk^2\operatorname{sn}^2 u,$$
$$xy''-yx'' = C''-\frac{Q}{n}k^2\operatorname{sn}^2 u.$$

Pour déterminer C, C′, C″, je supposerai $u=0$; il suffira ainsi de connaître les valeurs des fonctions $\Phi(u)$, $\Phi_1(u)$ et de leurs premières dérivées quand on pose $u=0$; or on obtient, par un calcul facile dont je me borne à donner le résultat,

$$e^{-i\nu}\Phi(u) = -in\frac{\operatorname{dn}\omega}{\operatorname{cn}\omega}+\beta\frac{\operatorname{dn}\omega}{\operatorname{cn}\omega}u+i\frac{n^2k^2\operatorname{cn}^2\omega+\beta^2\operatorname{dn}^2\omega}{n\operatorname{cn}\omega\operatorname{dn}\omega}\frac{u^2}{2}+\ldots,$$
$$e^{+i\nu}\Phi_1(u) = +in\frac{\operatorname{dn}\omega}{\operatorname{cn}\omega}+\beta\frac{\operatorname{dn}\omega}{\operatorname{cn}\omega}u-i\frac{n^2k^2\operatorname{cn}^2\omega+\beta^2\operatorname{dn}^2\omega}{n\operatorname{cn}\omega\operatorname{dn}\omega}\frac{u^2}{2}+\ldots;$$

on en conclut

$$C=\beta^2\frac{\operatorname{dn}^2\omega}{\operatorname{cn}^2\omega},\qquad C'=n\beta\frac{\operatorname{dn}^2\omega}{\operatorname{cn}^2\omega},\qquad C''=\beta\frac{n^2k^2\operatorname{cn}^2\omega+\beta^2\operatorname{dn}^2\omega}{n\operatorname{cn}^2\omega}.$$

Soient donc S l'aire d'un secteur, s la longueur de l'arc et R le rayon de courbure de l'erpoloïde; nous aurons

$$D_u S = n\left(\beta\frac{\operatorname{dn}^2\omega}{\operatorname{cn}^2\omega}-\delta k^2\operatorname{sn}^2 u\right),$$
$$(D_u s)^2=\beta^2\frac{\operatorname{dn}^2\omega}{\operatorname{cn}^2\omega}+\left(n^2-\delta^2-\frac{n^2k'^2}{\operatorname{cn}^2\omega}\right)k^2\operatorname{sn}^2 u-n^2k^4\operatorname{sn}^4 u,$$
$$R=\frac{n\operatorname{cn}^2\omega\left[\beta^2\frac{\operatorname{dn}^2\omega}{\operatorname{cn}^2\omega}+\left(n^2-\delta^2-\frac{n^2k'^2}{\operatorname{cn}^2\omega^2}\right)k^2\operatorname{sn}^2 u-n^2k^4\operatorname{sn}^4 u\right]^{\frac{3}{2}}}{\beta(n^2k^2\operatorname{cn}^2\omega+\beta^2\operatorname{dn}^2\omega)-Qk^2\operatorname{cn}^2\omega\operatorname{sn}^2 u}.$$

Ces formules donnent lieu à quelques remarques.

J'observerai, en premier lieu, qu'on tire de la première, en comptant l'aire à partir de $t = t_0$ où $u = 0$,

$$S = n\beta \frac{\mathrm{dn}^2\omega}{\mathrm{cn}^2\omega} u - n\delta\left[\frac{J}{K}u - \frac{\Theta'(u)}{\Theta(u)}\right] = nu\left(\beta\frac{\mathrm{dn}^2\omega}{\mathrm{cn}^2\omega} - \delta\frac{J}{K}\right) + n\delta\frac{\Theta'(u)}{\Theta(u)};$$

il en résulte que, u devenant $u + 2K$, le secteur s'accroît de la quantité constante

$$2n\left(\beta\frac{\mathrm{dn}^2\omega}{\mathrm{cn}^2\omega}K - \delta J\right),$$

ou, sous une autre forme,

$$2\sqrt{\frac{\delta - \alpha}{\gamma - \beta}}[(\gamma - \delta)\beta K - (\gamma - \beta)\delta J].$$

Je démontrerai ensuite que le trinome en $\mathrm{sn}\, u$ qui se présente dans l'élément de l'arc, et dont les racines sont réelles et de signes contraires, a sa racine positive comprise entre 1 et $\frac{1}{k}$. En faisant, en effet, $\mathrm{sn}\, u = 1$, puis $\mathrm{sn}\, u = \frac{1}{k}$, nous trouvons pour résultats les quantités

$$\frac{\alpha^2(\gamma - \delta)(\delta - \beta)}{(\gamma - \beta)(\delta - \alpha)}, \quad \frac{\gamma^2(\beta - \delta)}{\gamma - \beta},$$

dont la première est positive et la seconde négative. On verra sans peine aussi qu'en introduisant $\mathrm{dn}\, u$ au lieu de $\mathrm{sn}\, u$, il prend la forme suivante, qui est assez simple,

$$\frac{\gamma^2(\beta - \delta)}{\gamma - \beta} - [\gamma(\alpha + \beta - 2\delta) - \alpha\beta]\,\mathrm{dn}^2 u - (\gamma - \beta)(\delta - \alpha)\,\mathrm{dn}^4 u.$$

Enfin, et en dernier lieu, je remarquerai que les constantes qui entrent dans le dénominateur du rayon de courbure peuvent s'écrire ainsi

$$Q = \delta(\beta\gamma + \gamma\alpha + \alpha\beta) + 2\alpha\beta\gamma;$$

$$\frac{\beta(n^2k^2\,\mathrm{cn}^2\omega + \beta^2\,\mathrm{dn}^2\omega)}{\mathrm{cn}^2\omega} = \frac{\beta(\gamma - \delta)(\beta\alpha + \beta\gamma - \alpha\gamma)}{\gamma - \beta}\ (^1).$$

---

(1) Nous supprimons ici quelques lignes relatives à la formule donnant les points stationnaires, inexacte comme il a été indiqué dans la note de la page 313.

E. P.

XIX.

Après l'erpoloïde, je considère encore la courbe sphérique décrite par un point déterminé du corps pendant la rotation, et dont les équations sont

$$x = a\,\xi + b\,\eta + c\,\zeta,$$
$$y = a'\,\xi + b'\,\eta + c'\,\zeta,$$
$$z = a''\xi + b''\eta + c''\zeta.$$

Je remarquerai tout d'abord que les éléments géométriques, qui conservent la même valeur quand on passe d'un système de coordonnées rectangulaires à un autre quelconque, seront des fonctions doublement périodiques du temps. Si l'on pose, en effet,

$$D_t^n\, x = a\,\xi_n + b\,\eta_n + c\,\zeta_n,$$
$$D_t^n\, y = a'\,\xi_n + b'\,\eta_n + c'\,\zeta_n,$$
$$D_t^n\, z = a''\xi_n + b''\eta_n + c''\zeta_n,$$

les équations de Poisson donnent facilement

$$\xi_{n+1} = D_t\,\xi_n + q\,\zeta_n - r\,\eta_n,$$
$$\eta_{n+1} = D_t\,\eta_n + r\,\xi_n - p\,\zeta_n,$$
$$\zeta_{n+1} = D_t\,\zeta_n + p\,\eta_n - q\,\xi_n,$$

et ces relations permettent d'exprimer de proche en proche, pour toute valeur de n, les quantités ξ_n, η_n, ζ_n par des fonctions rationnelles et entières de a'', b'', c''. On trouvera, en particulier,

$$\xi_1 = b''\beta\zeta - c''\gamma\eta, \qquad \eta_1 = c''\gamma\xi - a''\alpha\zeta, \qquad \zeta_1 = a''\alpha\eta - b''\beta\xi,$$

et, par conséquent, en désignant par s l'arc de la courbe, nous aurons la formule

$$(D_t s)^2 = \xi_1^2 + \eta_1^2 + \zeta_1^2.$$

On obtient ensuite, pour le rayon de courbure R et le rayon de torsion R_1, les expressions suivantes

$$R^2 = \frac{(\xi_1^2 + \eta_1^2 + \zeta_1^2)^3}{u^2 + v^2 + w^2}, \qquad R_1 = \frac{u^2 + v^2 + w^2}{\Delta},$$

où j'ai fait, pour abréger,

$$u = \eta_1\zeta_2 - \zeta_1\eta_2, \qquad v = \zeta_1\xi_2 - \zeta_2\xi_1, \qquad w = \xi_1\eta_2 - \xi_2\eta_1,$$

$$\Delta = \begin{vmatrix} \xi_1 & \xi_2 & \xi_3 \\ \eta_1 & \eta_2 & \eta_3 \\ \zeta_1 & \zeta_2 & \zeta_3 \end{vmatrix}.$$

C'est à l'élément de l'arc que je m'arrêterai un moment, afin de tirer quelques conséquences de la forme analytique remarquable que présente la quantité $\xi_1^2 + \eta_1^2 + \zeta_1^2$. Nous avons, en effet, la relation

$$\xi\xi_1 + \eta\eta_1 + \zeta\zeta_1 = 0,$$

qui donne facilement

$$(\xi^2 + \zeta^2)(D_t s)^2 = (\xi^2 + \eta^2 + \zeta^2)\eta_1^2 + (\zeta\xi_1 - \xi\zeta_1)^2,$$

et, par suite, cette décomposition en facteurs imaginaires conjugués, où j'écris, pour abréger, $\rho^2 = \xi^2 + \eta^2 + \zeta^2$,

$$(\xi^2 + \zeta^2)(D_t s)^2 = (\zeta\xi_1 - \xi\zeta_1 + i\rho\eta_1)(\zeta\xi_1 - \xi\zeta_1 - i\rho\eta_1).$$

Or les valeurs de a'', b'', c'', à savoir

$$a'' = -\sqrt{\frac{\gamma - \delta}{\gamma - \alpha}}\operatorname{cn} u, \qquad b'' = \sqrt{\frac{\gamma - \delta}{\gamma - \beta}}\operatorname{sn} u, \qquad c'' = \sqrt{\frac{\delta - \alpha}{\gamma - \alpha}}\operatorname{dn} u,$$

conduisent à l'expression suivante

$$\begin{aligned} \zeta\xi_1 - \xi\zeta_1 + i\rho\eta_1 = {} & \alpha\sqrt{\frac{\gamma - \delta}{\gamma - \alpha}}(\xi\eta + i\rho\zeta)\operatorname{cn} u \\ & + \beta\sqrt{\frac{\gamma - \delta}{\gamma - \beta}}(\xi^2 + \zeta^2)\operatorname{sn} u \\ & - \gamma\sqrt{\frac{\delta - \alpha}{\gamma - \alpha}}(\eta\zeta - i\rho\xi)\operatorname{dn} u, \end{aligned}$$

et nous allons facilement en déduire les valeurs particulières des coordonnées ξ, η, ζ, pour lesquelles l'arc de la courbe sphérique, au lieu de dépendre d'une transcendante compliquée, s'obtient sous forme finie explicite. Je me fonderai, à cet effet, sur cette remarque, que le produit de deux fonctions linéaires

$$\Pi(u) = (A\operatorname{cn} u + B\operatorname{sn} u + C\operatorname{dn} u)(A'\operatorname{cn} u + B'\operatorname{sn} u + C'\operatorname{dn} u)$$

devient le carré d'une fonction uniforme si l'on a

$$A^2 k'^2 + B^2 - C^2 k'^2 = 0, \qquad A'^2 k'^2 + B'^2 - C'^2 k'^2 = 0.$$

A cet effet, j'observe que les formules

$$\operatorname{sn} 2u = \frac{2 \operatorname{sn} u \operatorname{cn} u \operatorname{dn} u}{1 - k^2 \operatorname{sn}^4 u},$$

$$\operatorname{cn} 2u = \frac{1 - 2 \operatorname{sn}^2 u + k^2 \operatorname{sn}^4 u}{1 - k^2 \operatorname{sn}^4 u},$$

$$\operatorname{dn} 2u = \frac{1 - 2k^2 \operatorname{sn}^2 u + k^2 \operatorname{sn}^4 u}{1 - k^2 \operatorname{sn}^4 u}$$

permettent d'écrire

$$\begin{aligned} &A \operatorname{cn} 2u + B \operatorname{sn} 2u + C \operatorname{dn} 2u \\ &= \frac{A + C - 2(A + Ck^2) \operatorname{sn}^2 u + (A + C) k^2 \operatorname{sn}^4 u + 2B \operatorname{sn} u \operatorname{cn} u \operatorname{dn} u}{1 - k^2 \operatorname{sn}^4 u}. \end{aligned}$$

Cela étant, soit, en désignant par g et h deux constantes,

$$\begin{aligned} A + C - 2(A + Ck^2) \operatorname{sn}^2 u + (A + C) k^2 \operatorname{sn}^4 u& \\ + 2B \operatorname{sn} u \operatorname{cn} u \operatorname{dn} u &= (g \operatorname{sn} u + h \operatorname{cn} u \operatorname{dn} u)^2, \end{aligned}$$

on verra que les quatre équations résultant de l'identification se réduisent aux trois suivantes

$$A + C = h^2, \qquad 2(A + Ck^2) = h^2(1 + k^2) - g^2, \qquad B = gh;$$

or l'élimination de g et h conduit immédiatement à la condition

$$A^2 k'^2 + B^2 - C^2 k'^2 = 0.$$

Soit de même ensuite

$$A' \operatorname{cn} 2u + B' \operatorname{sn} 2u + C' \operatorname{dn} 2u = \frac{(g' \operatorname{sn} u + h' \operatorname{cn} u \operatorname{dn} u)^2}{1 - k^2 \operatorname{sn}^4 u},$$

sous la condition semblable

$$A'^2 k'^2 + B'^2 - C'^2 k'^2 = 0;$$

nous en conclurons, pour $\sqrt{\Pi(2u)}$, l'expression suivante

$$\sqrt{\Pi(2u)} = \frac{(g \operatorname{sn} u + h \operatorname{cn} u \operatorname{dn} u)(g' \operatorname{sn} u + h' \operatorname{cn} u \operatorname{dn} u)}{1 - k^2 \operatorname{sn}^4 u},$$

ou, en développant,

$$\sqrt{\Pi(2u)} = \frac{gg' \operatorname{sn}^2 u + hh'[1 - (1 + k^2) \operatorname{sn}^2 u + k^2 \operatorname{sn}^4 u] + (gh' + hg') \operatorname{sn} u \operatorname{cn} u \operatorname{dn} u}{1 - k^2 \operatorname{sn}^4 u};$$

on en déduit ensuite facilement, si l'on change u en $\frac{u}{2}$,

$$2\sqrt{\Pi(u)} = \frac{2}{k^2} gg'(\operatorname{dn} u - \operatorname{cn} u) + (gh' + hg') \operatorname{sn} u + hh'(\operatorname{dn} u + \operatorname{cn} u).$$

Voici maintenant l'application de la remarque que nous venons d'établir.

XX.

Revenant à l'expression précédemment donnée des facteurs de $(D_t s)^2$, je pose

$$A = \alpha\sqrt{\frac{\gamma-\delta}{\gamma-\alpha}}(\xi\eta + i\rho\zeta), \qquad B = \beta\sqrt{\frac{\gamma-\delta}{\gamma-\beta}}(\xi^2+\zeta^2), \qquad C = -\gamma\sqrt{\frac{\delta-\alpha}{\gamma-\alpha}}(\eta\zeta - i\rho\xi),$$

$$A' = \alpha\sqrt{\frac{\gamma-\delta}{\gamma-\alpha}}(\xi\eta - i\rho\zeta), \qquad B' = \beta\sqrt{\frac{\gamma-\delta}{\gamma-\beta}}(\xi^2+\zeta^2), \qquad C' = -\gamma\sqrt{\frac{\delta-\alpha}{\gamma-\alpha}}(\eta\zeta + i\rho\xi),$$

et j'observe que, au moyen de la valeur $k'^2 = \frac{(\alpha-\gamma)(\beta-\delta)}{(\beta-\gamma)(\alpha-\delta)}$, nos conditions se présentent sous la forme suivante

$$\frac{\alpha^2}{\alpha-\delta}(\xi\eta + i\rho\zeta)^2 + \frac{\beta^2}{\beta-\delta}(\xi^2+\zeta^2)^2 + \frac{\gamma^2}{\gamma-\delta}(\eta\zeta - i\rho\xi)^2 = 0,$$

$$\frac{\alpha^2}{\alpha-\delta}(\xi\eta - i\rho\zeta)^2 + \frac{\beta^2}{\beta-\delta}(\xi^2+\zeta^2)^2 + \frac{\gamma^2}{\gamma-\delta}(\eta\zeta + i\rho\xi)^2 = 0.$$

Elles donnent immédiatement $\xi\eta\zeta = 0$; et nous poserons en conséquence:

1° $\quad \xi = 0, \quad \left(\frac{\gamma^2}{\gamma-\delta} - \frac{\alpha^2}{\alpha-\delta}\right)\eta^2 + \left(\frac{\beta^2}{\beta-\delta} - \frac{\alpha^2}{\alpha-\delta}\right)\zeta^2 = 0,$

2° $\quad \eta = 0, \quad \left(\frac{\alpha^2}{\alpha-\delta} - \frac{\beta^2}{\beta-\delta}\right)\zeta^2 + \left(\frac{\gamma^2}{\gamma-\delta} - \frac{\beta^2}{\beta-\delta}\right)\xi^2 = 0,$

3° $\quad \zeta = 0, \quad \left(\frac{\beta^2}{\beta-\delta} - \frac{\gamma^2}{\gamma-\delta}\right)\xi^2 + \left(\frac{\alpha^2}{\alpha-\delta} - \frac{\gamma^2}{\gamma-\delta}\right)\eta^2 = 0.$

Soit, pour abréger,

$$\begin{aligned} \mathrm{a} &= (\alpha-\delta)(\gamma-\beta)(\gamma\delta+\beta\delta-\gamma\beta), \\ \mathrm{b} &= (\beta-\delta)(\alpha-\gamma)(\alpha\delta+\gamma\delta-\alpha\gamma), \\ \mathrm{c} &= (\gamma-\delta)(\beta-\alpha)(\beta\delta+\alpha\delta-\beta\alpha); \end{aligned}$$

au moyen de ces quantités, qu'on verra facilement vérifier les relations

$$a + b + c = 0, \qquad \frac{a\alpha^2}{\alpha - \delta} + \frac{b\beta^2}{\beta - \delta} + \frac{c\gamma^2}{\gamma - \delta} = 0,$$

nous obtenons les trois systèmes de valeurs

1° $\xi = 0, \quad \eta^2 = c, \quad \zeta^2 = b,$

2° $\eta = 0, \quad \zeta^2 = a, \quad \xi^2 = c,$

3° $\zeta = 0, \quad \xi^2 = b, \quad \eta^2 = a.$

Maintenant je vais démontrer que, de ces diverses solutions, la première est seule réelle et répond à la question proposée.

Pour cela, je rappelle que les constantes α, β, γ, δ satisfont aux conditions

$$\text{(I)} \qquad \alpha < \beta < \delta < \gamma,$$

ou à celles-ci

$$\text{(II)} \qquad \alpha > \beta > \delta > \gamma,$$

et j'observe qu'on aura, dans les deux cas,

$$(\alpha - \delta)(\gamma - \beta) < 0, \qquad (\beta - \delta)(\alpha - \gamma) > 0, \qquad (\gamma - \delta)(\beta - \alpha) > 0.$$

J'ajoute à ces résultats les suivants

$$\gamma\delta + \beta\delta - \gamma\beta > 0, \qquad \alpha\delta + \gamma\delta - \alpha\gamma > 0, \qquad \beta\delta + \alpha\delta - \beta\alpha > 0,$$

qui donneront, comme on voit,

$$a < 0, \qquad b > 0, \qquad c > 0.$$

On peut écrire, en effet,

$$\begin{aligned}
\gamma\delta + \beta\delta - \gamma\beta &= \beta\delta + (\delta - \beta)\gamma,\\
\alpha\delta + \gamma\delta - \gamma\alpha &= \alpha\delta + (\delta - \alpha)\gamma,\\
\beta\delta + \alpha\delta - \beta\alpha &= \alpha\delta + (\delta - \alpha)\beta,
\end{aligned}$$

et, dans le premier système de conditions, on voit ainsi que les premiers membres sont tous positifs. Nous ferons ensuite, en passant au second système,

$$\begin{aligned}
\gamma\delta + \beta\delta - \gamma\beta &= \gamma\delta + (\delta - \gamma)\beta,\\
\alpha\delta + \gamma\delta - \alpha\gamma &= \gamma\delta + (\delta - \gamma)\alpha;
\end{aligned}$$

mais ces transformations faciles ne suffisent plus, à l'égard de la troisième quantité $\beta\delta + \alpha\delta - \beta\alpha$, pour reconnaître qu'elle est toujours positive comme les autres. Il est nécessaire, en effet, d'introduire une condition nouvelle, $\frac{1}{\alpha} + \frac{1}{\beta} > \frac{1}{\gamma}$, ayant son origine dans la définition des quantités $\frac{1}{\alpha}$, $\frac{1}{\beta}$, $\frac{1}{\gamma}$, qui sont proportionnelles aux moments principaux d'inertie. Nous écrirons, dans ce cas,

$$\beta\delta + \alpha\delta - \alpha\beta = \alpha\beta\delta\left[\left(\frac{1}{\alpha} + \frac{1}{\beta} - \frac{1}{\gamma}\right) + \left(\frac{1}{\gamma} - \frac{1}{\delta}\right)\right],$$

et le dernier résultat qui nous restait à établir se trouve démontré. Les valeurs réelles ainsi obtenues pour les coordonnées ξ, η, ζ, à savoir $\xi = 0$, $\eta = \sqrt{b}$, $\zeta = \sqrt{c}$, donnent, en prenant les radicaux avec le double signe, quatre points qui décrivent des courbes rectifiables, ou plutôt deux droites remarquables: $\xi = 0, \eta = \pm\sqrt{\frac{c}{b}}\zeta$, dont tous les points décrivent pendant la rotation du corps de telles courbes. Pour former l'expression de l'arc s, observons que, d'après l'égalité $a + b + c = 0$, on peut écrire $i\rho = \sqrt{a}$, ce qui donne les valeurs suivantes :

$$A = \zeta\alpha\sqrt{\frac{\gamma - \delta}{\gamma - \alpha}\,a}, \qquad B = \zeta\beta\sqrt{\frac{\gamma - \delta}{\gamma - \beta}\,b}, \qquad C = \zeta\gamma\sqrt{\frac{\delta - \alpha}{\gamma - \alpha}\,c}.$$

On a ensuite

$$A' = -A, \qquad B' = B, \qquad C' = C,$$

et nous en concluons

$$\begin{aligned}&(A\operatorname{cn}u + B\operatorname{sn}u + C\operatorname{dn}u)(A'\operatorname{cn}u + B'\operatorname{sn}u + C'\operatorname{dn}u)\\ &\quad = (B\operatorname{sn}u + C\operatorname{dn}u)^2 - A^2\operatorname{cn}^2 u.\end{aligned}$$

La condition $A^2 k'^2 + B^2 - C^2 k'^2 = 0$ conduit enfin à cette nouvelle transformation

$$\begin{aligned}&(B\operatorname{sn}u + C\operatorname{dn}u)^2 - A^2\operatorname{cn}^2 u\\ &\quad = (B\operatorname{sn}u + C\operatorname{dn}u)^2 - \frac{C^2k'^2 - B^2}{k'^2}(\operatorname{dn}^2 u - k'^2\operatorname{sn}^2 u)\\ &\quad = \left(Ck'\operatorname{sn}u + \frac{B}{k'}\operatorname{dn}u\right)^2,\end{aligned}$$

et il vient, en définitive, après quelques réductions, pour l'expression de l'arc de la courbe sphérique,

$$s = \gamma\sqrt{\frac{\beta-\delta}{\beta-\gamma}(\beta\delta+\alpha\delta-\beta\alpha)(\delta-\alpha)(\gamma-\beta)}\int k\,\mathrm{sn}\,u\,du$$
$$+\beta\sqrt{\frac{\gamma-\delta}{\gamma-\alpha}(\alpha\delta+\gamma\delta-\alpha\gamma)(\delta-\alpha)(\gamma-\alpha)}\int \mathrm{dn}\,u\,du,$$

puis, en effectuant les intégrations,

$$s = \gamma\sqrt{\frac{\beta-\delta}{\beta-\gamma}(\beta\delta+\alpha\delta-\beta\alpha)(\delta-\alpha)(\gamma-\beta)}\log(\mathrm{dn}\,u-k\,\mathrm{cn}\,u)$$
$$+\beta\sqrt{\frac{\gamma-\delta}{\gamma-\alpha}(\alpha\delta+\gamma\delta-\alpha\gamma)(\delta-\alpha)(\gamma-\alpha)}\,\mathrm{am}\,u.$$

Il en résulte que, u devenant $u+4K$, l'arc s'accroît de la quantité constante

$$2\pi\beta\sqrt{\frac{\gamma-\delta}{\gamma-\alpha}(\alpha\delta+\gamma\delta-\alpha\gamma)(\delta-\alpha)(\gamma-\alpha)}.$$

XXI.

Je terminerai cette étude de la rotation en indiquant encore un point de vue sous lequel on peut traiter la question et où l'on évitera le défaut de symétrie des méthodes précédemment exposées, qui donnent d'abord les quantités A, B, C ; puis, par un calcul différent, la quantité V, en séparant ainsi des expressions composées de la même manière avec les quatre fonctions fondamentales de Jacobi. Des transformations algébriques faciles des équations de la rotation, lorsqu'on suppose en général le corps sollicité par des forces quelconques, permettent, en effet, d'associer les composantes de la vitesse aux neuf cosinus ; elles seront le point de départ du nouveau procédé que je vais donner pour le cas où il n'y a point de forces accélératrices. Avant de les exposer, je rappelle d'abord les équations d'Euler

$$\mathrm{a}\,D_t p = (\mathrm{b}-\mathrm{c})qr + P,$$
$$\mathrm{b}\,D_t q = (\mathrm{c}-\mathrm{a})rp + Q,$$
$$\mathrm{c}\,D_t r = (\mathrm{a}-\mathrm{b})pq + R,$$

où les moments d'inertie sont désignés par a, b, c et celles de

Poisson, dont j'ai déjà fait usage,

$$D_t a'' = b'' r - c'' q,$$
$$D_t b'' = c'' p - a'' r,$$
$$D_t c'' = a'' q - b'' p,$$

puis

$$D_t A = B r - C q,$$
$$D_t B = C p - A r,$$
$$D_t C = A q - B p.$$

Cela étant, soit, comme précédemment,

$$v = a\ p + b\ q + c\ r,$$
$$v' = a' p + b' q + c' r,$$
$$v'' = a'' p + b'' q + c'' r,$$
$$V = A\ p + B\ q + C\ r;$$

en écrivant, pour abréger,

$$\Delta = p D_t p + q D_t q + r D_t r - (a'' p + b'' q + c'' r)(a'' D_t p + b'' D_t q + c'' D_t r),$$

nous aurons, comme conséquence, les relations suivantes, que je vais démontrer :

I.

$$A\Delta = V(D_t p - a'' D_t v'') + i D_t V\, D_t a'',$$
$$B\Delta = V(D_t q - b'' D_t v'') + i D_t V\, D_t b'',$$
$$C\Delta = V(D_t r - c'' D_t v'') + i D_t V\, D_t c'',$$

II.

$$V a'' = A v'' + i D_t A,$$
$$V b'' = B v'' + i D_t B,$$
$$V c'' = C v'' + i D_t C;$$

III.

$$i C D_t b'' = B r + i c'' D_t B,$$
$$i A D_t c'' = C p + i a'' D_t C,$$
$$i B D_t a'' = A q + i b'' D_t A;$$

IV.

$$i B D_t c'' = C q + i b'' D_t C,$$
$$i C D_t a'' = A r + i c'' D_t A,$$
$$i A D_t b'' = B p + i a'' D_t B.$$

A cet effet, je remarque que, en écrivant Δ sous la forme

$$\Delta = \tfrac{1}{2} D_t(p^2 + q^2 + r^2) - v'' D_t v'',$$

la condition $p^2 + q^2 + r^2 = v^2 + v'^2 + v''^2$ donne immédiatement

$$\Delta = v D_t v + v' D_t v'.$$

Observons encore qu'on tire des équations

$$v = ap + bq + cr, \qquad v' = a'p + b'q + c'r,$$

en employant les égalités $ab' - ba' = c''$, $ca' - ac' = b''$, l'expression suivante :

$$a'v - av' = b''r - c''q = D_t a''.$$

On a d'ailleurs immédiatement

$$D_t p - a'' D_t v'' = a D_t v + a' D_t v',$$

et ces résultats transforment l'équation

$$A\Delta = V(D_t p - a'' D_t v'') + i D_t V D_t a''$$

dans la suivante

$$\begin{aligned}(a + ia')(v D_t v + v' D_t v') \\ = (v + iv')(a D_t v + a' D_t v') + i(D_t v + i D_t v')(a'v - av'),\end{aligned}$$

qui est une identité.

Passons à l'égalité $Va'' = Av'' + iD_t A$; il suffit d'y remplacer les quantités V, v'', $D_t A$ par les expressions en A, B, C, p, q, r, ce qui donne

$$(Ap + Bq + Cr)a'' = A(a''p + b''q + c''r) + i(Br - Cq),$$

et par conséquent encore une identité, en l'écrivant ainsi

$$q(Ba'' - Ab'' + iC) + r(Ca'' - Ac'' - iB) = 0.$$

Enfin les équations

$$iAD_t c'' = Cp + iD_t C a'', \qquad iAD_t b'' = Bp + iD_t B a''$$

des systèmes III et IV conduisent, par un calcul semblable, en se servant des expressions de $D_t c''$ et $D_t b''$, aux mêmes égalités

$$Ab'' - Ba'' = iC, \qquad Ac'' - Ca'' = -iB;$$

elles se trouvent donc encore vérifiées ; or toutes les autres équations, dans les quatre systèmes, se démontreraient de même, ou se déduisent de celles que nous venons d'établir par un simple changement de lettres.

XXII.

J'applique maintenant ces résultats au cas où il n'y a point de forces accélératrices, et je pose à cet effet $p = \alpha a''$, $q = \beta b''$,

$r = \gamma c''$, $v'' = \delta$, ce qui donne d'abord

$$\Delta = \alpha^2 a'' \mathrm{D}_t a'' + \beta^2 b'' \mathrm{D}_t b'' + \gamma^2 c'' \mathrm{D}_t c'' = (\alpha - \beta)(\beta - \gamma)(\gamma - \alpha) a'' b'' c''.$$

Ayant ensuite

$$\mathrm{D}_t p - a'' \mathrm{D}_t v'' = \alpha(\gamma - \beta) b'' c'',$$

on voit que, en supprimant le facteur $(\gamma - \beta)\, b''\, c''$, l'équation

$$\mathrm{A}\Delta = \mathrm{V}(\mathrm{D}_t p - a'' \mathrm{D}_t v'') + i\,\mathrm{D}_t \mathrm{V}\, \mathrm{D}_t a''$$

devient simplement

$$\mathrm{A} a''(\alpha - \beta)(\alpha - \gamma) = \mathrm{V}\alpha + i\,\mathrm{D}_t \mathrm{V}.$$

Dans les trois autres systèmes, les réductions sont encore plus faciles, et nous nous trouvons ainsi amenés aux relations suivantes :

I.

$$\mathrm{A} a''(\alpha - \beta)(\alpha - \gamma) = \mathrm{V}\alpha + i\,\mathrm{D}_t \mathrm{V},$$
$$\mathrm{B} b''(\beta - \gamma)(\beta - \alpha) = \mathrm{V}\beta + i\,\mathrm{D}_t \mathrm{V},$$
$$\mathrm{C} c''(\gamma - \alpha)(\gamma - \beta) = \mathrm{V}\gamma + i\,\mathrm{D}_t \mathrm{V};$$

II.

$$\mathrm{V} a'' = \mathrm{A}\delta + i\,\mathrm{D}_t \mathrm{A},$$
$$\mathrm{V} b'' = \mathrm{B}\delta + i\,\mathrm{D}_t \mathrm{B},$$
$$\mathrm{V} c'' = \mathrm{C}\delta + i\,\mathrm{D}_t \mathrm{C};$$

III.

$$i\mathrm{C} a''(\alpha - \gamma) = \mathrm{B}\gamma + i\,\mathrm{D}_t \mathrm{B},$$
$$i\mathrm{A} b''(\beta - \alpha) = \mathrm{C}\alpha + i\,\mathrm{D}_t \mathrm{C},$$
$$i\mathrm{B} c''(\gamma - \beta) = \mathrm{A}\beta + i\,\mathrm{D}_t \mathrm{A};$$

IV.

$$i\mathrm{B} a''(\beta - \alpha) = \mathrm{C}\beta + i\,\mathrm{D}_t \mathrm{C},$$
$$i\mathrm{C} b''(\gamma - \beta) = \mathrm{A}\gamma + i\,\mathrm{D}_t \mathrm{A},$$
$$i\mathrm{A} c''(\alpha - \gamma) = \mathrm{B}\alpha + i\,\mathrm{D}_t \mathrm{B}.$$

La question est maintenant d'obtenir quatre fonctions A, B, C, V, qui vérifient à la fois les douze équations. Nous ferons un premier pas vers notre but, par un changement d'inconnues, en posant

$$\mathrm{A} = \frac{i}{k \operatorname{cn} \omega} \mathfrak{a}, \qquad \mathrm{B} = \frac{\operatorname{dn} \omega}{k \operatorname{cn} \omega} \mathfrak{b}, \qquad \mathrm{C} = -\frac{\operatorname{sn} \omega}{\operatorname{cn} \omega} \mathfrak{c}, \qquad \mathrm{V} = -in\mathfrak{v};$$

nous prendrons aussi la quantité u pour variable indépendante à la place de t ; enfin, en employant les expressions de a'', b'', c'', on trouvera les transformées suivantes de nos équations :

I.

$$ik \operatorname{cn} u \mathfrak{a} = \frac{i\alpha}{n} \mathfrak{v} - \mathrm{D}_u \mathfrak{v},$$
$$k \operatorname{sn} u \mathfrak{b} = \frac{i\beta}{n} \mathfrak{v} - \mathrm{D}_u \mathfrak{v},$$
$$i \operatorname{dn} u \mathfrak{c} = \frac{i\gamma}{n} \mathfrak{v} - \mathrm{D}_u \mathfrak{v};$$

II.

$$ik \operatorname{cn} u \mathfrak{v} = \frac{i\delta}{n} \mathfrak{a} - \mathrm{D}_u \mathfrak{a},$$
$$k \operatorname{sn} u \mathfrak{v} = \frac{i\delta}{n} \mathfrak{b} - \mathrm{D}_u \mathfrak{b},$$
$$i \operatorname{dn} u \mathfrak{v} = \frac{i\delta}{n} \mathfrak{c} - \mathrm{D}_u \mathfrak{c};$$

III. IV.

$$ik \operatorname{cn} u\, \mathfrak{c} = \frac{i\gamma}{n}\mathfrak{b} - D_u \mathfrak{b}, \qquad ik \operatorname{cn} u\, \mathfrak{b} = \frac{i\beta}{n}\mathfrak{c} - D_u \mathfrak{c},$$

$$k \operatorname{sn} u\, \mathfrak{a} = \frac{i\alpha}{n}\mathfrak{c} - D_u \mathfrak{c}, \qquad k \operatorname{sn} u\, \mathfrak{c} = \frac{i\gamma}{n}\mathfrak{a} - D_u \mathfrak{a},$$

$$i \operatorname{dn} u\, \mathfrak{b} = \frac{i\beta}{n}\mathfrak{a} - D_u \mathfrak{a}, \qquad i \operatorname{dn} u\, \mathfrak{a} = \frac{i\alpha}{n}\mathfrak{b} - D_u \mathfrak{b}.$$

Je ne m'arrêterai point aux calculs faciles qui donnent ces résultats, et je remarque immédiatement qu'il convient de les disposer dans ce nouvel ordre, à savoir

$$ik \operatorname{cn} u\, \mathfrak{a} = \frac{i\alpha}{n}\mathfrak{d} - D_u \mathfrak{d}, \qquad k \operatorname{sn} u\, \mathfrak{a} = \frac{i\alpha}{n}\mathfrak{c} - D_u \mathfrak{c}, \qquad i \operatorname{dn} u\, \mathfrak{a} = \frac{i\alpha}{n}\mathfrak{b} - D_u \mathfrak{b},$$

$$ik \operatorname{cn} u\, \mathfrak{b} = \frac{i\beta}{n}\mathfrak{c} - D_u \mathfrak{c}, \qquad k \operatorname{sn} u\, \mathfrak{b} = \frac{i\beta}{n}\mathfrak{d} - D_u \mathfrak{d}, \qquad i \operatorname{dn} u\, \mathfrak{b} = \frac{i\beta}{n}\mathfrak{a} - D_u \mathfrak{a},$$

$$ik \operatorname{cn} u\, \mathfrak{c} = \frac{i\gamma}{n}\mathfrak{b} - D_u \mathfrak{b}, \qquad k \operatorname{sn} u\, \mathfrak{c} = \frac{i\gamma}{n}\mathfrak{a} - D_u \mathfrak{a}, \qquad i \operatorname{dn} u\, \mathfrak{c} = \frac{i\gamma}{n}\mathfrak{d} - D_u \mathfrak{d},$$

$$ik \operatorname{cn} u\, \mathfrak{d} = \frac{i\delta}{n}\mathfrak{a} - D_u \mathfrak{a}, \qquad k \operatorname{sn} u\, \mathfrak{d} = \frac{i\delta}{n}\mathfrak{b} - D_u \mathfrak{b}, \qquad i \operatorname{dn} u\, \mathfrak{d} = \frac{i\delta}{n}\mathfrak{c} - D_u \mathfrak{c}.$$

Par là se trouvent mises en évidence trois substitutions remarquables, qui correspondent aux multiplications des quatre fonctions par $\operatorname{cn} u$, $\operatorname{sn} u$, $\operatorname{dn} u$, à savoir

$$\begin{pmatrix} \mathfrak{a} & \mathfrak{b} & \mathfrak{c} & \mathfrak{d} \\ \mathfrak{d} & \mathfrak{c} & \mathfrak{b} & \mathfrak{a} \end{pmatrix}, \qquad \begin{pmatrix} \mathfrak{a} & \mathfrak{b} & \mathfrak{c} & \mathfrak{d} \\ \mathfrak{c} & \mathfrak{d} & \mathfrak{a} & \mathfrak{b} \end{pmatrix}, \qquad \begin{pmatrix} \mathfrak{a} & \mathfrak{b} & \mathfrak{c} & \mathfrak{d} \\ \mathfrak{b} & \mathfrak{a} & \mathfrak{d} & \mathfrak{c} \end{pmatrix};$$

elles ont la propriété caractéristique de laisser invariables les quantités du type $(\mathfrak{a} - \mathfrak{b})(\mathfrak{c} - \mathfrak{d})$, et, si on les applique deux fois, chacune d'elles donne la substitution identique. Représentons les quatre lettres $\mathfrak{a}$, $\mathfrak{b}$, $\mathfrak{c}$, $\mathfrak{d}$ par X_s pour les valeurs 0, 1, 2, 3 de l'indice, en convenant de prendre cet indice suivant le module 4; elles s'expriment comme il suit

$$\begin{pmatrix} X_s \\ X_{3-s} \end{pmatrix}, \qquad \begin{pmatrix} X_s \\ X_{2+s} \end{pmatrix}, \qquad \begin{pmatrix} X_s \\ X_{1-s} \end{pmatrix}.$$

Si l'on adopte un autre ordre, en supposant que Z_s donne $\mathfrak{c}$, $\mathfrak{a}$, $\mathfrak{b}$, $\mathfrak{d}$ pour $s = 0, 1, 2, 3$, on retrouvera encore, sauf un certain échange, les mêmes fonctions de l'indice, à savoir

$$\begin{pmatrix} Z_s \\ Z_{2+s} \end{pmatrix}, \qquad \begin{pmatrix} Z_s \\ Z_{1-s} \end{pmatrix}, \qquad \begin{pmatrix} Z_s \\ Z_{3-s} \end{pmatrix}.$$

C'est cette disposition qu'il convient de garder, et semblablement nous désignerons les constantes $\frac{i\gamma}{n}, \frac{i\alpha}{n}, \frac{i\beta}{n}, \frac{i\delta}{n}$ par ε_s pour $s = 0, 1, 2, 3$; cela étant, nous pouvons comprendre, dans ces trois seules équations, le système de nos douze relations :

$$\text{(I)} \quad \begin{cases} ik \operatorname{cn} u \, Z_s = \varepsilon_s Z_{2+s} - D_u Z_{2+s}, \\ k \operatorname{sn} u \, Z_s = \varepsilon_s Z_{1-s} - D_u Z_{1-s}, \\ i \operatorname{dn} u \, Z_s = \varepsilon_s Z_{3-s} - D_u Z_{3-s}. \end{cases}$$

Le résultat relatif aux quantités X_s ne diffère de celui-ci qu'en ce que $ik \operatorname{cn} u$, $k \operatorname{sn} u$, $i \operatorname{dn} u$ se trouvent remplacés respectivement par $i \operatorname{dn} u$, $ik \operatorname{cn} u$, $k \operatorname{sn} u$; en désignant $\frac{i\alpha}{n}, \frac{i\beta}{n}, \frac{i\gamma}{n}, \frac{i\delta}{n}$ par η_s pour $s = 0, 1, 2, 3$, nous aurons, en effet,

$$\text{(II)} \quad \begin{cases} ik \operatorname{cn} u \, X_s = \eta_s X_{3-s} - D_u X_{3-s}, \\ k \operatorname{sn} u \, X_s = \eta_s X_{2+s} - D_u X_{2+s}, \\ i \operatorname{dn} u \, X_s = \eta_s X_{1-s} - D_u X_{1-s}. \end{cases}$$

Avant d'aller plus loin, je crois devoir montrer comment ces deux systèmes d'équations se ramènent l'un à l'autre, par un changement très simple de la variable et des constantes.

Je me fonderai, à cet effet, sur les formules de la transformation du premier ordre

$$\operatorname{cn}\left(iku, \frac{ik'}{k}\right) = \frac{1}{\operatorname{dn} u}, \quad \operatorname{sn}\left(iku, \frac{ik'}{k}\right) = \frac{ik \operatorname{sn} u}{\operatorname{dn} u}, \quad \operatorname{dn}\left(iku, \frac{ik'}{k}\right) = \frac{\operatorname{cn} u}{\operatorname{dn} u},$$

en les écrivant de la manière suivante, où j'ai fait, pour abréger, $l = \frac{ik'}{k}$,

$$\begin{aligned} k' \operatorname{cn}(iku, l) &= -\operatorname{dn}(u - K + 2iK'), \\ l \operatorname{sn}(iku, l) &= +\operatorname{cn}(u - K + 2iK'), \\ \operatorname{dn}(iku, l) &= -\operatorname{sn}(u - K + 2iK'). \end{aligned}$$

Changeons, en effet, u en $u - K + 2iK'$, et désignons par Z'_s ce que devient ainsi Z_s ; les équations (I) donneront celles-ci

$$\begin{aligned} ikl \operatorname{sn}(iku, l) Z'_s &= \varepsilon_s Z'_{2+s} - D_u Z'_{2+s}, \\ -k' \operatorname{dn}(iku, l) Z'_s &= \varepsilon_s Z'_{1-s} - D_u Z'_{1-s}, \\ -ik' \operatorname{cn}(iku, l) Z'_s &= \varepsilon_s Z'_{3-s} - D_u Z'_{3-s}. \end{aligned}$$

Soit encore Z''_s le résultat de la substitution de $\frac{u}{ik}$ au lieu de u, on trouvera, si l'on remarque que $il = -\frac{k'}{k}$,

$$l\,\mathrm{sn}(u,\,l)Z''_s = \frac{\varepsilon_s}{ik}Z''_{2+s} - D_u Z''_{2+s},$$

$$i\,\mathrm{dn}(u,\,l)Z''_s = \frac{\varepsilon_s}{ik}Z''_{1-s} - D_u Z''_{1-s},$$

$$il\,\mathrm{cn}(u,\,l)Z''_s = \frac{\varepsilon_s}{ik}Z''_{3-s} - D_u Z''_{3-s};$$

nous sommes donc ainsi ramené aux équations (II), en y remplaçant les constantes η_s par $\frac{\varepsilon_s}{ik}$, ce qui entraîne le changement de k en l.

Je vais montrer maintenant comment la théorie des fonctions elliptiques donne la solution de ces nouvelles équations auxquelles nous a conduit le problème de la rotation.

XXIII.

Je représenterai dans ce qui va suivre les fonctions $\Theta(u)$, $H(u)$, $H_1(u)$, $\Theta_1(u)$ par $\theta_0(u)$, $\theta_1(u)$, $\theta_2(u)$, $\theta_3(u)$, en adoptant une notation employée pour la première fois par Jacobi dans ses leçons à l'Université de Kœnigsberg, dont plusieurs auteurs ont depuis fait usage. L'une quelconque des quatre fonctions fondamentales sera ainsi désignée par $\theta_s(u)$, et je ferai de plus la convention que l'indice sera pris suivant le module 4, afin de pouvoir lui supposer une valeur entière quelconque. Cela posé, soit R_s le résidu correspondant au pôle $u = iK'$ de la quantité $\frac{\theta_s(u+a)e^{\lambda u}}{\theta_0(u)}$, où a et λ sont des constantes quelconques, et posons

$$\Phi_s(u) = \frac{\theta_s(u+a)\,e^{\lambda u}}{R_s\,\theta_0(u)}.$$

Nous définissons ainsi un système de quatre fonctions comprenant comme cas particulier $\mathrm{sn}\,u$, $\mathrm{cn}\,u$, $\mathrm{dn}\,u$ lorsqu'on suppose $a = 0$, $\lambda = 0$, mais qui, en général, ne sont point doublement périodiques, et se reproduisent multipliées par des constantes, lorsqu'on change

u en $u + 2K$ et en $u + 2iK'$ (1). On a en effet, en posant $\mu = e^{2\lambda K}$, $\mu' = e^{-\frac{i\pi a}{K} + 2i\lambda K'}$, les relations suivantes :

$$\Phi_s(u + 2K) = \mu(-1)^{\frac{1}{2}s(s+1)}\Phi_s(u),$$
$$\Phi_s(u + 2iK) = \mu'(-1)^{\frac{1}{2}s(s-1)}\Phi_s(u),$$

et, en passant aux valeurs particulières de l'indice, les multiplicateurs seront indiqués comme il suit :

$\Phi_0(s)$,	$+\mu$,	$+\mu'$,
$\Phi_1(s)$,	$-\mu$,	$+\mu'$,
$\Phi_2(s)$,	$-\mu$,	$-\mu'$,
$\Phi_3(s)$,	$+\mu$,	$-\mu'$.

L'étude de leurs propriétés pourrait peut-être former un chapitre nouveau dans la théorie des fonctions elliptiques, mais en ce moment je dois me borner à en tirer la solution que j'ai en vue du problème de la rotation. Je partirai de ce que les rotations $\Phi_s(u)$, ayant un pôle $u = iK'$ à l'intérieur du rectangle des périodes et pour résidu correspondant l'unité, peuvent jouer le rôle d'éléments simples à l'égard des fonctions qui ont les mêmes multiplicateurs. Telles seront, par exemple, les quantités

$$\operatorname{cn} u\,\Phi_s(u),\quad \operatorname{sn} u\,\Phi_s(u),\quad \operatorname{dn} u\,\Phi_s(u);$$

si l'on remarque qu'en mettant $2 + s$, $1 - s$, $3 - s$, au lieu de s, le facteur $(-1)^{\frac{1}{2}s(s+1)}$ se produit multiplié par -1, -1, $+1$, tandis que $(-1)^{\frac{1}{2}s(s-1)}$ est multiplié successivement par -1, $+1$, -1, on reconnaît en effet qu'elles ont respectivement les multiplicateurs des fonctions

$$\Phi_{2+s}(u),\quad \Phi_{1-s}(u),\quad \Phi_{3-s}(u).$$

(1) Peut-être pourrait-on, afin d'abréger, convenir de désigner les quantités de cette nature sous le nom de *fonctions doublement périodiques de seconde espèce*, les fonctions périodiques de première espèce correspondant au cas où les multiplicateurs seraient égaux à l'unité. Enfin les quantités telles que $\Theta(u)$, $H(u)$, ..., les fonctions intermédiaires de MM. Briot et Bouquet, où les multiplicateurs sont des exponentielles, recevraient par analogie le nom de *fonctions périodiques de troisième espèce*.

Nous voyons aussi qu'elles n'admettent que le pôle $u = i\mathrm{K}'$, dans le rectangle des périodes, de sorte que la décomposition en éléments simples s'obtiendra immédiatement au moyen de la partie principale des trois développements

$$\begin{gathered}\operatorname{cn}(i\mathrm{K}'+\varepsilon)\,\Phi_s(i\mathrm{K}'+\varepsilon),\\ \operatorname{sn}(i\mathrm{K}'+\varepsilon)\,\Phi_s(i\mathrm{K}'+\varepsilon),\\ \operatorname{dn}(i\mathrm{K}'+\varepsilon)\,\Phi_s(i\mathrm{K}'+\varepsilon).\end{gathered}$$

Or on a, sans aucun terme constant dans les seconds membres,

$$ik\operatorname{cn}(i\mathrm{K}'+\varepsilon) = \frac{1}{\varepsilon},\qquad k\operatorname{sn}(i\mathrm{K}'+\varepsilon) = \frac{1}{\varepsilon},\qquad i\operatorname{dn}(i\mathrm{K}'+\varepsilon) = \frac{1}{\varepsilon},$$

et par conséquent il suffit de calculer les deux premiers termes du développement de l'autre facteur $\Phi_s(i\mathrm{K}'+\varepsilon)$, c'est-à-dire le terme en $\frac{1}{\varepsilon}$, et le terme constant. J'emploie à cet effet la relation, sur laquelle je reviendrai tout à l'heure,

$$\theta_s(u+i\mathrm{K}') = \sigma\,\theta_{1-s}(u)\,e^{-\frac{i\pi}{4\mathrm{K}}(2u+i\mathrm{K}')},$$

où σ est égal à i pour $s=0$, $s=1$, et à l'unité si l'on suppose $s=2$, $s=3$, de sorte qu'on peut faire $\sigma = -e^{-\frac{i\pi}{4}(s+1)(s+2)(2s+1)}$. On en conclut l'expression suivante

$$\Phi_s(i\mathrm{K}'+\varepsilon) = \mathrm{A}\,\frac{\theta_{1-s}(a+\varepsilon)\,e^{\lambda\varepsilon}}{\theta_1(\varepsilon)},$$

A désignant un facteur constant, et par suite ce développement, que je limite à ses deux premiers termes

$$\Phi_s(i\mathrm{K}'+\varepsilon) = \frac{\mathrm{A}\,\theta_{1-s}(a)}{\theta_1'(0)}\left[\frac{1}{\varepsilon}+\lambda+\mathrm{D}_a\log\theta_{1-s}(a)\right].$$

Mais A doit être tel que le coefficient de $\frac{1}{\varepsilon}$ soit l'unité ; nous avons donc simplement

$$\Phi_s(i\mathrm{K}'+\varepsilon) = \frac{1}{\varepsilon}+\lambda+\mathrm{D}_a\log\theta_{1-s}(a),$$

et l'on voit que les parties principales des développements des fonctions

$$\begin{gathered}ik\operatorname{cn}(i\mathrm{K}'+\varepsilon)\,\Phi_s(i\mathrm{K}'+\varepsilon),\\ k\operatorname{sn}(i\mathrm{K}'+\varepsilon)\,\Phi_s(i\mathrm{K}'+\varepsilon),\\ i\operatorname{dn}(i\mathrm{K}'+\varepsilon)\,\Phi_s(i\mathrm{K}'+\varepsilon)\end{gathered}$$

se réduisent à cette seule et même expression dans les trois cas, à savoir

$$\frac{1}{\varepsilon^2} + [\lambda + D_a \log \theta_{1-s}(a)] \frac{1}{\varepsilon}.$$

La formule générale de décomposition en éléments simples nous donne en conséquence les relations suivantes

$$\begin{aligned} ik \operatorname{cn} u\, \Phi_s(u) &= [\lambda + D_a \log \theta_{1-s}(a)]\, \Phi_{2+s}(u) - D_u \Phi_{2+s}(u), \\ k \operatorname{sn} u\, \Phi_s(u) &= [\lambda + D_a \log \theta_{1-s}(a)]\, \Phi_{1-s}(u) - D_u \Phi_{1-s}(u), \\ i \operatorname{dn} u\, \Phi_s(u) &= [\lambda + D_a \log \theta_{1-s}(a)]\, \Phi_{3-s}(u) - D_u \Phi_{3-s}(u); \end{aligned}$$

et l'on voit qu'on les identifiera aux équations (I), obtenues dans le paragraphe précédent, en disposant des indéterminées a et λ de manière à avoir

$$\varepsilon_s = \lambda + D_a \log \theta_{1-s}(a).$$

Reprenons, à cet effet, les égalités données, paragraphe XV, page 303,

$$\alpha - \beta = in \frac{k^2 \operatorname{sn} \omega \operatorname{cn} \omega}{\operatorname{dn} \omega}, \qquad \alpha - \delta = in \frac{\operatorname{sn} \omega \operatorname{dn} \omega}{\operatorname{cn} \omega}, \qquad \gamma - \alpha = in \frac{\operatorname{cn} \omega \operatorname{dn} \omega}{\operatorname{sn} \omega},$$

en les écrivant d'abord de cette manière (*voir* p. 304) :

$$\frac{i\alpha}{n} + \frac{\Theta'(\omega)}{\Theta(\omega)} = \frac{i\beta}{n} + \frac{\Theta_1'(\omega)}{\Theta_1(\omega)} = \frac{i\gamma}{n} + \frac{H'(\omega)}{H(\omega)} = \frac{i\delta}{n} + \frac{H_1'(\omega)}{H_1(\omega)}.$$

Rappelons ensuite que les constantes $\frac{i\gamma}{n}, \frac{i\alpha}{n}, \frac{i\beta}{n}, \frac{i\delta}{n}$ ont été désignées par ε_s pour $s = 0, 1, 2, 3$, et elles prendront, en introduisant les quantités $\theta_s(\omega)$, cette nouvelle forme

$$\begin{aligned} \varepsilon_1 + D_\omega \log \theta_0(\omega) &= \varepsilon_2 + D_\omega \log \theta_3(\omega) \\ &= \varepsilon_0 + D_\omega \log \theta_1(\omega) = \varepsilon_3 + D_\omega \log \theta_2(\omega). \end{aligned}$$

Il en résulte que l'expression

$$\varepsilon_s + D_\omega \log \theta_{1-s}(\omega)$$

reste la même pour toutes les valeurs de s; par conséquent, on satisfait immédiatement à la condition posée en faisant

$$a = -\omega \qquad \text{et} \qquad \lambda = \varepsilon_s + D_\omega \log \theta_{1-s}(\omega).$$

XXIV.

Les résultats que nous venons d'obtenir montrent encore par un nouvel exemple combien la question de la rotation se trouve intimement liée à la théorie des fonctions elliptiques. C'est même à l'étude d'un problème de Mécanique qu'est due la considération de ces nouveaux éléments analytiques $\Phi_s(u)$, très voisins des fonctions $\varphi(x,\omega)$, $\varphi_1(x,\omega)$, $\chi(x,\omega)$, $\chi_1(x,\omega)$, employées au commencement de ce travail pour intégrer l'équation de Lamé, mais qui en sont néanmoins distincts et offrent un ensemble de propriétés propres. Il est nécessaire, en effet, d'attribuer à la constante λ quatre valeurs particulières pour en déduire ces dernières fonctions, et de là résultent, pour les multiplicateurs de chacune d'elles, des déterminations essentiellement différentes, tandis que la propriété essentielle qui réunit en un seul système les fonctions $\Phi_s(u)$, c'est d'avoir, sauf le signe, les mêmes multiplicateurs. Je me bornerai à leur égard à considérer, pour en donner l'intégrale complète, les équations différentielles auxquelles elles satisfont, équations linéaires et du second ordre comme celle de Lamé; mais auparavant je dois d'abord montrer comment les formules de Jacobi résultent de l'expression à laquelle nous venons de parvenir, $Z_s = N\Phi_s(u)$, où N désigne une constante. J'emploie, à cet effet, la valeur de R_s, qu'on obtient facilement sous la forme

$$R_s = \frac{\sigma\,\theta_{1-s}(a)\,e^{-\frac{i\pi a}{2K}+i\lambda K'}}{i\,\theta_1'(0)}$$

et où l'on doit faire $a = -\omega$. En se rappelant la détermination du facteur σ, et écrivant pour un moment

$$\Omega = \sigma\,\frac{e^{\frac{i\pi\omega}{2K}+i\lambda K'}}{i\,\theta_1'(0)};$$

nous obtenons ainsi

$$R_0 = -i\Omega\,\theta_1(\omega),\qquad R_1 = i\Omega\,\theta_0(\omega),\qquad R_2 = \Omega\,\theta_3(\omega),\qquad R_3 = \Omega\,\theta_2(\omega).$$

Or on a

$$A = \frac{i}{k\,\mathrm{cn}\,\omega}Z_1,\qquad B = \frac{\mathrm{dn}\,\omega}{k\,\mathrm{cn}\,\omega}Z_2,\qquad C = -\frac{\mathrm{sn}\,\omega}{\mathrm{cn}\,\omega}Z_0,\qquad V = -in Z_3;$$

de là résultent, si l'on remplace N par Ω N et les quantités θ_s par Θ, H, ..., les valeurs suivantes

$$A = \frac{iN}{k \operatorname{cn}\omega} \frac{H(u-\omega)e^{\lambda u}}{i\Theta(\omega)\Theta(u)} = \frac{N}{\sqrt{kk'}} \frac{H(u-\omega)e^{\lambda u}}{H_1(\omega)\Theta(u)},$$

$$B = \frac{\operatorname{dn}\omega N}{k \operatorname{cn}\omega} \frac{H_1(u-\omega)e^{\lambda u}}{\Theta_1(\omega)\Theta(u)} = \frac{N}{\sqrt{k}} \frac{H_1(u-\omega)e^{\lambda u}}{H_1(\omega)\Theta(u)},$$

$$C = \frac{\operatorname{sn}\omega N}{\operatorname{cn}\omega} \frac{\Theta(u-\omega)e^{\lambda u}}{iH(\omega)\Theta(u)} = \frac{N}{\sqrt{k'}} \frac{\Theta(u-\omega)e^{\lambda u}}{iH_1(\omega)\Theta(u)},$$

$$V = -inN\frac{\Theta_1(u-\omega)e^{\lambda u}}{H_1(\omega)\Theta(u)}.$$

Je ne m'arrête pas à la détermination de la constante N qui s'obtient comme on l'a déjà vu au paragraphe XIV, page 300, elle a pour valeur $H'(0)e^{i\nu}$, et nous retrouvons bien, sauf le changement de λ en $i\lambda$, les résultats qu'il fallait obtenir.

Je reviens encore un moment sur la désignation par $\theta_s(u)$ des quatre fonctions fondamentales de Jacobi, afin de la rapprocher de la notation qui résulte de la définition même de ces fonctions, par la série

$$\theta_{\mu,\nu}(u) = e^{-\frac{\mu\nu i\pi}{2}} \sum (-1)^{m\nu} e^{\frac{i\pi}{K}\left[(2m+\mu)u+\frac{1}{4}(2m+\mu)^2 iK'\right]}.$$

Supposant μ et ν égaux à zéro ou à l'unité, on a donc en même temps

$$\begin{aligned}
\Theta(u) &= \theta_0(u) = \theta_{0,1}(u),\\
H(u) &= \theta_1(u) = \theta_{1,1}(u),\\
H_1(u) &= \theta_2(u) = \theta_{1,0}(u),\\
\Theta_1(u) &= \theta_3(u) = \theta_{0,0}(u);
\end{aligned}$$

et, en premier lieu, je remarquerai que le système des quatre équations fondamentales

$$\begin{aligned}
\Theta(u+iK') &= iH(u)e^{-\frac{i\pi}{4K}(2u+iK')},\\
H(u+iK') &= i\Theta(u)e^{-\frac{i\pi}{4K}(2u+iK')},\\
H_1(u+iK') &= \Theta_1(u)e^{-\frac{i\pi}{4K}(2u+iK')},\\
\Theta_1(u+iK') &= H_1(u)e^{-\frac{i\pi}{4K}(2u+iK')},
\end{aligned}$$

peut être remplacé par la relation unique dont j'ai déjà fait usage, à savoir

$$\theta_s(u+i\mathrm{K}') = \sigma\,\theta_{1-s}(u)\,e^{-\frac{i\pi}{4\mathrm{K}}(2u+i\mathrm{K}')}.$$

On doit y joindre les suivantes

$$\begin{aligned}\theta_s(u+\mathrm{K}) &= \sigma'\,\theta_{3-s}(u),\\ \theta_s(u+\mathrm{K}+i\mathrm{K}') &= \sigma''\,\theta_{2+s}(u)\,e^{-\frac{i\pi}{4\mathrm{K}}(2u+i\mathrm{K}')},\end{aligned}$$

les facteurs σ, σ', σ'' ayant pour valeurs

$$\sigma = -e^{-\frac{i\pi}{4}(s+1)(s+2)(2s+1)}, \qquad \sigma' = e^{\frac{i\pi}{2}s(s-1)}, \qquad \sigma'' = e^{-\frac{i\pi}{4}s(s-1)};$$

puis celles-ci

$$\begin{aligned}\theta_s(u+2\,\mathrm{K}) &= (-1)^{\frac{1}{2}s(s+1)}\,\theta_s(u),\\ \theta_s(u+2i\mathrm{K}') &= -(-1)^{\frac{1}{2}s(s-1)}\,\theta_s(u)\,e^{-\frac{i\pi}{\mathrm{K}}(u+i\mathrm{K}')}.\end{aligned}$$

Je remarquerai enfin qu'en passant du système de deux indices à un indice unique on est amené à exprimer, d'une manière générale, s au moyen de μ et ν. Si nous avons égard à la convention admise que s est pris suivant le module 4, on trouve aisément l'expression

$$s \equiv -1-\mu+\nu+2\mu\nu.$$

Cela étant, soit de même

$$s' \equiv -1-\mu'+\nu'+2\mu'\nu',$$

et désignons par S la quantité relative aux sommes $\mu+\mu'$ et $\nu+\nu'$. Les admirables travaux de M. Weierstrass ayant montré de quelle importance est, pour la théorie des fonctions abéliennes, l'addition des indices dans les fonctions θ à n variables, où entrent $2n$ quantités analogues à μ et ν, on est amené, dans le cas le plus simple des fonctions elliptiques, à chercher l'expression de S en s et s'. M. Lipschitz m'a communiqué la solution de cette question par la formule élégante

$$\mathrm{S} \equiv -1-s-s'-2ss' \qquad (\operatorname{mod} 4),$$

et voici comment l'éminent géomètre la démontre. Écrivons l'égalité précédemment donnée : $s \equiv -1-\mu+\nu+2\mu\nu$ sous cette forme

$$2s+1 \equiv (2\mu+1)(2\nu-1) \qquad (\operatorname{mod} 8),$$

et remarquons qu'on peut poser, μ et ν étant zéro ou l'unité,

$$2\mu+1 \equiv 3^\mu, \qquad 2\nu-1 \equiv -7^\nu \pmod 8.$$

On en conclura

$$2s+1 \equiv -3^\mu 7^\nu \pmod 8;$$

or les relations analogues

$$2s'+1 \equiv -3^{\mu'} 7^{\nu'}, \qquad 2S+1 \equiv -3^{\mu+\mu'} 7^{\nu+\nu'} \pmod 8$$

donneront immédiatement

$$2S+1 \equiv -(2s+1)(2s'+1) \pmod 8,$$

et l'on en conclut l'équation qu'il s'agissait d'obtenir.

XXV.

Nous avons vu que le système des quatre fonctions représentées, en faisant $s=0, 1, 2, 3$, par l'expression

$$\Phi_s(u) = \frac{\theta_s(u+a)\,e^{\lambda u}}{R_s\,\theta_0(u)},$$

où a et λ sont des constantes quelconques et R_s le résidu correspondant au pôle $u=i\text{K}'$ de $\frac{\theta_s(u+a)\,e^{\lambda u}}{\theta_0(u)}$, conduit aux équations différentielles suivantes (§ XXIII, p. 331),

$$\begin{aligned}
ik \operatorname{cn} u\, \Phi_s(u) &= [\lambda + \text{D}_a \log \theta_{1-s}(a)]\, \Phi_{2+s}(u) - \text{D}_u \Phi_{2+s}(u),\\
k \operatorname{sn} u\, \Phi_s(u) &= [\lambda + \text{D}_a \log \theta_{1-s}(a)]\, \Phi_{1-s}(u) - \text{D}_u \Phi_{1-s}(u),\\
i \operatorname{dn} u\, \Phi_s(u) &= [\lambda + \text{D}_a \log \theta_{1-s}(a)]\, \Phi_{3-s}(u) - \text{D}_u \Phi_{3-s}(u).
\end{aligned}$$

Ces relations me paraissent appeler l'attention, comme donnant d'elles-mêmes des équations linéaires du second ordre, dont la solution complète s'obtient, ainsi que celle de Lamé, dans le cas de $n=1$, par des fonctions doublement périodiques de seconde espèce, ayant la demi-période $i\text{K}'$ pour infini simple. Pour y parvenir facilement, il convient de représenter les quantités $ik\operatorname{cn} u$, $k\operatorname{sn} u$, $i\operatorname{dn} u$ par U_1, U_2, U_3, de manière à avoir sous forme entièrement symétrique

$$\text{D}_u \text{U}_1 = -\text{U}_2 \text{U}_3, \qquad \text{D}_u \text{U}_2 = -\text{U}_1 \text{U}_3, \qquad \text{D}_u \text{U}_3 = -\text{U}_1 \text{U}_2.$$

Cela étant, si nous changeons successivement s en $2+s$, $1-s$, $3-s$, on obtiendra, en écrivant, pour abréger, Φ_s au lieu de $\Phi_s(u)$ et ε_s pour $\lambda+D_a\log\theta_{1-s}(a)$, ces trois groupes de deux équations, à savoir

$$\left\{\begin{aligned} U_1\Phi_s &= \varepsilon_s\ \Phi_{2+s}-D_u\Phi_{2+s},\\ U_1\Phi_{2+s} &= \varepsilon_{2+s}\Phi_s\ -D_u\Phi_s,\end{aligned}\right.$$

$$\left\{\begin{aligned} U_2\Phi_s &= \varepsilon_s\ \Phi_{1-s}-D_u\Phi_{1-s},\\ U_2\Phi_{1-s} &= \varepsilon_{1-s}\Phi_s\ -D_u\Phi_s,\end{aligned}\right.$$

$$\left\{\begin{aligned} U_3\Phi_s &= \varepsilon_s\ \Phi_{3-s}-D_u\Phi_{3-s},\\ U_2\Phi_{3-s} &= \varepsilon_{3-s}\Phi_s\ -D_u\Phi_s.\end{aligned}\right.$$

L'élimination successive des quantités Φ_{2+s}, Φ_{1-s}, Φ_{3-s} donne ensuite

$$\text{(I)}\quad D_u^2\Phi_s-(\varepsilon_s+\varepsilon_{2+s}+D_u\log U_1)D_u\Phi_s+(\varepsilon_s\varepsilon_{2+s}+\varepsilon_{2+s}D_u\log U_1-U_1^2)\Phi_s=0,$$

$$\text{(II)}\quad D_u^2\Phi_s-(\varepsilon_s+\varepsilon_{1-s}+D_u\log U_2)D_u\Phi_s+(\varepsilon_s\varepsilon_{1-s}+\varepsilon_{1-s}D_u\log U_2-U_2^2)\Phi_s=0,$$

$$\text{(III)}\quad D_u^2\Phi_s-(\varepsilon_s+\varepsilon_{3-s}+D_u\log U_3)D_u\Phi_s+(\varepsilon_s\varepsilon_{3-s}+\varepsilon_{3-s}D_u\log U_3-U_3^2)\Phi_s=0.$$

Nous avons donc trois équations du second ordre dont une solution particulière est la fonction $\Phi_s(u)$; voici comment on parvient à les intégrer complètement.

Faisons successivement dans (I), (II) et (III)

$$\Phi_s=X_1\,e^{\frac{u}{2}(\varepsilon_s+\varepsilon_{2+s})},$$

$$\Phi_s=X_2\,e^{\frac{u}{2}(\varepsilon_s+\varepsilon_{1-s})},$$

$$\Phi_s=X_3\,e^{\frac{u}{2}(\varepsilon_s+\varepsilon_{3-s})};$$

on aura pour transformées

$$D_u^2X_1-D_u\log U_1\,D_uX_1-(\delta_1^2+\delta_1D_u\log U_1+U_1^2)X_1=0,$$
$$D_u^2X_2-D_u\log U_2\,D_uX_2-(\delta_2^2+\delta_2D_u\log U_2+U_2^2)X_2=0,$$
$$D_u^2X_3-D_u\log U_3\,D_uX_3-(\delta_3^2+\delta_3D_u\log U_3+U_3^2)X_3=0,$$

en posant, pour abréger l'écriture,

$$\delta_1=\tfrac{1}{2}(\varepsilon_s-\varepsilon_{2+s}),\qquad \delta_2=\tfrac{1}{2}(\varepsilon_s-\varepsilon_{1-s}),\qquad \delta_3=\tfrac{1}{2}(\varepsilon_s-\varepsilon_{3-s}).$$

Je remarque maintenant que ces équations ne changent pas si, en remplaçant dans la première, la deuxième et la troisième, s par $2+s$, $1-s$ et $3-s$, on écrit dans toutes en même temps $-u$

au lieu de u. Par conséquent, on peut, d'une solution, en tirer une autre : la première, par exemple, qui est vérifiée en prenant

$$X_1 = \Phi_s(u)\, e^{-\frac{u}{2}(\varepsilon_s+\varepsilon_{2+s})},$$

le sera encore si l'on fait

$$X_1 = \Phi_{2+s}(-u)\, e^{+\frac{u}{2}(\varepsilon_s+\varepsilon_{2+s})}.$$

En employant les formules

$$\varepsilon_s = \lambda + D_a \log\theta_{1-s}(a), \qquad \varepsilon_{2+s} = \lambda + D_a \log\theta_{3-s}(a),$$

et mettant pour abréger θ_s au lieu de $\theta_s(a)$, on en conclut pour l'intégrale générale

$$X_1 = \frac{C\,\theta_s(u+a)}{\theta_0(u)}\, e^{-\frac{u}{2} D_a \log\theta_{1-s}\theta_{3-s}} + \frac{C'\,\theta_{2+s}(u-a)}{\theta_0(u)}\, e^{\frac{u}{2} D_a \log\theta_{1-s}\theta_{3-s}}.$$

Les solutions des deux autres équations seront semblablement

$$X_2 = \frac{C\,\theta_s(u+a)}{\theta_0(u)}\, e^{-\frac{u}{2} D_a \log\theta_s\theta_{1-s}} + \frac{C'\,\theta_{1-s}(u-a)}{\theta_0(u)}\, e^{\frac{u}{2} D_a \log\theta_s\theta_{1-s}},$$

$$X_3 = \frac{C\,\theta_s(u+a)}{\theta_0(u)}\, e^{-\frac{u}{2} D_a \log\theta_s\theta_{2+s}} + \frac{C'\,\theta_{3-s}(u-a)}{\theta_0(u)}\, e^{\frac{u}{2} D_a \log\theta_s\theta_{2+s}}.$$

XXVI.

Les relations qui nous ont servi de point de départ donnent lieu à d'autres combinaisons dont se tirent de nouvelles équations du second ordre analogues aux précédentes, et qu'il est important de former. On a, par exemple, comme on le voit facilement,

$$U_1(\varepsilon_s\Phi_{1-s} - D_u\Phi_{1-s}) = U_2(\varepsilon_s\Phi_{2+s} - D_u\Phi_{2+s}),$$

et l'on en conclut, en changeant s en $1-s$,

$$U_1(\varepsilon_{1-s}\Phi_s - D_u\Phi_s) = U_2(\varepsilon_{1-s}\Phi_{3-s} - D_u\Phi_{3-s}).$$

Joignons à cette équation la suivante

$$U_3\Phi_{3-s} = \varepsilon_{3-s}\Phi_s - D_u\Phi_s,$$

et l'on trouvera, par l'élimination de Φ_{3-s},

$$D_u^2\Phi_s-(\varepsilon_{1-s}+\varepsilon_{3-s}+D_u\log U_2U_3)D_u\Phi_s+(\varepsilon_{1-s}\varepsilon_{3-s}+\varepsilon_{1-s}D_u\log U_2+\varepsilon_{3-s}D_u\log U_3)\Phi_s=0.$$

De simples changements de lettres donneront ensuite

$$D_u^2\Phi_s-(\varepsilon_{3-s}+\varepsilon_{2+s}+D_u\log U_3U_1)D_u\Phi_s+(\varepsilon_{3-s}\varepsilon_{2+s}+\varepsilon_{3-s}D_u\log U_3+\varepsilon_{2+s}D_u\log U_1)\Phi_s=0,$$
$$D_u^2\Phi_s-(\varepsilon_{1-s}+\varepsilon_{2+s}+D_u\log U_1U_2)D_u\Phi_s+(\varepsilon_{1-s}\varepsilon_{2+s}+\varepsilon_{2+s}D_u\log U_2+\varepsilon_{1-s}D_u\log U_1)\Phi_s=0.$$

Cela posé, je fais dans la première, la deuxième et la troisième de ces équations, les substitutions

$$\Phi_s=Y_1\,e^{\frac{u}{2}(\varepsilon_{1-s}+\varepsilon_{3-s})},$$
$$\Phi_s=Y_2\,e^{\frac{u}{2}(\varepsilon_{3-s}+\varepsilon_{2+s})},$$
$$\Phi_s=Y_3\,e^{\frac{u}{2}(\varepsilon_{1-s}+\varepsilon_{2+s})}.$$

J'écris aussi, pour abréger,

$$\delta'_1=\tfrac{1}{2}(\varepsilon_{1-s}-\varepsilon_{3-s}),\qquad \delta'_2=\tfrac{1}{2}(\varepsilon_{3-s}-\varepsilon_{2+s}),\qquad \delta''=\tfrac{1}{2}(\varepsilon_{1-s}-\varepsilon_{2+s});$$

les transformées qui en résultent, savoir

$$D_u^2Y_1-D_u\log U_2U_3\,D_uY_1-\left(\delta_1'^2-\delta'_1\,D_u\log\frac{U_2}{U_3}\right)Y_1=0,$$
$$D_u^2Y_2-D_u\log U_3U_1\,D_uY_2-\left(\delta_2'^2-\delta'_2\,D_u\log\frac{U_3}{U_1}\right)Y_2=0,$$
$$D_u^2Y_3-D_u\log U_1U_2\,D_uY_3-\left(\delta_3'^2-\delta'_3\,D_u\log\frac{U_1}{U_2}\right)Y_3=0,$$

se reproduisent comme les équations en X, lorsqu'on change s en $2+s$, $1-s$, $3-s$ et u en $-u$, les quantités δ et δ', ainsi que les dérivées logarithmiques, changeant de signe. On en conclut immédiatement pour les intégrales complètes les formules

$$Y_1=\frac{C\,\theta_s(u+a)}{\theta_0(a)}\,e^{-\frac{u}{2}D_a\log\theta_s\theta_{2+s}}+\frac{C'\,\theta_{2+s}(u-a)}{\theta_0(u)}\,e^{\frac{u}{2}D_a\log\theta_s\theta_{2+s}},$$
$$Y_2=\frac{C\,\theta_s(u+a)}{\theta_0(a)}\,e^{-\frac{u}{2}D_a\log\theta_{2+s}\theta_{3-s}}+\frac{C'\,\theta_{1-s}(u-a)}{\theta_0(u)}\,e^{\frac{u}{2}D_a\log\theta_{2+s}\theta_{3-s}},$$
$$Y_3=\frac{C\,\theta_s(u+a)}{\theta_0(u)}\,e^{-\frac{u}{2}D_a\log\theta_s\theta_{3-s}}+\frac{C'\,\theta_{3-s}(u-a)}{\theta_0(u)}\,e^{\frac{u}{2}D_a\log\theta_s\theta_{3-s}}.$$

Ce sont donc les mêmes quotients des fonctions θ qui figurent dans les valeurs de X_1 et Y_1, X_2 et Y_2, X_3 et Y_3, les exponentielles qui multiplient ces quotients étant seules différentes. Cette circonstance fait présumer l'existence d'équations linéaires du second ordre plus générales, dont la solution s'obtiendrait en remplaçant, dans les expressions $CA + C'B$ des quantités X et Y, les fonctions déterminées A et B par Ae^{pu} et Be^{-pu}, où p est une constante quelconque ; voici comment on les obtient.

XXVII.

Considérons en général une équation linéaire du second ordre à laquelle nous donnerons la forme suivante

$$PX'' - P'X' + QX = 0,$$

où P et Q sont des fonctions quelconques de la variable u, et dont l'intégrale soit

$$X = CA + C'B.$$

Je dis que, si l'on connaît le produit de deux solutions particulières, et qu'on fasse en conséquence

$$AB = R,$$

nous pourrons obtenir l'équation qui aurait pour solution l'expression plus générale

$$\mathfrak{X} = CA\, e^{pu} + C'B\, e^{-pu}.$$

J'observe à cet effet que, le résultat de l'élimination des constantes C et C' étant

$$\begin{vmatrix} \mathfrak{X} & A & B \\ \mathfrak{X}' & Ap + A' & -Bp + B' \\ \mathfrak{X}'' & Ap^2 + 2A'p + A'' & Bp^2 - 2B'p + B'' \end{vmatrix} = 0,$$

le développement du déterminant donne pour l'équation cherchée

$$\mathfrak{P}\mathfrak{X}'' - \mathfrak{P}'\mathfrak{X}' + \mathfrak{Q}\mathfrak{X} = 0,$$

les nouvelles fonctions $\mathfrak{P}$ et $\mathfrak{Q}$ ayant pour expressions

$$\mathfrak{P} = AB' - BA' - 2ABp,$$
$$\mathfrak{Q} = A'B'' - B'A'' + (AB'' - 4A'B' + BA'')p - 3(AB' - BA')p^2 + 2ABp^3.$$

Or on a, quelles que soient les solutions particulières A et B, la relation

$$AB' - BA' = Pg,$$

en désignant par g une constante dont voici la détermination.

Donnons à la variable une valeur $u = u_0$ qui annule B dans cette équation et la suivante

$$AB' + BA' = R',$$

et soient P_0 et R'_0 les valeurs que prennent P et R'; on trouvera immédiatement la condition

$$P_0 g = R'_0.$$

La constante g étant ainsi connue, nous avons déjà la formule

$$\mathfrak{P} = Pg - 2Rp.$$

Pour obtenir $\mathfrak{Q}$, je remarque d'abord qu'on peut écrire

$$A'B'' - B'A'' = \frac{P'B' - QB}{P} A' - \frac{P'A' - QA}{P} B' = Qg,$$

puis semblablement

$$AB'' + BA'' = \frac{P'B' - QB}{P} A + \frac{P'A' - QA}{P} B = \frac{P'R' - 2QR}{P};$$

nous avons d'ailleurs

$$AB'' + 2A'B' + BA'' = R'',$$

par conséquent

$$AB'' - 4A'B' + BA'' = -\frac{2PR'' - 3P'R' + 6QR}{P},$$

et l'on en conclut la valeur cherchée

$$\mathfrak{Q} = Qg - \frac{2PR'' - 3P'R' + 6QR}{P} p - 3Pgp^2 + 2Rp^3.$$

Ce point établi, j'envisage, dans les équations différentielles en X_1, X_2, X_3, les expressions du produit AB, que je désignerai successivement par $R_1(u)$, $R_2(u)$, $R_3(u)$, en faisant

$$R_1(u) = \frac{\theta_1'^2(o)\,\theta_s(u+a)\,\theta_{2+s}(u-a)}{\theta_0^2(u)\,\theta_{1-s}(a)\,\theta_{3-s}(a)},$$

$$R_2(u) = \frac{\theta_1'^2(o)\,\theta_s(u+a)\,\theta_{1-s}(u-a)}{\theta_0^2(u)\,\theta_s(a)\,\theta_{1-s}(a)},$$

$$R_3(u) = \frac{\theta_1'^2(o)\,\theta_s(u+a)\,\theta_{3-s}(u-a)}{\theta_0^2(u)\,\theta_{1-s}(a)\,\theta_{2+s}(a)}.$$

Les formules élémentaires concernant les fonctions θ donneraient ces quantités pour chaque valeur de s, mais j'y parviendrai par une autre voie en conservant l'indice variable. Et d'abord, au moyen des relations

$$\theta_s(u+2\,\mathrm{K}) = (-1)^{\frac{s(s+1)}{2}}\,\theta_s(u),$$

$$\theta_s(u+2i\mathrm{K}') = (-1)^{\frac{(s+1)(s+2)}{2}}\,\theta_s(u)\,e^{-\frac{i\pi}{\mathrm{K}}(u+i\mathrm{K}')},$$

on obtient

$$\mathrm{R}_1(u+2\mathrm{K}) = -\,\mathrm{R}_1(u), \qquad \mathrm{R}_1(u+2i\mathrm{K}') = -\,\mathrm{R}_1(u),$$

$$\mathrm{R}_2(u+2\mathrm{K}) = -\,\mathrm{R}_2(u), \qquad \mathrm{R}_2(u+2i\mathrm{K}') = +\,\mathrm{R}_2(u),$$

$$\mathrm{R}_3(u+2\mathrm{K}) = +\,\mathrm{R}_3(u), \qquad \mathrm{R}_3(u+2i\mathrm{K}') = -\,\mathrm{R}_3(u).$$

Les fonctions $\mathrm{R}_1(u)$, $\mathrm{R}_2(u)$, $\mathrm{R}_3(u)$ possèdent ainsi la même périodicité que $\mathrm{cn}\,u$, $\mathrm{sn}\,u$, $\mathrm{dn}\,u$, par conséquent les quantités proportionnelles U_1, U_2, U_3, ayant le seul pôle $u = i\mathrm{K}'$ à l'intérieur du rectangle des périodes $2\mathrm{K}$, $2i\mathrm{K}'$, et pour résidu correspondant l'unité, peuvent servir, à leur égard, d'éléments simples. Employons maintenant l'équation

$$\theta_s(u+i\mathrm{K}') = \sigma\,\theta_{1-s}(u)\,e^{-\frac{i\pi}{4\mathrm{K}}(2u+i\mathrm{K}')},$$

où j'ai posé

$$\sigma = -\,e^{-\frac{i\pi}{4}(s+1)(s+2)(2s+1)},$$

et désignons par σ_1, σ_2, σ_3 ce que devient σ, et, changeant s en $2+s$, $1-s$, $3-s$, nous trouverons [1]

$$\mathrm{R}_1(i\mathrm{K}'+\varepsilon) = -\,\sigma\sigma_1\,\frac{\theta_1'^2(0)\,\theta_{1-s}(a+\varepsilon)\,\theta_{3-s}(-a+\varepsilon)}{\theta_1^2(\varepsilon)\,\theta_{1-s}(a)\,\theta_{3-s}(a)},$$

$$\mathrm{R}_2(i\mathrm{K}'+\varepsilon) = -\,\sigma\sigma_2\,\frac{\theta_1'^2(0)\,\theta_{1-s}(a+\varepsilon)\,\theta_{s}(-a+\varepsilon)}{\theta_1^2(\varepsilon)\,\theta_{1-s}(a)\,\theta_{s}(a)},$$

$$\mathrm{R}_3(i\mathrm{K}'+\varepsilon) = -\,\sigma\sigma_3\,\frac{\theta_1'^2(0)\,\theta_{1-s}(a+\varepsilon)\,\theta_{2+s}(-a+\varepsilon)}{\theta_1^2(\varepsilon)\,\theta_{1-s}(a)\,\theta_{2+s}(a)}.$$

Cela étant, comme on peut introduire à volonté un facteur constant dans la fonction R, je prends, au lieu des expressions précédentes,

---

(1) On démontre facilement qu'on a

$$\sigma\sigma_1 = +i, \qquad \sigma\sigma_2 = (-1)^{\frac{s(s-1)}{2}}, \qquad \sigma\sigma_3 = +i.$$

celles-ci, qui en diffèrent seulement par le signe ou le facteur $\pm i$, savoir

$$R_1(iK'+\varepsilon) = \frac{\theta_1'^2(0)\,\theta_{1-s}(a+\varepsilon)\,\theta_{3-s}(a-\varepsilon)}{\theta_1^2(\varepsilon)\,\theta_{1-s}(a)\,\theta_{3-s}(a)},$$

$$R_2(iK'+\varepsilon) = \frac{\theta_1'^2(0)\,\theta_{1-s}(a+\varepsilon)\,\theta_s(a-\varepsilon)}{\theta_1^2(\varepsilon)\,\theta_{1-s}(a)\,\theta_s(a)},$$

$$R_3(iK'+\varepsilon) = \frac{\theta_1'^2(0)\,\theta_{1-s}(a+\varepsilon)\,\theta_{2+s}(a-\varepsilon)}{\theta_1^2(\varepsilon)\,\theta_{1-s}(a)\,\theta_{2+s}(a)}.$$

Développant donc suivant les puissances de ε et faisant usage des quantités δ, précédemment introduites, qui donnent

$$\frac{\theta'_{1-s}(a)}{\theta_{1-s}(a)} - \frac{\theta'_{3-s}(a)}{\theta_{3-s}(a)} = 2\delta_1,$$

$$\frac{\theta'_{1-s}(a)}{\theta_{1-s}(a)} - \frac{\theta'_s(a)}{\theta_s(a)} = 2\delta_2,$$

$$\frac{\theta'_{1-s}(a)}{\theta_{1-s}(a)} - \frac{\theta'_{2+s}(a)}{\theta_{2+s}(a)} = 2\delta_3,$$

nous obtenons, pour les parties principales, les quantités

$$\frac{1}{\varepsilon^2} + \frac{2\delta_1}{\varepsilon}, \quad \frac{1}{\varepsilon^2} + \frac{2\delta_2}{\varepsilon}, \quad \frac{1}{\varepsilon^2} + \frac{2\delta_3}{\varepsilon},$$

et l'on en conclut les valeurs suivantes, qu'il s'agissait d'obtenir :

$$R_1(u) = 2\delta_1 U_1 - D_u U_1,$$

$$R_2(u) = 2\delta_2 U_2 - D_u U_2,$$

$$R_3(u) = 2\delta_3 U_3 - D_u U_3.$$

Ces résultats nous permettent de former les fonctions $\mathfrak{P}$ et $\mathfrak{Q}$; mais, pour la deuxième, le calcul est un peu long, et je me bornerai à en retenir cette conclusion, que dans les trois cas on parvient, en désignant par U une quantité qui soit successivement U_1, U_2, U_3, à des expressions de cette forme

$$\mathfrak{P} = \alpha U + \alpha' D_u U,$$

$$\mathfrak{Q} = \beta U + \beta' D_u U + \beta'' D_u^2 U,$$

où les coefficients α et β sont des constantes. Leur complication tient à ce qu'ils sont exprimés au moyen des quantités a et p qui figurent explicitement dans l'intégrale, et nous allons voir comment l'introduction d'autres éléments conduit à des valeurs beaucoup plus simples.

XXVIII.

Soient U et U_1 deux fonctions doublement périodiques de seconde espèce ayant chacune un pôle unique $u = 0$, et représentées par les formules

$$U = \frac{H(u+\alpha)e^{pu}}{H(u)}, \qquad U_1 = \frac{H(u+\beta)e^{qu}}{H(u)};$$

je me propose de former en général l'équation du second ordre, admettant pour intégrale l'expression

$$\mathfrak{X} = CU + C'U_1,$$

qui est

$$\begin{vmatrix} \mathfrak{X} & U & U_1 \\ \mathfrak{X}' & U' & U_1' \\ \mathfrak{X}'' & U'' & U_1'' \end{vmatrix} = \mathfrak{P}\mathfrak{X}'' - \mathfrak{P}'\mathfrak{X}' + \mathfrak{Q}\mathfrak{X} = 0,$$

en posant

$$\mathfrak{P} = UU_1' - U_1U', \qquad \mathfrak{Q} = U'U_1'' - U_1'U''.$$

Nommons pour un moment μ et μ' les multiples de A, ν et ν' ceux de B; on voit d'abord que les coefficients $\mathfrak{P}$ et $\mathfrak{Q}$ sont des fonctions de seconde espèce aux multiplicateurs $\mu\nu$ et $\mu'\nu'$, ayant de même pour seul pôle $u = 0$, qui est un infini double pour $\mathfrak{P}$ et un infini triple pour $\mathfrak{Q}$. L'équation $\mathfrak{P} = 0$ n'admet ainsi à l'intérieur du rectangle des périodes que deux racines, $u = a$ et $u = b$, et, en décomposant en éléments simples les fonctions de première espèce, $\frac{\mathfrak{P}'}{\mathfrak{P}}$ et $\frac{\mathfrak{Q}}{\mathfrak{P}}$, on aura les expressions suivantes,

$$\frac{\mathfrak{P}'}{\mathfrak{P}} = \frac{H'(u-a)}{H(u-a)} + \frac{H'(u-b)}{H(u-b)} - 2\frac{H'(u)}{H(u)} + \lambda,$$

$$\frac{\mathfrak{Q}}{\mathfrak{P}} = \frac{P\,H'(u-a)}{H(u-a)} + \frac{Q\,H'(u-b)}{H(u-b)} + \frac{R\,H'(u)}{H(u)} + S,$$

où P, Q, ... sont des constantes assujetties à la condition

$$P + Q + R = 0.$$

Les quantités a et b, que nous venons d'introduire, représentent donc, à l'égard de l'équation différentielle, des points que M. Weierstrass nomme *à apparence singulière*, $u = 0$ étant seul un point singulier. Ce sont les véritables éléments qu'il convient d'employer comme appropriés à la formation de l'équation différentielle, au lieu des constantes α, β, p, q qui entrent dans les fonctions A et B. Je me fonderai, à cet effet, sur le lemme suivant, qui donnera, par un calcul facile, la détermination des coefficients P, Q, ...

Considérons l'équation différentielle

$$y'' - f(u)y' + g(u)y = 0,$$

où les fonctions uniformes $f(u)$, $g(u)$ admettent seulement des infinis simples qui soient, d'une part, $u = 0$ et de l'autre $u = a$, b, c, ... Posons d'abord, en développant suivant les puissances croissantes de ε,

$$f(\varepsilon) = -\frac{2}{\varepsilon} + \mathrm{F} + \ldots, \qquad g(\varepsilon) = \frac{\mathrm{G}}{\varepsilon} + \ldots,$$

et en second lieu, pour les diverses quantités a, b, c, ...,

$$f(a+\varepsilon) = \frac{1}{\varepsilon} + f_a + \ldots, \qquad g(a+\varepsilon) = \frac{g_a}{\varepsilon} + g_a^1 + \ldots.$$

Si l'on a, d'autre part,

$$\mathrm{F} + \mathrm{G} = 0,$$

puis, pour toutes les quantités a, b, c, ...,

$$g_a^1 = g_a(f_a - g_a),$$

l'intégrale de l'équation proposée sera une fonction uniforme ayant pour seul point singulier $u = 0$, et, dans le domaine de ce point, les intégrales nommées *fondamentales* par M. Fuchs seront de la forme $\varphi_1(u)$ et $\frac{1}{u} + \varphi_2(u)$, où $\varphi_1(u)$ et $\varphi_2(u)$ représentent des séries qui procèdent suivant les puissances ascendantes entières et positives de la variable.

XXIX.

Ce sont ces belles et importantes découvertes de M. Fuchs dans la théorie générale des équations différentielles linéaires qui permettent ainsi d'obtenir les conditions nécessaires et suffisantes pour que l'intégrale complète de l'équation considérée soit une fonction uniforme de la variable. Il n'est pas inutile, à l'égard de ces conditions, de remarquer qu'elles se conservent, comme on le vérifie aisément, dans les transformées auxquelles conduit la substitution $y = ze^{-\alpha u}$, à savoir

$$z'' - [2\alpha + f(u)]z' + [\alpha^2 + \alpha f(u) + g(u)]z = 0.$$

J'observe encore qu'on peut supposer doublement périodiques les fonctions $f(u)$ et $g(u)$, en convenant que les quantités $u = 0$, $u = a$, $u = b$, ..., au lieu de représenter tous leurs pôles, désigneront seulement ceux de ces pôles qui sont à l'intérieur du rectangle des périodes. Soit donc, en nous plaçant dans ce cas,

$$f(u) = \frac{\mathfrak{P}'}{\mathfrak{P}},$$

$$g(u) = \frac{\mathfrak{Q}}{\mathfrak{P}},$$

ou bien, d'après la remarque qui vient d'être faite,

$$f(u) = 2\alpha + \frac{\mathfrak{P}'}{\mathfrak{P}},$$

$$g(u) = \alpha^2 + \alpha\frac{\mathfrak{P}'}{\mathfrak{P}} + \frac{\mathfrak{Q}}{\mathfrak{P}},$$

α étant une constante arbitraire. Je disposerai de cette constante de sorte qu'on ait

$$f(u) = \frac{H'(u-a)}{H(u-a)} + \frac{H'(u-b)}{H(u-b)} - 2\frac{H'(u)}{H(u)} + \frac{\Theta'(a)}{\Theta(a)} + \frac{\Theta'(b)}{\Theta(b)},$$

et par conséquent, d'après les formules connues,

$$f(u) = \frac{\operatorname{sn} a}{\operatorname{sn} u \operatorname{sn}(u-a)} + \frac{\operatorname{sn} b}{\operatorname{sn} u \operatorname{sn}(u-b)}.$$

Cela étant, il est clair qu'on peut écrire, avec trois indéterminées, A, B, C,

$$g(u) = \frac{A \operatorname{sn} a}{\operatorname{sn} u \operatorname{sn}(u-a)} + \frac{B \operatorname{sn} b}{\operatorname{sn} u \operatorname{sn}(u-b)} + C,$$

et nous tirerons sur-le-champ de ces expressions les valeurs suivantes :

$$F = -\frac{\operatorname{cn} a \operatorname{dn} a}{\operatorname{sn} a} - \frac{\operatorname{cn} b \operatorname{dn} b}{\operatorname{sn} b},$$

$$G = -A - B,$$

$$f_a = -\frac{\operatorname{cn} a \operatorname{dn} a}{\operatorname{sn} a} + \frac{\operatorname{sn} b}{\operatorname{sn} a \operatorname{sn}(a-b)},$$

$$g_a = A,$$

$$g_a^1 = -\frac{A \operatorname{cn} a \operatorname{dn} a}{\operatorname{sn} a} + \frac{B \operatorname{sn} b}{\operatorname{sn} a \operatorname{sn}(a-b)} + C.$$

Or la condition

$$g_a^1 = g_a(f_a - g_a)$$

conduit à

$$\frac{\operatorname{sn} b (A - B)}{\operatorname{sn} a \operatorname{sn}(a-b)} - A^2 - C = 0;$$

le second pôle $u = b$ donne semblablement

$$\frac{\operatorname{sn} a (B - A)}{\operatorname{sn} b \operatorname{sn}(b-a)} - B^2 - C = 0,$$

et l'on conclut enfin de l'équation $F + G = 0$

$$\frac{\operatorname{cn} a \operatorname{dn} a}{\operatorname{sn} a} + \frac{\operatorname{cn} b \operatorname{dn} b}{\operatorname{sn} b} + A + B = 0.$$

Je remarque immédiatement que cette dernière relation n'est point distincte des deux autres et qu'elle en résulte en les retranchant membre à membre et divisant par $A - B$. En l'employant avec la première, nous trouvons, par l'élimination de B,

$$A^2 - 2A \frac{\operatorname{sn} b}{\operatorname{sn} a \operatorname{sn}(a-b)} - \frac{\operatorname{sn}^2 a - \operatorname{sn}^2 b}{\operatorname{sn}^2 a \operatorname{sn}^2(a-b)} + C = 0,$$

ou encore

$$\left[A - \frac{\operatorname{sn} b}{\operatorname{sn} a \operatorname{sn}(a-b)}\right]^2 - \frac{1}{\operatorname{sn}^2(a-b)} + C = 0.$$

Remplaçant désormais C par $\frac{1}{\operatorname{sn}^2(a-b)} - C^2$, on voit qu'on aura

$$A = \frac{\operatorname{sn} b}{\operatorname{sn} a \operatorname{sn}(a-b)} + C,$$

et par conséquent

$$B = \frac{\operatorname{sn} a}{\operatorname{sn} b \operatorname{sn}(b-a)} - C.$$

Telles sont donc, exprimées au moyen de la nouvelle indéterminée C, les valeurs très simples des constantes A et B pour lesquelles, d'après les principes de M. Fuchs, l'intégrale complète de l'équation

$$y'' - \left[\frac{\operatorname{sn} a}{\operatorname{sn} u \operatorname{sn}(u-a)} + \frac{\operatorname{sn} b}{\operatorname{sn} u \operatorname{sn}(u-b)}\right] y'$$
$$+ \left[\frac{A \operatorname{sn} a}{\operatorname{sn} u \operatorname{sn}(u-a)} + \frac{B \operatorname{sn} b}{\operatorname{sn} u \operatorname{sn}(u-b)} + \frac{1}{\operatorname{sn}^2(a-b)} - C^2\right] y = 0$$

est une fonction uniforme de la variable avec le seul pôle $u = 0$.

Nous sommes assurés de plus, par une proposition générale de M. Picard (*Comptes rendus* du 21 juillet 1879, p. 140, et du 19 janvier 1880, p. 128), que cette intégrale s'exprime dès lors par deux fonctions périodiques de seconde espèce. Si donc on restitue, en faisant la substitution $y = ze^{\alpha u}$, une constante arbitraire dont il a été disposé pour simplifier les calculs, il est certain que la nouvelle équation différentielle contiendra, comme cas particuliers, toutes celles dont il a été précédemment question. C'est, en effet, ce que je ferai bientôt voir; mais je veux auparavant obtenir une confirmation de l'important théorème du jeune géomètre en effectuant directement l'intégration de cette équation et donner ainsi, avant d'aborder des cas plus généraux, un nouvel exemple du procédé déjà employé pour l'équation de Lamé dans le cas le plus simple de $n = 1$.

XXX.

Considérons la fonction doublement périodique de seconde espèce la plus générale, admettant pour seul pôle $u = 0$, à savoir

$$f(u) = \frac{H'(0)\,\Theta(u+\omega)}{\Theta(\omega)\,H(u)}\, e^{\left[\lambda - \frac{\Theta'(\omega)}{\Theta(\omega)}\right] u},$$

et proposons-nous de déterminer ω et λ de telle sorte qu'elle soit une solution de l'équation proposée. Soit, à cet effet, $\Phi(u)$ le résultat de la substitution de $f(u)$ dans son premier membre. Les coefficients de l'équation ayant pour périodes $2K$ et $2iK'$, on voit que cette quantité est une fonction de seconde espèce, ayant les mêmes multiplicateurs que $f(u)$, qui pourra, par conséquent, remplir à son égard le rôle d'élément simple. On voit aussi que les pôles de $\Phi(u)$ sont $u=a$, $u=b$, $u=0$, les deux premiers représentant des infinis simples et le troisième un infini triple. Nous aurons donc

$$\Phi(u) = \mathfrak{A} f(u-a) + \mathfrak{B} f(u-b) + \mathfrak{C} f(u) + \mathfrak{C}' f'(u) + \mathfrak{C}'' f''(u),$$

et la condition $\Phi(u) = 0$ entraîne ces cinq équations

$$\mathfrak{A} = 0, \quad \mathfrak{B} = 0, \quad \mathfrak{C} = 0, \quad \mathfrak{C}' = 0, \quad \mathfrak{C}'' = 0,$$

qu'il est aisé de former, comme on va voir.

Nous avons pour cela à décomposer en éléments simples les produits de $f(u)$ et $f'(u)$ par deux quantités de la même forme $\frac{\operatorname{sn} p}{\operatorname{sn} u \operatorname{sn}(u-p)}$, c'est-à-dire à chercher les parties principales des développements de ces produits, d'abord suivant les puissances de u, puis, en posant $u=p+\varepsilon$, suivant les puissances de ε. Or il résulte de l'expression de $f(u)$ qu'on a

$$f(u) = \chi(i\mathrm{K}'+u)\, e^{\lambda u},$$

$\chi(u)$ désignant la fonction considérée au paragraphe V, page 277, et par conséquent

$$\begin{aligned} f(u) &= \left[\frac{1}{u} - \frac{1}{2}\left(k^2 \operatorname{sn}^2\omega - \frac{1+k^2}{3}\right)u + \ldots\right] e^{\lambda u} \\ &= \frac{1}{u} + \lambda + \frac{1}{2}\left(\lambda^2 - k^2 \operatorname{sn}^2\omega + \frac{1+k^2}{3}\right)u + \ldots. \end{aligned}$$

On trouve ensuite

$$\frac{\operatorname{sn} p}{\operatorname{sn} u \operatorname{sn}(u-p)} = -\frac{1}{u} - \frac{\operatorname{cn} p \operatorname{dn} p}{\operatorname{sn} p} - \left(\frac{1}{\operatorname{sn}^2 p} - \frac{1+k^2}{3}\right)u + \ldots$$

et sans nouveau calcul, en remplaçant u par $-\varepsilon$,

$$\frac{\operatorname{sn} p}{\operatorname{sn}(p+\varepsilon) \operatorname{sn}\varepsilon} = \frac{1}{\varepsilon} - \frac{\operatorname{cn} p \operatorname{dn} p}{\operatorname{sn} p} + \left(\frac{1}{\operatorname{sn}^2 p} - \frac{1+k^2}{3}\right)\varepsilon + \ldots.$$

Ces développements nous donnent les formules

$$\frac{\operatorname{sn} p}{\operatorname{sn} u \operatorname{sn}(u-p)} f(u) = f(p) f(u-p) - \left(\lambda + \frac{\operatorname{cn} p \operatorname{dn} p}{\operatorname{sn} p}\right) f(u) + f'(u),$$

$$\begin{aligned} \frac{\operatorname{sn} p}{\operatorname{sn} u \operatorname{sn}(u-p)} f'(u) = f'(p) f(u-p) &- \frac{1}{2}\left(\lambda^2 - k^2 \operatorname{sn}^2\omega - \frac{2}{\operatorname{sn}^2 p} + 1 + k^2\right) f(u) \\ &- \frac{\operatorname{cn} p \operatorname{dn} p}{\operatorname{sn} p} f'(u) + \frac{1}{2} f''(u), \end{aligned}$$

et l'on en conclut, en faisant successsivement $p = a, p = b$, les expressions cherchées

$$\mathfrak{A} = \mathrm{A}\, f(a) - f'(a),$$

$$\mathfrak{B} = \mathrm{B}\, f(b) - f'(b),$$

$$\mathfrak{C} = \lambda^2 - \mathrm{A}\left(\lambda + \frac{\operatorname{cn} a \operatorname{dn} a}{\operatorname{sn} a}\right) - \mathrm{B}\left(\lambda + \frac{\operatorname{cn} b \operatorname{dn} b}{\operatorname{sn} b}\right) - \mathrm{C}^2 + \frac{1}{\operatorname{sn}^2(a-b)}$$

$$- k^2 \operatorname{sn}^2 \omega - \frac{1}{\operatorname{sn}^2 a} - \frac{1}{\operatorname{sn}^2 b} + 1 + k^2,$$

$$\mathfrak{C}' = \mathrm{A} + \mathrm{B} + \frac{\operatorname{cn} a \operatorname{dn} a}{\operatorname{sn} a} + \frac{\operatorname{cn} b \operatorname{dn} b}{\operatorname{sn} b},$$

$$\mathfrak{C}'' = 0.$$

Ces résultats obtenus, nous observons d'abord que $\mathfrak{C}'$ s'évanouit, d'après une des relations trouvées entre A et B; j'ajoute que l'équation $\mathfrak{C} = 0$ est une conséquence des deux premières; par conséquent, les cinq conditions se réduisent, comme il est nécessaire, à deux seulement, qui serviront à déterminer ω et λ. Nous recourrons, pour l'établir, à la transformation suivante de la valeur de $\mathfrak{C}$. Soit, pour abréger l'écriture,

$$\mathrm{G} = \left(\lambda - \mathrm{C} + \frac{\operatorname{cn} b \operatorname{dn} b}{\operatorname{sn} b}\right)\left(\lambda + \mathrm{C} + \frac{\operatorname{cn} a \operatorname{dn} a}{\operatorname{sn} a}\right),$$

$$\mathrm{H} = \left(\mathrm{A} - \mathrm{C} + \frac{\operatorname{cn} b \operatorname{dn} b}{\operatorname{sn} b}\right)\left(\mathrm{B} + \mathrm{C} + \frac{\operatorname{cn} a \operatorname{dn} a}{\operatorname{sn} a}\right);$$

on a identiquement

$$\mathfrak{C} = \mathrm{G} - \mathrm{H} + (\mathrm{A} - \mathrm{C})(\mathrm{B} + \mathrm{C}) - k^2 \operatorname{sn}^2 \omega$$

$$+ \frac{1}{\operatorname{sn}^2(a-b)} - \frac{1}{\operatorname{sn}^2 a} - \frac{1}{\operatorname{sn}^2 a} + 1 + k^2,$$

et plus simplement déjà

$$\mathfrak{C} = \mathrm{G} - \mathrm{H} - k^2 \operatorname{sn}^2 \omega - \frac{1}{\operatorname{sn}^2 a} - \frac{1}{\operatorname{sn}^2 b} + 1 + k^2.$$

les valeurs de A et B que je rappelle

$$\mathrm{A} = \frac{\operatorname{sn} b}{\operatorname{sn} a \operatorname{sn}(a-b)} + \mathrm{C}, \qquad \mathrm{B} = \frac{\operatorname{sn} a}{\operatorname{sn} b \operatorname{sn}(b-a)} - \mathrm{C},$$

donnant

$$(\mathrm{A} - \mathrm{C})(\mathrm{B} + \mathrm{C}) = -\frac{1}{\operatorname{sn}^2(a-b)}.$$

Nous obtenons ensuite, en faisant usage de ces expressions,

$$H = \left[\frac{\operatorname{sn} b}{\operatorname{sn} a \operatorname{sn}(a-b)} + \frac{\operatorname{cn} b \operatorname{dn} b}{\operatorname{sn} b}\right]\left[\frac{\operatorname{sn} a}{\operatorname{sn} b \operatorname{sn}(b-a)} + \frac{\operatorname{cn} a \operatorname{dn} a}{\operatorname{sn} a}\right]$$

$$= -\frac{1}{\operatorname{sn}^2(a-b)} + \frac{1}{\operatorname{sn}(a-b)}\left(\frac{\operatorname{sn} b \operatorname{cn} a \operatorname{dn} a}{\operatorname{sn}^2 a} - \frac{\operatorname{sn} a \operatorname{cn} b \operatorname{dn} b}{\operatorname{sn}^2 b}\right) + \frac{\operatorname{cn} a \operatorname{dn} a \operatorname{cn} b \operatorname{dn} b}{\operatorname{sn} a \operatorname{sn} b}.$$

On a d'ailleurs

$$\frac{1}{\operatorname{sn}(a-b)}\left(\frac{\operatorname{sn} b \operatorname{cn} a \operatorname{dn} a}{\operatorname{sn}^2 a} - \frac{\operatorname{sn} a \operatorname{cn} b \operatorname{dn} b}{\operatorname{sn}^2 b}\right)$$

$$= \left(\frac{\operatorname{sn} a \operatorname{cn} b \operatorname{dn} b + \operatorname{sn} b \operatorname{cn} a \operatorname{dn} a}{\operatorname{sn}^2 a - \operatorname{sn}^2 b}\right)\left(\frac{\operatorname{sn}^3 b \operatorname{cn} a \operatorname{dn} a - \operatorname{sn}^3 a \operatorname{cn} b \operatorname{dn} b}{\operatorname{sn}^2 a \operatorname{sn}^2 b}\right)$$

$$= -\frac{\operatorname{sn}^2 a + \operatorname{sn}^2 b}{\operatorname{sn}^2 a \operatorname{sn}^2 b} - \frac{\operatorname{cn} a \operatorname{dn} a \operatorname{cn} b \operatorname{dn} b}{\operatorname{sn} a \operatorname{sn} b} + 1 + k^2,$$

et la valeur de H qui en résulte, à savoir

$$H = -\frac{1}{\operatorname{sn}^2(a-b)} - \frac{1}{\operatorname{sn}^2 a} - \frac{1}{\operatorname{sn}^2 b} + 1 + k^2,$$

donne cette nouvelle réduction

$$\mathfrak{C} = G - k^2 \operatorname{sn}^2 \omega + \frac{1}{\operatorname{sn}^2(a-b)}.$$

C'est maintenant qu'il est nécessaire d'introduire les conditions $\mathfrak{A} = 0$, $\mathfrak{B} = 0$, c'est-à-dire $A = \frac{f'(a)}{f(a)}$, $B = \frac{f'(b)}{f(b)}$. Or, au moyen des valeurs de A, de B et de l'expression

$$\frac{f'(x)}{f(x)} = \frac{\Theta'(x+\omega)}{\Theta(x+\omega)} - \frac{H'(x)}{H(x)} - \frac{\Theta'(\omega)}{\Theta(\omega)} + \lambda,$$

$$= -k^2 \operatorname{sn} x \operatorname{sn} \omega \operatorname{sn}(x+\omega) - \frac{\operatorname{cn} x \operatorname{dn} x}{\operatorname{sn} x} + \lambda,$$

on en tire

$$\lambda - C = \frac{\operatorname{sn} b}{\operatorname{sn} a \operatorname{sn}(a-b)} + \frac{\operatorname{cn} a \operatorname{dn} a}{\operatorname{sn} a} + k^2 \operatorname{sn} a \operatorname{sn} \omega \operatorname{sn}(a+\omega),$$

$$\lambda + C = \frac{\operatorname{sn} a}{\operatorname{sn} b \operatorname{sn}(b-a)} + \frac{\operatorname{cn} b \operatorname{dn} b}{\operatorname{sn} b} + k^2 \operatorname{sn} b \operatorname{sn} \omega \operatorname{sn}(b+\omega).$$

Cela étant, une réduction qui se présente facilement donne

$$\lambda - C + \frac{\operatorname{cn} b \operatorname{dn} b}{\operatorname{sn} b} = \frac{\operatorname{sn} a}{\operatorname{sn} b \operatorname{sn}(a-b)} + k^2 \operatorname{sn} a \operatorname{sn} \omega \operatorname{sn}(a+\omega),$$

$$\lambda + C + \frac{\operatorname{cn} a \operatorname{dn} a}{\operatorname{sn} a} = \frac{\operatorname{sn} b}{\operatorname{sn} a \operatorname{sn}(b-a)} + k^2 \operatorname{sn} b \operatorname{sn} \omega \operatorname{sn}(b+\omega),$$

et nous pouvons écrire en conséquence

$$G = \left[\frac{\operatorname{sn} a}{\operatorname{sn} b \operatorname{sn}(a-b)} + k^2 \operatorname{sn} a \operatorname{sn} \omega \operatorname{sn}(a+\omega)\right] \times \left[\frac{\operatorname{sn} b}{\operatorname{sn} a \operatorname{sn}(b-a)} + k^2 \operatorname{sn} b \operatorname{sn} \omega \operatorname{sn}(b+\omega)\right].$$

Je considérerai cette expression comme une fonction doublement périodique de ω, ayant pour infinis simples $\omega = i\mathrm{K}' - a$, $\omega = i\mathrm{K}' - b$, et pour infini double $\omega = i\mathrm{K}'$. Elle présente cette circonstance que les résidus qui correspondent aux infinis simples sont nuls. En effet, des deux facteurs dont elle se compose, le premier s'évanouit en faisant $\omega = i\mathrm{K}' - b$, et le second pour $\omega = i\mathrm{K}' - a$. Il en résulte que le résidu relatif au troisième pôle $\omega = i\mathrm{K}'$ est également nul, de sorte qu'en décomposant en éléments simples on obtient

$$G = -D_\omega \frac{\Theta'(\omega)}{\Theta(\omega)} + \text{const.} = k^2 \operatorname{sn}^2 \omega + \text{const.}$$

Posons, afin de déterminer la constante, $\omega = 0$; nous trouverons finalement

$$G = k^2 \operatorname{sn}^2 \omega - \frac{1}{\operatorname{sn}^2(a-b)},$$

et de là résulte, comme il importait essentiellement de le démontrer, que l'équation $\mathfrak{C} = 0$ est une conséquence des relations $\mathfrak{A} = 0$ et $\mathfrak{B} = 0$.

XXXI.

La détermination des constantes ω et λ s'effectue au moyen des deux équations

$$\lambda - C = \frac{\operatorname{sn} b}{\operatorname{sn} a \operatorname{sn}(a-b)} + \frac{\operatorname{cn} a \operatorname{dn} a}{\operatorname{sn} a} + k^2 \operatorname{sn} a \operatorname{sn} \omega \operatorname{sn}(a+\omega),$$

$$\lambda + C = \frac{\operatorname{sn} a}{\operatorname{sn} b \operatorname{sn}(b-a)} + \frac{\operatorname{cn} b \operatorname{dn} b}{\operatorname{sn} b} + k^2 \operatorname{sn} b \operatorname{sn} \omega \operatorname{sn}(b+\omega),$$

que nous avons maintenant à traiter. En les retranchant et après une réduction qui s'offre facilement, elles donnent d'abord

$$k^2 \operatorname{sn} \omega [\operatorname{sn} b \operatorname{sn}(b+\omega) - \operatorname{sn} a \operatorname{sn}(a+\omega)] - 2\frac{\operatorname{sn} a \operatorname{cn} a \operatorname{dn} a + \operatorname{sn} b \operatorname{cn} b \operatorname{dn} b}{\operatorname{sn}^2 a - \operatorname{sn}^2 b} - 2C = 0,$$

et nous démontrerons immédiatement, le premier membre étant une fonction doublement périodique, qu'on n'aura, dans le rectangle des périodes $2K$ et $2iK'$, que deux valeurs pour l'inconnue. En effet, la fonction, qui au premier abord paraît avoir les trois pôles $\omega = iK' - a$, $\omega = iK' - b$, $\omega = iK'$, ne possède en réalité que les deux premiers, le résidu relatif au troisième, qui est un infini simple, étant nul, comme on le vérifie aisément. Ce point établi, nous donnerons, pour éviter des longueurs de calcul, une autre forme à l'équation, en employant l'identité suivante

$$\begin{aligned}&\operatorname{sn} b \operatorname{sn}(b+\omega) - \operatorname{sn} a \operatorname{sn}(a+\omega)\\&\quad = \operatorname{sn}(b-a)\operatorname{sn}(a+b+\omega)[1-k^2 \operatorname{sn} a \operatorname{sn} b \operatorname{sn}(a+\omega)\operatorname{sn}(b+\omega)],\end{aligned}$$

à laquelle je m'arrête un moment. Elle est la conséquence immédiate de la relation mémorable obtenue par Jacobi, dans un article intitulé : *Formulæ novæ in theoria transcendentium ellipticarum fundamentales* (*Journal de Crelle,* t. XV, p. 201, et *Gesammelte Werke*, t. I, p. 337), à savoir

$$\begin{aligned}&E(u)+E(a)+E(b)-E(u+a+b)\\&\quad = k^2 \operatorname{sn}(u+a)\operatorname{sn}(u+b)\operatorname{sn}(a+b)[1-k^2 \operatorname{sn} u \operatorname{sn} a \operatorname{sn} b \operatorname{sn}(u+a+b)].\end{aligned}$$

Qu'on change en effet a en $-a$, puis u en $a+\omega$, on aura

$$\begin{aligned}&E(a+\omega)-E(a)+E(b)-E(b+\omega)\\&\quad = k^2 \operatorname{sn}\omega \operatorname{sn}(b-a)\operatorname{sn}(a+b+\omega)[1-k^2 \operatorname{sn} a \operatorname{sn} b \operatorname{sn}(a+\omega)\operatorname{sn}(b+\omega)]\end{aligned}$$

et il suffit de remarquer que le premier membre, étant la différence des quantités

$$E(a+\omega)-E(a)-E(\omega), \qquad E(b+\omega)-E(b)-E(\omega),$$

peut être remplacé par

$$k^2 \operatorname{sn}\omega[\operatorname{sn} b \operatorname{sn}(b+\omega) - \operatorname{sn} a \operatorname{sn}(a+\omega)].$$

On y parvient encore d'une autre manière au moyen de la relation précédemment démontrée

$$\begin{aligned}G = &\left[\frac{\operatorname{sn} a}{\operatorname{sn} b \operatorname{sn}(a-b)} + k^2 \operatorname{sn} a \operatorname{sn}\omega \operatorname{sn}(a+\omega)\right]\\&\times\left[\frac{\operatorname{sn} b}{\operatorname{sn} a \operatorname{sn}(b-a)} + k^2 \operatorname{sn} b \operatorname{sn}\omega \operatorname{sn}(b+\omega)\right] = k^2 \operatorname{sn}^2\omega - \frac{1}{\operatorname{sn}^2(a-b)},\end{aligned}$$

car on en tire

$$\begin{aligned}&\operatorname{sn} b \operatorname{sn}(a+\omega) - \operatorname{sn} a \operatorname{sn}(b+\omega)\\ &\quad = \operatorname{sn}\omega \operatorname{sn}(b-a)[1 - k^2 \operatorname{sn} a \operatorname{sn} b \operatorname{sn}(a+\omega)\operatorname{sn}(b+\omega)],\end{aligned}$$

ce qui donne la formule proposée en changeant a en $-a$, b en $-b$ et ω en $\omega + a + b$.

Cela posé, soit $\upsilon = \omega + \frac{a+b}{2}$; faisons aussi, pour abréger, $\alpha = \frac{a+b}{2}$, $\beta = \frac{a-b}{2}$; nous trouverons, par cette formule,

$$\begin{aligned}&\operatorname{sn}\omega[\operatorname{sn} b \operatorname{sn}(b+\omega) - \operatorname{sn} a \operatorname{sn}(a+\omega)]\\ &\quad = -\operatorname{sn} 2\beta \operatorname{sn}(\upsilon+\alpha)\operatorname{sn}(\upsilon-\alpha)\\ &\qquad \times [1 - k^2 \operatorname{sn}(\alpha+\beta)\operatorname{sn}(\alpha-\beta)\operatorname{sn}(\upsilon+\beta)\operatorname{sn}(\upsilon-\beta)].\end{aligned}$$

Or, on voit que le second membre devient ainsi une fonction rationnelle de $\operatorname{sn}^2\upsilon$; on peut, en outre, supprimer au numérateur et au dénominateur le facteur $1 - k^2\operatorname{sn}^2\upsilon\operatorname{sn}^2\alpha$, de sorte qu'il se réduit à l'expression

$$-\frac{\operatorname{sn} 2\beta(1 - k^2\operatorname{sn}^4\beta)(\operatorname{sn}^2\upsilon - \operatorname{sn}^2\alpha)}{(1 - k^2\operatorname{sn}^2\alpha\operatorname{sn}^2\beta)(1 - k^2\operatorname{sn}^2\upsilon\operatorname{sn}^2\beta)}.$$

Remarquant encore qu'on a

$$\operatorname{sn} 2\beta(1 - k^2\operatorname{sn}^4\beta) = 2\operatorname{sn}\beta\operatorname{cn}\beta\operatorname{dn}\beta,$$

nous poserons, pour simplifier l'écriture,

$$\mathrm{L} = \frac{1 - k^2\operatorname{sn}^2\alpha\operatorname{sn}^2\beta}{k^2\operatorname{sn}\beta\operatorname{cn}\beta\operatorname{dn}\beta}\left(\frac{\operatorname{sn} a\operatorname{cn} a\operatorname{dn} a + \operatorname{sn} b\operatorname{cn} b\operatorname{dn} b}{\operatorname{sn}^2 a - \operatorname{sn}^2 b} + \mathrm{C}\right),$$

et l'équation en $\operatorname{sn}\upsilon$ sera simplement

$$\frac{\operatorname{sn}^2\upsilon - \operatorname{sn}^2\alpha}{1 - k^2\operatorname{sn}^2\upsilon\operatorname{sn}^2\beta} = -\mathrm{L}.$$

On en tire

$$\operatorname{sn}^2\upsilon = \frac{\operatorname{sn}^2\alpha - \mathrm{L}}{1 - k^2\operatorname{sn}^2\beta\,\mathrm{L}},\quad \operatorname{cn}^2\upsilon = \frac{\operatorname{cn}^2\alpha + \operatorname{dn}^2\beta\,\mathrm{L}}{1 - k^2\operatorname{sn}^2\beta\,\mathrm{L}},\quad \operatorname{dn}^2\upsilon = \frac{\operatorname{dn}^2\alpha + k^2\operatorname{cn}^2\beta\,\mathrm{L}}{1 - k^2\operatorname{sn}^2\beta\,\mathrm{L}},$$

et, si l'on fait

$$\mathfrak{L} = (\operatorname{sn}^2\alpha - \mathrm{L})(\operatorname{cn}^2\alpha + \operatorname{dn}^2\beta\,\mathrm{L})(\operatorname{dn}^2\alpha + k^2\operatorname{cn}^2\beta\,\mathrm{L})(1 - k^2\operatorname{sn}^2\beta\,\mathrm{L}),$$

ces valeurs donnent

$$\operatorname{sn}\upsilon\operatorname{cn}\upsilon\operatorname{dn}\upsilon = \frac{\sqrt{\mathfrak{L}}}{(1 - k^2\operatorname{sn}^2\beta\,\mathrm{L})^2}.$$

Nous ferons usage de cette expression pour le calcul de λ, qui nous reste à déterminer. A cet effet je reprends, pour les ajouter membre à membre, les équations

$$\lambda - C = \frac{\operatorname{sn} b}{\operatorname{sn} a \operatorname{sn}(a-b)} + \frac{\operatorname{cn} a \operatorname{dn} a}{\operatorname{sn} a} + k^2 \operatorname{sn} a \operatorname{sn} \omega \operatorname{sn}(a+\omega),$$

$$\lambda + C = \frac{\operatorname{sn} a}{\operatorname{sn} b \operatorname{sn}(b-a)} + \frac{\operatorname{cn} b \operatorname{dn} b}{\operatorname{sn} b} + k^2 \operatorname{sn} b \operatorname{sn} \omega \operatorname{sn}(b+\omega),$$

et j'obtiens, comme on le voit facilement,

$$2\lambda = k^2[\operatorname{sn} a \operatorname{sn} \omega \operatorname{sn}(a+\omega) + \operatorname{sn} b \operatorname{sn} \omega \operatorname{sn}(b+\omega)],$$

ou bien encore

$$\begin{aligned} 2\lambda = k^2[& \operatorname{sn}(\alpha+\beta) \operatorname{sn}(\upsilon-\alpha) \operatorname{sn}(\upsilon+\beta) \\ & + \operatorname{sn}(\alpha-\beta) \operatorname{sn}(\upsilon-\alpha) \operatorname{sn}(\upsilon-\beta)]. \end{aligned}$$

Maintenant, un calcul sans difficulté donne en premier lieu l'expression

$$\begin{aligned} \lambda = & \frac{k^2 \operatorname{sn} \alpha \operatorname{cn} \alpha \operatorname{dn} \alpha (\operatorname{sn}^2 \upsilon - \operatorname{sn}^2 \beta)}{(1 - k^2 \operatorname{sn}^2 \upsilon \operatorname{sn}^2 \alpha)(1 - k^2 \operatorname{sn}^2 \alpha \operatorname{sn}^2 \beta)} \\ & + \frac{k^2 \operatorname{sn} \upsilon \operatorname{cn} \upsilon \operatorname{dn} \upsilon (\operatorname{sn}^2 \beta - \operatorname{sn}^2 \alpha)}{(1 - k^2 \operatorname{sn}^2 \upsilon \operatorname{sn}^2 \alpha)(1 - k^2 \operatorname{sn}^2 \upsilon \operatorname{sn}^2 \beta)}; \end{aligned}$$

on en conclut ensuite la valeur cherchée, à savoir

$$\begin{aligned} \lambda = & \frac{k^2 \operatorname{sn} \alpha \operatorname{cn} \alpha \operatorname{dn} \alpha [\operatorname{sn}^2 \alpha - \operatorname{sn}^2 \beta - (1 - k^2 \operatorname{sn}^4 \beta) L]}{(1 - k^2 \operatorname{sn}^2 \alpha \operatorname{sn}^2 \beta)[1 - k^2 \operatorname{sn}^4 \alpha + k^2 (\operatorname{sn}^2 \alpha - \operatorname{sn}^2 \beta) L]} \\ & + \frac{k^2 (\operatorname{sn}^2 \beta - \operatorname{sn}^2 \alpha) \sqrt{\mathfrak{L}}}{(1 - k^2 \operatorname{sn}^2 \alpha \operatorname{sn}^2 \beta)[1 - k^2 \operatorname{sn}^4 \alpha + k^2 (\operatorname{sn}^2 \alpha - \operatorname{sn}^2 \beta) L]}. \end{aligned}$$

Cette expression devient illusoire lorsqu'on suppose d'abord $1 - k^2 \operatorname{sn}^2 \alpha \operatorname{sn}^2 \beta = 0$, c'est-à-dire

$$\alpha + \beta = a = iK',$$

ou bien

$$\alpha - \beta = b = iK',$$

puis en faisant

$$1 - k^2 \operatorname{sn}^4 \alpha + k^2 (\operatorname{sn}^2 \alpha - \operatorname{sn}^2 \beta) L = 0.$$

La première condition, ayant pour effet de rendre infinis les coefficients de l'équation différentielle, doit être écartée; mais la seconde appelle l'attention, et je m'y arrêterai un moment, afin d'obtenir la nouvelle forme analytique que prend l'intégrale dans ce cas singulier.

XXXII.

Remarquons en premier lieu que cette condition se trouve en posant

$$\operatorname{sn}^2 \upsilon = \frac{\operatorname{sn}^2 \alpha - \mathrm{L}}{1 - k^2 \operatorname{sn}^2 \beta \mathrm{L}} = \frac{1}{k^2 \operatorname{sn}^2 \alpha},$$

c'est-à-dire $\upsilon = \alpha + i\mathrm{K}'$, et donne par conséquent $\omega = i\mathrm{K}'$. Cela étant, je fais dans la solution de l'intégrale, qui est représentée par la formule

$$\frac{\Theta(u+\omega)}{\mathrm{H}(u)} e^{\left[\lambda - \frac{\Theta'(\omega)}{\Theta(\omega)}\right] u}, \qquad \omega = i\mathrm{K}' + \varepsilon,$$

ε étant infiniment petit, et je développe suivant les puissances croissantes de ε la différence $\lambda - \frac{\Theta'(\omega)}{\Theta(\omega)}$. Or, l'expression précédemment employée

$$2\lambda = k^2[\operatorname{sn} a \operatorname{sn} \omega \operatorname{sn}(a+\omega) + \operatorname{sn} b \operatorname{sn} \omega \operatorname{sn}(b+\omega)]$$

donne facilement

$$\lambda = \frac{1}{\varepsilon} - \frac{\operatorname{cn} a \operatorname{dn} a}{2 \operatorname{sn} a} - \frac{\operatorname{cn} b \operatorname{dn} b}{2 \operatorname{sn} b} + \ldots;$$

nous avons d'ailleurs

$$\frac{\Theta'(\omega)}{\Theta(\omega)} = \frac{\mathrm{H}'(\varepsilon)}{\mathrm{H}(\varepsilon)} - \frac{i\pi}{2\mathrm{K}} = \frac{1}{\varepsilon} - \frac{i\pi}{2\mathrm{K}} + \ldots,$$

et l'on conclut, pour $\varepsilon = 0$, la limite finie

$$\lambda - \frac{\Theta'(\omega)}{\Theta(\omega)} = \frac{i\pi}{2\mathrm{K}} - \frac{\operatorname{cn} a \operatorname{dn} a}{2 \operatorname{sn} a} - \frac{\operatorname{cn} b \operatorname{dn} b}{2 \operatorname{sn} b}.$$

Remplaçant donc $\Theta(u+i\mathrm{K}')$ par $i\mathrm{H}(u) e^{-\frac{i\pi}{4\mathrm{K}}(2u+i\mathrm{K}')}$, on voit qu'au lieu de la fonction doublement périodique de seconde espèce nous obtenons l'exponentielle $e^{-\left(\frac{\operatorname{cn} a \operatorname{dn} a}{2 \operatorname{sn} a} + \frac{\operatorname{cn} b \operatorname{dn} b}{2 \operatorname{sn} b}\right) u}$, qui devient ainsi une des solutions de l'équation différentielle. Nous parvenons à l'autre solution en employant, au lieu de $\upsilon = \alpha + i\mathrm{K}'$, la valeur égale et de signe contraire $\upsilon = -\alpha - i\mathrm{K}'$, d'où l'on tire $\omega = -2\alpha - i\mathrm{K}' = -a - b - i\mathrm{K}'$, et par conséquent

$$\lambda = \frac{\operatorname{sn}^2 a + \operatorname{sn}^2 b}{2\operatorname{sn}(a+b)\operatorname{sn} a \operatorname{sn} b}, \qquad \frac{\Theta'(\omega)}{\Theta(\omega)} = -\frac{\mathrm{H}'(a+b)}{\mathrm{H}(a+b)} + \frac{i\pi}{2\mathrm{K}}.$$

Des réductions qui s'offrent d'elles-mêmes en employant la formule

$$\frac{\mathrm{H}'(a+b)}{\mathrm{H}(a+b)} = \frac{\mathrm{H}'(a)}{\mathrm{H}(a)} + \frac{\mathrm{H}'(b)}{\mathrm{H}(b)} - \frac{\operatorname{sn} b}{\operatorname{sn} a \operatorname{sn}(a+b)} - \frac{\operatorname{cn} b \operatorname{dn} b}{\operatorname{sn} b}$$

donnent ensuite

$$\lambda - \frac{\Theta'(\omega)}{\Theta(\omega)} = \frac{\mathrm{H}'(a)}{\mathrm{H}(a)} + \frac{\mathrm{H}'(b)}{\mathrm{H}(b)} - \frac{\operatorname{cn} a \operatorname{dn} a}{2\operatorname{sn} a} - \frac{\operatorname{cn} b \operatorname{dn} b}{2\operatorname{sn} b} + \frac{i\omega}{2\mathrm{K}}.$$

La seconde intégrale devient donc

$$\frac{\mathrm{H}(u-a-b)}{\mathrm{H}(u)} e^{\left[\frac{\mathrm{H}'(a)}{\mathrm{H}(a)} + \frac{\mathrm{H}'(b)}{\mathrm{H}(b)} - \frac{\operatorname{cn} a \operatorname{dn} a}{2\operatorname{sn} a} - \frac{\operatorname{cn} b \operatorname{dn} b}{2\operatorname{sn} b}\right] u},$$

et l'on voit que, pour le cas singulier considéré, la solution générale est représentée par la relation suivante,

$$y\, e^{\left(\frac{\operatorname{cn} a \operatorname{dn} a}{2\operatorname{sn} a} + \frac{\operatorname{cn} b \operatorname{dn} b}{2\operatorname{sn} b}\right) u} = \mathrm{C} + \mathrm{C}' \frac{\mathrm{H}(u-a-b)}{\mathrm{H}(u)} e^{\left[\frac{\mathrm{H}'(a)}{\mathrm{H}(a)} + \frac{\mathrm{H}'(b)}{\mathrm{H}(b)}\right] u}.$$

XXXIII.

Un dernier point me reste maintenant à traiter; j'ai encore à montrer comment les équations différentielles obtenues aux paragraphes XVII et XVIII se tirent comme cas particulier de l'équation que nous venons de considérer, ou plutôt de celle qui en résulte si l'on change u en $u + i\mathrm{K}'$, à savoir

$$\begin{aligned} y'' &- [k^2 \operatorname{sn} u \operatorname{sn} a \operatorname{sn}(u-a) + k^2 \operatorname{sn} u \operatorname{sn} b \operatorname{sn}(u-b)] y' \\ &+ \left[\mathrm{A} k^2 \operatorname{sn} u \operatorname{sn} a \operatorname{sn}(u-a) + \mathrm{B} k^2 \operatorname{sn} u \operatorname{sn} b \operatorname{sn}(u-b) + \frac{1}{\operatorname{sn}^2(a-b)} - \mathrm{C}^2\right] y = 0. \end{aligned}$$

Je me fonde, à cet effet, sur ce que les deux déterminations de la quantité $\upsilon = \omega + \frac{a+b}{2}$ peuvent être supposées égales et de signes contraires, de sorte que, en désignant par ω et ω' les valeurs correspondantes de ω, on a la condition $\omega + \omega' = -a - b$. Qu'on se reporte maintenant aux expressions données au paragraphe XXV (p. 337) :

$$X_1 = \frac{C\,\theta_s(u+a)}{\theta_0(u)} e^{-\frac{u}{2} D_a \log \theta_{1-s}\theta_{3-s}} + \frac{C'\,\theta_{2+s}(u-a)}{\theta_0(u)} e^{\frac{u}{2} D_a \log \theta_{1-s}\theta_{3-s}},$$

$$X_2 = \frac{C\,\theta_s(u+a)}{\theta_0(u)} e^{-\frac{u}{2} D_a \log \theta_s\theta_{1-s}} + \frac{C'\,\theta_{1-s}(u-a)}{\theta_0(u)} e^{\frac{u}{2} D_a \log \theta_s\theta_{1-s}},$$

$$X_3 = \frac{C\,\theta_s(u+a)}{\theta_0(u)} e^{-\frac{u}{2} D_a \log \theta_s\theta_{2+s}} + \frac{C'\,\theta_{3-s}(u-a)}{\theta_0(u)} e^{\frac{u}{2} D_a \log \theta_s\theta_{2+s}}.$$

On voit aisément que les quantités qui jouent le rôle des constantes ω et ω' ont pour somme, successivement, $K + iK'$, iK', K. C'est, en effet, la conséquence des relations déjà remarquées

$$\theta_s(u+iK') = \sigma\;\theta_{1-s}(u)\, e^{-\frac{i\pi}{4K}(u+iK')},$$

$$\theta_s(u+K) = \sigma'\;\theta_{3-s}(u),$$

$$\theta_s(u+K+iK') = \sigma''\;\theta_{2+s}(u)\, e^{-\frac{i\pi}{4K}(2u+iK')}.$$

D'après cela, je ferai successivement $a + b = K + iK'$, iK', K; je poserai en outre, en changeant d'inconnue dans ces divers cas,

$$y = z\,e^{-\frac{u}{2} D_a \log \operatorname{cn} a}, \quad z\,e^{-\frac{u}{2} D_a \log \operatorname{sn} a}, \quad z\,e^{-\frac{u}{2} D_a \log \operatorname{dn} a}.$$

Or, en considérant, pour abréger, seulement le premier de ces cas, voici le calcul et le résultat auquel il conduit. La condition supposée $b = K + iK' - a$ donne d'abord

$$\operatorname{sn} b = \frac{\operatorname{dn} a}{k \operatorname{cn} a}, \quad \operatorname{sn}(u-b) = -\frac{\operatorname{dn}(u+a)}{k \operatorname{cn}(u+a)}, \quad \operatorname{sn}(a-b) = -\frac{\operatorname{dn} 2a}{k \operatorname{cn} 2a},$$

et nous obtenons, pour la transformée en z, l'équation suivante :

$$z'' - \left[k^2 \operatorname{sn} u \operatorname{sn} a \operatorname{sn}(u-a) - \frac{\operatorname{sn} u \operatorname{dn} a \operatorname{dn}(u+a)}{\operatorname{cn} a \operatorname{cn}(u+a)} - \frac{\operatorname{sn} a \operatorname{dn} a}{\operatorname{cn} a}\right] z'$$
$$+ \left[P k^2 \operatorname{sn} u \operatorname{sn} a \operatorname{sn}(u-a) - Q \frac{\operatorname{sn} u \operatorname{dn} a \operatorname{dn}(u+a)}{\operatorname{cn} a \operatorname{cn}(u+a)} + R\right] z = 0,$$

où j'ai fait, pour abréger,

$$P = A - \frac{\operatorname{sn} a \operatorname{dn} a}{2 \operatorname{cn} a}, \quad Q = B - \frac{\operatorname{sn} a \operatorname{dn} a}{2 \operatorname{cn} a}, \quad R = \frac{\operatorname{sn}^2 a \operatorname{dn}^2 a}{4 \operatorname{cn}^2 a} + \frac{k^2 \operatorname{cn}^2 2a}{\operatorname{dn}^2 2a} - C^2.$$

Soit maintenant

$$\mathfrak{P} = \operatorname{cn}(u+a)(1-k^2 \operatorname{sn}^2 u \operatorname{sn}^2 a) = \operatorname{cn} a \operatorname{cn} u - \operatorname{sn} a \operatorname{dn} a \operatorname{sn} u \operatorname{dn} u;$$

on trouvera d'abord que le coefficient de z' est simplement

$$D_u \log \mathfrak{P} = \frac{\mathfrak{P}'}{\mathfrak{P}}.$$

Représentons ensuite par $\dfrac{\mathfrak{Q}}{\mathfrak{P}}$ le coefficient de z; au moyen de la formule élémentaire,

$$\operatorname{sn}(u-a)\operatorname{cn}(u+a) = \frac{\operatorname{sn} u \operatorname{cn} u \operatorname{dn} a - \operatorname{dn} u \operatorname{sn} a \operatorname{cn} a}{1-k^2 \operatorname{sn}^2 u \operatorname{sn}^2 a},$$

nous obtiendrons

$$\begin{aligned}\mathfrak{Q} = {} & \mathrm{P} k^2 \operatorname{sn} u \operatorname{sn} a(\operatorname{sn} u \operatorname{cn} u \operatorname{dn} a - \operatorname{dn} u \operatorname{sn} a \operatorname{cn} a) \\ & - \mathrm{Q}\frac{\operatorname{sn} u \operatorname{dn} a}{\operatorname{cn} a}(\operatorname{dn} u \operatorname{dn} a - k^2 \operatorname{sn} u \operatorname{cn} u \operatorname{sn} a \operatorname{cn} a) \\ & + \mathrm{R}(\operatorname{cn} u \operatorname{cn} a - \operatorname{sn} u \operatorname{dn} u \operatorname{sn} a \operatorname{dn} a),\end{aligned}$$

ou bien, en réunissant les termes semblables,

$$\begin{aligned}\mathfrak{Q} = {} & (\mathrm{P}+\mathrm{Q})k^2 \operatorname{sn} a \operatorname{dn} a \operatorname{sn}^2 u \operatorname{cn} u \\ & - \left(\mathrm{P} k^2 \operatorname{sn}^2 a \operatorname{cn} a + \mathrm{Q}\frac{\operatorname{dn}^2 a}{\operatorname{cn} a} + \mathrm{R} \operatorname{sn} a \operatorname{dn} a\right) \operatorname{sn} u \operatorname{dn} u + \mathrm{R} \operatorname{cn} a \operatorname{cn} u.\end{aligned}$$

Soit maintenant $\mathrm{C} = \delta - \dfrac{\operatorname{sn} a \operatorname{dn} a}{2 \operatorname{cn} a}$; cette nouvelle forme de la constante donnera, après quelques réductions,

$$\begin{aligned}\mathfrak{Q} = {} & -k^2 \operatorname{cn} a \operatorname{sn}^2 u \operatorname{cn} u \\ & + \Big[\operatorname{sn} a \operatorname{dn} a\, \delta^2 + \operatorname{cn} a(1-2k^2 \operatorname{sn}^2 a)\,\delta \\ & \qquad + k^2 \operatorname{sn}^3 a \operatorname{dn} a - \frac{k^2 \operatorname{cn}^2 2a}{\operatorname{dn}^2 2a} \operatorname{sn} a \operatorname{dn} a\Big] \operatorname{sn} u \operatorname{dn} u \\ & - \left[\operatorname{cn} a\, \delta^2 - \operatorname{sn} a \operatorname{dn} a\, \delta - \frac{k^2 \operatorname{cn}^2 2a}{\operatorname{dn}^2 2a} \operatorname{cn} a\right] \operatorname{cn} u.\end{aligned}$$

Or, en faisant successivement $a = 0$, puis $a = \mathrm{K}$, on tire de là les équations

$$\begin{gathered}\operatorname{cn} u\, z'' - D_u \operatorname{cn} u\, z' - [k^2 \operatorname{sn}^2 u \operatorname{cn} u - \operatorname{sn} u \operatorname{dn} u\, \delta + (\delta^2 - k^2)\operatorname{cn} u]z = 0, \\ \operatorname{sn} u \operatorname{dn} u\, z'' - D_u \operatorname{sn} u \operatorname{dn} u\, z' - [\operatorname{cn} u\, \delta + \operatorname{sn} u \operatorname{dn} u\, \delta^2]z = 0;\end{gathered}$$

ce sont précisément les relations en X_1 et Y_1 des paragraphes XXV et XXVI, en supposant dans la première $\delta = \delta_1$ et dans la seconde $\delta = -\delta'_1$.

XXXIV.

Les fonctions doublement périodiques de seconde espèce avec un pôle simple, qu'on pourrait nommer *unipolaires*, donnent, comme nous l'avons vu, la solution découverte par Jacobi du problème de la rotation d'un corps autour d'un point fixe, lorsqu'il n'y a pas de forces accélératrices. Ces mêmes quantités s'offrent encore dans une autre question mécanique importante, la recherche de la figure d'équilibre d'un ressort soumis à des forces quelconques, que je vais traiter succinctement. On sait que Binet a réussi le premier à ramener aux quadratures l'expression des coordonnées de l'élastique, dans le cas le plus général où la courbe est à double courbure (*Comptes rendus*, t. XVIII, p. 1115, et t. XIX, p. 1). Son analyse et ses résultats ont été immédiatement beaucoup simplifiés par Wantzel ([1]), et j'adopterai la marche de l'éminent géomètre en me proposant de conduire la question à son terme et d'obtenir explicitement les coordonnées de la courbe en fonction de l'arc. Mais d'abord je crois devoir considérer le cas particulier où l'élastique est supposée plane et où l'on a, en désignant l'arc par s (*Mécanique* de Poisson, t. I, p. 608),

$$ds = \frac{2c^2\,dx}{\sqrt{4c^4 - (2ax - x^2)^2}}, \qquad dy = \frac{(2ax - x^2)\,dx}{\sqrt{4c^4 - (2ax - x^2)^2}}.$$

Soit alors

$$x = a - \sqrt{2c^2 + a^2}\sqrt{1 - X^2}, \qquad k'^2 = \frac{1}{2} + \frac{a^2}{4c^2};$$

on obtient facilement

$$ds = \frac{c\,dX}{\sqrt{(1 - X^2)(1 - k^2X^2)}},$$

de sorte qu'on peut prendre $X = \operatorname{sn}\left(\frac{s - s_0}{c}\right)$, s_0 étant une constante arbitraire. Mais il est préférable de faire $X = \operatorname{sn}\left(\frac{s - s_0}{c} + K\right)$;

([1]) Wantzel, enlevé à la Science par une mort prématurée à l'âge de 37 ans, en 1840, a laissé d'excellents travaux, parmi lesquels un Mémoire extrêmement remarquable, sur les nombres incommensurables, publié dans le *Journal de l'École Polytechnique*, t. XV, p. 151, et une Note sur l'intégration des équations de la courbe élastique à double courbure (*Comptes rendus*, t. XVIII, p. 1197).

nous parviendrons ainsi à des expressions mieux appropriées au cas important qui a été considéré par Poisson, où c est supposé une ligne dont la longueur est très grande par rapport à a, s et x. En premier lieu, les formules

$$\operatorname{cn}(z+K) = -k' \frac{\operatorname{sn} z}{\operatorname{dn} z}, \qquad k^2 = \frac{1}{2} - \frac{a^2}{4c^2}$$

donnent, pour l'abscisse,

$$x = a + \frac{\sqrt{4c^4 - a^4}}{2c} \frac{\operatorname{sn}\left(\frac{s-s_0}{c}\right)}{\operatorname{dn}\left(\frac{s-s_0}{c}\right)}.$$

La valeur de l'ordonnée, à savoir

$$2c^2 y = \int (2ax - x^2)\,ds = \int \left[a^2 - (2c^2 + a^2)\operatorname{cn}^2\left(\frac{s-s_0}{c} + K\right)\right] ds,$$

s'obtient ensuite immédiatement en employant la relation

$$\int_0^z k^2 \operatorname{cn}^2(z+K)\,dz = k^2 z + D_z \log \operatorname{Al}(z)_3.$$

Or ces formules conduisent comme il suit aux développements de x et y suivant les puissances décroissantes de c. J'emploie à cet effet la série

$$\frac{\operatorname{sn} z}{\operatorname{dn} z} = z + \frac{k^2 - k'^2}{6} z^3 + \frac{1 - 16 k^2 k'^2}{120} z^5 + \ldots,$$

et je remarque qu'en désignant par $F_n(k)$ le coefficient de z^{2n+1}, qui est un polynome de degré n en k^2, on a la relation suivante :

$$F_n(k') = (-1)^n F_n(k).$$

Nous en concluons facilement pour n pair l'expression

$$F_n(k) = \alpha_0 + \alpha_1 (kk')^2 + \alpha_2 (kk')^4 + \ldots + \alpha_{\frac{1}{2}n} (kk')^n,$$

et pour n impair

$$F_n(k) = (k^2 - k'^2)\left[\beta_0 + \beta_1 (kk')^2 + \ldots + \beta_{\frac{n-1}{2}} (kk')^{n-1}\right].$$

Cela étant, les formules

$$k^2 k'^2 = \frac{1}{4} - \frac{a^4}{16c^4} \qquad \text{et} \qquad k^2 - k'^2 = \frac{a^2}{2c^2}$$

montrent que le terme général $F_n(k)z^{2n+1}$, qui est de l'ordre $\frac{1}{c^{2n+1}}$, lorsqu'on remplace z par $\frac{s-s_0}{c}$, devient, si l'on suppose n impair, de l'ordre $\frac{1}{c^{2n+3}}$. Nous pourrons donc écrire, en négligeant $\frac{1}{c^8}$ dans la parenthèse,

$$x = a + \frac{\sqrt{4c^4 - a^4}}{2c^2}\left[s - s_0 + \frac{a^2(s-s_0)^3}{12c^4} - \frac{(s-s_0)^5}{40c^4}\right].$$

Remplaçons enfin le facteur $\frac{\sqrt{4c^4-a^4}}{2c^2}$ par $1 - \frac{a^4}{8c^4}$, et prenons $s_0 = a$; il viendra, avec le même ordre d'approximation,

$$x = s - \frac{s-a}{120c^4}[3(s-a)^4 - 10a^2(s-a)^2 + 15a^4].$$

Le développement de c^2y résulte ensuite de l'équation

$$\int_0^z k^2 \operatorname{cn}^2(z+K)\,dz = \frac{k^2k'^2}{3}z^3 + \frac{k^2k'^2(k^2-k'^2)}{3.5}z^5 + \frac{k^2k'^2(2-17k^2k'^2)}{5.7.9}z^7 + \ldots;$$

mettant $\frac{s-a}{c}$ au lieu de z et déterminant la constante amenée par l'intégration de manière qu'on ait $y=0$ pour $s=a$, on en tire, par un calcul facile,

$$2c^2y = as^2 - \frac{s^3+2a^3}{3} + \frac{(s-a)^3}{420c^4}[3(s-a)^4 - 14a^2(s-a)^2 + 35a^4].$$

Le second membre, dans cette expression de l'ordonnée, est exact aux termes près de l'ordre $\frac{1}{c^8}$, comme la valeur trouvée pour l'abscisse.

XXXV.

Les équations différentielles de l'élastique, dans le cas le plus général où la courbe est à double courbure, se ramènent par un choix convenable de coordonnées, comme l'a remarqué Wantzel, à la forme suivante,

$$y'z'' - y''z' = \alpha x' + \beta y,$$
$$z'x'' - z''x' = \alpha y' - \beta x,$$
$$x'y'' - x''y' = \alpha z' + \gamma,$$

où $x', y', z', x'', y'', z''$ désignent les dérivées par rapport à l'arc s de x, y, z et α, β, γ des constantes dont les deux premières sont essentiellement positives.

Cela étant, j'observai en premier lieu que, si on les ajoute après les avoir multipliées respectivement, d'abord par x', y', z', puis par x'', y'', z'', on obtient

$$\alpha(x'^2 + y'^2 + z'^2) + \beta(x'y - xy') + \gamma z' = 0,$$
$$\alpha(x'x'' + y'y'' + z'z'') + \beta(x''y - xy'') + \gamma z'' = 0.$$

Or la première de ces relations donne, par la différentiation,

$$2\alpha(x'x'' + y'y'' + z'z'') + \beta(x''y - xy'') + \gamma z'' = 0;$$

nous avons donc

$$x'x'' + y'y'' + z'z'' = 0,$$

d'où

$$x'^2 + y'^2 + z'^2 = \text{const.},$$

et l'on voit que, en prenant la constante égale à l'unité, on satisfera à la condition que l'arc s soit, comme on l'a admis, la variable indépendante.

Cela posé, et après avoir écrit les équations précédentes de cette manière,

$$\beta(xy' - x'y) = \gamma z' + \alpha, \qquad \beta(xy'' - x''y) = \gamma z'',$$

j'en déduis

$$\beta[(xy' - x'y)z'' - (xy'' - x''y)z'] = \alpha z'';$$

mais le premier membre, étant écrit ainsi,

$$\beta[(y'z'' - y''z')x + (z'x'' - z''x')y],$$

se réduit à

$$\beta[(\alpha x' + \beta y)x + (\alpha y' - \beta x)y] = \alpha\beta(xx' + yy'),$$

de sorte que nous avons

$$\beta(xx' + yy') = z'',$$

puis par l'intégration, en désignant par δ une constante arbitraire,

$$\beta(x^2 + y^2) = 2(z' - \delta).$$

Soit maintenant $z' = \zeta$; nous remplacerons le système des équations à intégrer par celles-ci,

$$\beta(x^2+y^2) = 2(\zeta - \delta),$$
$$\beta(xx'+yy') = \zeta',$$
$$x'^2+y'^2 = 1 - \zeta^2,$$
$$\beta(xy'-x'y) = \gamma\zeta + \alpha.$$

Or l'identité

$$(x^2+y^2)(x'^2+y'^2) = (xx'+yy')^2 + (xy'-x'y)^2$$

donne en premier lieu

$$\zeta'^2 = 2\beta(\zeta-\delta)(1-\zeta^2) - (\gamma\zeta+\alpha)^2,$$

et l'on trouve ensuite facilement

$$\frac{x'+iy'}{x+iy} = \frac{\zeta'+i(\gamma\zeta+\alpha)}{2(\zeta-\delta)};$$

ces résultats obtenus, les expressions des coordonnées en fonction de l'arc s'en déduisent comme il suit.

Soient a, b, c les racines de l'équation

$$2\beta(\zeta-\delta)(1-\zeta^2) - (\gamma\zeta+\alpha)^2 = 0,$$

de sorte qu'on ait

$$\zeta'^2 = -2\beta(\zeta-a)(\zeta-b)(\zeta-c).$$

Désignons aussi par ζ_0 une des valeurs de ζ, qu'on doit, d'après la condition $x'^2+y'^2+\zeta^2 = 1$, supposer comprise entre $+1$ et -1. Le facteur β étant positif, comme nous l'avons dit, le polynome $2\beta(\zeta-a)(\zeta-b)(\zeta-c)$ sera négatif en faisant $\zeta = \zeta_0$. Mais il prend pour $\zeta = +1$ et $\zeta = -1$ les valeurs positives $(\gamma+\alpha)^2$ et $(\gamma-\alpha)^2$; par conséquent, les racines a, b, c sont réelles, et, si on les suppose rangées par ordre décroissant de grandeur, a sera compris entre $+1$ et ζ_0, b entre ζ_0 et -1, et c entre -1 et $-\infty$. Remarquons aussi que, ayant pour $z = \zeta$ un résultat positif, il est nécessaire que cette constante δ soit supérieure à a ou comprise entre b et c. Mais la relation $x^2+y^2 = 2(\zeta-\delta)$ montre que la seconde hypothèse est seule possible, car dans la première x^2+y^2 serait négatif. Cela posé, puisque ζ a pour limites a et b, nous ferons

$$\zeta = a - (a-b)U^2;$$

soient encore

$$k^2 = \frac{a-b}{a-c}, \qquad k'^2 = \frac{b-c}{a-c};$$

on aura

$$(\zeta - a)(\zeta - b)(\zeta - c) = -(a-b)^2(a-c)\,U^2(1-U^2)(1-k^2U^2),$$

et de l'équation

$$\zeta'^2 = -2\beta(\zeta - a)(\zeta - b)(\zeta - b)$$

nous conclurons

$$U'^2 = \frac{(a-c)\beta}{2}(1-U^2)(1-k^2U^2).$$

Faisons donc $n = \sqrt{\frac{(a-c)\beta}{2}}$; puis, en désignant par s_0 une constante, $u = n(s-s_0)$, on aura

$$U = \operatorname{sn} u, \qquad \zeta = a - (a-b)\operatorname{sn}^2 u,$$

et par conséquent

$$n(z-z_0) = \int_0^u \zeta\, du = \left[a - (a-c)\frac{J}{K}\right]u + (a-c)\frac{\Theta'(u)}{\Theta(u)},$$

z_0 étant la valeur arbitraire de z pour $u = 0$.

Considérons, pour obtenir la valeur de $x+iy$, l'expression $\frac{\zeta' + i(\gamma\zeta + \alpha)}{2(\zeta - \delta)}$, qui en représente la dérivée logarithmique. C'est une fonction doublement périodique de la variable u, ayant pour pôles d'une part $u = iK'$ et de l'autre les racines de l'équation $\zeta - \delta = 0$. Mais des deux solutions $u = \pm\omega$ qu'on en tire une seule est en effet un pôle, comme le montre la relation

$$\zeta'^2 + (\gamma\zeta + \alpha)^2 = 2\beta(\zeta - \delta)(1-\zeta^2),$$

d'où l'on déduit

$$\zeta' = \pm i(\gamma\delta + \alpha),$$

en faisant $\zeta = \delta$. Il en résulte que, si nous prenons pour $u = \omega$ la valeur $\zeta' = +i(\gamma\delta + \alpha)$, on aura

$$\zeta' = -i(\gamma\delta + \alpha) \qquad \text{pour} \qquad u = -\omega,$$

la dérivée changeant de signe avec la variable. En même temps on voit que le résidu de la fonction qui correspond au pôle $u = \omega$ est $+n$; le résidu relatif à l'autre pôle $u = iK'$ est donc $-n$, et, par la décomposition en éléments simples, nous obtenons

$$\frac{\zeta' + i(\gamma\zeta + \alpha)}{2(\zeta - \delta)} = n\left[\lambda - \frac{\Theta'(u)}{\Theta(u)} + \frac{H'(u-\omega)}{H(u-\omega)}\right].$$

La constante λ se détermine en supposant $u = 0$ ou $\zeta = a$, ce qui donne immédiatement

$$\lambda = \frac{in(a\gamma + \alpha)}{a - \delta} + \frac{H'(\omega)}{H(\omega)},$$

et l'expression cherchée se conclut de la relation

$$D_s \log(x + iy) = n D_u \log(x + iy) = n\left[\lambda - \frac{\Theta'(u)}{\Theta(u)} + \frac{H'(u-\omega)}{H(u-\omega)}\right]$$

au moyen d'une fonction doublement périodique de seconde espèce

$$x + iy = (x_0 + iy_0)\frac{\Theta(0)\,H(\omega - u)\,e^{\lambda u}}{\Theta(u)\,H(\omega)}.$$

Dans cette formule, x_0 et y_0 désignent les valeurs que prennent x et y pour $u = 0$; elles sont liées par l'équation

$$\beta(x_0^2 + y_0^2) = 2(a - \delta)$$

et ne contiennent, par conséquent, qu'une seule indéterminée. En y joignant les constantes z_0, s_0 et δ, on a donc quatre quantités arbitraires dans l'expression générale des coordonnées de l'élastique. A l'égard de δ, nous avons vu que sa valeur doit rester comprise entre b et c ; de là résulte que $\text{sn}^2\omega$, déterminé par la formule $\text{sn}^2\omega = \frac{a - \delta}{a - b}$, a pour limites 1 et $\frac{1}{k^2}$. On peut écrire par suite $\omega = K + i\upsilon$, υ étant réel, et poser

$$x + iy = (x_0 + iy_0)\frac{\Theta(0)\,H_1(i\upsilon - u)\,e^{\lambda u}}{\Theta(u)\,H_1(i\upsilon)}.$$

Changeons i en $-i$, ce qui change λ en $-\lambda$; on aura

$$x - iy = (x_0 - iy_0)\frac{\Theta(0)\,H_1(i\upsilon + u)\,e^{-\lambda u}}{\Theta(u)\,H_1(i\upsilon)},$$

et ces relations, jointes à celle qui a été précédemment obtenue, à savoir

$$n(z-z_0)=\left[a-(a-c)\frac{J}{K}\right]u+(a-c)\frac{\Theta'(u)}{\Theta(u)},$$

donnent la solution complète de la question proposée.

XXXVI.

Les expressions des rayons de courbure et de torsion, R et r, se calculent facilement, sans qu'il soit besoin d'employer les valeurs des coordonnées, et comme conséquence immédiate des équations différentielles

$$y'z''-y''z'=\alpha x'+\beta y,$$
$$z'x''-z''x'=\alpha y'-\beta x,$$
$$x'y''-x''y'=\alpha z'+\gamma.$$

On trouve, en effet, après les réductions qui s'offrent d'elles-mêmes,

$$\begin{aligned}\frac{1}{R^2}&=(\alpha x'+\beta y)^2+(\alpha y'-\beta x)^2+(\alpha z'+\gamma)^2\\&=2\beta(\zeta-\delta)+\gamma^2-\alpha^2\\&=2\beta[a-\delta-(a-b)\,\mathrm{sn}^2 u]+\gamma^2-\alpha^2,\end{aligned}$$

puis

$$\begin{vmatrix}x' & x'' & x'''\\ y' & y'' & y'''\\ z' & z'' & z'''\end{vmatrix}=\alpha\beta(\zeta-\delta)-\beta(\alpha\delta+\gamma)+\alpha(\gamma^2-\alpha^2),$$

et, par conséquent,

$$\frac{1}{r}=\frac{\alpha\beta(\zeta-\delta)-\beta(\alpha\delta+\gamma)+\alpha(\gamma^2-\alpha^2)}{2\beta(\zeta-\delta)+\gamma^2-\alpha^2}.$$

Cette expression du rayon de torsion conduit naturellement à envisager le cas particulier où elle devient indépendante de ζ et a la valeur constante $r=\frac{2}{\alpha}$. La condition à remplir à cet effet étant

$$2\beta(\alpha\delta+\gamma)-\alpha(\gamma^2-\alpha^2)=0,$$

je remarque que, en remplaçant l'indéterminée ζ par $-\frac{\gamma}{\alpha}$, dans l'égalité

$$2\beta(\zeta-\delta)(1-\zeta^2)-(\gamma\zeta+\alpha)^2=-2\beta(\zeta-a)(\zeta-b)(\zeta-c),$$

le résultat peut s'écrire ainsi

$$(\gamma^2-\alpha^2)[2\beta(\alpha\delta+\gamma)-\alpha(\gamma^2-\alpha^2)] = 2\beta(\gamma+a\alpha)(\gamma+b\alpha)(\gamma+c\alpha),$$

par où l'on voit que l'une des racines a, b, c est alors égale à $-\frac{\gamma}{\alpha}$. Mais notre condition donne

$$\delta+\frac{\alpha^2-\gamma^2}{2\beta} = -\frac{\gamma}{\alpha};$$

ainsi l'on doit poser

$$\delta+\frac{\alpha^2-\gamma^2}{2\beta} = a,\ b \text{ ou } c,$$

et voici la conséquence remarquable qui résulte de là. Nous avons trouvé tout à l'heure

$$\frac{1}{R^2} = 2\beta[a-\delta-(a-b)\operatorname{sn}^2 u]+\gamma^2-\alpha^2,$$

ou plutôt

$$\frac{1}{R^2} = 2\beta\left(a-\delta-\frac{\alpha^2-\gamma^2}{2\beta}\right)-2\beta(a-b)\operatorname{sn}^2 u;$$

or cette expression montre que le premier cas, où l'on suppose

$$\delta+\frac{\alpha^2-\gamma^2}{2\beta} = a,$$

doit être rejeté, comme conduisant à une valeur négative pour R^2. Mais les deux autres peuvent avoir lieu et donnent successivement, en employant la valeur du module $k^2 = \frac{a-b}{a-c}$,

$$\frac{1}{R^2} = 2\beta(a-b)\operatorname{cn}^2 u,$$

$$\frac{1}{R^2} = 2\beta(a-c)\operatorname{dn}^2 u.$$

Le rayon de courbure devient donc, comme les coordonnées elles-mêmes, une fonction uniforme de l'arc, en même temps que le rayon de torsion prend une valeur constante. Ces circonstances remarquables me semblent appeler l'attention sur la courbe qui les présente; mais ce serait trop m'étendre d'essayer d'en suivre les conséquences, et je reviens à mon objet principal, en donnant une dernière remarque sur la formation des équations linéaires d'ordre quelconque dont les intégrales sont des fonctions doublement périodiques de seconde espèce, unipolaires ([1]).

XXXVII.

Soit, comme au paragraphe XXX (p. 347),

$$f(u) = \frac{H'(o)\Theta(u+\omega)}{H(u)\Theta(\omega)} e^{\left[\lambda - \frac{\Theta'(\omega)}{\Theta(\omega)}\right]u};$$

désignons par $f_i(u)$ ce que devient cette fonction quand on y remplace les quantités ω, λ par ω_i, λ_i; nommons enfin μ_i et μ'_i ses multiplicateurs. Si l'on pose

$$y = C_1 f_1(u) + C_2 f_2(u) + \ldots + C_n f_n(u),$$

l'équation différentielle linéaire d'ordre n, admettant cette expression analytique pour intégrale, se présente sous la forme suivante :

$$\begin{vmatrix} y & f_1(u) & f_2(u) & \ldots & f_n(u) \\ y' & f'_u(u) & f'_2(u) & \ldots & f'_n(u) \\ \ldots & \ldots\ldots & \ldots\ldots & \ldots & \ldots\ldots \\ y^n & f_1^n(u) & f_2^n(u) & \ldots & f_n^n(u) \end{vmatrix} = 0.$$

D'après cela, j'observe que, le déterminant étant mis sous la forme

$$\Phi_0(u)y^n + \Phi_1(u)y^{n-1} + \ldots + \Phi_n(u)y,$$

les coefficients $\Phi_i(u)$ sont des fonctions de seconde espèce, aux multiplicateurs $\mu_1\,\mu_2 \ldots \mu_n$, $\mu'_1\,\mu'_2 \ldots \mu'_n$, ayant le pôle $u = 0$, avec l'ordre de multiplicité $n+1$, sauf le premier $\Phi_0(u)$, où l'ordre de multiplicité est n. C'est ce qu'on voit immédiatement en retranchant la seconde colonne du déterminant de celles qui suivent, attendu que les différences $f_2(u) - f_1(u)$, $f_3(u) - f_1(u)$, ..., ainsi que leurs dérivées, ne sont plus infinies pour $u = 0$. Nous pouvons donc poser, comme je l'ai fait voir ailleurs (*Sur l'inté-*

([1]) On doit à M. de Saint-Venant un travail important sur les flexions considérables des verges élastiques, que l'éminent géomètre a publié dans le *Journal de Mathématiques* de M. Liouville (t. IX, 1844), et auquel je dois renvoyer; je citerai aussi, sur la même question, un Mémoire récemment publié par M. Adolphe Steen, sous le titre : *De elastike Kurve, og dens anvendelse i böjningstheorien*, Copenhague, 1879.

gration de l'équation différentielle de Lamé, dans le *Journal de M. Borchardt*, t. LXXXIX, p. 10),

$$\Phi_0(u) = \frac{G_0 H(u-a_1) H(u-a_2) \ldots H(u-a_n) e^{g_0 u}}{H^n(u)},$$

les quantités G_0, g_0, a_i étant des constantes, puis d'une manière semblable pour les coefficients suivants,

$$\Phi_i(u) = \frac{G_i H(u-a_1^i) H(u-a_2^i) \ldots H(u-a_{n+1}^i) e^{g_i u}}{H^{n+1}(u)}.$$

Il en résulte qu'en décomposant en éléments simples les quotients $\frac{\Phi_i(u)}{\Phi_0(u)}$, qui sont des fonctions doublement périodiques de première espèce, on aura

$$\frac{\Phi_i(u)}{\Phi_0(u)} = \text{const.} + \frac{A_1 H'(u-a_1)}{H(u-a_1)} + \frac{A_2 H'(u-a_2)}{H(u-a_2)} + \ldots + \frac{A_n H'(u-a_n)}{H(u-a_n)} + \frac{A_0 H'(u)}{H(u)},$$

avec la condition

$$A_0 = -(A_1 + A_2 + \ldots + A_n).$$

C'est donc la généralisation du résultat trouvé au paragraphe XXVIII (p. 343) pour les équations du second ordre, et il est clair qu'on peut encore écrire

$$\frac{\Phi_i(u)}{\Phi_0(a)} = \text{const.} + \frac{A_1 \operatorname{sn} a_1}{\operatorname{sn} u \operatorname{sn}(u-a_1)} + \frac{A_2 \operatorname{sn} a_2}{\operatorname{sn} u \operatorname{sn}(u-a_2)} + \ldots + \frac{A_n \operatorname{sn} a_n}{\operatorname{sn} u \operatorname{sn}(u-a_n)}.$$

La détermination des constantes A_1, A_2, ..., qui entrent dans ces expressions des coefficients de l'équation linéaire, par la condition que les solutions soient des fonctions uniformes, est une question difficile et importante, que je n'ai pas abordée au delà du cas le plus simple de $n=2$; je me borne à donner la forme analytique générale de ces coefficients et à observer que, chacune des fonctions $f_i(u)$ contenant deux arbitraires, l'équation différentielle en renferme en tout $2n$. Les remarques que j'ai à présenter ont un autre objet, comme on va le voir. Je me suis attaché à cette circonstance que présente l'équation de Lamé, $y'' = (2k^2 \operatorname{sn}^2 u + h)y$, de ne contenir aucun point à apparence singulière ; elle m'a paru donner l'indication d'un type spécial, à distinguer et à caractériser, de manière qu'on ait ses analogues, si je puis dire, pour un ordre quelconque. Introduisons donc la condition $\Phi_0(u) = \text{const.}$ pour amener la disparition des points à apparence singulière $u = a_1$, $a_2, \ldots, a_n$, et posons, à cet effet, les $n+1$ conditions

$$a_1 = 0, \qquad a_2 = 0, \qquad \ldots, \qquad a_n = 0, \qquad g_0 = 0.$$

J'observerai, en premier lieu, que, dans ce type particulier d'équations, le nombre des arbitraires se trouve réduit à $2n-(n+1)$, c'est-à-dire à $n-1$. Je remarque ensuite que, les fonctions $\Phi_i(u)$ ayant toutes les mêmes multiplicateurs, ces multiplicateurs seront nécessairement l'unité, puisque l'une d'elles, $\Phi_0(u)$, est une constante. C'est dire qu'elles deviennent des fonctions doublement périodiques de première espèce, ayant pour pôle unique $u = 0$, avec l'ordre de multiplicité maximum $n+1$. Nous avons, par conséquent, l'expression

$$\Phi_i(u) = a + b\frac{1}{\operatorname{sn}^2 u} + c\, D_u \frac{1}{\operatorname{sn}^2 u} + \ldots + h\, D_u^{n-1} \frac{1}{\operatorname{sn}^2 u},$$

que la considération suivante va nous permettre encore de simplifier.

Et, d'abord, il résulte des expressions de $\Phi_0(u)$ et $\Phi_1(u)$, sous forme de déterminants, qu'on a, en général,

$$\Phi_1(u) = -D_u\, \Phi_0(u).$$

La condition $\Phi_0(u) = \text{const.}$ donne donc

$$\Phi_1(u) = 0,$$

et l'on voit que l'équation d'ordre n, analogue à celle de Lamé, a la forme

$$y^n + \Phi_2(u) y^{n-2} + \ldots + \Phi_n(u) y = 0.$$

Je ferai maintenant un nouveau pas en appliquant l'un des beaux théorèmes donnés par M. Fuchs, à savoir que le point singulier effectif $u = 0$ doit être, dans le coefficient $\Phi_i(u)$, un pôle dont l'ordre de multiplicité ne dépasse pas i, pour que l'intégrale de l'équation différentielle soit une fonction uniforme de la variable. On a, en conséquence, les expressions suivantes des coefficients, en remplacant u par $u + i\mathrm{K}'$, afin de nous rapprocher autant que possible de l'équation de Lamé,

$$\Phi_2(u) = \alpha_0 + \alpha_1 \operatorname{sn}^2 u,$$
$$\Phi_3(u) = \beta_0 + \beta_1 \operatorname{sn}^2 u + \beta_2 \mathrm{D}_u \operatorname{sn}^2 u,$$
$$\Phi_4(u) = \gamma_0 + \gamma_1 \operatorname{sn}^2 u + \gamma_2 \mathrm{D}_u \operatorname{sn}^2 u + \gamma_3 \mathrm{D}_u^2 \operatorname{sn}^2 u,$$
$$\ldots\ldots\ldots\ldots\ldots\ldots\ldots\ldots\ldots\ldots$$

La question de déterminer les constantes α_0, α_1, ..., de manière à réaliser complètement la condition que l'intégrale soit une fonction uniforme, offre, comme on le voit, beaucoup d'intérêt. Elle a fait le sujet des recherches d'un jeune géomètre du talent le plus distingué, M. Mittag-Leffler, professeur à l'Université d'Helsingfors, et je vais exposer les résultats auxquels il est parvenu.

XXXVIII.

Considérons en premier lieu les équations du troisième ordre, que nous savons devoir contenir deux constantes arbitraires. Elles présentent deux types distincts, et l'un d'eux, découvert antérieurement par M. Picard, a offert le premier et mémorable exemple de l'intégration au moyen des fonctions elliptiques d'une équation différentielle d'ordre supérieur au second ([1]). C'est l'équation

$$y''' + (\alpha - 6k^2 \operatorname{sn}^2 u)y' + \beta y = 0,$$

a là quelle on satisfait de la manière suivante.

Soit

$$y = \frac{\mathrm{H}(u+\omega)}{\Theta(u)} e^{\left[\lambda - \frac{\Theta'(\omega)}{\Theta(\omega)}\right]},$$

et posons, comme au paragraphe V,

$$\Omega\ = k^2 \operatorname{sn}^2\omega - \frac{1+k^2}{3},$$
$$\Omega_1 = k^2 \operatorname{sn}\omega \operatorname{cn}\omega \operatorname{dn}\omega.$$
$$\Omega_2 = k^2 \operatorname{sn}^4\omega - \frac{2(k^2+k^4)}{3}\operatorname{sn}^2\omega - \frac{7 - 22k^2 + 7k^4}{45},$$
$$\ldots\ldots\ldots\ldots\ldots\ldots\ldots\ldots\ldots\ldots,$$

([1]) *Sur une classe d'équations différentielles* (*Comptes rendus*, t. XC, p. 128).

de sorte qu'on ait, pour $u = i\mathrm{K}' + \varepsilon$,

$$y = \mathrm{C}\, e^{\lambda\varepsilon}\left(\frac{1}{\varepsilon} - \frac{1}{2}\Omega\varepsilon - \frac{1}{3}\Omega_1\varepsilon^2 - \frac{1}{8}\Omega_2\varepsilon^3 - \ldots\right),$$

C désignant un facteur constant. Les quantités ω et λ se déterminent au moyen des relations

$$3(\lambda^2 - \Omega) + \alpha - 2(1 + k^2) = 0,$$
$$2\lambda^3 - 6\lambda\Omega - 4\Omega_1 - \beta = 0,$$

et il a été démontré par M. Picard qu'elles admettent trois systèmes de solutions, d'où se tirent trois intégrales particulières et par conséquent l'intégrale complète de l'équation considérée.

Le second type qu'il faut joindre au précédent pour avoir, dans le troisième ordre, toutes les équations analogues à celle de Lamé est

$$y''' + (\alpha - 3k^2\,\mathrm{sn}^2 u)y' + (\beta + \gamma k^2\,\mathrm{sn}^2 u - 3k^2\,\mathrm{sn}\, u\,\mathrm{cn}\, u\,\mathrm{dn}\, u)y = 0,$$

avec la condition

$$3(\alpha - 1 - k^2) + \gamma^2 = 0.$$

Il présente cette circonstance bien remarquable que, dans les trois intégrales particulières, la constante λ a la même valeur, à savoir : $\lambda = -\frac{\gamma}{3}$. Cela étant, ω s'obtient par la relation

$$2\lambda^3 - \lambda(3\Omega - 1 - k^2) - \Omega_1 - \beta = 0.$$

En passant maintenant au quatrième ordre, on obtient quatre équations A, B, C, D avec trois constantes arbitraires, et pour chacune d'elles les constantes ω et λ se déterminent ainsi que je vais l'indiquer.

A.

$$y^{\text{IV}} + (\alpha - 12k^2\,\mathrm{sn}^2 u)y'' + \beta y' + (\gamma + \delta k^2\,\mathrm{sn}^2 u)y = 0,$$

avec la condition

$$2\alpha - 8(1 + k^2) + \delta = 0.$$

Les relations entre ω et λ sont

$$4\lambda^3 - \lambda(12\Omega + \delta) - 8\Omega_1 + \beta = 0,$$
$$90\lambda^4 - (540\Omega + 15\delta)\lambda^2 - 720\Omega_1\lambda - 270\Omega_2 + 15\delta\Omega$$
$$- 30\gamma - 10\delta(1 + k^2) + 48(1 - k^2 + k^4) = 0.$$

B.

$$y^{\text{IV}} + (\alpha - 8k^2 \operatorname{sn}^2 u)y'' + (\beta + \gamma k^2 \operatorname{sn}^2 u - 8k^2 \operatorname{sn} u \operatorname{cn} u \operatorname{dn} u)y' + (\delta + \varepsilon k^2 \operatorname{sn}^2 u - \gamma k^2 \operatorname{sn} u \operatorname{cn} u \operatorname{dn} u)y = 0,$$

sous les conditions

$$4\varepsilon = \gamma^2, \qquad \gamma^3 + 8\gamma(\alpha - 2 - 2k^2) + 16\beta = 0.$$

On a ensuite

$$48(\lambda^2 - \Omega) + 12\lambda\gamma + 24\alpha + 3\gamma^2 - 64(1 + k^2) = 0,$$

$$120\lambda^4 - 720\lambda^2\Omega - 960\lambda\Omega_1 - 360\Omega_2 - 60(\lambda^3 - 3\lambda\Omega - 2\Omega_1)\gamma - 15(\lambda^2 - \Omega)\gamma^2 - 120\delta - 10(1 + k^2)\gamma^2 + 64(1 - k^2 + k^4) = 0.$$

C.

$$y^{\text{IV}} + (\alpha - 6k^2 \operatorname{sn}^2 u)y'' + (\beta - 12k^2 \operatorname{sn} u \operatorname{cn} u \operatorname{dn} u)y' + (\gamma + \delta k^2 \operatorname{sn}^2 u)y = 0,$$

avec la relation

$$12\gamma - \delta^2 - 2\delta[\alpha - 4(1 + k^2)] = 0.$$

Les équations en ω et λ sont

$$6(\lambda^2 - \Omega) + 2\alpha + \delta - 4(1 + k^2) = 0,$$

$$2\lambda^3 - \lambda(6\Omega - \delta) - 4\Omega_1 - \beta = 0.$$

D.

$$y^{\text{IV}} + (\alpha - 4k^2 \operatorname{sn}^2 u)y'' + (\beta + \gamma k^2 \operatorname{sn}^2 u - 8k^2 \operatorname{sn} u \operatorname{cn} u \operatorname{dn} u)y' + (\delta + \varepsilon k^2 \operatorname{sn}^2 u - 8k^4 \operatorname{sn}^4 u + \gamma k^2 \operatorname{sn} u \operatorname{cn} u \operatorname{dn} u)y = 0.$$

On a entre les constantes les deux conditions

$$8\alpha - 32(1 + k^2) + 4\varepsilon + \gamma^2 = 0,$$

$$4\beta + \gamma[\varepsilon - 4(1 + k^2)] = 0.$$

Ce dernier cas présente un second exemple de la circonstance remarquable qui s'est offerte dans l'une des équations du troisième ordre, la quantité λ ayant dans toutes les intégrales particulières la même valeur, à savoir $\lambda = -\frac{\gamma}{4}$. L'équation en ω est ensuite

$$90\lambda^4 - 15(\lambda^2 - \Omega)[3\varepsilon - 8(1 + k^2)] - 360\lambda^2\Omega - 360\lambda\Omega_1 - 90\Omega_2 - 90\delta - 30\varepsilon(1 + k^2) + 16(11 + 4k^2 + 11k^4) = 0.$$

XXXIX.

Les recherches dont je viens d'énoncer succinctement les premiers résultats ont été étendues par M. Mittag-Leffler aux équations linéaires d'ordre quelconque, dans un travail qui paraîtra prochainement. (*Annali di Mathematica*, II, t. XI, 1882, p. 65.) Il sera ainsi établi que la théorie des fonctions elliptiques conduit aux premiers types généraux, après celui des équations à coefficients constants, dont la solution est connue sous forme explicite. L'équation de Lamé

$$D_x^2 y = [n(n+1)k^2 \operatorname{sn}^2 x + h]y,$$

ayant été l'origine et le point de départ de ces recherches, doit d'autant plus appeler notre attention, et j'y reviens pour aborder un second cas, celui de $n = 2$, en me proposant d'en faire l'application à la théorie du pendule. Je traiterai ce cas par une méthode spéciale que j'expose avant d'arriver au cas général où le nombre n est quelconque, afin de réunir divers points de vue sous lesquels peut être traitée la même question. Reprenons à cet effet l'équation considérée au paragraphe XXX (p. 347) et dont nous avons obtenu la solution complète, à savoir

$$D_u^2 y - \left[\frac{\operatorname{sn} a}{\operatorname{sn} u \operatorname{sn}(u-a)} + \frac{\operatorname{sn} b}{\operatorname{sn} u \operatorname{sn}(u-b)}\right] D_u y$$
$$+ \left[\frac{A \operatorname{sn} a}{\operatorname{sn} u \operatorname{sn}(u-a)} + \frac{B \operatorname{sn} b}{\operatorname{sn} u \operatorname{sn}(u-b)} + \frac{1}{\operatorname{sn}^2(a-b)} - C^2\right] y = 0.$$

Soit $u = x + iK'$, et changeons aussi a et b en $a + iK'$ et $b + iK'$, de sorte que les constantes A et B deviennent

$$A = \frac{\operatorname{sn} a}{\operatorname{sn} b \operatorname{sn}(a-b)} + C,$$
$$B = \frac{\operatorname{sn} b}{\operatorname{sn} a \operatorname{sn}(b-a)} - C.$$

L'équation prendra la forme suivante,

$$D_x^2 y - \left[\frac{\operatorname{sn} x}{\operatorname{sn} a \operatorname{sn}(x-a)} + \frac{\operatorname{sn} x}{\operatorname{sn} b \operatorname{sn}(x-b)}\right] D_x y$$
$$- \left[\frac{A \operatorname{sn} x}{\operatorname{sn} a \operatorname{sn}(x-a)} + \frac{B \operatorname{sn} x}{\operatorname{sn} b \operatorname{sn}(x-b)} + \frac{1}{\operatorname{sn}^2(a-b)} - C^2\right] y = 0,$$

et aura pour solution la fonction de seconde espèce

$$y = \frac{H(x+\omega)}{\Theta(x)} e^{\left[\lambda - \frac{\Theta'(\omega)}{\Theta(\omega)}\right]x},$$

les quantités ω et λ étant déterminées maintenant par les conditions

$$\lambda - C = \frac{\operatorname{sn} a}{\operatorname{sn} b \operatorname{sn}(a-b)} - \frac{\operatorname{cn} a \operatorname{dn} a}{\operatorname{sn} a} + \frac{\operatorname{sn} \omega}{\operatorname{sn} a \operatorname{sn}(a+\omega)},$$

$$\lambda + C = \frac{\operatorname{sn} b}{\operatorname{sn} a \operatorname{sn}(b-a)} - \frac{\operatorname{cn} b \operatorname{dn} b}{\operatorname{sn} b} + \frac{\operatorname{sn} \omega}{\operatorname{sn} b \operatorname{sn}(b+\omega)}.$$

Cela posé, considérons le cas où $b = -a$; on trouve aisément, en chassant le dénominateur $\operatorname{sn}^2 x - \operatorname{sn}^2 a$, l'équation

$$(\operatorname{sn}^2 x - \operatorname{sn}^2 a) D_x^2 y - 2 \operatorname{sn} x \operatorname{cn} x \operatorname{dn} x D_x y$$
$$+ \left[\frac{2A \operatorname{cn} a \operatorname{dn} a}{\operatorname{sn} a} \operatorname{sn}^2 x + \left(\frac{1}{\operatorname{sn}^2 2a} - C^2\right)(\operatorname{sn}^2 x - \operatorname{sn}^2 a)\right] y = 0.$$

Particularisons encore davantage et, observant qu'on a

$$A = -\frac{1}{\operatorname{sn} 2a} + C,$$

faisons disparaître le terme en $\operatorname{sn}^2 x$ dans le coefficient de y, en posant

$$\frac{2 \operatorname{cn} a \operatorname{dn} a}{\operatorname{sn} a} = \frac{1}{\operatorname{sn} 2a} + C.$$

Ce coefficient se réduisant à une constante, l'équation précédente devient

$$(\operatorname{sn}^2 x - \operatorname{sn}^2 a) D_x^2 y - 2 \operatorname{sn} x \operatorname{cn} x \operatorname{dn} x D_x y$$
$$+ 2[3k^2 \operatorname{sn}^4 a - 2(1+k^2)\operatorname{sn}^2 a + 1] y = 0.$$

Soit donc, pour un moment,

$$\Phi(x) = \operatorname{sn}^2 x - \operatorname{sn}^2 a;$$

on voit qu'on peut l'écrire ainsi

$$\Phi(x) D_x^2 y - \Phi'(x) D_x y + \Phi''(a) y = 0,$$

et l'on en conclut, par la différentiation,

$$\Phi(x) D_x^3 y - [\Phi''(x) - \Phi''(a)] D_x y = 0.$$

Ce résultat remarquable donne, en remplaçant $D_x y$ par z,

$$D_x^2 z = \left[\frac{\Phi''(x) - \Phi''(a)}{\Phi(x)}\right] z = (6k^2 \operatorname{sn}^2 x + 6k^2 \operatorname{sn}^2 a - 4 - 4k^2) z :$$

c'est précisément l'équation de Lamé dans le cas de $n = 2$, la constante qui y figure étant $h = 6k^2 \operatorname{sn}^2 a - 4 - 4k^2$. Nous n'avons donc plus, pour parvenir à notre but, qu'à former l'intégrale de l'équation en y, c'est-à-dire à déterminer les quantités ω et λ au moyen des équations rappelées plus haut. Introduisons, à cet effet, les conditions $b = -a$, $C = \frac{2 \operatorname{cn} a \operatorname{dn} a}{\operatorname{sn} a} - \frac{1}{\operatorname{sn} 2a}$; on en tirera successivement, en les retranchant et les ajoutant,

$$\frac{\operatorname{sn}^2 \omega}{\operatorname{sn}^2 a - \operatorname{sn}^2 \omega} = \frac{\operatorname{sn}^2 a (2k^2 \operatorname{sn}^2 a - 1 - k^2)}{\operatorname{cn}^2 a \operatorname{dn}^2 a},$$

$$\lambda = \frac{\operatorname{sn} \omega \operatorname{cn} \omega \operatorname{dn} \omega}{\operatorname{sn}^2 a - \operatorname{sn}^2 \omega}.$$

De là nous concluons d'abord, pour ω, les expressions suivantes,

$$\operatorname{sn}^2 \omega = \frac{\operatorname{sn}^4 a (2k^2 \operatorname{sn}^2 a - 1 - k^2)}{3k^2 \operatorname{sn}^4 a - 2(1 + k^2) \operatorname{sn}^2 a + 1},$$

$$\operatorname{cn}^2 \omega = -\frac{\operatorname{cn}^4 a (2k^2 \operatorname{sn}^2 a - 1)}{3k^2 \operatorname{sn}^4 a - 2(1 + k^2) \operatorname{sn}^2 a + 1},$$

$$\operatorname{dn}^2 \omega = -\frac{\operatorname{dn}^4 a (2 \operatorname{sn}^2 a - 1)}{3k^2 \operatorname{sn}^4 a - 2(1 + k^2) \operatorname{sn}^2 a + 1}.$$

On a ensuite

$$\lambda^2 = \frac{\operatorname{sn}^2 \omega \operatorname{cn}^2 \omega \operatorname{dn}^2 \omega}{(\operatorname{sn}^2 a - \operatorname{sn}^2 \omega)^2} = \frac{(2k^2 \operatorname{sn}^2 a - 1 - k^2)(2k^2 \operatorname{sn}^2 a - 1)(2 \operatorname{sn}^2 a - 1)}{3k^2 \operatorname{sn}^4 a - 2(1 + k^2) \operatorname{sn}^2 a + 1},$$

et l'on voit que les constantes $\operatorname{sn}^2 \omega$ et λ^2 sont des fonctions rationnelles de $\operatorname{sn}^2 a$ ou de h. Nous remarquerons en même temps que $\operatorname{sn} \omega$ et, par conséquent, ω ayant deux déterminations égales et de signes contraires, le signe de λ est donné par celui de ω, en vertu de la relation $\lambda = \frac{\operatorname{sn} \omega \operatorname{cn} \omega \operatorname{dn} \omega}{\operatorname{sn}^2 a - \operatorname{sn}^2 \omega}$. Aucune ambiguïté ne s'offre donc dans la formule

$$y = C \frac{H(x + \omega)}{\Theta(x)} e^{\left[\lambda - \frac{\Theta'(\omega)}{\Theta(\omega)}\right] x} + C' \frac{H(x + \omega)}{\Theta(x)} e^{-\left[\lambda - \frac{\Theta'(\omega)}{\Theta(\omega)}\right] x},$$

et l'on en conclut, pour l'intégrale de l'équation de Lamé,

$$D_x^2 y = (6k^2 \operatorname{sn}^2 x + 6k^2 \operatorname{sn}^2 a - 4 - 4k^2)y,$$

l'expression

$$y = \mathrm{C}D_x \frac{\mathrm{H}(x+\omega)}{\Theta(x)} e^{\left[\lambda - \frac{\Theta'(\omega)}{\Theta(\omega)}\right]x} + \mathrm{C}' D_x \frac{\mathrm{H}(x-\omega)}{\Theta(x)} e^{-\left[\lambda - \frac{\Theta'(\omega)}{\Theta(\omega)}\right]x}.$$

Voici les remarques auxquelles elle donne lieu.

XL.

Nous allons supposer nulle ou infinie la quantité λ, en nous proposant d'étudier les circonstances qu'offre alors la solution de l'équation différentielle.

Et d'abord, on voit, par l'expression de λ^2, que le premier cas a lieu en posant les conditions

$$2k^2 \operatorname{sn}^2 a - 1 - k^2 = 0,$$
$$2k^2 \operatorname{sn}^2 a - 1 = 0,$$
$$2 \operatorname{sn}^2 a - 1 = 0,$$

qui donnent successivement $\operatorname{sn}\omega = 0$, $\operatorname{cn}\omega = 0$, $\operatorname{dn}\omega = 0$. Les valeurs de ω qui en résultent, à savoir, $\omega = 0$, $\omega = \mathrm{K}$, $\omega = \mathrm{K} + i\mathrm{K}'$, conduisent aux solutions considérées par Lamé, qui sont des fonctions doublement périodiques de la variable, avec la périodicité caractéristique de $\operatorname{sn} x$, $\operatorname{cn} x$, $\operatorname{dn} x$. Nous avons, en effet, pour $\omega = 0$ et $\omega = \mathrm{K}$: $y = D_x \operatorname{sn} x$, $y = D_x \operatorname{cn} x$. Il suffit ensuite d'employer les relations

$$\mathrm{H}(x + \mathrm{K} + i\mathrm{K}') = \Theta_1(x)\, e^{-\frac{i\pi}{4\mathrm{K}}(2x + i\mathrm{K}')},$$
$$\frac{\Theta'(\mathrm{K} + i\mathrm{K}')}{\Theta(\mathrm{K} + i\mathrm{K}')} = -\frac{i\pi}{2\mathrm{K}},$$

pour conclure de la valeur $\omega = \mathrm{K} + i\mathrm{K}'$ l'expression $y = D_x \operatorname{dn} x$.

Supposons maintenant λ infini, et soit à cet effet

$$3k^2 \operatorname{sn}^4 a - 2(1 + k^2) \operatorname{sn}^2 a + 1 = 0;$$

en désignant une solution de cette équation par $a = \alpha$, je ferai $a = \alpha + \eta$, $\omega = i\mathrm{K}' + \varepsilon$, les quantités η et ε étant infiniment petites. D'après la relation

$$\operatorname{sn}^2\omega = \frac{\operatorname{sn}^4 a(2k^2\operatorname{sn}^2 a - 1 - k^2)}{3k^2\operatorname{sn}^4 a - 2(1+k^2)\operatorname{sn}^2 a + 1},$$

on voit d'abord qu'on aura, en développant en série,

$$\varepsilon^2 = p\eta + q\eta^2 + \ldots,$$

p, q étant des constantes. Cela étant, nous développerons aussi λ suivant les puissances croissantes de ε, au moyen de l'expression

$$\lambda = \frac{\operatorname{sn}\omega\operatorname{cn}\omega\operatorname{dn}\omega}{\operatorname{sn}^2 a - \operatorname{sn}^2\omega} = \frac{\operatorname{cn}\varepsilon\operatorname{dn}\varepsilon}{\operatorname{sn}\varepsilon}\,\frac{1}{1 - k^2\operatorname{sn}^2(\alpha+\eta)\operatorname{sn}^2\varepsilon}.$$

Or, ayant

$$\frac{\operatorname{cn}\varepsilon\operatorname{dn}\varepsilon}{\operatorname{sn}\varepsilon} = \frac{1}{\varepsilon} - \frac{1+k^2}{3}\varepsilon + \ldots,$$

$$\frac{1}{1 - k^2\operatorname{sn}^2(\alpha+\eta)\operatorname{sn}^2\varepsilon} = 1 + k^2\operatorname{sn}^2\alpha\,\varepsilon^2 + \ldots,$$

on en conclut

$$\lambda = \frac{1}{\varepsilon} + \left(k^2\operatorname{sn}^2\alpha - \frac{1+k^2}{3}\right)\varepsilon + \ldots.$$

Employons maintenant l'équation

$$\frac{\Theta'(iK'+\varepsilon)}{\Theta(iK'+\varepsilon)} = \frac{H'(\varepsilon)}{H(\varepsilon)} - \frac{i\pi}{2K} = \frac{1}{\varepsilon} - \frac{i\pi}{2K} + \left(\frac{J}{K} - \frac{1+k^2}{3}\right)\varepsilon + \ldots;$$

nous obtenons cette expression, qui est finie, pour $\varepsilon = 0$, à savoir

$$\lambda - \frac{\Theta'(iK'+\varepsilon)}{\Theta(iK'+\varepsilon)} = \frac{i\pi}{2K} + \left(k^2\operatorname{sn}^2\alpha - \frac{J}{K}\right)\varepsilon + \ldots.$$

Enfin, je remplace, dans la solution de l'équation différentielle, la quantité $H(x+iK+\varepsilon)$ par

$$i\,\Theta(x+\varepsilon)\,e^{-\frac{i\pi}{4K}(2x+2\varepsilon+iK')};$$

il viendra ainsi

$$\frac{H(x+\omega)}{\Theta(x)}\,e^{\left[\lambda - \frac{\Theta'(\omega)}{\Theta(\omega)}\right]x} = i\,e^{\frac{\pi K'}{4K}}\,\frac{\Theta(x+\varepsilon)\,e^{g\varepsilon}}{\Theta(x)},$$

en faisant, pour abréger,

$$g = -\frac{i\pi}{2K} + \left(k^2\operatorname{sn}^2\alpha - \frac{J}{K}\right)x.$$

Or, en développant suivant les puissances de ε, on obtient, si l'on se borne aux deux premiers termes,

$$\frac{\Theta(x+\varepsilon)\,e^{g\varepsilon}}{\Theta(x)} = 1 + \left[\frac{\Theta'(x)}{\Theta(x)} + g\right]\varepsilon;$$

il suffira donc de remplacer la constante arbitraire C par $\frac{C}{\varepsilon}$, pour la limite cherchée, lorsqu'on pose $\varepsilon = 0$. Nous trouvons ainsi

$$\frac{1}{\varepsilon} D_x \left[\frac{\Theta(x+\varepsilon)\,e^{g\varepsilon}}{\Theta(x)}\right] = D_x\left[\frac{\Theta'(x)}{\Theta(x)} + g\right] = k^2(\operatorname{sn}^2\alpha - \operatorname{sn}^2 x),$$

où la constante $\operatorname{sn}^2\alpha$ est déterminée par l'équation

$$3k^2 \operatorname{sn}^4\alpha - 2(1+k^2)\operatorname{sn}^2\alpha + 1 = 0.$$

Ces deux solutions de l'équation différentielle, réunies à celles qui ont été obtenues précédemment, complètent l'ensemble des cinq solutions de Lamé, qui sont des fonctions doublement périodiques, ces deux dernières ayant, comme on voit, la périodicité de $\operatorname{sn}^2 x$.

XLI.

La théorie du pendule conique ou du mouvement d'un point pesant sur une sphère conduit à une application immédiate de l'équation qui vient de nous occuper. C'est M. Tissot qui a le premier traité cette question importante, par une analyse semblable à celle de Jacobi dans le problème de la rotation, et donné explicitement, en fonction du temps, les coordonnées du point mobile (*Thèse de Mécanique*, *Journal de M. Liouville*, t. XVII, p. 88). En suivant une autre marche, nous trouvons une autre forme analytique de la solution que j'ai indiquée, sans démonstration, dans une Lettre adressée à M. H. Gyldén et publiée dans le *Journal de Borchardt*, t. LXXXV, p. 246. Ces résultats s'établissent de la manière suivante.

Soient x, y, z les coordonnées rectangulaires d'un point pesant, assujetti à rester sur une sphère de rayon égal à l'unité ; les équations du mouvement, si l'on désigne par g la pesanteur et N la force accélératrice, seront [1]

$$\frac{d^2 x}{dt^2} + \mathrm{N} x = 0,$$

$$\frac{d^2 y}{dt^2} + \mathrm{N} y = 0.$$

$$\frac{d^2 z}{dt^2} + \mathrm{N} z = g,$$

$$x^2 + y^2 + z^2 = 1.$$

Elles donnent d'abord, comme on sait, en désignant par c et l des constantes,

$$\left(\frac{dx}{dt}\right)^2 + \left(\frac{dy}{dt}\right)^2 + \left(\frac{dz}{dt}\right)^2 = 2g(z+c),$$

$$y\frac{dx}{dt} - x\frac{dy}{dt} = l.$$

Cela étant, j'emploie la combinaison suivante,

$$(x+iy)\left(\frac{dx}{dt} - i\frac{dy}{dt}\right) = x\frac{dx}{dt} + y\frac{dy}{dt} + i\left(y\frac{dx}{dt} - x\frac{dy}{dt}\right) = -z\frac{dz}{dt} + il,$$

et je remarque que le carré du module du premier membre,

$$(x^2+y^2)\left[\left(\frac{dx}{dt}\right)^2 + \left(\frac{dy}{dt}\right)^2\right],$$

s'exprime par

$$(1-z^2)\left[2g(z+c) - \left(\frac{dz}{dt}\right)^2\right],$$

de sorte qu'on obtient, en l'égalant au carré du module du second membre,

$$(1-z^2)\left[2g(z+c) - \left(\frac{dz}{dt}\right)^2\right] = z^2\left(\frac{dz}{dt}\right)^2 + l^2,$$

ou bien

$$\left(\frac{dz}{dt}\right)^2 = 2g(z+c)(1-z^2) - l^2.$$

La variable z étant déterminée par cette relation, une première méthode pour obtenir les deux autres coordonnées consiste à di-

---

(1) *Traité de Mécanique* de Poisson, t. I, p. 386.

viser membre à membre les équations

$$(x+iy)\left(\frac{dx}{dt}-i\frac{dy}{dt}\right)=-z\frac{dz}{dt}+il,$$
$$x^2+y^2=1-z^2.$$

On obtient facilement ainsi les expressions qui conduisent aux résultats de M. Tissot, à savoir

$$x-iy=e^{-\int\frac{z\,dz-il\,dt}{1-z^2}},$$

puis, en changeant i en $-i$,

$$x+iy=e^{-\int\frac{z\,dz+il\,dt}{1-z^2}}.$$

Mais j'opérerai différemment; je déduis d'abord des équations différentielles, et les ajoutant après les avoir multipliées respectivement par x, y, z,

$$x\frac{d^2x}{dt^2}+y\frac{d^2y}{dt^2}+z\frac{d^2z}{dt^2}+\mathrm{N}=gz,$$

puis de l'équation de la sphère, différentiée deux fois,

$$x\frac{d^2x}{dt^2}+y\frac{d^2y}{dt^2}+z\frac{d^2z}{dt^2}=-\left(\frac{dx}{dt}\right)^2-\left(\frac{dy}{dt}\right)^2-\left(\frac{dz}{dt}\right)^2=-2g(z+c).$$

Nous avons donc

$$\mathrm{N}=g(3z+2c),$$

et, par conséquent,

$$\frac{d^2(x+iy)}{dt^2}=-g(3z+2c)(x+iy);$$

or on est ainsi amené à l'équation de Lamé, dans le cas de $n=2$, comme nous allons le voir.

Formons pour cela l'expression de z, et soit à cet effet

$$2g(z+c)(1-z^2)-l^2=-2g(z-\alpha)(z-\beta)(z-\gamma),$$

ce qui donne les relations suivantes :

$$\begin{aligned}\alpha+\beta+\gamma&=-c,\\ \alpha\beta+\beta\gamma+\gamma\alpha&=-1,\\ \alpha\beta\gamma&=c-\frac{l^2}{2g}.\end{aligned}$$

On sait que les racines α, β, γ sont nécessairement réelles, et qu'en les rangeant par ordre décroissant de grandeur α sera positive, β positive ou négative, et toutes deux moindres en valeur absolue que l'unité, tandis que γ sera négative et supérieure à l'unité en valeur absolue. Soient donc

$$k^2 = \frac{\alpha - \beta}{\alpha - \gamma},$$
$$u = n(t - t_0),$$
$$n = \sqrt{\frac{g(\alpha - \gamma)}{2}};$$

on aura

$$z = \alpha - (\alpha - \beta)\operatorname{sn}^2(u, k),$$

t_0 étant une constante et le coefficient n étant pris positivement. Introduisons maintenant la variable u dans l'équation du second ordre; elle deviendra

$$D_u^2(x + iy) = \frac{g}{n^2}[3(\alpha - \beta)\operatorname{sn}^2 u - 3\alpha - 2c](x + iy)$$

et, en simplifiant,

$$D_u^2(x + iy) = \left(6k^2\operatorname{sn}^2 u - 2\frac{\alpha - 2\beta - 2\gamma}{\alpha - \gamma}\right)(x + iy).$$

C'est donc l'équation de Lamé dont nous avons donné la solution complète au moyen de deux fonctions doublement périodiques de seconde espèce à multiplicateurs réciproques. Or une seule de ces fonctions doit figurer dans l'expression de $x + iy$, comme le montre la formule obtenue tout à l'heure

$$x + iy = e^{-\int \frac{z\,dz + il\,dt}{1 - z^2}};$$

par conséquent, nous pouvons immédiatement écrire

$$x + iy = \mathrm{C}D_u \frac{\mathrm{H}(u + \omega)}{\Theta(u)} e^{\left[\lambda - \frac{\Theta'(\omega)}{\Theta(\omega)}\right]u}$$

ou, sous une autre forme, en modifiant la constante arbitraire,

$$x + iy = \mathrm{A}D_u \frac{\mathrm{H}'(0)\,\mathrm{H}(u + \omega)}{\Theta(\omega)\,\Theta(u)} e^{\left[\lambda - \frac{\Theta'(\omega)}{\Theta(\omega)}\right]u};$$

maintenant il nous faut déterminer cette constante, ainsi que les quantités ω et λ.

XLII.

En posant la condition

$$6k^2 \operatorname{sn}^2 a - 4 - 4k^2 = -2\frac{\alpha - 2\beta - 2\gamma}{\alpha - \gamma},$$

et employant l'expression du module $k^2 = \frac{\alpha - \beta}{\alpha - \gamma}$, on trouve d'abord

$$\operatorname{sn}^2 a = \frac{\alpha}{\alpha - \beta}.$$

De là se tirent ensuite, après quelques réductions faciles où l'on fera usage de la relation

$$\alpha\beta + \beta\gamma + \gamma\alpha = -1,$$

les formules suivantes,

$$\operatorname{sn}^2 \omega = -\frac{\alpha^2(\beta + \gamma)}{\alpha - \beta},$$

$$\operatorname{cn}^2 \omega = +\frac{\beta^2(\alpha + \gamma)}{\alpha - \beta},$$

$$\operatorname{dn}^2 \omega = +\frac{\gamma^2(\alpha + \beta)}{\alpha - \gamma},$$

$$\lambda^2 = -\frac{(\alpha + \beta)(\beta + \gamma)(\gamma + \alpha)}{\alpha - \gamma}.$$

Cela étant, nous remarquerons en premier lieu que, d'après les limites entre lesquelles sont comprises les quantités α, β, γ, on obtient pour $\operatorname{sn}^2\omega$ et $\operatorname{dn}^2\omega$ des valeurs positives, tandis que $\operatorname{cn}^2\omega$ est négatif. Il en résulte que $\operatorname{sn}^2\omega$ est plus grand que l'unité et moindre que $\frac{1}{k^2}$, de sorte qu'on doit supposer

$$\omega = \pm K + i\upsilon,$$

υ étant réel et donné par ces expressions

$$\operatorname{sn}^2(\upsilon, k') = \frac{\beta^2(\gamma^2 - \alpha^2)}{\alpha^2(\gamma^2 - \beta^2)},$$

$$\operatorname{cn}^2(\upsilon, k') = \frac{\gamma^2(\beta^2 - \alpha^2)}{\alpha^2(\beta^2 - \gamma^2)},$$

$$\operatorname{dn}^2(\upsilon, k') = \frac{\beta - \alpha}{\alpha^2(\beta + \gamma)}.$$

J'observe ensuite qu'ayant $n^2 = \frac{g(\alpha-\gamma)}{2}$ nous pouvons écrire la valeur de λ^2 de cette manière,

$$\lambda^2 = -\frac{g(\alpha+\beta)(\beta+\gamma)(\gamma+\alpha)}{2n^2},$$

d'où l'on conclut facilement

$$\lambda^2 = -\frac{l^2}{4n^2}.$$

Les constantes ω et λ se trouvent ainsi déterminées, mais seulement au signe près, et deux autres relations sont encore nécessaires pour lever toute ambiguïté. La première résulte d'abord de la condition qui a été donnée pour la solution générale de l'équation de Lamé, à savoir

$$\lambda = \frac{\operatorname{sn}\omega \operatorname{cn}\omega \operatorname{dn}\omega}{\operatorname{sn}^2 a - \operatorname{sn}^2\omega},$$

et l'on en tire immédiatement

$$\lambda = -\frac{(\alpha-\beta)\operatorname{sn}\omega \operatorname{cn}\omega \operatorname{dn}\omega}{\alpha\beta\gamma}.$$

Nous obtiendrons tout à l'heure la seconde comme conséquence de l'équation considérée plus haut,

$$(x+iy)\left(\frac{dx}{dt} - i\frac{dy}{dt}\right) = -z\frac{dz}{dt} + il.$$

Mais voici d'abord la détermination de la constante A qui entre dans la formule

$$x+iy = \mathrm{AD}_u \frac{\mathrm{H}'(0)\,\mathrm{H}(u+\omega)}{\Theta(\omega)\,\Theta(u)} e^{\left[\lambda - \frac{\Theta'(\omega)}{\Theta(\omega)}\right]u}.$$

Soit, pour abréger,

$$\mathrm{F}(u) = \frac{\mathrm{H}'(0)\,\mathrm{H}(u+\omega)}{\Theta(\omega)\,\Theta(u)} e^{\left[\lambda - \frac{\Theta'(\omega)}{\Theta(\omega)}\right]u}.$$

Désignons par $\mathrm{F}_1(u)$ ce que devient cette fonction lorsqu'on change i en $-i$, et par A_1 la quantité conjuguée de A, de sorte qu'o

$$x+iy = \mathrm{A}\ \mathrm{F}'(u),$$
$$x-iy = \mathrm{A}_1 \mathrm{F}'_1(u),$$

et, par conséquent,

$$x^2+y^2=AA_1\,F'(u)\,F_1'(u).$$

Nous supposerons $u=0$, ce qui donne $z=\alpha$, dans l'équation $x^2+y^2+z^2=1$; il viendra ainsi

$$AA_1\,F'(0)\,F_1'(0)=1-\alpha^2,$$

ou encore, au moyen de la condition $\alpha\beta+\beta\gamma+\gamma\alpha=-1$,

$$AA_1\,F'(0)\,F_1'(0)=-(\alpha+\beta)(\alpha+\gamma).$$

J'emploie maintenant, pour y faire $u=0$, la relation

$$\frac{F'(u)}{F(u)}=\frac{H'(u+\omega)}{H(u+\omega)}-\frac{\Theta'(u)}{\Theta(u)}-\frac{\Theta'(\omega)}{\Theta(\omega)}+\lambda;$$

on en tire d'abord

$$\frac{F'(0)}{F(0)}=\frac{\operatorname{cn}\omega\operatorname{dn}\omega}{\operatorname{sn}\omega}+\lambda,$$

puis, au moyen de la valeur donnée précédemment de λ,

$$\frac{F'(0)}{F(0)}=\frac{\operatorname{cn}\omega\operatorname{dn}\omega}{\operatorname{sn}\omega}-\frac{\alpha-\beta}{\alpha\beta\gamma}\operatorname{sn}\omega\operatorname{cn}\omega\operatorname{dn}\omega=\frac{\operatorname{cn}\omega\operatorname{dn}\omega}{\operatorname{sn}\omega}\left(1-\frac{\alpha-\beta}{\alpha\beta\gamma}\operatorname{sn}^2\omega\right),$$

et enfin

$$\frac{F'(0)}{F(0)}=-\frac{\operatorname{cn}\omega\operatorname{dn}\omega}{\beta\gamma\operatorname{sn}\omega},$$

comme conséquence de la formule

$$\operatorname{sn}^2\omega=-\frac{\alpha^2(\beta+\gamma)}{\alpha-\beta};$$

mais l'expression de $F(u)$ donne immédiatement

$$F(0)=\frac{H'(0)\,H(\omega)}{\Theta'(0)\,\Theta(\omega)}=k\operatorname{sn}\omega,$$

et nous en concluons l'expression cherchée, à savoir

$$F'(0)=-\frac{k\operatorname{cn}\omega\operatorname{dn}\omega}{\beta\gamma}.$$

Changeons enfin i en $-i$; la constance $\omega=\pm K+i\upsilon$ deviendra

$$\omega'=\pm K-i\upsilon;$$

on a donc

$$\operatorname{sn}\omega' = \operatorname{sn}\omega, \qquad \operatorname{cn}\omega' \operatorname{dn}\omega' = -\operatorname{cn}\omega \operatorname{dn}\omega,$$

et par suite

$$F'(o)\,F'_1(o) = -\frac{k^2 \operatorname{cn}^2\omega \operatorname{dn}^2\omega}{\beta^2\gamma^2} = -\frac{(\alpha+\beta)(\alpha+\gamma)}{(\alpha-\gamma)^2}.$$

De cette expression nous tirons

$$AA_1 = (\alpha-\gamma)^2,$$

de sorte qu'on peut écrire

$$A \quad = (\alpha-\gamma)\,e^{i\varphi},$$

φ désignant un angle arbitraire.

Ce point établi, je reprends l'équation

$$(x+iy)\left(\frac{dx}{dt} - i\frac{dy}{dt}\right) = -z\frac{dz}{dt} + il,$$

qui devient, si l'on introduit, au lieu de t, la variable u,

$$(x+iy)\left(\frac{dx}{du} - i\frac{dy}{du}\right) = -z\frac{dz}{du} + \frac{il}{n},$$

et j'y fais $u = o$. En remarquant qu'alors $\frac{dz}{du}$ s'évanouit, on trouve

$$(\alpha-\gamma)^2\,F'(o)\,F''_1(o) = \frac{il}{n},$$

ce qui nous mène à chercher la valeur de $F''_1(o)$. Pour cela, je déduis de la relation employée tout à l'heure

$$\frac{F'(u)}{F(u)} = \frac{H'(u+\omega)}{H(u+\omega)} - \frac{\Theta'(u)}{\Theta(u)} - \frac{\Theta'(\omega)}{\Theta(\omega)} + \lambda$$

la suivante :

$$\frac{F''(u)}{F(u)} - \frac{F'^2(u)}{F^2(u)} = -\frac{1}{\operatorname{sn}^2(u+\omega)} + k^2\operatorname{sn}^2 u,$$

et j'en tire d'abord

$$\frac{F''(o)}{F(o)} = \frac{F'^2(o)}{F^2(o)} - \frac{1}{\operatorname{sn}^2\omega} = \frac{\operatorname{cn}^2\omega\operatorname{dn}^2\omega}{\beta^2\gamma^2\operatorname{sn}^2\omega} - \frac{1}{\operatorname{sn}^2\omega},$$

puis, après une réduction facile et au moyen de la valeur obtenue pour F(o),

$$F''(o) = -\frac{2k \operatorname{sn} \omega}{\alpha(\alpha - \gamma)}.$$

Cette expression restant la même lorsqu'on change i en $-i$, nous pouvons écrire

$$F''_1(o) = -\frac{2k \operatorname{sn} \omega}{\alpha(\alpha - \gamma)},$$

et, comme on a déjà trouvé

$$F'(o) = -\frac{k \operatorname{cn} \omega \operatorname{dn} \omega}{\beta\gamma},$$

nous en concluons

$$F'(o) F''_1(o) = \frac{2k^2 \operatorname{sn} \omega \operatorname{cn} \omega \operatorname{dn} \omega}{\alpha\beta\gamma(\alpha - \gamma)},$$

et, en employant la valeur de k^2, l'équation suivante,

$$(\alpha - \gamma)^2 F'(o) F''_1(o) = \frac{2(\alpha - \beta) \operatorname{sn} \omega \operatorname{cn} \omega \operatorname{dn} \omega}{\alpha\beta\gamma} = \frac{il}{n}.$$

Si on la rapproche maintenant de la relation déjà donnée

$$\lambda = -\frac{(\alpha - \beta) \operatorname{sn} \omega \operatorname{cn} \omega \operatorname{dn} \omega}{\alpha\beta\gamma},$$

on trouve immédiatement

$$\lambda = -\frac{il}{2n};$$

c'est le résultat que j'ai principalement en vue d'obtenir, afin d'avoir la détermination précise de la constante λ, qui n'était encore connue qu'au signe près.

En dernier lieu, et à l'égard de ω, on remarquera que la fonction $F(u)$ change seulement de signe ou se reproduit quand on met $\omega + 2K$ et $\omega + 2iK'$ à la place de ω. Et comme on peut obtenir un tel changement de signe pour la valeur de $x + iy$, en remplaçant φ par $\varphi + \pi$ dans l'argument du facteur constant A, il en résulte qu'il est permis de faire $\omega = K + iv$, au lieu de $\omega = \pm K + iv$, et de déterminer une valeur de v, comprise entre $-K'$ et $+K'$.

Or, de la relation

$$\operatorname{sn}^2(v, k') = \frac{\beta^2(\gamma^2 - \alpha^2)}{\alpha^2(\gamma^2 - \beta^2)},$$

se tirent deux valeurs égales et de signes contraires de cette quantité entre lesquelles il reste à choisir. C'est à quoi l'on parvient au moyen de la condition

$$\frac{il}{2n} = \frac{(\alpha - \beta)\operatorname{sn}\omega\operatorname{cn}\omega\operatorname{dn}\omega}{\alpha\beta\gamma},$$

qui prend, si l'on y fait $\omega = K + i\upsilon$, la forme suivante,

$$\frac{l}{2n} = -\frac{(\alpha - \beta)k'^2\operatorname{sn}(\upsilon, k)\operatorname{cn}(\upsilon, k')}{\alpha\beta\gamma\operatorname{dn}^3(\upsilon, k')};$$

or, γ étant négatif, on voit ainsi que υ aura le signe de l ou un signe contraire, suivant que la racine moyenne β sera positive ou négative. Dans le cas de $\beta = 0$, on a donc

$$\omega = K$$

et, par suite,

$$F(u) = k\,D_u\,e^{\frac{ilu}{2n}}\operatorname{cn} u:$$

c'est un exemple de ces fonctions particulières de seconde espèce qui ont été considérées par M. Mittag-Leffler dans un article intitulé *Sur les fonctions doublement périodiques de seconde espèce* (*Comptes rendus*, t. XC, p. 177).

XLIII.

Je terminerai par une remarque sur l'équation

$$\frac{il}{n} + \frac{\Theta'(\omega)}{\Theta(\omega)} = 0,$$

qui exprime que les coordonnées x et y se reproduisent, sauf le signe, lorsqu'on change u en $u + 2K$. Soit $\omega = K + i\upsilon$ et posons

$$i\,\Pi(\upsilon) = \frac{il}{n} + \frac{\Theta'(K + i\upsilon)}{\Theta(K + i\upsilon)};$$

cette fonction $\Pi(\upsilon)$, évidemment réelle, finie et continue pour toute valeur réelle de υ, a pour dérivé l'expression

$$\Pi'(\upsilon) = \frac{J}{K} - k^2\operatorname{sn}^2(K + i\upsilon),$$

qui est toujours négative. On a, en effet,

$$J < k^2 K,$$

comme conséquence des formules

$$K = \int_0^1 \frac{dx}{\sqrt{(1-x^2)(1-k^2x^2)}}, \qquad J = \int_0^1 \frac{k^2x^2\,dx}{\sqrt{(1-x^2)(1-k^2x^2)}},$$

et l'on sait d'ailleurs que $\operatorname{sn}^2(K + iv)$ est supérieur à l'unité. La fonction $\Pi(\nu)$, étant décroissante, ne peut s'évanouir qu'une fois; or on a, en désignant par a un nombre entier,

$$\frac{\Theta'(K + 2iaK')}{\Theta(K + 2iaK')} = -\frac{ia\pi}{K},$$

et par conséquent

$$\Pi(0) = \frac{l}{n}, \qquad \Pi(2aK') = \frac{l}{n} - \frac{a\pi}{K}.$$

Nous établissons ainsi l'existence d'une racine, puisqu'on peut disposer de a de manière que $\frac{l}{n} - \frac{a\pi}{K}$ soit de signe contraire à $\frac{l}{n}$. Mais c'est en déterminant les quantités c et l qu'il serait surtout important d'obtenir les cas où le mouvement du pendule est périodique, ces constantes représentant les éléments essentiels de la question. N'ayant pu surmonter les difficultés qui s'offrent alors, je me borne à donner de l'équation précédente une transformée où ces constantes se trouvent plus explicitement en évidence. Soit, à cet effet,

$$R(z) = 2g(z + c)(1 - z^2) - l^2;$$

on aura, en premier lieu,

$$K = \int_\beta^\alpha \frac{n\,dz}{\sqrt{R(z)}}, \qquad J = \int_\beta^\alpha \frac{n(\alpha - z)\,dz}{(\alpha - \gamma)\sqrt{R(z)}};$$

on trouvera ensuite

$$z = \alpha - (\alpha - \beta)\operatorname{sn}^2\omega = -\alpha\beta\gamma,$$

d'où

$$\omega = \int_{-\alpha\beta\gamma}^\alpha \frac{n\,dz}{\sqrt{R(z)}}, \qquad \int_0^\omega k^2 \operatorname{sn}^2 x\,dx = \int_{-\alpha\beta\gamma}^\alpha \frac{n(\alpha - z)\,dz}{(\alpha - \gamma)\sqrt{R(z)}}.$$

Enfin, en partageant l'intervalle compris entre les limites, en deux parties, l'une de $-\alpha\beta\gamma$ à β, et l'autre de β à α, l'équation se présentera, après une réduction facile, sous la forme suivante :

$$\frac{2l}{g}\int_\beta^\alpha \frac{dz}{\sqrt{R(z)}} = \int_\beta^\alpha \frac{z\,dz}{\sqrt{R(z)}}\int_{-\alpha\beta\gamma}^\beta \frac{dz}{\sqrt{-R(z)}} - \int_\beta^\alpha \frac{dz}{\sqrt{R(z)}}\int_{-\alpha\beta\gamma}^\beta \frac{z\,dz}{\sqrt{-R(z)}}.$$

La question qui vient d'être traitée termine les applications à la Mécanique que j'ai annoncées au commencement de ce travail, et j'arrive maintenant, pour la considérer dans toute sa généralité, à l'équation

$$D_x^2 y = [n(n+1)k^2 \operatorname{sn}^2 x + h]y,$$

dont la solution n'a encore été obtenue que pour $n=1$ et $n=2$. Au moyen des méthodes de M. Fuchs, permettant de reconnaître que l'intégrale est une fonction uniforme de la variable, et de l'importante proposition de M. Picard, que cette intégrale est dès lors une fonction doublement périodique de seconde espèce, la solution de l'équation de Lamé est donnée directement par l'application de principes généraux s'appliquant aux équations linéaires d'un ordre quelconque. J'exposerai néanmoins une méthode indépendante de ces principes ; je m'attacherai ensuite, et ce sera mon principal but, à la question difficile de la détermination, sous forme entièrement explicite, des éléments de la solution. La considération du développement en série, qu'on tire de l'équation proposée lorsqu'on suppose $x = iK' + \varepsilon$, aura, dans ce qui va suivre, une grande importance; voici, en premier lieu, comment on l'obtient.

XLIV.

Soit, pour abréger,

$$\frac{1}{\operatorname{sn}^2\varepsilon} = \frac{1}{\varepsilon^2} + s_0 + s_1\varepsilon^2 + \ldots + s_i\varepsilon^{2i} + \ldots,$$

les expressions des premiers coefficients étant

$$s_0 = \frac{1+k^2}{3},$$

$$s_1 = \frac{1-k^2+k^4}{15},$$

$$s_2 = \frac{2-3k^2-3k^4+2k^6}{189},$$

$$s_3 = \frac{2(1-k^2+k^4)^2}{675}.$$

Je dis qu'on vérifie l'équation

$$D_\varepsilon^2 y = \left[\frac{n(n+1)}{\operatorname{sn}^2\varepsilon} + h\right] y,$$

en posant

$$y = \frac{1}{\varepsilon^n} + \frac{h_1}{\varepsilon^{n-2}} + \ldots + \frac{h_i}{\varepsilon^{n-2i}} + \ldots.$$

La substitution donne en effet les conditions

$$\begin{gathered}(n-1)(n-2)h_1 = h + n(n+1)(h_1 + s_0),\\ (n-3)(n-4)h_2 = hh_1 + n(n+1)(h_2 + s_0 h_1 + s_1),\\ \ldots\ldots\ldots\ldots\ldots\ldots\ldots\ldots\ldots\ldots,\end{gathered}$$

et nous allons voir qu'elles déterminent de proche en proche les coefficients h_1, h_2, ... Mettons-les d'abord sous une forme plus simple; en éliminant la quantité h au moyen de la première, on aura, après une réduction facile,

$$i(2n-2i+1)h_i = (2n-1)h_1 h_{i-1} - m(s_1 h_{i-2} + s_2 h_{i-3} + \ldots + s_{i-1}),$$

où j'ai écrit, pour abréger, $n(n+1) = 2m$.

Or, le facteur $2n-2i+1$ ne pouvant jamais être nul, on voit que le coefficient de rang quelconque h_i s'obtient au moyen des précédents, h_{i-1}, h_{i-2}, ... En particulier, on trouve

$$\begin{aligned}h_2 &= \frac{(2n-1)h_1^2}{2(2n-3)} - \frac{ms_1}{2(2n-3)},\\ h_3 &= \frac{(2n-1)^2 h_1^3}{6(2n-3)(2n-5)} - \frac{m(6n-7)s_1 h_1}{6(2n-3)(2n-5)} - \frac{ms_2}{3(2n-5)}.\end{aligned}$$

Ce premier développement obtenu, nous en concluons immédiatement un second. Effectivement, le coefficient $n(n+1)$ ne change pas si l'on remplace n par $-(n+1)$, de sorte qu'en désignant par h'_1, h'_2, ... ce que deviennent h_1, h_2, ... par ce changement, l'équation différentielle sera de même satisfaite en prenant

$$y = \varepsilon^{n+1} + h'_1 \varepsilon^{n+3} + h'_2 \varepsilon^{n+5} + \ldots,$$

ou bien

$$y = \varepsilon^{n+1}(1 + h'_1\varepsilon^2 + h'_2\varepsilon^4 + \ldots).$$

Je remarque enfin qu'en substituant dans l'expression

$$D_\varepsilon^2 y - \left[\frac{n(n+1)}{\operatorname{sn}^2\varepsilon} + h\right] y$$

la partie de la première série représentée par

$$y = \frac{1}{\varepsilon^n} + \frac{h_2}{\varepsilon^{n-2}} + \ldots + \frac{h_i}{\varepsilon^{n-2i}},$$

tous les termes en $\frac{1}{\varepsilon^{n+2}}, \frac{1}{\varepsilon^n}, \ldots, \frac{1}{\varepsilon^{n-2i+2}}$ disparaissent, de sorte que le résultat ordonné suivant les puissances croissantes de ε commence par un terme en $\frac{1}{\varepsilon^{n-2i}}$. On en conclut qu'en supposant n pair et égal à 2ν, ou bien $n = 2\nu - 1$, on n'aura aucun terme en $\frac{1}{\varepsilon}$, si l'on prend dans le premier cas

$$y = \frac{1}{\varepsilon^{2\nu}} + \frac{h_1}{\varepsilon^{2\nu-2}} + \ldots + \frac{h_{\nu-1}}{\varepsilon^2} + h_\nu,$$

et dans le second

$$y = \frac{1}{\varepsilon^{2\nu-1}} + \frac{h_1}{\varepsilon^{2\nu-3}} + \ldots + \frac{h_{\nu-1}}{\varepsilon} + h_\nu \varepsilon.$$

Ce point établi, nous obtenons facilement, comme on va le voir, la solution générale de l'équation de Lamé.

XLV.

Je considère l'élément simple des fonctions doublement périodiques de seconde espèce, en le prenant sous la forme suivante,

$$f(x) = e^{\lambda(x - iK')} \chi(x),$$

où l'on a, comme au paragraphe V,

$$\chi(x) = \frac{H'(0)\,H(x+\omega)}{\Theta(\omega)\,\Theta(x)}\, e^{-\frac{\Theta'(\omega)}{\Theta(\omega)}(x - iK') + \frac{i\pi\omega}{2K}}.$$

Le résidu qui correspond au pôle unique $x = iK'$ sera ainsi égal à l'unité, et nous pourrons écrire

$$f(iK' + \varepsilon) = \frac{1}{\varepsilon} + H_0 + H_1\varepsilon + \ldots + H_i\varepsilon^i + \ldots.$$

Cela posé, je dis que les expressions

$$F(x) = -\frac{D_x^{2\nu-1} f(x)}{\Gamma(2\nu)} - h_1 \frac{D_x^{2\nu-3} f(x)}{\Gamma(2\nu-2)} - \ldots - h_{\nu-1} D_x f(x),$$

$$F(x) = +\frac{D_x^{2\nu-2} f(x)}{\Gamma(2\nu-1)} + h_1 \frac{D_x^{2\nu-4} f(x)}{\Gamma(2\nu-3)} + \ldots + h_{\nu-1} \quad f(x)$$

satisferont, suivant les cas de $n = 2\nu$ et $n = 2\nu - 1$, à l'équation différentielle en déterminant convenablement les constantes ω et λ.

Pour le démontrer, je remarque que, si l'on pose $x = i\mathrm{K}' + \varepsilon$, les parties principales de leurs développements proviendront du seul terme $\frac{1}{\varepsilon}$ qui entre dans $f(i\mathrm{K}' + \varepsilon)$, et seront, par conséquent,

$$\frac{1}{\varepsilon^{2\nu}} + \frac{h_1}{\varepsilon^{2\nu-2}} + \ldots + \frac{h_{\nu-1}}{\varepsilon^2}$$

et

$$\frac{1}{\varepsilon^{2\nu-1}} + \frac{h_1}{\varepsilon^{2\nu-3}} + \ldots + \frac{h_{\nu-1}}{\varepsilon}.$$

Disposons maintenant de ω et λ, de telle sorte que dans le premier cas le terme constant soit égal à h_ν et le coefficient de ε, dans le suivant, égal à zéro; nous poserons pour cela les conditions

$$\mathrm{H}_{2\nu-1} + h_1 \mathrm{H}_{2\nu-3} + h_2 \mathrm{H}_{2\nu-5} + \ldots + h_{\nu-1} \mathrm{H}_1 + h_\nu = 0,$$
$$2\nu \mathrm{H}_{2\nu} + (2\nu - 2) h_1 \mathrm{H}_{2\nu-2} + (2\nu - 4) h_2 \mathrm{H}_{2\nu-4} + \ldots + 2 h_{\nu-1} \mathrm{H}_2 = 0.$$

Et semblablement, dans le second cas, faisons en sorte que le terme constant soit nul et le coefficient de ε égal à h_ν, en écrivant

$$\mathrm{H}_{2\nu-2} + h_1 \mathrm{H}_{2\nu-4} + h_2 \mathrm{H}_{2\nu-6} + \ldots + h_{\nu-1} \mathrm{H}_0 = 0,$$
$$(2\nu - 1) \mathrm{H}_{2\nu-1} + (2\nu - 3) h_1 \mathrm{H}_{2\nu-3} + \ldots + h_{\nu-1} \mathrm{H}_1 - h_\nu = 0.$$

On a donc ces deux développements, à savoir :

$$\mathrm{F}(i\mathrm{K}' + \varepsilon) = \frac{1}{\varepsilon^{2\nu}} + \frac{h_1}{\varepsilon^{2\nu-2}} + \ldots + \frac{h_{\nu-1}}{\varepsilon^2} + h_\nu + \ldots,$$

puis

$$\mathrm{F}(i\mathrm{K}' + \varepsilon) = \frac{1}{\varepsilon^{2\nu-1}} + \frac{h_1}{\varepsilon^{2\nu-3}} + \ldots + \frac{h_{\nu-1}}{\varepsilon} + h_\nu \varepsilon + \ldots;$$

il en résulte que les deux fonctions doublement périodiques de seconde espèce

$$\mathrm{D}_x^2 \mathrm{F}(x) - [n(n+1)k^2 \operatorname{sn}^2 x + h] \mathrm{F}(x),$$

étant finies pour $x = i\mathrm{K}'$, sont par conséquent nulles. Nous avons ainsi démontré que l'équation se trouve vérifiée en faisant $y = \mathrm{F}(x)$, de sorte que l'expression

$$y = \mathrm{C}\,\mathrm{F}(x) + \mathrm{C}'\,\mathrm{F}(-x)$$

en donne l'intégrale générale.

XLVI.

La question qui s'offre maintenant est d'obtenir ω et λ au moyen des relations précédentes, qui sont algébriques en $\operatorname{sn}\omega$ et λ. Or, on est de la sorte amené à un problème d'Algèbre dont la difficulté se montre au premier coup d'œil et résulte de la complication des coefficients H_0, H_1, ...

Revenons, en effet, au développement déjà donné paragraphe V, à savoir :

$$\chi(iK'+\varepsilon) = \frac{1}{\varepsilon} - \frac{1}{2}\Omega\varepsilon - \frac{1}{3}\Omega_1\varepsilon^2 - \frac{1}{8}\Omega_2\varepsilon^3 - \frac{1}{30}\Omega_3\varepsilon^4 - \ldots,$$

où l'on a

$$\begin{aligned}
\Omega &= k^2\operatorname{sn}^2\omega - \frac{1+k^2}{3},\\
\Omega_1 &= k^2\operatorname{sn}\omega\operatorname{cn}\omega\operatorname{dn}\omega,\\
\Omega_2 &= k^4\operatorname{sn}^4\omega - \frac{2(k^2+k^4)}{3}\operatorname{sn}^2\omega - \frac{7-22k^2+7k^4}{45},\\
\Omega_3 &= k^2\operatorname{sn}\omega\operatorname{cn}\omega\operatorname{dn}\omega\left(k^2\operatorname{sn}^2\omega - \frac{1+k^2}{3}\right),\\
&\ldots\ldots\ldots\ldots\ldots\ldots\ldots\ldots
\end{aligned}$$

Les coefficients H_0, H_1, ... résultant de l'identité

$$\frac{1}{\varepsilon} + H_0 + H_1\varepsilon + \ldots = \left(1 + \lambda\varepsilon + \frac{\lambda^2\varepsilon^2}{2} + \ldots\right)\left(\frac{1}{\varepsilon} - \frac{1}{2}\Omega\varepsilon - \ldots\right)$$

seront

$$\begin{aligned}
H_0 &= \lambda,\\
H_1 &= \tfrac{1}{2}(\lambda^2 - \Omega),\\
H_2 &= \tfrac{1}{6}(\lambda^3 - 3\Omega\lambda - 2\Omega_1),\\
H_3 &= \tfrac{1}{24}(\lambda^4 - 6\Omega\lambda^2 - 8\Omega_1\lambda - 3\Omega_2),\\
&\ldots\ldots\ldots\ldots\ldots\ldots\ldots\ldots,
\end{aligned}$$

et l'on voit que, H_n étant du degré $n+1$ en λ, l'une de nos deux équations est, par rapport à cette quantité, du degré n, et la seconde du degré $n+1$. A l'égard de $\operatorname{sn}\omega$, une nouvelle complication se présente en raison du facteur irrationnel $\operatorname{cn}\omega\operatorname{dn}\omega$, qui entre dans Ω_1, Ω_3, Ω_5, ...; aussi paraît-il impossible de conclure de leur forme actuelle qu'elles ne donnent pour λ^2 et $\operatorname{sn}^2\omega$ qu'une seule et unique détermination. Et si l'on considère ces quantités comme des coordonnées, en se plaçant au point de vue de la Géométrie, on verra aisément que les courbes représentées par nos deux équations n'ont aucun point d'intersection indépendant de la constante h qui entre sous forme rationnelle et entière dans les coefficients. Il n'est donc pas possible d'employer les méthodes si simples de Clebsch et de Chasles qui permettent de reconnaître, *a priori* et sans calcul, que les points d'un lieu géométrique se déterminent individuellement en fonction d'un paramètre. Le cas de $n = 3$, qui sera traité tout à l'heure, fera voir en effet que les intersections des deux courbes se trouvent, à l'exception d'une seule, rejetées à l'infini. Mais, avant d'y arriver, je ferai encore cette remarque, qu'on peut joindre aux équations déjà obtenues une infinité d'autres, dont voici l'origine.

Nous avons vu au paragraphe XLIV que l'équation de Lamé donne, en faisant $x = i\mathrm{K}' + \varepsilon$, ces deux développements, à savoir :

$$y = \frac{1}{\varepsilon^n} + \frac{h_1}{\varepsilon^{n-2}} + \frac{h_2}{\varepsilon^{n-4}} + \ldots,$$

$$y = \varepsilon^{n+1} + h'_1\,\varepsilon^{n+3} + h'_2\,\varepsilon^{n+5} + \ldots.$$

Il en résulte que, si l'on pose de même $x = i\mathrm{K}' + \varepsilon$ dans la solution représentée par $\mathrm{F}(x)$, nous aurons, en désignant par C une constante dont on obtiendra bientôt la valeur,

$$\mathrm{F}(i\mathrm{K}' + \varepsilon) = \frac{1}{\varepsilon^n} + \frac{h_1}{\varepsilon^{n-2}} + \frac{h_2}{\varepsilon^{n-4}} + \ldots + \mathrm{C}(\varepsilon^{n+1} + h'_1\,\varepsilon^{n+3} + h'_2\,\varepsilon^{n+5} + \ldots).$$

On peut donc identifier ce développement avec celui que donnent l'une ou l'autre des deux formules

$$\mathrm{F}(x) = -\frac{\mathrm{D}_x^{2\nu-1} f(x)}{\Gamma(2\nu)} - h_1 \frac{\mathrm{D}_x^{2\nu-3} f(x)}{\Gamma(2\nu-2)} - \ldots - h_{\nu-1}\,\mathrm{D}_x f(x),$$

$$\mathrm{F}(x) = +\frac{\mathrm{D}_x^{2\nu-2} f(x)}{\Gamma(2\nu-1)} + h_1 \frac{\mathrm{D}_x^{2\nu-4} f(x)}{\Gamma(2\nu-3)} + \ldots + h_{\nu-1}\quad f(x)$$

lorsqu'on pose $x = i\mathrm{K}' + \varepsilon$. Bornons-nous, pour abréger, au cas de $n = 2\nu$, et représentons la partie qui procède, suivant les puissances positives de ε, par

$$\sum_0 {}_i\,\mathfrak{H}_i\,\varepsilon^i.$$

On trouve facilement, si l'on écrit

$$m_i = \frac{m(m-1)\ldots(m-i+1)}{1.2\ldots i},$$

l'expression

$$\mathfrak{H}_i = -(i+2\nu-1)_i \mathrm{H}_{i+2\nu-1} - (i+2\nu-3)_i h_1 \mathrm{H}_{i+2\nu-3}$$
$$-(i+2\nu-5)_i h_2 \mathrm{H}_{i+2\nu-5} - \ldots - (i+1)_i h_{\nu-1} \mathrm{H}_{i+1}.$$

Nous aurons donc, pour $i = 1, 3, 5, \ldots, 2\nu-1$, les équations

$$\mathfrak{H}_i = 0;$$

on trouvera ensuite, pour les valeurs paires de l'indice,

$$\mathfrak{H}_{2i} = h_{i+\nu},$$

et enfin, pour les valeurs impaires supérieures à $2\nu-1$,

$$\mathfrak{H}_{2i+2\nu+1} = \mathrm{C}h'_i.$$

Telles sont les relations, en nombre illimité, qui doivent toutes résulter des deux que nous avons données en premier lieu, à savoir :

$$\mathfrak{H}_1 = 0, \qquad \mathfrak{H}_0 = h_\nu;$$

on est amené ainsi à se demander si leurs premiers membres, $\mathfrak{H}_i$, $\mathfrak{H}_{2i} - h_{i+\nu}$, $\mathfrak{H}_{2i+2\nu+1} - \mathrm{C}h'_i$, ne s'exprimeraient point, sous forme rationnelle et entière, par les fonctions $\mathfrak{H}_1$ et $\mathfrak{H}_0 - h_\nu$. Mais je laisserai entièrement de côté cette question difficile, et j'arrive immédiatement à la résolution des équations relatives au cas de $n = 3$.

XLVII.

Ces équations ont été données au paragraphe XXXVIII, et sont

$$\mathrm{H}_2 + h_1 \mathrm{H}_0 = 0,$$
$$3\mathrm{H}_3 + h_1 \mathrm{H}_1 = h_2.$$

Si l'on met en évidence les quantités Ω, et qu'on fasse $h_1 = \frac{l}{2}$, ce qui donne

$$h = -4(1+k^2) - 5l,$$
$$h_2 = \frac{5l^2}{24} - s_1,$$

elles prennent la forme suivante :

$$\lambda^3 - 3\Omega\lambda - 2\Omega_1 + 3l\lambda = 0,$$
$$\lambda^4 - 6\Omega\lambda^2 - 8\Omega_1\lambda - 3\Omega_2 + 2l\lambda^2 - 2l\Omega = \frac{5l^2}{3} - 8s_1.$$

Cela étant, j'emploie ces identités, à savoir :

$$\Omega^2 - \Omega_2 = 4s_1,$$
$$\Omega\Omega_2 - \Omega_1^2 = \Omega s_1 + 7s_2,$$

et je remarque qu'on en tire, par l'élimination de Ω_1 et Ω_2, deux équations du second degré en Ω. Mais il convient d'introduire H_1 au lieu de Ω; en faisant alors, pour un moment,

$$a = 1 - k^2 + k^4,$$
$$b = 2 - 3k^2 - 3k^4 + 2k^6,$$

ces relations seront

$$36H_1^2 - 12lH_1 + 36l\lambda^2 + 5l^2 - 4a = 0,$$
$$72lH_1^2 - 6(5l^2 - a)H_1 + 72l^2\lambda^2 + b = 0.$$

Éliminons λ^2; elles donnent immédiatement

$$H_1 = -\frac{10l^3 - 8al - b}{6(l^2 - a)};$$

nous obtenons ensuite

$$\lambda^2 = -\frac{4(l^2 - a)^3 + (11l^3 - 9al - b)^2}{36l(l^2 - a)^2},$$

ou bien

$$\lambda^2 = -\frac{\varphi(l)}{36l(l^2 - a)^2},$$

si l'on pose, pour abréger,

$$\varphi(l) = 125l^6 - 210al^4 - 22bl^3 + 93a^2l^2 + 18abl + b^2 - 4a^3,$$

soit encore

$$\psi(l) = 5l^6 + 6al^4 - 10bl^3 - 3a^2l^2 + 6abl + b^2 - 4a^3$$
$$= \varphi(l) - 12l(l^2 - a)(10l^3 - 8al - b);$$

de la relation $\lambda^2 - 2H_1 = \Omega$ on conclura

$$\Omega = k^2 \operatorname{sn}^2\omega - \frac{1 + k^2}{3} = -\frac{\psi(l)}{36l(l^2 - a)^2}.$$

Enfin j'observe qu'on déduit des équations proposées la valeur de Ω_1 exprimée en Ω et λ, par cette formule,

$$2\Omega_1 = (\lambda^2 - 3\Omega + 3l)\lambda;$$

faisant donc

$$\chi(l) = l^6 - 6al^4 + 4bl^3 - 3a^2l^2 - b^2 + 4a^2,$$

nous parvenons encore à la relation

$$\Omega_1 = k^2 \operatorname{sn}\omega \operatorname{cn}\omega \operatorname{dn}\omega = -\frac{\chi(l)\lambda}{36l(l^2-a)^2}.$$

Le signe de λ se trouve ainsi déterminé par celui de ω, et la solution complète de l'équation de Lamé dans le cas de $n=3$ est obtenue sans aucune ambiguïté au moyen de la fonction

$$\frac{\mathrm{H}(x+\omega)}{\Theta(x)} e^{\left[\lambda - \frac{\Theta'(\omega)}{\Theta(\omega)}\right]x}$$

On n'a toutefois pas mis en évidence dans les formules précédentes les valeurs de la constante l qui donnent les solutions doublement périodiques, ou les fonctions particulières de seconde espèce de M. Mittag-Leffler, comme nous l'avons fait dans le cas de $n=2$.

Voici, dans ce but, les nouvelles expressions qu'on en déduit.

Posons, en premier lieu,

$$\begin{aligned}
\mathrm{P} &= 5l^2 - 2(1+k^2)l - 3(1-k^2)^2,\\
\mathrm{Q} &= 5l^2 - 2(1-2k^2)l - 3,\\
\mathrm{R} &= 5l^2 - 2(k^2-2)\,l - 3k^4,\\
\mathrm{S} &= 36l,
\end{aligned}$$

et, d'autre part,

$$\begin{aligned}
\mathrm{A} &= l^2 - (1+k^2)l - 3k^2,\\
\mathrm{B} &= l^2 - (1-2k^2)l + 3(k^2-k^4),\\
\mathrm{C} &= l^2 - (k^2-2)\,l - 3(1-k^2),\\
\mathrm{D} &= l^2 - 1 + k^2 - k^4;
\end{aligned}$$

on aura

$$\begin{aligned}
\lambda^2 &= -\frac{\mathrm{PQR}}{\mathrm{SD}^2},\\
k^2\operatorname{sn}^2\omega &= -\frac{\mathrm{PA}^2}{\mathrm{SD}^2},\\
k^2\operatorname{cn}^2\omega &= +\frac{\mathrm{QB}^2}{\mathrm{SD}^2},\\
\operatorname{dn}^2\omega &= +\frac{\mathrm{RC}^2}{\mathrm{SD}^2},
\end{aligned}$$

et enfin, pour établir la correspondance des signes entre ω et λ, l'équation

$$k^2 \operatorname{sn} \omega \operatorname{cn} \omega \operatorname{dn} \omega = -\frac{ABC\lambda}{SD^2}.$$

Cela étant, ce sont les conditions $P = 0$, $Q = 0$, $R = 0$, $S = 0$ qui donnent les solutions doublement périodiques, au nombre de sept, tandis qu'on obtient les fonctions de M. Mittag-Leffler en posant $A = 0$, $B = 0$, $C = 0$, $D = 0$. Mais je laisse de côté l'étude détaillée de ces formules, en me bornant à la remarque suivante, sur laquelle je reviendrai plus tard. Exprimons les quantités $k^2 \operatorname{sn}^2 \omega$, $k^2 \operatorname{cn}^2 \omega$, $\operatorname{dn}^2 \omega$, en partant de l'équation

$$k^2 \operatorname{sn}^2 \omega - \frac{1+k^2}{3} = -\frac{\psi(l)}{36 l (l^2-a)^2},$$

de cette nouvelle manière, à savoir :

$$k^2 \operatorname{sn}^2 \omega = \frac{12 l (l^2-a)^2 (1+k^2) - \psi(l)}{36 l (l^2-a)^2},$$

$$k^2 \operatorname{cn}^2 \omega = \frac{12 l (l^2-a)^2 (2k^2-1) + \psi(l)}{36 l (l^2-a)^2},$$

$$\operatorname{dn}^2 \omega = \frac{12 l (l^2-a)^2 (2-k^2) + \psi(l)}{36 l (l^2-a)^2}.$$

On conclura facilement de l'égalité

$$k^4 \operatorname{sn}^2 \omega \operatorname{cn}^2 \omega \operatorname{dn}^2 \omega = -\frac{\varphi(l)\chi^2(l)}{[36 l (l^2-a)^2]^3}$$

la relation que voici :

$$\psi^3(l) - 3.12^2 a l^2 (l^2-a)^4 \psi(l) + 12^3 b l^3 (l^2-a)^6 = \varphi(l)\chi^2(l).$$

Or elle conduit à cette conséquence, qu'en posant

$$y = \frac{\psi(l)}{12 l (l^2-a)^2},$$

on a

$$\int \frac{dy}{\sqrt{y^3 - 3ay + b}} = 2\sqrt{3} \int \frac{(5l^2-a)\,dl}{\sqrt{l\varphi(l)}};$$

c'est donc un exemple de réduction d'une intégrale hyperelliptique de seconde classe à l'intégrale elliptique de première espèce.

XLVIII.

La méthode générale que je vais exposer maintenant pour la détermination des constantes ω et λ repose principalement sur la considération du produit des solutions de l'équation de Lamé, qui viennent d'être représentées par $F(x)$ et $F(-x)$. Et, d'abord, on remarquera que, ayant

$$F(x+2K) = \mu F(x),$$
$$F(x+2iK') = \mu' F(x)$$

et, par suite,

$$F(-x-2K) = \frac{1}{\mu} F(-x),$$
$$F(-x-2iK') = \frac{1}{\mu'} F(-x),$$

ce produit est une fonction doublement périodique de première espèce, qui a pour pôle unique $x = iK'$. Voici, en conséquence, comment s'obtient son expression sous forme entièrement explicite.

Soit

$$\Phi(x) = (-1)^n \mu' F(x) F(-x),$$

le facteur μ' ayant été introduit pour pouvoir écrire

$$\begin{aligned}\Phi(iK'+\varepsilon) &= (-1)^n \mu' F(iK'+\varepsilon) F(-iK'-\varepsilon)\\ &= (-1)^n F(iK'+\varepsilon) F(iK'-\varepsilon).\end{aligned}$$

Cela étant et posant, pour abréger,

$$S = \frac{1}{\varepsilon^n} + \frac{h_1}{\varepsilon^{n-2}} + \frac{h_2}{\varepsilon^{n-4}} + \ldots,$$
$$S_1 = C(\varepsilon^{n+1} + h'_1 \varepsilon^{n+3} + h'_2 \varepsilon^{n+5} + \ldots),$$

nous aurons

$$F(iK'+\varepsilon) = S + S_1,$$
$$F(iK'-\varepsilon) = (-1)^n (S - S_1),$$

d'où, par conséquent,

$$\Phi(iK'+\varepsilon) = S^2 - S_1^2.$$

On voit ainsi que la partie principale de développement suivant les puissances croissantes de ε est donnée par le premier terme S^2, et ne dépend point de la constante C, entrant dans le second terme, que nous ne connaissons pas encore. Faisons donc

$$S^2 = \frac{1}{\varepsilon^{2n}} + \frac{A_1}{\varepsilon^{2n-2}} + \frac{A_2}{\varepsilon^{2n-4}} + \ldots + \frac{A_{n-1}}{\varepsilon^2} + \ldots;$$

les coefficients A_1, A_2, ... seront

$$\begin{aligned} A_1 &= 2h_1, \\ A_2 &= 2h_2 + h_1^2, \\ A_3 &= 2h_3 + 2h_1h_2, \\ &\ldots\ldots\ldots\ldots\ldots\ldots, \end{aligned}$$

et l'on en conclut que, h_i étant un polynome de degré i en h_1, il en est de même, en général, pour un coefficient de rang quelconque A_i. Maintenant l'expression cherchée découle de la formule de décomposition en éléments simples, qui a été donnée au paragraphe II. Nous obtenons ainsi

$$\Phi(x) = -\frac{D_x^{2n-1}\left[\dfrac{\Theta'(x)}{\Theta(x)}\right]}{\Gamma(2n)} - A_1\frac{D^{2n-3}\left[\dfrac{\Theta'(x)}{\Theta(x)}\right]}{\Gamma(2n-2)} - A_2\frac{D^{2n-5}\left[\dfrac{\Theta'(x)}{\Theta(x)}\right]}{\Gamma(2n-4)} - \ldots$$
$$- A_{n-1}D_x\left[\frac{\Theta'(x)}{\Theta(x)}\right] + \text{const.}$$

La relation élémentaire

$$D_x\frac{\Theta'(x)}{\Theta(x)} = \frac{J}{K} - k^2 \operatorname{sn}^2 x$$

donnera ensuite, sous une autre forme, en désignant par A une nouvelle constante,

$$\Phi(x) = \frac{D_x^{2n-2}(k^2 \operatorname{sn}^2 x)}{\Gamma(2n)} + A_1\frac{D^{2n-4}(k^2 \operatorname{sn}^2 x)}{\Gamma(2n-2)} + A_2\frac{D^{2n-6}(k^2 \operatorname{sn}^2 x)}{\Gamma(2n-4)} + \ldots$$
$$+ A_{n-1}(k^2 \operatorname{sn}^2 x) + A.$$

Pour la déterminer, nous emploierons, en outre de la partie principale de la série S^2, le terme indépendant de ε, qui sera désigné par A_n. En déduisant ce même terme de l'expression de $\Phi(x)$, et se rappelant qu'on a fait

$$\frac{1}{\operatorname{sn}^2\varepsilon} = \frac{1}{\varepsilon^2} + s_0 + s_1\varepsilon^2 + \ldots + s_i\varepsilon^{2i} + \ldots,$$

nous trouvons immédiatement

$$A = A_n - A_{n-1} s_0 - A_{n-2} \frac{s_1}{3} - \ldots - A_1 \frac{s_{n-2}}{2n-3} - \frac{s_{n-1}}{2n-1}.$$

Beaucoup d'autres expressions s'obtiennent par un procédé semblable en fonction linéaire de dérivées successives de $k^2 \operatorname{sn}^2 x$, celles-ci, par exemple,

$$D_x^\alpha F(x) D_x^\beta F(-x),$$

que je vais considérer dans le cas particulier de $\alpha = 1$, $\beta = 1$.

Soit alors

$$\Phi_1(x) = (-1)^{n+1} \mu' F'(x) F'(-x),$$

et désignons par S' et S'_1 les dérivées par rapport à ε des séries S et S_1, de sorte qu'on ait

$$F'(iK' + \varepsilon) = S' + S'_1,$$
$$F'(iK' - \varepsilon) = (-1)^{n+1}(S' - S'_1).$$

De la relation

$$\Phi_1(iK' + \varepsilon) = (-1)^{n+1} F'(iK' + \varepsilon) F'(iK' - \varepsilon),$$

on conclura cette expression, savoir :

$$\Phi_1(iK' + \varepsilon) = S'^2 - S'^2_1.$$

Faisant donc, comme tout à l'heure,

$$S'^2 = \frac{n^2}{\varepsilon^{2n+2}} + \frac{B_1}{\varepsilon^{2n}} + \frac{B_2}{\varepsilon^{2n-2}} + \ldots + \frac{B_n}{\varepsilon^2} + B_{n+1} + \ldots,$$

où le coefficient B_i est encore un polynome en h_1 de degré i, nous aurons

$$\Phi_1(x) = n^2 \frac{D_x^{2n}(k^2 \operatorname{sn}^2 x)}{\Gamma(2n+2)} + B_1 \frac{D_x^{2n-2}(k^2 \operatorname{sn}^2 x)}{\Gamma(2n)}$$
$$+ B_2 \frac{D^{2n-4}(k^2 \operatorname{sn}^2 x)}{\Gamma(2n-2)} + \ldots + B_n(k^2 \operatorname{sn}^2 x) + B,$$

et la constante sera donnée par la formule

$$B = B_{n+1} - B_n s_0 - B_{n-1} \frac{s_1}{3} - \ldots - B_1 \frac{s_{n-1}}{2n-1} - n^2 \frac{s_n}{2n+1}.$$

J'envisage enfin le déterminant fonctionnel formé avec les solutions $F(x)$ et $F(-x)$ de l'équation de Lamé, et je pose

$$\Phi_2(x) = (-1)^{n+1}\mu'[F(x)F'(-x) + F'(x)F(-x)].$$

La relation suivante, qui s'obtient aisément, et dont le second membre ne contient que des termes entiers en ε, à savoir

$$\Phi_2(iK'+\varepsilon) = 2(SS'_1 - S'S_1) = 2(2n+1)C + \ldots,$$

donne, comme on le voit, la proposition bien connue que cette fonction est constante; nous allons en obtenir la valeur en la mettant sous la forme

$$(2n+1)C = \sqrt{N},$$

que nous garderons désormais.

XLIX.

J'observe, à cet effet, que de l'identité

$$(SS' - S_1S'_1)^2 = (SS'_1 - S_1S')^2 + (S^2 - S_1^2)(S'^2 - S_1'^2)$$

on conclut immédiatement, entre les fonctions dont il vient d'être question, la relation suivante :

$$\frac{1}{4}\Phi'^2(iK'+\varepsilon) = \frac{1}{4}\Phi_2^2(iK'+\varepsilon) + \Phi(iK'+\varepsilon)\Phi_1(iK'+\varepsilon),$$

et, par conséquent,

$$\frac{1}{4}\Phi'^2(x) = N + \Phi(x)\Phi_1(x).$$

Elle fait voir qu'en attribuant à la variable une valeur particulière, en supposant, par exemple, $x = 0$, N s'obtient comme un polynome entier en h_1 du degré $2n+1$, puisque cette quantité entre, comme on l'a vu, au degré n dans $\Phi(x)$ et au degré $n+1$ dans $\Phi_1(x)$. Ce point établi, nous remarquons que, en posant la condition $N = 0$, le déterminant fonctionnel $\Phi_2(x)$ est nul, de sorte que le quotient $\dfrac{F(x)}{F(-x)}$ se réduit alors à une constante. Désignons-la pour un instant par A, on voit que le changement de x en $-x$ donne $A = \frac{1}{A}$; on a donc

$$A = \pm 1,$$

et, par conséquent,

$$F(-x) = \pm F(x).$$

Remplaçons ensuite x par $x + 2K$ et $x + 2iK'$: le quotient se reproduit multiplié par μ^2 et μ'^2; ainsi il faut poser $\mu^2 = 1$, $\mu'^2 = 1$, c'est-à-dire $\mu = \pm 1$, $\mu' = \pm 1$.

La condition $N = 0$ détermine donc les valeurs de h, pour lesquelles l'équation de Lamé est vérifiée par des fonctions doublement périodiques. Ce sont ces solutions, auxquelles est attaché à jamais le nom du grand géomètre, et dont les propriétés lui ont permis de traiter pour la première fois le problème difficile de la détermination des températures d'un ellipsoïde, lorsque l'on donne en chaque point la température de la surface. Elles s'offrent en ce moment comme un cas singulier de l'équation différentielle, où l'intégrale cesse d'être représentée par la formule

$$y = C\,F(x) + C'\,F(-x)$$

et subit un changement de forme analytique. Je me borne à les signaler sous ce point de vue, devant bientôt y revenir, et je reprends, pour en tirer une nouvelle conséquence, l'équation

$$\frac{1}{4}\Phi'^2(x) = N + \Phi(x)\,\Phi_1(x).$$

Introduisons $\text{sn}^2 x$ pour variable, en posant $\text{sn}^2 x = t$; on voit que $\Phi(x)$ et $\Phi_1(x)$, ne contenant que des dérivées d'ordre pair de $\text{sn}^2 x$, deviendront des polynomes entiers en t des degrés n et $n+1$, que je désignerai par $\Pi(t)$ et $\Pi_1(t)$. Soit encore

$$R(t) = t(1-t)(1-k^2 t);$$

la relation considérée prend cette forme

$$R(t)\,\Pi'^2(t) = N + \Pi(t)\,\Pi_1(t);$$

et voici la remarque, importante pour notre objet, à laquelle elle donne lieu.

Développons la fonction rationnelle $\frac{\Pi'(t)}{\Pi(t)}$ en fraction continue, et distinguons, dans la série des réduites, celle dont le dénominateur est du degré ν, dans les deux cas de $n = 2\nu$ et $n = 2\nu - 1$. Si on la représente par $\frac{\theta(t)}{\varphi(t)}$, le développement, suivant les puissances décroissantes de t, de la différence

$$\frac{\Pi'(t)}{\Pi(t)}\varphi(t) - \theta(t),$$

commencera ainsi par un terme en $\frac{1}{t^{\nu+1}}$, et, en posant

$$\Pi'(t)\varphi(t) - \Pi(t)\theta(t) = \psi(t),$$

on voit que, dans le premier cas, $\psi(t)$ sera un polynome de degré $\nu - 1$, et, dans le second, de degré $\nu - 2$. Cela étant, je considère l'expression suivante,

$$\mathrm{N}\varphi^2(t) - \mathrm{R}(t)\psi^2(t);$$

on trouve d'abord aisément, en employant la relation proposée et la valeur de $\psi(t)$, qu'elle devient

$$\Pi(t)[-\varphi^2(t)\Pi_1(t) + 2\varphi(t)\theta(t)\mathrm{R}(t)\Pi'(t) - \theta^2(t)\mathrm{R}(t)\Pi(t)],$$

et contient, par conséquent, en facteur, le polynome $\Pi(t)$. On vérifie ensuite qu'elle est de degré $n+1$ en t, dans les deux cas de $n = 2\nu$ et $n = 2\nu - 1$; nous pouvons ainsi poser

$$\mathrm{N}\varphi^2(t) - \mathrm{R}(t)\psi^2(t) = \Pi(t)(gt - g'),$$

et nous allons voir que ω est donné par la formule

$$\mathrm{sn}^2\omega = \frac{g'}{g},$$

où le second membre est une fonction rationnelle de h.

L.

Considérons dans ce but une nouvelle fonction doublement périodique définie de la manière suivante,

$$\Psi(x) = -\mu' f(-x)\mathrm{F}(x),$$

en faisant toujours

$$f(x) = e^{\lambda(x - i\mathrm{K}')}\chi(x),$$

de sorte que les deux facteurs $f(-x)$ et $F(x)$ soient encore des fonctions de seconde espèce à multiplicateurs réciproques. Nous aurons d'abord

$$\Psi(x)\Psi(-x) = \mu'^2 f(x) f(-x) F(x) F(-x),$$

et, en employant l'égalité, qu'il est facile d'établir,

$$\mu' f(x) f(-x) = -k^2(\operatorname{sn}^2 x - \operatorname{sn}^2 \omega),$$

on parvient à cette relation

$$\Psi(x)\Psi(-x) = (-1)^{n+1} k^2(\operatorname{sn}^2 x - \operatorname{sn}^2 \omega)\Phi(x),$$

dont on va voir l'importance. Formons à cet effet l'expression de $\Psi(x)$ qui s'obtiendra sous forme linéaire au moyen des dérivées successives de $k^2\operatorname{sn}^2 x$, puisque cette fonction, comme celles qui ont été précédemment introduites, a pour seul pôle $x = iK'$. Nous déduirons pour cela un développement, suivant les puissances croissantes de ε, de l'équation

$$\begin{aligned}\Psi(iK'+\varepsilon) &= -f(iK'-\varepsilon)F(iK'+\varepsilon)\\ &= \left(\frac{1}{\varepsilon} - H_0 + H_1\varepsilon - H_2\varepsilon^2 + \ldots\right)\left(\frac{1}{\varepsilon^n} + \frac{h_1}{\varepsilon^{n-2}} + \frac{h_2}{\varepsilon^{n-4}} + \ldots\right),\end{aligned}$$

développement que je représenterai par la formule

$$\Psi(iK'+\varepsilon) = \frac{1}{\varepsilon^{n+1}} + \frac{\alpha_0}{\varepsilon^n} + \frac{\alpha_1}{\varepsilon^{n-1}} + \ldots + \frac{\alpha_i}{\varepsilon^{n-i}} + \ldots,$$

en posant

$$\alpha_0 = -H_0, \qquad \alpha_1 = H_1, \qquad \ldots,$$

et nous observerons immédiatement que cette série ne contient point le terme $\frac{\alpha_{n-1}}{\varepsilon}$. On a effectivement, pour $n = 2\nu$,

$$\alpha_{n-1} = H_{2\nu-1} + h_1 H_{2\nu-3} + h_2 H_{2\nu-5} + \ldots + h_{\nu-1} H_1 + h_\nu,$$

puis, en supposant $n = 2\nu - 1$,

$$\alpha_{n-1} = -(H_{2\nu-2} + h_1 H_{2\nu-4} + h_2 H_{2\nu-6} + \ldots + h_{\nu-1} H_0).$$

Or on voit que, d'après les équations obtenues pour la détermination de ω et λ, au paragraphe XLV, le coefficient α_{n-1} est nul dans les deux cas. La partie principale du développement de

$\Psi(i\mathrm{K}'+\varepsilon)$, à laquelle nous joindrons le terme indépendant de ε, est donc

$$\frac{1}{\varepsilon^{n+1}}+\frac{\alpha_0}{\varepsilon^n}+\frac{\alpha_1}{\varepsilon^{n-1}}+\ldots+\frac{\alpha_{n-2}}{\varepsilon^2}+\alpha_n.$$

On en conclut, quand $n=2\nu$,

$$\begin{aligned}\Psi(x)=&-\frac{\mathrm{D}_x^{2\nu-1}(k^2\,\mathrm{sn}^2x)}{\Gamma(2\nu+1)}+\alpha_0\frac{\mathrm{D}_x^{2\nu-2}(k^2\,\mathrm{sn}^2x)}{\Gamma(2\nu)}\\&-\alpha_1\frac{\mathrm{D}_x^{2\nu-3}(k^2\,\mathrm{sn}^2x)}{\Gamma(2\nu-1)}+\ldots+\alpha_{2\nu-2}(k^2\,\mathrm{sn}^2x)+\alpha,\end{aligned}$$

la constante ayant pour valeur

$$\alpha=\alpha_{2\nu}-\alpha_{2\nu-2}s_0-\alpha_{2\nu-4}\frac{s_1}{3}-\ldots-\alpha_0\frac{s_{\nu-1}}{2\nu-1},$$

puis, dans le cas de $n=2\nu-1$,

$$\begin{aligned}\Psi(x)=&+\frac{\mathrm{D}_x^{2\nu-2}(k^2\,\mathrm{sn}^2x)}{\Gamma(2\nu)}-\alpha_0\frac{\mathrm{D}_x^{2\nu-3}(k^2\,\mathrm{sn}^2x)}{\Gamma(2\nu-1)}\\&+\alpha_1\frac{\mathrm{D}_x^{2\nu-4}(k^2\,\mathrm{sn}^2x)}{\Gamma(2\nu-3)}-\ldots+\alpha_{2\nu-3}(k^2\,\mathrm{sn}^2x)+\alpha,\end{aligned}$$

en posant

$$\alpha=\alpha_{2\nu-1}-\alpha_{2\nu-3}s_0-\alpha_{2\nu-5}\frac{s_1}{3}-\ldots-\alpha_1\frac{s_{\nu-2}}{2\nu-3}-\frac{s_{\nu-1}}{2\nu-1}.$$

Soit maintenant $\mathrm{sn}^2x=t$; les expressions auxquelles nous venons de parvenir prendront cette nouvelle forme, à savoir

$$\Psi(x)=\mathrm{G}(t)+\sqrt{\mathrm{R}(t)}\,\mathrm{G}_1(t),$$

où $\mathrm{G}(t)$ et $\mathrm{G}_1(t)$ sont des polynomes entiers en t des degrés ν et $\nu-1$ dans le premier cas, ν et $\nu-2$ dans le second. Observons aussi que, le radical $\sqrt{\mathrm{R}(t)}$ changeant de signe avec x, d'après la condition

$$\sqrt{\mathrm{R}(t)}=\mathrm{sn}\,x\,\mathrm{cn}\,x\,\mathrm{dn}\,x,$$

on aura

$$\Psi(-x)=\mathrm{G}(t)-\sqrt{\mathrm{R}(t)}\,\mathrm{G}_1(t);$$

nous concluons donc de l'égalité donnée plus haut

$$\Psi(x)\Psi(-x)=(-1)^{n+1}k^2(\mathrm{sn}^2x-\mathrm{sn}^2\omega)\Phi(x)$$

la suivante :

$$\mathrm{G}^2(t)-\mathrm{R}(t)\,\mathrm{G}_1^2(t)=(-1)^{n+1}k^2(t-\mathrm{sn}^2\omega)\,\Pi(t).$$

Cette forme de relation est bien connue par le théorème d'Abel pour l'addition des intégrales elliptiques, et l'on sait que les polynomes $G(t)$, $G_1(t)$, étant des degrés donnés tout à l'heure, se trouvent, à un facteur constant près, déterminés par la condition que l'expression

$$G^2(t) - R(t)\,G_1^2(t)$$

soit divisible par $\Pi(t)$. Il suffit, par conséquent, de nous reporter à l'équation obtenue au paragraphe XLIX, à savoir

$$N\,\varphi^2(t) - R(t)\,\psi^2(t) = \Pi(t)(gt - g'),$$

pour en conclure le résultat que nous avons annoncé

$$\operatorname{sn}^2\omega = \frac{g'}{g}.$$

Mais nous voyons, de plus, qu'on peut poser

$$\rho\left[G(t) + \sqrt{R(t)}\,G_1(t)\right] = \sqrt{N}\,\varphi(t) + \sqrt{R(t)}\,\psi(t),$$

ρ désignant une constante. Voici maintenant les conséquences à tirer de cette relation.

Je supposerai que l'on ait $n = 2\nu$; les polynomes $\varphi(t)$ et $\psi(t)$, dont les coefficients doivent être regardés comme connus et, si l'on veut, exprimés sous forme entière en h, seront alors des degrés ν et $\nu - 1$. Cela étant, revenons à la variable primitive en faisant $t = \operatorname{sn}^2 x$; on pourra mettre $\sqrt{R(t)}\,\psi(t)$ et $\varphi(t)$ sous la forme suivante, à savoir

$$\sqrt{R(t)}\,\psi(t) = -\,a\,\frac{D_x^{2\nu-1}(k^2\operatorname{sn}^2 x)}{\Gamma(2\nu+1)} - a'\,\frac{D_x^{2\nu-3}(k^2\operatorname{sn}^2 x)}{\Gamma(2\nu-1)} - \ldots,$$

$$\varphi(t) = +\,b\,\frac{D_x^{2\nu-2}(k^2\operatorname{sn}^2 x)}{\Gamma(2\nu)} + b'\,\frac{D_x^{2\nu-4}(k^2\operatorname{sn}^2 x)}{\Gamma(2\nu-2)} + \ldots.$$

Nous aurons donc cette expression de la fonction $\Psi(x)$,

$$\begin{aligned}\rho\,\Psi(x) = -\; & a\,\frac{D_x^{2\nu-1}(k^2\operatorname{sn}^2 x)}{\Gamma(2\nu+1)} - a'\,\frac{D_x^{2\nu-3}(k^2\operatorname{sn}^2 x)}{\Gamma(2\nu-1)} - \ldots \\ & + \sqrt{N}\left[b\,\frac{D_x^{2\nu-2}(k^2\operatorname{sn}^2 x)}{\Gamma(2\nu)} + b'\,\frac{D_x^{2\nu-4}(k^2\operatorname{sn}^2 x)}{\Gamma(2\nu-2)} + \ldots\right],\end{aligned}$$

où les constantes $a, a', \ldots, b, b', \ldots$ sont déterminées linéairement par les coefficients de $\varphi(t)$ et $\psi(t)$.

Or on en déduit, en faisant $x = i\mathrm{K}' + \varepsilon$ et se rappelant qu'on a supposé $n = 2\nu$, l'égalité suivante,

$$\rho\left(\frac{1}{\varepsilon^{n+1}} + \frac{\alpha_0}{\varepsilon^n} + \frac{\alpha_1}{\varepsilon^{n-1}} + \ldots\right) = \frac{a}{\varepsilon^{n+1}} + \frac{a'}{\varepsilon^{n-1}} + \ldots + \sqrt{\mathrm{N}}\left(\frac{b}{\varepsilon^n} + \frac{b'}{\varepsilon^{n-2}} + \ldots\right),$$

d'où nous tirons

$$\begin{aligned} \rho &= a, \\ \rho\alpha_0 &= b\sqrt{\mathrm{N}}, \\ \rho\alpha_1 &= a', \\ &\ldots\ldots \end{aligned}$$

Éliminons l'indéterminée ρ et remplaçons les coefficients α_0, α_1, ... par leurs valeurs du paragraphe L (p. 406); on aura ces relations

$$\begin{aligned} \lambda &= -\frac{b\sqrt{\mathrm{N}}}{a}, \\ h_1 + \frac{1}{2}(\lambda^2 - \Omega) &= \frac{a'}{a}, \\ &\ldots\ldots\ldots\ldots \end{aligned}$$

La première donne l'expression de λ, et nous reconnaissons, par cette voie, qu'elle ne contient d'autre irrationnalité que $\sqrt{\mathrm{N}}$. On obtiendrait la même conclusion dans le cas de $n = 2\nu - 1$, et c'est le résultat que j'avais principalement en vue d'établir, après avoir démontré que $\mathrm{sn}^2\omega$ est une fonction rationnelle de h. L'étude des solutions de Lamé qui correspondent aux racines de l'équation $\mathrm{N} = 0$ nous permettra, comme on va le voir, d'aller plus loin et d'approfondir davantage la nature de ces expressions de λ et $\mathrm{sn}^2\omega$.

LI.

On a vu au paragraphe XLIX (p. 404) que l'intégrale générale de l'équation différentielle n'est plus représentée, lorsqu'on a $\mathrm{N} = 0$, par la formule

$$y = \mathrm{C}\,\mathrm{F}(x) + \mathrm{C}'\,\mathrm{F}(-x),$$

le rapport $\frac{\mathrm{F}(x)}{\mathrm{F}(-x)}$ se réduisant alors à une constante, et, comme conséquence, nous avons établi que les multiplicateurs de la fonction de seconde espèce deviennent, au signe près, égaux à l'unité.

Suivant les diverses combinaisons des signes de μ et μ', nous pouvons donc avoir des solutions particulières de quatre espèces, caractérisées par les relations suivantes :

$$\begin{array}{llll}
\text{(I)} & F(x+2K)=-F(x), & F(x+2iK')=+F(x), \\
\text{(II)} & F(x+2K)=-F(x), & F(x+2iK')=-F(x), \\
\text{(III)} & F(x+2K)=+F(x), & F(x+2iK')=-F(x), \\
\text{(IV)} & F(x+2K)=+F(x), & F(x+2iK')=+F(x).
\end{array}$$

Toutes existent en effet, et les trois premières, où $F(x)$ a successivement la périodicité de $\operatorname{sn} x$, $\operatorname{cn} x$, $\operatorname{dn} x$, s'obtiennent en faisant, dans l'expression générale de cette formule, $\lambda = 0$, conjointement avec $\omega = 0$, $\omega = K$, $\omega = K + iK'$. Nous remarquerons, pour l'établir, que, les valeurs de l'élément simple

$$f(x) = e^{\lambda(x-iK')}\chi(x)$$

étant alors $f(x) = k\operatorname{sn} x$, $ik\operatorname{cn} x$, $i\operatorname{dn} x$, dans ces trois cas, les développements en série de $f(iK'+\varepsilon)$ ne contiennent que des puissances impaires de ε, de sorte que les coefficients désignés par H_i s'évanouissent tous pour des valeurs paires de l'indice. Des deux conditions obtenues au paragraphe XLV (p. 393), pour la détermination de ω et λ, à savoir

$$H_{2\nu-1} + h_1 H_{2\nu-3} + h_2 H_{2\nu-5} + \ldots + h_{\nu-1} H_1 + h_\nu = 0,$$
$$2\nu H_{2\nu} + (2\nu-2) h_1 H_{2\nu-2} + (2\nu-4) h_2 H_{2\nu-4} + \ldots + 2h_{\nu-1} H_2 = 0,$$

dans le cas de $n = 2\nu$; puis, en supposant $n = 2\nu - 1$,

$$H_{2\nu-2} + h_1 H_{2\nu-4} + h_2 H_{2\nu-6} + \ldots + h_{\nu-1} H_0 = 0,$$
$$(2\nu-1) H_{2\nu-1} + (2\nu-3) h_1 H_{2\nu-3} + \ldots + h_{\nu-1} H_1 - h_\nu = 0;$$

on voit ainsi qu'une seule subsiste et détermine la constante h, l'autre étant satisfaite d'elle-même.

Mais soit, pour plus de précision,

$$k\operatorname{sn}(iK'+\varepsilon) = \frac{1}{\varepsilon} + p_1\varepsilon + p_2\varepsilon^3 + \ldots + p_i\varepsilon^{2i-1} + \ldots,$$

$$ik\operatorname{cn}(iK'+\varepsilon) = \frac{1}{\varepsilon} + q_1\varepsilon + q_2\varepsilon^3 + \ldots + q_i\varepsilon^{2i-1} + \ldots,$$

$$i\operatorname{dn}(iK'+\varepsilon) = \frac{1}{\varepsilon} + r_1\varepsilon + r_2\varepsilon^3 + \ldots + r_i\varepsilon^{2i-1} + \ldots;$$

je poserai, dans le cas de $n = 2\nu$,

$$P = p_\nu + h_1 p_{\nu-1} + h_2 p_{\nu-2} + \ldots + h_{\nu-1} p_1 + h_\nu,$$
$$Q = q_\nu + h_1 q_{\nu-1} + h_2 q_{\nu-2} + \ldots + h_{\nu-1} q_1 + h_\nu,$$
$$R = r_\nu + h_1 r_{\nu-1} + h_2 r_{\nu-2} + \ldots + h_{\nu-1} r_1 + h_\nu;$$

puis, en supposant $n = 2\nu - 1$,

$$P = (2\nu - 1) p_\nu + (2\nu - 3) h_1 p_{\nu-1} + \ldots + h_{\nu-1} p_1 - h_\nu,$$
$$Q = (2\nu - 1) q_\nu + (2\nu - 3) h_1 q_{\nu-1} + \ldots + h_{\nu-1} q_1 - h_\nu,$$
$$R = (2\nu - 1) r_\nu + (2\nu - 3) h_1 r_{\nu-1} + \ldots + h_{\nu-1} r_1 - h_\nu;$$

cela étant, les équations

$$P = 0, \qquad Q = 0, \qquad R = 0$$

détermineront les valeurs particulières de h auxquelles correspondent les trois espèces de solutions que nous avons considérées, et l'on voit que dans les deux cas elles sont toutes du degré ν.

Il ne nous reste plus maintenant qu'à obtenir les solutions de la quatrième espèce dont la périodicité est celle de $\operatorname{sn}^2 x$, mais elles se déduisent moins immédiatement que les précédentes de l'expression générale de $F(x)$; il est nécessaire, en effet, de supposer alors la constante λ et $\operatorname{sn}\omega$ infinis; je donnerai en premier lieu une méthode plus directe et plus facile pour y parvenir.

Soit d'abord $n = 2\nu$; je remarque que toute solution de l'équation différentielle par une fonction doublement périodique de première espèce résulte du développement

$$y = \frac{1}{\varepsilon^{2\nu}} + \frac{h_1}{\varepsilon^{2\nu-2}} + \ldots + \frac{h_{\nu-1}}{\varepsilon^2} + h_\nu,$$

et sera donnée par l'expression

$$F(x) = \frac{D_x^{2\nu-2}(k^2 \operatorname{sn}^2 x)}{\Gamma(2\nu)} + h_1 \frac{D_x^{2\nu-4}(k^2 \operatorname{sn}^2 x)}{\Gamma(2\nu - 2)} + \ldots + h_{\nu-1}(k^2 \operatorname{sn}^2 x)$$
$$+ h_\nu - h_{\nu-1} s_0 - h_{\nu-2} \frac{s_1}{3} - \ldots - h_1 \frac{s_{\nu-2}}{2\nu - 3} - \frac{s_{\nu-1}}{2\nu - 1}.$$

Cela étant, disposons de h de manière à avoir

$$F(iK' + \varepsilon) = \frac{1}{\varepsilon^{2\nu}} + \frac{h_1}{\varepsilon^{2\nu-2}} + \ldots + \frac{h_{\nu-1}}{\varepsilon^2} + h_\nu + h_{\nu+1}\varepsilon^2,$$

ce qui donne la condition

$$\nu s_\nu + (\nu - 1) h_1 s_{\nu-1} + (\nu - 2) h_2 s_{\nu-2} + \ldots + h_{\nu-1} s_1 = h_{\nu+1};$$

je dis que la fonction doublement périodique

$$D_x^2 F(x) - [n(n+1)k^2 \operatorname{sn}^2 x + h] F(x)$$

est nécessairement nulle. Si, après avoir posé $x = iK' + \varepsilon$, on la développe en effet suivant les puissances croissantes de ε, non seulement la partie principale, mais le terme indépendant disparaîtront, comme on l'a vu au paragraphe XLIV (p. 392). De ce que la partie principale n'existe pas, on conclut que la fonction est constante; enfin cette constante elle-même est nulle, puisqu'elle s'exprime linéairement et sous forme homogène par le terme indépendant de ε, et les coefficients des divers termes en $\frac{1}{\varepsilon}$.

Soit ensuite $n = 2\nu - 1$; le développement qu'on tire de l'équation différentielle, à savoir

$$y = \frac{1}{\varepsilon^{2\nu-1}} + \frac{h_1}{\varepsilon^{2\nu-3}} + \ldots + \frac{h_{\nu-1}}{\varepsilon} + \ldots,$$

contenant un terme en $\frac{1}{\varepsilon}$, on doit tout d'abord le faire disparaître en posant $h_{\nu-1} = 0$, pour en déduire une fonction doublement périodique de première espèce, qui sera de cette manière

$$F(x) = -\frac{D_x^{2\nu-3}(k^2 \operatorname{sn}^2 x)}{\Gamma(2\nu - 1)} - h_1 \frac{D_x^{2\nu-5}(k^2 \operatorname{sn}^2 x)}{\Gamma(2\nu - 3)} - \ldots - h_{\nu-2} D_x(k^2 \operatorname{sn}^2 x).$$

Cela étant, et en nous bornant à la partie principale, on aura

$$F(iK' + \varepsilon) = \frac{1}{\varepsilon^{2\nu-1}} + \frac{h_1}{\varepsilon^{2\nu-3}} + \ldots + \frac{h_{\nu-2}}{\varepsilon^3};$$

il en résulte que, si on laisse indéterminée la constante h, le développement de l'expression

$$D_x^2 F(x) - [n(n+1)k^2 \operatorname{sn}^2 x + h] F(x),$$

après avoir posé $x = iK' + \varepsilon$, commencera par un terme en $\frac{1}{\varepsilon^3}$. Mais faisons $h_{\nu-1} = 0$; comme on peut écrire alors

$$F(iK' + \varepsilon) = \frac{1}{\varepsilon^{2\nu-1}} + \frac{h_1}{\varepsilon^{2\nu-3}} + \ldots + \frac{h_{\nu-2}}{\varepsilon^3} + \frac{h_{\nu-1}}{\varepsilon},$$

on voit que ce développement commencera par un terme en $\frac{1}{\varepsilon}$, qui lui-même doit nécessairement s'évanouir, et il est ainsi prouvé que, sous la condition posée, le résultat de la substitution de la fonction $F(x)$, dans le premier membre de l'équation différentielle, ne peut être qu'une constante. J'ajoute que cette constante est nulle, le résultat de la substitution étant, comme $F(x)$, une fonction qui change de signe avec la variable. Soit donc, dans le cas de $n = 2\nu$,

$$S = \nu s_\nu + (\nu - 1)h_1 s_{\nu-1} + (\nu - 2)h_2 s_{\nu-2} + \ldots + h_{\nu-1} s_1 - h_{\nu+1};$$

puis, en supposant $n = 2\nu - 1$,

$$S = h_{\nu-1},$$

on voit que les équations

$$P = 0, \qquad Q = 0, \qquad R = 0, \qquad S = 0$$

déterminent les valeurs de h auxquelles correspondent les quatre espèces de solutions doublement périodiques découvertes par Lamé, ces solutions ne se trouvant plus distinguées par leur expression algébrique, comme l'a fait l'illustre auteur, mais d'après la nature de leur périodicité. On voit aussi que la condition $N = 0$, d'où elles ont été tirées, se présente sous la forme

$$PQRS = 0,$$

et l'on vérifie immédiatement que le produit des quatre facteurs, dans les deux cas de $n = 2\nu$ et $n = 2\nu - 1$, est bien du degré $2n + 1$ en h, comme nous l'avons établi pour N au paragraphe XLIX (p. 403).

Voici maintenant le procédé que j'ai annoncé pour déduire les solutions de la quatrième espèce de la solution générale.

LII.

Je reviens à l'élément simple

$$f(x) = \frac{H'(0)\,H(x+\omega)}{\Theta(x)\,\Theta(\omega)}\, e^{\left[\lambda - \frac{\Theta'(\omega)}{\Theta(\omega)}\right](x - iK') + \frac{i\pi\omega}{2K}},$$

où λ et $\operatorname{sn}\omega$ sont des fonctions déterminées de h; je les suppose infinies l'une et l'autre pour une certaine valeur de cette constante, et je me propose de reconnaître ce que devient, lorsqu'on attribue à h cette valeur, l'expression de $f(x)$. Concevons, à cet effet, que λ soit exprimé au moyen de ω; je ferai

$$\omega = iK' + \delta,$$

ce qui donne, après une réduction facile,

$$f(x) = \frac{H'(0)\Theta(x+\delta)}{\Theta(x)H(\delta)} e^{\left[\lambda - \frac{H'(\delta)}{H(\delta)}\right](x - iK') + \frac{i\pi\delta}{K}}$$

Or nous avons, en développant suivant les puissances croissantes de δ,

$$\frac{H'(\delta)}{H(\delta)} = \frac{1}{\delta} - \left(s_0 - \frac{J}{K}\right)\delta - \frac{s_1\delta^3}{3} - \frac{s_2\delta^5}{5} - \ldots;$$

cela étant, pour que l'exponentielle

$$e^{\left[\lambda - \frac{H'(\delta)}{H(\delta)}\right](x - iK')}$$

soit finie lorsqu'on fera $\delta = 0$, on voit que λ doit s'exprimer de telle manière en ω qu'on ait, en supposant $\omega = iK' + \delta$,

$$\lambda = \frac{1}{\delta} + \lambda_0 + \lambda_1\delta + \ldots.$$

Cette forme de développement nous donne, en effet,

$$\lambda - \frac{H'(\delta)}{H(\delta)} = \lambda_0 + \left(\lambda_1 + s_0 - \frac{J}{K}\right)\delta + \ldots;$$

on a d'ailleurs immédiatement

$$\frac{H'(0)}{H(\delta)} = \frac{1}{\delta} + \left(s_0 - \frac{J}{K}\right)\frac{\delta}{2} + \ldots,$$

$$\frac{\Theta(x+\delta)}{\Theta(x)} = 1 + \frac{\Theta'(x)}{\Theta(x)}\delta + \ldots,$$

et nous en concluons l'expression

$$f(x) = e^{\lambda_0(x - iK')}\left(\frac{1}{\delta} + X + X_1\delta + \ldots\right),$$

où le terme indépendant de δ, qui sera seul à considérer, est

$$X = \left(\lambda_1 + s_0 - \frac{J}{K}\right)(x - iK') + \frac{i\pi}{2K} + \frac{\Theta'(x)}{\Theta(x)}.$$

Elle fait voir que les formules, pour $n = 2\nu$ et $n = 2\nu - 1$,

$$F(x) = -\frac{D_x^{2\nu-1} f(x)}{\Gamma(2\nu)} - h_1 \frac{D^{2\nu-3} f(x)}{\Gamma(2\nu - 2)} - \ldots - h_{\nu-1} D_x f(x),$$

puis

$$F(x) = +\frac{D_x^{2\nu-2} f(x)}{\Gamma(2\nu - 1)} + h_1 \frac{D^{2\nu-4} f(x)}{\Gamma(2\nu - 3)} + \ldots + h_{\nu-1} \quad f(x),$$

contiennent chacune un terme en $\frac{1}{\delta}$, qui est, pour la première,

$$-e^{\lambda_0(x-iK')}\left[\frac{\lambda_0^{2\nu-1}}{\Gamma(2\nu)} + h_1 \frac{\lambda_0^{2\nu-3}}{\Gamma(2\nu - 2)} + \ldots + h_{\nu-1}\lambda_0\right],$$

et, dans la seconde,

$$e^{\lambda_0(x-iK')}\left[\frac{\lambda_0^{2\nu-2}}{\Gamma(2\nu - 1)} + h_1 \frac{\lambda_0^{2\nu-4}}{\Gamma(2\nu - 3)} + \ldots + h_{\nu-1}\right].$$

Il est donc nécessaire, afin d'obtenir des quantités finies en faisant $\delta = 0$, que λ_0 satisfasse à ces équations

$$\frac{\lambda_0^{2\nu-1}}{\Gamma(2\nu)} + h_1 \frac{\lambda_0^{2\nu-3}}{\Gamma(2\nu - 2)} + \ldots + h_{\nu-1}\lambda_0 = 0,$$

$$\frac{\lambda_0^{2\nu-2}}{\Gamma(2\nu - 1)} + h_1 \frac{\lambda_0^{2\nu-4}}{\Gamma(2\nu - 3)} + \ldots + h_{\nu-1} \quad = 0.$$

Cela étant, les expressions de $F(x)$ se transforment de la manière suivante.

Soit, en général,

$$f(x) = e^{\lambda x} X,$$

en désignant par λ et X une constante et une fonction quelconques. On voit aisément que la quantité

$$A D_x^n f(x) + A_1 D_x^{n-1} f(x) + \ldots + A_n f(x),$$

si l'on admet la relation

$$A\lambda^n + A_1\lambda^{n-1} + \ldots + A_n = 0,$$

s'exprime, au moyen de la nouvelle fonction

$$f_1(x) = e^{\lambda x} D_x X,$$

par la formule

$$AD_x^{n-1} f_1(x) + (A\lambda + A_1) D_x^{n-2} f_1(x) + \ldots$$
$$+ (A\lambda^{n-1} + A_1\lambda^{n-2} + \ldots + A_{n-1}) f_1(x).$$

Dans le cas auquel nous avons été conduit, on tire immédiatement de la valeur de X l'expression

$$f_1(x) = e^{\lambda_0(x - iK')}(\lambda_1 + s_0 - k^2 \operatorname{sn}^2 x),$$

et nous obtenons par conséquent pour $F(x)$ le produit, par l'exponentielle $e^{\lambda_0 x}$, d'une fonction doublement périodique de première espèce, composée linéairement avec les dérivées de $\operatorname{sn}^2 x$. L'analyse précédente, en établissant l'existence de ce genre de solutions de l'équation différentielle, les rattache aux valeurs de h qui rendent à la fois infinies les constantes λ et $\operatorname{sn}\omega$; on voit aussi que, dans le cas particulier où λ_0 est nul, elles donnent bien les fonctions que je me suis proposé de déduire de la solution générale. Mais revenons à la première forme qui a été obtenue au moyen de la fonction

$$f(x) = e^{\lambda_0(x - iK')}\left(\frac{1}{\delta} + X + X_1\delta + \ldots\right).$$

Le terme $\dfrac{e^{\lambda_0(x - iK')}}{\delta}$ disparaissant, comme nous l'avons vu dans l'expression de $F(x)$, il est permis de prendre plus simplement à la limite, pour $\delta = 0$,

$$f(x) = e^{\lambda_0(x - iK')} X.$$

Cette fonction joue donc le rôle d'élément simple ; il est facile, lorsqu'on fait $x = iK' + \varepsilon$, d'obtenir son développement et d'avoir ainsi les quantités qui remplacent, dans le cas présent, les coefficients désignés en général par H_0, H_1, etc. Nous avons en effet, pour $x = iK' + \varepsilon$,

$$X = \left(\lambda_1 + s_0 - \frac{J}{K}\right)\varepsilon + \frac{H'(\varepsilon)}{H(\varepsilon)} = \frac{1}{\varepsilon} + \lambda_1\varepsilon - \frac{s_1\varepsilon^3}{3} - \frac{s_2\varepsilon^5}{5} - \ldots.$$

Multiplions par $e^{\lambda_0\varepsilon}$ les deux membres, et soit

$$e^{\lambda_0\varepsilon} X = \frac{1}{2} + S_0 + S_1\varepsilon + \ldots + S_i\varepsilon^i ;$$

nous trouverons

$$\begin{aligned}
S_0 &= \lambda_0,\\
S_1 &= \frac{\lambda_0^2}{1.2} + \lambda_1,\\
S_2 &= \frac{\lambda_0^3}{1.2.3} + \lambda_1\lambda_0,\\
S_3 &= \frac{\lambda_0^4}{1.2.3.4} + \lambda_1\frac{\lambda_0^2}{1.2} - \frac{s_1}{3},\\
&\ldots\ldots\ldots\ldots\ldots\ldots\ldots\ldots,
\end{aligned}$$

S_i étant, en général, un polynome du degré $i+1$ en λ_0, où n'entrent que des puissances impaires ou des puissances paires, suivant que l'indice est pair ou impair. Les conditions données au paragraphe XLV (p. 392) conduisent donc, dans les deux cas de $n=2\nu$, $n=2\nu-1$, en y joignant l'équation en λ_0 précédemment trouvée, à ces trois relations

$$\begin{gathered}
\frac{\lambda_0^{2\nu-1}}{\Gamma(2\nu)} + h_1\frac{\lambda_0^{2\nu-3}}{\Gamma(2\nu-2)} + \ldots + h_{\nu-1}\lambda_0 = 0,\\
S_{2\nu-1} + h_1 S_{2\nu-3} + h_2 S_{2\nu-5} + \ldots + 2h_{\nu-1}S_1 + h_\nu = 0,\\
2\nu S_{2\nu} + (2\nu-2)h_1 S_{2\nu-2} + (2\nu-4)h_2 S_{2\nu-4} + \ldots + 2h_{\nu-1}S_2 = 0,
\end{gathered}$$

lorsque l'on suppose $n=2\nu$, puis

$$\begin{gathered}
\frac{\lambda_0^{2\nu-2}}{\Gamma(2\nu-1)} + h_1\frac{\lambda_0^{2\nu-4}}{\Gamma(2\nu-3)} + \ldots + h_{\nu-1} = 0,\\
S_{2\nu-2} + h_1 S_{2\nu-4} + h_2 S_{2\nu-6} + \ldots + h_{\nu-1}S_0 = 0,\\
(2\nu-1)S_{2\nu-1} + (2\nu-3)h_1 S_{2\nu-3} + \ldots + h_{\nu-1}S_1 - h_\nu = 0
\end{gathered}$$

pour $n=2\nu-1$. Elles donnent le moyen d'obtenir directement, et sans supposer la connaissance de la solution générale, les trois quantités λ_0, λ_1 et h. Elles montrent aussi qu'on a en particulier la valeur $\lambda_0=0$, à laquelle correspondent les solutions de Lamé. Effectivement, lorsque λ_0 est supposé nul, on obtient

$$S_{2i}=0, \qquad S_1=\lambda_1, \qquad S_{2i+1} = -\frac{s_i}{2i+1};$$

cela étant, dans le cas de $n=2\nu$, la première et la troisième équation sont satisfaites d'elles-mêmes; la deuxième, devenant

$$-\frac{s_{\nu-1}}{2\nu-1} - h_1\frac{s_{\nu-2}}{2\nu-3} - h_2\frac{s_{\nu-3}}{2\nu-5} + \ldots + h_{\nu+1}\lambda_1 + h_\nu = 0,$$

ne détermine que λ_1. Il est donc nécessaire de recourir à l'une des relations en nombre infini qui ont été données au paragraphe XLVI (p. 394), sous ces formes,

$$\mathfrak{H}_i = 0, \qquad \mathfrak{H}_{2i} = h_{i+\nu}, \qquad \mathfrak{H}_{2i+2\nu+1} = C h_i.$$

» La plus simple est

$$\mathfrak{H}_2 = h_{\nu+1},$$

ou bien

$$-\nu(2\nu+1)H_{2\nu+1} + (\nu-1)(2\nu-1)h_1 H_{2\nu-1} + (\nu-2)(2\nu-3)h_2 H_{2\nu-3} + \ldots + 3h_{\nu-1}H_3 + h_{\nu+1} = 0,$$

et nous en tirons immédiatement

$$-\nu s_\nu - (\nu-1)h_1 s_{\nu-1} - (\nu-2)h_2 s_{\nu-2} - \ldots - h_{\nu-1}s_1 + h_{\nu+1} = 0,$$

ce qui est l'équation en h précédemment trouvée.

» En dernier lieu et pour le cas de $n = 2\nu - 1$, nos trois relations se trouvent vérifiées si l'on fait $h_{\nu-1} = 0$; on retrouve donc encore de cette manière le résultat auquel nous étions précédemment parvenu par une méthode toute différente. »

ÉTUDES DE M. SYLVESTER

SUR LA

THÉORIE ALGÉBRIQUE DES FORMES.

Comptes rendus de l'Académie des Sciences, t. LXXXIV, 1877, p. 974.

On doit à M. Paul Gordan, professeur à l'Université d'Erlangen, la belle et importante découverte, qu'à l'égard des formes à deux indéterminées, les invariants et covariants, qui sont, comme on sait, en nombre illimité, peuvent être exprimés tous par les fonctions rationnelles et entières d'un nombre essentiellement fini et limité d'invariants et covariants fondamentaux, nommés, pour ce motif, *Grundformen*. Cette proposition capitale vient d'être étendue par M. Sylvester aux formes les plus générales, quels que soient leur degré et le nombre de leurs indéterminées, et je me fais un devoir de reproduire les termes mêmes dans lesquels l'illustre géomètre m'a chargé d'annoncer sa belle découverte.

Baltimore. — Depuis mon dernier envoi, avertissez l'Académie que j'ai résolu le problème de trouver les *Grundformen* complètes pour des *quantités* quelconques avec n variables.

EXTRAIT

D'UNE

LETTRE DE M. CH. HERMITE A M. L. FUCHS.

Journal de Crelle, t. 82, 1877, p. 343.

Soit

$$Z(x) = \frac{H'(x)}{H(x)};$$

on peut à l'aide de cette fonction représenter toute fonction uniforme, ayant pour périodes $2K$ et $2iK'$, par une formule entièrement analogue à celle d'une fraction rationnelle décomposée en fractions simples, à savoir

$$\begin{aligned} F(x) = \text{const.} &+ AZ(x-a) + A_1 D_x Z(x-a) + A_2 D_x^2 Z(x-a) + \ldots \\ &+ BZ(x-b) + B_1 D_x Z(x-b) + B_2 D_x^2 Z(x-b) + \ldots \\ &+ \ldots\ldots\ldots\ldots\ldots\ldots\ldots\ldots\ldots\ldots\ldots \\ &+ LZ(x-l) + L_1 D_x Z(x-l) + L_2 D_x^2 Z(x-l) + \ldots, \end{aligned}$$

où les constantes A, B, ..., L sont essentiellement assujetties à remplir la condition

$$A + B + \ldots + L = 0.$$

C'est cette expression, dont j'ai fait usage dans bien des circonstances, que je vais employer à la recherche des coordonnées d'une cubique plane en fonction explicite d'un paramètre. Je pose à cet effet

$$\begin{aligned} x &= x_0 + A\,Z(t-a) + B\,Z(t-b) + C\,Z(t-c), \\ y &= y_0 + A'Z(t-a) + B'Z(t-b) + C'Z(t-c), \end{aligned}$$

avec les conditions

$$A + B + C = 0, \qquad A' + B' + C' = 0,$$

de sorte que les coordonnées x et y se trouveront des fonctions linéaires des deux différences : $Z(t-a)-Z(t-c)$ et $Z(t-b)-Z(t-c)$. Cela étant, je remarque que x^2, xy, y^2 étant des fonctions doublement périodiques uniformes aux périodes $2K$ et $2iK'$, s'expriment linéairement, d'une part par ces deux différences, et de l'autre par les dérivées $D_t Z(t-a)$, $D_t Z(t-b)$, $D_t Z(t-c)$. Et pareillement, si l'on considère x^3, x^2y, xy^2, y^3, il résulte de la formule générale qu'on aura seulement les dérivées secondes $D_t^2 Z(t-a)$, $D_t^2 Z(t-b)$, $D_t^2 Z(t-c)$, à joindre aux dérivées premières et aux deux différences. Ce sont donc huit fonctions en tout, entrant linéairement dans les neuf fonctions doublement périodiques, que je viens de former, et la relation du troisième degré entre les coordonnées x et y en est la conséquence immédiate. J'ajoute que ces coordonnées renfermant, en premier lieu, les constantes a, b, c, ou seulement $a-c$, $b-c$, car on peut mettre $t-c$ au lieu de t, puis les coefficients A, B, A', B', et enfin x_0 et y_0, contiendront huit arbitraires, de sorte qu'en y joignant le module de la transcendante, on aura bien le nombre maximum égal à neuf, des indéterminées d'une cubique plane quelconque.

Soit maintenant

$$\begin{aligned}
x &= x_0 + A\,Z(t-a) + B\,Z(t-b) + C\,Z(t-c) + D\,Z(t-d),\\
y &= y_0 + A'Z(t-a) + B'Z(t-b) + C'Z(t-c) + D'Z(t-d),\\
z &= z_0 + A''Z(t-a) + B''Z(t-b) + C''Z(t-c) + D''Z(t-d),
\end{aligned}$$

avec les conditions

$$\Sigma A = 0, \qquad \Sigma A' = 0, \qquad \Sigma A'' = 0.$$

Ces trois quantités d'une part, et celles-ci de l'autre, à savoir : x^2, y^2, z^2, xy, xz, yz, s'exprimeront en fonctions linéaires de $Z(t-a)-Z(t-d)$, $Z(t-b)-Z(t-d)$, $Z(t-c)-Z(t-d)$, et des quatre dérivées $D_t Z(t-a)$, etc. On a par conséquent sept fonctions, dans l'expression de neuf quantités, qui dès lors sont liées par deux équations, de sorte que les quantités considérées représentent bien l'intersection de deux surfaces du second ordre, et comme ci-dessus, on voit qu'elles contiennent le nombre d'arbitraires maximum que comporte une telle courbe, lequel est égal à seize.

Je reviens à la Géométrie plane pour considérer les courbes de Clebsch, dont les coordonnées sont des fonctions elliptiques d'un paramètre, que je prends sous la forme suivante :

$$x = x_0 + \mathrm{A}\,\mathrm{Z}(t-a) + \mathrm{B}\,\mathrm{Z}(t-b) + \ldots + \mathrm{L}\,\mathrm{Z}(t-l),$$
$$y = y_0 + \mathrm{A}'\mathrm{Z}(t-a) + \mathrm{B}'\mathrm{Z}(t-b) + \ldots + \mathrm{L}'\mathrm{Z}(t-l),$$

en supposant toujours

$$\Sigma\mathrm{A} = 0, \qquad \Sigma\mathrm{A}' = 0.$$

Le succès de la méthode précédente dans le cas de la cubique m'a fait tenter d'établir par la même voie que x et y satisfont à une équation algébrique d'un degré égal au nombre des transcendantes : $\mathrm{Z}(t-a)$, $\mathrm{Z}(t-b)$, ..., $\mathrm{Z}(t-l)$. Mais les choses se passent alors moins simplement. Considérez en effet les diverses fonctions homogènes de x et y, jusqu'au degré μ, dont le nombre sera $2+3+\ldots+\mu+1 = \frac{1}{2}(\mu^2+3\mu)$, et soit m le nombre des transcendantes. Toutes ces fonctions doublement périodiques s'expriment linéairement par les différences : $\mathrm{Z}(t-a)-\mathrm{Z}(t-l)$, $\mathrm{Z}(t-b)-\mathrm{Z}(t-l)$, ..., en nombre $m-1$, puis par les dérivées jusqu'à l'ordre $\mu-1$, des quantités $\mathrm{Z}(t-a)$, c'est-à-dire en tout par $m-1+m(\mu-1)$ fonctions. Afin donc de pouvoir effectuer l'élimination de ces fonctions, je pose la condition

$$\frac{1}{2}(\mu^2+3\mu) = m + m(\mu-1) = m\mu$$

qui me donne $\mu = 2m-3$, de sorte que je parviens par cette voie à une courbe d'ordre $2m-3$, au lieu d'obtenir l'ordre m. Le procédé qui réussit dans le cas de $m=3$, donne donc en général un degré trop élevé, et j'ai dû complètement y renoncer, comme méthode d'élimination. Mais l'existence, au moins, d'une équation de ce degré m se prouve très facilement. Considérez pour cela une droite arbitraire $\alpha x + \beta y + \gamma = 0$, dont les points de rencontre avec la courbe s'obtiennent en déterminant t par l'équation

$$\alpha x_0 + \beta y_0 + \gamma + (\mathrm{A}\alpha + \mathrm{A}'\beta)\mathrm{Z}(t-a) + (\mathrm{B}\alpha + \mathrm{B}'\beta)\mathrm{Z}(t-b) + \ldots = 0.$$

Le premier membre de cette équation est une fonction doublement périodique qui devient infinie pour les m valeurs

$$t = a, b, c, \ldots, l.$$

Elle ne peut donc s'annuler, d'après un théorème connu de la théorie des fonctions elliptiques, que pour m valeurs de t, dans l'intérieur du rectangle des périodes $2K$ et $2iK'$, et la courbe ne pouvant être coupée qu'en m points par une droite quelconque, est bien d'ordre m.

Ce même raisonnement appliqué à la polaire, dont les coordonnées sont

$$X = \frac{-y'}{xy' - x'y}, \qquad Y = \frac{x'}{xy' - x'y},$$

en détermine le degré.

Effectivement les intersections de cette seconde courbe avec la droite $\alpha X + \beta Y + \gamma = 0$ sont données par l'élément

$$-\alpha y' + \beta x' + \gamma(xy' - yx') = 0,$$

et vous voyez, que son premier membre est une fonction doublement périodique, admettant les infinis doubles $t = a, b, \ldots, l$, de sorte qu'on a $2m$ racines, et par suite $2m$ points d'intersection. Connaissant l'ordre de la polaire des courbes de Clebsch, $\delta = 2m$, le nombre d des points doubles de ces courbes en résulte immédiatement, comme conséquence de la relation $2d + \delta = m(m-1)$ donnée dans mon *Cours d'Analyse* (p. 385); on trouve ainsi par une voie facile la proposition fondamentale $d = \frac{1}{2}m(m-3)$ démontrée par Clebsch (t. 63 de ce *Journal*, p. 189).

Paris, 29 juin 1876.

P.-S. — La détermination des points d'inflexion de la cubique plane, et des points stationnaires de la quadrique dans l'espace, dépendent des équations suivantes :

$$\begin{vmatrix} Z'(t-a) - Z'(t-c) & Z'(t-b) - Z'(t-c) \\ Z''(t-a) - Z''(t-c) & Z''(t-b) - Z''(t-c) \end{vmatrix} = 0$$

et

$$\begin{vmatrix} Z'(t-a) - Z'(t-d) & Z'(t-b) - Z'(t-d) & Z'(t-c) - Z'(t-d) \\ Z''(t-a) - Z''(t-d) & Z''(t-b) - Z''(t-d) & Z''(t-c) - Z''(t-d) \\ Z'''(t-a) - Z'''(t-d) & Z'''(t-b) - Z'''(t-d) & Z'''(t-c) - Z'''(t-d) \end{vmatrix} = 0.$$

Je me suis proposé de calculer les déterminants qui forment les premiers membres, et j'ai trouvé les expressions suivantes. Soit pour abréger

$$\begin{aligned}\Phi(a, b, c) &= \mathrm{H}(a-b)\,\mathrm{H}(a-c)\,\mathrm{H}(b-c),\\ \Phi(a, b, c, d) &= \mathrm{H}(a-b)\,\mathrm{H}(a-c)\,\mathrm{H}(a-d)\\ &\qquad\mathrm{H}(b-c)\,\mathrm{H}(b-d)\\ &\qquad\mathrm{H}(c-d),\end{aligned}$$

le premier déterminant est

$$\mathrm{H}'(0)^5\,\frac{\Phi(a, b, c)\,\mathrm{H}(3t-a-b-c)}{[\mathrm{H}(t-a)\,\mathrm{H}(t-b)\,\mathrm{H}(t-c)]^3},$$

et le second

$$\mathrm{H}'(0)^9\,\frac{\Phi(a, b, c, d)\,\mathrm{H}(4t-a-b-c-d)}{[\mathrm{H}(t-a)\,\mathrm{H}(t-b)\,\mathrm{H}(t-c)\,\mathrm{H}(t-d)]^4}.$$

Les beaux résultats découverts par Clebsch sont la conséquence de ces expressions qui m'ont amené à considérer, en général, le déterminant à $n-1$ colonnes

$$\begin{vmatrix} \mathrm{Z}'(t-a)-\mathrm{Z}'(t-l) & \mathrm{Z}'(t-b)-\mathrm{Z}'(t-l) & \ldots & \mathrm{Z}'(t-k)-\mathrm{Z}'(t-l) \\ \mathrm{Z}''(t-a)-\mathrm{Z}''(t-l) & \mathrm{Z}''(t-b)-\mathrm{Z}''(t-l) & \ldots & \mathrm{Z}''(t-k)-\mathrm{Z}''(t-l) \\ \ldots\ldots & \ldots\ldots & \ldots & \ldots\ldots \\ \mathrm{Z}^{n-1}(t-a)-\mathrm{Z}^{n-1}(t-l) & \mathrm{Z}^{n-1}(t-b)-\mathrm{Z}^{n-1}(t-l) & \ldots & \mathrm{Z}^{n-1}(t-k)-\mathrm{Z}^{n-1}(t-l) \end{vmatrix}$$

où $a, b, \ldots, k, l$ sont n constantes. Si l'on pose comme précédemment

$$\begin{aligned}\Phi(a, b, \ldots, k, l) = \mathrm{H}(a-b)\,&\mathrm{H}(a-c)\ldots\mathrm{H}(a-l)\\ &\mathrm{H}(b-c)\ldots\mathrm{H}(b-l)\\ &\ldots\ldots\ldots\ldots\\ &\mathrm{H}(k-l),\end{aligned}$$

on trouve qu'il a pour valeur

$$\mu\,\mathrm{H}'(0)^{\frac{1}{2}(n-1)(n+2)}\,\frac{\Phi(a, b, \ldots, k, l)\,\mathrm{H}(nt-a-b-\ldots-l)}{[\mathrm{H}(t-a)\,\mathrm{H}(t-b)\ldots\mathrm{H}(t-l)]^n},$$

μ désignant un facteur numérique.

Paris, 29 décembre 1876.

EXTRAIT D'UNE LETTRE DE M. CH. HERMITE A M. BORCHARDT

SUR LA FORMULE DE MACLAURIN.

Journal de Crelle, t. 84, 1878, p. 64.

Les propriétés de la fonction de Jacob Bernouilli établies par M. Malmsten dans son beau Mémoire sur la formule

$$hu'_x = \Delta u_x - \frac{1}{2} h \Delta u'_x + \ldots$$

(t. 35 de ce *Journal*, p. 55) peuvent être obtenues par une autre méthode à laquelle m'ont conduit les recherches que vous avez publiées, t. 79, p. 339. Reprenant à cet effet l'équation de définition, à savoir

$$\frac{e^{\lambda x} - 1}{e^{\lambda} - 1} = S(x)_0 + \frac{\lambda}{1} S(x)_1 + \frac{\lambda^2}{1.2} S(x)_2 + \ldots,$$

de sorte que l'on ait pour x entier

$$S(x)_n = 1^n + 2^n + 3^n + \ldots + (x-1)^n,$$

je remplacerai d'abord λ par $i\lambda$, ce qui donnera

$$\frac{e^{i\lambda x} - 1}{e^{i\lambda} - 1} = \frac{e^{\frac{1}{2}i\lambda x}\left(e^{\frac{1}{2}i\lambda x} - e^{-\frac{1}{2}i\lambda x}\right)}{e^{\frac{1}{2}i\lambda}\left(e^{\frac{1}{2}i\lambda} - e^{-\frac{1}{2}i\lambda}\right)} = \frac{e^{\frac{1}{2}i\lambda(x-1)} \sin\frac{1}{2}\lambda x}{\sin\frac{1}{2}\lambda}$$

$$= \frac{\sin\frac{1}{2}\lambda x \cos\frac{1}{2}\lambda(x-1)}{\sin\frac{1}{2}\lambda} + i\frac{\sin\frac{1}{2}\lambda x \sin\frac{1}{2}\lambda(x-1)}{\sin\frac{1}{2}\lambda},$$

et l'on en conclura ces deux égalités, où je fais pour abréger $(n) = 1.2.3\ldots n$:

$$(1)\quad \frac{\sin\frac{1}{2}\lambda x \sin\frac{1}{2}\lambda(x-1)}{\sin\frac{1}{2}\lambda} = \lambda\, S(x)_1 - \frac{\lambda^3}{(3)} S(x)_3 + \frac{\lambda^5}{(5)} S(x)_5 - \ldots,$$

$$(2)\quad \frac{\sin\frac{1}{2}\lambda x \cos\frac{1}{2}\lambda(x-1)}{\sin\frac{1}{2}\lambda} = S(x)_0 - \frac{\lambda^2}{(2)} S(x)_2 + \frac{\lambda^4}{(4)} S(x)_4 - \ldots.$$

Ceci posé, la formule suivante dans laquelle B_1, B_2, etc., désignent suivant l'usage les nombres de Bernouilli

$$\log\sin\frac{1}{2}x = \log\frac{1}{2}x - \frac{B_1}{(2)}\frac{x^2}{2} - \frac{B_2}{(4)}\frac{x^4}{4} - \ldots - \frac{B_n}{(2n)}\frac{x^{2n}}{2n} - \ldots$$

conduit à une expression analytique des polynomes $S(x)_n$, qui met immédiatement en évidence les propriétés découvertes par M. Malmsten. En considérant d'abord la première de nos deux relations, on en déduit en effet

$$\begin{aligned}\log\frac{\sin\frac{1}{2}\lambda x \sin\frac{1}{2}\lambda(x-1)}{\sin\frac{1}{2}\lambda} = \log\frac{1}{2}\lambda x(x-1) &+ [1 - x^2 - (1-x)^2]\,\frac{B_1}{(2)}\frac{\lambda^2}{2}\\ &+ [1 - x^4 - (1-x)^4]\,\frac{B_2}{(4)}\frac{\lambda^4}{4}\\ &+ \ldots\ldots\ldots\ldots\ldots\ldots\\ &+ [1 - x^{2n} - (1-x)^{2n}]\,\frac{B_n}{(2n)}\frac{\lambda^{2n}}{2n}\\ &+ \ldots\ldots\ldots\ldots\ldots\ldots\end{aligned}$$

Posant donc

$$X_n = 1 - x^{2n} - (1-x)^{2n}$$

et observant que

$$X_1 = -2x(x-1),$$

nous avons cette formule

$$\frac{\sin\frac{1}{2}\lambda x \sin\frac{1}{2}\lambda(x-1)}{\sin\frac{1}{2}\lambda} = -\frac{\lambda}{4} X_1\, e^{\frac{B_1 X_1}{(2)}\frac{\lambda^2}{2} + \frac{B_2 X_2}{(4)}\frac{\lambda^4}{4} + \ldots}$$

dont voici les conséquences. Je remarque que le développement de l'exponentielle, suivant les puissances de λ, donnera pour le coefficient d'une puissance quelconque de cette indéterminée, une fonction rationnelle et entière des quantités X_1, X_2, $\ldots$, X_n, dont les coefficients seront tous positifs. On trouvera successivement, en effet,

$$S(x)_1 = -\frac{1}{4}X_1,$$

$$S(x)_3 = \frac{1}{16}X_1^2,$$

$$S(x)_5 = -\frac{1}{192}(2X_1X_2 + 5X_1^3),$$

$$S(x)_7 = \frac{1}{2304}(16X_1X_3 + 42X_1^2X_2 + 35X_1^4),$$

....

Or X_n qui s'annule pour $x=0$ et $x=1$, n'admet dans l'intervalle de ces deux racines, qu'un seul maximum, correspondant à la valeur $x=\frac{1}{2}$, comme le montre la dérivée

$$D_x X_n = -2nx^{2n-1} + 2n(1-x)^{2n-1}.$$

Cette valeur ne dépendant point de n, fournit par conséquent le maximum de toute fonction rationnelle entière et à coefficients positifs des quantités X_n, et il est ainsi prouvé que le polynome $(-1)^{n-1}S(x)_{2n+1}$, est positif quand la variable croît de $x=0$ à $x=1$, et acquiert sa valeur la plus grande pour $x=\frac{1}{2}$.

Je passe à l'équation (2) qui concerne les polynomes d'indices pairs, et en écrivant le premier membre sous la forme $\frac{1}{2}+\frac{\sin\frac{1}{2}\lambda(2x-1)}{\sin\frac{1}{2}\lambda}$, je développerai le logarithme de la quantité $\frac{\sin\frac{1}{2}\lambda(2x-1)}{\sin\frac{1}{2}\lambda}$. On sera ainsi amené à employer l'expression

$$X_n^0 = 1-(2x-1)^{2n},$$

qui permettra d'écrire

$$\log\frac{\sin\frac{1}{2}\lambda(2x-1)}{\sin\frac{1}{2}\lambda} = \log(2x-1) + \frac{B_1X_1^0}{(2)}\frac{\lambda^2}{2} + \frac{B_2X_2^0}{(4)}\frac{\lambda^4}{4} + \dots$$

et par suite

$$\frac{\sin\frac{1}{2}\lambda(2x-1)}{\sin\frac{1}{2}\lambda} = (2x-1)e^{\frac{B_1X_1^0}{(2)}\frac{\lambda^2}{2}+\frac{B_2X_2^0}{(4)}\frac{\lambda^4}{4}+\dots}.$$

Les polynomes X_n^0 possèdent la même propriété que les précédents de s'annuler pour $x=0$, $x=1$, et de n'admettre dans l'intervalle qu'un seul maximum correspondant à $x=\frac{1}{2}$. Il en est donc aussi de même de tous les coefficients des puissances de λ dans le développement de l'exponentielle, et en exceptant seulement $S(x)_0$, nous avons cette seconde proposition que les polynomes $\frac{(-1)^n S(x)_{2n}}{2x-1}$ sont positifs de $x=0$ à $x=1$ avec un seul maximum dans l'intervalle pour $x=\frac{1}{2}$.

La facilité avec laquelle les propriétés des polynomes $S(x)_n$ résultent de la forme trigonométrique de leurs fonctions génératrices conduit à employer ces mêmes fonctions pour établir la formule de Maclaurin. A cet effet je partirai de la formule élémentaire

$$\int U^{2n} V\,dx = U^{2n-1}V - U^{2n-2}V' + \ldots - UV^{2n-1} + \int UV^{2n}\,dx,$$

où U et V sont deux fonctions quelconques de la variable x, dont les dérivées d'ordre k sont désignées par U^k et V^k. Posons pour abréger

$$\Phi(x) = U^{2n-1}V + U^{2n-3}V'' + \ldots + U'V^{2n-2},$$
$$\Psi(x) = U^{2n-2}V' + U^{2n-4}V''' + \ldots + U\,V^{2n-1},$$

ce qui donnera

$$\int U^{2n} V\,dx = \Phi(x) - \Psi(x) + \int UV^{2n}\,dx;$$

en laissant arbitraire la fonction V, je prendrai

$$U = \frac{\sin\frac{1}{2}\lambda x \sin\frac{1}{2}\lambda(x-1)}{\sin\frac{1}{2}\lambda} = S(x)_1 - \frac{\lambda^3}{1.2.3}S(x)_3 + \ldots$$

et il sera facile d'obtenir les expressions de $\Phi(x)$ et $\Psi(x)$, si l'on met U sous la forme $\frac{\cos\frac{1}{2}\lambda - \cos\frac{1}{2}\lambda(2x-1)}{2\sin\frac{1}{2}\lambda}$. Ayant en effet

$$U^{2k} = (-1)^k\lambda^{2k}\,\frac{\cos\frac{1}{2}\lambda(2x-1)}{2\sin\frac{1}{2}\lambda},$$
$$U^{2k-1} = (-1)^k\lambda^{2k-1}\,\frac{\sin\frac{1}{2}\lambda(2x-1)}{2\sin\frac{1}{2}\lambda},$$

on trouvera

$$\Phi(x) = (-1)^n \frac{\sin\frac{1}{2}\lambda(2x-1)}{2\sin\frac{1}{2}\lambda}[\lambda^{2n-1}V - \lambda^{2n-3}V'' + \ldots - (-1)^n\lambda V^{2n-2}],$$

$$\Psi(x) = (-1)^{n-1}\frac{\cos\frac{1}{2}\lambda(2x-1)}{2\sin\frac{1}{2}\lambda}[\lambda^{2n-2}V' - \lambda^{2n-4}V''' + \ldots + (-1)^n \quad V^{2n-1}]$$
$$+ \frac{\cos\frac{1}{2}\lambda}{2\sin\frac{1}{2}\lambda}V^{2n-1}.$$

Maintenant désignons les valeurs de V^k pour $x = 1$ et $x = 0$, par V_1^k et V_0^k, de ce qui précède nous déduirons les formules

$$\Phi(1) - \Psi(0) = \frac{(-1)^n}{2}[\lambda^{2n-1}(V_1 + V_0) - \lambda^{2n-3}(V_1'' + V_0'') + \ldots],$$

$$\Psi(1) - \Psi(0) = \frac{(-1)^{n-1}\cos\frac{1}{2}\lambda}{2\sin\frac{1}{2}\lambda}[\lambda^{2n-2}(V_1' - V_0') - \lambda^{2n-4}(V_1''' - V_0''') + \ldots]$$
$$+ \frac{\cos\frac{1}{2}\lambda}{2\sin\frac{1}{2}\lambda}(V_1^{2n-1} - V_0^{2n-1}),$$

dont la première comme on voit renferme des sommes et la seconde des différences. Soit encore

$$\varphi(\lambda) = \lambda^{2n-2}(V_1 + V_0) - \lambda^{2n-2}(V_1'' + V_0'') + \ldots + (-1)^n \;\lambda(V_1^{2n-2} + V_0^{2n-2}),$$
$$\psi(\lambda) = \lambda^{2n-2}(V_1' - V_0') - \lambda^{2n-4}(V_1''' - V_0''') + \ldots + (-1)^n\lambda^2(V_1^{2n-3} - V_0^{2n-3});$$

en remarquant que le terme indépendant de λ disparaît dans la seconde formule, nous pouvons écrire

$$\Phi(1) - \Phi(0) = \frac{(-1)^n}{2}\varphi(\lambda),$$

$$\Psi(1) - \Psi(0) = \frac{(-1)^{n-1}\cot\frac{1}{2}\lambda}{2}\psi(\lambda),$$

et l'on en conclura, en prenant pour limites des intégrales zéro et l'unité, la relation suivante :

$$(-1)^n\int_0^1 \lambda^{2n}\frac{\cos\frac{1}{2}\lambda(2x-1)}{2\sin\frac{1}{2}\lambda}V\,dx$$
$$= \frac{(-1)^n}{2}\varphi(\lambda) - \frac{(-1)^{n-1}\cot\frac{1}{2}\lambda}{2}\psi(\lambda) + \int_0^1 \frac{\cos\frac{1}{2}\lambda - \cos\frac{1}{2}\lambda(2x-1)}{2\sin\frac{1}{2}\lambda}V^{2n}\,dx,$$

ou, plus simplement,

$$\int_0^1 \lambda^{2n}\frac{\cos\frac{1}{2}\lambda(2x-1)}{2\sin\frac{1}{2}\lambda}V\,dx = \frac{1}{2}\varphi(\lambda) + \frac{\cot\frac{1}{2}\lambda}{2}\psi(\lambda) + (-1)^n\int_0^1 UV^{2n}\,dx.$$

Elle donne parmi divers résultats la formule de Maclaurin que j'ai eue principalement en vue, et qui s'obtient, comme on va le voir, en égalant les termes en λ^{2n-1}. Posons en effet $V = f(x_0 + hx)$, d'où

$$V_1^k = h^k f^k(x_0 + h), \qquad V_0^k = h^k f^k(x_0);$$

le coefficient de λ^{2n-1}, dans la quantité $\frac{1}{2}\cot\frac{1}{2}\lambda\psi(\lambda)$, s'obtient au moyen de la série

$$\frac{1}{2}\cot\frac{1}{2}\lambda = \frac{1}{\lambda} - \frac{B_1\lambda}{(2)} - \frac{B_2\lambda^3}{(4)} - \frac{B_3\lambda^5}{(6)} - \ldots,$$

sous la forme suivante :

$$\begin{aligned} &-\frac{B_1 h}{(2)}[f'(x_0+h) - f'(x_0)] + \frac{B_2 h^3}{(4)}[f'''(x_0+h) - f'''(x_0)] - \ldots \\ &+ (-1)^{n-1}\frac{B_{n-1}h^{2n-3}}{(2n-2)}[f^{2n-3}(x_0+h) - f^{2n-3}(x_0)]. \end{aligned}$$

D'ailleurs, dans $\varphi(\lambda)$, le coefficient du même terme est simplement

$$V_1 + V_0 = f(x_0 + h) + f(x_0);$$

dans la fonction

$$U = \lambda\,S(x)_1 - \frac{\lambda^3}{(3)}S(x)_3 + \ldots,$$

son expression est $\frac{(-1)^{n-1}}{(2n-1)}S(x)_{2n-1}$; on est par conséquent amené à l'égalité

$$\begin{aligned} \int_0^1 f(x_0+hx)\,dx = \frac{1}{2}[f(x_0+h) + f(x_0)] &- \frac{B_1 h}{(2)}[f'(x_0+h) - f'(x_0)] \\ &+ \frac{B_2 h^3}{(4)}[f'''(x_0+h) - f'''(x_0)] + \ldots \\ &+ (-1)^{n-1}\frac{B_{n-1}h^{2n-3}}{(2n-2)}[f^{2n-3}(x_0+h) - f^{2n-3}(x_0)] \\ &- \frac{h^{2n}}{(2n-1)}\int_0^1 f^{2n}(x_0+hx)\,S(x)_{2n-1}\,dx \end{aligned}$$

qui se ramène à la forme habituelle, en remplaçant dans le premier membre l'intégrale $\int_0^1 f(x_0+hx)\,dx$ par $\frac{1}{h}\int_{x_0}^{x_0+h} f(x)\,dx$.

La proposition de M. Malmsten à l'égard de $S(x)_{2n-1}$ permet ensuite d'écrire

$$\int_0^1 f^{2n}(x_0 + hx)\,\mathrm{S}(x)_{2n-1}\,dx = f^{2n}(x_0 + \theta h)\int_0^1 \mathrm{S}(x)_{2n-1}\,dx,$$

θ étant compris entre zéro et l'unité. Quant au facteur $\int_0^1 \mathrm{S}(x)_{2n-1}\,dx$, il est donné par le coefficient de $\frac{(-1)^{n-1}\lambda^{2n-1}}{(2n-1)}$, dans le développement de l'intégrale

$$\int_0^1 \frac{\cos\frac{1}{2}\lambda - \cos(2x-1)\frac{1}{2}\lambda}{2\sin\frac{1}{2}\lambda}\,dx = \frac{1}{2}\cot\frac{1}{2}\lambda,$$

d'où la valeur

$$\int_0^1 \mathrm{S}(x)_{m-1}\,dx = (-1)^n \mathrm{B}_n,$$

de sorte que la formule ordinaire s'obtiendra en remplaçant dans le premier membre l'intégrale

$$\int_0^1 f(x_0 + hx)\,dx \qquad \text{par} \qquad \frac{1}{h}\int_{x_0}^{x_0+h} f(x)\,dx.$$

Paris, 7 avril 1877.

EXTRAIT D'UNE LETTRE DE M. CH. HERMITE A M. BORCHARDT

SUR LA

FORMULE D'INTERPOLATION DE LAGRANGE.

Journal de Crelle, t. 84, 1878, p. 70.

Je me suis proposé de trouver un polynome entier $F(x)$ de degré $n-1$, satisfaisant aux conditions suivantes :

$$\begin{array}{llll}
F(a)=f(a), & F'(a)=f'(a), & \ldots, & F^{\alpha-1}(a)=f^{\alpha-1}(a),\\
F(b)=f(b), & F'(b)=f'(b), & \ldots, & F^{\beta-1}(b)=f^{\beta-1}(b),\\
\ldots\ldots\ldots, & \ldots\ldots\ldots, & \ldots, & \ldots\ldots\ldots\ldots,\\
F(l)=f(l), & F'(l)=f'(l), & \ldots. & F^{\lambda-1}(l)=f^{\lambda-1}(l),
\end{array}$$

où $f(x)$ est une fonction donnée. En supposant

$$\alpha+\beta+\ldots+\lambda=n,$$

la question comme on voit est déterminée et conduira à une généralisation de la formule de Lagrange sur laquelle je présenterai quelques remarques. Elle se résout d'abord facilement comme il suit. Je considère une aire s, comprenant d'une part, a, b, $\ldots$, l, et de l'autre la quantité x; je suppose qu'à son intérieur la fonction $f(x)$ soit uniforme et n'ait aucun pôle; cela étant je vais établir la relation

$$F(x)-f(x)=\frac{1}{2i\pi}\int_s \frac{f(z)(x-a)^\alpha(x-b)^\beta\ldots(x-l)^\lambda}{(x-z)(z-a)^\alpha(z-b)^\beta\ldots(z-l)^\lambda}\,dz,$$

l'intégrale du second membre se rapportant au contour de s, et en même temps donner l'expression du polynome cherché $F(x)$.

Faisons pour abréger

$$\Phi(x) = (x-a)^\alpha (x-b)^\beta \ldots (x-l)^\lambda$$

et

$$\varphi(x) = \frac{f(z)\Phi(x)}{(x-z)\Phi(z)};$$

l'intégrale curviligne sera la somme des résidus de $\varphi(z)$ pour les valeurs $z = a, b, \ldots, l$ et $z = x$. Le dernier de ces résidus est évidemment $-f(x)$; à l'égard des autres, en considérant pour fixer les idées celui qui correspond à $z = a$, je vais le déterminer par le calcul du terme en $\frac{1}{h}$ dans le développement de $\varphi(a+h)$, suivant les puissances croissantes de h.

Observons d'abord qu'on a

$$\Phi(a+h) = h^\alpha (a-b+h)^\beta (a-c+h)^\gamma \ldots (a-l+h)^\lambda,$$

de sorte qu'en posant

$$\begin{aligned}&(a-b+h)^{-\beta}(a-c+h)^{-\gamma}\ldots(a-l+h)^{-\lambda}\\ &\quad = A + A_1 h + A_2 h^2 + \ldots + A_{\alpha-1} h^{\alpha-1} + \ldots,\end{aligned}$$

nous pouvons écrire

$$\varphi(a+h) = \frac{f(a+h)\Phi(x)}{(x-a-h)h^\alpha}[A + A_1 h + A_2 h^2 + \ldots].$$

Effectuons ensuite le produit des deux séries

$$f(a+h) = f(a) + f'(a)\frac{h}{1} + f''(a)\frac{h^2}{1.2} + \ldots + f^{\alpha-1}(a)\frac{h^{\alpha-1}}{1.2\ldots\alpha-1} + \ldots,$$

$$\frac{1}{x-a-h} = \frac{1}{x-a} + \frac{h}{(x-a)^2} + \frac{h^2}{(x-a)^3} + \ldots + \frac{h^{\alpha-1}}{(x-a)^\alpha} + \ldots;$$

il est clair qu'on aura pour résultat

$$\frac{f(a+h)}{x-a-h} = \frac{X_0}{x-a} + \frac{X_1 h}{(x-a)^2} + \frac{X_2 h^2}{(x-a)^3} + \ldots + \frac{X_{\alpha-1} h^{\alpha-1}}{(x-a)^\alpha} + \ldots,$$

X_i désignant un polynome entier en x du degré i. Il résulte que le résidu cherché, étant le coefficient de $h^{\alpha-1}$, dans le produit

$$\begin{aligned}&\Phi(x)[A + A_1 h + A_2 h^2 + \ldots + A_{\alpha-1} h^{\alpha-1}]\\ &\quad + \left[\frac{X_0}{x-a} + \frac{X_1 h}{(x-a)^2} + \frac{X_2 h^2}{(x-a)^3} + \ldots + \frac{X_{\alpha-1} h^{\alpha-1}}{(x-a)^\alpha}\right],\end{aligned}$$

aura pour expression

$$\Phi(x)\left[\frac{AX_{\alpha-1}}{(x-a)^{\alpha}}+\frac{A_1X_{\alpha-2}}{(x-a)^{\alpha-1}}+\ldots+\frac{A_{\alpha-1}X_0}{x-a}\right],$$

ou encore

$$(x-b)^{\beta}(x-c)^{\gamma}\ldots(x-l)^{\lambda}$$
$$\times[AX_{\alpha-1}+A_1X_{\alpha-2}(x-a)+\ldots+A_{\alpha-1}X_0(x-a)^{\alpha-1}].$$

C'est donc à l'égard de la variable x, un polynome entier de degré $\alpha+\beta+\ldots+\lambda-1=n-1$; il en est de même des autres résidus de $\varphi(z)$, et par conséquent leur somme que je désignerai par $F(x)$ est bien un polynome entier de degré $n-1$, dans la relation que nous venons d'obtenir

$$F(x)-f(x)=\frac{1}{2i\pi}\int_s \frac{f(z)\,\Phi(x)}{(x-z)\,\Phi(z)}\,dz.$$

Observez maintenant que l'intégrale du second membre, renfermant comme facteur, sous le signe d'intégration, la fonction $\Phi(x)$, s'annule ainsi que ses dérivées par rapport à x, jusqu'à l'ordre $\alpha-1$ pour $x=a$ jusqu'à l'ordre $\beta-1$ pour $x=b$, etc. Il est ainsi immédiatement mis en évidence que $F(x)$ est le polynome cherché, toutes les conditions à remplir se trouvant en effet satisfaites. Mais de plus, nous obtenons une expression de la différence entre la fonction et le polynome d'interpolation, sous une forme permettant de reconnaître qu'elle diminue sans limite, lorsque le nombre des quantités $a, b, \ldots, l$, ou bien les exposants $\alpha, \beta, \ldots, \lambda$ vont en augmentant. Effectivement, si nous admettons que tous les cercles passant par le point dont l'affixe est x et ayant pour centres les n points $a, b, \ldots, l$ soient contenus à l'intérieur de s, les rayons de ces cercles, c'est-à-dire les modules de $x-a$, $x-b$, ..., seront respectivement inférieurs aux modules des quantités $z-a$, $z-b$, ..., $z-l$, lorsque la variable z décrit le contour de l'aire.

Le module du facteur $\frac{\Phi(x)}{\Phi(z)}$ entrant dans l'intégrale curviligne peut ainsi devenir moindre que toute quantité donnée, lorsqu'on augmente le degré du polynome $F(x)$.

Cette considération est d'ailleurs exactement celle dont on fait usage à l'égard du reste de la série de Taylor,

$$R = \frac{1}{2i\pi}\int_s \frac{f(z)(x-a)^\alpha}{(x-z)(z-a)^\alpha}dz,$$

lorsqu'on veut établir la convergence de cette série pour des valeurs imaginaires de la variable. J'ajouterai cette remarque que la différentiation par rapport à a donne

$$\frac{dR}{da} = \frac{\alpha(x-a)^{\alpha-1}}{2i\pi}\int_s \frac{f(z)\,dz}{(z-a)^{\alpha+1}},$$

de sorte que la formule

$$f^{(\alpha)}(a) = \frac{1.2\ldots\alpha}{2i\pi}\int_s \frac{f(z)\,dz}{(z-a)^{\alpha+1}}$$

permet d'écrire

$$\frac{dR}{da} = \frac{(x-a)^{\alpha-1}f^{(\alpha)}(a)}{1.2\ldots\alpha-1},$$

et l'on en conclut, R s'évanouissant pour $a = x$, la forme élémentaire du reste

$$R = \int_x^a \frac{(x-a)^{\alpha-1}f^{(\alpha)}(a)\,da}{1.2\ldots\alpha-1}.$$

Après avoir rattaché à un même point de vue la série de Taylor et la formule d'interpolation de Lagrange, qui s'obtiennent, comme on voit, en posant

$$\Phi(x) = (x-a)^\alpha \qquad \text{et} \qquad \Phi(x) = (x-a)(x-b)\ldots(x-l),$$

je vais considérer un nouveau cas et faire

$$\Phi(x) = (x-a)^\alpha(x-b)^\beta.$$

Si l'expression des polynomes $F(x)$ devient alors plus compliquée, l'intégrale $\int_a^b F(x)\,dx$ donne, pour la valeur approchée de la quadrature $\int_a^b f(x)\,dx$, un résultat très simple, auquel on parvient comme il suit.

Nommons A et B les résidus correspondant à $z = a$ et $z = b$ de la fonction

$$\varphi(z) = \frac{f(z)(x-a)^\alpha(x-b)^\beta}{(x-z)(z-a)^\alpha(z-b)^\beta},$$

de sorte qu'on ait

$$\mathrm{F}(x) = \mathrm{A} + \mathrm{B},$$

je montrerai d'abord que les intégrales

$$A = \int_a^b \mathrm{A}\, dx, \qquad B = \int_a^b \mathrm{B}\, dx,$$

se déduisent immédiatement l'une de l'autre. Ces quantités sont en effet les coefficients de $\frac{1}{h}$, dans le développement des expressions

$$\int_a^b \varphi(a+h)\, dx = \frac{f(a+h)}{h^\alpha(a-b+h)^\beta} \int_a^b \frac{(x-a)^\alpha(x-b)^\beta\, dx}{x-a-h}$$

et

$$\int_a^b \varphi(b+h)\, dx = \frac{f(b+h)}{h^\beta(b-a+h)^\alpha} \int_a^b \frac{(x-a)^\alpha(x-b)^\beta\, dx}{x-b-h}.$$

Or écrivons pour un moment

$$(a, b, \alpha, \beta) = \frac{f(a+h)}{h^\alpha(a-b+h)^\beta} \int_a^b \frac{(x-a)^\alpha(x-b)^\beta\, dx}{x-a-h},$$

et permutons à la fois, d'une part a et b, et de l'autre α et β, ce qui donnera

$$(b, a, \beta, \alpha) = \frac{f(b+h)}{h^\beta(b-a+h)^\alpha} \int_b^a \frac{(x-a)^\alpha(x-b)^\beta\, dx}{x-b-h};$$

on voit que le second membre de cette égalité étant $-B$, on a simplement

$$\int_a^b \mathrm{F}(x)\, dx = (a, b, \alpha, \beta) - (b, a, \beta, \alpha).$$

Cette remarque faite, posons $m = \alpha + \beta$; la formule élémentaire

$$\int_a^b (x-a)^{p-1}(b-x)^{q-1}\, dx = (b-a)^{p+q-1} \frac{\Gamma(p)\,\Gamma(q)}{\Gamma(p+q)}$$

donne le développement

$$\begin{aligned}\int_a^b & \frac{(x-a)^\alpha(b-x)^\beta\, dx}{x-a-h} \\ &= \frac{\Gamma(\alpha)\,\Gamma(\beta+1)}{\Gamma(m+1)}(b-a)^m + \frac{\Gamma(\alpha-1)\,\Gamma(\beta+1)}{\Gamma(m)}(b-a)^{m-1} h \\ &\quad + \frac{\Gamma(\alpha+2)\,\Gamma(\beta+1)}{\Gamma(m-1)}(b-a)^{m-2} h^2 + \ldots.\end{aligned}$$

Faisons encore $h=(b-a)t$, on pourra l'écrire sous cette nouvelle forme

$$\frac{\Gamma(\alpha)\Gamma(\beta+1)}{\Gamma(m+1)}(b-a)^m\left[1+\frac{m}{\alpha-1}t+\frac{m(m-1)}{(\alpha-1)(\alpha-2)}t^2+\ldots\right].$$

Cela étant, nous effectuerons la multiplication par le facteur $(a-b+h)^{-\beta}$, ou plutôt par la quantité égale

$$(-1)^\beta(b-a)^{-\beta}(1-t)^{-\beta}.$$

Des réductions qui se présentent d'elles-mêmes montrent que le produit des deux séries

$$1+\frac{m}{\alpha-1}t+\frac{m(m-1)}{(\alpha-1)(\alpha-2)}t^2+\frac{m(m-1)(m-2)}{(\alpha-1)(\alpha-2)(\alpha-3)}t^3+\ldots,$$

$$1+\frac{\beta}{1}t+\frac{\beta(\beta+1)}{1.2}t^2+\frac{\beta(\beta+1)(\beta+2)}{1.2.3}t^3+\ldots$$

a la forme simple

$$\begin{aligned}T=1&+\frac{\alpha(\beta+1)}{\alpha-1}t+\frac{\alpha(\beta+1)(\beta+2)}{1.2(\alpha-2)}t^2+\frac{\alpha(\beta+1)(\beta+2)(\beta+3)}{1.2.3(\alpha-3)}t^3+\ldots\\&+\frac{\alpha(\beta+1)(\beta+2)\ldots(\beta+\alpha-1)}{1.2.3\ldots(\alpha-1)}t^{\alpha-1}+\ldots,\end{aligned}$$

de sorte qu'on a

$$\frac{1}{(a-b+h)^\beta}\int_a^b\frac{(x-a)^\alpha(x-b)^\beta\,dx}{x-a-h}=\frac{\Gamma(\alpha)\Gamma(\beta+1)}{\Gamma(m+1)}(b-a)^\alpha T.$$

Mais il est préférable, en gardant seulement les puissances de h, dont l'exposant est inférieur à α, et qui nous seront seules utiles, d'ordonner le second membre suivant les puissances décroissantes de cette quantité. On obtient ainsi

$$\begin{aligned}&\frac{1}{(a-b+h)^\beta}\int_a^b\frac{(x-a)^\alpha(x-b)^\beta\,dx}{x-a-h}\\&\quad=\frac{\alpha}{m}(b-a)h^{\alpha-1}+\frac{\alpha(\alpha-1)}{m(m-1)}\frac{(b-a)^2h^{\alpha-2}}{2}\\&\quad+\frac{\alpha(\alpha-1)(\alpha-2)}{m(m-1)(m-2)}\frac{(b-a)^3h^{\alpha-3}}{3}+\ldots.\end{aligned}$$

En dernier lieu, multiplions par le facteur

$$f(a+h)=f(a)+f'(a)\frac{h}{1}+f''(a)\frac{h^2}{1.2}+\ldots+f^{\alpha-1}(a)\frac{h^{\alpha-1}}{1.2\ldots\alpha-1}+\ldots;$$

pour former le coefficient du terme en $h^{\alpha-1}$, qui est la quantité cherchée, nous parvenons ainsi à l'expression

$$(a, b, \alpha, \beta) = \frac{\alpha}{m}(b-a)f(a) + \frac{\alpha(\alpha-1)}{1.2\ldots m(m-1)}\,\frac{(b-a)^2 f'(a)}{1.2}$$
$$+\frac{\alpha(\alpha-1)(\alpha-2)}{m(m-1)(m-2)}\,\frac{(b-a)^3 f''(a)}{1.2.3}+\ldots,$$

dont la loi est manifeste.

On obtient d'une autre manière cette formule, en partant de la relation

$$\int UV^m\,dx = \Theta(x) + (-1)^m \int VU^m\,dx,$$

où j'ai fait

$$\Theta(x) = UV^{m-1} - U'V^{m-2} + U''V^{m-3} - \ldots.$$

Prenons en effet $U = f(x)$, $V = (x-a)^\beta (x-b)^\alpha$, avec la condition $\alpha + \beta = m$, de sorte qu'on ait $V^m = 1.2\ldots m$. On en déduira en intégrant entre les limites $x = a$ et $x = b$

$$\int_a^b f(x)\,dx = \frac{\Theta(b)-\Theta(a)}{1.2\ldots m} + \frac{(-1)^m}{1.2\ldots m}\int_a^b f^m(x)(x-a)^\beta(x-b)^\alpha\,dx,$$

et il est aisé de calculer $\Theta(a)$ et $\Theta(b)$. Il suffit en effet d'avoir les dérivées successives de $V = (x-a)^\beta (x-b)^\alpha$ pour $x = a$ et $x = b$; or les premières s'obtiennent en faisant $x = a + h$, et sont données par les coefficients de $h^\beta(a-b+h)^\alpha$, les autres résultant semblablement de l'expression $h^\alpha(b-a+h)^\beta$, et l'on trouve ainsi

$$\frac{\Theta(a)}{1.2\ldots m} = \frac{\alpha}{m}(a-b)f(a) - \frac{\alpha(\alpha-1)}{m(m-1)}\,\frac{(a-b)^2 f'(a)}{1.2}$$
$$+\frac{\alpha(\alpha-1)(\alpha-2)}{m(m-1)(m-2)}\,\frac{(a-b)^3 f''(a)}{1.2.3}-\ldots.$$

Écrivons cette quantité de la manière suivante

$$\frac{\Theta(a)}{1.2\ldots m} = -\frac{\alpha}{m}(b-a)f(a) - \frac{\alpha(\alpha-1)}{m(m-1)}\,\frac{(b-a)^2 f'(a)}{1.2}$$
$$-\frac{\alpha(\alpha-1)(\alpha-2)}{m(m-1)(m-2)}\,\frac{(b-a)^3 f''(a)}{1.2.3}-\ldots;$$

on aura de même

$$\frac{\Theta(b)}{1.2\ldots m} = -\frac{\beta}{m}(a-b)f(b) - \frac{\beta(\beta-1)}{m(m-1)}\frac{(a-b)^2 f'(b)}{1.2}$$
$$-\frac{\beta(\beta-1)(\beta-2)}{m(m-1)(m-2)}\frac{(a-b)^3 f''(b)}{1.2.3} - \ldots,$$

et nous sommes ramenés à la formule précédemment obtenue. Mais on trouve, par cette méthode, que la différence entre l'intégrale $\int_a^b f(x)\,dx$ et sa valeur approchée est la quantité

$$\frac{(-1)^m}{1.2\ldots m}\int_a^b f^m(x)(x-a)^\beta(x-b)^\alpha\,dx,$$

où le facteur $(x-a)^\beta(x-b)^\alpha$ conserve toujours le même signe entre les limites de l'intégration.

Écrivant donc

$$\int_a^b f^m(x)(x-a)^\beta(x-b)^\alpha\,dx = f^m(\xi)\int_a^b (x-a)^\beta(x-b)^\alpha\,dx,$$

en désignant par ξ une quantité comprise entre a et b, on voit que pour une valeur donnée de m, l'approximation obtenue dépend du facteur

$$\int_a^b (x-a)^\beta(x-b)^\alpha\,dx,$$

ce qui conduit à déterminer α et β par la condition qu'il soit le plus petit possible. Or on trouve aisément que le minimum du produit $\Gamma(x)\Gamma(m-x)$ s'obtient en faisant $x = \frac{m}{2}$. Parmi les diverses formules qui se rapportent à la même valeur de m, c'est donc celle où $\alpha = \beta$, où figure par conséquent la dérivée de l'ordre le moins élevé de la fonction $f(x)$, qui conduit en même temps à l'approximation la plus grande.

En particulier on trouvera, pour $\alpha = \beta = 1$,

$$\int_a^b f(x)\,dx = \frac{1}{2}(b-a)[f(a)+f(b)] - \frac{1}{12}(b-a)^3 f''(\xi),$$

puis en supposant $\alpha = \beta = 2$,

$$\int_a^b f(x)\,dx = \frac{1}{2}(b-a)[f(a)+f(b)] + \frac{1}{12}(b-a)^2[f'(a)-f'(b)] + \frac{1}{720}(b-a)^5 f^{\text{IV}}(\xi).$$

Paris, 5 juillet 1877.

POST-SCRIPTUM.

J'ai réfléchi de nouveau à ces deux origines de la série de Taylor, suivant qu'on la déduit, au point de vue élémentaire, de l'intégrale définie

$$\int_x^a \frac{(x-u)^\alpha f^{\alpha+1}(u)}{1.2\ldots a}\,du,$$

ou bien sous un point de vue analytique plus étendu, de l'intégrale curviligne

$$\frac{1}{2i\pi}\int_s \frac{(x-a)^{\alpha+1} f(z)}{(x-z)(z-a)^{\alpha+1}}\,dz,$$

et j'ai pensé qu'il devait être possible pareillement d'arriver au polynome d'interpolation par une autre voie qui n'exigerait pas l'emploi des variables imaginaires et des intégrales curvilignes. C'est en effet ce qui a lieu, mais il faut recourir comme vous allez le voir à la considération des intégrales multiples.

En posant

$$\Pi(z) = (z-a_0)(z-a_1)\ldots(z-a_n)$$

j'envisage l'intégrale

$$\frac{1}{2i\pi}\int_s \frac{f(z)}{\Pi(z)}\,dz,$$

où la fonction $f(z)$ est supposée continue à l'intérieur de l'aire s, qui comprend tous les points ayant pour affixes $a_0, a_1, \ldots, a_n$.

Si l'on désigne par $f^n(z)$ la dérivée d'ordre n de $f(z)$ et qu'on fasse

$$u = (a_0 - a_1)t_1 + (a_1 - a_2)t_2 + \ldots + (a_{n-1} - a_n)t_n + a_n,$$

l'intégrale curviligne s'exprime comme il suit au moyen d'une intégrale multiple d'ordre n. On a

$$\frac{1}{2i\pi}\int_s \frac{f(z)}{\Pi(z)}\,dz = \int_0^1 dt_n \int_0^{t_n} dt_{n-1} \int_0^{t_{n-1}} dt_{n-2} \ldots \int_0^{t_2} f^n(u)\,dt_1,$$

et nous allons aisément le démontrer.

Il vient d'abord en effet

$$\int_0^{t_2} f^n(u)\,dt = \frac{f^{n-1}[(a_0-a_2)t_2+(a_2-a_3)t_3+\ldots+a_n]}{a_0-a_1} + \frac{f^{n-1}[(a_1-a_2)t_2+(a_2-a_3)t_3+\ldots+a_n]}{a_1-a_0},$$

puis successivement

$$\int_0^{t_3} dt_2 \int_0^{t} f^n(u)\,dt_1 = \frac{f^{n-2}[(a_0-a_3)t_3+(a_3-a_4)t_4+\ldots+a_n]}{(a_0-a_1)(a_0-a_2)} + \frac{f^{n-2}[(a_1-a_3)t_3+(a_3-a_4)t_4+\ldots+a_n]}{(a_1-a_0)(a_1-a_2)} + \frac{f^{n-2}[(a_2-a_3)t_3+(a_3-a_4)t_4+\ldots+a_n]}{(a_2-a_0)(a_2-a_1)},$$

$$\int^{t_4} dt_3 \int_0^{t_3} dt_2 \int_0^{t_2} f^n(u)\,dt_1 = \frac{f^{n-3}[(a_0-a_4)t_4+(a_4-a_5)t_5+\ldots+a_n]}{(a_0-a_1)(a_0-a_2)(a_0-a_3)} + \frac{f^{n-3}[(a_1-a_4)t_4+(a_4-a_5)t_5+\ldots+a_n]}{(a_1-a_0)(a_1-a_2)(a_1-a_3)} + \frac{f^{n-3}[(a_2-a_4)t_4+(a_4-a_5)t_5+\ldots+a_n]}{(a_2-a_0)(a_2-a_1)(a_2-a_3)} + \frac{f^{n-3}[(a_3-a_4)t_4+(a_4-a_5)t_5+\ldots+a_n]}{(a_3-a_0)(a_3-a_1)(a_3-a_2)},$$

en faisant usage des identités élémentaires :

$$\frac{1}{(a_0-a_1)(a_0-a_2)} + \frac{1}{(a_1-a_0)(a_1-a_2)} + \frac{1}{(a_2-a_0)(a_2-a_1)} = 0,$$

$$\frac{1}{(a_0-a_1)(a_0-a_2)(a_0-a_3)} + \frac{1}{(a_1-a_0)(a_1-a_2)(a_1-a_3)} + \frac{1}{(a_2-a_0)(a_2-a_1)(a_2-a_3)} + \frac{1}{(a_3-a_0)(a_3-a_2)(a_3-a_1)} = 0.$$

En dernier lieu, et sans qu'il soit besoin d'entrer dans des détails que la simplicité des calculs rend inutiles, on obtient pour l'intégrale multiple d'ordre n l'expression

$$\frac{f(a_0)}{\Pi'(a_0)}+\frac{f(a_1)}{\Pi'(a_1)}+\ldots+\frac{f(a_n)}{\Pi'(a_n)},$$

qui est en effet la valeur de l'intégrale $\frac{1}{2i\pi}\int_s \frac{f(z)}{\Pi(z)}\,dz$.

Appliquons ce résultat en supposant $a_0 = x$, et faisons pour abréger

$$\Phi(x) = (x-a_1)(x-a_2)\ldots(x-a_n);$$

si l'on désigne comme précédemment par $\mathrm{F}(x)$ le polynome d'interpolation de Lagrange, on trouvera

$$f(x)-\mathrm{F}(x) = \Phi(x)\int_0^1 dt_n \int_0^{t_n} dt_{n-1}\ldots\int_0^{t_2} f^n(u)\,dt_1,$$

la valeur de u pouvant être mise sous la forme suivante :

$$\begin{aligned} u = x t_1 + a_1 & (t_2 - t_1) \\ + a_2 & (t_3 - t_2) \\ + & \ldots\ldots\ldots\ldots \\ + a_{n-1} & (t_n - t_{n-1}) \\ + a_n & (1 - t_n). \end{aligned}$$

Je remarque ensuite qu'en différentiant la relation

$$\frac{1}{2i\pi}\int_s \frac{f(z)}{(z-x)\Phi(z)}\,dz = \int_0^1 dt_n \int_0^{t_n} dt_{n-1}\ldots\int_0^{t_2} f^n(u)\,dt_1$$

$\alpha - 1$ fois par rapport à a_1, $\beta - 1$ fois par rapport à a_2, ..., $\lambda - 1$ fois par rapport à a_n, nous obtiendrons dans le premier membre l'intégrale

$$\frac{1}{2i\pi}\int_s \frac{\Gamma(\alpha)\Gamma(\beta)\ldots\Gamma(\lambda)f(z)}{(z-x)(z-a_1)^\alpha(z-a_2)^\beta\ldots(z-a_n)^\lambda}\,dz,$$

qui se trouvera donc exprimée par l'intégrale multiple

$$\int_0^1 dt_n \int_0^{t_n} dt_{n-1}\ldots\int_0^{t_2} f^\sigma(u)\Theta\,dt_1,$$

où j'ai fait

$$\Theta = (t_2 - t_1)^{\alpha-1}(t_3-t_2)^{\beta-1}\ldots(1-t_n)^{\lambda-1},$$
$$\sigma = \alpha+\beta+\ldots+\lambda.$$

Nous parvenons ainsi, pour la formule plus générale d'interpolation, à l'expression suivante du reste

$$f(x) - F(x) = \frac{\Phi(x)}{\Gamma(\alpha)\Gamma(\beta)\ldots\Gamma(\lambda)} \int_0^1 dt_n \int_0^{t_n} dt_{n-1} \ldots \int_0^{t_2} f^{\alpha+\beta+\ldots+\lambda}(u)\Theta\, dt_1,$$

$\Phi(x)$ représentant le polynome $(x - a_1)^\alpha (x - a_2)^\beta \ldots (x - a_n)^\lambda$; c'est le résultat que je me suis proposé d'obtenir et qui me semble compléter sous un point de vue essentiel la théorie élémentaire de l'interpolation.

Bain-de-Bretagne, septembre 1877.

EXTRAIT D'UNE LETTRE DE M. HERMITE A M. LINDEMANN.

OBSERVATIONS ALGÉBRIQUES

SUR

LES COURBES PLANES.

Journal de Crelle, t. 84, 1878, p. 298-299.

Les formules que je crois d'une grande importance, par lesquelles vous représentez les coordonnées d'une courbe d'ordre m et de genre p, renferment-elles le nombre maximum de constantes arbitraires qu'elles comportent, c'est-à-dire

$$\frac{1}{2}m(m+3) - \left[\frac{1}{2}(m-1)(m-2) - p\right] = 3m - 1 + p?$$

Pour $p = 0$, les expressions des coordonnées étant

$$\xi = \frac{B}{A}, \qquad \eta = \frac{C}{A},$$

où A, B, C représentent des polynomes du $m^{\text{ième}}$ degré en t, on peut d'abord, si l'on remplace cette variable par la fonction linéaire $\frac{\alpha + \beta t}{1 + \gamma t}$, diminuer de trois unités, en disposant de α, β, γ, le nombre des constantes que contiennent ces formules. On peut encore dans les résultats de cette substitution

$$\xi = \frac{\mathfrak{B}}{\mathfrak{A}}, \qquad \eta = \frac{\mathfrak{C}}{\mathfrak{A}},$$

supposer égal à l'unité le coefficient de la puissance la plus élevée de t, dans le dénominateur $\mathfrak{A}$, par exemple; et ainsi le nombre des arbitraires se réduit à

$$2(m+1)+m-3=3m-1.$$

Pour $p=1$, les formules

$$\xi = \xi_0 + A_1 Z(t-t_1) + A_2 Z(t-t_2) + \ldots + A_m Z(t-t_m),$$
$$\eta = \eta_0 + B_1 Z(t-t_1) + B_2 Z(t-t_2) + \ldots + B_m Z(t-t_m)$$

mettent en évidence, d'une part les résidus, $A_1, A_2, \ldots, B_1, B_2, \ldots$, c'est-à-dire $2(m-1)$ constantes, à cause des conditions $\Sigma A = 0$, $\Sigma B = 0$, puis les quantités $t_1, t_2, \ldots, t_m$ qu'il faut réduire à $m-1$ arbitraires, puisqu'on peut remplacer t, par $t+t_1$, par exemple. Si l'on ajoute à ces constantes le module ainsi que ξ_0 et η_0, on trouve bien en définitive le nombre $3m$.

Après avoir appelé votre attention sur ce point, permettez-moi de vous dire de quelle manière j'exprime qu'une courbe

$$f(x,y)=0$$

admet δ points doubles. Je considère à cet effet les relations

$$u=f(x,y), \qquad \frac{df}{dx}=0, \qquad \frac{df}{dy}=0,$$

et j'observe que le résultat de l'élimination de x et y sera une équation en u, $\Pi(u)=0$ dont les racines représenteront les diverses valeurs que prend $f(x,y)$, quand on y remplace x et y, par les solutions des équations $\frac{df}{dx}=0$, $\frac{df}{dy}=0$. Par conséquent le nombre des points doubles est donné par le nombre des racines u qui sont égales à zéro. Ceci posé, nommons a, b, c, ..., k les coefficients de $f(x,y)$ et supposons que le terme indépendant des variables soit k. Il est évident que l'équation $\Pi(u)=0$ se formera au moyen du discriminant relatif à l'équation proposée, en y remplaçant k par $k-u$, de sorte qu'en représentant ce discriminant par $\Pi(a,b,c,\ldots,k)$, on aura

$$\Pi(u)=\Pi(a,b,c,\ldots,k-u).$$

Les conditions pour que la courbe $f(x,y)=0$ possède δ points doubles peuvent donc s'obtenir, au moyen du discriminant, sous la forme suivante :

$$\Pi = 0, \qquad \frac{d\Pi}{dk} = 0, \qquad \frac{d^2\Pi}{dk^2}, \qquad \ldots, \qquad \frac{d^{\delta-1}\Pi}{dk^{\delta-1}} = 0.$$

Paris, 13 juillet 1877.

EXTRAIT D'UNE LETTRE A M. GYLDÉN, DE STOCKHOLM.

SUR LE PENDULE.

Journal de Crelle, Bd. 85, 1878, p. 246.

J'ai remarqué que les coordonnées x, y, z de l'extrémité d'un pendule sphérique sont les dérivées de fonctions uniformes du temps dont voici les expressions. Considérons en premier lieu la valeur de z qui s'obtient immédiatement comme conséquence des équations fondamentales

$$x^2+y^2+z^2=1,$$
$$(D_t x)^2+(D_t y)^2+(D_t z)^2=2g(z+c),$$
$$y D_t x - x D_t y = h,$$

où c et h désignent des constantes dont la signification est bien connue et qui donnent comme on sait

$$(D_t z)^2=2g(z+c)(1-z^2)-h^2.$$

Nommons α, β, γ les racines rangées par ordre décroissant de grandeur, de l'équation du troisième degré

$$2g(z+c)(1-z^2)-h^2=0,$$

de sorte que α soit positive et moindre que l'unité, β moindre également que l'unité en valeur absolue et γ enfin négative et supérieure à l'unité en valeur absolue. Si l'on pose

$$k^2=\frac{\alpha-\beta}{\alpha-\gamma},$$
$$k'^2=\frac{\beta-\gamma}{\alpha-\gamma},$$
$$n^2=\frac{1}{2}g(\alpha-\gamma)$$

et

$$u = n(t - t_0),$$

on aura

$$\alpha - z = (\alpha - \beta) \sin^2 \operatorname{am}(u),$$

$$z - \beta = (\alpha - \beta) \cos^2 \operatorname{am}(u),$$

$$z - \gamma = (\alpha - \gamma) \Delta^2 \quad \operatorname{am}(u).$$

Or la formule

$$\int_0^u k^2 \sin^2 \operatorname{am}(u)\, du = \frac{\mathrm{J}u}{\mathrm{K}} - \frac{\Theta'(u)}{\Theta(u)}$$

permet déjà d'écrire

$$z = \mathrm{D}_u \left[\frac{\alpha k^2 \mathrm{K} - (\alpha - \beta)\mathrm{J}}{k^2 \mathrm{K}} u + \frac{\Theta'(u)}{k^2 \Theta(u)} \right].$$

Soit ensuite, en désignant par φ un angle arbitraire,

$$\mathrm{A} = \alpha \sqrt{(\gamma - \alpha)(\gamma + \beta)}\, e^{i\varphi},$$

et posons

$$\Phi(u) = \frac{\Theta(0)\, \mathrm{H}_1(u + \omega)}{\mathrm{H}_1(\omega)\, \Theta(u)}\, e^{\left[\lambda - \frac{\Theta'_1(\omega)}{\Theta_1(\omega)}\right] u},$$

on aura cette expression

$$x + iy = \mathrm{A}\mathrm{D}_u \Phi(u),$$

de sorte qu'en égalant les parties réelles et les coefficients de i, x et y seront, aussi bien que z, les dérivées de fonctions à sens unique. Voici maintenant la détermination des constantes ω et λ qui entrent dans la fonction $\Phi(u)$. Nous avons d'abord

$$\lambda^2 = -\frac{h^2}{4n^2},$$

puis ces formules

$$\sin^2 \operatorname{am}(\omega) = \frac{\beta^2(\alpha^2 - \gamma^2)}{\gamma^2(\alpha^2 - \beta^2)},$$

$$\cos^2 \operatorname{am}(\omega) = \frac{\alpha^2(\gamma^2 - \beta^2)}{\gamma^2(\alpha^2 - \beta^2)},$$

$$\Delta^2 \operatorname{am}(\omega) = \frac{\beta - \gamma}{\gamma^2(\alpha + \beta)}.$$

Elles font voir que ω est imaginaire, mais sans partie réelle, comme λ. Si l'on pose en effet $\omega = ia$, et qu'on emploie les relations

$$\sin \operatorname{am}(ix, k') = \frac{i \sin \operatorname{am}(x, k)}{\cos \operatorname{am}(x, k)},$$

$$\cos \operatorname{am}(ix, k') = \frac{1}{\cos \operatorname{am}(x, k)},$$

$$\Delta \operatorname{am}(ix, k') = \frac{\Delta \operatorname{am}(x, k)}{\cos \operatorname{am}(x, k)},$$

on obtient les valeurs

$$\sin^2 \operatorname{am}(a, k') = \frac{\beta^2(\alpha^2 - \gamma^2)}{\alpha^2(\beta^2 - \gamma^2)},$$

$$\cos^2 \operatorname{am}(a, k') = \frac{\gamma^2(\beta^2 - \alpha^2)}{\alpha^2(\beta^2 - \gamma^2)},$$

$$\Delta^2 \operatorname{am}(a, k') = \frac{\beta - \alpha}{\alpha^2(\beta + \gamma)},$$

et d'après l'ordre de grandeur des quantités α, β, γ, vous voyez qu'elles sont, en effet, toutes positives et moindres que l'unité. Mais une double indétermination subsiste à l'égard des signes de ω et λ; elle se lève par les formules suivantes. On a, en premier lieu,

$$\frac{\sin \operatorname{am}(\omega) \cos \operatorname{am}(\omega)}{\Delta^3 \operatorname{am}(\omega)} = \frac{ih}{n} \frac{\alpha\beta\gamma(\alpha - \gamma)}{2(\alpha - \beta)(\gamma - \beta)},$$

ce qui fixe le signe de ω, sa valeur absolue étant connue; je trouve ensuite qu'on doit prendre

$$\lambda = -\frac{ih}{2n}.$$

Vérifions, par l'élévation au carré, la formule relative à ω au moyen des expressions données pour $\sin^2 \operatorname{am}(\omega)$, $\cos^2 \operatorname{am}(\omega)$, $\Delta^2 \operatorname{am}(\omega)$. On trouve d'abord, dans le premier membre, la quantité

$$-\frac{\alpha^2\beta^2\gamma^2(\alpha + \beta)(\beta + \gamma)(\gamma + \alpha)(\alpha - \gamma)}{(\beta - \gamma)^2(\beta - \alpha)^2},$$

et le second, en remplaçant n^2 par $\frac{1}{2}g(\alpha - \gamma)$, devient

$$-\frac{h^2}{2g} \frac{\alpha^2\beta^2\gamma^2(\alpha - \gamma)}{(\beta - \gamma)^2(\beta - \alpha)^2};$$

il suffit, par conséquent, de vérifier la condition

$$\frac{h^2}{2g} = (\alpha + \beta)(\beta + \gamma)(\gamma + \alpha),$$

ce qui se fait immédiatement, en posant dans l'équation

$$2g(z+c)(1-z^2)-h^2=-2g(z-\alpha)(z-\beta)(z-\gamma),$$

$z=-c$, et remarquant qu'on a

$$\alpha+\beta+\gamma=-c.$$

Vous m'avez dit, Monsieur, dans votre dernière lettre, que la différentiation des fonctions elliptiques par rapport au module pourrait peut-être servir dans les importantes recherches auxquelles vous consacrez vos efforts pour l'application de ces fonctions à la théorie des perturbations. Voici à ce sujet les diverses formules que j'ai obtenues, et dans lesquelles j'ai posé pour abréger $\zeta=\frac{J}{K}$:

$$D_k \sin\mathrm{am}(x) = \frac{\cos\mathrm{am}(x)\Delta\mathrm{am}(x)}{kk'^2}\left[(\zeta-k^2)x-\frac{\Theta'_1(x)}{\Theta_1(x)}\right],$$

$$D_k \cos\mathrm{am}(x) = -\frac{\sin\mathrm{am}(x)\Delta\mathrm{am}(x)}{kk'^2}\left[(\zeta-k^2)x-\frac{\Theta'_1(x)}{\Theta_1(x)}\right],$$

$$D_k \ \Delta\mathrm{am}(x) = -\frac{k^2\sin\mathrm{am}(x)\cos\mathrm{am}(x)}{kk'^2}\left[(\zeta-k^2)x-\frac{H'_1(x)}{H_1(x)}\right].$$

Si l'on pose, en outre,

$$Z(x)=\int_0^x k^2\sin^2\mathrm{am}(x)\,dx,$$

on a aussi

$$D_k Z(x) = \frac{K}{k'^2}\left[x\Delta^2\mathrm{am}(x)-\sin\mathrm{am}(x)\cos\mathrm{am}(x)\Delta\mathrm{am}(x)-\cos^2\mathrm{am}(x)Z(x)\right].$$

M. C. O. Meyer avait déjà donné les trois premières, mais sous une forme différente et en prenant pour variable la quantité q au lieu du module, dans son Mémoire intitulé *Ueber rationale Verbindungen der elliptischen Transcendenten*, t. LVI de ce *Journal*, p. 321.

Paris, 8 octobre 1877.

SUR LA

THÉORIE DES FONCTIONS SPHÉRIQUES.

Comptes rendus de l'Académie des Sciences, t. LXXXVI, 1878, p. 1515.

J'ai l'honneur de faire hommage à l'Académie, au nom de l'auteur, M. le Dr E. Heine, professeur à l'Université de Halle, de la seconde édition d'un Ouvrage intitulé : *Sur les fonctions sphériques. Théorie et applications*. Ce sont les applications du calcul à la Mécanique céleste qui ont conduit à la découverte et à l'introduction en Analyse des fonctions auxquelles est consacré le beau et savant Ouvrage de M. Heine. Legendre et Laplace, dans d'admirables recherches sur la théorie de l'attraction des sphéroïdes et la figure des planètes, en ont donné les propriétés fondamentales, et elles ont été ensuite employées avec le plus grand succès dans beaucoup de questions importantes de Physique mathématique, et principalement dans la Théorie de la chaleur. Après ces deux grands géomètres, et en suivant la voie qu'ils avaient ouverte, Lamé est parvenu à ses belles découvertes qui ont étendu à la fois, comme on le sait, le champ des applications du calcul à la Physique et celui de l'Analyse pure. Coordonner, sous ce double point de vue, de nombreux et importants travaux, ceux de Dirichlet, de Jacobi, de nos illustres confrères Lamé et M. Liouville, de M. F.-E. Neumann, compléter la théorie sous un point de vue essentiel par l'introduction des fonctions de seconde espèce, montrer enfin par quels liens étroits elle se rattache aux fractions continues algébriques et à la série hypergéométrique de Gauss, tel est en peu de mots l'objet d'un Ouvrage auquel l'auteur a fait concourir tous les travaux de sa vie scientifique. Un point entièrement nouveau me semble devoir être particulièrement signalé à l'attention : c'est celui qui se rattache aux recherches de Lamé. Soient $a_1, a_2, \ldots, a_p$ des constantes, et $\mathfrak{I}(x)$ une fonction entière, composée de telle manière que l'une des intégrales de l'équation différentielle

$$(a) \qquad \frac{dy^2}{du^2} + \mathfrak{I}(x)y = 0,$$

où l'on suppose

$$du = \frac{dx}{\sqrt{x(x-a_1)(x-a_2)\ldots(x-a_p)}},$$

soit une fonction entière et du degré n de $\sqrt{x}$, $\sqrt{x-a_1}$, ..., $\sqrt{x-a_p}$. L'auteur appelle cette intégrale *fonction de Lamé* de première espèce, de degré n et d'ordre p. Il démontre l'existence et trouve le nombre de ces fonctions pour chaque ordre p (§ 135). Les intégrales de l'équation différentielle, qui s'évanouissent pour des valeurs infinies de x, forment les fonctions de seconde espèce. Pour $p = 2$, on a les fonctions ellipsoïdales E, introduites par Lamé lui-même; et, si l'on fait $a_1 = a_2$, elles se changent en fonctions sphériques de Legendre. Supposons ensuite que les produits $n\sqrt{x-a_1}$, $n\sqrt{x-a_2}$ soient finis pour n infini, on trouve (p. 413) les *fonctions du cylindre elliptique;* et, faisant en outre $a_1 = a_2$, on en conclut les *fonctions de cylindre de révolution*. Ces dernières, introduites par Fourier, en 1822, sont de première ou de seconde espèce et, dans le premier cas, ont la forme

$$\begin{aligned} J_\nu(x) &= \frac{x^\nu}{2.4\ldots2\nu}\left[1 - \frac{x^2}{2(2\nu+2)} + \frac{x^4}{2.4(2\nu+2)(2\nu+4)} - \ldots\right] \\ &= \frac{(-1)^\nu}{\pi}\int_0^\pi e^{ix\cos\varphi}\cos\nu\varphi\,d\varphi. \end{aligned}$$

L'auteur les représente ainsi

$$K_\nu(x) = (-1)^\nu \int_0^\infty e^{ix\cos iu}\cos i\nu u\,du = (-1)^\nu K_\nu(-x),$$

sous la condition que la partie réelle de ix soit négative; et, pour une valeur réelle de x, il égale $K_\nu(x)$ à la moyenne arithmétique, entre $K_\nu(x+oi)$ et $K_\nu(x-oi)$.

Pour toutes ces fonctions on a des théorèmes semblables, par exemple un théorème d'addition, comme celui de Laplace (voir p. 312, 333, 340, 346, 455, etc.).

Lamé a créé ses fonctions (*Journal de M. Liouville*, t. IV, p. 139) en intégrant par des produits $E(\rho_1).E(\rho_2)$ l'équation

$$\frac{d^2U}{d\varepsilon_1^2} + \frac{d^2U}{d\varepsilon_2^2} + n(n+1)U(\rho_1^2 - \rho_2^2) = 0;$$

et les fonctions du cylindre elliptique tirent leur origine de l'équation bien connue

$$\frac{d^2U}{du^2} + \frac{d^2U}{d\varphi^2} + \lambda^2(\cos^2\varphi - \cos^2 iu)U = 0.$$

Pour qu'elle admette une intégrale particulière de la forme $F(\varphi)F(iu)$, il faut poser

$$(b) \qquad \frac{d^2F(\varphi)}{d\varphi^2} + (\lambda^2\cos^2\varphi - l)F(\varphi) = 0.$$

Mais la constante l n'est pas définie comme la constante B de Lamé, par la condition que les fonctions F, du moins dans la première de leurs quatre classes, soient entières. La condition est alors que chaque intégrale de l'équation (b) soit une fonction périodique de φ, développable par la formule de Fourier. Si l'on représente les fonctions $F(\varphi)$, par exemple, dans la première de leurs quatre classes, par les séries $\Sigma\alpha_\nu \cos 2\nu\varphi$, la condition nécessaire est que α_ν s'évanouisse pour ν infini, et l'auteur démontre (p. 412) qu'elle suffit en même temps pour assurer la convergence de la série. Or α_ν est un polynome entier en l, du degré ν, et la condition $\alpha_\infty = 0$ donne une équation d'un degré infini. M. Heine démontre (§ 104) que chaque racine, jusqu'à une grandeur quelconque, peut être comprise entre des limites aussi rapprochées qu'on le veut, et parvient (p. 408) au résultat suivant :

Les constantes α_ν sont les dénominateurs N_ν des réduites de la fraction continue

$$\sigma = 1 - \cfrac{1}{-\frac{1}{2}bz - \cfrac{1}{b(1-z) - \cfrac{1}{b(4-z) - \cfrac{1}{b(9-z) - \dots}}}}$$

où $\lambda\sqrt{b=4}$, en prenant pour z les diverses racines de l'équation $N = 0$.

Les mêmes coefficients α_ν entrent dans le développement de $F(\varphi)$ suivant les fonctions J (p. 414), et, en y remplaçant les quantités J par les fonctions de deuxième espèce K, on a le développement des fonctions $F(\varphi)$ de deuxième espèce du cylindre elliptique.

On retrouve enfin les mêmes valeurs α_ν (p. 421), si l'on transforme, par une substitution orthogonale, la forme quadratique d'un nombre infini de variables,

$$b(1.x_1^2+4x_2^2+9x_3^2+\ldots)-2(x_0x_1+x_1x_2+x_2x_3+\ldots)$$

en une somme de carrés $z_0y_0^2+z_1y_1^2+z_2y_2^2+\ldots$, et ce résultat pouvait être prévu, d'après une proposition analogue concernant les fonctions de Lamé.

Dans les deux cas, le polynome homogène du second degré à transformer a la forme singulière

$$\Sigma a_i x_i^2 + 2\Sigma b_i x_i x_{i+1}.$$

La démonstration des théorèmes ainsi que les résultats dans la théorie de la transformation orthogonale sont plus simples à l'égard d'une telle forme singulière que dans le cas général. On peut mettre cette remarque à profit, Jacobi ayant démontré (*Journal de Crelle* et de M. Borchardt, p. 39 et 69, p. 290 et 1) que toute forme quadratique peut être réduite par des substitutions équivalentes à cette forme particulière, et une légère modification de la méthode de Jacobi permet de démontrer qu'on peut obtenir cette transformation au moyen d'une série de substitutions orthogonales très simples, les coefficients s'exprimant par des racines carrées (p. 480). Ces mêmes remarques ont été faites d'ailleurs par M. Kronecker dans un Mémoire publié dans les *Comptes rendus de l'Académie des Sciences de Berlin*, 1878, p. 105, et dont l'auteur a reçu communication pendant que s'imprimaient les dernières pages de son livre.

SUR L'INTÉGRALE $\int_0^1 \frac{z^{a-1}-z^{-a}}{1-z}\,dz$.

Atti della Reale Accademia delle Scienze di Torino, vol. XIV
(séance du 17 novembre 1878).

L'application des procédés élémentaires de l'intégration des fonctions rationnelles aux quantités

$$\int_{-\infty}^{+\infty} \frac{x^{2n}}{x^{2m}+1}\,dx \quad \text{et} \quad \int_{-\infty}^{+\infty} \frac{x^{2n}-x^{2p}}{x^{2m}-1}\,dx,$$

où m, n, p sont des nombres entiers, conduit facilement aux formules

$$\int_0^\infty \frac{x^{a-1}}{1+z}\,dz = \frac{\pi}{\sin a\pi}, \qquad \int_0^\infty \frac{z^{a-1}-z^{b-1}}{1-z}\,dz = \pi(\cot a\pi - \cot b\pi),$$

et si l'on suppose $b = 1 - a$, la seconde devenant

$$\int_0^\infty \frac{z^{a\cdot 1}-z^{-a}}{1-z}\,dz = 2\pi\cot a\pi,$$

on a sous forme d'intégrales définies les expressions des fonctions $\frac{1}{\sin a\pi}$ et $\cot a\pi$, pour des valeurs de l'argument comprises entre zéro et l'unité. Ces expressions peuvent servir de base à la fois à l'étude des fonctions circulaires et à celle des intégrales eulériennes, en établissant une transition naturelle entre la théorie des deux transcendantes et montrant le lien étroit qui les réunit. En ce qui concerne les fonctions circulaires, je m'attacherai principalement à la formule

$$\pi\cot a\pi = \frac{1}{a} + \frac{2a}{a^2-1} + \frac{2a}{a^2-4} + \frac{2a}{a^2-9} + \ldots$$

pour lever une difficulté singulière qu'elle présente, lorsque, en remplaçant a par ia, on suppose a infiniment grand. La limite du premier membre est, en effet, $-i\pi$ ou $+i\pi$, suivant que a croît positivement ou négativement, et depuis longtemps Eisenstein a fait la remarque que la série ne conduit point à cette limite et donne lieu ainsi à un paradoxe que je me propose d'expliquer. Relativement aux intégrales eulériennes, j'aurai surtout pour but, en suivant une indication rapidement donnée par Cauchy dans son Mémoire sur les intégrales prises entre des limites imaginaires (p. 45), d'obtenir la relation

$$\log\Gamma(a) = \left(a - \frac{1}{2}\right)\log a - a + \log\sqrt{2\pi}$$
$$+ \frac{1}{2}\int_{-\infty}^{0} \frac{e^x(2-x)-2-x}{x^2(1-e^x)} e^{ax}\,dx,$$

démontrée par le grand Géomètre dans les *Nouveaux Exercices d'Analyse et de Physique mathématique* (t. II, p. 386). Ces résultats se rapportant aux fonctions circulaires et aux intégrales eulériennes, vont s'offrir comme les conséquences successives d'une même analyse, qui mettra ainsi en évidence la liaison et l'enchaînement des théories des deux genres de fonction.

1. Je commencerai par faire voir que des relations

$$\int_0^\infty \frac{z^{a-1}}{1+z}\,dz = \frac{\pi}{\sin a\pi}, \qquad \int_0^\infty \frac{z^{a-1}-z^{-a}}{1-z}\,dz = 2\pi\cot a\pi,$$

la première est une conséquence de la seconde, et en découle par suite de l'égalité

$$\frac{2}{\sin 2a\pi} = \cot a\pi + \tang a$$

Ayant, en effet,

$$\int_0^\infty \frac{z^{a-1}-z^{-a}+z^{-\frac{1}{2}-a}-z^{-\frac{1}{2}+a}}{1-z}\,dz = 2\pi\left[\cot a\pi + \cot\left(\frac{1}{2}-a\right)\pi\right],$$

nous écrirons

$$z^{a-1}-z^{-a}+z^{-\frac{1}{2}-a}-z^{-\frac{1}{2}+a} = \left(1-z^{\frac{1}{2}}\right)z^{a-1}+\left(1-z^{\frac{1}{2}}\right)z^{-a-\frac{1}{2}},$$

de sorte que l'intégrale sera ramenée à la forme

$$\int_0^\infty \frac{z^{a-1} + z^{-a-\frac{1}{2}}}{1 + z^{\frac{1}{2}}} dz.$$

Cela étant, il convient d'y remplacer z par z^2 ; elle devient ainsi

$$2\int_0^\infty \frac{z^{2a-1} + z^{-2a}}{1+z} dz.$$

Or, il est visible que les deux quantités

$$\int_0^\infty \frac{z^{2a-1}}{1+z} dz \quad \text{et} \quad \int_0^\infty \frac{z^{-2a}}{1+z} dz$$

sont égales : la première se ramenant à la seconde par le changement de z en $\frac{1}{z}$. Si l'on remplace a par $\frac{a}{2}$, nous obtenons donc bien la relation

$$\int_0^\infty \frac{z^{a-1}}{1+z} dz = \frac{\pi}{\sin a\pi}.$$

D'après cela, je me bornerai pour abréger à considérer l'intégrale définie, qui représente la cotangente, et j'y introduirai encóre les limites zéro et l'unité, au lieu de zéro et l'infini, En faisant, en effet

$$\int_0^1 \frac{z^{a-1} - z^{-a}}{1-z} dz + \int_1^\infty \frac{z^{a-1} - z^{-a}}{1-z} dz = 2\pi \cot a\pi,$$

et remarquant, comme tout à l'heure, que la seconde intégrale se ramène à la première par le changement de z en $\frac{1}{2}$, nous aurons

$$\int_0^1 \frac{z^{a-1} - z^{-a}}{1-z} dz = \pi \cot a\pi.$$

Posons, en effet, $z = e^x$, et l'on se trouve amené à cette nouvelle forme

$$\int_{-\infty}^0 \frac{e^{ax} - e^{(1-a)x}}{1-e^x} dx = \pi \cot a\pi,$$

qui suffit à faire prévoir les rapports avec la théorie des intégrales eulériennes, dont je viens de parler. En représentant sur $S(a)_n$ la fonction de Jacob Bernouilli, de sorte qu'on ait pour a entier

$$S(a)_n = (a-1)^n + (a-2)^n + \ldots + 1^n,$$

nous avons en effet

$$\frac{e^{ax} - e^{(1-a)x}}{1-e^x} = 1 - 2a - 2\,S(a)_2 \frac{x^2}{1.2} - 2\,S(a)_4 \frac{x^4}{1.2.3.4} - \ldots$$
$$- 2\,S(a)_{2n} \frac{x^{2n}}{1.2\ldots 2n} - \ldots.$$

La formule relative à l'inverse du sinus, à savoir

$$\int_0^1 \frac{z^{a-1} + z^{-a}}{1+z}\,dz = \frac{\pi}{\sin a\pi},$$

ou bien

$$\int_{-\infty}^0 \frac{e^{ax} + e^{(1-a)x}}{1+e^x}\,dx = \frac{\pi}{\sin a\pi},$$

conduit à une remarque analogue, la quantité $\frac{e^{ax} + e^{(1-a)x}}{1+e^x}$ donnant la série

$$1 + 2\,\mathfrak{S}(a)_2 \frac{x^2}{1.2} + 2\,\mathfrak{S}(a)_4 \frac{x^4}{1.2.3.4} + \ldots + 2\,\mathfrak{S}(a)_{2n} \frac{x^{2n}}{1.2\ldots 2n} + \ldots,$$

où

$$\mathfrak{S}(a)_n = (a-1)^n - (a-2)^n + (a-3)^n - \ldots \pm 1^n,$$

lorsque a est entier (¹).

2. Le développement de la cotangente, sous forme d'une série infinie de fractions simples, est à bien des égards d'une grande importance en analyse, mais plus particulièrement peut-être, comme ayant offert le premier exemple d'un mode d'expression d'une fonction périodique où la périodicité se trouvait mise en évidence. Et c'est sous ce point de vue qu'elle a été l'objet des recherches d'Eisenstein en servant de point de départ à la théorie des fonctions

(¹) Les polynomes $\mathfrak{S}(a)_{2n}$ s'annulent pour $a = 0$, $a = 1$, et possèdent la même propriété que les polynomes $S(a)_{2n+1}$ de n'avoir entre ces limites qu'un seul maximum pour $a = \frac{1}{2}$.

elliptiques qu'a donnée l'illustre géomètre. Or la formule

$$\int_0^1 \frac{z^{a-1} - z^{-a}}{1-z}\,dz = \pi \cot a\pi$$

conduit immédiatement à ce développement. En remplaçant dans l'intégrale $\frac{1}{1-z}$ par l'expression

$$1 + z + z^2 + \ldots + z^{n-1} + \frac{z^n}{1-z},$$

on en tire en effet

$$\pi \cot a\pi = \frac{1}{a} + \frac{1}{a+1} + \ldots + \frac{1}{a+n-1}$$
$$+ \int_0^1 \frac{z^{a-1} - z^{-a}}{1-z} z^n\,dz - \frac{1}{1-a} - \frac{1}{2-a} - \ldots - \frac{1}{n-a}.$$

Nous représenterons pour abréger par S_n la somme des fractions simples, et par R_n le reste, de sorte qu'on ait

$$S_n = \frac{1}{a} + \frac{1}{a+1} + \ldots + \frac{1}{a+n-1} - \frac{1}{1-a} - \frac{1}{2-a} - \ldots - \frac{1}{n-a}$$
$$= \frac{1}{a} + \frac{2a}{a^2-1} + \ldots + \frac{2a}{a^2-(n-1)^2} - \frac{1}{n-a}$$

et

$$R_n = \int_0^1 \frac{z^{a-1} - z^{-a}}{1-z} z^n\,dz = \int_{-\infty}^0 \frac{e^{ax} - e^{(1-a)x}}{1-e^x} e^{nx}\,dx.$$

Je me propose maintenant d'établir que pour une valeur imaginaire quelconque de l'argument, $a = \alpha + i\beta$, R_n, ou plutôt son module, a pour limite zéro quand n croît indéfiniment. A cet effet je considérerai l'intégrale

$$\int_{-\infty}^0 \operatorname{mod}\left[\frac{e^{(\alpha+i\beta)x} - e^{(1-\alpha-i\beta)x}}{1-e^x} e^{nx}\right] dx,$$

qui est une limite supérieure de $\operatorname{mod} R_n$, et en distinguant deux cas suivant que α est négatif ou positif, je l'écris successivement sous ces deux formes :

$$\int_{-\infty}^0 \operatorname{mod}\left[\frac{e^{i\beta x} - e^{(1-2\alpha-i\beta)x}}{1-e^x}\right] e^{(n+\alpha)x}\,dx$$

et

$$\int_{-\infty}^{0} \bmod\left[\frac{e^{(2\alpha+i\beta)x} - e^{(1-i\beta)x}}{1-e^x}\right] e^{(n-\alpha)x}\, dx.$$

Cela posé, je dis, à l'égard de la première, que la plus grande valeur du module de $\frac{e^{i\beta x} - e^{(1-2\alpha-i\beta)x}}{1-e^x}$, entre les limites de l'intégrale, est donnée à la limite supérieure pour $x = 0$. Ce maximum étant donc $\sqrt{(2\alpha-1)^2+4\beta^2}$, nous pourrons écrire, en désignant par ε un nombre inférieur à l'unité,

$$\bmod R_n = \varepsilon\sqrt{(2\alpha-1)^2+4\beta^2}\int_{-\infty}^{0} e^{(n+\alpha)x}\, dx = \frac{\varepsilon\sqrt{(2\alpha-1)^2+4\beta^2}}{n+\alpha}.$$

Je mets, pour le démontrer, l'expression

$$\bmod^2\left[\frac{e^{i\beta x} - e^{(1-2\alpha-i\beta)x}}{1-e^x}\right] = \frac{1-2\cos 2\beta x\, e^{(1-2\alpha)x} + e^{(2-4\alpha)x}}{(1-e^x)^2},$$

sous la forme suivante

$$\left[\frac{1-e^{(1-2\alpha)x}}{1-e^x}\right]^2 + 4\left[\frac{\sin\beta x}{1-e^x}\right]^2 e^{(1-2\alpha)x},$$

et je remarque d'abord que la quantité $\frac{1-e^{(1-2\alpha)x}}{1-e^x}$, ou bien $\frac{1-z^{1-2\alpha}}{1-z}$ en prenant $z = e^x$, est toujours pour des valeurs de z inférieures à l'unité, au-dessous de la limite $1-2\alpha$, qu'elle atteint pour $z = 1$. On vérifie en effet l'inégalité

$$\frac{1-z^{1-2\alpha}}{1-z} < 1-2\alpha,$$

ou la suivante

$$1-z^{1-2\alpha} - (1-2\alpha)(1-z) < 0,$$

en observant que la dérivée du premier membre est la quantité positive $(1-2\alpha)(1-z^{-2\alpha})$. Ce premier membre va donc en croissant depuis la valeur négative 2α qui correspond à $z = 0$, pour aboutir à une valeur nulle à la limite supérieure $z = 1$, et reste par conséquent négatif dans l'intervalle.

Ce point établi, je passe à l'autre terme, j'y remplace $\sin\beta x$ par βx, ce qui en augmente la valeur, et après l'avoir écrit

$$4\left[\frac{\beta x\, e^{\frac{1}{2}x}}{e^x-1}\right]^2 e^{-2\alpha x},$$

ou encore

$$4\beta^2 \left[\frac{x}{e^{\frac{1}{2}x} - e^{-\frac{1}{2}x}}\right]^2 e^{-2\alpha x},$$

je remarque que la quantité $\frac{x}{e^{\frac{1}{2}x} - e^{-\frac{1}{2}x}}$ croît de zéro à l'unité lorsque x varie de $-\infty$ à o. C'est ce qu'on reconnaît immédiatement en développant en série le dénominateur, car on obtient ainsi l'expression

$$\frac{x}{e^{\frac{1}{2}x} - e^{-\frac{1}{2}x}} = \frac{1}{1 + \frac{1}{1.2.3}\frac{x^2}{4} + \frac{1}{1.2.3.4.5}\frac{x^4}{16} + \ldots}.$$

On en conclut, le facteur $e^{-2\alpha x}$ atteignant lui-même sa plus grande valeur pour $x = 0$, que pour ce second terme comme pour le premier, le maximum est encore donné en faisant $x = 0$, ce qui démontre le résultat annoncé.

Nous obtiendrons à l'égard de l'expression

$$\operatorname{mod}^2 \left[\frac{e^{(2\alpha+i\beta)x} - e^{(1-i\beta)x}}{1-e^x}\right] = \frac{e^{4\alpha x} - 2\cos 2\beta\, x\, e^{(1+2\alpha)x} + e^{2x}}{(1-e^x)^2}$$

une conclusion toute pareille, en la mettant sous la forme

$$\left[\frac{e^{2\alpha x} - e^x}{1-e^x}\right]^2 + 4\left[\frac{\sin \beta x}{1-e^x}\right]^2 e^{(1+2\alpha)x}.$$

Nous n'avons en effet qu'à considérer la quantité $\frac{e^{2\alpha x} - e^x}{1-e^x}$, ou $\frac{z^{2\alpha} - z}{1-z}$, la variable z croissant de zéro à l'unité; mais deux cas sont maintenant à distinguer. Supposons d'abord $2\alpha < 1$ de sorte qu'elle soit positive, nous prouverons qu'on a

$$\frac{z^{2\alpha} - z}{1-z} < 1 - 2\alpha,$$

ou bien

$$z^{2\alpha} - z - (1-2\alpha)(1-z) < 0,$$

en remarquant que le premier membre prend les valeurs $-(1-2\alpha)$ et o, pour $z = 0$, $z = 1$, et a pour dérivée la quantité positive

$$2\alpha(1 - z^{1-2\alpha})z^{2\alpha-1}.$$

Soit enfin $2\alpha > 1$, nous raisonnerons sur $\frac{z - z^{2\alpha}}{1 - z}$; et la condition

$$\frac{z - z^{2\alpha}}{1 - z} < 2\alpha - 1$$

se vérifiera absolument de même. Il est donc ainsi démontré que le maximum du module des deux expressions introduites, en supposant successivement α négatif et α positif, a pour valeur

$$\sqrt{(1 - 2\alpha)^2 + 4\beta^2},$$

de sorte qu'on a dans la première hypothèse

$$\operatorname{mod} R_n = \frac{\varepsilon\sqrt{(1 - 2\alpha)^2 + 4\beta^2}}{n + \alpha},$$

et dans la seconde

$$\operatorname{mod} R_n = \frac{\varepsilon\sqrt{(1 - 2\alpha)^2 + 4\beta^2}}{n - \alpha}.$$

Ces expressions, du reste, dans le développement en série de fractions simples de la cotangente, établissent en toute rigueur la convergence de cette série; elles montrent en effet que pour des valeurs aussi grandes qu'on le veut de α et β, mais finies cependant, R_n est nul si l'on suppose n infini. Mais on voit en même temps qu'on n'est point autorisé à faire usage de l'expression

$$\frac{1}{a} + \frac{2a}{a^2 - 1} + \frac{2a}{a^2 - 4} + \ldots$$

pour des valeurs infinies de l'argument; dans le domaine de ces valeurs, la définition de $\cot a\pi$ par la série offre en effet une lacune que la considération du reste permet seule de combler, comme nous allons le faire voir.

3. Je dis en premier lieu que la limite de S_n est indéterminée lorsqu'après avoir remplacé a par ia on suppose à la fois n et a infinis. Revenons en effet à l'expression

$$\begin{aligned} S_n &= \frac{1}{a} + \frac{2a}{a^2 - 1} + \ldots + \frac{2a}{a^2 - (n-1)^2} - \frac{1}{n - a} \\ &= \frac{1}{a} + \frac{2a}{a^2 - 1} + \ldots + \frac{2a}{a^2 - n^2} - \frac{1}{n + a}, \end{aligned}$$

et changeons a en ia, on en conclura

$$iS_n = \frac{1}{a} + \frac{2a}{a^2 + 1} + \ldots + \frac{2a}{a^2 + n^2} + \frac{i}{n + ia}.$$

Soit maintenant, en supposant a positif $\frac{1}{a} = dx$, désignons aussi par λ la limite du rapport $\frac{n}{a}$ lorsqu'on fait croître n et a indéfiniment, de sorte qu'on ait $\frac{n}{a} = ndx = \lambda$; nous pourrons écrire, en négligeant $\frac{1}{a}$ et $\frac{1}{n + ia}$,

$$iS_n = \frac{2\,dx}{1 + dx^2} + \frac{2\,dx}{1 + (2\,dx)^2} + \ldots + \frac{2\,dx}{1 + (n\,dx)^2}.$$

De cette expression résulte immédiatement, comme on voit, la valeur cherchée

$$iS_n = \int_0^\lambda \frac{2\,dx}{1 + x^2} = 2 \operatorname{arc\,tang} \lambda$$

qui dépend de la quantité entièrement arbitraire λ.

Ce point établi, cherchons ce que devient l'intégrale représentant le reste,

$$R_n = \int_{-\infty}^0 \frac{e^{ax} - e^{(1-a)x}}{1 - e^x} e^{nx}\,dx.$$

Pour cela je remplace a par ia, n par λa, ce qui donne d'abord

$$R_n = \int_{-\infty}^0 \frac{e^{iax} - e^{(1-ia)x}}{1 - e^x} e^{\lambda ax}\,dx,$$

puis en changeant de variable et posant $x = \frac{t}{a}$

$$R_n = \int_{-\infty}^0 \frac{e^{it} - e^{\left(\frac{1}{a} - i\right)t}}{a\left(1 - e^{\frac{t}{a}}\right)} e^{\lambda t}\,dt.$$

Maintenant on obtient pour a infini la valeur

$$R_n = -2i \int_{-\infty}^0 \frac{\sin t}{t} e^{\lambda t}\,dt = -2i \operatorname{arc\,tang} \frac{1}{\lambda},$$

et l'on en tire la relation

$$i(S_n + R_n) = 2\left(\operatorname{arc\,tang} \lambda + \operatorname{arc\,tang} \frac{1}{\lambda}\right) = \pi$$

ou encore

$$S_n + R_n = -i\pi.$$

Ce résultat lève entièrement, comme on voit, la difficulté d'analyse offerte par le développement en série de la cotangente.

4. L'expression de $\sin a\pi$ en produit de facteurs linéaires est immédiatement donnée en intégrant par rapport à a les deux membres de l'équation

$$\pi \cot a\pi = \frac{1}{a} + \frac{2a}{a^2-1} + \ldots + \frac{2a}{a^2-n^2} - \frac{1}{n+a} + R_n;$$

on obtient ainsi

$$\log \frac{\sin a\pi}{\pi} = \log a + \log\left(1 - \frac{a^2}{1}\right) + \log\left(1 - \frac{a^2}{4}\right) + \ldots$$
$$+ \log\left(1 - \frac{a^2}{n^2}\right) - \log\left(1 - \frac{a}{n}\right) + R_n,$$

si l'on pose

$$R'_n - \int_{-\infty}^{0} \frac{e^{ax} + e^{(1-a)x} - e^x - 1}{x(1-e^x)} e^{nx}\, dx.$$

Peut-être n'est-il pas inutile de donner encore pour R'_n une limite supérieure montant que cette quantité est nulle en supposant n infini, quelle que soit la valeur réelle ou imaginaire

$$a = \alpha + i\beta.$$

Posons à cet effet, pour abréger,

$$f(x) = \frac{e^{ax} + e^{(1-a)x} - e^x - 1}{x(1-e^x)};$$

je remarque qu'on peut écrire en ajoutant et retranchant $2e^{\frac{1}{2}x}$ au numérateur

$$f(x) = \frac{\left[e^{\frac{1}{2}ax} - e^{\frac{1}{2}(1-a)x}\right]^2}{x(1-e^x)} - \frac{\left[e^{\frac{1}{2}x} - 1\right]^2}{x(1-e^x)}.$$

On en déduit par une proposition connue,

$$\operatorname{mod} f(x) < \operatorname{mod} \frac{\left[e^{\frac{1}{2}ax} - e^{\frac{1}{2}(1-a)x}\right]^2}{x(1-e^x)} + \operatorname{mod} \frac{\left(e^{\frac{1}{2}x} - 1\right)^2}{x(1-e^x)},$$

c'est-à-dire

$$\operatorname{mod} f(x) < \frac{e^{\alpha x} - 2\cos\beta x\, e^{\frac{1}{2}x} + e^{(1-\alpha)x}}{x(e^x - 1)} + \frac{\left(e^{\frac{1}{2}x} - 1\right)^2}{x(e^x - 1)}.$$

L'expression suivante

$$\int_{-\infty}^{0} \frac{e^{\alpha x} - 2\cos\beta x\, e^{\frac{1}{2}x} + e^{(1-\alpha)x}}{x(e^x - 1)} e^{nx}\,dx + \int_{-\infty}^{0} \frac{\left(e^{\frac{1}{2}x} - 1\right)^2}{x(e^x - 1)} e^{nx}\,dx$$

est donc une quantité supérieure à l'intégrale $\int_{-\infty}^{0} \operatorname{mod} f(x) e^{nx}\,dx$ et à plus forte raison au module de R'_n. Or en considérant d'abord la seconde des intégrales qui y entrent et qu'on peut écrire ainsi

$$\int_{-\infty}^{0} \frac{e^{\frac{1}{2}x} - 1}{x\left(e^{\frac{1}{2}x} + 1\right)} e^{nx}\,dx,$$

je remarque que le maximum de la fraction $\frac{e^{\frac{1}{2}x} - 1}{x\left(e^{\frac{1}{2}x} + 1\right)}$ entre les limites de l'intégration est donné à la limite supérieure en faisant $x = 0$. Mettons en effet $-x$ au lieu de x, elle gardera la même forme, et l'inégalité

$$\frac{e^{\frac{1}{2}x} - 1}{x\left(e^{\frac{1}{2}x} + 1\right)} < \frac{1}{4},$$

ou bien celle-ci

$$4\left(e^{\frac{1}{2}x} - 1\right) < x\left(e^{\frac{1}{2}x} + 1\right),$$

se vérifie immédiatement par le développement en série, le coefficient de $\left(\frac{x}{2}\right)^{n+1}$ dans le premier membre étant

$$\frac{4}{1.2\ldots n+1} \quad \text{et} \quad \frac{1}{1.2\ldots n}$$

dans le second.

Passant maintenant à la première intégrale, j'emploie la décomposition suivante

$$e^{\alpha x} - 2\cos\beta x\, e^{\frac{1}{2}x} + e^{(1-\alpha)x} = \left[e^{\frac{1}{2}\alpha x} - e^{\frac{1}{2}(1-\alpha)x}\right]^2 + 4\sin^2\frac{1}{2}\beta x\, e^{\frac{1}{2}x},$$

qui nous conduit à deux termes, dont l'un $\dfrac{4\sin^2\frac{1}{2}\beta x e^{\frac{1}{2}x}}{x(e^x-1)}$ atteint encore son maximum pour $x=0$. Si on l'augmente en effet en remplaçant $\sin\frac{1}{2}\beta x$ par $\frac{1}{2}\beta x$, il se réduit à l'expression $\dfrac{xe^{\frac{1}{2}x}}{e^x-1}$, dont le maximum a été obtenu plus haut, et ce résultat joint au précédent montre qu'on peut poser, en désignant par ε un nombre plus petit que l'unité

$$\int_{-\infty}^{0} \frac{4\sin^2\frac{1}{2}\beta x\, e^{\frac{1}{2}x}+\left(e^{\frac{1}{2}x}-1\right)^2}{x(e^x-1)} e^{nx}\,dx$$
$$=\varepsilon\left(\beta^2+\frac{1}{4}\right)\int_{-\infty}^{0} e^{nx}\,dx=\frac{\varepsilon(4\beta^2+1)}{4n}.$$

Quant au dernier terme qui nous reste à considérer

$$\frac{\left[e^{\frac{1}{2}\alpha x}-e^{\frac{1}{2}(1-\alpha)x}\right]^2}{x(e^x-1)},$$

nous l'écrirons sous l'une ou l'autre de ces deux formes

$$\frac{\left[1-e^{\frac{1}{2}(1-2\alpha)x}\right]^2 e^{\alpha x}}{x(e^x-1)} \quad \text{et} \quad \frac{\left[e^{\alpha x}-e^{\frac{1}{2}x}\right]^2 e^{-\alpha x}}{x(e^x-1)},$$

suivant que α est négatif ou positif, en mettant en évidence, comme facteurs des exponentielles, des quantités ayant leur maximum pour $x=0$. En nous bornant par exemple à la première pour abréger, il suffit de la décomposer ainsi

$$\frac{1-e^{\frac{1}{2}(1-2\alpha)x}}{1-e^x}\times\frac{e^{\frac{1}{2}(1-2\alpha)x}-1}{x};$$

on retrouve en effet dans le premier facteur l'expression dont l'étude a été déjà faite, et l'on vérifie facilement que le second augmente de zéro à $\dfrac{1-2\alpha}{2}$, quand la variable augmente de $-\infty$ à 0.

De là résulte que nous pouvons poser

$$\int_{-\infty}^{0} \frac{\left[e^{\frac{1}{2}\alpha x}-e^{\frac{1}{2}(1-\alpha)x}\right]^2}{x(e^x-1)} e^{nx}\,dx = \frac{\eta(1-2\alpha)^2}{4}\int_{-\infty}^{0} e^{(n+\alpha)x}\,dx,$$

pour α négatif, et

$$\int_{-\infty}^{0} \frac{\left[e^{\frac{1}{2}\alpha x} - e^{\frac{1}{2}(1-\alpha)x}\right]^2}{x(e^x - 1)} e^{nx}\, dx = \frac{\eta(1-2\alpha)^2}{4} \int_{-\infty}^{0} e^{(n-\alpha)x}\, dx,$$

quand α est positif, η désignant un nombre < 1. Suivant ces deux cas, nous parvenons donc aux expressions suivantes que je me suis proposé d'obtenir :

$$\bmod R'_n = \frac{\eta(1-2\alpha)^2}{4(n+\alpha)} + \frac{\varepsilon(4\beta^2+1)}{4n}$$

et

$$\bmod R'_n = \frac{\eta(1-2\alpha)^2}{4(n-\alpha)} + \frac{\varepsilon(4\beta^2+1)}{4n}.$$

Elles donnent la formule

$$\sin a\pi = \pi a\left(1 - \frac{a^2}{1}\right)\left(1 - \frac{a^2}{4}\right)\cdots\left(1 - \frac{a^2}{n^2}\right)\frac{e^{R'_n}}{1 + \frac{a}{n}},$$

et par conséquent une démonstration rigoureuse du développement du sinus en produit d'un nombre infini de facteurs.

5. Les intégrales R_n et R'_n sont des cas particuliers de cette expression plus générale

$$\int_{-\infty}^{0} \Phi(x)\, e^{nx}\, dx,$$

qui offre des circonstances sur lesquelles l'attention a été appelée pour la première fois par l'étude des intégrales Eulériennes. Nous allons voir qu'elle donne lieu à un développement en série procédant suivant les puissances décroissantes de n, mais que cette série est nécessairement divergente pour toute valeur de cette quantité, si grande qu'on la suppose. Il en résulte qu'on ne peut en employer que les premiers termes, avec l'obligation d'avoir une limite supérieure du reste permettant d'apprécier pour quel nombre de termes il est le plus petit possible. Admettons que pour x infiniment grand et négatif, les quantités

$$\Phi(x)\, e^{nx}, \quad \Phi'(x)^{nx}, \quad \ldots, \quad \Phi^{i-1}(x)\, e^{nx}$$

s'évanouissent; ce développement limité à un nombre déterminé de termes, et le reste s'obtiennent comme conséquence de la formule élémentaire

$$\int \Phi(x)\, e^{nx}\, dx = \left[\frac{\Phi(x)}{n} - \frac{\Phi'(x)}{n^2} + \ldots \mp \frac{\Phi^{i-1}(x)}{n^i}\right] e^{nx} \pm \frac{1}{n^i} \int \Phi^i(x)\, e^{nx}\, dx.$$

On en tire en effet

$$\int_{-\infty}^{0} \Phi(x)\, e^{nx}\, dx = S_i \pm \frac{1}{n^i} \int_{-\infty}^{0} \Phi^i(x)\, e^{nx}\, dx,$$

en posant

$$S_i = \frac{\Phi(0)}{n} - \frac{\Phi'(0)}{n^2} + \frac{\Phi''(0)}{n^3} - \ldots - (-1)^i \frac{\Phi^{i-1}(0)}{n^i},$$

et nous allons voir que cette série prolongée indéfiniment est divergente, au moins dans tous les cas où $\Phi(x)$ n'est point une fonction holomorphe.

Soit en effet

$$\Phi(x) = A_0 + A_1 x + \ldots + A_k x^k + \ldots,$$

sous la condition que ce développement cesse d'être convergent à l'extérieur d'un cercle de rayon ρ. C'est dire que A_k est de la forme $\frac{a_k}{\rho^k}$, a_k tendant vers une limite finie lorsque k augmente indéfiniment. Or ayant

$$\frac{\Phi^k(0)}{1.2.3\ldots k} = \frac{a_k}{\rho^k},$$

on en conclut pour le terme général de S_i, cette expression

$$\rho \frac{1.2.3\ldots k\, a_k}{(n\rho)^{k+1}},$$

et la divergence est rendue ainsi évidente, puisque ces termes augmentent indéfiniment à partir d'une certaine valeur de k. Mais la conclusion que nous venons d'obtenir pourrait ne plus avoir lieu si $\Phi(x)$ était, dans toute l'étendue du plan, développable en série convergente. En supposant par exemple

$$\Phi(x) = A\, e^{ax} + B\, e^{bx} + \ldots,$$

et par suite

$$\int_{-\infty}^{0} \Phi(x)\, e^{nx}\, dx = \frac{A}{n+a} + \frac{B}{n+b} + \ldots,$$

il est clair que le second membre donnera lieu à une série convergente quand n sera supérieur en valeur absolue à la plus grande des quantités a, b, etc.

Les remarques précédentes s'appliquent aux intégrales R_n, R'_n. Et d'abord, en employant la relation donnée en commençant

$$\frac{e^{ax} - e^{(1-a)x}}{1-e^x} = 1 - 2a - 2\,S(a)_2 \frac{x^2}{1.2} - 2\,S(a)_4 \frac{x^4}{1.2.3.4} - \ldots,$$

on obtient pour S_i cette expression

$$S_{2i+1} = \frac{1-2a}{n} - \frac{2\,S(a)_2}{n^3} - \frac{2\,S(a)_4}{n^5} - \ldots - \frac{2\,S(a)_{2i}}{n^{2i+1}},$$

qui doit finir par devenir divergente, la fraction $\frac{e^{ax} - e^{(1-a)x}}{1-e^x}$ n'étant pas en général synectique. Mais si l'on suppose que a soit un nombre entier, elle change de nature; elle prend, suivant qu'il est négatif ou positif, l'une ou l'autre de ces deux formes

$$[1 + e^{2x} + e^{4x} + \ldots + e^{-2ax}\ ]\, e^{(n+a)x},$$

$$-[1 + e^{2x} + e^{4x} + \ldots + e^{(2a-2)x}]\, e^{(n-a)x};$$

et alors la série cesse d'être divergente en ayant une somme finie, lorsque n est en valeur absolue plus grand que a.

La théorie des intégrales Eulériennes, à laquelle j'arrive maintenant, va nous donner de nouvelles et importantes applications des mêmes considérations.

6. Nous rattacherons cette théorie à l'étude de l'intégrale

$$\int_0^1 \frac{z^{a-1} - z^{-a}}{1-z} dz,$$

en développant une idée jetée par Cauchy dans son Mémoire sur les intégrales définies prises entre des limites imaginaires (p. 45), et dont le grand géomètre se borne à tirer, lorsque n est un grand nombre, la formule de Laplace

$$1 = \frac{\sqrt{2\pi}\, n^{n+\frac{1}{2}}}{\Gamma(n)},$$

mais qui a une portée plus étendue, comme on va voir.

Revenons à la relation

$$\log\frac{\sin a\pi}{\pi} = \log a + \log(1+a) + \ldots + \log\left(1+\frac{a}{n-1}\right) + R'_n$$
$$+ \log(1-a) + \log\left(1-\frac{a}{2}\right) + \ldots + \log\left(1-\frac{a}{n}\right),$$

et intégrons les deux membres entre les limites $a = 0$ et $a = 1$. Les formules élémentaires

$$\int \log x\, dx = x(\log x - 1),$$
$$\int \log\left(1+\frac{x}{k}\right) dx = (x+k)\log\left(1+\frac{x}{k}\right) - x,$$

nous donnant

$$\int_0^1 \log a\, da = \int_0^1 \log(1-a)\, da = -1,$$

puis en général

$$\int_0^1 \left[\log\left(1+\frac{a}{k}\right) + \log\left(1-\frac{a}{k+1}\right)\right] da = (2k+1)\log\frac{k+1}{k} - 2,$$

on aura dans le second membre, pour la somme des intégrales des logarithmes, la quantité

$$-2n + 3\log 2 + 5(\log 3 - \log 2) + \ldots + (2n-1)[\log n - \log(n-1)],$$

ou bien en réduisant

$$-2n - 2\log(1.2.3\ldots n-1) + (2n-1)\log n.$$

On tire ensuite de l'expression de R'_n, à savoir

$$R'_n = \int_{-\infty}^{0} \frac{e^{ax} + e^{(1-a)x} - e^x - 1}{x(1-e^x)} e^{nx}\, dx,$$

par un calcul facile

$$\int_0^1 R'_n\, da = \int_{-\infty}^{0} \frac{e^x(2-x) - 2 - x}{x^2(1-e^x)} e^{nx}\, dx.$$

Dans le premier membre enfin s'offre la quantité $\int_0^1 \log\frac{\sin a\pi}{\pi}\, da$

que nous obtenons ainsi. Soit pour un moment,

$$f(a)=\int_0^1 \log\frac{\sin a\pi}{\pi}\,da;$$

on aura aisément ces relations

$$f(a)=f(1-a),$$
$$f(a)=f\left(\frac{a}{2}\right)+f\left(\frac{1-a}{2}\right)+\log 2\pi,$$

et nous conclurons de la seconde

$$\int_0^1 f(a)\,da=\int_0^1 f\left(\frac{a}{2}\right)da+\int_0^1 f\left(\frac{1-a}{2}\right)da+\log 2\pi.$$

Mais les deux intégrales du second membre sont égales, et l'on peut écrire par conséquent

$$\int_0^1 f(a)\,da=2\int_0^1 f\left(\frac{a}{2}\right)+\log 2\pi.$$

Remarquant ensuite que la première relation nous donne

$$\int_0^1 f(a)\,da=2\int_0^{\frac{1}{2}} f(a)\,da,$$

et qu'on a évidemment

$$\int_0^1 f\left(\frac{a}{2}\right)da=2\int_0^{\frac{1}{2}} f(a)\,da,$$

nous conclurons la valeur cherchée

$$\int_0^1 \log\frac{\sin a\pi}{\pi}\,da=-\log 2\pi.$$

Au moyen de ce résultat, on parvient à la relation suivante

$$-\log 2\pi=-2n-2\log[1.2.3\ldots(n-1)]+(2n-1)\log n$$
$$+\int_{-\infty}^0 \frac{e^x(2-x)-2-x}{x^2(1-e^x)}e^{nx}\,dx,$$

d'où

$$\log[1.2.3\ldots(n-1)]$$
$$= \left(n-\frac{1}{2}\right)\log n - n + \log\sqrt{2\pi} + \frac{1}{2}\int_{-\infty}^{0}\frac{e^x(2-x)-2-x}{x^2(1-e^x)}e^{nx}\,dx,$$

et nous allons en exposer les conséquences.

7. En premier lieu nous avons une démonstration rigoureuse de la formule de Laplace par cette remarque que le maximum de la fonction $\frac{e^x(2-x)-2-x}{x^2(1-e^x)}$ a lieu pour $x=0$, et a par conséquent pour valeur $\frac{1}{6}$. Afin de considérer des valeurs positives de la variable mettons en effet $-x$ au lieu de x, ce qui n'en change pas la valeur, et nous vérifierons sur le champ l'inégalité

$$2+x-(2-x)e^x < x^2(e^x-1),$$

par le développement en série, car on trouve pour le premier membre

$$2+x-(2-x)e^x = \frac{x^3}{6}+\ldots+\frac{n}{1.2\ldots n+2}x^{n+2},$$

tandis que le coefficient de x^{n+2} dans le second est $\frac{1}{1.2\ldots n}$ qui est évidemment supérieur à $\frac{n}{1.2.3\ldots n+2}$. Il suit de là qu'on peut écrire, en désignant par ε un nombre <1,

$$\int_{-\infty}^{0}\frac{e^x(2-x)-2-x}{x^2(1-e^x)}e^{nx}\,dx = \frac{\varepsilon}{6}\int_{-\infty}^{0}e^{nx}\,dx = \frac{\varepsilon}{6n},$$

et qu'on a par conséquent

$$\log\Gamma(n) = \left(n-\frac{1}{2}\right)\log n - n + \log\sqrt{2\pi} + \frac{\varepsilon}{12n}.$$

En second lieu j'établirai que si l'on remplace dans l'égalité

$$\log\Gamma(n) = \left(n-\frac{1}{2}\right)\log n - n + \log\sqrt{2\pi} + \frac{1}{2}\int_{-\infty}^{0}\frac{e^x(2-x)-2-x}{x^2(1-e^x)}e^{nx}\,dx,$$

le nombre entier n par une quantité quelconque a, et qu'on pose

$$F(a) = \left(a-\frac{1}{2}\right)\log a - a + \log\sqrt{2\pi} + \frac{1}{2}\int_{-\infty}^{0}\frac{e^x(2-x)-2-x}{x^2(1-e^x)}e^{ax}\,dx,$$

on aura $F(a)=\log\Gamma(a)$ quel que soit a.

J'observe à cet effet qu'on a d'abord

$$F'(a) = \log a - \frac{1}{2a} + \frac{1}{2}\int_{-\infty}^{0} \frac{e^x(2 - x) - 2 - x}{x(1 - e^x)} e^{ax}\, dx,$$

puis

$$F''(a) = \frac{1}{a} + \frac{1}{2a^2} + \frac{1}{2}\int_{-\infty}^{0} \frac{e^x(2 - x) - 2 - x}{1 - e^x} e^{ax}\, dx.$$

Or on obtient un développement en série de cette quantité, en remplaçant $\frac{1}{1 - e^x}$, dans l'intégrale, par la progression indéfinie $1 + e^x + \ldots + e^{nx} + \ldots$; les intégrales de chaque terme résultent de la formule suivante

$$\int_{-\infty}^{0} [e^x(2 - x) - 2 - x]\, e^{(a+n)x}\, dx = \frac{1}{(a + n)^2} + \frac{1}{(a + n + 1)^2} - \frac{2}{a + n} + \frac{2}{a + n + 1},$$

et l'on en conclut aisément cette expression

$$F''(a) = \frac{1}{a^2} + \frac{1}{(a + 1)^2} + \frac{1}{(a + 2)^2} + \ldots$$

qui est précisément $D_a^2 \log \Gamma(a)$. Les deux fonctions $F(a)$ et $\log \Gamma(a)$ ne pourront ainsi différer que par un binome du premier degré en a, et comme elles sont égales pour toutes les valeurs entières de a, on voit, comme nous avions pour but de l'établir, qu'elles sont identiques.

La découverte de l'équation que nous venons de démontrer est due à Binet qui l'a donnée dans son beau Mémoire intitulé *Sur les intégrales définies Eulériennes et leur application à la théorie des suites, ainsi qu'à l'évaluation des fonctions de grands nombres* (*Journal de l'École Polytechnique*, t. XVI, p. 123). Elle a été ensuite le sujet des recherches de Cauchy qui y a consacré une partie essentielle d'un travail d'une grande importance, publié dans le Tome II des *Nouveaux Exercices d'Analyse et de Physique mathématique*, p. 384, sous ce titre : *Mémoire sur la théorie des intégrales définies singulières, appliquée généralement à la détermination des intégrales définies, et en particulier à l'évaluation des intégrales Eulériennes*. L'analyse un peu longue du grand géomètre peut être beaucoup abrégée et rendue, comme on l'a vu, entièrement élémentaire, en suivant une voie qu'il avait lui-même ouverte, bien des années auparavant; et c'est l'étude de la courte indication donnée à ce sujet dans le Mémoire sur les intégrales infinies prises entre des limites imaginaires, qui m'a conduit aux recherches qu'on vient de lire.

EXTRAIT D'UNE LETTRE A M. BRIOSCHI.

SUR L'ÉQUATION DE LAMÉ.

Annali di Matematica pura ed applicata,
2e série, t. IX, p. 21-24.

. . . .

Vous ne serez donc pas surpris que je sois parvenu de mon côté à l'équation différentielle du troisième ordre

$$z''' + 3pz'' + (p' + 2p^2 + 4q)z' + 2(q' + 2pq)z = 0$$

dont les solutions sont les produits de deux solutions de l'équation du second ordre

$$y'' + py' + qy = 0;$$

mais je l'obtiens sous une forme un peu différente, en prenant pour point de départ l'équation

$$(1) \qquad 2Ay'' + A'y' = By.$$

Un calcul facile me donne

$$(2) \qquad 2Az''' + 3A'z'' + A''z' = 4Bz' + 2B'z,$$

et voici les conséquences que j'en tire. Faisant dans l'équation de Lamé, $\mathrm{sn}^2 x = t$, on obtiendra pour transformée l'équation (1), où l'on prendra

$$A = t(1-t)(1-k^2t),$$
$$2B = n(n+1)k^2t + h.$$

Les fonctions A et B étant ainsi de simples polynomes, du troisième et du premier degré en t, la différentiation d'ordre p de l'équation (2) donne

$$2Az^{p+3}+(2p+3)A'z^{p+2}+\left[\frac{5p(p+1)+2}{2}A''-2B\right]z^{p+1}$$
$$+[2p(p-1)(p-2)+9p(p-1)+6p-(2p+1)(n^2+n)]k^2z^p=0\,;$$

or on peut mettre le coefficient de z^p, sous la forme

$$(2p+1)(p-n)(p+n+1)\,;$$

il s'annule donc en faisant $p=n$, et en adoptant cette valeur, l'équation est satisfaite si l'on pose $z^p=$ const. L'équation (2) par conséquent admet pour solution un polynome entier en t de degré n, $z=F(t)$, et les conclusions auxquelles vous êtes parvenu pour $n=1$ s'étendent d'elles-mêmes au cas où n est quelconque. En effet, deux solutions y_1 et y_2 de l'équation (1) sont liées par la relation

$$y_2\frac{dy_1}{dt}-y_1\frac{dy_2}{dt}=\frac{C}{\sqrt{A}},$$

où C est une constante, et en y joignant la condition

$$\frac{d(y_1.y_2)}{dt}=y_2\frac{dy_1}{dt}+y_1\frac{dy_2}{dt}=F'(t),$$

on en déduira

$$y_2\frac{dy_1}{dt}=\frac{1}{2}\left[F'(t)+\frac{C}{\sqrt{A}}\right],\qquad y_1\frac{dy_2}{dt}=\frac{1}{2}\left[F'(t)-\frac{C}{\sqrt{A}}\right],$$

et par suite

$$\frac{1}{y_1}\frac{dy_1}{dt}=\frac{1}{2}\left[\frac{F'(t)}{F(t)}+\frac{C}{\sqrt{A}\,F(t)}\right],\qquad \frac{1}{y^2}\frac{dy_2}{dt}=\frac{1}{2}\left[\frac{F'(t)}{F(t)}-\frac{C}{\sqrt{A}\,F(t)}\right],$$

d'où enfin

$$(3)\qquad y=G\,e^{\frac{1}{2}\int\left[\frac{F'(t)}{F(t)}+\frac{C}{\sqrt{A}F(t)}\right]dt}+G'\,e^{\frac{1}{2}\int\left[\frac{F'(t)}{F(t)}-\frac{C}{\sqrt{A}F(t)}\right]dt},$$

en désignant par G et G′ deux constantes arbitraires.

Voici maintenant, à l'égard de la constante C, une remarque essentielle. On tire aisément de l'équation (2) la suivante

$$(4)\qquad A(2zz''-z'^2)+A'zz'=2Bz^2-N,$$

et ce résultat se vérifie sur-le-champ en différentiant et divisant les deux membres par z. Mais à la solution spéciale de cette équation qui est donnée en prenant pour z le polynome $F(t)$, correspond une valeur entièrement déterminée de N. Qu'on attribue en effet à la variable t pour valeur particulière une racine de l'équation $y_1 = 0$, nous aurons en même temps $z = 0$, $z' = y'_1 y_2$, donc $N = A(y'_1 y_2)^2$. Or en attribuant cette même valeur à t, dans l'équation

$$y_2 \frac{dy_1}{dt} - y_1 \frac{dy_2}{dt} = \frac{C}{\sqrt{A}},$$

vous voyez qu'on en conclut $C = \sqrt{A} y'_1 y_2$; nous parvenons par suite à cette expression $C = \sqrt{N}$, et tout se trouve par conséquent déterminé dans la formule (3) qui donne ainsi la solution complète de l'équation de Lamé.

Vous reconnaîtrez maintenant sans peine qu'en posant $N = 0$ on a les valeurs particulières de h auxquelles correspondent les solutions qui, à l'égard de la variable x, sont des fonctions doublement périodiques, mais en laissant de côté ce point, je vous indiquerai une dernière remarque. L'équation (4) montre qu'en supposant N différent de zéro, il est impossible d'avoir à la fois $F(t) = 0$ et $F'(t) = 0$, de sorte que la première équation n'a que des racines simples. Soit $t = \tau$ l'une quelconque de ces racines, et faisons

$$\frac{1}{F(t)} = \sum \frac{1}{F'(\tau)(t-\tau)}.$$

Si nous désignons par T la valeur de A pour $t = \tau$, de sorte que l'équation (4) donne

$$TF'^2(\tau) = N,$$

on en conclura

$$\frac{\sqrt{N}}{F(t)} = \sum \frac{\sqrt{N}}{F'(\tau)(t-\tau)} = \sum \frac{\sqrt{T}}{t-\tau},$$

et par conséquent

$$\frac{F'(t)}{F(t)} + \frac{\sqrt{N}}{\sqrt{A}\,F(t)} = \sum \left[\frac{1}{t-\tau} + \frac{\sqrt{T}}{\sqrt{A}(t-\tau)}\right] = \sum \frac{\sqrt{A}+\sqrt{T}}{\sqrt{A}(t-\tau)}.$$

Cette formule conduit de la manière la plus facile à l'expression de l'intégrale qui figure en exponentielle dans l'équation (3).

Faisant en effet $t = \operatorname{sn}^2 x$, $\tau = \operatorname{sn}^2 \omega$, on a

$$\frac{1}{2}\int \frac{\sqrt{A}+\sqrt{T}}{t-\tau}\,dt = \int \frac{\operatorname{sn} x \operatorname{cn} x \operatorname{dn} x + \operatorname{sn}\omega \operatorname{cn}\omega \operatorname{dn}\omega}{\operatorname{sn}^2 x - \operatorname{sn}^2\omega}\,dx$$
$$= \int \left[\frac{H'(x-\omega)}{H(x-\omega)} - \frac{\Theta'(x)}{\Theta(x)} + \frac{\Theta'(\omega)}{\Theta(\omega)}\right] dx$$

(voyez *Comptes rendus*, p. 1086). Soit pour plus de clarté ω_1, ω_2, ..., ω_n les n déterminations de ω qui correspondent aux diverses racines τ, et qui ont été choisies de telle sorte qu'on ait $\sqrt{T} = \operatorname{sn}\omega \operatorname{cn}\omega \operatorname{dn}\omega$, en excluant comme vous voyez la supposition $\sqrt{T} = -\operatorname{sn}\omega \operatorname{cn}\omega \operatorname{dn}\omega$, nous parvenons à ce résultat

$$e^{\frac{1}{2}\int\left[\frac{F'(t)}{F(t)} + \frac{\sqrt{N}}{\sqrt{A}F(t)}\right]dt} = \frac{H(x-\omega_1)H(x-\omega_2)\ldots H(x-\omega_n)}{\Theta^n(x)}\, e^{x\sum\frac{\Theta'(\omega)}{\Theta(\omega)}},$$

et il est clair qu'on aurait semblablement

$$e^{\frac{1}{2}\int\left[\frac{F'(t)}{F(t)} - \frac{\sqrt{N}}{\sqrt{A}F(t)}\right]dt} = \frac{H(x+\omega_1)H(x+\omega_2)\ldots H(x+\omega_n)}{\Theta^n(x)}\, e^{-x\sum\frac{\Theta'(\omega)}{\Theta(\omega)}}.$$

Cette méthode pour intégrer l'équation de Lamé se trouve dans les feuilles lithographiées de mon cours de 1872 à l'École Polytechnique (1)....

17 décembre 1877.

---

(1) *Voir* page 118 de ce Volume. E. P.

SUR UN THÉORÈME DE GALOIS

RELATIF AUX

ÉQUATIONS SOLUBLES PAR RADICAUX [1].

J.-A. Serret, *Algèbre supérieure*, t. II, 5e édition, p. 677-680.

Étant données deux quelconques des racines d'une équation irréductible de degré premier, soluble par radicaux, les autres s'en déduisent rationnellement.

Lemme I. — *Soient*

$$F(x) = 0$$

une équation irréductible de degré quelconque n, et

$$x_0, \quad x_1, \quad x_2, \quad \ldots, \quad x_{n-1}$$

ses n racines. Si toutes les fonctions des racines invariables par les substitutions de la forme x_k, x_{k+1} *ou* $\binom{k+1}{k}$ (les indices étant pris comme fait Galois, suivant le module n) *sont rationnellement connues, on pourra déterminer rationnellement une fonction entière* $\varphi(x)$ *du degré* $n-1$, *telle qu'on ait*

$$x_1 = \varphi(x_0), \quad x_2 = \varphi(x_1), \quad \ldots, \quad x_{k+1} = \varphi(x_k), \quad \ldots, \quad x_{n-1} = \varphi(x_{n-2}).$$

On a, en effet,

$$F(x) = (x - x_0)(x - x_1) \ldots (x - x_{n-1}),$$

(1) Cette Note a été publiée seulement dans l'*Algèbre supérieure* de J.-A. Serret, qui s'exprime ainsi (*loc. cit.*, p. 677) : « Il ne sera pas inutile de présenter ici une analyse remarquable que M. Hermite m'a communiquée, et qui a pour objet la démonstration de ce théorème de Galois. » E. P.

et, si l'on pose

$$\varphi(x)=\frac{F(x)}{x-x_0}\frac{x_1}{F'(x_0)}+\frac{F(x)}{x-x_1}\frac{x_2}{F'(x_1)}+\ldots+\frac{F(x)}{x-x_{n-1}}\frac{x_0}{F'(x_{n-1})},$$

il est évident que $\varphi(x)$ sera une fonction entière du degré $n-1$ en x et que ses coefficients seront des fonctions des racines invariables par les substitutions de la forme $x_k,\ x_{k+1}$; on voit aussi immédiatement qu'on a

$$\varphi(x_0)=x_1,\qquad \varphi(x_1)=x_2,\qquad \ldots,$$

ce qui démontre la proposition énoncée.

Lemme II. — *Si une équation irréductible de degré premier n est telle que toutes les fonctions des racines invariables par les substitutions de la forme $x_k,\ x_{k+1}$, et de la forme $x_k,\ x_{\rho^k}$, ρ désignant une racine primitive de n, soient rationnellement connues, on pourra déterminer rationnellement une fonction entière de $\varphi(x)$ de degré $n-1$, telle que l'on ait*

$$\begin{array}{l}
(x_1+\lambda x_\rho+\lambda^2 x_{\rho^2}+\ldots+\lambda^{n-2}x_{\rho^{n-2}})^{n-1}=\varphi(x_0),\\
(x_2+\lambda x_{\rho+1}+\lambda^2 x_{\rho^2+1}+\ldots+\lambda^{n-2}x_{\rho^{n-2}+1})^{n-1}=\varphi(x_1),\\
\ldots\ldots\ldots\ldots\ldots\ldots\ldots\ldots\ldots\ldots\ldots\ldots,\\
(x_n+\lambda x_{\rho+n-1}+\lambda^2 x_{\rho^2+n-1}+\ldots+\lambda^{n-2}x_{\rho^{n-2}+n-1})^{n-1}=\varphi(x_{n+1}),
\end{array}$$

les indices étant pris toujours suivant le module n et λ désignant une racine de l'équation binome $\lambda^{n-1}=1$.

Pour démontrer cette proposition, nous ferons voir que le système des équations linéaires ainsi posées entre les coefficients indéterminés de la fonction φ n'est pas altéré lorsqu'à la place d'une racine quelconque x_k on met x_{k+1} et aussi quand on remplace x_k par x_{ρ^k}.

Le premier point est évident, puisque chaque équation se déduit de la précédente en ajoutant une unité aux indices des racines, et qu'en opérant de la sorte sur la dernière on reproduit la première.

Le second point se vérifie aussi immédiatement par rapport à l'équation

$$(x_1+\lambda x_\rho+\lambda^2 x_{\rho^2}+\ldots+\lambda^{n-2}x_{\rho^{n-2}})^{n-1}=\varphi(x_0),$$

car la $(n-1)^{\text{ième}}$ puissance de la fonction linéaire

$$x_1+\lambda x_\rho+\lambda^2 x_{\rho^2}+\ldots+\lambda^{n-2} x_{\rho^{n-2}}$$

ne change pas quand on multiplie cette fonction par λ; or cela revient à multiplier les indices des racines par ρ, ce qui ne change pas non plus le second membre $\varphi(x_0)$. Mais les autres équations du système ne se comportent plus de même. Dans l'une quelconque d'entre elles

$$(x_{1+\alpha}+\lambda x_{\rho+\alpha}+\lambda^2 x_{\rho^2+\alpha}+\ldots+\lambda^{n-2} x_{\rho^{n-2}+\alpha})^{n-1}=\varphi(x_\alpha),$$

faisons $\alpha\equiv\rho^\mu \pmod{n}$, ce qui est possible, puisque α ne reçoit plus la valeur zéro; il viendra

$$(1)\quad (x_{1+\rho^\mu}+\lambda x_{\rho+\rho^\mu}+\lambda^2 x_{\rho^2+\rho^\mu}+\ldots+\lambda^{n-2} x_{\rho^{n-2}+\rho^\mu})^{n-1}=\varphi(x_{\rho^\mu}),$$

et, en multipliant les indices par ρ,

$$(2)\quad (x_{\rho+\rho^{\mu+1}}+\lambda x_{\rho^2+\rho^{\mu+1}}+\lambda^2 x_{\rho^3+\rho^{\mu+1}}+\ldots+\lambda^{n-2} x_{\rho^{n-1}+\rho^{\mu+1}})^{n-1}=\varphi(x_{\rho^{\mu+1}}).$$

Or la $(n-1)^{\text{ième}}$ puissance de la fonction linéaire

$$x_{\rho+\rho^{\mu+1}}+\lambda x_{\rho^2+\rho^{\mu+1}}+\ldots+\lambda^{n-1} x_{\rho^{n-1}+\rho^{\mu+1}}$$

ne change pas quand on multiplie cette fonction par λ; au lieu de l'équation (2), on peut donc écrire la suivante :

$$(x_{\rho^{n-1}+\rho^{\mu+1}}+\lambda x_{\rho+\rho^{\mu+1}}+\lambda^2 x_{\rho^2+\rho^{\mu+1}}+\ldots+\lambda^{n-2} x_{\rho^{n-2}+\rho^{\mu+1}})^{n-1}=\varphi(x_{\rho^{\mu+1}}).$$

Or, en remarquant que $\rho^{n-1}\equiv 1 \pmod{n}$, on reconnaît que celle-ci se déduit de l'équation (1) par le changement de μ en $\mu+1$.

Il suit de là que la substitution x_k, x_{ρ^k} ne fait que permuter circulairement nos équations, rangées, à partir de la deuxième, suivant l'ordre des valeurs croissantes de μ. En les résolvant par rapport aux coefficients de φ, on sera conduit à des fonctions rationnelles des racines, invariables par les substitutions x_k, x_{k+1} et x_k, x_{ρ^k}; de sorte que ces coefficients s'exprimeront bien rationnellement, comme nous l'avons annoncé. Notre lemme est donc démontré, et l'on en déduit le suivant :

Lemme III. — *Si une équation de degré premier est résoluble algébriquement, l'équation de degré moindre d'une unité, qu'on forme en divisant son premier membre par un de ses facteurs linéaires, appartient à la classe des équations abéliennes.*

En effet, relativement à l'équation de degré $n - 1$, qu'on obtient par la suppression du facteur $x - x_\alpha$, et dont les racines ont été représentées par

$$x_{1+\alpha}, \quad x_{\rho+\alpha}, \quad x_{\rho^2+\alpha}, \quad \ldots, \quad x_{\rho^{n-2}+\alpha},$$

on connaît *rationnellement* la fonction résolvante

$$(x_{1+\alpha} + \lambda x_{\rho+\alpha} + \lambda^2 x_{\rho^2+\alpha} + \ldots + \lambda^{n-2} x_{\rho^{n-2}+\alpha})^{n-1}.$$

Les trois lemmes que nous venons de démontrer permettent maintenant d'établir très aisément le théorème que nous avons en vue. Faisons pour un instant

$$x_{\rho^k+\alpha} = X_k.$$

Puisque nous connaissons (lemme III), en fonction rationnelle de x_α, l'expression

$$(X_0 + \lambda X_1 + \lambda^2 X_2 + \ldots + \lambda^{n-2} X_{n-2})^{n-1},$$

nous devons pareillement regarder comme connue toute fonction rationnelle des racines X_k, invariable par les substitutions de la forme X_k, X_{k+1}. Cela nous place dans les conditions du lemme I; ainsi nous pouvons former une fonction φ telle qu'on ait généralement

$$X_{k+1} = \varphi(X_k).$$

D'ailleurs, les coefficients de cette fonction s'exprimeront rationnellement par les quantités connues et la racine x_α; de sorte qu'en mettant cette racine en évidence nous aurons

$$X_{k+1} = \varphi(X_k, x_\alpha) \qquad \text{ou} \qquad x_{\rho^{k+1}+\alpha} = \varphi(x_{\rho^k+\alpha}, x_\alpha).$$

Or on peut prendre $\rho^k \equiv \beta$, β étant un entier arbitraire, mais essentiellement différent de zéro; il vient ainsi

$$x_{\rho\beta+\alpha} = \varphi(x_{\beta+\alpha}, x_\alpha).$$

Cette équation exprime précisément la relation que nous nous proposions d'établir; elle montre très facilement comment toutes les racines s'expriment de proche en proche, au moyen des deux racines arbitraires x_α, $x_{\alpha+\beta}$, et met immédiatement en évidence dans quel ordre elles naissent ainsi les unes des autres.

Il est aisé de démontrer que, réciproquement, la relation précédente, admise entre trois racines x_α, $x_{\alpha+\beta}$, $x_{\alpha+\rho\beta}$, entraîne la résolution par radicaux de l'équation.

A cet effet, soient θ une racine de l'équation binome $x^n = 1$, et

$$F(\theta) = (x_0 + \theta x_1 + \theta^2 x_2 + \ldots + \theta^{n-1} x_{n-1})^n$$

la fonction résolvante de Lagrange. D'après la propriété caractéristique de cette fonction, on pourra, sans altérer sa valeur, ajouter aux indices des racines un nombre entier arbitraire α, et écrire

$$F(\theta) = (x_\alpha + \theta x_{\alpha+1} + \theta^2 x_{\alpha+2} + \ldots + \theta^{n-1} x_{\alpha+n-1})^n.$$

Cela posé, soit β un autre nombre entier arbitraire, mais différent de zéro, et prenons β_0 de manière qu'on ait

$$\beta\beta_0 \equiv 1 \quad (\text{mod.}\, n);$$

on voit immédiatement qu'on a

$$F(\theta^{\beta_0}) = (x_\alpha + \theta x_{\alpha+\beta} + \theta^2 x_{\alpha+2\beta} + \ldots + \theta^{n-1} x_{\alpha+(n-1)\beta})^n,$$

et il est clair qu'en employant la relation

$$x_{\rho\beta+\alpha} = \varphi(x_{\beta+\alpha}, x_\alpha),$$

on pourra, par des substitutions successives, transformer le second membre en une fonction rationnelle Π de deux racines x_α, $x_{\alpha+\beta}$, de manière à avoir

$$F(\theta^{\beta_0}) = \Pi(x_\alpha, x_{\alpha+\beta})$$

pour une valeur quelconque de l'indice arbitraire α.

Cela étant, soit, comme plus haut, λ une racine de l'équation binome $x^{n-1} = 1$, la fonction

$$\begin{aligned}[&\Pi(x_\alpha, x_{\alpha+\beta}) + \lambda \Pi(x_\alpha, x_{\alpha+\rho\beta}) \\ &+ \lambda^2 \Pi(x_\alpha, x_{\alpha+\rho^2\beta}) + \ldots + \lambda^{n-2} \Pi(x_\alpha, x_{\alpha+\rho^{n-2}\beta})]^{n-1}\end{aligned}$$

conserve la même valeur quand on met $\rho\beta$ au lieu de β, c'est-à-dire qu'elle est indépendante de la valeur attribuée à β. Chacun des termes dont elle se compose est d'ailleurs indépendant de α; donc, en la transformant, au moyen de la relation

$$x_{\alpha+\rho\beta} = \varphi(x_{\alpha+\beta}, x_\alpha),$$

en une fonction rationnelle des deux seules racines x_α et $x_{\alpha+\beta}$, cette fonction devra se réduire à une quantité connue. Effectivement, si une fonction

$$u = \psi(x_{\alpha+\beta}, x_\alpha)$$

conserve la même valeur, quels que soient les indices α et β, le second indice étant différent de zéro, on peut écrire

$$n(n-1)u = \sum_{0}^{n-1}{}_\alpha \sum_{1}^{n-1}{}_\beta \psi(x_{\alpha+\beta}, x_\alpha),$$

relation dont le second membre est une fonction symétrique de toutes les racines $x_0, x_1, \ldots, x_{n-1}$.

Il résulte de là que nous pouvons regarder les $n-1$ quantités

$$\Pi(x_\alpha, x_{\alpha+\beta}), \quad \Pi(x_\alpha, x_{\alpha+\rho\beta}), \quad \ldots, \quad \Pi(x_\alpha, x_{\alpha+\rho^{n-2}\beta})$$

comme les racines d'une équation abélienne résoluble par l'extraction d'un seul radical de degré $n-1$. Or, ces quantités une fois obtenues, nous connaissons, pour toutes les valeurs de β, excepté $\beta = 0$, la puissance $n^{\text{ième}}$ de la fonction résolvante $F(\theta^{\beta_0})$; donc, par l'extraction de $n-1$ radicaux du $n^{\text{ième}}$ degré, nous aurons ces diverses fonctions résolvantes, et, par conséquent, les racines elles-mêmes. On sait d'ailleurs, par une observation d'Abel, que ces $n-1$ radicaux s'expriment rationnellement en fonction de l'un d'entre eux et des quantités sur lesquelles ils portent, quantités qui sont, comme nous venons de le dire, les racines d'une équation abélienne.

SUR LE CONTACT DES SURFACES.

Hermite, *Cours d'Analyse de l'École Polytechnique*, p. 139-149. Gauthier-Villars, 1873.

I. Une surface étant définie par l'équation $F(x, y, z) = 0$, les coordonnées d'un quelconque de ses points seront des fonctions de deux variables différentes, et devront s'exprimer de cette manière

$$x = \varphi(t, u), \qquad y = \psi(t, u), \qquad z = \theta(t, u).$$

Et si nous considérons une seconde surface dont tous les points se déduisent par une construction déterminée de ceux de la première, leurs coordonnées seront représentées pareillement par ces expressions où figurent les mêmes variables indépendantes t et u

$$X = \Phi(t, u), \qquad Y = \Psi(t, u), \qquad z = \Theta(t, u).$$

Cela étant, la théorie du contact repose encore sur la considération de la fonction $\delta = f(t, u)$, qui donne la distance de deux points correspondants, savoir

$$\begin{aligned}\delta &= [(X - x)^2 + (Y - y)^2 + (Z - z)^2]^{\frac{1}{2}} \\ &= \{[\Phi(t, u) - \varphi(t, u)]^2 + [\Psi(t, u) - \psi(t, u)]^2 + [\Theta(t, u) - \theta(t, u)]^2\}^{\frac{1}{2}},\end{aligned}$$

et nous dirons qu'en un point donné par les valeurs $t = a$, $u = b$, les surfaces ont un contact du $n^{\text{ième}}$ ordre, lorsqu'en posant $t = a + h$, $u = b + k$, la distance δ est infiniment petite d'ordre $n + 1$ par rapport à h et k. Mais il faut tout d'abord préciser ce qu'on entend par l'ordre d'un infiniment petit par rapport à deux autres. Nous imaginerons à cet effet que h et k dépendent d'une seule variable, en faisant par exemple $k = \omega h$, et supposant ω fini.

Cela posé, la quantité

$$\delta = f(a+h,\ b+\omega h)$$

pourra se développer en série suivant les puissances croissantes de h, et il sera désormais entendu qu'elle est infiniment petite d'ordre $n+1$, lorsque indépendamment de toute valeur attribuée à ω, les coefficients des puissances de h jusqu'à la $n^{\text{ième}}$ seront tous nuls. En admettant ce principe, on déduira sur-le-champ de la définition de l'ordre du contact à l'égard des deux surfaces, ces conséquences qu'il suffit d'énoncer :

1° Les trois différences $X - x$, $Y - y$, $Z - z$ doivent être chacune infiniment petites de l'ordre $n+1$;

2° Ces conditions restent les mêmes en changeant les axes coordonnés;

3° Elles subsistent si l'on change de variables indépendantes, en posant

$$t = f(\tau, \upsilon), \qquad t = f_1(\tau, \upsilon).$$

Ainsi en admettant qu'à $t = a$, $u = b$ répondent $\tau = \alpha$, $\upsilon = \beta$, et qu'on ait

$$a + h = f(\alpha + i,\ \beta + j), \qquad b + k = f_1(\alpha + i,\ \beta + j),$$

si les quantités $X - x$, $Y - y$, $Z - z$ sont infiniment petites d'ordre $n+1$ par rapport à h et k, elles seront infiniment petites du même ordre par rapport à i et j.

4° Prenant d'après cela pour variables indépendantes les coordonnées x et y, de sorte que les équations des surfaces deviennent

$$z = f(x, y),$$
$$X = \mathcal{F}(x, y), \qquad Y = \mathcal{F}_1(x, y), \qquad Z = F(x, y),$$

une des trois fonctions $\mathcal{F}$, $\mathcal{F}_1$, F détermine la nature de la seconde surface, les deux autres, $\mathcal{F}$ et $\mathcal{F}_1$ par exemple, la loi de correspondance de leurs points, et les conditions relatives aux différences $X - x$, $Y - y$ caractérisent les lois de correspondances compatibles avec la définition de l'ordre du contact. Quant aux conditions concernant les surfaces elles-mêmes, elles se déduisent des développements que donne la série de Taylor étendue à deux variables, savoir :

$$F(a+h,\ b+k)$$
$$= F(a,b) + \left(\frac{dF}{da} + \omega\frac{dF}{db}\right)\frac{h}{1} + \left(\frac{d^2F}{da^2} + 2\omega\frac{d^2F}{da\,db} + \omega^2\frac{d^2F}{db^2}\right)\frac{h^2}{1.2} + \ldots,$$

$$f(a+h,\ b+\omega h)$$
$$= f(a,b) + \left(\frac{df}{da} + \omega\frac{df}{db}\right)\frac{h}{1} + \left(\frac{d^2f}{da^2} + 2\omega\frac{d^2f}{da\,db} + \omega^2\frac{d^2f}{db^2}\right)\frac{h^2}{1.2} + \ldots;$$

on exprime en effet que la différence $Z - z$ est infiniment petite d'ordre $n+1$, en posant

$$F(a,b) = f(a,b),$$
$$\frac{dF}{da} + \omega\frac{dF}{db} = \frac{df}{da} + \omega\frac{df}{db},$$
$$\frac{d^2F}{da^2} + 2\omega\frac{d^2F}{da\,db} + \omega^2\frac{d^2F}{db^2} = \frac{d^2f}{da^2} + 2\omega\frac{d^2f}{da\,db} + \omega^2\frac{d^2f}{db^2},$$
$$\ldots\ldots\ldots\ldots\ldots\ldots\ldots\ldots\ldots\ldots,$$
$$\frac{d^nF}{da^n} + \frac{n}{1}\omega\frac{d^nF}{da^{n-1}db} + \ldots + \frac{n}{1}\omega^{n-1}\frac{d^nF}{da\,db^{n-1}} + \omega^n\frac{d^nF}{db^n}$$
$$= \frac{d^nf}{da^n} + \frac{n}{1}\omega\frac{d^nf}{da^{n-1}db} + \ldots + \frac{n}{1}\omega^{n-1}\frac{d^nf}{da\,db^{n-1}} + \omega^n\frac{d^nf}{db^n},$$

et considérant ω dans ce système de relations comme une indéterminée; il en résulte que le contact du premier ordre exige trois équations :

$$F(a,b) = f(a,b), \qquad \frac{dF}{da} = \frac{df}{da}, \qquad \frac{dF}{db} = \frac{df}{db};$$

le contact du second ordre six, car aux précédentes il faudra joindre celles-ci :

$$\frac{d^2F}{da^2} = \frac{d^2f}{da^2}, \qquad \frac{d^2F}{da\,db} = \frac{d^2f}{da\,db}, \qquad \frac{d^2F}{db^2} = \frac{d^2f}{db^2},$$

et en général le contact d'ordre n, $\frac{(n+1)(n+2)}{2}$ équations. C'est ce nombre qui donne à la théorie dont nous nous occupons son caractère propre, et éloigne, sauf le premier cas de $n=1$, toute analogie avec celle du contact de deux courbes, ou d'une courbe et d'une surface, comme on va le voir par les applications suivantes.

II. En premier lieu, nous envisagerons le plan

$$Z = aX + bY + c,$$

dont l'équation renferme trois coefficients, de sorte qu'on peut, comme pour la ligne droite à l'égard d'une courbe, obtenir, en un point quelconque

$$X = x, \qquad Y = y,$$

un contact de premier ordre avec toute surface $z = f(x, y)$. Ayant en effet

$$F(X, Y) = aX + bY + c,$$

les conditions

$$F(x, y) = f(x, y), \qquad \frac{dF}{dx} = \frac{df}{dx}, \qquad \frac{dF}{dy} = \frac{df}{dy}$$

donnent immédiatement

$$z = ax + by + c, \qquad a = \frac{dz}{dx}, \qquad b = \frac{dz}{dy},$$

et l'on retrouve ainsi l'équation déjà obtenue du plan tangent sous la forme

$$Z - z = \frac{dz}{dx}(X - x) + \frac{dz}{dy}(Y - y).$$

Nous remarquerons, avant de faire les applications de ce résultat, qu'en supposant parallèle au plan coordonné des XY le plan tangent en x, y, z à la surface $z = f(x, y)$, on a nécessairement

$$\frac{df}{dx} = 0, \qquad \frac{df}{dy} = 0.$$

Et si le plan des XY est lui-même tangent à l'origine des coordonnées, la fonction $f(x, y)$ ainsi que ses dérivées partielles du premier ordre s'annuleront pour $x = 0$, $y = 0$, de sorte que le développement par la série de Maclaurin de l'ordonnée z suivant les puissances croissantes de x et y commencera seulement aux termes du second degré, et sera de la forme

$$z = ax^2 + bxy + cy^2 + dx^3 + ex^2y + \ldots.$$

De là se déduirait que la distance au plan tangent d'un point d'une surface infiniment voisin d'un point de contact est un infiniment petit du second ordre. Mais d'une manière plus générale, comme par définition la distance δ de deux points correspondants A et B de deux surfaces, infiniment voisins de leur point de contact, est infiniment petite d'ordre $n+1$ lorsqu'elles ont un contact du $n^{\text{ième}}$ ordre, il en résulte *a fortiori* que la plus courte distance du point A de la première surface à la seconde, est aussi infiniment petite du même ordre.

Observons enfin qu'en supposant z une fonction implicite déterminée par la relation

$$f(x, y, z) = 0,$$

l'équation

$$Z - z = \frac{dz}{dx}(X - x) + \frac{dz}{dy}(Y - y)$$

reprend la forme sous laquelle nous l'avions précédemment obtenue. On a en effet

$$\frac{df}{dz}\frac{dz}{dx} + \frac{df}{dx} = 0, \qquad \frac{df}{dz}\frac{dz}{dy} + \frac{df}{dy} = 0,$$

d'où l'on tire

$$\frac{dz}{dx} = -\frac{\frac{df}{dx}}{\frac{df}{dz}}, \qquad \frac{dz}{dy} = -\frac{\frac{df}{dy}}{\frac{df}{dz}},$$

et en substituant il vient

$$(X - x)\frac{df}{dx} + (Y - y)\frac{df}{dy} + (Z - z)\frac{df}{dz} = 0.$$

Nous en conclurons pour la normale à la surface, c'est-à-dire la perpendiculaire élevée en x, y, z au plan tangent, les équations

$$\frac{X - x}{\frac{df}{dx}} = \frac{Y - y}{\frac{df}{dy}} = \frac{Z - z}{\frac{df}{dz}},$$

en supposant que les axes coordonnés soient rectangulaires.

III. Soit pour première application les surfaces données par l'équation

$$f(x - az, y - bz) = 0,$$

ou plus simplement

$$f(\alpha, \beta) = 0,$$

en posant

$$\alpha = x - az, \qquad \beta = y - bz.$$

On tirera de là

$$\frac{df}{dx} = \frac{df}{d\alpha}, \qquad \frac{df}{dy} = \frac{df}{d\beta}, \qquad \frac{df}{dz} = -a\frac{df}{d\alpha} - b\frac{df}{d\beta},$$

de sorte qu'en réunissant les termes en $\frac{df}{d\alpha}$ et $\frac{df}{d\beta}$, l'équation du plan tangent devient

$$\frac{df}{d\alpha}[X - x - a(Z - z)] + \frac{df}{d\beta}[Y - y - b(Z - z)] = 0.$$

Ce résultat fait voir que, quelle que soit la fonction $f(\alpha, \beta)$, ce plan contient la droite

$$X - x = a(Z - z), \qquad Y - y = b(Z - z).$$

Effectivement, l'équation proposée est celle des *surfaces cylindriques*, et le calcul met en évidence cette propriété du plan tangent, de contenir la génératrice qui passe par le point de contact.

Nous considérons en second lieu les *surfaces coniques* qui sont données par l'équation

$$f(\alpha, \beta) = 0,$$

en posant

$$\alpha = \frac{x - a}{z - c}, \qquad \beta = \frac{y - b}{z - c}.$$

On aura alors

$$\frac{df}{dx} = \frac{1}{z - c}\frac{df}{d\alpha}, \qquad \frac{df}{dy} = \frac{1}{z - c}\frac{df}{d\beta},$$

$$\frac{df}{dz} = -\frac{x - a}{(z - c)^2}\frac{df}{d\alpha} - \frac{y - b}{(z - c)^2}\frac{df}{d\beta},$$

et, par suite, pour l'équation du plan tangent, après avoir supprimé le facteur $\frac{1}{z - c}$,

$$\frac{df}{d\alpha}\left[X - x - (Z - z)\frac{x - a}{z - c}\right] + \frac{df}{d\beta}\left[Y - y - (Z - z)\frac{y - b}{z - c}\right] = 0.$$

Il contient donc encore la génératrice qui passe par le point de contact.

En dernier lieu, les équations de la normale aux surfaces de révolution

$$f(\alpha, \beta) = 0,$$

en faisant

$$\alpha = x^2 + y^2, \qquad \beta = z,$$

seront

$$\frac{X - x}{2xf'(\alpha)} = \frac{Y - y}{2yf'(\alpha)} = \frac{Z - z}{f'(\beta)},$$

et les deux premières se réduisant à $\frac{X}{x} = \frac{Y}{y}$, il en résulte que cette droite est dans le plan déterminé par le point (x, y, z) et l'axe des z, qui est l'axe de révolution de la surface.

IV. Une surface reçoit le nom *d'osculatrice*, lorsqu'on a disposé de toutes les constantes qui fixent sa position et déterminent sa nature, de manière à obtenir, avec une surface donnée, le contact de l'ordre le plus élevé possible. C'est là, comme on voit, l'extension naturelle de la notion qui s'est offerte dans la théorie du contact des courbes considérées sur un plan ou dans l'espace, et qui a reçu, dans le cas du cercle, une application d'une grande importance. Mais toute surface ne peut point devenir osculatrice d'une autre, comme toute courbe plane, quelle qu'elle soit, d'une ligne donnée. Il faut en effet que le nombre des constantes à déterminer soit un terme de la série

$$3, \quad 6, \quad 10, \quad 15, \quad 21, \quad \ldots, \quad \frac{(n+1)(n+2)}{2},$$

de sorte qu'il n'y a ni sphère, ni surface du second degré osculatrices, puisque leurs équations générales renferment repectivement 4 et 9 coefficients. En général, une surface du $m^{\text{ième}}$ degré en contient $\frac{(m+1)(m+2)(m+3)}{6} - 1$, ce qui conduit à poser l'équation

$$\frac{(n+1)(n+2)}{2} = \frac{(m+1)(m+2)(m+3)}{6} - 1,$$

dont il y aurait lieu ainsi de rechercher toutes les solutions en nombres entiers et positifs pour m et n. Mais l'Arithmétique supérieure ne donne à cet égard aucune méthode, et je me bornerai à remarquer qu'on y satisfait, par les moindres nombres, en prenant $m = 5$ et $n = 9$. Il n'y a donc aucune surface algébrique, de degré inférieur à 5, pouvant être osculatrice, de sorte que la théorie actuelle ne semble pas applicable au delà du plan et du contact du premier ordre. La considération suivante permettra cependant d'aller plus loin. En disposant des deux coordonnées d'un point d'une surface, on peut en effet ajouter deux constantes à celles qui déterminent une sphère, et par conséquent la rendre en ces points osculatrice du second ordre, puisqu'on aura le nombre voulu de six quantités arbitraires. En disposant d'une seule des coordonnées on ajoute une arbitraire aux neuf coefficients d'une surface du second degré, ce qui permettra de la rendre osculatrice du troisième ordre, non plus alors en un certain nombre de points, mais comme il le semble au premier abord, tout le long d'une ligne déterminée d'une surface quelconque. Nous allons traiter ces deux questions.

V. L'équation de la sphère étant

$$(X - a)^2 + (Y - b)^2 + (Z - c)^2 = R^2,$$

on obtiendra les dérivées du premier ordre

$$P = \frac{dZ}{dX}, \qquad Q = \frac{dZ}{dY}$$

par les relations

$$X - a + P(Z - c) = 0,$$
$$Y - b + Q(Z - c) = 0,$$

et celles du second

$$R = \frac{d^2 Z}{dX^2}, \qquad S = \frac{d^2 Z}{dX\,dY}, \qquad T = \frac{d^2 Z}{dY^2},$$

par celles-ci, qui s'en déduisent en différentiant successivement par rapport à X et à Y,

$$1 + P^2 + R(Z - c) = 0,$$
$$PQ + S(Z - c) = 0,$$
$$1 + Q^2 + T(Z - c) = 0.$$

Or les conditions du contact du second ordre avec une surface quelconque $z = f(x, y)$, au point $X = x$, $Y = y$, sont

$$Z = z, \qquad P = \frac{dz}{dx}, \qquad Q = \frac{dz}{dy},$$
$$R = \frac{d^2 z}{dx^2}, \qquad S = \frac{d^2 z}{dx\,dy}, \qquad T = \frac{d^2 z}{dy},$$

de sorte qu'en faisant

$$p = \frac{dz}{dx}, \qquad q = \frac{dz}{dy}, \qquad r = \frac{d^2 z}{dx^2}, \qquad s = \frac{d^2 z}{dx\, dy}, \qquad t = \frac{d^2 z}{dy^2},$$

nous les obtiendrons en remplaçant dans les relations précédentes, X, Y, Z, P, Q, R, S, T par x, y, z, p, q, r, s, t, ce qui donnera

$$\begin{aligned} x - a + y(z - c) &= 0, \\ y - b + q(z - c) &= 0, \\ 1 + p^2 + r(z - c) &= 0, \\ pq + s(z - c) &= 0, \\ 1 + q^2 + t(z - c) &= 0. \end{aligned}$$

Cela étant, les trois dernières conduisent immédiatement par l'élimination de c ou plutôt de $z - c$ aux deux équations de condition cherchées entre x et y, savoir

$$\frac{1 + p^2}{r} = \frac{pq}{s} = \frac{1 + q^2}{t},$$

et en chassant les dénominateurs,

$$\begin{aligned} (1 + p^2)s - pqr &= 0, \\ (1 + p^2)t - (1 + q^2)r &= 0. \end{aligned}$$

On donne le nom *d'ombilics* aux points de la surface $z = f(x, y)$, que déterminent ces relations, et que bientôt nous verrons s'offrir sous un autre point de vue. Je me bornerai en ce moment à les obtenir à l'égard de l'ellipsoïde

$$\frac{x^2}{a^2} + \frac{y^2}{b^2} + \frac{z^2}{c^2} = 1,$$

où ils ont un rôle extrêmement important dans l'étude géométrique des courbes tracées sur cette surface. En formant à cet effet les valeurs des quantités p, q, r, s, t, on trouve

$$p = -\frac{c^2 x}{a^2 z}, \qquad q = -\frac{c^2 y}{b^2 z},$$

$$r = -\frac{c^4(b^2 - y^2)}{a^2 b^2 z^3}, \qquad s = -\frac{c^4 xy}{a^2 b^2 z^3}, \qquad t = -\frac{c^4(a^2 - x^2)}{a^2 b^2 z^3},$$

et après quelques réductions, il viendra simplement

$$(a^2 - c^2)xy = 0, \qquad b^2(a^2 - c^2)x^2 - a^2(b^2 - c^2)y^2 - a^2 b^2(a^2 - b^2) = 0.$$

Ces relations sont identiques dans le cas où l'ellipsoïde se réduit à une sphère, comme on pouvait le prévoir; mais si les axes sont inégaux, et qu'on suppose

$$a > b > c,$$

nous parviendrons très aisément à ces solutions, les seules réelles, savoir

$$x = \pm a\sqrt{\frac{a^2 - b^2}{a^2 - c^2}}, \qquad y = 0, \qquad z = \pm c\sqrt{\frac{b^2 - c^2}{a^2 - c^2}}.$$

On en conclut que les ombilics sont les quatre points où les plans des sections circulaires deviennent tangents à la surface.

VI. Dans la seconde question, il s'agit de l'équation générale du second degré

$$\begin{aligned} F(X, Y, Z) = aX^2 + a'Y^2 + a''Z^2 + 2bYZ + 2b'ZX + 2b''XY \\ + 2cX + 2c'Y + 2c''Z + d = 0, \end{aligned}$$

et des conditions du contact du troisième ordre avec la surface quelconque $z = f(x, y)$. Alors il est nécessaire d'introduire, en outre des dérivées partielles du premier et du second ordre p, q, r, s, t, celles du troisième que je désignerai ainsi

$$g = \frac{d^3 z}{dx^3}, \qquad h = \frac{d^3 z}{dx^2\, dy}, \qquad k = \frac{d^3 z}{dx\, dy^2}, \qquad l = \frac{d^3 z}{dy^3}.$$

Cela étant, et sans répéter ce qui a été dit tout à l'heure à propos de la sphère, j'écrirai immédiatement ces relations

$$\begin{gathered} ax^2 + a'y^2 + a''z^2 + 2byz + 2b'zx + 2b''xy + 2cx + 2c'y + 2c''z + d = 0, \\ (b'x + by + a''z + c'')p + ax + b''y + b'z + c = 0, \\ (b'x + by + a''z + c'')q + b''x + a'y + bz + c' = 0; \end{gathered}$$

puis celles-ci, qui contiennent les dérivées du second ordre, et où je fais pour abréger

$$\omega = \frac{1}{2}\frac{df}{dz} = b'x + by + a''z + c,$$

savoir

$$\begin{aligned} \omega r + a''p^2 + 2b'p + a = 0, \\ \omega s + a''pq + bp + b'q + b'' = 0, \\ \omega t + a''q^2 + 2bq + a' = 0. \end{aligned}$$

On en tire, par la différentiation, ces quatre dernières équations, où entrent les dérivées partielles du troisième ordre, et qui ne contiennent plus que les coefficients a'', b, b', c'' sous forme homogène

$$\begin{gathered}\omega g + 3(a''p + b')r = 0,\\ \omega h + (a''q + b)r + 2(a''p + b')s = 0,\\ \omega k + (a''p + b')t + 2(a''q + b)s = 0,\\ \omega l + 3(a''q + b)t = 0.\end{gathered}$$

Voici la conséquence remarquable à laquelle elles conduisent; deux d'entre elles donnent

$$a''p + b' = -\frac{\omega g}{3r}, \qquad a''q + b = -\frac{\omega l}{3t},$$

et, en substituant dans les deux autres, la quantité ω disparaîtra comme facteur commun, de sorte qu'au lieu d'une seule équation de condition entre x et y, nous obtenons les deux suivantes ([1]):

$$\begin{gathered}3hrt - lr^2 - 2gst = 0,\\ 3krt - gt^2 - 2lrs = 0.\end{gathered}$$

Mais, en même temps, les inconnues a'', b, b', c'' entre lesquelles on n'a plus que deux équations, et par suite tous les coefficients de $F(X, Y, Z)$, s'exprimeront en fonction linéaire et homogène de deux indéterminées λ et μ, de sorte qu'on doit poser

$$F(X, Y, Z) = \lambda\Phi + \mu\Phi_1,$$

où Φ et Φ_1 sont des polynomes entièrement déterminés. Il s'ensuit qu'en un nombre fini de points de la surface $z = f(x, y)$, et non le long d'une ligne comme on l'avait d'abord présumé, nous obtenons un faisceau de surfaces, au lieu d'une surface osculatrice unique du second degré ([2]).

([1]) Elles expriment, comme on le vérifie aisément, que le polynome du troisième degré $g\lambda^3 + 3h\lambda^2 + 3k\lambda + l$ est exactement divisible par $r\lambda^2 + 2s\lambda + t$.

([2]) Il est remarquable qu'on trouve des lignes en appliquant cette théorie aux surfaces du troisième degré; ces lignes sont les 27 droites situées sur ces surfaces.

SUR LES

ÉQUATIONS DIFFÉRENTIELLES LINÉAIRES.

Bulletin des Sciences mathématiques, 2e série, t. III, 1879, p. 311-325.

C'est à Euler qu'est due la première méthode d'intégration de ces équations dans le cas où, les coefficients étant supposés constants, l'équation a la forme

$$\alpha y + \beta \frac{dy}{dx} + \gamma \frac{d^2 y}{dx^2} + \ldots + \frac{d^n y}{dx^n} = 0.$$

Cauchy a ensuite donné une seconde méthode, qui est celle que nous allons exposer.

A cette équation différentielle, Cauchy a rattaché l'équation algébrique suivante

$$\alpha + \beta z + \gamma z^2 + \ldots + z^n = 0,$$

obtenue en remplaçant les dérivées successives de la fonction y par les puissances de l'inconnue z, dont les exposants sont respectivement égaux aux ordres de dérivation. Soit $F(z)$ le premier membre de cette équation, que Cauchy a appelée l'*équation caractéristique* de l'équation différentielle proposée. Si nous envisageons l'intégrale suivante

$$y = \int \frac{e^{zx} \Pi(z)}{F(z)} dz,$$

où $\Pi(z)$ est un polynome entier en z à coefficients arbitraires, et si nous supposons cette intégrale effectuée en faisant décrire à la variable z un contour fermé tout à fait quelconque, nous allons montrer que cette intégrale est une solution de l'équation différentielle proposée.

Dans le cas particulier où le contour ne renferme aucun pôle de la fonction $\frac{e^{zx}\Pi(z)}{F(z)}$, c'est-à-dire aucun point qui ait pour affixe une racine de l'équation caractéristique, l'intégrale est nulle, et $y = 0$ est bien une solution de l'équation différentielle proposée; mais c'est dans le cas où le contour renferme des pôles que nous obtenons effectivement des solutions.

Pour démontrer ou plutôt pour vérifier ce théorème, formons les dérivées successives de l'intégrale par rapport à x; nous aurons

$$\frac{dy}{dx} = \int \frac{e^{zx} z \Pi(z)}{F(z)} dz,$$

$$\frac{d^2y}{dx^2} = \int \frac{e^{zx} z^2 \Pi(z)}{F(z)} dz,$$

$$\cdots\cdots\cdots\cdots\cdots\cdots,$$

$$\frac{d^ny}{dx^n} = \int \frac{e^{zx} z^n \Pi(z)}{F(z)} dz,$$

chacune de ces intégrales étant toujours supposée effectuée le long du contour fermé.

Substituons dans l'équation proposée; le premier membre devient

$$\int \frac{e^{zx}\Pi(z)}{F(z)} (\alpha + \beta z + \ldots + z^n)\, dz.$$

On voit que $F(z)$ disparaît comme facteur commun et que l'intégrale est celle de $e^{zx}\Pi(z)$, qui, effectuée le long du contour fermé, est nulle, puisque $\Pi(z)$ est un polynome entier. L'équation est donc vérifiée, ce qui démontre que, quel que soit le contour fermé d'intégration, l'intégrale

$$\int \frac{e^{zx}\Pi(z)}{F(z)} dz$$

est une solution de l'équation proposée.

Remarque. — $\Pi(z)$ étant un polynome de degré quelconque, il semble qu'il entre dans la solution un nombre quelconque de constantes arbitraires; mais il est facile de voir que ce nombre est au plus égal à n. En effet, on peut toujours, si $\Pi(z)$ est de degré supérieur à celui de $F(z)$, écrire identiquement

$$\frac{\Pi(z)}{F(z)} = \Phi(z) + \frac{\Psi(z)}{F(z)},$$

$\Psi(z)$ étant un polynome entier en z de degré inférieur à n, d'où l'on tire

$$\int \frac{e^{zx}\Pi(z)}{F(z)}dz = \int e^{zx}\,\Phi(z)\,dz + \int \frac{e^{zx}\,\Psi(z)}{F(z)}dz;$$

mais, en intégrant le long d'un contour fermé quelconque, on voit que la première intégrale s'évanouit, puisque $\Phi(z)$ est un polynome entier, et il ne reste que la seconde où $\Psi(z)$ renferme au plus n constantes arbitraires, puisque son degré est au plus égal à $n-1$.

Nous allons maintenant passer de l'expression de la solution sous forme d'intégrale à une expression sous forme explicite.

Soit S la somme des résidus de la fonction $\frac{e^{zx}\Pi(z)}{F(z)}$ qui correspondent aux racines du dénominateur affixes de points intérieurs au contour d'intégration.

L'intégrale aura pour valeur $2i\pi S$.

Calculons ces résidus.

Supposons d'abord que l'équation caractéristique n'ait pas de racine multiple, et décomposons la fonction $\frac{\Pi(z)}{F(z)}$ en éléments simples. On peut toujours supposer que le degré $\Pi(z)$ est inférieur à celui de $F(z)$; par suite, le résultat de la décomposition sera

$$\frac{\Pi(z)}{F(z)} = \frac{A}{z-a} + \frac{B}{z-b} + \ldots + \frac{L}{z-l}.$$

Faisons $z = a+h$ dans la fonction $\frac{e^{zx}\Pi(z)}{F(z)}$; elle devient

$$\frac{e^{x(a+h)}\Pi(a+h)}{F(a+h)} = e^{ax}\left(1 + \frac{hx}{1} + \frac{h^2x^2}{1.2} + \ldots\right) \times \left(\frac{A}{h} + p + qh + rh^2 + \ldots\right),$$

puisque le terme $\frac{A}{z-a}$ donne seul un terme en $\frac{1}{h}$. Le résidu sera donc égal à Ae^{ax}; on a donc pour première solution, en intégrant le long d'un contour qui ne contient que la racine a, $2i\pi Ae^{ax}$. En général, le contour pouvant contenir un nombre quelconque de pôles de la fonction $\frac{e^{zx}\Pi(z)}{F(z)}$, la solution générale sera de la forme

$$y = \mathrm{A}\, e^{ax} + \mathrm{B}\, e^{bx} + \ldots + \mathrm{L}\, e^{lx},$$

a, b, ..., l étant les racines de l'équation caractéristique, et A, B, ..., L, n constantes arbitraires qui peuvent être nulles et qui renferment le facteur $2i\pi$.

Supposons maintenant que l'équation caractéristique ait des racines multiples, et soit

$$\mathrm{F}(z) = (z-a)^{\alpha+1}(z-b)^{\beta+1}\ldots(z-l)^{\lambda+1}.$$

La formule de décomposition est alors

$$\begin{aligned}\frac{\Pi(z)}{\mathrm{F}(z)} = {} & \frac{\mathrm{A}}{z-a} + \frac{\mathrm{B}}{(z-b)} + \ldots \\ & + \frac{\mathrm{A}_1}{(z-a)^2} + \frac{\mathrm{B}_1}{(z-b)^2} + \ldots \\ & + \ldots\ldots\ldots\ldots\ldots\ldots\ldots\ldots \\ & + \frac{\mathrm{A}_\alpha}{(z-a)^{\alpha+1}} + \frac{\mathrm{B}_\beta}{(z-b)^{\beta+1}} + \ldots.\end{aligned}$$

Nous aurons, en faisant $z = a + h$,

$$\frac{\Pi(a+h)}{\mathrm{F}(a+h)} = \frac{\mathrm{A}}{h} + \frac{\mathrm{A}_1}{h^2} + \ldots + \frac{\mathrm{A}_\alpha}{h^{\alpha+1}},$$

les termes suivants ne contenant pas de puissances négatives de h; d'ailleurs,

$$e^{x(a+h)} = e^{ax}\left(1 + \frac{hx}{1} + \frac{h^2x^2}{1.2} + \ldots + \frac{h^\alpha x^\alpha}{1.2\ldots\alpha} + \ldots\right).$$

Pour avoir le résidu correspondant à $z = a$, c'est-à-dire le coefficient du terme en $\frac{1}{h}$ dans le développement de $\frac{\Pi(a+h)}{\mathrm{F}(a+h)}e^{x(a+h)}$, il suffit de multiplier les coefficients des termes qui se correspondent dans les seconds membres des deux égalités précédentes. On trouve ainsi pour expression du résidu, et par conséquent pour une solution de l'équation différentielle proposée,

$$2i\pi\, e^{ax}\left(\mathrm{A} + \frac{\mathrm{A}_1 x}{1} + \ldots + \frac{\mathrm{A}_\alpha x^\alpha}{1.2\ldots\alpha}\right).$$

La solution générale sera donc de la forme

$$\begin{aligned}& e^{ax}(\mathcal{A} + \mathcal{A}_1 x + \ldots + \mathcal{A}_\alpha x^\alpha) + e^{bx}(\mathcal{B} + \mathcal{B}_1 x + \ldots + \mathcal{B}_\beta x^\beta) + \ldots \\ & \qquad + e^{lx}(\mathcal{L} + \mathcal{L}_1 x + \ldots + \mathcal{L}_\lambda x^\lambda),\end{aligned}$$

et, comme

$$(\alpha+1)+(\beta+1)+\ldots+(\lambda+1)=n,$$

on voit que la solution générale contient n coefficients arbitraires.

Faisons une vérification dans le cas des racines simples.

Montrons d'abord que $y=\mathrm{A}e^{ax}$ est une solution; nous partirons de là pour vérifier la solution générale. Soit donc

$$\begin{aligned}
y &= \mathrm{A}\,e^{ax},\\
\frac{dy}{dx} &= \mathrm{A}\,a\,e^{ax},\\
\frac{d^2y}{dx^2} &= \mathrm{A}\,a^2\,e^{ax},\\
&\ldots\ldots\ldots\ldots\ldots,\\
\frac{d^ny}{dx^n} &= \mathrm{A}\,a^n\,e^{ax}.
\end{aligned}$$

Substituant dans l'équation différentielle, le premier membre devient

$$\mathrm{A}\,e^{ax}(\alpha+\beta a+\gamma a^2+\ldots+a^n).$$

Or le second facteur n'est autre chose que $\mathrm{F}(a)$; il est donc nul, puisque $\mathrm{F}(z)=0$ admet la racine a. Donc $y=\mathrm{A}e^{ax}$ est une solution.

Je dis que, si y_1 et y_2 sont des solutions, il en est de même de y_1+y_2.

En effet, si l'on a

$$\alpha y_1+\beta\frac{dy_1}{dx}+\gamma\frac{d^2y_1}{dx^2}+\ldots+\frac{d^ny_1}{dx^n}=0,$$

$$\alpha y_2+\beta\frac{dy_2}{dx}+\gamma\frac{d^2y_2}{dx^2}+\ldots+\frac{d^ny_2}{dx^n}=0,$$

il vient, en ajoutant,

$$\alpha(y_1+y_2)+\beta\frac{d}{dx}(y_1+y_2)+\gamma\frac{d^2}{dx^2}(y_1+y_2)+\ldots=0,$$

ce qui montre que y_1+y_2 est une solution. Il en serait de même de la somme d'un nombre quelconque de solutions de la forme $\mathrm{A}e^{ax}$, ce qui vérifie la solution générale

$$\mathrm{A}\,e^{ax}+\mathrm{B}\,e^{bx}+\ldots+\mathrm{L}\,e^{lx}.$$

Passons au cas des racines multiples. La vérification est moins immédiate. Nous considérerons, pour y parvenir, une transformée de l'équation différentielle proposée, dont la variable z sera liée à la variable y par la relation

$$y = e^{mx} z,$$

m étant une constante arbitraire. Formons les dérivées successives de y; on aura

$$\frac{dy}{dx} = e^{mx}(mz + z'),$$

$$\frac{d^2y}{dx^2} = e^{mx}(m^2 z + 2mz' + z''),$$

$$\dots\dots\dots\dots\dots\dots\dots\dots$$

On voit que, en substituant dans l'équation proposée, on obtient le produit de e^{mx} par une fonction linéaire de z et de ses dérivées.

Nous avons donc identiquement

$$\alpha y + \beta \frac{dy}{dx} + \ldots + \frac{d^n y}{dx^n} = e^{mx}(Gz + Hz' + \ldots + Lz^{(n)}).$$

Pour calculer les coefficients constants G, H, ..., L, remarquons que nous n'avons fait aucune hypothèse sur la nature de z, qui est une fonction quelconque de x. Faisons $z = e^{hx}$, h étant une constante; nous devons avoir identiquement, en divisant les deux membres par le facteur $e^{(m+h)x}$,

$$\alpha + \beta(m+h) + \gamma(m+h)^2 + \ldots + (m+h)^n = G + Hh + \ldots + Lh^n.$$

Le premier membre est $F(m+h)$; l'identité précédente devant avoir lieu quel que soit h, les coefficients G, H, ... doivent être égaux respectivement aux coefficients des puissances successives de h dans le développement de $F(m+h)$. On a donc

$$G = F(m),$$
$$H = F'(m),$$
$$\dots\dots\dots,$$
$$L = \frac{F^n(m)}{1.2\ldots n}.$$

L'équation transformée est donc la suivante :

$$e^{mx}\left[zF(m) + \frac{dz}{dx}F'(m) + \frac{d^2z}{dx^2}\frac{F''(m)}{1.2} + \ldots\right] = 0.$$

Supposons que m soit une racine simple de l'équation caractéristique; alors $F(m) = 0$. L'équation précédente commence par un terme en $\frac{dz}{dx}$; elle est donc vérifiée si l'on suppose que z est une constante A. L'équation proposée aura pour solution correspondante

$$y = A e^{mx}.$$

Si m est une racine double, on a $F(m) = 0$, $F'(m) = 0$; la transformée, commençant par un terme en $\frac{d^2 z}{dx^2}$, est vérifiée si l'on suppose que z est un binome du premier degré en x $(z = A + Bx)$. La solution correspondante pour l'équation proposée est

$$y = e^{mx}(A + Bx).$$

On verrait de même que, si m est une racine d'ordre de multiplicité $\alpha + 1$ de la caractéristique, on a pour solution de l'équation différentielle

$$y = e^{mx}(A + Bx + \ldots + Lx^{\alpha}),$$

A, B, ..., L étant des coefficients arbitraires.

Nous allons maintenant déterminer les constantes arbitraires que renferme la solution générale de l'équation différentielle linéaire, de façon que pour une valeur particulière de x, pour $x = 0$ par exemple, la fonction y et ses dérivées successives prennent des valeurs données.

Voici quelle était la méthode suivie avant que Cauchy eût donné une solution générale de ce problème. Prenons le cas où $F(z)$ n'a que des racines simples; la solution est de la forme

$$y = A e^{ax} + B e^{bx} + \ldots + L e^{lx}.$$

On forme les $(n-1)$ premières dérivées, on y fait $x = 0$, et, en égalant les valeurs qu'elles prennent aux valeurs données $y_0, y'_0, \ldots, y_0^{n-1}$, on obtient, pour déterminer A, B, ..., L, les n équations suivantes :

$$\begin{array}{l} A + B + \ldots + L = y_0, \\ Aa + Bb + \ldots + Ll = y'_0, \\ \ldots\ldots\ldots\ldots\ldots\ldots, \\ Aa^{n-1} + Bb^{n-1} + \ldots + Ll^{n-1} = y_0^{(n-1)}. \end{array}$$

Quand on passe au cas où l'équation caractéristique a des racines multiples, cette méthode est d'une application difficile, puisque les dérivées de y sont plus compliquées et que les diverses racines n'entrent plus de la même manière dans les équations à résoudre.

Cauchy a donné une méthode très simple, qui est la même dans le cas des racines simples et des racines multiples.

Reprenons la solution de l'équation différentielle sous la forme

$$y = \frac{1}{2i\pi}\int \frac{e^{zx}\Pi(z)}{F(z)}dz;$$

pour que cette intégrale soit la solution générale, il faut supposer que le contour d'intégration renferme à son intérieur tous les points dont les affixes sont des racines de $F(z)$, et, comme l'intégrale ne change pas de valeur quand on agrandit le contour, je supposerai que c'est un cercle dont le centre est à l'origine des coordonnées et dont le rayon sera très grand.

Il s'agit de déterminer les coefficients de $\Pi(z)$ de sorte que, pour $x = 0$, $\frac{1}{2i\pi}\int \frac{e^{zx}\Pi(z)}{F(z)}dz$ et ses $n-1$ premières dérivées prennent les valeurs données, que je supposerai être $y_0, y'_0, \ldots, y_0^{(n-1)}$; nous avons les n équations

$$\begin{aligned}
&\frac{1}{2i\pi}\int \frac{\Pi(z)}{F(z)}dz = y_0,\\
&\frac{1}{2i\pi}\int \frac{z\Pi(z)}{F(z)}dz = y'_0,\\
&\frac{1}{2i\pi}\int \frac{z^2\Pi(z)}{F(z)}dz = y''_0,\\
&\ldots\ldots\ldots\ldots\ldots\ldots\ldots,\\
&\frac{1}{2i\pi}\int \frac{z^{n-1}\Pi(z)}{F(z)}ds = y_0^{(n-1)}.
\end{aligned}$$

Pour obtenir ces diverses intégrales, développons $\frac{\Pi(z)}{F(z)}$ suivant les puissances décroissantes de la variable; $\Pi(z)$ étant en général de degré $n-1$, le premier terme du développement sera du degré -1 en z, et l'on aura

$$\frac{\Pi(z)}{F(z)} = \frac{\varepsilon_0}{z} + \frac{\varepsilon_1}{z^2} + \frac{\varepsilon_2}{z^3} + \ldots + \frac{\varepsilon_{n-1}}{z^n} + \ldots.$$

En effectuant le long du cercle de rayon infini les n intégrales précédentes, il suffira d'avoir égard dans chaque développement au terme en $\frac{1}{z}$, et nous nous trouverons immédiatement amenés aux relations

$$\begin{aligned} \varepsilon_0 &= y_0, \\ \varepsilon_1 &= y'_0, \\ &\ldots\ldots\ldots, \\ \varepsilon_{n-1} &= y_0^{n-1}, \end{aligned}$$

puisque les valeurs des intégrales sont respectivement

$$\varepsilon_0, \quad \varepsilon_1, \quad \ldots, \quad \varepsilon_{n-1}.$$

Nous connaissons ainsi dans le développement de $\frac{\Pi(z)}{F(z)}$ les coefficients des termes de degré égal ou supérieur à $-n$; cela suffit pour déterminer complètement $\Pi(z)$, puisqu'on a identiquement

$$\Pi(z) = F(z)\left(\frac{y_0}{z} + \frac{y'_0}{z^2} + \ldots + \frac{y_0^{n-1}}{z^n}\right)$$

et que $\Pi(z)$ doit être un polynome entier; par conséquent, $F(z)$ étant de degré n, on voit que les n premiers termes de la série sont seuls utiles à la détermination de ce polynome et qu'on obtient

$$\begin{aligned} \Pi(z) = {} & y_0(\beta + \gamma z + \delta z^2 + \ldots + z^{n-1}) \\ & + y'_0(\gamma + \delta z + \ldots + z^{n-2}) \\ & + y''_0(\delta + \varepsilon z + \ldots + z^{n-3}) \\ & + \ldots\ldots\ldots\ldots\ldots\ldots\ldots\ldots \\ & + y_0^{n-1}. \end{aligned}$$

On a donc $\Pi(z)$ par une méthode qui s'applique aussi bien au cas des racines simples qu'à celui des racines multiples. Cela étant, et pour obtenir explicitement la valeur de y, il suffira, connaissant $\Pi(z)$, de calculer les résidus de la fonction $\frac{e^{zx}\Pi(z)}{F(z)}$. Ce calcul, que nous avons effectué précédemment, n'exige, comme on l'a vu, que l'opération algébrique élémentaire de la décomposition de la fraction rationnelle $\frac{\Pi(z)}{F(z)}$ en fractions simples.

Comme application des formules obtenues dans la dernière Leçon pour l'intégration des équations linéaires à coefficients constants sans second membre, je prendrai l'équation

$$\frac{d^2y}{dx^2} + n^2y^2 = 0,$$

qui se rencontre dans les applications de l'Analyse à la Physique, et en particulier à l'Optique. Elle appartient à un type déjà étudié d'équations différentielles du second ordre; mais nous la traiterons suivant les procédés que nous venons d'expliquer.

L'équation caractéristique est $z^2 + n^2 = 0$; elle admet les deux racines $z = \pm in$. Si nous voulons que, pour $x = 0$, y et y' prennent certaines valeurs fixées d'avance, y_0 et y'_0, il faudra déterminer le polynome entier $\Pi(z)$ par la relation

$$\frac{\Pi(z)}{F(z)} = \frac{y_0}{z} + \frac{y'_0}{z^2} + \frac{y''_0}{z^3} + \ldots,$$

qui donne, en multipliant les deux membres par $F(z)$ et ne conservant dans le second que les termes ne contenant pas z en dénominateur,

$$\Pi(z) = y_0 z + y'_0.$$

La fonction $\frac{e^{zx}\Pi(z)}{F(z)}$, dont on doit calculer les résidus, est $\frac{y_0 z + y'_0}{z^2 + n^2} e^{zx}$; pour une racine z, son résidu est $\frac{e^{zx}\Pi(z)}{F(z)}$ ou $\frac{1}{2}\left(y_0 + \frac{y'_0}{z}\right) e^{zx}$; pour la racine $-z$, ce sera $\frac{1}{2}\left(y_0 - \frac{y'_0}{z}\right) e^{-zx}$. La somme de ces deux résidus est alors

$$\frac{1}{2} y_0 (e^{zx} + e^{-zx}) + \frac{1}{2} y'_0 \frac{e^{zx} - e^{-zx}}{z};$$

en y faisant $z = in$, on trouve l'intégrale cherchée

$$y_0 \cos nx + y'_0 \frac{\sin nx}{n}.$$

D'après la forme de l'équation différentielle, il est évident que, si l'on a une solution $y = \varphi(z)$, $y_1 = \varphi(x + c)$ sera encore une solution, c étant une constante quelconque. On profite de cette remarque pour mettre l'intégrale sous une forme telle qu'elle prenne des valeurs y_0 et y'_0, non plus pour la valeur $x = 0$, mais pour une valeur quelconque $x = c$; il suffit de prendre

$$y = y_0 \cos n x (x - c) + y'_0 \frac{\sin n (x - c)}{n}.$$

Cette intégrale, comme on voit, est une expression réelle, bien que les racines de l'équation soient imaginaires; or, en général, étant donnée une équation différentielle linéaire sans second membre et à coefficients constants, je dis que, si ces coefficients sont réels, ainsi que les quantités $y_0, y'_0, y''_0, \ldots$, on pourra mettre aisément l'intégrale sous forme explicitement réelle. En effet, a étant une racine imaginaire de l'équation caractéristique, on prendra sa conjuguée b et l'on considérera les deux termes $A e^{ax} + B e^{bx}$. A et B sont évidemment conjugués, puisque ce sont les résidus d'une même fonction réelle $\frac{\Pi(z)}{F(z)}$ pour deux racines conjuguées du dénominateur.

Supposons que $a = \alpha + i\beta$, $b = \alpha - i\beta$ et $A = P + iQ$, $B = P - iQ$; nous aurons

$$\begin{aligned} A\, e^{ax} + B\, e^{bx} &= A\, e^{\alpha x}(\cos\beta x + i \sin\beta x) + B\, e^{\alpha x}(\cos\beta x - i\sin\beta x) \\ &= e^{\alpha x}\cos\beta x(A + B) + e^{\alpha x}\sin\beta x(A - B)i \\ &= 2P\, e^{\alpha x}\cos\beta x - 2Q\, e^{\alpha x}\sin\beta x, \end{aligned}$$

quantité qui est en effet réelle.

Nous avons vu tout à l'heure que, étant donnée une solution de $\frac{d^2y}{dx^2} + n^2 y = 0$, en y changeant x en $x + c$, on a encore une solution. Cela se voit immédiatement sur la forme générale $y = A e^{ax} + B e^{bx} + \ldots$, car les différents termes se trouvent simplement multipliés par e^{ax}, e^{bx}, ce qui revient à changer les constantes A, B, qui sont arbitraires.

Équations linéaires à second membre et à coefficients constants.

Je supposerai que, ce second membre étant un polynome entier $f(x)$ de degré p, l'équation proposée soit

$$\alpha y + \beta \frac{dy}{dx} + \gamma \frac{d^2y}{dx^2} + \ldots + \frac{d^n y}{dx^n} = f(x).$$

Si je prends la dérivée d'ordre $p + 1$ des deux membres, je trouverai

$$\alpha \frac{d^{p+1}y}{dx^{p+1}} + \beta \frac{d^{p+2}y}{dx^{p+2}} + \ldots + \frac{d^{n+p+1}y}{dx^{n+p+1}} = 0,$$

que je sais intégrer et dont les solutions fourniront celles de la proposée. A la vérité, cette nouvelle équation est plus générale que la première; aussi devrons-nous particulariser le résultat obtenu.

L'équation caractéristique est

$$\alpha z^{p+1} + \beta z^{p+2} + \ldots + z^{n+p+1} = 0.$$

Le premier membre est z^{p+1} multiplié par le premier membre de l'équation caractéristique qui correspondrait à l'équation différentielle proposée sans second membre. On sait qu'une racine a d'ordre $(p+1)$ de l'équation caractéristique donne dans l'intégrale un terme $e^{ax}(g + hx + \ldots + x^p)$. Ici $a = 0$; on aura donc simplement un polynome de degré p, $F(x)$, auquel il faudra ajouter l'ensemble des termes correspondant aux racines simples ou multiples de l'équation caractéristique

$$\alpha + \beta z + \ldots + z^n = 0.$$

La valeur de y sera donc

$$y = F(x) + A\,e^{ax} + B\,e^{bx} + \ldots,$$

où la partie ajoutée à $F(x)$ représente la solution de l'équation proposée, privée de second membre.

Il s'agit maintenant de déterminer les coefficients de $F(x)$; on pourrait le faire en effectuant la substitution de cette valeur de y dans l'équation proposée, et il n'y aura qu'à s'occuper des termes produits par $F(x)$ et ses dérivées successives et identifier la somme de ces termes au second membre $f(x)$.

Mais nous donnerons le moyen de déterminer plus rapidement les coefficients de $F(x)$. Effectuons la division $\frac{1}{\alpha + \beta z + \gamma z^2 + \ldots}$, et représentons le quotient par $\alpha_0 + \beta_0 z + \gamma_0 z^2 + \delta_0 z^3 + \ldots$. Les coefficients $\alpha_0, \beta_0, \gamma_0, \ldots$ seront liés par les relations

$$(1) \quad \left\{ \begin{aligned} \alpha\alpha_0 &= 1, \\ \alpha\beta_0 + \beta\alpha_0 &= 0, \\ \alpha\gamma_0 + \beta\beta_0 + \gamma\alpha_0 &= 0, \\ &\ldots\ldots\ldots\ldots \end{aligned} \right.$$

Cela étant, je dis que

$$F(x) = \alpha_0 f(x) + \beta_0 f'(x) + \gamma_0 f''(x) + \ldots,$$

série qui s'arrêtera d'elle-même quand on arrivera à $f^{p+1}(x)$, qui est nul.

Pour vérifier cette valeur de $F(x)$, il suffit de faire la substitution comme il a été dit tout à l'heure; or on trouvera ainsi

$$\alpha\alpha_0 f(x) + (\alpha\beta_0 + \beta\alpha_0) f'(x) + (\alpha\gamma_0 + \beta\beta_0 + \gamma\alpha_0) f''(x) + \ldots,$$

qui doit être identique à $F(x)$, et cette condition est satisfaite d'après les relations (1).

Comme exemple, je prendrai l'équation linéaire du premier ordre

$$\frac{dy}{dx} + ay = f(x),$$

que nous savons déjà intégrer; nous allons ainsi retrouver le résultat précédemment obtenu. En appliquant la méthode qui vient d'être exposée, nous ferons le quotient

$$\frac{1}{a+z} = \frac{1}{a} - \frac{z}{a^2} + \frac{z^2}{a^2} - \ldots.$$

En posant alors

$$F(x) = \frac{f(x)}{a} - \frac{f'(x)}{a^2} + \frac{f''(x)}{a^3} - \ldots,$$

la solution générale sera

$$y = c\, e^{-ax} + F(x).$$

Remarque. — Dans un grand nombre de questions, on se sert, comme nous l'avons fait ici, d'une fonction $\varphi(x) = \alpha + \beta x + \gamma x^2 + \ldots$, dans laquelle les exposants de la variable correspondent à des indices de dérivation d'une fonction donnée $F(x)$. Lorsqu'on déduit ainsi de $F(x)$ la nouvelle fonction $\alpha F(x) + \beta F'(x) + \gamma F''(x) + \ldots$, cela s'appelle *opérer* sur $F(x)$ à l'aide de $\varphi(x)$.

En terminant, nous indiquerons, sans la démontrer, la conséquence suivante : *Lorsque l'équation caractéristique a toutes ses racines réelles, le nombre des racines réelles de* $F(x)$ *est au plus égal au nombre des racines réelles de* $f(x)$.

SUR

L'INDICE DES FRACTIONS RATIONNELLES.

Bulletin de la Société mathématique de France, t. VII, 1879, p. 128-131.

Soient U et V deux polynomes de degré n et $n-1$, que je supposerai premiers entre eux; je me propose de montrer, par une considération directe et entièrement élémentaire, que l'indice de la fraction $\frac{V}{U}$, entre les limites $-\infty$ et $+\infty$ de la variable, donne la différence entre le nombre des racines imaginaires de l'équation $U+iV=0$, où le coefficient de i est positif, et le nombre de ces racines où il est négatif. Soit, à cet effet,

$$U+iV=(x-a_1-ib_1)(x-a_2-ib_2)\ldots(x-a_n-ib_n),$$

et posons

$$U_1+iV_1=(x-a_2-ib_2)\ldots(x-a_n-ib_n),$$

de sorte qu'on ait

$$U+iV=(x-a_1-ib_1)(U_1+iV_1),$$

et, par conséquent,

$$U=(x-a_1)U_1+b_1V_1,$$
$$V=-b_1U_1+(x-a_1)V_1,$$

Je remarque d'abord qu'il résulte de ces relations que les polynomes U et U_1 sont premiers entre eux; car autrement U et V auraient un diviseur commun, contre la supposition faite. Cela posé, l'égalité

$$(U+iV)(U_1-iV_1)=(x-a_1-ib_1)(U_1^2+V_1^2)$$

donne, en égalant dans les deux membres les coefficients de i,

$$VU_1 - UV_1 = -b_1(U_1^2 + V_1^2)$$

ou bien

$$\frac{V}{U} - \frac{V_1}{U_1} = -\frac{b_1(U_1^2 + V_1^2)}{UU_1}.$$

Faisons croître maintenant la variable de $-\infty$ à $+\infty$; puisque les polynomes U et U_1 ne peuvent s'évanouir pour la même valeur, on voit que l'indice du premier membre sera la différence des indices des fractions $\frac{U}{V}$ et $\frac{U_1}{V_1}$, qui va s'obtenir immédiatement.

Supprimons, en effet, le facteur positif $U_1^2 + V_1^2$; nous sommes amené à la quantité $\frac{-b_1}{UU_1}$, dont la réciproque a un indice nul, de sorte qu'il suffit d'appliquer la proposition contenue dans l'égalité

$$\mathop{\mathrm{I}}_{x_0}^{x_1} f(x) + \mathop{\mathrm{I}}_{x_0}^{x_1} \frac{1}{f(x)} = \varepsilon,$$

où $\varepsilon = +1$ lorsque $f(x_0) > 0$, $f(x_1) < 0$, $\varepsilon = -1$ si l'on a $f(x_0) < 0$, $f(x_1) > 0$, et enfin $\varepsilon = 0$ lorsque $f(x_0)$ et $f(x_1)$ sont de même signe. Dans le cas présent, $x_0 = -\infty$, $x_1 = +\infty$; d'ailleurs U et U_1 sont de degrés n et $n-1$: il en résulte que ε sera $+1$ ou -1 suivant que b_1 sera positif ou négatif.

La proposition énoncée à l'égard de l'équation $U + iV = 0$, de degré n, se trouve ainsi ramenée au cas de l'équation $U_1 + iV_1 = 0$, dont le degré est moindre d'une unité, et, de proche en proche, on arrivera au cas le plus simple, à savoir

$$x - a_n - ib_n = 0,$$

où elle se vérifie immédiatement.

Une première conséquence à en tirer, c'est que, en désignant par I l'indice de $\frac{V}{U}$, c'est-à-dire l'excès du nombre de fois que cette fraction, en devenant infinie, passe du positif au négatif sur le nombre de fois qu'elle passe du négatif au positif, le nombre des racines imaginaires de l'équation $U + iV = 0$ dans lesquelles le coefficient de i est positif est donné par la formule $\frac{I + n}{2}$.

Supposons ensuite que, en changeant x en $x + i\lambda$, $U + iV$ devienne $U_\lambda + iV_\lambda$, et soit I_λ l'indice de $\frac{V_\lambda}{U_\lambda}$. Le nombre des racines de l'équation proposée dans lesquelles le coefficient de i est supérieur à λ sera $\frac{I_\lambda + n}{2}$; la formule $\frac{I_\lambda - I_{\lambda'}}{2}$ donnera donc, en supposant $\lambda < \lambda'$, le nombre des racines où le coefficient de i est compris entre les deux limites λ et λ'. La transformée déduite de l'équation $U + iV = 0$ par le changement de x en ix conduira d'ailleurs de la même manière au nombre des racines dont la partie réelle est dans un intervalle donné. Considérons encore l'équation en y obtenue en faisant

$$y = \frac{x - g}{h - x}$$

et la droite passant par les points dont les affixes sont g et h. L'indice relatif à cette nouvelle transformée donnera le nombre des racines de la proposée qui sont au-dessus ou au-dessous de cette droite, et, si nous remplaçons g et h par $g + k$ et $h + k$, de manière à définir une seconde droite parallèle à la première, la demi-différence des indices relatifs aux deux transformées représentera le nombre des racines comprises entre les deux parallèles.

En dernier lieu, je remarquerai que, si l'on suppose les quantités $b_1, b_2, \ldots, b_n$ toutes de même signe, on a

$$I = +n \quad \text{ou} \quad I = -n,$$

selon qu'elles seront positives ou négatives. Dans les deux cas, la fraction $\frac{V}{U}$ doit, par conséquent, passer n fois par l'infini lorsque la variable croît de $-\infty$ à $+\infty$; ainsi l'équation $U = 0$ a nécessairement toutes ses racines réelles. C'est donc un nouvel exemple qui s'ajoute, en Algèbre, à l'équation dont dépendent les inégalités séculaires du mouvement elliptique des planètes et qui a été l'objet du travail célèbre de notre confrère M. Borchardt. Je ne tenterai point de suivre la voie qu'a ouverte l'illustre géomètre en appliquant le théorème de Sturm à l'équation $U = 0$ pour obtenir, sous forme de sommes de carrés, les fonctions littérales dont dépendent les conditions de réalité des racines; mais je saisis l'occasion d'employer, pour démontrer directement la propriété que j'ai en vue, une méthode que Sturm a lui-même donnée dans une Note du *Journal de M. Liouville*, publiée à la suite d'un travail de M. Gascheau, intitulé *Application du théorème de Sturm aux transformées des équations binomes*, t. VII, p. 126 (*voir* aussi le *Cours d'Algèbre supérieure* de M. Serret, t. I, p. 183). J'introduis, à cet effet, la série entière des polynomes $U_1, U_2, \ldots, U_{n-1}$, en posant

$$U_k + iV_k = (x - a_{k+1} - ib_{k+1})(x - a_{k+2} - ib_{k+2})\ldots(x - a_n - ib_n),$$

et je remarque que la suite

$$U, \quad U_1, \quad U_2, \quad \ldots, \quad U_{n-1}, \quad 1$$

présente n variations pour $x = -\infty$ et n permanences pour $x = +\infty$. J'observe ensuite que trois fonctions consécutives quelconques, par exemple U, U_1, U_2, sont liées par la relation

$$b_2 U - [b_1(x - a_2) + b_2(x - a_1)]U_1 + b_1[(x - a_2)^2 + b_2^2]U_2 = 0.$$

Sous la condition admise à l'égard des quantités $b_1, b_2, \ldots$, on voit donc que, quand une fonction s'annule, la précédente et la suivante sont de signes contraires; il en résulte que, en faisant croître la variable de $-\infty$ à $+\infty$, des changements dans le nombre des variations de la suite considérée ne peuvent se produire qu'autant que c'est la première fonction qui s'évanouit. Puisqu'on perd n variations, il est donc démontré que le polynome U passe n fois par zéro; en même temps que nous voyons que, à l'égard de U, la fonction U_1 possède la propriété caractéristique de la dérivée, c'est-à-dire que le rapport $\frac{U}{U_1}$ passe toujours, en s'évanouissant, du négatif au positif, pour des valeurs croissantes de la variable.

EXTRAIT D'UNE LETTRE DE M. CH. HERMITE A M. BORCHARDT.

SUR UNE EXTENSION DONNÉE A LA THÉORIE DES FRACTIONS CONTINUES PAR M. TCHEBYCHEF.

Journal de Crelle, t. 88, 1879, p. 10-15.

M. Tchebychef m'a fait part, dans un entretien, d'un théorème arithmétique qui m'a vivement intéressé. Il a établi, dans un Mémoire publié en langue russe dans les *Mémoires de Saint-Pétersbourg* et dont sans lui je n'aurais jamais eu connaissance, cette proposition extrêmement remarquable, qu'il existe une infinité de systèmes de nombres entiers x et y tels que la fonction linéaire

$$x - ay - b,$$

où a et b sont deux constantes quelconques, soit plus petite en valeur absolue que $\frac{1}{2y}$. C'est, comme vous voyez, le résultat fondamental de la théorie des fractions continues, étendu à une expression toute différente, et qui ouvre la voie à bien des recherches. Dans une lettre adressée à M. Braschmann, et publiée dans le *Journal de Liouville*, 2e série, t. X, M. Tchebychef, appliquant cette même conception à l'Algèbre, considère l'expression

$$\mathrm{X} - \mathrm{UY} - \mathrm{V},$$

où U et V sont deux fonctions quelconques d'une variable x, et il détermine des polynomes entiers par rapport à cette variable, X et Y, tels qu'en ordonnant suivant les puissances décroissantes, le degré soit le nombre négatif le plus grand possible en valeur absolue. Les recherches de l'illustre géomètre sur la question sont extrêmement belles ; à bien des titres elles sont pour moi du plus grand intérêt, et voici une remarque à laquelle elles m'ont amené. Me plaçant d'abord au point de vue arithmétique, je suppose que a soit une quantité positive; les valeurs entières de x et y s'obtiennent alors comme il suit. Soient $\frac{m}{n}$, $\frac{m'}{n'}$ deux réduites consécutives du développement en fraction continue de a; posons

$$nb = \mathrm{N} + \omega, \qquad n'b = \mathrm{N}' + \omega',$$

en désignant par N et N′ des nombres entiers, par ω et ω' des quantités inférieures en valeur absolue à $\frac{1}{2}$. Soit encore, pour abréger,

$$\varepsilon = mn' - m'n = \pm 1;$$

on aura

$$\varepsilon x = m\mathrm{N}' - m'\mathrm{N}, \qquad \varepsilon y = n\mathrm{N}' - n'\mathrm{N}.$$

Ces formules donnent en effet

$$\begin{aligned}\varepsilon(x - ay) &= (m - an)\mathrm{N}' - (m' - an')\mathrm{N}\\ &= (m - an)(n'b - \omega') - (m' - an')(nb - \omega)\\ &= \varepsilon b + \omega(m' - an') - \omega'(m - an),\end{aligned}$$

de sorte qu'il vient déjà

$$\varepsilon(x - ay - b) = \omega(m' - an') - \omega'(m - an).$$

Employons maintenant la quantité λ qu'on nomme *quotient complet* dans la théorie des fractions continues et qui résulte de l'égalité

$$a = \frac{m'\lambda + m}{n'\lambda + n};$$

on aura

$$m - an = \frac{\varepsilon\lambda}{n'\lambda + n}, \qquad m' - an' = -\frac{\varepsilon}{n'\lambda + n}$$

et, par suite,

$$\omega(m' - an') - \omega'(m - an) = -\varepsilon\frac{\omega'\lambda + \omega}{n'\lambda + n},$$

quantité moindre, d'après les limitations de ω et ω', que

$$\frac{1}{2}\,\frac{\lambda+1}{n'\lambda+n}.$$

Mais cette expression décroît avec λ sous la condition $n'>n$, qui est ici remplie ; son maximum a donc lieu pour $\lambda=1$, et de là résulte qu'on peut poser

$$x-ya-b=\frac{\theta}{n'+n},$$

θ étant compris entre -1 et $+1$. Ce point établi, il suffit de remarquer qu'ayant

$$\varepsilon y=n\mathrm{N}'-n'\mathrm{N}=n(n'b-\omega')-n'(nb-\omega),$$

c'est-à-dire

$$\varepsilon y=\omega n'-\omega' n,$$

l'entier y est renfermé entre les limites

$$+\frac{n'+n}{2},\quad -\frac{n'+n}{2},$$

ce qui démontre le beau théorème découvert par M. Tchebychef.

Les expressions de x et y conduisent facilement à une conséquence qu'il n'est pas inutile de remarquer. Supposons qu'on ait $g-ah-b=0$, g et h étant entiers ; je dis qu'à partir d'une certaine réduite du développement de a en fraction continue, et pour toutes celles qui suivent, on trouvera constamment $x=g, y=h$. La théorie des fractions continues donnant en effet

$$a=\frac{m}{n}+\frac{\theta}{nn'},\qquad a=\frac{m'}{n'}+\frac{\theta'}{n'n''},$$

où θ et θ' désignent des quantités moindres que l'unité, on obtient, en substituant dans la valeur $b=g-ah$,

$$nb=ng-mh+\frac{\theta h}{n'},\qquad n'b=n'g-m'h+\frac{\theta h}{n''}.$$

Vous voyez donc que, quand n' dépassera $2h$, nous aurons

$$\mathrm{N}=ng-mh,\qquad \mathrm{N}'=n'g-m'h;$$

or en remplaçant dans les formules proposées

$$\varepsilon x = m\mathrm{N}' - m'\mathrm{N}, \qquad \varepsilon y = n\mathrm{N}' - n'\mathrm{N},$$

on en tire sur-le-champ

$$x = g, \qquad y = h.$$

Si l'on suppose $b = a^2$, cette remarque donne un algorithme pour la détermination des diviseurs du second degré des équations algébriques à coefficients entiers, lorsque le coefficient de la plus haute puissance de l'inconnue est l'unité.

Enfin, en passant de l'Arithmétique à l'Algèbre et considérant l'expression $\mathrm{X} - \mathrm{UY} - \mathrm{V}$, où U et V sont des fonctions quelconques dont la partie infinie est de la forme $\frac{a}{x} + \frac{a'}{x^2} + \ldots$, on obtient sous une forme toute semblable les polynomes X et Y qui donnent l'approximation la plus grande de la fonction V, par la formule $\mathrm{X} - \mathrm{UY}$. Désignons encore par $\frac{\mathrm{M}}{\mathrm{N}}, \frac{\mathrm{M}'}{\mathrm{N}'}$ deux réduites consécutives du développement de U en fraction continue algébrique ; faisons toujours $\varepsilon = \mathrm{MN}' - \mathrm{M}'\mathrm{N} = \pm 1$, et représentons la partie entière du développement d'une fonction $f(x)$ suivant les puissances descendantes de la variable par $[f(x)]$, on aura

$$\begin{aligned} \varepsilon\mathrm{X} &= \mathrm{M}[\mathrm{N}'\mathrm{V}] - \mathrm{M}'[\mathrm{NV}], \\ \varepsilon\mathrm{Y} &= \mathrm{N}[\mathrm{N}'\mathrm{V}] - \mathrm{N}'[\mathrm{NV}]. \end{aligned}$$

Soit, de plus, $\frac{\mathrm{M}''}{\mathrm{N}''}$ la réduite qui suit $\frac{\mathrm{M}'}{\mathrm{N}'}$ et posons semblablement

$$\begin{aligned} \varepsilon'\mathrm{X}' &= \mathrm{M}'[\mathrm{N}''\mathrm{V}] - \mathrm{M}''[\mathrm{N}'\mathrm{V}], \\ \varepsilon'\mathrm{Y}' &= \mathrm{N}'[\mathrm{N}''\mathrm{V}] - \mathrm{N}''[\mathrm{N}'\mathrm{V}]. \end{aligned}$$

En observant que $\varepsilon' = -\varepsilon$, on en déduira

$$\begin{aligned} \varepsilon(\mathrm{X}' - \mathrm{X}) &= (\mathrm{M}'' - \mathrm{M})[\mathrm{N}'\mathrm{V}] - \mathrm{M}'[\mathrm{NV}] - \mathrm{M}'[\mathrm{N}''\mathrm{V}], \\ \varepsilon(\mathrm{Y}' - \mathrm{Y}) &= (\mathrm{N}'' - \mathrm{N})[\mathrm{N}'\mathrm{V}] + \mathrm{N}'[\mathrm{NV}] - \mathrm{N}'[\mathrm{N}''\mathrm{V}]. \end{aligned}$$

Mais la loi de formation des réduites donnant, si l'on désigne par q le quotient incomplet,

$$\mathrm{M}'' = q\mathrm{M}' + \mathrm{M}, \qquad \mathrm{N}'' = q\mathrm{N}' + \mathrm{N},$$

vous voyez qu'on obtient

$$\varepsilon(X' - X) = \omega M', \qquad \varepsilon(Y' - Y) = \omega N',$$

en posant

$$\omega = q[N'V] + [NV] - [N''V].$$

Cette formule se simplifie, si l'on remplace dans le dernier terme N″ par sa valeur, et devient évidemment

$$\omega = q[N'V] - [qN'V].$$

De là se tire l'expression des polynomes X et Y sous forme de séries, telle que l'a donnée M. Tchebychef dans sa lettre à M. Braschmann, et je remplis l'intention qu'a bien voulu m'exprimer l'illustre géomètre en vous communiquant ce qui m'a été suggéré par l'étude de son beau travail.

La considération de la forme

$$f = (x - ay - bz)^2 + \frac{y^2}{\delta} + \frac{z^2}{\delta'},$$

où δ et δ sont des quantités variables essentiellement positives, qui donne une démonstration facile des résultats découverts par Dirichlet sur les minima de la fonction linéaire $x - ay - bz$, conduit également à la proposition de M. Tchebychef. Soit d'abord $\delta = t^2 u$, $\delta' = tu^2$, de sorte que l'invariant D ait pour expression $t^3 u^3$, je rappelle qu'un minimum de f, pour des valeurs entières des indéterminées, ayant pour limite supérieure le double de l'invariant, on a, quelles que soient les quantités positives de t et u,

$$(x - ay - bz)^2 + \frac{y^2}{t^2 u} + \frac{z^2}{tu^2} < \frac{\sqrt[3]{2}}{tu},$$

et par conséquent

$$(x - ay - bz)^2 < \frac{\sqrt[3]{2}}{tu}, \qquad x - ay - bz < \sqrt{\frac{2}{27}} \times \frac{1}{yz},$$

puis

$$y^2 < t\sqrt[3]{2}, \qquad z^2 < u\sqrt[3]{2}.$$

Cela posé, je remarque en premier lieu que, si la limite supérieure de z est inférieure à l'unité, on aura $z = 0$, et les minima obtenus en faisant croître t indéfiniment seront ceux de la fonction linéaire $x - ay$ que donne le développement de a en fraction continue.

Concevons ensuite qu'on fasse croître u, la valeur entière de z à partir d'une certaine limite ne sera plus égale à zéro, et il s'agit de prouver qu'en cessant d'être nulle elle devient égale à l'unité. Je me fonderai pour cela sur la remarque suivante : Considérant une forme définie à coefficients variables quelconques $f(x, y, z) = ax^2 + a'y^2 + a''z^2 + \ldots$; je suppose que, pour trois systèmes de valeurs infiniment voisines de ces coefficients, les minima soient

$$f(m, n, p), \quad f(m', n', p'), \quad f(m'', n'', p'');$$

je dis que le déterminant

$$\Delta = \begin{vmatrix} m & m' & m'' \\ n & n' & n'' \\ p & p' & p'' \end{vmatrix}$$

sera zéro ou l'unité.

Soit en effet D l'invariant de f, $AX^2 + A'Y^2 - A''Z^2 + \ldots$ la transformée qui en résulte en faisant

$$\begin{aligned} x &= mX + m'Y + m''Z, \\ y &= nX + n'Y + n''Z, \\ z &= pX + p'Y + p''Z, \end{aligned}$$

et dont l'invariant sera, par conséquent, $\Delta^2 D$. Comme, pour toute forme définie, le produit des coefficients des carrés des variables surpasse l'invariant, nous aurons $AA'A'' > \Delta^2 D$, ou bien

$$f(m, n, p) f(m', n', p') f(m'', n'', p'') > \Delta^2 D.$$

Mais on peut poser, en négligeant les quantités infiniment petites,

$$f(m, n, p) < D\sqrt[3]{2}, \qquad f(m', n', p') < D\sqrt[3]{2}, \qquad f(m'', n'', p'') < D\sqrt[3]{2},$$

et par conséquent

$$f(m, n, p) f(m', n', p') f(m'', n'', p'') < 2D.$$

Nous en tirons la condition $\Delta^2 < 2$, de sorte qu'on a bien $\Delta = 0$ ou $\Delta = \pm 1$.

Cela établi et revenant à la forme $f = (x - ay - bz)^2 + \frac{y^2}{t^2 u} + \frac{z^2}{tu^2}$, je considère t et u comme l'abscisse et l'ordonnée d'un point rapporté dans un plan à des axes rectangulaires, de sorte qu'à un système de trois entiers, qui donnent le minimum de f, correspond un ensemble de points ou une aire déterminée dans ce plan. De telles aires limitées par la partie positive de l'axe des abscisses s'offrent d'abord lorsqu'en faisant varier t, on suppose u assez petit pour avoir $z = 0$, et à deux aires contiguës appartiennent deux minima successifs de $x - ay$, ou bien deux réduites consécutives $\frac{m}{n}$, $\frac{m'}{n'}$ de a. Vous voyez qu'en un point de la ligne de séparation de ces deux aires voisines, les valeurs des quantités t et u présentent cette circonstance qu'une variation infiniment petite donne les minima correspondant aux deux systèmes m, n, 0 et m', n', 0. Suivons cette ligne jusqu'à son extrémité où elle aboutit à une nouvelle aire placée au-dessus des précédentes et à laquelle appartiennent les nombres m'', n'', p''. Nous introduirons, en supposant p'' différent de zéro, la condition que cette aire ne fasse plus partie de la première série où la troisième indéterminée est toujours nulle. Mais il en résulte que le déterminant

$$\Delta = \begin{vmatrix} m & m' & m'' \\ n & n' & n'' \\ 0 & 0 & p'' \end{vmatrix},$$

ayant pour valeur $\pm p''$, est lui-même alors différent de zéro ; or on a vu dans ce cas qu'il est en valeur absolue égal à l'unité, nous démontrons donc ainsi que $p'' = \pm 1$, ce qui établit bien l'existence du minimum découvert par M. Tchebychef. Enfin et comme conséquence de cette seconde méthode, la limitation précédemment obtenue $x - ay - b < \frac{1}{2y}$ se trouve remplacée par celle-ci : $x - ay - b < \sqrt{\frac{2}{27}}\frac{1}{y}$ où le coefficient numérique $\sqrt{\frac{2}{27}}$ est sensiblement plus petit que $\frac{1}{2}$.

Paris, le 22 mars 1879.

FIN DU TOME III.

ERRATA DU TOME I.

Page 168, lignes 18 et 19, *au lieu de* pour des valeurs entières des indéterminées, *lire* pour des valeurs entières des indéterminées, premières entre elles.

Page 179, ligne 9, *au lieu de* comme distincts, *lire* comme non distincts.

ERRATA DU TOME III.

				au lieu de	*lire*
Page 9,	ligne 2,	à partir d'en	bas	z_{m1}	z_{m-1}
» 35,	» 3,	»	haut	(1	(1)
» 55,	» 1,	»	bas	$(f \sin x, \cos x)$	$f(\sin x, \cos x)$
» 68,	» 7,	»	bas	$\int \sin^a \cos^b x\, dx$	$\int \sin^a x \cos^b x\, dx$
» 69,	» 4,	»	haut	$\int \sin^{a-2n} \cos^b x\, dx$	$\int \sin^{a-2n} x \cos^b x\, dx$
» 77,	» 2,	»	haut	$f(\sin x, \cos x$	$f(\sin x, \cos x)$
» 81,	» 3,	»	haut	$-\cot \frac{x-\mu}{2}$	$-\cot \frac{x+\mu}{2}$
» 122,	» 9,	»	bas	$\frac{dy}{dt} \frac{d \frac{1}{2\sqrt{x}}}{dx}$	$\frac{dy}{dt} \frac{d}{dx} \frac{1}{2\sqrt{x}}$
» 150,	» 8,	»	haut	$A\sqrt{A}$	$A\sqrt[n]{A}$
» 221,	» 8,	»	haut	$B(x)$	$B'(x)$
» 225,	» 3,	»	haut	$en(x-z)$	$cn(x-z)$
» 302,	» 1,	»	haut	$v + i\nu'$	$v + iv'$
» 357,	» 10,	»	haut	$e^{-\frac{i\pi}{4K}(u+iK_1)}$	$e^{-\frac{i\pi}{4K}(u+iK')}$
» 371,	» 9,	»	bas	$e^{\left[\lambda-\frac{\Theta'(\omega)}{\Theta(\omega)}\right]}$	$e^{\left[\lambda-\frac{\Theta'(\omega)}{\Theta(\omega)}\right]u}$
» 408,	» 7,	»	bas	$D_x^{2\nu 3}$	$D_x^{2\nu-3}$
» 415,	» 14,	»	bas	$\lambda_0^{2\nu 4}$	$\lambda_0^{2\nu-4}$
» 426,	» 9,	»	haut	$Sn^e(ix, k')$	$Sn^e(ix. k')$
» 433,	» 1,	»	bas	$+[\ldots\ldots]$	$\times[\ldots\ldots]$
» 448,	» 5,	»	bas	a^2	α^2
» 457,	» 7,	»	bas	$\frac{1}{2}$	$\frac{1}{z}$

TABLE DES MATIÈRES.

Pages

AVERTISSEMENT V

Sur l'extension du théorème de M. Sturm à un système d'équations simultanées 1

Intégration des fonctions rationnelles 35

Intégration des fonctions transcendantes 55

Sur l'équation $x^3+y^3=z^3+u^3$ 115

Sur l'équation de Lamé 118

On an application of the theory of unicursal curves 123

Sur l'irrationalité de la base des logarithmes hyperboliques 127

Sur une équation transcendante 131

Extrait d'une lettre sur l'expression $U \operatorname{Sin} x + V \operatorname{Cos} x + W$ 135

Extrait d'une lettre sur quelques approximations algébriques 146

Sur la fonction exponentielle 150

Extrait d'une lettre sur l'intégrale $\int_0^\pi \left(\frac{\sin^2 x}{1-2a\cos x+a^2}\right)^m dx$ 182

Extrait d'une lettre sur la transformation des formes quadratiques ternaires en elles-mêmes 185

Extrait d'une lettre sur la réduction des formes quadratiques ternaires ... 190

Extrait d'une lettre sur quelques équations différentielles linéaires 194

Extrait d'une lettre sur les nombres de Bernoulli 211

Extrait d'une lettre sur la fonction de Jacob Bernoulli 215

Sur les développements de $F(x) = \operatorname{Sn}^a x \operatorname{Cn}^b x \operatorname{Dn}^c x$ 222

Sur un théorème d'Eisenstein 232

Extrait d'une lettre sur le développement des fonctions elliptiques suivant les puissances croissantes de la variable 236

Extrait d'une lettre sur une formule de M. Delaunay 246

Sur l'aire d'un segment de courbe convexe 248

Sur un exemple de réduction d'intégrales abéliennes aux fonctions elliptiques 249

Sur une formule de Jacobi 262

Sur quelques applications des fonctions elliptiques 266

Études de M. Sylvester sur la théorie algébrique des formes 419

Extrait d'une lettre de M. Hermite à M. Fuchs 420

Extrait d'une lettre sur la formule de Maclaurin 425

Extrait d'une lettre sur la formule d'interpolation de Lagrange 432

Extrait d'une lettre sur les courbes planes 444

Extrait d'une lettre sur le pendule 447

Pages

Sur la théorie des fonctions sphériques.................................. 451

Sur l'intégrale $\int_0^1 \frac{z^{a-1} - z^a}{1 - z} dz$.................................. 455

Extrait d'une lettre sur l'équation de Lamé.................................. 475

Sur un théorème de Galois relatif aux équations solubles par radicaux... 479

Sur le contact des surfaces.................................. 485

Sur les équations différentielles linéaires.................................. 496

Sur les équations linéaires.................................. 509

Extrait d'une lettre sur une extension donnée à la théorie des fractions continues par M. Tchebychef.................................. 513

FIN DE LA TABLE DES MATIÈRES DU TOME III.

43600 Paris. — Imp. GAUTHIER-VILLARS, quai des Grands-Augustins, 55.

www.ingramcontent.com/pod-product-compliance
Lightning Source LLC
LaVergne TN
LVHW010830120826
845149LV00016B/125

* 9 7 8 1 4 1 8 1 8 5 0 6 0 *